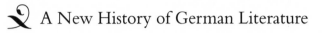 A New History of German Literature

HARVARD
UNIVERSITY
PRESS
REFERENCE
LIBRARY

A New History of German Literature

David E. Wellbery

EDITOR-IN-CHIEF

Judith Ryan

GENERAL EDITOR

Hans Ulrich Gumbrecht
Anton Kaes
Joseph Leo Koerner
Dorothea E. von Mücke

EDITORS

THE BELKNAP PRESS OF
HARVARD UNIVERSITY PRESS

Cambridge, Massachusetts
London, England 2004

Library of Congress Cataloging-in-Publication Data

A new history of German literature / David E. Wellbery,
    editor-in-chief ; Judith Ryan, general editor ;
    Hans Ulrich Gumbrecht . . . [et al.], editors.
p.   cm.—(Harvard University Press Reference Library)
Includes bibliographical references and index.
ISBN 0-674-01503-7 (cloth: alk. paper)
1. German literature—History and criticism.
I. Wellbery, David E.   II. Ryan, Judith.   III. Gumbrecht, Hans Ulrich.   IV. Series.
PT91.N49 2004
830.9 22—dc22   2004059590

♫ Contents

♃ Introduction

Every poem, according to a dictum of Paul Celan's, is datable ("Jedes Gedicht ist datierbar"). Although it may seem quite uncontroversial, this statement by one of the 20th century's most original poets implies a forceful critique of traditional literary history: a critique that proceeds not from a formalist rejection of history, but from a radicalization of the idea that literature is historical. The date each poem or work of literature bears is internal to the work itself, the temporal center around which it crystallizes. The meaning of literary texts—their capacity to testify to human experience and to resonate in the lives of their readers—is inseparably tied to the singularity of their moment, to their primary historical character as contingent events. Paradoxically, in the inherited form of literary-historical writing, it is just this character of literature that goes missing. Traditional literary histories treat individual texts and performances not as singular occurrences, but as illustrative instances of some force, tendency, or norm such as the spirit of an age or a nation, a class bias, or an aesthetic ideal. To grasp the historical character of a literary text is, according to this way of thinking, to see the individual case as typical of something else, and therefore as replaceable. This operation effaces literature's "datable" singularity and contingency. A major aim of *A New History of German Literature* is to find a mode of presentation that restores access to this dimension of literature.

Another way of stating this aim is to say that *A New History of German Literature* attempts to preserve the quality of "encounter" that characterizes the most exhilarating experiences of reading. Genuine encounters promote fascination and curiosity. They can even change the course of a reader's life by creating the desire for a deeper acquaintance with a writer or work. Walter Benjamin, whose ideas on history were an essential inspiration for this volume, stressed the importance to historical understanding of such momentary interruptions of the continuum of time, which he likened to a "tiger's leap" into the past. It seemed to the editors that such encounters have the best chance of happening when the presentation of works or events is focused on particulars. For example, Goethe, the towering figure of the German literary tradition, is to be met in these pages not in his monumentality, but at three or four telling moments of his career. We see him writing his *Werther,* censoring his own *Ro-*

man Elegies, declaring his *Faust* complete; in one entry, we even see him hiding behind a curtain to listen to F. A. Wolf lecture on Homer. This approach conveys the compelling intellectual interest of the material treated here, be it canonical or relatively unknown. Encounters in this sense—confrontations, recognitions, discoveries, even affronts—await the reader throughout these pages: encounters with the tradition of mystical writing from Meister Eckart to Angelus Silesius, with the writers' guild of the cobbler-poet Hans Sachs, with the difficult life of the 17th-century businesswoman and memoirist Glikl bas Yehuda Leib. The drama of the event catches Lessing, Germany's most important Enlightenment man of letters, in the act of misdating his great comedy *Minna von Barnhelm.* It shows us E. T. A. Hoffmann, author of the tale from which Freud would derive his theory of the "uncanny," deliberating on a murder case. In the redecoration of a church altar it reveals how thoroughly Luther's ideas changed the individual churchgoer's experience. Major authors are placed in unexpected contexts: Heinrich von Kleist is seen in connection with the emergence of guerrilla warfare in the resistance to Napoleon; Wilhelm Raabe's novel *Stopfkuchen* is read as a critique of colonialist politics; Kafka's story "The Judgment" is viewed in the context of international politics. Placed next to such major figures, relatively unknown writers ascend from the status of footnotes to that of engaging discoveries: Hans Staden, the 16th-century traveler to colonial Brazil; Salomon Maimon, whose autobiography charts the path from the Polish ghetto to Enlightenment Berlin; Irmgard Keun, the advocate of the "New Woman" during the Weimar Republic. A public controversy, such as the heated dispute surrounding the Hebrew studies of the Humanist Johannes Reuchlin, can bring the tensions within an intellectual movement to light. Differences of intellectual style are elicited through juxtaposition, as when Benjamin and Heidegger are each glimpsed in 1927. The strategy, in short, is to shun summary and cataloguing and to exploit, rather, the communicative potential of the anecdotal and the discontinuous for generating sudden illumination.

A New History of German Literature participates in the "reflective turn" in recent historiography. Its formal arrangement and selection of contents are motivated by a consideration of the conditions that spawned literary history as both an intellectual inquiry and a literary genre. Such self-scrutiny is especially appropriate to a volume that portrays German literary and intellectual traditions, since the historical treatment of literature is itself arguably a German discovery. But it also corresponds to a feature that distinguishes German culture from its European counterparts: a tradition of self-reflection that results in a remarkable—often exhilarating, on occasion ponderous—interpenetration of imagination and conceptualization. The idealizing cliché according to which Germany is a "land of poets and thinkers" (alliteratively fixed in German as "Land der Dichter und Denker") attests to this characteristic habit of thought. One of the unique aspects of *A New History of German Literature* is the effort to do justice to the reflective bent of German culture by including articles on such figures as the philosophers Leibniz, Kant, Hegel, Schopenhauer, and

Wittgenstein. This decision required an expansion of the traditional notion of literature as well as a recasting of literary history as an interdisciplinary endeavor.

The contention that literary history had its beginnings in Germany (shorthand for "German-speaking countries") is confirmed by the striking observation that opens Hippolyte Taine's influential *History of English Literature* (1864): "History, within a hundred years in Germany, and within sixty years in France, has undergone a transformation, owing to a study of literatures." Taine's remark dates the emergence of literary history as a field of inquiry within the last third of the 18th century, when a large-scale semantic transformation fundamentally altered inherited conceptions of tradition and change, fame and aesthetic value. As Reinhart Koselleck has shown, during this period the term "history," which had always allowed for a plural usage (for example, the "histories" of dynasties, institutions, voyages), acquired its modern meaning as a collective singular term referring to the overriding process that gives direction and sense to all individual patterns of change. The predominant experience was no longer one of permanence and of continuity with the past, but of accelerating alteration in all dimensions of communal life. This acute sense of historical difference, this deepening of the gulf between present and past, affected the apprehension of art and literature as well, rendering implausible any sense of enduring and universal aesthetic achievement. In this context, a new task arose: to understand cultural artifacts not as reflecting eternal values, but as the expressions of their age.

It is tempting to conjecture that Taine's dating of the transformation of historical thought was meant to be exact. In 1764, Johann Joachim Winckelmann's *History of the Art of Antiquity* had appeared, the book generally held today to be the foundational text of art history. Winckelmann's contemporaries quickly sought to extend his work to other realms. Already in the late 1760s, Johann Gottfried Herder began to sketch out a historical conception of culture that would embrace the entire range of human expression. His essay on Shakespeare (1773) demolished the notion of timeless artistic standards and derived the essential features of Shakespearean dramatic form from the conditions of his age. Herder insisted on understanding literary artifacts as interwoven with religious and political institutions and beliefs, with commerce, custom, and morality. This is not to say, of course, that literary history had not been practiced prior to Herder. The Enlightenment had conceived of it as a documentation of the progress of taste; the 17th century had created monuments of erudition that catalogued writers and works of the past; treatises on poetics such as those by Martin Opitz (1624) and Johann Christoph Gottsched (1730) had often included a survey of prior achievements. But such histories are hardly recognizable as anything that today might count as historical depiction. This is why Taine's remark is so suggestive. His still vivid sense that a *transformation* of the very notion of history had occurred a century before him captures the innovative force of Winckelmann's and Herder's contributions.

The intellectual revolution that would culminate in Hegel's thought that time and history are the very mode of existence and self-realization of what he called "Spirit" (*Geist*) required new discursive forms capable of capturing both the unity and diversity—the logic in movement—of cultural expression. The achievement of such forms is one of the major accomplishments of German Romanticism, to which we owe both the central concepts of modern literary criticism and the overview of European literary history still accepted today. In particular, August Wilhelm Schlegel, who delivered a series of influential lectures on the history of literature and art in Berlin in 1803–1804, and his brother Friedrich, who delivered similar lectures in Paris and Cologne (1803–1804) and later in Vienna (1812), share the credit for creating a capacious, philosophically grounded vision of European literary history. The operative word here is "European." Like Herder before them, the Schlegels were not primarily concerned with a nationally based history of German literature, although they highlighted such works as the *Nibelungenlied,* which in subsequent decades would take on the aura of a national epic. Their inquiries were cosmopolitan, concerned with the "Spirit," which appeared in various national guises and expressed itself in different idioms. There is a double lesson to be learned here: first, that the conception of literary history developed by the Schlegels does not stand alone, but is keyed to a general theory of poetics and, beyond this, to a philosophy of mind; second, that although they created the intellectual preconditions for a national history of literature, the Schlegels' own framework of inquiry was vigorously comparatist, their object of study what Goethe—and later Marx—would describe as *Weltliteratur* (world literature). An important intention of *A New History of German Literature* is to recover the double reference to theoretical inquiry and to the context of world literature that is built into the Romantic concept of literary history.

Neither Herder nor the Schlegels were professional literary scholars, nor did they address their works to an audience of students and fellow historians. The academic transformation of literary history is, rather, the accomplishment of the 19th century. By 1860, professorships in Germanic philology had been founded at every German-speaking university. Professional organizations were established, critical editions—even of recent writers—were produced, journals devoted to literary-historical research proliferated. Thus emerged the professionalized discipline of literary history. Nonetheless, some literary histories looked beyond the university context. For example, Gottfried Gervinus's five-volume *History of the Poetic National-Literature of the Germans* (1835–1842)—often considered the pioneering effort of the genre—was driven by a liberal political agenda, while the poet Joseph von Eichendorff's *History of the Poetic Literature of Germany* (2 vols., 1857) promoted a deeply nostalgic form of cultural conservatism. Increasingly, however, literary histories were keyed to the dual demands of university-based research and university-based education (primarily the preparation of high school teachers). As research generated further research, the ideal of historical synthesis became more and more unattainable. Every text recovered from obscurity, every case of literary influence demonstrated, every detail of a writer's life discovered, increased the complexity of the knowledge base that historical narrative was supposed to organize and make sense of. Thus, by the end of the century, the genre had abandoned its philosophical and political ambitions, restricting itself to providing a synopsis of current scholarly consensus. Literary histories became the narrative meta-texts of the disciplinary and educational apparatus that produced them, serving important functions such as outlining a framework for university and high-school curricula, supplying mnemonic devices useful in exam preparation, and establishing links to neighboring historical disciplines. Perhaps even more crucially, they consolidated a diffuse sense of "national" literary tradition and thus supplied an important tool for the transmission of cultural literacy. In this sense, the primary function of academic literary history was the production of cultural identity within the context of the nation-state.

With few exceptions, the genre of literary history looks very much today as it did at the end of the 19th century. Its basic form—an overriding narrative divided according to periods or movements; the treatment of individual texts as exemplifying large-scale historical tendencies—has remained intact regardless of changes in methodology and ideology. Indeed, one of the remarkable features of literary history as practiced from the late 19th century up to the present is that it has so blithely resisted the revolutionary transformations of narrative form initiated in modernism. At the same time, it has proved relatively immune to the philosophical critique of historicism, from Nietzsche to Heidegger and Benjamin. The reason this is so is that the genre's institutional context—university-based research and instruction within a state system of education—has itself remained quite stable, despite the social and political changes of the 20th century. *A New History of German Literature* seeks to accomplish quite different aims, however, making it both possible and necessary to transform the structure and content of literary-historical presentation. This transformation has left none of the major terms of our title untouched: neither "history," nor "German," nor "literature" means quite the same thing here as in the standard works.

We began with a different readership. Our forerunners since the late 19th century have typically addressed students and scholars of German literature. *A New History of German Literature* is certainly not intended to exclude this group—on the contrary!—but from the start we have also had the general or educated reader in mind. This reader we imagine as someone who may be motivated by desires other than successfully completing an examination or preparing a lecture. Perhaps it is a person who, having read a work by Schiller or Kafka, having seen an opera by Mozart or Wagner, has always wanted to learn more about the traditions from which those works emerged. Very likely it will be someone who has noticed that so many ideas crucial to the reinvigoration of humanistic inquiry during the past thirty years have their source in German-language works. Where is this reader's home? Under the conditions of international mobility, of modern book production and electronic communication, of ethnic diversity within the great cities of the world, the only possible answer to this question is: "Almost anywhere." Our vision is of readers with varying interests, who are curious, for whatever reason, about German literature and culture. We believe that the history of German literature is a vital resource wherever intelligence and imagination are devoted to exploring the complexities of the world made by human thought.

Three elements, then, are presupposed here. The first is what might be termed the archival simultaneity of German literature: works that originated in different historical contexts are *co-present*—today, in the age of the Internet, more than ever—in the various media of reproduction, storage, and distribution, ordered by library catalogues and search engines. The second element is the book's readers, a group held together by no national tradition, no disciplinary training, no particular profession. The third term in our equation is a range of curiosities rooted in serendipitous encounters, individual biographies, historical circumstances, particular passions and interests, chosen or inherited obligations. *A New History of German Literature* is intended to be useful within the configuration defined by these three elements. One might say—borrowing a term from computer science—that it is a random access history, providing multiple points of entry and allowing for various reading agendas. This volume has no single story to tell, but sets many stories in relation to one another. Its aim is to allow various types of curiosity to unfold, divergent patterns to emerge, different—and often dissonant—resonances to be heard.

To accomplish this end, we chose to rely on the fundamental organizational grid of every history: chronology. Thus, each entry is marked by a date, usually a year, sometimes a month or even a day. Each date marks an event, a particular happening, and our book as a whole presents the sequence of these events. In many cases, the dated event in question is the composition or publication of a text, but other sorts of events can serve as the focus of an entry as well: a visit by a noble personage, an invention, a court decision, a theatrical production. In every case the event was selected because it highlights a network of interconnections and brings into representation a complex historical field. With this strategy—gratefully adapted from *A New History of French Literature* (1989)—we have tried to approach the level of historicity that was so important to Celan: the singularity of the literary event.

Although "datable," the literary event is not fixed within a single temporal order or pattern of historical meaning. As Erwin Panofsky pointed out in an essay from 1927, every historical phenomenon "represents the intersection of numerous frames of reference that confront each other as products of different spaces and times and whose interaction in each instance leads to a unique result." Such interactions produce what Walter Benjamin called "constellations," configurations of historical facts that converge in a moment of sudden insight. Thus multiple paths radiate from each event to other events. Echoes, influences, and contrasts become perceptible. Sometimes these interconnections are chronologically proximate; sometimes they leap across centuries. The volume thereby offers multiple trajectories of reading determined by the subject matter and the pull of the reader's fascination. The linkages discovered will be historical, but there is no one history that gives them their definitive order. Why shouldn't this be the case? Why shouldn't an interest in Brecht lead to an interest in Grimmelshausen, a fascination with Hofmannsthal and Strauss to an appreciation of Schikaneder and Mozart?

A New History of German Literature departs from its apparent structure of the chronicle, however, in that each of the events marked by date and title also unfolds a particular theme, usually indicated in the entry's subtitle. Each entry is written in the form of an essay, literally an "attempt," almost an "experiment." The entries of this volume reflect not only the dynamics of their various subject matters, but also the particular interests of the individual contributors. This aspect of the book expresses the editors' assessment of the current state of literary-historical inquiry, in which various methodological paradigms coexist. It also reflects a basic fact of literary life: that works refract differently in different sensibilities, that individual texts respond to vastly different readings. We asked contributors to write according to their own best lights about what, in a given work, author, or event, spoke to them. They were required to construct their essays around a dated event, and to write an essay of a certain length, but the angle of thematic interest was left to the individual authors. This compositional strategy fit well with our vision of the book as an interdisciplinary forum on the traditions and ruptures of German culture and enabled us to include, along with essays by literary scholars, contributions by musicologists, philosophers, art and theater historians, historians of ideas, and specialists on cinema and popular culture. The result is a volume that displays the scope and richness of contemporary research devoted to the German past and present.

The variety of critical methods represented in *A New History of German Literature* is counterbalanced by a common set of themes that recur throughout the entire volume. The first bears on the changing conceptions of time and tradition that inform the self-understanding of writers and readers. Historical time is not a homogeneous medium that the historian can simply presuppose, but is itself in flux. The task is to grasp the ongoing reconstruction of the semantic frameworks within which time is experienced. Thus, many individual entries highlight particular ways of understanding temporality at particular historical moments and show how these conceptions determine the shape of the material they are presenting. In addition, we have included several entries that are specifically devoted to conceptualizations of time and history, from the *Weltchronik* of Rudolf von Ems to Hegel's proclamation of the "end of art," from Jacob Burckhardt's evocation of the Italian Renaissance to W. G. Sebald's melancholic meditation on the devastations of the Second World War. Finally, by refusing to map the manifold relations of historical reality onto what the novelist Robert Musil referred to as the "one-dimensional thread of narration," we have endeavored to preserve the novelty and surprise that characterize the historical present.

A second thematic strand that runs through the work bears on the larger linguistic, cultural, and political unities within which literary activity operates. Although the concept "German" defines the field from which we have made our selections, it is employed in a flexible way throughout the book. One of the features that distinguishes German history from that of France, England, and Spain, after all, is the relatively late achievement of a unified and centralized national state, in 1871. At least eight cities can boast of having been the German capital at one time or another, and the boundaries of Germany remained a matter of contention through most of the 20th century. Even if the concept "German" is used in the linguistic sense, it fails to do justice to the complexity of the literary-historical field. *A New History of German Literature* attempts to reflect the complexity inherent in the term "German" by highlighting political and linguistic variety, by considering the perspectives of outsiders and exiles, and by stressing the European—indeed, the global—context of German literary culture. For instance, because a book written by a French speaker in Swiss exile (Germaine de Staël's *De l'Allemagne,* 1810) shaped the international image of the German literary tradition in decisive ways, it is discussed in the volume. In general, we have tried to emphasize geographical diversity and shifting political contexts, stressing, for example, that the greatest German philosopher of the late Middle Ages, Nicholas of Cusa, spent much of his life in Rome as advisor to three popes; that Charles I, the founder of the first German university in Prague, was in contact with the Italian Humanist Petrarch; that the name of Alexander von Humboldt is memorialized across the maps of North and South America. Indeed, *Dr. Faustus* (1947), perhaps the most significant novelistic exploration of the German artistic tradition, was written by a resident of California and its allusions to contemporary events were often drawn from the pages of *Time* magazine.

The third major thematic concern of the volume is the changing configurations of the media of storage and transmission. There was a time when the term "literature" designated simply all that is written. With the Romantics, the term came to mean "imaginative writing," a definition that still delimits most literary histories. Contemporary scholarship, however, has complicated both these understandings considerably. Thus, entries on manuscript production and collecting, on Gutenberg's invention of moveable type, and on the normalization of a national language are included in this volume, as are entries on pictorial display, on poetic-musical forms, on the cinema and radio plays, even on television, museums, and public festivals. The idea is not merely to expand the canon of literary history, but to call attention to the evolution of literature.

These three topics take *A New History of German Literature* beyond the three parameters of traditional literary histories: continuous narrative time, the cultural space of the "nation," and imaginative writing. Our goal is to provide an account of German literary history that focuses on "the interaction of different spaces and times," that mirrors the fluctuations of linguistic and national identity characteristic of literary activity throughout its history, and that highlights the variety and interaction of media. This inclusiveness forced us to accept some rather painful exclusions as well, but selection is endemic to historical representation. Indeed, one of the virtues of the form of presentation chosen here is that it calls attention to the fact that other choices might have been made. As our title indicates, this is *a* history of German literature. It is a history, however, that does not impose a single order on the material, but rather traces many strands within it. The ideas of datable event, encounter, and constellation from which we have derived the volume's organizational strategy permit its readers to discover some of these different strands. In following their own itineraries of reading, they will be struck by historical patterns—echoes, influences, similarities, contrasts—that we have only been able to hint at in the cross-references suggested at the end of each entry. Readers will uncover more of these configurations each time they explore the book. The order of history this volume evokes is in fact an array of orders that is reorganized with every reading.

Bibliography: A New History of French Literature, ed. Denis Hollier (Cambridge, Mass.: Harvard University Press, 1989). Walter Benjamin, *Selected Writings,* gen. ed. Marcus Bullock, 4 vols. (Cambridge, Mass.: Harvard University Press, 1996–2003). ———, *The Arcades Project,* trans. Howard Eiland and Kevin McLaughlin (Cambridge, Mass.: Harvard University Press, 1999). Paul Celan, *Collected Prose,* trans. Rosemary Waldrop (Manchester: Carcanet, 1986). Reinhart Koselleck, *Vergangene Zukunft: Zur Semantik geschichtlicher Zeiten* (Frankfurt am Main: Suhrkamp, 1985). Niklas Luhmann, "Temporalisierung von Komplexität: Zur Semantik neuzeitlicher Zeitbegriffe," in Luhmann, *Gesellschaftsstruktur und Semantik,* vol. 1 (Frankfurt am Main: Suhrkamp, 1980), 235–300. Friedrich Meinecke, *Die Entstehung des Historismus* (Munich: Oldenbourg, 1936). Robert Musil, *The Man without Qualities,* trans. Sophie Wilkins and Burton Pike (New York: Knopf, 1995). Erwin Panofsky, "Reflections on Historical Time," trans. Johanna Baumann, *Critical Inquiry* 30:4 (2004): 691–702. Hippolyte Taine, *History of English Literature,* trans. H. Van Laun (New York: Holt and Company, 1875).

David E. Wellbery

A New History of German Literature

♌ 744

Bishop Boniface founds a monastery at Fulda, where—nearly two centuries later—magical formulae in Old High German are recorded on an empty codex page

The Charm of Charms

The small town of Fulda lies in the heart of Germany, less than a hundred kilometers northeast of Frankfurt am Main. The founding of a monastery there in 744 by the missionary Bishop Boniface, which marks the beginning of the town's history, is an important milestone in the life of the Christian Church as well as a foundational event in the history of the German nation. Boniface devoted the last decade of his life (he was slain, in 754, by worshipers of the Germanic gods in Frisia) to developing the monastery of Fulda with such care that it became the center for the Christianization of most of the area that is Germany today. His mission not only had the blessing of the pope; he also was able to count on military and political support from the Carolingians, the warrior clan which Charlemagne a while later transformed into a royal house. When Boniface founded the monastery of Fulda, he was about sixty years old, thirty years of which he had spent on the Continent, away from his native England. Almost immediately after his death, he came to be revered as a saint of the Christian Church, and a national tradition has long honored him as the "Apostle of the Germans."

It was in the monastery at Fulda, about two hundred years later, that the texts of two charms in alliterative verse were written on a blank leaf in a codex containing several texts required for celebrating Mass. Such overlapping of religions and cultures was typical for this historical period. Part of the remaining traces constitute a body of some three dozen charms, written in different layers—some very early—of Old High German. Linguists tell us that the two charms of the Fulda codex are written in the German—or Germanic—language of the time of Boniface. The magic rituals and deities they invoke belong to pre-Christian layers of Germanic culture. We do not know, however, what the intention of the monk who set these charms down into writing might have been. Neither do we know whether what he transcribed was a sequence of Germanic words that had previously existed only in oral transmission, nor whether he copied a text from an older manuscript now lost. It is likely that a persistent belief in the efficacy of Germanic charms was a strong enough reason to rescue them from oblivion. After all, several of the charms that have come down to us contain references to Christ, Christian saints, and apocryphal Christian narratives in place of names and settings from Germanic mythology. As in the case of a sacred oak dedicated to the Germanic thunder-god Dunar and felled by Boniface in 724, other places and functions of the Germanic religion were frequently graced with sacred Christian objects and endowed with Christian meanings.

And yet there are only a few things we can say with certainty about these so-called *Merseburger Zaubersprüche (Merseburg Charms),* which are named after the town of Merseburg, near Halle in Saxony, whose cathedral flourished in the 11th century and which still owns today the codex containing the two charms. First, they signify the moment of transition from Germanic culture to the German culture that arose from the convergence of Boniface's Christianizing mission and political centralization achieved by the Carolingians. Second, early medieval manuscripts from the Continent abound with texts, genres, and images of a similarly ambiguous character. German literary scholars of the 19th and early 20th centuries made much of the "Germanness" and even of the literary quality of the charms as a genre. Today, most specialists agree that, while the charms are indeed part of an initial stage of German culture, and while they afford us a glimpse of everyday life of that period, there is nothing specifically German or literary about them. The everyday situations described show a world in which the well-being of horses and watchdogs was essential for human survival. It shows a world in which much attention was paid to the flight of bees to the appropriate flowering plants; a world, finally, where the Christian religion has not yet completely dispelled the fear of demons, ghosts, or devils. But, rather than being specific to early German culture, such life conditions characterize many cultures we call "archaic"—and in this sense they do not belong to any particular historical period.

Here is the text of the longer, more mythology-laden—and also more transparent—of the two Merseburg charms:

> Phol ende Wuoadan   vuorun zi holza.
> du wart demo Balderes volon   sin vuoz birenkit.
> thu biguol en Sinthgunt,   Sunna era swister;
> thu biguol en Friia,   Volla era swister;
> thu biguol en Wuodan,   so he wola conda:

The Merseburg charms. The passage discussed in this essay begins on the second line from the top of the page. (Domstiftbibliothek Merseburg, Bildarchiv)

sose benrenki,   sose bluotrenki, sose lidirenki:
ben zi bena,   bluot zi bluoda,
lid zi geliden,   sose gelimida sin.

This brief document contains several details that have not yet been clarified satisfactorily and thus make any translation conjectural. For one thing, it is unclear what the very first word means—although it may well refer to an as yet unknown mythological character (this charm is one of only two early German texts that name Germanic deities). But when recited, the text will always have a solemnly somber sound and a vague impression of content not too far from the following translation: "Phol and Wuodan were riding through the forest. / At this Balder's colt dislocated its hoof. / So Sinthgunt was conjuring it, and Sunna, her sister, / so Friya was conjuring it, and Volla, her sister, / so Wuodan was conjuring it, who was well able to do so: / Dislocated bone like dislocated blood like dislocated members: / bone to bone, blood to blood / member to member, they shall be as if they were glued."

It is not difficult to describe how such charms function. They normally begin by invoking a mythological situation, mainly through verb morphology in the past tense, that centers almost always on a problem and its resolution. In this case gods ride through the forest, and the horse of one of these gods contracts a hoof injury which is subsequently healed through a ritual of conjuring. Then the text refers, in the present tense, to the situation in which it is being performed and in which a similar problem has come up—without being resolved thus far. In one line and without verb morphology it suggests three different types of "injuries" existing in the present. All are referred to by the word *-renki,* that is, "dislocation"—and against all of them the charm's magic powers may be used: dislocated bones, dislocated blood, dislocated members. Finally, and normally combined with verb forms in either the imperative or subjunctive mode, the text points to future situations in which—through the power of the charm—the present problem will be resolved. In this case all three types of problems will indeed be mentioned again in the third part, where the dislocated parts shall come together again "as if they were glued."

From a logical point of view, no charm can exist without these three levels, but the actual corpus shows multiple variations in contracting and expanding each of these levels, and in combining them. The key implication of the charms is that the second part of the mythological level, the part containing the solution to the problem, can be projected into the future, that is, into the future of the present in a yet unresolved situation. Rather than speaking of a "projection" of the mythological past into the future, however, we should speak of a fusion of the mythological past and the future. For the world of magic is a world where a return of the past, with all its objects, to the present and the future appears quite possible. The morphology through which the fusion of past and future, which leads to the return of the past, is marked in the text is not in the future tense but in the imperative or the subjunctive. The bones "shall be" as if they were glued—"gelimida sin" in the original text is a subjunctive form.

The primary function of the text is neither narrative, nor descriptive, nor expressive. Charms are certainly not about conveying a speaker's voice, nor are they about describing a situation or narrating a past. Charms are texts that are meant to achieve something. But unlike the examples commonly invoked by modern-day linguists or philosophers, when texts or even individual words "are" one or the other "action" the speaker-subject performs, the charms presuppose much more complex cosmic mechanisms. The interplay of verb morphemes in the charms is part of this complexity—whereas examples for textual performativity in present-day cultures are normally reduced to the present tense ("I promise," "I declare you wife and husband," and the like). The presupposed knowledge in the genre of the charm is about specific mechanisms underlying the act of conjuring and its power. This act implies that drawing an intense parallel between a past situation and a partially identical situation in the present will trigger—with mechanical necessity—their fusion in the future. Through this fusion the present situation becomes identical with the mythological situation and with the solution achieved.

But what does it mean to say that an intense parallelism must be established between a past situation and a present situation? It means, above all, that the magic text has to invoke, rather than describe, these situations. The words of magic texts, therefore, point to specific situations and to their elements as a substantial thing-reference instead of providing concepts that invite a listener to imagine the situations in question. What we see in our charm is typical of the genre: a large number of names of mythological characters in this very text.

Sometimes there are also place names, especially if the sameness of the place in which the solution happens and the place in which the magic ritual takes place is considered a precondition for the unfolding of its performative power. For names cannot help pointing to individual referents.

Another frequently used device of conjuring, although not part of our text, is demonstrative pronouns. They are complemented by adverbs and particles indicating specific places and points in time (in our charm *du* and *thu,* in lines 2–5) and, quite often, by exclamations and vocative forms (the final two lines). Charms always "speak" as if the past and future situations they invoke were in their immediate spatial and temporal presence—and this is indeed how they make them present, that is, how they produce the impression that these situations are becoming tangible. In the case of charms that were not written down and, above all, not recited in verse, the interplay of the complex structure of verb morphemes and the abundance of demonstrative forms were seemingly sufficient to produce the desired magic effect. Although we can, of course, never exclude that texts which, in manuscript, look like prose were performed in a more rhythmic fashion.

In addition to these two levels, it is possible to show how bound language, quite literally, can create the effect of fusion between the past and future dimension. By "bound language" we mean "rhythmic language," and as "rhythmic" we consider any text that, through patterns of recurrence, gives itself a form. What we mean by "form" here is a stable quality through which a text, for example, can point to itself and, simultaneously, to its environment, shaping its own identity within the same environment. To achieve a form in this sense constitutes a specific problem for texts since they are objects that can exist only as sequential unfolding. As time objects in the sense proper, texts seem to defy one stable form. What the various devices, subsumed under the concept "rhythm," do in order to give form to a text, is to shape the time of performance ("performance" in reciting or performance in "reading") in two ways: first, as a well-circumscribed, overarching present of the entire text and, second, as an overarching present with distinct internal structures and subdivisions.

As is typical for texts of Germanic origin, our charm produces rhythm mainly through alliteration, although scholars are far from agreed on how exactly this works. As one unifying principle, alliteration runs through the entire text, with different recurrent consonants giving different sound colors to different verses. Thus it is alliteration that produces the one overarching present. A second device that gives form to the text may be the alternation between longer and shorter lines. It is easy to see that the first five lines of the text (in the structure that editors since the 19th century have agreed upon), the verses invoking the mythological situation, all have roughly the same number of syllables. The single verse that invokes the present situation(s), the situation without solution, however, is longer than the verses of the first and of the third part. It is also the only verse that apparently has two caesuras. Finally, the two verses invoking the future scene in which the problem will be resolved are shorter than the verses of the first and of the second part. We could go one step farther and associate the alliterations based on the repetition of the same nouns in the final lines ("ben zi bena") with the goal of the charm to bring together again ("sose gelimida sin") what was out of joint.

But the most important aspect of the rhythmic structure of this charm is the formation of a paradox. This paradox consists in the fact that the entire text constitutes one form and one present, based on alliteration, while it has, at the same time, a clear internal separation into three parts. The separation seems based on different verse structures that occur in these three parts. If any fusion—not only a fusion of time—plays with the paradox of things being both separate and one, then the entire text, as it emerges from its recitation, constitutes one present within which and through which the three parts are fused. This impression that semantic contours and structures become blurred without disappearing completely corresponds to our actual experience of being exposed to incantatory language.

Things can get even more complicated with early German charms—for example, when additional layers of magic are implied and, at the same time, a more intense degree of textual contraction comes into play. A genre-specific tendency toward laconic forms probably made it easy for the users of the charms to memorize the texts. But in their sometimes extreme brevity, these texts may also have sounded like an order through which it was possible to keep hostile powers in check. In a manuscript that was probably written at St. Gall about the year 1000, there are only three lines—one title line in Latin and two verses in Old High German—that make up the so-called *Zürcher Haussegen (Zurich Home Blessing)*:

AD SIGNANDUM DOMUM CONTRA DIABOLUM
wola, wiht, taz tu weist,   taz tu wiht heizist,
Taz tu neweist noch nechanst   cheden chnospinci.

The following translation has been proposed: "How good, wight, that you know that your name is wight, / that you can neither know nor speak chnospinci." "Chnospinci" is a word that does not occur in any other text— and it must have been meant to appear unfamiliar to the users of this charm, too. A meaning can be construed, however, based on the diminutive form of a word close to the modern *Knospe* (bud). Such guessing would make "chnospinci" more or less synonymous with "wight"—and turn it into another potential name for the devil (or the evil spirit) to whom this charm is addressed. The magical knowledge presupposed here is, then, that having a specific name for a thing (or for an evil spirit) is having power over it. Consequently, this text suggests that the evil spirit does not know at least one of its names—which gives those who know the name power over him. But why would this magic name be "chnospinci"—of all possible words? The reason may simply be that a phonetically complex sound sequence fits the expectation for a magical word. But perhaps a more complex word also makes the im-

plication more convincing that the evil spirit will never be able to learn it—
and thus will never regain power over himself.

Charms were meant to function by producing a fusion between a mythological past and a present full of challenges. During transitional periods—a
foundational period in German culture—the genre seems to have survived by
keeping together the pagan culture of a pagan past and the present and future
of a Christian culture. In modern times, the German charms are as thoroughly
forgotten as the Germanic culture which began to recede by the 8th century,
as if it could no longer hold onto the Christian present, into a past that appears
much more remote to us than Greek and Roman antiquity. Yet, while charms
as a genre are far from any modern conception of literature, their magic mechanisms suggest a relationship of immediate tangibility to the things of the
world which Western poetry—somehow unknowingly—has always presupposed and cultivated, since its own Occitan beginnings in the late 11th and
early 12th centuries.

See also 800, 830, 930, 1027

Bibliography: Walter Haubrichs, "Zauber und Segen," in J. Heinzle, ed., *Die Anfänge: Versuche volkssprachiger Schriftlichkeit im frühen Mittelalter (ca 700–1050/60),* vol. I/1: *Geschichte der deutschen Literatur von den Anfängen bis zum Beginn der Neuzeit* (Frankfurt am Main, 1988), 412–436. "Zauber- und Segensprüche," in Walter Haug and Benedikt Konrad Vollmann, eds., *Frühe deut-sche Literatur und lateinische Literatur in Deutschland 800–1150,* Bibliothek des Mittelalters, vol. 1, Deutsche Klassiker Bibliothek, vol. 62 (Frankfurt am Main, 1991), 151–161, 1141–1168.

Hans Ulrich Gumbrecht

Circa 800

Charlemagne orders that the vernacular heroic poems be recorded at his Palace
School in Aachen

The Carolingian Renaissance

In 794, the twenty-seventh year of his reign, Charles, King of the Franks
and the Lombards and Patrician of the Romans (747?–814), settles at Aachen
for the remaining years of his life. In his *Vita Karoli Magni* (before 835; *Life of
Charlemagne,* ch. 22) Einhard the Frank (ca. 770–840) attributes this choice to
the local hot springs which allowed his former master to enjoy the benefits of
steam bathing, but evidently Charles had more substantial aspirations. His
realm, which now included almost all of what was to become France and Germany, as well as the middle Danube region, northern and central Italy, and
northeast Spain, could no longer be governed by a peripatetic warrior-king
and his court. So he decided to take up residence at the very core of the old
Frankish kingdom, not too far from the problem regions of his empire: the
Danish frontier, Saxony and the adjacent Slavic territories, Bohemia, and the
hideouts of the Avars. From here he could hope to launch the great work of
military, institutional, economic, and religious consolidation he apparently had

been planning for many years with his counselors, among whom were some of the most distinguished scholars of Europe.

When Charles sends out from Aachen his first fundamental edicts, the *General Admonition* and the *Double Edict of Commission,* in 789, "his" palace and the Palace Chapel are still under construction. Both are erected, at great expense, on the grounds of a royal villa with an oratory that dated back to his father Pippin's time. But however provisional the court's installation is at the first, the year 789 marks a turning point in the governmental history of Western Europe. As Charles announces in the preamble of the *Admonition,* henceforth his orders will be transmitted in written form, after having been summed up in "articles" *(capitula),* and their enactment will be enforced through special itinerant "commissioners" *(missi)* bearing his instructions. We know from one of his later admonitory letters that it took almost twenty years for all of his subjects to willingly obey laws that were not promulgated by the king in person (letter to his son Pippin, after 805; *Capitularia* 1, 212). Notwithstanding, Charles, who himself never learned to write, increasingly insists on having all official matters set down in writing—regulations and privileges as well as judicial evidence and periodical reports by *missi* and counts from all over his vast territory.

Aachen finally becomes the seat of the famous Palace School, at a time when most of its founding figures are no longer at the court. Paul the Deacon (d. ca. 797) has already returned to his convent at Monte Cassino; Paulinus (d. 802) and Theodulf (ca. 755–821) have left, the former to become the Patriarch of Aquileia, the latter to occupy the See of Orleans; and Peter of Pisa (d. before 799), being advanced in age, has gone back to his native country as well; only a few years later, even Alcuin (ca. 735–804) retires more and more to the Abbey of Saint Martin at Tours, which was conferred on him in 796. Still, though absent, the members of Charles's "academy" *(academici vestri)* continue to make their contributions to the king's great enterprise. At his departure, Paul is commissioned to obtain from Pope Hadrian a valid Sacramentary text to serve as master-copy *(authenticus)* for liturgical use throughout the Frankish realm. Moreover, "out of obedience," he sends from his monastery his new homiliary, which Charles subsequently imposes on all "the religious lectors subject to our dominion" in a circular letter written to that effect (*Letter to the Lectors,* after 786). Alcuin and Theodulf, competing with each other, undertake a thorough revision of the text of "all the books of the Old and New Testaments, corrupted by the ignorance of copyists," a project that the very same circular—a bit rashly, it seems—claims was carried out "long ago" *(iam pridem)* on Charles's orders.

In 794 the two rivals, together with Paulinus, who has come back from Italy for the occasion, are editing, in Charles's name, the statements of the Frankfurt synodal council on the sonship of Christ and the adoration of images. Peter, who had been the king's Latin tutor, is asked to make available a master copy of his adaptation of Donatus's *Ars minor,* in a last, revised version. So the temporary, then permanent dispersion of Charles's entourage prepares the ground for more independent contributions and, not least, for a lively exchange of letters and verse-epistles centered on the court at Aachen.

But, of course, the influence of Charles's original staff diminishes with time, as Alcuin in particular is to experience in the last years of his life, when the next generation takes over: Einhard, who through his artistic interests also makes himself useful as supervisor of public works at Aachen ("Bezaleel"); Angilbert (d. 814), poet ("Homer"), diplomat, and recognized lover of Charles's daughter Bertha; Fridugis (d. 834), at Charles's request author of a *Letter on the Nature of Nothing* (after 804; *De substantia nihili et tenebrarum*) and afterward arch-chancellor of Charles's heir, Louis the Pious.

Throughout this period, "David," as Alcuin customarily addresses his patron, is the undisputed head of the academy. In fact, Charles coauthors the productions of his academicians in almost the same manner as he does his own releases, which he could not edit without assistance. It is always he who takes the initiative, he who sets the topics and the approach to be taken. In Alcuin's somewhat flowery words, he "rouses" his crew "from [their] idleness by posing shrewd questions" (to Charles, 789; letter 136). When the work is accomplished in conformity with his intentions, the proposed text is read aloud to him *(recitari)*. He approves *(probat)* or rejects it, and returns the whole draft with a list of desired modifications (cf. Alcuin to Charles, April–May 799, letter 172). Naturally, this kind of collaboration is possible only thanks to Charles's tremendous capacity for grasping complex issues in oral transmission and his excellent textual memory. Alcuin can be confident that Charles understands even obscure biblical allusions, and the court is impressed by the king's unhesitating participation in the Latin liturgy of the Mass and the Divine Offices (Einhard, ch. 26).

Charles, for his part, upholds his own belated conversion to learning and literacy as a shining example to his subjects. "We summon whom we can, even by our own example, to master the studies of the liberal arts," he proclaims in his *Letter to the Lectors*. The king, the foremost student of his realm! Einhard's survey of the royal curriculum is overwhelming: grammar under Peter, all other liberal arts under Alcuin, including rhetoric, dialectics, and, the *Vita* adds enthusiastically, especially astronomy: "He applied himself to mathematics *(ars computandi)* and traced the course of the stars with great attention and care" (ch. 25). However, Charles's interest is never merely literary or scientific; at no time does he endorse the maxim his youthful admirer Lupus of Ferrières (ca. 805–after 862) adopts fifty years later, that "wisdom should be sought for its own sake" (to Einhard, ca. 835; letter 1). His foremost concern is the reform of the liturgy and the reorganization of the largely illiterate Frankish clergy, in order to ensure that God is worshipped in the right way, and in the same way, throughout his kingdom. Appropriately he alludes to his father's decision to "abolish the Gallican chant for the sake of unanimity with the Apostolic See and the peaceful harmony of God's Holy Church" (*General Admonition,* ch. 80).

Roman orthodoxy is the link that unites the manifold peoples under

Charles's dominion to form one *populus christianus.* Thus the stability of his realm depends, as it were, on the availability of the Gospel, the Psalter, and the Missal in their genuine versions in every monastery, on the unadulterated transmission of Christian doctrine through preaching in every parish, on the assiduous attendance of all the "faithful" *(fideles)*—in the double sense of the word—at services they fully understand. The provisions in chapters 70, 72, and 82 of the *General Admonition* are definite on these essentials and imply an extensive educational program. As the mandate *On Cultivating Letters* (between 794 and 800) points out several years later, whenever writing skills are deficient, it is to be feared that wisdom for understanding the Holy Scriptures too is less prevalent than it ought to be.

Charles's involvement in *computus,* calendar reckoning, also springs from a basic public need, the necessity to fix a reliable date for the celebration of Easter each year. His study of the art of political speech with Alcuin is a theoretical complement to his everyday official practice, as Alcuin suggests through the medium of the king's double in the opening lines of their jointly signed *Rhetoric of Alcuin and Charlemagne* (after 800). The former warrior does not even shrink from tackling intricate theological matters whenever he has to take a stand against the pretensions of the Greek Church or to prevent the infiltration of unorthodox beliefs from Visigoth Spain. Alcuin argues in the dedication letter to his major dogmatic work, the "sermon" *On Faith in the Holy and Undivided Trinity* (802; *De fide sanctae et individuae Trinitatis*), which he submits to Charlemagne, that "nobody should know better nor more than the emperor, whose knowledge *[doctrina]* may benefit all of his subjects" (letter 257). Charles was likely to agree, since "knowledge comes before action" *(On Cultivating Letters).*

However, even long before he accepts the title of emperor and is crowned by Pope Leo III on Christmas Day 800, Charles realizes that, in order to preserve his reign, he must provide a cultural as well as a religious foundation. Now that Rome is no longer the center of the (Western) Empire, Aachen must strive to be a "second Rome," even a better Rome, at any rate a different one—in political structures, legislation, representative architecture, and literary self-expression. In contrast to Rome's rigid centralism, Charles establishes a system of semi-autonomous kingdoms, parceled out to his sons and other members of his family in anticipation of future succession. He supplements his standardization of canon law, begun in the seventies, with a codification of the legal practice effective in the different parts of his realm. This was, of course, easier for Lombardy than for the original Frankish domain, as Einhard laments (ch. 29).

The layout of Charles's new residence at Aachen mirrors, at least ideally, the plan of the Roman Lateran, formerly the palace of Constantine and occupied since by the popes; the adjacent *basilica salvatoris* (the future San Giovanni in Laterano); and, in between, the equestrian statue of Marcus Aurelius, commonly called *caballus Constantini.* The octagonal construction of the Palace

Chapel was evidently inspired by Mediterranean churches such as San Vitale in Ravenna, and the royal hall seems to have been modeled on the ruins of the monumental basilica at Trier from Constantinian times. In their new historical context, however, these recognizable archetypes undergo significant modifications, as can best be seen in the unique arrangement of the Palace Chapel: from his throne in an upper gallery, the Frankish king looks down on the main altar, with the relics which have accompanied him in his battles, and on his men, who see him as he sees them. And Alcuin, who as early as 796 claimed to train his pupils in the liberal arts "for the advance of the Holy Church of God and the honor of your imperial kingdom" (to Charles, late 796; letter 121), is quite hopeful that under Charles's leadership "a new Athens" will be created in "France" *(Francia),* "indeed a far finer one," based on the teachings of Christ (to Charles, end of March 799; letter 170). There are, however, strong indications that Charles, particularly in the last phase of his reign, had in mind not only a Christian but also a Frankish Rome and Athens, a view not entirely in accordance with Alcuin's.

In a final chapter on Charles's activities (ch. 29), Einhard reports that, after his return from Rome in 801, the emperor dedicated himself, not very successfully, to harmonizing Frankish tribal laws and to compiling a vernacular grammar and nomenclature. He also gave orders to collect and write down the ancient songs of "the warlike deeds *[actus et bella]* of the kings of ancient times," to which he liked to listen during his meals (cf. ch. 24). None of these has survived, but the almost contemporary fragment of the *Hildebrandslied* (ca. 830; *Song of Hildebrand*) gives us an idea of what was lost—and maybe also of why the Frankish king attached so much importance to keeping alive this "barbarous" legacy of the past.

"Long ago he went to the east, he fled Otacher's hatred, away with Dietrich and many of his warriors" (trans. J. Knight Bostock; ll. 18–19)—this is how Hadubrand summarizes the fate of his father Hildebrand. These lines indicate that the fragment is related to the epic cycle of Theoderic's (mythical) flight and triumphant return to Ravenna. Now, notwithstanding his Arianism, Theoderic, king of the Goths and patrician of the Romans, is to Charles a distinguished forerunner, who prepared the "transfer of the Roman Empire from the Greeks to the Germanic peoples" *(translatio Romani Imperii a Graecis in Germanos)* in his own person—as Pope Innocent III was to define four hundred years later the event of Christmas Day 800. (In fact, the throne of Byzantium, usurped by the dowager Empress Irene since 797, was considered vacant in the West.) Consequently, Charles adorned the rotunda of his Palace Chapel with porphyry pillars taken from Theoderic's palace in the late nineties. Passing through Ravenna again on his way back to Aachen in May 801, the newly crowned emperor orders the statue of his precursor brought to Aachen and installed in the palace courtyard. We know from Alcuin's letters how much his patron enjoyed Virgil's poetry—"your Virgil" *(Virgilius vester),* he calls the great pagan poet disapprovingly, who nevertheless is Saint Augustine's great authority (to Charles, end of March 798; letter 145). Charlemagne might well have yearned for a new Virgil, who, inspired by the age-old songs of his people, would sing the past deeds of Dietrich/Theoderic, "who first from the east, exiled by fate, came to Italy to build, after many wars, a Germanic kingdom on Roman soil at Ravenna, whence came the Frankish Empire and the lofty palace of Aachen." The tragic encounter of father and son between two armies after an absence of sixty summers and winters, such as we glimpse it in the *Hildebrandslied,* could have constituted a conspicuous episode of this future epic.

See also 744, 830, 847

Bibliography: "Alcvini sive Albini epistolae," in *Epistolae Karolini aevi* II, ed. Ernst Dümmler = *Monumenta Germaniae Historica: Epistolae* IV (Berlin: Weidmann, 1895), partially trans. in Stephen Allott, *Alcuin of York—His Life and Letters* (York, U.K.: Sessions, 1974). *Einhardi Vita Karoli Magni,* ed. Oswald Holder-Egger (Hanover and Leipzig: Hahn, 1911), trans. Lewis Thorpe in Einhard and Notker the Stammerer, *Two Lives of Charlemagne* (Harmondsworth, U.K.: Penguin, 1969), 47–90. "Karoli Magni capitularia," in *Capitularia regum francorum* I, ed. Alfred Boretius = *Monumenta Germaniae Historica: Leges,* II, 1 (Hanover: Hahn, 1883), partially trans. P. D. King, *Charlemagne: Translated Sources* (Kendal: P. D. King, 1987). *Disputatio de rhetorica et de virtutibus sapientissimi regis Karli et Albini magistri,* ed. and trans. Wilbur Samuel Howell, *The Rhetoric of Alcuin and Charlemagne,* Princeton Studies in English 23 (Princeton, N.J.: Princeton University Press, 1941). Bernhard Bischoff, "The Court Library of Charlemagne," in Bischoff, *Manuscripts and Libraries in the Age of Charlemagne,* trans. Michael Gorman, Cambridge Studies in Paleography and Codicology 1 (Cambridge and New York: Cambridge University Press, 1994). Rosamond McKitterick, *Carolingian Culture: Emulation and Innovation* (Cambridge and New York: Cambridge University Press, 1994), esp. chapters by Giles Brown, Mary Garrison, Matthew Innes and McKitterick, Vivien Law, and Janet L. Nelson.

Karl Maurer

ℒ *Circa 830*

Sixty-eight lines of verse are copied onto the flyleaves of a theological manuscript in the Fulda monastery

Heroic or Vernacular Poetry?

The earliest fragment of German imaginative literature, sixty-eight lines of alliterative verse now known as *Hildebrandslied* or *Hildebrandlied (Song of Hildebrand),* was copied onto the flyleaves of a theological manuscript from Fulda about 830, by current paleographic estimates. No indications exist about the circumstances of composition. The copy is clearly the work of two scribes, perhaps an instructor and an apprentice, and is written in Carolingian minuscule, one of the triumphs of Charlemagne's school reforms. Interspersed are some characteristics that seem to reflect the Anglo-Saxon origin of the Fulda monastery, which was founded by the English missionary Saint Boniface in 744. The language itself contains an unusual mixture of North and South German (Bavarian) peculiarities that raise several, as yet unsolvable, philological questions. A generally held view, though not universally accepted, presumes that North German orthographic styles were superimposed on a Bavarian original, but there is no good explanation for how or why such a macaronic text was created in the first place.

No less baffling are the details of the narrative. The first line is elliptical, and the poem breaks off before the action is completed, so that the situation at the beginning and end is unclear. The opening could be construed to mean: "The warriors Hildebrand and Hadubrand met alone between two armies." They are obviously expected to do battle, but whether on behalf of their respective armies in a public showdown, like latter-day Horatii or Curiatii, or because of a chance meeting during a larger battle, or before battle, is not clear. Whatever the actual circumstances, the text proceeds to reveal that Hildebrand and Hadubrand are father and son, but do not recognize each other after long years of separation. Hildebrand inquires into his opponent's lineage and Hadubrand responds by stating that according to what he knows his father was a certain Hildebrand, who fled eastward with (or perhaps to join) Dietrich and to escape Odoacer's enmity. Hildebrand exclaims that Hadubrand had never addressed a kinsman as close as him, but Hadubrand accuses him of Hunnish trickery and rejects precious arm rings proffered on the tip of a spear. Hildebrand therefore mournfully concedes that he is compelled to fight, and the description of the battle proceeds for six lines until the text breaks off at the bottom of the second page.

How did the fight end? In a much later fragment of Icelandic verse, Hildebrand laments the killing of his own son, leading us to believe that this was also the outcome of the *Hildebrandslied*. But there are conflicting indications. Later German texts, *þiðreks saga* (a Norse reworking of German materials from the end of the 12th century) and a 15th-century ballad version ("Das jüngere Hildebrandslied") document a conciliatory outcome in which Hadubrand is defeated, identifies himself, and is embraced by his father. Nor is the story confined to Germanic literature. There are versions from many lands, notably Persia, Ireland, and Russia. In these texts, the son invariably dies at the hands of his father. The conciliatory variant, therefore, is generally considered to be a late, even vapid, distortion of the tragic original.

In Germanic territory, the earliest comparable account is the one in *þiðreks saga*. Here Hildebrand (Hildibrandr) spends twenty years in exile with his lord Dietrich (þiðrekr) at the court of the Hunnish king Attila, after Dietrich had been driven out of Italy by King Ermanaric (Jǫrmunrekkr). Eventually Dietrich reclaims his realm. Hildibrandr, who accompanies him on his return journey, learns on the road to Verona of the presence of his son Alibrandr. When they meet, a dialogue ensues, in the course of which both parties refuse repeatedly to identify themselves. The combat proceeds in several increments until Alibrandr feigns defeat and tries to deliver a trick blow. Hildibrandr subdues him and extracts his name with a demand that is tantamount to a concession: "If you want to save your life, tell me quickly whether you are my son

Alibrandr." This leads to recognition and reconciliation in this version of the story, but whether it constitutes evidence that the *Hildebrandslied* also ended in reconciliation remains open.

The account in *þiðreks saga* does, however, suggest a larger narrative context for the old lay, and several of the details in the two stories can be reconciled. Line 18 of *Hildebrandslied* states that Hildebrand went east with Dietrich. Line 27 makes it clear that he was militarily active, as in *þiðreks saga*. Lines 33–35 indicate that he received rewards from "the lord of the Huns," and line 50 clarifies that he spent "sixty summers and winters," that is, thirty years, abroad. Although this outline corresponds to the situation in *þiðreks saga*, we cannot be certain that the 9th-century narrative matches the 12th-century one in all details.

On one aspect we can be certain that they did not. In *þiðreks saga* Dietrich is driven into exile by the usurper Ermanaric, but in the *Hildebrandslied* we are told (line 18) "he fled from Odoacer's hostility" *(floh her Otachres nid)*. The mention of Odoacer's name leads to a historical revelation. Dietrich is for good reason identified with the great Ostrogothic king Theodoric (d. 526), who did, in fact, have dealings with Odoacer. The Germanic military leader Odoacer was proclaimed King of Italy in 476, but was dethroned and killed by Theodoric in 493. The *Hildebrandslied* reverses these events by allowing Odoacer to dethrone Theodoric. How and why Theodoric, in his legendary afterlife, became the hero of a story of exile and repatriation is not clear, but this recasting is not the only historical distortion. Later legend also has Dietrich and Hildebrand spend their exile years at the court of the historical King Attila, but this is chronologically impossible since Attila died in 453, forty years before Theodoric conquered Italy.

It is, nonetheless, generically significant that the *Hildebrandslied,* however unhistorical in detail, is embedded in early medieval history, which is a fundamental property of heroic poetry, the only well-attested genre from the early Germanic period, with traces in Old English and Old Norse as well. The best known of these traditions are the stories of Brunhild and Siegfried, and their sequel, the destruction of the Burgundians by the Huns. These legends are transmitted in several variants in the *Poetic Edda, þiðreks saga,* and the *Nibelungenlied*. Here, too, are traces of a historical foundation. The names of the Burgundian kings (Gunther and his brothers) are historically documented, Attila (Etzel) again figures prominently, and the destruction of the Burgundians can be correlated with an event chronicled in 435. As a work anchored in Ostrogothic history—a feature of Germanic heroic poetry—the *Hildebrandslied* can be classified as belonging to that genre. Its classification as heroic poetry has encouraged preference for a tragic outcome, since this too is a feature of Germanic heroic poetry.

Since such poetry is slightly better documented in Old English and significantly better documented in Old Norse than in German, there is a tendency to classify the *Hildebrandslied* with Germanic literary prehistory rather than with the history of Carolingian literature, where it would virtually stand alone. The vernacular literatures in Old High German and Old Saxon offer few points of comparison, but, given the survival of heroic verse elsewhere in the Germanic world, a rich vein of heroic verse in Germany can be supposed. Such a supposition gains credence through the assumption that the epic *Nibelungenlied* (ca. 1200) stands at the end of a long oral evolution of such stories.

Prominent in this oral tradition is a passage in Einhard's *Life of Charlemagne,* which may have been written shortly after the king's death in 814 or perhaps as late as 830, close to the date of our copy of the *Hildebrandslied.* According to Einhard (chapter 29): "Similarly he [Charlemagne] caused to be written down and preserved in memory the very ancient barbarian poems in which the deeds and wars of former kings were celebrated." Since this comment is part of a discussion of Charlemagne's interest in Germanic law codes and is followed by a note that he also initiated a grammar of his own native language (Frankish), it is reasonable to suppose that the poems referred to were in the vernacular. One scholar, Friedrich von der Leyen, tried to make an inventory list of the heroic poems that might have been transcribed in this collection and hypothesized that there were no fewer than twenty-five, of which only the *Hildebrandslied* survives.

In Germany only one remotely comparable literary document is still extant, a poem in 1456 Latin hexameters which is known as the *Waltharius.* Although its authorship and date are uncertain, most scholars place it somewhere in the 9th century. However, the *Waltharius* is not quite as devoid of context as the *Hildebrandslied* because there is a fairly substantial amount of Latin poetry from the Carolingian period. Stylistically the *Waltharius* fits in well with the poetry composed at the time of Charlemagne, which might well reflect an interest in native heroic poetry, a tradition of which the protagonist Walter of Aquitaine is as much a part as Hildebrand and Dietrich. Only, in this instance, the native poem was not transcribed in the vernacular but recast in Virgilian hexameters. Consequently, the *Waltharius* is not compressed and allusive, like the *Hildebrandslied,* but broadly epic and descriptive.

Once again, Attila the Hun figures at the center of the action. He descends like a whirlwind on the western realms, subduing the Franks, Burgundians, and Aquitanians, and takes hostage three noble youths, the Frank Hagano, the Burgundian princess Hiltgunt, and the Aquitanian prince Walter. Hagano soon escapes, leaving Walter and Hiltgunt behind. Walter, not unlike Hildebrand, distinguishes himself in Hunnish military service. In the meantime, he and Hiltgunt fall in love, as their parents had always intended, and together they plan their escape. With considerable wit and verve, they make their way west under cover of night. When they reach the Vosges Mountains, they encounter King Guntharius and a retinue of twelve Frankish warriors, as well as Hagano. After a series of epic combats, the finale of which seems a travesty of heroic style, the three survivors are reconciled. Walter marries Hiltgunt, and the couple rules happily in Spain for thirty years.

The cast of characters guarantees that this very readable poem is an offshoot of Germanic heroic traditions—Attila, Guntharius, Hagano, and Waltharius, all return to the stage in the *Nibelungenlied*. However, the happy, even comic, conclusion sets the *Waltharius* distinctly apart from other works in that tradition. While all Norse and English heroic poems end in tragedy, one, and possibly both, of the German works end on a harmonious note. Somewhat paradoxically, then, the *Waltharius* serves not so much to link the *Hildebrandslied* with the Germanic tradition as to reinforce the possibility that it too might be generically anomalous. This has considerable implications since putting in doubt the tragic tenor of the *Hildebrandslied* overturns the commonly held view of how German literature began. Perhaps half-consciously, it has been presumed that it originated under the sign of tragic ineluctability, a pagan cheerlessness destined only with time to yield to a Christian redemption theology in the texts that actually survive. It is, however, disconcerting to contemplate on how tenuous a thread hangs this view that Hildebrand was fated to kill his son.

This assumption may have something to do with the moment in modern German history when the *Hildebrandslied* was appropriated and magnified. Georg Baesecke's popular edition and introduction in the last months of World War II connected the first scholarly publication by the Grimm Brothers in 1812 with the *Freiheitskriege*—the wars of liberation from Napoleonic rule in Germany, Italy, and Spain. The Grimm brothers' edition was in fact entirely free of national and heroic strains, though these undercurrents gradually swelled in the course of the 19th century and culminated in Baesecke's patriotic exhortations in 1945. More recently, this type of rhetoric has yielded to interest in placing the *Hildebrandslied* within the cultural activity in the first great period of German letters, the Carolingian Renaissance, rather than a lost Germanic legacy.

It is easy to exaggerate the idea of heroism in the poem. Can heroism really be reconciled with a father's compulsion to kill his son—especially when the overriding obligation is set out as vaguely as in the *Hildebrandslied?* All attempts to rationalize the compulsion under which Hildebrand stands rest on conjectures about insult in heroic society or rules of formal combat between opposing armies which, in this case, bind father and son. Heroic life exerted a particular fascination in the 19th century, a matter that has been explored in some depth as it relates to the early reception of the character of Siegfried in the *Nibelungenlied*. But it is far from certain that a 19th-century model is appropriate for a 9th-century text. Ninth-century audiences may have been struck first by the fact that circumstances can be so compelling as to pit a father against his son rather than that Hildebrand fulfills the public expectation of a warrior at any cost. Public vindication may have been secondary to private horror.

In other words, the audience may have responded more to the sundering of family bonds than to the preservation of a warrior ethic. Family loss is indeed a universal theme in what we now call Germanic heroic poetry, and family affection generally dominates moral issues. Einhard often points to Charlemagne's predilection for heroic poems, and we may, therefore, ask what aspect Charlemagne himself responded to most. He, no doubt, valued heroic literature as a formidable military campaigner (in fact as well as in fiction), but what is less often remarked on is his emotional attachment to his family. That affection is detailed at some length in Einhard's *Life* (chapters 18–20).

The traditional theme of a chance confrontation between a father and son always contained a choice between a hard and a soft option. That the German tradition was more open to the soft option, and at an earlier date, is sufficiently demonstrated in the *Waltharius*. Perhaps the soft option was incorporated into the *Hildebrandslied* only at a later date, but we can never be certain that it was not already present in the lost conclusion of the poem we have. If not explicitly realized, it was at least present by implication. As long as family solidarity was a cultural value, the tragic option, most fully realized in Ferdowsi's *Book of Kings* (ca. 1000), was never proof against the thought of reconciliation.

It is precisely the irrationality and implausibility of a father-son battle to the death that has made a satisfactory interpretation of the text so difficult. Attempts to uncover something in early medieval thinking—honor, uncompromising heroism, guilt, higher obligation—that would make the paradox comprehensible, have yielded so far no compelling results. It may in fact be that contemporary listeners reacted with the same disbelief that is seemingly natural for us, or indeed that the poem was calculated to provoke mental resistance rather than acquiescence. Sooner or later that resistance produced the more palatable resolution in *þiðreks saga* and "Das jüngere Hildebrandslied." The actual modification of the plot may not have occurred in the 9th century, but the pressure for change is at the core of the poem. Listeners, then as now, would have argued for resolution, although we cannot know whether their demands were met. The human strain oscillates between tragic and comic dénouements, but only in German literature did the strain ultimately break the tragic mold once and for all to vindicate the integrity of the family. What the *Hildebrandslied* may most centrally be about is the tension between alternatives, rather than a particular outcome.

See also 744, 800, 930, ca. 1200, 1815

Bibliography: Jakob and Wilhelm Grimm, *Die beiden ältesten deutschen Gedichte aus dem achten Jahrhundert: Das Lied von Hildebrand und Hadubrand und das Weissenbrunner Gebet zum erstenmal in ihrem Metrum dargestellt und herausgegeben* (Cassel: Thurneisen, 1812). Facsimiles of the two MS leaves in Georg Baesecke, *Das Hildebrandlied: Eine geschichtliche Einleitung für Laien, mit Lichtbildern der Handschrift, alt- und neuhochdeutschen Texten* (Halle: Niemeyer, 1945). J. Knight Bostock, *A Handbook on Old High German Literature,* rev. K. C. King and D. R. McLintock (Oxford, U.K.: Clarendon, 1976), 43–82. Ferdowsi, *The Epic of the Kings: Shah-nama, the National Epic of Persia,* trans. Reuben Levy (Costa Mesa, Calif., and New York: Mazda Publishers/Bibliotheca Persica, 1996), 47–80. Peter Goodman, *Poetry of the Carolingian Renaissance* (Norman: University of Oklahoma Press, 1985).

Theodore M. Andersson

⟨ 847, October

Archbishop Rabanus Maurus convenes a synod to discuss conveying sacred doctrine to an illiterate populace

A Vernacular Gospel Harmony

The day is early October in the year 847. The place: Mainz on the Rhine, the *metropolis Germaniae*—or more precisely, the renowned ancient royal monastery of St. Alban's. The aging Rabanus Maurus, who resigned as abbot of Fulda five years earlier, has made peace with his adversary King Louis "the German" (833–876) and has been named archbishop and head of the Church of the East Frankish realm. The churchman wants to make another attempt to reform the Church in accord with Charlemagne's ideals by taking up where the synods of the year 813 left off. The delegates to this synod form two groups: the cloistered clergy with their abbots presiding, and the non-cloistered clergy led by their bishops. The discussion concerns how to convey sacred Church doctrine to that portion of the populace unable to read. The priests, at least, should be versed in the Gospels and the Church doctrines and should be able to read, understand, and preach them. Sermons should have the proper content, namely the foundations of the faith; they should also emphasize that good works will be rewarded in heaven and evil deeds lead to eternal damnation. They should also explain the Resurrection and the Last Judgment. At stake is the salvation of human souls, which is attained through educated, enlightened faith. The form of sermons, considered as instruments of education rather than ritual acts within the Mass, is also at issue. As the central tool for carrying the word of God to all the faithful, sermons must be accessible and understandable, whether the priest uses a Romance language or a Germanic tongue.

Rabanus's synod quoted from a council of 813 that had been inspired by Charlemagne in the last year of his life and gave impetus to use the vernacular as part of the pastoral obligation to preach the Gospel and to evangelize. However, the guidelines drawn up by the synod go a step further: priests who are members of the aristocracy—accustomed to owning their own churches, wearing swords and fine clothes, and participating in hunts and banquets—are barred from speaking or writing on any but sacred themes, just as monks are. As was stated in many pastoral directives of the time, priests were expressly prohibited from writing works containing scandalous language or humor and attending secular plays and concerts. They were enjoined not to tolerate profane jokes and games at their tables and to listen to sacred readings during meals instead.

The recommendation was all well and good, but where could this kind of material be found? Where were the poems in the vernacular on sacred themes that could compare with the popular heroic epics or minstrel lays? It is certainly no accident that almost at the same time as Rabanus's recommendations are devised, the Saxon epic *Heliand* is composed at the Fulda monastery where

Rabanus had been abbot. The *Heliand* is a monumental poem on the life and teachings of Christ in the form of traditional Germanic epics. The learned monks of Fulda had already produced a translation of the Gospel Harmony by the Syrian author Tatian, for use at the monastery school. Nor is it an accident that some twenty years later Otfrid of Weissenburg, a pupil of Rabanus, attempted to combine both injunctions—namely translating Christian teachings into the vernacular and applying Christian themes in poetry—in one biblical poetic work, which he subsequently dedicated to the East Frankish king, Louis the German. The result was the *Liber evangeliorum* (863–872; *Book of the Gospels*).

As in Late Antiquity, the intended audience of *illiterati,* people without training in theology, mentioned in both the Latin preface to the *Heliand* and Otfrid's vernacular introduction, made an epic treatment of the Bible necessary. The story had to be related in a vivid manner with scenes that could serve as the basis for pious meditation. Otfrid's inclusion of exegetical material in particular, following the model from Late Antiquity, gives the poetry a quality of edification not achieved by the biblical text alone. Otfrid not only invented a sophisticated system of correspondences and links between narrative (that occasionally rises to the level of devotional scenes) and theological exegesis; he also reflects on and attempts to justify the grammar and spelling of his Frankish tongue, which he calls "barbaric" as compared to Latin. While it does not conform to the rules of classical languages, it does possess its own *slithi* (regularity). This is also true of the rhyming meter that Otfrid certainly imported from oral poetry. It does not fulfill the requirements of ancient hexameters, but it far outshines its ancient model in content. In contrast to the biblical poetry of Late Antiquity, Otfrid's Christian poetry consists in hexameters of content; its true meter is the six ages of the world within which salvific history unfolds. To "walk in the law of the Lord" in these six ages, as called for at the start of Psalm 119, is to fill more than the six feet of hexameter verse. "Verse" of true Christian beauty fulfills itself not in metric regularity but in obedience to divine commandments; it derives its beauty from the seventh age of peace and contemplation in the hereafter, in the sight of God. The aesthetics of edification remains primary here, again as in the tradition of the biblical epics of Late Antiquity. The incorporation of exegetical meaning into the narrative establishes the primacy of devotion and relegates the logic required by the epic form to the background.

In the introduction to his poem on the gospels, Otfrid also introduces a political motive that makes the connection with the kingdom fully explicit. Next to the revered *edilzungen*—the noble, even holy tongues of the Greeks and Romans—he places the language of the Franks, which derives its *rectitudo* or "right measure" from the poem's sacred content. Had the Frankfurt Synod in 794 not established that God could be praised in any language? Now at last, three generations later, someone is taking up the challenge of Charlemagne's theologians, who had asked: "Why should Franks hesitate, why shouldn't they begin to sing God's praises in the Frankish language?" Otfrid adds a new argument to the self-justificatory rationale of the biblical poetry of Late Antiquity. He bases his argument on the historical position of the Franks, on the rank they occupy in both secular and salvation history. Franks share the same faith as the later Romans, but they are also the equals of the imperial Romans as soldiers and farmers, in economic and political power, as well as their god-given historical role. The *translatio imperii* (transfer of the empire) brings in its wake the *translatio studii* (transfer of education). Literature, too, particularly sacred poetry, is a representative feature of a ruling people. Otfrid wants the *Book of the Gospels* to be explicitly understood as "national" poetry, the poetry of the people of the Frankish Empire.

Who was this monk named Otfrid, who attempted to achieve three goals in his work: to transform the word of God into poetry, to supplant native poetry, and to turn the Frankish vernacular into a literary tool for the transmission of the message of the Scriptures? Born at the beginning of the 9th century, he took the vows of a Benedictine monk in the second or third decade of the century at the royal monastery of Weissenburg in the diocese of Speyer. At the monastery he was trained as a scribe; numerous official documents he wrote are preserved as copies. He himself notes that one of his teachers was the distinguished Carolingian scholar Rabanus Maurus, abbot of Fulda (822–842) and archbishop of Mainz (847–852). Otfrid must have been in Fulda during the 820s and 830s when learned monks collaborated under Rabanus's direction to produce the great biblical commentaries that unified the patristic exegetical tradition and to translate into Old High German the Gospel Harmony of the Syrian philosopher Tatian. The degree to which Otfrid was influenced by Rabanus's scholarship shows in the exegetical method of his *Book of the Gospels* and in the way in which he—now a *magister* and probably in charge of the monastery library at Weissenburg—increased the size of the book collection by acting as a scribe himself. Between 845 and 870 the size of the library doubled, and Otfrid personally participated in the production of one-third of the new manuscripts. Taking Rabanus's chain commentaries as his starting point, Otfrid developed a plan for a series of marginal glosses on the entire Bible, which created the foundation for more intensive study of God's word at the monastery school.

Otfrid's dedications of his work indicate that his scholarly reputation reached beyond the monastery walls. In addition to a dedication to the king, whose chaplain and chancellor, Grimald, was Otfrid's abbot (847–872), the poet wrote dedications to Liutbert, the king's archchaplain and archbishop of Mainz (863–889), and to Bishop Solomon I of Constance (839–871), who also had ties to the Frankish court. The last named he cites as his teacher along with Rabanus. Otfrid also had notable connections with the monastery at Saint Gall, where Grimald was also abbot. He was on good terms there with two leading figures of the time, Hartmuot and Werinbert. Hartmuot was dean and prior at Saint Gall from 849 to 872, and later abbot until 883, as well as head of the *scriptorium*. Under his leadership the library collection grew to more than four hundred volumes. Hartmuot also oversaw the copying of a Bible in eight volumes, giving Saint Gall the most modern biblical text of its day. Werinbert, the first Benedictine monk at the monastery, was himself a scribe and owner of a Virgil manuscript. He also taught at the monastery school, where he numbered Notker Balbulus (ca. 840–912), later a noted historian and poet of sequence plainchant, among his pupils. Otfrid also dedicated a copy of his Gospel Harmony to two fellow monks at Saint Gall in recognition of their learning.

What, in fact, is a Gospel Harmony? It is the first step toward transforming sacred history into epic, not by placing the statements of the four gospels side by side, but by evaluating the text and arranging it in chronological order. Tatian was the first to do this in AD 170. The original Latin translation of his work had been kept at Fulda since the time of Saint Boniface (d. 754), where it was translated into Old High German. Copies made at the great monastery east of the Rhine circulated throughout the Latin West. But unlike the author of the *Heliand,* Otfrid did not closely adhere to the model established by Tatian. He developed his own structure, based on modern theology and principles of rhetoric and narrative organization. His ordering of the material goes beyond pure epic and portrays the saving truth of the Christian mystery. In an *ordo artificialis,* Otfrid created five books with 140 chapters, which he interwove, in a magnificent and original manner, with the aspect of Christ's humanity derived mainly from the synoptic gospels (Saint Matthew, Saint Luke, and Saint Mark) and the divine nature of the Redeemer taken from Saint John.

One peculiar aspect of Otfrid's translation of the gospels into poetry is his narration of theology. In fact, Christ as he appears in the *Book of the Gospels* goes far beyond the biblical model, insofar as he comments on and interprets the plot. While the exegesis of God's word is thus woven into the main narrative, the work also contains a complex apparatus of commentary and interpretation. As a former student at the schools of Rabanus and at Fulda and a scholar concerned with improving the study of exegesis even at Weissenburg, Otfrid also sought to present to his readers and listeners a spiritual level of meaning. Here, too, he followed the tradition of older biblical poetry that strove to make the symbolic structure of the Holy Scriptures transparent despite extensive use of mysterious analogies. By presenting the spiritual meaning not only within the main narrative, but also in separate chapters with summaries of allegorical exegesis and instructions for the reader in the headings, he approached once more the Carolingian method of distinguishing the different levels of understanding.

Otfrid's genuine achievement, unique in the early medieval period, consists in the way he combined the narrative and exegesis of the sacred story without losing sight of the individual levels of meaning. The transformation of the prose narrative into epic poetry, bringing the events alive, was to serve the *aedificatio* (edification) of readers and hearers alike. However, edification cannot consist merely in the retelling of the narrated events. Care must be taken to prevent misunderstandings or even heresies from arising among the populace addressed. Otfrid's *Book of the Gospels* is a supreme product of Carolingian theology as it consistently seeks to allow its audience to share in the interpreted Word, which could only be achieved in the language of the people, and, at the same time, is concerned with mediation through the unique character of its exegesis. The poet thus surpasses in quality the commentaries of the school of Rabanus and most of Carolingian spiritual poetry in Latin. The aim of this work of edification is to present, interpret, and communicate the synthetic meaning of the Gospels, while the building blocks of the synthesis remain secondary. It is in its content, edifying the new, the inner man, and transforming life, that this poetry finds its essence.

See also 744, 800, 1027

Bibliography: Oskar Erdmann and Ludwig Wolff, eds., *Otfrids Evangelienbuch* (Tübingen, 1962). H. Butzmann, ed., *Otfrid von Weißenburg: Evangelienharmonie* (Facsimile edition of the Cod. Vindobonensis 2687 of the Austrian National Library; 1972). J. K. Bostock, *A Handbook on Old High German Literature,* rev. K. D. King and D. R. McLintock, 2nd ed. (Oxford, U.K., 1976), 190–211. Cyril Edwards, "German Vernacular Literature: A Survey," in *Carolingian Culture: Emulation and Innovation* (Cambridge, U.K., 1993), 141–170.

Wolfgang Haubrichs
Translated by Deborah Lucas Schneider

𝒬 930
The Icelandic Commonwealth is founded

Old Norse Literature

In 930 AD, give or take a year or two, Iceland invented itself as a nation. Discovered by Scandinavian seafarers a half century earlier, the northern terra nova proved attractive to those who, in the straitened political and economic conditions of the Viking Age, wanted free land to work out of reach of the long arm of monarchy. From about 870 on, a steady flow of settlers migrated westward from the mainlands. Although these migrants from diverse geographical areas managed to communicate across the language dialects they brought with them from their homelands, they did less well in matters of law, in which imported differences proved disruptive to the emerging community. According to an early historian, some leading citizens got together and sent a man named Ulfljót to Norway to study the laws of certain western districts with an eye to adapting them to Icelandic conditions. Because both peoples were still illiterate at the time, Ulfljót's study was a matter of observation, memory, and oral report. The result was a constitution that provided a uniform law, a fixed number of chieftaincies, and annual assemblies with legislative and judicial functions at both the district and national level, to be attended by all free men. At the first meeting of the national assembly or Althing in about 930, the so-called Icelandic Commonwealth came into being.

The importance of this singular development in the history of early European literature cannot be overstated. At a moment when the rest of the northern world was consolidating into national monarchies, the Icelanders in effect institutionalized a version of the political system of the tribal past—a system that, lacking an executive function, relied on private enforcement not only of the social rules but also of the official judgments of courts of law. Instead of a king, Iceland had one official, the Lawspeaker, who was elected for a three-year term and whose job it was to recite and explain the law as needed. Even more remarkable, perhaps, is the fact that this system lasted for more than three centuries—the Commonwealth Period—until Iceland passed under Norwegian sovereignty in 1262. It is hardly surprising that a culture that chose to preserve some version of the political structure, including the mechanism of feud, that prevailed in an earlier era throughout the Germanic world should also preserve recognizable versions of that world's literary traditions. When the Icelanders began writing, approximately a century and a half after adopting Christianity at the Althing near the year 1000, one of the things they wrote down were the tales of the legendary heroes and, indeed, of the pagan gods— subject matter that had long been eclipsed elsewhere in the Germanic world by Christian teaching, courtly culture, and Latin learning more generally.

This is not to say that Scandinavia in general and Iceland in particular remained untouched by mainstream medieval culture. On the contrary, European saints' lives, homilies, and other clerical and learned literature circulated in early Norse renditions, as did romances and other works popular in the medieval world. In fact, the very first sagas on native subjects were neither legendary nor secular, nor even in the Norse language. They were hagiographic biographies, in Latin, of the Christianizing kings of Norway, Óláfr Tryggvason and Óláfr Haraldsson. The turn toward vernacular and secular subjects was almost immediate, however, and for about a century, starting around 1200, there was an outpouring of vernacular and secular literature as prodigious in quality as it was in range and quantity. That this outpouring should have been mostly Icelandic surely attests not only to a clerical culture tolerant of the pagan past, but also to the peculiar social circumstances of that frontier nation.

A discussion of Norse poetry might usefully begin with the prose work *Snorri's Edda,* also known as *Prose Edda* or *Younger Edda.* Written by the giant of medieval Icelandic letters, Snorri Sturluson, the work presents itself as a skaldic *ars poetica.* (The meaning of the term "Edda," which appears in a colophon, is unclear. The word *skáld* is Norse for "poet" but is normally used to refer to practitioners of a particular kind of verse, on which more below.) The bulk of *Snorri's Edda* tells, in medieval question and answer form, the stories of the gods and the heroes. The ostensible reason for this remarkable recital of pre-Christian lore is to clarify the references of the periphrastic figures that are the cornerstone of Norse poetic diction. Thus the story of the creation of the world out of the body of a slain giant is told by way of explaining the kennings (poetic figures) "Ymir's flesh" for earth, "Ymir's blood" for sea, and the like. The story of Sigurð slaying the gold-hoarding Fafnir is similarly told by way of explaining kennings for gold like "metal of Gnita-heath" (where the hoard was found) and "burden of Grani" (Sigurð's horse). Just how much Snorri gleaned from oral tradition is not clear. It appears, however that he had recourse to a written collection of traditional poems (from some of which he quotes) and when such a manuscript, the *Codex Regius,* was eventually discovered, it was taken as something like Snorri's original and was thus named *Edda* (or *Poetic Edda* or *Elder Edda*) to distinguish it from Snorri's work, which then came to be called *Prose Edda* (or *Younger Edda* or *Snorri's Edda*).

Eddic poetry (most of which is contained in the Codex Regius) is the Norse variant of the Germanic alliterative tradition. Anonymous, generally epic in tone, and on traditional subjects, the Eddic poems tell or allude to stories of the violent creation and no less violent end of the world, of the adventures and wisdom of the gods (Oðin, Thor, Loki, Baldr, Freyr), and of the tragic lives of the legendary heroes (Helgi, Sigurð). Although Eddic verse deploys alliteration and stress in the Germanic manner—short verses bearing two stresses are paired into long verses by means of alliteration in two or three of the stressed syllables—it is distinguished from Anglo-Saxon and Continental relatives by reliance on dialogue, shorter lines, and grouping of lines into stanzas. Thus the third stanza of "Vǫluspá" (alliterations marked in boldface):

Ár var **a**lda   þat er **Y**mir bygði,
vara **s**andr né **s**ær   né **s**valar unnir;
i**ǫ**rð fannz æva   né **u**pphiminn,
gap var **g**innunga,   enn **g**ras hvergi.

It was long ago when Ymir lived,
there was neither sand nor sea, nor cool waves;
earth existed not, nor the heavens,
there was a yawning void, and grass nowhere.

Although Eddic poetry is thought of as the most archaic form of Norse verse, the oldest preserved poems are in fact skaldic. Formally, the difference is one of degree. Skaldic poetry is also alliterative, stanzaic, and kenning-reliant. But at some point about the 9th century, some poets began to do more: to observe syllable number, to introduce internal rhyme in regular patterns (usually half-rhymes in odd lines, full rhymes in even ones), to rigidify the alliteration scheme, and to vary these rules in an array of meters. The third section of *Snorri's Edda* lists, exemplifies, and explains 102 such meters. One of Snorri's explanations reads: "Here form is lacking in the first and third lines, but in the second and fourth are full-rhymes, while the chief stave, the one that determines the alliteration, is positioned in the second and fourth lines in such a way that it is preceded by one or two syllables, but in other respects it is like *dróttkvætt."* Two other characteristics of skaldic verse—its unnatural syntax and its elaborately periphrastic diction—may be seen as effects of the extreme metrical strictures. Skaldic poetry may be the most technically difficult verse form ever composed in a European language. Some skaldic poems feel more like solutions to puzzles than poetry, but the greatest of them—the long elegy composed by Egill Skallagrímson on the death of his sons, for example—are achievements of the highest order.

However, the skaldic innovation went beyond form. Insofar as the skalds, unlike the Eddic poets, whoever they may have been, could register themselves and their experience in the first person, they emerge as eyewitnesses and speaking characters from otherwise undocumented times and events. The names of some 250 skalds and about 40,000 lines of poetry (only a small fraction of the total) have come down to us. We know the poems from the sagas in which they are embedded ("The king's skald Glúmr Geirason composed this stanza after the death of Hákon . . ."). Their craft brought skalds into the courts of earls and kings all over northern Europe, and skalds were present at, and composed poems about, some of the major events in early Scandinavian history. Because skaldic verse was for four centuries an entirely illiterate phenomenon, composed orally and passed on by memory, and because its structure more or less dictated that it had to be remembered intact or not at all, the skaldic verse that survives is likely to be in the form of its first utterance. Some of those utterances were composed in the medieval period as forgeries of a sort—a practice that indicates the vitality of the craft, with all its pagan connections, up through the 13th century—but those dating from the Viking Age constitute a unique record of that period.

Skaldic poetry was also crucial to the development of the north's most original literary form: the long prose narratives known as the sagas. The Norse word *saga* itself (story or narrative, derived from *segja,* to say) suggests an oral origin, and there is no doubt that a good deal of the matter and much of the plain style of the sagas derive from oral tradition, even though the whole works that have come down to us are certainly the handiwork of (anonymous) 13th-century authors. There are several dozen sagas, which have been categorized, in the modern era, by subject matter (sagas of bishops, of saints, of "knights," adaptations of Continental romance, *chansons de geste,* and so on), of contemporary times, of legendary heroes, of kings, and of Icelanders. Of particular interest for the Germanic connection are the sagas of legendary heroes *(fornaldarsögur,* literally "sagas of ancient times," for example, *Vǫlsunga saga* and *Hrolfs saga kraka),* whose fantastic action-adventure plots are dotted with reflexes of archaic traditions, some dating from the Age of Migrations. As literature and as historical sources, however, the sagas that hold pride of place are the so-called classical sagas—the *konungasögur* (including, centrally, Snorri's *Heimskringla*) and the *Íslendingasögur* (for example, *Njáls saga, Laxdœla saga, Egils saga, Grettis saga,* and so on). Celebrated for their unadorned prose style and laconic dialogue, the classical sagas offer an unprecedented view into the politics of an emerging feudal monarchy (Norway) as well as the workings of law and power in a stateless society (Iceland). The kings' sagas, in particular, use skaldic poems as historical sources, and one subtype of sagas features the skalds themselves as heroes, as, for example, *Egils saga* and *Kormáks saga.* The tendency to refer to the sagas as Europe's first novels or only prose epics underscores their anomalous status in western literary history.

Because so much Norse literature was written after the fact—the classical sagas at least two centuries after the events they describe and the Eddas and related texts two centuries after the introduction of Christianity—its historicity and authenticity are often in question. These issues have been of central scholarly concern for the better part of the last century. It comes down to the role assigned to oral tradition. Where the neo-traditionalists assume a rich, conservative oral tradition that delivered to the medieval writers not only an archaic content but traditional forms, the inventionists assume a minimum of oral tradition, instead seeing the literature as the product, more or less fanciful, of self-conscious medieval authors. It is around the *Íslendingasögur* that the debate has been most vigorous, but the split between inventionist and traditionalist interpretations marks the discussion of the other parts of the literature as well.

The fact remains that the account of myth and legend in Norse literature rhymes with a variety of far-flung vestiges. The stories of the gods told in the Scandinavian sources (the two Eddas, skaldic poetry, Saxo Grammaticus's *Gesta Danorum*, some of the *fornaldarsögur*, the first part of *Heimskringla*, and stone carvings that show, for example, Oðin astride his eight-legged horse, his two ravens flying overhead, and Thor fishing up from the bottom of the sea the immense Midgard Serpent) are also referred to in the Latin histories of Tacitus, Jordanes, Rimbert, Adam of Bremen, and Ibn Fadlan, as well as in Old High German sources (notably the *Merseburger Zaubersprüche,* the *Wessobrunner Gebet,* and the *Muspilli*) and Old English sources (including, of course, in the words Tuesday, Wednesday, Thursday, and Friday, after Tyr/Tiw, Oðin/Woden, Thor, and Frigg). Also cited throughout the Germanic world is the story of the semi-mythic smith Vǫlund. The Norse sources—the Eddic poem *Vǫlundarkvida, Þiðreks saga,* and Gotlandic picture stones—tell how Vǫlund takes revenge on the king who captured and crippled him by killing his sons and raping and impregnating his daughter. That account makes sense of the first two stanzas of the elusive Old English poem *Deor,* as it does of some references in *Beowulf,* two references in *Waldere,* an allusion in the *Waltharius,* and the panel on the Franks' Casket (7th-century Northumbrian) that shows a bent-legged man at a smithy, under which lie two small, headless corpses. Without the matrix provided by the Norse materials, these and other German and English allusions would be little more than tantalizing fragments. Without the German and English references, in turn, the Norse stories would seem like local inventions. Together, they make a powerful case for the commonality of pre-Christian Germanic culture, and, once again, for the conservatism of Icelandic literary culture well into the Christian period.

At the center of early Germanic heroic culture is the cycle of Sigurð, Brynhild, and Guðrun (=Kriemhild). The Norse tradition has a full analogue in *Das Nibelungenlied* and other German sources. Legends about events in the Ostrogothic and Burgundian kingdoms in the 4th to 6th centuries came early to Scandinavia, where they underwent further evolution. The legend's popularity in the north is suggested by the range in age, genre, and distribution of the multitude of Norse references, depictions, and retellings. The Norse branch differs from the *Nibelungenlied* on many points of plot, and some larger elements are unique to the northern branch. Particularly striking are the differences in scope and tone between the Norse and German versions. Where the *Nibelungenlied* features nations, castles, and armies of thousands, the Norse sources, for all their talk of "kings," tell the stories of clans, homely halls, and small bands of men. Nor does the courtly grandeur of *Das Nibelungenlied* have any counterpart in the Norse variants, which remain firmly rooted in the hard-bitten, pared-down style of heroic tradition and stubbornly focus on the problem of conflicting obligations of kinship. Only in the first-person laments of Gudrun do the Norse sources go operatic, and then only in tone, not scale.

Moreover, the *Nibelungenlied* is a full epic, whereas the Eddic poems are quite short (ranging roughly from 50 to 300 long lines). Only the two prose renditions of the cycle, *Þiðreks saga* and *Vǫlsunga saga,* achieve epic length— perhaps in direct response to Continental long forms. Certainly the author-redactor of *Þiðreks saga* knew of such forms, given that his work is itself a translation into prose of German sources. If Scandinavia had developed a verse epic, it would surely have been on this subject. The fact that it did not, and that prose, rather than verse, was the vehicle for the long-form exercise, even when the sources were poetic, suggests either that Eddic poetry was by nature not amenable to such expansion or that the practice of Eddic poetry was no longer a going concern by the time the epic moment arrived. Whatever the reason, the Scandinavian verse tradition halted with the heroic lay, while the German verse tradition evolved from heroic lay to epic. A similar situation may be posited with respect to the *Beowulf* traditions, which grew to epic length only in England.

Norse literary activity did not stop with the demise of the Commonwealth in 1262. The greatest of the Icelandic sagas, *Njáls saga,* was written around 1280, and the production of *fornaldarsögur* continued well into the 14th century. But *Njals saga* has a retrospective feeling about it, as does *Grettis saga,* another late-century product, and the cartoonish *fornaldarsögur* have nothing of the intelligence or antiquarian spirit of the classical texts. Why periods of intense cultural activity come to an end is a question larger than early Iceland, but the fact that Iceland's literary lights dimmed at just the point when the country was absorbed into a medieval monarchy suggests just how important honor-based feud culture of the Commonwealth period must have been in sponsoring and sustaining, long after they faded elsewhere, the lore and forms of the tribal past.

See also 744, 830, ca. 1200, 1203 (Summer), 1400, 1457

Bibliography: The Poetic Edda, tr. and ed. Carolyne Larrington (Oxford and New York: Oxford University Press, 1996). Snorri Sturluson, *Edda,* tr. and ed. Anthony Faulkes (London: Dent; Rutland, Vt.: Tuttle, 1982). Carol J. Clover and John Lindow, eds., *Old Norse–Icelandic Literature: A Critical Guide* (Ithaca, N.Y.: Cornell University Press, 1985). John Lindow, *Norse Mythology: A Guide to the Gods, Heroes, Rituals, and Beliefs* (Oxford and New York: Oxford University Press, 2001).

Carol J. Clover

ᎏ *1027, August*

Empress Gisela visits Saint Gall

Monastic Scriptoria

"Empress Gisela, together with her son Henry, came to the monastery of Saint Gallus. She made benevolent gifts and received hospitality." With these words, the contemporary chronicler commemorated an extraordinary event: a visit by Gisela, wife of Emperor Konrad II, to Saint Gall. She was returning from Rome, where she had been crowned empress on March 26, 1027.

This was not the first imperial visit to Saint Gall. Some fifty years earlier, Otto I had visited the abbey with his wife Adelheid, his son, the future Otto II, and his daughter-in-law, Theophanu. Gisela, however, was the first Salian empress. Her visit demonstrated that the traditional good relations between the imperial rulers and Saint Gall would continue under the new Salian dynasty. It was a gesture of great promise for the monks—and Gisela did not leave empty-handed. The Saint Gall monk Ekkehart IV tells us in his *liber benedictionum* that Empress Gisela, eager for works by the famous scribe and teacher Notker, the German, had commissioned copies of the Psalter and the Book of Job. Notker, born around 950, and *magister* (teacher) at the school of Saint Gall, had died of the plague on July 28, 1022, leaving to his home monastery a remarkable body of works. From his letters to Bishop Hugh of Sion, we know that he set himself the task of preparing Latin texts for use in schools where German was the language of instruction. To adaptations of Latin texts according to the rules of the tractatus of Saint Gall, Notker added translations and commentaries in the Latin tradition that left many terms untranslated. The resulting bilingual style is typical of Notker's work. In his search for a deep understanding of spiritual literature, Notker covered the entire spectrum of the seven liberal arts, which he introduced into the canon of monastic teaching. He was the first to translate into German parts of Aristotle *(Categories; On Interpretation),* the *Consolatio Philosophiae* of Boethius, the *Andria* of Terence, and the *Bucolica* of Virgil, to mention only a few examples. Nearly all of these works are most likely unique copies, transmitted in the house tradition of Saint Gall without mention of the author, who was well known to the inhabitants at the monastery. Only Notker's Psalter received broad and continuing attention outside Saint Gall. The second book Gisela requested, Notker's commentary on Job, seems to be permanently lost.

Although the act of writing and copying books is not mentioned in Saint Benedict's monastic rules, Christianity itself seems to have produced such institutions: the central messages of Christendom are stored in a book. Special competence was required to make this book talk, a task that rested with literate scholars of the time. The word of God should be heard rather than read privately. "He that hath ears let him hear," says the Gospel of Matthew on three occasions (11:15, 13:9, 13:43). This written appeal to hearing points up the disparity between the literate recipients of the word of God and the illiterate, who will hear it only through a learned mediator. Benedict's insistence that every single monk should hold a private spiritual reading every day assured that monasteries cultivated literary competence. Books and the ability to read them thus became the foundation of Christian culture. Irish and Anglo-Saxon monks usually traveled with books in their luggage. Liturgical books were in constant use. Monastic *scriptoria* served this elementary need of religious life.

In addition to the transcription of basic liturgical books, the *scriptoria* produced and distributed copies of the Holy Scripture and exegetical works. However, the scribes did not confine themselves to works of Christian theology. The writings of pagan antiquity were copied as well. In fact, without the monastic scriptoria, the works of many ancient authors would not have survived. Cicero, Tacitus, and Suetonius are good examples. At the height of this monastic activity, from the 8th to the 12th century, when competing centers of learning emerged, monastic *scriptoria* were the sole suppliers of contemporary libraries. The right to exclusive control over distribution, preservation, and development of knowledge was a potential source of power and, therefore, of intense interest to secular rulers. In this context, Charlemagne's *renovatio imperii,* a framework standardizing texts and intensifying their production, was an attempt to make knowledge available and to channel its use toward consolidation of Carolingian rule.

Medieval Europe was dotted with monasteries and many of their *scriptoria* enjoyed great renown: Clonmacnois and Kells in Ireland, Lindisfarne (an Irish branch) and Canterbury in England, Fleury and Corbie in France, Montecassino and Bobbio in Italy, Fulda and Reichenau in Germany—to name just a few. Preeminent among them to this day is Saint Gall since most of the early medieval manuscripts produced there are still preserved in the monastery archives. These documents allow a fairly illuminating glance into the workings of medieval monastic *scriptoria*. A detailed architect's drawing of an ideal monastery (known as the "St. Galler Klosterplan"), dating to the time of Charlemagne, indicates that the preferred placement for the *scriptorum* was adjoining the monastic cathedral. It was to take the form of a two-story building with a library upstairs and a writing office below.

Hagiographic tradition dates the founding of Saint Gall to the year 612. Columban, an Irish missionary, had been active for many years in France and southern Germany. On his way to Italy, he left behind his pupil Gallus, who set up a small cell in a place that was then in the middle of nowhere. However, history usually places the establishment of Saint Gall in the year 719, when Otmar founded a monastery in that place. Books were always held in high esteem at the Saint Gall monastery. A spectacular instance of this was the rescue of the Saint Gall books during the Hungarian invasion in the year 926. The female hermit Wibroda, patron saint of libraries ever since, urged that the books be transported from Saint Gall to the neighboring monastic island of Reichenau. There they remained in safety until the Hungarians left. Although the right number of books was returned, records show that some volumes from Reichenau were accidentally brought to Saint Gall, while some from Saint Gall remained on the island. For this reason, many Saint Gall texts do not have an uninterrupted history.

The *Brevarium librorum,* a medieval catalogue of the books in the Saint Gall library from the years 884 to 888, lists some 294 manuscripts. Today we have about 450 original Saint Gall manuscripts, 300 of which were produced directly at the monastery. The number of books in those days has been estimated to have been about 1000 volumes. In addition, there were about 200 *codices dispersi* (disparate manuscripts) produced at Saint Gall, but transferred elsewhere, indicating lively commerce with other medieval centers of learning. Foreign productions were generously incorporated into the Saint Gall library, for example the earliest German dictionary (the *Abrogans* manuscript), or the Saint Gall Codex 857 (including the *Nibelungenlied, Parzival,* and other Middle High German classics). Although these texts were not originally copied in Saint Gall, they were kept and preserved there.

Another Saint Gall phenomenon is its specific writing and copying culture. Even in the 10th century, at a time of a serious halt in manuscript production throughout Europe, the monks of Saint Gall continued to write and copy (see Beat van Scarpatetti). The Saint Gall art of writing enjoyed international fame from the 9th century onward, ebbing only in the 13th century.

Saint Gall was obviously a well-functioning scriptorium, with competent scribes and a high output. Nevertheless, manuscripts remained extremely rare and precious, and Gisela's request for copies of Notker's Psalter and the Book of Job was a truly imperial wish. In Germany, unlike Italy, organized trade in manuscripts did not develop until the end of the 14th century, when paper was invented and became a relatively inexpensive material. By then, the newly established universities drastically increased demand for the written word. Still, buying and selling of manuscripts on a small scale had already been common in earlier days. We know that Charlemagne ordered in his will the numerous manuscripts in his possession to be sold for a "just price" and the proceeds given to the poor. In 1074, a single Mass book went for the price of an entire vineyard paid by Udalrich of Bozen to a priest from Benedictbeuren. Yet, about the same time the monks from Saint-Père-de-Chartres bought a book from a Langobardian colleague for what amounted to small change. In general, however, copying a manuscript required rich material and personal resources. When Bishop Hugh of Sion asked for a copy of Notker's writings, he was told first to supply parchment and pay the scribes to make sure he could cover the immense cost of copying.

However, Gisela certainly did not pay a penny for the manuscripts she requested. Reciprocal relationships between the monastery and the ruling king or emperor insured that the scriptorium would produce magnificent manuscripts for the royal house, and that the ruler would, in turn, sponsor the monastery. Many of the most famous medieval manuscripts owe their existence to this practice. Some of the most extravagant, beautifully illustrated books extant were not copied for reading but for veneration. The process of writing was of-

Illuminated initial showing merchant offering parchment to a monk. (Royal Library, Copenhagen)

ten described as a manner of worship: manuscripts were tangible expressions of spiritual and material values.

What exactly was involved in the making of a manuscript? Although Notker's Job is not preserved, let us try to reconstruct how a copy of the Psalter would have been produced during the empress's stay at Saint Gall. First, adequate writing material needed to be on hand. Most important—and most expensive—was the parchment, animal skin from sheep, pigs, or calves. On average, one animal hide supplied two folios of parchment, which, when folded in the middle to a double page, yielded four book pages. Several of these double pages were placed inside each other, and after being inscribed, they were bound into a codex. The usual way to describe a book was to indicate the number of double pages it contained: a group of three double pages was called a *ternio,* four double pages a *quaternio,* five a *quinio,* and so forth. However, Saint Gall manuscripts are paginated due to the personal preference of the 18th-century librarian Ildefons von Arx (1755–1833).

After the hide was dried, it was polished with pumice-stone and chalk to create a smooth surface and eliminate the difference between the inner, the flesh side, and the outer, the hair side, of the animal skin. Because the less flexible hair side tended to create a concave bend in the parchment, a good scriptorium would lay hair side on hair side and flesh side on flesh side so that the codex as a whole was not bent. Next, the sheets were ruled with lines using a metal stylus to make a slight indentation. None of this was simply mechanical work. Like the process of writing itself, the production of the necessary raw material had—at least ideally—a contemplative character.

The other materials required were goose quills and ink. The latter was produced with crushed branches of hawthorn and blackthorn soaked in wine. Ashes or iron sulfate intensified the color. The book cover was made of parchment. Medieval book covers served primarily as ornamentation. Since the manuscripts were not kept upright on shelves but laid horizontally, they did not need to be stabilized with rigid covers.

The process of writing itself was complicated. Medieval scribes wrote either standing at a high desk or squatting on a bench with the book on their knees. Holding the stylus was almost unbearable. Until the 16th century, scribes commonly used three fingers—forefinger, middle finger, and thumb—a practice believed to represent the Holy Trinity that kept these fingers straight. Unlike today's practice, the forearm was held upright, which was very tiring for the upper arm and shoulder. The result was an impersonal "school-script." What we admire today as aesthetic mastery was often the result of mere drill. Scribes in training suffered frequent beatings. The man who copied Saint Gall Codex 10 complains, "Just as an invalid desires to be cured, the scribe desires the book to end." An early 9th-century scribe in the monastery of Lorsch noted that he wrote with his feet chained so that he could not escape from his wearisome job.

On average, copying a codex would take about three or four months. In some instances, the work was divided among several scribes. Some cases of unusually rapid work were commemorated: Saint Nilus, for example, is said to have copied the whole Psalter in four days, though this is hardly credible. In 1004, the Boethius translation of Euclid was copied in Luxeuil in the span of four days, and the Milan Codex (Ambr. Bibl. 301) folio 100 recto to folio 108 recto, seventeen pages all told, was written in a single day. Medieval manuscripts, even those written under time constraints, were generally also proofread. Jodokus Metzler (1574–1639), basing his account on older sources, reports in his *Chronicon Sancti Galli* that Empress Gisela did not wait until the requested copies were finished. To the annoyance of the monks, she simply took off with the originals. Before she left, the monks, anxious to copy the manuscripts rapidly, reproduced the Psalter in only fourteen days.

Can we trust Jodokus Metzler's story? Both manuscripts, the Psalter and the Job, disappeared. If wax tablets were used instead of parchment, a single manuscript could have been copied in fourteen days. And given that it was easier to travel with parchment than with wax tablets, Gisela might well have decided to take the originals with her. She would not have been the first to take precious documents from the monastic library. When Otto I, known as the Great, visited Saint Gall in 973, his son, the future Otto II, took away several codices, according to a history of Saint Gall by Ekkehart IV *(Casus Sancti Galli).*

Empress Gisela's obsession with Notker's books might have come from her acquaintance with his pupil Ekkehart. The Psalter was one of the subjects Ekkehart taught at Mainz, and he may well have wanted to use his teacher's vernacular translations for didactic purposes. Of course, this remains in the realm of speculation. Notker's Psalter is the earliest German book, copied again and again in the course of several centuries. The shocking abduction of the Notker Psalter and the attempts by the monks of Saint Gall to salvage what they could by hastily drawing up a copy, stand at the beginning of the German written tradition.

Whatever can be made of the story of Gisela's visit to Saint Gall, it shows a scriptorium far from being a place of monotonous reproduction and more a place where spiritual and secular ambitions, monks, and empresses could meet. They played a central part in the social and political life of their time.

See also 744, 800, 847, ca. 1200, 1203 (Summer), 1400, 1457

Bibliography: Bernhard Bischoff, *Latin Palaeography: Antiquity and Middle Ages* (Cambridge, U.K., 1990). Johann Kelle, "Die S. Galler Deutschen Schriften und Notker Labeo," in *Abhandlungen der philosophisch-philologischen Classe der königlich bayerischen Akademie der Wissenschaften,* vol. 18 (Munich, 1890), 207–280. Notker der Deutsche, *Der Psalter.* Psalms 1–50, ed. Petrus W. Taxed (Tübingen: 1979). Beat von Scarpatetti, "Das St. Galler Scriptorium," in Peter Ochsenbein, ed., *Das Kloster St. Gallen im Mittelalter: Die kulturelle Blüte vom 8. bis zum 12. Jahrhundert* (Darmstadt, 1999), 31–67. Wilhelm Wattenbach, *Das Schriftwesen im Mittelalter,* 3rd ed.(Leipzig, 1896). Ekkehart IV, *Sankt Galler Klostergeschichten—Casus Sancti Galli,* trans. Hans F. Haefele, Ausgewählte Quellen zur deutschen Geschichte des Mittelalters, Freiherr vom Stein-Gedächtnisausgabe, vol. 10, 3rd ed.(Darmstadt, 1991); cited as CSG.

Stephan Müller

⟲ *1074–1119*

Revolts and restabilizations mark the history of Cologne after the reign of Anno II

The Mystical Exposition of a City

Cologne in the 11th century was one of the largest and most powerful cities in the known world. A full thousand years after *Colonia Agrippinensis,* the Roman colony on the left bank of the Rhine, was founded by Agrippa (39 B.C.) and thereafter was named in honor of its most famous daughter, the empress Agrippina (A.D. 50), Cologne lived up to its Roman past. In the middle of the century (about 1057), the scholar Meinhard of Bamberg exposes the pattern in which Cologne figures as the very *topos* of city life. "The multiform Colonia or, rather, Babilonia" is full of what young men cannot be warned enough against: the "smooth and silken bodies of the girls of Cologne." According to a venerable cliché, cities in the 11th century, like Paris or Cologne, were still represented in terms of the allegorical extremes of Jerusalem and Babylon.

The Early Middle High German *Annolied* (*Song of Anno;* hereafter *AL*) is one of the best, though most enigmatic, documents from this transitional phase in European intellectual history. After the period of the Dark Ages that divides Late Antiquity and the 12th-century medieval Renaissance, it is the first work of literature to come from a major city. It celebrates the city of Cologne from its Roman origins to the age after Anno II (d. 1075), the archbishop of Cologne and chancellor of the Holy Roman Empire who was one of the most controversial figures of his time. In its learned approach to world history, the song shows the early development of the bourgeois worldview, from monastic spiritual preoccupation and discipline to the *vita activa* of the modern world. Discovered in Breslau and published by Martin Opitz in 1639, the *AL* was carefully re-edited by Bodmer and Breitinger in 1745, in an edition proclaimed as the first critical edition of a German text prior to the 19th century. The work is remarkable in three respects: its extremely refined discursive economy of Latin and German texts, which bears far-reaching implications for legal and theological semantics and for political and poetical questions of the period; its elaborate rhetoric of intertextual relations and tropological substitutions, in which the figural repertoire is handled with utmost wit and virtuosity; and its ingenuity in managing conflict between episcopal and early bourgeois interests.

The type of discourse developed in the *AL* is a complex blend of textual strategies that are only understood. In any event, the presumably modern title of "Song" is misleading if understood in the sense of praise for individual merits. The *AL* is a historical discourse on the city of Cologne, focusing on Anno II and the history of his episcopal rule. Thirty-three out of forty-nine stanzas are completed before depiction abruptly shifts from world history to Anno's reign. What is striking about this beginning is the precise identification of the city's crucial role in the world-historical development of salvation. The city has played a crucial role in the development of that history ever since Saint Peter fulfilled his apostolic mission in Rome. It was there that "he erected the sign of the Holy Cross" and "took possession of the city" (stanza 32): not any city, but Rome, the center of the ancient world, and with it Cologne, in whose very name the colonial foundation of Rome is remembered, reiterated, and reinforced.

Thus the historical continuity from the *Colonia Agrippinensis* to the *fidelis filia Colonia,* the "true daughter Cologne" of the archbishops after Anno, both enables the historical narrative and legitimates the worldly power of the bishops. Under the "sign of the Cross," the post-Roman history of the city supersedes the Roman foundations, leaving imperial Rome behind as some sort of "middle age" between Caesar's world-historical mission and Cologne's "modern" existence. The *AL* offers a very keen and accurate description of the transformation of these foundations without dismissing them. On the contrary, reaching back to the freedom of the old Roman senate, the history of Cologne resumes what was given away in Late Antiquity.

The detailed emphasis on the "republican" heritage of the *civitas* of Cologne stands in latent contradiction to the new Christian *civitates* with the lord bishops. It is a most remarkable characteristic of the episcopal cities, notably those on the Rhine, that they allowed for an early and steady bourgeois development outside the feudal constraints of cities under worldly lords, though not without conflict with their own priestly rulers. The *AL* is situated in this conflicted terrain. The redactor seems to favor a strong "see" for Cologne's bishops among the secular *lantheirrin* (literally "landlords"), while also advocating a vigorous internal politics of the patrician families in response to the worldly power of the bishops. The *AL* is marked by, and clearly remarks upon, this situation. But the evidence is very thin and highly controversial.

Similarly unique and complex is the *AL*'s rhetorical use of typology as structure of representation. Here the *AL*'s transformation of the long tradition of biblical exegesis is fundamental. History as discourse *(historia)* is structured according to repertoire of types, functional slots that are filled time and again in the course of events. This typology ultimately centers on the founding events of Christ's salvation, which are actually called "anti-types" because they fulfill the promise figured in their Old Testament prototypes. The typological link between the city and the historical mission of Christianity enables the *AL* to project the Old Testament types of David, Job, and Moses onto the history of Cologne. The crux of this procedure—a *modus operandi* of far-reaching consequences for the development of literary forms—is the considerable abstraction needed to transcribe Old Testament types into a post-Roman rather than New Testament vision of the *City of God* to come. To ensure this transposition, not only are the types that inform history re-presented, but exegetical reflections on the typological principles that guide the discourse accompany the historical part of the *AL* and lead to its exemplary conclusion. The aim of the historical reconstruction is to produce an *exemplum* for the audience to contemplate, the *exemplum* of Anno's career. Thus, Anno assumes his typological significance within a history that exhibits the *civitas Dei* in its present state of imminence with both its empirical problems as well as its ethical norm.

Although the *AL,* composed contemporary with the controversy surrounding papal Investiture, certainly participates in many ways in the political semantics of the age, the most significant aspect of its *exemplum* is the "mystical exposition" it elaborates on the basis of typological exegesis. The term *expositio mystica* was used by the monk and mystic Rupert from the monastery of Deutz, located across the Rhine from Cologne. One of the important philosophers of his time, Rupert was probably the only scholar in spatial and temporal proximity to the *AL* who could have influenced such a complex product. Otherwise, the degree of learning that entered into this vernacular work is hard to account for. Rupert's notion of *expositio* provides a theoretical background for Anno's transfiguration in the text into a threefold figure of exemplarity. In contrast to what was empirically and historically known about the man Anno, the *AL* elevates his all too human deeds and exploits the well-known struggles of his life in order to establish the saintly type he is to embody, providing him, to this end, with the purifying torture of a terrible disease. In this an exemplarity is achieved that transcends the official, factual version narrated in the *Vita Annonis*.

As archbishop of Cologne and chancellor of the Holy Roman Empire, Anno was first of all exemplary as an eminent politician and source of pride for his city. The type he refers to is that of David, king and ruler, and as such he suffers according to "the holy Christ's image," the *imago Christi,* which, according to Rupert, constitutes the very "form" of imitation (stanza 39). The terrible fate of being betrayed by his own children, as David was betrayed by his son Absalom, leads to and gives the best available interpretation of Anno's darkest moment, the high treason committed against him by Cologne's citizens. The revolt against the city's father and bishop in 1074 arose from a conflict that had proved, if anything, the alienation of father and children, bishop and city. The second prefiguration of Anno's fate is Job, a typological significance that surpasses mere politics. In this tropological rather than historical dimension of meaning, Anno reassembles his children and returns to the community where he had failed as a father. Beyond the historical and moral levels of the allegory, there is a third signification, the anagogical perspective of the paradise to be regained.

Like the manifold senses of scriptural exegesis in general—both in the fourfold system and particularly in the mystical exposition according to the threefold version employed here—the *AL*'s exemplary conclusion barely hides a deepening split in biblical tropology, the fatal discrepancy between the moral and anagogical senses, between individual and collective eschatology. But whereas the next comparable text, the slightly later *Kaiserchronik (Emperors' Chronicle),* is entirely interested in collective eschatology, from the start the *AL* declares as its cause the anagogy of the individual fate. Recalling some lost precursors of the *Nibelungenlied,* the *AL*'s prologue effectively distances itself from the empty glory of heroic oral poetry—the battles and devastation of war, the breakdown of friendships, and the downfall of mighty kings—and confronts the vanity of feudal politics with the miraculous "signs" evoked by Anno in reference to the mountain on which he founded a monastery. The "Sigeberg" is glossed as a "mountain of victory" (prologue, stanza 1). As false as this etymology of Siegburg may be (the mountain is actually named after the river Sieg), it stresses the semiotic quality of the founding act: a sign erected in the succession of Peter's sign, the cross erected in Rome.

The key to reading the *AL* lies in this curious connection of individual eschatology with the city's salvational mission. Obviously, the practical interest in managing city politics is not everything. As the prologue suggests, there is more than a profane literary end to be achieved. But there is also more than just an interest in collective salvation. The practical interest in maintaining political stability is put into the perspective of another, more than collective interest: an individual desire for paradise. Just as the knowledge that went into the *AL* was achieved due to an overwhelming "desire for God," so too does the practical dimension of the Anno *exemplum* draw on a mystical interest that rests in God and his promised "land of paradise." Thus, it is by no means necessary to take the "signs" of Anno in the *AL* as symptoms of a sudden transformation of the man himself through the doubly dolorous fate of being estranged from his community and being ostensibly punished for his deeds through a detestable disease. These deeds and their striking consequence are meant to serve as a true "mirror" (stanza 34), much like the *Mirror for Magistrates* in Shakespearean England. The exemplary effect that turns the man Anno in his agony into the expiating "image of the holy Christ" (stanza 39) secures the political *exemplum* of the archbishop Anno and acknowledges it as an aspect of our individual path to heaven.

Read in light of city politics after Anno, the political semantics of the *AL* becomes prominent. The "broken friendships" of the prologue not only recall a heroic motif from earlier times, but also point to the language of contractual law, as the occasional reference to the legal term *amicitiae causa,* "for the sake of patronage," demonstrates (stanza 30). Also, the feudal tie between the lord bishop and his liegemen is explicitly mentioned in connection with Anno's relationship with the *ministriales* in his service (stanza 43). The growing bonds and shared interests between this group of liegemen and the merchant families of the city, whose growing economic importance made their rise to prominence inevitable, seem to be at the root of the conflict between bishop and city, beginning with the unhappy developments in Anno II's last years. The revolt of 1074, a year before Anno's death, not only overshadows Anno's memory in the city but looms large in the design of the *exemplum* as it is presented in the *AL*.

The revolt of Cologne in 1074 was one of the first of its kind. It had an enduring influence on the city and also signaled a far-reaching development in European social and political history. It recurred several times, and each recurrence was followed by compromises and redefinitions of the citizenry as an independent community, interacting with the overlord and bishop of the city. A similar revolt in 1119 is the last in a series across which spontaneous reaction against the archbishop's rule evolved into a rather well-defined "liberty." In fact, Frederick I, archbishop of Cologne and chancellor of the Holy Roman Empire, may have found himself addressed in the *AL,* if we assume it was written on the occasion of one such uprising. About 1119, the abbot of Siegburg, Cuno I, and his friend Rupert of Deutz were Frederick's closest counselors.

The traces of actual events are best deciphered in light of the *AL*'s awareness of the city's republican heritage. The "three hundred senators" are mentioned "because the Romans did not want kings" and knew how to guarantee discipline and honor on their own. Julius Caesar's military mission, though performed in the interest of his own power, was successful because of treaties rather than victories, and this included the establishment of the *colonia* in Cologne (stanza 18). The *libertas Romana,* evoked as the founding moment, was a commonplace established through the German commentary on Boethius's

Consolation of Philosophy by Notker of Saint Gall. Notker speaks of a conference called *senatus consultum* (consulting senate). He may have had the nearby city of Constance in mind, another bishop-ruled city on the Upper Rhine founded by Romans. Notker's word *einunga* for the conference of the senators is a translation of the Latin *coniuratio,* a sworn conspiracy. In the aftermath of the revolt of 1074, Cologne built the first city wall against its lord and bishop in 1106, after the peace movement of the *treuga Dei,* "Truce of God," had already found entrance into Cologne, and through Cologne into the empire, in 1083. Against the background of these events, and the concomitant development of liberties, the *coniuratio pro libertate* (conspiracy for liberty) took place in 1112 and made manifest what the *AL* presupposes as the given state of politics. It is this state of affairs that is opposed in the formula of the *fidelis filia Colonia* (loyal daughter Colonia), the church of Cologne.

The *AL's exemplum* focuses on Anno II's actions in 1074, which provide a mirror for his successors. How the revolt came about is difficult to determine. The bishop's administrative servants (as distinguished from the military ones) seem to have conspired with the merchants, and in the interest of the merchants; the confiscation of a merchant's ship for Anno's own political aims triggered a spontaneous reaction. Anno decided that only the severest punishment would be adequate, and in doing so he grossly underestimated the degree of the citizens' outrage. Anno's punishment of the ringleaders—he ordered them blinded—not only was a cruel misjudgment of the citizens and liegemen whose judge he indeed was (stanza 7), but seemed to betray his own blindness toward his episcopal duty. His focus on eyes became proverbial and caused a considerable disturbance during the dubious procedure of his canonization a hundred years later.

The *AL's* counterplot gives an account of what cannot very well be documented, the conversion from cruel judge to a saintly ruler. This entails the usual conversion dream, in which Anno finds "a stain on his breast" instead of the bishop's cross (stanza 42), as was the case among some of his more saintly predecessors. In the *AL* Anno proves his saintliness by interceding on behalf of his citizens with a marvelous, even ironic miracle. He restores to a liegeman the eyes he had lost in a dramatic case of blasphemy: one eye after the other "shot" out of his head, but this time Anno, the specialist in this matter, causes them to "grow again in their sockets" (stanzas 47–48). Suffice it to say that through this act of healing he was able to reverse his previous error. In perhaps the only portion of the text that deserved to be called narrative, the *AL* negotiates an unexpected ironic reversal, making palpable what Quintilian (freely translated) called "the inversion toward the contrary."

See also 1027, 1250, 1260, 1622–1624, 1952 (Spring)

Bibliography: *Frühe deutsche und lateinische Literatur in Deutschland 800–1150,* ed. Walter Haug and Benedikt Konrad Vollmann, Bibliothek deutscher Klassiker, vol. 62 (Frankfurt am Main: Deutscher Klassiker Verlag, 1991). Walter Haug, *Vernacular Literary Theory in the Middle Ages: The*

German Tradition, 800–1300, in Its European Context (Cambridge and New York: Cambridge University Press, 1997). Anselm Haverkamp, *Typik und Politik im Annolied: Zum Konflikt der Interpretationen im Mittelalter* (Stuttgart: Metzler, 1979). Edith Ennen, *The Medieval Town* (Amsterdam and New York: North-Holland Publishing, 1979).

Anselm Haverkamp

ᢙ 1147
Hildegard of Bingen writes to Bernard of Clairvaux

A Cosmological Vision

Sometime in 1147, an unknown German nun from the Benedictine establishment of Saint Disibod wrote to the great Cistercian abbot, Bernard of Clairvaux, asking his advice about her divinely inspired visions. (Although an abbess for all practical purposes and almost always referred to as such, Hildegard's complex relationship with her community of religious women and the male Cistercian house of Saint Disibod forbade her official use of the title.) Bernard was then at the height of his fame, preaching the Second Crusade against Islam to enthusiastic crowds throughout Europe. The pope, Eugenius III, was a Cistercian and Bernard's former pupil. Although active in ecclesial affairs and the Church's ongoing battle against infidels and heretics, Bernard was also widely known for his writings on the contemplative life. Hildegard turned to him because he was an important religious leader with both the understanding and the authority to legitimate not her visions, whose divine source she did not question, but the publication of these experiences: "Most good and kind Father, I have put myself in your soul so that you should reveal to me, in your answer, if it so pleases you, whether I must say these things openly or whether I must keep silent, for I experience great torments in this vision, not knowing what I must say of the things I have seen and heard. And sometimes, after the vision, I am confined to my bed with terrible sufferings, because I am silent, and I cannot even stand up." Bernard encouraged Hildegard and eventually intervened on her behalf with Pope Eugenius. When, in the winter of 1147–48, Eugenius was in nearby Trier presiding over a synod of bishops, he took the opportunity to procure a copy of the nun's still unfinished visionary book. He commanded that selections from Hildegard's visions be read publicly to the assembled bishops and subsequently endorsed them, sending the abbess a letter of approbation and encouragement for the continuation of her work.

The book was Hildegard von Bingen's *Scivias,* the first of her three visionary texts. In part because of Pope Eugenius III's approval, the abbess of Bingen was to become famous throughout 12th-century Christendom as a prophet, preacher, reformer, composer, poet, artist, and scientist. In addition to her visionary trilogy (*Scivias,* the *Book of Life's Merits,* and the *Book of Divine Works*), she wrote the first known morality play, two collections of scientific lore (which contain the first known female-authored account of sexuality and gynecology), a poetic song sequence, and a voluminous correspondence with important political, ecclesial, and monastic leaders as well as more humble interlocutors. In addition, Hildegard made four preaching tours of Germany and Swabia. Many of her prophetic sermons against corruption in the Church and the spread of heresy survive. Such a wide range of accomplishments is notable in any age, though perhaps more typical of the encyclopedic propensities of 12th-century intellectuals than of our own time.

Hildegard, however, was a woman. As such, she had few educational opportunities and was officially barred from public preaching or teaching. The medieval Church took literally the Pauline injunction against women speaking in church and extended it to ban women from interpreting scripture and teaching or preaching in any public forum. Although in the early Middle Ages a few powerful abbesses took on semi-sacerdotal functions, administering the sacraments and preaching to other women within their convents, these powers were increasingly restricted in the 12th and 13th centuries. However, through the authority vested in her as a visionary and prophet, Hildegard overcame the limitations the medieval Church placed on her sex, for prophecy was explicitly open to women as a charismatic gift with ample biblical warrant. Although only Hildegard's visionary trilogy was explicitly mandated by God, divine sanction of her charismatic gifts legitimated her life's work and enabled her to undertake that work in public. As Hildegard well realized, however, without ecclesial recognition of the divinely inspired nature of her prophecy, she would have remained without authority among her contemporaries.

According to the *Life of Saint Hildegard,* composed by Godfrey of Saint Disibod and Theoderic of Echternach (but also including memoirs Hildegard dictated as an aid to earlier biographers), Hildegard began to have visions in childhood. The youngest of ten children born to noble Rhenish parents, Hildegard was offered by her parents to the religious life when she was eight years old. Together with her older kinswoman, Jutta, and one or two other girls, she was later enclosed as a recluse at the monastery of Saint Disibod and took monastic vows. She discussed her visions with Jutta and the monk Volmar, but otherwise kept them hidden. After Jutta's death, she was chosen to be the teacher and leader of her small community, presumably on the basis of other, non-charismatic qualities.

As her letter to Bernard suggests, Hildegard underwent a crisis in her early forties when she was first commanded by God to "speak these things that you see and hear" (*Scivias,* Preface). She again confided in her teacher, Volmar, who supported her call. Yet fear of writing and the ridicule it might elicit continued to keep Hildegard silent, resulting, she tells us, in a serious illness. This is a pattern central to the lives of many female religious authors in the Middle Ages, for whom writing itself became the cure for divinely inspired illnesses. Hildegard, with the support of Volmar and Kuno, the abbot of Saint Disibod, finally overcame her fears and began to record her visions. Volmar was crucial to the production of her texts, becoming her friend and secretary. An image of

Hildegard at work in her scriptorium, which many scholars believe she herself designed, shows an idealized portrayal of their collaboration. From a representation of Hildegard's vision of the Trinity emerges an effulgence of light, which flows onto Hildegard's uplifted face. She is seated, writing on dark tablets apparently made of wax. Behind her stands another nun. Separated by a partition from Hildegard and facing her, a seated Volmar writes on white parchment. This image suggests that Hildegard first jotted down her visions on wax tablets and Volmar later copied them. The simultaneity of these actions in the image may be meant to represent Volmar's mediating participation in Hildegard's divinely inspired work.

As I have suggested, the approbation Hildegard sought from Bernard of Clairvaux was meant not to authorize her writings, but to provide the ecclesial protection required to safeguard her and her community. Hildegard records the divine mandate of her work in the preface: "O fragile human, ashes of ashes, and filth of filth! Say and write what you see and hear. But since you are timid in speaking and simple in expounding, and untaught in writing, speak and write these things not by human mouth, and not by the understanding of human invention, and not by the requirements of human composition, but as you see and hear them on high in the heavenly places in the wonders of God." Hildegard writes because God commands her to do so. Moreover, what she writes and the manner in which she writes it are divinely inspired. Almost every woman writing on religious topics in the Middle Ages recounts a similar divine injunction and promise, thereby proclaiming a charismatic origin for her words and legitimating them in the eyes of the Church. The claim is generally coupled with professions of ignorance and inability; thus Hildegard proclaims herself "untaught" in order to highlight the divine origin of her words.

Yet we should not take Hildegard's claims to ignorance literally. She was certainly taught to recite the Psalms by Jutta, and thus to read Latin. Although she did not have the formal education accorded to boys in cathedral and monastic schools (and to a few exceptionally privileged women like Héloïse in convents or with private tutors), she wrote a vibrant, if not always grammatical, Latin. As her work attests, she amassed an enormous amount of theological, scientific, and practical knowledge over the course of her life. In recognizing the strategic nature of Hildegard's assertion of ignorance and the authorizing power of her claim to divine authority, however, I do not think we should consider her visionary accounts as fictional. Hildegard clearly believed in her visions and their prophetic power and was spurred by them to write and teach.

Unlike Mechthild of Magdeburg and many other medieval visionaries, whose accounts of visionary experience are often grounded in dialogues between the soul and various heavenly figures, Hildegard's texts are predominantly visual. In a letter written late in her life to Guibert of Gembloux, Hildegard describes the nature of her visionary experience:

> In this vision, my soul, as God would have it, rises up high into the vault of heaven and into the changing sky and spreads itself out among different peo-

ples, although they are far away from me in distant lands and places. And because I see them this way in my soul, I observe them in accord with the shifting of clouds and other created things. I do not hear them with my outward ears, nor do I perceive them by the thoughts of my own heart or by any combination of my five senses, but in my soul alone, while my outward eyes are open. So I have never fallen prey to ecstasy in the visions, but I see them wide awake, day and night.

(First Letter to Guibert)

Striking about this account is its decidedly untraditional nature. Whereas Augustine and other theorists of visionary experience distinguish between various kinds of vision (for Augustine, the imaginative, intellectual, and spiritual) and argue that the highest form of vision is noncorporeal, Hildegard insists on the visuality of her experience. Unlike many visionaries, who describe themselves as ecstatically leaving their bodies when they receive revelations, Hildegard claims that she remains awake and alert (see Newman).

These visions serve as the core of Hildegard's great trilogy. The *Scivias,* completed in 1151, provides a comprehensive summary of the true doctrine of the Church, from creation through salvation. The *Book of Life's Merit* (1158) is predominantly ethical, offering a series of visionary debates between the vices and virtues, and the *Book of Divine Works* (1158–1163) centers on Hildegard's cosmological visions of the dynamic unity of all reality. Despite thematic differences, these three texts share a structure that points to their close interrelationship. The basic division of all three books comes from the individual visions. Each of these "vision texts" opens with a prophetic claim, generally "Then I saw," which is followed by a detailed, concrete description. Hildegard then goes on to explain her vision. The move from vision to interpretation is often marked by an assertion that she hears a voice from heaven, which is the source of these allegorical and didactic explanations.

Generally much longer than the vision itself, this interpretive section suggests the key role the visions played in Hildegard's theological reflections and arguments. For monastic male theologians like Bernard of Clairvaux, working within the commentary tradition, the Bible was the authoritative source; for Hildegard, as a woman barred from engaging in biblical exegesis, it was her visions that grounded and legitimated her theology. This authority also enabled her to incorporate into her interpretations of the visions brief expositions of scripture. Finally, each vision ends with an admonition to the reader.

Hildegard's theology is extraordinarily rich and diverse and cannot be easily summarized. Despite its singular mode of presentation and the liveliness and originality of her imagery, her substantive theological claims are fairly traditional, sharing important assumptions with the 12th-century world in which she lived and wrote. Light is both a defining image and theological reality: "The light that I see thus is not spatial, but it is far, far brighter than a cloud that carries the sun. I can measure neither height, nor length, nor breadth in it; and I call it 'the reflection of the living Light.' And as the sun, the moon, and the stars appear in water, so writings, sermons, virtues, and certain human actions take form for me and gleam within it" (First Letter to Guibert).

This light suffuses reality and is the source of the harmonious union of microcosm and macrocosm described in the *Book of Divine Works*. Following the prologue to the Gospel of John, Hildegard associates the living light with the creative and salvific Word that is Christ. Through her visions of the light and its reflection, Hildegard participates in that light. Although she shares this Johannine, neo-Platonic ontology with many of her contemporaries, Hildegard's experiential emphasis makes it concrete and personal. The essentially optimist view of reality provided by this ontology also shapes her understanding of the religious life, which she continually celebrates in her writing, music, and monastic leadership as a joyful participation in the divine light.

Lest this create too irenic a view of Hildegard's life and career, however, we should remember that her visions also legitimated action in the world, often leading her into conflict with political, religious, and monastic authorities. The institutional consequences of Hildegard's divinely ordained mission were established early in her public career (1148), when God commanded her to remove her nuns from the predominantly male monastery at Saint Disibod and found a convent at Mount Saint Rupert. Not only were many of the nuns and their families unhappy about this decision, which would entail significant hardship, but Kuno, the abbot of Saint Disibod, objected strenuously to the plan. Once again, illness overcame Hildegard until she was permitted to fulfill God's command. She later established a second, sister house at Eibingen.

In her letters and sermons, Hildegard fiercely denounced heresy and a disorganized and corrupt Church which, she claimed, enabled heresy to thrive. Using all the apocalyptic imagery at her disposal, in the *Scivias,* the *Book of Divine Works,* and in her sermons, she prophesied anticlerical riots and other ecclesial disasters if the leaders of the Church refused to heed the divine call for reform. In an amazing testament to the authority vested in Hildegard by her contemporaries, religious leaders did not resent or challenge her denunciations. Instead they asked her to preach and then requested copies of her sermons, using her charismatic gift as an instrument in their own fight against heresy and corruption. After Hildegard's death, these apocalyptic prophecies were the only portion of her work that was anthologized and widely disseminated, in the extremely popular *Mirror of Future Times*. These were thus the texts through which the "Sibyl of the Rhine" (a name first attached to Hildegard in the 14th century) was known to subsequent generations.

See also 1265, 1329, 1346

Bibliography: Peter Dronke, *Women Writers of the Middle Ages: A Critical Study of Texts from Perpetua (d. 203) to Marguerite Porete (d. 1310)* (Cambridge, U.K.: Cambridge University Press, 1984). Gottfried von Disibodenbert and Theodoric von Echternach, *Vita Sanctae Hildegardis,* ed. Monika Klaes, in *Corpus Christianorum: Continuatio mediaevalis* 126 (Turnhout, Belgium: Brepols, 1993). *Epistolarium,* ed. Lieven Van Acker, in *Corpus Christianorum: Continuatio mediaevalis* 91–91a (1991). *The Letters of Hildegard of Bingen,* trans. Joseph L. Baird and Radd K. Ehrman (New York:

Oxford University Press, 1994 and 1998), 2 vols. *Liber divinorum operum,* ed. Albert Derolez and Peter Dronke, in *Corpus Christianorum: Continuatio mediaevalis* 92 (1996). *Liber vite meritorum,* ed. Angela Carlevaris, in *Corpus Christianorum: Continuatio mediaevelis* 90 (1995). *Scivias,* ed. Adelgundis Führkötter and Angela Carlevaris, in *Corpus Christianorum: Continuatio mediaevalis* 43–43a (1978). *Scivias,* trans. Mother Columba Hart and Jane Bishop (New York: Paulist Press, 1990). Barbara Newman, *Sister of Wisdom: St. Hildegard's Theology of the Feminine* (Berkeley: University of California Press, 1987).

Amy M. Hollywood

✑ 1150

Otto von Freising records a meeting between the Armenian Bishop of Gabala and Pope Eugene III

Anthropology of the Crusades

In November 1145, just after the fall of Edessa, the Armenian Bishop Hugo of Gabala paid Pope Eugene III a visit at Viterbo. He described to those present the tribulations of missionary work and the perils of the Eastern Church. While he illustrated the amazing effects of Christian baptism by citing the miraculous case of heathen children who lost their innate bad smell after being christened, he also portrayed the military situation as precarious. Although Prester John, a so-called priest-king from the Far East and descendant of the Magi, had only recently defeated the Persians and Medes, his envisaged Jerusalem campaign failed because he was unable to cross the River Tigris. It was the aim of his journey, the bishop stated, to appeal for help from the Franco-Roman king beyond the Alps.

The historic meeting at Viterbo, recorded around 1150 by Otto of Freising in his *Chronicle,* offers insight into essential features of the Christian Crusade ideology: the belief in moral responsibility for the way of the world; the interpretation of missionary work as a purgational process; the parallel strategies of mission and war; the worldwide dimension of threat; but foremost, a strong identification with the Holy Land. The centrifugal movement of missionary work is juxtaposed with the movement of the Crusades, which is directed toward the center of the world, Jerusalem. The effectiveness of Christianity is obviously linked to the conquest of the land and its semantic center. The Crusades were a blatantly territorial enterprise, just as missionary work traditionally claims a spatial dimension, both metaphorically (sowing the word of God, superstition as a weed) and concretely (recultivation of the wilderness). The metaphor of cultivation can also be applied to the Crusades. In March 1147, Bernard of Clairvaux appealed to Emperor Conrad III to join the Second Crusade to "weed the world from the enemies of the name of Christ." But on several occasions the mission also used the protection of temporal power to free the space from those "savage" pagans who resist the "yoke of peace." From an ecclesiastical point of view, mission and Crusade are complementary enterprises against pagan "savageness," based on a specifically Christian way of perceiving oneself and others.

The Christian doctrine of man is based on two precepts: First, a sense of loss, that is, the memory of the perfection of paradise; and second, an expectation, that is, the hope of re-establishing the original state. Between these two poles, Christian philosophy of history constitutes itself as the doctrine of human sinfulness and the deliverance of man. The "split" nature of "fallen" man becomes manifest not only in the relation of body and soul, which is regarded as full of conflict, but also in the sinful nature of man. Based on the Christian doctrine of the soul, both the relation to the self and the relation to foreigners, particularly those of a different creed, are regarded as relations of rivalry. This results in ethical striving to overcome the self, or an "inner Crusade," but also in a struggle against a menacing external world. A major reason why the idea of the Crusade was so successful was that it combined both requirements. Thus, the expression used for Crusades at the time was (penitential) pilgrimage.

The Christian structure of conflict gains its full dimension in world history in Saint Augustine's vision of the struggle of the City of God with worldly states, which had a formative influence on Otto of Freising's *Chronicle* even in the 12th century (ca. 1150). Early vernacular pieces of historical poetry, such as the *Kaiserchronik* (after 1147; *Emperors' Chronicle*) or the *Rolandslied* (ca. 1170; *Song of Roland*), thus assume a distinctly Crusade-centered perspective on historical events like the history of the Christian emperors or Charlemagne's defeat at Roncesvalles, enhancing the idea that the world is divided into heathens and Christians. Heathens represent the anti-image of Christian self-perception: the epitome of idolatry, vice, monstrosity, and a milling mass of demons. It is the Crusaders' task to clear this universe the way peasants clear a forest. But heathens are also depicted as dangerous members of society itself. They are criticized not only for the classical vices which theology describes as sins, but also for genuinely feudal values: loyalty to country and family, noble pride, and courtly glamour.

Such convictions were an essential part of Crusade propaganda for two centuries (1098–1291). The negative testimony about heathens developed in numerous letters, tracts, sermons, poems, and songs, constituting a powerful, influential discourse. Internal religious, political, social, and personal crises are projected onto the Crusades, which become a great movement of integration for a torn Europe. That it was their function to keep peace at home by directing feudal violence abroad was obvious even to contemporaries. The political competition between Church and Empire, the rivalry between kingdoms, feuds among rulers and within the nobility—the entire articulation of intra-European social violence—were to be ended in favor of a concept of a common enemy. The Crusades become the vehicle for channeling the diverging dynamics of feudal society. With kings, rulers, nobility, clergymen, and common people alike joining the Crusades, the hierarchical structure of society comes to form a uniform organism.

In this war, church and feudal nobility find a common field of action; however, each party pursues its own interests. The attitude of martyrs, typical of the

Christian mission, corresponds to a willingness to die a hero's death. Each attitude, in its own way, is based on the experience of contingency and a view of life as a struggle. However, they are inscribed into different registers of memory. While martyrs sacrifice themselves for the salvation of their souls, warriors strive for post-mortal fame. Despite all efforts, the symbolic orders of church and nobility can be only superficially brought into harmony.

Thus, from the beginning, the Crusades were subject to the tension of rival interpretations. In the early 13th century, Walther von der Vogelweide wrote several lieder about the Crusades in which this division is made obvious. That they are normally divided into religious and political lieder shows a shift of emphasis away from the earlier enthusiasm for the Crusades. While the religious Crusade lieder mostly remain within the bounds of official Crusade propaganda, the political lieder focus on actual historical circumstances. The religious "Kreuzlied," for example, unfolds its argument in a traditional manner within the conflict between loss and reattainment of salvation. Assuming that Christ's act of redemption requires man's readiness to make sacrifices, both inward conversion and outward struggle are necessary. God's act of redemption aiming at the soul is juxtaposed with man's act of liberation directed at the Holy Land. By imitating Christ, the faithful are not only the aim of salvation, but also its executor. The Crusades are justified within the framework of the theology of sin, but they are also related to concepts of feudal law (reward, service). Such arguments form a steady background for Crusade poetry, for example, in metaphors of service or figures of sacrifice and *vanitas,* which foreground the purely instrumental nature of the body.

The political lieder, by contrast, juxtapose the religious program with harsh reality, using innuendoes of military defeat, excessive violence, squabbles over competence, and material interests. As Walther vehemently argues against papal claims to hegemony, the function of the Crusades has perceptibly shifted. They are being exploited for purposes of *Realpolitik.* The lieder are directed at internal matters: against failures of the emperor, the pope, of rulers and the knighthood in general. But as a political platform appears side by side with the religious platform, the feudal nobility advances claims to its own perspective on the Crusades. Unlike the *Rolandslied,* this point of view does not aim at imposing a martyr's attitude on the nobility. On the contrary, the idea of the Crusades is employed to advance the idea of empire. Walther's interpretation of the doctrine of the Divine Right of Emperors as a feudal system confirms this reassignment of the role of vicarage, or representation, traditionally assigned to the pope. In the face of the genuine and dangerous rivalry of feudal families, a political concept (empire) becomes the decisive criterion for the nobility to create a sense of community. The Crusades merely form the vehicle for safeguarding the territorial claims of imperial politics through an interpretation of history as occurring through God's saving grace.

In addition to theology and politics, Walther uses ad hominem argumentation. The "Elegie" starts out from a subjective perspective of resignation which, by citing phenomena like aging, moroseness, and social alienation, describes privation as a personal experience. The negative social findings are transferred to a cultural level, where the crisis is reflected in the decline of courtly manners. Obviously, the diagnosis of resignation asserts itself against all established forms of community building. No framework, be it social, cultural, or even natural, offers any reliable orientation. In the end they all prove to be merely different forms of mankind's misery in general. Therefore, Walther's lament again peaks in a general figure of *vanitas* which calls into question any claim to splendor or joy.

Against the background of this all-encompassing picture of decline, Walther offers the Crusades as the only way out for the leadership of his time. Obviously, the Crusaders partly overcome the division, for in contrast to the ascetic ideal of the Knights Templars, they manage to reconcile knightly glory with Christian readiness to make sacrifices. This is a possible way to salvation, which the arms-bearing Walther immediately reclaims from the privileged class. Even if the idea of *vanitas* in the end encompasses the projects of life and culture, these projects refer to models of community building in competition with the political model. Not only the sinful individual, but also the torn community and even nature itself, on whose symptoms of crisis Walther places great emphasis, want salvation.

Man's sinfulness and its consequences for body and soul correspond to the concept of an unbalanced natural world whose topography indicates the loss of salvation through wild growth and climatic variation. The Middle Ages reinterpret the climate theory of the ancient world to fit into hamartiology: the effects of the Fall of Man on space form a constant danger to man and environment. Just as a sinner threatens to corrupt nature by merely touching it, the untamed environment, in turn, has its effect on the physical and ethical state of man. Albertus Magnus, following Vitruvius, thus views the European scientific tradition and the continuing political power of the Roman Empire as indications of a climatic privilege, while to Guibert of Nogent the numerous heretical teachings and the sexual permissiveness of Eastern Christianity are attributable to the hot climate. There is a natural border drawn between the familiar and the alien. It is characteristic that the rhetoric of Urban II's Crusade sermon contains this climatic aspect as he contrasts the bravery of the European Crusaders with the cowardice of the Levantines. The Crusaders were all the more surprised when harsh reality forced them to correct this image of the enemy.

Space and different human types correspond to each other. From the perspectives of climate theory and *Heilsgeschichte* (Salvation History), the nature of alien peoples, especially in the far-off regions of the Earth, is exposed to pernicious influences: wild nomadic tribes, dwellers at the edge of the world, and apocalyptic peoples. Even toward the neighboring peoples, who have been Christianized only superficially, some ethical reservations are voiced. Danes, for example, according to Arnold of Lübeck, merely imitate German manners. Bohemians are accused of innate wickedness and, according to Otto of Freising, the war ethics of the Hungarians are just a feeble imitation of Franconian war virtues. Christian Europe views itself as surrounded by obstructive forces and inferior nations. Accordingly, Christian observers refer to Slavs, Normans, Irish, Welsh, Navarese, and Basques as uncultured savages living like beasts. The synonymous use of *barbarus* and *paganus* in the Middle Ages indicates a superimposition of cultural and ideological dissociation. Heathens, especially, are seen as the uncivilized antithesis to the Christians' self-image: cruel savages who openly demonstrate the consequences of the Fall of Man, products of the wild and savage space that spawned them. Thus, proselytizing and colonizing these peoples is described in the chronicles as "taming."

The epic poetry of the Crusades shows the external threat facing Christianity more clearly than the scholarly chronicles do by introducing uncivilized characters. These are an integral part of the heathen armies, like the dog-headed and pig-bristled warriors of the *Song of Roland,* or the damned warriors of Zernubel. In Stricker's *Charlemagne,* it is the dark-skinned Ethiopians who frighten Bishop Turpin. And while still fighting Paligan, Charlemagne exclaims: "Lord Christ, through your wounds / deliver us from these hounds" (*Karl,* 10085–6). The extreme portrayal of such enemies highlights the element of struggle in Salvation History and, at the same time, also shows how foreign ethnic groups were pictured in the Middle Ages and how this was expressed in language. All this gives a concrete image of the "animalized heathen," an image that, although already found in the Bible, is deduced mainly from an ancient climate theory viewed from a Christian angle. Thus, Bernard of Clairvaux's appeal to the Knights Templar exempts them from the accusation of murder by claiming that on the Crusades they will kill not men, but evil. This appeal is an indication that all this does not merely constitute epic imagination but has a real background.

Seen against this background, the Crusades are more than a feud or a war: they are a crisis extending into both Salvation History and cultural history and leaving an effect in space as well. Although salvation still depends, in this context, on the sinner's attitude, it may also emanate from a holy place. Palestine represents a place not only of commemoration and apocalyptic justice, but also of present miracles. Contemporary descriptions of the Middle East depict an exotic area at the center of the world, where wealth abounds and the climate is fertile and life-prolonging. Above all, however, there are visible and active traces of Salvation History. Some are natural, like the palm tree that bends toward the Holy Family on their flight to offer them fruit. Others are artificial, like a picture of the Virgin Mary at Damascus—which, travelers claim, literally has become flesh and secretes a redeeming liquid—that also confirms the miraculous force of the locale. The Middle East, therefore, proves to be an exceptional place where God's saving grace is still present and where even nature takes a stand in the competition of faiths.

Of course, it is Paradise that serves as the prototype for miraculous Palestine. Sacred sites such as Santiago de Compostela or simply the garden of a monastery or convent are also experienced as paradisiacal. Burchard consistently describes the fertile Damascus area as a "paradise on Earth." Just as pilgrims will experience a reflection of the paradisiacal beginnings, the Crusaders, so they are led to believe, will reach, at the eastern frontier of the empire, the Promised Land, to which they can then lay claim.

See also 1147, 1170, 1172, 1230

Bibliography: The Letters of St. Bernhard of Clairvaux, trans. Bruno Scott James (London: Burns Oates, 1953). Saint Bernard on the Song of Songs: Sermones in cantica canticorum, trans. and ed. by a religious of C.S.M.V. (London: Mowbray, 1952). Otto von Freising, The Two Cities (Historia de duabus civitatibus), trans. C. C. Mierow (London and Oxford: Oxford University Press, 1928). Otto, Bishop of Freising and Rahewin, The Deeds of Frederic Barbarossa (Gesta Frederici I. Imperatoris), trans C. C. Mierow (London and Oxford: Oxford University Press, 1953). Poems of Walther von der Vogelweide, trans. E. H. Zeydel and B. Q. Morgan (Ithaca, N.Y.: Thrift Press, 1952). Friedrich-Wilhelm Wentzlaff-Eggebert, Kreuzzugsdichtung des Mittelalters: Studien zu ihrer geschichtlichen und dichterischen Wirklichkeit (Berlin: de Gruyter, 1960).

Udo Friedrich

☙ 1157, March 22–31

Emperor Frederick I, known as Barbarossa, writes a letter containing the first recorded reference to the Holy Roman Empire

Imperial Spin Control

In the 18th century, Voltaire described the Holy Roman Empire of the German Nation, then just a few decades away from its dissolution in 1806, as being neither holy, nor Roman, nor an empire. In the second half of the 12th century, the imperial administration's policy team of scribes and *doctores* liked to cast it as all three. The empire was holy by declaration, a move that neatly circumvented a politically active and often adversarial Papacy. It was Roman by circuitous inheritance, for according to the notion of *translatio imperii* in imperial historiography, the emperorship had descended from Rome to Byzantium to France to Lombardy, and finally to Germany. It was the idea of transmigration that enabled Otto, Bishop of Freising and chronicler of world history and his nephew Frederick I's deeds, to refer to Charlemagne as the sixty-ninth emperor since Augustus (*Cities,* 353). Even though the goal of reestablishing a universal empire modeled on Ancient Rome tended to be more diplomatic bluster than actual policy, the German-run empire's irredentist rhetoric rankled its rivals. At the Synod of Saint-Jean de Losne in August 1162, John of Salisbury, the English churchman, diplomat, and author of *Policraticus,* archly demanded to know who had put the Germans in charge of running the world: "Quis Teutonicos constituit iudices nationum?" The imperial spin *doctores* had an answer: God.

For approximately the last two centuries, the fundamental political challenge in the West has been for the party in government to remain in government or for the opposition party to move out of opposition and into government. By contrast, the fundamental political challenge of the Middle Ages was

The Holy Roman Empire ca.1150

DENMARK
BALTIC SEA
NORTH SEA
Kolberg
POMERELIA
Lübeck
Rostock
Stettin
POMERANIA
Notec
Emden
POLAND
Groningen
Oldenburg
Bremen
Warta
FRIESLAND
Brandenburg
BRANDENBURG
Utrecht
Minden
Magdeburg
LUSATIA
Münster
Dessau
Wismar
Oder
Lubin
SAXONY
Brunswick
Halle
Breslau
SILESIA
Ghent
Antwerp
Cologne
Kassel
Leipzig
MEISSEN
Brussels
Liege
Aachen
Erfurt
OSTERLAND
THURINGIA
LOWER LORRAINE
Fulda
VOGTLAND
Prague
MORAVIA
Charleville
Luxembourg
Trier
Frankfurt am Main
Minden
Hannover
Pilsen
Brünn
Mainz
BOHEMIA
FRANCONIA
Nuremberg
UPPER LORRAINE
Mulhouse
Heidelberg
Regensburg
AUSTRIA
Colmar
Stuttgart
Passau
Linz
Vienna
Strasbourg
Augsburg
BAVARIA
Danube
SWABIA
Munich
Salzburg
STYRIA
HUNGARY
Dijon
Basel
Zurich
Saint Gall
Innsbruck
Graz
BURGUNDY
Bern
TYROL
CARINTHIA
FRANCE
Geneva
Trent
FRIULI
CARNIOLA
Lyon
KINGDOM OF ARLES
SAVOY
Milan
VERONA
Venice
Trieste
Turin
Po
Mantua
ADRIATIC SEA
Arles
LOMBARDY
Genoa
Ravenna
PROVENCE
ROMAGNA
ANCONA
Gulf of Lions
Ligurian Sea
Pisa
Florence
TUSCIA
SPOLETO
Corsica
Rome
PATRIMONY
KINGDOM of the TWO SICILIES

Holy Roman Empire, ca.1150
Boundaries of major states and regions

0   100 miles

The Holy Roman Empire, circa 1150

for a ruler to control the periphery of his realm from the center. The medieval Roman Empire existed in the fullest sense only where the emperor and his entourage of dukes, counts, and Imperial knights happened to be. So for the empire to achieve spatial plenitude, the emperor had to appear periodically in the various parts of his realm. He had to practice what modern executives call MBWA: management by walking around. To put it more abstractly, the center continually had to saturate the periphery. Between 1154 and 1186, Frederick I launched seven large-scale military campaigns against the empire's insubordinate periphery in northern Italy. These expeditions were in addition to Frederick's essentially uninterrupted peregrinations throughout the empire. The drama now commonly called *Ludus de Antichristo* (circa 1160; *The Play of Antichrist*), which portrays the expansionist reign and abdication of a Roman emperor—likely modeled on Frederick I—followed by the expansionist reign and subsequent dethronement of the Antichrist, is a celebration of the center's saturation of the periphery.

Little is certain about *Antichrist*'s origins. The only complete text of the minimal liturgico-political drama, a copy produced between 1178 and 1186, comes from a Benedictine monastery near the Tegernsee in Bavaria. Although 1186 thus represents a reliable *terminus ad quem*, it is unclear whether the Tegernsee manuscript is a transcription of the original or a copy of an earlier copy. Estimates of the drama's date of composition span almost the entire 12th century, with most scholars arguing for the years 1150 to 1170. The same vexing opacity obscures the question of *Antichrist*'s author or authors. The quality of the play's rhymed Latin couplets and their liturgical erudition (a significant portion are either direct quotations from the Vulgate or versified adaptations) point to a clergyman. The obvious guess—but it is only a guess—is that the playwright was a monk at the Tegernsee monastery. The dates and places of any performances are likewise guesswork. Was *Antichrist* staged at Frederick I's coronation as German King in Aachen in March 1152? Was it performed at the Regensburg Imperial Diet, held five months after Frederick's crowning as Roman Emperor in Rome in June 1155? Or was Gerhoh of Reichersberg referring to *Antichrist* when, in the early 1160s, he vilipended the practice of staging plays in churches and specifically mentioned dramas that feature an Antichrist figure? We will never know. That said, *Antichrist*'s more than one hundred stage directions and its numerous costume descriptions—both unique in medieval drama—are compelling evidence that its author at least contemplated a performance.

The source material for *Antichrist* comes from the Bible—Daniel, Revelation, and especially the epistles of John and Paul—and from eschatological myths like the 7th-century Pseudo-Methodius (*Visions*, 73–76) and Adso of Moutier-en-Der's "de ortu et tempore Antichristi" (circa 980; "On the Origin and Life of Antichrist," *Antichrist*, 100–110). The medieval myths typically envision a final King of the Romans who travels to Jerusalem to abdicate his rule after presiding over a century-long flourishing economy and after converting the Jews and the pagans to the true faith. His abdication makes way for

Antichrist's reign of deception and destruction, at the height of which the Son of Perdition is struck down by God on the Mount of Olives. In addition to the wide circulation of Antichrist myths such as Adso's, the protracted power struggle between the empire and the Holy See—and perhaps latent millennial anxiety—fostered an inflation of ideologically motivated Antichrist rhetoric in the 11th and 12th centuries. During the investiture controversy (1075–1122), the papal party decried Emperor Henry IV as the Antichrist. A poem by Walter of Châtillon warned that Frederick I's schismatic policies (he supported two antipopes, Victor IV and Pascal III) were precursors of the Final Enemy. Gerhoh interpreted the disease that decimated Frederick's army in Rome in 1168 as the triumph of God's people over Antichrist's legions. And Hildegard's mid-12th-century *Liber Scivias* offered a minatory—and obstetrically precise— vision of Antichrist's birth from the pelvis of the church.

Antichrist has a singularly elaborate and cartographically specific set. According to the play's meticulous stage directions, the Temple of the Lord in Jerusalem is stage-east flanked by the throne platforms (the seats or *sedes*) of the King of Jerusalem and of Synagoga, a personification of the Jews. Stage-west is the Roman Emperor's throne platform, flanked by those of the Kings of the Teutons and of the Franks. At the southern periphery are the seats of the King of the Greeks (representing Byzantium), the King of Babylon, and Gentilitas (personifying the heathens). The play begins with Gentilitas, Synagoga, and Ecclesia entering in succession chanting their particular credos. Gentilitas praises polytheism, Synagoga rejects salvation through Christ, and Ecclesia reminds heretics of the eternal damnation that awaits them. The following instructions for Ecclesia's entrance are an example of the play's rich detail: "Then Ecclesia enters, dressed in woman's garments and wearing a breastplate and crown; escorting her are Mercy, on the right, with oil, and Justice, on the left, with scales and a sword. Both are dressed in women's garments. From the right-hand side the Pope follows her with the Clergy and from the left the Emperor of the Romans with his army. Ecclesia sings the processional chant *Alto consilio,* with those who follow her responding to the individual verses" (69). The Kings of the Franks, the Greeks, and Jerusalem then take the stage with their armies. The set, the pageantry, the spectacle (a siege, four battles, and a massacre are enacted onstage), and the sheer number of performers are all of the awesome proportions that befit the drama's universal scope. For *Antichrist's* stage encompasses—geographically, theologically, and politically—nothing less than the entire medieval world.

After the processions and theological songs, the Roman Emperor announces his irredentist project:

> The writings of historians tell us
> That once the whole world was a Roman fief.
> The strength of early men accomplished this,
> But the neglect of their successors squandered it.
> Though under them the imperial power fell

The majesty of our might shall win it back.
Therefore each king [. . .] must do homage and swear fealty
Before his Emperor: that is our decree.

(70–71)

The emperor then proceeds to make the Kings of the Franks, the Greeks, and of Jerusalem—that is, all of Christianity—his vassals. Imperial messengers journey back and forth delivering the emperor's decree and the kings' replies; the Kings descend from their throne platforms and cross to the emperor's platform to pay homage and swear fealty. There are minor but politically significant variations among the three vassalage ceremonies. The King of the Franks, a potential rival, is at first obdurate (he remarks tartly that if the writings of the historians tell us anything, it is that *he* ought to be emperor) and must be defeated in an onstage battle. The militarily insignificant King of the Greeks, by contrast, succumbs peacefully. It is of greater significance, however, that the same fifty lines of sonorous verse and the same meticulously choreographed toing and froing are repeated three times in succession. These nearly identical ceremonies comprise about one fifth of *Antichrist,* underscoring the critical role medieval public rituals played in articulating political power relationships and binding the participants and their supporters to recognize the political order portrayed in—and established by—the ritual. Moreover, the pro-German potential audience doubtless would have found the thrice-repeated fulfillment of imperial enfeoffment fantasies intensely satisfying.

Medieval homage rituals symbolized a vassal's submission and surrender. The vassal knelt, placed his clasped hands into his lord's, and vowed henceforth to be his lord's man (Ganshof, 66–67). It is very likely that this ritual was intended to be enacted onstage during a performance of *Antichrist.* And in the play's spatially and temporally condensed context, the solemn spectacle of each king leaving his throne platform and crossing the stage to the emperor's underscores his submission. The journey to one's lord was a constituent part of the vassalage system. In contrast to the submission of homage, the medieval fealty ritual symbolized the exchange of mutual obligations. "Live through my grace, and keep your royal name," the emperor intones to his vassals in the play's staging of the fealty pact, "since you acknowledge me as the only Emperor" (73). In the fealty contract the lord typically promised protection in return for the vassal's *auxilium* (military support) and *consilium* (advice). Both military support and advice require the vassal's physical presence before his lord. Homage and fealty are thus a contractual way of making the periphery come to the center. Frederick I's mention at the outset represents just such a demand for his vassals' *auxilium* and their presence at the center. And in *Antichrist,* the emperor soon calls for his vassals' military assistance to battle the King of Babylon who besieges Jerusalem after the final fealty ritual is completed.

The Christian armies, led by the Roman Emperor, defeat Babylon. For a play written after the disastrous Second Crusade (1145–1148), in which the

European armies never reached Jerusalem, this moment is the emotional apex. But having reached a climax of imperial wish-fulfillment—the emperor has enfeoffed the Christian kingdoms and liberated the Holy City—the drama bows to eschatological exigencies. In consonance with the source material, the emperor enters the Temple in Jerusalem, lays down his crown and scepter, and abdicates:

> Receive, O Lord, my grateful gift, for I
> Resign my rule to Thee, the King of Kings,
> Through Whom kings reign, and Whom alone we call
> The Emperor and Ruler of us all.

(79)

After the emperor returns to his former realm (the play henceforth refers to him as the King of the Teutons), Antichrist takes the stage wearing a robe and cuirass, symbols of his sacerdotal and military treachery, and flanked by his "fifth columnists," Hypocrisy (whose mission it is to infiltrate the laity) and Heresy (whose mission it is to infiltrate the clergy). Under Antichrist's command, the Hypocrites depose the King of Jerusalem, who flees west across the stage to find refuge with the King of the Teutons. Antichrist is crowned in Jerusalem and in a geographical and ideological anti-Crusade, which begins in the East and moves to the West, he initiates his own round of demanding homage and fealty. The procedure from the play's first half—"shuttle diplomacy" culminating in vassalage rituals—is reenacted in all its details. But this time the fealty vows are disturbingly different. The Kings of the Greeks and the Franks are allowed to continue their reigns as long as they recognize Antichrist as the Creator of All Things, a heretical variation on the oath they swore to the emperor. The ceremony also has a nefarious twist. As the kings kneel in submission to receive their crowns, Antichrist draws the first letter of his name on their foreheads, invoking the mark of the beast from Revelation 13. If the intended audience was to thrill to the thrice-repeated Imperial vassalage rituals, the playwright now seeks to make them shudder at this sinister parody. Yet Antichrist's establishment of demonic vassalage relationships also demonstrates that he, too, is subject to the imperative to achieve political control by saturating the periphery from his usurped center in Jerusalem.

But the King of the Teutons, the former Roman Emperor, rejects Antichrist's demands for homage and defeats him in another onstage war. Thwarted by German martial prowess, Antichrist tries his luck with German credulity. He goes before the King of the Teutons and heals a lame man, cleanses a leper, and seemingly revives a soldier who the stage directions tell us is only pretending to be dead. The German King's faith waivers and he too finally swears homage to Antichrist. At this point the drama becomes brisk and giddy-paced. Babylon again wages war and is again routed, this time by Antichrist's army. The prophets Elijah and Enoch appear, strip away Antichrist's mask, and convert Synagoga to the true faith of the Holy Trinity. Enraged, Antichrist has Synagoga, the two prophets, and the Jews executed. There is a thunderclap, and Antichrist collapses onstage. Everyone returns to the faith, and the play abruptly ends. The final theologically correct atmospherics notwithstanding, Antichrist's reign is made possible by the Roman Emperor's abdication after his victory in the Holy City. When the deposed King of Jerusalem decamps following Antichrist's seizure of power, he grumbles that the King of the Teutons should never have surrendered his rule as Roman Emperor. A malevolence was bound to follow his departure, a "malum discessionis" as he puts it (*Ludus*, 24).

According to Paul's second epistle to the Thessalonians, Antichrist will not be revealed "except there come a falling away [*discessio*] first." For *Antichrist*'s author, both the empire and the emperor have an eschatological and political mission: they are the "power that holds [the man of sin] in check" (2 Thessalonians 2:6). *Antichrist*'s fantasy of imperial enfeoffment followed by the minatory disaster of antichristic enfeoffment comprise a spectacularly staged entreaty for the Roman Emperor's divinely ordained power to be projected onto the periphery in order to prevent—or at least postpone—the *discessio*.

See also 1147, 1150

Bibliography: Gerd Althoff, *Spielregeln der Politik im Mittelalter: Kommunikation in Frieden und Fehde* (Darmstadt: Primus, 1997). François L. Ganshof, *Feudalism,* trans. Philip Grierson (London: Longmans, 1952). *Ludus de Antichristo: Das Spiel vom Antichrist,* trans. Rolf Engelsing (Stuttgart: Reclam, 1968). Bernard McGinn, *Visions of the End: Apocalyptic Traditions in the Middle Ages* (New York: Columbia University Press, 1979). Otto, Bishop of Freising, *The Two Cities: A Chronicle of Universal History to the Year 1146 AD,* trans. Charles C. Mierow (New York: Columbia University Press, 1928). Otto, Bishop of Freising, and Rahewin, *The Deeds of Barbarossa,* trans. Charles C. Mierow (New York: Norton, 1966). *The Play of Antichrist,* trans. John Wright (Toronto: Pontifical Institute of Mediaeval Studies, 1967).

Sean Ward

♌ *Circa 1170*
Minnesingers begin imitating troubadours and trouvères

Phantom Ladies

The first German lyric poets came from the Danube region between Regensburg and Vienna and may have performed at the Vienna court of Duke Heinrich II of Austria (1146–1177). Although we know almost nothing about these early singers (the Lord von Kürenberg, Dietmar von Aist, the castellan [*Burggraf*] of Regensburg), they were certainly noblemen. Writing and performing songs was for them a leisure-time avocation, which links them to the court singers of France, the troubadours and trouvères. For about ten generations (1100–1300), unique in European cultural history, members of the ruling aristocracy produced great poetry, writing verse and composing melodies. The subject of these early lyrics, as of all minnesong, is love: courting, pledging loyalty, love fulfilled, jealousy, love lost. As Hartmann von Aue (about

1195) attests, these poets called themselves minnesingers, *minne* being the medieval German word for love. It is related to English "mind," suggesting that love is an intellectual activity, and to the Swedish word for "memory," love as emotion remembered.

Medieval poetry is not confessional, the poet does not explore his own feelings. Like a composer, he works with established genres that specify the subject, the way to deal with it, and the voice that is to speak. The voice in about one third of early poetry is a woman although all minnesingers known to us were men. Women's songs are found in the early poetry of many European cultures. This suggests that such songs, often lamenting the absent or faithless lover, are indigenous, much as dancing songs are. The first German lyric poet (exact dates of birth and death unknown), the Lord of Kürenberg, is also one of the masters of the German love poetry. In a surviving work of only fifteen strophes are four different voices: the demure woman longing for her lover, the dominant woman asserting her claim over the man, the macho knight who lures women as easily (with a flesh lure) as he does his hunting falcon, the subservient knight humbly yearning for his lady. In contrast to later minnesong, the woman here speaks freely of her need for love. She does so in her gown by the bed at night, on the castle rampart overlooking her domain, while watching the falcon, her lover, wheeling in the sky, free from the yoke of courtly discipline. Many of these songs consist of a single strophe or stanza. The original meaning of the German word *Lied* is "single strophe" *(daz liet)* while the plural *(diu liet)* denotes a gathering of stanzas, a song.

Coupling two single strophes gave rise to a song type called *Wechsel* ("Exchange") found only in German poetry. It links the monostrophe of the woman with that of the man. They speak about a love they share or remember, not to each other but to themselves. In their understated brevity, in their use of a few powerful symbols, in giving voice to the passionate woman, the earliest German love lyrics appeal most directly to the modern reader. Later minnesingers, like master Reinmar (dates unknown), "a scholastic of unhappy love," as the German Romantic poet Ludwig Uhland called him, are much harder to appreciate.

In contrast to later minnesingers writing in the French mode, the Danube school poets use a long verse (a pause separates three- or four-beat half lines), with four verses forming a strophe. Clearly meant to be sung, this strophe is used, about 1200, by the Passau cleric writing the *Nibelungenlied,* the first and greatest German heroic epic. The long verse goes back to Germanic alliterative poetry. Yet while based on native forms, the early lyrics are not devoid of French influence. The troubadour style manifests itself in the theme of love service: the knight is happy just to serve his lady whom he praises as the embodiment of physical and moral perfection.

The minnesingers who begin composing around 1170 along the Rhine and the Neckar rivers are familiar with the old Austrian poets, but they fix their gaze firmly on the West. They imitate the troubadours of southern France, writing in Occitan, and the trouvères of the north, writing in French.

All to the castle born, these new minnesingers gather at the court of the Hohenstaufen emperor Friedrich I whose son Heinrich (1165–1197) was himself a poet. Three of his love songs survive. The most accomplished singer of the Rhenish school, Friedrich von Hausen (d. 1190 on crusade), was cabinet secretary, in today's parlance, to the emperor. Like most courts of the time, the imperial court was peripatetic, moving often into France and Italy. This provided many social occasions to meet trouvères and troubadours. Heinrich, the royal minnesinger, had a French mother, Beatrix of Burgundy. In 1178, the archbishop of Arles crowned his father Friedrich King of Burgundy. Many French poets, among them Guiot de Provins (Friedrich von Hausen imitates one of his songs), joined the company of European princes in 1184 at the Mainz Pentecost festival where Emperor Friedrich knighted his son Heinrich, the minnesinger (then nineteen years old), and his brother. Heinrich von Veldeke (near Maastricht, d. ca. 1200), the first German poet to write in the trouvère style, took part in the festival and described it as the high point of European chivalry. After Heinrich was crowned King of Italy and Sicily in 1186, several of his fellow minnesingers (Friedrich von Hausen, Ulrich von Gutenburg, Bligger von Steinach) traveled with him to northern Italian castles whose lords where fond of hosting troubadours. Much of court culture was oral. Most noblemen did not know how to read or write. Thus, Heinrich and his fellow singers must have had an excellent command of French and a good ear, as just listening to the songs enabled them to imitate words, strophic form, and melody.

Most of the classical minnesingers, heirs to the Rhenish school, were also aristocrats. Professional poets of the age, wandering from castle to castle and singing for their supper, wrote didactic or instructional verse that taught the lessons of life, moral wisdom, and basic religion. Only Heinrich von Morungen (thirty-five songs) and Reinmar (fifty-three) left oeuvres of a size associated with professional poets. Heinrich appears to have earned his keep singing at the court of the Margraves of Meissen (in Saxony, north of Dresden). Reinmar was court poet to the dukes of Austria at Vienna. There he mentored the first great professional singer, Walther von der Vogelweide (ca. 1170–ca. 1230), who by conjoining minnesong and instructional verse became one of the immortal German poets.

Minnesingers were selective in the lyric forms they took over from the French. They ignored major parts of the troubadour repertory: the debate songs *(tenson, partimen),* the political songs *(sirventes),* songs lamenting the death of a patron or a colleague *(planh).* Of the song types favored by trouvères, they opted not to imitate the *pastourelle* (knight meets shepherdess) and dancing songs, usually featuring a refrain. Minnesingers were most fascinated by the centerpiece of the Romance repertory, the *grand chant courtois,* the song celebrating unrequited love. Yet in writing their *Minnelieder,* the Germans omitted certain features of the great court song. They did not give cover names *(senhal)* to their ladies and did not add closing verses *(envoi)* that mention the lady, friends, or a patron to whom the song is addressed. Lacking a social or historical context, the songs of high *minne* tend to be more theoretical and abstract. They dwell on the ideal of courtly love and love service.

In high minnesong, the lyrical voice switches resolutely to the first person. The singer, the male I, speaks obsessively about himself in probing what love is and what love means. There are two other protagonists. One is his lady, distant and unreachable, forever indifferent to his pleas. In contrast to the early lyrics, she no longer speaks. The other party is the people at the court, the audience, whom the singer befriends and tries to enlist in his cause. Endlessly frustrated, the singer analyzes himself, plays philosopher to his sad feelings: what is love, why am I unworthy of my lady's love, how can I improve myself to be worthy of her? He finds the answer in constant faith and unremitting service. He serves his lady the way, in feudal or lordship society, the vassal serves his lord. Metaphors of the feudal contract abound. His service consists of singing. He sings of his desires, of a love that keeps him enthralled, clouds his reason and sense, of the pain of yearning, and the hope of winning his lady's love, eventually. The lady is a phantom; she has virtually no physical features. Only sometimes do singers mention radiant eyes and red lips. In evoking Ovid's myth of the self-enchanted Narcissus, Heinrich von Morungen suggests that the singer is creating the lady in his own image. He must sustain this vision in order to write. The minnesinger, observed the poet Rilke, fears nothing so much as that one day his lady will say yes. That would be the end of his singing.

The courtiers are party to his song. As "friends," they share the singer's distress and support his pleas. As "spies" *(Merker),* they personify public morality and prevent him from approaching his lady. The singer finds himself locked in a paradox: While unrequited love (and thinking too much about himself) makes him sad, he is expected to make court people happy with his singing. The more profound paradox is social. In writing songs to an unattainable lady, aristocrats, who in real life had women aplenty, stylize themselves as vassals and plead for their lord's favor. This is more than a parlor game. By humbling themselves before an ideal, these noblemen profess faith in the new secular religion of courtesy and chivalry created in literature.

In addition to creating the high minnesong, minnesingers also take over three other French song types. In the crusading song, first written by trouvères, the singer has to decide whether to continue serving his unyielding lady or go on crusade as a soldier of Christ and serve God. The usual option is to bid the lady a reluctant farewell (Friedrich von Hausen). An alternative is to take the good lady along in the shrine of the heart and share the heavenly crusader reward with her (Albrecht von Johansdorf, ca. 1165–after 1209). Thematizing both *minne* and religious service (to the cross, the Virgin), the *Leich* (French *descort, estampie*) makes the greatest demands on the poet's skill as versifier and composer. This long poem consists of multiform short strophes, usually paired, called versicles. Although the first minnesingers under French influence compose *Leichs* (Ulrich von Gutenberg, dates unknown), most write only one as a formal, through-composed showpiece.

Quite different from these subjective forms, is the objective or narrative genre of the dawn song *(tageliet)*, the Occitan *alba* (morning light). It features two lovers, not married to each other, who must part at dawn after spending the night in "secret love." Here the woman speaks again, as she does in the early lyric. She is in fact much more vocal than her partner. Dietmar von Aist (dates unknown) wrote a dawn song not influenced by the alba, suggesting that the form is indigenous. The lament of lovers parting at dawn is found in love poetry throughout the world. In the alba, a watchman on the ramparts wakes the lovers and urges the man to leave. The German master of the genre is the great romancer Wolfram von Eschenbach (ca. 1170–ca. 1220). In his dawn songs, the watchman embodies the woman's conscience and the moral claims of society. Enormously popular, dawn songs continued to be written for three centuries.

Much of what minnesingers learned from their French colleagues concerns the craft of form: to alternate stresses and dips in a regular rhythmic pattern, to regulate the beginning (anacrusis) and the end (cadence) of verses, to build strophes with verses of different length, to devise new rhyme patterns, to compose an original tune. Imitating French verse was not easy. It is defined by the number of syllables (syllabic) while German (and English) verse alternates between stressed and unstressed syllables (rhythmic). German singers transposed French decasyllabic (ten-syllable) verse into dactyls, or triple measures. Alien to the German sense of duple rhythm, dactylic verse did not outlast the Rhenish school for long. It is easier to find rhymes in French than in German. The minnesingers, therefore, did not try to imitate the more complex French ways of rhyming. Eighty percent of German court lyrics are set in a tripartite form first used by Duke William IX of Aquitaine, the first troubadour (d. 1127). It gave rise to the sonnet and is still with us today. If you hum the "Star Spangled Banner," you will note that the first melody *(pes, Stollen)* is repeated *(contra-pes, Gegenstollen)*, thus forming what Dante called the *frons* (German *Aufgesang*). The second melody, set in a higher register, makes up the *cauda* *(Abgesang)*.

Aside from imitating the subject matter, the Rhenish minnesingers sometimes copied the strophic form of French songs in a process known as "contrafacture." Presumably they also borrowed the melody. But since melodies survive only for the French songs, this remains an assumption. Of Friedrich von Hausen's seventeen songs, seven are contrafactures of songs composed by three troubadours and three trouvères. As minnesingers devise their own strophic form and compose an original melody, this "tune" *(dôn)* becomes their intellectual property. The only "copyright" widely respected, it shows the enormous artistic importance medieval song poets attached to creating metrical and musical forms. When Gottfried von Strassburg (in his *Tristan* romance) praises the minnesingers as nightingales, he celebrates them as musical composers. This heritage is largely lost. The urban patrons of the great song collections (Zurich, Constance, perhaps Strasbourg, 1290–1340) chose not to transcribe the melodies.

Minnesingers exercised mind and memory to write songs, inventing lyrics and melody in the same process. Ulrich von Lichtenstein (ca. 1260) tells us that he composed songs while castle-bound in winter, while riding to tournaments in the summer, while lying on his sickbed, while riding as pilgrim to Rome, while languishing in prison. Manuscript variants suggest that the modern concept of a single authentic or authorized version did not exist. Singers would, at times, add strophes to an existing tune and try out different strophic sequences. Musical memory is more permanent; the melody aids in remembering the words. Troubadours speak of writing down their songs to send them to their lady or a patron. Living in an age without paper, they or their scribes would have inscribed them on wax tablets, on vellum (calf skin), or parchment (sheep skin) sheets or on rolls formed by sewing together such sheets. Yet until about 1250, when song collections begin to be compiled, songs were largely performed by heart, retained in and passed down from memory.

There is no evidence that minnesingers, as did gentry troubadours, hired minstrels *(joglars)* or professional singers *(cantadors)* to sing their songs. They presumably sang themselves before the assembled court, perhaps accompanying themselves on a drone instrument like the fiddle. Yet formal recitation was not the only way in which songs were disseminated. If literature mirrors life, courtiers would sing songs together after dinner, while taking a walk or riding a horse, before jousting, when dancing. Reading these songs on the printed page falsifies them. Singing a text slows it down, intimate sentiments become artfully enunciated public statements. Performing before an audience made singing a cabaret-like show, court theater, in which listeners, versed in the art, would participate. Medieval music groups have, for three decades, struggled to recreate this experience. Yet the melodies we have were notated at least a century, sometimes two or three, after the songs were composed. The single-line notation tells us little about rhythm and tempi and nothing about instrumentation. So the recordings we hear today are at best informed guesswork.

See also 1150, 1189, ca. 1200, 1203 (November 12), 1210, 1922 (February)

Bibliography: German and Italian Lyrics of the Middle Ages, ed. and trans. Frederick Goldin (Garden City, N.Y.: Anchor, 1973). Hans-Herbert S. Räkel, *Der deutsche Minnesang: Eine Einführung* (Munich: Beck, 1986). Joachim Bumke, *Courtly Culture: Literature and Society in the High Middle Ages,* trans. Thomas Dunlap (Berkeley and Los Angeles: University of California Press, 1991). *Deutsche Lyrik des frühen und hohen Mittelalters,* ed. Ingrid Kasten, trans. Margherita Kuhn (Frankfurt am Main: Deutscher Klassiker Verlag, 1995).

Eckehard Simon

♫ 1172, January

At the height of his power, Duke Henry the Lion embarks on a pilgrimage to the Holy Land

Religious Devotion and Courtly Display

Einhard reports in chapter 9 of his *Vita Karoli Magni (Life of Charlemagne)* that at the time of the Saxon wars, the Emperor Charlemagne also fought a campaign in Spain and conquered several cities and castles across the Pyrenees. While crossing the Pyrenees on the way back, his army was ambushed in a mountain pass by Basques, and his entire rear-guard was lost. Eggihard, the king's steward; Anselm, Count Palatine; and Roland, margrave of Brittany, were killed in the fighting. The attackers fled in the difficult terrain as night fell, and the deaths of Charlemagne's men remained unavenged.

This event of the year 778 is reported by other chroniclers as well. One late account, from the second half of the 11th century, is particularly noteworthy. The *Nota Emilianense* limits the historical events to a military encounter near Saragossa and expands the number of participants to include twelve nephews of the king. Six are mentioned by name: Roland, Bertran, Ogier, William of the Short Nose, Olivier, and Bishop Turpin. The site of the disaster is now the valley of Roncesvalles, and Roland is killed by Saracens instead of Basques. The changes obviously reflect a reworking of the events into legend, which then took literary form in the later *chansons de geste*. In this process the *gestes* of Charlemagne and William diverged.

The story of Roland remained part of the *geste* of Charlemagne and shortly after the turn of the century found its most significant literary expression in the *Chanson de Roland*. The oldest extant version is the Oxford manuscript (O) from the first half of the 12th century, where the story runs as follows: Charlemagne has been waging war in Spain for seven years. Saragossa alone remains to be conquered. King Marsilie decides to trick Charlemagne by pretending he wants to surrender. He declares himself willing to pay tribute and be baptized. Charlemagne confers with his vassals and twelve paladins, among them the knights Roland and Olivier and the pugnacious Bishop Turpin. They decide to accept the offer of surrender, and Roland proposes his stepfather, Guenes (Guenelun), as messenger. Guenelun fears for his life and vows to take revenge for the hatred that Roland has long harbored against him. He carries the message to the Saracens and secretly allies himself with them. As the Christians depart, Guenelun proposes that Roland be left behind with a small number of troops to guard the territory. The emperor is forced to accept the general decision but is tormented that night by ominous dreams, which soon become reality. King Marsilie attacks the Christian rear-guard, and in heroic defiance Roland refuses to summon back the emperor's forces. Only when his badly outnumbered troop is exhausted does he order the signal horn to be blown. The emperor returns, but it is too late. He laments the dead, among them Roland and Olivier, pursues the fleeing heathens, and destroys them. King Marsilie is already mortally wounded by the time Baligant, the supreme ruler of all heathen empires, comes to his aid. In a second battle, Charlemagne defeats the heathen reinforcements, in spite of being outnumbered. He sees to it that the fallen Christians are buried and returns home. In Aachen he holds a court of justice. Guenelun invokes his right to a trial by combat, and so God's judgment is sought. Guenelun loses and is drawn and quartered.

The epic concept is straightforward. The historical event remains recognizable (not the case in Germanic heroic sagas); the motives are outlined, and the outcome is interpreted. The destruction of the emperor's rear-guard in the Pyrenees is now explained as the result of betrayal, and the poet supplies the element of revenge (lacking in real life) in two battles, in conformity with the basic epic principle of intensification. Charlemagne acquires a mythical dimension as emperor of all Christendom.

When a German named Priest Konrad retells the story, he notes that his source was a "book in the French language" (ll. 9080f), "written in France" (9022f). Yet it cannot have been any of the known versions of the *Chanson de Roland,* since the German *Rolandslied (Song of Roland)* differs from them in many details. It most closely resembles the Oxford version, but the background story (31–360) is found neither there nor in any of the other extant versions. It is possible that Konrad either added it or might have worked from an expanded French version. Although his statement that he neither added nor removed anything is a stock phrase, it should be taken seriously. Whatever the form of the model, it did not include the interpretation given to the story by its German adapter.

For Priest Konrad the story of Charlemagne and his nephew and vassal Roland is a spiritual paradigm with clearly legendary elements. The men killed in Spain are knights of God and martyrs, followers in the path of Christ's suffering, and models in their unswerving faith. Priest Konrad is in all probability also the source of the Crusade motifs that appear in the ceremonial prayers, exhortations, and sermons. The struggle for power is now a struggle for the Christian religion. In the *Chanson de Roland,* the Christian knights are fighting for *la douce France* (sweet France); in the German *Song of Roland* their struggle is for the kingdom of heaven. This shift alters the motivation of the participants. Guenelun's demand for a trial by combat, which was traditional and lawful in the original version, is here declared illegal, and Guenelun himself is portrayed as a traitor, a "Judas" (1924ff). Roland faces the enemy not in heroic defiance, but with a martyr's steadfastness in his faith (3873ff).

Priest Konrad's *Song of Roland* lies at the intersection of religious and secular poetry. The archaic nature of its verse rhythm and rhyming techniques distinguishes it from early courtly poetry of the decade 1170–1180. In style it bears a close resemblance to the German *Kaiserchronik (Emperors' Chronicle).* However, the language of the manuscripts displays a puzzling mixture of High and Middle German characteristics. For this reason, the date and place of composition of *The Song of Roland* remain in dispute, despite the fact that the epilogue (9017–9094) contains unusually precise details about its origins.

The epilogue states that the poem was commissioned by a duke named Henry and his wife. She is identified as the daughter of a powerful king. The poet compares the duke with David, implying that he is the equal of a king in birth. He also praises Duke Henry as a man who has converted heathens and who is just in the eyes of God because he has already atoned for his sins through an act of penance that is clearly out of the ordinary (but remains unspecified). And finally the author, "Chunrat," speaks of himself and his literary task. He refers to himself as a "phaffe," a term equivalent to *clericus,* meaning a member of the clergy in general, not specifically a priest or monk.

These details are open to interpretation. The marriage of a Duke Henry to a king's daughter suggests the Guelph dukes Henry the Proud (1126–1138) or Henry the Lion (1155–1180). The Babenberg Duke Henry Jasomirgott (1143–1156) is also a possibility. All three were married to women of royal lineage. Thus Priest Konrad's *Song of Roland* could date from the first half, the middle, or the second half of the 12th century. Several indications have prompted scholars in recent years to settle on Henry the Lion, who took Mathilde, daughter of Henry II of England, as his second wife in 1168. His Crusades against the Wends in 1147 justify the reference to him as a "converter of the heathens," and his pilgrimage to the Holy Land in the year 1172 could be the act of atonement mentioned. The striking emphasis placed on his being equal in rank to a king and his marriage to a powerful royal house speak in his favor. Other documents, too, support the claim to quasi-royal status, chiefly Henry's own illuminated Gospels (from the Abbey of Helmarshausen). Both the words of the dedicatory poem and the miniature coronation portrait allege Henry's descent from Charlemagne. The *Song of Roland*—which would be better named the "Song of Charlemagne" after its protagonist—fits seamlessly into the "representational art" (in Karl Bertau's phrase) related to Henry the Lion. If the duke's wife played a role in making the French *Chanson de Roland* known to his court, Mathilde of the House of Plantagenet also seems the most likely candidate, for it is difficult to connect the wives of Henry the Proud and Henry Jasomirgott with such an occurrence.

In addition, literary interest in the traditional lore about Charlemagne can be connected with two other historical events that took place during Henry the Lion's reign. In the year 1165, as a result of the Staufen party's efforts, Charlemagne was canonized. The Guelph duke Henry the Lion appears to have actively supported and propagated the not uncontroversial proposal. And while the emperor is not called "sanctus" in the *Song of Roland,* the prologue does assert that he has attained eternal blessedness (12).

According to the epilogue, the translation and transmission of the poem were undertaken in honor of the empire (l. 9034). And here, too, the Guelph duke confidently allowed himself to be placed next to the Staufen emperor. His claim to imperial status was bolstered by demonstrative acts of piety, including his widely hailed pilgrimage to the Holy Land. Such displays of status and devotion gave this undertaking its particular stamp. They also included endowments and gifts, to which the highly edifying *Song of Roland* may have belonged. This would explain the consistent reinterpretation of the *Chanson de Roland* in religious terms (a feature that may not, as in the modern period, be attributed to the personal beliefs of the German author). It would also make the epilogue, which is strikingly unconventional in a literary sense, more understandable as an identification of the work's sponsor. In any case, Henry the

Lion is considered one of the first patrons of vernacular literature identified by name in European literary history, even if scholars disagree about whether other German texts, such as *Lucidarius* or the *Tristrant* of Eilhart of Oberg, can be traced back to him and his court.

Little is known about Priest Konrad's identity, as is the case for almost all medieval German authors. In earlier research, he was equated with the author of the *Emperors' Chronicle*. Later he was seen as only loosely connected with the literary circle of Regensburg, while recent scholars have attempted to identify him as a chaplain of Henry the Lion who worked in Brunswick. While such speculations fascinate us today, they remain without effect on literary history since, with few exceptions, the personality of a medieval author was of secondary importance to the texts he composed. The wishes of his patron who commissioned the work, the function the work was to serve, and the traditions in which the type of work was embedded played a more important role.

Priest Konrad is firmly anchored in the tradition of 12th-century German religious poetry, traces of which philologists believe to have identified in particular phrases of the *Song of Roland*. However, after the *Emperors' Chronicle* and Priest Lambrecht's *Alexanderlied (Song of Alexander),* both of which were written about the middle of the century, interest in narrative grew. This tendency was strengthened by the reception of French influence, which began at about this time and remained dominant for the next fifty years. Lambrecht's *Song of Alexander* and Konrad's *Song of Roland* mark the beginning of this highly significant change. The unconventionality of this process is apparent in Priest Konrad's statement in the epilogue that he first translated the French book into Latin (the literary language with which he was familiar) and only then, in a second step, from Latin into German (9080ff).

The *Song of Roland* is the first courtly verse epic in German, even though the style may strike us as old-fashioned in this context. The verse technique, for instance, lacks the refinement of classic courtly poetry. The language, usage, and intellectual scope of the poem also remain traditional. The author almost always uses the word *Ritter* ("knight"), which later came to be associated with specific social behavior, in its original limited and technical sense of "mounted warrior." Spiritual and worldly knighthood remain strict opposites and have not yet attained the higher unity that poets began to celebrate not long thereafter. This is determined by the nature of the material, for Priest Konrad's *Song of Roland* is a story about men, in which women play only marginal roles. Both Brechmunda, wife of King Marsilie, and Alda, Roland's betrothed, are victims. Priest Konrad found them represented as such in his model, and he leaves them in this role in his version. He omits Charlemagne's ambiguous declaration that he intends to take Bramimunde, the wife of his slain foe, to France as a prisoner and convert her "par amur" (3674). Instead he has the heathen queen convert to Christianity at once. The only element he adds to the brief scene in which the grief-stricken Alda dies is a prayer. When Heinrich von Veldeke (d. ca. 1200) completed his German version of the *Roman d'Eneas (Ro-*

mance of Aeneas), he added hundreds of lines to the tale of Aeneas and Livinia, turning it into its own little love story. Of course, the *Romance of Aeneas* already contained a strong love theme, even though it was written only fifteen years after the *Song of Roland.*

It appears that the *Song of Roland* was quickly copied and circulated, for most of the six existing manuscripts date back to the 12th century. But it entered on its triumphal course through medieval German literature only in the revised form by the 13th-century author known as "der Stricker." This modernization was so successful that, to judge by the abundance of surviving manuscripts, Stricker's *Charlemagne* was one of the most widely read German verse epics of the late Middle Ages. Konrad's *Song of Roland,* by contrast, was quickly forgotten. Its most obvious traces may be found in the *Willehalm* of Wolfram of Eschenbach (ca. 1170–ca. 1220), a German version of part of the *geste* of Wilhelm *(Aliscans).* Wolfram—probably writing in the second decade of the 13th century—sets the story of Margrave Willehalm of Provence against the historical background of the *Song of Roland,* as a kind of sequel. The author frequently alludes to the older poem and inserts many quotations from it into his work. Thus the constant presence of the older poem within the newer one makes the different spirit of the latter all the more evident. Whereas Priest Konrad uses edifying legends to convey an unqualified dualism, in which life and afterlife, heathens and Christians, good and evil confront each other as irreconcilable opposites, Wolfram introduces the possibility of doubt. The Saracens in *Willehalm* are not despicable heathens condemned by God, who can be slaughtered like dogs. Rather they are the Christians' equals in every respect, equipped with the same qualities, virtues, and ideals. Heathens, Jews, and Christians are all portrayed as children of God, who should spare each other. This depiction endows the warfare between Christians and non-Christians with a tragic dimension. Even the heathens' faith, which Wolfram still regards as a condemnable error, is treated with respect, in that Willehalm allows his royal foes to be buried according to their own religious rites.

Modern readers, for whom the attitudes expressed in Konrad's *Song of Roland* may seem alien, will find *Willehalm* more congenial. But literary historians realize that the more humane outlook is based on the aesthetics of its genre. Wolfram retells the *chanson de geste* with the tools and in the light of the courtly romance. This approach leads to contradictions that cannot be resolved solely by softening the crass oppositions. Here may be why Wolfram did not finish his *Willehalm.* However, medieval readers apparently took a much more naive attitude toward his work. The two 13th-century authors who added a preceding and a subsequent story do not seem discernibly impressed by Wolfram's humane view of heathens, though their poems were read and handed down with Wolfram's *Willehalm.* In eight of the twelve existing complete manuscripts, *Willehalm* stands between the *Arabel* (preceding history) of Ulrich von dem Türlin and the *Rennewart* (sequel) of Ulrich von Türheim, in which the battle between Christians and heathens is fought with the same rigor, just as if Wolfram's *Willehalm* had never existed.

See also 800, 1150, 1203 (November 12), 1230

Bibliography: Priest Konrad's Song of Roland, translated and with an introduction by J. W. Thomas (Columbia, S.C.: Camden House, 1994). John Ashcroft, "Magister Conradus Presbyter: Pfaffe Konrad at the Court of Henry the Lion," in D. S. Brewer, ed., *Literary Aspects of Courtly Culture* (Cambridge, U.K.: Cambridge University Press, 1994).

Dieter Kartschoke
Translated by Deborah Lucas Schneider

Ꮗ Circa 1175–1195

Herrad of Landsberg works on the *Hortus Deliciarum (Garden of Delights),* which depicts poets and intellectuals as transcribers of messages from the devil

The Archpoet and Goliard Poetry

The medieval Church offered excellent opportunities for professional advancement. But you had to be willing to travel. Nicholas Brekespear, for example, started life humbly in Hertfordshire around 1100, went to France to study, became abbot of a monastery near Avignon, was made Bishop of Albano, journeyed to Scandinavia as a papal legate, and ended up in Rome as Pope Adrian IV. Of course, not every churchman rose systematically through the sacerdotal ranks. In fact, many theology graduates never got a chance to launch their careers. The Church received them into the clergy, allowed them to wear the tonsure, but had no benefice for them. Some of these young jobless clerics took their Latinity and lyricism on the road to earn a living as poets and minstrels. Rome was not pleased. The mobility of its "top executives" notwithstanding, the medieval Church liked its people to stay put. It was particularly peevish about those who traveled without its consent. For clerics— beneficed or unbeneficed—were not allowed to leave their diocese without their bishop's written permission. As for the monastic orders, some were sedulously sedentary. Benedictines, for instance, took a vow of *stabilitas,* of never budging from where they had practiced their profession. To the Church's annoyance, its prodigal-poetical sons—known as wandering scholars or goliards—seemed to have taken a vow of vagrancy.

Though the problem of what to do with fugitive clergymen dates back to Saint Augustine's time, the designation *goliard* first appears in 13th-century church documents that warn bishops about "ribald clerics and particularly what are commonly called Goliards." The term's etymon is uncertain. It may be *gula,* Latin for "throat" and "gluttony" (from which English gets "gullet"), and likely a reference to the goliards' voluptuary lifestyle. Or it may be *Golias,* the Vulgate's spelling for Goliath, the Philistine champion felled by the smooth stone from David's sling. David was a shepherd, and so the sobriquet *Golias* came to be applied to sheep-thieves, criminals, and, by extension, vagabonds like the wandering scholars.

A vagrant in the Middle Ages was presumed guilty of crapulousness, sloth, and concupiscence. And being a poet, as the Alsatian abbess Herrad's *Garden of*

Delights indicates, did not necessarily add to one's reputation. The public authorities put wandering scholars—whose tonsure unmistakably identified themselves as members of the clergy—in a class with itinerant practitioners of illicit trades, such as jugglers, buffoons, and beggars. The town of Strasbourg resorted to a quota system: its ordinances allowed a maximum of four poets and singers at a time within its walls. As for the Church, it implored its bishops to be wary when granting the tonsure because often young men only sought to obtain it as a license for wandering. Still, goliards had several good reasons for wanting to remain at least nominally affiliated with the Church. Wearing the tonsure meant freedom from taxes, from military service, and, to a certain degree, from physical harm, since the penalty for striking a cleric was excommunication. The Church's Council at London conceded in 1200 that the threat of excommunication gave the clergy an unfair advantage in barroom dust-ups and ordered clerics to steer clear of taverns. More important, even vagrant churchmen arrested for disorderliness could be prosecuted only in a Canon court, which, for all Rome's ire at vagabondage, was likely to be more lenient than the secular judiciary.

One of the most famous and lyrically accomplished of the goliards, among whom were such figures as Hugh Primas of Orléans, Serlo of Wilton, and Walter of Châtillon, was a man known only as the Archpoet *(archipoeta)*. We do not know whether he granted himself this title or whether it had currency during his lifetime. The word is merely at the top of the so-called Göttingen manuscript dating from about 1200 and containing eight of his ten extant poems. (Two other medieval poets—Henry of Avranches and a certain Nicolas, both of whom lived in the 13th century—also laid claim to the moniker borne by their anonymous mid-12th-century forebear.) References to contemporary events in the Archpoet's works suggest that they were written between 1159 and 1165. All traces of the poet vanish thereafter. One of the verses announces defiantly that its author is a man and not a boy—making him somewhere between fifteen and twenty-five—so we can infer that the Archpoet was born around 1140.

A few meager facts about the Archpoet's life can be gleaned from his poems. Historians remind us that medieval society was tripartite, comprising warriors *(bellatores)*, the clergy *(oratores)*, and workers *(laboratores)*. The Archpoet had links to all three. He claimed to have been born into the first estate (but said he didn't become a knight because the military arts terrified him), was loosely attached to the second (but had no benefice), and was in danger of descending into the third (but said that as a scholar he shouldn't have to sully his hands digging ditches). We also know that he briefly studied medicine in Salerno and suffered from pertussis or perhaps tuberculosis—if we believe the complaints about his health to be genuine and not, along with many of the other self-descriptions, merely the attributes of the persona he adopts in his poems. The Archpoet's career is inseparable from that of his highly placed patron, Reginald (Rainald) of Dassel. Reginald was Emperor Frederick I's Imperial Chancellor and later the Archchancellor of Italy and Archbishop of

Cologne. The Archpoet probably visited many of the towns he mentions in his works (Cologne, Pavia, Novara, and Vienne) in his patron's entourage. Reginald was a generous sponsor—at his death, John of Salisbury mourned the passing of a second Maecenas—and rewarded the Archpoet's lyrical talents with horses, cloaks, and money. Fewer than 900 lines of verse by the Archpoet have survived. One reason for this paucity may be that the medieval copyist transcribed only those poems that were dedicated to or mentioned Reginald. In Umberto Eco's novel *Baudolino,* the medievalist and semiotician offers a different explanation. According to Eco's picaresque tale, the Archpoet's lyrics were actually written by the novel's eponymous hero as a favor to the Archpoet, who sought employment with Reginald. The poems were so few in number because Baudolino wrote only enough material to last the Archpoet, who in the novel suffers not from tuberculosis but from chronic writer's block, through his first year in Reginald's service.

Jacob Grimm, the Archpoet's first editor, wrote in 1843 that his works achieved the highest degree of perfection of which the Middle Ages were capable. The Archpoet's lyric brilliance and Grimm's praise notwithstanding, the thematic range of the Archpoet's extant works is fairly limited. They are almost all about wandering, wenching, gambling, and boozing. They generally culminate in a request for money, wine, or clothing. The Archpoet's poetic persona was a ship without a captain *(sine nauta navis),* who proposed, in a poem known as the "Confession of Golias," to die tight as an owl:

> Meum est propositum in taberna mori,
> ut sint vina proxima morientis ori.
> Tunc cantabunt lecius angelorum chori:
> "Sit Deus propicius huic potatori!"
>
> In a tavern's where I'll die—so I have decided;
> there my dying mouth and wine needn't be divided.
> Then the choirs of angels will joyfully be singing:
> "God have mercy on this man who was always drinking!"
>
> (Abcock, 116–117)

This stanza of the "Confession," a poem dubbed the "greatest drinking song in the world" (Waddell, 169), today adorns the website of a vineyard in Oregon. The poem's first five strophes were set to music by Carl Orff in *Carmina Burana* (1937).

How one interprets the Archpoet's name to a certain degree determines one's overall analysis of his oeuvre. Assuming he did call himself the Archpoet, did he claim to be the greatest poet? He was certainly derisive of his fellow bards: several of his poems contain jibes at his more sober colleagues whose lucubrations did not yield decent lyrics. Or is "Archpoet" a parody of his patron's title of "Archchancellor"? In *Baudolino,* Eco splits the difference: the novel's hero explains that the poet used the name "un poco scherzando e un poco pavoneggiandosi" ("half-jesting, half-swaggering," 82). The question of whether the Archpoet is a genuine panegyrist or a sarcastic critic is particularly important for one's reading of two of his better-known works, the poetic tribute to Emperor Frederick I's successful siege of Milan in March 1162 and the poetic refusal to write an epic poem about Frederick's campaign in Italy. The first work praises Frederick as Caesar Augustus's legitimate successor, as the divinely anointed Prince of princes. Frederick represents—that is, he makes present again—Charlemagne, for whose canonization the emperor had successfully lobbied in 1165. As in the roughly coeval *Play of the Antichrist,* it was the previous emperors' fecklessness *(desidia)* that had allowed the empire to become weak and people like the Lombards strong. In their hubris, the Lombards erected towering citadels like the Giants and earned God's wrath, visited upon them by His chosen ruler, Frederick. In three different formulations, the Archpoet predicts that Frederick will return the Roman Empire to its former glory. At the end of the poem, the Archpoet turns the focus of his praise on his patron, Chancellor Reginald, who, he says, paved the way for Frederick's victory over Milan. For all the Archpoet's bibulous playfulness, it seems implausible that the poem, as some critics propose, is a thinly veiled attack on Frederick's Italian policy.

Reginald had to be satisfied with this shortish, 130-line work because the Archpoet had the crust to refuse to write the *Fredericiade* that had been requested of him. The poet claims he was given only a week to complete it and reminds Reginald that it would have taken Lucan or Virgil five years to do the same for Aeneas—which flatteringly or, as some scholars claim, mockingly compares Frederick to the Trojan hero. (Another anonymous poet of the 12th century eventually supplied the desired epic: the *Carmen de gestis Frederici I imperatoris in Lombardia,* translated into English in 1994 as *Barbarossa in Italy.*) After softening the blow of the refusal to grant his patron's wish—he explains that he's too poor to sing about great men, nicely rhyming "mendicus" with "Fredericus"—the Archpoet turns his attention to touching his patron for a handout. He needs a steady supply of wine because his couplets are only as good as the vintage in his cup. As long as Bacchus is in charge of his cerebral citadel, Apollo will perform lyrical miracles. In the end, the poetic apology becomes a poem of thanks for earlier gifts and an entreaty for more of the same. Such emoluments enable the Archpoet to continue singing the praises of Reginald's great deeds.

The history of the Archpoet's reception, which began in the mid-19th century, has at times been marked by febrile nationalism. In the first half of the 20th century, several scholarly articles were devoted to determining whether the Archpoet was German, French, or Italian. The exclamatory title of one of these essays, Karl Langosch's 1935 "Der Archipoeta war ein Deutscher!" ("The Archpoet was a German!"), indicates the degree of scholarly acrimony. In the Middle Ages, some Italian universities divided their students into two bodies: those from north of the Alps *(tramontane)* and those from south of the Alps. The Archpoet, who studied briefly at Salerno, unknowingly started the 20th-century feud by employing this distinction in one of his many poetic attempts to bite Reginald's ear. He pointed out that they both came from north of the Alps: "As a Tramontane [*vir Transmontane*], you should help me; I'm Tramontane too" (Abcock, 87). In contrast to Langosch's efforts to secure the Archpoet for Germany, Ernst Robert Curtius, in 1940, appreciated the fact that the poet's Latin verses ultimately precluded a definitive judgment on their author's origins. And whether or not "tramontane" definitively indicates the Archpoet's nationality, it is at least possible that the contentious couplet is a playful reference to the Archpoet's student days.

It is perforce difficult to get a sense of the mellifluous insouciance of the Archpoet's lyrics in anything but their original Latin. Happily, leftover scraps of grammar-school or doctoral-reading-exam Latin will get you further with the Archpoet's verses than with those of Catullus or Virgil. The closing lines of what is thought to be the earliest of the Archpoet's extant works deal characteristically with the chief preoccupation of the poet's persona—petitioning Reginald to donate cash or clothing:

> Constantly I'm coughing, consumption is just in the offing;
> Pulse-beats scarce existent are a warning that death is not distant.
> Proof of my neediness is that my shoes are as poor as my dress is.
> Hence as is most meet I importune you with words of entreaty:
> Wearing such rags and tatters in your presence—believe me, it matters!
> So may success greet you as in largess you're mindful of me too.
>
> (Whicher, 105)

Felicitous English translations of the Archpoet's verse are by Helen Waddell, George Whicher, and, more recently, Fleur Adcock. The above rendering by Whicher succeeds in giving English readers a feel for the rhythm and rhyme scheme of the Archpoet's leonine hexameters—and in making the medieval bard sound a bit like Cole Porter: "If the Harris pat means a Paris hat, okay!"

Abbot Luan, founder of Clonfert monastery in Ireland, advised his monks to "dig and sow that you may have wherewith to eat and drink and be clothed, for where sufficiency is, there is stability, and where stability is, there is religion [*ubi stabilitas, ibi religio*]" (Waddell, 177–178). The Archpoet, like the other goliards, professed to be little interested in stability, preferring to get his drink and clothing from his patron.

See also 1157, 1596, 1815

Bibliography: Fleur Abcock, *Hugh Primus and the Archpoet* (Cambridge, U.K.: Cambridge University Press, 1996). *Barbarossa in Italy,* trans. Thomas Carson (New York: Italica Press, 1994). Peter Dronke, *The Medieval Lyric,* 2nd ed. (Cambridge, U.K.: Cambridge University Press, 1977). Peter Dronke, "The Art of the Archpoet: A Reading of 'Lingua Balbus,'" in W. T. H. Jackson, ed., *The Interpretation of Medieval Lyric Poetry* (New York: Columbia University Press, 1980). Umberto Eco, *Baudolino,* trans. William Weaver (New York: Harcourt, 2002; orig. Milan: Bompiani, 2000). W. T. H. Jackson, "The Politics of a Poet: The Archipoeta as Revealed by His Imagery," in Edward P. Mahoney, ed., *Philosophy and Humanism: Renaissance Essays in Honor of Paul Oskar Kristeller* (New York: Columbia University Press, 1976). *Die Lieder des Archipoeta,* trans. Karl Langosch (Stuttgart: Reclam, 1965). Helen Waddell, *The Wandering Scholars of the Middle Ages* (Mineola, N.Y.: Dover, 2000). George F. Whicher, *The Goliard Poets: Medieval Latin Songs and Satires* (Cambridge, Mass.: Harvard University Press, 1949).

Sean Ward

♌ *1177–1197*

The poet Heinrich composes the first animal epic in the German vernacular

A Satire of Courtly Literature

In *The Deeds of Frederick Barbarossa* (1158/1160; *Gesta Friderici*), Bishop Otto of Freising celebrates the upper Rhine region between Basel and Mainz as the "stretch of country" where the German Empire's "principal strength" lies. Both Frederick I (1152–1190) and his successor, Henry VI (1190–1197), favored the southwestern German lands, especially the lovely plain that unfolds between the banks of the Upper Rhine and the Vosges Mountains, the region known as Alsace. As rulers of a realm without an administrative center, these two Hohenstaufen emperors traveled in order to exert power and hold court at various locations. Their itineraries frequently led them through Alsace, and Henry VI made Hagenau, one of the region's foremost towns, his favorite residence.

In the same region, a certain Heinrich composed in the years between 1177 and 1197 the first animal epic in the German language, *Reinhart Fuchs* (*Reynard the Fox;* hereafter *RF*). In a string of episodes, *RF* features a fox who, by cunning, deceit, and slyness, dupes every fellow animal, including the most powerful of all, the lion king. Composed in 2266 verses of rhymed couplets, *RF* is itself modeled on a French narrative, the *Roman de Renart (RdR)*. In accordance with authorial practice in the vernacular, Heinrich, of whom nothing is known beyond his name, significantly reworked his model from a loose sequence of animal stories into a highly organized epic structure.

Unlike *Erec, Yvain, Tristan, Perceval,* and other courtly poems of French origin, medieval fox epics travesty what they reflect, courtly culture and its literary representation. Set against the lofty ideals of courtly literature, *RF* exposes a crisis of sociability. Its author warns against the secret underworld of polite human interactions. In *RF,* self-interest triumphs over honesty and loyalty and the rather likeable rogue Renart has metamorphosed into the evil Reinhart, who seriously challenges the divinely ordained social order.

The poem's vituperative tone can be understood as a scathing satire of the Hohenstaufen court. Reinhart's cunning serves to unmask the king's entourage as an assembly of simpletons, and the lion, King Noble (*Vrevil* in the German text), is portrayed as a tyrant whose lust for power is "beyond measure" (l. 1265). He destroys the ants' kingdom, an unprovoked act of aggression that will ultimately lead to his downfall. Indeed, the poet envisions the king's demise in a scene that is, within the tradition of fox epics, without parallel. Furthermore, oblique references within the text link *RF* to Alsace without mention of either Frederick or Henry. Could any contemporary listener or reader have failed to view this narrative as a poignant critique of imperial rule?

Animal stories work by dint of analogy between animal protagonists and their human counterparts. Animals display human traits while, by implication, humans appear beastlike. Unfolding the theme of deceit in a series of encounters between individual animals and the fox (sometimes involving human beings as the animal kingdom's enemies), the poem's structure permits its audience to see through the fox's intrigues while the duped animals often undergo painful experiences. "What did he think that he let himself be betrayed so often" (990f) notes the poet when the fox's ally, Isengrin, the wolf, is tricked once again. Reinhart's cunning also enables him to assume various roles throughout the poem—ally, courtier, lover, and medical counselor, to name only a few.

What emerges is anything but a peaceable kingdom. Reinhart's doings seem especially destructive in light of the fact that many episodes do not offer a motivation for his evil acts. "He did not know what he took revenge on" (281), comments the poet when, after having lured the raven into singing, Reinhart deprives this "nephew" not only of his cheese but also assaults the bird itself. In the end, he even attacks his ruler. "I hadn't done anything against him [the fox]" (2235), exclaims Noble shortly before his death. The fox's actions manifest an unchecked destructive urge. To be sure, Reinhart is not always successful in what he attempts to achieve (especially in the first episodes with small animals), but he reveals the corruption that lies beneath the smooth, sociable surface.

In fact, *RF* presents courtly sociability turned upside down. "Loyalty among relatives is great joy" (113–14), states the fox, as if quoting a common saying. With these words, he lures Chanticleer, the cock, into a trap. Though his words invoke loyalty, Reinhart is consistently disloyal. Loyalty, a key concept of courtly literature, is not simply a virtue. It is the glue that holds the social fabric of feudal society together. "Disloyalty," that is behavioral disloyalty as opposed to lip service, "is fashionable these days" (997), laments the poet. Because any society is predicated on a code of mutual obligation, this society is defenseless against selfish duplicity that detaches words from their meanings. Though Reinhart is not the only animal guilty of transgressions against the communal order, a double face has become his trademark. The fox's cunning wins out over the more transparent selfishness of his fellow animals.

Reinhart courts all animals by addressing them as relatives. The more intimate the social bonds that are being violated by the fox's betrayals, the greater the sense of social rupture. When Reinhart forms a close alliance with Isengrin, the wolf, he increases the social stakes considerably. Their common raids reap little success, result in many failures, and often show one of the allies at a disadvantage. Nevertheless, the two do not break their ties. Only when the fox violates the wolf's domestic sphere does their alliance go awry. When it is suggested that Hersant, Isengrin's wife, had an adulterous affair with Reinhart, Isengrin dismisses the rumor as unfounded. Not until Reinhart causes the loss of Isengrin's tail, in a later episode, does the wolf turn against his former ally. He announces a feud, and in the course of this conflict Reinhart rapes Hersant and escalates the conflict. Both the feud and the court trial that ensues turn out to be blunt weapons. They can neither restore the wolf's lost honor nor restitute the damaged social order.

Besides the celebration of the chivalrous code of honor and warfare, another primary theme in literary celebration of courtly sociability in the late 12th century was love. Lines such as "My heart is very wounded by your love" (426f) or "Love bestows high spirits" (843) evoke the lyrical apotheosis of erotic love in *Minnesang*. *RF* and the object of its parody obviously share this idiom. A verbal import from French like *amie* (1162; female lover) shows how deeply Heinrich was steeped in courtly ways. Not accidentally, these expressions are all linked to Reinhart, the courtier (441). As a sly courtier, the fox conceals his desire for Hersant from Isengrin. In his presence, eloquent but fickle words give way to silence: the highly cultivated speech of courtly sociability is thus portrayed as false and deceitful.

The poet's fixation on the object of his parody is particularly evident in one central episode, the rape of Hersant. No element of the plot breaks more radically with the carefully circumscribed code of courtly culture than the literary representation of sexual violence. Courtly poets hint at rape but mostly refrain from representing it. Yet in *RF,* rape manifests itself with brute force. Its depiction suggests that the discourse of love merely serves as a thin veneer over a graphic sexual aggression. Considering the rules of literary courtliness, this episode of Reinhart courting the she-wolf is introduced as an "outrageous story" (422), just as the poem as a whole is labeled outrageous (1). In this climactically structured narrative, the rape amounts to one of Reinhart's greatest provocations of the sociopoetic order to which he belongs.

Again and again, verbal communication provides treacherous access to a veiled reality. Rape becomes an act that disrupts the system of reliable signification on which communication itself is based. At the trial, the recounting of past events makes what *RF*'s audience knows is true seem dubious, that is, that Hersant was violated while she was trapped in a hole. But did the rape really happen? Crimel, the badger, immediately questions the accusation when it is first raised in court: How could a small animal like the fox have sexually violated a larger animal like a wolf? If, however, the sexual act occurred with mutual consent or "love," the badger insinuates, this would be "nothing strange since such things often occur" (1392f).

In the end the entire animal kingdom is gathered at the trial. Instead of portraying the court as a festive society, this scene shows it as a gathering where legal conflicts are resolved. Catering to current literary tastes, Heinrich invests his tale with an epic climax. In contradistinction to other fox epics, here the crowning scene is set at the end of the tale. The poet displays close familiarity with contemporary legal custom, according to which the accused, Reinhart, has to be summoned to court three times before a sentence can be imposed. The first two messengers are treated with abuse. Summoned a third time, Reinhart appears in court, where once again this trickster is able to turn the tables on his plaintiffs and persecutors.

Meant to expel the fox from the community, the trial takes the opposite turn. Plagued by an avenging ant in his brain, the lion king is in desperate need of medical relief, and Reinhart is quick to refashion himself as a medical counselor. The nonsensical cure he prescribes is concocted from the body parts of his enemies, whom the king readily sacrifices for the sake of his own health. The point is not that good rule went amiss because of the fox's mischief; all relations are corrupted from the very beginning in this poetic universe. Reinhart's mischievous behavior reveals what drives the world: self-interest. Thus, the alliance against the fox as the animal kingdom's archenemy is bound to disintegrate. At the mercy of his subject, Noble dies of the poisonous concoction Reinhart serves him. In a final act of senseless treachery, Reinhart poisons the same lion king who has done everything for the fox's cause. Together with the body politic, the king's body literally breaks to pieces.

Whereas courtly literature solemnizes a unified social world of nobles after a chivalrous hero has restored the community's honor, *RF* envisions the breakup of the social order and the ensuing social anarchy. Although cabal is a constitutive element of court life and is present in much of courtly literature, Heinrich universalizes the mechanism of simulation and dissimulation so that all social relations are tainted. *RF* is radical in both its uncompromisingly pessimistic vision of human sociability and its poetics of anti-courtliness.

Thus, in *RF,* a crisis of sociability is linked to the ascent of self-interest unchecked by communal codes of conduct, by individuality, one might say, if that wording did not unduly modernize a medieval concept of the self that is clearly viewed negatively. Reinhart is a solitary figure without friends, except for temporary allies who are destined to be duped by him. Yet the loner is not portrayed as marginal to society. That is precisely the problem. The individual and traitor resides within a nexus of social relations whose fabric his actions help undo. At the tale's end, after the king is destroyed, this antihero leaves the stage, triumphant but completely isolated.

The author of *RF* revels in the power of words to deceive, beguile, and make believe. It is the relationship between words and acts or objects—the lifeline of signification—that the poem shows in a state of disarray. The gullibility of Reinhart's fellow animals depends more than anything else on the dangerous potential of duplicity in verbal communication. Enclosed at the bottom of a well, Reinhart makes his ally Isengrin believe that he, in fact, lives in paradise and they should exchange positions. In episode after episode, the fox's rhetorically crafted words provide the key to duping his peers.

Not only human speech seems deceptive; literary language itself appears problematic. Heinrich ends his work with the insidious remark "This [story] may be false or wrong." Falseness, however, is firmly associated with the fox's deceitful doings throughout the poem. Approximately one hundred years after *RF* was first composed, in the second half of the 13th century, adapters copied and updated the poem (only in this smoothed-out version has the full text come down to us). They added a cognomen to the poet's name Heinrich, "the dissembler" *(der Glichesere),* as if to identify Heinrich with his protagonist, the cunning fox, thereby to distance themselves from the poem's dark vision.

In the development of secular German literature, the arrival of Reinhart the fox on the literary stage is a hallmark. Among other things, *RF* testifies to the emergence of a courtly literary matrix—a common language, common poetic structures, and a set of ideas shared by vernacular poets at the end of the 12th century. As much as this development offers a common ground of literary production and reception, it also offers a forum for literary debate. In this context, *RF* marks the advent of parody—a mirroring of one set of genres in another, yet within a shared literary purview.

As a literary figure, the all-too versatile Reinhart and his brothers have never really waned in popularity. The Low German *Reynke de vos* (1498) has proven the most influential version of the fox narratives (whereas only three medieval manuscripts extant today document an interest in *RF*). It was translated into High German, from there into Latin—in Hartmann Schoppe's widely read *Speculum vitae aulicae (Mirror of Courtly Life)*—and, in a multitude of versions, the sly fox has infiltrated almost all European languages. The stories of the deceitful trickster remained popular even after the allegorical age, and Reinhart lives on in children's literature to this day. In 1793, shortly after the execution of the French king Louis XVI, Johann Wolfgang von Goethe started to adapt the stories of a roguish fox for an updated version in hexameters. Goethe's version is based on Gottsched's translation of *Reynke de vos,* but even if he had been familiar with *Reinhart Fuchs* and had therefore known of King Noble's tragic end, it is unlikely that he would have retold *Reineke Fuchs* within the political context of the French Revolution. Rather, *Reineke Fuchs* offered Goethe a respite from the exigencies of modern life and politics—a turn toward the comfortable certainties of perennial moral truths, moderated by humor and irony.

See also 1170, ca. 1200, 1735, 1774, 1786

Bibliography: *Das mittelhochdeutsche Gedicht vom Fuchs Reinhart,* 2nd ed., ed. Ingeborg Schröbler, Altdeutsche Textbibliothek, 8 (Halle: Max Niemeyer, 1952). Heinrich der Glîchezâre, *Reinhart Fuchs: Mittelhochdeutsch und Neuhochdeutsch,* ed. Karl-Heinz Göttert (Stuttgart: Reclam, 1987). Thomas W. Best, *Reynard the Fox* (Boston: Twayne Publishers, 1983). Ferdinand Opll, "Friedrich Barbarossa und das Oberrheingebiet," in Rüdiger Krohn et al., eds., *Stauferzeit: Geschichte, Literatur, Kunst* (Stuttgart: Klett-Cotta, 1979). Kathryn Gravdal, "Law and Literature in the French Middle Ages: Rape Law on Trial in 'Le Roman de Renart,'" *Romanic Review* 82 (1992): 1–24. Klaus Düwel, "Reinhart/Reineke Fuchs in der deutschen Literatur," *Michigan Germanic Studies* 7 (1981): 233–248.

Helmut Puff

♌ 1184, Whitsuntide

The sons of Emperor Frederick Barbarossa come of age and are admitted into knighthood

The Courtly Festival

The celebration at Mainz on Whitsuntide 1184, hosted by the Holy Roman Emperor Frederick Barbarossa to mark the coming of age of his sons Henry and Frederick of Swabia, is a more telling reflection of Barbarossa's reign and aristocratic culture at the end of the 12th century than any other event. As a model to be emulated, the emperor's court radiated unequaled influence over the older *gentil* (aristocratic) society. The imperial court was the absolute center of political life, the place where most important political decisions were made, especially those concerning war or peace. It was also the social setting where nobility and clergy gathered and the life of the aristocracy played itself out against an agrarian background. Aristocratic culture reached its peak at Barbarossa's court. Refinement of manners, the art of hunting and sports, patronage of literature and music, all were part of a culture of festivals reflecting the hierarchical social order of the nobility. Contemporary chroniclers and poets regarded the 1184 court festival at Mainz as the high point of Barbarossa's reign. In fact, the written record suggests that courtly festivals were the focal point of medieval courtly culture and had a dimension that went beyond mere diversion or entertainment.

The celebration at the imperial court in Mainz has been described in detail by Gislebert of Mons in the *Hennegau Chronicle,* in which Count Balduin of Hennegau, Gislebert's overlord, plays the central role. Count Balduin travels to the imperial court with a large retinue and sets up a camp more lavish than that of any of the other princes, archbishops, abbots, dukes, margraves, counts palatine, other counts, noblemen, and *ministeriales,* come from all parts of the empire north of the Alps. Some seventy thousand knights, not counting the clerics and people of other estates, are assembled. At the festivities, it is the Count of Hennegau who carries the ceremonial sword, despite the fact that the most powerful princes of the empire have a better claim to this honor. Says Gislebert, "His name was greatly respected everywhere, and furthermore he was a new man at the court, where he had many princely and noble kinsmen."

The politics behind this distinction pales against the portrayal of Count of Hennegau as a courtly hero, whose status receives the emperor's symbolic confirmation on the occasion of his introduction to the court. The other noble guests, too, vie for enhancing their personal reputations and social standing with generous gifts for the emperor and his sons. In fact, these acts of self-interest seem to overshadow the actual reason for the celebration, which receives startlingly brief mention in Gislebert's account: "On Whit Monday the sons of the Holy Roman Emperor, Henry, King of Rome, and Frederick, Duke of Swabia, were received into the knighthood."

Emperor Barbarossa and his sons, from the *Welfenchronik*. (Bildarchiv Marburg/Fulda Library)

The tournament that follows is described in greater detail because it brings more honor to the Count of Hennegau:

> On Whitsunday and Whit Monday, after the morning meal, the sons of the emperor put on the tournament, in which some twenty thousand knights participated. It was a joust without arms *(gyrum sine armis);* the knights demonstrated the use of shields, lances, and banners, and were jousting without blows *(cursus equorum sine ictibus).* At these games Emperor Frederick himself condescended to demonstrate superior use of his shield, with Count Hennegau carrying his lance, although he was neither taller nor heavier than the other participants.

On the third day, a violent storm causes much damage to the guests' cabins and tents and brings the festivities to a close. The chronicler's description of the guests' departure is prefaced by a long listing of their names in the style of court reports. Acquisition of symbolic capital is central to the chronicler's description: emphasis is placed on the role of the emperor, the status of the guests, the honor of the representatives of Hennegau, and the assurance of *fama.* From a historiographical perspective, the coming of age of Barbarossa's sons would appear to be the central event, yet the description of their admission into knighthood remains disproportionately scant. However, such brevity is not a peculiarity of Gislebert's style. The records of other writers about inductions into the knighthood likewise tend to center on the guests and their participation in the festivities. Courtly society was the event as well as the intended audience of the ceremony and the authority by which it was to be judged.

It is no accident that celebrations were associated with important political, legal, dynastic, and genealogical decisions. The courtly celebration established laws and guaranteed relationships of value and rank, which became visible in the ceremonies, spread by *fama,* and then became anchored in the collective memory of the people by the extraordinary event. The repetition of such celebrations at particular times (in this case, Whitsuntide) as part of the ritual organization of the calendar points to the role these feasts played in how the aristocracy viewed itself.

Medieval courtly celebrations stand out within an "alarmingly profane and limited world" as an exceptional situation protected by ritual. They transcend the confines of everyday life, and are both the creation and realization of aristocratic cooperation, as well as a means of community formation and display of power. They arouse a sense of elation through observation and participation, through rich images for the eye, colorful sounds for the ear, through food and drink, odors and smells.

Festive demonstrations of power are thus a stylization of aristocratic and courtly life which can be perceived with the senses and which asserts the correspondence of the ontologically based social hierarchy: as a representation or "recalling to mind" of a cosmological order. These festivities are thus the polar opposite of the periodic release of the lower orders at carnival time during pre-Lent from their socially restrictive circumstances. The courtly festival, by contrast, serves to create order. Courtly harmony is understood as a significant divine endowment, a universal figuration of meaning at the foundation of all aristocratic values and forms of action. Thus festive displays and religious pageantry are structurally similar, and both are connected with Christian forms of collective establishment of meaning.

The description of the wedding of Aeneas and Lavinia in Heinrich von Veldeke's *Eneit* (based on the French *Roman d'Eneas)* has been understood as a point where literary depictions and historical documentation of festivals come together. The culmination and conclusion of this Middle High German Aeneas romance (1170–1180) suggest that the wedding ceremony, in which the old king gives away the bride, should also be read as a political celebration of the founding of the Roman Empire and the festive legitimating of territorial conquest. Veldeke's description corresponds in essential characteristics to the depictions of celebrations in Hartmann von Aue's *Erec* and Wolfram von Eschenbach's *Parzival*. Emphasis is placed on the great distance from which the nobles come by sea and by land, as well as on the great number of guests and the influx of minstrels and itinerant performers. Following a description of the music, the dancing and jousting, the wedding festivities of Aeneas and Lavinia are linked to the coming-of-age ceremony of Emperor Frederick Barbarossa's sons.

This comparison invokes the continuity of imperial rule, which alone enables a mirroring of Aeneas's wedding feast and the historical celebration at Mainz. It draws a line from Aeneas, the founder of Rome and, by extension, the Roman Empire, to the German emperors, the successors to the Roman tradition of the Caesars *(translatio imperii)*. The romance receives added value as it prefigures the historical celebration.

A typical literary example of a celebration occurs in Hartmann's *Erec*. The wedding of Erec and Enite, hosted by King Arthur at his court, is planned for Whitsuntide. This is the date of the annual Arthurian festival that forms a secular counterpart to the Christian Feast of Easter. The description of the celebration is clearly structured: Arthur sends letters and messengers to everyone he can reach, primarily the princes of his land, who cannot refuse an invitation of this sort. Hartmann follows his account of this invitation with an unusually impressive guest list. Although the list is fictitious and names no historical persons, it demonstrates all the more clearly the extent to which guests lend prestige and significance to a planned celebration. Count Brandes of Doloceste, alone, brings a retinue of five hundred men with him, all in regalia identical to his own. Then comes Maheloas, lord of the Island of Glass, whose land has never experienced a storm or been plagued by heat, cold, or insects. The ruler of another magical kingdom, the lord of the Island of Avalon, also is among the guests. In addition to dukes and counts, ten kings, "powerful and rich" in splendid trappings indicating their status, attend the festivities.

This exhibition corresponds to the kinds of public display of authority recounted in contemporary documents. When Thomas à Becket visited the court of King Louis VIII of France in Paris in 1158 to negotiate the marriage of the oldest son of King Henry II of England and Louis's daughter, part of his mission was to make an opulent display. Becket was accompanied by 200 mounted retainers of his own household and 250 on foot, all lavishly decked out. In addition to his horses and a selection of costly furs, tapestries, and carpets, he brought with him dogs, birds, and monkeys, carriages loaded with foodstuffs, the chancellor's musicians, and his own furniture and kitchen equipment. Pack horses carried gold and silver plates, clothing, books, and all the articles required to celebrate Mass.

While the two texts contain obvious differences, they nevertheless project a single principle: the demonstration of status, which provides impressive sensory evidence for a ruler's relative rank through display of opulent accoutrements. The reader or hearer learns from the procession of the guests that the most important potentates come from the highest mountains and most distant islands, from their own country but also from the ends of the earth.

King Arthur rides out personally to meet his guests and welcomes them most magnificently. They are entertained and housed in accordance with their status. The Archbishop of Canterbury presides over the religious ceremony. Hartmann makes only very brief mention of the actual festivities, but his remarks about the banquet set a special tone: "There were so many excellent knights present there that I cannot report to you that they fell on the food, for they gave more heed to conducting themselves with honor than to stuffing themselves." The didactic intent is impossible to overlook. In principle, rich food and drink belonged to and were emphasized in celebrations among both peasants and nobles. Perhaps it was precisely the desire to distinguish this banquet from peasant revelries that led Hartmann to emphasize his knights' courtly manners in voluntarily refraining from excessive eating and drinking. Hartmann mentions only in passing that the time between dinner and nightfall is filled with a tournament and dancing, conversations with the ladies, and performances by musicians, acrobats, and storytellers who have come near and far.

The host's power and benevolence are demonstrated by his *milte,* or the largess he extends to the traveling minstrels. Each of the three thousand entertainers is given 30 marks in gold. If one were to take this sum seriously, it would amount to 90,000 gold marks for the performers alone. The lavishly dispensed gold is complemented by gifts of clothing and horses, and this gift giving, the author recounts, does not stop until the festival ends fourteen days later. After that the minstrels and performers function as the king's messengers; they carry the message of this unparalleled celebration to the rest of the world: "They all spoke resoundingly about this wedding." The word "resound" indicates that the minstrels and performers can be seen as "loudspeakers" in the original sense of the word, that is, they proclaim the news of the celebration and of the host's munificence far and wide. The host's largess is thus not just generosity, but a manifestation of authority that legitimates the central court by means of contemporary "media."

Three weeks after this celebration, a great tournament is held for the diversion and pleasure of the noble lords. Erec gains the greatest glory and accompanies Arthur to the king's court where he meets Enite. The two leave together at once for his father's country where Erec is to assume the reign.

Seen as a whole, Hartmann's description of the celebration highlights three points. First, the celebration demonstrates and confirms status; in this case, King Arthur's foremost rank. The far reach of his invitations, the status of his guests, and signs of his own magical powers are elements in confirming his status. Second, the celebration serves the acquisition of symbolic capital, not only for the king and his nobles, but also for young Erec. Honor accrues from the uniqueness of the celebration itself, from the ruler's generosity, from the guests' apparel and accoutrements, the visibility and audibility of publicly exhibited power and authority, and finally from the news of the ceremony that is spread by the minstrels. Third, for Erec, this celebration constitutes his initiation; it introduces him to King Arthur's circle and establishes his *fama* as prerequisite for becoming a king himself.

As acts of courtly self-realization, celebrations reproduce and transmit courtly culture from generation to generation in forms that are old and, at the same time, always new. It thus becomes clear that the literary depiction of a celebration functions as more than mere diversion; it also forms the collective memory that connects and reconciles the ceremony actually experienced with an idealized one that predetermines the shape of both the real and the fictional versions. This goes a long way toward explaining why—even though literary accounts of celebrations do not display an identical dramaturgy—they do include largely identical elements or components that return on different occasions in different combinations or settings. These components include the arrival of the ruler, the tournament, the banquet, the initiation of a knight, and the departure. Here the order of elements seems to obey relatively fixed rules, even though before the late Middle Ages hardly any explicit codifications of these rules existed. The courtly celebration is a multi-media event that allows aristocratic rule and aristocratic opulence to be directly and immediately experienced, more through the senses than the intellect.

Literary descriptions of celebrations thus reveal the self-interpretation of the aristocracy as much as legends of the saints reveal contemporary views on theology. As descriptions of "a utopian and visionary vanishing point, which always becomes visible only through that process which passes through the negation of the ideality shining in this vanishing point" (Walter Haug), they become part of the collective memory.

See also 1189, 1203 (Summer), 1230

Bibliography: "Am Pfingstmontag wurden die Söhne des römischen Kaisers Friedrich, Heinrich, römischer König, und Friedrich, Herzog von Schwaben, in den Ritterstand aufgenommen," in *La Chronique de Gislebert de Mons,* ed. Léon Vanderkindere (Brussels, 1904), 157. Hartmann von Aue, *Erec,* ed. A. Leitzmann (Tübingen, 1985). ———, *Erec,* Middle High German text and translation by Thomas Cramer (Frankfurt am Main, 1984). Walter Haug, "Von der Idealität des arthurischen Festes zur apokalyptischen Orgie in Wittenwilers 'Ring,'" in *Das Fest*, ed. Walter Haug and Rainer Warning, *Poetik und Hermeneutik* 14 (Munich: Fink, 1989), 157–179.

Horst Wenzel
Translated by Deborah Lucas Schneider

ᡚ *1189*

Barbarossa launches the Third Crusade to prove the righteousness of Christian Europe

Hartmann's Poetry

In the prologue to his verse tale *Der arme Heinrich* (ca. 1190; *Poor Henry*), the "author" of the text introduces himself as Hartmann, a vassal in a place called Aue, and a learned knight who has read many books. These opening lines provide a considerable amount of information. The term *Ritter* (knight) covered a broad social spectrum in the 12th and 13th centuries, but the term *Dienstmann* (vassal) is more specific. Scholars agree today that this term identifies Hartmann as a member of the "ministerials," public servants mainly of common birth but promoted into the aristocracy by virtue of their intellect. The aristocracy's increasing need for able men to carry out administrative tasks gained them a limited amount of power. That Hartmann makes much of his education fits well into this picture. He worked "*ze Owe*" (in Aue), a place name that occurs frequently and thus cannot be precisely identified. Other indicators, chiefly linguistic, point to the Alemannic region—southwestern Germany and northern Switzerland. Furthermore, the hero's name in *Der arme Heinrich* is Heinrich von Aue and he comes from *Swâben* (Swabia). It is possible–although not definitely proven—that Hartmann was born into a family of ministerials in the service of the dukes of Zähringen near Fribourg, Switzerland.

Dating Hartmann's writings is likewise not easy. The only extratextual reference in his extensive work is to "Salatîn" (Saladin), Salah ad-Din Jusuf ibn Ajub (1138–1193), Sultan of Egypt and Syria. It was Saladin's capture of Jerusalem in 1187 that touched off the Third Crusade in 1189. But the precise reading of the lines in which this reference occurs is controversial. Most of Hartmann's love lyrics and crusade poetry, as well as his *Erec*, the first Arthurian romance in German, were most likely written in the 1180s. Three of Hartmann's major works probably date from the 1190s: the epic *Gregorius;* the second Arthurian romance, *Iwein;* and finally the legend *Der arme Heinrich*.

Hartmann may be considered one of the most versatile medieval German poets. He is at home in all genres—the longer narrative form of the verse romance as well as shorter forms of epic, and lyric poetry. In addition, he wrote a *Klage (Complaint),* a quarrel between the heart and the body that is difficult to assign to a specific genre, but is perhaps closest to the late medieval *minne* (courtly love). In all of these works, Hartmann brought new impulses to German literature. His love lyrics, while articulating what was known as *hoher sang* (elevated poetry) through praise of women and lovelorn laments, also contain astonishingly modern techniques, including playful parodying of the genre. The dialogue *Klage* is the first treatment of the creed of courtly love in German. It laid the groundwork for subsequent approaches to this topic, including Hartmann's own. Scholars have long concentrated on Hartmann's two Arthurian epics, *Erec* and *Iwein,* and quite understandably so. Hartmann was the first to make powerful epic material, which was already very popular in its French versions, accessible to German readers. He also created a structural model—doubling, mirroring, repetition, and variation—for many later Arthurian romances.

Both *Erec* and *Iwein* superimpose ideals and ideological concepts derived from courtly and knightly culture and socialization on an epic plot that is understood as exemplary. Both epics center on an intense struggle to bring the hero's social life and his private life into harmony. In the former he must exercise social responsibility, while in the latter he seeks individual self-realization as a "loving knight."

Hartmann's *Erec* is an adaptation of the Old French verse epic *Erec et Enide.* The adaptation is characterized by condensation and expansion, techniques that function not merely as rhetorical devices, but introduce new emphases that can certainly be regarded as intentional.

Prince Erec achieves his knightly goals at first with considerable ease. In particular, he acquires a beautiful wife with whom he enjoys the pleasures of sexual union. However, as Erec devotes himself more and more to his personal happiness, he neglects his duties as ruler, or more generally, his duties as a member of a social group. In the second part of the romance, Erec gradually learns to make up for these shortcomings by going through several stages. This learning process is symbolized, or allegorized, by initial separation from his beloved and eventual reunion, as well as a series of adventures Erec must endure to learn to become more altruistic.

Hartmann's second Arthurian romance, *Iwein,* displays fewer variations on Chrétien de Troyes's Old French text *Yvain.* The work has two fundamental themes: the protagonist Iwein must learn to be punctual and to help others. Like Erec, Iwein achieves his initial desires quickly. He marries Laudine, the widow of a ruler whom Iwein had killed earlier in a misunderstood attempt to save the honor of a member of Arthur's Round Table. Since he believes that a knight must constantly participate in tournaments, he asks his wife's consent to depart for a year. However, he fails to return at the agreed upon time and falls in with disreputable company. In the second part of the epic, Iwein must prove, as did Erec, that he can keep his word; he must also cease to engage in combat motivated by a false sense of honor. Hartmann thus renews the discussion of courtly norms and ideals he had initiated in *Erec.* He also uses a tale within the tale to relativize the characterization of King Arthur. Whereas Arthur had appeared in the prologue as an ideal figure, he now endangers his marriage and his kingdom by making a nonsensical promise which he believes he must keep. Only the "perfect knight" Gawain can restore stability to Arthur's world through courageous and selfless action.

Compared with Wolfram von Eschenbach's *Parzival,* which Mikhail Bakhtin terms "the first modern novel," Hartmann's *Erec* and *Iwein* represent relatively simple forms; in particular the polyphony and dialogic quality, which Bakhtin identifies as hallmarks of modernity, remain undeveloped. Nevertheless, the two first Arthurian epics represent significant departures from heroic epics with their relatively "flat" characters.

Like his minnesongs and his poetic dialogue, *Complaint,* Hartmann's two Arthurian epics have secular themes and the characters live in the secular world of the court. This is not the case in the two legends *Gregorius* and *Der arme Heinrich,* whose themes are religious and revolve around the questions of guilt and sin. Hartmann's audience probably came primarily from the secular upper class. He presents no theological doctrines to this audience, but offers various examples of personal responsibility within particular social settings. Such a characterization applies in principle to all of Hartmann's narrative works, but perhaps to *Der arme Heinrich* most of all. Even more than in *Gregorius,* the tale brings together disparate spheres—the secular milieu of the court (Henry's life at the start), an opposite noncourtly private world (the dependent steward's family), and the personal inner world of the main character—to create an affirmative panorama of humanity.

Gregorius, which survives in six manuscripts and several fragments, some from as early as the 13th century, is a tale of the "good sinner" (in the text's own phrase), whose guilt cannot be unambiguously determined either morally or within the theological category of sin. Although the offense in question is incest, in itself a grievous sin, medieval Church law held that ignorance could be grounds for absolution. While the central character, Gregorius, feels a profound sense of guilt, the narrator—and indeed the text as such—remains ambivalent. In any event the intention is to demonstrate how a person can commit a sin and find absolution. Gregorius himself is the offspring of an incestuous relationship between a brother and sister, who pay a heavy price for their sin. They leave the infant at the door of a monastery, where he is subsequently raised. However, he is unable to adapt to a purely spiritual, contemplative life and leaves the monastery to begin a new life as a knight. When he arrives in a country which, unbeknownst to him, is ruled by his widowed mother, he frees the land from an oppressor. Without knowing that they are mother and son, they fall in love and marry. When they finally realize their true relationship, both fall into deep despair. Gregorius seeks exile on an island in order to do penance. God does not leave him there, however, but destines him to become pope.

Like Hartmann's Arthurian epics, *Gregorius* is based on an Old French source, *La Vie du pape Saint Grégoire (Life of Saint Gregory the Pope).* Unlike his source, Hartmann places great emphasis on the contrast between the secular world (the knight's life) and the religious life. Gregorius is exposed to both spheres: in the secular world he falls into the most heinous sin without realizing it, acquiring a heavy burden of guilt, but the religious sphere offers him an exemplary life without guilt. Nevertheless, the text does not condemn the secular life as error per se. Rather Hartmann suggests that people in this world almost inevitably come to ruin, even when they have no evil intention, but that God's grace can save them no matter how grievous their sin.

Hartmann's *Gregorius* achieved long-lasting popularity. In about 1210, Arnold of Lübeck translated it into Latin under the title *Gesta Gregorii peccatoris (The Deeds of Gregory the Sinner)*. The legend continued to crop up in various versions into the 18th century, notably in the important late medieval collection *Der Heiligen Leben* (ca. 1400; *Lives of the Saints*). Thomas Mann used it as the basis for his novella *Der Erwählte* (1951; published in English as *The Holy Sinner*).

Hartmann's second narrative devoted to religious themes, *Der arme Heinrich,* occupies a special place within his work, as is demonstrated by the number of surviving versions. In contrast to the Arthurian epics and *Gregorius,* no direct source for *Der arme Heinrich* appears to have existed, although the author, or narrator, states that he searched in "many books." The plot of *Der arme Heinrich* can be quickly summarized: God strikes Henry of Aue, a member of a noble family, with leprosy. All attempts to heal the disease fail. Henry withdraws from the world of the court to the more natural, rustic world of the steward of his landed estate. The steward's young daughter looks after Henry— sometimes appearing childlike and naive, sometimes saintlike, but at other times with hints of eroticism. One day she learns that Henry could be cured by the blood from the heart of a virgin. Selflessly, she offers herself, obstinately resisting the vehement objections of her parents and Henry himself. Her willfulness makes her appear sinful, thus creating a situation that puts Henry and the girl to the test. After much hesitation, the two depart for Salerno, where the operation is to take place. As he observes the naked girl on the operating table, Henry weighs his own and her existence in the balance and, deciding in favor of her life, he breaks off the procedure. As a reward for this altruistic act, God restores Henry's health, enabling him to return to his original social environment. The ending differs considerably in the various versions: in some manuscripts, the two protagonists marry; in another, Henry enters a monastery after marrying the girl but apparently before the union is consummated; and in yet another manuscript, the tale ends without any wedding at all.

At this point, we need to ask what the custom was with respect to marriage between two people from different social estates. In the past, scholars often regarded the marriage between the aristocrat Henry and the "unfree" steward's daughter as a problematic misalliance, but this is not necessarily the case. For one thing, social mobility through marriage is historically well documented and may have been less problematic for late 12th-century audiences than for

20th-century philologists. But on a more fundamental level, one may see the marriage in *Poor Henry* simply as "part of an optimistic ending" that need not be considered as a reflection of actual social conditions of the time.

Hartmann's story raises puzzling questions for modern readers. How was leprosy understood in 12th-century medicine and theology? What cultural and ritual practices account for the apparently macabre theme of virgin sacrifice? Did the idea that leprosy could be cured by the blood of a virgin form part of 12th-century medical practice? What the text reveals is a strange association of traditions about the magical properties of blood and the actual practice of medicine in the 12th century. Salerno was a respected medical center from the 11th century on; books from the city were widely circulated and it is possible that Hartmann knew about them. However, none of these writings contain references to superstitious beliefs concerning the properties of blood. Connected with the medical tradition of Salerno is a legend about the origins of the didactic poem *De conservanda bona valetudine (On Maintaining Good Health)*. Robert, the son of William the Conqueror (11th century), is wounded by a poisoned arrow; he survives, but a fistula develops that will not heal. In Salerno, physicians tell him that he can only be healed if a person regularly sucks the poison from it. Robert does not believe at first that anyone could be found to perform this dangerous service until his wife does it at night. The structural parallels to *Der arme Heinrich* are obvious. Yet Hartmann diverges from medical practices of the day in several respects: while it was not customary for patients to be unclothed, the girl in *Der arme Heinrich* is naked as she prepares to sacrifice herself; and the idea that one person can be healed through the death of another was contrary to theological principles and the traditions of Salerno. Hartmann thus creates a highly individual mixture of ideas from ancient and contemporary medicine about the properties of blood and common customs.

The problematic theological and moral issues raised in *Der arme Heinrich* ensured it a broad reception, and the story has frequently served as a basis for subsequent literary works, including a retelling by Adelbert von Chamisso (1839), a novella by Ricarda Huch (1899), a play by Gerhart Hauptmann (1902), a "musical fable" by Gerhart Hermann Mostar (1928), and a radio play by Martin Beheim-Schwarzbach (1962).

See also 1150, 1184, 1943

Bibliography: Michael Batts, "National Perspectives on Originality and Translation: Chrétien de Troyes and Hartmann von Aue," in Martin H. Jones and Roy Wisbey, eds., *Chrétien de Troyes and the German Middle Ages: Papers from an International Symposium = Arthurian Studies* 26 (London: Institute of Germanic Studies, 1993), 9–18. David Duckworth, "Heinrich and the Godless Life in Hartmann's Poem," *Mediävistik* 3 (1990–1992): 71–90. ———, "Heinrich and the Knowledge of God in Hartmann's Poem," *Mediävistik* 5 (1992–1994): 57–70. Rod W. Fisher, "The Courtly Hero Comes to Germany: Hartmann's *Erec* and the Concept of Shame," *Amsterdamer Beiträge zur älteren Germanistik* 46 (1996): 119–130. Nigel Harris, "The Presentation of Clerical Characters in the *Vie du pape Saint Grégoire*," *Medium Aevum* 64 (1995): 189–204. William Henry Jackson, *Chivalry in Twelfth-Century Germany: The Works of Hartmann von Aue* (Cambridge: D. S. Brewer, 1994) = *Arthurian Studies* 34ss.

Thomas Bein
Translated by Deborah Lucas Schneider

℧ *Circa 1200*

The *Nibelungenlied* is composed in the Bavarian town of Passau

Contagious Violence

The *Nibelungenlied (Song of the Nibelungs)* tells the story of the murder of a Burgundian king and his brothers at a feast to which their sister, Kriemhild, had invited them. The tales retold in this epic are very old, dating back to the tribal migrations in the period called the Dark Ages. The epic combines material from several sagas, including those telling about the downfall of a Burgundian kingdom along the Rhine (A.D. 436–437), about Attila the Hun (died A.D. 453), Theoderic the Great (A.D. 455–526), and the hero Siegfried, who may have been a member of a Merovingian dynasty. As is customary in heroic sagas, very different sets of events are compressed chronologically and spatially, and linked to the actions of a few outstanding protagonists ("heroes"), resulting in memorable fables about elemental human passions: love, jealousy, envy, and the desire for revenge. For 700 years, the saga of the Nibelungs was passed down orally. In the beginning, it may have served to recall the fate of the kingdoms and their royal houses, later becoming a source for the origins of noble families who traced their lineage to the saga's heroes, and finally a history of events that shook the medieval political and social order to its foundations.

The bard who retold the saga in extended form, probably shortly before A.D. 1200, is thought to have lived near the court of the bishop of Passau. The poet did not have much freedom in shaping his material and was obliged to relate the story as it was preserved in the collective memory of the time. However, we know virtually nothing about the details of the version he worked from. He was free to add embellishments, shift accents, or alter the characters' motivation, but he could not change the basic plot. While there is a suggestion of a possible different outcome, he tells the story in the familiar manner, with the saga taking its ineluctable course: Kriemhild invites her brothers to Attila's court, concealing her real motive, and has them killed. But in *The Song of the Nibelungs* the murders are the culmination of a long story that at first appears to take a quite different turn. Kriemhild seems to be the heroine of a courtly romance, a princess living under the protection of her brothers at the royal court of Worms. Siegfried is a courtly knight, prince of Xanten, the son of a king in the Low Countries. He wants to marry Kriemhild and sets out for Worms to win her hand. Only when he arrives there do we learn from a remark by Hagen, the mightiest warrior in Worms, that Siegfried is a famous hero, who once wrested an enormous treasure from the kings of the Nibelungs' lands and killed a dragon. In Worms, he announces not that he wants to win Kriemhild as his wife, but rather that he has come to challenge King Gunther to a duel for control of his kingdom. The looming conflict is avoided when Siegfried is persuaded to change his mind and submit to the norms of behavior at Gunther's court. He gets a first glimpse of Kriemhild only after he has successfully fought on the Burgundian side in a war against the Danes and Saxons. King Gunther then demands that before Siegfried can marry he must assist the king in his own suit for Brünhild. This Brünhild is not easily won. She will accept as a husband only the man who can show he is stronger than she is and a better fighter; any suitor who competes with her and loses must die. Gunther is too weak for the contest and asks Siegfried to stand in for him, disguised in the magic cloak he had acquired with the treasure of the Nibelungs. To conceal the deception, Siegfried identifies himself as Gunther's vassal. In this manner, Gunther wins Brünhild's hand. When asked at the wedding ceremony in Worms, he is unable to explain why he gave his sister in marriage to a vassal of lower rank. Brünhild refuses to consummate the marriage until he has told her the reason. Once again Siegfried is called upon to take the king's place and wrestle Brünhild into submission in the bedroom with the express promise to Gunther that he will not violate her.

Siegfried subdues Brünhild a second time, and all seems well. Siegfried returns to rule Xanten with Kriemhild. But Brünhild's suspicions give her no rest. She persuades Gunther to invite the couple back to Worms. At a tournament Brünhild insults Siegfried by calling him a serf. If this claim were true, it would also make his wife, Kriemhild, a serf; Kriemhild gets even by proclaiming that Siegfried had been Brünhild's lover before Gunther. The king's attempt to settle the dispute fails, and from then on the Burgundians are resolved to kill Siegfried. With Gunther's approval, Hagen devises a plan. Under pretense that a war was imminent, he persuades Kriemhild to reveal to him the one vulnerable spot where Siegfried can be wounded. The war is then called off, and Hagen sneaks up behind Siegfried while they are out hunting and murders him. There is no doubt about who committed the crime, for when Hagen and Gunther approach the bier, Siegfried's wounds begin to bleed again. The grief-stricken Kriemhild knows to delay her revenge. She becomes outwardly reconciled with Gunther and has the Nibelungs' treasure transported to Worms. As she distributes the gold to acquire a retinue of warriors, Hagen intervenes once more. He steals the treasure and sinks it in the Rhine, while her brothers do nothing to help her. Kriemhild now gives herself over completely to her grief.

At this point the scene shifts abruptly to the court of Attila, king of the Huns. His wife has died, and he seeks to marry Kriemhild. Despite Hagen's warnings, the kings in Worms agree, and Kriemhild also gives her consent, after another suitor, Rüdeger, has made vague promises to come to her aid if she should ever need help. As queen of the Huns, Kriemhild wields enormous power. She persuades Attila to invite her relatives from the Rhine; once again they ignore Hagen's warning and accept. Their journey is accompanied by unfavorable omens. At Attila's court the situation is tense from the outset, and violence is narrowly averted on several occasions. But then Kriemhild orders her men to fall on the Burgundian retinue at a banquet. Hagen responds by killing the prince, Kriemhild's and Attila's son. A pitched battle ensues. The remaining characters are drawn in one by one: first Irinc, in exile at Attila's court; then Rüdeger, a relative of the Burgundians who feels legally bound to assist them; and finally Dietrich of Bern, who has tried to keep his retinue out of the fighting for as long as possible. When only Hagen and Gunther remain alive on the Burgundian side, Dietrich captures them both and hands them over to Kriemhild. The queen demands for the last time that they give back "what has been taken from her." Hagen interprets this as a reference to the treasure and refuses. In the hope that he would relent, Kriemhild orders Gunther executed first, but when Hagen remains silent she strikes his head off herself. Thereupon Hildebrand, another hero, hacks her to pieces.

At the core of the epic is the theme of betrayal and its opposite, loyalty *(triuwe)*. In the Middle Ages, a period of relatively weak and undeveloped political and social institutions, *triuwe* was a central principle of order, based on personal relationships thought to be stronger and more reliable than others. The concept of *triuwe* epitomized all the positive ties in the medieval family: between siblings, parents, and children, between man and wife, and among relatives in general. It also extended to the relationship between lord and vassal, allies and comrades in arms. The epic deals in part with cases in which such loyalty is maintained, but chiefly it is a story of betrayal, of loyalty undermined and perverted. Bonds of loyalty to one person or group can come into irreconcilable conflict with obligations to another person, or they can be misused, since their only guarantee is the character of the person involved. In the case of Kriemhild, her loyalty to her husband, Siegfried, inevitably leads to her betrayal of her kin. The principle on which the heroic world rests is thus deconstructed.

This occurs in the course of an epidemic of destructive violence. The heroic, violent world clashes with a courtly, peaceful one for the first time when Siegfried arrives in Worms and, rather than courting Kriemhild, issues a challenge to the ruler. The rules of courtly conduct prevent the outbreak of open conflict. The king treats Siegfried as a guest, placing "everything at his disposal." The duel for power becomes an athletic competition, a tournament, instead. The war against the Danes and Saxons provides a means to channel the violent impulse toward an outside group in the form of self-defense against an arbitrary attack. The resolution of this conflict takes an exemplary form in the victory celebration: The aggressors have been defeated and taken prisoner, yet the victors are generous and release them without sanctions. This pattern of looming violence and its tenuous deflection and dissimulation continues throughout the epic until, in the end, the last remnants of courtly civility are overturned by bloody vengeance. Ironically, the conflict between courtly and heroic codes, between symbolic status and superior physical force comes to light at the tournament, that is, in a situation in which all fighting has been reduced to a competition for the symbolic capital of honor.

In the queens' dispute over who ranks above the other, Kriemhild's courtly standards of honor conflict with Brünhild's heroic conception of political power. As the dispute escalates, Gunther's claim to being the legitimate holder of power is challenged, both as king and as husband, that is, subduer, of the queen. Up to this point, violence has been kept in check through courtly rituals or made invisible through Siegfried's use of his magic cloak or under cover of night. Now it emerges into the open; dangerous consequences threaten to follow, which the king hopes to avert by holding a trial. But since both Brünhild's and Kriemhild's interpretations are incorrect, an open discussion must necessarily fail, and the conflict descends again into the obscurity of concealed intrigues, ending in the treacherous murder of Siegfried. His corpse, placed by the killers at Kriemhild's door, where she will literally stumble over it, becomes an emblem of the latent violence that, although disavowed repeatedly, spins more and more out of control. Attempts to make peace continue, along with denial and cover-ups of the violence that has occurred, as seen in Kriemhild's reconciliation with Gunther, her recruitment of warriors loyal to her, disguised as hospitality; in Hagen's secret theft of the treasure hoard; and in the contradiction between the kings' leniency and imposition of punishments.

The final outbreak of violence at the court of Attila is ambivalent. Although celebrated by the heroes, the event, which they and Kriemhild have deliberately brought about, still marks the breakdown of all remaining forms of order. The truth emerges and the game of hide-and-seek comes to an end, but so do the last vestiges of mutual consideration and any possibility for peaceful relations. Hagen's murder of Attila's and Kriemhild's son signals an orgy of violence, in which blood flows instead of wine, and the hall resounds with the clash of weapons rather than music. One after the other, the protagonists are drawn into the fighting, until in the end only Dietrich, Hildebrand, and Attila remain. Heroic furor prevails over all attempts to make peace, at the cost of destroying the world as it had previously been constructed.

Once infected with this epidemic of violence, the figures undergo a complete transformation, even though the narrator does not make the changes in their psyche explicit. The courtly Kriemhild becomes adept at intrigue and betrayal; the weak king, whose claims to power rest solely on heredity, turns into a brave warrior; and Hagen, Siegfried's murderer, is transformed into an almost invincible hero. Even the positive figures—such as Dietrich of Bern or the margrave Rüdeger, the model of courtly behavior in the epic, who gives his feudal duty to Attila priority over his obligation to the Burgundian guests only reluctantly—become heroes in the end; they acquire *rehtes helden muot,* the "courage of a real hero," as they are swept into the frenzy of combat. Once Attila's surviving guests have left for Worms, the Burgundians are referred to more and more frequently as "Nibelungs." The inhabitants of the wild realm of saga conquered by Siegfried have infiltrated and infected the courtly world of Worms, so to speak, until the two merge into one.

It is striking that the poet should have linked the progression of the catastrophe with the abandonment of courtly manners. In this respect the *Song of the Nibelungs* takes up a stance in direct opposition to the contemporary courtly romance, although neither as a criticism of the latter's optimism nor as a confirmation of it *ex negativo*. Rather it makes a point of exposing what courtly romances omit: the fascination with violence and superior physical force, the hero's lack of ties to others, the selfish emotions under a veneer of courtly manners, the latent weakness of institutionalized rule, and contempt for mere appearances. As the catastrophic consequences of this abandonment of all rules of behavior are narrated, the process continues all the way to the annihilation of the established order. For the most part, the narrator refrains from commentary, withholding judgment and merely presenting the mechanisms of a growing inversion: from the courtly world at the beginning of the poem to the devastated battleground of the ending. However, he does not show them in a positive light. Gaining "the courage of a real hero" means lapsing into purely physical violence. The epic thus presents the ambivalent nature of the heroic world about the year 1200, at a critical moment of transition to a new political and social order, against the background of courtly society developing into a more complex civilization.

See also 830, 930, 1184, 1203 (Summer), 1876

Bibliography: Theodore M. Andersson, *A Preface to the Nibelungenlied* (Stanford: Stanford University Press, 1987). Michael S. Batts, ed., *Nibelungenlied: Paralleldruck der Handschriften A, B und C nebst Lesarten der übrigen Handschriften* (Tübingen, 1971). Edward R. Haymes, *The Nibelungenlied: History and Interpretation,* Illinois Medieval Monographs (Urbana, 1986). Jan-Dirk Müller, *Spielregeln für den Untergang: Die Welt des Nibelungenliedes* (Tübingen, 1998).

Jan-Dirk Müller
Translated by Deborah Lucas Schneider

✑ Post 1200

Classical Middle High German becomes the medium for a growing number of writers and readers and for an explosion in literary genres

A Literary Language?

While the question mark in the title of this entry might apply most directly to the adjective "literary," it also pertains to the date assigned to the entry and to the phrase "Middle High German." Thus one may properly question whether 1200 is a realistic demarcation point in the history of the German language. What exactly does the term "Middle High German" denote? Was it a language at all, and if so, was it a literary one? And how should "literary" be defined?

A good place to start in answering these questions is with the traditional term "Middle High German," which breaks down syntactically into three components. Middle High German is a kind of High German, and High German is a kind of German. So to begin with, what is German?

The use of the term "German," and its German equivalent *deutsch,* today refers to the Germanic speech varieties currently spoken within the national borders of Germany, Austria, Switzerland, Luxembourg, and Liechtenstein, plus related speech varieties in other nations where they are spoken by a linguistic minority (for example in France, Czechoslovakia, the United States). This was not always so, and certainly not in the Middle Ages. During the tenure of the language we are investigating here, there were numerous speech varieties called *deutsch* or in variants such as *duutsch, dietsch,* and the like, varieties that we would not designate as German at all. The most prominent of these is the language we now call Dutch, an interesting relic in the English language of the older terminology (the Dutch themselves now call their language *Nederlands,* reserving *Duits* for German in the narrower modern sense).

The term *deutsch,* deriving from a root meaning "people" in Germanic, originally found its meaning primarily in contrast to the word *welsch* ("foreign," especially Romanic or Celtic; compare the modern English and German words "Welsh," *Rotwelsch* [thieves' jargon], "Walloon"), and on a linguistic level in contrast to Latin. Thus in early documentations of the word in Latin texts (for example, in the Latin part of the *Strasbourg Oaths*), the term denotes something like "Germanic colloquial" rather than "reasonably unitary language spoken by a specific political or linguistic group." Though it eventually gained the latter meaning, in the period we are looking at *deutsch* still has a rather fuzzy wider range.

In spite of its widespread colloquial identification with the standard German language (a concept to be discussed below), High German is a linguistic term. It refers to any Germanic dialect that contains some part of the High German Consonant Shift, whereby, among other things, older $\star$p, $\star$t, and $\star$k (the asterisk indicates a "reconstructed" sound) become, under specifiable circumstances, the affricate consonants *pf, ts,* and *kch* or the fricative consonants *f, s,* or *ch* (I refrain here from using phonetic symbols). These sound changes, which account for correspondences like those between English *water* and German *Wasser,* or English *pepper* and German *Pfeffer,* are currently found to some degree in German dialects south of an imaginary east-west line passing through the village of Benrath on the Rhine north of Cologne (the term *Benrath line* is therefore sometimes used for this linguistic boundary). During the period under discussion here, this line ran further to the south than it does currently and had not yet attained its maximum eastward expansion into formerly Slavic territories.

High German is, of course, defined in opposition to Low German, the dialects north of the Benrath line that did not undergo the High German Consonant Shift. Middle High German must be similarly defined, this time temporally, against Old High German and New High German. Since language change is usually continuous and fairly gradual, isolating precise moments on the continuum is no easy task. In addition, the primary linguistic criterion for the break between Old High German and Middle High German, namely the (again, gradual) weakening of full vowels in unaccented syllables, is somewhat arbitrary (though we may argue that this weakening is indeed responsible for, or at least symptomatic of, an important set of changes that reshaped the language completely). Fortunately, this linguistic criterion is reinforced by a literary-cultural one. Between the end of an Old High German period actually documented by a significant body of texts and the beginning of a Middle High German period with an analogous volume of texts lie several generations of a surprising paucity of literary materials.

It should be borne in mind that this break is to some extent deceptive. All along, smaller prose texts of a private, pragmatic nature were written, mostly dealing with prayers and penance, heaven and hell. But as Kuhn (1958) notes, the quality of such *Gebrauchsliteratur* (utilitarian literature) escalated palpably in the mid-eleventh century, a process characterized by creditable attempts at versification. In addition, and more prominently, the first real literary monument cited by most scholars as the starting point for Middle High German is the *Ezzolied* (ca. 1060), a poetic reflection on sin and redemption by a Bamberg monk, probably on the eve of a pilgrimage.

The end of the Middle High German period rests on no such definitive textual or linguistic criteria. Accordingly, different scholars set the boundary between this period and the New High German period at varying points. While some argue for a date as late as 1500, a choice that positions Luther as the catalytic figure of the transition, most scholars place it at the end of the Late Middle High German period, at about 1350, though with some discomfort.

Assuming that we have now roughly characterized the spatial and temporal boundaries of Middle High German, we must ask what kind of a language it was. In what sense was it a language at all? The word that most obviously stands in binary opposition to the term *language* in modern English (and for that matter German) is *dialect* (German *Mundart*). In the non-technical understanding of this opposition, a dialect is a social or regional variant of a language, which is understood as a standard from which dialects deviate. Yet, applying this kind of understanding to Middle High German presents some difficulties. A glance at the handbooks of this language shows that, throughout this period, Middle High German is found in several flavors, correlated with geographical provenience, text genre, and social class. Moreover, these flavors often differed widely at all linguistic levels. It is unlikely that the speakers or writers considered themselves to be speaking or writing in variants of a single overarching unity we could call a standard.

However, there may have been at least some idea of such a unity. When modern scholars of Middle High German describe this language, they tend to concentrate on a type of Middle High German in use at the courts of southern (especially southwestern) Germany, or in imitation of those courts, primarily as a vehicle for the creation of literary works, the accepted canon of which was established in the early nineteenth century. This language variant is referred to by those scholars as the *höfische Dichtersprache* (courtly literary language), or more boldly, perhaps, as Classical Middle High German.

Although this literary language had a great deal more variation than one might expect of a standard language, its texts contain several centralizing tendencies. Classical Middle High German texts show to a certain extent a common preference for words and forms associated with courtly society (for example, *minne,* love; *muot,* state of mind; the borrowed French word *âventiure,* adventure). In addition, they share common syntactic and stylistic patterns arguably also correlated with the life of the court (for example, impersonal and passive constructions as signs of politeness and distance).

If these phenomena were the only unifying factors in Classical Middle High German, it would be difficult to defend it as a separate language. But these works also show a distinct convergence in the written representation of individual words (generally following a southwestern model). There is also an (increasing) avoidance of regionally idiosyncratic rhymes in favor of those which work in most German-speaking areas, either because they followed the preferred southwestern pattern or because the etymology of certain words ensured their rhyming in most German-speaking areas.

Such a convergence clearly depended on the existence of a self-aware, supra-regional literary community of people who read or heard each other's works, who agreed on, or at least argued about, aesthetic values, and who, in their very conscious competition to entertain courtly society throughout the German-speaking regions, arrived at similar linguistic structures. That this push toward a common idiom, while clearly felt, was not always followed, may be seen in the following quotation from Ebernand von Erfurt, who in around the year 1215 wrote his (religious) legend *Heinrich and Kunegunde:* "I was born of Thuringian background; if I had now turned away from that language, and forced my tongue to a different manner, what good would that do me? I believe that one behaves apishly, when one appropriates a language which one cannot use properly" (Paul, Wiehl, and Grosse 1989, 15).

The literature written in Classical Middle High German (primarily lyric and epic poetry) flourished in the period from about 1170 to about 1250 (though scholars quibble over the exact date span). One of the most famous, though not most typical, products was the *Nibelungenlied (Song of the Nibelungs),* written down sometime around 1200 by an anonymous, but probably clerical, author. Given this literary efflorescence, the date of 1200 suggested in the title is appropriate for an entry on Middle High German. But it is important to note that there is a reciprocal relationship between this date and the specific interpretation of the words in the rest of the title. That is, if Middle High German means Classical Middle High German as defined above, then 1200 is an obvious date for this entry.

The same reasoning applies equally well to justifying the word "literary." For if "Middle High German" means "Classical Middle High German," and Classical Middle High German is the language of those works adjudged in the early 19th century to be literary monuments, Middle High German was *by definition* a literary language.

Surely this is not a satisfactory answer to the question posed in the title.

What we would really like to know are the answers to questions such as these: Did anybody really *speak* something like the written language we call Classical Middle High German, and, if so, who? Did the notion of a unified German language become more of a reality during the Middle High German period, and, if so, how? How important in this process are texts outside the classical literary canon, and what do we mean by "literary" anyway?

Early 19th-century scholars, such as Jacob Grimm and Karl Lachmann, who first collected, edited, and published the classical texts, were convinced that their tendencies toward a common written language reflected similar tendencies in the speech of the courts. Lachmann especially assumed "that the poets of the 13th century, except for a few dialectal particularities, spoke a certain unchangeable High German, while uneducated writers allowed themselves other, sometimes older, sometimes more corrupt forms of the common language" (Paul, Wiehl, and Grosse 1989, 13). Subsequent scholars have concluded that this was overstated, even for the poets. Given the absence of real evidence concerning the spoken language, we can postulate at best some supra-regional tendencies toward linguistic convergence among a few social groups.

It could be argued that the true significance of the body of work written in Classical Middle High German is not its relative uniformity, but rather its relative secularity. Or to put it another way, the truly important thing that happened to the German language during the Middle High German period was not that it became more standardized (the later standard German language is by no means a straightforward continuation of Classical Middle High German), but that German, in whatever form, became, during this historical period, the medium for a growing number of writers and readers, from social groups that were either newly formed or greatly changed from earlier periods and, in consequence, the medium of an explosion of written works in a variety of genres hitherto unrepresented in the language.

Although the essays in this volume deal only with a select subset of the works written in some form of Middle High German, they convey a sense of this expansion. For the period from 1050 to 1170 (Early Middle High German), we find, besides works written in Latin, in German only the *Annolied,* which, despite substantial differences, like the *Ezzolied,* is the work of a cleric with a predominantly religious outlook. And indeed, clerical authorship and religious themes characterize the vast majority of works in German for the better part of the century following the *Annolied.* In a first wave of French influence, starting in the mid-12th century, however, we find increasing interest in more worldly topics, as in the *Song of Roland,* which, despite the fact that its translator was a cleric, deals with the adventures and manners of a secular, though pious, chivalry.

Within a very short period of time, the obvious audience for this kind of material (the nonclerical aristocracy of the feudal courts), following the French model and frequently reworking French material, began to produce many of its foremost poets: Hartmann von Aue, Wolfram von Eschenbach, and

Gottfried von Strassburg, who are the core writers of the Middle High German court epic (in a twenty- to twenty-five-year period!), show us a highly sophisticated secular literary genre in full bloom. In about the same span of time, also following French models, but increasingly forging its own way, we find a flowering of lyric poetry: *Minnesang,* Walther von der Vogelweide. About 1200, the *Nibelungenlied,* along with later, lesser poems, gives us a literary manifestation of older Germanic oral traditions (altered, of course, in conformity with contemporary taste).

Thus the year 1200 can be seen as a pivotal point in the history of the German language. We can say that German is in transition from a language used primarily for religious writings to one used for all manner of secular as well as religious purposes. In the course of the 13th century, we find, in addition to works in poetic genres new to the German language ("Der Stricker," "Geistliches Spiel," Ullrich von Lichtenstein's *Frauendienst,* Konrad von Würzburg), a veritable spurt in prose works. This increasingly includes now, not just utilitarian (religious) prose, but substantial works of history (Rudolf von Ems's *Weltchronik*), Arthurian legend, law (legal charters, city laws, local treaties, and the like), theology (especially sermons), medicine and mysticism (Mechthild von Magdeburg, Meister Eckhart), among areas important and trivial. German is used increasingly by an increasingly literate and increasingly bourgeois population.

It has often been noted, more than a little disapprovingly, that the relative uniformity of Classical Middle High German yielded to much more regional variability in the post-classical period. It has also been noted, though less often, that this increase in variability had to do with the enormous increase in the general use of written German (see Keller 1978, 254–255). Classical Middle High German was the artificial product of a small group of court literati; later Middle High German represents a genuine rebellion against the sway of Latin in many realms of life. It is debatable whether the development toward an eventual standard German was in any way impeded by this rebellion, rather the contrary.

In this context, let us return to the heading of this essay and concentrate on "Post 1200." Can Middle High German after 1200 be called a literary language? Of course, the answer depends partly on one's definition of literature. To what extent, for example, should one treat a work of history or of mysticism as literature? But whatever one's definition of literature might be, when one considers the enormous increase in the volume of texts in German in genres hitherto completely unrepresented in that language, the answer has to be "increasingly not," or "not only."

See also 1189, ca. 1200, 1203 (Summer), 1815

Bibliography: Adolf Bach, *Geschichte der deutschen Sprache,* 8th ed. (Heidelberg: Quelle & Meyer, 1965). Michael Curschmann, "Middle High German Literature," in *Dictionary of the Middle Ages,* vol. 8 (New York: Scribner, 1987). R. E. Keller, *The German Language* (Atlantic Highlands, N.J.: Humanities Press, 1978). Hugo Kuhn, "Frühmittelhochdeutsche Literatur," in *Reallexikon der deutschen Literaturgeschichte,* vol. 1 (Berlin: de Gruyter, 1958). ———, *Entwürfe zu einer Literatursystematik des Spätmittelalters* (Tübingen: Niemeyer, 1980). Hermann Paul, Peter Wiehl, and Siegfried Grosse, *Mittelhochdeutsche Grammatik* (Tübingen: Niemeyer, 1989). Gabriele Schieb, "Mittelhochdeutsch," in L. E. Schmitt, ed., *Kurzer Grundriß der germanischen Philologie bis 1500*, vol. 1 (Berlin: de Gruyter, 1970). Max Wehrli, *Geschichte der deutschen Literatur im Mittelalter: Von den Anfängen bis zum Ende des 16. Jahrhunderts*, 3rd ed. (Stuttgart: Reclam, 1997).

Orrin W. Robinson

♫ *1203, Summer*

Allies of Hermann of Thuringia besiege the forces of Philip of Swabia in Erfurt; the damage to the vineyards is said to be still visible about halfway through *Parzival*

Salvation through Fiction

The vineyards of Erfurt are granted only a few lines in Wolfram von Eschenbach's *Parzival* (1200–1210), where the damage they suffered provides a point of reference to the havoc wrought by a fictional battle Wolfram describes at some length (379.18–20). They remind us that the decade in which *Parzival* was written was a time of political upheaval in Germany. Two rival kings, Philip of Swabia and Otto IV, were engaged in a protracted struggle that laid waste much of the country. Hermann of Thuringia, who first supported Philip, changed sides no fewer than three times before the struggle ended with Philip's murder in 1208. The turmoil in early 13th-century Germany is but one particular instance of the endemic violence among the nobility of medieval Europe. It dominates Wolfram's *Parzival* as well. The story told is one of violence that pits knight against knight, with women as the prize. Clamide desires the hand of Condwiramurs; when she refuses he attacks her country. Parzival comes to her aid, defeats the attacker, and wins her hand. We learn of Parzival's prowess at arms in the prologue, which is the only attribute that warrants mention at his birth (4.14–17, 112.28–30). Parzival is above all a fighter. Occasionally Wolfram expresses reservations about the "foolish men" who "fight for no reason other than to win favor with fame" (538.2–4). But sustained critique is out of the question, since fighting is the activity by which male nobles define themselves as a gender and as a class. Even Wolfram himself claims to belong. "I am Wolfram von Eschenbach," he announces (114.12), and declares to be a knight (115.11). He insists that women should not love him for his songs (Wolfram also wrote *minnesongs*), but only if he can "earn the reward of their love with shield and spear" (115.16–17). He sets himself apart from those writers of romance, like Hartmann von Aue, who boast of their learning. "I don't know a single letter of the alphabet," he asserts in a famous line (115.27). Real men don't write, they fight.

Luckily, there were forces at work to contain the damage. The gradual concentration of power in the hands of the great princes (territorialization) enabled them to check the violence among lesser nobles. Very slowly the Church established the principles of indissolubility and monogamy, thus curbing the power of husbands to repudiate their wives or to take concubines. In the world of fiction, the violence of knights toward one another is regulated by a code of chivalry, the behavior of knights toward women by the ritual of love service. Knightly combat is performed as "service" for a lady for as long as she requires; when she is satisfied that the knight has proven his worthiness, she grants him the "reward" of her love. In *Parzival,* love service is the only paradigm available for conceptualizing the relations of men and women: rape is understood as a violation of love service (526.3–5); marriage is the continuation of love service, with the partners achieving sexual intimacy. There are more than a dozen important love service relationships in *Parzival,* and they are directly or indirectly responsible for nearly all the major developments in the plot. Wolfram, the knight-narrator, even suggests he is telling his story as a sort of love service (115.21–24, 337.23–30, 827.25–30).

While the actual violence of male nobles is hardly questioned, the means of regulating it are continually examined. Love is a constant concern. Characters suffer from love; they behave badly out of love; they are inspired by love to bold feats of arms and prodigious devotion. The narrator waxes eloquent about the power of love to upset order of any kind: men are made weak; women are dishonored; lords violate their vassals; souls are lost (291.1–292.4). And yet there is a good sort of love: "real love is true faithfulness" (532.10). In love, men and women are held to the same standard. They should be modest and faithful like Condwiramurs and Parzival, or Sigune and Schianatulander, who died in her service. True love is of such high virtue that even God must respect it. Sigune is only one of several women whose knight-servitors are killed before being granted their reward. By extending a love service relationship over too long a period, in which they retain the upper hand, these women lose their lovers altogether. Their anguish serves as an admonition to women not to hold out too long. Apparently the regulation of knightly violence, requiring women to exercise power for a time, generated some anxiety among the men.

The historical setting for codes of chivalry and love is the medieval court, one of the great achievements of the High Middle Ages. At the court, various aspects of life are refined and elaborated and turned into marks of distinction: eating is ritualized into a courtly feast; fighting is stylized into a knightly tournament; storytelling is elaborated into the performance of vernacular romance. These rituals set those who belong to courtly society apart from those who do not, and legitimate the power of those who can marshal the resources required to sustain such a way of life. The cultivation of courtliness is one of the ways in which noble violence was contained—both by redirecting its energies to less disruptive ends and by offering an alternative way for a man to distinguish himself. The ideal court was the fictional court of King Arthur, which was given its classic form by Chrétien de Troyes, the great French creator of Arthurian romance. He had already provided the models for two German romances—Hartmann von Aue's *Erec* (1180–1190) and *Iwein* (1195–1205)—before Wolfram took Chrétien's unfinished last work, the *Conte du Graal* (1180–1190), as the principal source for *Parzival.* How Wolfram came upon this source and who supported him while he wrote are matters about which we can only speculate. Arthur's court represents an ideal of courtly culture, both within the fictional world and beyond, and the hero's appearances at court mark milestones in his career. The Arthurian court also supplies a familiar cast of actors, whose qualities, established in previous romances, can be exploited in new contexts. Wolfram draws on this literary tradition to enter into a wider cultural conversation. At the moment when the German nobility elaborates its own secular culture, *Parzival* offers a complex reflection on the tensions between the violence that continued to define noble masculinity and the various protocols of courtliness that sought to restrain that violence in the interest of a new, more "civilized" class ideal.

Chrétien had already expanded the parameters of this conversation by adding to the *Conte du Graal* an explicit religious dimension centered on the Grail, which had been absent from his earlier romances. Wolfram greatly elaborates this dimension. He gives the Grail a place in salvation history, tracing it back to the rebellion of Lucifer. He also gives it a future, looking forward to the Christianization of India, which would make the Grail the imaginary center of a Christian world order. Although Parzival is destined to succeed his ailing uncle as Grail king, on his first visit to the Grail castle he fails to ask the crucial question that would bring relief to his uncle and allow Parzival to assume the kingship. When he is denounced a few days later at Arthur's court for his failure, he turns away from God. After four-and-a-half years in pursuit of knightly combat "without direction" (460.29), he finally abandons his "hatred toward God" (461.9) and acknowledges his sins under the guidance of another uncle, the hermit Trevrizent. Although Parzival's sins are linked to specific actions, they are sins of ignorance or omission, like his failure to ask the question at the Grail castle, rather than sins of malice or willfulness, indicating the inevitable human entanglement in sin. Parzival represents a new kind of Arthurian hero, one whose human sinfulness is part of the story. Even such a hero can be saved, however, as Wolfram assures us at the beginning of the prologue (1.3–9) and as Parzival demonstrates at the end of the romance.

Sigune, whom Parzival finds enclosed in a tiny cell in the forest reading her Psalter, and the hermit Trevrizent represent fictional types who can also be found in the historical thirteenth century: women and men who exchanged the noble world into which they were born for a life of pious asceticism. The 12th and 13th centuries were a period of great religious fervor. They witnessed the founding and rapid growth of new monastic orders, the rise of heretical movements, and the Crusades. The lay nobility, especially noble women, participated actively. One of the most illustrious examples is Elizabeth, the daughter-in-law of Hermann of Thuringia, who abandoned the court after her husband's death on a Crusade (1217) and devoted the rest of her short life to the care of the poor and the sick. She was canonized in 1235. The religious aspects in *Parzival* are no doubt a response to the concerns of the noble audiences for which it was written. It is important to recognize, however, that although Sigune and Trevrizent, like Elizabeth, abandon courtly society to lead more holy lives, Parzival never abandons knighthood, and that although the epic opens Arthurian romance to religious themes, it does not repudiate the world of King Arthur. In what are nearly the last lines of the romance, Wolfram proclaims it "a worthwhile effort" if someone can manage to "end this life so that God is not robbed of the soul on account of the sins of the flesh and who is nevertheless able to retain the favor of the world with dignity" (827.19–24). *Parzival* presents an elaborate case that no contradiction need exist between the quest for glory in this world and the search for salvation in the next.

Wolfram's inclination to reconcile potentially discordant elements is evident in the numerous structural, thematic, and rhetorical strands that hold together this very long narrative and give it its distinctive complexity and coherence. A single character may appear in several scenes: Parzival encounters Sigune four times in the course of the romance, and each encounter reflects a different stage in her transfiguration and in his relation to the Grail. A single attribute connects disparate domains: faithfulness or *triuwe* is the quality that defines proper love, that binds lord and vassal, and that describes God's relation to humankind. A series of references to the calendar, the church year, and the position of the planets makes it possible to sketch a very precise chronology that organizes much of the narrative. Over one hundred real place names (Chrétien has twelve), not only in Europe but in Asia and Africa as well, connect the fictional geography of Arthur to the real geography of Wolfram's contemporaries (Erfurt, for example) and raise questions about the boundaries between the two. There are 182 named characters in *Parzival* (four times the number in Chrétien's narrative), and of these, 119 belong either to the lineage of King Arthur or to that of the Grail family. Since Parzival belongs to both, there is hardly a character he encounters to whom he is not related. This adds intensity: the first knight he kills, Ither, turns out to have been a relative, which means that Parzival's entry into knighthood is, at the same time, an entry into sinfulness. It curbs violence: important knightly contests are called off when the opponents are discovered to be related. And it generates stories: Wolfram has added three thousand lines to the beginning of Chrétien's narrative, devoting them to the hero's parents and others of their generation. The romance is the story not just of a single hero but of lineages. The elaborate bonds that seem to connect even the smallest element of *Parzival* to every other element are a literary manifestation of the desire for completeness, the impulse to construct systems, the fondness for the *summa,* that has been said to characterize the 13th century.

The world Wolfram represents is one of extraordinary complexity, held together by extensive associations, not always readily apparent, of time, space, and consanguinity. One of Parzival's main tasks is to discover these associations and acknowledge his place within them. But this happens slowly. He does not even learn his name until after he has left home. He does not learn that Ither is a relative until years after he killed him. Parzival is a hero, as we are told in the prologue, who "took a long time to grow up and become wise" (4.18). Wolfram's listeners and readers must also learn to see the connections, and this too can take a long time because the connections are revealed to us, as to the hero, only gradually—a reticence that Wolfram elevates to a matter of principle. When Parzival first visits the Grail castle, we are no better informed about what is going on there than he is. Rather than enlighten us, the narrator informs us he will answer our questions "later, when the proper time comes" (241.5). "I narrate the bowstring," he declares, "not the bow" (241.8). Just as the bowstring, though straight, must be bent for the arrow to travel quickly, the narration must be bent by withholding information until the proper time comes to reveal it and then must quickly hit its target. The narration that hits the target most effectively is the one that reveals its secrets bit by bit.

It takes some effort to figure out what Wolfram means by a bowstring that is straight but bent, and this illustrates another reason it is difficult to discover the various strands that hold *Parzival* together. Wolfram loves unexpected images, circumlocutions, compressed syntax, made-up words, foreign words, puns, contradictions, jokes, and surprises. He jumps abruptly from a fictional battlefield to "the vineyard at Erfurt," which "still tells of the same affliction caused by trampling" (379.18–19). The vineyard itself speaks of its affliction, and it chooses to do so in a way that frustrates effortless comprehension. Wolfram's style attracted comment from his contemporaries. Gottfried von Strassburg said one needs a commentary to determine what is meant (*Tristan*, p. 105). But Wolfram is unapologetic. He announces in the prologue that his story "never ceases to flee and pursue, to evade and turn, to accord praise and blame; reason has done well by the person who is not thrown off by all the ways the dice are cast" (2.9–14). Then he raises the stakes: "Whoever merely pretends to offer companionship deserves the fires of hell" (2.17–18). This is a bold claim: whoever follows the twists and turns of Wolfram's story, whoever sees the complex connections generated by his dense language, will be saved. Whoever does not is damned. The audience thus is in the same spot as the hero. The process of getting beneath the surface to discover the connections that hold the world together is long and arduous, requiring patience, faith, and humility. But the one who perseveres will be saved in the end.

Over the next three centuries, *Parzival* proved to be by far the most influential of the great narratives written in German about the year 1200. Subsequent generations were drawn to the hermeneutic challenges it poses, to the promise of salvation through fiction it holds out, and, doubtless with some nostalgia, to the synthesis of courtly and Christian culture it represents with more complexity and conviction than any other text of the German Middle Ages.

See also 1189, 1210, 1876

Bibliography: Arthur Groos, *Romancing the Grail: Genre, Science, and Quest in Wolfram's* Parzival (Ithaca, N.Y.: Cornell University Press, 1995). Wolfram von Eschenbach, *Parzival*, ed. Karl Lachmann, rev. Eberhard Nellmann, trans. Dieter Kühn, 2 vols., Bibliothek des Mittelalters, 8 (Frankfurt am Main: Deutscher Klassiker Verlag, 1994). Wolfram von Eschenbach, *Parzival,* trans. A. T. Hatto (Harmondsworth, U.K.: Penguin, 1980).

James A. Schultz

♩ *1203, November 12*

Walther von der Vogelweide receives five gold coins for the purchase of a fur coat

Singer of Himself

The only extant historical record of Walther von der Vogelweide's existence is an entry of November 12, 1203, in Wolfger of Erla's books. The bishop of Passau recorded the unusually large gift of five gold coins to the poet ("Walthero cantori de Vogelweide") in Zeiselmauer, near Vienna, for the purchase of a fur coat. The appellation *cantor* makes Walther a professional singer. This coincides with Walther's own, rather novel, view of his status, which did not conform to established classifications. Although he aspired to become a court minnesinger, Walther's poems frequently lack the courtly conventions of the *minne* genre. He also wrote *Sangsprüche* and a *Leich,* a multistrophic, complex form, usually of religious content and meant to display poetic virtuosity. Minnesong had been the reserve of poets of wealth, high social standing, and political influence. By contrast, the *Sangsprüche,* gnomic didactic poems in a single strophe, were associated with itinerant minstrels of the lower strata of society. Walther combined the two genres and set new standards for both. While his minnesongs contain social criticism, some of his *Sprüche* approach the absoluteness of the *minne* ethos. Walther also redefined the *Sangspruch* by expanding it to multistrophic forms and turning it into a supple medium of political commentary.

All but a few earlier and contemporary minnesingers meant erotic satisfaction when talking about a reward *(lôn)* for their service and singing. Walther's *Sprüche* contain frank requests for financial rewards for his public services and his minnesongs. Wolfger listed Walther in the company of his entertainers *(ioculator episcopi)* and falconers. But unlike a typical minstrel, Walther did not receive worn clothes. In fact, he proudly claimed that he had never worn such garments. Nevertheless, the date of Wolfger's gift, the day after Saint Martin's, suggests a charitable donation to someone in need, analogous to the saint's legendary gift of half his coat to a shivering beggar.

Although the "I" predominates in Walther's poetry, his utterances in the first person are not immediately autobiographical. Rather they belonged to a series of set roles, each of them a *persona* the poet assumes for the rhetorical realization of the ideal of courtly society. The effectiveness of poetry rested on the speaker's integration within the universal order which constitutes the moral and theological horizon of the *Sprüche*. The author quotes pre-existing models and varies them according to the intended message, but generally remains within the confines of the overarching feudal ideology. Both *minne* and *Spruch* poetry were sung, whereby they underwent a certain alienation effect. The melody slowed the presentation and provided a uniform medium even for seemingly spontaneous utterances. Supporting the poetic message, the musical presentation turned it, at the same time, into a social act.

The persuasive power of many of Walther's *Sprüche* rests on the confluence of typological requirements and individual experiences. When Walther states that he is unable to return his host's welcome greeting for lack of a home of his own (31.23ff) and that he longs for an end to his unsteady life of wandering entertainer (*gougelfuore;* 31.29), the constant striving for a secure post at a patron's court, expressed in many of his *Sprüche* and minnesongs, resounds in this emotional iteration of a genre tradition. The poetic *persona* Walther assumes is often unfettered by the social boundaries of feudal society. The poetic "I" admonishes kings and princes, ridicules popes with a vengeance, and brazenly requests compensation for services rendered—all with the air, not of a supplicant, but of a superior moral and political authority. Inasmuch as they reflect concrete political events as well as his personal situation, Walther's *Sprüche* may be read as an objective biographical blueprint. Clearly, he was not a glamorous knight or advisor to the emperor, as Melchior Goldast claimed in the first printed edition of Walther's songs in 1604 and as the Baroque poet Martin Opitz repeated in his highly influential *Buch von der Deutschen Poeterey* (1624; *Book on German Poetics*). Neither was he the "singer of the *Reich,*" as much of the German scholarship in the 19th and early 20th century maintained. Rather, he was primarily a "singer of himself" *(Rühmkorf),* who pitted intellectual and moral preeminence against the social and political hierarchy based on lineage.

Inherent in the concept of minnesong is a competition regarding the highest praise of the lady, the object of *minne.* Reinmar's extreme refinement of the genre pushed the *minne* arrangement to the brink of paradox: if the lady granted his wishes, he would be disappointed because she would have cheapened herself; if she stayed aloof, his plight would continue without end. Walther suggests, however, that a kind of *minne* that causes grief does not deserve the name (69.6). He rejects the absolute position Reinmar accords the lady. The praise on which her status is based, he insists, depends on his singing (73.4); she dies with his death (*stirbe aber ich so ist si tôt;* 73.16 in manuscript E). Thus, Walther posits the *minne* discourse as constitutive of "the lady and the tradition she represents" (Groos 404), and not vice versa. He recognized minnesong, including its affirmative courtly function, as a performative speech act that creates the object of its utterance.

For Walther, the lady is no longer the immobile, absolute embodiment of courtly decorum and thus of feudal society. Perceiving the gulf between the courtly ideal and reality, he questions the assumed identity of social and ethical standing. If the worthiness of *minne* is not merely a function of the social standing of the adored woman but depends on the realization of the canonical virtues required of her, it follows that women of lower station can be models of *minne* as much as noble ladies. Walther put this novel insight into performative practice in a few songs reminiscent of contemporary Latin lyrics. Unlike many Latin poets, Walther is less interested in masculine and, on occasion, violent carnal gratification than in a new *minne* ideal of mutuality between partners. Situated in a space free of social conventions, a song such as the famous

"Under der linden" (39.11ff; Under the Linden Tree) suggests that the *minne* values of *staetekeit* and *triuwe,* constancy and faithfulness, were independent of the lovers' social station (also 50.13).

Whereas Reinmar's beautiful mourning self-consciously leads to the limits of the conventional discourse, Walther's poetry attains self-reflexivity with regard to the fundamental code of *minne,* including its moral and social dimensions. The lady, or rather the woman, is to make the subject of *minne,* the poetic "I," worthy by instilling in him the desire to abide by the proper ethos of feudal society. In return, the singer praises the woman's worthiness. To be deserving of such praise, the woman has to show moral steadfastness and a certain aesthetic discernment, particularly by appreciating the proper type of minnesong—as opposed to the new bawdy genre by the likes of Neidhart. Ironically, in a song ascribed to Reinmar in one manuscript, Walther outlines the paradox created by his own new *minne* ethos. In a time when Neidhart and his followers were gaining popularity and when *"minneclîche minne"*—a *minne* that deserves the name—was in decline, the true poet's song inevitably had to become *unminneclîche* (48.14f). Minnesong, Walther implied, had lost its specificity. It increasingly assumed the critical and didactic traits of the *Sangspruch.* In quite a few of Walther's songs, even the lady is no longer exempt from criticism.

Walther's *Preislied* (56.14ff) illustrates how cross-fertilization of minnesong and *Spruch* became a literary strategy. The song begins with a familiar topos, an exhortation to welcome the messenger who has news to tell. But already this typical opening contains an explicit rejection of Reinmar, who lamented that he was too unhappy to be bothered by inquiries of what news he had to tell. Walther was willing to give the people what they wanted, provided he received compensation for it (*miete, lôn;* 56.19f). In the third strophe (56.30), the poetic "I" boasts of his knowledge of the wider world and thus turns the fate of the wandering poet to his advantage. Having experienced different cultures and courts, the speaker can present himself as an informed judge in whose opinion German women and men and the German language and culture fare well. This praise becomes the perfect introduction for the poet's wish, thinly veiled by the fiction of the poetic "I," that he himself may live long in this land—an obvious attempt to gain permanent employ at a court. The strophes alternate between *minne* and *Spruch* themes. The direct mention of material compensation links the opening strophe with the *Spruch* tradition, while the following strophe in praise of German women is in keeping with the *minne* tradition. However, the singer's insistence that he wants to bring these women the news (*maere;* 56.23) that they are most precious without asking for a large reward (*âne grôze miete;* 56.25), immediately recalls the insistence in the first strophe that *maere* be compensated with *miete.* The next line strengthens this echo when posing the question: "What would I want as compensation?" (*Waz wolde ich ze lône?* 56.26). And the answer that the lady will greet him with regard (*grüezen schône;* 56.29) is only seemingly humble. In the courtly semiotic system, to receive the lady's *"blôzen gruoz"* (49.12) was more than a mere greeting or acknowledgment. It signified approval of the singer's *minne* service and, by extension, amounted to his acceptance at court. The poet's desire for recognition, as much as the alliterative linkage of *maere, miete,* and *minne,* created the nexus of *minne* and *Spruch* elements.

The protracted conflict between the worldly power and the Church, between *imperium* and *sacerdotium,* played an important role in Walther's *Spruch* poetry. He sided invariably with the worldly rulers—who were his patrons—and derided the Papacy. Accusations included simony, embezzlement, and dishonesty; Walther also indicted the clergy's excesses. Thomas of Circlaria, a cleric who was employed by the same Wolfger of Erla, now patriarch of Aquileja, in whose service Walther had received five gold coins, chastised Walther in a widely disseminated didactic poem, contending—without naming Walther—that he had "enchanted a thousand men / into ignoring / the command of God and pope."

In March 1212, Walther attended the court of Emperor Otto IV in Frankfurt, possibly as a member of the entourage of Margrave Dietrich of Meissen. Soon after, he turned his back on the emperor, apparently because, as he alleges, his services were not duly rewarded. Walther switched his allegiance to Frederick, whose generosity and politics of concessions toward the territorial rulers Otto could not match. In some of his subsequent panegyrics on the Hohenstaufen claimant, Walther made clear that for him, the singer dependent on the just ruler's generosity, it was less the tone than the reward—the *lôn*—that made the music. The niggardly, unlucky, and only physically tall Otto suffered Walther's vitriolic poetic revenge.

Never one to scold in moderation, Walther heaped ridicule on his erstwhile employer and claimed to have taken stock of Otto again, this time using his honor (*êre;* 26.36) as the measure. He found him wanting, like a badly cut garment (27.1). The brilliance of this mordant polemic consists in its rhetorical double nature. It is not only a powerful reprimand of one who did not honor the unwritten contract of *guot umb êre*—praise for a price—but also a panegyric on and defense of Frederick, who had been considered unfit to be king by his opponents because of his small stature. Needless to say, the concluding line declaring Frederick to be a giant of generosity was intended as a not-so-subtle reminder to live up to the poet's liberal praise. As if to prove that the reminder had been heeded, a *Spruch* of a few years later begins with a sigh of relief: "I have my fief" (*Ich hân mîn lêhen;* 28.31). These words seem to indicate that an aging Walther was awarded a fief by Frederick, perhaps around 1220, though his elevation to the rank of vassal is in dispute. Since the proclamation occurs in a literary performance, it may be entirely fictional, or at least proleptic. Aside from Walther's sigh of relief, there is no evidence of such a fief.

Walther remained a Hohenstaufen supporter. In April 1220, he appeared at Frederick's court in Frankfurt (cf. 29.15). After this date, the stations of his life are difficult to trace with any certainty. The so-called "Elegy" (124.1ff), a review of the (fictional) narrator's life, saturated with inconsolable melancholy, mentions "unpleasant news" from Rome, presumably a reference to Frederick's excommunication in 1227. The poem ends with praise of crusading and an implicit exhortation to join Frederick on his second Crusade attempt, which began in 1228.

About 1230 Walther died. A later document, the *Würzburg Manuscript* (E), produced about the middle of the 14th century, contains some of Walther's poetry and states, not without local pride, that he was buried in a courtyard of the Würzburger Neustift—a claim contested to this day.

When medieval literature was written down and collected about half a century after Walther's death, his poetry was canonized as among the best of the age. Works by Walther have survived in about thirty different manuscripts, although only eight contain *Spruch* poetry. A few texts have double or multiple attributions, perhaps because later singers performed Walther's popular songs. All the *minne* and *Spruch* poems were sung and had melodies, but only a few have a very rudimentary notation. Merely five of Walther's melodies are considered authentic (more than for most other German medieval poets). Numerous references to Walther by contemporary and younger poets, mostly in recognition of his minnesong, document the extent of his fame. Gottfried von Strassburg recognizes his contemporary as a great poet in his epic *Tristan*. After the death of the nightingale "of Hagenau" (presumably Reinmar), Gottfried states, "the one of the Vogelweide" should become the leader of the nightingales. He lauds Walther's accomplishments as a minnesinger, particularly his ability to find the right "melody of *minne.*" Wolfram von Eschenbach mentions Walther in his *Parzival* and *Willehalm*. Ulrich von Singenberg parodies him and composes an admiring obituary. Ulrich von Lichtenstein integrates an entire strophe of the *Preislied* (56.14ff) in a climactic passage of his *Frauendienst,* without mentioning the author (FD 780.7ff), an indication that Walther's praise of German women and culture was widely known and appreciated. By 1260, Walther appeared as a literary, quasi-mythical figure in the growing and loosely linked corpus of strophes that treats of a poets' competition on the Wartburg in Thuringia. Around 1300, Hugo von Trimberg worried that Walther might be forgotten: "*Her Walther von der Vogelweide, / swer des vergaeze, der tête mir leide*" (*Der Renner,* ll. 1187f). His fears were unfounded, for Walther remains today the most famous of the medieval German nightingales.

See also 1150, 1170, 1203 (Summer), 1275, 1300, 1622

Bibliography: Arthur Groos, "'Shall I Compare Thee to a Morn in May?': Walther von der Vogelweide and His Lady," *PMLA* 91 (1976): 398–405. George F. Jones, *Walther von der Vogelweide* (New York: Twayne Publishers, 1968). Peter Rühmkorf, *Walther von der Vogelweide, Klopstock, und ich* (Reinbek bei Hamburg: Rowohlt, 1975). Walther von der Vogelweide, *Leich, Lieder, Sangsprüche,* ed. Christoph Cormeau (Berlin: de Gruyter, 1996).

Peter Gilgen

ℒ *Circa 1210*

Gottfried's romantic poem of the ill-fated lovers Tristan and Isolde remains incomplete at the time of the poet's death

Love Exalted

Almost nothing is known about Gottfried von Strassburg, a German cleric who wrote the classic version of the romance of Tristan and Isolde, a poem of some nineteen thousand lines, in Middle High German rhymed couplets. The lyricism of his language places him next to Goethe and Rilke; his tragic conception of romantic love stands almost alone in the Western literary tradition; only Stendhal comes close among modern writers.

Gottfried's version of the romance was incomplete at the time of his death, ca. 1210. His poem brings the ill-fated lovers, bound to each other for life by a magic potion, to the point of their final separation, of Tristan's wanderings and marriage to another woman, whom he weds because she has the same name as the true Isolde. The poem breaks off before their tragic death and remains a fragment, unworthily brought to completion by two mediocre poets later in the 13th century.

The generations in the period 1150 to 1220 produced a brilliant new literature that projected refined aristocratic social values and ideals onto a rough-cut class of mounted warriors, who came to be known grandly as "knights," "chevaliers," "Ritter," and the values and ideals they held as "chivalric." This literature appealed to the aristocracy, lay and clerical, of all levels, from king to soldier, from archbishop to parish priest. Both genres—courtly love lyric and courtly romance—eventually deteriorated into a trivial and highly conventional form of entertainment at its worst. But at its best, it embraced two of the great projects of medieval aristocratic culture: the civilizing of the warrior class and the quest for a form of love that exalted and conferred virtue on the lovers, that is, that gave them inner worth and social prestige.

Literature takes the temperature and measures the pulse-beat of the age that produces it. What this age wanted and what distinguished it from other Western love literature or love philosophy was love that exalted through suffering. A famous real-life experience was the love affair of Peter Abelard (d. 1142) and his student Héloïse (d. 1164). Héloïse created an aura of tragic grandeur around her love for Abelard, maintaining it beyond his castration and her entry into monastic life. Another example was Christine of Markyate, an English visionary and hermit, whose biography records a series of love relations, rising from profane to sacred. At the high point, God himself asks Christina if she would wish her spiritual love, Abbot Geoffrey of St. Albans, to die for His sake. Her answer: yes, she would gladly kill her lover herself, in the name of a higher love just as Abraham was willing to sacrifice Isaac.

This love-death, or rather love-murder, is at the level of intensity of Héloïse's sacrifice of self for her love: "I found strength at your command," she writes to her castrated lover years after their scandalous affair ended, "to destroy myself. Even more, my love rose to such heights of madness that it robbed itself of what it most desired beyond hope of recovery." And she makes clear that she still values that love more than her own salvation.

This is as high as the temperature rises: a love so intense as to compel sacrifice of self, body, soul, and salvation, sacrifice even of the lover. This kind of love has the nimbus of a divine curse: infectious, crushing, and exalting. It creates an elite of emotional life, an amatory nobility, a select few who enter a deep realm of inexorable sorrow and yet glow with the aura of the adventurer in territory too remote and too exclusive for those who live trivial lives in pursuit of happiness. The inner world opens its most profound capacities in a love so deeply rooted, so unremitting and merciless that it costs the lovers' life.

In the course of the 12th century, the literature of courtly love moved along a spectrum from cooler settings to this kind of love. Some of the points along the way:

A courtier of King Louis VII of France, Andreas Capellanus, begins a glib tract on courtly love (ca. 1176) with a buzzword and a phrase bound to catch the reader's sympathies: "Love is a certain inborn suffering/sickness [*passio*]." But the pitter-patter of his discourse, often on the level of court gossip, dilutes this passion into irony and shallow jesting. It was not what the age needed.

Lancelot, in Chrétien de Troyes's version of the romance (ca. 1185), after being stripped of his honor, wandered through a landscape fashioned to humiliate him, while secretly reserving his honor through love service. But this was love-suffering as comedy. Marie de Champagne, the romance's patroness, had found in Chrétien a genial, witty narrator for her comedy of passion and abasement, but Chrétien's touch was light, and that was not what the age wanted.

Chrétien came closer in his last romance, *Perceval or the Story of the Grail,* in which the hero is condemned to wander for years for having failed the test at the grail castle. He is sustained only by the love of his wife. The old grail king, Anfortas, had sustained an incurable wound in the genitals, because he had violated the laws of the grail community and served a woman for her love. Here we are closer to that inner sanctum, because the love-suffering is deep and incurable. But it was also a punishment for love as a crime against morality, revealing love-suffering as an exalting fate reserved for an elect few. Left unfinished by Chrétien, the story received a more complete version from a German who was both a quirkier genius and a greater prude, Wolfram von Eschenbach. This story (and others of Chrétien's romances) rescued the exalting character of love by domesticating it in marriage, and while the sublimation of love into the grail quest filled bland cravings of the age for a spiritual worldly love, Chrétien and Wolfram set it at the lukewarm temperature of the later love of Dante for Beatrice and of Petrarch for Laura.

The temperature rises further in Gottfried's *Tristan* and the pulse beats harder in this triangle love relationship. Tristan is the nephew of Mark, the king of Cornwall, Isolde is the king's wife. The poet introduces his work as a love tragedy, whose lovers suffer so that we can benefit from their story: "If the two of whom this love-story tells had not endured sorrow for the sake of joy, love's pain for its ecstasy within one heart, their name and history would never have brought such rapture to so many noble spirits!"

Not only does this romance of state-shaking adulterous love bring rapture; it also endows the "noble spirits" with prestige and virtue: "Love is so blissful a thing, so blessed an endeavor, that apart from its teaching, none attains worth or reputation. In view of the many noble lives that love inspires and the many virtues that come from it, oh! that every living thing does not strive for sweet love" (187–194; trans. Hatto, p. 43). Tristan is the nephew of King Mark of Cornwall, and Isolde is his wife. How is it possible to reconcile the morality of marriage and civility with passion? Don't ask! It is a secret reserved for the few noble hearts who understand the principle of mystical election on which its love philosophy is based. The hero and heroine die of their love, but tragedy is not enough. Gottfried invests the love with a morbid imagery of poison, entrapment, and death. One of his most powerful metaphors of destructive love is the fatal wound. Tristan is conceived on the death-bed of his father, who was mortally wounded in combat. His beloved Blancheflur comes to him disguised as a physician, "doctors" him with the act of love, and he is miraculously cured. Tristan first finds his way to Isolde because of a poisoned wound to which only Isolde—the mother of the Princess Isolde—has the antidote. Sickness becomes a metaphor for desire; healing for its gratification. The magic potion is the king among poisons. When Tristan and Isolde drink it by predestined chance, their lady-in-waiting, Brangaene, tells them that they have drunk their death, to which Tristan responds, "Whether it be life or death, it has poisoned me most sweetly! I have no idea what the other will be like, but this death suits me well! If my adorable Isolde were to go on being the death of me in this fashion, I would woo death everlasting!" (12494–12502; trans. Hatto, p. 206). They fall in love like birds settling into the hunter's glue-trap; the more they struggle against it, the more tightly they become ensnared. Tristan is wounded and suffers pain and disorientation, as does Isolde: "She found this life unbearable" (11791). She struggled against the snare, "twisted and turned with hands and feet, and immersed them ever deeper in the blind sweetness of Love and of the man" (11803–11809; trans. Hatto, p. 196). They drank eternal love and their death at the same time, the narrative states repeatedly, serving up this brew vicariously and eucharistically to the noble hearts of the audience:

> For wherever still today one hears the recital of their . . . hearts' joy, their hearts' sorrow—*this is bread to all noble hearts. With this, their death lives on. We read their life, we read their death, and to us it is sweet as bread.*
>
> Their life, their death are our bread. Thus lives their life, thus lives their death. Thus they live still and yet are dead, and their death is the bread of the living.
>
> (230–240; trans. Hatto, p. 44; emphasis added by Hatto)

With these lines of the prologue, the nature of this love recedes into regions where—like the mysteries of faith—it is not accessible to reason: death gives life, sorrow brings joy; we live through their death and their love.

But such a love, beyond all reason, a love that overwhelms, tortures, devastates, and destroys, indifferent to law and social convention, and yet somehow redemptive and sacramental, satisfied the age's appetite for extremes of devotion and for suffering turned positive. Such passion transferred comfortably into religious life. As the example of Christina of Markyate illustrates, this transferal registers most clearly in women's religious experience. One can hear echoes (though not intentional—it is the shared language of noble love-suffering) of Gottfried's language in that of the mid-13th-century French mystic Marie D'Oignes, who expressed her love of Christ in constant weeping. Asked whether it was painful to cry so much, she answered, "These tears are my refreshment. Night and day they are my bread . . . They do not torment me with pain, but rather they rejoice my soul with a kind of serenity. They . . . fill the soul to satiety and soften it with a sweet anointing."

Gottfried borrowed abundantly from religious practices to deepen and sanctify the love of his characters. A remarkable episode Gottfried invents is the "cave of lovers." The lovers are banished from the court and live in a pastoral paradise, miraculously reserved for noble lovers. In an arcadian grove is a temple-like building with a crystalline bed in its center. The poet gives an allegorical reading of the architecture of this building drawn from a Christian ritual, the consecration of the church building. He calls his lovers *martaeraere*, "martyrs" or "sufferers," and their sylvan residence *klûse*, a term that denotes a hermit's cave. Their food in the cave of lovers, he explains, is not material, but the force that beams from their eyes, a spiritual substance more nourishing than physical food. The idea is borrowed from miracles of desert saints. The merging of religious elements with adulterous passion has long raised questions about the mind and motives of the poet. His inclination toward surrounding an adulterous love with sacred forms remains perplexing and unexplained.

The love affair takes up only the second half of the poem. The first ten thousand or so lines deal with Gottfried's other main concern: the character of his hero, his education, his talents. Here again we see Gottfried bending and breaking the conventions of the courtly romance. Tristan is not a chivalric knight, as are the heroes of Arthurian romance and the romances of antiquity. He is a polished courtier, musician, master huntsman, not only highly educated, but skilled in the courtier's art of self-fashioning. His debut at the court of King Mark of Cornwall is a showpiece of courtier self-presentation.

The sources of Gottfried's humanism take us into the origins of courtly romance. Since the late 10th and early 11th century, the cathedral schools of Germany and France had offered an education based on "literature and refined manners," *Litterae et mores,* a formula as central to education as our Letters and Science. The literature was largely classical with emphasis on Virgil, Horace, Cicero, and Martianus Capella; the manners were a Christian courtly adaptation of Roman social ideals known as *honestas, urbanitas,* and *facetia.* The code came to be known, since the late 11th century, as *curialitas,* or "courtliness," since it originated at the ruler's court. By the first half of the 12th century, the ancient humanistic curriculum was falling into disfavor. The old masters were replaced by teachers of logic. An uprooted generation of humanistically trained clerics sought new careers at worldly courts as tutors, chaplains, chroniclers.

The move from schools to courts created, or at least contributed to, the circumstances for one of the great cultural innovations of the 12th century: the rise of courtly literature. The first courtly romances were mainly adaptations of Greek and Roman epics, the so-called Romances of Antiquity—not surprisingly, since their clerical authors were schooled in ancient literature. The anonymous Old French *Roman d'Eneas* and *Roman de Thèbes,* and the *Roman de Troyes* by Benoît de St. Maure, are the earliest. They emerged in mid-century, but were followed in short order by the narrative form that became by far the most popular, the Arthurian romance, created by a French cleric named Chrétien de Troyes.

These early romances are charming, gentle love comedies. A knight performs "love service" to win the lady he loves, which, after trials and tribulations, he invariably does. The trials often involve the restoration of the knight's honor, lost through some neglect of his lady and of his courtly-Christian-chivalric moral obligations. The love that impels him turns him into a courtly gentleman, restores him to the good graces of his lady, whose love and castles he then commands, and places him within the greater social and celestial order.

Love has the force of educating knights to courtliness. In the romance, this code of manners forms an amalgam with traditional warrior values, the latter starkly subordinated to civilized and courteous behavior. The amalgam creates one of the longest enduring of Western social codes: chivalry, courtesy, *courtoisie, Höflichkeit.*

Gottfried shared the educational background of Benoît and Chretien. His "classicism" is in evidence in many passages. He concludes the poetic fireworks he shoots off to celebrate the knighting of his hero with a survey of contemporary German poets. He assigns a classical or pagan source of inspiration to each of them, and ends the passage with the longest, most elaborate invocation to Apollo and the muses (whose inspiration he reserves for himself) in medieval literature. Here Gottfried shows himself the finest stylist of Middle High German; in fact he raises this language to the highest level of elegance, refinement, and allusiveness it was to attain. He also shows himself an arbiter of taste and style. He passes judgment on his contemporaries, usually laudatory, in some cases subtly critical, and in one case bluntly attacks a poet who is undoubtedly Wolfram von Eschenbach, the author of *Parzival.* Gottfried leaves no doubt that his word as critic was respected and probably feared. In sum,

Gottfried von Strassburg brought humanistic learning and high style to the courtly romance, breaking radically with that often trivially optimistic form by introducing a dark and tragic vision of courtly love.

See also 1203 (Summer), 1876

Bibliography: Mark Chinca, *Landmarks of World Literature: Gottfried von Strassburg, Tristan* (Cambridge, U.K.: Cambridge University Press, 1997). C. Stephen Jaeger, *Medieval Humanism in Gottfried von Strassburg's 'Tristan und Isolde'* (Heidelberg: Carl Winter, 1977). *The Letters of Abelard and Héloïse,* trans. Betty Radice (Harmondsworth, U.K.: Penguin, 1974). Gottfried von Strassburg, *Tristan: Translated Entire for the First Time, with the Surviving Fragments of the 'Tristan' of Thomas,* trans. A. T. Hatto (Harmondsworth, U.K.: Penguin, 1974). Original text cited by line numbers from *Gottfried von Strassburg, Tristan,* trans. Rüdiger Krohn, 3 vols. (Stuttgart: Reclam, 1993).

C. Stephen Jaeger

✑ Circa 1230

A wandering poet known only as "der Stricker" composes the comic romance *Schwänke des Pfaffen Amis*

The Dual Economy of Medieval Life

The works of the author who called himself "der Stricker" ("the weaver") are generally assigned to the reign of Emperor Frederick II (1212–1250). He wrote in a German of southern Franconian coloring, and his main area of activity is thought to have been the duchy of Austria. He cannot be connected to a more precise location because his potential patrons and audiences cover a wide social and geographic spectrum—from the court of the Duke of Austria in Vienna and the landed aristocracy to urban patricians and the clergy. Der Stricker was most likely a wandering poet. His pseudonym is best understood as a metaphor: the Middle High German verb *stricken* means to weave, knit, or tie together, and *der Stricker* would thus be a "weaver" of tales, a maker of texts (the Latin word *textum* = a woven cloth or fabric). Although most of what is known about this weaver's identity comes from his own writings, he has a clear profile. Der Stricker was one the great innovators in medieval German literature. The verb *erniuwen,* "to renew/reform/innovate," sums up his literary achievement in a dual sense: renewal of past literary traditions and creation of new genres in vernacular literature. To the latter he added several forms: the *maere* or minor epic in prose; the *bîspel,* a type of short tale illustrating a moral; and the *Schwankroman* or comic romance. In addition, he produced two works in the prevailing large forms of courtly literature, *Charlemagne,* a *chanson de geste,* and *Daniel from the Blossoming Valley,* an Arthurian romance. All in all, he displays a range previously unknown in German literature.

The work *Schwänke des Pfaffen Amis (Jests of Priest Amis),* thought to date from about 1230, is a "romance" consisting of 2,300 lines in rhyming couplets that link a series of comic episodes to a single protagonist in what is essentially a biographical narrative. It is the first tale of its kind, although structural antecedents can be found in epic tales of animals, such as *Reinhart Fuchs.* The originality of *Priest Amis* accounts for its notable success; the work enjoyed widespread distribution well into the early era of printing. Subsequent writers, both of verse chronicles and courtly romances, therefore, could assume that references to the central character would be understood. The comic romance became a separate epic form and achieved its greatest refinement in the 16th century with the prose work *Ulenspiegel,* which explicitly mentions the Weaver, and later the *Lalebuch,* containing tales about the town of Schilda and its famously foolish citizens. *Priest Amis's* literary success cannot be attributed to a smooth, seemingly harmless, texture; rather it can be traced to the shifting refractions in a disconcerting tale of a disconcerting hero.

The story begins with Amis's bishop threatening to remove him from his parish in the English town of Tranis, because he suspects the priest of trying to turn the social hierarchy of the clergy upside down. Indeed, by the end of the tale, the priest attains a rank equal to the bishop's when the monks of a Cistercian monastery choose him as their abbot, assuring him of eternal bliss. Priest Amis achieves his goal by leaving his parish after the quarrel with his bishop and traveling through England, France, and Lorraine. After his return, he twice leaves Tranis again on journeys to Constantinople before finally coming home for good—first to his parish and then, by way of the Cistercian monastery, to God. The plot is based on the simple narrative pattern of exile and return. In this case, the repeated journeys of the protagonist suggest that the courtly romances about King Arthur and his court, the most important model in high courtly narrative literature for endowing experience with meaning, served as a point of reference. The Weaver used the symbolic structure of the courtly Arthurian romance, first developed by Chrétien de Troyes and Hartmann von Aue, in his own Arthurian romance, *Daniel from the Blossoming Valley.* In *Priest Amis,* however, the axiological coding of the pattern is fundamentally altered: Amis does not shine as a courtly knight, but as a swindler and thief. The story revolves entirely around lies and deception, and it goes without saying that the protagonist's goal is to increase not his virtue or honor, but his store of worldly goods. His victims are monarch and aristocrat, peasant and knight, man and woman, layman and cleric in equal measure.

As a result, *Priest Amis* has often been read as a parody of the courtly Arthurian romance and a critique of its idealistic ethics. It is not the courtly knight who leaves King Arthur's court here, but a sly, dishonest priest, who leaves his parish not in search of aristocratic *ere* (honor) but of material *gut* (goods). Furthermore, his actions are not honorable duels governed by rules and fought with knightly physical prowess, but by duping everyone intellectually inferior to him. Undefeated opponents he sends to the king; the riches he manages to acquire go to his parish. As a parody of courtly and knightly tales, the Weaver's comic romance is evidence of a deeply pessimistic or new realistic view of the world. This world of the first half of the 13th century, a world of social upheaval, economic changes, and political crises, would have offered many opportunities for satirical treatment of the traditional epic models' idealized image of the feudal aristocracy. But the world very often invites critical glances, and so to regard *Priest Amis* as simply a moralizing tale or parody of an established literary genre would trivialize it. The work is noteworthy not only for the contrasting references to earlier narrative forms and the ethical concepts of courtly romance, but also for the disconcerting tensions within the text itself. The central character is a priest who devises fraudulent schemes and has an insatiable appetite for worldly goods; a man who should represent truth and honesty serves as the source of all deceit. Such extremes of dissonance exist virtually nowhere else in German narrative literature of the time.

The protagonist's confrontation with the world effects no changes in him. Amis gains riches, but no new insights. From the start, he possesses all the knowledge and skills he needs to function as the hero of the tale, namely, the ability to see through others while preventing them from recognizing his own intentions. His game is one of deception, which from the outset depends not only on complete mastery of the rules in the world, but also on opportunities to exploit them. Amis succeeds in making them serve his own long-term material interests. However, the framework within which the hero acts is the prevailing order based on rules of a premodern culture that does not distinguish between faith and knowledge. Such a culture frequently has recourse to the category of miracles, and always reckons with the possibility that salvation can enter the world; it is also a culture in which economic forms of exchange have a complex overlay of noneconomic social ties. How this appears in the Weaver's text, and how Amis manipulates the rules and structures of his world, constantly deceiving others for the sake of material gain, can be illustrated here on the basis of a single episode.

The Weaver begins by relating a trick that Amis often employs on his travels: The priest sets out from Tranis as an itinerant preacher, carrying with him a holy relic, part of the skull of Saint Brendan. He goes from one village fair to another and asks *gebouren* and *vrouwen* (357; peasants and noble ladies) for donations to build a cathedral to the saint. Amis tells the ladies that naturally Brendan will accept donations only from women who have not committed the sin of adultery. He encodes the message in such a way that the women have little choice but to pay up: "Every woman who held back would have immediately set tongues wagging. People would have accused her of having secret lovers" (401ff). The encoding reckons with a logic according to which the qualification of the donor is substantially present in the act of giving and in the quality of the donation. And the calculation pays off. Crowds of women come forward, especially those who have committed adultery, of course, to make "the largest donation ever offered to a priest" as proof of their virtue (422ff). They even go so far as to borrow the money. Hence the episode shows a social order based on universal deception only the swindler Amis is able to perceive. He thus gains not only in material goods but also in personal prestige and reputation as a "holy preacher" through his pseudo-exculpation of society (480).

Amis's calculations always work out; luck never goes against him. The hero's exploits virtually replace a metaphysical Providence, for it is he alone who works miracles, assures salvation, and turns the wheel of fortune (1829). Yet, unlike the characters in some later comic tales, the Weaver's hero does not represent an anarchic or destructive force, disruptive of the existing order to no purpose. His rational calculations and cunning have a clear, transparent goal: the increase of his wealth. Thus Amis's deceptions do not act as a catalyst to expose the irrationality or corruption of the social order, as has been suggested. Even where such order might be dubious, as in the episode of Saint Brendan's relic, Amis does not disturb the social order; rather he stabilizes it through the effect of his scam. The priest's victims operate, it has been suggested, within a logical framework that recognizes only what exists in a given situation, whatever is immediately present and evident in a moment, be it the presence of salvation or an opportunity for financial gain. Amis, by contrast, makes his calculations in terms of situations and situational contexts. His cunning consists in distancing himself from whatever exists in a given situation. The protagonist is a unique figure in his environment, and also a lonely one. In this respect, too, he differs from the courtly knight, who may restore order to the world single-handedly, but always as a representative of court society. Amis does not work on behalf of either a collective or a court, but only for himself. He represents nothing more than what he himself is. But who is he, and why?

To answer this question, it is important to note that, according to the frame story, Priest Amis's primary motivation is not greed but its opposite, charity, his desire to distribute his wealth among others without limits, conditions, or distinctions. The comic episodes do not show unmitigated evil at work. The priest's scams have an ulterior motive, the continuation of his generosity. This generosity constitutes endless festivities, and it is the threat to these festivities that inspires the priest's forays. His journeys always remain connected with the permanent festivities, and Amis sends the spoils of his schemes home as soon as he acquires them. This implies that the party goes on uninterrupted back in Tranis, or rather vice versa: the epic foreground of the comic episodes also represents the backstage activity in support of the play of consumption and status being enacted in Tranis. Thus one could say that the romance reveals the "secrets" behind courtly displays of status, and the expense and skills required to maintain them.

As a ritual that makes no distinctions and has no fixed limits, generosity of any kind, including that of Priest Amis, must ignore the fact that medieval society, on the whole, is governed by the law of scarcity and short supply of goods. Amis's capacity for denial is negated when the number of his guests exceeds his ability to offer them food and gifts, and he must set out again to increase his wealth. On these journeys, he follows a different logic from that of charity. Because he must be greedy and acquisitive in order to give lavishly, he constantly makes claims on the property of others. Hence Amis's acquisition of goods on his travels through the world—in contrast to his generosity in Tranis—is economic in the strict sense; in fact it is based directly on the economization and monetarization of the transcendental. As the figure-ground pattern of this comic romance shows, riches have a very different status seen from the front and rear of conspicuous display and consumption. The Weaver's romance makes abundantly clear that the boundless wealth of feudal generosity and the permanence of the festivities are themselves a deception. The form of housekeeping practiced in Tranis rests on principles that must be kept invisible, namely strict calculations regarding time and money, long-term planning, mastery of the logics of immediacy and current circumstances, in addition to cunning use of situations and knowledge to deceive everyone else. Thus the text uncovers the scarcity of those resources on which all generosity depends; it shows the limits of wealth that idealistic literary depictions of feudal community, such as courtly romances and adventures, remove from the picture. The notion that generosity, the quintessence of successful courtly society, has nothing to do with economic exchange proves to be an illusion.

See also 1184, 1189, 1500 (Eulenspiegel)

Bibliography: K. Kamihara, ed., *Des Strickers "Pfaffe Amis"* (Göppingen: Kümmerle, 1978, 1990). Der Stricker, *Der Pfaffe Amis,* ed. and trans. into modern German by Michael Schilling (Stuttgart: Reclam, 1994). Sabine Böhm, *Der Stricker: Ein Dichterprofil anhand seines Gesamtwerkes* (Frankfurt am Main: Lang, 1995). Rupert Kalkofen, *Der Priesterbetrug als Weltklugheit: Eine philologisch-hermeneutische Interpretation des "Pfaffen Amis"* (Würzburg: Königshausen & Neumann, 1989). Hedda Ragotzky, *Gattungsneuerung und Laienunterweisung in Texten des Strickers* (Tübingen: Niemeyer, 1981). Stephen L. Wailes, "The Ambivalence of der Stricker's *Der Pfaffe Amis,"* *Monatshefte* 90 (1998): 148–160.

Peter Strohschneider
Translated by Deborah Lucas Schneider

♌ 1250

The death of Emperor Friedrich II initiates the last phase of Hohenstaufen rule

World History as Legitimation

Rudolf von Ems wrote his *Weltchronik (World Chronicle)* at the end of a turbulent epoch when many contemporaries felt human salvation was hanging in the balance. Horrible accusations were leveled against rulers whom Divine Providence had endowed with earthly power: "From the depths of the sea rises the monster spewing blasphemous names, . . . raging with the claws of the lion and the lion's maw. It opens its mouth to blaspheme the divine name and hurls the same shafts at God's habitation and the saints who dwell in heaven . . . Look upon the head, heart, and end of this beast: Friedrich, the so-called emperor!"

Friedrich II, apostrophized thus by Gregory IX, countered with assertions that the demonic visage of Antichrist belonged instead to the pope, that false Vicar of Christ occupying the chair of Saint Peter. It is he himself, the emperor claimed, who should be regarded as the reawakened lion from the tribe of Judah, since he now ruled the Holy Land again as the crowned king of Jerusalem. His subjects should honor him as a new David.

In the climactic battle between the Papacy and the Hohenstaufen emperors, the Bible was the weapon of choice. But this arrow could hit its target only if the bow of salvation history could be strung for the purpose. Understood as a revelation of God's plan for the salvation of the world, the Bible refers to both the past and the future, thus offering platforms that could be used either to justify a given political position on the basis of history or to attack the same position with reference to the visions of the Apocalypse. The Hohenstaufen dynasty emerged as the losing side from this battle. Friedrich II's act of having his nine-year-old son, Konrad, elected German—or as the actual title ran, Ro-man—king in Vienna in 1237, so that he could later become emperor, proved ineffective in the long run. Friedrich's will, written shortly before his death in 1250, also failed to achieve its goal. By 1248 Konrad was excommunicated and military offensives broke his hold on the Hohenstaufen's home territory of Swabia soon thereafter. After losing most of his power base in Germany, Konrad set out for southern Italy in 1251 to claim his kingdom of Sicily, but he died there in 1254. Hohenstaufen rule over the Holy Roman Empire thus came to a permanent end. Furthermore, Konrad IV never set foot in his king-dom of Jerusalem, for it had fallen back into the hands of the Muslims in 1244.

In the final phase of his rule, Konrad did not hesitate to seize on a favorable interpretation of salvation history and brandish it as a weapon. Shortly before his father's death, he commissioned the writer Rudolf von Ems to compose a chronicle in which the histories of creation, the biblical kingdoms, the Ro-man Empire, and Christianity were rendered in *tütsche getihte* (German verses; 21.687). To control the course of history by asserting its immutable laws, to promote the imperial office and merits—so emphatically refuted by some contemporaries—to a foremost place among world rulers, and thereby to cre-ate an overarching framework for advancing Konrad's claims to power and sta-tus beyond their apparent limitations, such was the potential hidden goal of the subject matter. A deft treatment could reveal to the world that the claims of the Hohenstaufens were the *rehte warheit* (genuine truth; 21.673).

With this tactic, Konrad followed a tradition of encouraging the writing of history about the Hohenstaufen court that had already produced works by such important authors as Otto von Freising and Godfried von Viterbo. What he required was an experienced writer, familiar with the Latin tradition of his-toriography, who was also a loyal subject. He found such a man in Rudolf von Ems, a member of a family of *ministeriales* (unfree knights) in the Vorarlberg re-gion who was educated in Latin and the liberal arts to a degree unusual for a layman. Early in his life, Rudolf had received a commission from Rudolf von Steinach, an unfree knight of the bishop of Constance, to write his first work, *Der gute Gerhard (Good Gerhard)*. Then Abbot Guido, head of the Cistercian monastery near Kappel (Switzerland) from 1223 to 1232, provided him with the Latin source for a second work of poetry, *Barlaam und Josaphat*. It appears that Rudolf also began a work about Alexander the Great in this period, but broke it off when, leaving the provincial backwaters behind, he made his way to the court of the Hohenstaufens and the world of dynastic politics sometime before 1231. There he met a circle of writers and patrons who won him over to a new agenda. Konrad von Winterstetten (d. 1243), procurator of the Duchy of Swabia and tutor of Friedrich II's sons Heinrich and Konrad, commissioned him to write a poem on the subject of *Willehalm von Orlens,* using a French source contributed by Johannes von Ravensburg. With this work, as well as the later *Alexander* and *World Chronicle,* Rudolf's literary ambition became completely absorbed by the project of princely instruction, not only for the edification of rulers such as Konrad, but also for bolstering the latter's political pretensions. When Konrad IV set out for southern Italy in 1251, Rudolf most likely remained in Germany.

The *World Chronicle*—a title conferred on it by literary historians—begins with the creation of the world and breaks off with the reign of King Solomon, although it was originally conceived to continue up to the author's own time, and indeed to the end of the world. The material thus appears to have been prescribed down to the last detail, since the Bible, which naturally served as the main source, was the "word of God," and, therefore, "said the truth" (*dú warheit seit;* 3.812). Poetic license was prohibited in this case. However, methods of exegesis, particularly those developed in the 12th century, allowed for various gradations of this truth. On the one hand, Rudolf aimed to reproduce the factual course of events accurately, to retell the stories related in Scripture in their literal and historical sense. On the other hand, he placed equal importance on extracting the spiritual meaning of what occurred, thereby leading the reader to the *rehtui warheit* (genuine truth; 3.791 and passim), the actual message behind the narrative. Rudolf intended to do more than just repeat an already familiar story. His aim was to clarify the inherent ordering principle of salvation history, which remained valid for all ages. Uncovering the truth in this way would clearly reveal the divine plan for Hohenstaufen rule.

The *World Chronicle* evinces two perspectives on time: diachronicity and synchronicity. Rudolf followed the Augustinian concept of a correspondence between the successive days of creation and the stages of salvation history; by the 13th century this had become the most common paradigm for historical analysis. He divided the course of history into six ages or worlds: from Adam to Noah, from Noah to Abraham, from Abraham to Moses, from Moses to David, from David to Christ, and from Christ to the Last Judgment. The only point on which he diverged from the traditional order was in marking a break after Moses, whereas ordinarily, in Christian exegesis, a single age was thought to extend from Abraham to David. Rudolf called each of his six epochs a *welt,* a world that reflected a qualitatively new mode of divine action toward mankind, and for added clarity he connected each with a central figure who represented a decisive *wandelunge* (transformation): Noah and his covenant with God, Abraham and his strengthening of the covenant, Moses and God's giving of the law, and David and the establishment of a Jewish kingdom.

The diachronic strand thus followed exactly the course of history as presented in the Bible. However, Rudolf also inserted into the presentation of each epoch long passages that conveyed the synchronous events taking place outside the confines of actual biblical history in the heathen empires. Thus, his account of the Babylonian confusion of tongues is followed by a detailed description of the regions assigned to the three sons of Noah; in the second world, he deals with the history of Assyria, Egypt, the empire of Nimrod, and the city of Trier; in the third world, Argivia and Greece are added to the aforementioned realms; in the fourth, this spectrum is expanded by the addition of Troy; and finally in the fifth world, Rudolf describes the Italy of Aeneas, Rome, and the origins of the Franks and Britons. His model and main source for these sections was the *Historia scholastica* of Petrus Comestor, which was written in the 12th century and was the most widely disseminated handbook of biblical history. But Rudolf not only supplemented this model, drawing on the *Etymologiae* of Isidore of Seville, the chronological tables of Eusebius in Saint Jerome's translation, and the *Pantheon* of Gotfried von Viterbo, he also tied together these authors' scattered observations in connected narratives that reached beyond the particular world under discussion and made visible genealogical continuities and successions of rule.

The combination of these approaches produced a highly complex, yet coherent structure due to the author's numerous cross-references, interspersed summaries, and clear, concise style. Rudolf repeatedly asserts his adherence to the prevailing standard of medieval historiography, which forbade poetic flights of fancy at the expense of factual truth and never permitted insertions of passages from exegetical commentary that would inhibit the narrative flow. Nevertheless, enough freedom remained for the author to demonstrate his literary skill, which followed compositional principles developed in the courtly romance. Rudolf organized his narrative into concrete episodes, centered on a principal figure, thus guiding the reader from one set of action to the next. In addition, concepts borrowed from the familiar courtly vocabulary enabled readers to recognize the coordinates of their own identity, despite the *undersheit der zît* ("difference in time") referred to again and again.

Even the fundamental division between the *rehtin ban* (true path) of biblical history and the *biwege* (by-ways) of synchronous events permitted drawing on an orientational framework familiar since Augustine and reshaped for historiographical purposes by Otto von Freising only a century before. This was the doctrine of "two citizenships"—in the *civitas Dei* (city of God) and in the *civitas terrena* (terrestrial city)—which Augustine understood as unbridgeable opposites. According to Otto of Freising, however, the two had already achieved some compatibility through the historical emergence of a *civitas permixta* (mixed city) since the time of Constantine. Rudolf incorporated this distinction into his conceptual framework, without, however, belittling "earthly citizenship."

The arrangement of the work follows those ordering elements of salvation history considered as revealed, thereby demonstrating not only that the account is factually accurate, but—even more importantly—that it transmits the *rehte warheit*. On the one hand, this created the textual basis for deriving *lêre* (edification) from history, that is to say, for extracting what is exemplary from the past. Thus the chronicle is set to achieve the aim of princely instruction as formulated in Gotfried von Viterbo's admonition to Konrad's grandfather Heinrich VI: "For it is impossible for kings and princes to reach the pinnacle of perfect rule and excellence of royal power if they are of the opinion that they do not need to either know the origin and course of the world or the dogmas of the Scriptures." On the other hand, the *rehte warheit* could be applied to the course of history in such a way that the laws of its order could be exhibited. Here was a case not of exemplification but of prefiguration, in which one historical event refers to another. At issue, after all, was the urgent contemporary problem of Hohenstaufen legitimacy, which was to be solved by showing that prior history had long ago set forth its solution.

To make this clear, Rudolf used a technique that deviated markedly from his usual style and, therefore, must have seemed conspicuous. At the start of the fifth world, which deals with David, whose *wandelunge* (transformation) consisted in the fact that "God gave his people kings," he takes up the problem of kingship as an aspect of the central path of history, not merely as one of its by-ways. At this point the poet inserts a panegyric, markedly atypical of his style, that is addressed not to David, as one might expect, but to Konrad IV himself. For the country to which he refers is Jerusalem, where Konrad *ist herre und kúnig genant* ("is called lord and king"; 21.585). The praise of the Hohenstaufen monarch continues—Sicily and Arles are under his rule, he is the "child of the Roman Emperor" (21.625)—and finally the genealogy of the Hohenstaufens and the list of their conquests are unfurled.

If the stringent order Rudolf observed in writing his history were not so apparent, one could take this passage as a formal flaw, for its theme actually belongs to the sixth world and should have been treated there at length. However, precisely at the point of the historical founding of David's kingdom it had to be made forcefully clear that the Roman king, Konrad IV, also the king of Jerusalem, was the direct descendant of David—the "new David." This title had also been applied to Frederick II in his lifetime, when the claim had been advanced that his ancestry from the house of David was equivalent to Christ's. But never before had such an assertion been supported through a demonstration encompassing the entire span of salvation history. By virtue of the particular way in which Rudolf marshaled his material, his historical chronicle provided the most credible justification of Konrad's position as the reigning Hohenstaufen. In his person he combined the two strands—carefully developed separately up to this point—of the central path and the by-ways. Thus, both the sacred and secular kingdoms are united in Konrad, the dynastic heir to Roman rule and simultaneously successor to David's royal title, proof positive that the Hohenstaufen monarch was the culmination and common destination of the two strands of history bearing on the *civitas Dei* and the *civitas terrena*. And from this it followed that Konrad held a rank above all other rulers, as indeed the Hohenstaufen faction claimed.

As a master shaper of the material of history, Rudolf succeeded in plucking the descendants of the monster from their apocalyptic damnation by presenting the course of salvation history so elegantly that their rule appears to be, not an arbitrary choice, but the *rehte warheit* as revealed by God Himself. Rudolf's own fate, however, was determined by the factual course of history, which had already rolled on ineluctably, far beyond the point where a conceptual revision of the past, no matter how bold, could effect it. In this respect, Rudolf played only an epigonal role, like his patron. Thanks to its lucid structure, however, his *World Chronicle* became a model for later German historians and one of the most widely read history books written in late medieval Germany, although often in the mutilated form of prose adaptions by authors who no longer understood the political background of the paean to Konrad IV.

See also 847, 1260

Bibliography: Rudolf von Ems, *Weltchronik,* ed. Gustav Ehrismann (Berlin, 1915).

Gert Melville
Translated by Deborah Lucas Schneider

🦎 *Circa 1260*
An Easter play is performed for the first time in German

Spiritual Drama in an Urban Setting

The Easter Play of Muri is the oldest documented Easter play in the German language. The surviving manuscript from the third quarter of the 13th century is thought to be roughly contemporaneous with the play's composition and original performance. Although such an old work may appear to have emerged out of nowhere, its language and unique form are surprisingly accomplished. The same is true for the thematic treatment of the material, which, before the play's discovery, was known only from the tradition of works in Latin.

In view of the work's notable literary merit, the fragmentary condition in which *The Easter Play of Muri* has survived is lamentable. Toward the end of the 15th century, when the script was apparently of no more use, the parchment was cut up by a bookbinder who glued it in four sizable pieces (about 15½ by 3¼ inches) to the wooden covers of a two-volume Latin Bible (Strasbourg, 1466); the text written on them was not discovered until 1840. The binder used four more small pieces (about 2½–3¼ by 5½–6½ inches) in the making of the books' spines; these were found in 1942. In 1527, the two volumes belonged to one Jakob Geilinger, who had been a citizen of Zurich since 1519 and served as chaplain at the great cathedral there from 1501 to 1546. Only later did the Bible become part of the library collection at the monastery of Muri in the Swiss canton of Aargau.

While the first fragments of the manuscript were named after the monastery where they were found, Muri was not its place of origin, as far as scholars can judge. Since features of the dialect in which it is written point to the present-day cantons of Aargau and Zurich and the volumes were presumably bound in Zurich, that city may have been the site where the Easter play was conceived and written. Paleographic evidence also points in this direction. Furthermore, the high literary quality of the play supports this assumption. This means that an appropriate interpretation of the play must take its urban setting into account.

Although only fragments have survived, Friedrich Ranke's argument that the original manuscript of *The Easter Play of Muri* must have been a parchment scroll more than six feet long seems quite plausible. It would thus have been comparable in size to the "Frankfurt Director's Scroll," which dates from the first half of the 14th century and has been preserved in its full length of almost 15 feet. Wooden rods were attached at both ends of the scroll, so that it could be unrolled and rewound as the play progressed. It enabled the director to give the actors and singers their cues and to oversee the production wherever it was performed. Hence the "Frankfurt Director's Scroll" contains not a full text, but only stage directions and the first lines of the actors' speeches and the hymns. In this respect the (presumed) original appearance of *The Easter Play of Muri* differs fundamentally inasmuch as it contained almost no stage directions and all Latin hymns are missing, except for references to the start of two Latin antiphons—the *Advenisti desiderabilis* from the scene of the descent into Hell, and the *Quis revolvet* from Mary's visit to the tomb. This circumstance, in combination with major errors of interpretation, has led to the mistaken view that the text represents the first medieval religious play to be written entirely in German. It is true that the surviving fragments of the scroll contain only spoken German text, in addition to indicating the speakers of the lines. In contrast to the Director's Scroll, these parchments contain the text written out, not just the first lines of each speech.

Nevertheless, the assumption that it was a play entirely in German is incorrect. Corresponding Latin hymns exist for a whole series of the German speeches and the single brief stage direction—*Post tonitrum* ("After a clap of thunder," to represent the Resurrection of Christ)—suggests the existence of a full set of stage directions in Latin. These directions probably indicated, as in other plays, at least one Latin hymn. Evidently the Latin hymns were not written out because they were familiar to the performers—clerics and members of the choir school—from church services. It was necessary to write down only what was unfamiliar and new, that is, the German-language text of the various spoken roles. Friedrich Ranke, therefore, speculated that what we have is a prompter's scroll, either for rehearsals or performances, in case actors forgot their lines. For this purpose the space on the scroll was used efficiently: The verse text is written in two columns, with the text on the reverse side running in the opposite direction from the front, so that when the end of the text on the front was reached, the scroll only had to be turned over for the reading to continue. Nevertheless the process of rolling and unrolling the scrolls must have been quite cumbersome, so they were later replaced by scripts in book form. Whether a director's scroll existed in addition to the text scroll of *The Easter Play of Muri* with stage directions and indications for Latin hymns, which were necessary to put on a performance, remains unclear. It is hard to imagine that the director would have worked from memory alone.

When only fragments of a work survive, questions inevitably arise about the length of the complete version and the relationship of the surviving pieces; any uncertainty about these matters will directly affect the interpretation of a text. Against all expectation, reconstruction of this scroll produced a positive result. Although text was lost in many places as the bookbinder cut up the scroll, the fact that he used the pieces of parchment in the binding of a two-volume set means that a continuous sequence of scenes was preserved in the eight fragments. Only the beginning and end of the play are missing. Scholars assume that the existing 612 verses represent slightly more than half of the original text.

The surviving sequence of scenes runs as follows: (1) setting up a watch at Jesus' sepulcher: in the presence of the Jews, Pilate negotiates with twelve knights for a guard to be posted at the sepulcher; Pilate sends both the guards and the Jews to the tomb, where the Jews give instructions to the watch. (2) Pilate's court I: Pilate issues a summons for a court to be held on the following morning. (3) The Resurrection accompanied by thunder: the guards flee from the tomb and discuss what has happened. (4) The guards and the Jews appear before Pilate: Pilate questions the guards; taking the Jews' advice, he bribes them to keep silent. (5) Pilate's court II: Pilate grants a peddler permission to sell his wares after paying a fee. (6) Peddler's scene: The peddler praises his wares. (7) Christ descends into Hell: He releases the souls there. (8) Purchase of ointment: Mary Magdalene and the other two Marys buy ointment from the peddler to embalm Jesus' body. (9) The Marys at the tomb: They are worried about how they will roll away the heavy stone; the angel announces the Resurrection to them and tells them to take the message to the disciples in Galilee. (10) Christ appears to Mary Magdalene. The end of the play probably contained the women's arrival in Galilee and their announcement of the Resurrection to the disciples (cf. scene 9), and Peter and John hurry to the tomb. The lost beginning is likely to have consisted of an opening scene and the placing of Jesus' body in the sepulcher.

This set of scenes corresponds to the Latin Easter plays of the 13th and 14th centuries, although *The Easter Play of Muri* cannot be linked directly to any of them. Most importantly, we do not know of any German-language model on which the author could have based his work. This makes the high literary quality of the play all the more astonishing. The careful copy prepared by two scribes and the accurate corrections—which some scholars have thought might even stem from the author—are striking in themselves. The second scribe placed the first letter of every line a little to the left in a manner reminiscent of the layout in manuscripts of courtly literature. The use of rhymed couplets with four stresses also points in this direction, as do the care taken to use only pure rhymes, the technique of broken rhyme— the first line of a couplet ends the speech of one character, and the second line is spoken by a different character—up to and including stichomythia and the artful construction of dialogue. And when the peddler hawks his aphrodisiacs for lovers *(minnere geile)* and cosmetics, sashes, handbags, and rings for young ladies, and even refers to love songs, the atmosphere has obviously taken on an aristocratic, courtly character. While the author must have been a cleric, since he was thoroughly familiar with Latin Easter plays, obviously he also knew the traditions of courtly literature.

In the past, it had been proposed that *The Easter Play of Muri* was an example of courtly drama; it was even interpreted as a presentation of "courtly theology" for an aristocratic laity. If this hypothesis were correct, then the traditional genres of courtly literature—that is, minnesong, didactic songs and poetry, romance, and heroic epic—would have to be extended to include religious drama which, after it was detached from Latin Easter services, is otherwise considered to have been a specifically urban genre.

Modern scholars have distanced themselves from such sweeping conclusions, and rightly so, for works that scholars long regarded as "courtly" owe their attributes to the literary situation of the period. Where else could learned literary German in the mid-13th century be found, if not in courtly literature? On the other hand, one should be careful not simply to equate the terms "courtly" and "aristocratic," as is still the case in some of the more recent studies of *The Easter Play of Muri*. The urban literature of this period clearly reflects courtly influences; one could even say it arose through the adaptation of aristocratic literature by the lay and clerical elites in cities. The extensive literary oeuvre of one Conrad of Würzburg (ca. 1230–1287), who found patrons in Basel and Strasbourg, offers the best proof. Given this background, one should avoid creating an anachronistic dichotomy between "courtly" versus "urban" and try to understand the function of the unarguably courtly elements in this play in the context of a performance setting likely to have been urban. In any event, the number of at least twenty-nine performers in the surviving scenes, the need for a choir familiar with the liturgical hymns, and the probability that the director belonged to the clergy, all suggest that *The Easter Play of Muri* was performed in a city, perhaps, as noted above, Zurich.

To indicate the intention and significance of the play, we should briefly consider the tenth scene, the last of the surviving scenes. At its center stands Mary Magdalene (who, by the way, was venerated in Zurich from the 12th century on as the city's patron saint), to whom Christ appears. It begins with the actual appearance (based on John 20:11–18); then, after a break indicated by a rhyming couplet, there follows a speech by Mary Magdalene of more than 120 lines, the longest single speech of the (surviving) play. The monologue opens with an apostrophe to Christ based on her firm faith in him as the divine son of the Virgin Mary, who rules heaven and earth. She bemoans the ordeal of the crucifixion, which she witnessed with her own eyes, and at the same time, she rejoices in having been permitted to see him risen from the dead. In this salvific context, Mary Magdalene confesses, in an emotional and moving lament, her great sinfulness, which exceeded that of all others. (This is reminiscent of the early Middle High German lament for sins committed.) Full of trust, she then addresses the redeemer of humankind. As she shifts from "I" to "we," she begins to speak for the audience as well. Using the dogmatic argument that the death of the son was necessary to attain eternal life for humankind, she requests of Christ that she herself may be saved, again shifting to the "we"-form at the end. In the brief reply that has been preserved, the risen Christ accepts Mary Magdalene's lament, prayer, and repentance. For the spectators, she becomes an effective exemplification of the necessity to take responsibility for one's sins. Mary exemplifies the path of faith, confession, and repentance that reliably leads to God, the Redeemer. Her monologue is a form of salvific instruction for the audience.

Much in the play suggests that the impulse behind *The Easter Play of Muri* was a new form of piety propagating the then-powerful poverty movement associated with the mendicant orders (Joachim Heinzle). *The Easter Play of Muri* offers valuable literary evidence of this movement, even though it had no recognizable influence on the future tradition of medieval German Easter plays. We must look at later plays and their occasionally copious stage directions to gain at least some impression of how *The Easter Play of Muri* was performed. It is certain that the play was no longer performed in a church, in the manner of Easter ceremonies, but in the open air—perhaps in front of a church, or in the market square. The strongest indication that the play was not put on inside a church is not so much the length of the text as the number of actors needed and the variety of the scenes. These require a considerable amount of movement, and thus a more spacious setting.

In this space various stands would have been built to represent the various locations *(loca),* such as Pilate's house, Jesus' tomb, the peddler's market stall. It was customary in medieval religious plays for the entire cast to be present for the duration. They either remained at their stand when they were not participating in a scene—for example, Pilate during the scene in which the women buy ointment—or they moved about from one stand to another—for example, the watchmen from Pilate's house to Jesus' tomb and, after the Resurrection, back to Pilate's stand. This style of production is known as simultaneous staging, in which the action moves from one stand to another.

Lack of evidence makes it impossible to say whether *The Easter Play of Muri* was staged on ground level with spectators on all sides, or on a raised platform, which would have distanced the audience from the performance but offered a better view. Of course, one can also imagine staging the play on ground or street level with various stands—Pilate's house, for instance—on individual platforms. In any event, simultaneous staging involved the spectators, who surrounded the scene, much more in the action of the play than the modern proscenium stage. On the simultaneous stage, the events of salvation history were not simply reenacted as a form of reminder; they were directly present. The spectators became witnesses of the salvific events in the play, or even became part of these events, from which no one could withdraw. This is the didactic function of religious plays as represented most admirably in the literary adaptation of *The Easter Play of Muri*.

See also 1250, 1450

Bibliography: *Das Osterspiel von Muri nach den alten und neuen Fragmenten,* ed. Friedrich Ranke (Aarau, 1944). *Das Osterspiel von Muri: Faksimiledruck der Fragmente und Rekonstruktion der Pergamentrolle,* ed. under the auspices of the Canton of Aargau (Basel, 1967). *Das Innsbrucker Osterspiel: Das Osterspiel von Muri, Mittelhochdeutsch und Neuhochdeutsch,* ed. and trans. Rudolf Meier (Stuttgart: Reclam, 1962), 113–155. Bernd Neumann, "Osterspiel von Muri," in *Literaturlexicon: Autoren und Werke deutscher Sprache,* ed. Walter Killy (Gütersloh and Munich: Bertelsmann, 1991), 9: 20ff. Max Wehrli, "Osterspiel von Muri," in *Die deutsche Literatur des Mittelalters,* ed. Kurt Ruh (Berlin and New York: de Gruyter, 1989), 119–124.

Johannes Janota
Translated by Deborah Lucas Schneider

℔ *Circa 1265*

The Beguine Mechthild von Magdeburg defends herself against an unnamed critic

A Vision of Flowing Light

In Book VI of *Das fliessende Licht der Gottheit (The Flowing Light of the Godhead),* Mechthild von Magdeburg (ca. 1208–ca. 1282) responds to an unnamed critic of an earlier part of the text, providing evidence that portions of the *Flowing Light* were circulated before the entire manuscript was completed. "I said in one passage in this book," Mechthild writes, "that the Godhead is my Father by nature. You do not understand this, and say: 'Everything that God has done with us is completely a matter of grace and not of nature.'" Mechthild refuses to bow before such learned critique. "You are right," she replies to her imaginary interlocutor, "but I am right, too" (VI.31).

The passage in question appears early in Mechthild's book, in the midst of an extended allegorical dance between the soul and her beloved. The senses warn the soul against the blazing heat emanating from the Godhead, in which they will lose all their capacities. But the soul replies,

A fish in water does not drown.
A bird in the air does not plummet.
Gold in fire does not perish.
Rather, it gets its purity and its radiant color there.
God has created all creatures to live according to their nature.
How, then, am I to resist my nature?
I must go from all things to God,
Who is my Father by nature,
My Brother by his humanity,
My Bridegroom by love,
And I his bride for all eternity.

(I.44)

Against the learned quibbles of her adversary, Mechthild insists that there is an aspect of the soul that shares in the divine nature, even though the soul too is fallen and requires divine grace to be redeemed.

Mechthild introduces here a mystical theme that had also been suggested by her contemporary Hadewijch (fl. ca. 1250) and was later elaborated by Marguerite Porete (d. 1310) and the German Dominican preacher Meister Eckhart (d. 1327). Mechthild, Hadewijch, and Marguerite Porete wrote in different Northern European vernaculars and it is unlikely that they knew each other's work. However, all three were Beguines. Given the divergences of their writings (and their commonalities with those of other, non-Beguine, contemporaries), one cannot argue for a distinctive Beguine theology. Yet the particularities of this form of religious life and the challenges faced by the Beguines as semi-religious women may shed light on Mechthild's work and on the emergence of the theologically innovative concept of the "precreated soul" found in the texts of all three Beguines.

Beguines were semi-religious women, living alone or in groups, who embraced poverty, chastity, and devotion without joining one of the official orders. The first signs of the movement are found in the hagiographies of late 12th- and 13th-century women, usually solitaries, from the southern areas of the Low Countries. The movement eventually spread throughout Northern Europe and took on a wide variety of institutional forms. In the Germany of Mechthild's times, Beguines generally lived in communal houses, supporting themselves through the dowries with which they entered the beguinage, gifts, and manual labor. In many cities of the Low Countries, Beguines were an important part of the workforce of the textile industry. In addition to spinning, weaving, and embroidering, Beguines also served as nurses and teachers of young girls.

Like the Franciscan and Dominican orders, which emerged at about the same time, the women who chose this form of life were driven by a desire to imitate the life of Christ and of the apostles by choosing poverty and service to the world. Underlying all three movements was a desire to rearticulate contemplation and action through Christ-like engagement with others, which they believed would generate true contemplation and union with God. The ideals of all three movements were tempered by the Church hierarchy, yet the Beguines posed a particular challenge to ecclesiastical leadership because they were women. Central to medieval ideology was the belief that women were sexually dangerous to themselves and others. Therefore strict cloistering, or separation from the world, was required for a woman who wished to devote her life to God. The Beguines, who refused to be cloistered, were almost immediately accused of immorality and hypocrisy.

A second, related challenge was posed by the Beguines' desire to embrace evangelical poverty; many early Beguines are depicted in *Lives* as wishing to support themselves through begging, as Francis and his early followers did. This was immediately decried as unacceptable for women, and male confessors or others in authority forbade such unseemly activities, as hagiographers of early Beguines testify. Rather than seeing it as a mark of apostolic piety, critics immediately attributed Beguine mendicancy to laziness and unwillingness to work. Throughout the 13th and 14th centuries attempts were made to organize the Beguines into houses with sufficient endowments to support themselves, so that Beguines would not wander the streets uncontrolled (as the popular image of the begging Beguine suggested). Manual labor, however, continued to be an important part of Beguine life.

In the face of such strong opposition and demands for changes in the Beguine ideal, many women internalized their calling for evangelical poverty and spiritualized the demand for work and engagement with the world. Mechthild understood her work as her writing and, like many Beguines depicted in 13th- and 14th-century hagiographies, the care for her spiritual children, including souls in purgatory released through suffering, tears, and petitions to Christ (II.8, III.15, and V.8). She frequently speaks of her life as one of pain and "exile." Like her conception of work, this image is closely tied to her Christology and her understanding of life as a Beguine, which is consciously patterned on that of Christ. While most scholars assume that Mechthild lived in a community of Beguines (and sections of her book offering advice to other Beguines might suggest this to be the case), she really placed great emphasis on the solitary, painful, and lonely nature of her chosen path.

At about the age of twelve, Mechthild tells us, she was "greeted by the Holy Spirit" and such experiences continued throughout her life. As a young woman, she desired "to be despised through no fault of my own. Then for the sake of God's love I moved to a town where no one was my friend except for one person. I was afraid that because of him holy contempt and God's pure love would be withdrawn from me. But God nowhere abandoned me and let me experience such delightful sweetness, such holy knowledge, and such incomprehensible wonders that I found little enjoyment in earthly things" (IV.2). Mechthild clearly equates her solitude and earthly abandonment with the receipt of divine gifts. Through suffering with Christ in his exile, one is united with him and shares the delights of the heavenly realm.

Since we have little historical evidence of Mechthild's life, we cannot determine whether her exile and loneliness were meant only spiritually or literally. The little we do know comes from Mechthild's book itself, the Latin translation of the *Flowing Light* (produced shortly after Mechthild's death, it does not include the seventh book, written in her final years at the convent of Helfta), and the anonymous prologues to these texts. She was born about 1208 into a noble family, although the level of nobility is unclear. What is certain, given the imagery and stylistic sophistication of her work, is that Mechthild was well versed in the German high courtly literature of the 12th and 13th centuries. She claims not to know Latin or to be trained in theology, yet occasionally cites liturgical Latin. Her probably rudimentary knowledge was gained, no doubt, through daily participation in the devotional life of the Church.

Mechthild brings her knowledge of courtly literature to her visionary and ecstatic experiences to create a unique, vibrant theology. God's love and the union of the soul and the divine through love is the theme that pervades Mechthild's entire book and gives it its overarching framework. God and the soul interact in a dialectical relationship. The first books oscillate between representations of God's presence and absence and the soul's resulting ecstasy and agony. The soul's delight in the experience of God's "greeting" is so great that all earthly pleasures become sources of pain. But the experiences of joy and suffering are intimately related, for God becomes present to the soul through the embrace of exile and the pain of God's absence. Mechthild's Christology grounds her account, for it is only in suffering with Christ in his humanity that one can be joined with him in his divinity (to paraphrase a line from Mechthild's contemporary Hadewijch).

The dialectical relationship of ecstasy and agony, God's presence and God's absence, receives a resolution later in the *Flowing Light*. Here Mechthild draws out the implications of her claim that the soul shares in God's nature; because of the soul's uninterrupted unity with God, God is present to the soul even when it does not experience his extraordinary gifts. Mechthild contrasts Mary, the mother of God, with Mary Magdalene to illustrate this development of the soul's understanding: "Mary, our lady, spoke with her thought to our Lord as often as she wished, and so his Godhead sometimes answered her. Therefore, she bore her suffering in a seemly manner. For this, Mary Magdalene was unprepared. When she did not see our Lord with fleshly eyes, she was without comfort, and her heart bore all the while great sorrow and discomfort" (V.23).

Unlike Mary Magdalene, who was disconsolate without the physical presence of Christ, Mary understood that God was continually present to the soul, and she remained at peace after Christ's death. Mechthild argues that the goal of the soul should be to become, like Mary, well ordered: "Love, your departure and your arrival are both alike welcome to the well-ordered soul" (V.30).

Mechthild makes use of a wide variety of genres to express this theological view of her experience and the teachings that emerge from it: the religious genres of vision, hymn, sermon, spiritual instruction, prayer, liturgy, litany, and prophecy; the courtly genres of love poetry, allegorical dialogue, messenger's song *(Botenlied),* and the exchange *(Wechsel);* and miscellaneous other genres, such as autobiography, drama, epigrammatic poetry and wisdom literature, anecdote, letter, parody, nursery rhyme, and polemics. Many parts of the text, therefore, seem to fit only uneasily within the theological framework. Yet for Mechthild, her teachings on a wide range of topics expressed in many different forms all emerge from her experience of the divine and the theological meaning she gave to that experience. Thus not only must Mechthild suffer with Christ in his exile; she must also work with Christ, a work that often entails or engenders more suffering. The abundance of her teachings, whether grounded in visionary experience or presented in literary forms (and often, presumably, in her own voice), is an overflow of the divine love she experiences in and as

Christ. Her understanding of the relationship of the soul and God provides the underlying unity of her diverse, seemingly unstructured writing.

The Beguines were suspect not only for their way of life. Throughout the 13th century, they were increasingly charged with theological errors and heresy. Therefore, Mechthild was in need of an extraordinary authorization for her work. Like the great 12th-century visionary Hildegard von Bingen, Mechthild opens her book with the legitimating words of God: "This book I hereby send as a messenger to all religious people, both the bad and the good; for if the pillars fall, the building cannot remain standing; and it signifies me alone and proclaims in praiseworthy fashion my intimacy." Mechthild, like Hildegard, claims that God is the author of her book:

> "Ah, Lord God, who made this book?"
> "I made it in my powerlessness, for I cannot restrain myself as to my gifts."
> "Well then, Lord, what shall the title of the book be, which is to your glory alone?"
> "It shall be called a flowing light of my Godhead into all hearts that live free of hypocrisy."

Mechthild argues that love flows of necessity from the heights down into the depths. She, who is most lowly, becomes the vessel through which God speaks to the world. With a new set of images, Mechthild reasserts the dialectic between ecstasy and suffering, God's presence and God's absence, which governs the text as a whole.

Despite her humility and lack of learning—or rather *because* of her lowliness—God chooses Mechthild as the conduit through which he speaks to the world. Her writing is a work that God commands she undertake in loving union with Christ. This work entails suffering, just as Christ's work did. She must recount the delights and agonies of the soul, offer prophetic denunciations of corruption and hypocrisy in the Church, recount her visions of purgatory, offer advice to contemporaries, and engage in a multitude of other literary and spiritual tasks. Her work is not confined to the production of the *Flowing Light,* for she must also pray, weep, and suffer for the souls in purgatory and for her spiritual children. Not only her book, but her entire life and her experience are unified in her developing theological vision.

In addition to claiming prophetic authority of one who speaks God's word as miraculously given to her, Mechthild also justifies her speaking out by reasoning that, if all souls are united with God "by nature" as well as by "grace," and if the well-ordered soul is fully present to God even when charismatic gifts are absent, then any soul grounded in God can be said to be speaking in God's name. By hinting at an alternative to charismatic authorization—the one form of legitimation open to women within the medieval Church—Mechthild poses a potential threat to the ecclesial hierarchy and its control over scriptural interpretation, dogmatic utterances, and theology. Priests must be ordained, and charismatic authority, to be accepted as legitimate, must be approved by the church hierarchy. But how is that hierarchy to judge if a soul is "well ordered" and speaking out of its "natural" unity with the divine? If such souls no longer require the grace provided by the Church, would such ecclesial approbation even be recognized or required? By agreeing that God is the soul's father both by nature and by grace, Mechthild stops far short of such radical claims. Yet, as her anxious critic in Book VI suspects, the seeds for them lie within her work.

Mechthild never directly challenged the church hierarchy. She had a powerful ally and protector in her Dominican confessor, Heinrich of Halle, and thus does not appear to have been persecuted. It was Marguerite Porete who radicalized Mechthild's view of the creature's "natural" unity with God in her concept of the free, simple, and annihilated soul. The implications of this view are fully realized in the authorizing strategies of *The Mirror of Simple Souls,* for Marguerite does not claim visionary or prophetic gifts. Rather, the soul depicted in her book claims to speak as God because, as simple and free, it is God. For these audacious claims, and her refusal to bow to church authority, Marguerite paid with her life.

See also 1147, 1329

Bibliography: Caroline Walker, *Jesus as Mother: Studies in the Spirituality of the High Middle Ages* (Berkeley: University of California Press, 1982). Amy Hollywood, *The Soul as Virgin Wife: Mechthild of Magdeburg, Marguerite Porete, and Meister Eckhart* (Notre Dame, Ind.: University of Notre Dame Press, 1995). Mechthild of Magdeburg, *The Flowing Light of the Godhead,* trans. Frank Tobin (New York: Paulist Press, 1998). Mechthild von Magdeburg, *Das fliessende Licht der Gottheit, nach der Einsiedler Handschrift in kritischem Vergleich mit der gesamten Überlieferung,* ed. Hans Neumann (Munich: Artemis, 1990 and 1993), 2 vols.

Amy M. Hollywood

♌ 1275, January 16

The Styrian politician and poet Ulrich von Lichtenstein dies

Truth and Fiction

Most lives of medieval writers are shrouded in mystery. Even in the case of poets as celebrated as Walther von der Vogelweide or Wolfram von Eschenbach, little is known about how they lived, what position in society they occupied, or the circumstances under which they wrote their poems. Historical sources, such as chronicles, deeds, and other official records, say almost nothing about literary activities. Autobiographical references in the poets' works are sparse. What a surprising difference it is then to see how Ulrich von Lichtenstein presents himself! His name occurs in more than ninety 13th-century historical sources; even the exact date of his death is known: 16 January 1275. Ulrich was a member of a powerful clan of *ministeriales* (unfree knights) in Styria, Austria, where he held a series of important offices. In 1244 he signed documents as *Truchsess* (chancellor of the ruler's court); from 1267 to

1272 he served as marshal, and in 1272 as a judge and representative of the ruler in a court of law. Yet none of these documents mentions his literary activities. Cultural life and public political life were distinctly kept separate.

Nonetheless, Ulrich was known as an important poet in his time. He left two outstanding epic works, *Frauendienst* (The Service of Women), composed in stanzas, and *Frauenbuch* (Book of Women), in rhymed couplets. In addition, several *minne* songs from his hand have survived. These songs are contained in the famous Great Heidelberg Song Manuscript (C), but they are also integrated, with slight variations, into the narrative text of *Frauendienst*. This combination of epic-narrative literary elements and lyric-reflective elements represents an enormous poetic innovation; yet virtually no other writers emulated it in the German-speaking regions. The form is reminiscent of the *vidas* and *razos*, familiar from manuscripts of lyric poetry originating in the southern French region of Provence. The *vidas* construct a fictitious biography of a poet; the *razos* offer commentaries on the poems, identifying the occasion of their composition and their function or use. Scholars assume that Ulrich was familiar with such texts and that they inspired his *Frauendienst*. But *Frauendienst* goes far beyond the forms of Provençal lyric poetry and introduces fundamental structural innovations. Not only does Ulrich combine the epic and the lyric in a unique manner, he also weaves another kind of text into his narrative: *büechelin* ("little books") and shorter *brieve* ("letters" or "reports"). These texts within the text represent fairly extensive messages of love and admiration for the ladies to whom *Frauendienst* pays homage.

In addition, *Frauendienst* can be seen as the first autobiographical novel in German. The first-person speaker, who is identified in the text itself by the name *von Liehtenstein her Uolrich* ("of Lichtenstein Master Ulrich"), is at once protagonist and author of the entire narrative. Just as elements of fiction, poetic heightening, and nonauthentic matter frequently characterize modern autobiographies, so too should *Frauendienst* be read as a novelistic autobiography and not as historical reality (Ulrich Müller).

In the considerably shorter *Frauenbuch,* the author again gives his name: *ich Uolrĭch von Liehtensteine* ("I, Ulrich of Lichtenstein"), and the appellation allows the first-person subject to function as both author and fictional character here as well. In contrast to *Frauendienst,* however, *Frauenbuch* tends toward allegory, suggesting that the experiences recounted are less real and less autobiographical.

Ulrich's *Frauendienst,* written about the middle of the 13th century, is documented today in three manuscripts, all fragmentary in part. This highly comic tale opens with Ulrich's entry into the knighthood, whereupon he offers his devoted service to the mistress of a distant female relative (even though he is already married). Ulrich presents himself as a man in the grip of undying love, completely dependent on the object of his desire. He gives up more and more of his own identity, endures both physical and mental torment, all to no avail. Frustrated, he at last abandons his pursuit of the adored lady. Several years later, Ulrich chooses a new beloved, and again we follow his tireless efforts to win her favor. Ulrich's mood, nevertheless, remains cheerful throughout: "vil hohes muotes man mich sach, / ze freuden stuont gar min gedanc" ("I was seen in very high spirits, / my thoughts were only on joy," verse 1752). Step by step, Ulrich relinquishes his role as courtly servant of love, and the text concludes with reflections on the proper life of men and women.

As author, Ulrich gives his text a title—something very rare in medieval poetry: "Ditz buoch sol guoter wîbe sin. / in hat dar an diu zunge min / gesprochen vil manec süezez wort. / [. . .] vrowen dienst ist ez genant: / da bi so sol ez sin bechant" ("This text is meant for good women. To them my tongue has offered many sweet words. [. . .] It is called 'Service of Women'; under this title it shall become known"; 1850). Courtship and praise of women occupy several levels in *Frauendienst*. One consists of love songs like those familiar from traditional minnesong. Ulrich transposes these love lyrics into an epic world, where, in contrast to traditional minnesong addressed to a largely imaginary woman, the songs become part of a real courtship. He has the songs recited to his lady and sends copies for her to read as a mode of communication. He also composes love letters in short prose and longer essays or booklets on the theory of courtly love, which he has delivered to her. By embedding traditional minnesong in a pseudo-realistic literary world, Ulrich reveals himself as a connoisseur of both traditional and contemporary literary styles. He is thoroughly familiar with all types of lyric poetry and displays great skill in making intertextual arrangements.

Ulrich attempts to impress his lady by participating in tournaments as part of his love service. One such event, the tournament at Freisach, is depicted in highly realistic manner, and mentions names of people known to have existed. These passages have led earlier scholars to regard the text as a genuine historical document. This is not the case, however—at least not in an absolute sense. Historical details in the *Frauendienst* should be regarded as aesthetic elements. Wolfram von Eschenbach had already scattered tiny historical elements throughout his *Parzival,* thereby drawing his audience out of the distant, mythical world of King Arthur and the Holy Grail, perhaps with the aim of inviting the reader to draw connections between the real world and the world of literature. Ulrich greatly increased the use of this technique of introducing actual people or historical events, such as political disorder in Bohemia or the death of Duke Frederick II. He, thereby, effects an authenticity that contrasts dramatically with some of Ulrich's grotesque courting exploits, for instance, drinking water in which his lady has washed her hands or even cutting off a finger to prove his love. This contrast may be the key to understanding the entire text as a complex juxtaposition of literary construction and historical reality.

An important episode is Ulrich's Venus journey. Disguised as Dame Venus, he embarks on a long journey in his lady's honor, traveling from Italy to Vienna and Bohemia and finally back to Vienna. In the course of this journey, Ulrich fights numerous battles, all in service to his lady. A key aspect of this episode is its playful approach to gender identity. In the Heidelberg Song Manuscript, this is depicted visually: an illustration shows a rider with an upright lance and shield, wearing a helmet with its visor down—so no face is visible—and mounted on a horse adorned in rich trappings. The knight's helmet is decorated with a rather large female torso representing Dame Venus in a flowing gown; she holds an arrow (symbolizing love) in her right hand and a torch in her left. Ulrich's masquerade is explained by the fact that it is easier for a woman to gain access to other women. But the Venus journey must also be seen as part of Ulrich's exaggerated homage to women: the ultimate means of conquering a woman for a man is to become a woman oneself. All the same, this apparently most radical of all methods does not lead to genuine success either. After enduring myriad humiliations in the course of the journey—such as living as a leper and being urinated on—he is finally granted an audience by his lady. The meeting does not go well, however, and Ulrich abandons his quest for her favor. When he has recovered from this defeat, Ulrich embarks on a second quest, this time for a new lady's favor. In structural symmetry with the Venus journey of part one, the narrative center of the second service is the Arthur journey. Here, too, Ulrich takes on a second identity. This time he plays the role of King Arthur, a figure anchored in the literature of the time and in the collective memory of the cultural past. Unlike his journey as Venus, Ulrich's journey as Arthur takes the form of a political manifestation. Once again, the narrative is interspersed with actual historical details. Given that King Arthur was by no means always seen as a flawless ideal, this part of the text may have been designed as a way of creating ironic distance to the protagonist's actions.

In the end, Ulrich sums up his literary achievement: "You must really believe me: I had been a knightly knight for thirty-three years when this book was read aloud again, so that I finished composing it. Now let the ladies judge whether or not I have sung and related their worthiness in it" (verse 1845). Here is a break with Ulrich's use of the first-person pronoun: On the one hand, he says "I" as protagonist of the story; on the other hand, the speaker is also the historical poet Ulrich von Lichtenstein, who has devised the whole entertainment with roles for both author and hero.

Scholars have been hard pressed to arrive at a consistent interpretation of this text. One basic problem lies in the complex mixture of actual elements, fictitious elements designed to appear real, echoes of other works of literature, and intertextual jests. The text as a whole cannot be categorized as either a burlesque or a historical account. Its charm lies precisely in its shifting quality, in its ability to remain a puzzle. The reader is constantly pulled back and forth between real and invented worlds, between the historical Ulrich von Lichtenstein, the politician, and the author-hero Ulrich, who inhabits the realm of literary tradition.

Ulrich's second work, *Frauenbuch,* is preserved in only one late manuscript, the *Ambraser Heldenbuch* (Ambras Book of Heroes), dating from the beginning of the 17th century. Like *Frauendienst,* the title *Frauenbuch* is documented in the text itself: "der frawen puech es hayssen sol" ("the book of women it shall be called," verse 2125). In contrast to *Frauendienst,* this is a reflective, static text, where action is held to a minimum. Almost philosophical in nature, it takes the form of a debate between a woman and a man, in which they develop the positions of the gender culture of the 14th century. As in *Frauendienst,* Ulrich's identity is split; he is the author of the debate, described as a gift to his lady, and he is the narrator of the work, who is also a literary figure drawn into the debate by the couple. Finally, of course, Ulrich is the creator of this entire literary construction.

Although *Frauenbuch* is dominated by a male perspective and informed by male cultural beliefs, its author deserves great credit for articulating the problems and fears of women in many situations—hardly a common position for a 13th-century writer. Many of the woman's arguments no doubt reflect genuine and painful experiences of women in real, everyday life—dealing with men who drink and beat their wives; men who are secret homosexuals or at least bisexuals; men who deliberately try to compromise women's reputations; and much more. Ulrich deals here with extramarital and erotic relations in a matter-of-fact way, absent of moralizing overtones.

At the end of the fictional debate, a judge is brought in to decide who has won. This form of resolution is familiar from *minne* allegories of the later 13th and 14th centuries. In the *minne* court of the *Frauenbuch,* the judge is one Ulrich von Lichtenstein. While he decides that women should be subservient to men, he also lauds the female sex for its nobility of spirit. The text concludes with a love lament and hyperbolic praise of the lady in whose service the work had been undertaken.

Frauenbuch has always been unjustly overshadowed by *Frauendienst.* A highly complex text that links literary tradition and historical details with astonishing sophistication and subtlety, *Frauenbuch* is an important source for both literary and cultural historians. Ulrich reveals himself here as a master of all forms of minnesong in the first half of the 13th century, and evokes a great variety of concepts and ideologies by using just a few key terms. In addition, his treatment of relations between men and women goes far beyond the realm of literature and offers glimpses of everyday reality and the problems in relationships between the sexes in that culture.

See also 1170, 1189, 1203 (Summer), 1203 (November 12), 1670 (Grimmelshausen)

Bibliography: Ulrich von Liechtenstein, *Frauendienst,* ed. Franz Viktor Spechtler (Göppingen, 1987). ———, *Frauenbuch,* ed. Franz Viktor Spechtler (Göppingen, 1989). Jan-Dirk Müller, "Lachen—Spiel—Fiktion: Zum Verhältnis von literarischem Diskurs und historischer Realität im *Frauendienst," Deutsche Vierteljahrsschrift für Literaturwissenschaft und Geistesgeschichte* 58 (1984): 38–73. Elke Brüggen, "Minnelehre und Gesellschaftskritik im 13. Jahrhundert: Zum Frauenbuch Ulrichs von Lichtenstein," *Euphorion* (1989): 72–97. David F. Tinsley, "Die Kunst der Selbstdarstellung in Ulrich von Lichtensteins Frauendienst," *Germanisch-Romanische Monatsschrift* 40 (1990): 129–140. Ulrich Müller, "Männerphantasien eines mittelalterlichen Herren: Ulrich von Lichtenstein und sein Frauendienst," in *Variationen der Liebe: Historische Psychologie der Geschlechterbeziehung,* ed. Thomas Kornbichler and Wolfgang Maaz (Tübingen, 1995), 27–50.

Thomas Bein
Translated by Deborah Lucas Schneider

🥲 *1300*
Hugo von Trimberg finishes writing *Der Renner*

Poetry, Teaching, and Experience

In the year 1300—when Boniface VIII was pope (1294–1303) and Albrecht I of Habsburg was German king (1298–1308)—Hugo von Trimberg finished a didactic poem of some 24,600 lines called *Der Renner (The Runner)*. The dates of medieval works of literature can often only be determined through references in the text itself since other evidence is usually lacking; the same holds true for biographical information about many authors. Hugo von Trimberg is no exception. He inserted a few autobiographical passages at strategic places in his works—the beginning, the end, or the transition to a new topic—following a 13th-century custom of injecting the poet's persona into the work. Michel Zink, commenting on French poetry of that era, termed this device "literary subjectivity." An early example of this can be found in the aphorisms of Walther von der Vogelweide. The poet no longer simply speaks for a group nor plays a familiar role such as that of the lover; rather, he gradually assumes the contours of an individual with his own personal experience.

As his poem indicates, Hugo von Trimberg had been a teacher and headmaster at the church school of Saint Gangolf in Teuerstadt near Bamberg for forty years at the time he finished *Der Renner*. He taught Latin grammar and read works of ancient and more recent Latin authors; he was neither a priest nor a member of the nobility. He may have adopted his name in honor of the Trimberg family, whose castle was located close to Oberwerrn near Schweinfurt, the village of his birth. He was probably born between 1230 and 1240, and must have lived until at least 1313, for a later addition to *Der Renner* mentions the death of King Henry VII of Luxembourg, who died in that year. Hugo most likely never ventured beyond Upper Franconia. Although he had a good knowledge of the Latin language and literature, he never attended a university. He must have had a long life by medieval standards, for his poem reflects the experience of old age.

In the prologue, the author mentions physical infirmities and noises in his head, an indication, he believes, that death is not far off. Hugo himself gave no title to the work he had begun. With great modesty he refers to the extensive poem as a "small book." He hopes it will remind friends of him and prompt them to pray for his soul—thereby doing good for their own souls. In this manner he introduces the decisive function of poetry—edification—right at the start. Hugo never loses sight of eternal life as the greatest goal of all Christians. He claims authorship to seven books in German and "five and a half" in Latin, but does not cite their titles. Of his books in the vernacular, only *Der Renner* has come down to us. By profession, Hugo was an *auctorista,* that is, a specialist in the literary canon of his age. This role is reflected in his *Registrum multorum auctorum (Register of Many Authors)* of 1280. Hugo reproduced this reading list for his pupils in the rhyming couplets popular among 12th-century itinerant scholars. Such rhyming verses had two advantages: they were easy to learn by heart, and they stood out from the verses of the authors cited, who followed classical Roman metrics of long and short syllables rather than stressed and unstressed. As the pupils recited and memorized passages of the *Register*, it was obvious which parts were by Hugo and which were quotations from the authors they were studying. Manuscript volumes were precious objects and the parchment on which they were written was costly, which meant that often several texts from various sources were included in one codex. For this reason it was practical to have pupils memorize both the opening verses of Latin poems most frequently taught and a little information about the qualities of the authors; this approach enabled them to recognize when a new text began and provided some orientation about the writer. Hugo divided writers into three categories: (1) "ethical" writers for older pupils, such as the Romans Virgil and Claudian; (2) "modern" authors strongly influenced by the ancients, like Alanus of Insulis or Walter of Châtillon; and most important, (3) theological writers. Ethical works for younger pupils, such as animal fables or the aphorisms attributed to Cato, rounded out Hugo's canon. Although the Roman authors were heathens and thus lacked the light of revelation, they could still illustrate the proper way to live. The ethical dimension of literature was all that counted. Like the *Register*, Hugo's calendar poem *Laurea sanctorum (Wreath of Saints)* is a catalogue, this time of saints and their feast days. In the preface, the author says he bound together "lilies and roses with the violets." Even today the term "anthology" is based on the image of collecting flowers. Just as edifying—although for modern tastes somewhat more entertaining—is the *Solsequium* (1284; *Heliotrope*), a collection of didactic stories for preachers. Its readers, Hugo hoped, would turn toward the light of God, just as the heliotrope follows the sun.

In *Der Renner*, Hugo uses related imagery, comparing himself to a harvester and to a bee. The poem, in rhyming couplets, shares several characteristics with Hugo's surviving works in Latin. It was compiled from many sources; it instructs, by means of examples and fables, what to do and what not to do, cites rules for conduct from Roman authors or Church Fathers, and reveals an overpowering urge to instruct. However, *Der Renner* is more complex, original, and monumental than any other of Hugo von Trimberg's works. This is due chiefly to the poem's allegorical framework. The first-person narrator finds himself in a pleasant landscape of flowering meadows. There, in a valley surrounded by tall mountains, he sees on a small knoll a tree with blossoms that become pears in the twinkle of an eye. Some pears drop into the grass, others into a thorn bush, a deep well, or a puddle of water. Following the allegory, Hugo presents the correct way to interpret it. Each element of the landscape is to be understood metaphorically in relation to the larger theme, which is man's fall from grace. From this fall comes man's need for redemption and hence, the sacrificial death of Christ. Out of the knoll (Adam) grows the tree (the sinner Eve) from which the pears (human beings) originate. If their way of life is godless, the wind of curiosity blows them into the thorns of pride, the well of greed, or the puddle of other sins. If they live in a manner that pleases God, however, they fall into the grass of repentance. The mountains of death surround and enclose the deceptively beautiful vale of tears that is the world. This allegorical landscape stands for the physical world while it determines, at the same time, a scale of values; unfortunately, the human being at the center is burdened by the weight of sin.

The temporal framework of *Der Renner* runs from Adam's fall to the Last Judgment; the organizing principle is provided by the seven deadly sins. However, since Hugo combines anger and envy in a single part, they are treated as six "distinctions." Hugo's treatment of the sins follows a hierarchical order. Pride and greed weigh most heavily, whereas gluttony, lust, anger, envy, and sloth follow from these principal vices. In his associative style of argumentation, Hugo shows how the various sins are linked. Thus gluttony and drunkenness go together with a love for gambling, since people indulge in all of these vices in taverns, and in gambling the sin of greed, which always lurks at the root of all evil, becomes evident once again. As he describes the various vices, Hugo seizes the opportunity to inject some criticism of the social estates: the nobility's pride, the clergy's excesses and lack of education, and the merchants' acquisitiveness. Hugo's language is filled with vivid similes: an evil man sits on his wealth like a hen on her eggs; the devil builds his nest on the "aristocracy of the Holy Spirit," the clergy, like a stork on a barn; vain women disguise their appearance more artfully than a dishonest horse trader his nags. He is particularly critical of romances that glorify King Arthur's court, which he regards as a canvas of lies. Thomasin of Zirclaria, by contrast, justified romances and recommended Hartmann's protagonists Erec and Enide as models of behavior for young people in his didactic poem "The Foreign Guest" (ca. 1215; *The Foreigner from Italy*). But whereas Thomasin wrote exclusively for an aristocratic audience, Hugo's aim was much broader. German authors found favor in Hugo's eyes when they ridiculed the faults of powerful men, as Walther von der Vogelweide or the mastersinger known as "the Marner" did in their aphorisms. Hugo especially liked to quote from "Modesty" (ca. 1230; *Lebensweisheit* [*Life Wisdom*]), which Freidank composed in aphorisms resembling proverbs.

Hugo's vision of society, like his canon of Latin literature, reveals clear conservative tendencies. Even though he lived in an urban milieu, he despised many of the changes connected with the rise of towns in the 13th century, such as increased social mobility, long-distance trade, a monetary economy, and the development of specialized fields of knowledge at universities. After the Bible, which he regarded as the source of all wisdom, his favorite authors, whom he quotes frequently, were Saint Augustine, Pope Gregory the Great, and Saint Bernard of Clairvaux. The dialectics of scholasticism left no direct traces in his work. Tournaments and academic disputations, the fashions of his day, he regarded as equally foolish activities. It is no accident, however, that *Der Renner* should stand at the end of a century of *summas* and *specula,* as encyclopedias were then called. Thomas Aquinas (1225–1274) had summed up all the theological knowledge of his time in question-and-answer form; in about 1257, Vincent of Beauvais had prepared a reference work in Latin for the clergy, summarizing all available information about nature, the sciences, and history; and Dante's teacher Brunetto Latini had produced his *Tresor* (ca. 1266), the first lay encyclopedia in French. Even though Hugo did not follow the scholastics' meticulous organizing methods in *Der Renner,* his aim was the same kind of inclusiveness in the area of lay education.

Hugo follows his discussion of the deadly sins with an excursus summarizing the order of creation with respect to nature, particularly the characteristics of animals, based on Thomas of Cantimpré's *De naturis rerum* (1228–1244; *On the Nature of Things*). The final section of the poem points the way toward blessedness via confession, repentance, penance, and good works. Hugo regarded the moral decline he perceived all around him as evidence that the coming of the Antichrist and the end of time were near. Like many of his contemporaries, Hugo believed he was living in a late time. His entire work is pervaded by praise of the past and laments about the chaos of the present. Confusion *(werre)* and the world *(werlt)* were for him inseparably connected, even related concepts. The labyrinthine structure of *Der Renner* mirrors this disorderly world through digressions, omissions, anticipations, and cross-references.

Hugo often makes the transition from one section or excursus to another with the words, "Jetzt müssen wir aber weiter rennen / und unseren Herrn besser erkennen" (But now we must go on running / and come to know better our Lord). From this couplet, Michael de Leone (d. 1355), prothonotary of the archdiocese of Würzburg and canon of the Neumünster Church, or Cathedral, of Saint Kilian, created the title for Hugo's poem in the hope that the book would "run through the whole country." The learned jurist de Leone not only included *Der Renner* in his "house book," a compendium of useful texts with a connection to the region of Franconia, he also wrote a detailed table of contents that made it easier to find particular passages. Roughly half of the sixty-four extant manuscripts of *Der Renner* follow Michael de Leone's version. The number of surviving copies is particularly large for a medieval text in German; this and the copious cycles of illustrations, found in thirteen manuscripts from the 15th century, indicate that Hugo von Trimberg was in tune with the pulse of the times and found an attentive audience, especially in the cities. In many of the surviving manuscripts, readers' comments are found in the margins and noteworthy passages are underlined, showing that they were read with great care. Many also contain condensed or augmented versions of the text. In the medieval period, new elements could be added to the allegorical framework, as Hugo himself did when he reworked a later version of his poem, or some stories it contained could be omitted. Readers did not necessarily have to read *Der Renner* from the first verse to the last, but were free to choose from among different episodes, aphorisms, or stories as they pleased, just as its author plundered Latin collections in order to enrich his text. Reading and writing were closely related; excerpting and compiling belonged together; the boundaries between author, adapter, and copyist were fluid. Hugo notes that he had collected two hundred books, an impressive library in the 13th century for a private person of no great means. Knowing that few people could afford such a collection, he tried to offer his readers its quintessence in a single volume.

The success of *Der Renner* was probably what led to its later appearance in print as "a fine and useful book" (Frankfurt 1549). Hugo's moral lessons were still appreciated at the time of the Enlightenment. In 1779, Gotthold Ephraim Lessing studied various manuscripts containing medieval animal fables. He came to appreciate the clarity of Hugo's style and planned an edition of several fables along with some passages of his literary criticism. As Lessing was unable to carry out his plan, Johann Gottfried Herder took it up and included some of the fables in his *Zerstreute Blätter (Scattered Leaves)*, asserting that the German nation had a duty to recall the "old moral tales and fables of its forefathers." Ironically, interest in *Der Renner* waned in the early 19th century, just as the Romantics were discovering their fascination with medieval literature and the new discipline of German studies was being established at universities. The *Nibelungenlied,* which acquired the status of a national epic, the poetry of the minnesingers, and the courtly romances matched the Romantics' expectations of orderly literary composition better than Hugo's discursive allegory. By then even Goethe had gone on record against allegorical literature, objecting that it always subordinated the particular to the general. As literature was striving to become an autonomous discipline, it dispensed with explicit moral instruction. The success of Romanticism had the consequence that *Der Renner* was from then on known only to specialists. Yet, it had been precisely Hugo's fondness for compilation, digression, and aphoristic platitudes that gained him such extraordinary popularity in late medieval times.

See also 1189, 1203 (November 12), 1767, 1784

Bibliography: Hugo von Trimberg, *Lateinische Werke,* I: *Das Solsequium,* ed. Erich Seeman (Munich, Callwey, 1914). ———, *Der Renner,* ed. Gustav Ehrismann (Tübingen, 1908); rev. ed., afterword by Günther Schweikle (Berlin: de Gruyter, 1970). Inés de la Cuadra, *Der "Renner" Hugos von Trimberg: Allegorische Denkformen und literarische Traditionen* (Hildesheim: Olms-Weidmann, 1999). Rudolf Weigand, "Textgenetische Edition: Zur Neuausgabe des 'Renner' Hugos von Trimberg," in *Editionsberichte zur mittelalterlichen deutschen Literatur,* ed. Anton Schwob (Göppingen: Kümmerle, 1994).

Max Grosse
Translated by Deborah Lucas Schneider

♌ 1329, March 27

Pope John XXII condemns portions of Meister Eckhart's work as heretical

Mysticism and Scholastic Theology

Few dates in the life and work of the Rhineland mystic Meister Eckhart are more certain than March 27, 1329. On this date, a papal Bull condemned seventeen of the mystic's statements as heretical and eleven as "suspect of heresy."

Although Eckhart did not live to see the Bull, its content would have come as no surprise to him. Eckhart had already defended the propositions rejected in the Bull, as well as numerous others, during the initial stages of his trial in Cologne. What motivated the proceedings against Eckhart has long been a subject of controversy. Internecine disputes within Eckhart's Dominican order as well as the rivalry between Dominicans and Franciscans might have led to the initial denunciation against him in 1325. His own involvement with the Beguines, a movement of lay sisters presumed heretical, might also have raised suspicions.

Among the propositions Eckhart was called to defend was his notion of the birth of the Word in the soul, which is believed to derive from Beguine spirituality. Whether this idea was inspired by the Beguines or by another source was not discussed at Eckhart's trial. His inquisitors objected mainly to his formulating this idea in his vernacular sermons and treatises, which reached a wider lay public. Eckhart was among the first churchmen to be tried for statements made in Latin *and* in the vernacular. The importance of this detail is borne out by a letter the pope attached to his Bull, in which he recommended that Eckhart's teachings should not be disseminated to a lay public. Although scholars have focused primarily on Eckhart's Latin writings, it is in the vernacular works that he makes his boldest assertions—assertions regarding the detachment of God as well as the detachment necessary for man to achieve oneness with God. Eckhart's accusers perceived in these claims an attack on the primacy of the Trinity; but these claims also earned him his modern reputation as the precursor of negative theology.

Eckhart was born about 1260 in Tambach in Thuringia and received his schooling at a Dominican monastery in Erfurt. In the 13th century, the Dominicans enjoyed enormous intellectual growth and fame. Thomas Aquinas, a member of the order, was at work on the *Summa Theologica,* which was to encompass the sum total of all learning. Among notable Dominicans in the German-speaking world (then called the Province of Teutonia) were Albertus Magnus and Dietrich von Freiberg. Eckhart met Albertus Magnus in all likelihood in Cologne while completing his general studies there. He then went on to study theology at the University of Paris, where he earned the degree of Master in 1302. From 1294 to 1298, he served as prior of Erfurt and vicar of Thuringia, a post previously held by Dietrich von Freiburg. The oldest known text we have from Eckhart, *The Discourses of Instruction,* dates from this period. These discourses on monastic life were meant for the novices in Eckhart's care as prior of Erfurt.

In the years that followed, Eckhart held posts in Paris, Saxony, Alsace, and Bohemia, a fact that is all the more astonishing given the arduousness of medieval travel. In 1303, he became a teacher of theology at the University of Paris. Later that year he was appointed Provincial of Saxony, where he remained until being named vicar general of Bohemia in 1307. In 1311, Eckhart returned to Paris, after the general chapter of the Dominicans refused his nomination to the post of Provincial of Teutonia. This refusal presaged Eckhart's later difficulties with the Church. From 1314 on, he was responsible for the convents of his order in Alsace and parts of Switzerland. It was in this period that Eckhart encountered the vibrant spiritual life of the Beguines. He then returned to Cologne, where he was called before the Inquisition in 1326. Eckhart died sometime in 1328, while awaiting a call for a hearing with the pope in Avignon.

Nowhere is Eckhart's thought more negative than in its treatment of the oneness of God. To distinguish God from the rest of creation, Eckhart resorts to such formulas as "God is not being or goodness" (DW 1.148, Walshe 2.151); "God is a being above being *(ein vber swebende wesen)* and a nothingness above being *(ein vber wesende nitheit)*" (DW 3.442); or "God works beyond being . . . he works in non-being" (DW 1.145, Walshe 2.150). In each of these statements, Eckhart seems to deny God a particular predicate, be it the predicate of being or of goodness or, finally, a manifest place of operation. But what is at stake in these denials is not a determination of God; rather, it is a determination of the categories in which God can be thought. Whatever can be said of creatures cannot be said of God, since creatures do not originate in themselves. They originate in God. Because they owe their entire being to something they are not, they are burdened by a deficiency, or what Eckhart calls in one sermon a "not": "In so far as a *not* adheres to you, to that extent you are imperfect" (DW 1.89–90, Walshe 1.117).

This "not" is the negation "creatures bear within themselves" insofar as they are not the source of the being they possess. Consequently, they can never be more than any one thing. Their nothingness apart from God limits them to this or that mode of being. God, by contrast, exists in all things as the one who cannot be divided, however differentiated creation may be. To this extent, he constitutes a "negation of negation." God is a negation of the nothingness of creatures in and of themselves. As such, he transcends the multitude of beings that he creates. But he also, and perhaps more important, transcends all words and concepts. Words, like creatures, are multiple in nature, for they, too, are created out of nothing. Consequently, the one means for expressing God is to differentiate him from the plurality of words and concepts referring to finite things.

To the extent that creatures are nothing in and of themselves, they represent the one thing that is other than God in the universe. In the sermon "Unus Deus," Eckhart remarks, "Outside of God there is nothing but—nothing" (DW 1.358, Walshe 2.337). Creatures, inasmuch as they come to be within God, generate a rift in him, dividing God from himself by emerging out of nothing in his very midst. To overcome this division, creatures must detach from their nothingness apart from God, which is to say from their creaturely existence. Then, and only then, do they reattach God to himself in his fullness and oneness as the sole being or substance. God not only transcends his creation, he also is immanent in it as its ground or foundation.

Among the most controversial ideas Eckhart had to defend at his trial was that of the "something in the soul" which is identical with God. This "something in the soul" is neither created nor creatable and, to this extent, differs from all created phenomena. For everything that exists is created by God, with the exception of God himself, who has no creator or cause. Insofar as this something is uncreated and uncreatable, it is one with God. Nothing determines it or, in other words, it has no external cause.

During the proceedings at Cologne, Eckhart retracted this claim on the grounds that if God were present in the soul in his uncreatability, his purity would be violated. The notion of "something in the soul," nonetheless, is fundamental to Eckhart's mysticism and ontotheology, since it is this precept that ensures the creatures' ability to restore God to his original unity. They do so by detaching themselves as beings who repeatedly seek in others what they lack in themselves. In the treatise "On Detachment," Eckhart emphasizes that detachment has no aim, in contrast to all other works, which are merely means to an end: Since detachment does not seek anything apart from itself, it is able to attain unity, that is, negate division. Detachment lets being be, apart from all predicates; that is, it lets the very Being that grounds all creation surface in its original, indivisible state.

In himself, God remains unknown to himself, since such knowledge would divide him from himself. Specifically, it would divide him into a subject and object, each of which would be like the other, yet separate. Instead of denying God the possibility of knowledge, Eckhart elevates it in him; in the act of knowledge, God is divided into the persons of the Trinity. The vehicle for God's knowledge is his son inasmuch as he is also the Word: "He is a Word of the Father. In this same Word, the Father speaks himself, all the divine nature and all that God is, just as He knows it" (DW 1.15–16, Walshe 1.59). God expresses himself in his son, *as he knows himself*, which is not himself in his entirety, but rather as he recognizes himself at any moment. To this extent, his knowledge is subject to time. He pronounces what he knows of himself at any moment or instance.

For this reason, Eckhart insists that God does not beget his son once, but perpetually in the soul of the believer, who detaches from everything. In this continual birth, Eckhart is able to resolve the disparity between God's finite (or temporal) knowledge and his infinite (or atemporal) being. God's knowledge is as inexhaustible as his being is infinite, as long as he continues to beget his son in the soul of the believer. In the sermon "Ave, gratia plena," Eckhart interprets the opening verse of the Gospel of John as a statement about a beginning that occurs again and again in each individual believer. We are each the Word of God insofar as God draws us from himself as the vehicle through which he reveals or expresses himself. At the same time, we are more than the Word, since we continue to dwell in God, even as he pronounces or begets us.

The believer is at once born and unborn, as Eckhart often says, since he is not only a testament to his father, but also an integral part of him. In the father, the work of begetting the son continues without cease in what Eckhart often describes as a reciprocal process: "In the same moment that He bears his only-begotten Son into me, I bear him back into the Father" (DW 1.383, Walshe

2.64). The father begets the son, who begets the son in him, thereby ensuring that whatever issues from the father is also returned to him.

By returning the son to the father, the son becomes a father as well, as Eckhart indicates in another passage of this same sermon: "[The Father] has been ever begetting me, his only begotten son, in the very image of his eternal Fatherhood that I may be a father and beget him of whom I am eternally begotten" (DW 1.382–383, Walshe 2.64). What Eckhart separates into two moments here is, in fact, one: the father begets the son in the believer, as the believer begets the son in him, since the two are identical, save for their grammatical positions. Grammatically, there must be a begetting father and a begotten son, who can exchange positions, but never be in the same position at the same moment. Grammar necessitates that there be a Trinity, a Father (or subject) and a Son (or predicate) united in the copula that is the Holy Spirit. What subtends the Trinity is nonetheless the One, what Eckhart calls in his perhaps most negative moment, "A non-God, a non-spirit, a non-person, a non-image" (DW 2.448, Walshe 2.335).

See also 1265, 1600, 1929 (Autumn)

Bibliography: Amy M. Hollywood, *The Soul as Virgin Wife: Mechthild of Magdeburg, Marguerite Porete, and Meister Eckhart* (Notre Dame, Ind.: University of Notre Dame Press, 1995). Josef Koch and Josef Quint, eds., *Meister Eckhart: Die deutschen und lateinischen Werke* (Stuttgart: W. Kohlhammer, 1936). Niklaus Largier, ed., *Meister Eckhart: Werke*, 2 vols.; texts constituted and trans. by Josef Quint (Frankfurt am Main: Deutscher Klassiker Verlag, 1993). M. O'C. Walshe, *Meister Eckhart: Sermons and Treatises*, 3 vols. (Shaftesbury, Dorset: Element, 1979).

Rochelle Tobias

𝒬 1346

Johannes Tauler preaches to Dominican nuns on detachment, poverty of spirit, and mystical union

Acknowledging the Divine

In a sermon about a short passage from the Gospel of Luke (19:5, "In domo tua oportet me manere," "I must abide in thy house"; *Sermon* 49, ed. Vetter, 377–380), Johannes Tauler mentions the wisdom of a pagan king who summarized the mystical vision with the following words: "God is a darkness in the soul, beyond all light, and he is known only to the mind which does not know by itself" (378). With this quotation, the sermon—delivered in 1346, on the day of the church festival at the monastery of St. Gertrude in Cologne—brings the traditional Christian concept of mystical union of soul and God together with the pagan, neo-Platonic idea of the soul's ascent toward divine peace and felicity.

Despite its scholarly philosophical and theological background, the sermon to the nuns of St. Gertrude is not merely a didactic discourse about salvation, mystical unity, and eternal beatitude. Rather, the listening nun—or reader of the sermon—is to be captivated by a subtle rhetorical structure that is shaped to lead toward acknowledgment of the divine "darkness" within herself. Tauler's rhetorical strategy of an allegorical reading and interpretation of a passage from the Gospel exemplifies his conception of spiritual transformation. Through an allegorical reading of the texts, he shows that there is no single, finite meaning to the Gospel and that every meaning, as soon as it is named and grasped, has to be understood as another in an infinite series of allegorical images incapable of naming the divine darkness. Tauler thus highlights not only the main precepts of the German mystical tradition—the convergence of the temporal and the eternal in the presence of God deep inside the soul—but also the art of preaching as it was then developing. Preaching, in this context, is thus—prefiguring from afar the *rhetorica sacra* of post-Tridentine culture—an engagement of the listening soul, guiding human understanding toward acknowledgment of God's presence.

Lâzen (to let go) and *gelâzenheit* (detachment), key terms in Meister Eckhart's sermons of the early 14th century and in Henry Suso's defense of Eckhart's thought in his *Büchlein der Wahrheit* (1328–1330; *Booklet of Truth*), are reinterpreted in this late sermon of Johannes Tauler in a specific way and for a specific audience, the nuns of St. Gertrude. However, he did not only preach to nuns and Beguines in his lifetime. His teaching was not restricted to this level of pastoral care. During his periods of activity in Strasbourg, Basel, and Cologne in the second quarter of the 14th century, he most likely spoke in more open spaces as well—to monks, to nuns, and to lay people—offering a reading of the scriptures inspired primarily by the intellectual traditions of the Dominican school of Cologne, the mystical movements along the Rhine, and early Christian asceticism. It was in this context that the long history of reception and veneration of Tauler had its beginning. It started with the movement of the *Gottesfreunde* (friends of God) and the ex-banker Rulman Merswin in Basel, who considered the Dominican father their eminent teacher, and it ended only in the 19th century. Martin Luther and Saint John of the Cross in the 16th century and Pietist circles in the 17th and 18th centuries were among the most devoted readers of Tauler's sermons.

In the sermon to the nuns of St. Gertrude, Tauler mentions and discusses the key elements of his teaching: spiritual renewal; the relation between external deeds and spiritual perfection; the ascent of the soul and the return into the "darkness" of the divine "bottom of the soul"; the divinization of man; and the "foolishness" of the ascetic turn in the eyes of the world. Tauler takes the day and the yearly ritual of the church festival as the rhetorical starting point of his discourse and goes on to discuss the value of religious symbols (the festival itself), of signs, deeds, and rituals of piety, and their significance for salvation and the renewal of the soul.

In a manner reminiscent of Meister Eckhart's rigorous criticism, Tauler undermines the value of these external elements and emphasizes a more spiritual focus on the radical interiority of the encounter between man and God. In one remarkable passage, he points out that external signs of religious piety and good deeds do have a specific function as background for "preparation," "calling," "remembrance," and "seduction" in the life of the soul. Ascetic practices (prayer, fasting, self-castigation), too, have this function, since they prepare the soul for its way. External elements that represent a pious and devoted lifestyle are thus not means toward salvation but parts of a memorial structure that prepares the soul as it becomes immersed in reading the Scriptures.

In another sermon about Luke 5:1 (*Sermon 41*, ed. Vetter, 170–176), Tauler explains the dynamics of this practice of memory, the soul's immersion in Scriptures, and the inscription of the Scriptures within the soul. Through the contemplation or meditation of the Scriptures, the soul not only deciphers a message but also imagines the Scriptures within itself. This involves an active imagination and passionate reenactment of the biblical images and is the first step in the transformation of the life of the soul. The commemorative signs, as they are used in everyday religious life and especially in the lives of the nuns Tauler addresses here, are thus linked to a pedagogy of the soul and to an allegorical reading of the Scriptures. The function of these signs consists not of a literal representation of the meaning of the Scriptures but of an endless, repetitive imaginary inscription of the Scriptures into the soul, into the space of memory, imagination, and passion. At this stage, the life of the soul becomes more and more a living image, an allegory of the Scriptures.

As Tauler points out in a second part of the sermon, this step must be taken and transcended in the course of divinization. Referring to verses from Psalm 103:3 ("qui ponis nubem ascensum tuum, qui ambulas super pennas ventorum," "who maketh the clouds his chariot, who walketh upon the wings of the wind"), the preacher speaks of three levels: preparation of the lower forces of the soul for the good through imitation of Christ (the "wings of the dove"); preparation of the higher forces, namely intellect and love (the "wings of the eagle"); finally "return to the origin" (the "wings of the winds"). This return into the divine darkness or abyss transcends the stage where the soul perceives itself through the allegorical images of Scripture and engages in imaginary imitation. It also transcends discursive reason and any natural way of understanding and loving, since it ends in a unity beyond names and meaning.

In his conception of the return of man and his union with God at the bottom of his soul, Tauler uses expressions inherited from Meister Eckhart (man returns to the state "when he was not yet created," ed. Vetter, 378) and from the traditions of negative and mystical theology, above all from Dionysius the Pseudo-Areopagite, who was especially popular among Dominican theologians in 14th-century Germany. Hence, he refers to this "bottom of the soul," to this "darkness"—paradoxically: light within the light, darkening all the other lights—to this "abyss" where man encounters God and becomes himself *gotfoermig* (divine).

In the sermon's third part, the preacher explains through another allegorical image taken from the Gospel of Luke (19:4)—Zacchaeus climbing a dead fig tree in order to see Christ—the "foolishness" of the desire to "see God" in the eyes of the world. This reference to the figure of the fools of Christ introduces the last part of the sermon and the concept of "true detachment." Here, again, we move from the literal meaning of the Scriptures—Zacchaeus's desire to see God and to be one with him—through an allegorical reading toward a spiritual understanding of the biblical text.

The preacher not only uses Luke's Gospel but also makes reference to visionary illustrations in the *Scivias* of Hildegard von Bingen (1141–1150). As Tauler points out, these illustrations were found on the walls of the monastery of St. Gertrude in Cologne as well. We know from passages in the works of Henry Suso and others that these types of illustrations and images of piety formed an integral part of the meditative practices of medieval monastic spirituality. Here, Hildegard's visionary painting is used for a reading of the Scriptures that explains the meaning of "detachment" and of the "pure poverty of spirit." Tauler shifts from the image of Zacchaeus, who wishes to see God, to the impossibility of seeing God with our worldly eyes, and ultimately to the visionary painting. He insists that vision in a literal sense is not an adequate response to the desire to see God. Rather, the visionary image and the biblical text have the specific character of an allegory that always hides the true, spiritual meaning, ultimately the unity of man and God at the "bottom of the soul."

The illustrations in Hildegard's book and the paintings on the wall are thus identical with the meaning of the words of Christ asking Zacchaeus to come down from the fig tree. In each case "seeing God" is not to be understood literally; rather it is attained by means of images that guide the soul and—in case of the sermon—the listener. These biblical and visionary images affirm the presence of a deeper meaning, but they deny, at the same time, the possibility of grasping the hidden meaning (the *sensus spiritualis* or *mysticus*) in positive terms. In other words, allegorical images teach the finitude of human understanding, and the use of allegorical images is in practice an acknowledgment of this finitude. "Detachment" is another word for this gesture of acknowledgment, since all it means is the gesture of giving up the desire to know and to name the divine. Detachment, Tauler concludes, is the affirmation of this finitude, the "foolishness" in the eyes of the world, and the return to the "house" where the hidden, ineffable sense of the Scriptures and the bottom of the soul converge.

In the concluding passages, Tauler illustrates his interpretation of Scriptures through the visionary paintings of Hildegard of Bingen at the St. Gertrude monastery, and establishes a perspective where the theological concept of union with God, the *theosis* ("divinization") inspired by Dionysius the Areopagite, coincides not only with the philosophical ideas of felicity and freedom, but also with the specific meaning the allegorical reading of the Scriptures had for medieval women mystics. Mechthild of Magdeburg, Hadewijch of Anvers, and Marguerite Porete—to name just a few—had developed their own way of reading Scriptures through infinite allegorization and by rewriting the texts. Tauler most likely knew Mechthild's *Das fliessende Licht der Gottheit* (*The Flowing Light of the Godhead*), as he was familiar with the writings of Hildegard of Bingen and of Mechthild of Hackeborn. His style of preaching was inspired by these traditions and by the ways these women conceived of the exemplary meaning of the scriptural texts, especially the Song of Songs, and of ascetic texts with a paradigmatic value, especially *Lives of the Desert Fathers.*

Since historical research into German mysticism began in the 19th century, Tauler has often been seen as a preacher whose sermons criticize speculative theological and philosophical ambitions. However, a generation younger than Eckhart von Hochheim, Tauler was—together with Henry Suso in the 14th and with Nicolaus of Cusa in the 15th century—one of the very few medieval interpreters of Eckhart's thought. The concepts of "detachment" and of the "birth of God in the soul," as well as aspects of his notions of the "bottom of the soul" and of freedom, should be understood in the light of Eckhart's works.

However, it would be wrong to view Tauler's work only in the context of pastoral care and with respect to Eckhart. His sermons clearly reflect his own genuine philosophical and theological interests and his various intellectual pursuits. He quotes not only from authors of the German Dominican School—Albertus Magnus, Dietrich von Freiberg, and Eckhart von Hochheim—but also from the "pagan masters" Plato, Aristotle, and Proclus. His fascination with Proclus—whom Tauler might have known through Berthold von Moosburg, the author of an *Expositio super Elementationem Theologicam Procli* (ca. 1330–1350; *Commentary on the Elements of Theology by Proclus*)—is visible in a series of late sermons delivered at Cologne (after 1336, possibly in 1346). In his discussion with Berthold, Tauler picks up certain concepts from Proclus that confirm the orientation of his own thought, especially the understanding of the "bottom of the soul" in terms of negative theology and of the unity of man and God as a "quiet, silent, sleeping, divine, unintelligible darkness" (*Sermon* 60d, ed. Vetter, 300) or as a "divine mania" (*Sermon* 64, ed. Vetter, 350). He identifies the neo-Platonic concept of an unintelligible unity that underlies intelligibility, freedom, and felicity with the Christian promise that the "kingdom of God is within you" (Luke 17:21; cf. *Sermon* 60d, ed. Vetter, 301). Thus Tauler proposes a specific response to the question of what it means to conceive of "spiritual philosophy"—to use a term of Henry Suso—and of "Christian wisdom" as an art of living inspired by the ascetic ideals and models of the imitation of Christ and by the pagan philosophers who were rediscovered during the 13th and 14th centuries.

See also 1147, 1265, 1329, 1600

Bibliography: Johannes Tauler, *Sermons,* ed. Maria Shrady (New York: Paulist Press, 1985); *Die Predigten Taulers: Aus der Engelberger und der Freiburger Handschrift sowie aus Schmidts Abschriften der ehemaligen Strassburger Handschriften,* ed. Ferdinand Vetter (Berlin: Weidmann, 1910). Richard Kieckhefer, "John Tauler," in Paul E. Szarmach, ed., *An Introduction to the Medieval Mystics of Europe* (Albany: State University of New York Press, 1984).

Niklaus Largier

⟁ *1354*

Charles IV meets Petrarch in Mantua on the way to his coronation in Rome

The Emperor and the Poet

On September 26, 1354, Charles IV of Luxembourg, son of John I of Bohemia and nephew of Henry VII, set out from Nuremberg on a journey across the Alps. Eight years earlier he had been crowned Holy Roman Emperor at Reims, with the consent of his former tutor, Pope Clement VI, and had established his court in Prague. Now he was on his way to Rome for a second, more exalted crowning that fired the imagination of Italian proponents of a Roman imperial rebirth. Prominent among them was Petrarch (Francesco Petrarca, 1304–1374), who, as early as in a letter of 1351, had been urging upon Charles a gesture of this kind. If his project of reviving the cultural glories of Augustan Rome was to be complete, the poet laureate needed a princely double. What Virgil was to Augustus Caesar, what Ennius was to the elder Scipio Africanus (according to the fiction of the *Africa*), Petrarch, the modern Ennius and Virgil, would be to a contemporary redeemer-hero. The only uncertainty was the prince's identity. The first monarch he cast in this role was not Charles, but King Robert II of Naples. It was around Robert that Petrarch built his carefully choreographed laureation ceremony in Rome in 1341: the first such ceremony, the poet contended, since the time of Statius. But Robert died, and so Petrarch had little choice but to shift his hopes to another candidate. His choice fell on the Roman tribune Cola di Rienzo, whose 1347 revolution tendered the promise, however momentary and illusory, of a new imperial golden age. When Cola's experiment collapsed, Petrarch's attention turned to Charles, and with Charles they would remain for the ensuing decades.

The 1351 epistle was followed by others in 1352 and 1353 (the last a reaction to an apologetic reply to Petrarch's first letter penned by Charles but, as fate would have it, polished by Cola di Rienzo, imprisoned in Prague in the wake of his flight from Rome). Their message remained the same: "Rome calls out for her bridegroom, Italy calls out for her deliverer and longs to feel your feet treading upon her soil" (*Familiar Letters* X, 1, 27). Historical examples were marshaled to argue for dispatch: Africanus, Nasica, Claudius Nero, and Julius Caesar. Italy was feminized; Charles was masculinized, called upon to live up to the virile imperial ideal. Petrarch saw Italy dismembered, her individual body parts fought over by Guelphs (proponents of the pope), Ghibellines (proponents of the emperor), and regional tyrants like Petrarch's Milanese patrons, the Visconti. The solution was the Papacy's recommitment to its sacred mission and the resurrection of imperial institutions that would be accomplished by the descent of a political messiah from the North. All this underscores a basic fact of European history: from the Middle Ages onward (even for Romans) the road to imperial Rome passed through Germany. Italy and Germany were wedded—literally wedded, because of the explicit gendering of the two nations—in an imperial imaginary that extended from the High Middle Ages to the Axis of World War II.

The fall of 1354 was unusually harsh and Charles did not reach Mantua until early November. There he was greeted by another epistle in which Petrarch jumped the gun, proclaiming him "now king not just of Bohemia but of the world, now Roman emperor and now truly Caesar" (*Familiar Letters* XIX, 1, 2). An invitation from Charles was soon forthcoming and Petrarch set out from Milan for Mantua along "a road that was less earth-like than like diamond and steel" (*Familiar Letters* XIX, 3, 9). On December 15, poet and emperor stood face to face. The fateful encounter lasted nearly a week, ending in an amicable deadlock. Petrarch provides a full account in a letter to Lello di Piero Stefano, a Roman noble of the Colonna circle. Charles's welcome was "more than cesarean" (*Familiar Letters* XIX, 3, 11), after which their conversations and confabulations (*colloquendo et confabulando; Familiar Letters* XIX, 3, 11) occupied entire days, from dawn to dusk. Less a meeting of minds than a polite debate on the relative merits of the active and the contemplative life, the dialogue hinged on the topics of imitation and fame.

Charles's aims were at once practical and idealistic. He wished to inform himself about Petrarch's literary career, projects, and ambitions, and to enroll the illustrious man of letters in his circle of courtiers. He also wished to secure the Tuscan's company for help in his dealings with various Tuscan city states and so that he might view the Eternal City of Rome through the eyes of one of her greatest students and apologists. Last but not least, he dreamt that his actions and life might be immortalized much as Petrarch (following the model of Suetonius) immortalized the greatest men of ancient times in his *De viris illustribus*. Charles requested a copy of the latter work, to which Petrarch (by his own account) replied that the work remained incomplete, adding, "In your case, Caesar, your worthiness for this literary gift and title will depend not upon the effulgence of your name nor upon a mere crown; rather, your actual deeds and valorous spirit will raise you to the ranks of illustrious men by living a life that posterity will read about just as you read about the ancients" (*Familiar Letters* XIX, 3, 13). Charles's approbation was supposedly registered with a twinkle in the eye.

As the crisp rejoinder indicates, Petrarch's intent in coming to Mantua was less to curry favor—he was not lacking in powerful patrons—than to recruit Charles for his antiquarian cultural-political project. Greatness was cast in an eternally fixed political and aesthetic mold, so the challenge for Petrarch was to provide his chosen prince with proper models and with an understanding of how to translate images of past actions into living historical realities, which is to say, of how to practice the Humanist art of *imitatio*. The lesson was administered through the gift of a series of late imperial gold and silver coins, along with verbal summaries of the lives of the emperors depicted upon them—so lifelike in the case of Augustus Caesar, or so Petrarch claims, that the image seemed to be breathing (*Familiar Letters* XIX, 3, 14).

With the vividly embossed images and no less vividly presented exemplary biographies came exhortations to action: "O Caesar, behold your predecessors, behold those whom you must strive to imitate and to revere, those according to whose principles and in whose image you must mold yourself" (*Familiar Letters* XIX, 3, 15). Only by following the greatest examples from antiquity will Charles find a place in Petrarch's pantheon of illustrious men; only by bringing them back to life will he fulfill the Humanist dream of giving rise to a living, modern antiquity. For ten centuries, the coins of the realm had been corrupted by dross. The imprint of ancient heroism had become blurred. The time had come to purify them, to remint them, and to stamp them anew.

Charles welcomed the gifts and erudite lessons but shifted the topic of conversation to the poet's life and future plans. Under the veil of curiosity lurked a provocation to debate the relative merits of the solitary life versus the life of action, which is also to say, of bookish versus practical wisdom. Petrarch rose to the bait, warning his interlocutor that there was no subject on which he had meditated at greater length and alluding to his recent treatise *De vita solitaria* in which definitive proof was offered that the former "transcends the glory and magnificence of your empire" (*Familiar Letters* XIX, 3, 18). Unfazed, the emperor quipped that, if it ever reached him, *De vita solitaria* would be swiftly consigned to the flames; the poet quipped back that he would see to it that Charles never received the book. The banter was playful, but at issue was a serious matter: the question of the limits of Petrarch's antiquarianism and cult of Augustus, and of how such a stance might be properly interpreted in contemporary terms.

The impasse in no way hindered subsequent contacts. Bard and emperor met again in early January 1355, when the latter entered Milan and was crowned monarch of Italy in the Church of Saint Ambrose. Petrarch even escorted the royal entourage on its way out of the Lombard capital, all the while rejecting repeated invitations to continue on with Charles to Rome. Letters of recommendation for Lello di Piero Stefano and of praise for the Humanist chancellor Johannes von Neumarkt greeted the travelers as they threaded the Tuscan hills. Discordant notes were sounded only in the wake of the coronation in Rome on April 5, when, as had been secretly agreed upon in advance with Pope Innocent VI (unbeknownst to Petrarch), the emperor beat a hasty retreat across the Alps. Deeply vexed, the poet reacted bitterly: "What a noble deed you have wrought, great Caesar, by means of your long-delayed entry into Italy and your hasty withdrawal! You bear away with you crowns of iron and gold and the barren name of empire. They call you the Roman emperor but you are, in fact, king of Bohemia and little more" (*Familiar Letters* XIX, 12, 6). In the same letter, the kingdom in question was dismissed as a "barbaric realm" (XIX, 12, 2) and the departure labeled shameful *(infami)* and inglorious *(inglorio)*.

However, the kiss-off proved temporary. For all his antiquarian idealism, Petrarch was also a canny realist. A year and a half later he found himself at

Charles's court in Prague, representing the Visconti family interests. He renewed his bonds with the emperor, solidified his friendship with Johannes von Neumarkt, earned the esteem of both Prague's Archbishop Ernest and the young Empress Anna (Anna von Schweidnitz), and emerged with the titles of Count Palatine and Councilor after little more than a month. Subsequent years saw exchanges of letters on literary matters. In 1361 Charles tendered a formal invitation to join his court, which Petrarch rejected, but seized as an occasion to renew their dialogues. "You summon me to Germany and I summon you to Italy," he wrote in one of numerous hortatory epistles; "your authority is greater than mine, my cause is greater than yours" (*Familiar Letters* XXIII, 8, 5).

Political circumstances shifted in the ensuing years in favor of Petrarch's cause, but without the dreamed-of world-historical consequences. Threatened by the ascendancy of various regional *condottieri* and by the growing power of the Visconti, the Papacy felt cornered, and determined that it had no alternative but to link arms with its imperial rival. With papal consent, Charles traveled once more across the Alps in the spring of 1368, this time—precisely as Petrarch had urged—flanked by his armies. His mission was the one long prescribed by the author of the *Africa:* to bring peace to Italy by reestablishing the empire's sway. Yet there was an unexpected twist. Charles's principal target was not the corrupt Papal Curia but Petrarch's Milanese patron Galeazzo Visconti. The bard was caught in a bind, a bind reinforced by Galeazzo's demand, acquiesced to by Petrarch, that he attempt to mediate the dispute. The poet's embassy came to naught, the imperial forces were humiliated at Ostiglia, and an entente was established via alternative channels. Petrarch ignored Charles's ceremonial entry into Rome in the fall of 1368, ignored his peacemaking efforts with Pope Urban V, and only reluctantly, and after many demurrals, paid any heed to Urban's invitations to relocate to the reborn Eternal City. His letters to Charles cease from this time forward or at least all traces of them were edited out of the meticulously crafted *Familiar Letters.*

If Petrarch's flirtation with the Bohemian court ended in embarrassed silence, the embarrassment was his alone. On the German side, there may have been resistance to his policy injunctions, but not to the models of eloquence, patronage, and cultural-historical retrieval that he embodied and espoused. Charles's reluctance to reenact the role of Scipio Africanus or Augustus on the 14th-century political stage was exceeded by his eagerness to cast Prague in a humanist mold. His was a cosmopolitan court whose refinement set the model for subsequent German courts: a court that served as the focal point for a newly founded university (1348); that favored the presence in the Bohemian capital of artists and artisans, such as the Parler brothers, who were instrumental in the construction of a magnificent cathedral; that commissioned a distinguished Italian traveler, John of Marignola, to compose a history of Charles's reign as a complement to the monarch's autobiography; and a court whose chancellor, Johannes von Neumarkt, promoted reforms to both Latin and vernacular usage that shaped the practices of German chanceries for centuries to come. Johannes was also an avid Petrarchan, extensively acquainted with the poet's opus, including the *De viris illustribus,* the *Bucolicum carmen (Bucolic Song),* and the *Remedia utriusque fortunae (Remedies for Fortune Fair and Foul),* copies of which he solicited personally from the author. He dutifully inscribed Petrarch's Latin epistles into the two formularies he redacted for the imperial chancery as models for all future correspondence, inspired by the desire, as his mentor put it, "to transform our predecessors' effeminate and enervated style . . . by restoring its manly and wholesome qualities" (*Familiar Letters* XXIII, 14, 2). And he initiated a similar castigation and reform of the German vernacular whose first fruits may be found in Johannes von Tepl's *Ackermann aus Böhmen (The Plowman from Bohemia).*

It was the nature and the implications of the last of these reforms that ignited a firestorm among early 20th-century German historiographers and linguists. There was no denying the scope of Petrarch's influence in Prague from where it radiated outward by the end of the 14th century. Manuscripts of his writings soon abounded in German libraries, vernacular translations began to appear in the course of the 15th century, and the first non-Italian biography of the poet was penned before the end of the century by a German, Rudolph Agricola. The more serious bone of contention was the degree to which Petrarch influenced the rise of Early New High German: the literary language Luther used for his vernacular translation of the Bible, universally considered the origin of modern standard German. At issue was the ineradicable Germanness of Lutheran and post-Lutheran linguistic and literary traditions, championed by the nationalist and racialist schools of historiography, for whom the hypothesis of Italian influence was anathema. Their archenemy was one of the leading Petrarch scholars of the time, Konrad Burdach. Burdach's studies began with Cola di Rienzo, but subsequently turned to Petrarch. He not only documented meticulously the poet's importance to developments in Germany, but also suggested a seminal role that the Prague-based Petrarch cult might have played in the genesis of Early New High German. Burdach was relentless in his championing of positivistic *Geschichtsforschung* (historical research) against the sort of romanticized or subjectivist *Geschichtsschreibung* (historical narrative) practiced by the likes of Ernst Kantorowicz. He debunked both the medievalists who denied any relevance of the Italian Renaissance in German cultural history and the likes of Ludwig Woltmann, the author of *Die Germanen und die Renaissance in Italien (Germans and the Italian Renaissance),* who claimed that Petrarch was really a German and that the Italian Renaissance was a Germanic phenomenon, the delayed result of the barbarian invasions of northern Italy. However real the importance of German noble families may have been, Burdach underscored the Renaissance's essential Italianness: "Humanism and the Renaissance derived their true vital essence from notions of an autochthonous Latin race and of Ancient Rome as the original, deeply rooted Italian civilization, and set out to propagate the unfettered development of the national vigor and distinctive religious, moral, and artistic characteristics of the people to which these attributes belonged" (*Riforma—Rinascimento—Umanesimo,* 118).

See also 1401, 1500 (Dürer)

Bibliography: Francesco Petrarca, *Familiarum rerum libri,* in *Opere,* ed. Mario Martelli (Florence: Sansoni, 1992). ———, *Briefwechsel mit deutschen Zeitgenossen,* ed. Konrad Burdach and Paul Piur (Berlin: Weidmann, 1933). ———, *L'Africa,* ed. Nicola Festa, Edizione Nazionale vol. I (Florence: Sansoni, 1926). Frank L. Borchardt, "Petrarch: The German Connection," in Aldo Scaglione, ed., *Francesco Petrarch, Six Centuries Later,* North Carolina Studies in the Romance Languages and Literatures 3 (Chapel Hill, N.C.: UNC Chapel Hill and Newberry Library, 1975), 418–431.

Jeffrey T. Schnapp

℣ 1382

The Cambridge Codex, the oldest known document of Yiddish literature, is written and later deposited in a *genizah* in Cairo

The Emergence of Yiddish Literature

When Leo Fuks published in 1957 a series of Germanic texts from the late 14th century that were written in Hebrew characters, he caused a stir among scholars both of Yiddish and of Middle High German. The texts were part of a manuscript that is commonly referred to as the Cambridge Codex, after the place where it is kept. Although the codex became more widely known in the second half of the 20th century, it was first discovered in the late 19th century among a large number of documents in the *genizah* of the Ezra Synagogue in Fostat, Cairo (Egypt).

A *genizah* ("treasure hoard") is a place where documents written in Hebrew letters are kept before they are disposed of. By Jewish law any kind of profanation of the name of God is forbidden, including the destruction of the written form of God's name. Therefore, all writing that includes the name of God, and by extension all writing in the Hebrew alphabet, has to be ritually buried in a Jewish cemetery. It became the practice in the Jewish world to reserve a special place in the synagogue as a *genizah* where parchments and papers were collected before burial. In the Ezra Synagogue, the *genizah* was a small storeroom without a door or windows, accessible only through a hole in the wall which was reached with a ladder. Because the room was so inaccessible, texts were never removed for burial and were allowed to accumulate from the time the synagogue was built in the 9th century. Travelers to Cairo in the 18th century reported having seen the room, but not having been able to inspect its contents more closely. It was in the 19th century that some travelers succeeded in obtaining items from the *genizah* which they brought back to Europe. This led the Cambridge scholar Solomon Schechter to try to obtain the entire contents for the University of Cambridge; he managed to buy nearly all of the remaining material, some hundred thousand fragments.

Since 1896, the year when Schechter brought the *genizah* finds to England, the Cambridge Codex has been discovered at least twice. First to recognize the importance of the collection was the French scholar Ernest-Henri Lévy, who transcribed the manuscript into normalized Middle High German and planned to publish a critical edition. Unfortunately, he was murdered by the Nazis and the manuscript of his edition was lost. The second discovery was made by Leo Fuks, Judaica librarian in Amsterdam, who published a series of articles in international journals on the Cambridge Codex, announcing his edition as "the oldest known literary documents of Yiddish literature." In 1957 Fuks's edition was published, and within a decade it was followed by several other editions of texts from the codex as well as a flurry of articles and books. Yiddish scholars hailed the publication of the oldest Yiddish texts, Germanists threw themselves on heretofore unknown Middle High German texts, and a controversy was born. The extreme positions in the debate can be summed up in the following theses: (1) a Germanic text in Hebrew characters has to be defined as Yiddish; (2) the texts are in Middle High German, differing from other Middle High German texts only in the alphabet used; by extension, (3) the texts are mere adaptations, little more than transcriptions of German works in the Hebrew alphabet.

The codex comprises seven texts: four epic poems about biblical figures and topics, *Moshe Rabeynu (Our Teacher Moses), Gan eden (The Garden of Eden), Avrom ovinu (Our Patriarch Abraham),* and *Yosef hatsadik (Joseph the Righteous);* an untitled fable about an old lion; a list of names in the weekly portions of the Torah (Pentateuch) read in the synagogue with a glossary of the stones in the high priest's breastplate; a long fragment of an epic poem from the Middle High German *Kudrun* cycle. This last text, the so-called *Kudrun* fragment, received special attention from scholars of Middle High German literature. As part of a German literary tradition, it fit into German literary history and also added something to it. Also part of the codex is an epic poem, the beginning of which is missing, entitled *Dukus Horant (Duke Horant),* for its principal hero.

Although Cairo's dry climate had been favorable to the conservation of the manuscript, the codex is damaged, pages are missing, and some parts are illegible. Since Fuks did not use the most modern techniques in reading the damaged passages, his edition left room for improvement. Scholars also had different views on what was the proper transcription system to use. Fuks's edition contained photographs of the manuscript, accompanied by a transcription in Hebrew characters, as well as a transliteration and a translation of the text into modern German. Whereas Fuks had automatically assumed the texts to be in Yiddish, others determined that the texts were in Middle High German and, although written in Hebrew characters, not specifically Yiddish. The transliterated text was difficult to decipher, and new editions in transcription (for example, Ganz et al., *Dukus Horant,* 1964) made the texts more easily accessible to Germanists. By choosing other letters or combinations of letters to correspond to the Hebrew characters and by filling in the vowels which were unmarked or marked by characters that could be pronounced in several ways according to the original orthography, the editors made the text look more familiar to those used to reading Middle High German.

Yiddish is a Germanic language based on High German dialects that originally came into being on German language territory. Since it was in contact with German (dialects) at various stages of its development, it is sometimes difficult to demarcate the borders clearly between Yiddish and other Germanic dialects and languages, especially in literary texts. The difficulties of definition are also expressed in the different names given to the language of such texts in Hebrew characters: Old Yiddish, Jewish Middle High German, Judeo-German, Hebrew-German, Germano-Judaic. The development of the Yiddish language has not been researched as thoroughly as that of other European languages, and its historical development is still being charted.

The language we call Yiddish originated in the period between the 9th and the 12th century in the Rhine area. The oldest known sentence in this language—which was found in a festival prayer book written in Worms in 1172, but which was not yet known at the time when the debate over the Cambridge Codex first began—is evidence that Yiddish is basically a Germanic language, but with Hebrew and Aramaic elements as an organic component. Early glosses and translations of biblical texts contain Romance elements as well, many of which survive in the language to this date and are at present under investigation. Whereas the Romance elements were (and are) rarely recognized as such by Yiddish speakers, the Semitic elements were, and this consciousness was reinforced by their use in Hebrew and Aramaic prayers and blessings recited several times a day, their use in religious study, and typographical distinctions. The Hebrew and Aramaic elements are written according to their historical writing system (a consonantal system), whereas all other elements are written more or less phonetically. The Cambridge Codex already adheres to this convention.

The texts in the Cambridge Codex do not contain Hebrew or Aramaic elements, with the exception of a single word and the titles of the biblical epics. This led some Germanists to conclude that all the texts were written in Middle High German and even that this was evidence that Yiddish had not yet begun its development in the 14th century. They did not consider the fact that these were refined literary texts, obviously part of an established tradition modeled on literary German. Literary texts in German of the period are not expected to reflect spoken German. In Yiddish the literary language was probably even further removed from the spoken language: the hybrid character of Yiddish was not considered aesthetic, because it mixes languages. Throughout the history of Yiddish literature, we find texts by authors who avoided the use of Hebrew elements. Hebrew names of persons and places, however, are kept in their Hebrew form. This is also the case in the Cambridge Codex. The paucity of Hebrew elements, therefore, cannot be the determining characteristic of the language.

The most extreme theory was proposed by an American Germanist, James

Marchand, who stated that medieval Yiddish literature was basically Middle High German literature in transcription. Other scholars, most notably the Israeli professor of Yiddish Chone Shmeruk, refuted this convincingly and placed the texts in a Jewish tradition that had borrowed from surrounding German culture.

The content of the Cambridge Codex illustrates the two main influences on Yiddish literature: Hebrew and Western traditions. Cultural contacts between Christians and Jews are illustrated by tales like the fable of the old lion, for example. It imitates a Hebrew fable from *Berechiah ha-Natronai ha-Nakdan* (France, late 12th or early 13th century), which contains elements common to versions of this fable in different European traditions and shows motivic and formal influences (rhymes, versification) from German literature. *Dukus Horant,* however, is most likely a straight adaptation of a German epic. The German text at the basis of *Dukus Horant* is not known, so *Dukus Horant* represents a variant of the German *Kudrun* epic that is lost in any other form. The adapter or transcriber took out some of the Christian references, but not all.

Adaptations and transcriptions of popular German texts are also known in the centuries following, when literary Yiddish was still quite close to literary German and many Ashkenazic Jews lived on German language territory. It is safe to assume that these speakers of Yiddish had no serious problems understanding German texts. Since the attention of Germanists was mainly focused on *Dukus Horant* and since most of them studied the Cambridge Codex in transcription and few were familiar with post-biblical Jewish narrative traditions, it was probably inevitable that someone would come up with the theory that there was nothing Jewish about the texts.

In an article published in 1962, J. Marchand and F. C. Tubach presented an edition of *Yosef Hatsadik* with a discussion of its place in German literature. Their edition identifies the text as written in a Central German dialect and transcribes it accordingly as the putative original would have been written. Although the poem does have a Yiddish (Hebrew) title that uses the common epithet for Joseph, the righteous, they renamed it *Der keusche Joseph (Chaste Joseph)*. By transcribing the text according to the rules of German and replacing its Hebrew title, the editors removed the two most saliently Jewish characteristics of the text. In 1977 Chone Shmeruk refuted Marchand and Tubach's argument for a non-Jewish origin of the poem by pointing out the acrostic embedded in it. Clearly highlighted in the manuscript by lines consisting of fine points leading to the letters that form the acrostic, it consists of Hebrew letters and spells out the author's name (corrupted, but clearly recognizable as such). The acrostic had already been noted by other editors of the text and was hard to miss for anyone who studied the photographs in Fuks's edition. The language and literary form of the poem show clear German influences, but the motifs that form the main content can all be traced to Jewish sources. Like most of pre-modern Yiddish literature, leaving adaptations aside, *Yosef Hatsadik* expresses Jewish traditions and the Jewish way of life, which includes influences from the culture of the non-Jewish neighbors. The adaptations of non-Jewish texts provide samples of the reception of non-Jewish (in this case German) texts by the Yiddish-speaking audience.

The Cambridge Codex has led to fierce debates among scholars of Yiddish and of German, but it has also brought the two disciplines closer together, since the texts it contains are a testimony to medieval Jewish literary activity that combined German and Hebrew traditions.

See also Post 1200

Bibliography: Jerold C. Frakes, *The Politics of Interpretation: Alterity and Ideology in Old Yiddish Studies* (Albany: State University of New York Press, 1989). Leo Fuks, *The Oldest Known Literary Documents of Yiddish Literature (circa 1382),* 2 vols. (Leiden: Brill, 1957). P. F. Ganz, F. Norman, and W. Schwarz, *Dukus Horant* (Tübingen: Max Niemeyer 1964). Chone Shmeruk, "The Hebrew Acrostic in the *Yosef Hatsadik* Poem of the Cambridge Yiddish Codex," *Michigan Germanic Studies* 3 (1977): 67–81. Erika Timm, "Die 'Fabel vom alten Löwen' in jiddistischer und komparatistischer Sicht," *Zeitschrift für deutsche Philologie* 100, Sonderheft Jiddisch (1981): 109–170.

Marion Aptroot

⤳ Circa 1400

Nuremberg becomes a hub of commercial activity and a center of book publishing and collecting

The Culture of the Book

Nuremberg in the 15th century was unrivaled among German cities as a center of literary activity. No other city of the time could lay claim to having produced the first pocket watch or the first globe, or to being the first town outside Italy to own a paper mill. The connection between an innovative book culture and thriving commerce may not be obvious until one realizes that the drive and demand for excellence that marked Nuremberg commerce were also basic to its literary preeminence.

Nuremberg was famous for its armor, its fine weapons of tempered steel, and a variety of handmade artifacts. The stamp "N" on a product guaranteed the quality of its workmanship. In part all this was possible owing to Nuremberg's location at the crossroads of twelve trade routes, which made it a center of international commerce. The routes fed raw material to this city of roughly fifty thousand, a population surpassed only by Cologne and Augsburg at that time. Nuremberg artisans transformed the raw materials into a variety of goods, which were then funneled along the same routes to citizens of European cities and communes eager to pay for "Nürnberger" quality. What worked in trade also served the intellectual life of the city, for along the same routes traveled ideas, manuscripts, new methods of bookmaking, and styles in art to Nuremberg, where they were noted, processed, reproduced, and again disseminated throughout Europe just like other goods and with the same emphasis on quality.

However, the city was not simply a manufacturing and trading center; it was also the de facto capital of the Holy Roman Empire of the German nation in this period. It was in Nuremberg where the emperor stored his treasure, garrisoned the imperial regiments, and was a frequent resident. So it was only natural that government business was conducted at Nuremberg too and that officials traveled to the city from all over the country. Governments, parliaments, and courts all needed legal scholars, historians, scientists, philosophers, entertainers—in short, a population dedicated to the production, consumption, and exchange of ideas, manuscripts, and books. All this goes by way of saying that the culture of the book in the 15th century had long since moved from its monastic venue to the highly competitive marketplace. Nuremberg book printing houses in no way resembled the secluded monastic scriptoria portrayed in Umberto Eco's novel *The Name of the Rose*. By the 15th century, writing of all kinds—manuscripts, correspondence, legal or political or religious texts, how-to books of practical advice, informative calendars, the earliest almanacs, containing single-sheet broadsides of ballads, poems, or political tracts—had long since become a commercial matter, an artisanal and an intellectual métier, very much dependent on a flourishing economy for success. Printing only accelerated this trend, even as the competition between printed and handwritten books intensified.

With the advent of printing in Nuremberg in 1469, the city quickly became a center of the industry in Germany. The printer and book trader Anton Koberger came to dominate the business after 1470, keeping twenty-four presses working, with more than one hundred employees. He established an international book trade, and built warehouses for his stock in Paris, Lyon, Vienna, Ofen, Breslau, Krakow, Venice, and Milan. Nuremberg editions from his presses were famous for their fine quality. They also illustrated the close link between manuscript collecting and publishing. One of Koberger's justly celebrated productions was the 1483 edition of a 9th-century German Bible. He also produced a sumptuous bilingual (German-Latin) edition of Hartmann Schedel's *Weltchronik (History of the World)* with 1,809 woodcut illustrations, as well as an Apocalypse with illustrations by Albrecht Dürer. Koberger's industrial approach to book production drove smaller printers, who were unable to compete, out of the city, and in some cases out of Germany altogether.

The central role Nuremberg played in irrevocably changing the book culture illustrates both the nature of that culture in the 15th century and how closely intertwined manuscripts and printed books were during this period. Rather than being regarded as a technological breakthrough, a revolution, the invention of movable type was taken in stride, as simply a more efficient way of producing books. It meant that a greater number of more or less identical copies of a book could be produced in a short time and at considerably less expense than was the case for the traditional hand-copied codex. Of course, the printed book tried to emulate the manuscript, as cheaper goods usually try to copy more elegant and expensive products. Manuscript books, or at least a segment of that market, in turn, became more elaborate and decorative, so as to be clearly distinguishable from cheaper emulators.

Initially, movable-type printing affected primarily the business side of book production, by creating competition between traditional stationers who produced fancy manuscript books, and printer-stationers, who sought to manufacture cheaper versions. Printing had little apparent effect at first on the actual product. No new literary genres were created in the 15th century as a result of its advent. At best, one might point to the broadside or single-sheet publication containing, in addition to woodcut illustrations, a poem, a ballad, a sentiment, or political or religious expressions of some kind. These mass-produced, inexpensive publications—an early manifestation of popular culture—offered printers a quick return for relatively little investment of either time or labor (unlike more ambitious printing projects). While they did not represent a new kind of literature, they did exploit the intimate link between book production and commerce, thereby revealing print technology's potential for creating what today is called a mass market.

Nuremberg's rapid rise to preeminence as a printing capital—similar to Lyon in France—highlights the fact that long before the turn of the 15th century, long before printing, Nuremberg was an important center of intellectual activity and consequently for production and collection of manuscripts. Literary activity in Nuremberg flourished during the period immediately preceding the introduction of printing in large part because the city had become an important center for Humanist studies in Germany, but also thanks to its political and commercial importance.

Prominent families could afford to send their sons to study in Italy, where they copied and had copied classical and vernacular works of all kinds—literary, historical, philosophical, and scientific. Nuremberg's Humanists were prolific collectors of manuscripts from the mid-14th century on. Their libraries contained intellectual works of high culture as well as more personal items such as university notes, commentaries by the Humanists themselves on the works they collected and studied, and even, in the case of Hartmann Schedel—author of the *Weltchronik* mentioned above—domestic writings, such as recipes.

Hartmann Schedel and his much older cousin Hermann typify Nuremberg Humanist collectors. They traveled extensively in Italy, where they made countless copies of works they needed or wanted. Most of the manuscripts dating from this period were made, in the manner of the Schedels' collection, by scholars, in connection with their own studies. Illustrative of the fact that in the later 15th-century readers used manuscripts and incunabula interchangeably for their collections and research, Schedel's library—one of the largest private collections in Europe with more than six hundred volumes at the time of his death in 1514—contained printed books and codices side by side. Moreover, his library catalogue rarely distinguishes between volumes as *liber scriptus* (manuscript) or *liber impressus* (printed). However, the catalogue does make a distinction between parchment *(in pergameno)* and paper, since works written on vellum had a greater monetary value than those written or printed on paper. Most interesting in Schedel's library, from the standpoint of the print-manuscript dichotomy, were the volumes that were so much a mixture of handwriting and printing as to make it impossible to categorize them.

The kinds of manuscripts and books to be found in Nuremberg libraries reflect a great variety of interests in ancient and modern history, literature, philosophy, theology, and science, as well as more pragmatic concerns. Alongside classical authors such as Plato, Aristotle, Tacitus, and Cicero were practical handbooks, such as the *Volkskalender* (folk calendar), a kind of almanac full of technical information pertaining to ways of calculating time, to astronomy, astrology, remedies, folklore, and other kinds of practical information for daily life. Folk literature, such as the pre-Lenten plays *(Fastnachtsspiele)* performed by artisans after parades and other activities that mark the carnival season, began to be collected at this time. More than a hundred *Fastnachtsspiele* from Nuremberg still exist; they show a progression from anonymous composition to more carefully crafted texts by such well-known Nuremberg poets as Hans Rosenplüt (b. ca. 1400), who is also known for his *Spruch auf Nürnberg (In Praise of Nuremberg)*, a long poem celebrating the glories of the city.

Such were the kinds of works to be found in private collections. Comparing the record of one of these, Hartmann Schedel's personal library, with more than six hundred volumes in 1514, allows us to measure the difference between private collections and the still rare municipal libraries of the period. Here again, Nuremberg was in the vanguard, having had the first Ratsbibliothek, or municipal library, in Germany. City records mention the existence of a library as early as 1370. This was not a free-standing institution, but a room in the Rathaus (city hall) where books were stored and consulted. Since the records of the holdings in the 14th century were lost to fires, we cannot be certain what kinds of manuscripts were deposited in the library. Many of them undoubtedly pertained to law. Yet we find mention of aldermen or burgesses *(Ratsherren)* bequeathing their libraries to the city. These were varied collections that supplemented the legal volumes supplied by the municipality for use by its judges and lawyers. The *Rat* (city council) regulated every aspect of life within the municipality. While the members of the council numbered only forty-two, they were drawn from the patrician upper class, consisting of three to four hundred economically successful families, businessmen, lawyers, doctors, and the like, who accounted for 6 to 8 percent of the population.

Given the concentration of wealth and power in the hands of a relatively small, homogeneous element of the larger population—the artisan class, which comprised some 50 percent of the population of Nuremberg, was excluded from power—the *Ratsherren* were likely to be similar in outlook and taste, formed as they were in the Humanist tradition. That leading citizens were so keen to bequeath their manuscripts to the Ratsbibliothek shows an awareness on their part of the importance of Humanist works in promoting an image of the city as a center of learning and culture.

Even though the early records of Nuremberg's municipal library have been lost, we can still trace the role of burgesses' donations in the first half of the 15th century. On March 4, 1429, Dr. Konrad Kornhofer, provost of Saint

Lorenz, deeded his library over to the Ratsbibliothek. It consisted of philosophical, theological, and scientific works. The donation could not be accommodated in the existing space, so a new room had to be added to the Rathaus. By 1432, the books, which had been stored in kegs, were being bound. Ten desks were provided, to which a certain number of the books were chained, while the rest were stored in containers on the walls. During the renovation that was undertaken by Ratsherr Hans Tucher from 1486 to 1488, the number of desks was increased to thirty-three and storage space for the increased holdings also had to be expanded. By this time there were 371 books and manuscripts, all duly catalogued, but far short of the 600 or so in Hartmann Schedel's personal library.

The increased inventory derived not only from legacies, but also from the council's active acquisition by commissioning specific kinds of books. In 1478, the council requested a German translation of Aeneas Silvio Piccolomini's *De miseria curialium* from Walther von Hirnkofen. Ten years later, it asked a Benedictine monk, Sigismund Meisterlin, to write a chronicle of the city. It also soon recognized the benefits of printing for the increase of the holdings of the library by the simple expedient of directing Nuremberg printers to donate copies of their published books.

The collections attracted scholars who in turn brought forgotten manuscripts to light. Conrad Celtis, a major Humanist figure in 15th-century Nuremberg, discovered the early medieval plays by the German noblewoman and nun Hroswitha in a monastery just outside of Nuremberg. His edition of Hroswitha's plays was adorned with preliminary sketches for illustrations by Albrecht Dürer, though the working drawings were apparently not from the master's hand. Nicholas of Cusa, who spent time in Nuremberg in the 1440s, had discovered manuscripts by Tacitus and Plautus as early as 1427, the latter containing twelve previously unknown comedies by the Latin playwright. The juxtaposition of the discovery of Hroswitha's and Plautus's manuscripts in close proximity to Nuremberg was important for the light it shed on how Hroswitha might have come by the Plautine models for her own plays.

We must presume that the link between the thirst for texts among the Humanists that inspired such finds and their own production of new texts was a close one. From the 1440s on, Nuremberg also became the center of activity for such notable figures as Aeneas Silvio Piccolomini, who was instrumental in bringing Humanism to Germany and who, as private adviser to Emperor Friederich III, resided in Nuremberg for a time in the 1440s. During his stay, he wrote an erotic comedy, *Chrysis,* in the style of Terence and a love story, *De duobus amantibus historia*. At the same time, Nicholas of Cusa, also in Nuremberg, wrote a treatise on astronomy that traces the movements of the earth relative to the sun in a manner that suggests he foresaw Copernicus's discovery of a solar-centered universe, though he did not feel he had sufficient evidence to announce a view so counter to Church doctrine.

By the 1460s we find a growing interest in near-contemporary indigenous and foreign secular works in vernacular languages. Heinrich Schlüsselfelder translated Boccaccio's *Decameron* in 1460, for example. In the previous decade the patrician Wölflin Lochamer compiled the *Lochamer Liederbuch,* a book of lyric songs and verses. History, and particularly local history, also became an increasingly important focus. In 1493, Hartmann Schedel wrote his *Weltchronik,* at the exact center of which he placed a laudatory description of Nuremberg. Translated into several languages and sold throughout Europe, the *Weltchronik* promoted Schedel's view of Nuremberg as central to what was then regarded as world culture. Conrad Celtis, another key Humanist figure, wrote his own meditation on Nuremberg, the *Norimberga,* published finally in 1502, though completed earlier. As though presaging Weber's *Protestantism and the Rise of Capitalism* (and, indeed, Nuremberg was one of the first important cities to embrace the Reformation), Celtis notes both the spirituality of the city and the intensity of its material acquisitiveness. Nurembergers in their drive for profits, he said, were like bees looking in flowers everywhere for treasures and riches to bring back to their city.

What we have seen in this brief survey of the book culture in 15th-century Nuremberg is that collecting books and manuscripts served multiple functions for different groups of readers. How these different, but overlapping, groups used their books shows us just how narrow our modern understanding of the book has become. Whereas a modern reader conceives of a book as having a specific content, within a book culture like Nuremberg's, a book's content was something to be worked on by its user. The notion of the book was much more holistic than today, encompassing not only content produced by an original writer, but additions by readers, and the meanings created by the page layout, as evidenced by works like Schedel's *Weltchronik,* which left empty pages at the end for the reader to fill in at will. Books, both printed and copied, were read, studied, commented on by their owners, and traded for yet others in a lively exchange. In short, the prominent burghers engaged in bibliophilia used their acquisitions to express themselves in an active and productive way that is hardly conceivable in our own day. Manuscript collecting, book printing, buying, and selling, Humanist studies, papal and imperial politics, writing of all kinds, and commerce were inextricably intertwined in Nuremberg. Perhaps of no other place at that time, even of Lyon, can it be said that book culture was a metaphor for the life of a city.

See also 1027, 1457, 1500 (Dürer), 1515

Bibliography: John L. Flood and William A. Kelly, eds., *The German Book, 1450–1750: Studies Presented to David L. Paisey in His Retirement* (London: British Library, 1995). Hermann Jantzen, *Literaturdenkmäler des 14. und 15. Jahrhunderts* (Berlin and Leipzig: de Gruyter, 1919). *L'humanisme allemand, 1480–1540: XVIIIe Colloque International de Tours* (Paris: Vrin; Munich: Fink, 1979). Christoph Reske, *Die Produktion der Schedelschen Weltchronik in Nürnberg* (Wiesbaden: Harrassowitz, 2000). Hartmann Schedel, *Chronicle of the World: The Complete and Annotated Nuremberg Chronicle of 1493* (Cologne and New York: Taschen, 2001). Ellen Shaffer, *The Nuremberg Chronicle: A Pictorial World History from the Creation to 1493* (Los Angeles: Dawson's

Book Shop, 1950). Adrian Wilson, *The Making of the Nuremberg Chronicle* (Amsterdam: Nico Is-rael, 1976).

Tracy Adams and Stephen G. Nichols

✑ Circa 1401

Johannes von Tepl sends a batch of literary exercises to his friend Petrus Rothers in Prague

A Dialogue with Death

In the early 15th century, the head of the Latin school in the town of Saaz in northern Bohemia, Johannes von Tepl, sent one of his pupils to Prague to deliver samples of the schoolmaster's literary output—a prose dialogue in the vernacular and some short Latin poems—to Petrus Rothers. A friend of von Tepl's since childhood, Rothers was an influential figure in the Jewish community of Prague. All this is known from the letter, written in Latin, that the schoolmaster sent with the compositions, in which he assures Rothers of his friendship and provides a brief description of the enclosed German dialogue. In a conventional gesture of understatement, he mentions the limitations of German prose, which was still considered underdeveloped at the time. Von Tepl also mentioned such rhetorical elements of his text as the construction of sentences and the use of figures of speech.

This letter is one of relatively few surviving documents in which a medi-eval author comments on a vernacular work of his own. However, readers hoping for help in understanding specific aspects of the text will be disap-pointed. Von Tepl's sole reference to the subject—the "inevitable fate of death"—is so brief that, had the work been lost, it would have been impossible to infer much about its contents. He also mentions the formal aspects of the work in such an oddly abbreviated fashion that it would not even be possible to identify it as a dialogue. The letter itself is, in fact, a highly stylized literary product, and it survived as part of the collection. Its aim was not so much to explain the accompanying text as to demonstrate the writer's mastery of rhet-oric, his ability to combine standard rhetorical elements with such enormous skill that they seemed to acquire a life of their own. Since von Tepl was a se-nior administrative official, working where clerical and lay institutions met, he knew how to write documents in the official government style, but he was also familiar with the standard works of Latin grammar, dialectics, and rhetoric. He displays this familiarity in the letter by concealing rather than revealing the nature of the dialogue in order to arouse his old friend's curiosity. "The atten-tive reader," he assures Petrus Rothers, will find in it "all the peaks of rhetoric that are possible in this awkward language."

And indeed the vernacular text, referred to in the heading of the letter as *libellus ackerman* (little book of the plowman), and known since then as *Der Ackermann aus Böhmen (The Plowman from Bohemia)*, contains almost all the rhetorical devices mentioned. It also stands in the tradition of official chancellery style, which, under the influence of Johann von Neumarkt, chancellor to Emperor Charles IV, placed new emphasis on rhythmical periods even in the German vernacular. Johannes von Tepl was familiar with the chancellor's German prayers and his prose translations into German. The *Buch der Liebkosung (Book of Caress),* a translation of the pseudo-Augustinian *Soliloquiae animae ad deum,* provided him with memorable phrases. The *Plowman* indeed corresponds to the work of rhetorical art as announced in the author's letter—but in a much broader sense than the letter indicates. As the argument unfolds, the rhetoric of the German text becomes emotionally charged over the "inescapable fate of death." The widower and Death confront each other in thirty-two exchanges. The former describes himself as a plowman of the pen, that is, a writer, with an attitude of despairing lament and furious accusation, while the latter defines himself as ruler of the earth, displaying an attitude of simulated ignorance and pedantic superiority. Not until the thirty-third chapter is the alternation between partial agreement and brusque opposition resolved by divine judgment. In the concluding prayer, the grieving man resigns himself to the inevitable.

When interest in the *Plowman* began to revive in the 19th century, the event referred to in the text, the death of Margaretha, was assumed to reflect an episode of bereavement in the author's life. The historical evidence makes this seem unlikely, however. Documents show that the wife of Johannes of Tepl was named Clara, not Margaretha, and that she survived her husband along with several of their children, who were already grown when Johannes died in 1415. Margaretha might be a love of his youth whose full identity has not been discovered, or simply a fictional "pearl" *(margarita),* a jewel among women similar to Petrarch's Laura. In any event, the notion that von Tepl gave direct literary form to his own grief is misleading. The *Plowman* does not represent, as has been claimed, the first modern experience of death. It is a work of literature, containing references to the real world but also based on numerous sources in both Latin and the vernacular. Its specific modernity lies in the way the author combined this material and rendered it dynamic in its rhetoric and argument.

A general model for a dialogue about mastering one's fate was provided by three texts in particular. *De remediis fortuitorum,* a little collection of maxims taken from Seneca and assembled in the early Middle Ages, contrasted brief descriptions of misfortunes (including the loss of a wife) and stoic aphorisms of a general nature, thereby offering components that could be used for Death's side of the argument. The biblical book of Job, if not read simply as a demonstration of idealized patience, shows the limits of consolation in this world and the significance of a direct connection to God. Boethius's *Consolatio philosophiae* shows how a person in despair can find consolation in cosmology and ontology. Johannes of Tepl is known to have read it with his pupils in Saaz and refers to it explicitly in the *Plowman.*

The despairing farmer must debate a special opponent, however, namely death itself. Death personified had appeared earlier in Medieval Latin disputations, such as the *Dialogus mortis cum homine* from the 12th century and the

14th-century *Tractatus de crudelitate mortis.* Johannes von Tepl owned a manuscript in which the *Tractatus* was included, and he appears to have marked important passages with little drawings of a pointing hand. However, he modified these passages to fit the situation of the characters in his dialogue, as he adapted his borrowings from tradition in general to make them fit the argumentative strategy of the two debaters. The idea that death is part of the law of nature he took from Seneca and Stoic philosophy, for example, and passed it on to Death as an argument that fails to convince the plowman. He also reduced the notion of the brevity and insignificance of human life, borrowed from Lothat of Segni's rhetorically brilliant *De miseria humanae conditionis,* to the problem of human restlessness.

It becomes evident in the first few exchanges that it is this process of transformation, the reworking of objective general statements to make them subjective, on which the inner dynamic of the *Plowman* rests. The plowman apparently initiates a trial for murder and abduction with his opening accusation, but his indictment is muddled, so that essential facts become clear only as the discussion continues. He brings in legal language, but does so not just to create a rational frame for argument, but to appeal to the only authority who could prevail over death—namely God. For it is to God to whom the plowman addresses his laments, even though in the debate he must deal with another interlocutor.

He must acquire an understanding of the paradoxical figure of Death, who represents the event that separates the living husband from his beloved wife, and who, at the same time, mediates his relationship to her. The exchange begins when the plowman allows himself to be drawn into Death's attempts to rationalize. He gets Death to define himself and even presses him into the role of adviser and comforter. Yet by resisting the comfort of stoicism, which aims to control and dampen the emotions, the plowman realizes his right to grief and memory as a special part of human existence. In *memoria,* he sees his lost beloved preserved alive.

In the last third of the dialogue, the plowman broadens his perspective to include the universal and a possible future. However, this change does not signify acceptance of Death's position. In an emphatic tribute to humankind (ch. 25), the plowman explicitly rejects the origin of Death in the Garden of Eden, and implicitly rejects the very idea of mortality. He is concerned with the condition of humanity before the Fall, not with Christian history of the world since. In the end, the widower even tries to entrap Death in a contradiction, in hopes of seeing him roast in Hell for all eternity (ch. 30).

This rhetorical leap is made plausible within the text, because the plowman reacts to a position that itself possesses subjective qualities. In an earlier passage, central to the dialogue, Death denies having any substantiality at all, pointing out that he is "nothing" but "nevertheless something" (ch. 16). But this "something" turns out to be the power of argument. The figure of Death becomes a presence through language and thereby gains a paradoxical profile by having simultaneously to establish and cancel itself out. Death is permitted to be independent and stubborn. He resembles an arrogant teacher, who tries to force his pupil, the plowman, into an inconsistent position, using aphorisms and proverbial turns of phrase, often ironically. At the same time, the plowman's adversary departs from the framework of traditional Christian meditation on death and thereby nourishes human resistance.

Death does not appear here as a known entity, but rather as something experienced in the fluctuation of the arguments. In the form of words, he becomes the Other, thus making it possible to plumb the experience of loss as a tension between denial and acceptance. Arguments that would neutralize grief through references to Christian faith in life after death therefore had to be avoided. Of course, Johannes von Tepl assumes the presence of God throughout, but at no point does he mention the dichotomy between this world and the hereafter, which is so central to all Christian *consolatio*. He makes no explicit reference in the dialogue to either Christ's incarnation and passion or the traditional explanation of death as punishment for a fallen, sinful humanity. Death in the *Plowman* justifies his existence primarily in the stoic sense as *lex humana,* thereby proving himself the appropriate dialectical counterpart to a subject who is rebelling against the unalterable, who demands permanent happiness in this world, and vigorously defends his right to a full life.

God's judgment in chapter 33 concerns the plowman's attempt to ignore that the life granted to human beings on earth is of limited duration, not his attempt to understand it as being of particular dignity and freedom. The concluding hymnic prayer revokes neither the right to grief nor the notion of human dignity and cosmic renewal; instead, it sets a goal for the experiential process of the text. The plowman's interlocutor is now not the God who appears in the text, but God on high, the absolute partner in dialogue, who replaces the simultaneously familiar and unfamiliar interlocutor Death. In prayer—in contrast to the dialogue—a greater Thou becomes palpable, who compensates for the absence of the human partner. The prayer makes palpable that power of the Creator which surpasses the ability of human language to represent it, and which, by providing the plowman with insight into his existence as God's creature, opens him to acceptance of mortality.

What the *Plowman* attempts as a whole can be understood, in the sense of Mikhail Bakhtin, as "inner dialogicity of the word." The text is a dialogue with respect to the traditions that are quoted, taken up, connected, and transformed. And it is a dialogue with respect to the divergences and convergences between the individual speakers (accuser, Death, God, and speaker of the prayer). In intertextual terms, the prose oscillates between discourses of theology and moral philosophy; intratextually, however, it oscillates between otherness and non-otherness in the relationship of the figures, between recognition of the loss experienced and efforts to recover the imagined lost object imaginatively. This oscillation opens the possibility for a textual subject that spans the various positions and, seen in historic terms, allows the *Plowman* to depart from the schematic rigidity and goal-oriented one-sidedness dominant in so many disputations and didactic debates of the period. But unlike later humanistic dialogues, this does not occur through imitation of the forms of spoken language. It is only through the creation of inner connections between the blocks of dialogue that the speakers' situation becomes more than an artificially constructed opposition, and this is achieved because the rhetoric of the text does not exhaust itself in formal play between the figures of the debate, but becomes a means of expressive movement.

Human dignity and freedom, the right to grief, the aspiration to find happiness in this world, and the anthropological function of rhetoric are all themes that unfold in the letters, dialogues, and treatises of Italian Humanists in the period around 1400. Like the *Plowman,* their aim is not to establish a fundamentally new world view, but to throw off the constraints of a view of human life dominated by theology, or at least to relegate it to the background. In intellectual laboratory experiments, human nature is given free rein over a limited terrain, which brings with it an expansion of horizons and an increase in philosophical possibilities that cannot be ignored in the long run. This free space, closely connected with the openness of dialogue, gives the *Plowman* its air of modernity and probably also helps to explain its fascination for later generations.

In the 15th and 16th centuries, the little book numbered among the most popular non-pragmatic texts in German-speaking areas. It was frequently reissued during times of plague and served as a literary aid in overcoming the trials of life. It was read in both monastic and humanist circles, and writers were often tempted to borrow from it or expand on it. Early translations into Czech and Latin also appeared. The succinct definitions of death were quoted in sermons and morality plays. In the process, the language was altered to more familiar patterns. Writers and printers de-emphasized the stylistic and rhythmic originality of the text; readers and anthologists smoothed out the intellectual audacity to enhance its practical usefulness, while adapters and imitators took the edge off the paradoxical figure of Death, reducing it to the traditional *memento mori.* The pessimistic discourses of the age treated human beings as flawed and sinful. The plowman's rebellion, by contrast, dealt with loss and liberating self-assertion in the here-and-now.

It was precisely this self-assertion that gave the book its popular appeal in the modern period. The prose work from Bohemia, an *ars vivendi* presented dialectically, became a paradigm for the modern individual's search for meaning, a model for overcoming loss and grief. After World War I, as it was turned into a novel, adapted for the stage and radio, and was included in anthologies, the *Plowman* gained extraordinary resonance. It even acquired a political dimension. German speakers exiled from Czechoslovakia after World War II cited it in the name of cultural continuity as a legitimation of their claims to the region. Generalizing its message as a call to resistance against what they perceived as the injustice of the times, they used its modern aspect as an instrument of political regression. This, too, testifies to the powerful social energy that can emanate from one small book.

See also 1354, 1457, 1927

Bibliography: Johannes de Tepla Civis Zacensis, *Epistola cum Libello ackermann und Das Büchlein Ackerman,* ed. Karl Bertau, 2 vols. (Berlin and New York: de Gruyter, 1994). *Die Ackermann-Handschriften E und H,* ed. Werner Schröder, 2 vols. (Wiesbaden: Reichert, 1987). Johannes von Tepl, *Der Ackermann,* ed. with commentary by Christian Kiening (Stuttgart: Reclam, 2000). Gerhard Hahn, *Der Ackermann aus Böhmen des Johannes von Tepl* (Darmstadt: Wissenschaftliche Buchgesellschaft, 1984). Christian Kiening, *Schwierige Modernität: Der "Ackermann" des Johannes von Tepl und die Ambiguität historischen Wandels* (Tübingen: Niemeyer, 1998).

Christian Kiening
Translated by Deborah Lucas Schneider

♉ 1437

Nicholas of Cusa receives a divine revelation as he sails back to Italy from Byzantium

The Beginning of Modern Thinking

Whether Nicholas of Cusa's narration in the letter that dedicates *De docta ignorantia* (1440; *On Learned Ignorance*) to Cardinal Giuliano Cesarini is an authentic report or a self-stylization, the dedicatory gesture itself gives meaning to what he says. Significantly, Nicholas uses the standard allegory of Christian didacticism that refers to human life as a sea journey, while his description of a sudden revelation is a clear allusion to the Augustinian concept of illumination. Even the fact that Nicholas received this illumination while on his way back from the capital of the Eastern Roman Empire seems significant. The subject of *On Learned Ignorance,* a treatise he wrote in the course of two years after his return, is basically philosophical, but its outlook is decidedly Christian. It stands in the tradition of Augustine as well as of Greek thinkers of the classical and the Hellenistic period, whose works, as he says, he came to know during his stay in Byzantium.

Nicholas was born in 1401, in a small village on the Moselle River, the name of which, according to prevailing custom, he adopted as his surname. He was educated by the Brothers of the Common Life in Deventer, Holland, where he came in contact with the *devotio moderna,* that is, medieval mysticism. He went on to study mathematics, philosophy, canon law, and theology at various universities, each of which marked a significant stage in his intellectual development. In Heidelberg, he came into contact with Occamist nominalism; in Padua, he learned some Greek, which later facilitated his reception of Platonism and Neoplatonism; and in Cologne, he received training in traditional Scholasticism. From there, he embarked on a brilliant ecclesiastical career which eventually earned him the rank of cardinal. He spent the last decades of his life mainly at the Roman Curia, where he was a privileged counselor of the popes Eugenius IV, Nicolas V, and Pius II. He died in Italy in 1464.

When Nicholas speaks of himself as a "German" in the prologue of *On*

Learned Ignorance, he refers to his regional origin. But the stage on which he performed his life was all of Western Europe, he wrote in Latin, and the intellectual authorities to which he was indebted were the great names of the Western tradition. He himself was considered one of the leading European intellectuals in his time. Even less than the literary texts that, after all, are written in specific idioms, the philosophical texts of the premodern era cannot be assigned to a rubric of national culture. The code Nicholas draws on and develops in his writings is neither specifically German nor universal, but the code of Western thought.

As a leading figure in the Church and as a diplomat, Nicholas dedicated himself to a single-minded mission, which also framed his philosophical and theological endeavors as one of the most influential participants at the Council of Basel (1431–1443). His objective was reconciliation with the heretics of the pre-Reformation period, primarily the Hussites of Bohemia. It was the same motive that prompted him, against fierce opposition from the Western Church, to initiate a theological colloquy with the most prominent representatives of the Eastern Orthodox Church. Foremost on his mind was the prevention of a religious war he saw looming, and which was to become reality in the wake of the Lutheran Reformation (1517) and the Counter-Reformation (Council of Trent, 1545–1563). To achieve this goal, he proposed a "world model" that would be acceptable to all parties and would reunify the various tendencies of Christian dogma. It even included the disciples of Islam within a "general consensus."

It is the formulation of this objective that makes Nicholas's thinking strikingly modern, and can almost be seen as close to 18th-century deism or even pantheism. Not by the sword, but through argumentation (1433, *De concordantia catholica [On Concord within the Church]*; 1454, *De pace fidei [On Religious Peace]*) would he achieve his goal. He reduced traditional religion to its rational core, disposing of what could be considered, from a modern view, as peculiarly premodern aspects of Christian belief embodied in ritual. Nicholas saw traditional concepts of the divine as reducing God to a "creature," and the attendant religious practices as "idolatry" (*De docta ignorantia* I, c. 26). Since he does not limit his critique to then-current forms of popular devotion, such as pilgrimages and veneration of saints, it may well be that he also aimed to overturn the view of the Eucharist as transubstantiation.

Yet, Cusanian rationalism, on occasion, borders on mystical experience, while keeping its distance from conventional mysticism by adhering to the mode of rational argumentation. The title of Nicholas's most important work, *On Learned Ignorance,* refers to this dichotomy: the highest level of (philosophical) knowledge is the consciousness of ignorance, of humankind's inability to attain essential knowledge. However, this consciousness is not achieved by turning away from intellectual endeavor. Rather, in order to be realized as the highest possible level of cognition, it requires unceasing striving for knowledge.

Nicholas's choice of this title is also a hint at the traditions of his own thinking. The formula of "learned ignorance" is Augustinian. And the valorization of ignorance as the highest level of (philosophical) knowledge is a major feature in the works of two of his most prominent precursors: William of Occam and Petrarch. The author of *On Learned Ignorance* shares with Augustine, Occam, and Petrarch the conceptual basis of his theory of knowledge as nonknowledge: a most pointed monotheism. This differentiates his argument from the original Socratic formula. The theorem is to be understood as referring first of all to theology: if there is one and only one God, this God is beyond the capacities of human conceptualization. He cannot be grasped by the differential terms of language and logic. God is the "coincidence of the contradictories" *(coincidentia contradictoriorum),* the Absolute beyond all understanding.

By defining God in exclusively negative terms, Nicholas goes far beyond the concept of ineffability found in Scriptures. He proposes a version of Christian belief free of the traces of the tribal deity of the Old Testament and, to a certain extent, of the anthropomorphic features of the New Testament God. At the same time, his method remains rigorously logical. He even betrays a preference for the pure symbols of mathematics as the appropriate vehicle for knowledge. This hybridization of nonknowledge, or ineffability, and precision of articulation is a principal reason for the fascination Nicholas has exercised on 20th-century thinkers such as Ernst Cassirer, Karl Jaspers, Joachim Ritter, Hans Blumenberg, and Niklas Luhmann.

Nicholas's modernity emerges clearly when we consider the value he places on the earthly and the material. Of the two books that Christian tradition considers sources of revelation—Scripture and Creation—Nicholas relies almost exclusively on the "book of nature." The reduction of religious dogma to abstract principles, which he had carried out in the interest of doctrinal consensus, dramatically diminishes the relevance of the Bible and directs attention to the material world. From a Cusanian standpoint, a notion of the divine, however faint, is attainable, if at all, only via cognition of the created. The Bible's stature is further diminished by the fact that Nicholas's general thesis contests a literal understanding of the biblical text as revelation. If God is ineffable and beyond all that language can express, the biblical text cannot be the authoritative articulation of God's essence.

One of the most startling features of *On Learned Ignorance*—half a century before Columbus and Magellan and 150 years before Kepler and Copernicus (both of whom were familiar with Nicholas's cosmological speculations)—is the deviation from Christian cosmological thinking, derived from the Aristotelian-Ptolemaic order, and the scriptural image of the universe as an edifice. Since God is the ineffable immensity and the universe, as a divine creation, reflects this immensity, Nicholas concludes: (1) the earth, as the highest in value of all created things, must have the most perfect of all forms, the sphere; (2) God, like the point without extension that constitutes the center of a geometrical form, must be the conceptual center of creation; (3) the earth moves like the other stars and, due to its shape, its track is that of a circle. In short, by speculative reasoning alone, Nicholas arrived at a notion of the universe as an infinite space within which our globe is no longer the center, but one mobile planet among many others, some of which too may be endowed with life.

But perhaps the most striking element in Nicholas's cosmological speculation is his contention that all propositions concerning the world are to be regarded as approximations. All human descriptions of the world are endlessly perfectible approximations of its true and perfect "quiddity" (essence); the latter remains, in the final analysis, unattainable by the natural and the mathematical languages at our disposal. In a text entitled *De coniecturis* (1442; *On Conjectures*), Nicholas amply elaborates on the tentative character of all formalized descriptions of the given world, as these relate to essential truth in the manner of conjectures. Such conjectural knowledge, however, is given a most positive, even optimistic assessment. Since creation stems from God and since human beings represent its highest level—a "created god" (*deus creatus,* II, c. 2), so to speak—the subject and the object of cognition are structurally isomorphic. This means that cognition of the world may, at the same time, be cognition of the self. This idea may even be thought to foreshadow the philosophy of subjectivity as developed by Kant and his successors.

But it seems more important to emphasize that Nicholas, though in the mode of philosophical speculation, was the first to give expression to the concept of the provisional character of cognition and the falsifiability of all descriptions, that is, to principles that would become the basis of systematic empirical research, hence of modernity in the strict sense of the term. Nicholas himself undertook some initial steps toward empirical description in his work *De staticis experimentis* (1450; *On Experiments with the Scale*). Thus it is perhaps not surprising that—some 250 years after Nicholas and without naming him explicitly—John Locke, the philosophical father of empiricism, would include the notions of conjectural knowledge and "learned ignorance" as basic components of his epistemology (*An Essay Concerning Human Understanding* [1690] IV, 2).

Nicholas of Cusa's *On Learned Ignorance* presents, in crystalline form, a basic pattern of the intellectual history of the West. If monotheism means, epistemologically speaking, that there is one and only one essential truth, then this might explain the intellectual restlessness, the permanent quest for the one and only truth that differentiates Western thought from polytheism and pantheism. But when this God is elevated, as in the writings of Augustine, William of Occam, and Nicholas of Cusa, to a level of omnipotence and ineffability, only then does the idea emerge that human knowledge is always a provisional approximation. A quest for truth together with an awareness of the always imperfect—hence infinitely perfectible—character of knowledge in the end breaks the dogmatic chains implied in the doctrine of the "one and only truth." Nicholas's contribution to the emergence of modern thought from the spirit of monotheism goes beyond those of his predecessors on one particular point. The distance from the mythical ground of Christian belief achieved through Nicholas's use of logical formalization entails the demise of the doctrine of original sin. In fact, that doctrine is not mentioned at all in Books I and II of his text and, in the "Christological" Book III, where he cannot avoid mentioning it, Nicholas develops an emphatic understanding of redemption that suggests a worldly optimism. The post-lapsarian corruption of reason in Augustine gives way in Nicholas to a notion of the imperfection of knowledge that nonetheless allows for an asymptotic approximation of the truth.

In later writings, such as *De beryllo* (1458; *On the Beryl* or *On the Spectacles of the Mind*) and *De venatione sapientiae* (1463; *On the Quest for Wisdom*), Nicholas went a step further. He argues that, if God is the coincidence of opposites *(coincidentia oppositorum),* the truth about the created (as the "resplendence of God") likewise exceeds what can be said within the confines of Aristotelian logic. Nicholas accords this thought with his concept of conjectural knowledge by reactivating the Platonic differentiation between reason and intellect. Reason, as the virtue inevitably linked to the principle of noncontradiction, is confined to the realm of limited conjectural knowledge. The intellect, as the Godlike part of the human being, he now argues, distancing himself from what he had said in *On Learned Ignorance* (II, c. 2), is able to conceive the essential truth of the created (not of the creator), which, however, can only be found beyond the principle of noncontradiction. This hybrid form of thinking, in which mathematical rigor, an awareness of the limitations of formalized languages of description, and a philosophical suspension of the principle of noncontradiction are interlaced, is reminiscent of attempts to transcend the limits of logic in our time. It also suggests the historical contexts to which such attempts owe their genesis. And it can even help us to understand that, in the final analysis, the postmodern critique of reason is something very different from the mythic or mystical thought of non-Western provenance that critics accuse it of being.

See also 1329, 1346, 1790, 1796–1797

Bibliography: Nicolai de Cusa, *De docta ignorantia libri tres,* Opera omnia Nicolai de Cusa iussu et auctoritate Academiae Litterarum Heidelbergensis ad codicum fidem edita, vol. 1, ed. Ernst Hoffmann and Raymond Klibansky (Leipzig and Hamburg: Meiner, 1932). ———, *De docta ignorantia / Die belehrte Unwissenheit,* bilingual Latin-German edition, ed. Paul Wilpert and Hans Gerhard Senger (Hamburg: Meiner, 1964–1977). ———, *On Learned Ignorance,* trans. Jasper Hopkins (Minneapolis, Minn.: The Arthur J. Banning Press, 1981). Hans Blumenberg, *The Legitimacy of the Modern Age,* trans. Robert M. Wallace (Cambridge, Mass.: MIT Press, 1983). Ernst Cassirer, *The Individual and the Cosmos in Renaissance Philosophy,* trans. Mario Domandi (Oxford, U.K.: Blackwell, 1963). Jasper Hopkins, *A Concise Introduction to the Philosophy of Nicholas of Cusa* (Minneapolis: University of Minnesota Press, 1978). Karl Jaspers, *Nikolaus Cusanus* (Munich: Piper, 1964). Joachim Ritter, *Docta ignorantia: Die Theorie des Nichtwissens bei Nikolaus Cusanus* (Leipzig and Berlin: Teubner, 1927).

Joachim Küpper

☙ *1442, May*

Oswald von Wolkenstein refutes accusations of confusing literature and reality

Poetic Transformations of the Self

The noble knight Oswald von Wolkenstein was one of many people involved in the so-called Villanderer Almstreit, a legal battle over the use of a
pasture in the South Tyrol Alps that began in the 14th and was not solved until
the early 19th century. As he approached the age of sixty-six, Wolkenstein
proved an unyielding adversary in his fight against an alliance of equally unyielding peasants. Now at the end of May 1442, Oswald von Wolkenstein has
good reason to be scared. A man from the hostile group in the region of
Ritten, whom Oswald had captured, has confessed to an attempt on Oswald's
life! What can Oswald do to guard against future attacks by other members of
this party? Lacking time (and the help of something comparable to our modern police), he reverts to means that seem typical not only for the late medieval
period but also for Oswald. In the course of an adventurous and checkered career as a judge, diplomat, traveling salesman, and—most of all—as a poet and
politician, he had acquired remarkable skills, especially a talent to "do things
with words." He decides to post his prisoner's confession in the center of the
town of Brixen. This bill of indictment, as it were, proves effective indeed, but
not in the intended way. It is torn down immediately and motivates a campaign of counterpropaganda that calls Oswald's accusations simply "a poetic
invention." For a moment Oswald seems in danger of getting trapped by his
reputation as a poet! To establish the trustworthiness of his point of view, he
draws up a second document reasserting his accusation and repudiating the
poetic argument. He affirms his creative talents, but protests energetically that
in this particular affair it would be insane to doubt the truth of his words. To
add weight to his argument, he curses his opponents: if they don't acknowledge the truth of what he says, they will end up in the devil's black asshole.

The aged Oswald von Wolkenstein appears to us in such a lively, not at all
bloodless episode because, among medieval poets, he has the best-documented
life. Some one thousand references to his life invite, almost urge, a biographical
approach to the study of this poet and artist. Even his contemporaries recognized his special talent of melding reality and literary fiction, just as modern
scholarship has spun a variety of direct and indirect threads between Oswald's
life and his literary work. One such thread is the fine line between the author's
artistic imagination and his pragmatic interests in the real world.

Oswald von Wolkenstein was probably born in 1376 in the Alpine province
of Tyrol as the second son of a prosperous, influential family. His ambitious nature involved him early on in a struggle for property and reputation in which
he had to overcome the severe disadvantage of being the second born after his
brother Michael. He traveled near and far in search of riches but was obviously
more successful at increasing his knowledge and erudition than at accumulat-

ing a fortune. It was not until the yearned-for division of the Wolkenstein estates in 1407 that Oswald finally was able to lead a life of luxury. Among other estates, he received one-third of the profitable castle Hauenstein, which also made him a *ministerialis* of the bishopric of Brixen and gained him the respected position of *Hauptmann* (captain), through which he became involved in legal affairs. Two remarkable monuments testify to his success: a life-size memorial stone and a lavish chapel dedicated to Saint Oswald. A few years after marrying his beloved Margaret of Schwangau, Oswald dedicated a second chapel to Saint Margaret.

Not satisfied with the recognition he had gained, Oswald aspired to still greater influence within the Tyrolean nobility. His chance to play an important role came as a rebel leader in a dispute of the landed gentry with the Habsburg duke of Austria and Tyrol, Frederick IV, over territorial claims. The gentry's position was strengthened by King Sigmund and his strategic policies in Tyrol. This was especially advantageous for Oswald, since his diverse talents qualified him for the imperial service. He distinguished himself especially during the Council of Constance (1414–1418) when he was dispatched on many successful diplomatic missions throughout Europe. One of these brought about the end of the Great Schism, which had lasted from 1378 to 1417 when three pretenders laid claim to the Papacy at the same time. Within the next years, however, Oswald ran into several disasters closer to home. His relentless fights for enlarging his inheritance put him at odds with the Hauenstein party, to which belonged not only his former lover Anna Hausmann but also Frederick IV. Oswald was imprisoned twice and most likely tortured, as his recently discovered remains indicate. Nevertheless, Oswald managed to overcome these ordeals and finally reach relative tranquility and peace with a prominent position in the regional government and as undisputed head of his large family. He died in Meran on August 2, 1445.

"If I remained silent any longer, I would completely fall into oblivion; after a few years nobody would remember me. Therefore, I shall start to sing again, if I can." Thus starts a late, quite amusing poem on the twelve stages of drunkenness. Oswald composed this song (Kl 117.1–5; "Kl" is an abbreviation for the edition by Klein) some time after 1438 in order to keep alive his reputation as an artist. The sum of what he had achieved on stages in and around Brixen, Constance, and Heidelberg was in need of, what he called, further "investment." Since his audiences were familiar with his personal affairs, they no doubt appreciated the dense net of allusions in his work. Thus Oswald's poetry can justifiably be examined from an economic angle that sees his artistic performances, as it were, as the capital that contributed to his social welfare.

The late song about drunkenness was eventually added to a project the author had launched a few years earlier to save his work from oblivion: the collection of his lyrics in two fairly expensive codices. Both codices were accompanied by transcriptions of the melodies he composed for them; 134 texts were collected in all. Each of these impressive volumes opens with a portrait of the poet—the first authentic portraits of a German writer. As these pictures and the history of the codices tell, it was he, the one-eyed yet sharp-sighted noble-man Oswald von Wolkenstein, who personally supervised the text collections. However, not all utterances of his alter ego were recorded, because not all the songs were deemed worthy of being remembered.

Oswald's principle of selection was highly effective not only in the delivery but at the very moment of poetic conception as well. A look at his chosen themes illustrates the point. As a poet free from the influence of patrons, he had the privilege of singing only about things that cast a favorable light upon him and were pleasing to his audience. So, why should he speak about the great battle of Agincourt between England and France in 1415 or the Turkish threat to Christianity in Europe? These events were already important and he felt free to neglect them. Oswald favored themes of common local inter-est and often selected a more advantageous perspective than cruel reality would suggest. This can be demonstrated with one of Oswald's most popular songs: the "Greifensteinlied," Kl 85. The historic background of this war song with its foot-stomping rhythm (just listen to one of its many modern record-ings!) describes—bluntly stated—the flight of Oswald and his brothers from Castle Greifenstein when it was besieged by Duke Frederick IV in the spring of 1418: "'Get on!' said Michael of Wolkenstein, 'Let us chase!' said Oswald von Wolkenstein. 'Quickly here!' said Lienhard von Wolkenstein, 'all of them have to flee from Greifenstein!'" (Kl 85,1–4). Oswald reworked a bitter defeat into a heroic poetic triumph!

Many of Oswald's poems abound with erotic metaphors telling of the plea-sure of physical love, though Oswald would not be a poet of high reputation if a further ingredient were not added to this age-old prescription for good po-etry. Indeed, he provides something fresh in the form of plays on words, the double meaning of which is nourished by the things that made up his world. Sexual connotations are artfully hidden, or rather offered, behind various ta-bleaux of everyday life.

A masterpiece of double-speak is found in the song Kl 76. The idyllic scen-ery resembles Kl 92, but here the male is a subjective poetic self through whose eyes the amorous adventure is presented. Kl 76 tells of a girl who cuts grass for her geese with the help of the male narrator. Their labors are listed in a literally correct way, giving the impression at first glance that the poem is primarily a faithful rendering of rural life. A careful reading, however, reveals the sexual undertones of many terms: "A grass cutter in the cool dew with white, bare and lovely feet made me happy on a green pasture; her brown-haired sickle did it / when I helped her to move the grating onward, to press it against the laths by leading and sinking it in" (Kl 76,1–9).

Similar *double-entendres* can be detected in some of Oswald's many *Tagelieder (Dawn Songs)*—traditional courtly songs about the mournful departure of a knight at daybreak after a blissful night with his beloved lady. These songs also contain another feature typical of Oswald: an almost excessive exploitation of a basic theme through a series of artistic variations. Oswald was the most prolific and most creative poet of *Tagelieder*. He enriched this traditional genre by blending it with elements of *Marienlieder*—songs about the Virgin Mary. He apparently performed these in such a subtle way that, in Kl 40, the adored woman sways between the poet's lover and the Virgin. This text can be read and understood easily in both ways.

Probably the most significant principle of Oswald's poetry is his exemplary self-stylization, shown at its best in his autobiographical sketches. Here all kinds of events are exploited for the unconstrained staging of Oswald's self. Be it kings or popes, battles or councils, princesses or his sweetheart, everything and everybody is accompanied, or even dominated, by a poetic self that readily adopts a variety of poses. It appears in serious and in jesting guises, although the latter are more frequent and most effective. Kl 19 offers perhaps the best example. Number twenty-two of the twenty-eight strophes depicts the historic reception of King Sigmund in Paris in the spring of 1416: "In Paris there stood many thousand people at their dwellings, on the lanes and roads, children, men and women, building a vast crowd, two miles in length. All of them watched Sigmund, the Roman King, and called me a clown in my fool's costume" (Kl 19,169–176).

For Oswald to risk standing in the limelight—in the text by appearing at the most effective point in the strophe—may be one thing, but how he could bear such prominence in the danger zone between fiction and reality without looking ridiculous to his critical audience and tarnishing his reputation is quite another. The answer may be found in the principle of self-stylization mentioned above, which permitted Oswald freely to link the literal traditions he had learned with the experiences of his historic self. He did so by drawing generally valid insights from personal episodes, regardless of whether they were pleasant or unpleasant. The principle of exemplary self-stylization worked either way and only the deep truth within counted.

Kl 18 is an entirely autobiographical poem that usually serves to start scholarly essays about Oswald von Wolkenstein. Here it is mentioned toward the end not so much to inform the reader that Oswald, who left home at the age of ten, was now, after thirty years of travels, filled with troubles and triumphs, ready to settle down; but rather to show that even in this specific, naturally egocentric poem, where the poetic self is not at all expected to justify its prominence, he again aspires to something higher or more general. Line 93 admonishes young people in love to keep in mind the author's past woes. Here again, the historic Oswald stylizes his life as being somehow exemplary. Apart from this marginal effort to transcend itself, Oswald's lyric self in Kl 18 makes use of yet another principle. Unlike his other techniques, this may be regarded more as an attitude as it is expressed in the last lines of his most discussed poem: "I, Wolkenstein, certainly have lived foolishly in tallying worldly things that long. I also concede not to know when I'm going to die, after which nothing more valuable will accompany me than the fruits of my good deeds. If I then should have served God well according to his orders, I would be little afraid of hell's blazing flames" (Kl 18, 107–112). Not only in these lines, but throughout his numerous pious and didactic poems—which make up more than half of his entire work—Oswald expresses his grievous desire to find favor with God for the sake of his soul and the souls of his listeners. Behind this principle of salvation is more than the common medieval outlook Oswald shared with some of the few personalities to whom he explicitly or indirectly refers, among them Dante, Boccaccio, and Petrarch. It is an attitude that has already transcended its initial literary confinement. The poetic self has apparently stepped out of its role-bound cage and attached itself more vitally and closely to the author than ever before. Or should the at times desperate cries in Oswald's texts be seen merely as mimed calls for rescue in the tradition of the *memento mori* motif? In this particular instance, the answer is clearly no. Oswald's poetic self indeed intended a complete breakthrough to its creator, and as a medium of God-fearing reflection was made to serve the historic man much like the chapels he had built and the Masses he had ordered to be sung for him.

From a cultural perspective, Oswald's stepping out of anonymity, leaving behind a faceless artistry, prefigures the dawning of a new age. Yet, this attitude was still accompanied by the medieval concept of trust in an almighty God who grants a stable social order and eternal life for all of His obedient servants. On the threshold of a new era, literature and music were for Oswald a medium to give expression to the most exalted emotions and ideas.

See also 1170, 1354

Bibliography: Karl Kurt Klein, ed., *Oswald von Wolkenstein: Die Lieder,* 3rd ed. (Altdeutsche Textbibliothek 55; Tübingen, 1987). Oswald von Wolkenstein, *Sämtliche Lieder und Gedichte: Ins Neuhochdeutsche übersetzt von Wernfried Hofmeister* (Göppinger Arbeiten zur Germanistik 511; Göppingen, 1989). Alan Robertshaw, *Oswald von Wolkenstein: The Myth and the Man* (Göppinger Arbeiten zur Germanistik 178; Göppingen, 1977). Werner Marold, *Commentar zu den Liedern Oswalds von Wolkenstein,* ed. Alan Robertshaw (Innsbrucker Beiträge zur Kulturwissenschaft, Germanistische Reihe 52; Innsbruck, 1995).

Wernfried Hofmeister
Translated by Deborah Lucas Schneider

⚘ Circa 1450

Hans Rosenplüt, the first artisan poet, writes plays for the Nuremberg Carnival

Fastnachtsspiele

On February 25, 1474, the Nuremberg City Council instructs Councilman Franz Rummel to see to it that "fish and wine" are presented to "the Turkish emperor" *(dem türckischen keiser).* The Council is welcoming Otman Kalixt, who arrived in the city the previous day in the entourage of Emperor Friedrich III and his fifteen-year-old son Maximilian. This was the first time Maximilian saw Nuremberg and its ancient imperial castle. Otman Kalixt came as Maximilian's companion. He was alleged to be the brother of Sultan Mehmed, the infamous sacker of Constantinople (1453). Chroniclers report that he had sought refuge in Rome to escape Mehmed's fratricidal rage and was baptized by the pope, who then "gave" him to Friedrich III. It is remarkable that the Nuremberg City Council and the scribe recording the events would routinely call him "the Turkish emperor." This is likely due to the popularity of *The Turk's Carnival Play* (334 verses, Keller 39), written by Hans Rosenplüt in 1455, toward the end of his life. In this, the first political play in the German language, the Turkish emperor comes to Nuremberg with a cabinet of advisers to reform the empire and restore peace and justice. The Christian empire, the "Great Turk" proclaims in eloquent German verses, is corrupt and divided against itself. Nobles fail to protect peasants and merchants, brigands make highways unsafe, the rich defraud the poor, people lie in court and bribe judges, the Church sells offices, and taxes and tolls burden everyone. The ruler of the infidel, therefore, predicts a "reformation" for the year 1456: the common people will rise up against the ruling gentry.

The Turk was the most popular of Rosenplüt's carnival plays. Between 1455 and 1494, Nuremberg scribes copied it into seven different manuscripts, more than they did with any other of the fifty-five or so plays attributed to him. Carnival turns the world upside down. So the idea that the Great Turk, who evoked apocalyptic terror throughout the West, should come to reform the Holy Roman Empire befits the topsy-turvy carnival mind. The curious figure of Otman Kalixt, "the Turkish emperor," explains how Rosenplüt came to write this carnival play in the first place.

Hans Rosenplüt was the first of Germany's artisan and city poets. Like the most famous artisan poet, the prolific cobbler Hans Sachs, he earned his living as a craftsman, but found his true calling in entertaining the energetic, well-educated townspeople of Nuremberg, which was then approaching the zenith of its economic and cultural power. Nuremberg records first mention Rosenplüt in 1426 when he, as "day worker" in the armor or chain mail industry *(sarwürht)*, pays two pounds to become a citizen. Only a year later the city licenses him as master chain mail smith. He therefore must have been apprenticed in another town and served his obligatory years as itinerant journeyman before settling in Nuremberg. It is, however, not likely that he wandered in from very far. The dialect Rosenplüt writes in is that of the Nuremberg area. This holds true even for his first written work, a report in verse that describes, much as a reporter would today, the defeat the Hussites of Bohemia inflicted on the imperial army at Tachau in August 1427. It is, therefore, not too far-fetched to assume that he was born, around 1400, in a Franconian town near Nuremberg.

Sensing, perhaps, that the future belonged not to body armor but to the cannon, Rosenplüt, in the early 1430s, changed his trade to that of brass founder *(rotschmyd)*. The City Council put his expertise to civic use by engaging him, from 1444 on, as artillery engineer *(Büchsenmeister)* in charge of operating and serving wall and gate cannons. The location of the houses Rosenplüt rented or owned in Nuremberg shows that he gradually gained social prominence both as craftsman and author. On June 4, 1460, his daughter picks up the last salary the city paid him as artillery engineer. Rosenplüt probably died that summer.

Starting in 1429, municipal bookkeepers begin referring to Rosenplüt by the alternate name Hans Schnepper. This appears to be a pen name he officially adopted. *Schnepperer,* the name with which he "copyrights" many of his works in the closing verse, means "eloquent poet." He was indeed an excellent wordsmith, capable of using literary German at all stylistic levels, from plain verse to highly embellished poetry. Rosenplüt was familiar with the literature of his time. Since he knew some Latin, basic theology, and astronomy, he must have had formal schooling. His fondness for peppering his high-style poems with technical musical terms suggests that he attended a music school *(schola cantorum).* Yet Rosenplüt, newly arrived, was largely a self-made man, ambitious, extremely hard working, alert to the city around him, and skilled at marketing his mail shirts and guns as well as his poems and carnival plays. As the "Great Turk" play shows, he was a champion of city life and a critic of the landed aristocracy who felt the threat of the burgeoning economic power of cities. In "Spruch von Nürnberg" (1447; In Praise of Nuremberg), Rosenplüt praises the city as the ideal place for human activities. He contrasts Nuremberg, the shining city on a hill, where order, justice, and peace are guaranteed by a wise City Council, with the chaotic countryside ruled by the fading aristocracy.

Although his sympathies are with Nuremberg's working people, he has, in his six historical poems, nothing but praise for the oligarchic City Council through which the "leading families" *(Geschlechter)* controlled all aspects of Nuremberg's life, not even permitting craftsmen, like Rosenplüt, to organize into guilds. Rosenplüt wrote many such *Sprüche, Reden,* or *dits,* as the form is known in French, a genre that reached a particular flowering in the hands of Nuremberg's artisan poets. The Sprüche are short to medium-length poems in verse couplets. Aside from reporting events, they teach basic knowledge about the world, rules of conduct, a religious truth, or a moral lesson. He also wrote eleven verse tales, the equivalent of the modern short story. As is traditional in the *fabliau,* most of Rosenplüt's verse tales are comedies about adultery. The graphic descriptions of sex make them come closest to the carnival plays.

As is true for most medieval plays, the authors of carnival plays are not identified. Only in one play (various heralds invite all to a great festival held by the king of England; Keller 100) is Rosenplüt's name embedded in the closing verse. Yet even in his lifetime, between 1455 and 1458, a Nuremberg scribe, perhaps known to the master, compiles the first extant carnival play collection (M). He assigns all forty-nine plays to Rosenplüt: *Vasnacht Spil Schnepers.* An examination of style and diction confirms his verdict. Scholars now attribute fifty-five Nuremberg carnival plays dating from before 1460 to Rosenplüt and his circle.

Medieval plays were not meant to be dramatic literature; they were libretti written for performance and their form followed function. Thus the way

Rosenplüt wrote his carnival plays was determined by how they were staged. During carnival, on Fat Tuesday (Mardi Gras) and the days preceding, groups of young men—apprentices and journeymen of the various trades, pupils of town schools, as well as sons of merchants and patrician families—entered the houses where carnival parties were being held. This practice survives today (albeit at Christmas) in the Mummers' plays of northern England. Carnival gave license. It was the one time of the year when social barriers fell and people of different classes mixed freely.

The players first created a theater by pushing aside benches and tables. The presenter *(Vorläufer)* opened (prologue) and closed (epilogue) this space by addressing the revelers gathered around: forgive the interruption, please be quiet, you are about to see; good-bye and good night, take care of your house, apologies for rude words, but it's carnival, see you again next year. Actors appeared in costume and men frequently dressed as women (a common carnival disguise), painting their faces and covering them with veils. But there were no sets, only a few hand props. The room was dark, lit only by torches and candlelight, giving license to lascivious behavior, in word and gesture. Carnival plays rely on words for comic effect; they are verbal theater. Since the players were interrupting dinner and had to visit other houses that night, the plays also had to be short. The great majority of Rosenplüt plays (ca. 80 percent) consist of two hundred or fewer verses, too short for a complicated plot.

Theater means something different in a society without professional actors and theater buildings, where stage-struck neighbors perform in houses, in the town hall, at street corners, or on scaffolds in the marketplace. The verbal carnival plays, therefore, must be seen in the context of nonverbal performances, the street theater of the Nuremberg carnival. Mummers ran through the streets in peasant or moor's costume. Morris dancers performed acrobatic leaps while revelers dressed as peasants held back the crowd. Escorted by town guards on horseback, the cutlers *(Messerer)* danced with swords (Nuremberg's swords and knives were the best), forming various figures. Linking themselves with leather rings, the butchers danced the *Zämertanz* to the beat of drums. This dance was tied to a masked procession known as *Schembartlauf* (Bearded Mask Run). First the butchers, then the sons of upper-class families donned identical masks and costumes (Wild Men, Wild Women, He-Devils, She-Devils), paraded through the streets pulling a *tabliau vivant* float (to be burned in the marketplace,) and firing gunpowder from musket barrels.

The fifty-five carnival plays attributed to Rosenplüt can be divided, by structure and content, into three forms. Fewer than 20 percent dramatize a story. In fact, most stories are really episodes, like the "Great Turk" coming to Nuremberg, or a quack physician, a comic character also popular in religious drama, diagnosing the illnesses of woeful peasants by examining their urine in a glass (Keller 85). Most stories dramatized are comic *fabliaux* familiar through Chaucer's *Canterbury Tales.* In "The Play of Aristotle" (Keller 17), the philosopher bears the brunt of the joke. As tutor to a king (not Alexander the Great as in most versions), he gives dubious lessons to the princes on how to tell character from facial features. His boast about being a chaste scholar, immune to female charms, entices the queen to seduce him by flashing her legs. As the instantly converted "slave of love," the philosopher allows the queen to ride him like a horse for all to see.

In the second major form, the court play, which makes up one-fifth of the repertory, plaintiffs bring complaints before judge and jury, who give the accused a chance to defend themselves. Court cases make good theater in all societies. Most of the complaints the court hears concern adultery. The accused are nearly always husbands who invent fabulous excuses. Like most medieval writers, Rosenplüt is fond of allegory. In two court plays (Keller 72, 73), the personified figures of Carnival and Lent are cited to the bar. Sometimes judges are asked to decide a question, such as if and when a young man should marry (Keller 41). The answers are not very helpful. This goes for all verdicts judges render after asking jurors to state their views. In many cases, the judge simply postpones the case. Many verdicts are no less grotesque than the complaints. At times, the court sentences men to supply judge and jurors with food and wine in carnivalesque quantities. Here Rosenplüt may be taking a stab at corruption in Nuremberg courts and their habits of postponing cases to maximize fees. But he actually attacks legal and social injustices much more vehemently in his historical and didactic *Sprüche*.

More than half the plays attributed to Rosenplüt conform to a type known as "revue" *(Reihenspiel)*. In the simplest form, one speaker after another, mostly peasants passing in "revue," tells the spectators why he is dressed in a funny way or how he succeeded or failed in sexual escapades (Keller 45). The revue can take the form of a contest, as when ten lovers compete for an apple awarded to him (shades of Aristotle), whom love led to act most foolishly (Keller 14). In the third subtype, speakers address a central figure. Various suitors—a knight, a peasant, a preacher, an artisan—court a young woman who chooses to marry the scribe—clerks have soft hands and a way with words (Keller 70).

Carnival celebrates the body. The dominant themes in Rosenplüt's plays are love and sex. A stock character is the comic peasant, dating back to Neidhart (d. ca. 1240) as a literary figure. He is addicted to bodily functions, not only to sex, but to eating, drinking, and defecating, and he personifies the carnival fool. Nuremberg carnival revelers often ran through the streets disguised as peasants, perhaps expressing the city dweller's disdain for the country bumpkin. In his didactic poems, Rosenplüt tends to praise the peasant as a righteous tiller of the soil. For the verbal theater, Rosenplüt and his colleagues invented a vast array of images and metaphors for bodily functions—especially for the sexual organs and how they interconnect—drawn from the worlds of manual labor, commerce, food, farming, and music.

Carnival revelers, no doubt, put on sketches before Rosenplüt arrived in Nuremberg in 1426. Visits to fellow citizens' homes to perform plays is first attested to as a Christmas custom. Christmas plays from the town of Constance and the province of Styria show that this practice was flourishing by 1420.

Nuremberg did not invent carnival plays. They existed as early as 1370 when chance copies of two plays were made (the St. Paul Neidhart play from Swabia and a north German farce [Keller 122]) about seven women lusting after the same man, a comic take on Isaiah 4:1). Subsidy, permit, and infraction notices from municipal records give testimony to the staging of carnival plays on marketplace scaffolds in several towns before Nuremberg: Arnhem on the Lower Rhine (starting in 1395), Butzbach, Hessen (1417), Hall in Tyrol (1426), Lübeck (1430), Baden in Switzerland (1432).

Rosenplüt took a carnival custom, perhaps unscripted, and raised it to the level of literature. He did the same with two other traditional Nuremberg literary forms. One was a short, witty epigramlike poem called "Priamel" (Preamble), which became synonymous with Rosenplüt (about 140 were ascribed to him), although he probably wrote only the most literate and clever of them. The other was a New Year's custom similar to the "Knock, knock, who is there?" routine. Going from house to house, young people knocked on doors to prompt the house owner to respond to a question. Such *Klopf-ansprüche* (knock demands) are also unique to Rosenplüt. By converting unscripted popular customs to literature, Rosenplüt succeeded in reaching less educated townspeople who normally did not (or could not afford to) read. Starting about 1455, the carnival plays Rosenplüt and his associates wrote for staging enter handwritten books as reading texts. This explains why about 110 pre-1500 carnival plays from Nuremberg, including the Rosenplüt repertory, survive while almost none from the other forty or so towns where carnival plays were staged have come down to us.

See also 1260, 1400, 1500 (Eulenspiegel)

Bibliography: Adelbert von Keller, ed., *Fastnachtspiele aus dem fünfzehnten Jahrhundert,* 4 vols. (Stuttgart, 1853, 1858; repr. Darmstadt: Wissenschaftliche Buchgesellschaft, 1965). Jörn Reichel, *Der Spruchdichter Hans Rosenplüt* (Stuttgart: Steiner, 1985). Ingeborg Glier, "Rosenplüt, Hans," "Rosenplütsche Fastnachtspiele," in Kurt Ruh et al., eds., *Die deutsche Literatur des Mittelalters: Verfasserlexikon,* 2nd ed., vol. 8 (Berlin: de Gruyter, 1990).

Eckehard Simon

1457

Gutenberg publishes the Mainz Psalter, the first work printed with movable type

An Information Revolution

Johannes Gensfleisch, better known as Johann Gutenberg, was a tinkerer. Before he invented a practical and profitable method of printing with movable type, he successfully marketed other inventions. One was a little mirror he sold to the thousands of pilgrims who came to Aachen for the periodic display of Charlemagne's great relics collection, in the belief that viewing the articles imparted grace. The crowds gathering on those days were so large that actually catching a glimpse of the precious objects was very difficult, and so Gutenberg's mirror came in handy. Pilgrims could hold the mirror above the crowd to deflect the images of the relics onto their own eyes and hearts and so share in the blessing. Gutenberg's little gadget had one aspect in common with his epoch-making invention of printing: something exclusive and difficult to access—in one case an intangible experience, in the other a written manuscript—was multiplied by technical means to bring its benefits within reach of more people. Of course, the premise was mistaken. Just as grace ceased to be grace if manufactured and replicated at will, so the written medium, once rare and expensive, was cheapened when mass production made it available, in principle at least, to everyone.

Mass printing also had unexpected consequences. In the 16th century, King Philip II of Spain ordered fifteen thousand breviaries from printers in Antwerp with the official text—recently approved by the Council of Trent—of offices and prayers for the canonical hours. The king intended to have the breviaries distributed to the entire clergy in his enormous realm, so they could fulfill their obligation of saying the prayers in exactly the same way. Through printing it was possible to standardize their daily approach to God, whose agent, in this case, was the absolutist state. Standardized texts could help bring about standardization of practices in various areas and give governments and other authorities greater control over the most private spheres, even a person's relationship with God.

The time was ripe for Gutenberg's innovation. Interest in written documents had risen sharply in the 15th century. For rulers, administrators, merchants, and tradesmen, writing was an almost indispensable instrument in their work. As literacy increased, particularly in cities, the demand for affordable manuscripts grew. For centuries, the clergy had been the custodian of written knowledge and erudition, but now lay people too were in need of written materials—instructions for the practice of crafts and trades, reading material for entertainment, and missals for private devotions were in high demand. Expensive, ornate manuscripts lost ground to simpler documents often intended for the writer's own use. Availability of cheaper materials also helped to reduce costs. In 15th-century Germany, writing paper was imported mostly from Italy or Spain, but by the end of the century paper mills sprang up in northern Europe as well in response to the rapidly growing demand. Paper is better suited than parchment for printing, as it is more elastic and absorbent, but even before Gutenberg, parchment was already being replaced by paper.

A relatively efficient production method had long been in use at universities, where portions of a text used for instruction were distributed to several scribes. In addition, commercial writing firms *(scriptoria)* flourished. Although proprietors still accepted commissions, they also tried to keep popular titles in stock. In addition, they maintained a crew of scribes who copied different parts of one text. While the traditional method had one monk copy an entire manuscript, the process was now speeded up and the output standardized. In absolute terms, however, the output was still extremely small, and single copies remained very expensive. Individual commissions to professional scribes continued to predominate. The documented cost of a Bible commentary for a wealthy cleric in Hamburg shows that long books were luxury items whose cost was equal to the annual earnings of people in most professions. Gradually a market developed for shorter texts, but the output was limited, and the demand for some items—such as blank forms for indulgences, official proclamations, and the like—still outstripped supply.

Attempts were made before Gutenberg to mechanize writing. The most significant invention had been wood-block printing, developed in China and the Arab countries. At first this technique was employed in Europe mainly for decorative cloth prints, but later it came to be used for making playing cards and Christian devotional images. The oldest surviving block prints are one-sided and depict the lives of Jesus and the saints. Less often they bear nonreligious images, frequently accompanied by a short explanatory text. The prints were sold to pilgrims, to churchgoers, at fairs, and from house to house. From 1430 or 1440 on, the process was used to make books by pasting two wood-block prints together to create a page. However, because the printing process made indentations on the paper, a sheet could not be printed on both sides. Surviving block-print books depict the dance of death, the *Ars moriendi,* and the *Biblia pauperum*. Such books continued to be produced after the invention of printed type. Their disadvantage was that two entire blocks had to be carved for each double-sided page, which Gutenberg's invention overcame by reassembling single letters over and over again.

The inventor of movable type was born Johannes Gensfleisch sometime between 1400 and 1403 in the city of Mainz. No details of his education are known, nor where he spent his early years. He was well versed in Latin and may have attended the university at Erfurt, in the territory ruled by the Elector of Mainz. In any event, he was also skilled in metalworking. In 1434 Gutenberg lived in Strasbourg, where he engaged in several enterprises of an unclear nature, but for which he developed ideas and others supplied the money—albeit with only mixed success. He may have been working on a printing process in the late 1430s, although no printed work from his time in Strasbourg is known to have survived. At some point between 1444 and 1448, he returned to Mainz, where he opened a print shop at the address from which he borrowed the name Gutenberg, by which he is known today.

In 1450, he tried to get a loan by demonstrating a technique for reproducing text on paper and parchment. The oldest prints that can be precisely dated are from 1454. The process was fully developed by 1457, when the Mainz Psalter was printed. The entire process consisted of type design, production of the type by pouring molten metal into forms, setting of single pages, and three-color printing in black, red, and blue. This procedure created three new professions: typecasters, typesetters, and printers, who continued to work in more or less the same manner until 1800. In principle, it had become possible to create printed materials in any quantity and quality desired.

The first type designs imitated the form of letters in manuscripts, which varied depending on their position in a word, and included marks for abbreviations, connecting strokes, and strokes over the letters *m* and *n* (like tildes) to indicate that they should be read as doubles. This meant that at first several hundred separate casts were required. Printing was originally referred to as "a new form of writing," since the term "artificial [= artful] writing" was already in use for the special calligraphy taught by writing masters. The first type-casters used particularly attractive manuscripts as their models. They copied large ornate initials and other decorative elements as well as ordinary letters. In the early years, parchment was still used frequently to make a printed book last as long as a high-quality manuscript. The practice of noting the origin and date of a work was also taken over from manuscripts.

Gutenberg's most famous achievement was his 42-line printed Bible. The type design was copied from a manuscript in a particularly beautiful hand. Forty-five thousand letters and three typesetters were required to complete the task, as well as twenty workmen, some of whom later became printers in their own right. Work on the Bible began in the early 1450s and lasted three years. It is estimated that some 180 copies were made in all, of which 30 or 35 were made on parchment and the rest on paper. The skins of five thousand calves were need for the parchment copies. Aeneas Silvius Piccolomini (later Pope Pius II) reported in a letter from Frankfurt in 1455 that he had seen some of the printed Bibles in the autumn of 1454 and that the printing quickly sold out. The first printed Bible was, nevertheless, a luxury item.

Like much of manuscript production before, printing was at first supported by public commissions. In addition to works for which manuscript copies had been in demand—such as Bibles and liturgical, theological, and canonical texts, for which regular demand could be expected to continue—polemical works, such as the *Turkish Calendar* and blank forms for indulgences, were also printed.

Promoting the new technology proved difficult. Soon disagreements arose among the inventor, his employees, organizers, and financial backers. Gutenberg quarreled with Johann Fust, a Mainz merchant to whom he owed large sums of money. Fust won a lawsuit in 1455 and took possession of the equipment Gutenberg had offered as collateral for the loan: the presses, the type, and perhaps also some of the printed Psalters. Gutenberg ended his association with Fust and borrowed more money elsewhere. His plans to mechanize further collapsed for lack of money. Gutenberg continued printing, mainly small items; his few larger projects included Hieronymus Balbi's *Catholicon* and the 36-line Bible. His financial situation remained precarious; he lost more of his possessions and appears to have been working at someone else's printing shop in Eltville in the 1460s. He died in Mainz in 1468.

Johann Fust and Peter Schöffer, Gutenberg's former journeyman, on the other hand, achieved great commercial success. They concentrated on providing books chiefly for high-ranking members of the clergy in Central Europe and farther East. Soon others outside their original circle began setting up shop as printers. The first printed works in the vernacular were made in Bamberg. In 1461, Albrecht Pfister, former secretary of the bishop there, brought out an edition of the *Ackermann aus Böhmen (The Plowman from Bohe-*

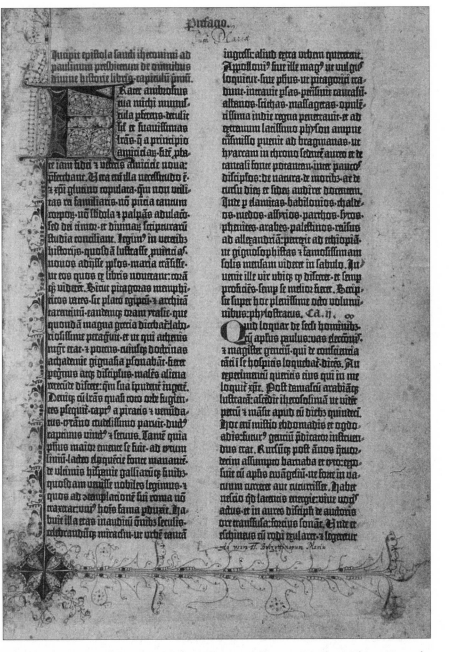

Page from a Gutenberg Bible. (Harry Elkins Widener Collection, Houghton Library, Harvard College Library)

mia) and Boner's collection of fables, *Der Edelstein (The Jewel)*. Otherwise, the oldest printing presses were located mainly in the Rhine area, but others soon sprang up in commercial centers like Augsburg (1468) and Nuremberg (1470). Most printers working abroad at the time were Germans.

From about 1473 on, printing spread rapidly throughout Europe. In about 1481, printers were working in the Netherlands, southwestern Germany, and northern Italy. By 1500 the most important centers had shifted to Venice and also Paris, where the first press was established in 1470. By that time about 60 print shops operated in Germany, mostly in the southwestern region, and more than 250 in all of Europe. It has been estimated that about 20 million books had been produced by the end of the 15th century. The Protestant Reformation shifted the concentration of printers to central and northern Germany, so that by the middle of the 16th century Frankfurt had overtaken Augsburg and Strasbourg as the printing and bookselling capital.

Besides religious texts that were traditionally in demand, other kinds of books gained in popularity: schoolbooks, books for private devotions, works on law, how-to books for cooking, distilling, and making herbal medicines. Instruction books appeared for various trades and crafts and for entertainment, in addition to newspapers, political and religious proclamations, and calendars. The early folios were replaced by smaller and more convenient formats, like the octavo volumes produced by Aldus Manutius in Venice.

The reproduction of text by technical means was immediately recognized as a significant innovation with far-reaching implications. In dedicatory letters and colophons, printing was celebrated as a gift from God, an invention that elevated the contemporary world above the ancient world and Germans above other nations. Writers praised the speed of production, the low cost, and the proliferation of written materials, which made important works widely available and improved communication among scholars. Printing also guaranteed that branches of art and science falling into disuse would be preserved.

From the start, book printing required the investment of large amounts of capital, and its rise was connected with the development of a new economic order. The importance of universities as centers of manuscript production declined. Although some university towns became centers of printing, others lacked printing shops for a long time, and presses flourished in towns that had no universities. In the early years, many monasteries added printing shops to their scriptoria, but their capacity remained small.

As a rule, the printing trade was not integrated into the prevailing medieval guild system, which was focused on protecting the livelihood of its members. Printers were thus not subject to guild regulations. The first printers came from various professions; few of them had previously worked as scribes or copyists. They tended to come from the better-paid crafts related to book decoration. Many had been goldsmiths, since technical skills were needed. Some were merchants, and many were members of the clergy or university faculties. The predominance of men with a university education ceased in the second generation. The investors were often physicians, patricians, and wealthy clerics. Print shops were family businesses; 62 percent of printers were related to other families in the same trade or to scholars, teachers, and later to preachers. As in other trades, marriage within the group was common, and the businesses changed hands as often through the remarriage of a printer's widow as through inheritance by sons.

Even the most impressive output from famous copyist workshops, like that of Vespasiano da Bisticci in Florence, could not match the numbers of a single print edition. The leading printers of the 1480s in Augsburg were among the wealthiest men in the city, although others barely eked out an existence. It seems that at first, they tended to err on the side of caution in the size of their print runs; Gutenberg's Bible quickly sold out, for instance. But soon overproduction became a problem, and many businesses failed. Sometimes different printers published the same titles, producing an oversupply. In the case of expensive works, like the Bible, a miscalculation could mean ruin.

Information about the size of print runs is inconclusive, as it is based on scattered accounts that happened to survive. From the 1480s on, print runs of one thousand and even two thousand copies are reported, and with the coming of the Reformation, the print runs increased further. Luther's *Open Letter to the Christian Nobility of the German Nation* appeared in a first edition of four thousand copies and was reprinted several times. As early as 1468–1470, publishers began to advertise, printing up their programs or lists of books in stock, including those of other printers. In the 16th century, they shifted to catalogues in book form.

Although the first printers imitated the highest-quality manuscripts in format, ornamentation, and binding, they could produce far more cheaply than the scriptoria. According to Elizabeth Eisenstein, in 1483 the Ripoli Press in Florence charged 3 florins per *quinternio* for printing Marsilio Ficino's translation of Plato's *Dialogues*. A scribe might charge 1 florin for the same work. The difference is that the scribe produced one copy, whereas the Ripoli Press produced 1,025. Nevertheless, longer books still remained unaffordable for most people. Prices for single copies are hard to determine, since the price given does not indicate whether the book in question was bound or unbound, provided with more expensive red headings, or illustrated. The low price for books when compared to manuscripts in the early days has probably been exaggerated. However, we do know that by about 1470, books cost between 50 to 80 percent less than manuscripts, and prices continued to fall, dropping by half again between 1470 and 1490. Competition kept prices down, and drove many printers into bankruptcy. Tax lists document that sometimes a printer was ruined by a single project. Furthermore, at the start of the 16th century, the trade suffered a general crisis that led to the collapse of many businesses.

New sales networks were created, and finally regular book fairs (Frankfurt) were organized. Venice owed its preeminent position to a well-developed trading network in the writings of classical authors and Humanists. Usually the people who produced books also sold them, often along with other commercial goods. One press might turn out a book under another firm's imprint; the second firm might then take charge of sales in its own region. Frequently publishers employed printers in other towns. And publishers appear to have produced different editions for local and distant markets—as in the case of early prints from the town of Ulm.

The original investment required was enormous, but so were the profit margins once a shop was established. This explains the publishers' interest in secrecy and the bitter lawsuits. After Fust and Schöffer had repossessed Gutenberg's best equipment with the help of the courts, they were able to supplant him in the marketplace. No effective patent protection existed, and protection from pirated editions was also insufficient. Licensing was possible for a particular book or a typeface, for a manufacturing process, or for such special areas as musical scores and materials in non-European languages. But licensing protected the printer, not the author. Enforcement depended on the effectiveness of the licensing authority. In many cases, if local officials were lax, licenses were simply counterfeited.

Specialization eventually provided a certain degree of protection. In the early years, between 1470 and 1490, the leading printers offered a wide selection of works in both German and Latin. Even at that time, however, they tended to emphasize particular categories. Thus in the imperial cities of Augsburg, Nuremberg, and Ulm in the South, the output was mainly in the German vernacular, while Cologne specialized in traditional literature for universities, and Basel in humanistic literature in Latin. Somewhat later Wittenberg became a center for the theological texts of the Reformation. Early modern narrative works came chiefly from Strasbourg and Augsburg until Frankfurt took their place in the mid-16th century.

During the early decades, printed books changed their appearance considerably. Mechanical and manual processes—for initials, rubrics (headings in red ink), and illustrations—existed side by side until even the last were mechanized, usually in the form of printed type and woodcuts. Up to the early 16th century, customers often chose their own more or less costly ornamentations and bindings. The belief that the upper classes, the traditional supporters of manuscript production, rejected printed books can thus be regarded as a legend. All the same, printing did not immediately replace other methods of text production, for copying was a pious work, and doing the writing oneself was certainly cheaper than buying a book. There are thus numerous surviving examples of hand-written copies of printed books from the 15th and 16th centuries.

Although title pages and page numbers were lacking in the beginning, they soon became the norm. And gradually the appearance of books became standardized in format, page size, number of lines, typefaces, orthography, punctuation, abbreviations, and front- and backmatter, such as a table of contents and index. Manuscripts from university copyist workshops often served as models. Printers like Aldus Manutius pointed proudly to improvements in their books' appearance. The varieties of type were reduced to upper- and lowercase letters and a few special characters. In manuscripts, the use of abbreviations and ligatures had saved space and money; now they were too expensive, since they made it necessary to stock several forms of each letter. Planning was difficult in any event, for printers were as yet unaware of the statistical frequency of letters. They had to invent techniques for keeping margins even, filling lines, and for hyphenation, and the various stages of the printing process had to be coordinated.

Not infrequently printers solved technical difficulties by altering text. Contemporaries found this unreliability all the more vexing since mechanical production had been expected to reduce the number of errors and variations between copies. The fact that all texts printed from one mold were exactly identical first filled people with amazement. When the Bishop of Brixen, Nicholas of Cusa, demanded uniform wording for the celebration of the Mass and prohibited the alteration of missals and texts for other church services under pain of excommunication, he could hope at best to suppress intentional alterations, for unintentional deviations that crept in during the copying process could not be controlled. The advent of printing changed this in a way that contemporaries found uncanny. Surviving records show that clerics in Regensburg were paid to go through the text of the new printed missal (1485) copy by copy to check for errors. They discovered, to their great surprise, that every copy was exactly the same and precisely matched the model—a miracle!

However, uniformity also created new pitfalls. In 1505, Erasmus of Rotterdam complained in his edition of Lorenzo Valla's *Adnotationes* to the New Testament that while scribes could make errors, they made them only one at a time, whereas print multiplied a single mistake many times. On the other hand, print errors could be corrected at a central location, while a copyist was limited to emending the single text in front of him. The more ambitious print shops hired scholars as proofreaders, like the jurist Sebastian Brant in Basel. A proofreader's tasks resembled those of an editor. Authors were not normally asked to read proofs of their own works. Errata lists were added to books and could be referred to for later editions. The new medium permitted the development of textual criticism, making it possible to conceive the idea of an original text that stood behind all its material representations. Classical philology was born.

In Germany, the most important by-product of increased uniformity was the development of standard German. The regional differences noticeable in the language of early printed works were evened out in the 16th century. The relationship between the sounds of German and their written form became standardized as well. Spelling rules developed, and publishers brought out German-language textbooks to teach elementary reading, writing, and grammar. In the 16th century, the spread of the Protestant Reformation from Wittenberg had a further standardizing effect on the written language in central Germany, in competition with southern or high German usage (as practiced by the imperial chancellery, for example). The dominance of the southern and central German book market accelerated the decline and disappearance of low German (northern German dialect) in print.

In contrast to scribes, who prepared a single manuscript for one purchaser, printers had to appeal to as large an audience as possible. The prefaces and dedications of very early printed works praise them as generally instructive or entertaining, or suggest they will be useful to people working in a variety of professions. Early printed works addressed a readership with diffuse interests, ready to consume anything and everything on the market. Much extraneous material was often included at first but dropped from later editions. From the point of view of consumers, distinctions between genres or eras, such as fiction and nonfiction, or modern and ancient authors, were of secondary importance. A romance about the Trojan War was considered as much a part of world history as a chronicle of contemporary events, and as instructive as a political tract. Narratives of all kinds were listed under the heading *historia,* independent of their particular form and function and the degree to which they dealt with real events, for histories, containing the experiences of other people, were deemed useful to readers in their own lives.

The advent of printing brought fundamental changes to the organization of knowledge, public communication, and the social role of writing, as some critics of printing recognized early on. On the one hand, it became possible to collect successive stages of traditional knowledge and to compare and contrast them; the entire body of lore handed down on a subject could be surveyed as a whole. A process began of accumulating information in a given field, fixing it in print, and seeing the boundaries of knowledge expand. The fact that information could become out of date ceased to be an argument against the utility of having it appear in writing. On the other hand, a printer's desire to make a profit often determined what information would become available. Commercialization was sometimes achieved at the expense of craftsmanship. The most significant development, however, was a shift of power in society. The privileged few who had been in charge of the craft of writing for centuries lost control of it. Writing ceased to be the exclusive domain of scholars and frequently fell into the hands of unscholarly, and thus, it was felt, illicit, users. The authorities responded by prohibiting access to written works—particularly the Bible—by the laity.

The development of book printing was accompanied by the implementation of stricter censorship. In 1485, in one of the earliest edicts on the subject, the Bishop of Mainz decreed that anyone caught printing German translations of biblical and liturgical books would have his press confiscated and be excommunicated. The German language could not express the subtle shades of meaning in Latin and Greek theological works, he declared, and laymen, the unschooled, and women were incapable of grasping the correct meaning. Translations of any work must, therefore, be submitted to scholars at the university in either Mainz or Erfurt for pre-censorship before being published. The Papacy had already created institutions within the Church to oversee censorship (Cologne 1479). They often dealt with single works, such as Giovanni Pico della Mirandola's 900 theses, which was banned by Innocent VIII. The intent was usually protection of Church monopoly on doctrinal teaching and interpreting Scriptures.

Opposition to this doctrine arose a few decades after the bishop's edict, when the leaders of the Reformation demanded universal access to the Bible—in translation, of course. Censorship also became an important instrument in the battle between denominations. A list of banned books *(index librorum prohibitorum)* was announced for Catholic territories for the first time in 1559.

Even before 1500, some had proposed using printed books for religious instruction of common people. Those who could read would use them directly, and the illiterate would listen as they were read aloud. Before publication of Luther's Bible translation in 1534, 156 printed versions of the Bible in Latin and 17 in German were in existence. When the Reformation made education of the laity one of its goals, the art of printing appeared as a God-given vehicle for promoting Church reform. The priesthood of the faithful, based on private ownership of the Holy Scriptures, was conceivable only if the Scriptures were universally available. Despite later attempts by the orthodoxy to regulate ownership, personal study of the Bible remained at the core of Protestant piety. With the publication of Luther's translation of the New Testament in Wittenberg in September 1522, the foundation of the Protestant faith became accessible to the general public. It appeared in large editions, but the first—consisting of four thousand copies, with twenty-one illustrations by Lukas Cranach—had sold out by December. Twelve more editions followed before publication of Luther's complete Bible translation in 1534. By 1523, his New Testament had been printed twelve times in other cities, seven times in Basel alone. There were ten printings of his complete Bible with 117 woodcuts before the appearance of the 1546 edition, the last to be published in Luther's lifetime. It has been estimated that between 1522 and 1546 altogether 380 different printings of either the entire Bible or portions of it were made; some of them were Catholic versions based on Luther's translation. A total of three hundred thousand copies are thought to have been printed of the thirty works Luther wrote between 1517 and 1520. A mass movement developed, unimaginable in scope at the time of earlier reformers like Jan Hus and John Wycliffe. Without the public resonance made possible by the invention of printing, Luther's posting of his ninety-five theses in 1517 would have remained a local event connected with the start of a new term at the university in Wittenberg. Many of his works—*On Secular Authority, An Open Letter to the Christian Nobility, On Trade and Usury, To the Councilors of All German Cities*—took the form of letters supposedly written to individuals, but in fact addressed to the public, like pamphlets expressly written to influence the denominational struggle. Some of them were presented as face-to-face conversations even though the message was intended for a disparate audience. By creating a public interested in and supportive of the aims of the Reformation, the new medium revolutionized medieval society and the culture of information.

Printing also led to profound changes in other sectors of culture. The arcane knowledge of the Renaissance can be understood as a reaction to the vulgarization of knowledge. Cabbala, hieroglyphics, *corpus hermeticum,* secret writing (cf. *Steganographia* by John Trithemius), and even popular narratives about magic, such as the tale of Faust, represent attempts to protect an exclusive zone of secrecy in the face of so much knowledge that had become available to all. Sebastian Brant's lament in *The Ship of Fools* about the glut of writing was anticipated in the Hebrew Bible: "Of making many books there is no end" (Ecclesiastes 12:12). By his time, however, Brant was protesting against a spread of information that had in fact become unstoppable.

See also 1027, 1401, 1492, 1500 (Dürer), 1523, 1596

Bibliography: Konrad Burger, *The Printers and Publishers of the XVth Century* (London, 1902). Elizabeth L. Eisenstein, *The Printing Revolution in Early Modern Europe* (Cambridge, U.K.: Cambridge University Press, 1983). Michael Giesecke, *Der Buchdruck in der frühen Neuzeit: Eine historische Fallstudie über die Durchsetzung neuer Informations- und Kommunikationstechnologien* (Frankfurt am Main: Suhrkamp, 1991). Rudolf Hirsch, *Printing, Selling and Reading 1450–1550* (Wiesbaden: Harrassowitz, 1974). Jan-Dirk Müller, "Der Körper des Buchs," in Hans Ulrich Gumbrecht and K. Ludwig Pfeiffer, eds., *Materialität der Kommunikation,* 2nd edition (Frankfurt am Main: Suhrkamp, 1995). Sandra Hinderman, ed., *Printing the Written Word: The Social History of Books circa 1450–1520* (Ithaca, N.Y., and London: Cornell University Press, 1991).

Jan-Dirk Müller
Translated by Deborah Lucas Schneider

♄ 1478

Jakob Fugger takes over his family's banking business as world trade expands from the Far East to the New World

Fortunatus Maps the World and Himself

Published in 1509 and written by an unidentified author, most probably a writer living in southern Germany, the prose narrative *Fortunatus* enjoyed bestseller status in its time and in the centuries that followed. Its success was due not only to its plot, which resonated with a new reading audience of wealthy merchants and bankers, but to its grand geographical sweep across the far reaches of the known world—from Ireland to Indonesia. By 1500 the towns of southern Germany were in the forefront of economic activity, and Augsburg, the city in which *Fortunatus* was published, was a major center of trade and commerce. At the time when Jakob Fugger assumed direction of his family's banking house there in 1478, European commerce was rapidly expanding toward both the West and the East. Between 1467 and 1540, the accumulated wealth in Augsburg alone grew twentyfold. In the course of forty years, the Fuggers, originally a family of weavers, increased their capital by a factor of seventy—an achievement that afforded them a life of luxury and enabled them to become the financiers of emperors. The Welsers, another prominent Augsburg merchant family, acquired massive riches, only to lose all within three generations. The author of *Fortunatus* captures this transience of

wealth, and the magical, even demonic power of money in the symbolic structure of his tale.

In this early prose novel various socio-economic and cultural discourses are
woven together: issues of capitalism and mercantilism, of travel and discovery
as well as a new conception of the individual—what might be called "the experiencing self"—imbued with all the anxieties and insecurities of the emergent merchant class. These themes are developed through two narrative strategies. First, the protagonist's fortunes are mapped across a topographical grid
that spans from West to East, with the West representing the socio-economic
world and the East the realm of fantasy. Second, the geographic metaphor is
anchored in two salient symbols—a magic purse, which Fortunatus acquires
from Lady Luck, and an enchanted hat, which he steals from the Sultan of
Egypt—both of which correlate with the novel's geographical and psychological space.

The novel's eponymous protagonist is an impoverished patrician's son from
Cyprus, whose quest for wealth, knowledge, and esteem takes him to the limits
of the known world. While the range of Fortunatus's travels is perhaps not surprising for a narrative written during a period of expanding trade and exploration, one wonders why, in a text written by a German author and based most
probably on German sources, the main character is a Cypriot. And why does
the story locate key moments—the beginning, midway point, and ending—on
the isle of Cyprus? Although some scholars have speculated on links between
Cyprus and possible patrons of the novel, or between the island and the cities
of Augsburg and Nuremberg, no convincing evidence for these hypotheses has
been found. The result of the narrative's focus on Cyprus, however, is the creation of a neutral, domestic space situated between West and East. From this
starting point, Fortunatus undertakes two journeys: first he traverses Europe
and then explores the Orient.

The isle of Cyprus is introduced in the very first line of the preface. In fact,
it is the island, not the protagonist, that is the subject of the first three sentences
of the narrative. Though the island's culture is Christian, it is bordered on three
sides by Islamic areas, and is thus a point of interface of two religions. In economic terms, the narrative recognizes the island's importance as a crossroads
for traders and pilgrims. However, its location on the contemporary world
map is also significant for the novel's narrative architecture, organization, and
plot development as well as thematic and symbolic structure. The East-West
dichotomy is delineated geographically by Fortunatus's itinerary and by the
character himself, who sees the world not so much in terms of "us" and
"them" but "das halbe tayl" and "das ander tayl"—the one half and the other.

Throughout his journeys, Fortunatus is always a stranger in foreign lands.
His experience of alienation is the theme that links the scattered stations of his
adventures. By locating the protagonist's origins in Cyprus, the narrator creates
an objective observer whose position is neither entirely western nor entirely
eastern, and whose point of view is solely that of the *Kaufmann,* or merchant.
Fortunatus is as much an observer of otherness in the British Isles as he is in
India. Unlike the protagonists of other travel literature from this period,

Fortunatus expresses anxieties associated with his experiences of the foreign. His reflections on the topic of otherness suggest that new issues are at stake here.

His first journey takes Fortunatus on a long westward loop. Alone and penniless, he leaves Cyprus to find his way in the social world. Yet nowhere in society—among the servants, merchants, or aristocrats—does he find acceptance. In due course, he encounters Lady Luck, who grants him limitless wealth in the form of a self-replenishing bag of money. Money, the privileged signifier, determines the nature of the protagonist's interactions with others. Yet, despite his enormous wealth, he never becomes integrated into the social world. He remains a stranger, always an outsider. Since money, rather than its carrier, is valued, it is money—and the greed and avarice it provokes—that determines social relationships. In effect, monetary transactions reshape a social space previously arranged according to religious and feudal norms.

Fifteen years of wandering take Fortunatus to Ireland—then the farthest western edge of the known world—and back again to his home in Cyprus. There he marries and has two sons. Despite twelve years of domestic and social good fortune, he feels compelled to explore "das ander tayl," the part of the world that lies east of Cyprus. However, his second journey has a motivation different from the first. Fortunatus goes to the East not in response to the demands of the real world—money, food, and power—but to satisfy an inner longing. In this narrative, as in others of the period, the realm of desire and fantasy is situated in the East.

Even as it was being "discovered," mapped, and reported about, the East remained, in the late medieval European mind, a conglomeration of the real and the imaginary: it was the realm of the Bible, but also of imagined vast riches, of wondrous places, and monstrous human races. Whereas Fortunatus's western itinerary was closely based on travel reports, for the second journey, the author turned to the iconic medieval text of eastern travel: the fictitious and fantastical 14th-century tale *The Travels of Sir John Mandeville,* to which he refers directly ("das buoch Johannem de Montevilla"). Only Alexandria, the powerful Arab trading center and portal to the Orient, is depicted in any way realistically. Fortunatus's eastern travels begin and end in this city. Following the model of fact-based *Reiseberichte* (travel reports), the text is chiefly concerned with details that would have interested an audience of merchants and bankers: docking procedure, warehousing of goods, currency exchange rates, translators, and travel permits. In Alexandria, money continues to speak, defining networks of power and human relationships. In contrast, the middle section of Fortunatus's eastern sojourn—from Persia to Indonesia—offers little in the way of facts and figures. Instead, the author relies on the trope of the fantastical East and mobilizes stock motifs of wonder and excess. If *Fortunatus* was written after the Portuguese had tracked the route around Africa to India in 1498, then the author chose not to make mention of their findings.

Curiously, India figures more prominently in the narrator's descriptions than any other region. Borrowing from Mandeville the division of India into three main regions, he elaborates at length on its climatic extremes. Yet, at the same time, he confesses to an inability to represent the vastness of this land, its customs, and its wonders. For the first time the author concedes to limitations of his narrative and language for evoking what lies beyond the realm of familiar experience. He relies on the conventional formula of India as a vast, mysterious place of great wealth, but he resists occupying this space—as one would expect—with the fantastical peoples, flora, and fauna that animate the writings of Herodotus, Pliny, and Mandeville, and crowd the edges of the medieval *mappae mundi*. The *Fortunatus* narrator omits these bizarre creatures, pointing instead to *Mandeville* as a substitute for description. The place of Fortunatus's desire is thus an imaginary realm of excess that demands, but also defies, description.

Even here, however, in this most fictional of spaces, the narrator does not abandon his overall concern with the very real experience of being foreign while also encountering the foreign. In a remarkable display of empathy, the narrator incorporates the notion of reciprocity into his text. We—the narrator tells us—are as strange to the Indians as they are to us. He even imagines the problems the inhabitants of India might encounter when traveling westward: cold and lacking in fruit, "our country" would seem bizarre to them; not knowing the customs, they would trade good for bad, and perhaps even be regarded as fools by their hosts. In this respect, *Fortunatus* breaks with *Mandeville*. The latter uses astronomy to establish a hierarchy of racial characteristics that is inextricably tied to workings of the cosmos: the Indians, according to Mandeville, are under the sign of Saturn, and thus have a propensity for lethargy and cowardice, while Europeans, influenced by the moon, are destined to seek and explore new lands. *Fortunatus* avoids such stereotypes and ascribes the Indians' reluctance to travel to a psychology common to people in both halves of the world. Anxiety associated with travel to foreign places and an encounter with the unknown is presented as universal. The narrator's concern with perception—how one is perceived within and outside of one's own social and cultural context—is sustained by his attempt to create an Indian point of view.

As it moves back to Alexandria, the narrative reverts to a fairly realistic portrayal of economic life, with one exception. As guest of the Sultan of Egypt, Fortunatus steals the ruler's most prized possession, a magic hat, which has the power to transport its wearer to whatever place he wishes. Pretending to try it on, Fortunatus literally disappears with it. He is immediately transported back to Cyprus, where he lives out his life in possession of both the magic purse and the enchanted hat.

If Fortunatus's itineraries can be considered analogous to a mapping of the self, along West-East coordinates, then the magic bag and hat, which Fortunatus acquires in the two parts of the world respectively, can and should be interpreted in the context of the novel's geographic construction of the self. The magic purse contains money—the universally understood medium of exchange, the novel's privileged signifier. Its role in the story reminds us of the familiar adage "money talks" and in *Fortunatus* money does in fact function like language as it shapes the subject's identity and his position within the socio-economic network. The magic hat represents the East, the theater of his fantasy. It enables Fortunatus to travel without boundaries or hindrances, and frees him not only from what he experiences as "boredom" but also allows him to escape from the obligations and restrictions of the social and domestic world. And while the purse is filled with self-replenishing money, the intermediary between self and society, the hat is a carrier without fixed content, symbolizing paucity—an emptiness which fantasy seeks to fill. The money is taken out of the bag while fantasy is inserted into the magical cap. What the hat offers is the product of its wearer's own imagination in much the same way as the geographical East functions as an empty space into which the western imagination projects its dreams of excess, wonder, and danger.

In keeping with the overall tendency to view this early modern novel as an expression of the new merchant class mentality, scholars generally interpret the enchanted hat as equivalent to the magic purse: the former symbolizing wealth and social integration, and the latter, international trade. But *Fortunatus* is more than a mere exploration of economic interconnections, of wealth lost and gained or, for that matter, of the merits of wisdom versus wealth. In an age that saw the emergence of the individual, this tale of a wandering merchant-adventurer attempts to explore, however tentatively, its protagonist's psyche, his experience of wealth, his encounter with a new social order and, through travel, with foreign worlds. It is a transitional work, one that represents a new economic order and geographical worldview through a new literary genre, the prose narrative. In a two-pronged effort to portray the external and internal worlds of its merchant protagonist, the novelist employs realistic description, symbolic geography, and fairy-tale motifs while creatively shifting Fortunatus's origins to neutral ground. From Cyprus, Fortunatus maps his self across the two halves of the world, navigating first—with the help of the magic purse—the labyrinth of social and financial relationships in the West, and second, the space represented by the enchanted hat, the realm of desire and fantasy in "das ander tayl der welt," the East.

See also 1457, 1596, 1647

Bibliography: Hans-Gert Roloff, ed., *Fortunatus: Studienausgabe nach der Editio Princeps von 1509* (Stuttgart: Philipp Reclam, 1996). Thomas Cramer, *Geschichte der deutschen Literatur im späten Mittelalter* (Munich: Deutscher Taschenbuch Verlag, 1990). Hannes Kästner, *Fortunatus, Peregrinator Mundi: Welterfahrung und Selbsterkenntnis im ersten deutschen Prosaroman der Neuzeit* (Freiburg: Rombach, 1990). Jan-Dirk Müller, *Romane des 15. und 16. Jahrhunderts* (Frankfurt am Main: Deutscher Klassiker Verlag, 1990). Renate Wiemann, *Die Erzählstruktur im Volksbuch Fortunatus* (Hildesheim: Olms, 1970).

Debra Prager

1492, November 7

A meteor strikes the earth near the western border of the Holy Roman Empire

The Ship of Fools

The early modern era may well be said to have started with a bang. About noon on November 7, 1492, a meteor thundered through the air and hit the ground near Ensisheim, a small town in Alsace and the administrative seat of the Habsburg Empire's westernmost territory. In premodern reckoning, a meteor was a portent, a divine message encoded in stone. In order for this message to become legible, the stone's meaning had to be deciphered as indicated by the time and place of the meteor's fall, its size, weight, and shape. Sebastian Brant (1457–1521), dean of the faculty of law in nearby Basel, and Johann Bergmann von Olpe, a local printer, were quick to respond to the challenge. Shortly after the event, they published a bilingual broadside in Latin and German. Judging by its wide dissemination and manifold literary echoes, this publication must have struck a nerve among contemporaries. Since popular prophecies had predicted the end of the world for 1492, the meteor lent itself to a great apocalyptic vision. Brant, however, defused all expectations of impending disaster. By focusing on the German Empire's political fate instead, he gave his interpretation a surprising, even comforting twist. The author of the broadside prophesied trouble for the empire's neighbor to the west, France, and hinted, ever so cautiously, at golden days for the "German nation" if only her future ruler, Maximilian I (1459–1519), lived up to the divine call to arms signaled by the meteor.

Broadsides were recent innovations. Adorned with woodcut illustrations, these one-page publications covered current events before the advent of newspapers. News had to be adapted to a universal order that was regarded as unchangeable. Thousands of miles west of Ensisheim, Christopher Columbus faced a similar dilemma as he scanned Cuba for evidence that it was what reliable authorities had led him to expect, namely Cipangu (Japan). When news of the Spanish and Portuguese discoveries reached Brant in 1494, he dismissed it on moral grounds as something that could not be true. The gulf between the old and the new, between well-established sources of information and experiential knowledge, invited commentary and, as a corollary, provoked an almost insatiable appetite for published information of all kinds.

The broadside about the meteor was not the last of Brant's and Bergmann von Olpe's successful collaborations. Two years later, they launched a more ambitious project: *Das Narrenschyff* (1494; *The Ship of Fools*), a 315-page panopticon of foolishly un-Christian ways of behavior, divided into 113 chapters and illustrated with 114 woodcuts. *The Ship of Fools* became an unprecedented and lasting success. At a time when writings in German were hardly noticed, let alone translated into other languages, this work became extremely popular among early modern readers in the empire and beyond. The book's sweeping success is evident in the number of editions that poured from print shops in London and Paris, Lyons and Lübeck in subsequent years and even centuries. The original edition alone was reprinted six times between 1494 and 1512. Starting in 1494, the year of the book's first publication, unauthorized editions, with some deviations from Brant's text, began to appear. In 1497, Jacob Locher Philomusus (1471–1528), one of Brant's students, translated *The Ship of Fools* into Latin under the title *Stultifera navis*. More heavily inflected toward Humanism than Brant's German text, Locher's Latin version paved the way for dissemination of the satire in French, Dutch, English, and other vernaculars.

Overall, sixty-nine editions of *The Ship of Fools* are known to have been printed between 1494 and 1600.

Brant had a tremendous influence on other contemporary writers. One of the era's most celebrated preachers, Johann Geiler von Kaysersberg (1445–1510), delivered a series of sermons based on Brant's satire that were published in Latin and subsequently translated into German. His compatriot Thomas Murner (1475–1537) adapted the figure of the fool in his own writings. Reformation pamphlets popularized Brant's literary style and by the mid-16th century a new edition reshaped Brant's pre-Reformation satire for Protestant readers. Numerous authors, Johann Fischart (1546/47–1590) and Friedrich Dedekind (1524–1598) among them, emulated *The Ship of Fools*. In *Laus stultiae* (1509; *The Praise of Folly*) even the great Erasmus (1466/69–1536) took up Brant's central theme, though without acknowledging his precursor.

Why did *The Ship of Fools* become a bestseller in the early modern period? The book's success, no doubt, rests on the fact that Narragonia, the fool's realm (*Narr* is German for fool), straddled many segments of early modern culture and society—a society deeply fragmented along lines of class and levels of education. *The Ship of Fools* bridged several of these segments, forging a synthesis of culturally diverse elements. A legal scholar by profession, Brant belonged to a milieu in which German and Latin were part of everyday usage, but Latin was considered the only proper medium for academic debate. Yet, he penned *The Ship of Fools* in the vernacular.

The poem attracted a wide array of readers. Part of the book's appeal may have been due to the way it crossed boundaries of communication. Scholars, for instance, were able to immerse themselves in what were regarded as the commoners' ways, while less educated readers could confront scholarly erudition. Even the illiterate were informed and entertained by the woodcut images that contributed so much to the book's success.

No figure was better suited to bring together such a diverse readership than the fool. Both literati and illiterati could rally around the notion of *docta ignorantia,* learned ignorance, a paradox bracketing the practical wisdom of the uneducated and the futility of any attempt to grasp the supreme wisdom of God's creation. In this blend of the religious, the ethical, and the humorous, Brant employed registers that set his concept of folly apart. In the early modern period, the fool and madman symbolized man's position in the eyes of an omnipotent God. At the same time, the buffoon in multicolored garb was a popular figure in urban carnival rituals across Germany. Tellingly, the first edition of *The Ship of Fools* is linked to urban rituals by dating its appearance as "the Shrovetide which one calls the Fool's Festival" (366). Although devotional handbooks, such as John Lydgate's *The Order of Fools* (ca. 1460), had used the image of the fool as symbolic of humankind before, it was Brant who first depicted the entire human race as an assembly of fools.

Like early modern society, Brant's assembly of fools is highly stratified. Their ranks include the excessive reader, the flatterer, the one who serenades women, and the one who refuses to reckon with human mortality. A great number of types of sins are presented as follies, some relatively petty, like effeminacy among men, others grave, like usury and blasphemy. Far from merely criticizing or ridiculing, however, Brant teaches how to improve oneself by learning from a negative example. As each chapter explores one specific folly, the sequence of the chapters is only loosely structured. The image of the ship itself provides narrative unity: the reader embarks on a vessel destined to travel the great sea of life. Weighed down by the increasing number of fools, the ship—it is implied—must inevitably sink.

Many scholars have seen the ship of fools as a reflection of early modern society as a whole. Yet, several of the graver sins, such as theft and sodomy, are not included in the catalogue of follies. Some actions, it seems, set their perpetrators so far apart from Christian society that they defied representation. Translators and redactors added new stations to the journey and expanded the echelons of fools to fill in presumed gaps in the text's rendering of contemporary society. In Brant's narrative, for example, women serve mostly as objects of men's follies, while Badius Ascensus published an entire volume on what he saw as women's foibles.

Situated at the border of the empire, the upper Rhine valley was an ideal area for intricate cultural mediation. In the 15th century, this highly urbanized, prosperous region had become a hub of international commerce, technological innovation, and educational reform. The Church Councils held in Constance (1414–1418) and Basel (1431–1449) intensified contacts between clerics from south and north of the Alps. Frequent encounters with Italian scholars, who had developed advanced philological skills, sparked interest in the study of ancient languages and texts among their northern counterparts. At the same time, these encounters also gave rise to notions of a distinct, glorious German nation that would prove itself through its arts and letters. The technology of print by movable type, first developed between Strasbourg and Mainz by Johannes Gutenberg (ca. 1397–1468), seemed to substantiate the claim of German superiority. Many towns in the upper Rhine valley seized the opportunity to attract the new trade. Albrecht Dürer (1471–1528) traveled to Alsace to study with Martin Schongauer (1450–1491), a pioneer in elevating etching to high art. When he found the master had died, Dürer moved on to Basel, where he designed woodcuts for various printers, including most of the illustrations for *The Ship of Fools*.

In the mid-15th century, Basel, a city of ten thousand, was granted the papal privilege of founding a university. When it opened its gates in 1460, the university at Basel gained renown for its innovative curriculum and rapidly emerged as one of the early centers of Humanism north of the Alps. In 1475, Brant, a native of Strasbourg, became a student there. Later, he joined the faculty of law and developed an acute interest in the practicalities of legal life. He worked as a lawyer and settled, among other things, marital disputes. As a docent, he also lectured on poetry, the art of speaking and writing Latin eloquently, a much-needed skill for lawyers. In 1501, he accepted a nonacademic position in Strasbourg as legal advisor to the town council, and after 1503, as city scribe. In other words, Brant's training in law disposed him toward mediating between cultural spheres.

While he was pursuing his studies in Basel, Brant also benefited from the splendid library of the local Carthusian monastery, unparalleled in the entire empire. Like many of his colleagues, Brant also worked as proofreader and consultant for the local presses, many of which had an excellent reputation throughout Europe for their publication of Latin, Greek, and Hebrew texts. Basel was fortunate in that the intellectual resources of the monastery and the university, combined with the presence of a local paper industry and the arrival of printers and publishers in the region, made possible some of the most ambitious projects in the early history of printing. In 1490, Brant himself launched an auspicious publishing career with a highly successful textbook for legal scholars. His subsequent oeuvre comprises diverse texts and genres, such as Latin textbooks, editions of law codes, and Latin poetry, not to mention broadsides and chronicles. Significantly, his list of publications includes texts in Latin and German. Often, however, these works were issued in bilingual editions. Even *The Ship of Fools,* though composed entirely in German, is situated at an intersection of languages and cultures.

Brant's writings shift freely between a great variety of styles. Sayings with a proverbial ring give way to informative passages, humorous digressions alternate with sententious didactics. Quotations from the German literary tradition enter this complex fabric just as easily as references to Greek and Roman mythology. Written in a meter modeled after Latin poetry, *The Ship of Fools* projects the effect of a Roman satire in German guise. German neologisms and Latinate terms merge to form a highly flexible idiom, creating overall an extremely lively effect.

Although the text is replete with learned allusions, the accompanying woodcuts convey a sense of immediate accessibility. Indeed, the book's appeal rested to a large degree on its illustrations, the majority of them brilliantly executed by the young Albrecht Dürer. One principal challenge was the need for rendering abstract concepts like rudeness in visual form. Aware of the images' crucial importance, Brant took an active role in the design of the woodcuts. Ultimately, however, the relation between text and image in *The Ship of Fools* is one of consonance and dissonance, a tension that must have been appealing to readers willing to decode a message delivered in two media.

The images thus tell a story of their own. The woodcut for chapter 72, for example, invokes, but also suspends, the laws of perspective. Endowed with crown and bell but angered by the fool, the sow reaches with its tail for a ship in full sail in the background. This detail connects the single fool with the foolish journey, aptly demonstrating how the individual fool's behavior is connected to a larger order and its impending demise.

The chapter illustrated by this woodcut focuses on the "coarse fool," specifically on the rules of polite behavior, by deriding offensive words and acts. This idea was so intriguing to contemporaries that it inspired a whole new genre of literature known as *Grobianische* or Saint Ruffian's literature. Like other chapters in *The Ship of Fools,* chapter 72 opens with a summarizing motto ("Vile, scolding words do irritate, / Good manners thereby will abate / If sow-bells rung from morn to late," 238), followed by a woodcut and, finally,

Illustration from *The Ship of Fools,* attributed to Albrecht Dürer. (Copyright © 2002 by the University Libraries, University of Houston)

a poem on the same theme. As a whole, this chapter is predicated on a complex rhetoric of reversal. The world is portrayed upside down: the sow is made king while the fool is brought in close touch with an unclean animal. The elements that indicate order, such as the cult of Saint Ruffian, are revealed as signs of disorder. Such satire is necessarily ambivalent. It immerses itself and takes pleasure in things to be rejected. The reader must work diligently to discern the didactic message beneath the humorous surface. Motto, illustration, and text overlap, yet they differ significantly as they heighten the sense of creative dissonance. This intricately crafted versatility made *The Ship of Fools* a literary and stylistic model for generations to come and initiated early modern readers into a specific way of reading the world. Brant's contemporaries hailed him, not without reason, as a new Virgil or a German Dante.

However, the bookish ship and foolish travelers are by no means part of contemporary popular culture. True, the book resides in a culturally significant space replete with reflections on popular rituals, but, even with its playful entertaining style, it is primarily a storehouse of erudition and a work of didacticism. In the spirit of northern Humanism, Brant advocates individual reform: "Well-ordered love for other men / Means: With yourself you must begin" (199). Every human is potentially a fool and all of human society an assembly of fools, even if many try to evade this truism: "A fool is all the more inclined / To think he's witty when men mock / And make of him a laughing stock" (227). It is, therefore, only logical that, within the realm of Narragonia, Brant presents himself as wearing the fool's cap. Is this author-fool the ultimate truth or just another disguise? And how are we to trust the teachings of a fool among fools if we intend to avoid shipwreck?

See also 1437, 1457, 1500 (Dürer), 1515–1517, 1570, 1860

Bibliography: Sebastian Brant, *Das Narrenschiff: Faksimile der Erstausgabe Basel 1494,* ed. Dieter Wuttke (Baden-Baden: Valentin Koerner, 1994). *The Ship of Fools by Sebastian Brant,* ed. and trans. Edwin H. Zeydel (New York: Columbia University Press, 1944). Gonthier-Lewis Fink, ed., *Sébastian Brant, son époque et "la nef des fols"* / *Sebastian Brant, seine Zeit und das "Narrenschiff": actes du colloque international Strasbourg* 10–11 mars 1994 (Strasbourg: Institut d'Études Allemandes, 1995). Joachim Knape, *Dichtung, Recht und Freiheit: Studien zu Leben und Werk Sebastian Brants, 1457–1521* (Baden-Baden: Valentin Koerner, 1992). Edwin H. Zeydel, *Sebastian Brant* (New York: Twayne, 1967).

Helmut Puff

ᎧᏔ *1500*

Germany's most famous jester and rogue, Till Eulenspiegel, steps onto the world's stage at a time when German itself is changing

A Philosophical Rascal?

In February 1500, as Cesare Borgia celebrated his triumph over his northern Italian enemies by staging an elaborate parade witnessed by hundreds of thousands who had also journeyed to Rome for the Christian Jubilee festivities that year, an unknown German author—he may have been Hermann Bote—put pen to paper in Strasbourg to compile the adventures of a professional rogue. His modestly sized book, with its ninety-five adventures of Till Eulenspiegel, *Ein kurzweilig lessen von Dil Ulenspiegel* (first publications: 1508?, 1510, 1512, 1515; *An Amusing Reading of Till Eulenspiegel;* the modernization "Eulenspiegel" first appears in later 16th-century editions), had about it from the beginning an aura of mystery. What was its intention? What did it mean?

The mystery was matched only by its popularity. This soon assumed the proportions of a tidal wave. It became a powerful literary sea-change, and its imaginative power continues. It rolls along to this day in fact, centuries later, with a public dazzle matched only by the mesmerism of Faust and Hamlet—far more impressive creations, or so the serious-minded may wish to believe. Their preference, however, seems acceptable only if one disregards the Eulenspiegel phenomenon itself. Few Germans over the past five hundred years have refused the happy invitation to set out with this supreme late medieval and Renaissance jester on his odd and hilarious adventures. Even fewer know nothing about him—his crudity, his truth-seeking, his compassion, his sadism, his purity of mission, his callousness, his absurdity, his occasional saintliness, his unique independence. In the end, the complex clown who has become a German national hero, or anti-hero, has influenced the world at large, not to mention his own German culture, more decisively and remarkably than Cesare Borgia, who fancied himself a reincarnation of Julius Caesar and who also played the rogue, if with bloodthirsty doses of Machiavellian deceit. Eulenspiegel by contrast goes on enchanting his German and international audience (for his tales have been translated into scores of languages) with an insuperable blitheness. It may be fair to say that he has helped to shape modern Germany's national character and even contributed to the country's political unification.

To get some grip on this amazing *succès de scandale,* while gaining some insight into Eulenspiegel's bizarre career, or clearing up its mystery, one needs to take stock of the history of rogues and jesters, of the transformation of Renaissance and Reformation Germany by the newly invented printing press, and of shifts just coming about, with some perhaps spurred on by Eulenspiegel's adventures themselves, in German as it was spoken and written during his tumultuous 16th century. One also needs to take stock of modern prudishness. Since the 19th century most versions of Eulenspiegel's adventures have been censored, cleaned up, toned down, smoothed out, and finally, in a burst of risible hypocrisy, relegated to the category of children's literature. Satire has been crumpled into slapstick, mockery into nonsense. The result is a misunderstanding, especially among most Germans, of Eulenspiegel's entirely adult sophistication.

Goethe himself supplies an important clue to his amazing game with the world: "Eulenspiegel: all the chief jests of the book depend on this: that everybody speaks figuratively and Eulenspiegel takes it literally." This insight applies to about half the tales in the book. In most of the rest, Eulenspiegel's literal interpretation of what people say colors, alters, and transforms the action, to produce a succession of absurdities.

At first his behavior may seem only ridiculous, which is to say meaningless, or cruel, or childish, as when in tale 37 he smashes through the roof of a blacksmith's house because he has ordered him to get up and out of the place; or when in tale 81 he kills and skins an innkeeper's dog, offering her its skin as payment for a jug of beer (from which at her bidding he has allowed the dog to take a gulp or two) because she tells him that each of her guests must pay for everything he drinks with whatever collateral he has. Rapidly, however, no doubt because of the sheer number of tales insisting on literal interpretations of speech, and because this develops into a puzzling force in its own right, one realizes that something more than an infantile desire to tease and annoy is afoot. One comes to see that Eulenspiegel is out to make mock of the sloppiness of ordinary conversation, or of anybody's speech in the heat of the moment, or of the general run of humanity's imprecise linguistic struggles when it attempts through some shorthand or other of phrasing—through idioms, say, or slang—to communicate a state of mind, rather than mere information. Eulenspiegel is fascinated by the fact that people rarely mean what they say. He is amazed at their conscious and unconscious self-deceptiveness. He is also astonished, or such at least is his pose, at what appears to be the inevitability of their linguistic stumblings-about. Indeed, he devotes his life and roguish career, during which he travels from one country, or German principality, to another, along with his wild excursions into France, Poland, and Italy, to exposing the frustrating dishonesty of language itself as it condemns everyone to babbling in misleading metaphors, or euphemisms, or pompous psychological evasions.

It is in this unique sense that he surely needs to be understood as a philosophical rascal, or even as an unrecognized but early and interesting linguistic philosopher. If he plays his often vicious tricks on the vainglorious, deflating their pretensions simply by taking them at their word, his real passion is to humiliate, by exhibiting its emptiness, the falsity of their styles of speech. At the same time, he sets out to illuminate the frequent idiocy, in its literal sense of irrelevance, of all spoken language. This would include the pleas of the desolate and virtuous. It embraces the often garbled prayers of the innocent. In Eulenspiegel's view, hypocrisy and bitter human conflicts enter the world not simply by way of egotism, greed, and mendacity, but through confused and emotion-driven talk. What he and his exploits demonstrate—and his demonstration also has about it in the end the air of a philosophical speculation—is that linguistic self-deception is unavoidable, if only because of the human need to convey feelings, attitudes, and convictions, or to do so most of the time, rather than data, instructions, and propositional announcements, or those types of supposedly logical assertions that are either true, false, or senseless because they consist of bad grammar. It would be a mistake, however, to imagine that this outlook places him in the camp of trendy modern philosophical relativists who argue that because words can be understood only in terms of other words, they make no real references to the outside world and their meanings are elusive or slippery. His own clear conviction is that words have definite meanings in their proper contexts, but that under pressure, or for psychological reasons, most people ignore them. Indeed most people cannot help doing so, if only because they are human.

Eulenspiegel's adventures thus amount to a brilliant scoffing at the human predicament itself, and his satire also has its theatrical and vulgar dimensions. Pomposity and pretentiousness require posing and acting, and to counter them he too assumes an amazing variety of roles in more than thirty-six of the tales: as page boy to a knight, barber's apprentice, artist, scholar, wandering monk, salesman of religious relics, washer of pelts, abbess's scribe, dying man, black-smith's boy, shoemaker's apprentice, brewer's apprentice, furrier's apprentice, tanner, carpenter, optician, cook, horse-dealer, and sacristan. His jeering recognizes neither class differences nor class sympathies. He cultivates neither loyalties nor friendships. On occasion, as in tale 70, when he rescues twelve blind men from an unscrupulous innkeeper, he exhibits a surprising compassion.

On the other hand, in this loosely organized picaresque novel that traces his life from his birth to his death, he never plays, or admits to playing, the rogue. Nor, in any of the eighty-seven superb woodcuts accompanying the earliest editions of the tales, some of which are by Albrecht Dürer's most famous pupil, Hans Baldung Grien, can he be seen in some rogue's costume, or, for that matter, in any of the medieval or Renaissance outfits of clowns and jesters (most often he wears peasant clothes, or those of a hunter). To be sure, to admit to roguishness would be to defeat his purposes. It would belie his ultimate pose as the innocent dupe traduced by other people's bumptiousness. Beyond this, it would render repulsive (as it did to the prudish of the last century) rather than satirical the unsettling malodorousness of many of his jests. His frequent satirical weapon is shit. In over fifteen tales he employs it to nose-bracing effect. When a hypocritical priest announces that indeed his church belongs to him and no one else, and that he can drop a fearsome pile in the middle of it if he likes (tale 12), Eulenspiegel bets him a barrel of beer that he cannot, and wins his bet when, on measuring the priest's immediate deposit, he shows it to be far from the middle. The owner of a bathhouse (tale 68) is delivered a mound of shit in one of his cleansing tubs because, as Eulenspiegel puts it, "Isn't this a house of cleansing? I needed cleansing more inside than outside—otherwise I wouldn't have come in here."

Though scatology as a satirical weapon is traceable into Aristophanes' early comedies, which the author of the *Eulenspiegel* had most likely not read, it generally combines with sex (as with Aristophanes) in the bawdy literature of later ages. The Eulenspiegel book itself emerges from a tradition of jest books, or *Schwankbücher*, in which both commingle. Poggio Bracciolini's *Facetiae* (1438–52), published in Nuremberg in the 1470s, one of the sources for a number of the Eulenspiegel tales, blends scatology, sex, and satire into a brisk stew, as do the *Facecie del Gonella* (Bologna, 1506), *Le cento novelle antiche* (also known as *Il novellino;* ca. 1290?), and *Les repues franches* (before 1493), which are themselves likely models for some of Eulenspiegel's adventures. Closer to home, however, the two German *Volksbücher* (folkbooks, or more accurately, popular books) that may have provided the plots for several of his escapades, *Die Geschicht des Pfaffe vom Kalenberg* (ca. late 15th century; *The Story of the Priest of Kalenberg*) and Der Stricker's mid-13th-century jest poem *Schwänke des Pfaffen Amis (Jests of Priest Amis),* deliver on the sex, often treating it as fun, but not, or far less often, on the scatology. What is striking about Eulenspiegel's stories is that the hero's or anti-hero's liberality with shit (many of the rest of his tales refer to excrement as well) is unalloyed with allusions to sex. A sole exception is to be found in tale 38, in which he tells a priest that he has slept with his servant girl. Even here, however, the title describes his confession as false.

A bracing excremental vision begins to emerge through these exploits. It is both devilish and devastating. It matches the power of Eulenspiegel's skepticism about honest language. The complexity of his personality—and this, surely, is what continues to attract his millions of readers—announces itself with a scathing jocosity. Eulenspiegel thus bears comparison with Swift's Gulliver, whose own interest in deceptive and pompous blathering, and whose similarly excremental view of human corruption, lead him, for instance, into dousing a fire at the Lilliputian palace by urinating on it.

Is the Eulenspiegel book, despite the literary sources for as much as 30 percent of the tales, and with some reaching into folk literature from as far away as India, the work of a single author? Was Eulenspiegel himself a real person? These questions continued to provoke hot scholarly disputes in the 19th and 20th centuries. Today they seem more or less settled. The once-fashionable belief that folk literature, and even *Schwankliteratur* (jest literature), emerged in some mysterious way "from the people" (a notion that once appealed to the Nazis, who, because of Eulenspiegel's cool indifference to all social institutions and allegiances, otherwise had no use for him) is now dismissed.

On stylistic grounds alone, moreover, the book seems the product of a single clever mind. In affirmation of its philosophical and excremental themes, its descriptive sentences are nearly devoid of figures of speech, such as metaphors, similes, and hyperboles, while its dollops of conversation abound in them. This unique split becomes a consistent feature of N.'s (as the anonymous author calls himself) unifying method. Recent efforts, however, actually to identify N., who tells us that he is writing in 1500, with Hermann Bote (ca. 1467–ca. 1520), a Low German satirical author of repute, and this on the basis of an acrostic buried among the initial capital letters of the last chapters, seem far-fetched. The "acrostic" appears only if one fiddles with the evidence, while N.'s attitudes toward clerical and other sorts of venality are not so much original—another claim made on Bote's behalf—as typical of 15th-century Catholic Humanists. The Eulenspiegel book and its author, whoever he may have been, belong in fact to a broad satirical humanist tradition that includes Sebastian Brant's *Das Narrenschiff* (1494; *The Ship of Fools*) and Erasmus's *In Praise of Folly* (1509; in Latin). The vigor and sinuosity of N.'s prose reflect a smart terseness coming into German itself two decades before the Reformation and Martin Luther's tour-de-force translation of the Bible.

Doubts must also be raised about whether an "actual" Eulenspiegel ever existed. In his preface the author tells us that Eulenspiegel died in 1350. Strenuous 19th-century efforts to locate his grave in Mölln and Lüneburg, and to trace his name through local records, turned up nothing definite. These efforts now seem pointless as well: so many of Eulenspiegel's exploits derive from literary sources that one cannot avoid seeing him for the most part as simply a sublime literary creation. In addition, his name has clear if dispute-provoking meanings. "Ul'n speghel" is a Low German expression for "wipe one's arse." Ulenspiegel, or Eulenspiegel itself, may be translated as "owl glass or mirror." In the 15th century and earlier, the owl was associated with wickedness, the devil, wisdom (though only by implication), and crafts such as printing.

"Ulenspiegel" or "Eulenspiegel" perhaps means that the wandering rogue is out to offer the world a "mirror of the stupid and wicked," though the book never mentions this interpretation.

No such murkiness surrounds its early success and influence. Published by the well-known Johannes Grüninger of Strasbourg, perhaps in a now lost edition before 1508, and hence making its appearance when printing itself was expanding the readership of Europe by reaching vast numbers of people for the first time (Grüninger himself published at least 139 books, and probably over 200, many of them illustrated, during his forty-year career), by the end of the 20th century Eulenspiegel had run into over 380 editions in German alone. Within seventy years of its debut, it had come out in Dutch, Flemish, Latin, Danish, Polish, Czech, and probably Italian. Over twenty public statues and other *Denkmäler* (monuments) in Germany, Flanders, and Holland, some of them recent, commemorate the notorious German rogue's adventures. His literary reputation aside, Eulenspiegel may today be most familiar through Richard Strauss's celebrated orchestral tone poem *Till Eulenspiegels lustige Streiche* (1895; *Till Eulenspiegel's Merry Pranks*), whose fifteen-minute rondo neatly captures his repetitious foolishness, mischief, courage, and scorn. Tales 8 and 3 seem even to have influenced Nietzsche's *Also sprach Zarathustra* (1883; *Thus Spake Zarathustra*, pt. I, 3–8), in which a rogue-jester behaves much as he does. Eulenspiegel's vitality thus continues to reach into many fields, and the shrewd gangster-nobleman Cesare Borgia, whose militaristic *imperium* simply vanished with his capture and death at the age of thirty-one in 1507, might easily have been astonished, if not baffled.

See also 1230, 1457, 1492, 1596, 1882

Bibliography: Ein kurzweilig lesen von Dyl Ulenspiegel gebore uss dem land zu Brunsswick. Wie er sein leben volbracht hatt. xcvi seiner geschichten (Strasbourg: Johannes Grüninger, 1515), anon. text, British Library, cat. no. C.57 C.23. (Note: despite Grüninger's announcement of ninety-six tales, there are only ninety-five.) Facsimile of Grüninger's edition, Edward Schröder, ed. (Leipzig: Inselverlag, 1911). Paul Oppenheimer, ed. and trans., *Till Eulenspiegel: His Adventures* (Oxford, U.K.: Oxford World's Classics, 1995. ———, *Till Eulenspiegel: His Adventures* (New York: Routledge, 2001), with a full scholarly treatment.

Paul Oppenheimer

1500

Jacopo de Barbari introduces Albrecht Dürer to a method of drawing the human figure according to a canon of proportion

A New Science of Beauty

Hailed by his contemporaries as a "Second Apelles" and esteemed for his exceptional learning, Albrecht Dürer (1471–1528) subsequently gained unequaled iconic status in German culture and is often regarded as the most significant and influential artist of the Northern Renaissance. This assessment is primarily based on his work as a painter, printmaker, and master draftsman. However, it is Dürer's now almost forgotten writings in the theory of art that attest most clearly to his outstanding scientific and mathematical accomplishments, as well as to his profound interest in general aesthetic questions. Trained in Northern European workshops where the medieval view of the artist as craftsman was still predominant and where young apprentices were instructed by practical and empirical methods, Dürer soon came to feel the limitations of this approach. Contact with the art and theory of the Italian Renaissance (his first journey to Italy was in 1494–95) convinced him of the necessity of a theoretical, scientific foundation for his artistic practice. He started to search for universally valid rules and general teachable principles, and besides questions of perspectival accuracy, his particular concern was the representation of the human body.

In the year 1500, the Venetian painter Jacopo de Barbari (ca. 1440/50–1516), who resided at the time in Dürer's hometown, the Imperial Free City of Nuremberg, introduced Dürer to a classical approach to the nude—depiction of which was only slowly regaining artistic dignity. In an unpublished draft of the dedication to *Vier Bücher von menschlicher Proportion* (1528; *Four Books on Human Proportion*) addressed to his friend Willibald Pirckheimer, who later edited the work, Dürer recounts his fascination with the art of constructing the human body based on mathematical rules when Barbari showed him "the figures of a man and woman, which he had drawn according to a canon of proportions." Dürer adds that he would rather have come into possession of this method than of a kingdom, but the Italian refused to share his knowledge. "Accordingly, I went ahead on my own and read Vitruvius, who writes somewhat about the human figure. Thus . . . I took my start, and since then, from day to day, have I followed up my search according to my own notions" (Rupprich I, 102). Encouraged by Humanist friends, including Pirckheimer and the neo-Latin poet Conrad Celtis (1459–1508), Dürer familiarized himself with numerous classical and contemporary Italian sources. Parallel to his theoretical studies, he began to collect statistical data from living models. The philosophical-religious assumption behind Dürer's scientific measuring approach to nature holds that the beauty of the human body is a microcosm of the harmonic order of the universe based on numeric relations, a medieval inheritance of a Greek tradition that extends from the Pythagoreans and Polyclitus's *Canon* through Plato and the neo-Platonists. Dürer epitomized this in several allusions to a verse from the apocryphal book *The Wisdom of Solomon,* an amalgam of Greek philosophy and Jewish religion absorbed into medieval Christian thinking: "But Thou hast ordered all things in measure and number and weight" (11:20).

According to Dürer's own testimony, by the year 1512 he had taken the measurements of some two or three hundred individuals, exceeding even the anthropometrical studies of his Italian contemporaries with which he had become more familiar during his second cisalpine sojourn (1505–1507). By eliminating particularities and extreme deviations, he arrived at a limited number of standard body types, which he presented in the first of the *Four Books on Human Proportion.* This complex work, published six months after Dürer's death and soon translated into Latin, French, Italian, Spanish, and Dutch, offers a synopsis of his extensive geometrical-mathematical knowledge as well as his anthropometrical research.

Originally, Dürer had planned to publish his findings as part of an encyclopedic painter's manual with the projected title *Ein Speis der Malerknaben* (*Food for Young Painters;* begun as early as 1508/9). Conceived as the first work of art theory in the German language, it was intended as a handbook for workshops and apprentices, offering instruction in the treatment of proportion, perspective, and color. Dürer's commitment to the education and well-being of younger artists is revealed in his plan to address such questions as the proper diet and boarding of apprentices, and even to offer cures for melancholic conditions caused by overwork. This project (of which only fragmentary drafts are preserved) was never executed. Instead, Dürer decided to treat the conceptual problems of perspective and proportion separately. A projected section on the use of color failed to come to fruition due to his death shortly before his fifty-seventh birthday.

Although Dürer's main effort went into his proportion studies, he decided that his treatise on perspective should be published first as a necessary mathematical foundation. *Unterweisung der Messung* (*The Manual of Measurement*), published in 1525, is the first literary document in German that treats of representational problems in a scientific manner. Designed as a textbook of applied mathematics for artists and artisans, it even influenced astronomers like Galileo and Johannes Kepler. Practical considerations of another kind prompted Dürer to delay publication of his proportion studies even further. In 1527, he responded to the Turkish threat to German cities with the publication of an instructional manual on fortifications of towns and castles, *Unterricht zur Befestigung der Städte, Schlösser und Flecken* (*Treatise on Fortifications*).

Dürer's *Proportionslehre*, written in the vernacular and copiously illustrated, marks the beginning of German scientific prose. This innovative literary and art theory text is formulated in language that aims for clarity, technical precision, and vividness. Conveying concrete scientific detail as deftly as it does abstract philosophical ideas, it represents a linguistic accomplishment comparable to Luther's contemporary Bible translation. Dürer frequently draws on religious prose and seemingly following Luther's maxim that one must "look at the mouth of the people," enriches the chancery style *(Kanzleisprache)* of his time with everyday expressions and graphic terms, such as "snail line" for spiral or "boar's teeth" for angles formed by circular arches. Some of these terms accord with artisan conventions; others are of Dürer's own coinage. Only partially revised for print by the artist himself, this work documents his artistic and intellectual development during its long gestational process. The comprehensive treatise reflects Dürer's contact with the intellectually charged atmosphere of Renaissance Italy and his ability not only to absorb but also to modify and radically transform classical and Italian concepts as he attempted to establish a new German art.

Of the four books, three are concerned with human proportion. The fourth proceeds to a theory of motion and—recalling geometrical procedures described in the *Treatise on Measurement*—proposes instruction methods on how to alter the posture of the figures described in the other books. The first book (essentially completed by 1512/13) reflects in a unique way Dürer's dialogue with scientific models of classical antiquity. Combining standardized empirical data and certain normative principles of geometric construction—the rule of increasing proportion, for example, reveals the influence of Euclid—it presents the proportions of five male and five female body types. Each is described in detail and illustrated with woodcuts showing the outlines of nude figures in profile, front and rear view. The models, ranging in height from seven-head-length ("stout and rustic") to ten-head-length ("long and thin"), are depicted upright and are complemented by exemplary proportions of the hand, foot, head, and the proportions of a child. As in Vitruvius, who in turn refers to older canons like that of Polyclitus, the measurement of each part of the body is expressed as a fraction of the whole.

In the second book (largely finished by 1523), Dürer employs a different method for capturing the human figure, one that attests to his engagement with the sophisticated Italian dialogue between scientific theory and art. He appropriates and slightly modifies a method described by Leon Battista Alberti (*De Statua*, 1464). Instead of expressing the length of individual body parts as fractions of the whole, Dürer introduces a basic measuring unit, the *Meßstab* (ruler), equal to one-sixth of the length of the body. The *Meßstab* and its decimal subdivisions make it possible to express individual lengths as multiples of one basic module in integers. The shift from a predominantly geometric to a predominantly arithmetic approach indicates an increased degree of standardization and abstraction. By introducing an additional eighteen figures in the second book, Dürer goes beyond the standard types in the first and offers a greater variety of physical types.

In the third book, Dürer introduces various methods and drafting devices, like the circular curve, which, by way of geometrical projection, allow variations of the basic body types detailed in the first two books. Labeled with descriptive names like "verkerer" (modifier) or "weler" (selector), some of these devices distort human proportions in a way that approximates the effect of concave and convex mirrors. Dürer takes particular care to demonstrate how geometric principles applied to the head can lead to grotesque facial distortions. Possibly influenced by Leonardo da Vinci's physiognomy studies, these counterexamples to the beautiful laid the ground for Dürer's philosophical reflections on beauty, nature, art, and the role of the artist at the end of the third book.

This passage, known as the "aesthetic excursus," urges moderation in the use of distortion. For educational purposes only, Dürer explains, he has included exaggerations bordering on the unnatural. In his regular work, however, every artist should strive for the most faithful representation of nature: "From Nature one can learn the truth of things. Therefore observe it diligently, be guided by it, and do not depart from Nature arbitrarily, presuming you can do better by yourself, because you would be mistaken" (Rupprich, III, 295). Nature defines the limits of artistic manipulation, and the more accurate an artist's approach to nature is by way of imitation, the better and more artistic his work will be.

This invocation of nature as supreme authority for the artist indicates the degree to which Dürer had changed his original views on representation. Specifically, it implies a rejection of the classically inspired idealization of the human figure that characterized his early proportion studies and found its most poignant artistic expression in the engraving of the perfect couple "Adam and Eve" (1504). Two underlying assumptions informed this and other works from Dürer's early period. The first was that the depiction of beauty must ignore the specificity of the individual. The second, mercilessly ridiculed in Francis Bacon's essay "Of Beauty," was that beautiful bodies consist of the combination of selected beautiful parts. While these earlier ideals are still apparent to some extent in the standard types of the first book, their influence wanes as Dürer presents a wider variety of models and becomes increasingly concerned with figures that diverge from the norm.

The excursus in its final version formulates Dürer's aesthetic position after he has already abandoned the concept of ideal beauty in favor of a more complex notion of "relative beauty" (Panofsky). Stating that our aesthetic perception is temporal, and that beauty, known in its fullness by God alone, cannot be captured in one universal canon because it resides in a variety of different forms, Dürer no longer aimed to create perfect bodies, but to create artistically perfect bodies. These bodies may range widely in appearance, reflecting the diversity in nature, but they need to conform to the principle of *Vergleichung* (balance) that guarantees the harmonic relation between their parts. For the secret of artistic perfection, Dürer refers the reader once more to the authority of nature: "For verily, art is embedded in nature; he who can extract it has it" (Rupprich, III, 295). Dürer's usage of the term *Kunst* (art) connotes the theoretical know-how, the knowledge of certain representational techniques that are not in contradiction to but derived from nature.

Subsequently, however, Dürer introduces an idea that originated in Italian Renaissance thought and proved most influential for the theory of artistic creativity. The experienced artist who has already "replenished his mind by much painting from life" can "draw forth/create" (Dürer plays on the dual meaning of the German verb "schöpfen") new artworks from his "secret treasure of the heart" (Rupprich, III, 296), a phrase based on Luther's translation of Matthew 12:35. Through this new understanding, Dürer casts the artist as a second creator under God and anticipates the modern redefinition of the role of the artist as genius. In Dürer's artistic work emphasis on the individuality of the artist and his skill finds expression in his self-portraits, the self-confident display of his initials AD, and in his practice of dating and signing even sketches.

The proportion books gained importance in German literature primarily due to the aesthetic excursus, not the details of Dürer's proportion studies. Perceived as a turning point in the tradition of German aesthetics, Dürer's ideas on artistic inspiration, nature, and beauty influenced many art theorists and creative writers from the late 18th century to the present. The 20th-century German philosopher Martin Heidegger, for example, used Dürer's statement about extracting art from nature as a springboard for his own philosophical inquiry, *The Origin of the Artwork* (1935). In his essay "Von deutscher Baukunst" (1772; On German Architecture), the young Goethe expresses his appreciation of Dürer's art over and against the frivolous and artificial virtuosity of Rococo aesthetics. Dürer's work exemplifies the characteristic, which, like the sublime and the picturesque, is set apart from the classical concept of the beautiful. According to Goethe, who valued the proportion books highly, characteristic art, the genuine expression of the creative genius, is often truer and greater than beautiful art itself. The Romantics revered Dürer, whom Friedrich Schlegel anointed as "the Shakespeare of painting," with an enthusiasm previously reserved for the literary genius. With Dürer as their model, they proclaimed a revival of a truly German art, invoking anew the century-old opposition of the Italian and northern traditions, personified by Raphael and Dürer, respectively, and asserting the superiority of the latter. The Romantics' appreciation of Dürer, like that of the young Goethe, was governed by a belief in the validity of multiple artistic expressions and found its most decisive poetic formulation in the works of Wilhelm Wackenroder and Ludwig Tieck. Their collaborative *Herzensergießungen eines kunstliebenden Klosterbruders* (1796; *Effusions from the Heart of an Art-Loving Monk*) praises the verisimilitude of Dürer's art, particularly where it diverges from classical notions and develops an alternative aesthetic program. The degree to which Dürer's art gained cult status is evidenced perhaps most poignantly in Tieck's novel *Franz Sternbalds Wanderungen* (1798; *Franz Sternbald's Wanderings*). Reinventing Dürer as the cultural hero of an idealized German past, Wackenroder's and Tieck's apotheosis of *alt-deutsche Kunst* laid the foundation for the nationalistic Dürer cult of the late 19th and early 20th century. With a more ironic sensibility, the Realist Swiss writer Gottfried Keller contrasts Dürer's creativity and wholeness with the deplorable reality of the protagonist's life in his novel *Der grüne Heinrich* (1855; *Green Henry*). Here, a carnival procession, in which Dürer's appearance is modeled on the famous "Christomorph" self-portrait of 1500, suggests that the ideal Dürer represented has become fragmented in modern times.

See also 1450, 1457, 1515–1517, 1523, 1774, 1800 (January), 1848 (September 12), 1927

Bibliography: Dürer: Schriftlicher Nachlaß, 3 vols., ed. Hans Rupprich (Berlin: Deutscher Verein für Kunstwissenschaft, 1956–1969). *The Writings of Albrecht Dürer,* trans. and ed. William Martin Conway (New York: Philosophical Library, 1958). Giulia Bartrum, *Albrecht Dürer and His Legacy: The Graphic Work of a Renaissance Artist* (London: The British Museum Press, 2002). Jan Białostocki, *Dürer and His Critics: 1500–1971* (Baden-Baden: Koerner, 1986). Reinhard Heinritz, ed., *Dürer und die Literatur: Bilder—Texte—Kommentare* (Bamberg: Universität Bamberg, 2001). Joseph Leo Koerner, *The Moment of Self-Portraiture in German Renaissance Art* (Chicago and London: University of Chicago Press, 1993). Erwin Panofsky, *The Life and Art of Albrecht Dürer,* 2 vols., 4th ed. (Princeton, N.J.: Princeton University Press, 1955).

Doris McGonagill

♌ *1515, Ash Wednesday*

Hans Sachs is accepted into the guild of Mastersingers at Würzburg

A Cobbler-Poet Becomes a Master Author

In a "mastersong" *(Meistersang)* dated 1516, Hans Sachs (1494–1576) reports that a song he sang probably a year earlier at a Würzburg competition won him the title of "Hans Rosengart." The Würzburg mastersong must have narrated an event that took place at a nearby inn a couple of days before that competition. In the version of 1516, the only one available today, Sachs recalls how he sang about his profession as a cobbler for the innkeeper's wife, receiving a coat in return; after performing the song at the inn, he went on to Würzburg, where he presented it at the Ash Wednesday meeting of the singer's guild. This was the first time that Hans Sachs inserted his name into a mastersong.

The towns that he may have visited during these years as an itinerant apprentice shoemaker *(schuknecht),* such as Nuremberg, Mainz, Augsburg, and Munich, are known to have had schools of mastersinging where poets would compete in contests known as *Singschulen* by performing compositions based on elaborate metrical rules. The 1516 mastersong describes the details of Sachs's profession (the kinds of leather he bought, its daily preparation) according to a set schema or "tone" *(Ton)* of twenty-two verses, with five in each of the first two stanzas and twelve in the last. Sachs's wish that the Würzburg guild's fame will grow—"den wünscht Hans Sachs / das ir lob wachs / gancz ewig unzubrochen" (Hans Sachs wishes that their praise grow eternally unbroken)—confirms the emergence of his poetic identity alongside his life as a cobbler. The narrative shows that both crafts—shoemaking and poetic production—share the central feature of accomplished skill in a trade. In this sense, Sachs's status as an author is embedded within a social and ethical context that embraces tradition and the adherence to fixed forms.

Würzburg, like other northern Bavarian towns in the early days of the Reformation, was a scene of civic unrest. Incited by Martin Luther's call for greater immediacy between the word of God and the people, the rebellion of the citizens against the ruling bishop would reach its climax in the Peasant Revolt of 1525. Unlike certain cities, among them Nuremberg, which were ruled by direct authority of the emperor, Würzburg was a bishopric with a regional ruler. Luther's teaching—that princely laws should accord with divine will and that people should resist and depose princes who did not follow the Gospel—showed the lower and middle classes that new orders of society were possible. This threshold moment was the environment of Hans Sachs's mastersongs.

Why did the art of mastersinging come to flourish in cities like Nuremberg and Würzburg? How was Hans Sachs, who also wrote numerous carnival plays *(Fastnachtsspiele)* and a famous poem praising Luther as a nightingale spreading the Gospel (1523; *Die Wittembergisch Nachtigall [The Wittenberg Nightingale]),* drawn to a tradition which, although aristocratic in origin, was sustained by municipal craftsmen, who strictly adhered to the code of their artistic guild?

To answer these questions, it is useful, as Hugo Kuhn has suggested, to locate Sachs and his work within the various literary modes of production in the sixteenth century. Sachs's production could be regarded as "serial": subordinating content and questions of interpretation to traditional formal recipes enabled him successively to generate a variety of texts that are contained within a stable framework. This stabilizing effect is produced by the "master aesthetics" that have periodically emerged throughout the literary history of continental Europe. By according the forms and patterns invented by past masters the status of ideal norms, such an aesthetic provided an island of continuity during times of social, ethical, and religious change. Thus, through participation in a poetic guild as well as through the practice of his cobbler's craft, Hans Sachs was able to establish an identity as "master" of his own work. And this discipline made possible an enormously productive career: when he died at the age of eighty-one, Sachs left behind more than six thousand works; lyric poems on religious, political, historical, and farcical themes *(Spruchgedichte);* plays, rhymes, and prose dialogues.

Our knowledge of the formal strictures of mastersinging comes from several songbooks, such as the Colmar manuscript (ca. 1460); the *Schulzettel* (1540; *School Notes),* a compilation of the Nuremberg mastersinger statutes or rules *(Tabulatur),* and the *Gemerkbüchlein (Record Book of Markers),* which contains competition minutes from 1555 to 1561. Mastersingers composed using pre-existing *Töne,* a term encompassing a tune and the specific rhyme and meter of the text that goes with it. Writing their own lyrics while using the *Töne* of famous poets from the 13th to the 15th centuries, mastersingers often produced numerous poems in a single *Ton.* The practice of using pre-existing *Töne* continued even when singers such as Sachs's predecessor Hans Folz (1435/40–1513) started to invent their own. A mastersong is formally consistent: the meter of a particular *Ton* does not vary from song to song, and each song has a metrical and musical AAB structure. The mastersingers performed alone, without musical accompaniment, following specified restrictions (for example, each verse, containing no more than thirteen syllables with an end rhyme, had to be sung in one breath). Although many of Sachs's lyrics convey a desire to sing "naturally" (he says in one that a song should not sound "uncomfortable" *[unpequemlic]),* the guild rules nonetheless limited the poetic potential of the mastersong. In one of Sachs's first mastersongs (1515) he speaks of the challenge of both performing competitively and pleasing his audience:

> Mein herz das mag nit rue han,
> darum so wil ich heben an,
> zu singen hie auf diesem plan,
> wiewol ich nit kan iederman
> singen und das im freude geit;
> es ist mir leit,
> seit ichs nit kan volbringen.

My heart, that may not find rest
on that account I thus begin
to sing here on this spot
although I may not sing for everybody
so as to give him joy
I am sorry
since I cannot accomplish this.

(Goedeke, I, 4, May 13, 1515)

Admitting he cannot please everyone, Sachs enumerates the various subjects that the singer should know to suit his audiences. He envisions mastersinging as a communal practice. While performing a *Ton* demands an awareness of formal rules, Sachs also expresses the desire for a good holistic "tone," a quality that usually means a tacit understanding between audience and performer. Thus, a tension exists in mastersinging between the desire for a popular and familiar *Ton* and one that stays within formal constraints, although at the price of sounding "unnatural."

The 16th-century Nuremberg *Schulordnung* helps us imagine Meistersinger competitions in Sachs's day. In staged ceremonial events, on a black-shrouded cubicle *(Gemerk)*, judges or "markers" *(Merker)* scored the success of a performance according to its conformity to the rules. The judges noted every error, declaring the singer with the fewest errors the winner. Bestowed with a silver chain portraying King David, patron of the Meistersinger, the winner would serve as marker at the next competition. Competitions involving religious songs (in Nuremberg, conformity with Lutheran doctrine was an additional requirement) were held on a holiday or on Sunday, while secular songs were sung at mastersingers' drinking festivals *(Zechsingen)* at an inn.

In addition to its Lutheran content, mastersinging appealed to a broad audience through its ritual homage to old masters such as the troubadours Walther von der Vogelweide, Frauenlob, Der Marner (ca. 1230–70), and Regenbogen (d. 1318). Many *Töne* were attributed to these masters. Sachs and other competitors were artisans from various trades—bakers, tailors, surgeon-barbers, nailsmiths, weavers, and illuminators. This fact highlights the communal nature of the art as well as its ties to a lay public. In a mastersong like the one cited above, Sachs expresses his desire to please his audience; in another, he lists in a technical fashion the items that would be penalized in competition. In a later poem *(Spruchgedicht)*, however, Sachs refers to the strain of conforming to the needs of his time:

Ach Gott, wie ist verderbt all Welt,
wie stark ligt die untreu zu felt,
wie hart ist grechtigkeit gefangen
wie hoch tut ungrechtigkeit prangen . . .
wie ist gemeiner nutz so teuer . . .

O God, how corrupted is all the world
how strong is faithlessness in the battle
how grimly is justice held captive
how greatly injustice flaunts itself . . .
how scarce is common interest . . .

(Goedeke II, 5, June 2, 1530)

Sachs is the most famous mastersinger today not exclusively for the merit of his work (which some critics have labeled repetitive), but because of his abundant industry and his keen awareness of his writings as a coherent, albeit heterogeneous, body of work. In short, he fashioned an authorial identity for himself. He classified his various works and published them, capping his achievement with an autobiographical review of his career, *Summa all meiner Gedicht* (1567; *Summation of All My Poems*). Finally, he collected all his work, carefully noting the dates of completion, in thirty-four manuscript volumes, and compiled a *Register,* a general index, listing the beginning verse of each work. Hans Sachs was the archivist of his own career, which, for that very reason, became his "own." Comparing Sachs's early Würzburg mastersong with his *Summa,* we can trace a transformation in his poetic identity. His spontaneous performance for the innkeeper's wife is canonized in the Würzburg guild competition, where he earns his poetic name. In the retrospective account of the *Summa,* that incidental triumph is absorbed into the overarching continuity of a life's achievement.

Sachs's multifaceted career as cobbler-poet, guild member, and publisher of his own work has parallels in the broader context of continental Europe. In both Spain and France during the later 14th and 15th centuries, professional poets from aristocratic circles performed their work and produced single-author songbooks. The "I" in these works has a dual function, referring both to the situation of courtly performance and to the clerk or composer of a body of written work now rendered independent of the performance context. Sachs's archival creation of his poetic persona bears comparison with the autobiographical *Voir dit* (1364) of the French poet-musician Guillaume de Machaut as well as the printed songbook *(cancionero)* of the Castilian poet Juan del Encina (1496). As the courtly performance context receded into the historical past and thus became idealized, poets and musicians of the late Middle Ages increasingly emphasized editorial control, as well as craft and skill as virtues independent from their immediate effect on a live audience. An artifact of this development is the emergence of an authorial persona embodied in the archivized written work.

Hans Sachs's life and work have been taken up by later authors, among them Goethe, who used the cobbler-poet as a mask for his own poetic ideas in the poem "Hans Sachsens poetische Sendung" (1776; Hans Sachs's Poetic Mission). But by far the best-known treatment of Sachs is Richard Wagner's opera *Die Meistersinger von Nürnberg* (1862; *The Mastersingers of Nuremberg*). Wagner's Hans Sachs is a poet who judges the rules of his art according to the criterion of expressive vitality, questioning "whether in the dull course of habit / their strength and life doesn't get lost" (act I, scene iii). Wagner interprets Sachs less as an innovator than as a spiritual conservator of an idealized German culture. In *Die Meistersinger,* Sachs promotes the renewal of mastersinging through the introduction of new *Töne,* and argues that the public, rather than the experts, should judge competitions. The knight Walther is conferred the title of master at the end of the opera because of his originality as an artist, while his main competitor, Beckmesser, is capable only of futile pedantry. Clearly Wagner aims to idealize a national past through the glorification of ritual and tradition. He celebrates a notion of German popular culture *(Volkskultur)* that, for other romantics as well, seemed to have found its purest embodiment in 16th-century Nuremberg. This romantic canonization of Sachs has influenced both literary-historical and musicological scholarship. Today it is clear that it is greatly anachronistic to apply the concept of *Volkskultur* to the mastersingers. The cultural lessons to be learned from their art have little to do with expression and everything to do with the complex intertwining of authority, discipline, and the emergence of a professional poetic identity.

See also 1203 (November 12), 1523, 1537, 1774, 1876

Bibliography: Hans Sachs, *Werke,* ed. Adalbert von Keller and Edmund Goetze, 26 vols. (Tübingen: Literarische Verein, 1870–1908). ———, *Dichtungen von Hans Sachs,* ed. Karl Goedeke and Julius Tittmann, 3 vols. (1870–1871). ———, *The Early Meisterlieder of Hans Sachs,* ed. Frances H. Ellis (Bloomington: Indiana University Studies, 1974). Peter Blickle, *Communal Reformation: The Quest for Salvation in 16th Century Germany,* trans. T. Dunlap (Atlantic Highlands, N.J.: Humanities Press, 1992). Horst Brunner, *Die alten Meister: Studien zu Überlieferung und Rezeption der mittelhochdeutschen Sangspruchdichter im Spätmittelalter und in der frühen Neuzeit* (Munich: Beck, 1975). Hans Ulrich Gumbrecht, "L'auteur comme masque: Contribution à l'archéologie de l'imprimé," in Marie-Louise Ollier, ed., *Masques et déguisements dans la litterature médiévale* (Montreal: Presses de l'Université de Montréal, 1988), pp. 185–192; *Table ronde,* pp. 277–295. Hugo Kuhn, *Entwürfe zu einer Literatursystematik des Spätmittelalters* (Tübingen: Niemeyer, 1980). A. Taylor, *The Literary History of Meistergesang* (New York: MLA, 1937). Michael Walter, *Hitler in der Oper: Deutsches Musikleben 1919–1945* (Stuttgart: J. B. Metzler, 1995).

Marisa Galvez

ᷱ 1515–1517
The first modern academic satire rallies support for Johannes Reuchlin

The Mysteries of the Kabbalah and the Theology of Obscure Men

The first great academic satire of modern times, the *Epistolae obscurorum virorum* or *Dunkelmännerbriefe (Letters of Obscure Men),* appeared between 1515 and 1517. It was inspired by the German Humanist and Hebraist Johannes Reuchlin's passionate defense of the study of Hebrew against attacks by Johannes Pfefferkorn, a converted Jew who called for the burning of the Talmud, and his allies, the Dominican theologians and some like-minded Humanists in Cologne. However, the satire transcended its occasion in more than one way. Like many later academic satires, the *Letters* created a new literary language from the debris of current academic jargon. Crotus Rubeanus and Ulrich von Hutten, the young Humanists who wrote the bulk of these collaborative texts, deftly deployed their enemies' vivid terms and techniques, savagely attacking their targets.

In recent years, scholars have come to realize that this satire was as deliberately overdrawn as the academic novels of Mary McCarthy and David Lodge. Some of the "obscure men," notably Ortwin Gratius, a Cologne scholar who repeatedly figures as letter recipient, were not scholastic theologians, but Humanists who rejected Jewish studies. And prominent Humanists like Erasmus and his English friend John Colet, who also lacked Reuchlin's taste for Hebrew studies and mysticism and defended him only in the most colorless terms, found the uncompromising wit of the *Letters of Obscure Men* as distasteful as the text's victims, or at least so they claimed. Nonetheless, although the *Letters,* as polemical weapons, tend to simplify the historical situation, they and other texts suggest something vital about Reuchlin's career and the wider intellectual world of his time. Both had reached a crisis in the second decade of the 16th century, a crisis that was directly relevant to the issues raised in the *Letters.*

During the Middle Ages, the Holy Roman Empire had boasted few institutions of higher learning. Germans with intellectual ambitions, like Albertus Magnus, were compelled to go to Paris or other scholastic centers, if they hoped to master and teach the corpus of ancient and modern texts that served as authorities in scholastic debate. In the 14th and 15th centuries, however, universities began to spring up all over the empire, from the Charles University in Prague to the University of Cologne in the Rhineland. Certain courts, especially those in Vienna and Munich, also became centers of intellectual activity. As in Italy during the same period, the spikily technical philosophy and theology of late scholasticism and the classicizing rhetoric and philology of the Humanists developed rapidly side by side. Even though each of these intellectual forms had its own adherents and occasional quarrels broke out between them, for the most part they enjoyed a moderately peaceful coexistence. The scholastic method, which treated ancient texts as if they had been written to serve contemporary needs and took Latin translations of the Bible, Aristotle, and much else as authoritative sources, dominated the higher faculties of law and theology. Professors in these faculties had far greater social and political power and far higher incomes than the classical scholars in search of unknown classical texts and scribbled Latin verse and oratory, and whose methods were chiefly employed in secondary schools and in the lowest faculty, that of arts. Clashes took place, especially when the Humanists offered to teach a new form of dialectic not geared toward preparing students for the formal study of theology or law. Nevertheless many learned men found it possible to combine traditional scholastic forms of learning with the new pursuits of the Humanists. Johannes Trithemius, the abbot of the Benedictine house at Sponheim, where he built a great library, helped Conrad Celtes to publish the Latin sacred dramas of Hroswitha, which proved that the classical tradition had flourished in medieval Germany, and emulated the scholastic natural philosopher Albertus Magnus by producing a detailed survey of the occult literature of the Latin-Arabic tradition.

Johannes Reuchlin (1454/5–1522) grew up as a characteristic figure in this peaceful, expansive, intellectual landscape. He studied scholastic dialectic and Roman law at Basel, Orléans, and Poitiers—following the established medieval tradition of professors staying in one place and students moving from school to school. Once trained, he served his ruler, Eberhard the Bearded of Württemberg, as a counselor and diplomat, as Roman lawyers traditionally had, and worked as one of the Swabian League's three-man tribunal in Tübingen. He also did *pro bono* work for private clients, among them the Dominican order. Though Reuchlin charged few, if any, legal fees, his career proved lucrative: it won him both noble status and wealthy wives. Yet even as he climbed the Roman lawyers' ladder of preferment, Reuchlin pursued his humanistic interests. In 1477, he studied Greek at Paris with George Hermonymus, the indispensable if unsatisfactory tutor who also helped Guillaume Budé find his footing in Greek letters. He wrote not only legal opinions, but a Latin dictionary and some comedies. And he adopted a standard Humanist second identity when he published his classicizing works under the Greek name Capnion, "smoke," a literal translation of his German name.

By the last decades of the 15th century, German scholars had begun to long for Italy, where they could visit Roman ruins and inscriptions firsthand, meet the heroes of Italian scholarship, and collect books and antiquities. Most of them brought home notebooks filled with erudition and nostalgic memories of the cultured life at Italian courts and cities. Reuchlin's trip in 1490 enabled him to do something even more distinctive: to find an intellectual vocation. In the Florence of Lorenzo de' Medici, the Humanists Marsilio Ficino and Giovanni Pico della Mirandola had become convinced that the most profound truths about life, the universe, and everything else lay hidden, not in the extant works of Plato and Aristotle, but in their sources. Ficino collected and translated the works of learned barbarians, such as the dialogues of the Egyptian sage Hermes Trismegistus and the verses of the Persian Zoroaster (these were in fact late texts in Greek, though the Hermetic corpus at least contained genuine elements of Egyptian thought and ritual). Pico cast his net even wider. For him, one of these traditions from outside the Greek and Roman world— the Kabbalah, or Jewish tradition of mystical contemplation, often connected with a spiritual exegesis of the Scriptures—offered the highest promise of revelation. It explained the structure of the universe, revealed the doctrine of the Trinity, and provided powerful knowledge about the sacred names of God and much else.

Captivated by the ancient promise of barbarian wisdom and revelations of the Jewish tradition, Reuchlin, already an accomplished Greek scholar, devoted himself to the study of Hebrew. He mastered the language far more systematically than Pico had and published a series of epoch-making books: above all, a treatise in 1494 *On the Wonder-Working Word;* a Hebrew grammar of 1506, the *Rudiments;* and a massive, somewhat frightening analysis titled *The*

Art of the Kabbalah, which appeared in 1517. In these books, Reuchlin argued with erudition and flair that Hebrew must take its place beside Latin and Greek in the canon of skills and languages that every scholar needed to master for Christians to gain access to powerful, occult knowledge. This knowledge centered on the realization, which Reuchlin owed to Pico, that the Kabbalah could unlock the true, Christian meanings of the Old Testament. But it also stretched to include revelations about many other fields, for example, the names and functions of the angels, and the best ways of invoking the power of talismans.

As Reuchlin slowly made his way through Hebrew manuscripts and formulated his interpretations of them, the intellectual ecology of the Holy Roman Empire underwent rapid and radical changes. Humanism began to define itself as an intellectual movement whose members shared a program, or at least some elements of a program, for the reform of the university and society. One of its least contentious planks was a shared opposition to scholasticism. Erasmus, Lefèvre d'Etaples, and other Humanists insisted that theology itself must rest not on the Latin Vulgate, the standard Latin version of the Bible, but on the original texts—the Greek New Testament and, by implication, the Hebrew Old Testament. They sharply criticized traditional theologians for their misunderstandings of the biblical text, and asserted that only a grammatical and philological approach, like their own, could yield true readings. Many theologians—including several Dominicans whose German stronghold was Cologne—issued a sharp response to this challenge to their professional authority. Grammarians without formal training in theology, they countered, could not hope to explicate the Bible correctly.

The occasional friction between 15th-century Humanists and Scholastics thus gave way to a series of thunderstorms. Polemical works of very different kinds—from the highly literate satire of Erasmus's *Praise of Folly* and Thomas More's *Utopia* to formal treatises and theological denunciations—carried these debates across Europe. Suddenly, one had to choose, or so it seemed, between the cause of "good letters" and that of traditional learning. Reuchlin, for all his legal erudition, knew in which camp he belonged. He sent Erasmus a manuscript of the Greek New Testament, which the Dutch Humanist needed for his new translation and edition of the text, and which appeared in 1514. He also energetically collaborated with Erasmus on one of the latter's scholarly projects, a massive edition of the works of Saint Jerome. A stream of letters to scholars across the empire and beyond established Reuchlin's claim to membership in the elite of the European Republic of Letters.

Even as Reuchlin took sides in what was becoming an intellectual war between Scholastics and Humanists, however, a second set of polemics, one far more vicious and intractable than the first, was boiling up around him. The denizens of the Holy Roman Empire had resorted for centuries—like Christians elsewhere in Europe—to magic of all sorts. Sometimes they drew on Christian sources of power like the Eucharist. Often, however, they used Jewish or Judeo-Christian magical objects and practices: for example, amulets inscribed with Hebrew names and characters. The Jews, who were widely believed to own the keys to this kingdom of occult power over men and angels, developed a reputation for magical prowess. At the same time, magic itself came under intense scrutiny as Dominican inquisitors developed a powerful theory. Witches, they claimed, were not innocent, cunning men and women who practiced traditional incantations to help their fellow rustics save their crops and find lost animals, but conspirators who had joined the Devil in his effort to undermine Christian society. The first great trials of witches and sorcerers were staged. In the second half of the 15th century, Christians began to accuse Jews of engaging in a particularly diabolical form of magic: the sacrifice of Christian children to obtain the blood presumably required to make unleavened bread. The use of torture produced confessions, and trials resulted in numerous convictions and crowd-pleasing executions. Vividly illustrated broadsides, shrines celebrating miraculous victories over the enemies of Christianity, and judicial opinions confirmed that the Jews, like the witches, were the enemies of mankind. The magical Jews whom Pico and Reuchlin had viewed with such interest had become dangerous figures, easily denounced and discredited.

Enter a converted Jew named Johannes Pfefferkorn, one of many who found in the dominant faith an escape from an identity that had become dangerous. He served as expert adviser to the persecutors and in illustrated pamphlets, each more vehement and intricate than the last, he revealed secrets of supposed Jewish rituals like the cleansing of sin on Yom Kippur. He won the support of the emperor's pious sister Kunnigund, and soon obtained an imperial mandate to suppress Jewish books by collecting and burning them. Pfefferkorn's zealous purging of libraries found approval far beyond the circle of the Scholastics in Cologne who feared a challenge to their monopoly on biblical studies. Plenty of Humanists, from Hartmann Schedel to Ortwin Gratius, believed the blood libel and joined Pfefferkorn in denouncing the Jews. But when he consulted Reuchlin for expert legal advice, the great Hebraist showed himself appalled by his book-burning campaign.

No Philo-Semite, Reuchlin prized Jewish learning for its confirmation of Christian truths and hoped to see the Jews convert. But he could not accept the wholesale destruction of Jewish learning. Urged on by Jews who appealed for protection, Reuchlin—one of four imperial commissioners appointed to examine Jewish books for blasphemies—rose to defend his Jewish fellow citizens of the empire and their right to possess and study their own books. A series of polemical exchanges in print ensued, each more vehement and intractable than the last. Basing himself on the principles of Roman law, Reuchlin stoutly maintained his position in appeal after appeal. Though he eventually lost his suit in Rome in 1520, he survived the defeat unimpaired, except in financial terms. He spent his remaining years partly in private life in Stuttgart, partly as professor of Greek and Hebrew in Ingolstadt and Tübingen. He died in 1522.

As Reuchlin's opponents stepped up the pressure, he came to see himself not only as a fairly isolated votary of Jewish mysticism and magic, but also as a tribune of good letters, like Erasmus himself. He appealed for solidarity and support to the Dutch Humanist and other influential proponents of the new culture. Eventually he assembled and published two anthologies of eloquent Latin letters in his own support, entitled *Letters of Famous Men,* carefully purged of all elements that might provoke the ire of more conservative readers. Reuchlin's effort to portray himself and his Hebrew studies as part of the wider humanistic movement did not meet with anything like uniform success. Erasmus, for example, expressed his concern that the revival of Hebrew studies might lead to a revival of the Jewish religion, which might be a threat to evangelical Christianity. Accordingly, though he warmly defended the character of his saintly and erudite German friend, he did not support Reuchlin's views on Hebrew and Kabbalah.

Erasmus's restraint, however, had less impact than Reuchlin's consistent efforts to position his work, and far less than Crotus Rubeanus's and von Hutten's explosive satire, which portrayed Reuchlin as the innocent victim of ignorant scholastic persecutors. Especially after 1517, when Martin Luther's denunciation of the Mass and proclamation of the freedom of the will led to the outbreak of the Protestant Reformation, Reuchlin came to be seen as a hero of Protestantism and good letters. From his nephew Phillip Melanchthon onward, Protestants who studied and taught Greek and Hebrew admired him, usually without reservation. They loved telling their students about his learning, his Spartan diet, and his wonderful library. And they saw to it that every respectable Protestant university employed a competent professor of Hebrew. To that extent, the wider views of the controversy developed by Reuchlin, and even those represented in the *Letters,* carried the day.

Yet Reuchlin's scholarly apotheosis, his rise to the pantheon of great Christian Humanists, was paradoxical in the extreme. For these same years witnessed the dramatic career of the historical Faust and the rise of a new learned magic. Daring scholars like Trithemius and Henry Cornelius Agrippa of Nettesheim, the speculative practitioners of magic and cryptography who laid the literary foundations of the new discipline, drew heavily on Reuchlin's works. He supplied them with much that was of value: a historical charter that legitimized their work as the continuation of an ancient Jewish learned tradition; an exegetical method that enabled them to find the messages and names of angels they needed in the Old Testament; and, most important of all, a series of bountiful instructions for the making of amulets and the formulation of effective prayers. The enemy of the *viri obscuri,* the hero of good letters, the intrepid philologist who showed his contemporaries the way to Hebrew, as well as Greek, sources of Christian tradition, also ended up as one of the founders of what Agrippa called "occult philosophy."

Renaissance magicians like John Dee consulted Reuchlin and later scholars who recycled his discoveries every time they tried to speak with angels. Philosophers from Giordano Bruno and Tommaso Campanella down to Henry More and Isaac Newton pursued the implications of the Christian Kabbalah for their new philosophy of nature. In the end, it seems clear that the obscure men had a point. For all his firm Christian faith and deep commitment to decorum and tradition, Reuchlin was an intellectual radical, one whose work shook the foundations of the established curriculum. Those who read him usually did justice only to isolated aspects of his thought. But his friends and enemies alike were right when they treated Reuchlin's learned books as the origin of an intellectual crisis.

See also 1492, 1500 (Dürer), 1523, 1551, 1596

Bibliography: R. Po-chia Hsia, *The Myth of Ritual Murder: Jews and Magic in Reformation Germany* (New Haven: Yale University Press, 1988). James Overfield, *Humanism and Scholasticism in Late Medieval Germany* (Princeton: Princeton University Press, 1984). Johannes Reuchlin, *Recommendation Whether to Confiscate, Destroy, and Burn All Jewish Books,* trans. and ed. Peter Wortsman, critical introduction by Elisheva Carlebach (New York: Paulist Press, 2000). Erika Rummel, *The Case against Johann Reuchlin: Religious and Social Controversy in Sixteenth-Century Germany* (Toronto: University of Toronto Press, 2002). ———, *The Humanist-Scholastic Debate in the Renaissance and Reformation* (Cambridge, Mass.: Harvard University Press, 1995).

Anthony Grafton

♎ *1522*

Martin Luther returns to Wittenberg and engages in a debate about idolatry with his follower, Andreas Bodenstein von Karlstadt

Martin Luther and the Whole Man

In order properly to situate the significance of Luther's teachings within the history of Western thought, we must counter a central and pervasive misreading of his theology. Indeed, in many ways, it is this misreading itself that is crucial to the development of Western thought, since it lies at the heart not only of the radical reform movements Luther rejected in his own day, but also of that mingled sense of asceticism and worldly calling with which a "Protestant ethic" (Max Weber) precipitated modern social and economic forms. We may situate the "origin" of this misreading in a controversy of 1522. Hastily leaving the sanctuary in Wartburg to which he retreated following the 1521 Diet of Worms, Luther returned to Wittenberg in March 1522 in order to tackle the iconoclasm of his follower, Andreas Bodenstein von Karlstadt. In their debate about the status of images within Christian worship we find both a succinct expression of Luther's theology and that decisive misreading of his theology that even today shapes our reception of Luther's work.

Beginning, perhaps, with Hegel's treatment of Luther in *The Philosophy of History,* modern readers have tended to characterize Luther's eminence in terms of his consummate individualism. According to this modern bias, Martin Luther's emphasis on a doctrine of justification by faith alone (solafideism) is fundamentally an individualistic one, reconfiguring Christian spiritual life around the inner man. For such readers, Luther inaugurates a new subjectivism that privileges the inner life at the expense of the merely external. In place of an externalist adherence to creed and practice, Luther focuses on the internal workings of God's grace. According to such a view, Luther's solafideism dispenses with the corporate emphasis of the medieval church and its objective forms of worship in favor of a religious practice grounded in individual conscience.

This is the view that Roland Bainton adopts in his influential 1950 biography of Luther, *Here I Stand*. As the biography's title suggests, for Bainton the hallmark of Luther's reform lies in its celebration of an embattled individual conviction: "Here I stand," Luther declared at the 1521 Diet of Worms, which ultimately resulted in his excommunication; "I cannot do otherwise." For Bainton, Luther's declaration marks a new Christian piety, one that can only be articulated in terms of the stand one takes over and against a largely hostile external world.

While there is no question that the dichotomies of inner and outer are essential to Luther's solafideism, such views mistakenly identify Luther's focus on inwardness with the stand-alone integrity and autonomy that our culture ascribes to the modern individual. Whence the increased interest among scholars in Luther's doctrine of "the whole man"—a doctrine which twentieth-century readers have increasingly perceived as central to Luther's teaching. *Totus homo peccator, totus homo justus:* man is both wholly sinner and wholly saint, Luther writes; he exists, in other words, as a total moral entity, neither his sin nor his salvation occurring piecemeal. For Luther, the New Testament concept of the "flesh" encompasses our lived, human totality: our flesh is not then a mere outer wrapping or extraneous shell to be stripped away on the road to salvation. It is, instead, the whole of us. We are saved in our entirety. And yet, since our salvation is imputed to us by an all-merciful God and not earned by our works, we remain the greatest of sinners.

For modern scholars, this doctrine of the whole man indicates the ways in which Luther rejects a traditional New Testament dualism between flesh and spirit. Such a dualism, it is argued, dooms fallen man to heteronomy as opposed to autonomy, to the captivity of a self divided between utterly separate, utterly distinct realms. "For the flesh lusteth against the Spirit, and the Spirit against the flesh: and these are contrary the one to the other: so that ye cannot do the things that ye would" (Gal. 5:17). We cannot do as we would because another law, a law besides the spiritual law of God, rules our members (cf. Romans 7): within the Neoplatonic framework of the New Testament, the strife between flesh and spirit amounts to a strife between mind and body, or material and immaterial realities.

Modern readers of Luther's "whole man" have rightly argued that Luther rejects such Neoplatonic dualism—but they have done so under the false assumption that Luther's whole man transcends dualism altogether. For such readers, Luther's redefinition of flesh as encompassing man in his entirety, mind, body, and soul, is central to his vision of a fully embodied, instead of dualistically riven, Christian life. Luther, it is argued, thus combats a medieval tradition of spiritualism that embraces both the moderate Neoplatonic reforms of an Erasmus and the iconoclastic asceticism of his radical followers. Both types of reform begin with the strictest of New Testament dualisms—"It is the spirit that gives life, the flesh is of no avail" (John 6:63), a favorite phrase with reformers of all stamps—and such reformers accordingly emphasize the dangers of a religion caught up in the "mere externals" of ritual and icon. Salvation, for these reformers, requires that we transcend the flesh—while Luther's doctrine of the whole man, it is argued, promotes a cheerful integration of matter and spirit. We are not far here from the Hegelian vision of Luther as the starting point for the modern freestanding individual. By rejecting dualism, it is suggested, Luther rejects the heteronomous terms of a world divided between consciousness and matter, spirit and flesh.

This reading of Luther's divergence from other reformers, however, mistakes the matter on both sides. In the first place, while Luther's doctrine of the *totus homo* does critique a traditional dualistic view, it does not reject dualism per se but only deepens it. Rather than banish dualism or promote a more integrated worldview, Luther's vision instead entails a still sharper—indeed a total—sense of the rift between flesh and spirit. In his view, the two are utter incommensurables. Luther's "whole man" is anything but whole, anything but undivided; to be all sinner, all saint, all at once, is to be profoundly cleft. In his essential embodiment, the inward man of Lutheran faith is neither autonomous nor freestanding. Where traditional dualism defines two opposed realms of flesh and spirit, it does so in order to assert the autonomy of the former vis-à-vis the latter. Luther's whole man, in contrast, is defined by the very contention between the two realms, a strife that even the saints must experience. Founded upon the inward assurance of God's grace—upon the inward workings of God's spirit within us—Lutheran faith consists, then, in a radically external gift that can never be incorporated or assimilated into the self since it is nothing like the self. For this reason, Luther often speaks of the "alien word" of God: when God's Word lives in us as an unshakeable confidence in our salvation, it does so by remaining unassimilable, utterly alien. Luther's inward man, thus, is not that "ich" of the Worms declaration ("Hier steh ich"), that *terra firma* of independent and subjective conviction, but something more akin to a shifting ground of contestation—a battle site, even—where the strife between self and Other, flesh and spirit entails that any gains will remain ever "incomplete" and inadequate.

Readers insisting on the "wholeness" of Luther's "whole man" miss the irreparable breach that defines him. At the same time, such readers also miss the ways in which a traditional dualism tends to repair any such breach. At stake in this tradition is not the denigration of the carnal but its elevation in the very name of transcendence. "What I utterly condemn," Erasmus writes in his 1503 *Enchiridion militis christiani,* in the context of the veneration of saints, "is the fact that they [i.e. saint-worshipers] esteem the indifferent in place of the highest, the nonessentials to complete neglect of what is essential. What is of smallest value spiritually they make the greatest." This language of hierarchies—of high and low, indifferent and essential—reveals Erasmus's commitment to a dualist tradition. Transcendence, for him, entails a dependence on the very materiality it would overcome. All the while arguing against a doctrine of works, against the externalization of religion, Erasmus nonetheless treats the flesh as the very vehicle—the Jacob's ladder, as he puts it—by means of which we scale the heavens.

For Luther's radical followers, in contrast, no Jacob's ladder joins flesh to spirit. Nonetheless, like Erasmus, they too end up elevating the inessential flesh—albeit in purely negative terms. For these writers the prohibited, unavailing flesh becomes a fetish object, granted a supreme importance, as Luther points out, in its very denial. Papist, iconoclast, and Humanist alike end up, as Luther puts it, "drowning in the flesh." In their insistence on the autonomy of spirit vis-à-vis the flesh, such traditional dualists deny the very force of the strife between the two realms and, paradoxically, lose sight of the New Testament opposition altogether. They, and not Luther, are the non-dualistic thinkers, for ultimately their spirituality becomes indistinguishable from the flesh it denies.

Nowhere does Luther argue more persuasively for this strange collapse of dualism than in his response to Andreas Bodenstein von Karlstadt and the Wittenberg iconoclast movement. Karlstadt had been in Luther's camp since the beginning; in 1519 it was he who challenged Johann Eck, a sharp critic of Luther's Ninety-Five Theses, to a public disputation on Luther's behalf (known as the Leipzig Disputation), and it was he who led the reform in Wittenberg when Luther went into hiding following the Diet of Worms. During Luther's year-and-a-half absence, students and townsmen—agitated by radical members of Luther's monastic order—engaged in a number of small riots against the use of images, culminating in late January 1522 in the city council's decision to remove images from all houses of worship. Three days after this council decision, Karlstadt's pamphlet, *Von Abtuhung der Bylder Und das keyn Betdler unther den Christen seyn sollen (Concerning the Abolition of Images and That No Beggar Shall Be among Christians)* appeared, initiating the Reformation's first significant discussion of iconoclasm. In February, townspeople took the matter into their own hands and broke into a parish church. When Luther returned from hiding a month later, the terms of the debate had already been established.

Karlstadt's main contention against images returned to a concern the Church had officially resolved as early as 787, at the Second Nicene Council: the problem of the image as idol. "That we have images in churches," Karlstadt declared in the opening thesis of *Von Abtuhung der Bylder,* "is wrong and contrary to the First Commandment: 'Thou shalt not have strange gods'" (qtd. Christensen 29). For the early Church, however, idolatry had not been an issue. Instead, the need to assimilate pagan artifacts had harmonized with a strongly incarnationist perspective: God had already shown that the earthly world was a fit vessel to embody the sacred. At Nicaea, this view became settled doctrine: the ecumenical council of bishops ruled that, although true worship belongs to God alone, the veneration of images is acceptable since such honor is immediately passed on to its archetype. As likenesses of corporeal things, images could allow man to reach higher, incorporeal truths. For the Second Nicene Council, in other words, the image functioned as a rung in Jacob's ladder, its materiality become transparent in the ascent to the realm of spirit.

For Karlstadt, however, this early defense of images mistook the relationship between flesh and spirit. Drawing heavily on John 6, Karlstadt argues a strict doctrine of the unavailing flesh. The Word of God, he maintains, is spiritual and it alone profits the believer. No image of Christ could bring us close to Christ, Karlstadt argues, since, as Christ himself said, such was the work of God alone: "no man can come unto me, except it were given unto him of my Father" (John 6:65). Indeed, the flesh could only teach us about the flesh, about how Christ looked, and how he died, and not at all about *why* he died: "all those who worship God in images worship in lies, and think of God in semblances and external reports" (qtd. Christensen 33).

In his own 1522 sermons and later treatise, however, Luther counters Karlstadt by reminding him that the crucial step lies not in outlawing images, but in teaching their insignificance: "one pleases God alone through faith" (LW 40, 84). Karlstadt, of course, had also based his position on the doctrine of justification by faith alone; it is thus not Karlstadt's point of departure that Luther rejects. Indeed, in general, Luther's strategy in this debate is not so much to dismiss the iconoclasts as too extreme in their assumptions, as it is to chastise them for not being extreme enough. In certain ways, Karlstadt and his followers are indeed extreme; the rioting they encourage horrifies Luther, and he fears that their violent measures will only accustom the masses to rebellion, as was already the case with Thomas Münzer's followers in Allstedt (cf. LW 40, 88–90, 104). Nonetheless, while their practical measures might be extreme, their theology, Luther argues, simply revisits a papist doctrine of works, promoting a new type of mortification that entails seeking its own worldly death of the flesh (LW 40, 81). In their zeal to implement a doctrine of solafideism, the iconoclasts paradoxically end up replicating the self-mortifying asceticism of the medieval church. To strive for the death of the flesh in this life "means teaching works and the free will all over again" (LW 40, 81).

The problem, Luther argues, lies not with iconoclasm per se but rather with its legislation. Insofar as iconoclasm finds its impetus in the First Commandment, the injunction against images must be understood not as a law in itself but as adjunct to the Law of Laws: Thou shalt have no other gods. Here Luther's Humanist training reveals itself as he insists on a contextualized reading practice, one that situates the commandment with respect to the "whole text." So far Luther is in agreement with Karlstadt: at the heart of the matter is the problem of strange gods. And yet, as Luther points out, Karlstadt's prohibition against images establishes a new legalism to be followed without the free conscience that alone heralds our loving fulfillment of God's law. Karlstadt's iconoclasm is thus dangerously superficial, stripping away external problems while it fills the very heart with idols. A genuine iconoclasm, Luther suggests, would in contrast destroy those idols in the heart. But without God's grace, those idols are indestructible. The only way to abolish our false gods is through faith in the one true God.

Ultimately, Karlstadt's teaching reveals the impossible bind of solafideism. If only faith can save us, then, it is true, the flesh is of no avail. And yet, to imagine that one can dispense with this unavailing flesh is only to adopt a false trust, a *falsch vertrawen,* that mires us ever more deeply in sin. The flesh cannot save us, but to seek to renounce it will surely damn us, for "to ensnare the conscience with laws in these matters is death for the soul" (LW 40, 90–91). What Karlstadt's "abomination" shares with the papacy is not simply a doctrine of works but a strategy of fetishization. To deny the flesh is only to make its hold on us absolute; it is to turn the dead letter into a spiritual law. It is to transform the merely flesh into the deadly fetish.

Images, Luther writes elsewhere, are "neither here nor there, neither evil nor good, we may have them or not as we please" (LW 51, 81–82; qtd. Christensen 47). As with all matters of the flesh, the trouble doesn't merely arise when, like the papists, we imagine using these "minor, external things" to our spiritual advantage. Equally problematic is any insistence that such things work to our spiritual detriment. Whether prescribed or prohibited, whether used or rejected in our efforts to be holy, the flesh becomes our idol. As such, it is no longer an external, minor thing, but instead the absolute and inward fetish that defines us. Both sides, iconoclast and papist, seek to resolve that New Testament strife of flesh and spirit—the one side through ascetic renunciation, and the other by surmounting the flesh on the way to spirit. The two sides fail equally, delivering themselves to a flesh whose claims are the more insistent, the more intractable for the effort. Both sides, iconophobic and iconophilic, radical reformer and papist, drown in a flesh that has taken the place of God.

For Max Weber, it is such fleshly "drowning" that, in its Protestant guise, characterizes that "ethic" so crucial to the rise of capitalism. Weber argues that an iconoclastic worldview makes possible the notion of worldly calling and enables the rationalization of one's conduct in the world. In this way, Protestant asceticism and its injunctions against idolatry work paradoxically against themselves, since they ultimately lead to a capitalist spirit of time management and acquisition. In no way did Martin Luther anticipate this most worldly consequence of Karlstadt's iconophobia. But it is equally fair to say that Luther's theology was similarly unprepared for the world a Karlstadtian asceticism would help to create. Given his doctrine of a whole man utterly riven between the embodied world of space and time and the world of God's word—a doctrine that, impossibly, forecloses participation in the world at the same time that it precludes transcendence—it seems in hindsight inevitable that Luther's (mis)readers would ultimately prove more influential than Luther himself.

See also 1523, 1570, 1666, 1670 *(collegia pietatis)*

Bibliography: *Martin Luthers Werke: Kritische Gesamtausgabe* [WA] (Weimar: H. Böhlau, 1883–). *Luther's Works: American Edition* [LW], vols. 1–30 ed. Jaroslav Pelikan; vols. 31–54 ed. Helmut T.

Lehman (Philadelphia: Fortress Press, 1955–1976). Roland H. Bainton, *Here I Stand: A Life of Martin Luther* (New York: New American Library, 1950). Heinrich Bornkamm, *Luther and the Old Testament,* tr. Eric W. Gritsch and Ruth C. Gritsch (Philadelphia: Fortress Press, 1969). Carl C. Christensen, *Art and Reformation in Germany* (Athens, Ohio: Ohio University Press, Wayne State University Press, 1979). Heiko A. Oberman, *Luther: Man Between God and the Devil,* tr. Eilenn Walliser-Schwarzbart (New York: Doubleday, 1982.)

Lisa Freinkel

♫ 1523

In the preface to his translation of the Old Testament, Martin Luther assails contemporary German usage

Luther's Bible and the Emergence of Standard German

"But this Martin Luther didn't just give us freedom of movement, he also gave us the means for movement; for he gave the Spirit a Body. He gave the Word to Thought. He created the German language. This happened through his translation of the Bible" (Heine 1973, 38–39). In this quotation from the great poet Heinrich Heine, himself a converted Jew, we see one of the main strands of thought concerning Martin Luther's contribution to the history of the German language. That this opinion was not restricted to literati but was also held by language scholars can be seen in a quote from one of the fathers of *Germanistik,* Jacob Grimm (admittedly a younger Jacob Grimm), in the introduction to the second (1822) edition of his *Deutsche Grammatik (German Grammar).* After essentially dismissing, for historical-grammatical purposes, most works written in German between the 13th and 18th centuries, Grimm is careful to note that the writings of Martin Luther are *not* included in this evaluation. Indeed, Luther's language, because of its noble, almost miraculous purity, also because of its mighty influence, must be considered to be the "kernel and basis of the New High German language-foundation" (36).

This remarkable conjunction of the linguistic with the religious can be found not just among Luther's supporters, but also among his detractors. One of his foremost contemporary Catholic critics, Hieronymus Emser, responds in one of several open letters to Luther's claim that the New Testament does not mention priests and bishops: "Now I am disconcerted with the monk for this reason, that our priesthood, in Latin *sacerdotium,* in his translation is not called a priesthood any more, *episcopus* not a bishop, *presbyter* not a priest, and the gobbledygook Doctor not only wants to teach us a new faith, but also a new German" (Enders 1892, 137–138).

Equally extreme, though less religiously motivated appraisals of Luther's contributions have not been lacking either, both pro and con. The scholar Wolfgang Jungandreas (1947) is often cited as an all too ardent admirer of Luther's influence on the German language (see especially p. 71), while the oft-reprinted work of Arno Schirokauer has frequently been criticized as going too far in the other direction. Notable about many of these assessments is the use of emotion-laden labels for Luther and his biblical language which reflect the evaluators' own religious and aesthetic prejudices and detract attention from the larger areas of agreement. They also discourage any attempt to discuss the nature of the questions they try to answer, and even less to answer them with a close look at the evidence.

Vocabulary and doctrinal differences aside, Emser found Luther's Bible translation to be so good that he plagiarized it for his own Catholic Bible. And while Jungandreas entitles the relevant section of his book "Luther as the Creator of the New High German Literary Language," the facts we actually find discussed in that section have led other scholars to the more modest appellations of "mediator," "expediter," or "catalyst."

As for posing the questions correctly, a good place to start would be with the phrase "Luther's translation of the Bible." On the face of it, this expression implies that a single man is responsible for the contents of a single work. Yet we know that this simplifies the case. While he was acknowledged by all his collaborators to be the genius in charge (Kluge 1918, 60–61), he did in fact have close collaborators who concerned themselves with every aspect of the Bible translation throughout the many editions published in Luther's lifetime. Among these collaborators must also be counted the printers who published his work and whose preferences clearly influenced Luther in the course of his endless revisions.

This brings up the second point. Luther's Bible was a work in progress throughout his life, a work that underwent thousands of changes during that period. In addition, after its first appearance in Wittenberg (in 1522 in the form of the September Testament, a translation of the New Testament), it was quickly reprinted, in both approved and pirated editions, and many of these editions imposed more or less important changes on the language of their model (this is most obvious in its translations into Low German). Thus, at least as far as language is concerned, one can hardly speak of a monolithic "Luther Bible."

This more complex understanding makes the question of Luther's influence on the German language more complex as well. In general, it seems sensible to break this question down into at least the following sub-questions: (1) Did the fact that Luther translated the Bible into German make a difference in the history of the German language, especially with regard to its standardization? If so, why? (2) Did the specific linguistic phenomena in Luther's own Bible translation influence the direction of that standardization? If so, which ones? (3) Where did these linguistic phenomena come from, and to what extent was their choice or their combination Luther's own?

As to the first question, I believe there is general agreement. Luther's Bible translation, along with his other German writings and the writings of others participating in the ferment of the Reformation, broadened irrevocably the range of registers and functions for which German, rather than Latin, was the preferred linguistic vehicle. Yet, if German was the appropriate language for most functions in the new Germany, some degree of standardization became urgent. In addition, the overwhelming popularity of Luther's Bible had a tremendous effect on the number of books printed in German, which, in turn, put special pressure on the printers, for economic reasons, to attempt some kind of supraregional language.

Why was Luther's Bible so popular? Even such a skeptic about Luther's originality as Schirokauer acknowledges the crucial factor: Luther had both the desire and the literary talent to convey to people of every station, but especially the common people, the message of the Christian Bible in their own language.

It really should come as no surprise that translating the Bible well was more important to Martin Luther than to his predecessors. His theological premises actually pushed him in that direction. If the relationship of a human being to God was to be mediated by no other human being (for example, popes or priests), but was supposed to be as direct as possible, and the Bible was the Word of God, then it was in every human being's interest to be able to understand the Bible. Two things, at least, follow from this: (1) the Bible should be as widely distributed as possible; (2) it should be available in a way that makes people want to read it, and that people understand.

If these objectives are combined, as they were in Martin Luther, with an extraordinary ear for language and a literary talent unparalleled in his place and time, the results can be, and were, equally extraordinary. Luther was obsessed with the right way to translate the Bible, as evidenced in his many letters to colleagues and friends and, therefore, also with the "proper" way of writing and speaking. His judgment on the preachers and writers of his day can be seen in the following quotation from the 1523 preface to his Old Testament translation: "And I have read no book nor letter up to now in which the right kind of German language can be found. Nobody tries to speak proper German either, especially not the chanceries of the lords and the hack preachers and puppet writers, who allow themselves to think that they have the power to change the German language." On the level of style, there is no question that Luther served as an important model to his contemporaries and continues to serve as one up to the present day. He released written German from the dry forms of the chancery and brought it closer to its spoken roots. Many of the metaphors and proverbs in his Bible translation belong to the core treasury of the modern language.

Yet surely it takes more than this to be the "creator" or "father" of the German language. What of the form of language? What of its syntax, its vocabulary, its inflectional categories, its spelling, even its pronunciation? What was Luther's influence on all of these? Obviously these questions cannot be answered without looking at standardizing tendencies in German before, during, and after Luther's time, and asking what would have been different had Luther not lived.

For quite some time before Luther, strong tendencies were at work toward a supraregional standard written language, especially in the primarily south-eastern chanceries of the Holy Roman Empire. These tendencies reached a high point under the Emperor Maximilian I (1459–1519) and his power-ful chancellor Niclas Ziegler, whose writing practice was disseminated in a stream of imperial documents throughout the German-speaking regions. Although this emergent southeastern standard deliberately avoided spell-ings, forms, and words that betrayed a narrow dialect origin, it still showed more general characteristics of southeastern German dialects—spelling, vocab-ulary, and inflection were necessarily influenced to some extent by regional speech.

Despite the regional idiosyncrasies, "gemeines Deutsch" (common Ger-man) invariably influenced the chancery of the Saxon electors. By Luther's time, the written language of east-central Germany had already absorbed nu-merous linguistic characteristics of the southeastern German "standard," nec-essarily giving up many linguistic features characteristic of the spoken dialects of that region. It is thus incorrect to assume, as many scholars have, that the language of Luther's Bible was somehow a direct outgrowth of the spoken dia-lects of east-central Germany, and that Luther established the language of Meissen–Upper Saxony as the standard German language. Regardless of the extent of Luther's influence, the emerging Standard German was, and to a great extent still is, a written language.

What did Luther himself say about the form of his language? The most fa-mous quote is from his *Tischreden* (*Table Talk*): "I don't have a certain, special, individual language in German, but use the common German language, so that both the Over- and the Netherlanders can understand me. I speak accord-ing to the Saxon chancery, which all princes and kings in Germany follow; all imperial cities, princely courts write according to the Saxon chancery and that of our prince, and that's why it is the most common German language. Em-peror Maximilian and Elector Friedrich of Saxony have thus pulled the Ger-man languages together into one certain language in the [Holy] Roman Em-pire." Given the earlier quotation from his Old Testament introduction, Luther is obviously talking about form here, not style. But it is also clear that, despite obvious differences, he discerns some kind of overarching unity in the writing traditions of the southeastern and Saxon chanceries, a unity arrived at before Luther himself came onto the scene.

Yet Luther was clearly also aware of the differences, and of the fact that in his own writings, especially the Bible translation, choices frequently had to be made, between words, forms, and spellings. And it is here that many scholars see his major contribution to the emerging standard. As a mediator between north and south, Luther obviously chose those phenomena he felt would gain his Bible the widest acceptance throughout the German-speaking realm. Of-ten his choice fell on southern forms, in line with the already widespread ac-ceptance of those forms. But in numerous other cases, for example, when a widely accepted northern word presented itself as the alternative to an equally widely accepted southern word, he chose the northern form.

Once made, the choice did not necessarily stick. Thus, although Luther initially followed the southeastern practice of dropping a final weak -*e* vowel in word roots and grammatical endings, in his Bible translation he ultimately reintroduced this vowel in line with east-central German written (and spoken) practice. This so-called *Luther'sche* -*e* (Lutheran -*e*) has contributed importantly to the preservation of the inflectional system (for example, plural or subjunctive markers) that distinguishes New High German from other Germanic dialects.

A comparison of Luther's Bible with a contemporary (southeastern) Catholic one reveals that, where the two make different choices, Luther's is usually much more in line with the modern standard language (Kluge, 33–35). This is certainly not to say that Luther always made the correct choice (a teleological notion one frequently encounters in these discussions); for example, Luther holds to a vocalic distinction between the preterite singular and preterite plural of many strong verbs that has been abandoned in the standard language, and had been abandoned by numerous contemporaries of Luther (thus Luther has *steig, stigen* "he, they climbed" as opposed to the modern *stieg, stiegen*).

The linguistic level in modern German most often cited as showing the influence of Luther's Bible is the lexicon, including both word choice and word formation. It is far less easy to show any direct influence in the areas of syntax or inflection (the syntactic patterns he used can be found in many contemporaneous writings, the "Lutheran -*e*" was not just Luther's, and then there are the wrong choices such as *steig*). In a fairly recent (1990) article, von Polenz has made an interesting case for Luther's central role in the (northern-oriented) pronunciation principles of the German literary language, based not so much on his written Bible translation as on his own oral practice and that of his students.

On the whole, there seems little justification for calling Luther the "creator" or "founder" of the modern German language. But there is also little justification for the position taken by Schirokauer and others that Luther was basically irrelevant to the formation of the standard language. Moreover, one should keep in mind that it has now been more than 450 years since the last edition of the Bible was printed that Luther personally oversaw. Although in its time, it surely came closer to a living standard language than any other book, languages change. As early as the 17th century, some of the language Luther used was perceived as rare or obsolete (and thus hard for common folk to understand). Despite some revisions this situation has only gotten worse since then. The interesting question is, what should be done about it? Revise Luther's text extensively in the light of the modern language, even retranslate, or leave it as it is (with some apparatus allowing modern readers to decipher it)? It seems clear that Luther personally would have chosen the first option. While he certainly was capable of using a sacral style in his biblical passages, a style that often deliberately evokes a poetic feeling of ritual and even antiquatedness, he would hardly have wanted the whole Bible to end up conveying that feeling. Certainly he wanted the common folk to understand it.

See also 1457, 1515, 1522, 1815, 1824

Bibliography: Heinrich Bach, "Wo liegt die entscheidende Wirkung der 'Luthersprache' in der Entwicklung der deutschen Standardsprache?" in Herbert Wolf, ed., *Luthers Deutsch: Sprachliche Leistung und Wirkung* (Frankfurt am Main: Lang, 1996), 126–135. Werner Besch, *Sprachlandschaften und Sprachausgleich im 15. Jahrhundert* (Munich: Franke, 1967). Joachim Dückert, "Das Grimmsche Wörterbuch und Luther," in Wolf, ed. *Luthers Deutsch,* 149–159. Ernst Ludwig Enders, *Luther und Emser: Ihre Streitschriften aus dem Jahre 1521,* v. 2 (Halle an der Saale: Niemeyer, 1892). Jacob Grimm, *"Deutsche Grammatik:* Vorrede," in *Vorreden zur deutschen Grammatik* (Darmstadt: Wissenschaftliche Buchgesellschaft, [1822], 1968). Heinrich Heine, *Historisch-kritische Gesamtausgabe der Werke,* Manfred Windfuhr, ed., vol. 8 (Hamburg: Hoffmann und Campe, 1973). Wolfgang Jungandreas, *Geschichte der Deutschen und der Englischen Sprache,* v. 2 (Göttingen: Vandenhoeck & Ruprecht, 1947). Friedrich Kluge, *Von Luther bis Lessing,* 5th ed. (Leipzig: Quelle & Meyer, 1918). Peter von Polenz, "Martin Luther und die Anfänge der deutschen Schriftlautung," in Wolf, ed., *Luthers Deutsch,* 221–235. Arno Schirokauer, "Frühneuhochdeutsch," in Arno Schirokauer, *Germanistische Studien* (Hamburg: Hauswedell, 1957).

Orrin W. Robinson

☙ 1537
The town of Dinkelsbühl installs texts behind its altars

The Image of the Word

In 1537, four years after it embraced the Protestant faith, the town of Dinkelsbühl redecorated the altars of its churches. In the great parish church dedicated to Saint George, the retable of a Last Supper painting was erected, captioned in gold by the biblical text of the Institution. In the Hospital Church just around the corner, a similar altarpiece was installed, which is still in place today. The retable is known only from descriptions: an oblong wooden panel displaying, on three fields, the Institution flanked by the Ten Commandments. The hospital's records list payment "to Beckerle to make the altar, 2 florin; 5 day-wages work at the altar, 7 pounds; 5 day wages, 4 pounds; and further eight florin to Wolf, painter of the panel, to gild and make [it]" (Bürckstümmer, I, 86). Given how far and in between commissions for church ornaments were in Dinkelsbühl at the time, Beckerle and Wolf—a carpenter, perhaps, and a painter-sculptor—no doubt welcomed the task even though their craft was making pictures, not words.

The idea for this altarpiece was conceived by Matthias Rösser, the hospital's administrator and indefatigable leader of church reform in Dinkelsbühl. In 1525, when Rösser was mayor and master of the Guild, he led a campaign against the city's corrupt Catholic priest and, after a setback in the wake of the Peasant Wars, he had worked with like-minded guildsmen and clergy to win the city council to his cause. By 1537, both the Georgskirche and the Hospital Church had Protestant pastors and preachers. By then, revenue from the monasteries went to the council; church services were held largely according to the Lutheran rite; pastors had full authority in religious matters and received their call from the city rather than from the bishop; and burghers went to Wittenberg for religious education.

But it was from Luther himself that Dinkelsbühl derived the form of the retables. In 1530, at the Diet of Augsburg, Luther had delivered a sermon on Psalm 111, in which he advised "whoever might want to have panels set up on the altar" should paint the Last Supper, along with the words, in big, gold letters, "The gracious and merciful Lord instituted a remembrance of his miracle" (Luther, *Werke,* vol. XXXI/1, 415). Like the picture he imagined, with its programmatic pairing of images and labels, Luther's statement about church pictures resists exegesis because it already *is* exegesis. To modern-day audiences who, like Luther, seek to explain everything, it may seem self-evident that altars should be decorated with images that reenact the biblical event. But it is well to remember that Luther's is the earliest known northern European text that explicitly states a general preference for the subject matter of altarpieces. As such, it was part of the campaign he launched from the Coburg fortress in 1530, and institutionalized in the Augsburg Confession, to replace practices based on custom with practices grounded in Scripture, and generally to explicate acts and objects whose motivations had been left unstated. Moreover, though the Last Supper seems the obvious subject for a retable, it was rare in the North, occurring only on some altars dedicated to specific mysteries, but almost never found, before 1530, on a high altar. The first surviving high altarpiece designed in this manner was none other than the great retable painted in the shop of Lucas Cranach the Elder for the city church in Wittenberg. Dedicated in 1547, this crucial ensemble, displayed in the church of Luther's own ministry, served both to commemorate the reformer, who died in 1546, and to proclaim, in the face of Catholic armies encamped at the city's gates, that Luther's religion was not a sect but a church.

Lutheran retables pictured a new, revolutionary frontality. This is especially true for the word-altarpiece in Dinkelsbühl. Long before they embraced Lutheranism, the burghers of that town, led by Rösser, had agitated against their exclusion from the altar. Already in 1503, the town council complained that of the countless private Masses performed for money, only a few were openly recited, and that priests did not participate in the festive church processions organized by the laity, who milled about idly in worldly clothes. As early as 1522, the Catholic priest, Bastian Süßler, was pressured into administering the sacrament of the Eucharist in both manners. These lay communions in the vernacular were performed intermittently on special days, until 1531/32, when they were briefly forbidden. During those bitter months, most citizens refused the customary Easter communion in protest. The German Mass became official in Dinkelsbühl in 1534, except for the Hospital Church itself, which tolerated Catholic services for some years afterward. In 1537, then, the word-altarpiece was erected behind an altar in the middle of the nave, traditionally reserved for the lay altar. It was there that—in Dinkelsbühl, begrudgingly—commoners had received Holy Communion from time to time. Until the 17th century, the choir of the Hospital Church retained its late Gothic Marian retable, a remnant, perhaps, of the parallel Catholic services that had been held in this church. The Virgin's missing crown suggests that, at some point, this ensemble sustained an iconoclastic blow.

What did the new ensemble say about the altar it backed? In place of image, relic, or host, the triptych enshrined the text of the institution of Holy Communion as paraphrased in Luther's *German Mass*. These are precisely the words that the Catholic Church had formerly withheld. Now facing the congregation, so that everyone can read them for themselves, they focus communion on the laity, defining its activity as reading, understanding, and believing. In place of a priesthood of God's deputies, speaking Mass unintelligibly in low tones for (or rather, before) the parishioners, the entire laity is now, as this altarpiece announces, a congregation of priests. For as Luther put it, "All Christians are of a priestly estate" (*Werke,* VI, 407).

Openly displayed and legible to anyone who can read, the writing hails the individual as a comprehending mind. It inserts the ordinary person into the central, but formerly prohibited, connection between word and gesture on which the representative power of the Church had been founded. In the Catholic Mass, the priest intones the effective sentence from a book that—mentally and materially—he alone possesses. Published on an altarpiece, and built into a culture that, through the institutions of catechism and school, endeavors to make subjects into readers, this sentence now places everyone before the Mass. In 1537, the citizens of Dinkelsbühl suddenly inhabited the public sphere of representation that had formerly been the monopoly of the Church.

Dinkelsbühl's textual altarpiece erased what went before. Unlike the lost retable of the Georgskirche, it does not feature a Last Supper panel. In its present state, the ensemble does not gloss over this omission, but trumpets it through its physical form. The concave segments fixed on both sides, together with the molding that spans the top, give the altarpiece the unmistakable shape of a predella that has been stripped of its image-bearing corpus. The sculpted and gilded words display what a previous priesthood had withheld. The altarpiece that can been seen in the Hospital Church today may well have been damaged at some point. A report by the church custodian Johannes Melchior Wildeisen, dating from about 1645, states that the retable in the Georgskirche had been "of the same sort" as the one "still in use" in the Hospital Church, and that the former was "made with a painted piece, the Last Supper" (Bürckstümmer, I, 82). Whether this "and" adds what the Hospital Church's altarpiece, in 1645, also had is unclear from Wildeisen's wording. A much over-painted painting of the Last Supper that was recently discovered in the Hospital Church may well be the original altarpiece panel, although when and why it was removed remains a mystery. In any case, the writing is the only surviving surface behind the altar: letters written "in reserve" on the toppled idol's base.

But what sort of spectacle do evenly sculpted letters, layered in gold, provide? While a reading eye scans them from left to right and top to bottom, the carved inscriptions form a diffuse center through their greater density in the middle panel, and through the symmetry of their triptych format. Since the writing occupies the framework of a figure in a shrine, it becomes itself a display of shiny, recursive shapes standing out from a dark background. Through their contributions to the printed book, the instrument of Scripture's new dispensation, wood-block cutters and type inventors (whose products Wolf had to imitate) could justly hail their craft for advancing a word-based faith. In 1537, writing was in and of itself a work of beauty.

In the middle panel of the altarpiece, in the interval following Christ's words about the bread—"Do this in my memory"—the carver chiseled, in high relief, not a period or comma but an object: a single blossom. Placed off-center and thus registering the contingency of patterns shaped by writing, this little flower is hardly a substitute for the carved, polychrome effigies it historically replaced. But the gaze fixes on it nonetheless, arrested by its appearance as a thing. From a distance where reading is impossible, the flower halts the eye through its isolated glint. From up close, it is read rather than viewed, and thus punctuates the biblical text and separates the words about the bread from the words about wine. Christ's order to "do this" and "remember" finds time to be performed and experienced in the pause the blossom inserts. After the bread has been blessed and elevated—Luther retained this crucial gesture of late medieval liturgy—the wine, too, is lifted, blessed, and poured; the flower will have affirmed that, in Dinkelsbühl, the chalice is also the layman's to receive. Far from being a mere thing distinct from language and devoid of inner meaning, the little rose on the altarpiece signals interiority itself, where meaning unfolds as sentiment in the heart.

If this is a reading, it violates the expected bandwidth of the written text. To an eye accustomed to writing, letters yield their meaning too effortlessly to be construed as figures, nor are the surrounding rubrics easily taken for texts. Friedrich Schleiermacher, the founder of modern hermeneutics who renewed Luther's faith, banned from poetry all verses "that look like an ax or bottle" (Schleiermacher, 580). Picture-poems to him convey messages through their external form and, therefore, violate the primacy of inner meaning that hermeneutics assumes—religiously—for language. Lutherans, by contrast, wished to exhibit writing as a beautiful emblem of all the truths it conveyed. In 1586, the Danish reformer Jacob Madsen termed the letters of the alphabet a "treasury" and "delicious hoard" which, present from the beginning and surviving until the world's end, contain within themselves all "spiritual and mundane learning" (Arvidsson, 195). In the same year, Peder Trellund crafted for the parish church in Holbjerg, Denmark, a retable, now in the Historical Museum in Copenhagen, of nineteen plaquettes in different colors, sizes, shapes, and materials. Each tablet showcases a biblical verse or saying, and each is written in a distinctive scriptural style. Cursive, antiqua, and micrography vie with each other in virtuoso calligraphy and carving, while the content of all these bits of writing—the pious texts themselves—are barely readable from any distance.

Where Master Wolf of Dinkelsbühl gave the iconoclastic texts some measure of aesthetic appeal, Trellund conceals the text kernels beneath their exuberant inscription. The heterogeneity of both the writing and the material from which writing can be made (soapstone, copper, wood, gold, and the like) belong to a forgotten phase in the historical transition from script to print. In 1580, a retable of nothing but inscriptions would have celebrated Protestantism's "new dispensation" of the word. And that dispensation depended on the printed book, specifically on Luther's German Bible, which, through the unprecedented ease of reading it facilitated and through its existence in thousands of identical copies, makes us forget—indeed renders (so to speak) immaterial—the stuff of which it is made. Carving biblical verses in stone, letter by tiny calligraphic letter, reflects a condition of writing, and through it, of communicating, distinct from the modern hermeneutic settlement, where that which counts is the message, not the medium. This a priori medial condition is not confined to eccentric objects like the Holbjerg and Dinkelsbühl retables; it obtains for countless works of Reformation art, where texts overwhelm the images they inscribe. In 1606, in the village church of Türkheim near Ulm, a local pastor ordered 195 biblical quotations painted on the walls, forty of them in Hebrew; and in 1649, the preacher and pedagogue Balthasar Schupp outfitted Hamburg's Church of Saint Jacobi with 229 choice sayings.

The iconic character of writing even finds expression in early editions of the German Bible itself. The still-current practice of printing the key bits of text—or "text kernels"—in a special type goes back to Luther's editor Georg Röhrer. In the revised German Bible of 1541, Röhrer introduced a system of setting some words in Antiqua, others all in upper-case Fraktur, and the rest in ordinary mixed Fraktur. In an afterword, Röhrer explains that wherever scripture speaks of Christ, it is set in upper-case Fraktur, whereas passages referring to evil or death are set in Antiqua. On the opening page of the Song of Songs, for example, we find the "I" in "I am black" in Antiqua, whilst in "I am like you" it is capitalized in Fraktur. Not different words but the different graphic supports for words give each sentence its underlying value. It is said that Luther rejected Röhrer's system as "sheer nonsense." Yet he ordered his translations and vernacular writings to be set in Fraktur probably because he believed that it, and not Antiqua, which was reserved for Latin texts, was the inscriptive vulgate for German readers and a font, or "Schriftbild," untainted by paganism and Rome. More crucially, Röhrer's foregrounding of some words over others agreed with Luther's exegetical method and with evangelical doctrine, which held that scripture should be interpreted by means of scripture alone. Printing text kernels—or a "canon in the canon"—in a special type merely reified the fact that the Bible's clarity depended on iconic features of writing. For how else could a text that had been obscure for centuries display those passages that now unlock its meaning? Already in his first Bible translation of 1522—the *September Testament*—Luther engineered Scripture's legibility and through it its capacity to be its own interpreter *(scriptura sui ipsius interpres)* by means of typography and layout. Even before it was carved in wood or stone, the biblical "text kernel" displayed writing as image.

In his visits to parish churches in Saxony in 1528, Luther found God's word poorly taught and rarely understood, even by village pastors. To teach the local ministry what to teach, Luther sought ways of setting forth what should be grasped at the end of an interpretive process not yet begun. Both his large and small catechisms extracted from Scripture and its "kernels" a second-order norm. And in a spirit of conciseness that would occupy Protestant pastors for centuries, Luther would further reduce these to thumbnail sketches—some but four lines long—that summarized catechism itself. Formerly, everything began with the priest, whose ordination linked him to Christ's first disciples; now religion started with catechism, which prepared an understanding of the faith that alone was the way to salvation. In the Wittenberg Church Ordinance and in his *German Mass* (both 1526), Luther states that, prerequisite to the communion, "a crude, basic, simple, good catechism is necessary" (Sehling, I, 12). The Preface to the Large Catechism recommends that no one be admitted to the altar who had not given public proof of his knowledge of doctrine. In the Schmalkaldic Articles (1537), he keeps confession for the purpose of preliminarily "interrogating and instructing" on their grasp of faith. What began as a voluntaristic ideal—the laity approaching the altar bound only by their conscience—became obligatory in teaching and testing. Parishioners in Dinkelsbühl and Ilstorp were expected to know the texts displayed in their church by heart and to be able to recite them on command. In some Lutheran regions, being a citizen depended on passing literacy exams, the set text of which was Luther's Small Catechism. From being a visual conduit to the sacred realm, the altarpiece had become a standardized test for admission to the secular state. The odd little object in Dinkelsbühl is, therefore, an important relic for the history of both art and literature.

See also 1523, 1670 *(collegia pietatis)*, 1800 (January), 1897

Bibliography: Bengt Arvidsson, *Bildstrid, Bildbruk, Bildlära* (Lund, 1987). Christian Bürckstümmer, *Geschichte der Reformation und Gegenreformation in der ehemaligen freien Reichstadt Dinkelsbühl (1524–1648),* 2 vols. (Leipzig, 1914–1915). August Gebessler, "Stadt und Landkreis Dinkelsbühl," *Bayrische Kunstdenkmale* 15 (Munich, 1962). Martin Luther, *Werke,* Kritische Gesamtausgabe (Weimar, 1980–1983). Emil Sehling, ed., *Die evangelischen Kirchenordnungen des 16. Jahrhunderts* (Leipzig, 1901–1913). Friedrich Schleiermacher, *Pädogogische Schriften,* ed. C. Patz (Langensalza, 1876).

Joseph Leo Koerner

৭ 1551

In Paris, Petrus Lotichius Secundus publishes a book of Latin elegies that explore his experiences in the Schmalkaldic War

Make Poetry, Not War

German literature, especially of the 16th and 17th centuries, teems with Latinate family names. Many names of German or other origin were Latinized by simply appending an *-ius* suffix—for example, Justus Georg Schottelius,

Georg Wicelius, Andreas Wissowatius. Other Latinate names were calques based on the meanings of underlying vernacular names or people's origins or occupations—for example, Johannes Agricola, Andreas Gryphius, Adam Olearius, Christian August Vulpius.

Petrus Lotichius Secundus, henceforth Lotichius, was born on November 2, 1528, in Niederzell, near Schlüchtern in Hesse. His parents were Hans (Johannes) and Elisabeth Lotz. How then did a boy named Peter Lotz acquire the portentous moniker with which this paragraph began? The family name was Latinized in 1548 on the advice of Philipp Melanchthon (1497–1560), a Humanist, Hellenist, and Lutheran whose own name rendered in Greek the components of his German family name. Secundus became part of Peter's Latin name to differentiate him from his uncle and teacher, Petrus Lotichius (1501–1567), the abbot of the monastery at Schlüchtern.

All the information at our disposal indicates that the parents of Lotichius were humble peasants, but his uncle—despite not having himself received the quality and quantity of education he coveted for his nephews—attained a level of learning that enabled him to have ties with leading intellectual figures of his day. Although Lotichius later occupied a professorship of medicine and botany at the University of Heidelberg, where his name now holds a place of pride on the wall of the Alte Aula (old auditorium), and although a 19th-century novel about him by one Otto Müller is called *Der Professor von Heidelberg,* his main achievement was not in scholarship, but in the composition of highly regarded Latin verse. He published nothing in German, and indeed none of his Latin books was even printed in Germany in his lifetime. His reputation rests almost entirely on the Latin elegies he began publishing in 1551.

While the questions "what is German?" and "what is Germany?" no longer lead to wars as in the past, the question "what is a German author?" might still elicit strong and varied reactions from literary historians. Lotichius, although he could be called a neo-Latin or a Renaissance Latin poet, qualifies as a German author not because he wrote in German but because German is his native tongue and, more important by far, because he grappled in his Latin poetry with the conflicting aspirations of poetry and scholarship that characterized German Humanism as well as the harsh realities of the military and political conflicts in Germany that resulted from the Reformation and Counter-Reformation.

By Lotichius's time, German was a well-established literary language, as can be seen in Martin Luther's translation of the Bible, published in a first complete version in 1534 and revised several times until shortly before his death. However, Latin still enjoyed a special prestige as an international, even global, language of culture among both Protestants and Catholics. The French essayist Michel de Montaigne (1533–1592), a contemporary of Lotichius, learned Latin as a toddler and did not acquire French until he was six, which renders topsy-turvy the usual associations of mother tongue or native language. Also in France, Joachim Du Bellay (1522–1560), who died in the same year as Lotichius, published his first collections of sonnets and other lyrics in

French in 1549 and 1550, and his Latin poems as well as his *Antiquités de Rome* and *Regrets* in 1558. But unlike Montaigne and Du Bellay, Lotichius chose to write exclusively in Latin and not even sporadically in his spoken language.

Why a young man such as Lotichius chose classical Latin as opposed to the new vernacular German to express himself in elegies lamenting the horrors of war, the frustration it creates for the pursuit of poetry and scholarship, and the powerful and abiding melancholy of lost love is hard to determine. The fact is that he conveyed with great ease in Latin the details of his life and feelings. Nothing that happened in the 16th century seems to have been beyond his ken: in words that would have been familiar to Virgil or Cicero he expresses even the operation of cannons.

The term that best describes the aesthetics of much of Renaissance Latin literature is *imitatio*. By writing elegies, Lotichius availed himself of the complex presuppositions about elegy that survived from Roman literature and that connected this form on the one hand to lament and on the other to love. From Augustan elegists, he drew resources for discussing love as well as warfare, particularly in Tibullus, and exile, in Ovid. The paradoxes of the Roman elegy and of neo-Latin precursors, such as Petrus Angelus Bargaeus (1517–1596), who also wrote in this genre, were Lotichius's primary models. His writings predated the publication of Pierre de Ronsard's (1524–1585) elegies in French (1565), although he may have known Ronsard's *Odes* and *Amours,* which were first printed in 1550 and 1552, respectively. Despite his commitment to faithfully adhering to the constructions and vocabulary of Classical Latin, and despite the aura of timeless serenity he sought to convey through his style, Lotichius was anything but detached from contemporary political and military preoccupations. The backdrop to the major events of his time was the dispute that pitted Luther and other reformers against the emperor and the Counter-Reformation.

In the mid-1540s, Lotichius looked to a very promising future. He studied Latin literature in the circle of Jacob Micyllus [Moltzer] (1503–1558) at Frankfurt and for a year at the University of Marburg. But then Germany began to unravel. When Marburg became untenable for Protestants, Lotichius went to Magdeburg. There, the eighteen-year-old joined the forces of Johann Friedrich, the Elector of Saxony, on the side of the Schmalkaldic League against Emperor Charles V. The Schmalkaldic League, so called after the Saxon town of Schmalkalden in Thuringia where the League was formed on December 31, 1530, gave its name to the Schmalkaldic War (1546–1547). Lotichius was a soldier in the war for seven months, from November 1546 until May 1547, when the League was defeated in the Battle of Mühlberg. Despite its brevity, the war had a profound impact on Lotichius. His father and one of his brothers died, while he himself suffered a serious illness.

Throughout the war, Lotichius was billeted in Magdeburg and environs, one of the safest stations since a full-scale battle did not take place there until late 1550, at the beginning of the Princes' War. Yet, Lotichius was plagued by occasional fears and even more by a sense of frustration since his life as a soldier kept him from realizing his aspiration of becoming a man of letters. It was largely from this torment that he wrote the poems of war and peace "Carmina militiae facta meae" (Poems Made Out of My Soldiering), in which he explores the tensions between military service and service to the Muses. Whether or not he believed the sword to be mightier than the pen is hard to gauge, but there can be no doubt that he preferred the power of poetry to the horrors of war and the concomitant realization of the transience of human life.

The short-lived peace following the Schmalkaldic War allowed Lotichius to resume his studies of the arts at Erfurt and Wittenberg and renew his contact with Humanists and classicists such as Melanchthon and Joachim Camerarius (1500–1574). As the peace threatened to dissolve in a new round of fighting, Lotichius made a decision with grievous consequences. From mid-1548 until late 1549 or early 1550, he had a love relationship in Wittenberg with a woman he called Claudia in his verse. Underestimating the strength of his passion or overestimating his ability to forget or control it, he left Germany for France at the end of 1549 as tutor to the nephews of Daniel Stibar (d. 1555), the canon of Würzburg. However, the woman he left behind haunted him for many years. His longing for her was perhaps most acute in 1551 during his stay in Paris.

On the surface, the time in Paris seemed a relief from the moral dilemma caused by his repugnance for a soldier's life and his obligation to support the political cause he had aligned himself with. During his leisure hours, he revised earlier drafts (which are not extant) of poems he wrote during the Schmalkaldic War. In late spring or early summer 1551, at the age of twenty-two, his first book of poetry (elegies together with *carmina*) was printed at the prestigious publishing house of Michel Vascosan in Paris. Its implicit opposition to the emperor made it impossible for the book to be printed in most cities in Germany; but this same stance made the elegies appealing to the French.

The book opens with a dedicatory letter to Stibar, who sponsored his trip to France. In the letter, Lotichius mentions hearing of renewed strife in Germany and describes his decision to revise the poems he first composed in 1547 during the Schmalkaldic War because of their fresh relevancy. Toward the end of his life, less than a decade after his stay in Paris, Lotichius again made sweeping changes to these poems so that most of them took on a very different form from the one in the first printing of 1551.

While he was in Paris, Lotichius, having already determined to pursue an advanced degree in medicine, studied astrology and botany. He also wrote the first five poems in the second book of elegies, as well as a few minor poems. Later in the year 1551, he moved with his charges to Montpellier, where he registered as a medical student. His studies of medicine in Montpellier and elsewhere failed to protect him five years later in February or March 1556 against a mishap in Bologna that might have been laughable, had it not damaged his health and severely curtailed his life. By agreeing to swap plates at a dinner, Lotichius inadvertently consumed part of a poisonous love potion that was meant for a friend. If his early biographer is to be believed, a recurrence of the illness induced by this potion was the cause of his death in 1560.

By then Lotichius had composed three more books of elegies. Book Two comprised poems from the years in France, Book Three from the years in Italy (1554–1556), and Book Four from the years in Heidelberg. He subjected his poetry to numerous revisions, but none more thorough than those of the poems from the Schmalkaldic War (Book One). These revisions were the logical consequence of the doubts Lotichius expressed about the quality of the first published form of these poems in a letter to Camerarius of July 1551, just as his book was coming into print.

The first *Opera omnia* of Lotichius's poetry was published, together with a laudatory biography, just over a quarter of a century after his death in Leipzig in 1586 by his friend Joannes Hagius (Johannes Hagen). It seems appropriate that Lotichius's elegies should have received their final form posthumously through the efforts of family and friends. After all, the poems originated in a world of men who shared a Latin education as well as a cult or culture of friendship based on Latin literature and values associated with it. This culture of friendship is evident in the original dedications to the 1551 elegies, all but one of which are directed to friends or mentors, such as Melchior Zobel, a friend and fellow student at Wittenberg who also served in the army; Johannes Alt, a comrade who had returned to Hesse without enlisting; and Micyllus, a mentor. But the clearest evidence of the ties that bound Humanists across even national, ethnic, and political lines can be found in a war anecdote in the elegies about German Protestant soldiers receiving merciful treatment from an Italian officer who claims to be related to the neo-Latin poet Iacopo Sannazaro of Naples (1456–1530). The ability to read and write in Latin in no way deprived the Humanists of their national or religious identities; and yet, unlike German and other vernaculars, Latinity constituted a passport that opened the doors to literary and intellectual circles throughout Western Europe.

See also 1515–1517, 1523, 1609, 1786

Bibliography: Peter Burmann, ed., *Petri Lotichii Secundi Poemata omnia,* 2 vols. (Amsterdam, 1754); in the absence of a more recent edition, this one contains the fullest commentary and collection of supporting materials. Petrus Lotichius Secundus, *Elegiarum liber* (Paris, 1551). ———, *Poemata* (Leipzig, 1563); Lotichius's final revision of the elegies and other poems, published posthumously by Camerarius. Katherine Anne O'Rourke Fraiman, "Petrus Lotichius Secundus Elgiarum liber primus: Edited with an introduction, translation, and commentary," Ph.D. diss., Columbia University, 1973. Walther Ludwig, "Petrus Lotichius Secundus and the Roman Elegists: Prolegomena to a Study of Neo-Latin Elegy," in *Classical Influences on European Culture A.D. 1500–1700,* ed. R. R. Bolgar (Cambridge, U.K., 1976), 171–190. Wanda Merchant, "Petrus Lotichius Secundus," in James Hardin and Max Reinhard, eds., "German Writers of the Renaissance and Reformation 1280–1580," *Dictionary of Literary Biography* 179 (Detroit, 1997), 124–128. Stephen Zon, *Petrus Lotichius Secundus: Neo-Latin Poet,* American University Studies, Series 1: Germanic Languages and Literatures 13 (New York, Frankfurt am Main, and Bern: Peter Lang, 1983).

Jan Ziolkowski

℥ 1557

Hans Staden publishes his *Warhaftig Historia,* dedicated to Landgrave Philipp of Hesse and introduced by Johann Dryander, professor of medicine at Marburg

A German Mamluk in Colonial Brazil?

Together with André Thevet's *Les Singularités de la France Antarctique* (Paris, 1557) and Jean de Léry's *Histoire d'un Voyage faict en la terre de Brésil* (Geneva, 1578), Hans Staden's *Warhaftig Historia und beschreibung eyner Landtschafft der Wilden/Nackten/Grimmigen Menschenfresser Leuthen, in der Newenwelt America gelegen* (Marburg 1557; *True History and Description of a Landscape of Savage, Naked, Fierce, Cannibalistic People Located in the New World America*) is one of the most remarkable narratives that ended the early period of European Americana dominated by Christopher Columbus's and Amerigo Vespucci's letters. Yet while the accounts of Staden, Léry, and Thevet are all based on travel experiences in Brazil at the time the French were seeking to break the Portuguese monopoly there (1555–1560), the publication of Staden's book alone was not motivated by the colonial project of a *France Antarctique*. Both the singular composition and the successful printing history of Staden's book can be traced to this conjunction of a colonial experience and a non-colonial context of publication. His narrative and ethnography of colonial Brazil is shaped by both the traveler's unique cross-cultural experience among the Tupinamba Indians and by the restrictions imposed on authorship in Protestant Hesse.

In the 16th century, German imprints represented a surprising share among European Americana, a fact that suggests that the link between the new print technology and colonialism was more complex and diverse than has previously been assumed. Germany was not among early modern colonial powers and, except for the Welser enterprise in Venezuela (1528–1546), was never directly engaged in the colonization of the Americas. New World narratives traditionally issued from presses in Augsburg, Strasbourg, and Nuremberg, merchant centers connected to Iberian overseas ventures by both dynastic politics and finance. However, the popularity of German travel accounts in pamphlets, cosmographies, and collections did not dissipate with the end of the personal union of the Habsburgs during the reign of Charles V, nor with the decline of the banking houses of Fugger and Welser. Printed within the boundaries and under the auspices of a Lutheran prince, Philipp of Hesse, who had no business interests overseas, the *Warhaftig Historia* became an extraordinary publishing success and went through numerous editions, translations, and reprints.

On the German book market, physicians and Protestant reformers assumed the task of transmitting the earliest news from America to a broad lay audience. Published in Reformation Hesse, edited and introduced by Johannes Dryander, professor of medicine at the Protestant university of Marburg, Staden's book stands in this tradition of German New World imprints. It is no accident that physicians, who played a prominent role in the elaboration of new empirical methods of inquiry, would turn to editing travel literature, especially about new worlds. In the absence of textual sources, empirical study of New World wonders in their own right was necessary. The editions and translations of travel collections into the vernacular issued by Jobst Ruchamer (Nuremberg, 1508), Michael Herr (Strasbourg, 1534), and Lorenz Fries (Strasbourg, 1525–1531) exemplify the contribution physicians made in popularizing New World reports. The reformulation of the genre's representational tasks was marked by the tension between an impulse toward systematization and methodology and an emphasis on the authority of firsthand narratives. Before the physician and Humanist Theodor Zwinger published *Methodus apodemica* in Basel (1577; *Method for Travelers*), Dryander responded to the paradoxical task of systematizing empirical knowledge by dividing Staden's travel book into a personal narrative *(Historia)* and an impersonal description *(Beschreibung)*. Although the French anthropologist Claude Lévi-Strauss has called Jean de Léry's *Histoire* the first "breviary of the ethnographer," it is Staden's book and its mixture of travel narrative and systematic description that most clearly anticipates the textual structure of modern ethnographies.

In the hands of Protestant publicists, America was reinterpreted as a new Revelation. Cosmographic writing, traditionally a commentary to the book of Genesis, now was seen as empirical evidence for an actively present Providential God. Thus the Protestant postulate of an active God entailed a theological justification for empirical observation and reconceptualized firsthand narratives as potential venues of divine Revelation. However, this conceptual shift also created the rhetorical problem of reconciling personal and divine testimony. One solution resorted to allegorization, as illustrated by the recasting of Hans Staden's return to Hesse as an exemplary narrative of personal salvation. In the theological debate over America, which had enormous implications for monogenetic theory and the doctrine of original sin, confessional differences determined the lines of interpretation. Catholics held that the tarnished body of the Roman Church should be restored through missionary work; Martin Luther saw in the experience of the New World proof *ex negativo* of the election and redemption of believers not fallen from Grace, a view presupposed by the narrative frame of exemplarity that shapes Staden's account. Deepened insight into divine creation was the aim of Sebastian Franck's cosmography (Tübingen, 1534), as well as its revised edition by Sigmund Feyerabend (Frankfurt, 1567) and the reprints of travels by Levinus Hulsius (Nuremberg, 1598–1650). The most famous collection, Theodore de Bry's *America* (Frankfurt, 1590–1635), used its lavish iconography and recycling of New World reports, including the *Historia*, for anti-Catholic propaganda. With its oddly ambivalent image of American Indians, it would inextricably weave together travel writing and religious dissent and establish the basis for the Enlightenment invention of the "noble savage."

Both reformers and physicians helped to establish cannibalism as an emblem of America, and particularly of Brazil. An entry in a German bookseller's catalogue at the Frankfurt book fair of 1567 refers to the *Historia* as the

"Menschenfresserbuch" (book of cannibals), indicating that its popular appeal derived in part from this aspect of the narrative. The English minister and editor Samuel Purchas, refusing to "glutton" his readers with such "savage arguments," and reproaching the traveler for "telling . . . only his tragedies," banished the *Historia*, already "englished," from his vast collection (*Purchas his Pilgrims*, London, 1625). Although Staden's book fed European readers' appetites for the exotic, it moved away from the alimentary cannibalism established early on by Columbus and Vespucci and disseminated by Fries's *Carta Marina* and Sebastian Münster's *Cosmographia* (Basel, 1544). Images of a butcher chopping up bodies or roasting dismembered parts had singled out America as the land of cannibals on every map. The *Historia* subverts this view, reflected in the narrator's conventional expectation of being killed and eaten right away, by emphatically transferring cannibalism to the realm of customs. Elaborate descriptions of the rites and ceremonies of capture, captivity, and execution of enemies revive the chivalric notion of a cannibalism of vengeance. References to the ritual as a "feast" and "merrymaking" relate it to the festivals of European popular culture. In contrast to comparisons between Tupinamba cannibalism and the Catholic Eucharist proliferating in the pamphlets of Protestant satirists of the theophagic Roman liturgy, and echoed in Michel de Montaigne's famous essay "Of Cannibals" (Bordeaux, 1590), in Staden's *Historia* cannibalism figures as a "carnival." Whether a reminiscence of medieval Catholicism or a marker of Protestant self-fashioning, the *Historia*'s borrowing from the ritual reversals and oppositional practices of European carnivals in its depiction of Tupinamba cannibalism, if only occasionally, undercuts the sensationalist attributions announced in the book's title. The conventional representation is contradicted by the assertion that, except for their nakedness and their sun-tanned skins, "the Tupinamba are a fine people . . . just like the people here at home" (*WH*, 162).

The title page of Staden's small quarto shifts the novelty of its subject matter from the "discovery" of America to the "Revelation" of its meaning within the territorial state of Hesse. Within this framework, the travel writer figures as both the recipient and the vehicle of divine Revelation. Responding to the lack of a previously established context for such a report and to the new demands of Protestant cosmography, the title's emphasis on the discursive authority of the narrator also privatizes the traveler. It is allegedly through his own experience and at his expense that the report is issued. Nonetheless, the credibility of the *Historia* also relies on the dual authority of the lordly dedicatee, Landgrave Philipp of Hesse, and the scholarly editor, professor of medicine Johannes Dryander. In this sense, the double reference to the figure of the private traveler and to the institutional realms of the absolutist state signals the constitutive paradox of Hans Staden's book. The travel account, whose first-person narrator acquires unprecedented amplification, is also subject to extraordinary surveillance and control.

In the long, authorizing preface, the physician-editor states that the returning traveler was interrogated and scrutinized by local authorities, including himself and the prince. Presented as a token of the traveler's gratitude for his salvation and as a gift to the landgrave, the book itself stands as material evidence for the complex process of social reconciliation. As a form of public confession, fully congenial with a profession of faith, the *Historia* effects the traveler's reintegration into the religious community. By framing the *Historia* as an exemplum of justification by faith, Staden brings the narrative into compliance with the principle that the choice of belief and worship is a prerogative of the prince. This endows the narrative with great political significance. The transformation of a mercenary soldier into a pious author and loyal subject is thus both the precondition and the effect of Staden's book. Yet, although the book's publication is predicated on the normative interpretation of the traveler's return as salvation, the text itself is not exhausted by its function as an exemplary tale. The *Historia* contains claims that move away from the prolegomena of the book and acquire specific meaning only with reference to colonial Brazil.

The *Warhaftig Historia* comprises reports about two voyages. On his first voyage (1547–1548), Hans Staden leaves Lisbon as a gunner on a Portuguese commercial vessel. On his second voyage (1549–1555), the traveler sets sail from Seville in Spain to Rio de la Plata in Argentina. After suffering shipwreck and wandering for two years in the wilderness, he becomes the chief commander of a Portuguese fort off the coast of São Vicente, one of the earliest colonial settlements in Brazil. Upon completing two years in the service of the Portuguese king, Dom Manuel, the traveler is captured by the Tupinamba Indians. Thus, it is the specific historical situation of local warfare and European competition, including the alliances between Portuguese and Tupiniquim, French and Tupinamba, which lead to the traveler's captivity. Eventually he avoids being killed by performing native roles and adhering to Tupinamba forms of life; he changes his identity from that of a Portuguese enemy to that of a French friend of the Tupinamba. As a consequence of his success in mobilizing divine forces through prayer and of the felicity of religious claims he proffers in the native language, he is recognized by the Tupinamba as someone imbued with prophetic powers. In the end, the traveler is granted permission to sail back to Europe on a French ship.

In the experience of the *Historia*'s protagonist, we can observe a parallel to the so-called Brazilian Mamluk. Usually born of a Portuguese or Mamluk father and an Indian mother, this figure underwent a double acculturation process, straddling a Christian and native way of life. In travelogues of the East, such as Ludovico di Varthema's widely translated *Itinerario* (Rome 1510), the term designated Christians and others who converted to Islam. In the *Historia,* the term Mamluk acquires the specific meaning of someone who merges two different cultures. It is eloquently exemplified by the ambivalent figure of the traveler-narrator, assimilated to the native way of life, while striving to keep his Christian identity. The reversals of European perceptions that result from this position are depicted not only in the captivity narrative, but also in the plentiful original woodcut illustrations in Staden's book. One of the most suggestive images shows the traveler-narrator standing in a canoe observing a European caravel from the same perspective as the Indians, from whom he is distinguished only by his beard. Although the traveler's attempts to deny that he is a Portuguese enemy are rebuked with irony by his captors, his performance among the Tupinamba warriors in a battle against former Portuguese friends, in which he makes proper use of native weapons and language, marks the beginning of his status reversal. His new identity, earned through acts of warfare, healing, and prophecy, is at once distinguished from and conflated with his Christian identity. In the healing sessions, the traveler combines distinctive Tupinamba practices with the power attributed to his words of prayer. As he slips into the roles of Tupinamba healer and prophet, he seems not only to have taken on the perspective of others, but also to have made them his own. Of course, the overriding narrative of the *Historia* is oriented toward the traveler's return to Protestant Hesse, and thus implies that the traveler is not a crossover. This in no way diminishes the claim that the traveler has contingently become, if not Tupinamba, at least a Mamluk "skilled and experienced in both the Savage and Christian people's tongues and motions" (*WH*, 74).

Although controlled by the Hessian authorities of prince and university, the travel narrator's discursive authority rests on both his self-fashioning as pious author and his ability to mobilize divine forces in the language of the Tupinamba. It is not by faith alone, but by his cross-cultural experience and active translation of his God's power, that the traveler is transformed from a Portuguese prisoner into a friend and prophet of the Tupinamba. Although the exemplarity of the *Historia* as a tale of salvation depends on the normalizing frame outlined in the preface, it reaches beyond this frame toward new possibilities of identity formation. In the traveler's closing words, "I have given him [the skeptical reader] information enough; let him follow my tracks, for the world is closed to none whom God assists" (*WH*, 198). Officially legitimated as a testimony of salvation, Hans Staden's *Historia* discloses a space for the wild stories of a German Mamluk in colonial Brazil.

See also 1478, 1622, 1647/1656, 1797

Bibliography: Rudolf Hirsch, "Printed Reports on the Early Discoveries and Their Early Reception," in Fredi Chiapelli et al., eds., *First Images of America: The Impact of the New World on the Old* (Berkeley: University of California Press, 1976). Michael Harbsmeier, "Neue Welten," in *Wilde Völkerkunde: Andere Welten in deutschen Reiseberichten der Frühen Neuzeit* (Frankfurt am Main and New York: Campus, 1994). Wolfgang Neuber, "Die Drucke der im Original deutschen Amerikareiseberichte bis 1715: Synopse, Bibliographie und marktgeschichtlicher Kommentar," *Frühneuzeit-Info*, vol. 2, no. 1 (1991): 76–83, and vol. 2, no. 2 (1991): 12–34. Silvia Schmitz, "Reisende Helden: Zu Hans Staden, Erec und Tristan," in Thomas Kramer, ed., *Wege in die Neuzeit* (Munich: Fink, 1988). Hans Staden, *Hans Stadens Warhaftige Historia,* ed. and trans. Reinhard Maack and Karl Fouquet (Marburg: Trautvetter & Fischer, 1964). ———, *The True History of His Captivity, 1557,* ed. and trans. Malcolm Letts (New York: McBridge, 1929).

Luciana Villas-Bôas

${\mathcal{Q}}$ *1570*

Johann Fischart's polemical treatise against the Jesuit Jacob Rabe inaugurates his
work of satire, Protestant engagement, and political vision

Ethical Utopianism and Stylistic Excess

A few years before he translated François Rabelais' *Gargantua* (1575)—
the work for which he is best known—into German, Johann Fischart (1546–
1590) published the first of many polemical treatises against the Roman Catholic Church, and especially against the Jesuits, under the title *Nacht Rab oder
Nebelkrähe. Von dem uberauß Jesuwidrischen Geistlosen schreiben unnd leben des
Hans Jacob Gackels, der sich nennt Rab* (1570; *Night Raven or Hooded Crow: On the
Exceedingly Stupid and Antichristian Life and Writings of Hans Jacob Rooster, Also
Known as Raven*). Printed shortly after his return from a study trip to Italy in
the newly established print workshop of his sister's husband, Bernhard Jobin,
this text marks the start of Fischart's career as a prolific writer, polemicist, and
compiler. The attack on Jacob Rabe, a Jesuit, is an early example of Fischart's
unique rhetorical style, his religious and political engagement, and highly productive collaboration with the printer Jobin.

Fischart's denunciation of Rabe, which appeared at a time of fierce discussions surrounding the election of a new bishop in Strasbourg, employs a range
of rhetorical strategies. He satirizes the practices and habits of the Jesuits; he recounts anecdotes and rumors; and he appeals to and provokes anti-Catholic
sentiment in his characterization of Rabe and Jesuits in general. His choice to
publish the text anonymously inaugurates a lifelong practice of publishing
sometimes anonymously, sometimes under a pseudonym, and sometimes under his own name. The tradition of compilation, montage of anecdotes, and
denunciation had existed since the early days of the Protestant Reformation.
Fischart, however, together with the printer Jobin and graphic artist Tobias
Stimmer, developed it further. This team produced not only polemical treatises
but also several series of pamphlets and fliers which exploit the abundant technical possibilities, rhetorical force, and publicity opportunities inherent in
print media. Fischart provided the narrative and explanation to Stimmer's illustrations critical of the Roman Church (1577, *Der Gorgonisch Meduse Kopf;
Medusa's Gorgon Head*) or, time and again, the order of the Jesuits. His reports
on the fate of the Huguenots in the religious wars in France, *Reveille Matin:
oder Wacht frü auf* (1575; *Morning Call: Or, Wake Up Early*), as well as his attacks
on Catherine de Medici show his ardent religious and political engagement.

Scholars have pointed out that Fischart's work—in contrast, for example, to
Paracelsus's—does not follow medieval patterns of allegorical thought based,
essentially, on similitude and analogy. Instead, Fischart's writings combine
practices of semiological dissociation and reconfiguration that anticipate a
modern attitude toward the world of signs. Irony, satire, comedy, and the
carnevalesque also combine, on a more general level, with his distinctive practices of translation, compilation, and adaptation. By taking full advantage of the

print media and collaborating closely with a printer and a graphic artist, as did many others in the 16th century, Fischart bolsters his imaginative language and extensive use of source material with early modern configurations of text and image. His writings thus incorporate multiple layers of intertextuality and innumerable polyhistorical, encyclopedic elements from a long, mainly humanist and classical tradition.

While Fischart explores new possibilities of language and textual play, his efforts nonetheless remain within an ethical framework. Specifically, he emphasizes a new orientation toward the everyday world, an orientation authorized and governed by Protestant ideals. This is visible in *Das Glückhafft Schiff von Zürich* (1577; *The Lucky Ship from Zurich*), which celebrates the friendship between the citizens of Zurich and Strasbourg. It highlights the freedom both cities enjoy and, perhaps more importantly, the status of the citizen of a reformed city-community. In Fischart's utopian view of elaborate, subtle imagery, the citizen is virtuous, free, and rational; these same qualities can also be seen as a stabilizing factor in his distinctive tendency toward semiotic and textual play and montage.

The emblem of Fischart's image of the new Protestant citizen was the new and "astounding" astronomical clock of the Strasbourg Cathedral, designed by the Strasbourg mathematician Konrad Dasypodius and painted by Tobias Stimmer. The rationality and orderly structure the clock represents may seem incongruous with Fischart's own polemical, associative, sometimes carnevalesque style. (The style of the "German Rabelais" was rediscovered much later by Herder and the Romantics and inspired such writers as Jean Paul and Arno Schmidt.) This incongruity, however, is at most superficial and in fact belies an essential connection between the Protestant orderliness of Fischart's utopian normativity and the playful character of his writing. The pleasures Fischart cultivated with the freedom of word play and of playing with texts and traditions are grounded in an ethics of unity and self-discipline. The clock represents the utopian, Protestant principles—piety, everyday ethics, and citizen life—that inform and, one might even say, constitute the underpinnings of Fischart's style, even in the most outrageous moments of rhetorical disassemblage, playful construction, and satirical expression for which he is famous. Tellingly, in the *Glückhafft Schiff von Zürich,* this clock figures as the most remarkable monument in the city of Strasbourg shown to the visitors from Zurich, overshadowing even the cultural significance of the cathedral and, implicitly, that of the ecclesiastical order of work and time. The importance of this clock, and its emblematic status in the city, as Fischart portrays it, is further highlighted in a pamphlet published in 1574, which explains the functioning of the clock based on a pictorial representation by Stimmer.

Fischart's polemical, aggressive defense of his Protestant convictions, which appears also in other texts, including a translation and adaptation of the Dutch *Biencorf der H. Rommschen Kercke* (1579; *The Beehive of the Holy Roman Church*), goes hand in hand with his attempts to cultivate and propagate the new virtues of biblical piety, for example in *Neue Künstliche Figuren Biblischer Historien*

(1576; *New Artful Illustrations of Biblical Stories*). Toward this end, he produced household manuals for the reformed citizen, for instance his *Anmanung zu Christlicher Kinderzucht* (1578; *Exhortation to Christian Child-Rearing*) and the *Philosophisch Ehzuchtbüchlein* (1578; *Philosophical Treatise on Marriage*). Both texts treat of issues concerned with a new ethics in everyday Christian life that focus not only on reformed religious precepts but also on a way of life supported and evaluated by reason, "vernunftgenäm." The terms in which Fischart attempts to define the project of Protestant reform almost anticipate the positions of the 18th-century Enlightenment. The *Ehzuchtbüchlein,* for example, is a compilation and montage of texts from numerous classical and Humanist sources, including Plutarch, Erasmus, Alciato, and Gesner. However, rather than merely referring to prior sources of authority, the *Ehzuchtbüchlein* amalgamates an entire philosophical tradition. Fischart's innovative approach—translating, adapting in the vernacular, and reassembling innumerable source texts—redefined the status of those texts and combined a Humanist emphasis on reason, a reformed Christian point of view, and the science of that time, especially 16th-century works on nature (Gesner's *Historia animalium,* Heusslein's *Vogelbuch,* Forer's *Thierbuch* and *Fischbuch*).

Fischart seems unconcerned with the norms of Humanist poetics, religion, and man, but compiles treatises and narratives from a range of exemplary sources. His fusion of these elements implicitly draws its authority from the Protestant vision of a new unity of nature, religion, and reason that should guide domestic and public life. Fischart's adaptation and substantial amplification of Mathias Holtzwart's *Flöh Hatz / Weiber Tratz* (1577; *Fleas A-Flitter / Wives A-Twitter*) can be understood in this light. The flea's-eye view allows him to talk about aspects of the human body, of social disputes, and of gender, but also to introduce, by means of satire, what amounts to a new Protestant self-discipline and normativity.

Fischart's inventiveness in handling language and source materials is most clearly visible and significant in his adaptation of Rabelais' *Gargantua* under the German title *Affenteuerliche und Ungeheuerlich Geschichtschrift vom Leben, Rhaten und Thaten der for langen Weilen vollenwolbeschraiten Helden und Herrn Grandgusier, Gargantoa, und Pantagruel Königen inn Utopien und Ninenreich* (1575; *Adventurous and Fantastic Stories of the Life, Thoughts, and Deeds of the Long-Famous Heroes and Sirs Grandgusier, Gargantua, and Pantagruel, Emperors in Utopia and Nowhereland;* since the second edition, 1582, with the title *Affentheuerlich Naupengeheuerliche Geschichtklitterung; Adventurous and Fantastic Story-Hodge-podge*). Although Fischart translated only the first book of Rabelais' text, he altered and added so much material to this early modern tale told through the eyes of giants that his German version turned out three times as long as the original French. Seduced by Rabelais' ironic style, Fischart amplified it, exploring the semantic possibilities of each word, constructing serial structures, moving through paradigms of similes, synonyms, and oppositions, and experimenting with neologisms, onomatopoesis, and rhymes. The same approach is found on the level of the narrative, where Fischart adds exemplary narratives from medieval and classical archives, gleans materials from historical and encyclopedic works, and vastly exaggerates numbers, parts, and qualities. These gestures reflect the experience of an avid reader and writer, but they also confuse the reader time and again—much more than in Rabelais— with an excess of body, language, knowledge, and play. Unbound language, plays with words and images, compilation and allusion, such are the pleasures and joys of this *Geschichtklitterung.* In several instances, just a few lines of Rabelais' *Gargantua* balloon into an entire chapter in Fischart, most significantly in the fifth chapter on Grandgouschier's marriage, entitled "Mit was wichtigen bedencken unser Held Grandgouschier zu der Ehe gegriffen, und sich nicht vergriffen" (With what significant reservations our hero Grandgouschier aimed for marriage and did not miss his mark). In his expansion of the text, Fischart promulgates an ethics of marriage and sexuality, praising the conjugal life as a preeminent source of virtue. Such references to ethics and virtue, once again, evoke the orderliness, piety, and utopianism that are the anchor of the transgressive textual pleasures that Fischart contrives. The tale of the adventures of the giants, King Grandgouschier, Queen Gargamelle, and especially of their son Gargantua—although essentially identical in Rabelais and in Fischart—is thus both amplified and moralized in the latter.

Fischart's style might appear to support an argument—in a reading more suitable to the Baroque (and also to James Joyce or Arno Schmidt)—that his styles and methods undermine the highly normative and prescriptive character of his Protestant engagement. Ultimately, however, his experimentation is controlled and overshadowed by a rigorous religious and rational moralism. Indeed this moralism is what gives Fischart's satire, irony, and playfulness authority. The liberation or unmooring of poetic language and the elaborate mannerisms that Fischart employs can be seen as reflecting the same norms that allow for eliminating ambiguity; and it is precisely a Catholic ambiguity that he criticizes in his polemics against the "diabolical" practices of the Jesuits (from the above-mentioned *Nacht Rab* to *Die wunderlichst unerhörtest Legend und Beschreibung des abgeführten, quartirten, gevierten und viereckechten vierhörnigen Hütleins,* 1580; *The Most Amazing Incredible Story and Description of the Four-Time, Fourfold, Four-Cornered, Four-Horned Hat*). By grounding his work of semiotic play in rational Protestant ideals—both in his own style and in the way he manipulates the exemplars of tradition—Fischart eliminates the latent "demonic" or "magical" character of language. Language and tradition, seen as purely representational, that is, as nonessential and contingent, are made available to forms of play that, for Fischart, would be suspect within a Catholic semiology wherein each sign maintains an intrinsic, essential, and thus potentially treacherous, set of connections. Fischart's attack against Aretino, who in the *Ehzuchtbüchlein* represents a highly decadent convergence of libertinage, Humanism, and Catholicism, testifies to this radical refusal of rhetorical ambiguity.

The same can be said about Fischart's translation of Jean Bodin's *De Daemonomania Magorum* (1581, *Vom ausgelasnen wütigen Teuffelsheer; On the Unruly Rabid Devil's Chase*). Interpreters of Fischart's works have found it hard to understand why this enlightened Protestant author should have translated a manual on the hunt of witches and witchcraft. They frequently sought an explanation in the fact that Fischart had been employed as a lawyer at the imperial court in Speyer since 1581 and needed to produce a text that would further his career. But Fischart's interest in Bodin's text can just as well be explained in terms of the significance of ambiguity—and, moreover, its exclusion and elimination—in his work as a whole. Fischart's interest in a scientific treatment and analysis of witchcraft, for which Bodin is a prime example, fits his emphasis on the convergence of reformed piety, reason, and community. Bodin also identifies and excludes those elements from the community Fischart explicitly excludes in *Geschichtklitterung* and in *Ehzuchtbüchlein* as well—namely whatever undermines the normative basis of the social body. The French jurist accomplishes this by locating elements and places of semiotic ambiguity—the hiding places of witchcraft—and by identifying the elements and places where the demonic power of signs threatens the real unity of meaning that is grounded in the binding ethics of citizen and community.

Fischart's peculiar practices of writing, compilation, experimentation, and rhetorical amplification seem at first glance to contradict such a logic of exclusion. However, his highly theatrical staging of the play of signs, of meanings, and of exemplary narratives is possible only on the basis of this exclusion of ambiguity. A utopian unity of Protestant ethics, beyond textual play, forms that play's very foundation. On the other hand, this also allows for the remarkable qualities of *Geschichtklitterung* through which the experience of the world and of language take on the character of discovery, unbridled with regard to language, bound however by the ethics of reformed citizenship.

See also 1260, 1784, 1796 (10 June)

Bibliography: Johann Fischart, *Geschichtklitterung (Gargantua): Text der Ausgabe letzter Hand von 1590,* ed. Ute Nyssen (Düsseldorf: Karl Rauch, 1963. ———, *Sämtliche Werke,* ed. Hans-Gert Roloff, Ulrich Seelbach, W. Eckehart Spengler (Bern: Peter Lang, 1993-). Christian Hoffmann, "Bücher und Autographen von Johann Fischart," *Daphnis* 25 (1996):489–579. Peter Fuss, "Von den Zeichen der Welt zur Welt der Zeichen: Semiologische Konzepte bei Paracelsus und Fischart," *Wirkendes Wort* 52 (2002):333–360. Josef K. Glowa, *Johann Fischart's Geschichtklitterung: A Study of the Narrator and Narrative Strategies* (New York: Peter Lang, 2000). Walter Haug, "Zwischen Ehezucht und Minnekloster. Die Formen des Erotischen in Johann Fischarts *Geschichtklitterung,*" in *The Graph of Sex and the German Text: Gendered Culture in Early Modern Germany 1500–1700,* ed. Lynne Tatlock (Amsterdam and Atlanta: Rodopi, 1994), 157–177. Wilhelm Kühlmann, "Johann Fischart," in *Deutsche Dichter der frühen Neuzeit (1450–1600): Ihr Leben und Werk,* ed. Stephan Füssel (Berlin: Erich Schmidt, 1993), 589–612. Jan-Dirk Müller, "Von der Subversion frühneuzeitlicher Ehelehre: Zu Fischarts *Ehzuchtbüchlein* und *Geschichtklitterung,*" in *The Graph of Sex and the German Text: Gendered Culture in Early Modern Germany 1500–1700,* ed. Lynne Tatlock (Amsterdam and Atlanta: Rodopi, 1994), 121–156. Jan-Dirk Müller, "Texte aus Texten: Zu intertextuellen Verfahren in frühneuzeitlicher Literatur, am Beispiel von Fischarts *Ehzuchtbüchlein* und *Geschichtklitterung,*" in *Intertextualität in der Frühen Neuzeit: Studien zu ihren theoretischen und praktischen Perspektiven,* ed. Wilhelm Kühlmann und Wolfgang Neuber (Frankfurt am Main: Peter Lang, 1994), 63–109. Ulrich Seelbach, *Ludus lectoris: Studien zum idealen Leser Johann Fischarts* (Heidelberg: C. Winter, 2000). Florence Weinberg, *Gargantua in a Convex Mirror: Fischart's View of Rabelais* (New York: Peter Lang, 1986). Gerhild Scholz Williams, "Die

Wissenschaft von den Hexen: Jean Bodin und sein Übersetzer Johann Fischart als Demonologen," in *Knowledge, Science, and Literature in Early Modern Germany*, ed. Gerhild Scholz Williams and Stephan K. Schindler (Chapel Hill and London: University of North Carolina Press, 1996), 193–218. Rüdiger Zymner, *Manierismus: Zur poetischen Artistik bei Johann Fischart, Jean Paul, und Arno Schmidt* (Paderborn: Ferdinand Schöningh, 1995).

Niklaus Largier and Karen S. Feldman

 1594

The romance *Pariz un Vyene* is printed in Verona

Highlight of the Yiddish Renaissance

The romance of Paris and Vienna—she the king's daughter, he the son of a mere count—is written with sophistication, wit, psychological insight, and absolute mastery of style and form. This makes it difficult to understand how the text—doubtless the most important work of Old Yiddish literature and one of the great works of sixteenth-century European literature—disappeared from view for centuries. The marginality of Yiddish cannot be the only cause, since the text was also lost to Yiddish reading audiences. Since only fragments and a copy of the narrative that was missing the first third were known for most of the twentieth century, the work did not appeal to a larger modern audience. Although its literary qualities were recognized, plans for publication came to naught.

In 1986 Anna Maria Babbi, an Italian scholar of Romance literature, found a complete copy of the Yiddish version in the library of the Episcopal Seminary in Verona while researching the tradition of the courtly romance *Paris e Vienna*. Within two years the first edition in facsimile made the work available to a somewhat wider audience. With the appearance of two complementary scholarly editions in 1996, it is finally accessible to those who read Yiddish or German, but translations are still lacking. The copy discovered in 1986 was the first complete copy to be found, but not of the first edition. This book was printed in Verona in 1594, but it is documented that it had already appeared in Sabbionetta in 1556, which may not have been the only earlier edition, and it had since been printed in Prague. By the seventeenth century, however, it seems to have disappeared from Yiddish reading materials. The main reason may have been that it was primarily written for an Italian Yiddish audience, an audience that had grown considerably during the fifteenth century when Jews fled Germany in high numbers. Its rapid decline started in the first half of the sixteenth century because some Yiddish speakers adopted Italian as their mother tongue, others emigrated to Eastern Europe. There the prospects of making a living were better, but the Jewish culture which had developed in Renaissance Italy could not be maintained under different conditions. The other well-known Italo-Yiddish romance, *Bovebukh* (*The Book of Bovo*, originally titled *Bovo de Antona, Bovo of Antona*, a distant adaptation and artfully rewritten version of *Sir Bevis of Hampton*), did survive. It may have been more successful because of its surprising and complicated story line, which kept audiences enthralled well into the nineteenth century, despite the work's being severely truncated through numerous cheap reprints. *Pariz un Vyene* may have been forgotten because it no longer met the preferences of the Yiddish-speaking audience, an audience which mainly bought religious and ethical works.

The story of Paris and Vienna must have originated in the fourteenth century, probably in France. It was extremely popular in the late Middle Ages. Many versions have come to us, in thirteen languages. The Yiddish version is based on one of the printed Italian prose versions; the author, however, preferred to put the text into rhyme. Although it is more common for literatures to start with verse and evolve to prose, in Yiddish literature long rhymed epics were still fashionable in the mid-sixteenth century, especially if the narrative material was manifestly non-Jewish. The author uses the rhyme scheme of the specifically Italian stanza form, the *ottaverime,* which consists of eight verses with the rhyme scheme *abababcc.* After *Bovebukh* this is the second Germanic text in *ottaverime.* The rhymes of the sextet *(ababab)* are alternately masculine and feminine, thus following the tradition of the (internal and verse-final) rhymes in German medieval epics. The author incorporates Hebrew and Italian forms and does this with seemingly effortless grace, and humor in the playful use of enjambments.

The larger structure of the romance consists of ten cantos which determine not only the external form but also the internal rhythm. The introductions of the cantos are inspired by those of Ariosto's *Orlando furioso (The Frenzy of Orlando,* 1516). At the end of cantos 3, 6, and 8 the poet uses the conventions of Italian epics such as *Orlando furioso,* stating that he is tired and that he has to rest, or that his throat has become dry and irritated, leaving him about to cough (canto 3) or wanting for a drink (canto 4). Our author is more sophisticated and witty when he reacts to the actions of the characters of his story: once he leaves a group of men because they deafen him with their cries, each praising his beloved woman over others (Canto 2: stanza 103.7–8):

> Zi haten ayn geschray, das zi mikh varen dertaben;
> Drum los ikh zi, biz zi ouz-geshrien haben.

> They produced such a noise, that they deafened me,
> That is why I'll leave them, until they've stopped shouting.

Or he can't continue because he is disappointed by the behavior of Dolfin, Vienna's father (canto 5). The author's wit also comes to the fore when he demonstrates he is getting drawn into the action, e.g., when he asks the participants in a tournament to wait, until he has fetched Paris and his friend Odoardo (stanza 90.7), or when he tells us he has to look for Paris in the Far East "before he has completely disappeared" (538.1–8). Aspects of the story line receive an extra dimension since the organization of the romance is related to the flaws of characters and authors alike, hence to the human condition in general.

The Italian influences are not just found in the basic narrative material and the conventions of the epic genre chosen by the author, but also in the integration of certain topics such as the female use of cosmetics (175.5–180.8). Ridiculing the actions women take to look better and the ensuing results was a topos in Italian literature. The trade in cosmetics was mainly in the hands of Jewish women and this may have contributed to the author's detailed knowledge of such affairs. He enumerates an impressive number of beauty products, describes how women make their hair look like gold, pluck their eyebrows, and give men the impression they see "clear white snow under the hot sun." But in the morning, when they aren't wearing high heels and elaborate clothes, before they've put on lots of paint, they present a different sight.

Pariz un Vyene entices not only through its poetic form and adventurous story line, but most of all because of the wit with which it is written. The original narrative contained two humorous scenes. The Yiddish version is the only one of the numerous retellings of the story of Paris and Vienna that exploits the possibilities the plot and the characters offer for making sudden and unexpected remarks that shed light on the comical aspects of almost any human quality. This is sometimes done by using coarse, even scatological, language and imagery, at other times through remarks stemming from the author as a persona or by the use of sayings and stopgaps. The author speaks directly to his audience not only at the beginning and end of each canto, but sometimes even in the middle of the action, often commenting on the action itself. On different occasions the author confides in us, recalling his own unhappiness in love; on others he pretends he can still change the course of events; and toward the end he climbs back on his misogynistic hobbyhorse (708.4–716.2).

The most successful humorous elements are found in the actions and language of the characters and the way they are described. Whereas one would expect that King Dolfin, the man who hinders the marriage of Paris and his daughter Vienna would be the butt of all ridicule and that the two lovers would be spared, this is not the case. At first Dolfin is described like a king we know from fairy tales; during the course of the story he is sometimes ridiculed, at other times he is nasty and then again more sympathetic, but he is never described without irony. The changes in mood and character make the structure of the action, including the psychological changes, more complex and even the king is regarded with sympathy when all ends well. Yakom, Paris's father, is also a confidant of Dolfin and caught between two fires: he is both a faithful vassal and a loving father. The author of *Pariz un Vyene* has used the comical potential of his weakness. Paris is the perfect hero—he is intelligent, beautiful, strong, courageous, independent, educated, a gifted musician, singer, dancer, huntsman, and jouster—and gets ample opportunity during the course of the action to display his prowess; Vienna is beautiful and can sew, embroider, read and write. Both, however, have their flaws and their deviousness and recourse to ruse—inspired by the problems caused by Dolfin but coming easily to both—are described with much irony. It is the plausibility of the characters and the action and the subtle irony with which they are treated that distinguish *Pariz un Vyene* from contemporary works.

With all its Italian influences, *Pariz un Vyene* is very much a work of Jewish literature. This is not just a matter of the Hebrew alphabet and the use of Yiddish by an author who could read Italian and who is addressing an audience that probably could do so too. The language is lively, idiomatic Yiddish with Italianisms as well as elements from the archaic language of Yiddish Bible translation. The contents of the text have been rid of Christian content in a subtle manner and every now and again Jewish elements are introduced. We find Jewish elements in the language: Paris feels as if he is in *gan eden* (the Garden of Eden, Heaven) one moment (40.8), then again as if he is an *ovl* (person in mourning according to the Jewish ritual, 540.7), and after the wedding "citizens, knights and counts" wish the happy couple *mazel tov* (congratulations, 702.1–6). That is not to say that the impression is ever given that the protagonists, members of the aristocracy, are or could be Jewish.

The narrative material on which *Pariz un Vyene* is based is clearly not Jewish, but the author and his audience could feel affinity with it, especially with the central problem of the story: the choice of a partner in marriage. In the Jewish tradition parents select a partner for their daughters, but girls can't be forced to marry someone they do not want. Because of this, the author was able to criticize the practice of parents forcing their will on their children as social critique and not as a direct attack on the religion. Since Vienna is the daughter of a king and Paris the son of a count, their social status makes their union well nigh impossible. At first, Paris hides his love for Vienna because he has no hope of marrying her; later, when the two have declared their love, her father poses the greatest obstacles. The negotiations in preparation of the marriage fail and Paris and his father lose their social status altogether. The two lovers consider eloping, but nothing comes of it (a good thing in view of the Jewish audience, since that would have been a clear contravention of Jewish law). Vienna uses her prerogative to refuse any candidate proposed by her parents. Eventually, Vienna's father gives permission for the marriage after his concern for the happiness of his daughter turns out to be nothing more than worries about her social and pecuniary position. The topic of marriage between partners of different social backgrounds and that of marriage for love and the problems encountered on the way is one that appealed to audiences, both Jewish and non-Jewish. In this romance it doesn't conflict with Jewish law in such a way as to hurt the sensibilities of the audience.

The most explicitly Jewish elements in the text are found in the prologue and the epilogue, in the form of references to the coming of the Messiah. The coming of the Messiah not only conjures up images of the Jewish Diaspora. In the epilogue we find a description of a man riding a "grey goat with long ears" (a comical description of a donkey) and sounding a horn, calling the Jews to prepare for Jerusalem and leading them there (716–717). The person announcing the coming of the Messiah is, of course, the prophet Elijah, and that leads us to the question of the authorship of *Pariz un Vyene*. The great mastery of the anonymous author leads to speculations about his identity. Although he states in the preface that he is a student of Elijah Bahur, it is very possible that this is a mystification of Elijah Levita Bahur (Yiddish: Elye Bokher) himself. There are good arguments for the authorship of Elijah Levita. Elijah Levita was born in Ipsheim near Neustadt on the Aisch (Germany) and emigrated to Northern Italy in the early 1490s. There he made a living as a Hebrew teacher and copyist of Hebrew manuscripts and became one of the most influential Hebrew grammarians and lexicographers. He lived and worked in Padua, Rome (where he was the house teacher of a cardinal), and Venice. Over the course of his life he wrote not only important works of Hebrew grammar and lexicography, but also a couple of Yiddish lampoons. In 1506–07 he wrote the *Bovebukh* (first printed in 1541 in a reworked version). He was steeped both in Jewish lore and Italian Renaissance culture. The brilliant use of the verse forms could point in the direction of Elijah Levita, since their successful use in *Bovebukh* would have given him practice. The problems he had gotten himself into with the rabbinate since the publication of his lampoons and his reworking of the non-Jewish *Bovo de Antona* into a Jewish courtly romance may have led him to publish another such work anonymously or pseudonymously.

See also 1515–1517, 1570, 1690, 1792

Bibliography: Ludovico Ariosto, *Orlando Furioso*, ed. and trans. Barbara Reynolds (London: Penguin, 1975–77). Elia Levita, *Elia Bahur Levita, Paris un Viene, Francesco Dalle Donne, Verona 1594*, ed. Valerio Marchetti et al. (Bologna: Università degli studi di Bologna, 1988) [facsimile edition with an introduction by Jean Baumgarten]. *Pariz un' Vyene*, ed. Chone Shmeruk and Erika Timm (Jerusalem: Israel Academy of Sciences and Humanities, 1996) [edition in the Hebrew alphabet with a commentary in Hebrew]. *Paris un Wiene: Ein jiddischer Stanzenroman des 16. Jahrhunderts von (oder aus dem Umkreis von) Elia Levita*, ed. Erika Timm (Tübingen: Max Niemeyer, 1996) [edition in transcription with explanatory footnotes and a commentary in German; these two editions are complementary].

Marion Aptroot

ℒ 1596, December 18

A medical student inspired by reading about Faustus is accused of attempting to make a pact with the devil

To Explore the Secrets of Heaven and Earth

Just in time for the Frankfurt book fair of 1587, the Lutheran publisher Johann Spies (d. 1623) brought out the first edition of what would become known as the *Faustbuch* (Faustbook) under the title: *Historia von D. Johann Fausten, dem weitbeschreyten Zauberer und Schwartzkünstler . . . (The history of Dr. Johann Faustus, the renowned sorcerer and black magician . . .)*. The author of this work is unknown, although the publisher states in his preface that the manuscript was given to him by a friend and the text claims to be based on the life and writings of a notorious historical figure. The book became an instant bestseller. Its superb English translation provided a key source for Christopher Marlowe's play *Doctor Faustus*, which was first performed in 1594. Subsequently, the *Faustbook* inspired numerous other literary works, among them

Goethe's *Faust* play in two parts (completed in 1832) and Thomas Mann's novel *Doktor Faustus* (1947).

Although there are no extant writings by any historical figure that could be associated with the protagonist of the *Faustbook,* a handful of historical documents testify to the existence of a scholar and magician whose exploits are likely to have provided the fodder for the Faust legends the published *Faustbook* draws on. A certain Georgius of Helmstadt, who had been enrolled at the University of Heidelberg and called himself Doctor Faustus, was rumored to have died violently in southern Germany sometime between 1530 and 1540. Georg Faust had been known as an astrologer, physician, and natural philosopher, always on the move, expelled by the authorities in various cities (Ingoldstadt, Nuremberg, Wittenberg), and scorned by Humanist scholars and theologians as a vainglorious charlatan, imposter, and braggart. But he was also respected and sought out by princely courts and influential families (Franz von Sickingen and the Hutten family) and even by religious authorities, such as Georg III, the Bishop of Bamberg, who hired him to draw up an astrological chart.

His assumed name, Faust, might reflect an attempt to fashion himself as successor to either the famous 4th-century Manichean Faust, an opponent of Saint Augustine (354–430), who was also reputedly skilled in magic, or to Saint Clement's father, a magician who distinguished himself through the devilish tricks he played on Simon Magus (1st century). The Latin Faustus—meaning "auspicious"—could also have been one of many pompous cognomens this character chose for himself, such as Hemitheus Hedelbergensis ("the demigod of Heidelberg"). Philipp Melanchthon (1497–1560) mentions a certain Johann Faust, an infamous knave, who died a violent death and whose body appeared to have been mutilated by the devil. Whatever his precise historical identity or identities, the notoriety of the figure was amplified by the vehement scorn heaped upon him by Martin Luther, who, although not knowing him personally, singled him out as an instrument of the devil in his immensely popular *Tischreden oder Colloquia Doct. Martin Luther* (1566; *Table Talks or Conversations of Doctor Martin Luther*). It was this association with the devil that fueled the proliferation of published legends about Faustus, which peaked in the 1570s when the German witch craze was approaching its climax. By 1585, when the Calvinist Hermann Witekind (1522–1603) published his *Christlich bedencken und erinnerung von Zauberei (Christian Reflection and Recollection on Magic)* under the pseudonym Augustin Lerchheimer, in which Faustus appears as an emblem of intellectual pride, the time was ripe for a book-length account of the life and death of this legendary scholar who had made a pact with the devil.

The sixty-eight short chapters in the 227-page octavo volume of the *Faustbook* are divided into four segments. The first part (chapters 1–17) tells of Faust's lowly birth, his upbringing by a wealthy, childless cousin in Wittenberg, his enormous intelligence, and his attainment of the degree of doctor of theology. All this highlights Faust's transgressive thirst for knowledge, which leads him finally to conjure up the devil. The disputations with Mephistopheles (the spirit of the devil) culminate in Faust's signing the infernal pact with his own blood. A conversation about hell concludes the first part.

At the beginning of the second part (chapters 18–32), Faust is presented as an astrologer and astronomer who converses with Mephistopheles about cosmology, meteorology, and creation, but it also narrates Faust's presumed journeys down into hell and up to the stars. This part also contains an account of Faust's travels, ranging from various German lands to Constantinople, Egypt, and India. His journey concludes with the ascent of a high mountain peak from where he can see the bright, fiery light barring humankind's return to the Garden of Eden.

The third part focuses on the protagonist's various adventures. He performs magical tricks and pranks both at the courts of the mighty (most prominently the Emperor Charles V) and among peasants, horse traders, and Jews. His sexual exploits culminate in his fathering a son with Helen of Troy, whose devastatingly beautiful image he had conjured up for his students on Whitsunday.

The eight chapters constituting the fourth and final part of the *Faustbook* are devoted to the last year of Faust's alliance with the devil and detail his anxious anticipation of death. To Faust's lamentations, Mephistopheles responds with taunting rhymes and frivolous proverbs that border on nonsensical platitudes ("every sausage has two ends"), all of which only deepen Faust's melancholia. On the eve of the night when the devil is scheduled to fetch his soul, Faust gathers his students around him, tells them about the pact and his imminent death, and admonishes them not to follow on his path. During the night the students and an innkeeper hear a violent storm and frightening noises emanating from Faust's study. The book ends with a description of the remains of Faust's body, found on a dung-heap in front of the inn.

By the end of the *Faustbook,* the reader might be tempted to sympathize with this extraordinary sinner, who, at the end of his infamous life, expresses such remorse. Just such a sympathetic response is prefigured in Faust's students, who urge him to "call upon God, desiring Him, for the love of His sweet son Jesus Christ's sake, to have mercy upon him" (*Faustbook,* 179). But the narrator solicits this compassion in order to state forcefully and with greater theological precision the reason for Faust's damnation. He remarks that, although Faust had promised his students to pray and seek God's mercy, he acted, in fact, like Cain, who "also said his sins were greater than God was able to forgive; for all his thought was on his writing: he meant he had made it too filthy in writing it with his own blood" (ibid.).

Faust is not just a victim of the devil, but the victim of his own presumptuous trust in his pact with the devil. He loses the possibility of salvation by exempting himself from the power of God's grace. Thus, the *Faustbook* ends by driving home the Lutheran doctrine of justification: neither the frequency nor the gravity of sins, nor the power of good works, determines the possibility of salvation, but solely faith in God's grace.

Although the narrative is dotted with frequent moralistic asides, demonstrating an unmistakable Lutheran bias, there is no apparent overarching frame that integrates the disparate episodes of Faust's adventures within a sequentially unfolding demonstration. Faust's curious exploits as a magician read as if they were a concatenation of trickster stories and tall tales arbitrarily linked together. Whether Faust exchanges a devious horse trader's animal for straw or whether he causes noisy, drunken peasants to lose their voice for a while, whether he makes antlers grow on the head of a sleeping knight or punishes a rude peasant by making him believe he has eaten up his wagon full of hay, horses included, his magical powers are put to use primarily for playing pranks on the vain, the bawdy, the ungrateful, or the deceptive. In most of these cases, Faust has the reader's chuckle on his side. Moreover, some magic is acceptable within the narrated universe of the tales, provided its manipulations are limited to the victim's perceptions and do not intervene in the order of material reality. Not the actual practice of magic but the pact he concludes with the devil makes Faust into a magician in the first place and constitutes his fundamental transgression. His magical skills are merely on loan. They are exclusively defined by his contract with the devil, who, in exchange for Faust's soul, provides the knowledge-hungry doctor with twenty-four years of service.

The distinct narrative realization of Faust's pact with the devil constitutes the uniqueness of the *Faustbook* not only thematically, but also conceptually, compositionally, and stylistically. Before the sixth chapter, which introduces the contract, the narrator inserts three detailed colloquia between Faust and Mephistopheles. In the first, Faust tells Mephistopheles that he wants one of the devil's spirits to become an obedient servant in all of his inquiries. But Mephistopheles counters that it is up to his Lord Lucifer to grant this request, that the world of the devils harbors secrets never revealed to humans, and that, should his desire be granted, Faust would have to pay with the loss of his soul. Though Faust initially reacts angrily to this objection, by the second colloquium he has significantly revised his demand: "His request was none other but to become a devil, or at the least a limb of him, and that the spirit should agree unto these articles as followeth: 1. That he might be a spirit in shape and quality. 2. That Mephistopheles should be his servant and at his commandment" (*Faustbook,* 96). Whereas the formulation in the first colloquium specifies the spirit's function as Faust's informant and research assistant, in the second colloquium Faust demands to become a spirit himself, a medium of unmediated, unobstructed access to knowledge.

To a certain extent, the move from the first to the second formulation merely highlights the theological implications of Faust's transgressive desire to know things hidden from ordinary human beings; it is equivalent to the hubristic aspiration to become like God. And in this way Faust actually acts "not unlike that enemy of God and His Christ, that for his pride was cast into hell," as the narrator comments in the third colloquium (*Faustbook,* 97). Within this logic, there is no need to specify what kind of spirit Faust desires to become, it can only be an evil, devilish spirit, and thus the devil can happily agree to base his contract with Faust on such a stipulation. But besides its moral and theological significance, the reformulation of Faust's demand spells out another aspect of his desire for unlimited access to knowledge. For by stating his desire "to be a spirit in shape and quality," spirit is defined not merely as a means for attaining something else, but as an end in itself. The emphasis is shifted from the possession of knowledge to the process and experience of accessing knowledge. In this sense, Faust's desire to shed the limitations of the mortal human body, as bound by space and time, and to become a spirit may be seen as a figurative expression of access to knowledge that was then becoming available to the learned scholar, who, thanks to the emergent print culture, could effortlessly read in heathen books and contemplate strange signs and maps. This cultural fantasy might also be captured in the image of flight, itself analogous to the experience of dreaming: "Taking to him the wings of an eagle to explore the secrets of heaven and earth."

This way of understanding the nature of Faust's transgression is supported by the events narrated in part two. Rather than orally conveying to Faust the information he seeks, the devil sends his adept on a series of breathtaking flights. He satisfies Faust's desire to become a pure spirit through a curious fusion of experience, dream, and hallucination. First, Beelzebub promises to take Faust on a journey through hell, for the duration of which he must remain silent. Whereas Faust believes that, along with flying monsters, he is actually soaring through the smoke and fire of hell, the reader is told that Faust is merely dreaming in his armchair. And, although Faust awakes with doubts as to the reality of his journey, he nonetheless records it in a narrative found enclosed in a book after his death. This piece of documentary evidence suggests that the entire armchair experience was perhaps the illusory product of a reader's imagination.

The second journey, in which Faust travels through the heavens, is described in a letter likewise found among Faust's papers. His marvelous journey began as, unable to fall asleep, he pored over certain astrological charts and wondered about the true nature of the firmament. At the conclusion of his lengthy report about the planetary system, he invites his correspondent to verify his account by consulting his own books on astronomy (only in the conclusion to chapter 25 of the German *Faustbook*).

Faust's final grand journey is again undertaken by means of air transport. This time the devil commandeers a winged dromedary. Except for a few lively anecdotes—Faust spying on the pope or cuckolding the Turkish emperor—this travelogue largely consists of a tedious list of country and city names and stale descriptions of standard sights, all copied from Hartmann Schedel's by-then somewhat outdated *Weltchronik* (1493; *Chronicle of the World*). Again a book lies at the source of Faust's exploratory flight.

To the extent that the German *Faustbuch* departs from the orally transmitted legends surrounding its main figure, it does so in the first two parts and at the very end, where the book's major innovation becomes discernible. This consists in the contextualization of the Faust material within a theological framework as well as in the construction of a skillfully feigned documentary that reflects on its own medial status as an artifact of print culture. In this sense, the *Faustbook* is intertwined with the two major cultural transformations that took place in Germany during the early modern period and which are associated with the names of Luther and Gutenberg.

See also 1457, 1523, 1831, 1943

Bibliography: Historia von D. Johann Fausten | dem weitbeschreyten Zauberer und Schwartzkünstler | Wie er sich gegen dem Teuffel auff eine benandte zeit verschrieben | Was er hierzwischen für seltzame Abentheuwer gesehen | selbs angerichtet und getrieben | biß er endtlich seinen wol verdienten Lohn empfangen. Mehertheils auss seinen eygenen hinderlassenen schrifften | allen hochtragenden | fürwitzigen und Gottlosen menschen zum schrecklichen Beyspiel | abscheuwlichen Exempel | und treuwhertziger Warnung zusammen gezogen . . . (The history of Dr. Johann Faustus, the renowned sorcerer and black magician; how he sold himself to the devil for a specified term, what curious exploits he devised and practiced during that term, until he finally received his well-deserved reward. For the most part gathered from his own posthumous papers and published as a terrible and horrific example and a sincere warning to all the arrogant, curious and ungodly; Frankfurt am Main: Johann Spies, 1587), rpt. in Romane des 15. und 16. Jahrhunderts, with notes and commentary by Jan-Dirk Müller (Frankfurt am Main: Deutscher Klassiker Verlag, 1990), 831–986, 1319–1430. Faustbook: A Critical Edition Based on the Text of 1592, ed. John Henry Jones (Cambridge, U.K.: Cambridge University Press, 1994). Christopher Marlowe, Doctor Faustus: A- and B-texts (1604, 1616), ed. David Bevington and Eric Rasmussen (Manchester and New York: Manchester University Press, 1993). Hans Henning, "Faust als historische Gestalt," Jahrbuch der Goethe Gesellschaft, Neue Folge, vol. 21 (Weimar 1959):107–139. ———, "Das Faust-Buch von 1587: Seine Entstehung, seine Quellen, seine Wirkung," Weimarer Beiträge 6 (1960):26–58. Frank Baron, "Faustus on Trial: The Origins of Johann Spies's Historia in an Age of Witch Hunting," Frühe Neuzeit, 9 (Tübingen: Niemeyer, 1992).

Dorothea E. von Mücke

☙ *1600*

Jakob Böhme finds divine illumination in the light reflected from a pewter dish and begins a prolific career in mysticism and theosophy

Signatures of Divinity

In 1600, the life of the twenty-five-year-old Jakob Böhme (1575–1624) seemed exemplary only in its ordinariness. A devout Lutheran, he had acquired the rights of citizenship in the small town of Görlitz, located halfway between Dresden and Breslau (Wrocław), where he had established himself as a cobbler. His professional and civic status was bolstered by auspicious events at home. He was newly married to a butcher's daughter, had bought a house, and, in January 1600, the first of his four children was born. Yet instead of leading a life filled with the usual mix of middling joys and worries, Böhme was beset by what years later he described as a "hard melancholy and sadness." This peasant son with minimal schooling, whose travels had been limited to those of a journeyman and who now found himself ensconced behind a shoemaker's bench far from Europe's centers of learning, fell into deep despair because he believed that "the heaven is many hundreds or thousands of miles from this earth, and that God dwells only in that heaven," a belief he found confirmed in the measurements of "many *Physici*." The feeling of remoteness from God prompted

Böhme to look "into the depths of the world, and the sun and the stars, as well as the clouds, and rain and snow," where he found a lot of things to be perturbed about: "That in all things there was evil and good, in the elements as well as in the creatures, and that the godless fare as well in this world as the pious, and that the barbaric peoples dwell in the best lands, and that luck is probably with them more than with the pious." Instead of forging a life whose elements were propitiously gathering before him, he was seized by profound anguish about the insignificance of "the little spark of humanity" against the immensity of the heavens and the earth (*Aurora,* 19, 3–8).

Yet it was this depressed shoemaker who came to produce a body of work of enormous intellectual abundance and impressive eccentricity spanning theology, philosophy, alchemy, and theosophy. The influence his work exercised in both longevity and breadth is amazing. Traces can be found in religion, from Pietism and Quakerism to more recent speculative theology; in philosophy, from Leibniz to Schelling; in literature, from Milton to the Romantics and to Yeats; and even in science, among esoterically inclined practitioners such as Newton. His turn from simple cobbler to "first German philosopher," as Hegel claimed, is due to a singular experience that, in his own words, "broke through the gates of Hell," lifted his melancholy, and bathed him in the light of knowledge (*Aurora,* 19, 11). This event was set off when a beam, reflected from a pewter dish, caught his eye one day in 1600. Its "gentle jovial sheen" introduced the young Böhme, as his friend and admiring biographer Abraham von Franckenberg informs us, "to the innermost ground or center of secret nature" (Böhme, *Sämtliche Schriften* 10:11). To dispel what he suspected may have been a flight of fancy or a simple optical illusion, Böhme left the house, exited the town through a nearby gate, crossed the river Neisse, and ambled about in a meadow. But, according to Franckenberg, the vision, far from lifting, became ever clearer, "so that he could, as it were, look into the heart of all creatures and into what is innermost in nature by means of the represented signatures and figures, lineaments and colors" (ibid.). Böhme beheld something very specific in these signatures and figures, something wondrous and monstrous in equal measure, namely what he repeatedly called "the innermost birth of the divinity," which enveloped him with a love like that binding bride and groom (*Aurora,* 19, 11). At this moment of supreme religio-sexual consummation, the cobbler of Görlitz, who once worried that God's perch in heaven was too far for comfort, was transformed into the Christian mystic, able to comprehend a hidden order behind the seemingly capricious distribution of light and dark, good and evil, believers and heathens. "What feeling of triumph there was in the spirit," he reports about his illumination, "I cannot write or say" (ibid.).

Böhme's inability to "write or say" anything at all about his triumph resulted, of course, in nearly four thousand tightly printed pages of prose on every conceivable topic under—and prominently including—the sun. He wrote in a muscular German, though admirers and editors gave his books Latin titles by which they are known in scholarship. Neither the ineffability of his experience nor his less-than-ideal working conditions were able to hold him back.

His business continued to demand his attention, and for several years he had to contend with a ban on writing that a Lutheran pastor had managed to impose on him on charges of heresy. Yet he wrote, compulsively and frantically, about "where every thing has its origin, how it exists and how it becomes, and how it will be at the end of this time; also whereof the kingdom of God and of Hell are made" as promised by the subtitle of his first book *Aurora, oder Morgenröte im Aufgang* (1612; *Aurora, or The Rising Dawn*).

While his rambling reflections, by turns insightful and bizarre, range over an astounding variety of issues, we find that Böhme's illumination, which by his own account lasted no more than a quarter hour, not only contains most of those issues *in nuce,* but also announces the specifically Böhmian way in which standard mystical topics are filtered through philosophy, alchemy, and science. The crucial moment of illumination is literalized and anchored in material reality, and despite its extraordinary effect, Böhme's beam of light obeys lawful principles of reflectivity that optical physicists would study throughout the 17th century. What is more, as the reference to Jupiter suggests, the gleam in the pewter dish owed its existence to a newly configured planetary model that, while still home to recondite astrological lore, acknowledged the centrality of the sun as the sole source of light and heat (*Aurora,* 25, 67). Yet this light, originating at a great distance and from the largest of astral bodies, permeates even the smallest things, and illuminates "the heart of all creatures." The pewter dish can be said then to have served Böhme as both telescope and microscope (albeit with certain psychedelic distortions): it permits him to gaze into the farthest reaches of a heliocentric universe and, simultaneously, into the "innermost of nature." That he did not see what years later Galileo and van Leeuwenhoek would observe through their instruments may be easily guessed, for as Böhme does not tire of repeating, he is not interested in the myriad appearances of nature—those are the devil's work—but in the "root from which they were made" (*Aurora,* 25, 45). This interest in the root, too, is present in his moment of illumination, namely in his odd claim to have spied "the innermost birth of the divinity." While his writings repudiate the flesh for being remote from true divinity in true mystical fashion, they are awash with fleshly metaphors of conception, birth, and growth. "The entire body of this world is like a human body," he writes (*Aurora,* 25, 22), endorsing an organic homology that would rouse the interest of Romantic poets and philosophers.

There is one other thing we can glean from Böhme's mystical experience: just as it allows us to observe how large conceptual complexes from cosmogony, natural philosophy, alchemy, and reproductive biology are interlaced with theological quandaries in a manner characteristic of Böhme's writings, it also points to an important lack, namely the lack of certainty. A penumbra of doubt hovers over this and many other details of his life, in part because we must rely on Franckenberg's adulatory, and therefore unreliable, biography. More important than the uncertainties surrounding matters of fact are those attending matters of interpretation, and for these Böhme alone is responsible: wholly distinct, at times entirely contradictory accounts of the same ideas populate his writings, not infrequently on the same page. They often give the impression that he wishes to press everything, perhaps due to a desire to replicate the moment of illumination, into one sentence. The 18th-century scientist Georg Christoph Lichtenberg has a generous way of characterizing Böhme's permissive attitude toward comprehensibility: his writings, Lichtenberg says, are "a sort of picnic, where the author supplies the words (the sound) and the reader the meaning" (*Schriften und Briefe*, 1: E 104). For this reason, there are many different Jakob Böhmes —a fact allegorized by the large number of ways his name is rendered, in both German and English (Behm, Behmont, Behmen, etc.). The more common reaction to such polysemy has been exasperation. Heinrich Heine, who never read Böhme because, he explains, "I don't like to be taken for a fool," tells of how Charles I of England, smitten with Böhme's ideas, sent a scholar to Görlitz to study the great cobbler's writings. "This scholar was luckier than his royal master," Heine quips. "For while the latter lost his head at Whitehall thanks to Cromwell's axe, the former only lost his mind in Görlitz thanks to Böhme's theosophy" (*Zur Geschichte der Religion und Philosophie in Deutschland*, p. 64).

The formidable difficulties in reading Böhme are due, at least in part, to his interest in the heterodox brew of religious and intellectual tendencies and tensions simmering around him. The period of his greatest productivity coincides with the early years of the Thirty Years' War (1618–1648), the most devastating sectarian conflict in the history of the German lands. Böhme liberally helps himself to Lutheran, Calvinist, crypto-Calvinist, Anabaptist, Paracelsian, Schwenckfeldian, Kabbalist, alchemical, and astrological offerings. Yet he also creates his own narrative of "where every thing has its origin, how it exists and how it becomes," for the grandest ambition of Böhme's writings is to provide a capacious mythopoetic account of God's mysterious self-differentiation into nature, and of the seemingly unaccountable appearance of errors, that is, of evil, in creation. Because any distinction entails a lack (for something must be excluded from the entity being distinguished) and because in Böhme's conception God cannot suffer from lack, his God is both everything—"all-powerful, all-knowing, all-seeing, all-hearing, all-smelling, all-tasting, all-feeling" (*Aurora*, 10, 61)—and, for the same reason, nothing, since in true totality there can be no distinctions. "One cannot say of God that He is this or that, evil or good, that He has differences within Himself," Böhme writes in his late book *De Electione Gratiae* (1623; *On the Election of Grace*), contradicting the Lutheran doctrine of the essential goodness of God. For this purely undifferentiated divine nothingness, Böhme coins the term *Ungrund*, "Unground." "He is the Unground in Himself," he continues, "He is Nothing and Everything, and is a unified will, in which the world and all of creation lies, in Him everything is equally eternal without beginning" (1, 3).

God does not tarry in this unmarked expanse beyond space, time, and sensibility, and the reason he does not has to do with Böhme's idea of signature, an idea that lies at the heart of his reception by the Romantics. (The idiosyncracy and tendentiousness of this conception has recently been demonstrated by

Paola Mayer.) Originating in the Paracelsian esoteric tradition, the signature is the true external manifestation of a thing's internal essence. "There is no thing in nature . . . which does not also reveal its inner form *[Gestalt]* externally, be-cause the inner always works toward revelation," Böhme writes in *De Signatura Rerum* (1622; *On the Signature of Things,* 1, 15). The concept of signature, then, has important semiotic as well as ontological implications. It guarantees that appearances, far from misleading us, can be taken as authentic signs of what is true. In the signature, man "may also learn to recognize the essence of all be-ings *[das Wesen aller Wesen]* . . . for nature has given each thing its own lan-guage according to its essence and its structure" (1, 16). The adequacy of signs and things, ratified by the idea of signature, prompts Böhme to posit a "lan-guage of nature" through which "each thing . . . always reveals itself and repre-sents what it is good and useful for, for each thing reveals its mother" (1, 17). That Romantic poets, such as Blake, Tieck, Novalis, and Coleridge, would be enthralled by such a concept goes without saying.

Beyond its importance for semiotics, the idea of signature plays a key onto-logical, indeed cosmogonic, role in Böhme's thought. The fact that a funda-mental congruence of essence and appearance obtains in the signature of things is, in Böhme's account, ultimately due to the fact that God does not rest in his purely undivided nothingness, but differentiates himself and, by self-im-pregnation, as it were, gives birth to the world of things. "Nothingness hungers for Somethingness," Böhme writes in *Mysterium Magnum* (1623; 3, 5), imbuing the philosophical abstractions with bodily longing. In God there is nothing but that hungry will, and it is the will that prompts him to reveal himself, and to observe himself in this self-revelation (*On the Election of Grace,* 1, 9). As Hegel astutely recognizes in his *Lectures on the History of Philosophy,* the struc-ture of this tripartite movement—undifferentiated nothingness, differentiation, observation of difference—is inherently dialectical and congenial to Hegel's thinking—though he faults Böhme for his "barbaric" presentation at least a half dozen times. Though such a view has the advantage of claiming Böhme for one of modernity's great philosophical projects, it runs the risk of over-looking Böhme's specificity. For the triple jump lands him directly inside the Christian notion of Trinity. God is neither a structural abstraction nor can he be glimpsed directly by reading the signature of things—this is where Böhme's thought diverts from pansophism. As he emphasizes in all of his writings, God can only be known in Christ.

The fact that, for Böhme, the idea of the signature of things is woven into the narrative of God's self-revelation by means of a specifically Christian thread foregrounds his self-understanding as a mystic and his motivation as a writer. For why after all write four thousand pages if the triumph of illumina-tion cannot be put into words? It is the Christian system of beliefs that lends Böhme's writings their peculiar force. To see in him a forerunner of the con-ceptual thought of idealism would miss the prophetic urge that gives shape not only to his ideas and to his language, but, more importantly, to the entire theo-sophical project. "In myself, paradise shall be," he writes in a haunting passage.

"Everything that God the Father has and is shall appear in me . . . all colors, force, and virtues of His eternal wisdom shall be revealed in and through me as His likeness; I shall be the revelation of the divine world and a tool of God's spirit, in which He plays with Himself as with His signature, with this echo that I am: I shall be . . . the stringed instrument of His spoken word and His echo" (*Of the Signature of Things*, 12, 13). What this exceptional cobbler means to reveal in his frenzied writings is—legible only to those who have seen the light—God's own signature.

See also 1789 (June 2), 1800, 1824, 1828 (Winter)

Bibliography: The Works of Jacob Behmen, The Teutonic Philosopher (London, 1764–1781). Jacob Böhme, *Sämtliche Schriften*, ed. Will-Erich Peuckert (Stuttgart: Frommanns Verlag, 1955–1961), rpt. of the 1730 edition, cited by chapter and paragraph number. Heinrich Heine, *Zur Geschichte der Religion und Philosophie in Deutschland*, vol. 8/1 of *Historisch-kritische Gesamtausgabe der Werke*, ed. Manfred Windfuhr (Hamburg: Hoffmann und Campe, 1979). Georg Christoph Lichtenberg, *Schriften und Briefe*, ed. Wolfgang Promies (Munich: Hanser, 1968–1974). Paola Mayer, *Jena Romanticism and Its Appropriation of Jakob Böhme: Theosophy—Hagiography—Literature* (Montreal: McGill-Queens University Press, 1999). Andrew Weeks, *Boehme: An Intellectual Biography of the Seventeenth-Century Philosopher and Mystic* (Albany: State University of New York Press, 1991).

Michel Chaouli

ℒ 1609

The Munich production of Jakob Bidermann's *Cenodoxus* effects the conversion of fourteen nobles from the Bavarian court

Jesuit Theater and the Blindness of Self-Knowledge

As the anonymous editor of Jakob Bidermann's *Ludi theatrales sacri* (1666), the posthumously published collection of his plays, recounts in the foreword ("Praemonitio ad lectorem"), the 1609 performance of the author's first play *Cenodoxus* at the Munich Jesuit college must have been truly remarkable. As a Jesuit stronghold, the Munich college housed nearly one thousand students and educated many members of the Bavarian elite. Its stage transcended its purely educational function and was by then the main theater of the Munich court. Not surprisingly, the audience at this performance, produced by Bidermann himself, included many important nobles of the Bavarian court and patricians of the city of Munich. The comic scenes in the first three acts roused the spectators to such laughter, the seats almost collapsed under them. But as the play progressed, merriment turned into shock and terror as they witnessed the unfolding of Cenodoxus's eternal damnation and descent into hell. By the end of the play, few in the audience were not trembling as they contemplated the punishment their own sins would merit if divine judgment were passed on them. The play's impact was immediate and lasting. Fourteen nobles of the Bavarian court underwent the Spiritual Exercises of Saint Ignatius, the meditation practices on which the Jesuit order was founded, and subsequently fundamentally changed their way of life. But the effect of this performance did not end there. Among the penitent was the actor who played the protagonist, the doctor of Paris, Cenodoxus. After completing the Ignatian Exercises, he entered the Society of Jesus where he led a pious and devout life until his death in the odor of sanctity. As the anonymous editor remarks, the play accomplished more in a few hours than a hundred sermons.

Whether the events recounted in the foreword, written two generations later, were historically true or a promotional ploy to advertise Bidermann's collected dramatic works, must remain unsettled. However, this little anecdote reveals much about the artistic function and status of Jesuit theater. As the comparison with the religious sermon indicates, Jesuit theater stood in the service of the *propaganda fidei* of the Society of Jesus, the spearhead of post-tridentine Catholic reform, and was not conceived as a self-sufficient work of art. Despite their professed allegiance to Aristotelian poetics, Jesuit dramatists, in practice, subordinated all elements of theatrical representation to the maximization of pedagogical efficacy. Not the adherence to poetological rules was important, but the saving of souls, as Ignatius never tired to admonish. Thus the generic hybridity of Bidermann's play, subtitled a "Comico-Tragoedia," had a precise psychological purpose. Due to laughter's cathartic function, plays with such comic components produced, as the "Praemonitio" observed, an especially large "spiritual harvest." As heaven and hell were part of the spiritual landscape in which the individual's soul sought its salvation, the classical unities of time and place were deemed too constrictive. Similarly, the dramatic plot was driven less by the logic of action than by the eternal battle between good and evil. In this sense Jesuit drama was fundamentally undramatic, as it merely unfolded this timeless dichotomy. The personifications of virtues and vices as well as other heavenly and infernal representatives owed their dramatic existence to this pastoral motivation as much as to the visualization techniques of the Ignatian Exercises. In general, Jesuit dramatists paid particular attention to the extralinguistic components of their theatrical performances in order to maximize their impact. They exploited all resources of the Baroque stage to embellish and intensify the spoken Latin word with dance, musical interludes, complex pictorial programs, and other special theatrical effects. In fact, since many spectators were not proficient enough in Latin, they were dependent on the dramatic action and these supplementary devices for understanding the theatrical sermons. The affective persuasion was aimed as much at the actors as at the spectators, transcending the border between stage and audience, fiction and reality. As an integral part of the rhetorical training at Jesuit colleges, the plays afforded the students an opportunity to practice spoken Latin as well as training in declamation and deportment, in preparation for the public careers for which they were destined. School plays thus were never mere representations of extra-theatrical, even if fictional, events. They were demonstrations of rhetorical power and skill. In other words, school theater always also displayed itself. Moreover, since heresy arose, as the Italian Jesuit Possevino argued, from a deficit of *humanitas,* the practice of the *bonae litterae* functioned as a therapeutic device to purge actors and audience of their sins. Such a theatrical *purgatio vitiorum* drew not only on the psychagogic techniques of the Ignatian Exercises, but prepared—as the aforementioned anecdote makes clear—its recipients to follow their *vocatio ad religionem*.

The vice Bidermann's play *Cenodoxus* seeks to purge is already advertised by the speaking name of its protagonist—Greek for "vainglory" (Galatians 5:26, Philippians 2:3) paired with pride and hypocrisy. The play dramatizes the legend of the unnamed Doctor of Paris whom popular tradition associated with the founding of the Carthusian Order by Saint Bruno. Cenodoxus, famous for his prodigious learning as well as his extraordinary virtue, dies. As his funeral is being prepared, the corpse rises up three times on three consecutive days to announce his accusation, judgment, and condemnation by the heavenly tribunal. Horrified by the condemnation of such a luminous example of Christian learning and virtue and unable to comprehend the rationale of God's judgment, Bruno and six companions renounce all worldly pursuits and proceed to establish a monastic order distinguished by its austere asceticism and reclusiveness. This drama of conversion and foundation not only echoes the conversion of Ignatius of Loyola and the subsequent founding of his own reform order, but, in turn, aims to effect such a turn-about in its performers and spectators. Not coincidentally, the theatricalization of vainglory or pride functions as the spiritual purgative. The sin of pride is as ancient as the world and yet genuinely modern.

Most importantly, it is a specifically Jesuit vice. In the medieval system of seven deadly sins, *superbia* was the main sin and source of all others. Because it was the sin that caused Lucifer to fall, Saint Augustine termed it the "beginning of sin." In his eyes, it was rooted in a "craving for undue exaltation . . . , when the soul abandons Him to whom it ought to cleave as its end, and becomes a kind of end to itself" (*City of God* XIX.13). Pride and vainglory are thus inextricably linked, as the proud one no longer lives and works for the glory of God but solely for his own. This primeval vice experienced a renaissance in the figure of the Humanist scholar whose thirst for knowledge, pride in his skills, and desire for fame seemed for many to perpetuate that first act of disobedience when man strove to be like God by tasting from the tree of knowledge.

For Bidermann, who as a young man had been an enthusiastic reader of Justus Lipsius, the brand of neo-Stoic self-reliance and constancy, parodied in the dying scene of Cenodoxus, reeked particularly of the pride of a man who seeks to gain salvation independent of God. Therefore, Bidermann's drama of the vainglorious Doctor of Paris was literally to be understood as a condemnation of certain aspects of the urbane Humanism embodied by intellectuals from Erasmus to Lipsius. As Bidermann's own adolescent sympathies for the latter indicate, the Jesuit spirit was particularly susceptible to vainglorious desires, not least because it was that vice that haunted the order's founder, Ignatius, until the end of his life. As a former soldier who desired nothing more than military honor and glory, Ignatius was so acutely aware of the temptations of self-glorification that he chose a personal motto, namely "ad maiorem Dei gloriam" ("For the greater glory of God"), as constant reminder of who alone deserved all glory. For an order that had quickly risen to the status of an elite unit within the *ecclesia militans et triumphans,* vainglory was the ultimate temptation and thus perversion.

This may explain the force of Cenodoxus's deterrent example since he cultivates his own fame and glory instead of heeding the principle on which the Ignatian Exercises were founded: "The human person is created to praise, reverence and serve God Our Lord, and by so doing to save his or her soul" (Ignatius, *Personal Writings,* 289 [23]). Cenodoxus loses his soul because none of his good works, which he performs in abundance, follows this universal epideictic. Lastly, vainglory is a particularly theatrical sin, and, conversely, it is the sin that theater itself is always in danger of committing. When Cenodoxus—under the direction of the personified vice Hypocrisy—"acts" virtuously, he merely plays to the audience, and he ceases to do so when he feels unobserved. Not only did Cenodoxus usurp God's position as the recipient of glory, he also introjected and displaced the preexistent divine gaze. Instead of being cognizant of the gaze of God's unsleeping eye, he always observes himself acting in order to ensure that his performance plays well with his mundane audience.

Like so many other Jesuit plays, Bidermann's *Cenodoxus* is metatheater, a theater that is not only an ostentatious display of its own theatricality, but a systematic reflection on it. An even more obvious example would be his play *Philemon Martyr,* which dramatizes the martyrdom of the actor Philemon. Thus Cenodoxus has to be read as an allegory for the actor, if not theater itself. For antitheatrical polemicists, from the Church Fathers on, hypocrisy is the *déformation professionelle* of the actor (*hypocrites* is the Greek word for "actor") who cannot but simulate and dissimulate, even offstage. And not coincidentally, the "Praemonitio ad Lectorem" remarks on the danger that those in the Society of Jesus concerned with theatrical performances might seek personal ovation rather than their own and the audience's salvation. Theater's insistent visuality must not distract the mind from spiritual things. It must never become an end in itself, but must always direct those involved toward the ultimate end: God. The practitioners of the theater are thus in the position of Cenodoxus. They must be "ever vigilant that their works don't displease God by pleasing others."

Characteristic of Cenodoxus's theatrical vice is the moment of (self-)delusion. Despite his luminous intellect and constant self-observation, Cenodoxus remains blind to his vaingloriousness until it is too late. He genuinely believes that the pious and holy life he is leading will be sufficient to effect his salvation. His turn toward himself (termed *incurvatio* by Saint Augustine), which makes all reflection and knowledge of the self possible, inevitably diverts him from God and renders him ignorant of the sinfulness of this perversion. In other words, he is capable of seeing himself, but not of seeing himself seeing, and more importantly, not seeing God. Moreover, he does not recognize that the insinuations of Hypocrisy (Hypocrisis) and Self-Love (Philautia) are of satanic origin, and consequently he does not heed the admonitions of Conscience (Conscientia) and his guardian angel Cenodoxophylax. Incapable of distinguishing good and evil, Cenodoxus is subject to a dilemma central to Jesuit spirituality. Motivated by his own spiritual crises, Ignatius's Exercises are devised as a psycho-technique to discern good and evil spirits and thus to be able to make life choices in accordance with God's will.

Ignatius states: "There are three sorts of thought processes in me, one sort which are properly mine and arise simply from my free will and choice, and two others which come from outside, one from the good spirit and the other from the bad" (*Personal Writings,* 291 [32]). As simple as this sounds, the problem is always that the bad angel may "assume the form of 'an angel of light'" (*Personal Writings,* 352 [332]), that feelings of consolation and spiritual joy may be induced by the enemy, and so forth. Ignatius's own biography and the wide variety of techniques he used for the "discernment of different spirits" indicate that the individual subject can never be entirely sure of having made a correct distinction and "put off self-love, self-will and self-interest" (*Personal Writings,* 320 [189]).

Bidermann's play addresses (and resolves) this existential dilemma with the epistemological resources of theater by externalizing and transposing it into the intersubjective realm: a technique that Ignatius anticipates in the *Spiritual Exercises* when he suggests that the subject should imagine himself as another and examine that person's decision objectively. In order to create a similar constellation, Bidermann introduces multiple observational levels into *Cenodoxus.* On the first and lowest level, Cenodoxus's conduct is observed by himself as well as people around him, who are, however, equally blind to his sinfulness. This *theatrum mundi* is, in turn, observed by the extraterrestrial forces of good and evil. The observational hierarchy between these two levels is indicated by its asymmetry. Whereas the *dramatis personae,* specifically Cenodoxus, can hear the allegorical figures, he can neither see nor recognize them for what they are. In fact, he takes the insinuations of Self-Love and Hypocrisy to be his own "thought processes."

Similarly, Bruno and his companions witness Cenodoxus's damnation by the heavenly tribunal, but are unable to comprehend its rationale. Only the real audience is in the position to discern the good and evil spirits and thus can recognize Cenodoxus's sin. In that sense, the spectators differ from Bruno and his companions, who serve as their proxies on stage. Intradramatically, it is the comic scenes that take up—albeit implicitly—and parody the blindness of the human actors and thus provide a metatheatrical commentary of the tragic events. But the audience also observes the inability of the *dramatis personae* to observe themselves and each other—which is their own position once they leave the theater and are no longer in the privileged position of an observer observing blind observers. In that sense, they are like Bruno. And in that sense, his subsequent conversion is exemplary—as the purported reaction to the 1609 performance demonstrates. Thus, Bidermann's *Comico-Tragoedia* observes the existential blindness of the subject observing itself and its actions; a blindness that outside the theater only faith can cure.

See also 1515–1517, 1647, 1767

Bibliography: Jacob Bidermann, *Cenodoxus,* ed. and trans. D. G. Dyer (Austin: University of Texas, 1974). ————, *Cenodoxus,* German translation by Joachim Meichel (1635), ed. Rolf Tarot (Stuttgart: Reclam; 1965). ————, *Ludi theatrales sacri,* 2 vols., Munich 1666; reprint, ed. Rolf Tarot (Tübingen: Niemeyer, 1967). Saint Ignatius of Loyola, *Personal Writings,* ed. and trans. J. A. Munitz and P. Endean (London: Penguin, 1996). Marjorie O'Rourke Boyle, *Loyola's Acts: The Rhetoric of Self* (Berkeley: University of California Press, 1997).

Christopher J. Wild

ℒ *1622–1624*

At the beginning of the Thirty Years' War, two small works on the refinement of the German language lay the groundwork for vernacular literature

Conversation, Poetic Form, and the State

In the early phase of a war that was to last thirty years, two works were published to which we now trace the beginnings of German as a literary language. At first glance, the juxtaposition of these texts seems odd. In the town of Köthen, seat of Prince Ludwig of Anhalt, appeared a little work about the aims of an association founded five years earlier and known as the Fruchtbringende Gesellschaft (Fruit-Bearing Society). Prince Ludwig had imported the idea from northern Italy where, in the small states and principalities, members of the social and governing elite made it a practice to meet for elegant conversation on literary and scholarly matters in private societies called *accademie.* The medium of these societies was language, spoken language, that is, the vernacular. In a world where Latin was the language of scholars and universities, the act of speaking in Italian or German about Italian or German art and culture constituted nothing less than a political program.

In 1624, only two years after the *Kurtzer Bericht der Fruchtbringenden Gesellschaft Zweck und Vorhaben (Brief Report on the Purpose and Aims of the Fruit-Bearing Society)* appeared, the *Buch von der deutschen Poeterey (Book of German Poetics)* was published in Breslau, the urban center of Silesia. Its author was Martin Opitz, a twenty-six-year-old writer and academic, not particularly successful in his university career but known in intellectual circles for his agile wit. It was also the era of territorial state building and Opitz had done quite well in the political arena as a diplomat and administrator for rulers of small principalities. With the ambitiously titled *Book of German Poetics,* he now aspired to provide a new foundation for a literature in the German language. To be sure, his was not the first such attempt in the German-speaking regions. Opitz mentions some of his most important forerunners, particularly Ernst Schwabe von der Heide, who had written a book of poems and rules for poetry (now lost) in 1616. Nevertheless, the *Book of German Poetics* marked a real beginning, as all Opitz's serious rivals, such as Zincgref and Weckherlin, were forced to admit. In a sense, Opitz created an institution that merited recognition and thus had an effect on the style and character of the works that followed.

The two founding documents of a literature in German in the 17th century are as closely related in content as they are in date of publication. Both mark the beginning of initiatives promoting the vernacular language. For in 1620 no language that might solidify the national identity of a populace was as yet in existence. Instead there were many different contexts of knowledge and usages in which powerful and educated men read and wrote vernacular German, French, or Italian side by side with Latin, which was still the language of scholars throughout Europe. Which language people employed depended on their status, class, and profession. Reading, writing, and speaking were separate, indeed divergent, modes of language use. The statutes of the Fruit-Bearing Society and the *Book of German Poetics* fused these levels according to two alternative conceptions. The members of the academy wished to elevate the language they already spoke and make it more refined. They had learned it because it was spoken in the region where they were born, mainly by servants and playmates, and only sometimes by their parents. Opitz, for his part, was concerned with formal mechanisms users would first have to master and could be used only by adults of a certain standing and education.

People who wanted to create a set of rules for their own vernacular language and literature had to borrow them from Latin grammar and poetics. Opitz's poetics thus began with the time-honored rhetorician's approach to writing: choosing the "matter" *(res)* and then adapting the "words" *(verba)* to it. This process has a nontrivial premise. Rhetoricians and writers on poetics did not believe that nature contained an unlimited number of topics, nor did they regard words as components that could be combined at will. There were established forms that were governed by their own laws. Rhetoricians took theirs directly from the law courts, selecting forms that were accepted in court proceedings. Writers on poetics started from the genres of ancient literature: epic and tragedy, comedy and satire, epigram and eclogue.

Opitz expounds guidelines for form, the place where the matters that can be invented and the words that can be chosen intersect, limiting himself to forms of lyric poetry. On the subject of rhyme, for example, Opitz teaches that whereas rhymes in Latin are either very exceptional effects or even errors, they are fundamental to poetic form in Italian and French, and also in German. Thus, he links genres directly with linguistic peculiarities of vernacular languages and their literary history. The aim is not so much to imitate or reproduce a model than for each language to distinguish itself from other modern languages.

Opitz saw the recent history of poetic forms in the German language connected with his own first attempts at writing poetry in German. However, his own works, which he cites as models for particular rhyme schemes or verse forms, were either not yet published at all or not by him. Zincgref, his friend from their student days in Heidelberg and rival, had published some of Opitz's poems that same year without the latter's knowledge. Opitz, therefore, may have intended the quotations from his own work in the *Book of German Poetics* to serve as corrected or emended versions. But no matter what Opitz's intention might have been, by introducing his own work as prescriptive he clearly took up positions that differed from his actions in the past. His own language acquired the status of a region undergoing colonization. For one must not forget that he also used his poetics and the literary language constructed according to it as weapons in a war against regional dialects, especially against his own Silesian dialect, as when he notes that the word *hören* (to hear) may not be used as a rhyme for *verkehren* (to associate with).

The Fruit-Bearing Society's aim seems to have been similar to that of Opitz. The *Brief Report on the Purpose and Aims of the Fruit-Bearing Society* states that a society should be founded "in which one would speak and write in good pure German and otherwise, in the same group, would undertake to elevate our mother tongue (as nature obliges each of us to do) in a useful and constructive fashion" (8). Such too is the purpose of a treatise on language and poetics. The *Brief Report* merely expresses it more concisely and in more modern terms, for the princes and officials used the vocabulary of natural law, familiar to them from the writings of Melanchthon and from Justus Lispius's political theory. Language is a gift to the people from God and nature, and like such other God-given gifts as family, native country, and indeed one's own self, it obliges one to preserve and cultivate it as duty requires.

However, cultivating one's own language is merely a means to the real end of an academy. When the founders of the society gathered, states the *Brief Report,* "mention was made of various academies, which were established both for maintaining good faith and encouraging good morals, as a useful exercise of every people's vernacular language." The actual aim of an academy was thus not focused on the semiotic structure of language. Its primary purpose was to further social contact and communication, both in its pragmatic and ethical dimensions ("morals") and in its linguistically performative aspects ("exercise of the vernacular language"). Good faith—*fides*—is both the prerequisite and the goal of this program. Furthermore, *fides,* that is, reliability and predictability in social and linguistic interactions, is a category of modern natural law. Both the prerequisite and the aim of academies—institutions of social contact—were the same: meaning what one says and taking responsibility for one's own actions.

Thus, just as in the Accademia della Crusca (founded in 1583), to which Prince Ludwig had been admitted in 1600, the meetings of the Fruit-Bearing Society served to bring together the elite of the new German centers of power and administration. In Köthen, this included reigning princes and civil servants who were also members of the aristocracy. Bourgeois members were fewer, but they might be admitted if they had attained senior positions in the bureaucracy or could make particular contributions to the academy's scholarly aims. In any case, under Ludwig's leadership, membership in the governmental elite played a greater role than noble lineage. The decision to require the vernacular language as the code for practicing social communication and the good faith connected with it must be seen in this context.

Around 1600, the elites of the princely courts functioned in areas in which the foremost language employed was the vernacular: in financial dealings, diplomatic and statistical correspondence, and legal decrees. One can, therefore, describe the purpose of academies as follows: Academies encoded the social communication of the governmental elite in the vernacular languages which had been prescribed for administrations and law courts since the 15th century in Italy and since the 16th century in France and Germany.

The main concern of Opitz's work on language and poetics, that is, prescriptive regulation of his own language, served cultivation of a code guaranteeing *fides*—reliability and accountability in social interactions. However, the code itself could overshadow the purpose of the encoding. The Italian dictionary brought out by the *Crusca* in 1612 was famous. Despite the fact that the academy in Köthen commissioned no such works, it counted among its members the philologist and literary figure Philipp Harsdörffer, who became secretary of the society, and Schottelius, who would publish his writings on grammar and lexicography in mid-century. The role language played in academies varied. In the Deutschgesinnete Genossenschaft (Brotherhood of the German-Minded), founded in about 1643, learned research on history and language became the dominant activity, while in the Pegnesischer Blumenorden (Flower Order of the Pegnitz), founded in 1644, literature and poetry played an increasingly important role. Of course, it is in the nature of academies that prescriptive efforts on behalf of a vernacular language could relegate other aims to the background. Instituting linguistic communication presumes the existence of the language in which it is encoded.

For precisely this reason, the document issued in Köthen and calling for refinement of the German language was not written in Latin as was Opitz's earlier *Aristarchus,* published in the same year. From the beginning, the Fruit-Bearing Society recognized the importance of using the vernacular ceremonially by devising an *impresa* for each new member and presenting it to him on admission. The *impresa* resembled an emblem or coat of arms, and consisted of a new name or designation, a motto, and an image; it could also contain an explanatory rhyming verse. When Opitz was admitted, the *impresa* alluded to the earlier custom of crowning poets while replacing it with the modern honor of induction into a learned society. Opitz received the epithet "der Bekrönte" (the crowned one); his motto was "mitt Diesem" (with this one), and in the foreground was a laurel tree and laurel wreath. In fact, the *Brief Report* conveys the impression that creating an epithet, motto, and image for each member was the society's chief activity. It was Prince Ludwig of Anhalt himself who designed the insignias, and after senior members had debated various suggestions and botanists and poets had submitted expert opinions, a new member was given a choice between several epithets and images. This led to further discussions on topics such as in which poetic form the explanatory verse should be couched; who would find a picture of the chosen object and prepare the copper engraving. And finally, the palace gardens in Köthen played a role, since all the epithets given to members were related to the cultivation and uses of plants. In the very act of admitting its members, the Fruit-Bearing Society fulfilled the purpose for which it had been founded: to foster conversation and literature in the German language. It appears almost symbolic of this closed circle of self-reference that the books published by the society at irregular intervals contained the society's own *impresa,* consisting of its designation as the "Fruit-Bearing Society," its motto, "useful in everything," and the image of a coconut tree, followed by a list of its members.

It is evident that German Baroque literature owes its beginnings to the interplay of two independent chains of events: efforts to create first of all a set of rules for the German language, and secondly a set of reliable and predictable conventions for social and linguistic interactions. The fact that both events—publication of the *Brief Report* and of the *Book of German Poetics*—occurred in close succession is related to political developments. In the winter of 1618, the Bohemian estates rebelled against the Catholic dynasty of the Habsburgs and declared Frederick V, the Elector Palatine and head of the Protestant Union, King of Bohemia. These events are connected to Opitz, since Heidelberg, where the poet spent a year important for his literary development as a student in 1619, was the capital of the Palatinate. There is also a connection to the Fruit-Bearing Society, since Christian von Anhalt, Frederick's most important adviser, was a brother of the academy's founder.

The rule of the Protestant King of Bohemia ended with his defeat at the Battle of the White Mountain near Prague in 1620, two years before publication of the *Brief Report* and four years before the *Book of German Poetics.* The Protestants' defeat, traditionally seen as the first stage in the Thirty Years' War, is now viewed as a failed attempt at founding a nation-state. In fact, Frederick's brief reign offered an alternative state to the Catholic Habsburg Empire. In addition to being Protestant, political power was vested in the estates more than in an absolute monarch. Frederick also sought to reorganize the educational system, drawing on Melanchthon's university reforms and Wolfgang Ratke's plans for school reform in Anhalt. In addition, he borrowed ideas—associated with Justus Lipsius and the House of Orange—from Dutch political theory and the reorganization of the Dutch army.

It seems clear that the founding of the Köthen academy and Opitz's literary reforms should be regarded as substitute or imitative actions that gained meaning from this political constellation. Nonetheless, identifying the political context does not reduce the tensions between the two programs and their ambiguous relationship to one another. Rather, both Opitz's poetics and the statutes of the academy were components of the overriding historical event—the attempt to establish a modern state within the German Empire, which ignited the Thirty Years' War.

See also 1515, 1523, 1551, 1638, 1657

Bibliography: Martin Opitz, *Gesammelte Werke,* ed. George Schulz-Behrend, vol. I: *Aristarchus sive De contemptu linguae Teutonicae;* vol. II: *Buch von der deutschen Poeterey* (Stuttgart: Hiersemann, 1968, 1978). Fürst Ludwig von Anhalt-Köthen, *Werke,* vol. I: *Kurtzer Bericht der Fruchtbringenden Gesellschaft Zweck und Vorhaben; Der Fruchtbringenden Gesellschaft Nahmen/Gemählde/ und Wörter* (1622), ed. Klaus Conermann (Tübingen: Niemeyer, 1992).

Rüdiger Campe
Translated by Deborah Lucas Schneider

✑ 1638

Twenty years into thirty years of war, Friedrich von Logau publishes 200 epigrams, with 3,360 to follow

Sense and Intellect

The opening epigram of Friedrich von Logau's (1604–1655) collection of *Reimen-Sprüche* (1638; *Rhyme Dicta*) traces the heritage of the Muses back to Jupiter, thereby legitimizing the poet's bloodline. The second takes on Momus, the carping critic of Greek myth banned from Olympus, the third Zoilus, another faultfinder. In the next, Logau laces into those who would lament the fallen heroes of his age: "Lament no more than this, that you're incapable of laments" (6). The tone of the volume is set. The young German nobleman Logau is to be the Momus of his age.

He implies that he alone possesses the poetic skill to address grand and small issues properly. A fifth poem wishes a young couple peace and fecundity on their marriage amidst times of "war and killing" (4)—marriage as the antidote to war. The next presents a pastoral scenario, while another has Fama, an allegorical voice, ironically addressing the current lack of agricultural productivity in a kind of reverse pastoral:

> In peace and stillness fully lies the land—
> Pasture's Sabbath day; fields so quiet lie
> And suffer not from plowman's brutal hand—
> No tyrant plow wounds deeply now and nigh. (6)

A ditty on flax follows and soon thereafter Logau offers thoughts on the pleasures of wine. And so it goes, as this formulator of epigrams generates rhymes on topics reflecting the conventions of the ancient form as well as the interests and concerns of his readers:

> This book it is the moon,
> Readers are its sun;
> So that at solar noon, moon
> reflects the other one. (26)

Logau's readers are a collective muse. His pseudonym, Salomon von Golaw (Golaw being an anagram of Logaw/u), implies that he is a latter-day Solomon, a critical voice and purveyor of wisdom, as in the Book of Wisdom from the Apocrypha.

The *Reimen-Sprüche* and the greatly expanded *Sinn-Gedichte* (1654; *Epigrams*) cemented their author's literary reputation. Born in Silesia, then an eastern border territory of the Holy Roman Empire, Logau lost his father, a member of the landed gentry, early on; he and his mother moved to Brieg, a nearby city centered on the court of a petty prince. Friedrich entered into the service of the duchess as a page even while completing schooling typical of the age: Latin, rhetoric, poetics, dialectics, philosophy, history, each set off against earnest Protestant piety, a Christian Humanist curriculum at its best. Subsequent education in law in Altdorf, a preeminent university of the empire, took him away from home to Nuremberg, one of Germany's greatest cities. Yet the firstborn returned to assume ownership of his father's Silesian estate in the 1630s, the decade during which the territory absorbed the brunt of the Thirty Years' War:

> Deserted fields, my devastated grounds I greet!
> As I survey you all, with dewy tears we meet,
> For you now are no more: Mars, that god,
> Murd'rous Mars, your lands he has down trod! (55)

Despite the war, ducal Brieg itself remained physically intact if not unaffected by dynastic gyrations. Logau was graced with posts in the chancellery, positions endowing him with security, prestige, and sufficient time to compose his 3,560 epigrams.

Friedrich von Logau's education would have exposed him to the works of his precursors. Martial's epigrams were standard educational fare during the early modern era, providing inspiration for German Neo-Latinist scholars. To emulate the writers of antiquity by composing epigrams was, thus, appropriate and culturally patriotic. Furthermore, Scaliger's Humanist poetics described the form so authoritatively that Martin Opitz, the German popularizer of Italian Renaissance literary theory, simply translated the Italian's definition of the epigram for his seminal German-language poetics of 1624. Logau elevates Opitz by equating him with Virgil, the poet of poets (428), and he paraphrases Scaliger on the title page of the *Sinn-Gedichte* (3). The title renders the compound word as "sense poem," as a text both fraught with meaning *(Sinn)* and as one exercising the intellect *(Sinn)* of the reader.

> Logau's epigrams possess a decided edginess:
> If my verses are not all good and always right;
> Well, the readers aren't always all ways bright. (43)

Epigrammatic wordplay cuts across languages, as in the double meaning of *Laus.* Latin for "praise" and German for "louse," these oddest of bedfellows are conjoined in meaningfully contrived play:

What Latin says for praise [*laus*], in German's footloose, free:
Laus tickles, hopes are raised; louse bites—sharp injury. (51)

When "Hofe-Leben" (life at court) is juxtaposed to "Hoffe-Leben" (life defined by unfulfilled hope), or when "Soldat" (soldier) becomes "als Tod" (as dead), Logau's deft deconstructions surprise, even as he unlocks and enhances the potential of the German language (31, 57).

Logau's manipulation of contents and words—the *res et verba* of early modern poetology—abets the satiric intent of the author. In the introduction to the 1654 imprint he maintains that "Sinn-Gedichte" are "kurtze Stichel-Gedichte," that is, "short satirical poems," or "words selected to represent all manner of things" for the purpose of raising an awareness of human shortcomings (2). There is nothing particularly new here, yet that Logau skewers large and small foibles *in German* in 200 poems (and then in an additional 3,360) marks his achievement as out of the ordinary.

Even though it remains unclear when he commenced jotting down his poems, internal evidence indicates that the epigrams in both collections are arranged in chronological order of composition as a kind of literary diary. There is an epigram to the year 1637 (63), one to 1638 (65), and others up until 1653 (619). There are numerous poems on war and soldiering and life at court, as well as on wine, women, song, death, taxes, virtues, sins, praise, and damnation. Little escapes Logau's attention as each human character or event passes in review. Yet, the courtier-poet takes care to direct his satire at types, not individuals:

> Fools have power over wise men: each transaction, each affair,
> Which the fools so badly muddle, wise men's wit must needs repair.
>
> (Schoolfield 219)

Logau's literary diary cajoles and warns, observes and comments carefully from behind a mask of sententious propriety:

> At court one talks of Truth not all too much a lot;
> he who could, would not; he who would, could not. (637)

Ultimately, Logau's literary artistry is wedded to rhetorical effect and affectation; life is but a play:

> A play from younger years I think of here and now,
> In which I played the king, while others manned the plow.
> And when the play was done, my kingship fell away,
> And I became again just who I am today. (28)

The deft poetic touch evidenced in the *Reimen-Sprüche* was sufficient to assure Logau's ritual induction into the foremost literary society of the era, the Fruit-Bearing Society (Fruchtbringende Gesellschaft). In 1648, he was granted membership and given the name "Der Verkleinernde," a singular honor that was the inspiration for a twenty-four-line poem (273). His designated name did not refer to his mastery of the diminutive poetic form (the verb *verkleinern* means "to make smaller, to reduce"), but rather honored his gracious humility, a courtly trait he likened to a supple bush unassumingly bowing before the wind (636).

Although his reputation was secure within 17th-century literary culture, it would likely have evaporated with time had it not been for Gotthold Ephraim Lessing (1729–1781), the prime mover of the German Enlightenment. He rescued Logau from neglect by republishing the *Sinn-Gedichte* in 1759. He announced the project in three self-serving epistolary reviews: "Soon we will see one of our best older poets emerge . . . As witty as Logau is, as tender, as sophisticated, as naive, he can also be so *galant!*"(77). Logau is identified as a "classic writer," as both a latter-day Martial and a forerunner of the Enlightenment(111). The didactic thrust of the epigram and the form's appeal to the intellect *(Sinn)* surely favored the revival of Logau's work, not to mention that young Lessing himself exhibited a facility for such verses.

Lessing's editorial project was an interpretive *Rettung,* the rescue of a kindred spirit. He and Karl Wilhelm Ramler (1725–1798) rearranged Logau's sequence, relocating poems on the nature of poetry and readership to the first and last positions in each of the twelve books. This framing makes the edition into a sort of poetics by exemplification, to which the philologist Lessing appends an extended Dictionary (352–411). He offers up-to-date explanations of hundreds of words and usages to ensure the 18th-century reader's appreciative understanding of the "modernity" of Logan's texts. *Sinn,* for example, is defined as "the genius, sensibilities, intellect, the capable mind" (399), all the exemplary traits of rationality. So understood, Logau's lines profess allegiance to "enlightened" values and the purpose of poetry:

> What my mind [*Sinn*], my pen has borne and seen the light of day,
> It shall stand, even if turned down, whatever one may say. (228)

The truth of Logau's pronouncement about the staying power of his epigrams was borne out by Lessing's continued attention to the poetic form. Lessing's essay *Zerstreute Anmerkungen über das Epigramm* (1771: *Musings on the Epigram*) opens with possible translations of the word *Epigramm* into German, predicting that Logau's usage *Sinngedicht* would prevail. Martial is held up as a model, even as Lessing comes to define the form's aesthetic dynamic in terms of *Erwartung* (anticipation) and *Aufschluss* (resolution; 188, 744–746). Lessing's extended theoretical musings, constantly tested on literary texts, "rescue" the form by giving it poetic legitimacy. Implicitly, he claims that Logau measures up to the likes of Martial, thereby ensuring him a place in the canon of German literature.

Since Lessing, the epigrams of Logau have been repeatedly anthologized. While many may be thematically bound to the religious conflict of the 17th century—"Lutheran, Popish, Calvinistic, all of these confessions three / Stand before us, yet we wonder where then Christendom may be" (Schoolfield 219)—the conventions of the form allow for clever observations transcending the historical reality of the Thirty Years' War:

> World this war has waged for more than twenty years;
> Now peace shall come again revoking all our fears.
> World waged this war for peace! Now just imagine that!
> We've won again what we once had before we ever fought. (118)

The wit pleases even as it enunciates an ironic truth, yet Gustav Eitner, the positivist scholar on whose edition study of Logau still relies, was at least as taken by the poet's supposed virtue as by his literariness. Eitner reads the epigrams as autobiographical statements revealing an exemplary morality, nobility of mind, and strength of purpose in times of depravity and war (719). Eitner's 1872 edition reduces Logau's work to a moral statement in the spirit of the Wilhelminian ideology of *Bildung*.

Subsequent editions of the *Sinngedichte* in 1972, 1974, and 1984 reflect the revival of scholarly interest in 17th-century German literary culture. The rich palette of topics explored by Logau documents the vital engagement of writers with the variegated context of their age. It is hardly coincidental, then, that Günter Grass seizes on the person and poetry of Logau—along with his fellow poets—in delineating the problematic interplay between politics and literature.

The action of Grass's cautionary tale *Das Treffen in Telgte* (1979; *The Meeting at Telgte*) is set in a community located on the road between the two cities in which the Treaty of Westphalia is being negotiated. The year is July 1647; the place, an inn; the players, twenty German writers of the 17th century, who gather to hammer out their own instrument of peace: "There they would sit until everything, the distress of the fatherland as well as the splendor and misery of poetry, had been discussed" (13). As much a commentary on the interminable war of the 20th century (1914–45) as on the Thirty Years' War, as much a parable of the ineffectuality of these intellectuals in advising politicians as anything else, Grass's novel stages a war of words. (The year 1647 alludes to the year 1947, the founding date of a postwar group of writers calling themselves Gruppe 47, which Grass met with regularly.) *Treffen* signifies both "meeting" and "battle," and both it is, with Logau in the midst of the fray: "Logau's curiosity about the meeting proved stronger than his scorn for the assembled poets" (5).

Grass has each writer read from works-in-progress, subjecting themselves to critique. Through it all, Logau is styled as the facile formulator of maxims to suit every occasion (20, 33, 37) as well as the champion of terse expressiveness (60, 68, 82) and subversive sarcasm (88, 98). His turn comes (as Grass cites actual epigrams): "The Belittler was his title in the Fruit-bearing Society. And Logau spoke with his trusted succinctness. Sarcastically and too irreverently for some of the listeners' taste, he said more in two lines than a long dissertation could have unsaid. About the religions, for instance: 'Lutheran, Papist, Calvinist—these faiths exist all three. But who can tell us just what is Christianity?' Or in view of the coming peace: 'When peace is made amid such devastation, Hangmen and jurisconsults will dominate the nation'" (74). It is a performance met with general approbation by the circle of poets, and the story's anonymous narrator who witnesses the meeting hints, by negative association, that he might just be Logau: "How do I know all this? I was sitting in their midst, I was there . . . Who was I? Neither Logau nor Gelnhausen" (84). Grass's statement privileges Logau, a factor accounting for the poet's crucial role as critic of the manifesto. Gelnhausen is another name for Simplicissimus, the protagonist of Grimmelshausen's picaresque novel on the Thirty Years' War, and a spirited observer of the poets' meeting in Telgte. The anonymous narrator (Grass?) styles himself as (n)either Logau (n)or his creation Simplicissimus—Logau was alleged to be the author of Simplicissimus, a work actually written by Grimmelshausen.

The meeting of the poets in Telgte has been convened to formulate a statement to the politicians negotiating the peace. On completion of the script it is read aloud and revealed to be both conceptually diffuse and stylistically abominable. It is Logau who excoriates his colleagues: "No! he cried several times . . . No! Before and after. Absolutely: No! . . . Pitiful, hypocritical, cried Logau, who, relinquishing expressive brevity, casting off the irony that makes for succinctness, was angry enough to make a long speech aimed at stripping sentence after sentence of its verbal frumpery . . . Logau's speech inspired gloom rather than disorder . . . Once again the poets were certain of their impotence and their inadequate knowledge of political forces" (122–23).

Brutally honest Logau delivers his ruthless assessment, one which effects change for the better (126), but as the inn in Telgte burns down behind the fleeing poets, the final revision goes up in flames: "The manifesto! . . . Where? Who? . . . The German poets' appeal for peace had been forgotten . . . on the long table. In defiance of all reason, Logau wanted to run back . . . to save the screed! Czepko had to hold him. And so, what would in any case not have been heard, remained unsaid" (131). Grass's cautionary tale centers on an imagined Logau with his death-defying commitment to engaged literariness, a fitting accolade at the last.

See also 1622, 1767, 1958

Bibliography: Friedrich von Logau, Erstes Hundert Teutscher Reimen-Sprüche Salomons von Golaw (Breslau: David Müller, 1638).———, Salomons von Golaw Deutscher Sinn-Gedichte Drey Tausend (Breslau: Caspar Klossmann, 1654), rept. as Friedrichs von Logau Sämmtliche Sinngedichte, ed. Gustav Eitner (Tübingen: Litterarischer Verein, 1872); page references are to Eitner's edition. Gerhard Dünnhaupt, "Friedrich von Logau," in Personalbibliographien zu den Drucken des Barock, 2nd ed. (Stuttgart: Anton Hiersemann, 1991), 4: 2584–88. "Friedrichs von Logau Sinngedichte: Zwölf Bücher," in G. E. Lessing, Sämtliche Werke, vol. 7, Karl Lachmann, Franz Muncker, eds. (Stuttgart: Göschen, 1891), 125–411. Günter Grass, The Meeting at Telgte, trans. Ralph Manheim

(New York: Harcourt Brace Jovanovich, 1981). *The German Lyric of the Baroque in English Translation,* ed. George C. Schoolfield (Chapel Hill: University of North Carolina Press, 1961).

Richard Erich Schade

℥ 1647

Adam Olearius publishes a firsthand account of Muscovy and Safavid Persia, the most popular Baroque travel narrative

The Dramaturgy of Travel

How would a European traveler in 17th-century Persia cure a scorpion sting? One could follow the treatment of the locals, who first tied a little piece of copper to the wound, and later put honey and vinegar on it. For tarantula bites, they also claimed that the spider should be killed and placed on the wound, so that the poison would return to its source. Toward the end of the Thirty Years' War, the learned German traveler Adam Olearius (1599–1671) provided this kind of practical travel advice in the descriptions of his travel experiences abroad, first in the *Offt Begehrte Beschreibung der Newen Orientalischen Reise* (1647; *The Oft-Requested Description of the New Oriental Journey*), then in a considerably expanded second edition, *Vermehrte Newe Beschreibung der Muscowitischen und Persischen Reyse* (1656; *Expanded New Description of the Muscovite and Persian Journey*). A bestseller in the author's lifetime, it is the only major German Baroque non-devotional work to have been translated from German into other foreign languages during the 17th century. A sense of the author's concerns and writing style can be gained from the following short selection:

> The Persian city of Kāshān is an important commercial center, with a thriving, international bazaar, wonderful caravanserais, a magnificent *maidan* (city square), and large, beautiful houses. The surrounding area engages in viniculture, fruit cultivation, and has very fertile fields. There is a problem, however:
>
> No city in all of Persia is so plagued by vermin as Kāshān, especially by scorpions . . . We found a number of them in our sleeping quarters, the ones which are black as coal, as long and thick as a finger, and are supposed to be the most poisonous . . . Out of the entire group I was the only one who had to experience such misery firsthand . . . On the return trip, during the night, I was stung by a scorpion in the neck, near my throat. A blister half the size of a finger appeared right away and burned as though coals had been placed there . . . I still felt the pain many years thereafter during the fall season . . . but I don't want to imply that it was caused by the sun being in the sign of Scorpio.

(Vermehrte Newe Beschreibung, 494–496)

This description of Kāshān situates the author squarely within his time, namely at the juncture between the Renaissance, with its emphasis on the classical tradition, and the rational, more "scientific" method of inquiry that is associated with the European Enlightenment. The landscape is objectively observed, together with the native methods of treatment while popular superstition is not entirely discounted, as seen by the mention of the zodiacal influence. The fauna are minutely described and characterized—a process that is applied to the region's inhabitants as well—and their dangerous, exotic qualities are underlined. However, in the case of the black scorpions, the menace is ultimately tamed, and put on display in the Western forerunner of the modern museum. As the author notes, he took a scorpion back home and "now it lies in oil in the Gottorf cabinet of curiosities" (*Vermehrte Newe Beschreibung,* 495). The engraving accompanying this passage depicts a cityscape of Kāshān, and includes the prominent front and back view of a tarantula in the cartouche, as well as several scorpions that seem to be hiding on and alongside it.

This account of a trading expedition to Persia via Muscovy, lasting from 1635 to 1639, under the auspices of the small northern German duchy of Holstein-Gottorf, tells its story through both verbal and visual means. In true Baroque style, the *Expanded New Description* is a scholarly proto-ethnography, containing information on geography, biology, linguistics, history, and natural history. The section on Persia, and the author's various activities there, highlights the peculiar structure of a Baroque travel account and explains its popularity, not only in the German-speaking lands, but across Europe as well.

New and compelling about Olearius's narrative is that he actually traveled to the areas he describes. Although several contemporary accounts concerning Persia, its land, and its inhabitants had appeared in the early 17th century, most were written by learned armchair geographers who had never journeyed to the country. Olearius's text still draws on the traditional image of the region as it was constructed in the works of such classical authors as Xenophon, Herodotus, and Quintus Curtius Rufus. But he also provides eyewitness information about the lands, peoples, flora and fauna he encountered, and then either substantiates or corrects widely held notions about the area.

While Olearius's travels took him to Muscovy and Persia, accounts written by German travelers in the age of exploration and incipient colonial expansion span the globe. Closer to home, descriptions of the Holy Land abound, as well as of the Ottoman Empire, whose military prowess was a constant source of both fear and fascination for a Europe threatened by Ottoman expansion, until the Turkish defeat at the gates of Vienna in 1680. Firsthand accounts range from the German soldier Hans Staden's description of his capture and eventual escape from the Tupinamba Indians of Brazil (1557; *Wahrhaftige Historia und beschreibung eyner Landschaft der Wilden Nackten Grimmigen Menschenfresser Leuthen, in der Newenwelt Amerika gelegen; The True Story and Description of a Landscape of the Savage, Naked, Fierce Cannibalistic People, Located in the New World of America*) and extend to Jesuit missionary accounts of the far-off lands of China and Japan, which emphasize the martyrdom of heroic priests as defenders of the faith.

The story of the Holstein expedition to Persia begins in 1633, at the midpoint of the Thirty Years' War, when Duke Frederick III, ruler of the duchy of Holstein-Gottorf, sought to convince Shah Safī I of Persia to export his country's silk products via the Volga, through Muscovy and the Baltic regions, to Gottorf; from there it would be sold throughout Northern Europe. The Ottoman monopoly on the trade carried exorbitant tariffs. In 1635, after coming to an agreement with Czar Michael, the first Romanov, the duke's embassy set out for the Shah's capital in Esfahān, accompanied by the celebrated poet Paul Fleming (1609–1640) and about one hundred support personnel. Adam Olearius—born Adam Öhlschlegel in 1599, the son of a tailor, and a distinguished graduate of the University of Leipzig in philosophy and the natural sciences—was chosen to chronicle the mission as its official secretary.

After a long, hazardous journey the travelers returned home in 1639. Along the way, they had to contend with hostile Cossacks, Dagestani Tatars, and Uzbeks, as well as shipwrecks on the North Sea and the Caspian Sea. The trouble paid off when soon afterward, a delegation from Shah Safī arrived in Gottorf to discuss details of the proposed agreement, express the Shah's friendship to the Duke, and invite further contact. As it turned out, the few bales of silk, which the Persian emissaries presented to Duke Frederick as a gift from the Shah, were the only amounts of the precious material that ever made it to Gottorf. Several factors contributed to the failure of the venture: the long, dangerous route; the high tariffs extracted by the Czar, as well as by the Swedes, who controlled shipping along the Baltic; the presence of rival Dutch trading companies in Esfahān; and most significantly, the fact that Persia did not produce enough silk to make the venture profitable.

The success of Olearius's account came in large part from his skillful use of visual and verbal material. Along with the numerous engravings (ca. 120 out of 800 folio pages), "drawn from life," the most practical and lasting result of the trip was the production of superior maps of the areas traveled. They improved and corrected previous depictions, many of which still adhered to the Ptolemaic system of the world.

The *Expanded New Description* includes large, detailed foldout maps of Moscow and the course of the Volga. The exactitude of this map, which maintained its validity until well into the 18th century, so impressed Czar Michael that he later attempted to enlist Olearius's services. Olearius's map of Persia and the Caspian Sea, the "Nova Delineatio Persiae," is a fascinating cartographic text that shows the influence of Islamic learning gleaned especially from Timurid and Persian sources.

An examination of the engraved frontispiece on the title page of one of Olearius's editions shows the specific interplay of image and text. The introductory image of a typical Baroque publication can be seen as a kind of portal or gateway to the written description that follows. The recondite imagery and allegorical figures of the frontispiece are learned signifiers belonging to the microcosmic visual world that reflects and prefigures the verbal description, which forms the body of the work.

Thus the frontispiece acts as a visual microcosm of the book—the textual macrocosm—it introduces, and the title-page is meant to intrigue the reader

Frontispiece to the first edition of Olearius's travel narrative. (University of Chicago Library)

through a complex set of images—taken from classical coins and medals, from devices and emblems, from Egyptian hieroglyphs and medieval treatises, which, however, can only be fully decoded by reading the book. Nature in all its manifestations—animal, vegetable, and mineral—must be displayed on a stage, be it the "stage" of the title page or the compartments of a cabinet of curiosities into which the exotic objects are placed for people to examine. Most Renaissance and Baroque title-pages were modeled on classical architecture: an arch or gateway, resting on a platform or plinth, symbolized the formal entrance to the work, a design that recalls the structures of allegorical tableaux used for triumphal entries into Italian and Dutch Renaissance cities honoring the hero of the day.

The frontispiece to the first edition of the travel account *The Oft-Requested Description of the New Oriental Journey* (Schleswig, 1647) presents a mixture of realistic and fantastic images about the journey to Muscovy and Persia. The architectural frame—festooned with swags of exotic fruits—is crowned with a profile portrait of Olearius within an oval cartouche, from which a cloth of honor has been drawn back. A Persian silk carpet with a floral pattern—representing the economic incentive for the journey—partially conceals the title of the work. The author's name below the title stands out unobscured. The carpet and the cloth of honor serve a similar function, in that they uncover the author's image on the entablature as well as his inscribed name and the title of his magnum opus. The illusionist fabrics denote not only an act of uncovering, but of discovery as well. As in a theater, the curtains are pulled back on the top and middle registers to reveal the true subject of the work, which, appropriately, is located in the center, a paradisiacal scene, flanked by exotic natives standing on plinths. These "natives" are on the right of a Russian boyar, a servant half-hidden behind him, standing above a scallop-shaped cartouche depicting Saint George slaying the dragon. On the left, a Persian nobleman holds a hooded falcon in his right hand; below him is the symbol of Persia, a lion and a rising sun.

In the Garden of Eden scene a leopard in the foreground sniffs at a hare; a lion lies with a lamb (as in the biblical citation); and in the background, an elephant leans against a palm tree. What is implied in this frontispiece is the presence of Adam—that is, of Adam Olearius, whose image and name are found just above the Garden scene. Adam's function is to name—and illustrate—the exotic wonders and foreign objects for his Western audience. He contributes to the information contained within the universe, thus fulfilling a quasi-religious function: his role as scholar and explorer is to add to the knowledge of the world, and as a New Adam, he too is helping to re-create the lost paradise on earth (in word and image) through his encyclopedic travel account.

Besides preparing the different accounts of the journey, editing the poetic works of his prematurely deceased friend Paul Fleming, and working on a (never published) Persian-Turkish-Arabic dictionary, Olearius had many other duties in Gottorf which kept him extremely busy until his death in 1671. Duke

Frederick appointed him court librarian and charged him with cataloguing and expanding the ducal collection. At the same time, Olearius built an astrolabe, a microscope, a telescope, and his crowning achievement, a giant globe, which was later presented to Peter the Great. All these achievements gained Olearius the sobriquet "the Holstein Pliny."

As the Persian delegation was making ready to leave Gottorf in 1639, several delegates defected, among them the secretary, Hakwirdi. This was to prove most fortunate for Olearius, since he was now able to perfect his knowledge of Persian, as well as check the information he had acquired abroad with a cultured native informant. Most importantly, Hakwirdi helped Olearius to translate the celebrated Persian poet Saʿdī's *Gulistān* (1258), under the title *Persianischer Rosenthal* (1654; *Persian Valley of Roses*), which found a most favorable resonance among the German literary public.

Olearius was writing in the period after the publication of Martin Opitz's *Buch von der deutschen Poeterey* (1624; *Book of German Poetics*)—a poetics that emphasized the importance of the German language—and in the era of *Sprachgesellschaften* (language academies charged with fostering the development of the German language). In *Persianischer Rosenthal,* the entire enterprise of translation is cloaked in highly metaphoric language. Olearius notes that it was the head of the Fruchtbringende Gesellschaft (Fruit-Bearing Society) himself who asked him to translate the *Gulistan* into German, and not into Latin. Nationalist sentiment is underlined in the idea that "our German language that used to lie beneath the dust of contempt now shines forth once again" (*Persianischer Rosenthal,* B2v).

Olearius's translation of Saʿdī, along with his travel account, find their echo in the works of the most influential German Baroque authors, such as Jakob von Grimmelshausen (1668; *Simplicius Simplicissimus*), Daniel Caspar von Lohenstein (1673; *Ibrahim Bassa* and *Ibrahim Sultan*), and Andreas Gryphius (1657; *Catharina von Georgien*) and, in the following centuries, in the works of Montesquieu (1721; *Lettres Persanes*). Even Goethe—when discussing the sources of his *West-östlicher Divan* (1819; *West-East Divan*), a cycle of poems steeped in the oriental tradition—acknowledges an intellectual debt to our traveler, when he praises the "integrity of the excellent Olearius," who "gives us extremely enjoyable and educational travel accounts." After this brief overview of the intrepid traveler's life and work, we may agree with Goethe that "we are loath to break off here, because we too wanted to give ample thanks to this man for the good things which we owe him" ("Noten," 243).

See also 1478, 1515, 1622, 1647 (Gryphius), 1797, 1831

Bibliography: *The Travels of Olearius in Seventeenth-Century Russia,* trans. Samuel Baron (Stanford, Calif.: Stanford University Press, 1967). Elio Brancaforte, *Visions of Persia: Mapping the Travels of Adam Olearius* (Cambridge, Mass.: Harvard University Department of Comparative Literature, 2003). John Emerson, "Adam Olearius and the Literature of the Schleswig-Holstein Missions to Russia and Iran, 1633–1639," in *Études safavides,* ed. Jean Calmard (Paris: Institut français de recherche en Iran, 1993). Johann Wolfgang von Goethe, "Noten und Abhandlungen zu besserem Verständnis des *West-Östlichen Divans*," in *Werke, Hamburger Ausgabe in 14 Bänden*, ed. Erich Trunz (Munich: DTV/Beck, 1988), vol. 2. Adam Olearius, *Offt begehrte Beschreibung Der Newen Orientalischen Reise* (Schleswig: Zur Glocken, 1647). ———, *Persianischer Rosenthal* (Schleswig: Johann Holwein, 1654). ———, *Vermehrte Newe Beschreibung der Muscowitischen und Persischen Reyse (1656)*, ed. Dieter Lohmeier, *Deutsche Neudrucke 21* (Tübingen: Niemeyer, 1971). ———, *The Voyages & Travels of the Ambassadors*, trans. John Davies (London: Thomas Dring and John Starkey, 1662).

Elio Brancaforte

🎵 1647

As the Thirty Years' War draws to a close, Andreas Gryphius returns to Silesia after several years of study abroad

Anatomy and Theology, Vanity and Redemption

In the preface to his second play, *Catharina von Georgien (Catherine of Georgia)*, Andreas Gryphius (1616–1664) notes that by the time the text was finally published in 1657, it had been incarcerated in his study longer than the play's heroine in the dungeons of the Persian Shah. If his 17th-century biographer Siegmund von Stosch is to be believed, Gryphius completed his first martyr drama a decade earlier, on the eve of the signing of the Peace of Westphalia (1648), upon returning to his native, war-ravaged Silesia from several years of travel and study throughout Europe. He studied six years at the most famous Protestant university in Leiden (1638–1644). Previously awarded a Master's degree and crowned poet laureate by his Silesian patron George Schönborner, Gryphius was entitled to teach "collegia" there himself, and as a Baroque polymath, he lectured on a wide range of subjects including metaphysics, natural philosophy, geography, trigonometry, logic, and astronomy.

Intrigued by Leiden's famous anatomical theater, second only to Padua's, Gryphius conducted several public dissections there and even held a "Collegium Anatomicum Practicum" in 1643. The corpse on the dissection table, often an executed criminal, provided, as Stosch remarks, the perfect "excerpt and model of the universe," an emblem of a war-torn Europe completely out of joint. The theater's space itself was a forceful reminder to its Baroque audience of the vanity and frailty of man steeped in original sin, as it was adorned with skeletons and props of vanity alongside familiar moralizing inscriptions such as "Nosce te ipsum" (Know thyself), "Pulvis et umbra sumus" (We are dust and shadows), "Nascentes morimur" (We are born to die).

However, the previous use of the building that housed the Leidener *theatrum anatomicum* adds a complementary and more redemptive dimension to anatomical dissection in early modern culture. When the Board of Curators decided, at the urging of the newly appointed chair of anatomy, Pieter Pauw, to establish a permanent anatomical theater in 1591, they chose the Beguinage chapel that had earlier belonged to the lay sisterhood of the Beguines. Where the altar had once stood, now stood the dissection table, and where the priest had previously broken bread, the divine body, during the Eucharistic sacrifice, the anatomist now celebrated the glory of God by rending the human body during the liturgy of public dissection.

Analogous to the Holy Communion, the mystery of incarnation lay at the heart of this sacred anatomy. Clothed in human form, the Son was sent to redeem fallen humanity from the bondage of mortality by permitting His own humiliation and sacrifice as a common criminal. A striking emblem of sinfulness and vanity, the corpse displayed in the anatomical theater also recalls Christ's execution as a criminal and becomes a figure of redemption. Similarly, the allegory of vanity so central and ubiquitous in the Baroque mourning play (Barockes Trauerspiel) dialectically gives rise, as Walter Benjamin observed in *The Origin of German Tragic Drama* (1925), to an allegory of resurrection and redemption.

The scenario of the prologue to *Catharina von Georgien* visually re-creates such an anatomical theater of vanity. The stage directions describe the scene as littered with corpses, crowns, scepters, and swords, the insignia of earthly power ("voll Leichen-Bilder/Cronen/Zepter/Schwerdter etc.") sandwiched between heaven and hell. Surrounded by these props of vanity, Eternity reminds the audience that all things temporal, contrary to their appearance, are in fact nothing and further exhorts her listeners to turn toward God before it is too late—much as Gryphius doubtlessly emphasized in his public oration "de rerum omnium vanitate" ("regarding the vanity of all things") in Leiden. Eternity's hasty departure, though, hints at the representational dilemma at the core of Gryphius's tragedies, namely the radical incongruity between eternity and temporality. While Eternity has no place in the realm of the temporal, she is replaced by the play's heroine, who exemplifies a lesser, more human form of eternity, that is, constancy, as the subtitle "Oder Bewehrete Beständigkeit" (Or Proven Constancy) indicates. With the figure of Catharina, Gryphius replaces the neo-Stoic concept of constancy based on an ethics of self-reliance with a more Christian version, one that is simultaneously grounded in human vulnerability and divine grace. Replicating Christ's passion in her violent death by torture at the hands of the Persian Shah, the Christian martyr Catharina joins, like the Word become flesh, time and eternity. Gryphius's Protestant tragedies demonstrate that the mystery of incarnation in all its hermeneutic opacity can be grasped only by faith (*sola fide*).

Seeking to establish a German dramatic tradition, writing in German and independent of foreign models, Gryphius put into dramatic practice the formal prescripts regarding subject, language, and meter of both comedy and tragedy that his fellow Silesian Martin Opitz had presented in *Buch von der deutschen Poeterey* (1624; *Book of German Poetics*). During his travels through Europe, Gryphius became acquainted with much of contemporary tragedy, especially the neo-Latin dramas of the Jesuit theater and the Dutch dramas of Joost van den Vondel (1587–1679) and P. C. Hooft (1581–1647). He translated Vondel's biblical tragedy *Gebroeders* (1640) and the hagiographical play *Felicitas* (1620) of the Jesuit Nicolaus Caussin as literary exercises in the 1640s and even taught a Collegium Tragicum at Leiden in order to develop his own tragic

German lands and the Holy Roman Empire after the Peace of Westphalia, 1648. The German lands were a mosaic of principalities, duchies, archbishoprics, and other dominions.

style. Gryphius, however, proudly declared his independence from foreign models in the preface to his first tragedy, *Leo Armenius,* written in 1646 and published in 1650.

In the same preface, he proclaimed that *Catharina von Georgien* would improve upon the flawed example set by Corneille's *Polyeucte* and set a new model for martyr drama. While Gryphius continued to adhere to the prescription of Renaissance poetics, which demanded history as a topic for tragedy dramatizing the mutability of fortune and the downfall of kings, his tragic representation of a Christian version of history was meant not only to fortify the spectator against future misfortune, but to have a cathartic effect as well, by liberating the audience from its fetishistic attachment to the temporal and redirect it toward the divine—just as the allegory of Eternity attempts in the prologue of *Catharina von Georgien.*

In a dialectical—or according to Benjamin—allegorical fashion, the theatrical representation of human misfortune and misery upheld redemption accessible only through faith in the infinite grace of God. Gryphius's religious drama thus had a profoundly consolatory effect as it focused on God's grace mediated through the Word made flesh, the coming of the Son. Guided by his religious beliefs, the devout Lutheran Gryphius thus placed the mystery of incarnation—that the Word was made flesh—at the center of dramatic production.

Gryphius's Christo-centrism accords the genre of the martyr drama particular significance. The dramatization of the martyr's superhuman fortitude became a model for ideal behavior of persecuted Christians and encouraged believers of various denominations to remain constant and to defend their respective faiths in post-Reformation Europe. The visual immediacy and theatrical ostentation with which *Catharina von Georgien* was staged at the court of Duke Christian of Wohlau in 1655 further impressed the audience with the presence of God's redemptive force, despite the ecclesiastical body's irreparable division after a century of religious war. The subject Gryphius chose for his first martyr drama, however, did not come from the classical canon of Christian martyrs the Jesuits exploited in their Counter-Reformation propaganda. Instead he chose to dramatize contemporary events.

Catharine of Georgia's martyrdom had taken place in 1624, slightly more than two decades before its dramatic rendition. The French chronicler Claude Malingre, Sieur de Saint-Lazare (1580–1653), recounts the fate of the Georgian queen in the sixteenth piece ("Histoire de Catherine Reyne de Georgie et des Princes Georgiques mis à mort par commandement de Cha-Abas Roy de Perse") of his *Histoires tragiques de notre temps* (Paris, 1635). Catharina travels to the Persian court to further her son Tamaras and to negotiate favorable conditions for her country, geographically and politically wedged between the powerful enemies Turkey and Persia. Chah Abas falls in love with her and pressures her to marry him and to convert to Islam. But Catharina remains steadfast in her Christian faith. Angered by her refusal, Chah Abas imprisons and subjects her to endless tortures. The intervention of the Russian czar on her behalf inaugurates the tragic conflict, forcing Abas either to free and thereby lose her or to keep and thereby kill her. By choosing the latter, he accedes to Catharina's desire for a martyr's death by insisting on spiritual and sexual integrity. The queen's fate resonated with Gryphius's Silesian audience not only spiritually, but politically as well. They saw in Catharina's situation and that of her small country, Georgia-Gurgistan, a conspicuous resemblance with their own homeland. As part of the Holy Roman Empire, the predominantly Protestant Silesia was recatholicized in the course of the Habsburg Counter-Reformation politics. Andreas Gryphius was also particularly sensitive to the precarious position of the Protestant Silesian estates, whose legal representative (Landsyndicus) to the Catholic emperor he was to become later in 1650. By politicizing sexuality and sexualizing politics, Gryphius fashioned Catharina's spiritual and sexual integrity into an emblem for the political inviolability of Silesia itself.

Catharina's chastity has as much theological as political significance, for while her sexual abstinence calls into question the patriarchal authority of the Persian Shah, it also represents the sexual constancy characteristic of the Christian martyr. Rather than marrying a Muslim ruler, she chooses martyrdom that betrothes her to Christ. Instead of choosing the love of temporal things, she chooses the love of things eternal.

Situated between these two alternatives, between the earthly and the heavenly, her person functions literally as a medium and her chaste body becomes a battlefield where divine and temporal powers clash. Despite the haunting sense of distance between the divine and the human, which Benjamin observed for the 17th century in general and for Lutheranism in particular, the image of Catharina's unconscripted body offered the Baroque spectator the possibility of joining these antithetical spheres. Virginity as an ideal, which was first articulated by the Patristic writers in Late Antiquity (intimate knowledge of whose writings Gryphius's funeral orations amply document), is ultimately grounded in the central mystery of Christian faith, the Word made flesh. As one Patristic treatise phrased it, a virgin is "the Holy Spirit given a body."

Catharina remains as constant in her faith as in her chastity. Constancy and its presentation are only means to a higher end, what Gryphius terms in the preface "die Ehre Gottes auszustreichen" (to strike out—in the sense of "highlight"— God's honor). To bear testimony to God, to sanctify His name in order to honor Him is the martyr's primary aspiration. Stemming from Greek legal language, the terms "martyr" and "martyrdom" mean "witness" and "testimony" or "bearing witness" respectively, at trial or otherwise. Similar to the Eucharistic utterance, "this is my body," martyrdom always implies an act of speech. Consistent with Protestantism's preoccupation with Holy Scripture, the Lutheran Gryphius figures the speech act of martyrdom as an act of writing, as the highlighting, "Ausstreichen," of God's honor and name with Catharina's blood as ink and her chaste body as the pure writing surface. This act of writing, the "Ausstreichen," becomes coextensive with the cut of the anatomical scalpel which destroys the fragile human frame as it reveals the majesty of God, in the moment when Gryphius stages Catharina's torture in all its gruesome, bloody detail, as the pictorial documents of the 1655 production suggest. "Ausstreichen" and its other variant "heraus streichen," which Gryphius employs a few lines later in the same preface, recalls the dialectical movement that engenders the allegory of resurrection. Through this inscription "the divine is given a body" displacing other contesting worldly inscriptions. Paradoxically, God's *Ehre* (honor) is simultaneously crossed out and erased in its "incarnation," since this act of writing, in which God guides the hand of Chah Abas and the executioner, destroys the "writing pad," and thereby itself. The inscription of God's honor is, therefore, simultaneously its erasure.

This graphic manifestation of the divine comes only at the expense of the erasure of the actual living body. With the loss of the living body, however, the divine loses its place and withdraws. Thus, the theatrics of anatomical dissection, as it was practiced in Leiden, and Gryphius's theatrics of martyrdom share the same paradoxical phenomenology. To quote from a sermon by Martin Luther of the year 1517: "Homo abscondit sua ut neget, Deus abscondit sua ut revelet." In contrast to man, God does not hide himself in His invisibility, but rather in the visibility of the Word become flesh. Inversely, the divine shows itself only in the opacity of the corpo-real—a corpo-real that must be obliterated, "ausgestrichen," by the cuts of the anatomical scalpel or the *arma martyrii*.

See also 1522, 1609, 1622–1624, 1927 (March)

Bibliography: Andreas Gryphius, *Catharina von Georgien* (Stuttgart: Reclam, 1975). Andreas Gryphius, *Gesamtausgabe der deutschsprachigen Werke, Trauerspiele III,* ed. Hugh Powell (Tübingen: Niemeyer, 1966). Walter Benjamin, *The Origin of German Tragic Drama,* trans. John Osborne (New York: Verso, 1998).

Christopher J. Wild

♫ *1657–1686*

Three very different works by Johannes Scheffler, Catharina Regina von Greiffenberg, and Quirinus Kuhlmann use poetry to treat Christian themes

Poems as Way-Signs

These 17th-century texts—Johannes Scheffler's *Geistreiche Sinn- und Schluß-reime,* Catharina Regina von Greiffenberg's *Geistliche Sonette,* and Quirinus Kuhlmann's *Der Kühlpsalter*—all use poetic forms to treat Christian themes, but their authors could not be more different. Scheffler (b. 1624) came from a noble family and was raised in Lutheran Breslau (Wroclaw). He studied medicine and practiced as a physician. During the Habsburg campaign to recatholicize the Protestant cities of Silesia, he publicly converted to Catholicism (12 June 1653) and changed his name to Johannes Angelus, and he later became a priest (29 May 1661). He took part in many Counter-Reformation ceremonies and published numerous polemical writings in his lifetime. He died in Breslau in 1677. Greiffenberg was born into a Protestant noble family in Counter-Reformation Lower Austria in 1633, and dedicated her life to God. As the Habsburgs exerted more religious pressure and the Turkish wars overran Lower Austria, she moved to Nuremberg, where she had already made contacts with poetic circles during a previous visit in 1663–1665. She remained in that city from 1680 until her death in 1694. Kuhlmann was born into a merchant family in Breslau in 1651. He studied law and later traversed Europe, attracting, and then alienating, admirers with his eschatological prophecies. In Istanbul he made an unsuccessful attempt to convert the Sultan. He was burned at the stake for heresy, conspiracy, and blasphemy in Moscow on 4 October 1689.

These are only three of a long line of 17th-century writers who created a huge corpus of poetry on religious themes. Among the best-known are the Jesuit Friedrich Spee von Langenfeld, the Capuchin friar Laurentius von Schnüfis, the Saxon court preacher Johann Ulrich König, the parson Johann Rist, and laypeople such as Martin Opitz, Daniel Czepko von Reigersfeld, Friedrich von Logau, Anna Owena Hoyers, Simon Dach, Paul Gerhardt, Johann Klaj, Paul Fleming, Andreas Gryphius, Prince Anton Ulrich zu Braunschweig-Lüneburg. But these three authors are, despite their differences, often mentioned in one breath, usually accompanied sometime before or after by the word "mystic." It is difficult to see what common features they may have. Certainly all three avoid the most communal of Christian poetic forms, the hymn. Their poems manifest a close personal relationship with the Christian deity, but that could also be said of most of the authors listed above. What apparently sets writers apart as mystic is a certain degree of inscrutability. Each of these poets produced inscrutability—often linked in discussions of mysticism with the term "ineffability." There are, however, many ways of being inscrutable.

Scheffler, usually referred to by his pseudonym Angelus Silesius, published pastoral songs of love between the soul and Christ (1657; expanded ed. 1668), a vivid description of Last Things (that is, death, judgment, heaven, and hell; 1675) and fifty-five Catholic polemical tracts, starting with a defense of his conversion. But he is best known for his pocket-size book of epigrams, *Cherubinischer Wandersmann* (Cherubic Wanderer), in mostly rhymed couplets (1657; pirate ed. 1657; new ed. 1675; expanded ed. 1675). Logau and Spee wrote epigrams in German, and the form was popular in Latin as well, for the concentration of a complex idea into a concise form allowed for the display of wit. Many of Angelus's epigrams are based on a *concetto*, whose layers of meaning must be peeled away. The *concetto* works by grafting two structures of meaning onto each other, and the interpretation consists in working out the structural similarities:

> Das Hertz ist GOttes Herd. (1.66)
> Wo GOtt ein Fewer ist
> so ist mein Hertz der Herd Auf welchem Er das
> Holtz der Eittelkeit verzehrt.

> The heart is the hearth of God. (1.66)
> If God is a fire, then my heart is the hearth
> on which he consumes the wood of vanity.

God is associated with fire (for example, the Burning Bush in Exodus 1), and many of Angelus's poems discuss what happens when God comes to dwell in the heart of the individual Christian. The analogy goes beyond assimilating the image schema "container/contained" (God is "in" the heart like a fire in the fireplace), to add another element to the concept "hearth": "wood." Here the extension of the analogy allows Angelus to discuss the process of purification that happens when the soul allows God to enter. Note that the analogy is couched not in a simile ("like a fire"), but in a logical framework: insofar as God is said to be a fire, God's presence in the heart is active and purificatory, and the wood is what is consumed.

This process of purification leads, for Angelus, to a state where the Christian becomes like God, or even (so to speak) becomes what God is:

> GOtt lebt nicht ohne mich. (1.8)
> Ich weiß daß ohne mich GOtt nicht ein Nun kan leben /
> ★Werd' ich zu nicht, Er muß von Noth den Geist auffgeben.

> God does not live without me. (1.8)
> I know that God cannot live without me for an instant;
> ★If I disappear, he must give up the ghost.

Such an assertion can quickly lead to accusations of heresy, and the asterisk in the second line leads to a note referring us to the preface, where other visionaries, including John the Evangelist and Bernard of Clairvaux, are cited for the orthodoxy of the expression. The preface claims that these first epigrams were written quickly, in a fit of divine inspiration, and Angelus published his book with two testimonials by members of the ecclesiastical hierarchy.

In fact, the doctrine of deification had already drawn criticism (Gerson) in the 14th and 15th centuries, providing what Jaroslav Pelikan calls "a vulnerable point of mystical theology." Angelus belongs to this (somewhat controversial) tradition. Through Abraham von Franckenburg, Scheffler was familiar with the works of Jacob Böhme, Mechthild of Magdeburg, Bridget of Sweden (ca. 1303–1373), and Johannes Tauler.

Like Tauler, Angelus infuses his theology with an active dose of passivity:

> Das höchste ist Stille seyn. (2.19)
> Geschäfftig seyn ist gutt; Viel besser aber Bethen:
> Noch besser Stumm und stil für Gott den Herren trethen.

> Being still is the highest thing. (2.19)
> Being active is good; but praying is much better.
> Better still is appearing before God silent still.

Here Angelus draws on a long tradition of Christian mysticism: John of the Cross (1542–1591) and Tauler had also emphasized interiority and growth of God in the soul, in a theological tradition leading back through Meister Eckhart to Albertus Magnus (ca. 1206–1280).

This tradition is acutely aware of the impossibility of describing God, and attempts to find other ways to define him negatively. The ingenious concetti and paradoxes resemble brain teasers, pushing at the bounds of possible parsing and interpretation:

> Wer älter ist als GOtt. (2.33)
> Wer in der Ewigkeit mehr lebt als einen Tag /
> Derselbe wird so Alt / als GOtt nicht werden mag.

> Whoever is older than God. (2.33)
> Whoever lives longer than one day in eternity
> becomes older than God can be.

This is as hard to understand literally as it is to interpret. Consequently there are several ways of translating the couplet. The mind strains to imagine what such an experience might be like. Probably the only way to know is to experience it. In that sense, the poem points beyond meaning to something else we cannot (yet?) discern.

Where Angelus must stress his orthodoxy in his preface, Greiffenberg is occluded from hers. Instead, her book of spiritual sonnets announces on the title page that it was published "without her knowledge" by her "cousin" Hans Rudolph von Greiffenberg, Freyherr zu Seyßenegg. His preface stresses the usual combination of the useful and pleasurable, with "proper and true poetry" defined as "useful inner content and a high and pleasurable display of words." But since poetry is in itself divine, the best poetry is Christian. The prefatory matter also defends the female author by listing famous female poets.

Greiffenberg's work has obvious poetic qualities. She uses repetitions and assonances in the manner of her Nuremberg associates. Like them, she coins new words, usually for *amplificatio,* as when her poem "Longing for glorious eternity" (p. 248) explains:

> Ach ich meyn die Ewig-Ewig-Ewig-Ewig-Ewigkeit /
> in die der belebend Tod wird entleibend einverleiben.

> Oh! I mean etern-etern-etern-etern-eternity
> into which life-giving death incorporates us, unbodying us.

Here Greiffenberg uses sentences that seemingly make no sense. But the strange new noun is merely an expansion of a previously existing one, itself formed in German from an adjective that is reduplicated to create a new word. The paradoxes of the line that follows dissolve if one recalls the central paradoxes of Christian theology: the God-Man who dies to be resurrected so that when believers die, their immortal souls can be separated from their mortal bodies, but only to be resurrected in the flesh for later eternal life.

Greiffenberg displays the whole Marinist array of metaphors and epithets, often compacting them into compounds made possible by German word formation. This refrain, for instance (p. 243), has a stanza rhyme scheme like a sonnet, but consists of alternating lines of 9 and 8 trochees:

Freud'-erfüller / Früchte-bringer / Vielbeglückter Jahres-Koch /
Grünung-Blüh und Zeitung-Ziel / Werkbeseeltes Lustverlangen!
lange Hoffnung / ist in dir in die That-Erweisung gangen.
Ohne dich / wird nur beschauet / aber nichts genossen noch.

Joy-fulfilling, fruit-bearing, happy cook of the year,
  bloom of the greening and goal of the seasons, the longing-for-joy, inspired by
    the task!
In you, long hope turns into the proof of the deed.
Without you, one can only look, but not taste.

The poem allows a display of technical virtuosity on the oft-attempted theme of autumn but turns the topic to the contrast between beginnings and endings, and then to God, who alone understood at the beginning the working out of completion. The theological treatment of Providence shades off into Predestination, but without giving the disputatious topic a particular sectarian cast. The difference between the heavenly and earthly gardens, stressed at the end, reminds us of the Garden of Eden and the events there that caused humanity to need Grace.

Greiffenberg's oeuvre is voluminous. Besides the book of sonnets and poems, she produced many books of religious contemplations: twelve each on "The Most Holy and Most Salvific Suffering and Death of Jesus Christ" (1672, rpt. 1683), "The Most Holy Incarnation, Birth, and Youth of Jesus Christ" (1678, rpt. 1693), and "The Most Holy Life of Jesus Christ" (1693). These are masterpieces of Baroque prose, similar in their dramatic intensity and verbal density (though not humor) to the Viennese sermons by Abraham à Sancta Clara (1644–1709). She also published an epic, "The Victory Column of Repentance and Faith" (1675), and other works. Her metaphors are often bold to the point of being literally unfathomable, as when she refers to God as the one who can moisten the stars with the juice of his wisdom, but they remain within the tradition of Christian devotional language.

Kuhlmann's *Kühlpsalter* is autobiographical and visionary. Its very name combines a promise ("Psalm of refreshment") with a play on Kuhlmann's name, and his strong sense of God's activity in the world merges the spiritual and biographical elements. Kuhlmann's interactions with various Protestant sects are portrayed as their rejection of him as God's prophet. But the work (like Augustine's *Confessions*) also has the form of a prayer. Its form, the emphasis on a struggle between a protagonist and his enemies, the frequency of laments, and the large role given to God's favor, all reflect the Psalms. When God's retribution against sinners is stressed, eschatological elements from Revelations are often cited.

Kuhlmann also delights in paradoxes and wordplay—including new words made by recombining old ones, or based on names from the Hebrew Bible— and in the number symbolism common to Jewish and Christian traditions. For example, his 75th Psalm involves the Persons of the Trinity in the cosmic drama of the Fall, depicted as the soul's and Adam's separation from God, and the ensuing attempts at reunification. The creation of Adam is described in series 1, first "refreshing-first-month-part," strophe 5 ("The golden ABC of the Eightfold and the First Beginning"):

> Es hatte GottGottGott sich Adam eingehaucht,
> Nach seiner Ewikeit, nach seinem Ebenbild:
> Der Adem war in ihm, der Gottes Adem selbt,
> Aus welchem alles kam, was ie zum wesen kam.
> Der Brodem brodmete nur ewigewigst fort,
> VVi er die VVelt gebrodmet aus.
> Sein grund war ohne grund, wird stets ungründlicher,
> Vann er gleich ist ungründlich offenbahr.
> Das ewig waristwird zeugt ewig istwirdwar,
> VVeil ewig wirdwarist das Ewigewigewigst.

> GodGodGod has breathed himself into Adam,
> According to his Eternity, according to his Image:
> The Breath was in him, the Breath of God itself [or: himself],
> from which [or: whom] everything came which ever came into being.
> The vapor just vapored out eternally-most-eternally
> As it had vapored out the world.
> His foundation was without foundation, becomes ever more unfathomable
> Even though he is also unfathomably revealed.
> The eternal was-is-will-be eternally engenders is-will-be-was
> Because eternal will-be-was-is [is] the Eternal-eternal-most eternal.

(Note: The original is slightly more readable than the translation.) The poem draws on both the human likeness to God in Genesis 1:27 and the breath of life in 2:7, as well as the vapor in 2:6. God's presence in humankind is emphasized, but even more strongly urged is God's unfathomable way of being. Stylistically, the writer produces the effect of mystery by pushing both syntax and semantics to their limits. He not only coins many new nouns from combinations of verb-tenses, but he makes the word "eternally" (ewig) to serve itself as an intensifying adverb. There is a pun on Adam and God's spirit or breath (*Adem,* modern spelling *Atem*).

Kuhlmann asserts in strophe 14 of this series (third part), "The bite of the Serpent loses its power in the soul that passively followed the example of Jesus." In its "most quiet quietness," Faith kills "death in death" (str. 19) and triumphs. At this stage, all sorts of separations disappear, and the soul is able to "see without pictures the pictures in the Writ" (str. 20), even in passages that were unclear to the Prophets. This soul, however, is contrasted to the soul that merely "dies in dying," which God will not help (str. 21). These strophes contain many biblical allusions, for example, to Jesus's parable (Matthew 25) of the Wise and Foolish Virgins with its imagery of waiting. Kuhlmann's poems, like medieval Latin devotional poetry or the liturgy, consist of a complex fabric of references to biblical passages which themselves have become key texts for Christian theology and hermeneutics. The allusions create a vast web of concepts linked together by the history of Christian homiletics, theology, mystical writing, and their exegesis.

Boyer reminds us that the meaning of most discourse is "massively underspecified" by its linguistic features, thus requiring completion from background knowledge and schemas. The Bible is all the harder to interpret definitively because so many commentators, convinced of its importance, have tried to interpret it, providing a vast number of schemas for interpretation. Kuhlmann recontextualizes large parts of the Bible in his conviction that, as a prophet of God, his own life was intricately bound up with the plan of salvation, including the Hebrew prophets and their rejection, the life and death of Jesus, and the rectifying Judgment to come.

What use are these texts to us today? From a consumer's perspective, they can be enjoyed as literature. For admirers of extraordinarily dense writing, thorough use of metaphorical structures, wordplay, and lyrical craftsmanship, they more than repay close attention. To the historian, they open a perspective on the mentality and the world of people in a bygone era. But, since they were produced within particular discursive and social contexts and addressed to particular audiences, they can hardly serve as unmediated records of personal experience. All make more sense in a general Christian context. But Angelus's work improves with a knowledge of Christian negative theology, Greiffenberg's with a knowledge of Opitzian poetics, and Kuhlmann's with profound biblical learning and a strong sense that the Second Coming is nigh. Few readers today combine an appreciation of early modern poetry with the requisite background, so these poets may not find the audience they deserve.

See also 1265, 1329, 1346, 1600, 1622, 1638

Bibliography: Angelus Silesius, *Cherubinischer Wandersmann,* Louise Gnädinger, ed. text of rev. ed. (Stuttgart: Reclam, 1984). Pascal Boyer, *The Naturalness of Religious Ideas: A Cognitive Theory of Religion* (Berkeley: University of California Press, 1994), esp. 245–246. Catherina Regina von Greiffenberg, *Sämtliche Werke,* Martin Bircher and Friedhelm Kemp, eds. 10 vols. (Millwood, N.Y.: Kraus Rpt., 1983), Sonette = vol. 1. Quirinus Kuhlmann, *Der Kühlpsalter,* ed. Robert L. Beare, 2 vols. (Tübingen: Niemeyer, 1972). George Lakoff, *Women, Fire, and Dangerous Things: What Categories Reveal about the Mind* (Chicago: University of Chicago Press, 1987). Jaroslav Pelikan, *Reformation of Church and Dogma (1300–1700),* vol. 4, *The Christian Tradition: A History of the Development of Doctrine* (Chicago: University of Chicago Press, 1978), cit. p. 66. Biblical chapters and verses are cited from the Authorized Version.

Emery Snyder

♌ 1662

Kaspar Stieler obtains his first position as a secretary at court

Learning and News in the Baroque

In 1695 the well-known author Kaspar Stieler entered into a protracted debate about the merits of newspapers with a work exemplifying several aspects of early modern European literature that are at odds with our own cultural practices. Stieler's career as a court official was an important trajectory for 17th-century writers, and his book—entitled *Zeitungs Lust und Nutz (The Pleasure and Usefulness of Newspapers)*—participates in the two genres of polemic and handbook.

The polemic at hand involved the role of newspaper, then a growing new medium. News had always been spread by messengers and the slow passing of information between communities through itinerant merchants. News circulated in manuscript form, and professional newsmongers made their appearance. The next step was small printed books and single sheets. In England and Germany, coffee houses became centers for the dissemination and discussion of news. These, along with courts, administrative officials, and the clergy, were the subscribers of the first news periodicals. The German-speaking world had monthly newspapers since 1609. By the middle of the century, many imperial cities had weekly newspapers, several of which lasted only a few years. Still, the *Historical and Political Mercury* ran from 1694 to 1723, and the *European State Chancellery* ran from 1697 to 1760.

In some ways, the Holy Roman Empire, with its hundreds of small states and cities, was an ideal setting for newspapers. In England, newspapers were forbidden by the crown, and did not become important until the civil wars of the 1640s. In France, the state was quick to take control of the nascent medium through three publications: the *Gazette* for political events, the *Journal des Savants* for science, and the *Mercure* for court life and the fine arts. Germany had seen the adversaries on both sides in the Thirty Years' War (1618–1648) use newspapers for propaganda, but the lack of a dominant administrative center precluded a single official organ. Newspapers were published by postmasters and printers. The empire had more than fifty such enterprises by 1700, most semiweekly, and the total circulation reached perhaps 300,000 people. Most of these dealt with current political events, although there were also long-running scholarly and scientific periodicals.

In the late 17th century, many European intellectuals became concerned about the breakdown of social boundaries. Despite sumptuary laws, newly rich members of the artisan and merchant sectors tried to gain status by imitating noble fashions in clothing, art, and personal style. Comedies of the period satirize upwardly mobile commoners, and social conservatives in Britain and the empire deplored the inroads made by French food, dress, manners, and language. A large group of works satirized the "political" commoners who pretended to talk knowledgeably of wars, court intrigues, and high politics, even though their information was imperfect and their relationship to the subject matter practically nonexistent. The German sociologist Jürgen Habermas claims that the invention of a "public sphere" where all citizens can discuss public affairs was crucial for democracy, but for many 17th-century observers allowing merchants to discourse about public affairs distracted them from their real social function and encouraged them to agitate about matters that were none of their business. Newspapers, which allowed information about state matters to circulate to anyone who could get hold of an issue, were seen as dangerous, and German authors advocated their suppression in many publications from 1629 to 1679. Others defended the newspapers, claiming that by allowing information to circulate, they would free the sovereign from dependence on information channels at the court, allowing him to find out if corrupt officials were oppressing his subjects. Some, including Jan Amos Comenius and Christian Weise, even suggested that newspapers should be used in schools and universities to teach contemporary history.

Polemics could be written only by those with enough education and authority to command an audience, enough leisure to write books, and enough means and contacts to publish regularly. Professors had been carrying on polemics since the 12th century and clergymen since the beginning of Christianity. In Stieler's period, they were joined by two groups to which he also belonged, bureaucrats and professional writers. Polemical writing also requires a subculture defined well enough for readers to follow a particular dispute. Printers who were able to spot such a niche market and encourage a polemical exchange stood to gain considerable sums of money, as did authors interested in exploiting the book market.

Stieler's own career demonstrates how education allowed one to attain such a position. He was born into a family of apothecaries in Erfurt on 25 March 1632. He attended the practical school for merchant children, from where he transferred to a classical school on the Humanist model. He learned Latin, the language of instruction at the universities. Stieler's studies of medicine and law at various universities were interrupted only by war. He did a stint as private tutor, and traveled for three years in Holland, France, Spain, Italy, and the Swiss Republic. He thus absolved the "grand tour" taken by earlier scholars or contemporary aristocrats.

In 1662, at age thirty, Stieler obtained his first court position as secretary. Until 1689, he held several other positions, including that of councilor, at various courts. During this period he also raised a family with his wife, the daughter of an imperial postmaster (this marriage allied him with other important officials). He spent the last years of his life as a private scholar and author; he died on 24 July 1707. As secretary at Jena, Rudolstadt, Eisenach, Weimar, and Holstein-Wiesenburg, Stieler produced works in many genres: court entertainment, lyrics, plays, letters, and professional documents. At thirty-six, his literary reputation won him entry into the Fruchtbringende Gesellschaft (Fruit-Bearing Society), the largest of the learned "academies" and known particularly for its cultivation of the German language. Yet his best-known work, a collection of poetry entitled "Venus in Armor," was published anonymously in 1660 and remained anonymous for 237 years. He spent his life as a court functionary, culminating in 1705 in his elevation to the hereditary nobility. His career informs the works for which Stieler was known in his lifetime, his handbooks.

Handbooks can be thought of as another version of the Baroque cultivation of erudition. They are usually impressive in length (one of Stieler's is longer than two thousand pages), in format (often folios), and in exhaustiveness of the subject. Although their structure often involves theoretical categorization, their content centers on practical knowledge for daily use. These tomes are hard to read from cover to cover, but work very well as reference works. They usually contain a good index and cross-references in the margins to a particular topic. Stieler put an immense amount of labor into preparing such compilations, including revisions. After 1673, he published a book every year under the (fairly public) pseudonym he was given on his admission into the Fruchtbringende Gesellschaft —der Spate (the spade).

Stieler's handbooks treat of a great number of subjects, but all have to do with the world of the absolutist court. Only five years after assuming his first secretarial post, he published *The German Art of the Secretary* (1673–1674), which was successful enough to be reprinted several times (1681, 1705, 1726). In 1679 he published another epistolary work, *The Ever-ready Secretary,* which went through two more editions.

These two works include much advice on letter writing, including official and love letters. They also discuss the duties of a court secretary, among them those which are today performed by a secretary of state or foreign minister. To address a letter, one needs information on the relative status of addressee and sender, which was expressed in the proper titles as well as presentational details like spacing and handwriting. Stieler instructs the reader in court practices, ciphers, invisible ink, weights and measures, legal affairs, notaries, and the imperial postal system. In 1678 his *German Lawyer* (2nd ed., 1691) appeared. In 1680 he published a reworking of Baltasar Kindermann's *German Orator* from 1660 (2nd ed., 1688). In 1683 he brought out a manual for military inspectors, in 1684 a collection of useful anecdotes called *The Silhouette of the World.* He also found time to write a poetic handbook which remained unpublished. In 1691 appeared his groundbreaking *Family Tree and Growth of the German Language,* or *German Thesaurus.* This work, which combined speculative linguistic history, a grammar of German, and a large dictionary (60,000 words in 2672 columns), was part of a program endorsed by the academies for describing, fixing, and improving the prestige of the German language. So when his work on news, *The Pleasure and Usefulness of Newspapers,* appeared in 1695 (2nd ed., 1697), Stieler was already a well-established author who lived in part on the income from his books.

Stieler begins this book with a defense of curiosity as an inborn human desire for knowledge. Opponents of too much knowledge had often treated curiosity as a sin. He proposes a value-neutral theory of media, in which only individual newspapers are good or bad. Stieler uses the word "Zeitung," which can be translated as "newspaper," but is related to the English word "tiding" and carries a more general meaning. (I will translate it as "news.") His discussion of news revolves around the social function of circulating information rather than the printed form itself. Seeking to establish the dignity of news, he invokes God, who published *his* news through the prophets and apostles. The state too benefits from circulation of information, allowing the monarch to stay informed about what is happening in his realm. But news also must be printed and be available for purchase, says Stieler, so that it will circulate widely. But the content should also be regulated, untrustworthy newspapers should be banned, and news writers and publishers should take an oath of office and give assurances to the appropriate authorities. Stieler stresses the impartiality of news. By this he means it should not reflect the views of a court faction or party. (In fact, newspapers that overtly carry personal or party positions became prominent only in the 18th century.) Avoiding a parochial slant on the news is related to its broader mission, as Stieler sees it. It is possible, he says, to gain access to information from all over the world while sitting at home. Geographic vistas can be superseded by temporal ones. A reader who understands the current world from the news will be better prepared to understand history.

Like poetry, news achieves the twofold Horatian goal of being useful and pleasant. The uses are manifold: knowledge of the world, which shows God's glory and the continual action of Providence (for example, in earthquakes); useful reflections for courtiers; preventing boredom; pleasing by novelty; and publishing honor. Stieler also devotes attention to the professionals who produce news. He notes that reporters work hard trying to find information and evaluate its worth, as opposed to the makers of almanacs, who merely steal and reprint old information. Stieler thus distinguishes news from other informational literature available to readers unschooled in the languages of scholarship. This distinction is seen in the newspapers' content. Stieler rejects items that do not satisfy curiosity because they are dated, have been printed before, or have no narrative closure. The occasional description of a little-known place is permissible because it does satisfy curiosity, but news about faraway exotic places will be useless to the readers. Proper names provide crucial information, and the news writer must distinguish the important from the trivial, and exclude that which is not fit to print. This category includes information that is merely private or concerns the lower classes. Furthermore, Stieler warns against the publication of "dangerous and awkward items" that might hurt the honor and reputation of a monarch. Since publishers are subjects too, they must obey the authorities who wish to insert false information.

Stieler describes the audience of news very generally as "any one who can read or hear," a class that includes the blind. But the ability to understand is also important, so the audience excludes small children. Those with a professional need to know are obviously included, but not all private persons are excluded. Servants, peasants, and manual laborers would do better to read the Bible. News encompasses the world of interest to an audience defined as "unmarked": items should be neither too intimate with the highest personages, nor too low or too local. This avoidance of "marked" categories extends to style, which should contain obviously regional, class-bound, or foreign words and ideas.

Not all members of this broad audience can understand the news. Stieler instructs them how to read a newspaper. Readers should treat news reports critically. For this they need a background knowledge of Europe's prominent persons, their coats of arms and family trees, as well as geography, history, some foreign languages, and political judgment. The appendices to Stieler's handbook supply much of this information: foreign words, current rulers, important locations, and basic heraldry. The necessary background knowledge is not impossible to come by, and thus does not create an insuperable barrier to reading news. Stieler's definition of news subsumes a variety of criteria: a general communicative type (narrative), function in society (information, satisfaction of a basic human need), production by a specific social group defined by function (reporters, publishers), relationships to related discourse (history, almanacs), formal markers of the discourse type (lack of "order"), restrictions as to content (particular information about matters of public interest) and style (superregional), specification of the physical medium (printed paper) and the conditions of circulation (availability on the open market), and relationship to different sorts of claims to truth (facts rather than meanings, plausible rather than absolutely true).

Although Stieler's book was part of a long-running debate, and he devotes a whole chapter to refuting the various claims of the anti-newspaper writers, it is not brief, addressed to one opponent, or abusive in the tradition of polemics. It is a handbook like his other books. Perhaps he responded to a publishing opportunity with one of his usual products, but the topic is also closely implicated in his overall project.

Stieler grew up in a world of hierarchies, where most people stayed within the social class they were born into and learned through apprenticeships. Like some Humanists before him, he moved from the mercantile sphere to hereditary nobility via education. But where the Humanists stressed the role of the liberal arts and the dignity of the scholar, Stieler's topics centered on everyday work. Where the Humanists claimed that training in the arts and sciences produced better people and better officials, Stieler helped turn the practical knowledge of officialdom into a learned discipline. His books make professional arcana accessible to anyone who can read German. We can thus see him as moving from a social world defined by status to one defined by function. A functional employee requires know-how, not social prestige. The public sphere needs information, and in a world before democracy, the court and the administration were the public sphere. The professional know-how provided by handbooks must be supplemented with current information of the sort found in handbooks, which, in turn, must be supplemented by current information from the news. Reading the news is another essential skill of the educated public official who works in the domain of circulating information.

See also 1515, 1622, 1647, 1986

Bibliography: Joad Raymond, *The Invention of the Newspaper: English Newsbooks 1641–1649* (New York: Oxford University Press, 1996). Kaspar von Stieler, *Zeitungs Lust und Nutz,* ed. Gert Hagelweide (Bremen: Schünemann, 1969).

Emery Snyder

1666, February

By order of Friedrich Wilhelm I, King of Prussia and Elector of Brandenburg, Paul Gerhardt is removed from the office of deacon at Saint Nicolai Church in Berlin

"Commit your way to the LORD"

In 1662 and 1664, attempting to quell increasing tensions between the Lutheran and the Reformed Churches, King Friedrich Wilhelm I (1640–1688) issued two edicts demanding that the conflicting parties observe tolerance. Leaders of both communities were required to declare their adherence to this principle. Whereas the Reformists viewed the edicts as securing the peaceful growth of their church in Brandenburg, the Lutherans saw the king's intervention as an unwarranted interference in religious matters that threatened to divide the Lutheran Church and dilute the purity of the Lutheran Creed. Among the Lutherans who refused to abide by the king's edict was Paul Gerhardt (1607–1676), who was subsequently removed from his pastoral office. Gerhardt had no intention of promoting doctrinal conflict and was entirely amenable to peaceful coexistence with the other religious community. However, he objected to signing a document he saw as contravening his obligation to the Lutheran Church and infringing on his freedom of conscience. This appeal to conscience must be understood in its historical specificity. Gerhardt saw himself as acting not on the basis of personal convictions, but on the basis of commitment to Truth, which is to say: the Bible and its interpretation according to Lutheran orthodoxy.

In the very month of Gerhardt's dismissal, the composer and musical director of Saint Nicolai Church, Johann Georg Ebeling (1637–1676), commenced publication of a complete edition of Paul Gerhardt's devotional songs and poems. Gerhardt had already acquired a reputation as a poet of devotional songs and Ebeling's predecessor Johann Crüger (1598–1662) had set several of his songs to music. The second edition of Crüger's *Neues vollkömmliches Gesangbuch Augspurgischer Confession* (1640; *New Complete Songbook according to the Augsburg Confession*), which appeared in 1647 under the title *Praxis pietatis melica,* contained eighteen of Gerhardt's songs. And this canonization continued well beyond Ebeling's edition of 1666. Even today the main section of *Das evangelische Kirchengesangbuch (Hymnal of the Protestant Church in Germany)* contains no fewer than thirty of Paul Gerhardt's songs. But Gerhardt's impact was by no means restricted to the development of the official church service. Indeed, in the second volume of his edition, Ebeling emphasized that the songs were meant to promote Christian devotion not merely in church but in the privacy of the home as well. By the time of his death in 1676, Gerhardt had composed 136 songs, 4 of them in Latin. Some of these were written for such important events as funerals or weddings, others address a specific time of day or a significant date in the church calendar; still others are songs of praise and consolation.

After receiving his theological training in Wittenberg, Paul Gerhardt became pastor of the Lutheran Church in Mittenwalde, in Berlin. Following his dismissal from the prestigious Saint Nicolai Church, he became a pastor in the town of Lübben, where he spent the last ten years of his life. Although he left no doubt as to his dedication to the Lutheran Church into which he had been ordained, Gerhardt's work as a poet does not represent a direct continuation of the tradition of religious songs established by Luther himself. Rather, it is firmly situated within the context of popular piety that had emerged in the spiritual revival of the early 17th century and, after the conclusion of the Thirty Years' War, had again become a prominent feature of Protestant religious life. The central notion of this pietism holds that religious devotion is rooted in the practical piety of lived experience rather than in official doctrine and ritual. Johann Arndt (1555–1621), whose enormously influential *Vier Bücher des Wahren Christentums* (1606; *Four Books on True Christianity*) combined detailed explanations of basic Christian beliefs with a rich set of spiritual exercises, coined the term "praxis pietatis" for this religious attitude. Arndt's *Four Books* enjoin the reader to meditate on his or her relationship to God, to sin, and to the work of redemption within the confines of both natural and domestic life. This new emphasis on lived experience and each individual believer's devotional practices gave rise to the publication of many new prayer- and songbooks meant for private and domestic use. Among these was Arndt's own *Paradies-Gärtlein* (1612; *Little Garden of Paradise*), and Paul Gerhardt based six of his songs on prayers from this book. Indeed prayer, praise, and consolation are the most common speech situations evoked by Gerhardt's poems.

Many of Gerhardt's poems go back to traditional, mainly biblical texts, among them twenty-five psalms, of which "Du meine Seele, singe" (Psalm 146: "Praise the Lord! Praise the Lord, O my soul!") is one of the best known. Also the Latin passion salves—hymns attributed in Gerhardt's time to the founder of the Cistercian Order, Bernard de Clairvaux (1090 or 1091–1153), that focus on individual aspects of Christ's body in agony—provide the basis for seven Passion songs. The last of these, "O Haupt voll Blut und Wunden" ("Oh Sacred Head! now wounded"), is known today throughout the world from Johann Sebastian Bach's *Saint Matthew Passion*. Gerhardt's poetic achievement rests on his manner of transforming these traditional materials by recasting the resonant biblical symbolism in a remarkably simple syntax and concrete diction. His rhetoric favors parallelism, repetition, reversal, gradation, and climax. Even for the gravest topics, he adhered to the plain style or *sermo humilis*. To the extent that the meter of his verses generally follows the natural accent of prose, his poetic work adheres to Martin Opitz's reform. Gerhardt's oeuvre displays a richness of strophic forms, ranging from simple four-verse models to complex stanzas of twelve verses. Clarity and comprehensibility are guaranteed by limiting each stanza to the development of a single complete thought, as recommended in the influential poetic theory of August Buchner (1591–1661). In brief, Paul Gerhardt's poetry stands out for its artful simplicity and theological precision, features that made it accessible to a broad audience.

Johann Heinrich Feustking, publisher of the 1707 posthumous edition of Gerhardt's work, noted that his edition was prepared on the basis of the author's own manuscripts as well as a printed copy, corrected in the author's own hand. This remark points to Gerhardt's craftsmanship in even the smallest detail of his compositions. But this poetic handiwork is part of a larger vocation, as can be gleaned from a poem dedicated to Gerhardt's fellow poet and theologian Joachim Pauli (1636–1708):

> Unter allen, die da leben,
> Hat ein jeder seinen Fleiß
> Und weiß dessen Frucht zu geben;
> Doch hat der den größten Preis,
> Der dem Höchsten Ehre bringt
> Und von Gottes Namen singt.
>
> Unter allen, die da singen
> Und mit wohlgefaßter Kunst,
> Ihrem Schöpfer Opfer bringen,
> Hat ein jeder seine Gunst;
> Doch ist der am besten dran,
> Der mit Andacht singen kann.
>
> Among all those who live
> Each one has his own endeavor
> And knows to deliver its fruit;
> But he, Who brings Honor to the Highest
> And sings of God's name,
> Receives the greatest praise.
>
> Among all those who sing
> And with well-formed art
> Bring offerings to their Creator,
> Each one has His favor;
> Yet, only he is best off
> Who can sing with devotion.

(Brunner, 241)

Although each individual has a specific talent, the ultimate goal of human endeavor must be the glory of the Lord. Among the many gifted poets engaged in praising their Creator, all will have their share of grace, and yet those who sing with true devotion will be "best off." Climax, gradation, and comparison are carefully calibrated in this complex, economical reflection on the best use of poetic talent and its rewards. Theologically, Gerhardt treads a fine line between the Calvinist belief in predestination and the Catholic notion of works. Thus the artist can neither work himself into God's favor by way of artful creations, nor will his artistic accomplishments prove his special status as one of the elect. Rather, the intensity and authenticity of his devotion are both something the poet needs to strive for and part of God's grace that is given to him. *Andacht* (devotion) is the ground and the goal of artistic activity.

The first-person singular of Gerhardt's poems covers the entire spectrum from the individualized to the corporate, ritual "I" of collective prayer and song. Yet, even when the first-person pronoun marks an individual experience, that individuality is always woven into the truths of codified dogma. Many of Gerhardt's songs begin with an apostrophe to the soul and heart to sing, an encouragement to open the self to the beauty and wonder of creation. Then, in the dialogue between the speaking "I" and the addressed soul, the meditation gradually transcends the enclosure of the self and approaches an understanding of the work of redemption. Thus Gerhardt's best-known summer song begins:

> Geh aus mein Herz und suche Freud
> In dieser lieben Sommerzeit
> An deines Gottes Gaben;
> Schau an der schönen Gärten Zier
> Und siehe, wie sie mir und dir
> Sich ausgeschmücket haben.

> Open yourself my heart and seek joy
> In this beloved summer time
> In the gifts of your God;
> Look at the beautiful gardens' ornament
> And see how for me and you
> They have adorned themselves.

The delighted contemplation of the flora and fauna in all their richness of detail, ranging from the fullness of the summer foliage, the lark's flight, and the song of the nightingale to the hen's taking her little chicks out, the stork's building his nest, and the swift deer's leap in the meadow, culminates in the fifth stanza in a natural artwork—at once painting and symphony—of joy:

> Die Bächlein rauschen in dem Sand
> Und malen sich und ihren Rand
> Mit schattenreichen Myrten;
> Die Wiesen liegen hart dabei
> Und klingen ganz vom Lustgeschrei
> Der Schaf und ihrer Hirten.

> The little brooks murmur in the sand
> And paint themselves and their border

With myrtles full of shade;
The meadows lie right next to them
And fully resound with the jubilation
Of the sheep and their shepherds.

But the song does not restrict itself to a worldly celebration of nature and summer. The second section—stanzas 6 to 10—considers the rich fruits of summer
(honey, wine, and wheat) not for their own sake, but as evidence of God's
boundless generosity. Finally, in the song's third and final section, the bounty of
summer is understood as prefiguring the greatest of gifts, that of redemption
and of life to come. The concluding prayer of the poem begins as follows:

Hilf mir und segne meinen Geist
Mit Segen, der vom Himmel fleußt,
Daß ich dir stetig blühe!
Gib, daß der Sommer deiner Gnad
In meiner Seele früh und spat
Viel Glaubensfrücht erziehe!

Help me and bless my spirit
With blessing that flows from heaven,
That I shall always blossom for you!
Grant that the summer of your grace
Within my soul early and late
Will produce many fruits of faith!

Paul Gerhardt's place in the history of Protestant piety is due not only to his
songs of praise but also, perhaps even more powerfully, to his songs of consolation in times of suffering when human hope seems exhausted. Perhaps no
other poet of the 17th century refers to the cross as often—eighty-eight times
in 134 songs. In more than half of these, the term signifies not the cross of
Christ's crucifixion, but "Christenkreuz," the cross of suffering to be borne by
every Christian (Krause, 283). The catalogue of suffering is copious, extending
from anxiety, calamity, death, and destitution to scorn, separation, sorrows,
tears, war, and the unholy wrath of princes. Gerhardt's songs envision a God
for whom all suffering has a good reason and end, be it to awaken the voice of
conscience, to strengthen the community of believers, or to encourage communion with the suffering of Christ as he bore his Cross. Especially in the latter sense that fuses Christian suffering with the Cross of Christ, Gerhardt's
songs build on the passion mysticism of its times. And yet, it is important to
note that Gerhardt's poems never suggest equivalence between individual suffering and the suffering of Christ. On the contrary, his passion songs always
emphasize the paradox of Christ's utterly undeserved suffering (Krause, 291).

The main tenor of Gerhardt's songs of consolation lies in an utter trust in
God's might, mercy, and wisdom, as expressed in "Befiehl du deine Wege,"
based on Psalm 37:5, "Commit your way to the LORD." The purity of this poetic expression has found great resonance among Christian believers through-

out the centuries. Thus the Protestant theologian Dietrich Bonhoeffer (1906–1945) acknowledged the great theological and personal importance Gerhardt's songs had for him during his last years in the concentration camp. But the imperative to trust absolutely in God's ways has also provoked harsh criticism. The theologian Dorothee Sölle (1929–2003) has made the point that, for the modern believer, the notion of a good paternalistic God has become obsolete. And in a literary context, Bertold Brecht (1898–1956) implicitly accuses Gerhardt's piety of promoting an unthinking, irresponsible subjection to authority by parodying "Befiehl du deine Wege" in one of his "Hitler Chorales." Nevertheless, throughout German literary history, Paul Gerhardt's songs have had their ardent admirers, ranging from Christian Fürchtegott Gellert (1715–1769), Matthias Claudius (1740–1813), and Friedrich Schiller (1759–1805) to Conrad Ferdinand Meyer (1825–1898), Theodor Fontane (1819–1898), Gottfried Benn (1886–1956), and Gertrud von le Fort (1876–1971). Most recently, Günter Grass (b. 1929) provided a fictional portrait of Gerhardt in *Das Treffen in Telgte* (1979; *The Meeting in Telgte*), which narrates a meeting of roughly twenty poets, musicians, and publishers in the year 1647. But the most significant aspect of Paul Gerhardt's poetic afterlife is certainly the fact that his songs are still sung by Protestant worshipers today, who often know nothing more of him than the name at the top of the hymnal page.

See also 1622, 1670 (*collegia pietatis*), 1895, 1949, 1958

Bibliography: Paul Gerhardt, *Dichtungen und Schriften,* ed. Eberhard von Cranach-Sichart (Munich: Paul Müller, 1957). Christian Brunners, *Paul Gerhardt: Weg, Werk, Wirkung* (Berlin and Munich: Buchverlag Union, 1993). Sven Grosse, *Gott und das Leid in den Liedern Paul Gerhardts* (Göttingen: Vandenhoeck & Ruprecht, 2001). Gerhard Krause, "Christuskreuz und Christenkreuz bei Paul Gerhardt," in *Theologia Crucis, Signum Crucis: Festschrift für Erich Dinkler,* ed. Carl Andresen and Günter Klein (Tübingen: J.C.B. Mohr, 1979), 283–302. Hermann Petrich, *Paul Gerhardt: Ein Beitrag zur Geschichte des deutschen Geistes; Auf Grund neuer Forschungen und Funde* (Gütersloh, 1914). Winfried Zeller, "Paul Gerhardt," in Winfried Zeller, *Theologie und Frömmigkeit: Gesammelte Aufsätze,* ed. Bernd Jaspert (Marburg: N. G. Elwert Verlag, 1971), vol. 1, 154–164.

Dorothea E. von Mücke

♆ 1670

At the Frankfurt and Leipzig book fairs, Grimmelshausen's publisher announces the forthcoming publication of *Trutz Simplex oder Ausführliche und wunderseltzame Lebens Beschreibung der Ertzbetrügerin und Landstürzerin Courasche*

Hermaphroditism and the Battle of the Sexes

When Johann Jacob Christoph von Grimmelshausen (b. 1621?) died in 1676, a statement from the foreword to his last publication—the second part of the *Wunderbarliches Vogel-Nest* (1675; *Magical Bird's Nest*)—became his literary last will and testament. His purpose as a "Simplician author," he noted, was moral and religious edification, but he had also "included many ridiculous anecdotes, as he had also done in describing the adventuresome life of

Simplicissimus." With this definition of his "Simplician" style, the author of *Der abentheurliche Simplicissimus Deutsch* (1668; *The Adventures of Simplicissimus*)—without question the greatest literary work written in German during the seventeenth century—acknowledges the necessity of sweetening the "bitter medicine" of his didactic message with the "sugar coating" of farce and hilarity. He conceives of himself as a physician not of the body but of the soul, thus aligning his style with the traditional Horatian notion that literature delights *(delectare)* as well as edifies *(prodesse)*. At the same time Grimmelshausen's remarks stress his own unique achievement, the creation of the unmistakable "Simplician" narrator. That this characterization of his authorial intentions also includes Grimmelshausen's briefer picaresque novel *Trutz Simplex oder Ausführliche und wunderseltzame Lebens Beschreibung der Ertzbetrügerin und Landstürzerin Courasche* (1672; *Spite Simplex, or Detailed and Wonderfully Strange Life History of the Archfraud and Runagate Courage*) is revealed by a remark at the end of the preface to *Bird's Nest* according to which all of his "Simplician writings"—the novel *Simplicissimus,* its continuation *(Continuatio),* his briefer novels *Courasche* and *Springinsfeld* (1670), both parts of the *Bird's Nest*—"hang together and neither the entire *Simplicissimus* nor any of the aforementioned small treatises can be adequately understood apart from this connection." But just wherein the "connection" among all these books consists—Grimmelshausen specialists have proposed numerological and allegorical solutions—remains a puzzle to this day.

The novel *Courasche* appeared in 1672, between the deaths of Rembrandt and Molière, under an anagrammatic pseudonym. It is tied to its predecessor, the six-book *Simplicissimus,* by an episode occurring near the end of the latter. The narrator-hero Simplicissimus finds himself in a bath with a lady, whose morals soon prove to be "more mobilis than nobilis" and whom he therefore "attempts politely to get rid of." The dubious lady in question is none other than Courasche, and the combined insult and indiscretion of the account of her given in *Simplicissimus* prompt her to publish her own "memoirs." To this end, she kidnaps a writer, whose name just happens to be an anagram of Grimmelshausen, and "everything about the person of Courasche is dictated into the author's pen." The concept of authorship oscillates here between fiction and reality: the figure of the first-person narrator—the renegade Courasche—makes use of the author who, at the same time, creates this very figure in his act of writing. This dialectic between narrator and author illustrates why the Romantics, who made such ironies a principle of art, would take a keen interest in Grimmelshausen after he had been neglected by the Enlightenment, just as the complex network of characters and the twisted plot of Grimmelshausen's narrative anticipate the intricate construction of Romantic novels such as Clemens Brentano's *Godwi* (1801).

The intertextual link between *Simplicissimus* and *Courasche* is taken up in the twenty-fourth of the latter's twenty-eight chapters, when Courasche offers her version of the encounter at the baths. Far from rejecting her, she claims, Simplicissimus "sailed with full wind into the dangerous harbor of my ample desires," a docking of his lustful ship that costs him a case of syphilis. Moreover, she later manages to convince him that she—the "barren" one—has borne him a child, passing off on him the illegitimate offspring of her chambermaid. It was no doubt Courasche's barrenness that inspired Bertolt Brecht's adaptation of Grimmelshausen's character in his *Mutter Courage und ihre Kinder* (1941; *Mother Courage and Her Children*). Just as the sterility of the 17th-century Courasche is the precondition of her picaresque career in prostitution, the protagonist's loss of her children in Brecht's play underlines its pacifist message. It would seem, then, that *Courasche* records the victory of the female protagonist over the male narrator-hero of the predecessor novel. And indeed Courasche's memoirs, as she often emphasizes, are written against Simplicissimus, which explains the initial component of its title: *Trutz Simplex (Spite Simplex)*. But this overturning of the traditional gender hierarchy is itself overturned in the subsequent volume of the "Simplician" cycle, *Der Seltzame Springinsfeld* (1670; *The Strange Springinsfeld*). There Simplicissimus offers, as it were, a synthesis of their respective viewpoints, claiming often to have "lain with the chambermaid" during the time he was "caressing" Courasche and thus actually to be the father of the child the latter thought to foist off on him. In the battle of the sexes, the male has the last word, but only after having suffered considerable humiliation in Courasche's memoirs. This interweaving of the three novels suggests that at least one of the connections holding Grimmelshausen's Simplician writings together involves the questions of sexual identity and gender attribution.

Grimmelshausen's idea of creating a female protagonist probably derives from the anonymous German translation of an Italian version (1615) of a picaresque novel originally published in Spain in 1605: *Landstörtzerin Ivstina Dietzin Picara genandt (Renegade Ivstina Dietzin, called Picara)*. The picaresque novel was not well established in the German-speaking lands and Grimmelshausen's exercise in the genre has the distinction of being its artistically innovative high point as well as its end. Whereas the earlier text starts off with a learned allegory, *Courasche* takes up the battle of the sexes with a forceful gesture of defiance. The opinion of nobles and clerics that, in her advanced age, she has seen the error of her ways and in writing her memoirs intends to express remorse is enough to make Courasche "laugh herself to pieces." Concern for the salvation of her soul might have helped her in her youth, but now it's too late and she is willing to risk perdition—a blasphemous assertion in the 17th century. Cynical and yet sublime, she recalls the terrible humiliations she suffered during her peregrinations through the Thirty Years' War, as when a group of soldiers, "having forgotten all shame and Christian honor, stripped me naked and cast a handful of peas onto the ground, which I had to pick up as they thrashed me with birches." Her unyielding pride—also illustrated in the emblematic illustration appearing on the novel's frontispiece—has been bought at a high price. She has fallen low, usually due to the fault of men, but as she commences her memoir, her self-awareness as a woman is unshakable.

With this ostentatious affirmation of her vitality and sexuality, Courasche mocks the male delusion that she, weak and frail, is preparing herself for death. For such thoughts she has "one member too few, and two too many," a sexual allusion she ironically glosses as a lack of remorse together with an excess of greed and envy. Indeed, throughout her life she had wanted to affirm her biological sex. When on their wedding night she challenges one of her several husbands to a battle "for the pants," her victory soon turns into failure as the townspeople ridicule her husband and force her into the socially suspect position of the masculine woman. This alienation from her own sexual identity is already announced in the title of the second chapter, with which the narrative action begins: "The Maiden Lebuschka (hereafter called Courasche) Happens into the War and Calls Herself Janko." By giving his protagonist the name Lebuschka, Grimmelshausen recalls the Bohemian national heroine Libussa—later the title figure of the 1872 drama by Franz Grillparzer—and therewith the mythic background of a struggle between male and female rulers. But we also notice that between her feminine and masculine names an ambivalent third term appears, on the one hand designating an attitude (courage) connoted as male and on the other hand euphemistically referring to the female genitals. For the memoirist informs us that a soldier had "groped her 'courasche,' where no man's hand had ever come before." Grimmelshausen's use of a term drawn from the language of soldiers to signify the vulva creates a verbal hermaphrodite, and this sexually ambiguous name becomes the heroine's trademark.

During the Bohemian campaign—Grimmelshausen's depiction of the Thirty Years' War is based here, as in *Simplicissimus,* on contemporary chronicles—she has "her hair cut and puts on men's clothes" in order to avoid the threat of rape. Similar hermaphroditic moments can be found in *Simplicissimus.* In one episode Simplicissimus finds himself "transformed from a young man into a young woman," a masquerade that attracts the amorous attentions of a cavalry officer, his wife, and their servant. The "labyrinth," from which the desired boy/girl can find no escape, is an appropriate emblem for this metaphorical hermaphroditism. Alienated from himself in the ambiguity of sexual identity, Simplicissimus resembles Courasche, who reports that she rides "not like the other officers' wives on a woman's saddle, but on a man's, and, although I sat side-saddle, I nevertheless bore pistols and a Turkish saber beneath my thigh, . . . and I wore pants beneath a thin taffeta skirt so that I could in a moment change my position and present a young male rider" (*Courasche,* ed. Bender, 38). The saber on the female thigh speaks for itself and makes the mixture of clothing—as in *Simplicissimus*—a cipher of hermaphroditism. In fact, Courasche sometimes considers declaring herself a "hermaphrodite" so that she can wear trousers in public and pass for a young man. Thus, Simplicissimus and his female counterpart constitute an hermaphroditic intertextuality, and this feature must be considered an important aspect of the connection that holds the cycle of Simplician writings together. Under social pressure—as an alleged hermaphrodite she would have to be examined by "medicos and mid-wives"—Courasche justifies her nonconformism by citing the example of the Amazons, who "fought against their enemies as gallantly as men." But by choosing this model, she remains caught in the sphere of hermaphroditism, for the Amazons are, etymologically speaking, the "ones without breasts," that is, dispositionally masculine. Thus, Courasche fails to achieve the ideal of the opposite sex. Just as she doesn't pass in her efforts to be a "guy" *(Kerl)*, her appeal to these warrior women likewise prevents her from realizing herself as female.

Courasche's tactical decision to achieve her aims by feigning hermaphroditism seems to confirm, as is often thought today, that early modern Europeans were relatively casual in their attitude toward this phenomenon. At baptism, the father and the godfather provisionally fixed the sex of the hermaphroditic infant. Having achieved the age of marriage, the individual could then him- or herself decide for one of the two possibilities. Alterations of this official choice and not the anatomical mixing of the sexes, Michel Foucault has argued, led to most of the documented condemnations of hermaphrodites during the Middle Ages and the Renaissance. While Courasche's aversion toward doctors and midwives may stem from the fact that they could easily disprove her claim to be a hermaphrodite, it also points to a function of the medicine and biology of the Baroque period that, according to Foucault, only begins in the 18th century, namely to determine the "true sex," the monosexuality, of the affected person. In practice, Courasche emphatically reserves this right for herself, although biologically she is not a hermaphrodite at all, nor does she really wish to be one. While the novel several times compares her to a goddess—Venus and Aphrodite are mentioned by name—there is no equivalent naming, let alone "embodiment," of Hermes. To invoke the heuristic idea of Herm-Aphroditism, Grimmelshausen restricts himself to employing a hermetic vessel—"a small sealed glass jar"—as a magical motif. What Courasche would like to be is entirely Venus-Woman or, just as unambiguously, a man. However, the circumstances of war force her into the masquerade of social hermaphroditism, which thwarts her life as a woman, paradoxically in order to protect her womanhood. Later she pretends to be a biological hermaphrodite, but only in order to attain the utopia of masculinity, the privileged sex. When she wishes "not to be a woman," or that she could be a man and "spend [her] days in warfare," then she seems to anticipate the lyrical voice of Annette von Droste-Hülshoff's famous poem "Am Turme" (1842; At the Tower). Long before the introduction of mixed-gender armies, this speaker, acutely aware of the discrimination she is subject to, longs to be "just a part of a soldier," or "at the very least a man." Grimmelshausen's *Courasche* takes its place in the history of the struggle for equality of the sexes.

In any case, from the start Courasche seeks an unequivocal gender status, something that—in Foucault's opinion at least—will only in subsequent centuries become a clearly formulated, and regrettable, aim. Above all, Courasche affirms her natural sex and gender, as her "spiteful" reckoning with Simplicissimus and the lords of nobility and church demonstrates. In the context of the history of ideas, her determined stance represents the division of the hermaphroditic spherical beings of Plato's *Symposium* as well as the separation of the sexes in the biblical story of creation. Filled with a desire to grow together again—"uniting their original nature," as Plato says—the separated human halves symbolize the yearning love of the sexes. This is the deeper meaning of Venus-Courasche's unfulfilled life as a woman. At times she is too dominant; at times the men—like the elusive Hermes-Mercury—escape her grasp, through quarrels, flight, or death. In this sense, hermaphroditism in *Courasche* not only thwarts the achievement of a univocal sexual identity, but is itself thwarted as the image of a reunification of the sundered sexes to be achieved interpersonally.

In accord with this latent hermaphroditic structure, Grimmelshausen's Simplician writings as a whole are undecided and ambivalent. This is finally because they are rooted in a historical epoch of transition and ambiguity. The inherited Ptolomaic cosmology, still supported by the Church, competes with the views of Copernicus, Kepler, and Galileo. Elements deriving from the Middle Ages combine with others anticipating the Enlightenment. In the political and social sphere, absolutism establishes its hegemony only to witness the growing influence of the middle classes. The Protestant North that emerged from the Reformation is confronted with a Counter-Reformation coming from the Catholic South, but also produces symbiotic cultural landscapes such as German-Polish Silesia. The Peace of Westphalia of 1648, which brought the Thirty Years' War to an end, threatens the privileged position of the emperor by strengthening France as well as the territorial principalities of Germany. Since the Humanism of the Renaissance, an emphatic notion of the individual is available, but it exists in tension with the strict hierarchy of baroque collectivities. Finally, while in some cases women share intellectual leadership with men, persecution of witches, in which the battle of the sexes is most terrifyingly manifest, spreads. In this time of upheaval it fell to a man to create a female figure marked by a comprehensive hermaphroditism and thereby representative of the era. The result is that the protagonist of Grimmelshausen's small picaresque novel *Trutz Simplex oder Ausführliche und wunderseltzame Lebens Beschreibung der Ertzbetrügerin und Landstürzerin Courasche* is one of the most striking and memorable female characters in German literature.

See also 1275, 1670 (Pufendorf), 1837, 1949, 1958

Bibliography: Hans Jacob Christoph von Grimmelshausen, *Courage, the Adventuress and The False Messiah,* trans. Hans Speier (Princeton: Princeton University Press, 1964). ———, *Mother Courage,* trans. Walter Wallich, illustrations by Fritz Wegner (London: Folio Society, 1965). ———, *The Runagate Courage: Spite Simplex or the Detailed and Wondrously Strange Life History of the Archfraud and Runagate Courage,* trans. Robert L. Hiller and John C. Osborne (Lincoln: University of Nebraska Press, 1965). ———, *Gesammelte Werke in Einzelausgaben: Lebensbeschreibung der Ertzbetrügerin und Landstörzerin Courasche,* ed. Wolfgang Bender (Tübingen: Niemeyer, 1967). ———, *Lebensbeschreibung der Ertzbetrügerin und Landstörzerin Courasche,* ed. Klaus Haberkamm and Günther Weydt (Stuttgart: Reclam, 1971). Kenneth Negus, *Grimmelshausen* (New York:

Twayne, 1974). Michel Foucault, *Herculine Barbin: Being the Recently Discovered Memoirs of a Nineteenth-Century Hermaphrodite* (New York: Pantheon, 1980).

Klaus Haberkamm

❧ 1670
The *collegia pietatis* is founded in Frankfurt am Main

"The Entirety of Scripture Is within Us"

In 1670 a group of men began to gather regularly in the study of Philipp Jakob Spener (1635–1705), a Lutheran theologian and later senior minister in the predominantly Protestant city of Frankfurt am Main. These meetings, soon to be called *collegia pietatis* and *exercitia pietatis,* enabled the circle of friends to support each other in their spiritual growth. Apart from church services, the Protestant Church had never before tolerated organized gatherings of lay-people. Although the initial meetings were attended primarily by Spener's colleagues, they were soon opened to people of all social ranks and ages, students of theology, lawyers, doctors, merchants, craftsmen, married as well as single people. Even women could attend, although they could not participate in the discussions, which were devoted to a particular biblical passage or to a book of religious edification. Bible study groups such as this are common among German Pietist communities to this day. It was in the cities of Darmstadt and Frankfurt around 1677 that the term "Pietists" was first used to refer to those church members who took part in the *collegia pietatis.* The term, at first intended as derisive, was quickly appropriated by the Pietists themselves.

Religious edification based on intensive Bible study could ultimately be achieved only through increased literacy. Spener's original plan was to set up some social programs for the alleviation of poverty. It was his student August Hermann Francke (1663–1727) who was responsible for institutionalizing Pietist reforms. In this context, he invented an entire educational system ranging from literacy programs for the poor to a "Pädagogium regium" to educate Prussian officers, high-ranking bureaucrats, and teachers. Another important aspect of pietist literacy was the cultivation of biographical and autobiographical writing and, especially in the 18th century, of friendship and letter writing. The influence Pietism was to have on German-speaking culture can be considered as the development of a supple interface between the printed word and the experience of the individual. Pietism linked the mysticism of the Baroque era to the reading and writing practices that were to dominate bourgeois print culture.

The book that contributed most to the intensification of devotional practices that were to become the basis of Pietism was the how-to manual of religious edification, *Vier Bücher vom wahren Christentum* (1610; *Four Books of the True Christianity*) by Johann Arndt (1555–1621). Though Pietism had its roots in the popular religiosity of the 17th century, Spener's *Pia Desideria oder Herzliches Verlangen nach gottgefälliger Besserung der wahren evangelischen Kirchen*

(1675; *Pia Desideria; or, Heartfelt Longing for God-Pleasing Improvement of the True Evangelical Churches*) is generally held to be the founding document of German Pietism. Spener's aim was to rejuvenate a Protestant Church that, following the Thirty Years' War, had become eroded by internal theological battles. Dry theological debates were to be replaced by religion as lived experience. Spener turned to mystical writers and invoked the historical authority of the early Christian community. The minister, for example, was no longer to be primarily an authority on biblical interpretation, but a living example of the faith.

In contrast to the radical religiosity of the Puritans in England, German Pietism, in the wake of Spener, was an attempt to avoid separatist tendencies by integrating a mystical tradition into official church culture. Nevertheless, the potential for separatism was high, even within mainstream Pietism, due to the Pietist critique of the external aspects of the Christian Church. Most of the radical Pietist sects that separated from the official Lutheran or Reformed Church, however, did not last very long. The most important exception is the Pietist community of the Moravian Brothers, a movement that goes back to the Francke pupil Count Nikolaus Ludwig von Zinzendorf (1700–1760), who established a community of believers on his estate at Herrnhut in 1722. The Moravian Brothers, or *Brüdergemeinde*, distinguished themselves through their international outlook, their missionary activities, and their social experiments. They had a strong influence on the Enlightenment and on the young Goethe, whose early friendship with Susanne von Klettenberg (1723–1774) is said to have inspired both the fictional "Confessions of a Beautiful Soul" in *Wilhelm Meister's Apprenticeship* and the mystical figure of Makarie in *Wilhelm Meister's Journeyman Years*.

Spener's *Pia Desideria* was addressed primarily to his fellow ministers and leaders of the Protestant Church. In the introduction, Spener points out that, whereas in former times Church reforms were initiated and organized by a council, he hoped that the printed dissemination of his ideas would now lead to a productive exchange among responsible theologians and ministers. His emphasis on religious praxis, on the actuality of a pious life rather than erudition in sophisticated doctrinal points, together with the urgent appeal for a better Church constitute the core of the *Pia Desideria*. Theologically speaking, Spener's speculation about the historical position of the Protestant Church and his hopes for the imminent future, which he expressed in the second part of the *Pia Desideria,* were remote from Lutheran orthodoxy, and were rather risky in the sense that they approached then-popular chiliastic hopes.

The truth of an individual's spiritual experience as something that has to be respected and accepted in its own right introduces powerful arguments in favor of religious freedom and tolerance. It threatens the role and position of Bible and Church by handing over the principal authority to the individual believer. The union of all true Christians, wherever they might be found, became a natural task for the Pietists. Not church membership but the experience of conversion, spiritual rebirth, and the pious life that followed it were thought to be the basis of religious community. Consequently, treatises, prayers, songs, and especially autobiographical writings by Roman Catholic nuns, monks, and laypeople were included within the Pietist canon. The integration of these texts into Protestant religious life signaled a decisive departure from orthodox tradition. Among the advocates of this opening of the Protestant tradition to mystical writers were Johann Arndt, Johann Henrich Reitz (1655–1720), and Gottfried Arnold (1666–1715).

Taking up Spener's remarks from the *Pia Desideria,* Gottfried Arnold studied the early Christian community's liturgy and government. His publications range from religious poetry and songs to a systematic description of mysticism and its tradition, and include the very controversial *Unparteiische Kirchen- und Ketzerhistorie* (1699/1700). This *Impartial History of the Church and of Heresy* represents a significant step toward the development of historiographical method. Arnold used the term "impartial" in the title to denote a position for the historian that is not congruent with any particular religious confession. Both heretics and church followers are subjected to a critical scrutiny that considers lived religiosity rather than doctrinal position as its standard of evaluation. The lives of individuals, often in the form of spiritual autobiographies, are reprinted in Arnold's history and serve as illustrations of the general historical development. Arnold argues—against Luther—that the decline of Christianity should not be blamed on the Papacy alone, but on all alliances between Church and State that result in an entrenched class of priests, dogmatic rigidity, and the predominance of worldly concerns.

Arnold's *Impartial History* gives a prominent place to the insights and lives of religious women of the latter part of the 17th century. He reprints at length Jane Lead's treatise on the nature of visions as well as the biographies of Antoinette Bourignon and Anna Vetter. He does not depict these women as spiritual leaders—although this title could certainly be claimed for both Bourignon and Lead—but merely as divinely inspired visionaries and exemplars of a pious life that does not shun exile and persecution. The overall picture that emerges from Arnold's *Impartial History* betrays a drift toward an atomistic individualism detached from any communal context. The work was widely read throughout the 18th century. In its effort to hold onto Christianity while rejecting its institutionalized aspects, it expressed the attitude toward religion that became dominant in the German Enlightenment. In a narrower sense, however, Arnold's influence was constrained by chiliastic hopes—typical for the period around 1700—that could not be sustained over time. His focus on the so-called heretics within the Church and his attempts to rehabilitate them in light of the authenticity of their piety need to be understood in conjunction with his condemnation of any form of dogmatism and sectarianism. Thus, although one must not judge and condemn an individual believer for divergence from official doctrine, any attempt at formalizing one's own belief, and of gathering followers, amounts to sinful sectarianism, or, in biblical terms, an attempt to steal the bride from her rightful bridegroom.

Beginning in 1699/1700, Johann Henrich Reitz started to publish, in ever-expanding editions of the *Historie der Wiedergebohrnen* (*History of the Reborn*), a collection of biographical and autobiographical narratives of spiritual rebirth, which became an enormous commercial success. By mid-century, ten thousand copies had been sold. Reitz advertised his collection as both grounded in experience and appealing to the reader's own experience. A single spiritual autobiography could not be exemplary because God's ways are not uniform. The highly specific and individual nature of true faith makes it important to provide a wide spectrum of conversion narratives that represent the multiplicity of God's "process with the souls of his children." He goes on to say in the preface, "Then any reader can see and perceive, in this history, as in a living mirror, his own image and figure, conformity and difference, what is lacking, or how far he is still removed from the realm of God." The assembled confessional narratives, with all their "anxiety and labor, sighs and tears, hope, doubt and fear," enable the reader to participate in an inner spiritual drama. As Reitz notes, however, this is not just a drama of the human heart, but of God's work of redemption and revelation: "One can see from that how the entire heaven with all its secrets, indeed, how the entirety of Scripture is within us: Hell, Heaven, Adam, Christ, Cain, Abel, Sin, Justice, Judgment, Death, Life, Darkness and Light." Of course, in order to elevate the confessions to the status of scriptural fragments and records of divine intervention, Reitz must dismiss certain literary and scholarly standards as inappropriate to them. They might not be learned or rhetorically sophisticated, but in their clumsy and simple language they far surpass the Ancients, expressing true learning and insight into the "essence of things" not in "art and order" but in "words full of spirit and life."

Reitz offers his collection to his readers as a much needed alternative forum to worldly gatherings. In this way, the very activity of reading becomes analogous to Spener's *collegia pietatis:* an authentic exchange of experience, an imaginary dialogue, a shared participation in a Christian life opposed both to abstract doctrine and to worldly entertainment. The reader is invited to learn by participating in the lived experience expressed in this collection. Long before the advent of 18th-century sensibility and its habit of absorbed novel reading, Reitz offers a model for the cultivation of interiority and authenticity that is centered on the private encounter of reader and book.

Both Arnold's *Impartial History* and Reitz's *Historie* situate confessional discourse at the heart of Pietism. In Arnold's case, the individual heretics' visions, dreams, and religious insights, supported by narratives about their lives, become an occasion for studying the worldly corruption, intrigue, and rigidity of the established Church and its officials. Reitz's emphasis falls exclusively on the testimonial status of the individual confessions with regard to the providential order. In his preface, Reitz develops a model through which the autobiographical material compels the reader to engage in self-examination. He draws attention to the actual articulation and textual features of the conversion narratives primarily in terms of an anticlassical aesthetic that values the nonstudied, artless immediacy of expression. He would, of course, not go so far as to seek an ideal of originality in those departures from rhetorical or stylistic standards; nor would he present the individual narrators as "authors" whose ideas are to be considered on their own, apart from the biographical persona of the writer.

The writers of the conversion narratives stand out exclusively for their piety, their authentic belief, their intensely felt insight into the necessity and truth of Scripture. They are, one might say, not of interest as senders of a message, but merely as receivers. The most salient example can be found in the second edition of Reitz's *Historie,* in the spiritual biography of Gottfried Arnold. Reitz briefly summarizes Arnold's education and activities as a scholar and professor of history, mentions a few of Arnold's publications, and praises their value for spiritual edification. Nevertheless, the only first-person account he includes in Arnold's spiritual biography is the latter's explanation of his resignation from his position as professor of history at the university and his growing "disgust for the arrogant, vainglorious rationality of academic life." Isolated from the learned community of scholars, even the learned Gottfried Arnold is integrated into the virtual community of the pious, who merely testify to the multiplicity of God's ways in calling each of his children. The cultural and literary-historical significance of Pietist confession lies in its validation and cultivation of individual experience. The practices of self-observation that arose from these experiential accounts, however, did not feed immediately into the more secular forms of individualized psychology, which emerged only in the latter half of the 18th century. In other words, the psychologizing of religious autobiography that we witness in Goethe's "Confessions of a Beautiful Soul" has no equivalent beyond the fictional realm in its presumed Pietist sources.

See also 1657, 1666, 1774

Bibliography: Primary works. Johann Arndt, *Vier Bücher vom wahren Christentum* (Magdeburg, 1610). ———, *Of true Christianity four books: Wherein is contained the whole oeconomy of God towards man; and the whole duty of man towards God* (London: Joseph Downing, 1720–1744). Gottfried Arnold, *Unparteiische Kirchen- und Ketzerhistorie vom Anfang des Neuen Testaments bis auf das Jahr Christi 1688;* reprint of the 1729 Frankfurt edition (Hildesheim: Olms, 1967). Johann Henrich Reitz, *Historie der Wiedergebohrnen: Vollständige Ausgabe der Erstdrucke aller sieben Teile der pietistischen Sammelbiographie (1698–1745) mit einem werkgeschichtlichen Anhang der Varianten und Ergänzungen aus den späteren Auflagen,* ed. Hans-Jürgen Schrader (Tübingen: Max Niemeyer Verlag, 1982). Philipp Jakob Spener, *Pia Desideria oder Herzliches Verlangen nach gottgefälliger Besserung der wahren evangelischen Kirchen samt einigen dahin einfältig abzweckenden christlichen Vorschlägen* (1675). ———, *Pia desideria,* ed. and trans. Thedore G. Tappert (Philadelphia, Pa.: Fortress Press, 1964). *Secondary works.* Martin Brecht, ed., *Geschichte des Pietismus,* vol. 1: *Der Pietismus vom siebzehnten bis zum frühen achtzehnten Jahrhundert;* vol. 2: *Der Pietismus im achtzehnten Jahrhundert* (Göttingen: Vandenhoeck & Ruprecht, 1993–1995). Gerhard Kaiser, *Pietismus und Patriotismus im literarischen Deutschland* (Frankfurt am Main: Athenäum, 1973). Dorothea von Mücke, "Experience, Impartiality, and Authenticity in Confessional Discourse," *New German Critique* 79 (Winter 2000): 5–35. Johannes Wallman, *Der Pietismus* (Göttingen: Vandenhoeck & Ruprecht, 1990).

Dorothea E. von Mücke

ℒ *1670*

Samuel Pufendorf, after his history of the states of the Holy Roman Empire is banned from German universities, accepts a position at the University of Lund in Sweden

Natural Law

In Heinrich von Kleist's play *The Broken Pitcher* (1808), an elderly character remarks offhand, "The world, our proverb says, gets ever wiser; and everyone, of course, reads Pufendorf." Pufendorf's most important work, a massive Latin treatise, *De jure naturae et gentium (On the Law of Nature and of Nations)*, appeared in 1672. Most audiences today, even in Germany, would probably not catch the reference, but Kleist may well have thought that his contemporaries would. For well over a century, Pufendorf was the most widely studied writer in Europe on natural law, morality, political theory, legal philosophy, and international law. Current German law still embodies some of his recommendations concerning the structure of a legal system. But aside from scholars, who study his impact on the history of modern thought about his subjects, not many people remember him today.

Samuel Pufendorf, born in 1632 in Saxony, was the son of a poor Lutheran pastor. While studying at Leipzig and Jena, he decided not to enter into his father's profession. In 1658 he assumed the position of tutor to the children of Sweden's minister to Denmark, and when war broke out between those two countries, he was imprisoned. There he wrote his first book, an attempt to demonstrate the principles of politics in geometrical fashion. The *Elementa jurisprudentiae universalis (Elements of Universal Jurisprudence)* was published in 1660. In the following year, Pufendorf began teaching international law at the University of Heidelberg. His most important publication during the Heidelberg years was a historical analysis of the states within the decaying Holy Roman Empire. Published in 1667 under a pseudonym, the book was so critical of the German political structure that it was banned from German universities. In 1670 he moved to the University of Lund, in Sweden. There he completed *On the Law of Nature and of Nations* as well as a short summary of it for students, *De officio hominis et gentium* (1673; *On the Duty of Man and Citizen*). This brilliant textbook went through more than one hundred editions in Latin and was translated into every European language.

In 1677 the king of Sweden appointed Pufendorf his official historian. During his time in Sweden, he published several historical works and a treatise on religious toleration and the relations between church and state. He dedicated the latter to Frederick William I, the ruler of Prussia, who in 1688 summoned him to Berlin to serve as his historian. Angered, the Swedish king held onto one of Pufendorf's manuscripts. Pufendorf's trip to Sweden to retrieve it, in 1694, ended in disaster. Scandinavian weather was too much for him, as it had been for Descartes and for Grotius. He died of illness contracted on the return journey, leaving a widow with very little money.

In 1648, when Pufendorf was sixteen, the Peace of Westphalia ended a thirty-year period of devastating warfare. The religiously motivated strife had destroyed innumerable villages, ruined agriculture, and depopulated large parts of the German-speaking lands. In England, civil war, centered on religious differences, continued for another dozen years. Rulers throughout Europe had to cope with fierce sectarian struggles as they tried to consolidate their power. The emergence of the modern nation-states and a growing intolerance for sectarian differences increased the need for rethinking the principles that had traditionally shaped individual conduct and public law.

Pufendorf's *Law of Nature and of Nations* was by far the most detailed and comprehensive of numerous 17th-century attempts to address the problem. In it, he offers a way of justifying morality he thought would be acceptable to every religious confession. A theory that puts morality on a sound footing, he argues, also provides the best view of political authority. He further claimed that his principles could be extended to develop the basic elements of international law, particularly the laws of war and peace. His system was structured to meet the specific problems of his era.

Despite the damage done by religious hatred, atheism was not openly acceptable in the 17th century. Hence one crucial problem social theorists of the time faced was how to show that God's existence was essential to human life while, at the same time, minimizing the danger that sectarian differences would carry over into disagreements about morality and politics. Pufendorf tried to solve the problem with two basic claims.

First, he holds that we must analyze moral obligation in terms of divine commands. Aristotle was wrong to think that nature gives ends to all things, and that these suffice to guide human action. Physical events can help us or harm us; they can be naturally good or bad. But recognition of good and evil alone does not tell us what we ought to do. God has given us commands to govern our action, and these are the original source of morality. Having created a physical universe, Pufendorf says, God *imposed* moral properties on it. Morality is not a matter of advising people to do what is for their own good. It involves obligating someone to do something, like it or not. To obligate someone is to issue a justifiable command backed by the threat of punishment for disobedience. Only God is in a position to issue commands that are binding on all humankind. And morality is constituted by precisely such norms. God is central to our lives because in acting as we morally should, we are obeying him.

Second, Pufendorf points out that since no one can command God, there can be no moral obligations binding on him. He is essentially unrestricted in his laying down laws for us. We therefore cannot understand his reasons for imposing on us the morality we have. The Christian revelation has not been given to all humans, so we cannot base morality on it. The only way we can hope to learn God's will is by looking at the evidence he has given us. We must consider our nature as showing how he meant us to live. To discover natural law, we must study human nature.

The knowledge we need is ordinary, empirical knowledge. It is not affected by our religious beliefs. It consists of facts that, Pufendorf thinks, no one can deny. We are weak beings with many needs. The world can supply the things we need, but we must cooperate in order to get them. We tend to be quarrelsome and selfish, but we also need one another's help and enjoy one another's company. From this we can infer that God wills us to live sociable lives. Because he gave us reason, we are unlike other animals in two crucial respects. We have language, and we are able to understand and share rules and laws. We must conclude, then, that God wills us to live together under laws that govern all reasonable beings.

The chief obstacle is our insufficient sociability. So the first divine command that reason discovers is that we must increase our sociability. We are enjoined to do whatever makes us better able to live together peacefully under the laws. This is the first law of nature, and all others are derived from determining what we need to do in order to carry out this law.

Pufendorf begins by considering the simplest sort of social life, a condition without conventions or laws, with no one in authority over anyone. Following a long tradition, he calls this "the state of nature." All humans in this state face the same task of increasing their sociability. Once we discover how these common problems can be solved, we recognize the laws God wills for everyone. Pufendorf thinks, moreover, that once he sees why people want to leave the state of nature for a society under government, he can also determine what kind of political regimes are justifiable.

Even the first people were under obligation to obey God. Solitary or not, they had to have control over material objects in order to survive. God, of course, owns the entire creation; but he gave everything in the world to humans. He did not assign shares. That was up to human decision. We come to realize that physical possession does not suffice for a secure social life. We need a way of being sure that no one will take anything from us when we are not guarding our possessions. So we invent a variety of ways of assigning things to particular people—of giving them property rights. God dictates only that such parceling out should take place. He leaves it to us to decide whether property rights should be held by individuals or groups.

However the first humans came into existence, it is plain that the sexual impulse is one of our strongest drives. God thus meant us to live in families. The law of nature does not require monogamy, but it plainly requires for one person to be in charge in each family. To Pufendorf it was obvious that the male, being stronger and wiser than the female, should rule. Children, slaves, and servants as well as wives must obey him, and the husband must take good care of them all.

God's laws assign rights even under conditions where a central authority to enforce them is lacking. Pufendorf thinks of humans in the state of nature as slowly developing tools and skills to serve their needs, as becoming increasingly agricultural and then starting to trade surplus crops for things they need or want but do not grow or make themselves. Commerce develops from these simple beginnings into complex forms of interaction. The pleasure we take from the company of others also leads to the development of different forms of society, and eventually to the arts and to luxury. All this begins and grows without governments; but it cannot endure.

In contrast to Aristotle, Pufendorf holds that humans are not naturally sociable. We are not law-abiding by nature. Some people develop sociability but many never do. As property rights become more important, people come to realize that something needs to be done to protect those rights against those who disregard them. Man is the greatest help to man, Pufendorf says, but also the greatest threat. Governments are human devices constructed to cope with the dangers of violation of rights, first from those within a society and eventually from other societies.

Governments possess authority, not mere strength. To create authority, the will of many must concur in assigning power to a person or group. Governments, therefore, must arise from consent or contract. One of several pacts needed to constitute a state specifies the kind of government to which consent is given. The law of nature imposes no limits on what might be a legitimate form of government. Those who live under a regime thereby signify their implicit consent to it. If rulers propose bad laws or become corrupt, the citizens cannot appeal to the contract in order to oust them. Bad government is like bad weather; it just has to be endured.

Rights for one person are meaningless, Pufendorf holds, unless they impose duties on others. And rights as well as duties arise from laws: first God's laws, then those imposed by the magistrate. Pufendorf spells out in great detail the many forms the command to increase sociability takes under different conditions of social life. He works out natural-law principles for positive laws concerning marriage, children, inheritance, contract, punishment, the distribution of honors and offices, international treaties, the exchange of ambassadors, the treatment of prisoners, and the conduct of war. The particulars of human legislation will vary from time to time and from society to society. Since God commands that we have rulers, all positive laws reflect God's will to some extent. But the magistrate never needs to appeal to God or revelation to find out what laws should be enacted.

At first sight it seems that protection of individual rights is all that matters to Pufendorf. But this is too simple. Sociability is a character trait. It is for Pufendorf the basic virtue, and its increase is the first order of law. Moreover the rights and duties the laws impose on individuals are meant to improve all of society. Pufendorf is no utilitarian. He never speaks about the greatest possible happiness. But rulers should strive to enact laws that will benefit the whole. We must obey their laws as well as God's out of respect for authority, not out of fear of sanctions. Although Pufendorf believes that our free will enables us to do so, he also thinks that people are selfish and that few will act out of respect for the law. Harnessing their energies to a system of individual rights designed for the good of all, therefore, is the best we can do.

Although Pufendorf centers his system on law, he also assigns an important role to love. He takes sociability itself as a form of love. And within his system of law, he distinguishes two kinds of rights and duties, the perfect and the imperfect. Perfect rights are entitlements that can be stated with considerable precision, and performance of the duties related to them can be exacted by force. Imperfect rights cannot be precisely specified, and performance of the duties tied to them must spring from love and so cannot be compelled. Perfect duties are duties of justice. Typical are those which arise from a contract. Imperfect duties are duties of love, exemplified in obligations to charity and gratitude. Society cannot exist unless most people carry out their perfect duties, but their performance entails no special merit. Duties of love, by contrast, make society pleasanter. The more we do of imperfect duty, the more merit we acquire—merit that Pufendorf thinks might even carry weight with God.

Pufendorf's theory of morality as arising from divine command was the first extended attempt to see how the worldview of the new physics would allow for the existence of norms that are central to a distinctively human life. His elaboration of the contrast between perfect and imperfect duties was drawn on by most major moral philosophers up to and beyond the time of John Stuart Mill. His learned and meticulous consideration of positive law gave his *Law of Nature and of Nations* unrivaled authority as a work of jurisprudence. His hypothetical history was used by many later writers. Its influence is evident, for example, in the thought of Jean-Jacques Rousseau and Adam Smith. His insistence that morality requires obedience to universal law for its own sake and that free will enables us to act from that motive raised questions that Kant eventually thought he had to answer. It is unlikely, of course, that there will again be a time when we all read Pufendorf. But he deserves to be a little less forgotten.

See also 1622–1624, 1670 (Grimmelshausen), 1790, 1806

Bibliography: Samuel von Pufendorf, *On the Law of Nature and of Nations,* trans. C. W. Oldfather and W. A. Oldfather (Oxford, U.K.: Oxford University Press, 1934). ———, *On the Duty of Man and Citizen,* ed. James Tully, trans. Michael Silverthorne (Cambridge, U.K.: Cambridge University Press, 1991). ———, *On the Natural State of Men,* trans. Michael Seidler (Lewiston, N.Y.: Edwin Mellen Press, 1990). ———, *Political Writings,* ed. Craig L. Carr, trans. Michael Seidler (Oxford: Oxford University Press, 1994). H. Denzer, *Moralphilosophie und Naturrecht bei Samuel Pufendorf* (Munich: Beck, 1972). J. B. Schneewind, *The Invention of Autonomy* (Cambridge, U.K.: Cambridge University Press, 1998), esp. chaps. 7 and 23.

J. B. Schneewind

𝒬 *1689–1690*

Daniel Caspar von Lohenstein's novel *Arminius* becomes all the rage among student groups

The Baroque Novel and the Romance Tradition

In March 1731, Georg Christian Gebauer, member of the Saxon feudal court and professor of feudal law at Leipzig, reminisced about his school days:

> I was about fifteen years old when one of my classmates revealed to me and to others that he had become the happy possessor of the long yearned-for *Arminius*. We couldn't wait for each other to read it; so we sat down in groups of three and four, with someone reading aloud, and no one missed a word or got distracted. If one of us was so overcome by pleasure that he had to say something, the others earnestly joined in his admiration, as if the success or failure of the book depended on our remarks.

This gripping book was a novel of more than 3000 pages written by one Daniel Caspar von Lohenstein (1635–1683), son of an imperial official and himself a bureaucrat. Lohenstein had studied law in Leipzig and Regensburg after schooling in Breslau, then toured Switzerland and Holland. For a time he was active as a lawyer and city official in Breslau and later became a senior official in the tiny state of Oels. There he found time to translate a treatise by Balthasar Gracián (1601–1658) and write plays and many occasional lyrics. In his lifetime, as now, Lohenstein was much better known for his school dramas. Eight editions of his works appeared between 1680 and 1748, most included his dramas and poetry, but not his novel, perhaps because of its huge size.

The novel's action takes place 1600 years earlier, when the Germanic peoples were engaged with the Romans and Celts in war, settlement, and trade. It centers on the "Magnanimous General Arminius or Herrmann, presented for the love of the fatherland with his noble Thussnelda as a brave protector of German freedom, in a useful story of politics, love, and heroism" *(Grossmüthiger Feldherr Arminius oder Herrmann, als Ein tapfferer Beschirmer der deutschen Freyheit nebst seiner Durchlauchtigen Thussnelda in einer sinnreichen Staats-, Liebes- und Helden-Geschichte dem Vaterlande zu Liebe . . . vorgestellet . . .).* The settings range from the forests of Germany to the city of Rome and the hills of Armenia. There are dozens of characters and the plot, too complicated to summarize, is interspersed with generous doses of historical detail.

The proportion of plot to information can be gauged from the novel's opening. It begins with presenting the Germans as a counterforce to the Romans: "Rome had already grown so large that it was superior to its own power, and nothing lacked but something to measure its strength" (1). Several pages sketching the state of the empire are followed by a transition:

> The world and Germany suffered under this yoke, so that once the Dalmatians had been overpowered, no one drew arms against the Romans but the valorous Duke Melo with his Sicambrians and Angrivarians; at this time a band of Ger-

man leaders (whom Quintilianus Varus had assumed to be opposing the apparently rebellious Melo) arrived to see the valorous Herrmann, Duke of the Cheruscii, and following his persuasive exhortations, had assembled their military leaders in the forest of the German Fortress on the Lippe River. The sun was just entering Libra, and the day had already turned golden—after midnight there would be a full moon—as Duke Herrmann had the leaders led into the grove of the goddess Thanfana.

Although this passage seems to promise the beginning of the actual narration, it is followed by a long description of the grove, some Germanic cosmology, more scenery, the verses inscribed above the cave door, the history of the grove, and some comparative ethnography. Even the sentence that finally launches the action includes description and cosmology as a character is introduced: "The priest Libys, a very old man whose ice-gray hair represented the mildew of time, yet whose lively face represented the immortality of the soul, stepped out of the cave toward the German heroes, and occasioned an uncommon respect for himself as well as the holy place; although the Germans always respected priests more than kings . . ." This continual postponing of narrative, so annoying to the modern reader, constitutes a major strategy of the novel, and is largely responsible for its size. The plot is put on hold while we read poems, attend ceremonies, enjoy a pastoral play, and learn about the customs of the Armenians.

If this novel is expansive in scope, it has plenty of contemporary competitors. The French novel *Astrée* by Honoré d'Urfé (1567–1625), with its nobility dressed as shepherds, love letters written on tree bark, host of characters, and complex amorous entanglements in five volumes, was read with delight in Germany as well. *Polexandre et Ericlée* (1619; 5 vols.) by Marin Le Roy Gomberville (1600–1674) was hugely popular all over Europe, as were Madeleine de Scudéry's *Grand Cyrus* (1649–1653) and *Clélie* (1654–1660) in ten volumes each. These and other works like them were available in German translation. Members of the court around Duke Anton Ulrich of Braunschweig-Wolfenbüttel were so taken with *Astrée*, they gave each other Astrean nicknames and produced two huge novels of their own: *Die Durchleuchtige Syrerin Aramena* (1669; *The Noble Syrian Lady Aramena*) and *Octavia* (1677–1707). Another German entrant, Andreas Heinrich Buchholtz's *Des Christlichen Teutschen Gross-Fürsten Herkules und der Böhmischen Königlichen Fräulein Valiska Wunder-Geschichte* (1651, later editions until 1728; *The Amazing Story of the Christian German Potentate Hercules and the Bohemian Royal Lady Valiska*) runs 881 pages with more than four hundred characters. All these novels are set in the ancient world. Grimmelshausen and Philipp von Zesen both wrote novels based on the biblical story of Joseph.

The models for these novels were the Greek "romances" (2nd–4th century CE). In the 1550s, translations of Longus's *Daphnis and Chloe*, Achilles Tatius's *Leucippe and Clitophon*, and Heliodorus's *Ethiopian Story* made them available to those without Greek, and set off a boom of adaptations and imitations. The works became bestsellers and Heliodorus was often ranked with Homer in

Renaissance discussions of narrative. Versions showing the best scenes as pictures with a short explanatory text functioned much like comic strips and have many analogues in Renaissance paintings and tapestries.

A decent work on the romance model should have at least one instance of each of the following ingredients:

- —a couple deeply in love, but not yet safely united in matrimony;
- —a character who has been brought up by foster parents but is really someone much more important;
- —a malefactor who is thoroughly wicked;
- —a malefactor who turns out to have good motives and can be redeemed;
- —a malefactor who falls in love with a heroine;
- —a character who seems to be on the side of the protagonists but is really working for his own ends;
- —pirates or bandits who kidnap a main character, preferably female;
- —a big battle scene;
- —an instance of utter despair causing a main character to contemplate suicide;
- —a setting sufficiently remote in place or time to allow for exotic elements and motivate lengthy descriptions;
- —a prediction sufficiently fuzzy to allow for several interpretations;
- —a wise figure who manages to untangle some of the confused elements of the story;
- —a happy ending in which the prophecy is clarified, the hidden information revealed, and the couple reunited and married.

All these elements are found in Heliodorus; the best results are produced by including three or four of the elements, arranged in subplots that interrelate and interrupt each other in the course of the action. Those wishing to imitate Longus should also include a few rustic characters of naive charm, ideally with some sexual titillation.

The romance narratives work by postponing narrative closure: when the couple is about to be reunited, some disaster intervenes to separate them, or some subplot takes precedence. Often the author teases with threats of premature closure: we see the heroine being killed, and the hero growing despondent; but it turns out to have been a clever conjuring trick, or a case of swapped clothing. The action moves toward striking scenes: picturesque occasions provoke long descriptions of processions, buildings, or ceremonies, and moments of high emotion provoke long speeches where rhetorical fireworks function as psychological analysis and models for imitation.

Obviously the writers of these works drew a great deal on Homer and Greek tragedians, and influenced subsequent genres including melodramas, soap operas, and movies like *Star Wars*. Perhaps the most obvious parallels occur in operas, famous for convoluted and implausible plots and scenes of high emotion culminating in a solo aria. Many Baroque operas and plays are drawn from these novels, their imitations, or their cousins like Ariosto's *Orlando furioso* (1536).

In fact, most major genres of 16th- and 17th-century European narrative are related to these romances. Stress the rustic aspects, and draw upon Theocritus and Virgil's *Eclogues,* and you get pastoral novels like Jorge de Montemayor's *Diana* (1559; German trans. by Harsdörffer, 1646, many German imitations), and Sir Philip Sidney's *Arcadia* (1580) in English. Keep the complicated plot, but replace the upper-class characters with marginal figures like those in Petronius's *Satyricon* (ca. 50 CE) or *The Life of Lazarillo de Tormes* (1554), and you get picaresque novels, like Alemán's *Guzmán de Alfarache* (1599) or Grimmelshausen's *Simplicissimus* (1668–69). Mix all these with recent versions of chivalric epics like Garci Rodríguez de Montalvo's *Amadis of Gaul* (1508, German trans. 1583), and you get a work like Cervantes's *Don Quixote* (1605–1615; German trans. 1648). Even narratives that do not fit clearly into any of these genres, like Philipp von Zesen's *Adriatische Rosemund* (1645), can be linked to the romance plots of the Greek models, and the genres of narrative can be seen as a system of oppositions (Guillén).

German authors often transformed the Greek and French models into more didactic forms. Buchholtz's *Herkules und Valiska* is strongly Christian, and Lohenstein's novel inflects several features of his models in other didactic directions. The love plot still dominates, but Arminius and Thussnelda are married halfway through the book and other couples dominate the ending. The novel was completed and published posthumously, and Benjamin Neukirch's preface interprets the love story as a sugar coating for "useful arts and serious matters of state, particularly about the customs and nature of Germany." Lohenstein's goals can thus be seen as predominantly social.

The experience of reading the book would have been more social. As the examples of the schoolboys and courtly gatherings show, early modern novels were often experienced in groups. Nobles and students made up the primary reading public and the novel appeals to this audience in several ways. The author clearly sought to exemplify moral behavior through the acts of the characters, repeatedly identified as both German and noble. Long discussions among the actors on how to behave in various situations have been related to early modern theories of morals, politics, and statecraft, especially the controversy over whether ends can justify means for people in power.

Given the large population movements in Late Antiquity, the inhabitants of modern Spain, Italy, France, and England could justly regard the Germanic speakers of Roman times as their ancestors. It is also clear from archaeology that Celts, Slavs, and Germanic peoples made up the gene pool of Germania. Nonetheless, since the rediscovery of Tacitus's *Germania* (c. 100 CE) in 1455, German-speaking scholars have tended to lay claim to these ancient peoples as exclusively and particularly German. Seventeenth-century historiography often assimilated Celtic and Germanic culture and language, widening the range of fanciful identification. According to the doctrine of *translatio imperii,* the Habsburg Empire was the legitimate heir to the Roman Empire, so even the Roman characters in Lohenstein's novel represented plausible figures for projection and emulation. By deploying conflicts and alliances between Germans and Romans, *Arminius* invokes and buttresses this legitimizing historiography.

If the Greek models already provided interesting geographic and anthropological anecdotes, Lohenstein took exoticism to the level of erudition. He incorporated most of the extant information on the ancient Germans, using materials from Tacitus, Georg Spalatinus's *Historia Armanii Germanorum contra Romanos Ducis* (1535; rpt. 1673), and a host of classical authors. Another feature of Lohenstein's models is supercharged in the roman à clef. John Barclay's *Argenis* (1621; German trans. by Opitz, 1626) was republished with a key in 1630. Keys for the novels of Gomberville and Scudéry were circulated soon after their publication, and many novels, including those of Eberhard Werner Happel, claimed to be based on real events. Buchholtz's *Herkules und Valiska* includes disguised incidents from the Thirty Years' War. But Lohenstein outdoes them all. A series of portraits in a hunting lodge introduces all twelve Habsburg emperors as backstory. Arminius is modeled on the reigning Emperor Leopold, and one section provides a history of Germany since the Reformation. *Arminius* thus functions as a textbook for ancient and modern German history as well as for morality, leadership skills, and literary style.

Although, as Gebauer noted as an adult, the schoolboys were more interested in the plot, these didactic elements of the novel were praised in reviews—in periodicals such as the *Acta eruditorum,* and by figures like Thomasius and Lessing—just as the style was singled out for imitation in Christian Schröter's *Gründliche Anweisung zur deutschen Oratorie* (1704; *Thorough Instruction in German Oratory*). Lohenstein's novel of 1689 enjoyed such prestige that its original Leipzig publisher reissued it in 1731, forestalling a planned pirate edition to be funded by subscription in Bern. For the reissue, Gebauer added notes, some reworking, a numbering system, and a full index allowing for easy locating of ancient German customs, moral facts, and information about human behavior. An abbreviated version, *Arminius enucleatus (Arminius Deshelled),* was brought out by Johann Christoph Männling in 1708, partly for the benefit of those who could not afford the two folio volumes of the original. Where a modern reader would want the plot without the digressions, this edition cut the story and kept the useful information. It thus serves as a handbook of commonplaces, including the best facts and observations for recycling in the reader's own speeches and writings.

Yet even in its first edition, Lohenstein's novel marked the end of an era. The decades between 1685 and 1715 were a watershed in European culture, when the modern book market, literature, and fiction came into being (Simons). But, as recent scholarship has shown (McKeon, Doody), modern realist fiction is unthinkable without the romance model as its countermodel. Fielding's *Tom Jones,* Goethe's *Wilhelm Meister,* the novel of manners, and the modern-day bodice ripper all derive from its plot structure and attention to the working of the human psyche. Modernist and postmodern novels reintroduced into fiction many elements of fantastic plot, vast temporal and geographic sweep, and the encyclopedic urge. Lohenstein's novel is hardly a good read for our times, but it demonstrates how a strong reworking of existing literary models, coupled with a concern for current moral concerns and the desire for a page turner, can produce a bestseller that has a lasting impact across multiple generations.

See also 1670 (Grimmelshausen), 1806, 1818

Bibliography: Margaret Anne Doody, *The True Story of the Novel* (New Brunswick, N.J.: Rutgers University Press, 1996). Claudio Guillén, *Literature as System* (Princeton, N.J.: Princeton University Press, 1971). Tomas Hägg, *The Novel in Antiquity* (Berkeley: University of California Press, 1983). Daniel Caspar von Lohenstein, *Grossmüthiger Feldherr Arminius . . .*, ed. Benjamin Neukirch, 2 vols. (Leipzig: Gleditsch, 1689–1690; rpt. Hildesheim: Olms, 1973); microfilm in German Baroque Literature reel 404, no. 1309; ed. Georg Christian Gebauer, 4 vols. (Leipzig: Gleditsch, 1731; also microfilm in German Baroque Literature, reel 406, no. 1310). Johann Christoph Männling, ed., *Arminius enucleatus*, 2 vols. (Leipzig: Jenisch, 1708). Michael McKeon, *The Origins of the English Novel, 1600–1740* (Baltimore: Johns Hopkins University Press, 1987). B. P. Reardon, ed., *Collected Ancient Greek Novels* (Berkeley: University of California Press, 1989). Olaf Simons, *Marteaus Europa, oder Der Roman, bevor er Literatur wurde: Eine Untersuchung des deutschen und englischen Buchangebots der Jahre 1710 bis 1720* (Amsterdam: Rodopi, 2001).

Emery Snyder

♉ *1690*

After her husband's death, Glikl bas Yehuda Leib begins to write her memoirs

Life's Balance Sheet

When Glikl bas Yehuda Leib, a well-known Jewish businesswoman and mother of fourteen, died in 1724, a Yiddish manuscript on which she had been working for three decades was given to her grieving family. The narrative contained in that manuscript commences with the year 1690–91, when she decided to begin her memoirs; from there it circles back to selected episodes of her life, among them her birth in 1646, her marriage to Chaim Segal at fourteen, and her almost three decades of business partnership with him, until his sudden death in 1689. The narrative then continues beyond the years when she first began writing, recording Glikl's decade of widowhood, her second marriage to the banker Cerf Levy in 1700, Levy's death in 1712, and Glikl's subsequent financial struggles; the memoir's final episode is set in 1719, five years before Glikl's death at the age of 78. When in 1896 David Kaufmann published the *Memoirs of Glueckl von Hameln* in the Latin alphabet, one of the richest surviving autobiographical records of the life of an early modern Jewish woman was made publicly available for the first time. Glikl, however, might well have objected to Kaufmann's use of the onomastic convention that linked her so firmly to the town of Hameln. In fact, she has little positive to say about the town in her *Memoirs,* considering it provincial compared to Hamburg, the bustling port city where she was born and raised, and in which she spent most of her life. Hameln's best feature, in her eyes, was her first husband. Though Chaim Segal himself was certainly known by the name of his hometown, as was typical of Jews engaged in international commerce, this was hardly a naming standard. Many Jews were known by nicknames derived not from places of origin, but from physical features (the *Memoirs* mention a "Tall Nathan," a "Fat Shmuel," and a "Fine Shmuel") or significant life events ("Shot Jacob" had survived bullet wounds inflicted by highwaymen). Depending on context, women were called by their patronymic, their matronymic, or their husband's name (as in "Glikl Reb Chaim's").

Glikl might have been uncomfortable with being nominally tied to a single town for other reasons as well. First, personal affairs and business requirements kept her constantly moving. Furthermore, Glikl understood herself as being in exile and lived in the hope of a messianic redemption that would bring the Jews to the Promised Land. Finally, contemporary Jewish communities were often uprooted by war or government decree. The first historical event mentioned in Glikl's *Memoirs* is the Jews' expulsion from Hamburg in 1649; one of the last is Louis XIV's order preventing Jewish merchants, Glikl's stepson among them, from reentering Alsace before giving up their holdings in Lorraine. All these factors combined to make the link between individuals and their locations highly tenuous. Hardly less complex was Glikl's sense of time. Though she would have used the Christian calendar for business dealings with non-Jews, her *Memoirs* unfold—as did her life—in keeping with the Jewish calendar. Thus she dates the beginning of her *Memoirs* as the year 5451, and not the corresponding year 1690–91. In Glikl's case, then, the three dimensions within which the memoirist charts a life—space, time, and personal identity—are variously layered, shot through with historical contingencies, and informed by tradition.

In giving shape and consistency to this complex life, Glikl drew on two contemporary generic traditions. She claims she began writing the *Memoirs* to help banish "melancholy thoughts" (*Memoiren,* 3) during the sleepless nights following her husband's sudden and painful death from gastrointestinal complications following a fall. However, she also clearly states that her primary reason for writing is to provide her children with knowledge of their father. In doing so, she intends to give them not merely a historical record, but also a work of moral and practical instruction. By situating the writing of the *Memoirs* within an extended contemplation of mortality, both her husband's and more indirectly her own, she links her *Memoirs* to the contemporary genre of the ethical will, a long text addressed to a decedent's survivors. In fact, Glikl refers explicitly to one of the best-known ethical wills, Avraham Horovitz's Hebrew *Yesh Nokhalin* (1615), a work that, given her limited knowledge of Hebrew, she probably heard read aloud in a Yiddish translation. Glikl's *Memoirs* also draw strongly upon the tradition of popular pietistic Yiddish literature. Works in this genre, addressed to the uneducated—or, as one book's title page famously had it, "to women and men who are like women"—were designed both to combat impiety and to replace such secular adventure works as the *Bove Bukh* (published 1541), which at that time continued to enthrall Jewish audiences. In Glikl's *Memoirs,* the *Brantspigl* (1596) and the *Lev Tov* (1620), both examples of this tradition, are explicitly cited.

Glikl's citations from these precedent texts show her not merely as a traditionalist relying upon others' works for their acknowledged moral authority, but as the creator of a multilayered composition in which the cited texts contribute added meaning both to the narrative details and to the overriding structure. For example, the first story Glikl cites at length, taken from the *Yesh Nokhalin,* describes an imprisoned physician who tells his visiting family that his unbroken spirits stem from a potion combining seven herbs. When asked the nature of these seven herbs, he identifies them as trust, hope, knowledge of sin, acceptance of fate, faith in God's forgiveness, knowledge that things could be worse, and the possibility of divine intervention. Glikl introduces the story by briefly commenting on how divine punishments repay human misdeeds. After retelling the narrative, she remarks: "One can learn much from this story. My beloved children, I may not go further, for were I to come to all the story's depths, ten books would not be sufficient. Read the German *Brantspigl* or the *Lev Tov;* there one can learn, in the books of morals one can find everything" (11). Glikl's esoterically minded comment suggests that the story bears a special relevance to the *Memoirs'* offer of moral guidance. Perhaps the seven herbs correspond to the seven books of Glikl's *Memoirs* themselves, with each moral-spiritual herb applying to the topics and events discussed within the respective books. Thus the final herb, a reminder of the possibility of divine intervention, corresponds to the seventh book's strangely supernatural tone, its descriptions of poltergeist-like activity within the synagogue, and its final sustained episode—the near-catastrophic collapse of the women's section in the synagogue and the mysterious salvation of the rabbi's wife and daughter by six tall veiled women. Glikl relates a tale of miraculous salvation near the work's end not simply because it occurred towards her life's end, but because it provides a thematic coda to the moral lessons she has promulgated from the beginning.

Such an interpretation, of course, presupposes that Glikl's citation of other texts as well as her presentation of real-life events are part of a considered strategy to produce a literary work of remarkable complexity. This assumption accords with recent research showing that Glikl deliberately reworked her manuscript throughout her life rather than simply adding new events and observations to an unedited stack of pages. Certainty is impossible since we lack an autograph copy; but the hypothesis seems plausible, especially since the chronology of the *Memoirs* is extremely problematic, which seems to undermine its function as a historical record. If, however, the text is seen primarily as an ethical work, a response to the world's problems shaped by traditional forms, then such temporal inconsistencies become relatively insignificant. All that matters is the hope that the children will not repeat the sins and errors of the parents. In such a context, the traditional stories provide a framework of meaning within which Glikl's bitter personal experience assumes the status of a moral lesson to be passed on to her children. Glikl's *Memoirs* present complex, multivalent events with deceptive simplicity.

Glikl's narrative of the messianic frenzy unleashed among European Jews in 1666 by Sabbatai Zevi is a case in point. Many felt that the messianic era was at hand, but the rampant enthusiasm was soon deflated when Sabbatai Zevi converted to Islam. Describing the community's disillusionment, Glikl interweaves personal and communal experience in a graphic comparison: "We had hoped like a woman who sits on the birthing stool and suffers through her labor with great pains, believing that after all her pain and labor she will be able to rejoice with her child; but after all her pain and labor nothing emerges but wind" (74–75). The account then expands by fusing the experience of the event within her family with issues of commerce, morality, and polity:

> Some, sadly, sold all their possessions, house and home, and all hoped that every day they would be redeemed. My father-in-law—he should rest in peace—lived in Hameln. He, too, abandoned his dwelling place and his court and his house and his furniture, all his possessions, let everything stand as it was and went to the city of Hildesheim to live. He sent here to us in Hamburg two big barrels with all sorts of linens. And in them were all sorts of things to eat—peas, beans, smoked meat, and other sorts of dried fruit, which could be preserved. For the good man—he should rest in peace—thought that one could simply travel from Hamburg to the Holy Land. These barrels stood for well over a year in my house. Finally he was afraid that the meat and other things would spoil. Then he wrote us that we should open the barrels and take out the foodstuffs so that the linens would not be ruined. As it was, they stood there for three years and he always thought that he would need them for his trip. But such did not please the Highest. (75–76)

Here Glikl shows both the impact of communal events on her family and the way in which the community's theological miscalculation had a commercial dimension. The sinful acceptance of the false messiah is expressed in the rash decision to sell property, presumably well below market value. Glikl's description of her father-in-law's preparations also displays a nuanced understanding of the believer's psychology. But the same passage includes a metaphorical dimension as well: as the pure, stainless linen is placed alongside perishable food, pure spirit and corruptible flesh are united in the same vessels. Glikl's account suggests that, even when the "food" is treated so as to prevent spoilage, a misdirected motive such as excessively urgent or incorrectly focused messianic longing may yield both spiritual and economic ruin.

Although the complex interweaving of economic, moral, and spiritual perspectives pervades Glikl's *Memoirs,* it is especially conspicuous in connection with the central theme of debt. For Glikl a business debt is sacred and must always be repaid. Conversely, the refusal to return borrowed capital or the willful ignoring of contractual obligations is variously interpreted by Glikl as either a moral transgression of the nonpaying debtor or a heavenly prescribed punishment for the lender's prior sins. In this sense, sudden economic reversals, sometimes catapulting an individual into financial ruin, are analogous to other destructive contingencies that afflict Glikl's family, such as outbreaks of plague or robberies of business associates even on supposedly safe roads. In the *Memoirs* such violent disruptions of the normal pattern of moral and economic life are seen as challenges in the face of which the traditionalist can prove her faith in divine justice. Certainly one of the crucial moral and ethical questions animating the *Memoirs* is that of theodicy. Why is a fair and just lender cast into bankruptcy when a debt is not paid? Why do good people die suddenly and painfully? Why are the righteous often poor and the unscrupulous, who go unpunished, often rich? Glikl addresses these disturbing questions by invoking traditional religious explanations. But such passive acceptance of destiny often seems to coexist uneasily with the activist, mercantile sensibility the *Memoirs* also evince.

Particularly important to Glikl—and closely tied to the generic concept of an ethical will—is the relationship of debt and obligation between parents and children. Glikl strongly feels she owes her children an assured position in life, that it is her duty to ensure they are well married and to provide them with the capital necessary to establish themselves economically. Her efforts to fulfill her parental obligation constitute much of the *Memoirs'* narrative content, much as the writing of the *Memoirs* itself serves to meet her parental responsibility of providing her children with the moral and spiritual tools that a successful life requires. The repayment of the children's resulting debt to the parents, as Glikl conceives of it, is always to be paid forward, to the succeeding generation, never back. This theme's strong connection to the *Memoirs'* project is indicated by its compositional prominence; it is highlighted both at the work's beginning and at its end. One of the first stories Glikl tells is of a mother bird who kills all her fledglings but one. Why? Because those she slays promise to care for her in her old age, while the one she spares vows to care only for her own children. Near the end of the *Memoirs* she records that financial reversals in her old age compelled her to move in with her children. Her views on the debt relations between the generations would lead her to consider such dependence an unwarranted imposition.

Glikl claims to be a remarkable businesswoman and notes proudly how her first husband had always consulted with her about business decisions in his trading of gold, silver, pearls, currency, and other commodities. After his death, she loaned and exchanged money across Europe and established a store in Hamburg, from which she dealt with an international clientele, selling and trading pearls, local products, and stockings she herself manufactured. But her mercantile instincts often failed her. In one of the few instances reported by her in which her husband actually listens to her advice, it turns out to be bad. Moreover, her own most significant commercial judgment, her decision to remarry, proves an unmitigated disaster. Two years after their marriage, her second husband went bankrupt, through no fault of his own. This event brings about a financial downturn for Glikl that would continue long after his death a decade later. Similarly, Glikl's asseverations of her own financial rectitude are belied by recent research documenting her failure to pay taxes owed to the city of Hamburg and to the Altona Jewish community when she changed her communal affiliation in order to remarry. But this is just to say that in early modern Europe it was not easy for a Jewish woman, who at times was her family's sole provider, to maintain both her financial balance sheet and her moral and spiritual equilibrium. In her *Memoirs* Glikl chronicled her tireless efforts to achieve that goal and in doing so fashioned a work of compositional subtlety that delicately juxtaposes traditional forms with keen historical observations.

See also 1515–1517, 1670 (Grimmelshausen), 1710, 1913, 1946/1947

Bibliography: Glueckel von Hameln, *Die Memoiren der Glückel von Hameln 1645–1719,* ed. David Kaufmann (Frankfurt am Main: Kaufmann, 1896). [In Western Yiddish, Latin alphabet. Citations are from this edition and are translated by the author.] ———, *The Life of Gluckel of Hameln, 1646–1724,* trans. Beth-Zion Abrahams (New York: Yosseloff, 1963). ———, *Zikhroynes,* ed. Shmuel Rozhanski, trans. Yosef Bernfeld (Buenos Aires: Musterverk fun der yidisher literatur, 1967). [Modern Yiddish translation, Hebrew alphabet.] Natalie Zemon Davis, *Women on the Margins: Three Seventeenth-Century Lives* (Cambridge, Mass.: Harvard University Press, 1995), 5–62. Michael Stanislawski, *Autobiographical Jews* (Seattle: University of Washington Press, 2004).

Jeremy Dauber

♌ 1710

Leibniz's *Theodicy* is published

"The Case of God Defended"

The only philosophical book Gottfried Wilhelm Leibniz published in his lifetime (1646–1716) was his *Essais de Théodicée sur la bonté de Dieu, la liberté de l'homme, et l'origine du mal* (1710; *Theodicy: Essays on the Goodness of God, the Freedom of Man, and the Origin of Evil),* which appeared in Amsterdam and was soon followed by French, Latin, German, and Dutch editions. With books on mathematics, law, diplomacy, and international politics to his credit, Leibniz, in 1710, was no stranger to publishing, but neither was publication his main venue of influence. In the tightly knit intellectual world of 17th-century Europe, a philosopher could achieve recognition through conversations, correspondence, interventions in discussions at court, and short papers in learned journals, rather than making a career, as Kant or Hegel would later, through a series of major books addressed to the entire reading public. Most of Leibniz's writings took the form of letters, privately circulated papers, or personal jottings (these last fortunately preserved after his death), and their publication took place long after the controversies or occasions that had stimulated the intellectual activity.

Leibniz's *New Essays on Human Understanding* appeared in 1765, fifty years after their author's death and seventy-five years after the work to which they were a response, John Locke's *An Essay Concerning Human Understanding* (1689), was published. A first collected edition of Leibniz's philosophical writings had to wait until 1768. His manuscript notes, catalogued in the late 19th century and made available on microfilm in the mid-20th, are slowly emerging in book form thanks to a dedicated succession of editors and transcribers. The exception to this pattern of delayed publication, the *Theodicy,* was thus for decades the main source for the signal influence throughout German-speaking lands of the philosophy of Leibniz and Christian Wolff.

Like the *New Essays* with their aim of correcting Locke's psychology, the *Theodicy* is a response to another's work. Certain articles of Pierre Bayle's *Historical and Critical Dictionary* (1697) had proposed challenges to dogmatic theology. God's omnipotence was incompatible with the free will of created beings, or if these beings were not free, then they could not reasonably be condemned for sinning. Moreover, an entirely beneficent God would not have created evil, and an all-powerful one could have prevented it from arising. Thus the traditional predicates of God—as supremely good, powerful, and wise—were incompatible with one another. By revealing the latent conflicts of faith and reason, Bayle (1647–1706), a Huguenot exile from France, hoped to advance the cause of religious tolerance. "All that reason can do is to show man his darkness and impotence and his need for another revelation, the revelation of Scripture" (*Dictionnaire,* "Manichéens"). "Who will not admire and deplore the fate of our reason? See the Manicheans, with their utterly absurd and contradictory hypothesis, giving an account of experience that is a hundred times preferable to that of the orthodox [Christians] who hold to the so just, so necessary, so uniquely truthful supposition of a good and all-powerful first principle!" ("Pauliciens"). Despite its fideistic design, Bayle's work was read as arguing the incoherence of Christianity. Condemned by both Catholic and Protestant theologians, read and debated avidly throughout Europe, it was of particular interest in the German courts where Leibniz served as advisor and diplomat. From the *Dictionary*'s first appearance, Leibniz combated its views on necessity, freedom, and fate, a position no doubt reinforced by Bayle's coolness toward Leibniz's system of "pre-established harmony" between body and soul. The *Theodicy* attempts to answer all of Bayle's objections with a comprehensive theory that expounds the nature and the purpose of the creation.

The first of the great German philosophers was trained as a lawyer and his *Theodicy* is explicitly cast in the form of a brief for the defense: "The case of God defended on the basis of his justice, which is here reconciled with all his other perfections and the whole of his actions" (*Théodicée,* Appendix 1). A God of infinite power would seem to have unlimited responsibility for what goes on in the world. Leibniz must show that in permitting evil to exist, God neither restricts his power nor lessens his goodness, and that the freedom of creatures is compatible with the foresight of the creator. The result must vindicate both divine authority and human responsibility.

These were not new problems in Christian theology, as Bayle's historical entries show—indeed they are as old as the Book of Job—but the 17th-century sciences posed them in different ways. The philosophers René Descartes, Thomas Hobbes, and Baruch Spinoza, among others, suggested that all motion can be explained by physical laws. How the law-bound character of physical action consorts with spontaneous thinking or willing was a problem that each philosopher approached in his own way, but the motif of a division of realms—a deterministic physical world for the body and a world of free choice and potential error for the soul—runs through the cosmology, epistemology, and ethics of each. Specific problems having to do with the nature of the mind, the legitimacy of political authority, and the mode of existence of God arise on the boundary of the two realms in such a way that the relation between body and soul is a test case for all.

If Bayle's *Dictionary* sharpened the contradiction between freedom and necessity in order to show contemporary rationalism —whose great successes lay in extending the domain of physical law—at war with the prerequisites of morality and theology, Leibniz sought to reconcile the opposites and show that the conflict between them is merely on the surface. The right perspective to adopt, Leibniz contends in the *Theodicy,* is that of the Creator. By creating the world, God established an immense interrelated set of "simple substances" or "monads," each of which undergoes successive states or "perceptions"; the successive states of these monads are all interrelated, so that a change to any one of them will be in some way perceived by all, each being a mirror or "expression" of the universe. (The metaphysics of the *Monadology* and *Theodicy* is thus the earliest theory of the world as made up solely of information.) A state of the world is a state of correlation among all the monads composing it. A particular state of the world is brought to actuality through a choice God makes among all the possible states, and this choice is to be explained in terms of a final cause: God's desire to bring about the best of the many possible worlds or states of the world.

Such a demanding account of final causes forestalls criticism. One cannot say that an event is good or bad without knowing its relation to other simultaneous and future events whose possibility correlates with that event's possibility, and, beyond that, the relation of that event's "compossibility set" to the final state of the world in view of which God is presumably choosing all intermediate states. The theory also aspires to rendering nonsensical the objection that a world in which Caesar did not cross the Rubicon, for example, is preferable to the world in which he did. For the condition of any individual monad at any moment is so imbricated with the past and future states of that monad, and with the states of all the other monads composing the correlative states of the world, that its condition follows necessarily from the choice that God makes of the best world. There is thus no room for exceptions or miracles, which would, as exceptions, call into question the wisdom of God as legislator.

A fabric of metaphysical necessity, founded in the choice of the best, would thus replace the commonsense idea of choices and alternatives with good and bad results. In anticipation of any criticism that his system leads to fatalism, Leibniz casts his vision as one of internal, spontaneous necessity rather than external constraint.

> By nature every simple substance has perception and . . . its individuality consists in the perpetual law that establishes the sequence of perceptions that are attached to that substance (these perceptions giving rise to one another naturally), to represent the body that is assigned to it, and, by representing that body, to represent the whole universe, according to the point of view that belongs to that simple substance, without the substance's needing to receive any physical influence from the body . . . From which it follows that the soul has in itself a

perfect spontaneity, so that in its actions it depends on nothing but God and itself. (*Théodicée,* 91)

At the creation of the world, God put into the monadic formula of Julius
Caesar the predispositions that would lead him to cross the Rubicon as well as
the predispositions required in all other monads for that event to occur. But
the crossing of the Rubicon is attributable to no one but Caesar, who performed it as a spontaneous playing-out of his nature.

Bodies and physical objects are accounted for in this system as "well-
founded phenomena," accountable mirages that proceed as sensory side effects
from the interaction of monadic substances. "From the moment that confused
thoughts exist, we have the senses and we have matter: for these confused
thoughts arise from the interrelation of all these things according to time and
extension. That is why in my philosophy there is no such thing as a reasonable
creature with no organic body, and there is no created spirit totally detached
from matter" (*Théodicée,* 181). Events affecting them are explained as consequences of efficient causes, while events affecting monads (and among monads,
human souls) follow directly from the final causes pursued by God in choosing
the best. Between these two realms of causation, there is no communication,
only synchronized parallelism as in a marionette theater.

> In the beginning, God created the soul in such a way that it must produce and
> represent for itself in due sequence everything that occurs in the body; and the
> body, as well, in such a way that it must perform spontaneously whatever the
> soul orders it to do. As a consequence, the laws that bind together the thoughts
> of the soul in the order of final causes, and according to its series of perceptions,
> must produce those images which encounter and match with the impressions
> of bodies on our organs; and moreover, the laws of movement in the body,
> which follow one another in the order of efficient causes, combine with one
> another and tally so well with the thoughts of the soul that the body is brought
> to act in such time as the soul may desire.
>
>   And far from constituting an obstacle to freedom, nothing could be more fa-
> vorable to it . . . It is as if someone who knew everything that I will command a
> servant to do tomorrow, in the course of the whole day, were to construct an
> automaton with the exact appearance of this servant, programmed to do what-
> ever I might ask of him tomorrow exactly according to schedule. This would
> not hinder me from commanding freely whatever I might desire, although
> there would be nothing at all free in the action of the automaton serving me.
>   (*Théodicée,* 138–139)

The problem of freedom is recast here in the form of a rhetorical chiasmus. Secure in the knowledge of his essential freedom, the master (the soul) issues orders all day to a robot valet (the body) who has been previously programmed
with an infallible algorithm synchronized with the precisely predicted actions
of this master, whose acts of free commanding then become the indication that
the master is the automaton of his automaton; but the master does not seem to
share in this knowledge, since he continues to speak of "commanding freely

whatever I might desire." From the point of view of God, the master's commanding must be a hollow linguistic display—though it is the one thing that differentiates master from servant, or soul from body.

Moreover, ordinary language operates a further chiasmus on the philosophical chiasmus. "It is, however, a fact that in common speech, which describes things according to their appearances, we must say that the soul in some way relies on the body and its sense-impressions, somewhat as we adopt the language of Ptolemy and Tycho Brahe in ordinary usage, though we may think like Copernicus, when we speak of the 'rising' and 'setting' of the sun" (*Théodicée,* 140). The body and soul, though elements within distinct causal series, are fashioned by God to behave as if they were connected. A complicated farce allows the soul to act as if it were really giving orders to the body and ordinary language allows us to speak as if the soul depended on the body for its knowledge of the outside world. Almost as a presage of Hegel's drama of master and slave, and of Marx's inversion of Hegel's hierarchies of order, Leibniz's perspectivalism situates the truth at the end of a series of linguistic misprisions, dictated by partial and limited points of view.

If the divine point of view reconciles these partial versions of the world, their point of contact is the phrase "as if." In the longer term, Leibniz's *Theodicy* survives not because of its theory of optimism (crudely but memorably ridiculed by Voltaire in *Candide*) but for its formulation of what Kant would later call "teleological reason." Take the end of the *Monadology:*

> Minds, again, are images of Divinity itself, of the very Author of nature; they are capable of knowing the system of the universe and of imitating some part of it in architectonic tokens; each mind being like a little divinity in its own department.
>
> It is this that makes the Minds capable of entering into a sort of Society with God . . . This City of God, this truly universal monarchy, is a moral world in the natural world, and the loftiest and most divine of all God's works . . .
>
> As we established earlier that a perfect harmony reigns between the two natural kingdoms (that of efficient and that of final causes), so here we must note a further harmony between the physical kingdom of Nature and the moral kingdom of Grace, that is, between God considered as architect of the machine of the universe, and God considered as monarch of the divine city of Minds. (*Monadology,* paras. 83–87)

Eighty years after the *Theodicy,* the Kingdom of Ends likewise emerges in the midst of the Kingdom of Nature (or of Means) at the end of Kant's examination of teleological judgment. But Kant's image of the Kingdom of Ends arises from "*moral* teleology supplement[ing] the deficiency of *physical* teleology, and for the first time establish[ing] a *theology,*" in "a moral argument for the existence of God [which] does not, strictly speaking, merely, as it were, supplement the physico-teleological so as to make it a complete proof. Rather it is a distinct proof which compensates for the failure of the latter to produce conviction" (Kant, *Critique of Judgment,* 111, 154). One can conceive of this kingdom but not cognize it; one can demonstrate the necessity of such a conception for the purposes of practical reason without being able (or entitled) to derive the conception from anything observable in nature. Although Kant almost never mentions Leibniz, the *Critique of Judgment* may well be read as a correction of the *Theodicy,* a replacement of the *Theodicy*'s theology and physics by aesthetics and epistemology. Leibniz's harmony between final and efficient causes yields in Kant to a lapse of continuity between argumentative modes between pure and practical reason. Kant's "as if" implies a "but we can never be certain that it is." The conciliatory divine point of view gives way to an enduring contingent, fictive relation between end—as glimpsed in theology, morality, and art—and means. A certain pathos in the Kantian account of beauty and finality derives from the chanciness of the relation between the natural world as given and the prerequisites that the moral world must establish for itself. A similar pathos sets the tone for much later writing on art, for example Schiller's *Letters on the Aesthetic Education of Man*. But such thought would have been incomprehensible to Leibniz, for whom we are always already (and happily) part of the Kingdom of Ends.

See also 1735, 1790, 1792 (August 26), 1828 (Winter)

Bibliography: Gilles Deleuze, *Le pli: Leibniz et le Baroque* (Paris: Minuit, 1988). Immanuel Kant, *Critique of Judgement,* tr. James Creed Meredith (Oxford, U.K.: Oxford University Press, 1952). Gottfried Wilhelm Leibniz, *Essais de Théodicée* (Paris: Garnier-Flammarion, 1969). ———, *La Monadologie,* ed. Emile Boutroux (Paris: Delagrave, 1982). ———, *Philosophical Papers and Letters,* ed. and trans. Leroy E. Loemker (Dordrecht, the Netherlands: Reidel, 1972). Benson Mates, *The Philosophy of Leibniz: Metaphysics and Language* (New York: Oxford University Press, 1986). Friedrich von Schiller, *On the Aesthetic Education of Man,* ed. and trans. Elizabeth M. Wilkinson and L. A. Willoughby (Oxford, U.K.: Oxford University Press, 1967). Michel Serres, *Le système de Leibniz et ses modèles mathématiques* (Paris: Presses Universitaires de France, 1968). Norbert Wiener, *Cybernetics, or Control and Communication in the Animal and the Machine* (Cambridge, Mass.: MIT Press, 1948).

Haun Saussy

1729

The Swiss physician Albrecht von Haller publishes a poem on the Alps that combines learned observations of natural history with poetic celebration of a sublime landscape

A Scientist and Poet

When Friedrich Schiller, in his play *Die Räuber,* had Franz Moor condemn the 18th century as an "ink-dripping seculum," the youthful robber's spite seemed to fit no one better than the Swiss author Albrecht von Haller (1708–1777). The sheer bulk of Haller's writing is so staggering that from the perspective of Weimar Classicism it could be understood only as an involuntary loss of ink rather than as conscious production. There is reason to believe, however, that this dictum was also a case of sour grapes, for Haller had succeeded in all three areas in which Schiller had attempted to establish himself:

he was the foremost natural scientist of his time, he was one of the most powerful academics in Europe, and he was a much admired poet.

Haller's fame grew from all three of these occupations. Recognition as a poet came first: after his studies of medicine in Tübingen, Leiden, London, and Paris, Haller settled in his native Bern as a practicing physician and began to publish poems. The unusually joyful love song *Doris* (1730), inspired by marriage to his first wife, Mariane Wyss, became famous enough to find its way into Klopstock's ode *Der Zürchersee* (1750; *The Lake of Zurich*). An extended botanical excursion into the Swiss Alps yielded not only the plan for a complete inventory of Swiss plants (the *Enumeratio methodica stirpium Helvetiae indigenarum* of 1742), but also the poem *Die Alpen* (1729; *The Alps*). Like all of Haller's poetic and scientific work, *Die Alpen* looks both back and forward: back to the baroque tradition of expansive learnedness (the poem has footnotes) and artful construction (it is written in alexandrine verse); forward to the celebration of nature in Klopstock's poems, and to the revival of didactic poetry in Goethe's *Die Metamorphose der Pflanzen (Metamorphosis of Plants)*. The repetitiveness and symmetry of the meter with its heavy caesura in the middle of each line encouraged the use of noun-agglomerations and the tendency to sententiousness:

> Die Ehr-sucht teilet nie, was Wert und Huld verbunden,
> Die Staatssucht macht sich nicht zur Unglücks-Kupplerin:
> Die Liebe brennt hier frei und scheut kein Donner-Wetter,
> Man liebet für sich selbst und nicht für seine Väter.

> Ambition never parts what worth and favor have bound together; desire for the trappings of luxury does not bring about unhappy matches; love burns freely here and fears no thunderstorm: people love for their own sake and not for that of their fathers. (127–130)

In many instances, though, Haller breaks through the metrical schema and approaches the suppler madrigal verse which he will employ in the poems *Über den Ursprung des Übels* (1734; *On the Origin of Evil*) and *Unvollkommenes Gedicht über die Ewigkeit* (1736; *Unfinished Poem on Eternity*). These Janus-like qualities also characterize the content of *Die Alpen*: there is much evocation of the sublimity of the mountains—a sign of the grandeur of God—but there is also the proto-romantic praise of the simplicity of the peasants' life and of their uncorrupted customs, as well as condemnation of the sinful city. The patricians governing the city of Bern had clearly felt the sting of this indirect criticism when they prevented Haller from obtaining a university position commensurate with his qualifications.

Of particular interest is Haller's moving *Trauer-Ode beim Absterben seiner geliebten Mariane (Elegiac Ode on the Death of His Beloved Mariane)*, written after the death of his first wife in 1736. Literary historians detect in it the first tones of the lyrical subjectivity and concentration on lived experience that announce the era of Klopstock and Goethe. However, this view of Haller as the patron saint of German lyrical poetry is tempered by the fact that Mariane died of a venereal infection transmitted by Haller (as did his second wife, Elisabeth). Ever the anatomist, Haller had verified the diagnosis through an autopsy.

Although Haller never considered himself a poet, he published *Die Alpen* in his *Versuch Schweizerischer Gedichte (Offering of Swiss Poetry)* together with the philosophical poems such as *Die Falschheit menschlicher Tugenden (The Falseness of Human Virtues), Über den Ursprung des Übels,* and *Unvollkommenes Gedicht über die Ewigkeit,* and painstakingly reworked the collection for each of its eleven editions. Criticized by Gottsched and others for the impurities of his vocabulary and for the density of his grammar, Haller gradually eliminated what he recognized as mistakes in meter and rhyme; but he insisted on the particular character of the German spoken and written by the Swiss, and defended the right of ethnic poetry to deviate from the dictates of (Saxonian) High German.

The deaths of his wives, combined with strong Pietist convictions detectable already in the poems, led to an extraordinary darkening of Haller's views. In his diaries (*Tagebuch seiner Beobachtungen über Schriftsteller und über sich selbst,* 1787; *Diary of Observations on Writers and on Himself*) he subjected his conscience to the merciless self-scrutiny we know from Pietist sources such as Karl Philipp Moritz's *Anton Reiser.* The remainder of physical and theological delight in the world that still permeated *Die Alpen* vanished into the bleak view of a universe in which creation enjoyed no special relation with God and in which the fundamental problem of the 18th century—the problem of theodicy—could find no answer. Haller became one of the great melancholics of the Enlightenment, a disposition that was certainly not helped by the enormous amounts of opium he took in his later years. He expressed growing alienation from his own time in three novels about the best political constitution (*Usong,* 1771; *Alfred,* 1773; *Fabius and Cato,* 1774), as well as in a series of apologetic writings, such as the *Briefe über die wichtigsten Wahrheiten der Offenbarung* (1772; *Letters on the Most Important Truths of Revelation*) and the *Briefe über einige Einwurfe nochlebender Freygeister wieder* [sic] *die Offenbarung* (1775–1777; *Letters on Some Objections of Surviving Freethinkers against the Revelation*).

Haller, who in 1736 had followed an invitation to join the medical faculty of the young university of Göttingen, brought his bleak view of the universe to natural science. If creation shows signs of divine rationality (but no promise of salvation), it is important to discover the blueprint and to understand the functioning of the animal machine (but not to describe its interaction with other parts of the cosmos). Unlike Goethe, for whom anatomy was the science of death and physiology the science of life, Haller conceived of physiology as *anatomia animata* with the task of explaining the structure as well as the function of the animal body. The insuperable distinctions lie not between life and death, but between the body and the soul: Haller's major hypothesis was that the forces that move the body originate in the body and disappear with it. It is no accident that he chose as his first and main areas of investigation phenomena that had previously been proposed as media of the soul: blood circulation, heart function, and respiration. Haller's experiments sought to falsify the animistic and vitalistic assumption that the principle of bodily life is, however tenuously, related to the soul and to the will. Animism and vitalism posed a huge threat to Haller's dualistic framework because they assumed a degree of autonomy for life that would make it independent from, or identical with, its creator. While from the perspective of Goethe and Schelling, dualism appears only as a restriction, it must be remembered that only in this way could the animal body become the object of "value-free," that is, non-philosophical, and non-theological, scientific scrutiny.

Haller undertook a systematic survey of the animal body to chart its two fundamental forces, irritability and sensitivity. He had observed that muscles, such as the heart, would contract if stimulated by incision, electricity, or chemical agents. This reaction—irritability—was involuntary and not transmitted by nerves; it was restricted to muscular tissue and would persist long after the muscle was removed from the living body. Haller counted the heart, the diaphragm, the bladder, and the uterus among the most irritable organs. The manifestations of sensitivity, on the other hand, could be observed only indirectly, as expressions of discomfort and pain in the subject when areas of sensitivity were stimulated. Sensitivity was proportional to the degree of innervation and characterized, among others, the skin, the tongue, the stomach, and the eye. Irritability and sensitivity are not mutually exclusive, but there are parts of the body, Haller argued, that have one and not the other. Haller presented his findings to the Academy of Science in Göttingen in 1752 and published them a year later in his epoch-making essay *De partibus corporis humani sensibilibus et irritabilibus (On the Sensible and Irritable Parts of the Human Body)*.

The essay is remarkable because it manages to address a highly charged problem—the relation of body and soul, with all of its theological and philosophical implications—on a purely experimental level. The repeated and repeatable physiological experiment has taken the place of the conclusion by analogy or by reference to earlier authorities. This utterly modern reliance on experimentation, however, came at a high price: the necessary experiments involved the "stimulation" and vivisection of hundreds, if not thousands, of animals. Although the cruelty he had to exert was hateful even to himself, Haller asserted that the gain for humanity would outweigh the pain for the animals. With his dispassionate descriptions of prickings, burnings, lacerations, electrocutions, and cauterizations Haller in *De partibus* reveals himself as a contemporary of de Sade, and this tone was to become the disquieting obverse of the triumphalist discourse of the life sciences. There can be little doubt that the screams in Haller's laboratory carried over into his poetry, and into his philosophical and theological views. Nonetheless, he continued to publish his scientific research at an astonishing pace: twenty-five treatises in the five years between 1739 and 1744 alone, some of them consisting of more than ten thousand pages.

Haller remained adamant in rejecting all vitalistic interpretations of his findings—interpretations, such as Herder's, that would either claim autonomy for the bodily forces or suggest a direct influence of the soul upon the body—but he could do so only by applying his dichotomies on an ever smaller scale. The distinction between the soul and the body recurs in the distinction between sensitivity and irritability within the body, and each of these realms again displays the same distinction: the nerves are themselves not sensitive, nor is the flesh of the muscles irritable. This structure of argumentation in which nature is conceived as a Russian doll, each shell encapsulating a smaller but similar shell, is not uncommon in 18th-century science—think of Newton's theory of absolute space that contains all other spaces—and it appealed to the period's fascination with the sublime, the infinitely small and the infinitely large. But it is a static view that does not conceive of nature as a source of productive and innovative forces, and that consequently assigns to the natural sciences the task of repetitive uncovering rather than that of comprehensive understanding. The generation of scientists after Haller (many of them his students) would reject this passive view and instead call on philosophy and poetry to produce a fuller, "livelier" image of nature. The concept of *Bildung* (formation or development), which came to dominate scientific, philosophical, and literary discourse beginning in the 1780s and 1790s, was born from discontent with Haller's type of science.

The debate about biological generation, which erupted in the last years of Haller's life, shows this discord between the generations in sharpest contrast. The young scientist Caspar Friedrich Wolff had argued that the theory of encapsulation, which held that each embryo is encapsulated in the ovum of the previous generation and is awakened to life (by "the foul stench of the male semen," as Haller opined), did not explain and in fact denied generation. To this position of "nothing new under the sun" Wolff opposed the theory of epigenesis: the mixture of male and female semen, guided by a formative force *(Bildungskraft)*, accounted for both the novelty and the regularity of natural generation. The assumption of a formative force (partly spiritual, partly physical) was abhorrent to Haller, who used his scholarly and institutional connections to combat the potentially immoral hypothesis. His own student and successor Johann Friedrich Blumenbach would bring widespread acceptance of epigenesis only a decade after Haller's death.

Haller's dominant position as a scientist and intellectual throughout Europe is unthinkable without the University of Göttingen. Founded in 1734, Göttingen was the first truly modern university in Europe and became the model not only for Wilhelm von Humboldt's reform of the Prussian high schools and universities, but also for many universities in the United States. The most visible sign of this modernity was the decreed equality among the four faculties. No longer were the theologians permitted to censor the members of the juridical, philosophical, or medical faculty (to which Haller belonged), but instead inter-faculty disputes had to be conducted by rational argumentation alone. This policy had far-reaching and lasting effects on the profile of the university: the historical sciences emerged as the common foundation of both theology and jurisprudence (with the beginning of historical Bible sciences

[Bibelwissenschaften] and the comparative history of law *[Rechtsgeschichte]*; philological accuracy became the standard of scientific method in the humanities; and a theory of historical and empathetic interpretation (hermeneutics) was developed that allowed access both to the scriptures and to secular literatures. In the sciences, mathematics was liberated from its ancillary position, and medicine, through the foundation of clinics and proper modes of instruction, could finally dispel its former aura of charlatanism and cruelty.

Haller took full advantage of these reforms. His laboratories and his botanical garden were well organized, and he involved his doctoral students in his ongoing research. None of his experimental work in *De partibus,* for example, would have been possible without this large-scale organization of science. In 1747 he founded the *Göttinger Gelehrten Anzeigen (Göttingen Scholarly Review),* the first journal in which the long-windedness of traditional scholarly publications was cast away in favor of concise articles and reviews. Haller himself is believed to have contributed up to ten thousand book reviews to the *GGA*. He was also a leading member of the Königliche Gesellschaft der Wissenschaft zu Göttingen (Royal Scientific Society at Göttingen), where scholars from all four faculties could present cutting-edge research without fear of misunderstanding or repression.

Despite these favorable conditions and the unwavering support of the university's curator, Gerlach von Münchhausen, Haller seems to have desired nothing more than to join the patriciate of his Swiss hometown. He left Göttingen for Bern in 1753 after he had been allotted a humble administrative position there. During his remaining years he continued to publish mountains of books (his published surveys of anatomical, medical, botanical, and chirurgical writings collect more than fifty-two thousand titles), but under the assaults of pain, opium, and the scholarly attacks of a younger and more optimistic generation, his life became deeply unhappy. Maintaining his spirit of dispassionate observation, he allegedly accompanied the last contractions of his heart with the words: "it beats, it beats, it beats—no longer."

See also 1789, 1792 (August 26), 1799, 1824, 1831, 1912 (March)

Bibliography: Albrecht von Haller, *Versuch Schweizerischer Gedichte* (Göttingen: Vandenhoeck, 1762, repr. Bern: Lang, 1969). Albrecht von Haller, *De partibus corporis humani sensibilibus et irritabilibus;* German: *Von den empfindlichen und reizbaren Teilen des menschlichen Körpers,* ed. Karl Sudhoff (Leipzig: J. A. Barth, 1922).

Helmut Müller-Sievers

♌ 1735

An M.A. dissertation by a 21-year-old student at the University of Halle introduces the term "aesthetics" into the vocabulary of European philosophy

Aesthetic Orientation in a Decentered World

Alexander Gottlieb Baumgarten (1714–1762) entered the University of Halle in 1730 as a student of theology, but soon shifted to philosophy. Following the publication of his master's thesis, *Meditationes de nonnullis ad poema pertinentibus* (1735; *Reflections on Poetry*), he served first as a lecturer, then as an associate professor in Halle until 1740, during which time he also published a volume on metaphysics that Kant would later use as the basis of his own lectures on the subject. From 1740 until his death, Baumgarten held a professorship at the University Viadrina in Frankfurt on the Oder, where he regularly lectured on the *disciplina aesthetica*. These lectures served as the basis for Baumgarten's magnum opus, *Aesthetica,* which, however, remained incomplete, probably due to the author's long battle with tuberculosis. The two volumes of the *Aesthetica* that appeared in 1751 and 1758 represent only a fraction of the work as Baumgarten had conceived it.

Baumgarten's overall philosophical project can be understood as the effort to overcome the dualism of reason and sense experience characteristic of the rationalism of Christian Wolff (1679–1754), the student and popularizer of Leibniz who dominated early 18th-century thought. The neologism Baumgarten introduced in the 116th paragraph of his master's thesis—"aesthetica" as the "science of perception"—is defined in opposition to logic, the science of what is known. But in the first paragraph of *Aesthetica,* he glosses the term more generously, calling aesthetics the science of sensible knowledge and the theory of the liberal arts (what we would today term the humanities). His further qualification of aesthetics as an "ars analogi rationis" (an art analogous to reason) foregrounds the parallelism between sensation and rationality. The arts and sciences are seen to complement one another; their common denominator is the formation of meaning.

It is important to recall that Baumgarten's notion of "art" is quite distinct from the fervent notion we are today accustomed to. In Baumgarten's time, the word embraced the mechanical arts as well as the fine arts and was commonly used in its plural form. Only at the end of the 18th century would "art" become the collective singular term that designates a restricted class of highly valued, non-practical cultural artifacts. This means that the science of aesthetics, as Baumgarten conceives it, covers the entire field of human skills insofar as they are rooted in our sensuous faculties and shape and articulate perceptions. For this reason, several recent theorists committed to the expansion of aesthetic inquiry beyond the sphere of art objects have called for a return to Baumgarten's more capacious delineation of the aesthetic field. Indeed, what Baumgarten had in view was the entire domain of our bodily experience and activity, our lives in space and time, our worldly practices. And it was his conviction that a set of cultural priorities that neglects the cultivation and, as he liked to phrase it, "perfection" of this domain—for example, by privileging logic as the sole access to truth—was doomed to failure. To be sure, our sensuous perceivings and doings are based on naturally given abilities ("aesthetica naturalis"), but this natural component can be expanded, deepened, and refined through an "ars aesthetica," the practice of articulating, organizing, and communicating our sensations. On this view, aesthetics is crucial to a healthy and well-ordered society.

In a student transcript of one of his lectures on aesthetics, Baumgarten argues that those who claim that the fear of God must be transmitted to humanity through supernatural instruction fail to consider that certain kinds of improvement are possible only through the human arts. Illustrative examples and poignantly expressed or well-constructed stories are indispensable to the process of socialization. This belief in the socializing power of literary expression seems to place Baumgarten in the vicinity of Johann Christoph Gottsched (1700–1766), the most important theoretician of literature in the German lands during the first decades of the 18th century. But Gottsched's early Enlightenment conception was based on the hierarchical notion of the mental faculties he had taken over from Wolff and adhered very much to a top-down schema. Thus, in his *Versuch einer Critischen Dichtkunst für die Deutschen* (1730; *Essay Concerning a Critical Poetics for the Germans*), which remained the authoritative treatise on poetics until at least 1751, the year of its greatly revised fourth edition, Gottsched argued that literature is valuable solely for the masses ("den großen Haufen"), since they are incapable of deducing moral maxims from rational principles. He even claimed that a poet must be schooled in philosophy so that he will be capable of explaining things truthfully and, indeed, constructing his work according to logical rules. Each poem is grounded in a moral principle, which it clothes in images that make it accessible even to the unlearned. Placed in the hands of an elite, art becomes a handmaiden for the moral edification of the uneducated populace.

Just as absolutist rulers consolidated their power by claiming to work for the economic benefit of all, enlightened critics such as Gottsched urged that the public critique of art by an educated few secured the common good in the realm of morality and education. The role thereby attributed to literature reflects the same belief in rationality evinced in the absolutist project of maximizing happiness through centralized planning. In all this we can discern nothing of Baumgarten's view of the artist as one who possesses a special skill for presenting the world concretely and intuitively. And it is precisely this skill that Baumgarten wants to improve in all human beings. Rather than employing sensate representations as a device for the moral management of a segment of the population, as Gottsched's theory aimed to do, Baumgarten proposed to enhance and refine the sentience of all human beings. In this respect, his aesthetic theory—although addressing a much broader field of practices and representations—anticipates the aesthetic humanism of Schiller.

To be sure, several contemporaries had kindred cultural agendas. In 1725 the philosopher Georg Bernhard Bilfinger (1693–1750) called for a theory of sensuality. From roughly 1740 on, this philosophical effort found counterparts in literary and poetic theory. In that year, the Swiss Johann Jakob Breitinger (1701–1776) published a treatise on the nature, uses, and ends of similes (*Gleichnisse*) that called for a logic of the imagination; and his own *Critical Poetics,* published in the same year, emphasized (with a view to Milton) the poet's capacity to invent marvelous alternative worlds. In 1747, the playwright

Johann Elias Schlegel (1719–1749), stressing the role aesthetic representation plays in human culture, argued that the theater's combination of ethical efficacy with pleasure is inimitable by other forms of representation. Lessing, in whose work Enlightenment criticism in the German-speaking world achieves its zenith, argued less than ten years later that the effect of aesthetic representation is not any specific change in ethical behavior, but rather a change in the overall disposition of its audience. Although written in Latin and articulated in a deductive-scholastic manner, Baumgarten's aesthetic theory participates in a broad transformation that, by the middle of the 18th century, had seized the literary culture at large.

This new interest in the sensate faculties can be conceived, in the terms of Erich Auerbach, as a shift from a vertical to a horizontal cultural orientation. This shift clearly informs Baumgarten's *Aesthetica,* which emphasizes factual—temporal and spatial—connections, the so-called "nexus rerum" (nexus of things). At the threshold of modernity, theory that merely contemplates the eternal order of the world is replaced by a practice that changes the world. Yet this reorientation brings about new ordeals. Horizontal cultures tend to isolate individuals, severing their ties with others. Vertical cultures orient subjects toward a fixed point outside space and time, a transcendent being or substance that centers the world as a whole, whereas horizontal cultures produce a world without fixed points of reference and thus require a renegotiation of the self's relation to others. If the subjectivity of the individual is no longer sustained by a transcendent being, then philosophy must propose an alternative support structure.

Baumgarten finds this support in a textual or aesthetic culture, in which individuals center themselves through artistic creation and interpretation. To this end, he defines the "facultas fingendi" (poetic faculty) as the faculty humankind employs in conjunction with the imagination to integrate perceptions into an orderly whole. Since our representations are initially a scattering of past impressions and current perceptions, they must be combined into unities in order to make sense. The production of an artifact is therefore necessarily creative, the result of an act of *poiesis.* The highest, most valuable representation is one with a perfected order that helps center the human gaze. Hence Baumgarten's definition of beauty (which he does not distinguish from truth) as the "perfection of sensate cognition." Such beautiful or perfected representations need to be placed before our eyes ("ab oculos ponere possit") in order to provide human beings with that centering of subjectivity that had previously been the function of the transcendent being. Baumgarten ascribes to the soul a natural disposition to think beautifully, that is, to integrate representations, to invest the perceptual field with an immanent order. The highest form of human existence is the "felix aestheticus" (the fortunate or happy aesthetic practitioner), who, by integrating perceptions into an ordered whole or "perfectio composites," embodies self-governance and openness to the world.

Baumgarten's exploration of the realm of aesthetic experience expands into a provocative vision of the human soul and its relations with the world. Like Locke and Leibniz before him, he emphasized the soul's reflective self-relation. Selves reflected in themselves view the world according to their position in it. This relationship to reality begins with the so-called obscure (not consciously distinguished) ideas. In contrast to Leibniz, Baumgarten accords obscure ideas a foundational function: they make up the "fundus animae," the ground out of which human insights arise. A similar revaluation can be discerned in his use of the notion of "confused" ideas and judgments, the judgments of sense. When he employs this term in his *Meditationes philosophicae,* he does not wish to imply, as Gottsched, for example, did, that such representations should be submitted to the clear and distinct judgments of the rationally minded critic. His aim is to improve confused judgments in and of themselves. Thus, he implicitly challenges the epistemological bias according to which confused judgments are the mother of error. For confusion—an apprehension in which the features of things are given to us interfused with one another—is in fact the resource upon which every discovery of truth must draw. When we refer to aspects of phenomena not clearly distinguished from one another, we begin to orient ourselves in the world. Nature does not leap from murkiness to clear and distinct thinking. The path from darkness to the clarity of midday passes, according to one of Baumgarten's most memorable metaphors, via the dawn. Within the crepuscular domain of confused representations the primary coordinates of human orientation in the world are drawn.

Baumgarten's use of the notion of confused representation anticipates later developments in the philosophy of art. The term designates a range of qualities such as ambiguity, complexity, and density. Precisely because they are confused, aesthetic objects display "fecunditas" (wealth, abundance). Thus, aesthetic representations have their own kind of clarity, a feature Baumgarten designates in his dissertation as "extensive clarity," as opposed to the "intensive clarity" of rational concepts whose defining features are distinguished one from another. Extensive clarity, which Baumgarten later calls "ubertas aesthetica" (aesthetic wealth based on vivid and forceful perceptions), brings about a "perceptio praegnans," a pregnant or fecund perception that is impossible to convey with the distinctness characteristic of rational discourse. This notion of a representation that cannot be reduced to an abstract linguistic formulation is taken up by Kant in the *Critique of Judgment,* where it receives the name "aesthetic idea." And it lives on in discussions among 20th-century Gestalt psychologists bearing on the "Prägnanz" of especially salient perceptual configurations. The reflective stance assumed by the subject toward such fertile presentations focuses the attention on the process through which meanings emerge from and retreat into the primordial givenness of the world to our sensate experience. Scanning the interfused manifold of salient perceptions, the mind grasps something of its own movement in situating itself within the world.

The emphasis on orientation goes hand-in-hand with what might be called Baumgarten's philosophy of perspectivism. In a key paragraph of the *Metaphysica,* in which he defines some of his chief concepts, Baumgarten writes, "My soul is a force that perceives this world according to the position of my body." Thus, whenever he adapts the concepts of clear and distinct perception to his own argumentative uses, Baumgarten tends to relate them to spatial and temporal phenomena, thus undermining their traditional hierarchical connotations. I can infer from the position of my body in the world why I perceive certain things in a confused fashion, others more clearly, and still others distinctly. That is, the varying degrees of cognitive clarity are functions of the body's location and orientation. As in the works of Leibniz, Baumgarten's philosophical perspectivism is reflected in his frequent use of such terms as "perspicuity."

Perhaps even more telling is his use of the notion of horizon, which in the first half of the 18th century was customarily rendered as *Gesichtskreis* (circle or range of vision). Herder, an early admirer, noted that Baumgarten set himself apart from other philosophers of his generation by not abandoning the shared horizon of healthy eyes. Moreover, whenever Baumgarten speaks of sight and eyes—and he does so often—he almost always highlights the sense of focusing the gaze within the medium of representations, including representations conveyed by signs. Signs have the special function of initiating a mode of thinking in which, by reflecting on the signs and its relation to them, the subject procures itself, as it were, as a conscious being. Even more importantly, Baumgarten extends this subject-sign relation into the past and the future. The signs we place before our eyes here and now enable us to represent past states of mind and thus to construct a coherent sense of ourselves over time, a narrative of our own identity. This is why the "facultas fingendi" (poetic disposition) becomes for Baumgarten the crucial factor in the self-organization of the modern subject and, more generally, of modern culture. The repetitious insistence that we perceive the world according to the position of our bodies can thus be understood to reflect a conception of the subject as a punctiform being whose eyes master and totalize the field of vision. This imagined mastery depends on the subject's apperception of itself as a self-conscious observer whose identity is supported by narratives and histories. Only on the basis of a concentrated look at texts, then, is the subject capable of grasping itself as a self-conscious subject.

See also 1710, 1767, 1790

Bibliography: Alexander Gottlieb Baumgarten, *Reflections on Poetry,* trans. Karl Aschenbrenner and William Holter, including a facsimile of the Latin original (Berkeley: University of California Press, 1954). ———, *Aesthetica,* facsimile of the original 1751–78 edition (Hildesheim: Georg Olms, 1961).———, *Metaphysica,* facsimile of the 1779 seventh edition (Hildesheim: Georg Olms, 1963).

Jochen Schulte-Sasse

♫ *1750*

The king of Denmark grants Friedrich Gottlieb Klopstock a pension enabling him to complete his epic poem *Der Messias*

Reading for Feeling

In German, "Klopstock" sounds like the name of a teacher in a comedy who is known for beating (low German *kloppen,* high German *klopfen*) his pupils with a stick (German *Stock*). That is probably why Clemens Brentano entitled one of his fairy tales *Schoolmaster Klopfstock and His Five Sons.*

"Klopstock!" exclaims Lotte in a central scene of Goethe's *Sorrows of Young Werther* (1774). No more is required for Werther to be "swept away" by "the stream of emotions that she poured over me with this password," and he weeps, letting "the most rapturous tears" fall on her hand. The name has clearly become a completely de-semanticized metonymy. It calls up the memory of reading the "splendid ode" "Die Frühlingsfeier" (Celebration of Spring) of Friedrich Gottlieb Klopstock (1724–1803), and sets in motion the flow of fluids—from Lotte's mouth to Werther and from his eyes to her hand. Werther's tears are the physical reaction to his rush of emotions, and to the exhilarating loss of differentiation not only between emotion and consciousness but also between past reading and present experience. This state of intense, but undifferentiated, awareness is what Klopstock called feeling. It is a feeling without an object, not even a feeling of self-awareness, but simply feeling as such.

The same kind of spectacular effect has also been ascribed to reading Klopstock's *Messiah.* In Johann Martin Miller's novel *Siegwart,* for instance, which enjoyed great success when it was published in 1776, two lovers read the poem together, as they had done repeatedly in the past: "Resting her head in her hand, Therese looked down at *The Messiah.* At once her soul was powerfully stirred; the thought of the imminent separation gripped her completely. Her heart began to pound; one sigh followed another, and Kronhelm heard teardrops falling on the page. He grasped her hand; she drew it over to touch the book, and he felt it was wet." Feeling must be shared, but it can communicate only through fluids. And if circumstances and propriety allow this communication to reach only the book that caused the feeling, a hand must intervene to help the other person understand the real message.

Klopstock reported that he had finished a complete outline of *The Messiah* and begun work on the poem itself by 1742, shortly before his eighteenth birthday. He felt encouraged and buoyed by his reading of Johann Jacob Bodmer's German translation of Milton's *Paradise Lost,* which had been published that same year. After some early attempts at poetic prose, Klopstock shifted to hexameters and finished the first canto in 1746. The following year, he was persuaded by friends at the University of Leipzig to publish the first three cantos in their journal *Neue Beiträge zum Vergnügen des Verstandes und des*

Witzes (New Contributions to Delight the Mind and Spirit). They appeared anonymously in 1748. The entire poem eventually filled four volumes of five cantos each. Volume one was completed in 1751, volume two in 1755, and volume three in 1768. Volume four finally appeared in 1773. While working on the later volumes, Klopstock continued to alter and revise, so that the first uniform edition was not published until 1780. Even then, he continued rewriting, until publication of his complete works in 1799.

The first three cantos were the first of Klopstock's writings to find their way into print. In 1750, the King of Denmark offered the penniless young poet an "honorary pension" so he could devote himself entirely to finishing *The Messiah*. The only condition attached was that Klopstock should reside in Copenhagen. The stipend was paid without interruption from 1751 until his death. It continued after the poet moved from Copenhagen to Hamburg in 1770, and even extended beyond 1773, the year he had finished *The Messiah* and the ostensible purpose of the grant had been fulfilled. As it turned out, this single work provided its author with a secure income for fifty-two years.

It goes without saying that the exalted theme of *The Messiah* called for "sublime style" throughout. Thus the demanding work is characterized by complex syntax, bold neologisms (including several newly coined verbs of motion), and "words of power"—everything, in other words, that Johann Jacob Breitinger had demanded of a style that would "touch the heart" in his *Critical Poetics* (1740). Semantically, too, everything aims at a sublime effect: There are flights with angels through a universe filled with suns; views from interstellar space onto a tiny earth (where, nevertheless, events of infinitely great importance are taking place); corridors running from the North Pole to the center of the earth; earthquakes and eclipses; eschatological combat with the forces of Hell (conducted and decided by the Messiah and God alone by means of devastating glances and glowing bullets); and the astounding physical abilities of masses of angels and seraphim, one of whom, "a thousand times a thousand miles distant," *hears* "anxiously the slowly rising blood of the mediator at prayer / Flow from vein to vein" (canto V, 574–577). For stretches, one could almost say, this is epic cinema with a touch of science fiction. Yet, the poetically decisive effect occurs not on the level of style or semantics, but on a pragmatic level. Critics and literary theorists, such as Breitinger, did not recognize this because it was unprecedented at the time; there was no model for it.

To achieve the full effect of the text required it to be read aloud, as was customary at the time, and though unstated, was taken for granted. As the body is conditioned by the variable rhythm of the hexameters and the brain is fully absorbed in making sense of the idiosyncratic syntax and semantics, the listeners are unsettled, even overpowered, by the successive creation, displacement, and demolishment of distinctions that occur as the poem unfolds.

A fundamental element is repetition, just as *The Messiah* itself is a repetition of the New Testament narratives that have been repeated every year in every church for centuries. Their wording was familiar to Klopstock's readers and was a constant presence in the background. Through the scene in which Moses explains the meaning of the cross to Abraham, Klopstock establishes the leitmotif for the work: "Of course, all that I will tell you / You already know, but it is good, to see / Once-seen truth again" (IX, 247–249). He creates the greatest effect by first erasing the distinction between the biblical text and a re-encounter with it through the use of a direct quotation, and then immediately re-creating the distinction by deviating from the familiar phrasing. In the Gospel according to Saint John, for example, Luther relates the death of Jesus on the cross with the words "und neigte das Haupt und verschied" ("and bowed the head and expired"). In the last verse of the tenth canto, however, Klopstock words it "und er neigte sein Haupt und starb" ("and he bowed his head and died"). There is no metrical reason for this deviation, since the biblical quotation could fit perfectly into the hexameter rhythm. The blatant, almost brutal, violation of the biblical phrasing turns the repetition into something new, which owes its power to the original with which it contrasts: an immediate confrontation with the fact, to which listeners had become blunted through countless repetitions. The effect is enhanced all the more since this verse is incomplete (the only instance in the entire work); it has only four stresses instead of the required six. For readers or listeners who have internalized the hexameter rhythm through reading the poem aloud, the abrupt end of the verse comes as a shock. The missing final two feet of the line convey speechlessness in face of the dead Messiah, a lack of words that is not described but simply occurs, and is imposed on the reader.

Of course, the poem has much to communicate about shock and horror, about the joy and rapture of those who witness the Passion and Resurrection, but the speaker who describes and relates these events communicates his own degree of emotion by pragmatic rather than semantic means. The speaker continually shifts position in relation to the world that is being created in the text. Rather than remaining in one place, he first creates a distinction between himself and the world of the text and then blurs or erases it, over and over again, in unpredictable shifts. Spatial distinctions become irrelevant, for the speaker can be everywhere—heaven, hell, and earth—and can traverse infinite distances in the transition from one line to the next.

Distinctions of personal identity are preserved or annulled as the situation requires—the speaker is just as much at home in the thoughts and dreams of other people as in the sphere of the visible. Temporal distinctions are enlarged or reduced or even suspended "on stage," so to speak, in the presence of the audience. Essentially the story is told in the past tense, but the speaker can also shift easily into the present tense in direct speech, which thereby becomes both concurrent and non-concurrent in relation to a single event. The pivotal point is the temporal adverb *itzt* or *itzo* (now), which occurs with the past and present tense and signals the shift of temporal perspective from close-up to far off, or vice versa, in the same way that the temporal conjunction *indem* (while) indicates a series of simultaneous events.

The way Klopstock manages the distinctions between passages of direct speech and the world of the text simulates God's relationship to the world, as the Messiah makes evident in the first use of direct speech of the first canto. Jesus' prayer on the Mount of Olives, a conversation with God the Father in heaven, conjures up the state of being before time began, when Father, Son, and Holy Spirit were together "in the stillness of eternity, alone, and without living creatures." But even then, they already decided to redeem the creatures not yet created: "Filled with our divine love / We looked down on the people / Who did not yet exist." The poem proceeds from this point—still in the past tense—to a future that still awaits the Son as he prays to "the hill I saw already full of the blood of the Covenant." Starting from the beginning of time, the speech catches up with and overtakes itself, and proves to be a repetition of the conversation that took place earlier between the three persons of the Trinity. It then shifts from the future described in the past tense to the present and the present tense, only to leap again—with the help of several occurrences of the temporal adverb *schon* (already)—into the future, when the passion begins in the Garden of Gethsemane. Here the temporal distinction collapses, and the figure praying on the Mount of Olives becomes co-present with the future petitioner in Gethsemane, who will be himself: "I see the nocturnal garden / before me already; I fall on the dusty ground / and pray to you, Father, sweating and writhing in agony." The human speaker, who resumes speaking after the Messiah, finally pulls the rug out from under himself completely, first by asserting that the heavenly Father's answer (a repetition with variations of the concluding words of the Son) was "inaudible to the angels, heard only by the Son and Himself," and then going on to quote it in full.

In his shorter lyric poems, Klopstock employs the same techniques of blurring distinctions of various kinds, with the aim of creating an overpowering effect. The culmination is a paradoxical denial of the poem's written form, that is, an attempt to demolish the difference between direct experience and reading. This is exemplified in "The Celebration of Spring," the "splendid ode," to which Werther's Lotte refers obliquely by naming its author. This hymn is written in free verse, a form Klopstock first introduced into German literature. The words are presented as spoken outdoors in the present, and the speaker endeavors to draw the readers ever more closely into the unfolding action. Addressing the readers in the plural, the person speaking asks persistently if they perceive the approaching storm: "Seht ihr den Zeugen des Nahen den zückenden Strahl? / Hört ihr Jehovas Donner? / Hört ihr? Hört ihr ihn, / Den erschütternden Donner des Herrn?" ("Do you see the witness of the near One, the flashing streak? / Do you hear Jehovah's thunder? / Do you hear? Do you hear it, / the jarring thunder of the Lord?") Once the attempt to make the discrepancy between the situation of the speaker and the readers disappear has succeeded, and the storm has passed, the poet evokes two other situations and combines them with the unified situation of speaking and reading: "Siehe, nun kommt Jehova nicht mehr im Wetter, / In stillem, sanftem Säuseln /

Kommt Jehova" ("See, Jehovah comes no more in the storm, / In a still small rustling / comes Jehovah," a reference to the form in which God reveals himself to Elijah on Mount Horeb); "Und unter ihm neigt sich der Bogen des Friedens" ("And below him curves the arch of peace," a reference to the rainbow God sent after the flood as a sign of his renewed covenant with humanity). It is the merging of these elements—the threefold opening and closing of discrepancies between situations—that generates "feeling."

By the time the collected *Odes* (1771) and the final volume of *The Messiah* (1773) appeared, the era in which Klopstock's difficult and highly artificial texts could achieve popularity was almost past. Only few readers responded warmly to the last volume of *The Messiah,* probably because the author outdid himself in the concluding canto 20, capping the already lofty tone of the verse in hexameters with triumphal choruses of such complex metrical patterns that the language could be made to fit in places only at the price of incomprehensibility. The intense reading experience of the first two volumes of *The Messiah* was by then available in less demanding and more modern form, namely in novels. The process Klopstock advanced so effectively required from the outset both powerful techniques and the protection the epic's religious theme offered to overcome church opposition. Later neither was necessary. By the middle of the 18th century, the general public gained ready access to fictional writings. General permission to commute between two worlds was granted—a decisive event in the history of human consciousness, because entering a second, fictional world and lingering there always involves a temporary distancing of the self from the real world, with unforeseeable consequences. Nevertheless, various social groups independently reached the conclusion that the pleasure to be gained from reading novels outweighed the potential dangers—a conclusion that could be supported, in the early days, by pointing to Klopstock's *Messiah.* By the 1770s warnings about the rise of "reading mania" were limited to avoiding excess, and the reading of fictional texts in German was introduced into the curriculum of secondary schools. Reading fiction had received society's approval as long as a way was found to domesticate and control it.

Klopstock had probably lost most of his readers even before 1770, except for the "noble few" he had addressed in the proem of *The Messiah.* In these circles, his later works continued to be read most attentively. The veneration they felt for the poet was directed at least as much at his person as at his work. Both in and outside Germany, the respect and admiration Klopstock won for *The Messiah* lasted, as shown by the vote of the French National Assembly to declare him a *citoyen français* in 1792 and his election as a foreign member of the *Institut National* in 1802. The funeral following his death on March 14, 1803, was a public event. A long cortège accompanied the mortal remains of the poet of *The Messiah* from Hamburg to the neighboring Danish town of Altona (a part of the German city today); the bells of all the churches in Hamburg tolled, and more than five thousand people lined the streets as the procession passed.

See also 1735, 1774, 1792 (August 26)

Bibliography: Friedrich Gottlieb Klopstock, *Werke und Briefe,* historical-critical edition, ed. Horst Gronemeyer et al. (Berlin and New York: de Gruyter, 1974–). ———, *The Messiah,* trans. Joseph Collyer, 4th ed. (London: J. Dodsley, T. Caslon, and F. Newbery, 1769–1771).

Klaus Weimar

᷎᷁ *1758*

In London, Johann Georg Hamann undergoes a religious conversion

Questioning the Enlightenment

In 1761 Johann Georg Hamann (1730–1788) wrote his famous essay "Aesthetica in nuce: Eine Rhapsodie in kabbalistischer Prosa ("Aesthetics in a Nutshell," as the English-speaking world inevitably translates it, "A Rhapsody in Cabbalistic Prose"). One year later the essay was published in a collection of pieces entitled *Kreuzzüge des Philologen (The Philologist's Crusades).* Literary historians have rarely been at a loss to mark the essay's irrefutable, unassailable significance in the timeline of German letters. "Aesthetics in a Nutshell," they tell us, is explained by what it clearly points to—what it points to in the past and what it points toward in the future. Hamann's passionate attack against the Enlightenment makes him, as only the hindsight of posterity can see, the father of Storm and Stress and ultimately of German Romanticism.

Using "Aesthetica in nuce" to tell a simplistic historical tale is like contemplating a solar eclipse in a vessel full of water. But what happens if we look, not only to what "Aesthetica in nuce" so famously and openly proclaims, the now time-honored clichés of the Storm and Stress along with its opposition to the reason, abstractions, and murderous threats to Nature of the Enlightenment? What happens if we also look to the way in which Hamann writes his text, the way in which the text performs, and, in turn, the way it forces the reader to perform? What "Aesthetica in nuce" produces is a radical reconception of language, and of language in relation to theology, a theology fraught with unexpected uncertainties; also, not insignificantly, a rethinking of the premises on which literary history is constructed.

Two years before "Aesthetica in nuce," Hamann had composed *Socratic Memorabilia* (1759), dedicated to his close friend Johann Christoph Berens (1729–1776) and to Immanuel Kant. In a later work, "Metacritique of the Purism of Reason" (1784), Hamann mocked Kant for failing to take into account that "the entire ability to think rests on language" and that "language is also the *crux of misunderstanding of reason with itself*" (Dickson, 522). Back in 1758, after Hamann's tumultuous religious conversion in London, Berens and Kant attempted to save Hamann's soul for the Enlightenment. Far more accessible than "Aesthetica in nuce," both in its point of departure and its prose, the earlier essay, much of which is cast in a veneer of autobiographical anecdote, draws analogies between Socrates, Jesus, and Hamann himself, and also between their accusers and the Enlighteners. Although *Socratic Memorabilia* ostensibly addresses language as a critical issue (naming, representation, figuration, interpretation), the illusion of narrative and direct polemic carries the reader along.

With "Aesthetica in nuce," Hamann's attack on the Enlightenment takes a more difficult turn. What are we to make of a writer who from then on seems compelled to write only on the occasion of, or in response to, other writings? "Aesthetica in nuce" clearly positions itself as a polemic against Johann David Michaelis's commentary on Robert Lowth's (1710–1787) *De sacra poesi Hebräorum* (1758). And Hamann assails not only Michaelis, but also various Enlightenment figures—Lessing, Mendelssohn, Voltaire, and others. Very little in the essay is not a commentary in many indirect ways on something or someone. Much of the text is in the footnotes, often expansive notes that do not necessarily elucidate the passage to which they refer. Moreover it seems that every other turn of phrase, even in the body of the text, is a reference to or an echo of a biblical or classical passage. Besides works from antiquity, Hamann presupposes an equally impossible, detailed knowledge of the works of his contemporaries or near contemporaries.

To grasp what is involved in this citational strategy, consider Hamann's take on Genesis: the production of God's divine creation is in images, guaranteeing a reassuring place for the human reader. Just as a typological textual practice—of the sort often attributed to Hamann—projects a harmonious and productive interrelation of images, so the divinely created world that Hamann describes in "Aesthetica in nuce" speaks of an unproblematic transition from the divine to the human interpreter:

> **Poetry** is the **mother-tongue** of the human race; as **gardening** is older than farming: **painting,**—than writing: **song**—than declamation: parables—than arguments. . . .
>
> The **senses** and the **passions** speak and understand nothing but **images. In images** the entire treasure of human **knowledge** is contained. . . . The first **explosion** of creation, and the first **impression** of its historian; the first **manifestation** and the first **enjoyment** of nature unite in the **word: "Let there be light!"**
>
> **Speaking** is **translation**—from a **tongue of angels** into a **human tongue.** (Dickson, 411–413)

If poetry is the mother tongue of the human race, if parables are older than conclusions, this is because God spoke to man in images and, ever since, the entire treasure of human knowledge has consisted precisely therein. And yet strangely, perhaps incomprehensibly, Hamann also has this to say: "in nature, we have only **jumbles of verse** and *disjecti membra poetae* left for our use. It is for the **scholar** to gather these; for the **philosophers** to interpret them; to imitate them—or even bolder—to bring them to their destiny is the **poet's** modest part" (Dickson, 412–413). A nature made up of fragments of poetry, but of broken pieces of poets as well. What might it mean that as scholars we must gather, as philosophers interpret, and as poets imitate these broken pieces? Some commentators have noted that "Aesthetica in nuce" resembles the *cento* of the decadent period of Roman literature. This type of writing takes its name from a patchwork garment. A patchwork of citations, in orgiastic rapidity, then, a long, repeatedly disrupted prosopopoeia, a series of personifications, in which Hamann's persona endlessly and abruptly changes. If this is the case, "Aesthetics in a Nutshell" is hardly as self-contained as its title implies.

Let us take the initial motto of "Aesthetica in nuce" as the critical test case of Hamann's mode of writing. The epigraph is just where we might expect to read "in a nutshell" what Hamann has to say: "Spoil of dyed stuffs embroidered, / two pieces of dyed work embroidered for [the neck of the looter]" (Judges 5:30). The fragment of verse comes from one of the historical books of the Old Testament, a book from which Hamann cites repeatedly in "Aesthetica in nuce." Why this repeated return to that part of Judges known as the "Song of Deborah"?

Hamann relates this tatter of biblical text explicitly to prosopopeia and it is from this point of view that the motto has been interpreted. In whose voice, the question is inevitably raised, does Hamann speak when he cites the Book of Judges? The "Song of Deborah" (Judges 5) tells of the struggle of the tribes of Israel against the forces of the Hazorite Sisera. Barak leads the triumphant troops and yet it is a woman who smites Sisera. At the hands of Yael, who lures him into her tent, Sisera falls. As the mother of Sisera awaits her son, she explains away the agonizing delay by imagining the booty with which he will return. "'Are they not finding and dividing the spoil: to every man a girl or two, for Sisera, plunder of dyed garments, plunder of garments embroidered and dyed, two pieces of dyed embroidery for the neck of the looter'" (Song of Deborah, Judges 5). The phrases Hamann cites as the opening, and perhaps critical, lines of "Aesthetica in nuce" are the last in this passage. In what way might this motto give us the summation of what is to come?

Much is at stake here. There is Hamann's promise of encapsulation, in a nutshell, also his practice of prosopopeia, writing in the voice of another. And, given the biblical story, it is also a question of spoils, of what one brings back from a battle won, what it means to assume a position of triumph. Still, following, as these lines of the motto do, on the narration of Sisera's violent death, it is no less a passage about delusions of victory, perhaps about the delusions of typological booty, seeming to redeem a past text through an act of citation and personification.

Let us follow this performance one step further in the essay's culminating statement, Hamann's fourth and critical allusion to Judges. Here he sums up the entire essay, passing judgment on the vanity of "Aesthetica in nuce" and, at the same time, calling forth the fulfillment of God's ultimate judgment. That final word appears as an "Apostille," a gloss, in which Hamann offers us a first reading of his essay and a judgment of it as well.

What might we expect from this interpretation of the interpreter? That

Hamann points us in the right direction with clarity? That he casts an all-enclosing structure over the whole? That, while we find ourselves in reading Hamann driven here and there, he will finally nail things down for us? Of "Aesthetica in Nuce: a Rhapsody in Cabbalistic Prose" he writes: "Everything in this aesthetic nut tastes of **vanity!**—of **vanity!**—The **Rhapsodist**[*] has read, observed, thought, sought, and found pleasant words, faithfully quoted, like a merchant's ship has obtained and brought his provisions from afar." Hamann goes on to offer two ways in which the rhapsodist, having found his sources far away and cited them, uses them to fabricate his writing. "The rhapsodist has ordered together **sentence** after **sentence,** as one counts the **arrows** on a **battlefield;** and marked out his **figures** as one measures out the **pegs** for a **tent.** Instead of **pegs** and **arrows,** he has, with the **petits-maîtres** and **pedants** of his time, written ★ ★ ★ ★ ★ ★ ★ and - - - - - - - - **obelisks** and **asterisks**" (Dickson, 431).

These are the two gestures, it seems, that constitute, and somehow explain, "Aesthetica in nuce." On the one hand, Hamann has piled sentence upon sentence, a building of the logical linearity of propositions, which guide the reader to the source of words that come from far away. On the other, in the rhapsodist's second manner of composition, he marks out his figures in a circle, just as one gauges the position for the pegs of a tent. He produces a circle, a figure that is going neither here nor there. And then Hamann gives us, it seems, the literal meaning of his figures. He equates the arrows and pegs with asterisks and dashes, ★★★★★ and - - - -, which in apposition he calls asterisks and obelisks. In the body of an 18th-century text, as in the first edition of "Aesthetica in nuce," asterisks direct us to the footnotes, notes that are marked by the same sign at the bottom of the page. Like the arrows of sentences built one on another, the asterisks of "Aesthetica in nuce" seem to set us in the right direction, pointing toward illumination and explanation, bringing us to references, biblical and otherwise, apparently provided by those nourishing notes.

But if the asterisks mark the footnotes that promise an unproblematic delivery from far away of the explanations of textual opacities, how shall we read those figures marked out like the pegs of a tent? The final footnote of "Aesthetica in nuce" further explains the significance of these signs. *"Asterisks illuminate; obelisks murder and stab."* The passage invites us back to Judges, which continues to provide a key of sorts to Hamann's difficult attack on the Enlightenment. "Then Yael, Heber's wife, took a tent peg and took a hammer in her hand, and went softly to him and drove the peg into his temple, and he went down into the ground" (Judges 4:21). And yet this tension between the illuminating asterisks of footnotes, which seem to complete knowledge, and the violence of obelisks/pegs that return us to Yael's murderous, if righteous, act, is not the complete explanation. What threatens in the figure of the tent peg? Rather than getting its typological nourishment solely from the distant text of Judges and bringing it back from far away, it is in Hamann's own domain that the "nail of the tent" (*Werke,* 1:81) is found most tellingly. It is in his own works that we find an alternative to the easy redemptive rewards of typological reading.

Is "Aesthetica in nuce" a typological text or are we to read it as a cabbalistic rhapsody stitched together like a *cento* in which the source of the text is of puzzling relevance to its significance? Is "Aesthetica in nuce" a crusade conducted to bring back meaning from far away, or does it meander like a nomadic language? How are all these questions of reading implicated in Hamann's tale of a divine creation in which we inhabit a world of nothing but images, spoken by God, the translation of which is left to the human reader? If one listens carefully to these last lines, the rhapsode speaks, the interpreter of interpreters. Hamann reads. But he does not simply read Judges, nor for that matter does he simply perform reading as judgment. He reads himself reading "The Song of Deborah."

Only three years before he drafted "Aesthetica in nuce," and while in the throes of his religious conversion in 1758, Hamann, as he tells it, goes through the Holy Bible for the second time. As he rereads, he writes his *Biblical Meditations*. There the tale of Sisera and Yael is the object of a long, if less than straightforward, meditation. As in the closing page of "Aesthetica in nuce," so in the *Biblical Meditations,* it is a question of figuration uneasily marked out. How, Hamann asks, are we to think the typology of Jesus? In the proto-images of Jesus, those who preceded him in the Old Testament, we see, counter-intuitively, images of the tyranny of the serpent rather than Christ-like figures of suffering. Hamann, understandably, is overwhelmed by Yael's violence as emissary of God. In the turmoil of his interpretation of Holy Scripture, God's emissaries and Satan, the sentinels against evil and its perpetrators, even God himself and Satan, become entirely interchangeable and indistinguishable. In this scramble of prose, Hamann, as reader, identifies, not with Yael, "blessed among women," but with that weary sleeping enemy of Israel, Sisera, nailed firmly and grotesquely to the earth.

In 1758, as he is caught in the jumble of verses from Judges, the grounding of Hamann's prose in the verses of the Old Testament brings about not closure but a total disordering of typological structures. Confronted with the task of reading the images penned by God, Hamann sinks wearily into a pathos of defeat and victory. But writing in 1761, in "Aesthetica in nuce," he figures the task of interpreting quite differently and opens up a religion that, in its uncertainty, liberates. Thus "Aesthetica in nuce" does not presuppose or nostalgically long for a definitive reading practice or a certainty of judgment. Hamann attacks certain illuminations in the name of a radical Christianity that often seems to point to a final judgment, but also often draws the reader into its unencompassable figures. No simple questioning of the Enlightenment, Hamann's attack in "Aesthetica in nuce" performs a radical rethinking of language and commentary.

See also 1767, 1778, 1784, 1790

Bibliography: Eric A. Blackall, *The Emergence of German as a Literary Language* (Ithaca, N.Y.: Cornell University Press, 1978). Gwen Griffith Dickson, *Johann Georg Hamann's Relational Metacriticism* (Berlin and New York: Walter de Gruyter, 1995). Johann Georg Hamann, *Sämtliche*

Werke, vol. 2, ed. Josef Nadler (Wuppertal: R. Brockhaus Verlag, 1999). ————, *Sokratische Denkwürdigkeiten, Aesthetica in nuce,* ed. with a commentary by Sven-Aage Jørgensen (Stuttgart: Philipp Reclam, 1968). Johann Wolfgang von Goethe, *The Autobiography of Johann Wolfgang von Goethe,* trans. John Oxford (New York: Horizon Press, 1969). Hans-Martin Lumpp, *Philologia crucis* (Tübingen: Max Niemeyer, 1970). James C. O'Flaherty, *Hamann's Socratic Memorabilia: A Translation and Commentary* (Baltimore: Johns Hopkins University Press, 1967).

Carol Jacobs

♫ 1765, February 8

Frederick the Great of Prussia issues a groundbreaking edict on infanticide that abolishes public shaming of women

"Educating Paper Girls" and Regulating Private Life

Published in 1771, Sophie von La Roche's epistolary novel *Die Geschichte des Fräuleins von Sternheim: Von einer Freudin derselben aus Original-Papieren und andern zuverläßigen Quellen gezogen (The History of Lady Sophia Sternheim: Extracted by a Woman Friend of the Same from Original Documents and Other Reliable Sources)* proved to La Roche's German contemporaries not only that a woman could write fiction but that she could do so with great success. The story of the young noblewoman Sophia von Sternheim's removal from the shelter of her parents' rural estate to a corrupt, provincial German court, her subsequent abduction, sufferings, and eventual vindication and marriage to the upright English Lord Seymour went through eight editions by 1783. Clearly patterned on the epistolary novels of the English writer Samuel Richardson, the history of Lady Sophia combined the edifying tribulations of Richardson's doomed heroine Clarissa (1748) with the victory of his earlier protagonist Pamela (1740), whose moral steadfastness enables her to rise above calumny and win her man. *Sternheim's* English settings and characters, as well as literary precedents, appealed to the rising Anglophilia of Continental readers. Like La Roche, well-read Germans romanticized Britain as the true homeland of the late Enlightenment, condensed in its appeal to *Tugend* or virtue: a public spirit and applied humanitarianism, coupled with personal sincerity, spontaneity, and naturalness of taste and sentiment.

Like many works of fiction by women at the time, *Sternheim* appeared anonymously, but under the aegis and editorship of the well-known poet Christoph Martin Wieland, who just happened to be La Roche's cousin and former fiancé as well as close friend. Wieland equipped the text with a condescendingly approving foreword and footnotes whose intrusive arrogance inspired immediate derision, but further sympathy for the author. Once the work's success was assured, the facts of its authorship by a previously unpublished forty-year-old mother of five who had spent her adult life as a court hostess and high ministerial official's wife in Mainz and Baden-Württemberg quickly emerged. The admiration of a younger literary generation, including Lenz, Herder, and Goethe, transmuted into friendships and correspondences that nourished La Roche's reputation for the rest of her long career.

Sternheim's blockbuster status, which La Roche followed up with a string of solid, sometimes groundbreaking, works in several genres, including the novel of marriage *Rosaliens Briefe an ihre Freundin Mariane von St*** (1779; *Rosalie's Letters to Her Friend Mariane von St***), an advice manual, *Briefe an Lina: Mütterlicher Rath für junge Mädchen* (1795; *Letters to Lina: Motherly Advice for Young Girls*), travel narratives, and a memoir, has led literary historians to dub the woman whom the readers of her time called "Mama La Roche" the mother of German women's fiction. This characterization invokes not just a personal stereotype, but also a mythology of female literary productivity that La Roche herself actively encouraged. According to the details she and Wieland disseminated, she started to write her first novel in 1767 during the loneliness and depression that had befallen her after her two daughters had been sent away to French convent schools. This move was apparently forced on her by the preferences of her husband's aristocratic patron, Graf Stadion, and by the old-fashioned customs of his Catholic court, of which she and her husband were leading, but also properly deferential, members. Her belated, well-publicized dissatisfaction with this custom allied La Roche, herself a product of the academic-professional middle class, with the rising bourgeois ideology of familial intimacy, which championed close emotional and educational involvement of parents, particularly mothers, with their offspring. Robbed, as she presented it, of her own children, she turned to the emotional solace and occupational compensation of writing, by setting out, in a now-famous phrase, "to educate a paper girl"—"ein papierenes Mädchen erziehen." Thus Sophie the writer gave birth to Sophie the character—and vice versa. It is difficult to separate La Roche's deprivation and helplessness from the cultivated pathos of her authorial self-stylization.

The novel appeared at a time when the public was primed to accept a woman writer and her fictional creations or alter-egos as a uniquely apposite medium for the transmission and inculcation of personal virtue. This willingness became, in turn, a springboard into the literary market for La Roche and other women—provided they kept to their assigned pedagogical function and niche. *Sternheim* was a product of the time in history when the German states began to rethink and reorganize the traditional regulation of sexual conduct and domestic arrangements of their subjects, who were just beginning to regard themselves as citizens.

In 1765, the year before Sophie von La Roche had sent her last daughter off to a Strasbourg convent school, Friedrich the Great of Prussia, in one of the initial groundbreaking legal edicts that culminated in the codified reforms of Prussia's Allgemeines Landrecht (1794), relieved women from public shaming penalties, like the pillory and other community-enforced rituals of public penitence for private offenses like fornication, adultery, or out-of-wedlock pregnancy. By 1781, La Roche's own home regions, Baden and Bavaria, had both instituted legal reforms that either decriminalized or substantially mitigated the harshest corporal punishments for the whole category of "carnal" delinquencies.

On the surface, a whole universe seemed to separate blunt juridical considerations of adultery, incest, and infanticide from the cloying propriety and high-flying protestations of *Sternheim* and other contemporary sentimental fiction. Yet the legal and the literary texts are complementary epiphenomena, products of the same epochal shift in the regulation of sexuality, gender relations, and domestic arrangements then under way in Europe. Popular fiction, together with the unit and affective dynamics of the nuclear family (which such fiction glorified), assumed part of the socializing function formerly monopolized by state and church. It promoted compliance in the private sphere not through public humiliation or physical coercion, but through compelling imaginative stories with which a mass readership could identify while imitating and internalizing virtuous behavior. The maternal preceptor was a natural prototype of fictional authority. Wieland spells this out in the foreword to *Sternheim* by modeling his own most heartfelt response as reader to his friend's "paper girl" in terms of parental approval: "If only—I thought in a hundred places—if only my daughters would learn to think and act like Sophie Sternheim! If only heaven would let me experience the bliss of seeing in my daughters this unvarnished sincerity of the soul, this ever constant goodness, this delicate sense of the true and the beautiful; and—springing from an inner source—this exercise of every virtue . . ." (Baguss-Britt translation, 46; all citations are from this version).

Sophia Sternheim is an example for other young women as an embodiment of a thoroughly internalized propriety that has become her second nature. Although she came by her uprightness through active altruism, critical self-appraisal, and suffering, it appears gracefully unforced, artless and innate—which makes her all the more lovable and an effective agent for socialization. In Wieland's and La Roche's appeal to the reader, Sophia Sternheim's wanderings, like the circulation of her letters, and her moves to various host households as the story unfolds, creates an ever-widening, benevolent circle of response and emulation. Compared to the dynamism of this virtue in action, physical virtue, for this heroine, is curiously of negligible significance. Technically, she loses hers to Lord Derby, the man she believes herself married to, although she does not love him, and the marriage ceremony is in fact a sham he arranged. And yet this loss, though traumatic, neither dooms her to the tragic end of a Clarissa, nor does it destroy her matrimonial prospects, or disqualify her as moral icon. La Roche's pointed refusal to equate female virtue with female virginity underlines the extent to which female excellence in her novel has been dematerialized, as it were, uncoupled from the possession of specifiable properties and recoded as transformative agency.

In *Lady Sophia Sternheim*, La Roche presents a feminine ideal that invites her readers to form a strong identification. Herder's fiancée, Caroline Flachsland, told him that she encountered in Sophia her "complete ideal of a woman." "I spent delicious, wonderful hours reading it! Oh how far I am still removed from my ideal!" (Baguss-Britt, Introduction). Sophia invites this response, in part, because she herself epitomizes authentic responsiveness. Her own comments attest, even if rather awkwardly, to this trait, as in "You know, my Emilia, that my face always mirrors the motions of my soul" (108). Sophie's inability to dissimulate puts her at odds with the life at the court to which her aristocratic relatives take her after her father's death. The court is *the* realm for dissimulation and studied inauthenticity, where reputation is grounded in (keeping up) appearances. While the courtiers engage in vacuous frivolity and vicious intrigue, the heroine longs for productive study and diligence. And yet, in this degenerate setting, Sophia shines all the more brightly. Even Derby, the Mephistophelean arch-plotter, testifies to her allure: "Everything charming I have ever seen in others of her sex is as nothing compared with the enchanting aura of sensibility that was diffused over her whole person" (108). Moreover, the epistolary form of the novel enhances this aura of genuineness. Sophia's letters to her friend Emilia, which constitute most of the novel, sustain the illusion of emotional immediacy, the moment-by-moment access to the flow and permutations of feeling.

The letters also document the protagonist's innocence, which prevents her from suspecting what the rest of the court knows, namely, that her aunt and uncle plan to further their family's influence by making their lovely niece into the next mistress of the principality's debauched ruler. As the courtiers prepare to enjoy the entertaining spectacle of the innocent's sacrifice, Derby, all the more attracted by the challenge of the competition, plots to possess her himself, while the noble Lord Seymour, who has loved her from afar, turns away from her in desperation after being convinced that she is a willing participant in her family's scheme. Thus Seymour is not only susceptible to entrapment by misleading appearances, but, even more seriously, he is guilty of a lack of trust in both his beloved and his own, never completely extinguished, belief in her. Sophia too commits an act of inauthenticity by letting wounded pride and horror undermine her self-possession, when, in the shock of discovering her relatives' intentions, she accedes to Derby's marriage proposal in order to flee family and court, even though she admits that the most she feels for her husband-to-be is pallid gratitude. Their lapses, and the high price Sophia pays for them, drive home the novel's message that failure to honor the strength of one's most deeply rooted responses constitutes self-betrayal.

Finally, literate women *and* men admired Sophia Sternheim and identified with her because she is a literate heroine. As an only child reared in the quiet isolation of a rural estate, she is the sole object of her parents' pedagogical enthusiasm and as a result receives a superb education in the humanities and modern languages from her father and in household management from her mother. Sophia's faith in the redemptive power of education carries her through her trials; as she urges the parents of a bankrupt family she has taken under her wing: "Consecrate all you have to your children's education!" (138). However temporary, reduced, or endangered her circumstances in the second half of the story may be, when she has been abandoned by Derby, discovered the subterfuge of her marriage, and is residing, under the pseudonym of Mme Leiden (Madame Suffering) with various friends and benefactresses, she inevitably finds the means to teach, as well as the means to write. Her skills are a resource for herself and for others. She repays one patroness by designing and instituting the curriculum of a school founded to give poor girls a basic education along with breadwinning skills. Just as importantly, teaching helps Sophia to retain the ultimate value, *self-possession,* by exercising compassion through philanthropy in settings where she has nothing else left to give. In the peasant hut in Scotland, to which she is abducted and where she is held hostage indefinitely after Derby has discovered her whereabouts in England and become afraid she might frustrate his plans to marry an unsuspecting heiress, she passes the time with giving elementary instruction in writing and needlework to the children of the area's few, desperately poor and isolated inhabitants. Among them is her jailors' daughter, who turns out to be Derby's child by another woman he seduced, abandoned, and sent north to die in imprisoned anonymity. Sophia has every reason to suspect that this is her intended fate as well. Indeed, she is only rescued and reunited with her husband-to-be, Lord Seymour, who, by an improbable string of coincidences is acquainted with the noblewoman with whom Sophie has taken refuge, after Derby's murderous manservant throttles her on the heath and leaves her for dead in a locked shed. The brutish world of *Sternheim's* Scottish episode anticipates, in its abruptly imposed, almost hallucinatory oppressiveness, the gothic novel. And yet, amid violence and squalor, Sophia asserts, "Thus deprived of what men call well-being, I enjoy the true gifts of heaven: serenity of soul and the pleasure of doing good—both fruits of true humanity and tested virtue" (223).

Sophie von La Roche herself sought all her life to exemplify her most popular creation's creed. Her career as a writer, like that of many of her writing female contemporaries, began as an occupation imbued with idealistic enthusiasm and ended as need-driven drudgery. Her prosperity as well as her social position evaporated when her husband lost his aristocratic patron and then his last position in Trier. By the time she started publishing her periodical *Pomona—Für Teutschlands Töchter* (*Pomona—For Germany's Daughters*) in 1783, she was the sole support of her family. Deprived in her last years of even a widow's pension, La Roche was compelled, almost until her death in 1807 in Offenbach, to churn out memoirs, tales, and compilations. A late work like *Mein Schreibtisch* (1799; *My Writing Desk*) shows La Roche recycling her own observations and compositions, along with favorite quotes from other writers, lists, scribbled reading notes, and even recipes. At the same time, the book offers the self-portrait of a woman trying to summon the grace, gratitude, and dignity demanded by her own ideal of womanly stoicism (*Gelassenheitsideal*) to an existence of genteel poverty and social marginalization. In the closing paragraph, she assures her readers that, although fate had destroyed her fortune and time her figure, "My soul has learned the worth of all earthly things . . . I know no jealousy, no hatred, no unrest, think only of the good, and have no greater wish than to remain in a condition to help the suffering and to read many more books."

See also 1773, 1774, 1781, 1784, 1931

Bibliography: Sophie von La Roche, *Die Geschichte des Fräuleins von Sternheim,* ed. with an afterword by Barbara Becker-Cantarino (Stuttgart: Metzler, 1985). ———, *The History of Lady Sophia Sternheim,* trans. with a critical introduction by Christa Baguss-Britt (Albany: State University of New York Press, 1991). ———, *Mein Schreibtisch,* 2 vols. (Leipzig: Heinrich Gräff, 1799; copy in possession of the University of Berlin). Helga Meise, *Die Unschuld und die Schrift: Deutsche Frauenromane im 18. Jahrhundert* (Frankfurt am Main: Helmer, 1992). Jeannine Blackwell and Susanne Zantop, *Bitter Healing: German Women Writers from 1700 to 1830* (Lincoln: University of Nebraska Press, 1990).

Chris Cullens

ﬡ 1767

Lessing misdates his comedy *Minna von Barnhelm* to make it coincide with the end of the Seven Years' War

A Woman's Design on Soldiers' Fortune

In the summer of 1870, at the height of the Franco-Prussian War, which led to the founding of the German Empire, Theodor Fontane reviewed a Hoftheater production of Lessing's comedy *Minna von Barnhelm* for the renowned *Vossische Zeitung.* Although he refers to the play as one "we have become accustomed to regarding as quintessentially Prussian," Fontane is disappointed that it did not live up to the patriotic fervor of the day. *Minna von Barnhelm,* written and first performed in 1767, gained its Prussian reputation from its setting against the backdrop of the Seven Years' War (1756–1763), in which the Prussian King Frederick II ("the Great") had prevailed against a powerful alliance that included France and the neighboring Kingdom of Saxony. The war and the upstart king who waged it had stirred patriotic feelings in many German middle-class intellectuals who wished to see their cultural aspirations matched by a great political cause. In his autobiography *Dichtung und Wahrheit* (1812; *Poetry and Truth*) Goethe lauds *Minna's* "perfect northern German national character," and calls it "the first theater production to grow out of a significant life context."

The author of this contemporary or national comedy, Gotthold Ephraim Lessing (1729–1781), was raised in Saxony as the son of an orthodox Lutheran pastor. Instead of pursuing his father's career as expected, he turned to the stage as a playwright and gained a reputation as a prolific writer on a variety of subjects, ranging from literature and dramaturgy to archeology, semiotics, and the key theological issues of the Enlightenment. Like so many 18th-century intellectuals, Lessing broke with the conventions of his social milieu and joined the cosmopolitan "republic of letters," which aspired to realize the Enlightenment ideal of free intellectual exchange articulated by Kant in his 1783 essay "Answer to the Question: What Is Enlightenment?" This context privileged literature and the arts for their socializing potential. It offered a fictional space for experimenting with new values and modes of living. The idea of a community of equals gave rise to the project of a German Nationaltheater, the first in-dependent repertory theater, with which Lessing became involved as critic and dramaturg. The result was *Hamburgische Dramaturgie* (1767–1769; *Hamburg Dramaturgy*), one of the seminal texts in German (and, arguably, European) the-ater history.

Lessing's lifelong preoccupation with the stage cannot be separated from his overarching concern with human enlightenment, which pervades all his writings and is best captured by the title of his late essay "Über die Erziehung des Menschengeschlechts" (1780; "On the Education of Humankind"). For Lessing, universal pedagogy did not exclude, but rather presupposed, concern for the local and the particular, which in the pre-nationalist era was meant by "national." A key issue of Enlightenment thinking was the problematic rela-tion between the universalism of reason and the particularism of inherited conventions, between the worlds of achievement and of tradition. As he bat-tled orthodox Lutheran theologians in a heated dispute that produced his last drama, *Nathan der Weise* (1779; *Nathan the Wise*), Lessing referred to the stage as his "old pulpit" from which he sought a free discussion of religious questions. The phrase suggests more than the drama's potential to disseminate a secular message of tolerance and universal brotherhood, which is most commonly as-sociated with the *Humanitätsdrama*. Rather, and crucially, *Nathan* enacts, in its very dramaturgy, the institution of the aesthetic as a means of establishing a new social ethic for the modern, autonomous individual, an individual who must be liberated from blind genealogical—ethnic, religious, feudal, and so on—allegiances.

Despite the wit and playfulness that have ensured its popularity over centu-ries, *Minna von Barnhelm* is no less concerned with human bonding and human autonomy. It is as much a drama of emancipation from social and gender de-terminations as it is a comedy about two lovers who lose and find each other in a period of chaos. Lessing transforms the familiar motif of love's triumph over contingency and social obstacles (father, tradition, the law) into a com-plex psychological negotiation. *Minna*'s aim is nothing less than the mutual recognition of man and woman on the basis of empathy and equality.

The comedy is set in 1763, just after the Seven Years' War. Major von Tellheim, a Prussian officer wounded in the war and discharged from the mili-tary for an alleged crime, feels compelled by his current disgrace and destitu-tion to break his engagement to Minna, a beautiful, wealthy Saxon. Minna, baffled at Tellheim's failure to contact her after the war, has set out on her own in search of him. As the action opens, chance brings the couple together, but Tellheim blocks Minna's affections, insisting repeatedly that his conscience and honor will not permit him to let her share his misfortune. However, Minna disregards the code of the aristocratic officer class—and, by implication, the demands of society at large—as firmly as Tellheim subscribes to it. Her sole criterion is unconditional love; if the army and the king have taken everything from him, she argues, what luck to gain everything back in her person. When

Tellheim becomes even more obdurate, she turns the tables on him, pretending to have been disowned by her uncle and guardian because of her engagement to an enemy officer, that is, a Prussian. Tellheim immediately falls for her ruse, insisting they marry now that Minna is allegedly impoverished herself. But now Minna refuses, and when Tellheim's honor is restored (he generously loaned money to occupied Saxons), she carries the deception further, eager to "teach him a lesson." She breaks off the engagement, throwing Tellheim's very words back at him: "Equality alone is the firmest bond of love" (*Minna,* 5.9). Minna's scheme nearly goes awry when Tellheim becomes convinced she had come to Berlin to break the engagement. In the nick of time, Minna's uncle arrives and welcomes his new son-in-law, her intrigue is disclosed, and the lovers are reunited with the blessing of both king and guardian.

The happy ending frames the subtle and sophisticated, but risky and slightly sadistic play staged by the heroine. This play within the play opens up Tellheim's soul, offering Minna and the audience alike "the sight of his whole heart" (*Minna,* 5.12). While she is playing with him, Minna writes a new comedy within the conventional comedy, one that supersedes the latter by transforming a stock dramaturgical type into a complex individual character. With his solipsistic fixation on lost honor and narcissistic self-deprecation, Tellheim falls at first glance within the comedic tradition of stubborn eccentrics ridiculed by other characters and the audience. Through Minna's brilliant role reversal his rich interior life is revealed and he comes to look at himself from the outside. Comic role-play, consciously performed, frees the individual from externally imposed and alienating roles by permitting a distanciated self-reflection. Comedy thus gives birth to the emancipated individual.

The play's pedagogical aim is more complex, however. Underlying Tellheim's rigid fixation on "the specter of honor" (*Minna,* 4.6) is a deep sense of responsibility, principle, and generosity. Yet it is precisely these moral qualities, which are colored by another, deeper flaw, toward which Minna directs her "lesson." Tellheim's masculine ego does not permit him to imagine himself bound to a wife of superior social standing; he does not want "to owe his whole fortune to a woman" and her "blind affection" (*Minna,* 4.6). For all his nobility of character, the major's illusory notion of integrity and self-sufficiency prevents him from accepting from others what he readily offers. The target of *Minna von Barnhelm,* and Minna herself, is not just an obsolete social code; it is the central value of enlightenment. Tellheim needs to be cured of an excess of autonomy as much as of honor.

But Tellheim is not the only figure guilty of this illusion of completeness. Minna too falls prey to it, if to a lesser extent, when she fails to take either Tellheim's predicament or his perspective seriously and blithely presumes that she alone can compensate for his loss. Both partners need to undergo a similar learning trajectory, to put themselves into the other's shoes and see with the other's eyes. Most crucially, they must unite in the awareness that human frailty is the condition of mutual dependency. If equality is the precondition for true love, insight into mutual frailty is the precondition for true equality. The balance of fortune achieved at the play's conclusion is nothing more than the theatrical mise-en-scène of this equality.

Lessing's principle of *Mitleid,* or sympathy, which fundamentally transformed the tragic genre, here finds its way into comedy. The concept of "bourgeois tragedy" that emerged under his influence (and that of his French contemporary Denis Diderot, whose dramatic and dramaturgical works Lessing translated) turned away from a hierarchical baroque and classicist tradition aimed at evoking the spectator's admiration. It invaded what had been the purview of comedy, the private sphere of the family and emotional intimacy, and restored them to new prominence as the subject matter in which all humans could recognize themselves. Psychological *Einfühlung,* or empathy, was the powerful maxim for the emerging middle-class theater directed against the French-dominated aristocratic culture. In Minna's game, sympathy, the intended effect of the tragic action on the audience, becomes the vehicle of a comical prank aimed at the happy solution of a potentially tragic conflict. Deceived by Minna's feigned misery, Tellheim's heart is opened by "compassion, the daughter of love" (*Minna,* 5.5), though this compassion also restores him to the position of benefactor, that is, it restores his male ego. *Minna von Barnhelm* demonstrates that the ethics of tragedy—opening oneself to the suffering of one's fellow humans—must be complemented by an ethics of comedy— opening oneself to and humbly accepting the contingent gift of happiness. Both aspects must come together to constitute the ideal reciprocity on which an equal relationship should be built.

Not only does *Minna von Barnhelm* use the tools of tragedy to create an enlightened comedy, but the play makes the transition from war to peace the central stake of a comedy that disarms (heroic) tragedy altogether. The hero's pathetic injury graphically illustrates this disarmament; far from being the triumphant token of his heroic feats, Tellheim's disabled right arm manifests the demise of the warrior and the dawn of peaceful civility. (Incidentally, the arm handicap produced a line of successors, from Goethe's *Götz von Berlichingen* [1772], the "knight with the iron hand," to Major von Crampas in Fontane's *Effi Briest.*) But civility needs to be constantly bolstered against the continuing threat of an inner, psychological state of war. In tracing belligerent attitudes and behavioral patterns into the recesses of the soul (Minna herself is not free from aggressive, even cruel traits) and, at the same time, alleviating them through comical gestures and witty rhetoric, Lessing's play as a whole performs a civilizing, indeed feminizing, function.

The age of Enlightenment and tragedy make for incompatible bedfellows. Tragic death is scarcely plausible for a thinking that views the world and history not as subject to firm metaphysical rule, but as open to an infinite process aspiring to human perfection. Thus, Lessing's own groundbreaking bourgeois tragedies, *Miss Sara Sampson* (1755) and *Emilia Galotti* (1772), indict bourgeois moral rigidity for producing catastrophic consequences. From the perspective of pedagogic perfectibility, tragedy indicates failure and is avoidable in princi-

ple. Comedy implies the necessity of compromise and reconciliation in its generic law, a compromise realized through devices of theatrical distanciation,
role splitting, and self-reflection—not to mention the anti-authoritarian gesture endemic to the genre. In *Minna,* comedy challenges the value absolutism
of the tragic tradition, be it heroic or bourgeois, and prevails over it, not by ridicule and exclusion, but by a sympathetic, integrative laughter, by laughing
with, not *at* (see *Hamburg Dramaturgy,* 29). The theater of comedy becomes the
place of peace.

Lessing's affinity for comedy is further shown in *Nathan the Wise,* the most
famous scene of which recalls Minna's intrigue. In *Nathan,* the Jewish hero responds to the Muslim monarch's demand to know the one true religion by
telling the parable of an empowering ring secretly replicated by a father so he
may bequeath it to all three of his sons (*Nathan,* V, 5–7). An aesthetic construct
thus takes the place of a lost metaphysical truth. The duplicated rings, however,
act as tokens of paternal love that imbues the sons with a zeal for brotherly
bonding and moral achievement. Nathan's tale also is a stand-in for a theoretically unachievable truth which is achieved on the moral level when the Muslim and the Jew bond in friendship. This bonding is paralleled in the final
scene as members of different ethnicities and religions recognize themselves as
belonging to one family and, silently embracing, form a ring that echoes the
protagonist's story. Lessing's aesthetic play, which is grounded in comedy, does
not do away with the idea of an ultimate truth, but rather transforms it into
practiced morality.

In *Minna,* rings are similarly important as a symbol of bonding, losing, and
regaining. By pure chance, Minna gets hold of the engagement ring Tellheim
has been forced to sell. She hands it back to him as if returning her own ring.
Under the pretense of its dissolution, then, the engagement is actually confirmed and renewed. The moment of Tellheim's deepest despair is the very
moment of his bliss—it only remains for him to see it (*Minna,* V, 12). Like the
father's ring in Nathan's parable, the engagement ring in *Minna* symbolizes an
original state of bonding that needs to be recognized and actively pursued.
The original engagement is repeated under conditions of mobility and liquid-
ity. Money is the play's pervasive symbol for these conditions; it interweaves a
sentimental discourse of the heart with a capitalist one of credits, debts, and
exchange. Passing through the medium of an exchange economy is the precondition for freely choosing a partner, yet paradoxically, this act simultaneously transcends the economy of exchange on which it depends.

The cover page of Lessing's comedy cites its full title, *Minna von Barnhelm or
Soldiers' Good Fortune (Minna von Barnhelm oder das Soldatenglück),* followed by a
bit of misinformation: "Written in the year 1763." In a whim of his own,
Lessing rewrites a date in political history as a marker of literary history. In his
idiosyncratic chronology, the year of the Peace of Hubertusberg that ended the
Seven Years' War likewise terminates the age of heroic tragedy, of honor, and
of soldiers' fortune—at least in one sense of the word. For the German word
Glück is ambiguous, meaning both luck and happiness. In its death throes is the

volatile world of *fortuna* as conceived by the Baroque, a world of vanity that had to be endured and surpassed for the greater good of a transcendent world. But far from a secularized safe haven, the emerging world of immanent happiness remains even more precarious and subject to a contingency ever poised to destroy, just as it may ensure, human happiness. In a never-ending process, happiness must be pursued and defended; the human autonomy to which the Enlightenment aspired must be mitigated by a trust in providence and the humility to accept its own limitations.

See also 1647, 1774, 1781, 1790, 1897

Bibliography: Gotthold Ephraim Lessing, *Werke,* vol. 9: *Gedichte, Fabeln, Lustspiele,* ed. Herbert G. Göpfert (Munich: Hanser, 1970). ———, *Nathan the Wise, Minna von Barnhelm, and Other Plays and Writings,* ed. Peter Demetz (New York: Continuum, 1991). Horst Steinmetz, ed., *Lessing—ein unpoetischer Dichter: Dokumente aus drei Jahrhunderten zur Wirkungsgeschichte Lessings in Deutschland* (Frankfurt am Main and Bonn: Athenäum, 1969).

Helmut J. Schneider

🦎 *1768, June 8*

Johann Joachim Winckelmann is murdered in Trieste

Becoming Greek

"That Winckelmann died young is also, for us, a good thing," wrote J. W. Goethe in his "Skizzen zu einer Schilderung Winckelmanns" (1805; Sketches for a Portrait of Winckelmann). In fact, the German antiquarian—whom many have called the first art historian—was fifty-one at the time of his death, but that did not prevent Goethe from comparing him to Achilles, wandering amongst the shades, "an eternally striving youth" (70) who exerted a powerful thrall on the present from beyond the grave. Somehow, J. J. Winckelmann, born the son of a shoemaker in the culturally unprepossessing Brandenburg town of Stendhal, had managed to make such an impression on his generation that he might well still seem a youthful presence in 1805.

From the time of the publication of his *Gedancken über die Nachahmung der griechischen Wercke in der Mahlerey und Bildhauer-Kunst (Reflections on the Imitation of Greek Works in Painting and Sculpture)* in 1755, Winckelmann had been greatly admired for his learning and for his passionate devotion to Greek culture. What made him famous, however, was less his publications than his life and untimely death. There was something spectacular, for late Enlightenment intellectuals, about a man who suffered thirty years of isolation, dependency, and privation in the North, then found recognition, cultural riches, and independence in the ancient Mediterranean capital. That the antiquarian's triumph should have found a sudden and violent end at the hand of an Italian thief gave the fairytale a ghoulish finale, and his admirers a sense of common loss. "One doesn't learn anything when one reads [Winckelmann]," Goethe later remarked, "but one becomes something" (Johann Peter Eckermann, *Gespräche mit Goethe,* 224). What one became was a member of the Graecophile, male-oriented, aestheticizing German intellectual elite—but one fully conscious, too, of the inevitably utopian and tragic qualities of this commitment.

The theme of "becoming" was central to Winckelmann's life and legacy. Winckelmann's contemporaries made much of his inauspicious beginnings. Born in 1717, just five years after Jean-Jacques Rousseau, the German writer had to climb a similarly difficult road toward recognition, one that fostered the development of a similarly half-boastful, half-obsequious persona, and a keen longing for freedom and autonomy. Although Winckelmann, like Rousseau, issued trenchant critiques of the churches and of court society, he depended throughout his life on precisely these institutions for patronage. From the Reformed Church Winckelmann received his early education; he funded his later studies of theology, medicine, and classical literature by serving as a tutor to aristocratic families. In 1748, he obtained the position of librarian at the estate of Count Heinrich von Bünau in Nöthnitz near Dresden, which gained him access to books, artifacts, friendly artists, and more affluent patrons. In 1754, he was awarded a small pension by the Duke of Saxony, and, after agreeing to convert to Catholicism, was released to live independently in Rome. He arrived in Rome in 1755, the same year his *Reflections* became a literary sensation in Germany. In the Holy City, he became a highly respected expert and tour guide; his small pension, however, did not give him the full intellectual independence he craved. Nor did he gain the entrée into high society necessary for his work, since the collections of antiquities remained in private hands. To make ends meet, he took up a series of commissions, becoming, in 1757, librarian to Cardinal Archinto, in 1758, librarian-secretary to Cardinal Albani, and in 1763 Commissioner of the Antiquities of the Apostolic Chamber under Clement XIII. These positions finally gave him social status and access to Rome's great collections, and his fame grew as his knowledge expanded. In 1764, he published *Geschichte der Kunst des Alterthums (History of the Art of Antiquity)*. Begun as a handbook for visitors, this work was immediately hailed as the most comprehensive study of ancient art to date. For the next four years, the last of his life, he enjoyed international renown. His death occurred after he had aborted a trip back to Germany, where a hero's welcome was awaiting him. On reaching Vienna, he found himself psychologically unable to return to the place of his dismal younger years, while he was also pining for Rome. During a stopover in Trieste, on the way back to the Eternal City, he was strangled by a penniless Italian cook. Francesco Arcangeli was caught, tried, and convicted, but would not admit to having had homosexual relations with the eminent scholar—possibly to avoid being burned alive and having his ashes scattered to the winds (though he was, in the end, broken on the wheel).

The news of Winckelmann's murder traveled quickly, and, as Goethe testified, struck a circle of young proto-romantics "like a clap of thunder from a clear blue sky." Winckelmann was for these young Germans a sort of contemporary Horatio Alger, an ordinary young man who had overcome poverty and adversity by dint of genius, meritorious work, and adherence to admirable principles. Genius meant something like possession of original passions and perspectives; Winckelmann certainly had that. As for meritorious work, this meant the pursuit, despite its hardships, of secular, rather than theological, knowledge, the aim of which was the unfolding of the unique individual, the cultivation, or *Bildung,* of a complete, autonomous self. The principles Winckelmann followed, or at least was thought to have followed, are outlined in the first four subheadings Goethe inserted into his *Sketches:* Antiquity, Paganism, Friendship, and Beauty. Though Winckelmann invented none of these terms, it was through activating them in his writings, and especially in the pageantry of his life, that he came to shape German cultural history in his wake.

Antiquity: Reacting, in part, to 17th-century debates about the superiority of the ancients versus the moderns, Winckelmann, in *Reflections,* took a clear position in favor of the ancients; the only way a nation, and especially a fragmented cultural nation like Germany, could become great, he argued, was by imitating the Greeks. In no way should this be a slavish sort of imitation, as the Dutch painters imitated nature, or Bernini imitated Renaissance models. Rather, the nation must learn to combine the natural and the ideal in the manner of the Greek artist, who created a perfect Helen of Troy by blending together the best attributes of several women.

Winckelmann's emphasis on Greece, especially on 5th-century Athens, a fragmented, youthful nation unified by cultural feats, and his desultory treatment of ancient Rome, seen as an imperious and unimaginative state based on force, was quite unusual in the mid-18th century, and bespoke a desire for distance from an aristocratic humanism focused on Latin eloquence. Winckelmann underscored the simplicity, youthfulness, and originality of Greek culture, and championed Greek art, poetry, and philosophy. His Graecophilia caught on very quickly and came to have a lasting effect on German cultural institutions. German intellectuals, especially Protestants, often saw themselves, after Winckelmann, as culture-loving Greeks, over and against the power-hungry Romans, played at various times by the Austrians, the French, the Catholics, and the English.

Paganism: Winckelmann was not, strictly speaking, a pagan, but his reverence for all things Greek, and his entirely mercenary conversion to Catholicism in 1755, made him seem emancipated from Christianity's thrall. For Winckelmann, the gods were actually present in the sculptures representing them; they were real participants in the everyday, and an integral part of the healthy culture of the Greeks. Here, the body and the soul were not separate, and the nude human form, far from being an object of revulsion, was worshiped; indeed, it was the study of beautiful nude youths exercising at the Gymnasium, Winckelmann wrote, that prepared Greek artists to create beautiful art. For Goethe and his generation of enlightened, anticlerical readers, Winckelmann's indifference to Christianity and reverential account of Greek religious practices had something particularly thrilling. Paganism represented their most cherished values: self-reliance, the wonders of the here-and-now, the universe as a work of art, the close relationship between nature and spirit, and the need for knowable, rational gods. Regrettably, however, this world of pagan harmony, in which the aesthetic and the religious, the natural and the ideal, were all united, had gradually fallen apart, and would not, it seemed, return. After Winckelmann, numerous German intellectuals, most notably the poet Friedrich Schiller and, in a different way, the philosopher G. W. F Hegel, reenacted this tragic demise of Greek paganism, the disappearance of this aesthetic primal unity in favor of a much less satisfying sensuous system of beliefs.

Friendship: In his letters from Rome, Winckelmann portrayed himself as a man transported from a Germanic hell into a sunlit southern heaven. But, though surrounded by Rome's aesthetic delights, the scholar seemed perpetually to lack soul mates. In his letters to friends, he lamented their absence and called on them to come and stay, not only to study the antiquities, but to pursue that one-on-one male relationship which Winckelmann, following in particular Homer's *Iliad* and Plato's *Phaedrus,* found so ennobling. Winckelmann's friendship ideal was a mixture of the homoerotic classical ideal, the Renaissance humanist ideal of a republic of letters, in which like-minded scholars of all ranks and religions share knowledge and information, and an emerging, anti-aristocratic conception of friendship as a nonhierarchical relationship based on a communion of souls. This friendship could only occur between two men, because only they could cultivate a fully selfless, disinterested love. In his insistence on same-sex male friendship, Winckelmann differs from Rousseau. But like Rousseau, Winckelmann appealed to his audience in a language that seemed newly expressive of the individual soul, filled with longing for freedom and community.

Beauty: Beauty is perhaps the most important keyword for understanding Winckelmann and his oeuvre. He cherished beauty in his friends and surroundings, and wanted his studies of antiquity, above all, to contribute to the birth of a new (Germanic) form of artistic beauty. According to Winckelmann, beauty meant the perfect unity of nature and ideal, as captured in the idealized human form. Here, Winckelmann demonstrated most clearly his debt to the tradition of humanism, in which the improvement and celebration of man— not of God—was to be the focus of human endeavor. In privileging the beauty of the Greek male nude, Winckelmann transformed humanism into an aesthetic theory that would shape German discussion of the beautiful ever afterward. For Winckelmann, the most beautiful works of art were the white, freestanding classical sculptures that had adorned the Greek city-states. They displayed, he famously proclaimed, "noble simplicity and silent grandeur." This affection for pure, white forms he bequeathed to the 19th century, the era, par excellence, of what later critics called "plaster-cast antiquity."

But if Winckelmann believed that Greek sculpture represented timeless beauty, he was, as a scholar, also keenly aware of historical changes in artistic ideals and practices. His *History of the Art of Antiquity* begins with the Egyptians and ends with the Romans, separating Greek art as well into periods of youth, maturity, and decay. Political institutions shape artistic production, he argued. The freedom of the Greek city-state made possible the production of artistic beauty. Drawing on Montesquieu's discussion of the effects of climate on political forms, and on recent French works on natural history, Winckelmann argued that climate and even physiognomy shape artistic forms. The Eskimo, living in an extremely cold environment and possessing what Winckelmann claimed to be particularly ill-proportioned faces, made art in a peculiar, and not very beautiful, way. The contradictions here between a historicized understanding of creative practices and a static conception of Greek ideal beauty, between an embryonic social history of art and a theory about race as a determinant feature, were apparent to neither Winckelmann nor many of his followers—though numerous knowledgeable antiquarians immediately pointed out that Winckelmann's chronology of Greek forms did not really correspond to his history of Greek political development. His theories about the political and climatic conditions appealed to Herder, Hegel, and Burckhardt, while early archaeologists took up his history of forms, a division of labor that made Winckelmann's legacy more diffuse, but also more powerful, in years to come.

Finally, we must evoke a term that Goethe failed to list in his catalog of Winckelmann's impressive attributes: Germanness. Winckelmann was devoted to the creation of a German cultural republic in which men like himself, not tradition-oriented "scribblers" or superficial Francophiles, would define the future. But, of course, in Winckelmann's lifetime, German culture was only beginning to gain recognition. Writing in German, living in Italy, Winckelmann was perfectly placed to articulate a patriotism that appealed especially to the disgruntled educated elite, eager to rid their localities of French aristocratic pretensions and to establish secular cultural institutions. In a letter of 1760, Winckelmann called Prussia "this nation of despotism and slavery" (quoted in Disselkamp, 150) and attacked it for its suppression of art and science. He offered two remedies for Germany's cultural backwardness: the enlightenment of princes and, more importantly, the imitation of the Greeks. The latter's republican simplicity, naïve sensuality, and aesthetic nobility would be an ideal counterweight to the baroque, Frenchified, imperial power. If the princes paid little attention, the bureaucrats, especially after Wilhelm von Humboldt's brief though pivotal service as Prussian Minister of Culture from 1809 to 1810, did, indeed, begin to infuse German cultural institutions with Winckelmann's ideas. This pairing of Greece with Germany has a long and complicated history, but unquestionably, its origins lie in Winckelmann's longings for reform of German culture and the achievement of the right sort of German state.

Winckelmann in Rome represented an emerging cultural nation to be reckoned with, but his decision to turn back after reaching Vienna in 1768 demonstrates that he himself had not yet, either practically or psychologically, achieved the harmonious union between the modern German and the ancient Mediterranean *Geist* he so passionately desired. His career poignantly illustrates the 18th-century German intellectual elite's sense of its outsider status, its youth, and its belatedness. Moreover, his death added to this sense of belatedness a layer of tragedy: for Winckelmann died trying to reach not Germany but Rome, a clear suggestion for those who saw his life as exemplary that Germans would always be, in some sense, strangers in the classical world.

They might "seek Greece with the soul," as Friedrich Hölderlin put it, but would never quite feel at home. In Goethe's *Faust,* part 2, the protagonist seduces Helen of Troy, but she refuses to stay with him, and he is left holding only her veil. In Thomas Mann's *Death in Venice,* an aging German artist succumbs to a forbidden passion for a youth whose beauty springs directly from Winckelmann's description of Greek sculpture. In both cases, German *Geist* longs to overcome its isolation by uniting with the sensuous beauty of the classical Mediterranean, and in both cases, it fails. In shaping this attempt, and in raising this failure to the level of a literary and cultural trope, J. J. Winckelmann set his seal on German cultural history.

See also 1789, 1808, 1828 (Winter), 1831, 1860, 1912 (June)

Bibliography: Johann Joachim Winckelmann, *Geschichte der Kunst des Altertums* (Darmstadt: Wissenschaftliche Buchgesellschaft, 1993). ———, *Gedanken über die Nachahmung der griechischen Werke in der Malerei und Bildhauerkunst* (Baden-Baden: Heitz, 1962; facsimile of the 2nd edition, Dresden 1762). ———, *Reflections on the Imitation of Greek Works in Painting and Sculpture,* trans. Elfriede Heyer and Roger C. Norton (La Salle, Ill.: Open Court, 1987). Johann Wolfgang Goethe, *Skizze zu einer Schilderung Winckelmanns,* ed. Jochen Golz (Frankfurt am Main: Insel, 1994). ———, *Werke,* Weimarausgabe, (Weimar: Commissioned by Grand Duchess Sophie von Sachsen, 1887–1919), vol. 27. Alex Potts, *Flesh and the Ideal: Winckelmann and the Origins of Art History* (New Haven, Conn.: Yale University Press, 1994). Martin Disselkamp, *Die Stadt der Gelehrten: Studien zu Johann Joachim Winckelmanns Briefen aus Rom* (Tübingen: Niemeyer, 1993). Henry Hatfield, *Winckelmann and His German Critics, 1755–1781* (New York: King's Crown Press, 1943). Suzanne L. Marchand, *Down from Olympus: Archaeology and Philhellenism in Germany, 1780– 1970* (Princeton, N. J.: Princeton University Press, 1996). Johann Peter Eckermann, *Gespräche mit Goethe in den letzten Jahren seines Lebens,* vol. 1, ed. E. Merian-Genast (Basel: Birkhäuser, 1945). Lionel Gossman, "Death in Trieste," *Journal of European Studies* 22 (1992): 207–240.

Suzanne L. Marchand

☽ *1773, July 2*

Students at the University of Göttingen burn the works of Christoph Martin Wieland, accusing him of being a "lascivious" poet

Wieland's Cosmopolitan Classicism

Christoph Martin Wieland's (1733–1813) chief contribution to German literature is a new kind of urbanity combined with literary erudition. He was equally at home in ancient Greek and Roman literature as in more contemporary Italian, Spanish, French, and English writings. His translations of Shakespeare and his exquisite verse narratives, novels, and essays served as models to a younger generation of writers. In retrospect, it seems astonishing that this urbane German representative of European literary and cultural traditions should have been so aggressively attacked by the young writers of the Storm and Stress and the early Romantic periods, who, after all, belonged to a generation of *soi-disant* progressives. Heinrich Wilhelm von Gerstenberg (1737– 1823) expressed the commonly held view of this generation: "Who did Wieland not try to be? Now Shaftesbury, now Milton, then Young, Rowe,

Richardson; now Crébillion, then Hamilton, at other times Fielding, Cervantes, Helvetius, Yorik, and in passing even something of Rousseau, Montaigne, Voltaire." Intended as a dismissal, Gerstenberg's comment demonstrates that Wieland had an exceptional knowledge of literary traditions. Goethe understood this. In the essay "Fraternal Commemoration of Wieland," he states that Wieland's abundant talents were similar to those of his "twin" Shaftesbury, but far exceeded them, "since what the Englishman teaches and aims for in principle, the German achieves poetically and rhetorically in verse and prose." This achievement was due in no small part to Wieland's command of French style, that well-known combination of "serenity, wit, esprit, and elegance." In his *Briefe an einen jungen Dichter* (1782; *Letters to a Young Poet*), Wieland pointedly calls for a synthesis of classical, French, and English styles. He encouraged a contemporary literature that, like Goethe's *Iphigenie,* brings together "the communion with nature that is the very soul of Shakespeare's works with the beautiful simplicity of the Greeks and the art and taste so profoundly claimed by the French." As Goethe stressed, Wieland was "against everything that had come to be understood under the term 'philistinism'—stagnant pedantry, narrow provinciality, petty manners and morals, poor judgment, unjustified prudishness, shallow comforts, pretentious dignity, and however else one wishes to term this legion of monsters."

Wieland was denounced as a *poeta doctus,* a cosmopolitan, a representative of the Enlightenment, of the Rococo, of the culture of form and grace. He was attacked for being too artful, witty, sensual, eudaemonistic, and un-German. These attacks, directed against him as the influential editor of the *Teutscher Merkur,* had a lasting effect. Wieland's journal, ironically named "the factory," contains clear and rather blunt essays denouncing the excessive German nationalism that had taken hold since Klopstock and the Storm and Stress period. These essays, which lack the ironic indirection of his novels, eviscerate chauvinistic slogans and expose to ridicule this "wandering about, lost in the woods of the old Germans, affecting in bardic songs a national character that has long since ceased to be ours." In opposition to a "national poetry," he advanced the idea of "world literature"; in opposition to chauvinism, an enlightened ideal of liberal cosmopolitanism.

Wieland's essays, novels, and narrative verse are concerned with the education *(Bildung)* of consciousness—hence his ironic detachment, his Apollonian distance, his program of "ridendo dicere verum" (speaking the truth with laughter). "We live," Wieland wrote, "in an ocean of phenomena, ideas, and phantoms; we are deluded by them in innumerable ways, but our aim is to be as little deluded as possible" (*Teutscher Merkur,* January 1788). Everything is a question of perspective. "The true seer," he writes in *Schach Lolo,* "is he who sees things from the right point of view." Like Laurence Sterne, he believed that people are moved less by facts than by opinions. "Facts are whatever one makes of them," says the protagonist of *Die Geschichte des weisen Danischmend* (1775; *The History of the Wise Danischmend*). "Seen from every new viewpoint, something different appears; and in ten cases to one, the alleged fact upon which one had so confidently built an opinion turns out to be in essence only a hypothesis." Wieland relativizes ideologies and jargon with a play of opinions, opinions with irony, and irony with "innate grace." Goethe put it well in "Commemoration": "This brilliant man liked to play with his opinions, but—as his contemporaries will agree—never with his convictions."

"Truth," Wieland wrote in a *Teutscher Merkur* essay in 1788, "is neither here nor there; it is everywhere. No one reveals it completely; everyone sees only a little bit of it, from behind, or else the hem of its robe; from a different point of view; in a different light." He believed in the value of communication, in the exchange of opinions, in tolerance and openness toward experiment. This did not mean relativism as a program, but a critique of every kind of rigid ideological one-sidedness that galled his natural tendency for enjoyment of life and love of humanity. Long before Nietzsche, this skeptical idealist registered the collapse of moral systems and the emergence of a political and cultural vacuum and did everything he could to hold off the demise of culture and to confront the danger of "an expanding barbarism." He admitted, however, that "in the end one is threshing empty hay, cupping water in a sieve, writing in the sand." Despite his skepticism—and he distrusted even the humanistic ideals of his time—he did not stop "speaking the truth with laughter" and appealing to the reason of his fellows. The Socratic irony he shares with Lichtenberg, Jean Paul, Heinrich Heine, Thomas Mann, and, in some ways, Robert Musil is a decisive element of his novels and also his narrative verse.

To achieve an art of living inspired by aristocratic tradition—"the perfect harmony of all the faculties," the reconciliation of egoism and altruism, sensuality and spirituality—Wieland took up principles from classical Greece and Rome. As early as 1767, in his verse narrative *Musarion,* he advances the notion that became definitive for German classicism: "What nature designs, art fulfills." One's true existential destiny is achieved only through art. In *Grazien* (1769), he counters the popular aesthetic category of the sublime: "For without the Graces and the Amoretti, who accompany them, even the Muses cannot make beauty complete." And, in *Beiträge zur geheimen Geschichte des menschlichen Verstandes und Herzens* (1770; *Contributions to the Secret History of the Human Understanding and Heart*), he anticipates Friedrich Schiller's concept of aesthetic education: "As he leaves the sculptor's hand, man is little more than potentiality. He must develop himself, educate himself, put the final polish on whatever it is that splendor and grace have showered upon him—in a word he must in some measure be his own second creator." It is thus no coincidence that with *Geschichte des Agathon* (1766–1767; *History of Agathon*), Wieland produced a philosophical *Bildungsroman* that became a model for novels from Goethe's *Wilhelm Meister* to Adalbert Stifter's *Nachsommer.* Wieland leads his protagonist through the vicissitudes of life, emphasizing their ideological conflicts.

The manner in which Agathon develops the potential of his nature is portrayed with great skill through encounters with characters from antiquity. Although Wieland owes much of his narrative technique to English writers, especially to Fielding, his psychological elegance and manner of creating an erotic atmosphere betray the inspiration of French models. As Gerstenberg remarked, Wieland is not only the German Shaftesbury, he is also the German Crébillion.

Despite these borrowings, Wieland invents a new genre with his novel *Agathon* and the almost contemporaneous verse narrative *Musarion*. Lessing describes *Agathon* in the sixty-ninth entry of his *Hamburgische Dramaturgie* as "unquestionably one of the most distinguished works of our century, but as regards the German reading public written much too soon." To which he adds, without envy: "It is the first and only novel for the thinking mind with a taste informed by classical antiquity." As Wieland's biographer Friedrich Sengle remarks, it cannot be sufficiently emphasized that "Wieland's importance for the epic form is like that of Lessing for the history of drama and Klopstock's for the development of lyric poetry."

Wieland's *Musarion* enacts with wit and sensuousness the essence of his philosophy of aesthetic education, the "philosophy of grace." In style and substance, *Musarion* combines the frivolous lightness of the *Comische Erzählungen* with the cultivated philosophical discourse of *Agathon*. Goethe remarked in *Dichtung und Wahrheit* when he read this perfect poem as a student in Leipzig, he "thought he saw the ancient world come alive and fresh." In a dedication to the then-famous poet, playwright, and author of *Singspiele* Christian Felix Weisse (1726–1804), Wieland states that in *Musarion* he portrayed the "embodiment of his spirit." "Musarion's philosophy," he confesses regarding his charming protagonist, "is that on which I base my life; her mode of thought, her principles, her taste, her moods are mine." Indeed, the work is a kind of didactic poem in which comic and epic elements are employed to express the author's worldview. With erotic, sensual, witty, and resourceful refinement, Musarion guides her disappointed lover, Phanias, toward a philosophical middle path, away from the extreme ideological positions that had deluded him. This middle path is conveyed in a new form developed from traditional models of the European Rococo and Enlightenment.

Musarion is structured like a three-act comedy. The first book provides an ironic sketch of the disappointed lover, Phanias, whose changed appearance reflects his recent philosophical conversion. Hitherto always clad in the latest fashions, he now appears in the garb of a cynic, shabbily dressed, with a long beard and uncombed hair. He has turned his back on the city and become an ascetic misanthrope, renouncing sensual pleasure for the sake of a virtuous life. With a wink to the reader, the author warns that Phanias's supposed "new way of thinking" has brought him only "grief" and "trouble." Furthermore, Amor is about to challenge his new convictions. Wieland portrays Musarion—the eponymous heroine in whom the Muses and the Graces are united—with a flair for erotic and spiritual allure unknown in his time. It is not surprising that Phanias, this ascetic apostle of virtue, immediately tries to flee from her. But Musarion easily succeeds in overcoming his resistance. With a lecture on conduct that criticizes his extreme devotion to dreamy enthusiasm, she displays her superior refinement and verbal skills. Like Minna von Barnhelm in Lessing's comedy, Musarion not only criticizes the behavior and convictions of the male protagonist, she does so while pursuing him on her own, risking not only her reputation but also having "her hair undone." The lovely woman explains that she wants to spend the night at Phanias's modest country house. Phanias is ill at ease with this proposition, since he already has two house guests, Kleanth the Stoic and Theophron the Pythagorean, but Musarion easily counters his objections. The narrator reports, not without a touch of *Schadenfreude,* that "evicted Amor creeps so softly, as upon the tips of flowers, / from her eyes into his heart" (598–600).

While in the first book Phanias's mental state is explained as the consequence of unrequited love, in the second book Musarion exposes the rigorous philosophies of his friends as ridiculous illusions and so much wind. At their very first meeting with Musarion they become ludicrous figures. Instead of engaging one another's arguments, they "tear each other's hair" (645) and wrestle each other to the ground. Musarion does not hesitate to suggest, with a smile, that the performance of the two wrestlers is really just a physical exercise to strengthen the mind. In her debate with the philosophers, Musarion's superiority becomes transparently clear and Phanias grows ashamed of his friends. He sees how Musarion's "wit, free-spirited gaiety," and grace turn the emptiness of their quixotic idealism upside down. She transforms the "light philosophical meal . . . into a little Bacchanal" (997–999) that rapidly demolishes the house of cards constructed by the two philosophers. Not only does her critical realism falsify their theories, it also brings them back to earth from their "extraterrestrial journeys" (943). While Kleanth, at the end of the third half-dozen bottles, devotes himself to the god of wine, Theophron succumbs to the charms of the frivolous slave Cloe, whom Musarion has brought along for the purpose of just such a didactic demonstration.

The third book constitutes the high point of the narrative in which Musarion initiates Phanias into her philosophy of grace: "Whatever nature and destiny so generously give to us, / we should enjoy with pleasure, and gladly renounce the rest" (1409–11). The pedagogical discourse is a simultaneous discourse on love, in which Phanias speaks for the romantic ideal of love as exclusivity, whereas Musarion denounces every kind of extreme enthusiasm and passion. Her principle, she explains, is "serene, gentle joy"—grace, not passion. She defines her love for Phanias with this simile: "As I love the Graces, as I love the Muses, / so do I love you" (1140–41). For Wieland, the Horation *aurea mediocritas* is the decisive measure, not only in a philosophy of life, but also in matters of love.

Eighteenth-century German texts exhibit as a rule a strategy for the avoidance of sensual or eudaemonistic concepts and perspectives; love is associated with reason, or else it is sublimated into a friendship of souls or into a concept of education. By combining the modern French and ancient semantics of love, Wieland dissolved the dichotomy between rational-idealistic accounts and sexual love *(amor concupiscentiae).* German literature may have denounced

French models of love as aristocratic, but Wieland attempted—never without encountering grave opposition—to make sexuality an acceptable part of bourgeois morals. The difficulty of revising a social code that spiritualized and idealized physical love is revealed in Goethe's *Werther,* Schiller's *Kabale und Liebe,* and, later, in the novels and novellas of the Romantics. It is not surprising that the author of *Musarion, Comische Erzählungen, Idris und Zenide* (1768), and *Agathon* should have been denounced by the "Hain Bund" (Brotherhood of the Forest Grove), a student group in Göttingen, as a "poet of lasciviousness" as they committed his books to the flames.

As Musarion's philosophy of grace demonstrates, Wieland was concerned with a "balance between enthusiasm and detachment" (letter to Weisse, March 15, 1769). He conceived of Socratic irony as an antidote to all forms of extremism and urged understanding indulgence for the imperfections of human nature. It is a pity that this skeptical critical realist, who took the world for neither an Elysium nor a hell (*Musarion,* 1424) and urged moderation in ideology, aesthetics, and politics, never gained greater popularity. In retrospect one may say that he remained, like Goethe, his younger and more famous friend, an "un-German classicist." Indeed, they both belonged to the "Order of Cosmopolitans." In an essay published in the August 1788 issue of *Teutscher Merkur,* Wieland wrote: "Cosmopolitans bear their title (citizens of the world) in the most specific and eminent sense. They perceive all peoples of the earth as so many branches of one single family and the universe as a state in which they are citizens sharing with innumerable other rational beings the aim of pursuing perfection within the general rules of nature, and in which every one in his own particular way is responsible for his own wellbeing." This humanist vision, which even today remains utopian, is the core of Wieland's aesthetic and political program.

See also 1750, 1767, 1786, 1792 (August 26)

Bibliography: Christoph Martin Wieland, *Musarion and Other Rococo Tales,* trans. Thomas C. Starnes (Columbia, S.C.: Camden House, 1991). ———, *Werke in zwölf Bänden,* ed. Gonthier-Louis Fink et al. (Frankfurt am Main: Deutscher Klassiker Verlag, 1986–). John A. McCarthy, *Christoph Martin Wieland* (Boston: Twayne, 1979). Friedrich Sengle, *Wieland* (Stuttgart: Metzler, 1949).

Walter Hinderer

♌ 1774, January–March

During six weeks of somnambulant writing, Goethe produces *Die Leiden des jungen Werther,* establishing his literary fame

Pathologies of Literature

Among the three books in the monster's hovel in Mary Shelley's gothic horror story *Frankenstein* (1818) is a French translation of Johann Wolfgang von Goethe's first novel, *Die Leiden des jungen Werther* (1774; *The Sorrows of Young Werther*). Shelley's creature finds in Goethe's compact epistolary fiction a literary rendering of his own situation. The touching depiction of "gentle and domestic manners" mirrors the family idyll he clandestinely observes; the novel's "lofty sentiments and feelings" echo his unappeasable yearning; and Werther's suicide, which elicits the monster's tears, anticipates the sad ending of his own story (*Frankenstein*, 124). With his adulation of the hero and lachrymose compassion for his suffering, the monster joins scores of readers who went before him. In the decades following its publication, Goethe's novel achieved undisputed status as the purest literary expression of sentimental emotion. By placing the book in the hands and heart of a monster, Mary Shelley subverts this widespread appraisal and exposes the violent undercurrent of 18th-century sentimentalism. Her diagnosis of sentimental love as a pathological condition draws on the resources of the predecessor text. Goethe's *Werther* is itself a study in tormented ambivalence, the tracking of an imagination and a desire that oscillate between idyllic harmony and monstrous aggression.

Goethe's best-known work, *Werther* was reprinted some fifty times and was widely translated during the poet's lifetime. However, from the beginning, the reception of the novel was polarized. While established rationalist writers, such as the shrewd Berlin bookseller Friedrich Nicolai, thought its effusiveness puerile and its restraint from moral judgment irresponsible, the younger generation was enthusiastic in the extreme. The paradox of imitated authenticity, still today a prominent feature of youth culture, found in the "Werther-fashion" unleashed by the novel one of its earliest historical manifestations. The protagonist's discontent with pretension, pedantry, and hierarchy, his love of nature, and his superabundant compassion congealed to an affective style. His idiosyncratic costume, a blue frock coat and yellow vest, became a much-replicated uniform. This identificatory behavior even spilled over into a wave of suicides, still sufficiently alive in the public mind in 1813 to provoke a professor of medicine in Göttingen, Friedrich Benjamin Osiander, to condemn the novel's poisonous influence. To Goethe the turbulence surrounding his work was generally annoying. During his travels in Italy (1786–1788), culturally the most significant such sojourn in German history, he adopted a pseudonym to shield himself against the omnipresent, intrusive curiosity about the novel's author. Rare were such satisfactions as that occasioned by his meeting with Napoleon on October 2, 1808, during which the emperor, who claimed to have read the novel seven times, interrupted the urgent business of war and politics to discuss with the author a question bearing on the hero's motives. Even the "incarnation of the world spirit," as Hegel had apotheosized Napoleon two years before, was preoccupied with *Werther*.

Two episodes in Goethe's life served as source material for the novel's plot. As a young lawyer at the Imperial Cameral Court in Wetzlar, from May through September 1772, Goethe met a certain Charlotte Buff and her fiancé, later husband, Johann Christian Kestner. His unrealizable affection for the bride-to-be turned to anguish and motivated his return to his native Frankfurt. But there too a triangular relationship developed. This time it involved the recently married Maximiliane Brentano (daughter of the novelist Sophie von La

Roche and, subsequently, the mother of the romantic writers Clemens and Bettina Brentano). In early 1774, the Frankfurt constellation flared up, compelling Goethe's withdrawal. Immediately following this embarrassing episode, Goethe began writing the novel, completing it in an astonishing six weeks. In his autobiography *Dichtung und Wahrheit* (1812–1813; *Poetry and Truth*), he recalls the process of composition, no doubt accurately, as unconsciously driven, "somnambulant."

In addition to the two congruent amorous events from his own life, a third complex, psychologically and aesthetically crucial, exerted a ghostly influence on this furious creative activity. On November 2, 1772, Goethe received a letter from Kestner, which related in detail the circumstances surrounding the suicide four days previously of the young assessor Karl Wilhelm Jerusalem, a somewhat directionless man of literary aspirations, who was hopelessly in love with a married woman. Several details from this letter, among them the fact that Jerusalem borrowed from Kestner the pistol with which he took his life, find their echo in the novel.

In his autobiographical recollections, Goethe employs two contradictory metaphors to capture the effect of Jerusalem's suicide on the compositional process. The similarity between Jerusalem's situation and his own impelled him to "breathe into the work . . . that glowing fire that allows for no distinction between the poetic and the real." Jerusalem's tragic death suddenly crystallized the entire arrangement of the novel in his mind, much as "water in a vessel that stands just at the freezing point is transformed, at the slightest perturbation, into solid ice" (*Werther*, 934–936). Whatever its historical veracity, this dual characterization does reflect a structural tension inherent in the finished work. Goethe's novel is an icy fire, at once a vehicle for empathetic identification and an artistic arrangement of unparalleled compositional rigor. Just this combination of passion and detachment makes the novel's neglect of moral guidelines, which its rationalist critics found so objectionable, both possible and necessary.

Goethe's *Werther* diverges significantly from the pattern of the sentimental novel established by Samuel Richardson's *Pamela* (1742) and *Clarissa* (1747–1748). The compendious correspondences of the standard form are reduced to the letters and fragmentary notes by the title character. The drama of tangled motivations and elaborate stratagems that unfolds in the epistolary novel across a multivolume format is replaced with Werther's desperate concentration on the momentary fluctuations of his inner life. This formal innovation is related to Goethe's break with the ideological project of the sentimental novel-in-letters. The novels by Richardson, Gellert, Rousseau, and La Roche were organized according to the model of "persecuted virtue." The narrative centered on the moral challenge posed to the heroine by a voluptuary whose aim, however embellished with soulful overtones, was a successfully completed seduction. The resolution of this conflict inevitably involved morally driven renunciation, occasionally sealed by the transfiguring death of the heroine. But Werther's beloved Lotte (the nickname for Charlotte) is, although certainly virtuous, not a beleaguered heroine, her husband, Albert, has none of the paternal features of his Rousseauean counterpart, and Werther himself is anything but a libertine. Goethe's novel addresses an altogether different field of cultural conflict from that of its predecessors. Reconciling virtue and erotic attraction was no longer an issue; rakish sexuality had been effectively domesticated; marriage based on the emotional attunement of two individuals had rendered sacrifice on the altar of virtue obsolete. Goethe's transformation of the epistolary novel in *Werther* reveals that the new ideal of family-centered love harbored unforeseen psychological perils.

In research on the history of the family, it has become a commonplace to locate the emergence of childhood—conceived as a separate sphere of experience, a kind of emotional cocoon—in the latter half of the 18th century. The implosion of the family into the nuclear triad of father-mother-child, the ascendance of the mother to the role of first educator, and the maternal monopolization of care in general, the consequent emotional-erotic charging of primary socialization, and, disciplinarily speaking, the pedagogical magnification of childhood as a domain of inquiry and manipulation from Rousseau forward: all these interlocked historical developments contributed to a reorientation of the literary imagination toward the deepest strata of personal history. *Werther* is one of the earliest, and most radical, exemplifications of this tendency. It is no accident that Goethe's protagonist identifies so insistently with children, borrowing from them the direction of his desire. He reads Homer as if listening to a "cradle song" and spoils his "heart" as if it were a "sick child" (*Werther*, 7). Werther's subjectivity is imbued with the affective dynamics of the passage through childhood, and his particular pathology derives from the conflicts becoming an adult has left, virulently unresolved, within him. Goethe's remarkable achievement in *Werther* is to have shaped a pattern of narrative coherence that rests not on the intricacies of plot (the novel's story is spare, a mere scaffold), but on the logic of an image repertoire, the roots of which reach back to the threshold of infancy.

In one of his countless notebooks, Goethe's contemporary Georg Christoph Lichtenberg remarks sardonically: "Werther—a heart with testicles." The anatomical concreteness of the observation cuts through to the latent agenda of Werther's sentimental effusions. The visions of a terrestrial paradise and of domestic harmony that his letters lavishly evoke are sexually motivated. But Werther's desire does not aim for coital union. It is more childlike and innocent, and yet profoundly sexual. Some one hundred and thirty years before Freud set forth his discovery of infantile sexuality in *Drei Abhandlungen zur Sexualtheorie* (1905; *Three Essays on the Theory of Sexuality*), Goethe created in *Werther* a protagonist whose love life is dominated by the subliminal fantasy of oral gratification. Out of this impossible wish grows Werther's no less impossible passion for Lotte. Her familial position—she lives with her widowed father and cares for her eight young siblings—predestines her for the role of maternal imago. When Werther sees her for the first time, she stands surrounded by the children, who, with outstretched arms, reach for the bread she distributes among them. His attention is captured by the "pink ribbons" affixed to Lotte's dress "at the arms and breast" (*Werther,* 15). Through the detail of the ribbon, which a fragmentary sketch of the novel even qualifies as "flesh-colored," the domestic idyll is transformed in Werther's eyes into the shimmering suggestion of the mother's liquid gift. As the story unfolds, the image repertoire that clusters about Lotte increasingly tantalizes Werther with the promise of exquisite oral pleasure. A pet canary picks morsels of food from her lips; as she sings at the clavichord, she seems to drink in the tones that swell forth from the instrument. The series culminates in the novel's single transgression: the kiss that necessitates Werther's break with Lotte and sends him, ecstatically satisfied, to his grave. In lines written to Lotte just before his self-inflicted death, Werther returns to his first vision of her, almost seeming to grasp the formative significance of the encounter: "From the first moment I saw you, I knew I could not leave you! Let this ribbon be buried with me; it was a present from you on my birthday. How eagerly I swallowed everything in!" (86).

Werther's aversion to the literary culture of his time is uncompromising. He casts off the ballast of his personal library; a young man conversant in the latest literary fashions strikes him as a web of quotations; and for the new pastor's wife, who assiduously follows all the current theological debates, he has nothing but loathing. These views respond to fundamental changes in the structure of cultural transmission and participation that had become flagrantly evident by the final third of the 18th century. In the twenty years surrounding the publication of *Werther* (1764–1785), book production doubled. Five thousand new titles appeared in 1780, with belletristic writing—above all, novels—leading the field. In his famous essay "Answer to the Question: What Is Enlightenment?" of 1783, Kant describes the circulation, discussion, and correction of published opinion as the vehicle of intellectual and social progress. Others were less sanguine. Even the resolute advocate of Enlightenment ideals Moses Mendelssohn noted critically that the preeminence of print had undermined inherited forms of cultural authority, diluted interpersonal relations, and effectively created a society of "alphabetical humans." "Books," the romantic writer Novalis remarked at the century's end, "are a modern species of historical being—but a most significant one. Perhaps they have replaced traditions" (*Schriften,* III, 586). The sense of deprivation engendered by this evacuation of cultural tradition is registered in *Werther* in the episode with the new pastor's wife. Her devotion to an abstract religion of print leads her to order two magnificent nut trees in front of the parsonage to be cut down. For Werther, this act symbolizes the ruthless destruction of genealogical and spiritual continuity.

The generation that broke into print in the 1770s sought to replenish the desiccated cultural environment by returning to the lived immediacy of pre-literate forms. The critical writings of Goethe's mentor Johann Gottfried Herder polemically juxtapose the values of genius, nature, and originality, the axiological triptych of Storm and Stress, with a moribund, commercialized

Frontispiece to the 1775 edition of *Werther,* engraving by Daniel Berger after Nikolaus Chodowiecki. The vignette below Lotte's idealized portrait shows Werther arriving at the house while she is serving bread to the children. (Goethe-Museum, Düsseldorf)

culture going back to Gutenberg's epoch-making invention. Werther's literary preferences reflect this generational sensibility, but also reveal its illusory character. The "nature" Werther discovers in his slim personal canon, and which he projects onto the world around him, is a concoction of print-transmitted data. Together with Lotte, he experiences the passing of a thunderstorm as the scene of a Klopstock ode; the patriarchal customs of the Old Testament seem to him embodied in the sight of a girl drawing water from a spring; Homer's world rises up before his imagination as he prepares a simple open-air meal. Finally, his reading aloud from his *Ossian* translations culminates in the tragic kiss that seals his destiny. Even where no explicit reference to a literary text is made, Werther's letters are laced with subcutaneous allusions—for example, to the idylls of the Swiss writer Salomon Geßner or to Rousseau's *Julie*. Werther's avid reading has so thoroughly suffused his psychic life that he, a sentimental Don Quixote, cannot keep fiction and perception apart.

Werther's "sickness unto death" derives from his captivation with a plethora of imaginary substitutes that progressively hollow out the world around him. The theme was not unique to Goethe. During the period extending from the first publication of *Werther* roughly to the century's end, the pedagogical establishment waged a campaign against excessive, uncontrolled reading. *Lesesucht* (reading addiction) was held to be a rampant syndrome. Perhaps the most famous case was a fictional one. For the title figure of Karl Philipp Moritz's novel *Anton Reiser* (1785) the consumption of books, foremost among them Goethe's *Werther*, has the effect of an opiate, affording temporary escape from the misery of his circumstances, but leaving him acutely depressed when the magic vanishes. Werther's prototype Jerusalem, of whom Kestner's letter notes that "there was hardly a novel he hadn't read" (*Werther*, 910), may have been a victim of the reading mania. According to the pedagogues, frantic ingestion of novels, particularly among adolescents and women, resulted in loss of purchase on the objective world, confusion of reality and fiction, inconsolable melancholy, dissolution of the sense of self. The addicted reader was eventually engulfed by the vacuous world of his own overstimulated imagination.

This is what happens to Werther. His pathology takes shape at the interface of medium and youthful psyche, at the point where the proliferation of print-conveyed images blends with desires rooted in the earliest phases of socialization—hence the implacable, suicidal logic of the novel's image repertoire. Dominated by the *Songs of Ossian*, Werther's world becomes an echo chamber of phantom voices. His visions of natural plenitude and oral gratification are transformed into the horrific fantasy of an omnivorous world-mouth. At this point Mary Shelley's diagnosis of sentimentalism is confirmed: "It is as if a curtain had been drawn from before my eyes, and, instead of prospects of eternal life, the abyss of an ever-open grave yawned before me . . . I stagger on in sheer anxiety. I see nothing but an all-consuming, all-devouring monster" (*Werther*, 52–53).

In preparing the revised edition of *Werther* that appeared in 1787 as the first volume of his collected writings, Goethe introduced several modifications. Idiosyncrasies of language were normalized, the other figures of the novel's love triangle, Lotte and Albert, were rendered psychologically more complex, the external perspective of the "editor" was endowed with greater authority, and a subplot eventuating in murderous aggression was introduced as a counterpoint to Werther's story. In the metaphorical terminology of *Dichtung und Wahrheit,* the collective thrust of these alterations was to dampen the "glowing fire that allows no distinction between the poetic and the real" by more sharply delineating the "icy" aspect of artistic arrangement. In the ensuing decade, this solution to the problem of empathetic identification became a central tenet of aesthetic theory. Formal differentiation and inner purposefulness—such was the consensus among Moritz, Kant, Schiller, and Wilhelm von Humboldt—insulated the artwork from the sphere of real needs and thus blocked its consumption as an imaginary substitute. Within the disinterested aesthetic enclave, the free play of the imagination could unfold as preparation for moral autonomy, not as its subversion.

This theoretical development sheds light on the specificity of the novel's historical moment. The writing and initial reception of *Werther* occurred within a vacuum of control mechanisms, a liminal phase of cultural evolution in which neither the earlier moral prescriptivism of the Enlightenment nor the later circumscription of the aesthetic sphere in classicism was available as a normative guide for the literary imagination. Under such deregulated conditions, the literary medium acquired unprecedented suggestive power, engendering pathological effects remarkable for both their breadth and their virulence. *Die Leiden des jungen Werther* is at once a symptom of this cultural configuration and its most penetrating analysis.

See also 1750, 1765, 1775, 1782, 1784, 1790, 1792 (August 26), 1899

Bibliography: Johann Wolfgang von Goethe, *Goethe's Collected Works,* vol. 9: *The Sorrows of Young Werther, Elective Affinities, Novella,* trans. Victor Lange and Judith Ryan, ed. David E. Wellbery (New York: Suhrkamp, 1987). ⸺, *Sämtliche Werke, Briefe, Tagebücher und Gespräche,* section I, vol. 8: *Die Leiden des jungen Werther, Die Wahlverwandtschaften, Kleine Prosa, Epen,* ed. Waltraud Wiethölter (Frankfurt am Main: Deutscher Klassiker Verlag, 1994). Novalis, *Schriften: Die Werke Friedrich von Hardenbergs,* ed. Paul Kluckhohn and Richard Samuel in collaboration with Hans-Joachim Mähl and Gerhard Schulz (Stuttgart: Kohlhammer, 1960–1968). Mary Shelley, *Frankenstein, or The Modern Prometheus* (London: Penguin, 1994).

David E. Wellbery

᠊ᠬ᠊ *1775*

Lavater's *Physiognomische Fragmente* traces the profile of an age in which the discourse of reason meets with an exuberance of imaginary speculations

Taking Individualism at Face Value

On the eve of the invasion of Switzerland by French troops in 1797, the Zurich theologian and pastor Johann Caspar Lavater (1741–1801) published a pamphlet, "Traum von den Heiligen Felix und Regula" (1797; "Dream of the

Saints Felix and Regula"), about the situation of the Church in times of political uncertainty. He traces its history in Zurich back to the legend of Felix and Regula, two Christian martyrs who were beheaded during the Roman occupation and subsequently became the patron saints of the city. Legend has it that they picked up their heads and staggered to the spot where later the Grossmünster (cathedral) was built, which became the center of Zwingli's reform movement in the 16th century, and the site of the Carolinum, the minster school where Bodmer and Breitinger had been Lavater's teachers. At a crucial point in his dream, Lavater asks one of the martyrs if that miracle of carrying their heads as shown in the city seal was true or at least had the semblance of truth. Regula's severed head smiles meaningfully: "Tell me, my dear, what do you think? People say you are very curious about such things."

What may have turned into a physiognomist's nightmare turns into something like Lavater's glory. For the site where the two martyrs died is, as Regula points out, "next to your public library" on whose shelves he placed the first volume of his *Physiognomische Fragmente zur Beförderung der Menschenkenntnis und der Menschenliebe (Physiognomical Fragments, Designed to Promote the Knowledge and Love of Humankind)* in 1775. The city seal showing Felix and Regula with their heads tucked under their arms is thus presented as something like a seal of approval affixed to his books on physiognomy with their pictures of disembodied heads and faces.

Lavater's idiosyncratic style pulls together different strands of narrative in which history inspires vision, fact is based on dream, and miracles reveal truth. At the time of the pamphlet's publication, Lavater was a celebrity, attracting visitors and admirers from all walks of life and from all across Europe. The authorities in Zurich had always been skeptical of this restless pastor, philosopher, prophet, and patriot with a wide circle of influential friends among intellectuals and at foreign courts. They were scandalized by his accusations against magistrates of fraud, bribery, or social injustice, and in 1799 his outspoken resistance to the French protectorate even led to his temporary exile to Basel. While his friends and the public at large may have admired Lavater for his courage and righteousness, they were alarmed by his increasing mysticism and obscurantism. Kant accused Lavater of *Schwärmerey* (enthusiasm), a term that became a hallmark in the age of sensibility. He argued that Lavater's ideas as such were not really incongruous with orthodox doctrine, but that, as a *Schwärmer,* he extended them far beyond the realm of experience, thus rendering them untenable as arguments. This is certainly true of Lavater's interest in para-psychological phenomena. His meetings with Cagliostro, his fascination with Mesmerism, and his participation in spiritualistic sessions conducted by Prince Karl von Hessen-Kassel and his circle in Copenhagen provoked a series of scandals that exposed Lavater to ridicule or contempt and gradually estranged him from friends such as Goethe and Herder. While his naïveté made him an easy victim for charlatans like Cagliostro, Lavater's explorations of the boundaries between the occult and the scientific, between orthodox doctrines of religion and magical experience were an integral part of his belief in the

continuity between the visible and the invisible world. For him these were instances of a rite of passage between the two worlds, proof of a "real experience
of transcendence," as Horst Weigelt has called it. In all his speculative thoughts,
Lavater saw himself as a true believer in Christ as a figure of eternal life and
guarantor of resurrection. Members of the spiritistic circle in Copenhagen,
whose sessions Lavater attended, were convinced that they could communicate with Christ through a medium. Ultimately, these occult practices are in
line with the series of portraits of Christ in the concluding section of *Physiognomische Fragmente* where Lavater seeks to present the human face as the first
and last medium that shows the resemblance of man to the Son of God. As a
preacher, letter writer, and physiognomist, in his formal as well as informal
contacts with friends, in everything he did, Lavater acted as a media manager.

The medium Lavater understood best was that of print. The rapid rise of
publishing in the second half of the 18th century created a new public space, a
republic of letters, and it almost seemed that Lavater lived right in the printer's
shop. Every letter he exchanged with his correspondents, every word he spoke,
wrote, or received was—however private it may have been—immediately
published when he considered it necessary or beneficial. His *Geheimes Tagebuch
von einem Beobachter seiner Selbst* (1771–1773; *Secret Diary of a Self-Observer*),
published three years before the famous diary in Goethe's *Werther*, was first circulated in manuscript form among his friends for immediate response. When
it was published, it turned the intimacy of self-observation into a public spectacle. Lavater's desire to go public was not restricted to his own person. Not
everyone, however, appreciated being exposed to public scrutiny and judgment. When Lavater translated parts of Bonnet's *La palingénésie philosophique*
(1769; *Philosophical Rebirth*), a work of natural philosophy that argues that both
body and soul will be reborn after death and that God reveals the truth of this
through miracles, he dedicated the translation to the Jewish philosopher Moses
Mendelssohn, asking him to refute the work or convert to the Christian faith.
In his usual naive and aggressive way, Lavater compromised Mendelssohn,
whose delicate position made a public response dangerous. When he finally
did send a letter in which he refuted Lavater's proselytizing argument and
made a strong plea for tolerance between the religions as a basis on which any
philosophical argument should be conducted, Lavater immediately published
the letter, continuing the embarrassment and causing more difficulties.

Lavater's urge to publish never slackened. When he was shot and seriously
wounded in 1799 by a French soldier in front of his house, the physician dressing his wounds was working almost alongside the printer issuing the circular
letter that communicated the incident to his friends at home and abroad.
Lavater died in 1801, never recovering from his wound. He did not die as a
martyr but as someone who made even his own death a topic of moral instruction and public debate.

Although Lavater is the author of some longer works, all of his publications
have the character of miscellanies. This is also true for the four volumes of his
Physiognomische Fragmente, which he originally planned to publish as a weekly

journal. In 1772, he published an essay, "Von der Physiognomik ("Of Physiognomy"), in which he distinguished individual character from the accidental nature of fate. Encouraged by its favorable reception, Lavater planned an illustrated edition with 16 sheets of text and 24 plates. The project soon grew to enormous proportions, and when the last of the four folio volumes was issued in 1778, the work totaled 188 sheets of text, 343 plates, and 488 vignettes. Between 1782 and 1803 a French edition was published, with texts largely rewritten by Lavater himself and augmented by still more illustrations.

Although Lavater claims that he would like to restore physiognomics to the status of the "most human and most divine science," the fragments focus on an interpretation of individual faces rather than the construction of a scientific system. He refers repeatedly to the face and its features as letters of a divine alphabet the physiognomist is called upon to read and decipher. In this sense, *Fragmente* is presented as a moral semiotics in which ethics and aesthetics are closely interrelated.

Three postulates constitute Lavater's theory of physiognomic correspondences: 1. The character of a person can be recognized in his or her physical appearance. 2. The better a person is morally, the more beautiful he or she is. 3. The truth of any observation or experience that can be deduced from a system of signification attains the status of science.

As Lichtenberg remarked in his critical essay "Über Physiognomik; wider die Physiognomen" (1778; "On Physiognomics; against the Physiognomists"), Lavater and other physiognomists were trying to read in the human face what astrologists had been trying to read in the heavens. While the latter think they can predict someone's fate from the constellation of the planets at the moment of birth, the former speculate on the face as an indicator of character. The connection between astrology and characterology has a long tradition, and Jean d'Indaigne's *Chiromantia* (1522), the first illustrated book on physiognomy, is an example of its revival in the Renaissance.

Another aspect that shaped the physiognomical tradition is the comparison of the human head and face with those of animals. Already Aristotle's *Physiognomonica* of the 3rd century B.C.E. contains examples of such analogies that became part of medieval lore. They also form the basis of Giambattista della Porta's *De humana physiognomia* (1602) and the painter Charles le Brun's *Traité de la physionomie de l'homme comparé à celle des animaux* (1698; *Treatise on the Physiognomy of Man Compared to That of the Animals*), two works that had a profound impact on modern concepts of physiognomy. Even though Lavater admired della Porta's work and *Fragmente* contains extensive sections on animals, Lavater ultimately rejected the direct comparison of human and animal character. Le Brun's handbook for painters studies the face as a mirror of emotions and affections in the context of an increased interest of the fine arts in the representation of passion.

Distinguishing between physiognomics and pathognomics, between the bone structure and the expression of emotion, Lavater emphasizes the relative importance of the former over the latter. Physiognomics is the "capital base," as he puts it in monetary terms, on which pathognomics accrues its "interest." Le Brun's work also contains sketches mapping out the geometrical relationships that exist between the shape and size of different heads and facial features, initiating the interest 18th-century anthropological science took in physiognomics. The Dutch natural scientist Petrus Camper, a contemporary of Lavater's, measured the cranium to assess human intelligence, and although Lavater was never comfortable with a translation of character or mental faculties into sets of mathematical data, he does introduce his own mechanical measuring device, the *Stirnmesser,* in the last volume of *Fragmente.* In his vitriolic satire on the aberrations of the new physiognomists, Lichtenberg calls the distance between the surface of the body and the depth of the human soul "unfathomable" *(unermesslich).* Kant accuses those who think they can read God's signature in someone's face of "impudence" *(Anmassung).* No measurement can account for the individual character of man.

Lavater's *Fragmente* does not promote science, nor does its success rest on the pious use of Christ as an icon of physiognomical study. Two aspects are responsible for the work's huge cultural and literary significance in the 18th century: the cultivation of friendship and love as expressions of individual identity and the silhouette, or shadow, as a new form of popular art. They are closely interrelated. The subtitle of *Fragmente* refers to philanthropy—in the sense of "love of humankind"—as one motive for studying physiognomics. Love and friendship became two powerful paradigms of personal as well as communal relationships for the rising middle class, transcending the limits of social status and decorum as defined by the waning aristocracy. Lavater's championing of character over fate can be read to have political implications, replacing the sense of a mythic political destiny with the promise of success based on individual virtue and merit. Whatever credit one might give the pious physiognomist for espousing democratic ideas, he definitely, and most directly, did promote the art of tracing shadows according to the method perfected around 1760 by Etienne Silhouette, the finance minister of King Louis XV.

The phrase *portrait à la Silhouette* had a derisory ring to it at the French court, where the minister promoted this art form to reduce the enormous cost of portraits in oil by celebrated artists. To Lavater, however, the silhouette constituted an art closest to nature, free of any aesthetic coloring or idealization. He encourages the production of silhouettes as some form of tactile learning about physiognomics in *Fragmente,* and in a later passage he emphasizes the do-it-yourself quality of the process— "selber machen" became something of a motto for this new popular art form. *Fragmente* boosted a fashion that took 18th-century Europe by storm. The amateur artists of a broad, educated middle class not only became experienced physiognomists of sorts but they also suddenly owned the means of producing portraits that before, as tokens of heritage or respectability, were almost exclusively hanging on the walls of the aristocracy or wealthy families. The silhouette anticipated the photograph as a form of mechanical representation. It could easily be enlarged or reduced and often silhouettes were included in the letters exchanged between family members, friends, or lovers.

Goethe's *Werther* made this practice famous. The novel puts both the rebellion against the court and the new art of the portrait as profile at the center of its narrative, marking a momentous step in the representation of the silhouette as a symbol, or performance, of creating individual identity. Failing in his attempt to draw a picture of Lotte, Werther produces her silhouette, which from then on becomes some kind of fetish he invests with the drama of his love and the shadow of death it eventually casts on his life. On Lotte's wedding day, he contemplates a ritual burial of her portrait. The night before he is buried, he sends her the silhouette as a testament. The amorous discourse of Werther's letters fits the very nature of the silhouette. Both are individual expressions in which the letter writer and the addressee, the artist and the subject communicate or correspond in an attempt to create and interpret identity. It is not surprising that Lavater was most enthusiastic when he read the manuscript of the novel on his first visit with Goethe in 1774. It was then, one might conjecture, that he secured Goethe's assistance for his physiognomical project.

Fragmente is a work of collaboration. All his life Lavater was building and entertaining a vast network of friends and acquaintances whom he asked in the 1770s to contribute to the vast physiognomical archive of texts, portraits, and engravings from which he selected the best specimens for publication in *Fragmente.* Herder, Sulzer, Merck, Lenz, Wieland, the Stolberg brothers, and, at an early stage, even Nicolai and Lichtenberg were among the contributors. Goethe provided a poem, "Lied eines physiognomischen Zeichners" (Song of a Physiognomical Artist), and a few other texts in volumes 1 and 2. In his autobiography *Dichtung und Wahrheit* (1811; *Poetry and Truth*), Goethe relates how Lavater beseeched all his friends to draw a portrait of Christ and send it to him. This obsession and Lavater's constant proselytizing, culminating in his scandalous challenge to Mendelssohn, finally led to a total rupture between Goethe and the pastor from Zurich.

Lavater found himself increasingly isolated from the literary community that had once admired him as a champion of the Storm and Stress movement and a figure of the genius. He never really understood or accepted that Goethe and those around him considered their involvement with him as a phase in their emotional and literary development, and he was deeply hurt when he saw himself ridiculed in Goethe's *Xenien* (1797; *Xenias*). Goethe's scorn exerted great influence and expedited the harsh judgment with which Lavater's work was met within German literature in the 19th century. The French edition secured him a more favorable reception in France, notably in the works of Balzac and Stendhal.

See also 1774, 1784, 1789

Bibliography: Johann Caspar Lavater, *Physiognomische Fragmente zur Beförderung der Menschenkenntnis und der Menschenliebe,* 4 vols. (Leipzig: Weidmanns Erben und Reich, 1775–1778);

———, *Essays on Physiognomy, Designed to Promote the Knowledge and Love of Mankind,* trans. Henry Hunter, 3 vols. in 5 (London: Printed for John Murray, Henry Hunter, and Thomas Holloway, 1789–1795).

Fritz Gutbrodt

ℒ *1778, February*
Jakob Michael Reinhold Lenz tries halfheartedly to commit suicide

The Confusions of Genre

Ever since the appearance of Georg Büchner's novella *Lenz* (1839), the 18th-century playwright, poet, moral philosopher, and writer of short fiction Jakob Michael Reinhold Lenz (1751–1792) has become an emblem of the marginal and the excluded in the pantheon of German literature. Büchner portrayed Lenz as an incipient realist, whose thought was a potential, but stunted, alternative to a German classical aesthetic that was to become the core of the myth of German *Bildung* and culture. Besides Büchner's there is another equally fundamental account, one that portrays Lenz as the young Goethe's alter ego. Goethe's own negative assessment of Lenz in *Dichtung und Wahrheit (Poetry and Truth)* represents a settling of accounts with his own youth, a belated rejection of the generational rebellion known as the *Sturm und Drang* (Storm and Stress).

A close companion of the young Goethe in Strasbourg, Lenz shared the fate of others whose genius went counter to Goethe's later aesthetics and politics; like Hölderlin and Kleist, he was rejected by the great Olympian of Weimar classicism. Lenz ostracized after his still mysterious fall from grace at the Weimar *Musenhof* (Court of the Muses) in 1776; Lenz gone mad in 1778, the key episode Pastor Oberlin recorded and Büchner fictionalized; Lenz, forgotten and unknown, who died in a Moscow street in 1792; Lenz, in Goethe's words, a shooting star which passed without effect on German life and literature: that was Goethe as failure, as ruin, as idiosyncratic talent, shipwrecked on the shoals of life and art—a living composite of *Werther* and *Tasso,* as it were. With such works, Goethe had succeeded in overcoming the inherent dangers of *Sturm und Drang*'s excess of subjectivity and formlessness, sexual desire, linguistic anarchy, and narcissism. Goethe's work stood for literature as a form of self-purging therapy on the road to classical maturity. Lenz failed where Goethe succeeded. German literary historiography needed Lenz as foil to its Goethe myth, and if he hadn't existed, he would have had to be invented.

What then is Lenz's real place in the literature of his time? With his major plays and the challenging dramaturgical theory *Anmerkungen übers Theater (Notations about Theater),* Lenz's literary achievement lies in the productive confusion of dramatic genres, the radical transformation of the *bürgerliches Trauerspiel* (domestic tragedy), the breakdown of classical rhetoric and an Enlightenment concept of language, and finally the subversive use of language, mimicry, and gesture that has struck many as peculiarly modern, if not avant-garde. His writing is haunted by the irreconcilable conflict between literary ambition and a desire for social reform regarding sexuality and education, power relations and the hidden injuries of class. It is energized by a belief against belief that literature can transcend compensatory gratification and emancipate human beings from the repressive, frozen social order of the absolutist state. But his literary work also marks an early awareness of the dialectic of enlightenment. In Lenz's work, enlightenment appears not simply as the high road to freedom and autonomy, but as part of the apparatus of repression, mutilation, and tutelage from which it promised relief.

Der Hofmeister (The Tutor), Lenz's first play, written in 1772, is the paradigmatic text for this tension-ridden constellation. Published anonymously in Leipzig with Goethe's help in 1774, the only play performed in the author's lifetime, it must be seen, not as a failed masterpiece, but as a masterpiece as failure: deliberate failure of the author to adhere to literary traditions and failure of German social and literary conditions to generate the kind of tragic drama that was this playwright's most ambitious goal. Designated a comedy, Der Hofmeister is a literary puzzle of the first order that confused the critics with its mixed message, hybrid construction, and flouting of all dramaturgical models.

Given the Sturm und Drang's enthusiasm for Shakespeare and the enormous success of Goethe's Götz von Berlichingen the previous year, critics, like Schubart, thought Der Hofmeister was another play by "our Shakespeare, the immortal Dr. Göthe [sic]," and they welcomed it as revitalizing German comedy after Lessing. In his correspondence though, Lenz also called the play a Trauerspiel (tragic drama), and an early manuscript version designated it a Lust- und Trauerspiel (comic and tragic drama). Such waffling between genres has significant implications for the interpretation of a text, especially since Lenz paid close attention to the issue of genre and its public function. The issue of genre already haunted the critic C. H. Schmid, who suggested that a play in which a father goes raving mad, a daughter loses her honor, prisons and beggars' huts appear on stage, mutilations, drownings, and castrations abound, made many a French tragedy look like comedy.

Surely, the subtitle "The Advantages of Private Tutoring" is ironic and implicitly takes issue with Rousseau's Émile (1762). Furthermore, Lenz spoke from experience. He had served as tutor to two traveling Prussian noblemen during his stay in Strasbourg. Filled with an insatiable desire for independence, the author experienced tutoring as indentured servitude. For Lenz pedagogy concerns the fate of the pedagogue as much as it concerns the pupil. Der Hofmeister carries its title for good reason.

The first act of the play depicts the existence of the private tutor in all its misery. The theology student Läuffer has been employed as private tutor on the country estate of the noble but dumb-witted, blustering Major von Berg and his conceited, ill-tempered wife. He is charged with instructing the couple's lazy son "in all the sciences, civilities, polite manners" (I:2), even though the father wants his son to be a soldier like himself. Just as the mother spoils Leopold rotten, the father pampers the tragedy-loving daughter Gustchen with whom the tutor is "to do some Christianity . . . every morning" (I:4). Both parents constantly interfere with the education of their children, harassing poor Läuffer with their contradictory demands and treating him no better than a servant.

Läuffer's only alternative to tutoring—employment at the public school in town—is blocked by the Major's brother, the enlightened Councilor Berg, who directs the school and uses every opportunity to sing the praises of public education and the enlightened state. However, his views—though close to Lenz's own—are revealed as so much highfalutin rhetoric. Councilor Berg is unable to persuade his brother to abandon private tutoring for his children. His language vacillates between empirical insight and abstract posturing, as he attacks private tutoring in a conversation with Läuffer's pastor father:

> Idling his days away and expecting to be paid for it? Loafing away the noblest hours of the day with a young gentleman who has no wish to learn but whom he can't afford to offend, and pining away like a slave on a chain the remaining hours that would be devoted to the necessities of life, eating and sleeping; hanging on the whims of her ladyship and conning the crotchets of his lordship; eating when he's full and fasting when he's hungry, drinking punch when he wants to piss, playing cards when he's got the runs. Without freedom life goes downhill backwards; freedom is man's element as water to a fish, and a man who surrenders his freedom poisons the noblest spirits of his blood, nips in the bud the sweetest of life's pleasures, and does himself to death. (II:1)

Lenz's characters are sharply drawn in language and habits. But the more they appear as recognizable figures, the more they approach caricature. They resemble marionettes on a string of clichés, proverbs, and quotations, parroting socially typical discourses that limit their range of imagination and action. The ideals of freedom and autonomy, central to Lenz's anthropology, are buried under the rubble of *idées reçues* and the compulsion of automatic reflexes.

The dramatic conflict is triggered by the disadvantages of private tutoring for life. More out of boredom than great passion, Läuffer and Gustchen enter into a sexual relationship that results in Gustchen's pregnancy, scandal, and the separate flight of the "lovers" from the Major's estate. Gustchen ends up giving birth in a beggar's hut in the forest, and Läuffer finds a tenuous refuge with the bizarre village teacher Wenzeslaus, in whom sexual repression and authoritarian pedagogy are parodied as the downside of the Protestant Enlightenment and Prussian public education.

At this stage, the spectator expects to be confronted with tragedy as it follows the typical seduction scene of the *bürgerliches Trauerspiel*. Seduction, murder, infanticide, suicide or capital punishment—these are some of the stations of 18th-century bourgeois tragedy that invariably ends with the death of the woman. None of that in *Der Hofmeister*. Lenz subverts the model in three significant ways.

First he de-dramatizes the plot by interlacing grotesque and roguish scenes from student life in Halle, revolving around Gustchen's cousin Fritz, the councilor's son. These scenes of students' pranks, amorous adventures, and burlesque happenings are reminiscent of the crude German popular theater or the *commedia dell'arte* rather than tragedy proper. Secondly, Lenz transforms bourgeois tragedy by way of a gender reversal and a happy ending. Whereas in the *bürgerliches Trauerspiel* the aristocrat typically seduces the bourgeois girl, thereby collapsing gender and class domination, in Lenz the adolescent girl is high-born and the lover of lower social extraction. The threat to Läuffer from the raving-mad Major, who bursts into his hide-out trying to shoot him, is, therefore, much more poignant than the threat from a still loving father to Gustchen, who is ultimately forgiven.

But the subversion of the domestic drama does not end here. Lenz does not present the relationship as love across class boundaries or as a sexual power relationship dominated by the male. Gustchen's pregnancy results from a one-time eruption of repressed sexual instincts. Throughout their relationship, they remain strangers to each other. This elusive love relationship becomes possible only through substitution of literary illusion for lived reality in the minds of the protagonists. Gustchen imagines Läuffer as her Romeo, and Läuffer is lost in thoughts about the medieval monk Abélard who, after abducting and marrying his pupil Héloïse, was castrated by her avenging relatives. The respective literary role-playing only highlights the characters' inability to communicate with each other. Significantly, the class barrier between the lovers pertains only in Läuffer's reference to the Abélard story, not in Gustchen's dreamy reflection about Romeo and Juliet. Not surprisingly, bodily harm is in store for Läuffer alone, who, in a fit of repentance, castrates himself when he receives the false news that Gustchen is dead. But even Läuffer's castration is not presented as the tragic self-inflicted suffering of the bourgeois victim. The act of self-mutilation is just another eruption rather than an act of ascetic renunciation of the pleasures of the flesh. Läuffer, in his passive drifting and merely reactive behavior, is no tragic hero. Thus he too gets his un-tragic ending, appropriate for the comedy form. Horrifying Wenzeslaus, the castrate marries the naive peasant girl Liese, who fantasizes about "learned gentlemen" and happily forgoes the pleasures of motherhood: "A fine thing it would be if I got children into the bargain. My father has ducks and chickens enough that I have to feed every day" (V:10).

Lenz concludes his comedy not with one, but with two happy endings: one featuring Läuffer and Liese (V:10), the other assembling all the upper-class characters in a final tableau of multiple family reconciliations, engagements, and marriages (V:11 and 12). Here the barrier between social classes becomes literary form, denying the happy ending of enlightened comedy in which social flaws are corrected and universal reason prevails. But just as Läuffer's soul marriage is not really a happy ending since it rests on his bodily mutilation, the reconciliation of Gustchen and Fritz, who magnanimously adopts the child he did not father, only rewrites gender domination, when he exults over Gustchen's guilt feelings.

In the play's excess of concluding family reconciliations, Lenz parodies enlightened comedy as a form. Nobody has learned anything at all. At the same time, this comedy persistently broaches the tragic. But tragedy is vitiated by the bathetic and thoroughly non-tragic social conditions that do not allow for a real tragic hero to emerge. Tragedy, for Lenz, requires an autonomous, freely acting hero, impossible in Lenz's social and literary vision of Germany in the 1770s. Werther ends in suicide and even ironhanded Götz von Berlichingen, the epitome of freedom and autonomy in *Sturm und Drang* drama, is an amputee and dies a broken man.

Lenz's practice and theory of drama may be more pertinent to his times than critics have often claimed. His *Anmerkungen übers Theater,* tentative and exploratory as they are, should not be rigorously applied to his plays, but they explain his preference for comedy. His argument is historical, not normative. In a polemic against Aristotle, and implicitly against Lessing, both of whom he accuses of elevating social determination to tragic destiny, he argues that comedy is required by prevailing German social and literary conditions. Tragedy, centered on the autonomous individual, the hero who alone controls his fate, was Lenz's lofty goal, but remained beyond his grasp. In that sense too, *Der Hofmeister* is a masterpiece as failure, in a historical situation in which comedy alone, according to Lenz, would satisfy the need of the German public. German playwrights, Lenz argues, are expected to write tragicomedy because the *Volk* for whom they write is itself a disparate mixture of culture and coarseness, morality and savagery. Lenz's project, which draws on the traditions of German popular theater, is a project of national pedagogy, and in that sense similar to Lessing's attempt to create a national theater in the 1760s, but equally doomed and perhaps even more misguided in its high hopes.

What Lenz puts on stage is the *Trauerspiel* of concrete social and cultural conditions; not what individuals do, but what is done to them marks the core of *Der Hofmeister.* It remains unclear how this type of comedy could ever prepare the ground for modern tragedy as Lenz imagined it. Is laughter liberating or is it not more the kind that gets stuck in the throat? Tragedy, though not the Lenzian kind, became the future of the German theater from Schiller and Kleist to Hebbel and Wagner. Tragedy of the free, autonomous individual as Lenz demanded it was a powerful utopia, but ultimately an ill-defined goal for a future theater—another phantasm of the Enlightenment.

In Lenz's work, Enlightenment optimism, as it still determined Lessing's empathy-based theory of the *bürgerliches Trauerspiel,* was replaced by melancholic pessimism toward German social and literary conditions. This darker side of the *Sturm und Drang* resulted from the deepened sensibility for the weaknesses and failures of rational Enlightenment in the real world. In Lenz's plays, it finds its most uncompromising dramaturgic shape as a critique of the Enlightenment and its major dramatic forms, which nevertheless remains true to the Enlightenment's ideal of freedom and autonomy. *Der Hofmeister* occupies the center of a movement that exhausted itself within a few years and whose most clear-sighted representative was the playwright and poet Jakob Michael Reinhold Lenz.

See also 1767, 1774, 1792 (August 26), 1835

Bibliography: Jakob Michael Reinhold Lenz, *The Tutor—The Soldiers,* trans. and with an introduction by William E. Yuill (Chicago: University of Chicago Press, 1972). ————, *Werke und Briefe in drei Bänden,* ed. Sigrid Damm (Munich: Hanser, 1987). Sigrid Damm, *Vögel, die verkünden Land: Das Leben des Jakob Michael Reinhold Lenz* (Berlin and Weimar: Aufbau Verlag, 1985). Andreas Huyssen, *Drama des Sturm und Drang* (Munich: Winkler, 1980). Hans-Gerd Winter, *J. M. R. Lenz* (Stuttgart: Metzler, 1987).

Andreas Huyssen

✑ 1781, 1810

Friedrich II of Prussia and Anna Louise Germaine de Staël expound opposing views of German literary culture

From Enlightenment Universalism to Romantic Individuality

In 1781, King Friedrich II of Prussia (1712–1786), also known as Frederick the Great, committed his views on the state of German literature to paper in a treatise entitled *De la littérature allemande (On German Literature)*. Some thirty years later, Madame Germaine de Staël (1767–1855) completed her much lengthier *De l'Allemagne* (1810; *On Germany*). The two texts are in many respects incommensurable. Friedrich addresses a primarily German-speaking audience, urging a program of linguistic reform; de Staël addresses a French-speaking readership and suggests that German literature can show her compatriots how to overcome the slavish imitation of the ancients. By juxtaposing these two texts, however, we can learn much about the changing status of the German language and of German literature within this historically important span of time. This transformation, it becomes clear, is related not only to literary developments, but also to a shift in the conceptualization of what constitutes a nation-state.

As ruler of Prussia, Friedrich played a major role in establishing and maintaining the borders of his state. His strategic brilliance enabled him to retake Silesia during the War of the Austrian Succession and to triumph over a powerful alliance during the Seven Years' War. In *De la littérature allemande,* however, the strategies he recommends for nation building relate to language rather than military might. In order to become a nation-state, Germany has to follow the universal pattern of development already witnessed in modern nations such as England and France. One essential step is the unification of a national language through the elimination of differences in regional dialect. Another is the attainment of linguistic clarity and harmony. Unfortunately, German writers, abetted no doubt by German syntax, tend to sacrifice clarity to obscurity in the construction of their sentences: "Many of our authors are pleased with a diffuse style; they pile parenthesis on parenthesis, and often you find only at the end of the entire page the verb on which depends the meaning of the whole sentence." Aside from sentence structure, Friedrich is concerned with the misuse of metaphor. He concedes that metaphors can provide insight and energy, but German writers have shown a preference for metaphoric deviations from the path of transparency and precision, as in phrases such as "Your Majesty shines like a carbuncle on the finger of our times" (431–432). As for harmony, Friedrich goes so far as to suggest that certain unpleasant sounds, like the "mute and disagreeable" final syllables of verbs such as *sagen* (to say), *geben* (to give), and *nehmen* (to take), might be made more harmonious by their transformation into *sagena, gebena,* and *nehmena,* although he concedes that such changes can hardly be effected by fiat (437).

As these examples suggest, language in *De la littérature allemande* is not considered as an organic unity. If a language, such as German, is somehow lacking, then it can and should be changed for the better. Friedrich's view of language is typical of the Enlightenment. Although we have come to consider language as a force that creates our world, for Friedrich language is *exterior* to both thought and things. Concerning the exteriority of language to the former, Friedrich asserts that "clarity is the first rule" for those who write and speak, because it is a matter of "painting one's thoughts and expressing one's ideas by words" (429). As to the exteriority of language to the world, Friedrich reminds a pettifogger, "We are no longer in the century of words, but in that of things" (445). Three terms to which Friedrich has frequent recourse are "polish," "perfection," and "fixedness." The latter two terms point directly to a universality of language that is determined by the real nature of the world to be represented and the immutability of rational thought. "Polish" indicates the processes by which any remaining distortions might be rubbed out.

With respect to aesthetics, the central term in *De la littérature allemande* is "taste" (*goût* in French). This concept assumes permanent standards by which any given work can be judged. Here Friedrich fears that current literary trends only trumpet the bad taste of his countrymen. What is Goethe's *Götz von Berlichingen* as far as the monarch is concerned? First and foremost a "detestable imitation" of the worst model: Shakespeare. Enthusiasm for the latter highlights the sorry state of literary affairs in Germany (441). In spite of the title of his treatise, Friedrich barely discusses historical or contemporary literature written in German. Gellert, Gessner, and a few others are mentioned. Praise is reserved for Cornelius von Ayrenhoff's now obscure comedy *Der Postzug* (1769; *The Mail Coach*). Although writers of genius may be responsible for the purification and clarification of the idiom at a later date, Friedrich implies that to attempt this now would be premature.

Concerning how to change this situation, Friedrich settles on education, and above all translation, as preliminaries to any possible future German literature. The French, English, and Italians have succeeded to a greater degree than the Germans in perfecting their languages through the translation of Greek and Latin. The lengthy discussion of education that caps the treatise closes with yet another exhortation to translate: "The general result of all that I have just made clear to you is that we should zealously apply ourselves to the translation into our language of all the classical authors in both ancient and modern languages; this will gain for us the dual advantage of forming our idiom and of rendering knowledge more universal" (450). At one level, this statement simply underlines Enlightenment esteem for knowledge in a form accessible to all. Friedrich is, after all, the prototype of the enlightened despot, who brought Voltaire to his court in an advisory capacity. On another level, one sees the historically specific construction of language that informs Friedrich's treatise: translation will help repair the defects of the German language, bringing it in line with the universal. This explains Friedrich's use of French, the current *lingua franca* of Europe. But Friedrich also shares the view of French as the living language that most transparently expresses logic and reality. Ironically, he bemoans the fact that the development of the German language, and thus the German nation, has been retarded by the unwillingness of scholars to use and polish their own idiom. This paradox aside, what is clear is that, given his conception of language, the German nation, when it does come into being, will be a nation like any other worthy of the name: united by a logical, descriptive, and, ideally, harmonious tongue.

Madame de Staël was certainly not unexposed to Enlightenment thought. Her mother, Suzanne Necker, was a celebrated *salonnière* and an intimate of the likes of Diderot. De Staël's views in *De l'Allemagne,* however, reveal the impact of the French Revolution, in which her father, the financier and politician Jacques Necker, played an active role, and the subsequent rise of Napoleon. De Staël detested Napoleon's expansionist nationalism, of which she considered Friedrich II, because of his annexation of Poland, a dangerous precursor. The dislike was mutual. Napoleon had her exiled from France for her public criticism of his policies. *De l'Allemagne* played an important role in this animosity. Although censors had already removed material they considered objectionable, the police ordered the destruction of the initial pressing. The text was declared anti-French and indeed contained many passages that could be construed as attacks on the emperor. Added fuel to the fire was no doubt de Staël's Genevan extraction (Napoleon's Corsican birth notwithstanding).

De Staël's own position on such matters was that the boundaries of nations are natural and should be inviolable. They are defined not by politics but by geography, climate, and, above all, linguistic unity. In *De l'Allemagne* she divides Europe into three national groups: the Latin, Germanic, and Slavonic races (1:13–14). Each group has its specificity, and each group can be further subdivided (for example, the Germanic includes the nations of England and Germany proper). Central to understanding such particularity is the understanding of national literatures. If Friedrich's *De la littérature allemande* hardly considers literature per se, it is equally telling that de Staël's *De l'Allemagne,* the title of which promises a general overview of Germany, puts enormous emphasis on literary production. The corollary to this linkage of nation and literature is the necessity of learning national languages. Where Friedrich insists that foreign works must be translated into German in order to transform the latter, de Staël starts from the premise of untranslatability. In the chapter entitled "Why do the French not do justice to German literature?" she begins with the following answer: "I could respond in an entirely simple fashion to this question by stating that very few people in France know German, and that the beauties of this language, above all in poetry, cannot be translated into French" (2:7). If de Staël is initially reticent, it is not because it is not true or important that most French do not know German. Rather, the matter is more complex: "It would all the same be a very superficial treatment of the question if one stopped with the statement that the French are unjust with respect to German literature because they are not familiar with it: they have, it is true, prejudices against it, but these prejudices are determined by the confused sentiment of the pronounced differences that exist between the ways of seeing and feeling in these two nations" (2:8–9). Nation, language, and literature thus merge as elements of a single, bounded system. De Staël replaces Friedrich's notion of translation as the potential for modeling one's language on universals with the quest for hermeneutic penetration: to understand another nation is to get inside it through its language and literature.

De Staël also notes that German literature has only come into its own in the previous twenty years. In this interim have appeared those works of Goethe, Schiller, Tieck, and others which de Staël sees as embodying the romantic heritage. She follows Friedrich and August Wilhelm Schlegel here (the latter served as tutor to her children and was himself a translator of Shakespeare). Although de Staël did not invent the term "romantic," *De l'Allemagne* was in large part responsible for spreading its specific use to France and elsewhere. For the French, *romantique* meant "fantastic." German Romanticism is set in opposition to classical literature, which draws on Greco-Latin sources (usually described as "pagan"). *Romantic* now describes poetry, "the origin of which were the songs of the troubadours, that which is born of chivalry and Christianity" (2:128). For de Staël, German literature had flourished of late because writers had learned to tap indigenous sources. In this respect, two key terms in de Staël's work are "genius" and "originality"—although these words must be grasped in their multivalency. "Genius," a term that, especially since the *Sturm und Drang* (Storm and Stress), had emphasized the struggles of the artist with constricting aesthetic rules, denotes in de Staël three distinct but related concepts. First, it describes the particularity of a given linguistic and national group. Second, it refers to the artist who draws fresh inspiration from the former (the term "enthusiasm" is resurrected). Third, it is the aspect of a given work of art that manifests the specific relation between artist and nation. Regarding the latter two meanings, Goethe and *Faust* are cited as the prime examples. "Originality" designates, as its etymology suggests, a return to origins, but it also marks the incipient value of innovation. For de Staël, future and past, artist and nation, difference and sameness exist in a dynamic tension. In contrast to Friedrich, for de Staël it is the mediation of the universal through the particular that fosters aesthetic creation and appreciation.

By elevating romantic literature, de Staël targets Friedrich's equating of Greco-Latin literature and universality. In fact, she explicitly contrasts her use of the term "classical" with an alternative use of the term as a "synonym of perfection" (2:129). Greek and Latin texts are certainly to be appreciated insofar as they express their own national-cum-linguistic genius, but they are no longer considered fit models for imitation. In fact, imitation and perfection in Friedrich's sense are associated with morbidity in *De l'Allemagne*. The examination of recent German literature does not simply involve a break with the past, however. It initiates a polemic on the future of French literature: "Romantic literature is the only one that is capable of being yet perfected, because, having its roots in our own soil, it is the only one that can grow and revivify itself; it expresses our religion; it expresses our history; its origin is ancient but not antique" (2:138–139). Thus, when de Staël has recourse to the concept of perfection, she separates it from Enlightenment universality and reintroduces it in an open-ended, nation-specific sense. Risking contradiction—is French literature not beholden to its Latin roots?—de Staël claims that French literature has much to learn from German literature because, in spite of linguistic, cultural, and political differences, France too shares—but has shunned—the romantic heritage of northern Europe: "The literature of the ancients is for the moderns a transplanted literature. Romantic or chivalric literature is indigenous to us, and it is our religion and our institutions that have made it blossom" (2:134). Although German literature should no more be imitated than Greek or Latin, the study of it will create a "movement of emulation" whereby the power to create one's own literature can be acquired (3:290). De Staël also maintains that, even if French classicism has produced masterpieces, "however perfect they may be, they are rarely popular, because they do not adhere, in present times, to anything national" (2:135). By turning away from its roots, French literature has, in effect, betrayed what de Staël designates as the true audience of literature: the people, imagined as the natural repository of a national spirit rather than a recalcitrant force to be shaped into national subjects. If de Staël bemoans the fact that Germany is not politically unified as yet, she does so because she considers the German nation to be already both an incipient and a present reality. In this respect, *De l'Allemagne* is, to use a term borrowed from the historian Hans Kohn in his discussion of de Staël, one of the "foundational texts of cultural nationalism."

See also 1774, 1786, 1792 (August 26), 1796 (April), 1800 (January), 1831

Bibliography: Frédéric II, roi de Prusse, *Oeuvres philosophiques* (Paris: Fayard, 1985). Madame de Staël, *De l'Allemagne*, 5 vols. (Paris: Librairie Hachette, 1958). Heinrich Heine, *The Romantic School and Other Essays*, ed. Jost Hermand and Robert C. Holub (New York: Continuum, 1985). John Claiborne Isbell, *The Birth of European Romanticism: Truth and Proganda in Staël's 'De l'Allemagne,' 1810–1813* (Cambridge, U.K.: Cambridge University Press, 1994). Hans Kohn, *Prelude to Nation-States* (New York: Van Nostrand Company, 1967).

James A. Steintrager

ᏽ *1782*

Karl Philipp Moritz calls for contributions to a "Magazine for Empirical Psychology"

Anton Reiser, *Case History, and the Emergence of Empirical Psychology*

In the spring of 1782, a remarkable essay appeared in the renowned journal *Deutsches Museum*. Its author, the twenty-three-year-old Karl Philipp Moritz, had hitherto published a few poems and short essays on pedagogy and linguistics. The "Proposal for a Magazine of Empirical Psychology" ("Vorschlag zu einem Magazin einer Erfahrungsseelenkunde") sounded an altogether different note. Addressed to "all observers of the human heart," it called for the creation of a new field of inquiry, capable of completing the Enlightenment project (793). According to Moritz, the modern spirit must turn upon itself and create a science of man subtle enough to bring the concrete individual—replete with passions and memories, quirks and idiosyncrasies—within the purview of empirical knowledge. *Erfahrungsseelenkunde* would accomplish this task by modeling itself after the only discipline that had ever shown interest in the particular. As a "moral doctor," the coming psychologist should apply the techniques of medical diagnostics (observation, inductive reasoning) to the study of mental phenomena. In one respect, however, psychology would be even more conjectural than medicine. Whereas medicine had its handbooks, institutions, and traditions, *Erfahrungsseelenkunde* was an emergent science that was still defining its object, methods, and disciplinary boundaries. Empirical richness was initially more important than conceptual stringency and scientific rigor. The new journal would provide an uncensored public forum for the gathering of intimate observations and personal experiences. All readers, regardless of "class and position," were thus urged to contribute short sketches about themselves and their world.

Moritz's call did not fall on deaf ears. Between 1783 and 1793, more than one hundred contributors from all walks of life—educators, priests, teachers, doctors, judges—filled the pages of the magazine with childhood memories, stories of misfits, dreams, reflections on language, and other *curiosa*. Moritz's journal afforded a fascinating glimpse into the inner life of the educated classes in Germany at the close of the 18th century. Although grounded in a widespread interest in anthropology, the *Magazin* initiated a new style of reasoning, leading to a radical rewriting of the soul. Moritz no longer saw the human mind as an atemporal substance with universal features; for him it was a singular constellation of ideas which an individual had acquired over time. The study of the mind, therefore, had to follow two paths of inquiry simultaneously: to attend to the behavioral oddities and idiosyncrasies that characterize a specific human being, and to make these features legible by tracing them back through time to the moment of their formation. Both aspects depict a human being as a singular case, and present the case history as the form best suited for revealing the particularity of the self through the narration of specific experiences and detours that comprise a life.

Moritz's autobiographical novel *Anton Reiser* is his most intricate case history. The book, which appeared in four volumes between 1785 and 1790, tells the story of a failed formation. Marked by poverty and a narrow religious upbringing, Anton (Moritz's alter ego) escapes his oppressive family only to become a captive of his overactive imagination. Moritz clearly conceived his novel as a documentation of *Erfahrungsseelenkunde:* he published selections of it in his journal, subtitled the book version a "psychological novel," and wrote several programmatic prefaces outlining the purpose of the new genre. The psychological novel aimed "to direct man's attention upon himself, and make his individual existence more important to him." It recounted the "inner history of a human being," not in order to entice the reader's fancy, but to focus his "imaginative faculties" on the innocuous circumstances and trivial details that shape a person's character (*Anton Reiser,* 86). By reversing traditional hierarchies of meaning, psychological description reveals that "the texture of a human life consists of an infinite number of details, which become important through their interconnection, however insignificant they might seem in themselves" (186).

Attention to detail is one aspect of Moritz's new narrative ethos; the other is an air of scientific objectivity. The narrator of *Anton Reiser* is indeed a "moral doctor" who dissects the mental habits of his patient with "cold-blooded attention" and analytical distance ("Proposal," 802). It is no exaggeration to say that Moritz's novel comprises two very distinct texts: a hot narrative, consisting of Anton's book-inspired fantasies, and a cold diagnostic commentary, which examines the social causes and psychological mechanisms behind Anton's illusions. This lack of empathetic identification distinguishes Moritz's psychological novel from other contemporary attempts to narrate the self. Whereas autobiography and *Bildungsroman* tell developmental stories that culminate in the protagonist's ability to recount his own life and merge with the narrator, Moritz's case history insists on strict separation of narrated and narrating self. Instead of leading toward reconciliation, *Anton Reiser* is, in the words of a contemporary reviewer, a "historical anatomy and meteorology of the soul."

The book's divergence from existing literary patterns is highlighted in a passage in which the adolescent Anton, inspired by his consumption of novels, considers writing his biography: "It always began like the many books he had read which were modeled after *Robinson Crusoe,* namely that he was born in Hanover in this or that year, from poor yet honest parents. It was supposed to go on like that" (*Anton Reiser,* 240). This is precisely *not* the beginning Moritz chooses. *Anton Reiser* begins before the hero's birth, with a lengthy description of his parents' religious beliefs and quarrels. Anton's life-long melancholy is traced to the two aspects that mark his childhood: his parents' disregard of him, which leaves him with deep-seated doubts concerning his own existence, and his father's religiosity, in which he finds an imaginary substitute for his worldly misery. This pattern of real neglect and illusory compensation structures the entire novel. *Anton Reiser* tells the story of a dual pathology: the pathology of late 18th-century social systems (family, school, economy), which marginalize and oppress the underprivileged Anton, and the pathology of a hypertrophic imagination that derails the subject with phantasmagoric scenes of wish fulfillment.

Religion is not the first of Anton's imaginary substitutes, but it shapes the structure of his fantasies and the direction of his desires. Anton's father adheres to the doctrines of Jeanne Guyon, a 17th-century French Quietist, whose writings outline an essentially mystic type of faith. Central to Guyon's belief was a complete renunciation of the self as a precondition for its boundless union with God. Moritz's novel translates this religious scenario into the language of late 18th-century anthropology. Anton oscillates between melancholy and enthusiasm, between a crushing sense of nothingness and ecstatic omnipotence brought about by his identification with an idealized Other. His fantasies articulate not so much a desire to play an active role, as most critics have claimed, as his wish to be seen. Whether he is engaged in a dialogue with God, or dreams of becoming a preacher or actor, Anton's reveries always stage him as the sole object of the approving gaze of an imaginary master. In this sense, even his theatrical illusions—which dominate the second half of the book—operate within the two configurations that characterized his earliest experience: his parent's disregard, and the Guyonian model of the self's ecstatic union with a loving God.

In the literature on the German tradition of autobiography, it has become a truism to point out the religious—and more precisely, pietistic—roots of introspection. *Anton Reiser* suggests a more complex picture. Religion here figures not as a matter of faith but as the cause of mental suffering. Viewed in psychological terms, it is demoted to the status of imaginary surrogate, a compensatory fantasy that affords Anton momentary relief from his misery but throws him into deep melancholy as soon as its illusory quality becomes evident. The more he suffers from his oppressive circumstances, the more his battered self flees into the fictitious counterworld of religion, games, and, above all, novels. Anton's illness is a cultural one. His symptoms—weak self-confidence, melancholy, confusion of reality and fantasy—are exacerbated by his consumption of novels, which he "devoured with insatiable desire" (109) and an intense enjoyment that "compensated to some extent for all the displeasure of real life" (94).

In depicting the pathological effects of excessive reading, Moritz joins the ranks of countless contemporary pedagogues who denounced the dangers of this habit. But *Anton Reiser* also suggests, if implicitly, a cure for this disease. The book's diagnostic framework provides an antidote to the protagonist's passionate stories. In turning his own life into a case history, Moritz becomes his own moral doctor, actively analyzing the social causes and psychological mechanisms he had suffered before. Moritz's psychological project thus becomes an attempt at self-healing through knowledge.

But there is a third factor that disturbs both the high-blown logic of Anton's self-created novels and the analytical consistency of the case history, that is, the world of contingent objects—of opaque bodies, unpredictable events, and recalcitrant details—that punctuate the narrative and thwart all attempts at sense-making. To begin with, there is Anton's frail body, which constantly intrudes into, and interferes with, his narcissistic fantasies. For instance, just before he is to perform in the long-awaited leading part in a play, Anton is thrown into utter despair by the sudden loss of his hair. His shabby clothes have a similarly stigmatizing effect, turning his desire for public recognition into shame at being seen. But nowhere does the world of objects unleash its destructive dynamic more fully than in the chance events that permeate the entire book and exert an enormous influence on the protagonist: "All of Reiser's impending sorrows in school derived from a single, hastily turned page in the director's copy of Cicero's *Book of Duties*" (242). Moritz's microscopic narrative radicalizes 18th-century realism to the point where it loses its rhetorical and ideological consistency. If, from Defoe onward, the minutiae of everyday life served to authenticate the ideal biography of the protagonist, in *Anton Reiser* their contingent force derails every attempt at biographical consistency. This means that Moritz's novel breaks with two metaphysical tenets that structure most contemporary narratives of the self, especially in Germany: (1) the assumption of a complementarity between the subject and the world, and (2) the teleological pattern of the individual's life history. Suffused with unforeseeable accidents and inert social structures, the world of Moritz's novel undercuts any development. Hence the strangely static quality of Anton's biography, which remains locked in a pattern of repetition and undulation: "One easily sees that the circumstances that combined to imbue his person with importance gave his vanity far too much food. A small humiliation was once again necessary, which indeed was not long in coming" (192).

On one level, Moritz's novel seems to make good on its claim to provide nothing but "observations . . . of the real world" down to the most insignificant details. But this realism is over-determined, and the author's reconstruction of his own life is driven by more than scientific rigor. This excess is already detectable in the quotation above, which emplots Anton's bad luck in terms of the intervention of a cosmic force that punishes him for his vanity. Chance no longer appears as senseless contingency but as the manifestation of a moral—and thus meaningful—universe. And this is no isolated instance. Throughout the novel, the narrator draws on both the semantics of fate and the fortuna motif—a language that is clearly at odds with the analytical intentions of the case history. Thus it happens that Moritz's seemingly scientific novel follows a pre-modern and baroque pattern, and that the repetitiveness of Anton's life is given two mutually exclusive explanations: a psychological one, linked to the fixation of character traits derived from earliest childhood, and a moral-ontological one, which appeals to a world in which pride goes before a fall. It is as if Moritz, in depicting his own life as a story of repetition and failure, wanted to break, at all cost, with the mechanism of narcissistic identification that had caused him so much psychic suffering. In other words, there is an excessiveness and cruel quality about the analytical gaze of the moral doctor. Moritz himself suggests as much in a passage in the "Proposal": "As soon as I realize that I am not given any role, I place myself in front of the stage and become a calm, cold observer. As soon as my own condition becomes onerous, I cease to be interested in myself and regard myself as an object of observation, as if I were a foreigner, whose bad luck I hear talked about with cold-blooded attention" (802). Perhaps the strange modernity of Moritz's novel derives precisely from this radically anti-autobiographical impulse, from the desire to write the self, not in order to make sense of one's past experiences and close the gap between narrated and narrating self, but to widen the difference between life and discourse, and to create out of past defeats a new identity as *author* of oneself.

What is omitted from this story, however, is Moritz's own genesis as an author. In pathologizing Anton's fantasies as compensatory forms of wish fulfillment, the narrator disregards their productive and critical dimension. Anton does not simply dream himself into a better world; his games and fantasies are a way of symbolically appropriating and working through the experiences of his life. Take for instance the following description: "Walking in the fields, he made an occasional mental distinction, and allowed two opposing armies of yellow and white flowers to advance. He named the largest of them after his heroes, and gave his own name to one of them. Then he incorporated a kind of blind fate, and with eyes shut and a stick in his hand, batted as many flowers as he could. When he opened his eyes, he examined the destruction. Here, there was a hero lying, over there, another lay massacred; and with a feeling at once melancholic and pleasurable, he saw himself among those killed in action" (104).

Is there another 18th-century work that so openly describes the aggressiveness of an eight-year-old? And yet, Anton's destructive game is also a creative act, for through it, he not only transforms the painful experience of passivity into an active role but also represents his own suffering to himself. The product of a symbolic appropriation, his game is a creative achievement, an invention that destroys the world in order to rearrange it into an imaginary medium of self-expression. And this is no isolated instance. Anton tenaciously refuses to accept the world on its own narrow terms. His productive imagination becomes the source of constant restlessness and critical dissatisfaction with the social status quo, that is, a source of newness. In this sense, Moritz's psychological case history exceeds its own interpretive framework and points to future literary and political developments. In fact, on one occasion, the narrator himself seems to say as much: "Once a house really did burn down in his hometown, and he felt, amidst all the terror, a sort of secret wish that the fire might not be extinguished immediately. This wish had nothing to do with malicious joy but was caused by an obscure premonition of great changes, emigrations, and revolutions, where all things would assume an entirely different form, and the existing monotony disappear" (105).

See also 1670 (*collegia pietatis*), 1774, 1792, 1899

Bibliography: Karl Philipp Moritz, *Werke,* vol 1: *Dichtungen und Schriften zur Erfahrungsseelen-kunde,* ed. Heide Hollmer and Albert Meier (Frankfurt am Main: Deutscher Klassiker Verlag, 1999).————, *Anton Reiser: A Psychological Novel,* translated and with an introduction by Ritchie Robertson (London and New York: Penguin Books, 1997).

Andreas Gailus

♄ 1784, October 12

Goethe encourages Johann Gottfried Herder to complete his philosophical history of humankind

The Universal and the Particular

On October 12, 1784, Goethe writes a letter to his former mentor Johann Gottfried Herder (1744–1803), urging him to persevere in his immense project *Ideen zur Philosophie der Geschichte der Menschheit* (1784–1791; *Ideas on the Philosophy of the History of Humankind*). This encouragement was both welcome and needed. The vast scope of Herder's undertaking, ranging from zoology to anthropology, from comparative botany to world geography, required his acquaintance with several rapidly expanding fields of inquiry. To accomplish this task within the span of a human life seemed impossible. Indeed, Herder's would be one of the last efforts to provide a comprehensive account of both the natural world and human civilization. Herder sought to unite within a single narrative the history of the planet and its place in the solar system, of its plants, animals, and, most importantly, its peoples. The sheer ambition of this project reflects the 18th-century aspiration of achieving for both the natural and cultural domains something akin to Newton's discovery of a fundamental law (gravity) operative in the entire inanimate world. The elaboration of such basic laws, it was felt, would supplant earlier religious and metaphysical models. Herder's radical naturalization of history stemmed from his belief in Spinoza's equation of God and nature, which held that God's design for the world and the course of nature coincide.

Herder's *Ideas* can be seen as an attempt to reformulate and expand his previous work *Auch eine Philosophie der Geschichte zur Bildung der Menschheit* (1774; *Another Philosophy of History for the Education of Humankind*), the first sketches of which date to his youth. In fact, *Ideas* is in many respects the culmination of a broad spectrum of research Herder had conducted since the late 1760s. In a famous essay on Shakespeare of 1773, for example, he had dealt a blow to all normative conceptions of literature by showing how literary works take shape within particular cultural contexts. His examination of the origin of lyric poetry demonstrated its connection with primitive religious beliefs and his collection of folk songs made a range of cultural expressions accessible to Europeans for the first time. Herder's great discovery, one might say, bears on the complex interweave of cultural forms and values and on their irreducibly historical character. In *Ideas* he attempted to survey this historical and cultural diversity and, at the same time, to grasp the underlying unity.

Although Herder draws on scientific knowledge, especially geography and climatology, he does not fully subscribe to the methodology of the natural sciences. On the contrary, what distinguishes his style of thought is the fusion of scientific inquiry with poetic license. His employment of the rather imprecise vitalist notion of *Kraft* (force, power) to designate the all-pervasive form of organization in nature exemplifies this tactic. In an anonymous and ironically dismissive review of the first part of Herder's *Ideas,* Kant sharply criticized such metaphorically dilated terminology and insisted on the strict maintenance of methodological boundaries for all forms of scientific inquiry. Dismayed and embittered by Kant's criticisms, Herder took solace in Goethe's supportive words.

In Herder's writing, elements such as intuition, feeling, and poetic figuration, which Kant rejected as inimical to scientific investigation, combine with conceptual thought to generate stunningly original insights into the patterns and progress of human culture. Most crucial among these poetic devices is certainly the analogy between organic growth and historical development. History displays an incomprehensible wealth of particularities, but in Herder's view all cultures and eras are characterized by a pattern of flowering and decay. However, this pattern does not amount to pointless repetition. Rather, each cultural phase is destined to actualize a unique aspect of what Herder calls *Humanität* (humanity). Humanity is the mandate of all individuals and peoples, and its progressive realization is the very meaning of history.

The concept of *Humanität,* which Herder also celebrated in his *Briefe zur Beförderung der Humanität* (1793–1797; *Letters on the Promotion of Humanity*), encompasses all those attributes that make us human. Herder introduces this distinctly human capacity with the rather bold and startling assertion that humans are "the first beings set free by creation" ("Der Mensch ist der erste Freigelassene der Schöpfung"). Release from natural (causal) determination into a life imbued with freedom and choice unites all members of the human race. The fruits of human freedom are voluntary social commitments, such as marriage, friendship, loyalty, and various forms of government. Contrary to animals, which nature produces complete, humans must make their world and in doing so make themselves. This is Herder's gloss on the Enlightenment notion of perfectibility. By nature imperfect and unfinished, human beings "perfect" themselves by forging the conventions, instruments, and practices within which human potential is realized. From this point of view, the development of human culture can be understood as a second, genuinely human genesis.

The concept of humanity links Herder's views to the neo-humanist thought of German Classicism, which emerged simultaneously with the writing of *Ideas* and flourished particularly in the 1790s. But Herder diverges from his contemporaries, such as Schiller, in two essential respects. As we have seen, he was very much a naturalist in the sense that he recognized no duality between nature and spirit. For him, the force or *Kraft* that expresses itself, for example, in the forms of organic nature likewise informs human action and utterance. The second characteristic feature of Herder's neo-humanism is the central importance he attributes to language. As he never tires of pointing out, even our unique natural endowments—for example, the brain, the senses, the human hand, erect posture— would have remained ineffective without human language. Speech is the driving mechanism *(Triebfeder)* that makes possible the practical use of all those physical advantages over the mute creatures. A minute physiological peculiarity—"a little air through a narrow gap"—gives us the capability of signifying ideas with sounds, thereby laying the foundation for all specifically human achievements. As the mother's "pupil," the infant trains its "finest senses," eye and ear, and through the education thus acquired develops "reason, *Humanität,* a human way of life." Herder even traces the notion of reason *(Vernunft)* back to its auditory origin *(vernehmen,* "to hear"). Reason is not an innate faculty, an inward capacity, but emerges within the continuous activity of human education *(Bildung).* Religion too is a product of this (self-)educative process, which always searches for ultimate causes and lends them an anthropomorphic shape.

The treatment of language in *Ideas* reveals an interesting shift of emphasis vis-à-vis Herder's famous prize essay of 1772, *Abhandlung über den Ursprung der Sprache (Treatise on the Origin of Language).* In the earlier text, the connection between the aspects of a thing perceived by the senses and its name was guaranteed by an onomatopoetic theory of designation, but in *Ideas* this connection is severed and language is viewed as thoroughly arbitrary. We can see here an attempt to discredit the notion that pure thinking can lead to substantial insights, a thesis that, according to Herder, Kant wrongly espoused. Our "poor reason," Herder claims, does its accounting with pennies, numbers, empty sounds, "for that there exists an essential connection between language and thoughts, let alone with the things themselves, nobody really believes who knows even only two languages." There are many languages and in each of them reason is satisfied simply by engaging in a shadow play with arbitrary tokens. Why? Because "reason itself is only in possession of inessential characteristics and in the end it does not really matter which signs it uses to designate." Were language able to express the essential nature of things, we would acquire godlike status or arrive, says Herder, "in the land of truth." Yet we stand twice removed from this land because what we know of a thing is only "a superficial, truncated symbol of the thing, clad in another arbitrary symbol." The linguistically inspired debunking of the claims of reason later found expression in Herder's attack on Kant, *Metakritik zur Kritik der reinen Vernunft* (1799; *Metacritique to the Critique of Pure Reason),* a text which today, depending on the theoretical preferences of the commentator, is considered as either woefully misguided or surprisingly prescient.

In addition to his aversion to the notion of reason as a purely conceptual faculty, Herder had a second, equally significant, motivation for accentuating the arbitrary character of linguistic signs in *Ideas.* He believed that, much as the circulation of paper money stimulates economic productivity, so does trafficking in arbitrary signs enhance intellectual inventiveness. The same thought is dramatized in the first act of *Faust II,* where the introduction of paper currency is correlated with an allegorical style of poetic writing, and Goethe may have had Herder in mind when he conceived the scene. The importance of commerce for Herder is evident in the economic metaphors so prominent throughout his writings. In his view, mutually beneficial international trade is the best guarantor of peace and social justice as well as the motor of economic and intellectual progress. This notion plays an especially important role in the descriptions of peoples and their civilizations in the later sections of *Ideas.* For example, the observation that Chinese is an essentialist, pictographic language unleashes a virulent denunciation of Chinese civilization, its laws, art, and commerce. The most scandalous aspect of Chinese culture is its resistance to economic as well as linguistic exchange. Such institutionalized stasis, in Herder's view, stultifies speculative-creative innovation, be it conceptual or commercial, and therefore paralyzes the humanizing dynamic of history itself.

Herder's evaluation of China—which was certainly not atypical for the late 18th and early 19th centuries—leads to what is perhaps the most vexing issue in *Ideas,* the question of the universal and the particular. While the process of acculturation is universal, the specific forms of cultural development, its expressions in a particular time and place, are necessarily various. This variety manifests itself in the arts and traditions of peoples, but also in the development of each individual human being. Herder endeavored to accord each civilization its cultural autonomy and inveighed against the application to all cultures of standards derived from one in particular. For this reason, he is still revered today in many Slavic countries for having helped them to appreciate the legitimacy of their indigenous achievements. While respect for individual cultures follows from Herder's organic model of historical development in *Ideas,* it also represents his engagement in the fight against colonial racism and economic exploitation. The poetic character of his descriptions stands in sharp contrast to the more scientific geological accounts and serves as instruction for the empathetic reader. In the preface to *Ideas,* Herder expresses his hope of finding such congenial readers, the "invisible *commercium* of minds and hearts."

Although Herder insisted that individual cultures should be appreciated on their own terms, he nonetheless posited a common "culture of humanity." This insistence was partly a defense against the critique of relativism but more importantly his major argument in the battle against all theories of polygenesis. In addition to the culture of humanity, Herder holds out two other regulative concepts for the development of historical cultures: *Bildung,* or cultivation, and the paradigmatic humanity of Christ. These normative ideals, however, remain vaguely defined yardsticks for the overall evaluation of individual cultures. More important as standards for concrete assessment are the aesthetic criteria Herder employs to judge the various civilizations. H. B. Nisbet has enumerated many concepts in *Ideas* that derive from aesthetics, among them the notion of the harmony of the universe, the form of the world, the Golden Mean, and the great chain of being, but the most frequently employed aesthetic criterion for intellectual perfection and physical beauty is the classical Greek rendering of the human body. Thus in the China chapter of the third part of *Ideas,* considered above in connection with language and commerce, Herder reverses the terms of approbation made famous by Winckelmann—"noble simplicity and quiet grandeur"—and characterizes the Chinese aesthetic as one of dissolute grandeur and vain splendor.

However, such moments of Eurocentric blindness are rare in *Ideas* and, as in the case of China, often reflect complex political and intellectual disputes in late 18th-century Europe. More important today are Herder's untiring efforts in *Ideas* to champion respect for cultural differences, even if these differences remain incommensurable with European standards. Herder's attention to the aesthetic side of science, its metaphoricity, has also taken on renewed relevance in contemporary debates. Finally, Herder's recognition of the centrality of language as a mode of world-making anticipates a major premise in modern thought. Herder himself saw his work at the very outset conditioned by the age in which he wrote and he considered the ideas he set forth not as eternal truths, but as provisional and ephemeral leaves released into the great wind of time.

See also 1790, 1799, 1828 (Winter), 1831

Bibliography: Johann Gottfried Herder, *Werke,* vol. 6, *Ideen zur Philosophie der Geschichte der Menschheit,* ed. Martin Bollacher (Frankfurt am Main: Deutscher Klassiker Verlag, 1989). ———, *Outlines of a Philosophy of the History of Man,* trans. T. Churchill (London: Hansard, 1800). H. B. Nisbet, *Herder and the Philosophy and History of Science* (Cambridge, U.K.: Modern Humanities Research Association, 1970). Robert E. Norton, *Herder's Aesthetics and the European Enlightenment* (Ithaca, N.Y.: Cornell University Press, 1991). John Zammito, "'Method' versus 'Manner'? Kant's Critique of Herder's *Ideen* in the Light of the Epoch of Science, 1790–1820," in *Herder Jahrbuch/Herder Yearbook,* eds. Hans Adler, Wulf Koepke, and Samson Knoll (Stuttgart and Weimar: Metzler, 1998).

Hansjakob Werlen

1785, August
F. H. Jacobi hastily composes his "Spinoza Büchlein," setting off the famous pantheism controversy

The Limits of Enlightenment

During a few weeks in August 1785, in feverish haste, Friedrich Heinrich Jacobi (1743–1819) threw together a short book to which he gave the rather bland title *Über die Lehre des Spinoza in Briefen an den Herrn Moses Mendelssohn (Concerning the Teachings of Spinoza in Letters to Moses Mendelssohn).* This brief tract—the "Spinoza Büchlein" (Spinoza Booklet), as many called it—was no literary or philosophical masterpiece. It was an odd pastiche of religious confession, textual exegesis, personal correspondence, and philosophical dialogue, all sprinkled with lavish quotations from Hamann, Herder, Lavater, and the

Bible. Hamann dubbed the book a monster, consisting of "Spinoza's head, Herder's body, and Goethe's toes." Yet, for all its flaws, the book was bound to become a *succès de scandale,* for it contained one stunning piece of news: Lessing was a Spinozist! According to Jacobi, this was not mere gossip but what Lessing had personally confessed to him in the summer of 1780 at Wolffenbüttel. Since, in late 18th-century Germany, Spinozism had connotations of atheism and fatalism, revealing Lessing's confession was sure to prove sensational. Lessing had been the most revered figure of the *Aufklärung* (Enlightenment); and now it turned out that he might be an atheist and fatalist.

Jacobi rushed his book into print because he wanted to beat Moses Mendelssohn to press. For several years, Jacobi had been corresponding with Mendelssohn about Lessing. He had informed Mendelssohn about his conversations with Lessing, assuming that Mendelssohn would keep this news confidential. An intimate friend of Lessing almost all his life, Mendelssohn was puzzled, surprised, and worried by Jacobi's revelations. If published, they could damage Lessing's reputation. That Lessing had often flirted with Spinozism, Mendelssohn knew very well; but the question was what Spinozism meant to Lessing, and Mendelssohn was convinced it did not amount to simple atheism and fatalism. In the summer of 1785, Reimarus wrote to Jacobi the disturbing news that Mendelssohn planned to publish his own version of Lessing's Spinozism. For Jacobi that meant only one thing: Mendelssohn was going to scoop him. Not only was Mendelssohn making unauthorized use of his conversations with Lessing, he was making public his version of Lessing's Spinozism first. So, indignantly and urgently, Jacobi pasted his materials together into a book. As fate would have it, Jacobi beat Mendelssohn to press by a narrow margin. *Briefe* appeared in September 1785; owing to publishing delays, Mendelssohn's tract, *Morgenstunden (Morning Hours),* appeared in October.

Thus began the so-called pantheism controversy between Jacobi and Mendelssohn. Jacobi had rightly calculated the effect of his book. Referring to the effect of *Briefe* on the public, Goethe later wrote of "an explosion" and Hegel of "a thunderbolt out of the blue." The controversy began with a bitter exchange of pamphlets. Eager to defend Lessing's reputation, Mendelssohn quickly wrote a riposte to *Briefe,* his *An die Freunde Lessings* (1786; *To Lessing's Friends*). Not to be outdone, Jacobi replied to Mendelssohn's insinuations with his *Wider Mendelssohns Beschuldigungen* (1786; *Against Mendelssohn's Accusations*). He then reformulated his position in *David Hume über den Glauben, oder Idealismus und Realismus* (1787; *David Hume on Faith, or Idealism and Realism*) and in a second edition of *Briefe* (1789), which nearly doubled in size with the addition of eight appendices. While the scandal and acrimony were raging, tragedy struck. Mendelssohn became so upset by the dispute and so eager to divest himself of it, he insisted on hand-delivering the manuscript of *An die Freunde Lessings* to his publisher; such was his haste and anger that he left without his overcoat, caught a cold, and died January 4, 1786. In the *Berlinische priviligierte Zeitung,* Karl Philipp Moritz blamed Jacobi for Mendelssohn's death. A heated debate ensued concerning Jacobi's role in the tragedy. To some,

Mendelssohn's death was very symbolic: the *Aufklärung* was murdered and Jacobi had the blood on his hands.

Although it began as a dispute between Jacobi and Mendelssohn, the pantheism controversy soon spread, involving virtually every intellectual in late 18th-century Germany. Among the notables who took part in the dispute, whether publicly or privately, were Goethe, Kant, Herder, and Hamann. Several younger writers made their debuts on the polemical stage: K. H. Heydenreich, the aesthetician, K. L. Reinhold, the spokesman for Kant, Thomas Wizenmann, the defender of Jacobi, and A. L. Rehberg, the conservative publicist. The controversy was also a crucible for the young Romantics, who developed much of their philosophical outlook by taking part in it. The letters and notebooks of Hölderlin, Schelling, Schleiermacher, Friedrich Schlegel, and Novalis reveal their close reading of Jacobi's *Briefe*. The pantheism controversy reached its height in the late 1780s, only to be soon eclipsed by the outbreak of the French Revolution. But the issues it raised continued to preoccupy thinkers well into the 19th century. Fichte, Hegel, and Kierkegaard also formed their philosophical views by taking sides in the dispute.

It is difficult to imagine a controversy whose cause was so incidental— Jacobi's disclosure of Lessing's Spinozism—and whose effects were so great. The pantheism controversy gave rise to new intellectual forces in Germany. One of its most striking results was the reversal in the fortunes of Spinozism. For more than a century the academic and ecclesiastical establishment had treated Spinoza "as a dead dog," as Lessing once put it. Decrying Spinoza's atheism and fatalism had become a ritual de rigueur, an easy way of proving one's orthodoxy. Spinozism stood not only for atheism and fatalism but for all those progressive causes the establishment loathed and feared: religious toleration, freedom of speech and press, separation of church and state, and republicanism. There were so many attacks against Spinoza that a hefty *Catalogus scriptorum Anti-Spinozanorum* was published in Leipzig, and Trinius counted some 120 enemies of Spinoza in his *Freydenkerlexicon (Lexicon of Freethinkers)*. However, when the pantheism controversy finally waned, the intellectual scapegoat of Germany had become its patron saint. Since Lessing was the most revered thinker of the *Aufklärung,* his credo had given courage and a stamp of legitimacy to every closet Spinozist. Many of the major thinkers of Goethe's time—Goethe himself, Novalis, Schleiermacher, Herder, Schlegel, Hölderlin, and Schelling—now joined ranks with Lessing, declaring their allegiance to, or at least sympathy with, Spinzosim. Thanks to the controversy, pantheism soon became, as Heine later put it, "the unofficial religion of Germany."

Another remarkable result of the controversy was the breakthrough of Kantianism, its final triumphal entry on the intellectual scene in Germany. Before the onset of the controversy, Kant had made some progress in gaining recognition. He had a few worthy disciples. There were lectures and commentaries on his work, and the *Allgemeine Literaturzeitung* had begun to champion his cause. But the critical philosophy was still far from a popular success. Kant's influence was confined to select circles in only a few universities. It was much too obscure and technical to be understood by the general public. Worst of all, it had been dismissed by some of the leading philosophers of the day—Garve, Mendelssohn, and Feder—as a relapse into Humean skepticism or Berkeleyian idealism. But the pantheism controversy quickly made Kant's philosophy fashionable. The decisive breakthrough came in the fall of 1786 with the publication of Reinhold's *Briefe über die kantische Philosophie (Letters concerning Kant's Philosophy),* an elegant popular exposition of the main tenets of Kant's philosophy. *Briefe* had created, to quote a friend of Kant's, "a sensation." But it is important to see the secret of Reinhold's success. He established the relevance of the critical philosophy to that dispute foremost in the public eye: the pantheism controversy.

How did Jacobi's book unleash such forces? How did such a slight, eccentric book have such profound consequences? The source of the book's power ultimately lay in Jacobi's challenge to the *Aufklärung.* It must be said that Jacobi had a daunting polemical talent, a sure knack for provoking people to address central philosophical issues. What so deeply disturbed his contemporaries was his attack upon the most basic article of faith of the *Aufklärung:* the authority of reason. Lessing was really just a pawn in Jacobi's long-planned campaign against the *Aufklärung* in Berlin. In revealing Lessing's credo, he sent out a warning about the dangerous consequences of all rational inquiry: atheism and fatalism. Lessing had a reputation for being the boldest and most radical of all the *Aufklärer,* a virtual Socrates on the Spree, who was willing to follow his reason wherever it might lead him, regardless of the consequences for social convention, political allegiance, or religious belief. Hence his Spinozism had a powerful symbolic significance. It meant that reason, when pushed to its limits, undermines morality and religion. Jacobi was confronting the *Aufklärer* with a drastic and dramatic dilemma: they had to choose between either a rational atheism and fatalism or a nonrational leap of faith in God and freedom. There could not be a middle path, though, where reason somehow demonstrates the fundamental principles of morality and religion. This was to say in effect that the main preoccupations of the *Aufklärung*—a natural morality and religion—were a waste of time, a mere illusion.

Of course, Jacobi's case against the *Aufklärung* did not rest upon mere innuendo and scandal. There is a confusing welter of arguments in *Briefe,* most of them merely suggested, but all of them very troubling. Jacobi struck out wildly in all directions, never stopping to marshal his forces in an orderly phalanx. He implied that reason is conditioned by historical forces and its principles simply reflect a specific culture. He suggested that reason is directed by will and is not impartial because it is dependent upon our natural needs. He also indicated that since reason comprehends only timeless relations between concepts, it is incapable of understanding real time itself. Whatever shook the *Aufklärer* out of their dogmatic slumber was good enough for Jacobi.

One argument in Jacobi's chaotic polemic gained particular notoriety. Its starting point was his bold claim that Spinozism was the paradigm of rationalism, the model of all philosophy. The spirit of Spinozism, he told Lessing, is nothing less than the maxim *a nihilo nihil fit* ("nothing comes from nothing"). Jacobi saw this maxim as a version of Leibniz's principle of sufficient reason that states "nothing happens unless there is a sufficient reason for it." Spinoza's philosophy is the paradigm of reason, Jacobi contended, because it refuses to limit this principle, applying it to every event in the universe. This means that for any event to happen, there must be some prior event that determines it into action, such that it cannot happen otherwise. Hence there cannot be a first cause of the universe, a creation from nothing; and there cannot be freedom in the sense required by moral responsibility, the power to act otherwise. In other words, a radical rationalism that refuses to limit the principle of sufficient reason must end in atheism and fatalism. Leibniz's philosophy, Jacobi added, is only an incomplete and inconsistent Spinozism because it fails to take its principle of sufficient reason to the same conclusions.

Jacobi saw the real challenge of Spinozism in its radical naturalism, and more specifically, in its principle that everything in the universe must be explained through mechanical causes. He equates Spinozism with a radical naturalism that denies the existence of anything supernatural, and that explains all events as following strict laws, such that everything happens of necessity and cannot be otherwise. His critique of the rationalism of the *Aufklärung* was so troubling to his contemporaries precisely because he was pointing out the increasingly visible consequences of the new sciences: the more inquiry advances, the more the realm of the supernatural disappears.

Although Jacobi saw Spinoza's philosophy as the model of a radical rationalism, he was at pains to insist that this was not his own philosophy. Rather than accepting Spinoza's atheism and fatalism, he made a *salto mortale* to uphold his moral and religious faith. Like Pascal, Jacobi held that our most basic moral and religious beliefs cannot be demonstrated, yet they are certain because they rest upon an immediate experience. All demonstration had to end in some self-evident belief, which had to rest upon feeling, insight, or inspiration. It is indeed only through immediate experience that we can have knowledge of existence, of the reality of things outside us. The real task of philosophy is to show the limits of reason and to point to, to gesture at, this reality. Jacobi declared in some famous lines, which resonated far and wide: "In my view the greatest service of the inquirer is to disclose existence, to reveal it . . . Explanation is only a means, a path toward the goal, the immediate but never the final end. His last goal is that which cannot be explained: the indissolvable, the immediate, the simple."

Although Jacobi's philosophy and polemic struck his age like a bombshell, it must be said that his view was not entirely new. There were some notable precedents for it. Earlier in the 18th century, some of the more radical Pietists, most notably Joachim Lange and Johann Budde, had argued that Wolff's rationalism, if it is only consistent, leads straight to the atheism and fatalism of Spinozism. The only escape from such consequences, they argued, was to recognize the sovereignty of faith over reason, or the authority of revelation over demonstration. In basing his polemic upon Spinoza, in arguing that Leibniz's philosophy was inconsistent Spinozism, and in stressing the importance of faith over reason, Jacobi followed in the footsteps of Lange and Budde. Still, there are important differences between Jacobi and his Pietist forebears. First, Jacobi intended to uphold not the literal authority of Scripture, but the role of personal experience. Rather than being an orthodox Lutheran, Jacobi was more a Pietist with roots in the Radical Reformation. Second, and more importantly, he did not mean to defend the state church or Protestant establishment. He made his stand against the *Aufklärung* not to undermine freedom of conscience, but to support it. It is important to see that this was Jacobi's motivation for his critique of the *Aufklärung,* if only because Jacobi's anti-rationalism has so often been interpreted as an instance of reactionary politics.

That Jacobi's intentions in attacking the *Aufklärung* were to defend liberal values becomes clear from an earlier essay he wrote in 1782, "Etwas, das Lessing gesagt hat" (Something That Lessing Said), which was a prelude to his later dispute with Mendelssohn. This essay too latches on to the figure of Lessing, but only to hold him up as an example of why the Enlightenment must not betray its fundamental principles of freedom, of conscience, and the press. The occasion for Jacobi's essay was the latest reforms of Joseph II of Austria, intended to abolish the traditional rituals and institutions of the Church to make it more useful to society. Jacobi saw the enlightened despotism of Joseph as a striking instance of "tyranny of reason" *(Alleinherrschaft der Vernunft),* the attempt to justify arbitrary restrictions of liberty in the name of reason. Jacobi's later attack on the Berlin *Aufklärer* in 1786 was essentially an extension of his critique of the Josephine reforms in 1782. Jacobi was suspicious of the Berliners—Mendelssohn, Gedike, Engel, Nicolai, and Biester—because they were in league with that other great enlightened despot, King Friedrich II of Prussia. There were striking instances of how these *Aufklärer* were willing to persecute in the name of reason. They saw Jesuits and Papists under every bed and they did not hesitate to appeal to the state to eliminate them.

For all the extraordinary success of Jacobi's *Briefe,* in the end, the book backfired. Jacobi's warning against Spinozism ultimately made Spinozism the religion of the intellectuals. Rather than damning Spinozism as atheism and fatalism, his contemporaries celebrated it as the only solution to the growing conflict between religion and science. For them, Spinozism was not only naturalism but pantheism. If it equated God with nature, it also identified nature with the divine. Everything was now part of the infinite whole, and God had finally come down to earth, manifesting his presence everywhere, in the rocks, trees, and stars, and in the inmost recesses of the human heart. It was left to old believers like Jacobi to pray to a supernatural being beyond the earth. His *salto mortale* did not appeal to the new generation of the 1790s.

See also 1670 *(collegia pietatis)*, 1767, 1782, 1790, 1796–1797, 1828 (Winter), 1831

Bibliography: F. H. Jacobi, *Werke*, ed. F. H. Jacobi and Friedrich Köppen (Leipzig: Fleischer, 1812). ———. *The Main Philosophical Writings and the Novel Allwill*, trans. George di Giovanni (Montreal: McGill-Queen's University Press, 1994). Moses Mendelssohn, *Gesammelte Schriften, Jubiläumsausgabe*, ed. Alexander Altmann et al. (Stuttgart: Frommann, 1971). David Bell, *Spinoza in Germany from 1670 to the Age of Goethe* (London: University of London Modern Languages Publications, 1984). Heinrich Scholz, ed., *Die Hauptschriften zum Pantheismusstreit zwischen Jacobi und Mendelssohn* (Berlin: Reuther & Reichard, 1916).

Frederick Beiser

⚘ *1786, September 3*

Following his return from Italy to Weimar, Goethe begins to compose his *Römische Elegien,* part of a project to create a new form of erotic poetry

Self-Censorship and Priapic Inspiration

Strictly speaking, Goethe's *Roman Elegies* are neither Roman nor elegiac. Though set in Rome, they were actually written in Weimar between the fall of 1788 and spring of 1790. Like Rilke's *Duino Elegies,* they take their name from the place where they were conceived. The title by which they are known today dates from the 1806 edition of Goethe's collected works. First published in 1795 in Schiller's journal, *Horen,* the collection was simply called *Elegien.* In the only extant manuscript version, dating from 1790–91, the poems bear the heading *Erotica Romana.* Although written in the form of elegiac distichs, these poems are an unabashed celebration of the human body and a hedonistic representation of sexual love. They mark one of the most palpable metamorphoses in Goethe's poetry. Whereas his previous lyrical works may justifiably be labeled "poetry of desire" (N. Boyle), the *Roman Elegies* are aptly described as poetry of fulfillment. As such, they represent a high point in the history of erotic poetry, unrivaled in their literary sophistication and full-blooded humanity.

Although Goethe discouraged speculation on a biographical model for this set of love poems—noting pointedly that the true poet creates "something good out of very little" (Eckermann, April 8, 1829)—investigation into the identity of his Roman lover continues unabated (R. Zapperi). Yet the woman behind Faustina of the *Elegies* remains obscure. Internal and other indirect evidence (letter to Duke Karl August, December 29, 1787) suggests that she was a young widow willing to play the well-defined role of the *mantenuta,* the kept woman, and to be his partner in what proved to be a remarkably successful act of self-therapy. Above all, however, the *Elegies* reflect the kind of intimacy and sensuality Goethe found in Christiane Vulpius, a twenty-three-year-old local woman who became his mistress soon after his return to Weimar, and with whom he lived openly. With Christiane he continued the sexually uninhibited life he had grown accustomed to in Rome. The scandal caused by this liaison foreshadowed the indignation of large segments of Weimar society over the publication—against the advice of the duke—of the *Elegies.* Christiane bore him five children, of whom only the oldest, August, survived. It was not until 1806 that Goethe legitimized their relationship.

Notwithstanding their apparent biographical over-determination, the *Roman Elegies* are by no means cast in a confessional mold. Rather, they bear all the earmarks of a programmatic statement about the problematic status of erotic poetry in a post-classical epoch. Written in a highly self-conscious style, they never let us forget that the lovers' idyll in 18th-century Rome is constructed from classical mythology, mediated through the poems of Catullus, Tibullus, and Propertius—the canonical triumvirate of precursors Goethe chose as models for his project of reviving the love poetry of the Roman masters.

While in Rome, Goethe also renounced his ambition to perfect his talent as a pictorial artist, instead rededicating himself to poetry and writing. Thus in the *Roman Elegies,* for the first time in his work, the experiencing self is cast as a poet—a writer from a northern country traveling in Italy—rather than as a painter, as in such poems of the 1770s as "Künstlers Morgenlied" (Artist's Morning Song). Indeed, in a discarded version of the elegy "Fraget nun wen ihr auch wollt" (Ask now whomever you want), that poet is identified as the author of *Werther.* The decisive shift, though, is thematic: from the uncertainties of creativity, which form the thematic focus of the earlier poems about art, Goethe now turned to questions of representation.

The *Roman Elegies* extend and even transgress the boundaries traditionally observed in the representation of sexuality. In ancient Rome, the poet was free to speak about all stages of erotic encounter, the famous *quinque lineae amoris* (Aelius Donatus): seeing *(visus)*, addressing *(allocutio)*, touching *(tactus)*, kissing *(basium)*, copulating *(coitus)*. In the Middle Ages and the Early Modern period, the poet was generally restricted to four of the five classical stages. Writing explicitly about all five and doing so in a serious rather than farcical vein constituted a deliberate breach of one of the firmest taboos in Western poetry. Specifically, Goethe's *Elegies* defy the Christian condemnation of sexual intercourse practiced for pleasure *(voluptas)*, rather than, as a conjugal duty *(debitum)*, for procreation. That position, first articulated by Saint Paul and Saint Jerome, was still official in Goethe's time. If, as the Hegelian Karl Rosenkranz defined it, obscenity consists in the intentional violation of the reigning norms of modesty *(Scham)*, the *Roman Elegies* had to be viewed as obscene; they were duly decried as "heathen."

Even in the standard twenty-part cycle, which represents a truncated version of Goethe's original project, there is no mistaking the heathen spirit of these poems. Taking their cue from the familiar palindrome *Roma—Amor,* the *Elegies* elaborate the interdependence of erotic and aesthetic sensation ("Seeing with vision that feels, feeling with fingers that see"); they espouse as ideal the instant gratification of desire, for this is how the gods loved "in the heroic age." And they celebrate—in the most emblematic moment of the entire cycle—the nexus between poetic and sexual creativity:

> Often I even compose my poetry in her embraces,
> Counting hexameter beats, tapping them out on her back
> Softly, with one hand's fingers.

We are indeed justified, then, in viewing the *Roman Elegies* as a "manifesto of heathen sensuality" (J. Williams). It cannot be overlooked, however, that in order to arrive at the twenty-part cycle eventually sanctioned for publication, Goethe had to exercise self-censorship. The true character and full extent of his heathen project was camouflaged and largely obscured by the secretion of four elegies, which led Goethe to rearrange the sequence of the poems and change the basic design of the cycle.

These four additional elegies are best accounted for by assuming that they were all part of the original conception of a substantial body of erotic poems to signal a profound aesthetic re-orientation, in the wake of the journey to Italy, and to prepare the way for the larger project of cultural reform that came to be known as Weimar Classicism.

Two of these elegies were excised when Schiller raised a red flag about some risqué passages. Rather than publish them in fragmentary form, with lines omitted, Goethe decided to drop them altogether. The first, "Mehr als ich ahndete schön" (More than I foresaw beautiful) evokes with wonderful vividness the pleasures of the "echten nacketen Amors" (of genuine naked love); the second, "Zwei gefährliche Schlangen" (Two dangerous snakes), ponders the ubiquitous dangers of venereal disease. Two additional elegies, which affect an emphatically heathen posture and are considerably more daring, were withheld even from Schiller. Nor did Goethe include them in the fair copy of the *Erotica Romana* he intended to publish. These two elegies form a self-referential duo, reflecting on the *Roman Elegies* as a whole and on the vicissitudes of erotic poetry in a post-classical age. In the first, "Hier ist mein Garten bestellt" (Here my garden is tended), the poet invokes Priapus, the phallic god of fertility, to be the guardian of his poetic garden, and instructs him to teach all hypocrites who turn up their noses at his poems a deft sodomitic lesson. In the second, Priapus himself is moved to speak. He gives thanks to the honest poet for having restored him to his rightful place among the gods. As a reward for his vindication by the poet of the *Roman Elegies,* Priapus promises to grant him fabulous sexual and poetic potency.

It appears that the structural function of the two Priapic elegies was to serve as Prologue and Epilogue and to provide an emphatically heathen frame for the *Erotica Romana.* With all the extant elegies restored to their proper place, the *Roman Elegies* may thus be seen as a twenty-four-part cycle. In Goethe scholarship, however, there is no agreement as to the authentic shape of the *Roman Elegies.* Most scholars favor the twenty-part cycle, since this is the version to which Goethe gave his approbation. Others argue for the authenticity of the twenty-four-part cycle, invoking Goethe's well-known complaint about the tyranny of convention that prevents the poet from saying with propriety things that were permitted to the ancient Greeks (Eckermann, 25 February 1824). There is no denying, as Karl Otto Conrady has noted, that it makes a big difference whether the *Roman Elegies* are read in the truncated or in the complete version. That difference is thrown into sharp relief when the *Elegies* are printed, as some scholars have done (H. Haile, 1979; Luke/Vaget), in what was most likely their intended sequence.

As soon as we accept the Priapic frame as an integral part of the cycle, some key references take on a new and more precise meaning. Thus the opening and concluding elegies add considerable weight to the allusion at the center of the cycle "Euch, o Grazien" (To you, oh Graces) to the "glorious son" of Bacchus and Cythere, that is, Priapus, who is absent from the workshop of the modern artist but actually should stand next to that artist's other gods. Likewise, the god invoked at the end of "Eines ist mir verdrießlich" (One thing distresses me) can now only be Priapus, or rather Love in its Priapic incarnation. Most importantly, the "Genius" addressed at the beginning, "Saget, Steine, mir an" (Tell me, you stones) can be read as a metaphor for Priapus, rather than as *genius loci*. In short, if we accept the Priapic frame, we can more confidently define the goal of the *Roman Elegies* as the recovery of Priapus for the modern world; explicitly and implicitly, Priapus informs the cycle as a whole.

Recognizing the Priapic program of these poems further allows us to see the *Roman Elegies* as part of a larger project aimed at the creation of a new, honest love poetry. To that end, concurrently with the composition of his *Elegies*, Goethe studied the notorious *Carmina Priapea*. This bore further fruit in *Venetian Epigrams,* written during a two-month stay in Venice in the spring of 1790 and still one of his "least read and least appreciated" works (M. K. Flavell). Characteristically, it was Nietzsche (*The Case of Wagner,* section 3) who recognized in *Venetian Epigrams,* with their concise and irreverent and sometimes aggressive comments, a "kindred free spirit" and who thus came to their defense. Some of the most irreverent epigrams are of a sexual nature and culminate in polemical confrontations of the crucified god of Christianity and the indomitable phallic god, Priapus.

This polemical confrontation forms the core of Goethe's most daring poem, *Das Tagebuch (The Diary)* of 1810—yet another text Goethe decided to withhold from publication. This elaborate 192-line poem appears to take its cue from the conclusion of the *Roman Elegies,* that is, Priapus's promise of unfailing sexual and poetic prowess. *The Diary* is a rumination on the inexplicable failure of this supposedly fail-safe gift and thus revisits the poetic issues underlying the *Roman Elegies.* Once again, Goethe uses the encounter between a traveling writer and a young woman as the narrative vehicle to reflect on the interdependence of the act of love and the act of writing, the two exemplary manifestations of human creativity. Like the *Elegies* in their original conception, this poem has a twenty-four-part structure and employs a framing device.

Written in ottava rima, it is set in the contemporary world of 1800, complete with traveling merchants, traffic accidents, welcoming inns, attractive waitresses.

From the vantage point of *The Diary,* the dilemma of the modern erotic poet becomes fully apparent. He had but two choices: to write poems in a contemporary idiom and form, while treating only conventionally acceptable subject matter; or to write poems presenting daring subject matter, while veiling and legitimizing them by using classical forms. Goethe explored the first option in two remarkable poems of 1788, "Der Besuch" (The Visit) and "Morgenklagen" (Morning Laments), that paint scenes of discreet domestic eroticism. He explored the second option in the *Roman Elegies.* Impermissible to the modern poet was a third option: to treat daring material in an authentically modern idiom. Goethe eventually availed himself of this option in *Das Tagebuch,* but only at the price of self-censorship.

Bertolt Brecht once complained in his *Journals* (8 March 1941) about the lack in German culture of a truly liberated "refined sensuality"; but he allowed for two notable exceptions: Mozart and Goethe. The composer of *Don Giovanni* and of *Così fan tutte* seems not to have expressed himself on the subject, but the author of *Roman Elegies* did indeed regard himself as a "liberator," as we know from his brief essay of 1830, *Further Advice for Young Poets.* There is abundant evidence in his work to justify this proud self-characterization, and some of the most striking and compelling testimony is to be found in his erotic poetry.

See also 1774, 1792 (August 26), 1831, 1882, 1922 (February), 1928

Bibliography: Johann Wolfgang von Goethe, *Sämtliche Werke, Briefe, Tagebücher und Gespräche,* 40 vols. (Frankfurt am Main: Deutscher Klassiker Verlag, 1987–): *Gedichte* in vols. 1 and 2, ed. Karl Eibl. ———, *Erotic Poems,* verse trans. David Luke, Introduction by Hans Rudolf Vaget (Oxford and New York: Oxford University Press, 1997). Harry G. Haile, "Goethe, Erotica Romana," ed. and tr. Harry Haile, *Boston University Journal* 27 (1979): 3–19. Karl Otto Conrady, *Goethe,* 2 vols. (Königstein/Taunus: Athenäum, 1982). M. Kay Flavell, "The Limits of Truth-Telling: An Examination of the 'Venezianische Epigramme,'" *Oxford German Studies* 12 (1981): 39–68. Hans Rudolf Vaget, *Goethe: Der Mann von sechzig Jahren* (Königstein/Taunus: Athenäum, 1982). Elizabeth M. Wilkinson, "Sexual Attitudes in Goethe's Life and Works," in E. M. Wilkinson, ed., *Goethe Revisited* (London: Calder, 1984): 170–184. Nicholas Boyle, *Goethe: The Poet and the Age,* vol. 1: *The Poetry of Desire (1749–1790)* (Oxford, U.K.: Clarendon, 1991). John R. Williams, *The Life of Goethe: A Critical Biography* (Oxford, U.K.: Blackwell, 1998). Roberto Zapperi, *Das Inkognito: Goethes ganz andere Existenz in Rom* (Munich: Beck, 1999).

Hans Rudolf Vaget

ℒ 1788

Adolph Freiherr von Knigge publishes *Über den Umgang mit Menschen*

A Snapshot of Civil Society

"Every person counts in this world just as much as he makes himself count." With this remarkable statement of liberal individualism Adolph

Freiherr (Baron) von Knigge (1750–1796) began his celebrated and influential handbook for navigating civil society, *Über den Umgang mit Menschen* (1788; *On Intercourse with People*). Few people would have been better equipped for such an undertaking than Knigge, who combined experience at various north German courts with a successful career as an independent writer. The indebtedness of his father's estate and the insecurity of tenure at court had forced Knigge to pursue a bourgeois career as a novelist, and it was not until late in his life that he became a state official in his native state of Hanover. Knigge's fictional works, modeled on the English social novels of Henry Fielding, were hugely popular—one conservative critic complained that they were "announced, made known, and recommended by the most beloved German journals" (Grolman, 103).

Knigge's popularity frightened conservatives because of his indefatigable championing of the radical Enlightenment. In the 1780s, he was the main recruiter for the *Illuminati,* a secret society dedicated to transforming German society and its states by training a cadre of influential men in the principles of radical Enlightenment. Knigge left the *Illuminati* in 1783 in protest against its secrecy and, especially, its imperative hierarchy. But he never abandoned the vision of a society transformed by the action of enlightened individuals. For a while, he despaired that great change would occur in his lifetime. The French Revolution, however, filled him again with hope and allowed him to voice more explicit political goals: constitutional government based on popular sovereignty and (male) democratic participation. Knigge was among a handful of Germans who remained ardent champions of the Revolution, even after the beheading of Louis XVI and the ensuing Reign of Terror. However, he was not a bloodthirsty revolutionary. The French people, in his view, had been forced onto a path of violence by their recalcitrant government. He still hoped that in Germany progressive reforms could achieve the same results without violence.

Knigge wrote the first edition of *Umgang* in 1788, one year before the French Revolution began. Successive editions—there were five before his death in 1796—contained ever more radical political assertions. But at base, *Umgang* was a pre-Revolutionary project strongly rooted in the *Illuminati* vision of change through willful individual action. In place of secrecy, he advocated open communication in the public sphere, and instead of speaking to an educated elite, Knigge directed his advice to the common man, the *Rechtschaffene* (upright man), who aspires to a place in civil society.

Umgang is based on two principles: completeness and practicality. "I believe one could not easily find a single relation in social life about which I have not had something to say," he concluded (*Umgang* 1790, 1:405). Completeness is what, in Knigge's view, sets his work apart from previous advice books. His attempt to comprehend an entire society is indeed *Umgang*'s most remarkable feature from the historical perspective, for it is the first book to provide a snapshot of civil society at its birth.

For all his fascination with Enlightenment utopias, Knigge wanted *Umgang* to be a useful handbook for the pursuit of happiness. Its table of contents clearly lays out the whole range of social situations, personalities, and potential problems one might encounter, so the reader can quickly find the advice he needs. Practicality had three consequences, which some later critics used to misrepresent the work. First, usefulness required Knigge to describe and, therefore, accept the social world as it was, even while deploring the circumstances. He also warns against unduly high expectations, for example, of social advancement; happiness thrives on moderation. Such passages make Knigge sound much more conservative than he actually was. Second, practicality demanded a full range of descriptions and advice. Typically, he begins with the positive characteristics of a class of people, moves to the main section on potential difficulties, and gives particular, situational advice, usually giving several reasons for his recommendations. The result often seems contradictory and the logic behind it can only be recognized in the creative tension between the whole and its parts. Finally, as a handbook, *Umgang* is self-consciously devoted to empiricism. "There are many things in this world which cannot be learned except through experience" (*Umgang* 1796, 2:141). In the spirit of self-examination typical of the age, Knigge offers many examples of his own *faux pas* at court to illustrate common errors in social interaction.

Knigge strenuously denied that *Umgang* was a *Complimentirbuch* (book of comportment; *Umgang* 1788, 1:9). He wanted to distance his work from the older literature on courtly behavior, and although that genre, along with the English moral weeklies of the early 18th century, the *Tatler* and the *Spectator,* laid the foundations for his project, *Umgang* belongs to a different world. It does not lay down static rules of comportment, nor does it aim at cynical manipulation of others; rather it seeks to analyze why problems in social communication arise and how one might overcome them. "It is important for anybody who wants to live in the world with people to adapt to the customs, tone, and mood of others," Knigge wrote (*Umgang* 1788, 1:24). At the same time—and this distinguishes his advice from earlier works—one must "act independently! Do not deny your principles, status [*Stand*], birth, or education; in this way neither your social superiors nor inferiors will be able to withhold their respect" (*Umgang* 1788, 2:7). This balance between individualism and social obligation was what Knigge wanted to teach.

The moral basis of his endeavor came straight from the early Enlightenment, the moral-philosophical writings of Christian Thomasius (1655–1728) and especially Christian Wolff (1679–1754). Wolff had taught that the pursuit of personal happiness coincides with and indeed propels the social good because both are expressions of Reason. The enlightened individual, therefore, wills what is good and just, which, in turn, produces abiding happiness. During Knigge's lifetime, the philosopher Immanuel Kant (1724–1804) blasted Wolff's optimistic assumption. Only duty, never personal happiness, provides the basis for moral action. Such a view undermined Knigge's conviction that "he acts in conformity with Reason, properly, well, virtuously, and dutifully, when his ac-

tions . . . further his happiness as an isolated being and as a part of the whole"
(*Über Eigennutz,* 1:18). Knigge explicitly rejected Kant's critique, and thus
Umgang preserves an early Enlightenment foundation even as it moves into the
modern world of individualism and civil society.

Knigge's extraordinary combination of moral philosophy and practical advice was instantly successful. Critics were sensitive to the problem Kant raised
and wondered if it were possible to unite morality with egotism, but they still
praised *Umgang* for its completeness, usefulness, wit, style, and entertainment
value. With the third edition (1790), Knigge finally found the proper logical
form for his bulky work, which thereafter followed the moral philosophers'
progression from duties to the self, to relations with family and neighbors, and
finally to the larger world. Beginning as early as 1801, however, editors sought
to cash in on Knigge's popularity and bowdlerized and falsified his carefully
thought-out work. One of the most prolific editors boasted that "almost no
page has remained without re-working, sometimes it was only necessary to
smooth out a wrinkle, or easily to expunge an excrescence, sometimes, however, a fundamental transformation was necessary" (Gödeke, 79n1). Nine-
teenth- and 20th-century readers did not know Knigge's original work. What
they devoured as "the Knigge"—his name became synonymous with advice
books in general—was, in fact, the comportment book which he purposely
did not write. In the history of German publishing, no work has had as contrary a fate. In part, it was its utilitarian design that was at fault; editors wanted
to bring Knigge's useful advice "up-to-date." But more important, political
changes—in the outlook of the middling strata, in liberalism, in the relation of
state to society—account for the complete misunderstanding of his individual
emancipatory, but socially grounded, goals.

Knigge never specified what he meant by *bürgerliche Gesellschaft* (civil society), but his conception of it is clear from his account. As for most of his contemporaries, it was for him the organized substratum or aspect of the state.
Civil society consisted of groups, some of them the old estates, such as the nobility or clergy, some religious communities like Jews, others occupational,
though economic life was remarkably unimportant in Knigge's social concept.
Rather, he understood civil society primarily as a sphere of communication:
the "first art" necessary to living in it was "the art of making oneself understood, thus speaking and writing" (*Allgemeines System,* 13). *Umgang* presents civil
society as the arena of constant interaction and social exchange. Although many
social groups or institutions (for example, the court) were part of the early modern world of absolutism, they now jostled with newer occupational groups and
societies, and Knigge expected readers of middling strata inevitably to have dealings with people of all stations. These interactions resulted in the continuous
exchange of information and opinions among classes, in continuous movement, and, therefore, in unending change. The seeming certainties of the old
order, the *Ständegesellschaft* (society of estates) were dissolving. Knigge advised
his readers to "learn to live with contradiction" (*Umgang* 1788, 2:322) and to

treat their enemies "with benevolence, objectivity, understanding, [and] care" (*Umgang* 1788, 2:174) since society was populated not simply with friends, but with rivals and foes. Above all, the diversity of civil society required tolerance. "We must be fair enough not to demand that everybody follow our customs, but instead, we must let everybody go his own way" (*Umgang* 1788, 1:81).

Both the competitive pressures of civil society and its boundless possibilities led Knigge to another principle: moderation. The "middle way" (*Umgang* 1788, 1:60) protected the denizens of civil society from its dangerous extremes. By adopting this hoary moral recommendation, Knigge opened himself to vitriolic criticism from 19th-century Romantics, for whom the advice "let go of your desire to rule, to play a brilliant main role" (*Umgang* 1790, 1:86) epitomized the unheroic, the domestic, small caliber of conventional bourgeois life. Later bourgeois self-criticism found a welcome target in Knigge's practicality.

Thirty years before the philosopher Georg Wilhelm Friedrich Hegel (1770–1831) set down the same observations in his *Philosophy of Right* (1820), Knigge noted that the ties of natural love—in the family or locality—and deference that had hitherto bound people and estates together were dissolving. They were being replaced by short, goal-oriented encounters that produced clashing interests, antagonistic groups, and ultimately different communication structures. Knigge was troubled by these developments, and some modern critics have seen this as evidence of his conservatism. Yet, he did not elevate the family or friendship above civil society. Instead, he took the liberal route. He expanded the sphere of the individual, which then became the haven from both civil society *and* the private worlds of family, marriage, and friendship. Throughout *Umgang*, Knigge repeats that one must avoid personal dependence on—the money, favor, or pity of— others. In this regard, he understood equality literally: "Let us accept or demand favors from others as little as possible . . . It ends the balance in the intercourse, robs freedom, and hinders unlimited choice" (*Umgang* 1788, 1:45). Friendship was equally subject to this rule—"everything which harms equality among friends is harmful to friendship," Knigge wrote (*Umgang* 1790, 2:217). Even within marriage, Knigge established distance between the spouses. The wife should never learn of her husband's doubts or momentary weakness, so his independence and freedom are preserved. It is in this interior sphere where no one penetrates that self-reflection and self-constitution take place. That Knigge should have associated this strictly with males, whom he addressed in *Umgang,* is not a sign of his conservatism, as many modern readers imagine, but of his liberalism, whose conception of individualism was, with rare exceptions, strictly masculine. And individualism, reconciled with social obligation in a complex way, was Knigge's aim.

Umgang was meant to be the handbook for the already enlightened, whose rational desires were congruent with the social good. Where the enlightened individual might occasionally falter, he would soon be corrected by social interaction, since that was based upon social communication that only operates by way of empathetic understanding of one's fellow social beings. *Umgang* provided the psychological and sociological information needed to achieve empathy. Its rules were not conventional; they were keys to recurring social situations, from which it was possible to devise the proper (always changing) rules of social intercourse. In this way, the individual, propelled by rational desire to achieve happiness, joins society and changes it for the better.

Soon after Knigge's death, fellow liberals began to misunderstand his project. The Romantics among them preferred a heroic to a merely modestly successful individual. Early in the 19th century, many liberals adopted an increasingly narrowed view of civil society for which Knigge's democratic construal of the just man was too broad. They saw *Umgang* fit for social inferiors with merely "a middling level of education" (Wilmsen, 64). Civil society was a closed club to which such people did not belong. Borrowing reactionaries' criticism of Knigge as a secret agitator, because of his involvement with the *Illuminati,* liberal critics excoriated the baron's putative "courtliness" and his lack of theory. His situational ethics offended the universal morality the educated bourgeoisie had taken as its identifying social characteristic. In this way Knigge became lost and the emancipatory, democratic, and modern foundations of *Umgang* were, until very recently, forgotten—and are still often misunderstood. Thus, liberalism itself destroyed one of the most remarkable sources of liberal thinking in German history.

See also 1735, 1790, 1828 (Winter)

Bibliography: Ernst-Otto Fehn, Paul Raabe, and Claus Ritterhoff, eds., *Ob Baron Knigge auch wirklich todt ist? Eine Ausstellung zum 225. Geburtstag des Adolph Freiherrn Knigge* (Wolfenbüttel: Herzog August Bibliothek, 1977). Karl Ludwig Friedrich Gödeke, "Introduction," *Über den Umgang mit Menschen,* 12th ed. (Hanover: Hahn, 1844), reprinted in Michael Schlott, ed., *Wirkungen und Wertungen.* Karl-Heinz Göttert, *Knigge oder: Von den Illusionen des anständigen Lebens* (Munich: Deutscher Taschenbuchverlag, 1995). Ludwig Adolf Christian von Grolman, "Ob Baron Knigge auch wirklich todt ist?" *Magazin der Kunst und Litteratur* 4, vol. 3 (July–September 1796): 100–106; reprinted in Michael Schlott, ed., *Wirkungen und Wertungen.* Wolfgang Hardtwig, "Die Lebensbilanz eines verhinderten Umstürzlers: Adolph Freiherr von Knigges Werk *Über den Umgang mit Menschen,*" in Schlott, ed., *Wirkungen und Wertungen.* Adolph Freiherr von Knigge, *Ausgewählte Werke in zehn Bänden,* ed. Wolfgang Fenner (Hanover: Fackelträger Verlag, 1991–1996). ———, *Allgemeines System für das Volk: Zur Grundlage aller Erkenntnisse für Menschen aus allen Nationen, Ständen und Religionen in einem Auszuge herausgegeben,* in *Ausgewählte Werke,* vol. 8, 9–30. ———, *Practical Philosophy of Social Life, or The Art of Conversing with Men, after the German of Baron Knigge,* 2 vols., trans. P. Will (London: T. Cadell, Jr. & W. Davies, 1799; 1st American ed., 1805). ———, *Über den Umgang mit Menschen,* 1st ed. (Hanover: Schmidtsche Buchhandlung, 1788). ———, *Über den Umgang mit Menschen,* 5th ed. [orig. 1796], reprint, ed. Karl-Heinz Göttert (Stuttgart: Philipp Reclam, 1991). ———, *Über Eigennutz und Undank: Ein Gegenstück zu dem Buche Über den Umgang mit Menschen* [1796], ed. Gert Ueding (Tübingen: Klöpfer, Meyer, 1996). Michael Schlott, ed., *Wirkungen und Wertungen: Adolph Freiherr von Knigge im Urteil der Nachwelt (1796–1994): Eine Dokumentensammlung* (Göttingen: Wallstein Verlag, 1998). Friedrich Philipp Wilmsen, "Introduction," *Umgang,* 9th ed. (Hanover: Hahn, 1817), reprinted in Schlott, ed., *Wirkungen und Wertungen.*

Isabel V. Hull

♌ 1789, June 2

Lichtenberg observes nature, society, and himself in brief compass

The Disciplines of Attention

On the Tuesday after Pentecost in 1789, Georg Christoph Lichtenberg (1742–1799), a professor of experimental physics at the University of Göttingen, was surprised by a thunderstorm in his garden (II. 241/J1315). He confided his detailed observations of the strong north wind, the dark wreath of clouds that appeared six degrees above the horizon against the general white-gray color of the sky, the distant thunder heard around eight o'clock, and numerous other minutiae to his waste-books *(Sudelbücher)*. In these notebooks, which Lichtenberg filled with thousands of entries in the period between 1765 and 1799, observations of natural phenomena and experiments stand cheek-by-jowl next to ribald anecdotes and epigrams, shrewd comments on people and mores, mathematical puzzles, sketches of faces and experimental apparatuses, speculations on the causes of everything from the weather to volcanoes, reading notes, descriptions with prices of the latest books and scientific instruments, philosophical ruminations on science, human nature, and politics, and a good deal else. The most striking qualities of these compulsive jottings are their miscellaneous character and their brevity. Eventually they would serve as the admired model for the German philosophical aphorism in a distinguished lineage stretching from Novalis to Schopenhauer to Nietzsche. But for Lichtenberg himself, the *Sudelbücher* belonged to a different genre, that of sharp-edged, compact observation. The subject matter of these observations was an early summer thunderstorm, the French Revolution, which Lichtenberg dubbed "experimental politics" (I.699/L322), country girls flocking to Göttingen to wait upon the well-heeled students, thermometer readings, human physiognomy, ice crystals on the window, his own nervous maladies. What mattered was the laserlike intensity of attention with which he excised the event or object from its mundane context, magnified and multiplied in detail, and framed by a succinct, distinct consciousness.

Lichtenberg evidently never intended his waste-book entries for publication, although they provided the raw material and early inspirations for some works that eventually found their way into print. He understood his notebooks as the ore from which pure metal could eventually be refined (I.372/E150). He made no effort to spell out private abbreviations and coded references or to distinguish his own reflections systematically from excerpts copied from the works of other authors. Nor is there any record that he ever read from his waste-books aloud to friends, family, or colleagues. The notes he wrote down every evening, starting at age twenty-three, were a dialogue with himself, perhaps even as an act of self-discovery or self-invention. But they are distinct in content and format from the sporadic diaries in which he recorded on a daily basis medical symptoms, family affairs, and social gatherings. The waste-book entries, by contrast, are occasionally personal, but almost never domestic. They are seldom dated, except when a meteorological or astronomical observation is at issue. When he refers to his parlous state of health, it is almost always as departure point for a more general remark or hypothesis. Writing was for him a quest not for an authentic self, but for "the slumbering system" of thought otherwise only dimly perceived by its originator (I.653/J19). The waste-books bear the stamp of Lichtenberg's personality, but they are not confessions.

Nor are they aphoristic in the sense Lichtenberg himself would recognize. In keeping with the Hippocratic revival in late 18th-century German medicine, Lichtenberg understood aphorisms in the ancient Greek sense, as definitions and tenets of a science memorably and tersely expressed for students to memorize. As the editor of four editions (1784, 1787, 1791, 1794) of his Göttingen predecessor Erxleben's textbook *Elements of Natural Philosophy* (1772; *Anfangsgründe der Naturlehre*), and one of the university's most popular lecturers, Lichtenberg also reflected on the principles of effective pedagogy, including the utility of aphorisms. He criticized a physics textbook for its lack of "aphoristic brevity and precision of expression," and in one of the many to-do notes in the waste-books resolved to write "aphorisms for physics every day . . . with the most apt examples available" (II.302/J1647). Although his appreciation of the aphorism as a didactic tool—as well as his respect for the pithy wisdom of biblical proverbs—may have contributed to his literary preference for short forms, he never referred to his waste-book entries as "aphorisms." He rather called them pointers *(Fingerzeige)*, notes, penny truths, piggy-bank excerpts *(Exzerptenbuch-Sparbüchse)*, or, most often, observations *(Bermerkungen)*. The term "aphorisms" as applied to the content of the waste-books was the invention of the editors of the posthumous selections from remnants of Lichtenberg's manuscript, which were edited in their entirety only in 1968–1971 by Wolfgang Promies. Hence Lichtenberg's reputation as an aphorist depends largely on the post hoc projections of later editors and scholars keenly aware of the genre's subsequent history, especially in German.

Yet there was at least one explicitly aphoristic tradition Lichtenberg knew and admired: Francis Bacon's vision of a reformed natural philosophy as set forth in numbered aphorisms in *Novum organum* (1620; *New Organon*). In *The Advancement of Learning* (1605), Bacon recommended aphorisms as an antidote to hasty "reduction of knowledge into arts and methods" on grounds of flexibility: "But as young men, when they knit and shape perfectly, do seldom grow to a further stature; so knowledge, while it is in aphorisms and observations, it is in growth; but when it once is comprehended in exact methods, it may perchance be further polished and illustrated, and accommodated for use and practice; but it increaseth no more in bulk and substance."

Bacon's writings powerfully impressed late 17th- and 18th-century naturalists committed to the study of natural particulars through observation and experiment. Aphorisms, numbered lists, and tables, all forms Bacon employed, filled the annals of Enlightenment scientific societies like the Royal Society of London and the Akademie der Wissenschaften zu Göttingen (Lichtenberg was a member of both). Lichtenberg once proposed an almanac for physicists that would have these short literary forms inscribed in its pages: columns in which to register barometer, thermometer, and wind readings day by day; facing blank pages for noting additional observations (II.210/H20). Like Bacon, who was apostrophized in the waste-books as a "storehouse of light" (I.809/J1111), Lichtenberg worried that reigning scientific theories might harden into dogma, and that the facile generalizations to which the human intellect is all too inclined will obliterate the evidence of fact. His waste-book entries are punctuated at regular intervals with injunctions to doubt this or that scientific shibboleth: "To doubt things that are now believed without further investigation, that is everywhere the chief thing" (II.233/J1276). Even mathematics, which Lichtenberg praised as the foundation of physics, can mislead through excessive abstraction. However beautiful mathematical laws of nature might be, "close up, it's all not true" (II.333/J1843). For Lichtenberg, and many of his contemporaries, the art of Enlightenment science was learning to see nature close up.

Lichtenberg's observations exemplify a psychology of inquiry cultivated by 18th-century naturalists like René Antoine de Réaumur, Albrecht von Haller, André De Luc, and Charles Bonnet, all of whom are repeatedly cited in the waste-books. Lichtenberg's own preferred term for his jottings, *Bemerkungen*, captures its chief element with a shared root: the ability to remark, to focus attention *(merken, Aufmerksamkeit)*. Unlike *Beobachtung*, the usual German rendering of the English "observation" and a word quite current in 18th-century German scientific prose, *Bemerkung* suggests a directed gaze, an active, analytic intensity of regard. The item has not only been observed; it has been noted. The disciplines of attention Lichtenberg and his colleagues practiced and theorized about worked in multiple ways to single out objects as worthy of sustained investigation, isolate them from the continuous flow of experience, subject them to an exacting mental, often literal, dissection into a mosaic of details, and describe them in a few pages or even a few sentences. Above all, attention served to imbue these objects with value and pleasure great enough to justify the considerable expenditure of time and resources demanded by a program of observations that could stretch out over years and, in a period in which libraries and instruments were usually the private property of researchers, consume fortunes.

Each achievement of disciplined scientific attention was hard won. Throughout the late 17th and 18th centuries, wags and moralists like Joseph Addison and Jean de La Bruyère had ridiculed scientific virtuosi for their preoccupation with the lowly and the trivial—the habits of insects, colored shadows, the nature of cold (all topics of Lichtenberg's observations). In contrast to the noble objects of the ancient science of astronomy, these new scientific objects were widely regarded as unworthy of an educated gentleman's scrutiny, and even as a dangerous distraction from more weighty civic, religious, and familial obligations. Many naturalists also subscribed to a psychology that made close observation of particulars, whether the craters of the moon or copulating flies, a strenuous, unpleasant task. They followed Bacon in the belief that the human mind naturally ascends to the level of abstraction and generalization. When forced to attend to empirical details without respite, the intellect succumbs to vertigo and fatigue. Hence the prevalence of wonders in the annals of early scientific societies with Baconian predilections: only a marvel, it was thought, could rivet the attention long enough for a sustained inspection of particulars. By the time Lichtenberg began writing his waste-books in the 1770s, three generations of naturalists had poured their best efforts into transforming the most humdrum, and sometimes revolting, objects into wonders for the scientific cognoscenti. This alchemy of converting base metals into gold was performed by feats of channeled attention. After Bonnet had observed a solitary aphid every day for about a month from about 5:30 a.m. to 11:00 p.m., duly recording all data in a table, he mourned its passing as if it had been a family member. Réaumur informed his more squeamish readers that they had only to look long and hard at insects to discover splendors more ravishing than any fairy tale. Through regimens of attention, Enlightenment naturalists had become connoisseurs of a remarkable range of natural phenomena, from comets to polyps, capable of remarking the finest nuances and most minute differences, and of appreciating their delights.

The techniques of scientific attention were bodily, instrumental, literary, and moral, and Lichtenberg's observations show all to excellent advantage. The demands made on 18th-century observers were often heroic, taxing the body and straining the senses. Lichtenberg spent sleepless nights tracking the path of a comet, sustained numerous electrical shocks, and made himself ill breathing inflammable air. Even under conditions of extreme fatigue and discomfort, attentive observers were expected to remain alert and in possession of their senses, in both meanings of that phrase—not only to observe accurately, but also to judge the quality of the observations made under trying circumstances. Conducting experiments on the speed of sound while nauseous, Lichtenberg took care to note which time measurements were reliable and which "somewhat uncertain" (II.256/J1391-2). Like connoisseurs of artworks, connoisseurs of naturalia tune sensory acuity to a high pitch through the vigilant exercise of attention.

Lichtenberg remarked on the fact that his clock chimed the hours a third higher when it stood in his chamber (II.245/J1335), that the flames of his tallow candle revealed "a single thin threadlet" (II.531/949), that the hammering of boards onto the roof of the St. John's Church in Göttingen on July 26, 1793, sounded "quite odd" (II.461/K339), and countless other details plucked from the blur of his daily routine. Since scientific instruments refined the senses still further, Lichtenberg met every new invention and their makers with enthusiasm. His waste-books are peppered with excited notes about the latest barometer or repeating circle. He joked that God ought to order the trumpets for the Last Judgment from the master instrument maker Ramsden in London (I.759/J747).

The sine qua non of sterling observation was fastidious attention to detail in word and deed. And since deeds were ultimately reduced to words in the naturalists' reports, it was above all the techniques of description that certified attentiveness. Lichtenberg called for the coinage of new words to occasion greater distinctions, noting that German collapses the English words "color" and "pigment" into the single word *Farbe* (I.301/D464). He also delighted in metaphor as a natural way of extending language to cover novelties and discover analogies. In addition to precise, differentiated language, sharp observation developed its characteristic literary forms in the 17th and 18th centuries, almost all of them short. There is a suggestive parallel between the act of arbitrary attention required to carve out a fragmentary observation from the continuum of experience, and the equally arbitrary brevity of an entry in a table, a list, or a waste-book that reports the observation.

In principle, both observation and description could go on at length, heaping detail upon detail. Yet the very nature of perception forces a distinction between foreground and background, between the spotlight focus defined by attention and its nebulous penumbra. Lichtenberg poked fun at a laconic chemistry article with a title of three-and-a-half lines and a text of four-and-a-half (I.935/L598). His waste-book entries seldom exceed a few sentences, and some are no more than a few words. Even the most laconic entries are more terse than fragmentary, the essential compressed into smallest compass. Although the numbering of the entries is the work of editors, the spaces between the entries on the page create a list effect, as four square opposed to continuous narrative as the pinpoint observation is to continuous experience.

It is speculative but nonetheless intriguing to posit yet another parallel between the habits of excerpting passages from reading material and of circumscribing observations from experience. Lichtenberg's waste-books also served as commonplace books (especially the *Keras Amaltheias,* or "cornucopia" notebook), filled with notes and quotations from his reading. Since the Renaissance, schoolboys had been taught to fill notebooks specially designated for this purpose with choice morsels from their reading, as an *aide-mémoire* and source of apposite quotations in set themes and speeches. Since the habit of excerpting and quoting, also familiar from florilegia and collections of adages, tends to decontextualize the commonplace entry, there is a certain analogy with the fragmentation of experience into observations. There is also some evidence that the practice of keeping commonplace books led to the kind of combination and recombination of items that Bacon had foreseen for the facts of natural history—independent and even in defiance of the intentions of the original author. Although it is a leap from reading practices to observing practices, the ingrained habits of excerpting, ordering, and recombining the entries of commonplace books might have served as a pattern for excising and collecting observations. There is something about the miscellaneous, overflowing, and decontextualized quality of Lichtenberg's waste-book entries, in which excerpts from books often mix with excerpts from nature on the same page, a practice strongly reminiscent of the stimulating jumble of 18th-century natural history cabinets.

Lichtenberg's attitude toward reading and its relationship to observation was marked by ambivalence. He loved books, read them, wrote them—reading and writing were "like eating and drinking" to him (I.68/B81). The waste-books testify abundantly to his gluttonous reading habits, with summaries, excerpts, critical remarks, recommendations, and lists of still more books to buy. Yet he feared that reading might interfere with or replace seeing, and cautioned that much reading makes for pedants, much seeing for wisdom (II.182/H30). His distrust of reading stemmed from a deeper, more pervasive concern about the blunting effects of habit and convention on sharp observation. The concerted attempt to refresh and focus attention on the new, the overlooked, and the hidden runs like a scarlet thread through the waste-books. He believed that most discoveries were made by chance because people are taught to think and see like their teachers (II.244/J1329). His own favorite method for seeing "something that no one else has yet seen and that no one has yet thought of" (II.251/J1363) was the analogy, in the root sense of the continued proportion, A:B::C:D—if silence is the acoustical equivalent of the color black in optics, what are the acoustical equivalents of white and mirror (II.285/J1543, II.464/K249)? Lichtenberg's analogies overleap all boundaries between nature and art, science and literature, the serious and the comic. Even his doctrine of analogy characteristically arches the intellectual and the jocular: "To find relationships and similarities between things that no one else sees. In this way, wit can lead to inventions" (II.225/GPH86).

Like analogy, attention does not respect boundaries. For Lichtenberg, it was a tool for inner as much as for outer observation, for the progress of moral as well as natural philosophy. He praised the Yoricks of this world (after the character in Lawrence Sterne's novels *Tristam Shandy* and *Sentimental Journey*) as the "observatories of the Philosophical Faculty," fully comparable to those that housed the instruments of astronomers (I.116/B268). During a crisis of despair while traveling in England in 1771, he marveled bitterly (in English) at the inattention of his companions: "Inward pain, the monster which is gnawing my bowels and brain, and which one would think, could not possibly escape any ones observation, because of his immense bigness, yet may be covered with a smile, and lurk unobserved under the transparent veil of a face" (II.611/TB 1171.19). Here the moral as well as the intellectual import of attention for Lichtenberg stands revealed. The entire method of his waste-books, so seemingly unmethodical in their hodge-podge plenitude, was "a strict attention to one's own thoughts and sensations" combined with "the most strongly individualized expression of the same, through carefully chosen words, that one writes down immediately," thereby laying up "a store of observations" (II.169/G207). When Lichtenberg finally emerged from his "Slough of Despond" in 1772, he returned to the notebook in which he had described his monster of inward pain, and added a postscript: "Thank God my Heart is perfectly well after a fundamental cure. . . . I do not know whether it is weak- or sharp-sightedness that makes me see things different from what they appear to other people" (II.615/TB1771.26).

See also 1729, 1799, 1853, 1882

Bibliography: Georg Christoph Lichtenberg, *Schriften und Briefe,* 4 vols. (vols. 1 and 2 contain the *Sudelbücher*), ed. Wolfgang Promies (Munich: Hanser, 1968–1972) [all references in text are to this edition]. ————, *The Waste Books: Selections,* trans. R. J. Hollingdale (New York: New York Review Books, 2000). Joseph P. Stern, *Lichtenberg: A Doctrine of Scattered Occasions* (London: Thames and Hudson, 1959). Franz H. Mautner, *Lichtenberg: Bildnis seines Geistes* (Berlin: De Gruyter, 1968). Albrecht Schöne, *Aufklärung aus dem Geist der Experimentalphysik: Lichtenbergsche Konjunktive* (Munich: Beck, 1983). Friedemann Spicker, *Der Aphorismus: Begriff und Gattung von der Mitte des 18. Jahrhunderts bis 1912* (Berlin: De Gruyter, 1997).

Lorraine Daston

✑ *1790*

Kant publishes *Kritik der Urteilskraft,* completing the three great critiques he wrote during the 1780s

The Experience of Freedom

Immanuel Kant (1724–1804) was *Privatdozent* (lecturer) and then professor of philosophy at Albertina University in Könisgberg from 1755 until his retirement in 1797. His work *Kritik der Urteilskraft (Critique of the Power of Judgment),* published in 1790, is the last of the three great critiques he wrote during the 1780s, the other two being the monumental *Kritik der reinen Vernunft* (*Critique of Pure Reason* 1781; second edition, 1787) and *Kritik der praktischen Vernunft* (*Critique of Practical Reason* 1788). This extraordinary decade also saw the publication of his *Grundlegung zur Metaphysik der Sitten* (1785; *Groundwork for the Metaphysics of Morals*) and *Metaphysische Anfangsgründe der Naturwissenschaft* (1786; *Metaphysical Foundations of Natural Science*). In spite of their systematic appearance, the critiques were not planned as a trilogy. Kant originally had in mind a single critique as the foundation of his philosophy and wrote the second only when his derivation of the moral law from the freedom of the will in *Groundwork* met with resistance. Although Kant had touched on aesthetics in his lectures on logic, metaphysics, and anthropology since the early 1770s, the decision to write the third *Critique* seems to have been made only in December 1787, when he suddenly realized how to connect aesthetics and teleology. Just what the intended connection between these two subjects is remains one of the contested questions in the interpretation of Kant's work.

For all his engagement with the natural science, metaphysics, and moral philosophy of his time, Kant harbored a lifelong love of literature and had extensive knowledge of the vast literature on aesthetics and artistic and literary theory that was produced in the 18th century. Sources and targets for his views on aesthetics include the sense-of-beauty school of the British philosophers Anthony Ashley Cooper, third Earl of Shaftesbury and Francis Hutcheson as well as the German rationalist aestheticians Alexander Gottlieb Baumgarten, Georg Friedrich Meier, and Moses Mendelssohn, all influenced by Gottfried Wilhelm Leibniz. The contrast between the beautiful and the sublime was introduced by Joseph Addison in his famous essays "On the Pleasures of the

Imagination" in *The Spectator* in 1712 and given canonical form by Edmund Burke in his *Philosophical Enquiry into the Origin of Our Ideas of the Sublime and Beautiful* in 1757. The development of the idea of genius was popularized by Alexander Gerard's *Essay on Genius* of 1774, which was translated into German as early as 1776. Correspondingly, the three main parts of the first half of the third *Critique* are the "Analytic of the Beautiful," the "Analytic of the Sublime," and the treatment of the fine arts and genius in the untitled third part.

In the "Analytic of the Beautiful," Kant analyzes the judgment of taste in four "moments": (1) in its quality—our pleasure in beauty and the judgment of taste that we make on its basis are disinterested (§§4–5); (2) in its quantity—the judgment of taste legitimately claims universal subjective validity for the pleasure that one feels with regard to a beautiful object (§§6–9); (3) in its relation—the pleasure in beauty is related to purposiveness in the form of an object rather than being a reflection of the perfection of the object for any concrete purpose (§§10–17); and (4) in its modality—the judgment of taste is exemplary, in the sense of being a model for others (518–522; see also §31–34).

The heart of Kant's argument is in the second moment. Here he posits that it is reasonable to expect agreement in judgments of taste, even though they are based on the feeling of pleasure, the most subjective of our mental states, because our pleasure in beauty is a product of the free and harmonious play between our imagination and understanding that is induced by the experience of an object. Our imagination and understanding can be expected to work the same way as long as they are not disturbed by interfering factors such as concerns about utility and possession. This is the closest Kant comes to an *a priori* principle of taste, and is defended in what he calls the "deduction of pure judgments of taste" (see §21 and 35–38). By free and harmonious play of imagination and understanding, Kant seems to have in mind the sense of unity and coherence we may have from experiencing a rich range of sensations, images, and associations induced by an object even when the organization of that manifold of material is not dictated by any concept that is applied to the object. Such an experience is felt to satisfy the general objective of the understanding to find unity in experience without adhering to its usual way of guaranteeing unity by subsuming the manifold of impressions under a determinate concept. It is pleasurable precisely because of the apparent contingency of its occurrence. This theory of free play steers between Hutcheson's reduction of the feeling of beauty to a purely sensory capacity and the Leibnizians' reduction of aesthetic experience to an indistinct form of conceptual cognition. One of Kant's most influential, yet controversial, arguments is in the second "moment" (see especially §14). The proper object of a judgment of taste, he claims, is only the perceptible form of the organization of an object in space and time, as contrasted to such features of its matter as color or tone as well as to any representational content that a work of art may have. This has had a tremendous influence in some quarters, for example, Clive Bell's notion of "significant form" in his essay *Art* (1914) and Clement Greenberg's ideology of abstract painting in *Art and Culture* (1961). But Kant's assertion of this kind of narrow formalism seems to have no basis in his own premises, other than in his desire to increase the probability of agreement in judgments of taste. Indeed, it rests upon a sleight of hand with Kant simply switching from talking about "the form of purposiveness" (§11) to "purposiveness of form" (13). Moreover, as will be seen, in his theory of the fine arts, Kant presents a much more liberal conception of the factors that can properly enter into our experience of art.

Like the "Analytic of the Beautiful," the "Analytic of the Sublime" is also organized around the four "moments" of quantity, quality, relation, and modality, although the role of this division tends to disappear beneath another one that has no parallel in the treatment of beauty, namely Kant's separation of the "mathematical" and the "dynamical" sublime. The experience of the mathematical sublime occurs when we attempt to grasp something immeasurably large, such as the starry skies above, as a single absolute whole. The understanding, which ordinarily takes in a whole by reiterating an arbitrarily chosen unit as many times as necessary, is frustrated in the attempt to grasp such a vista as a single absolute whole. However, the very fact that imagination even tries to do this reveals to us that we possess a faculty of reason, whose task it is to seek the unconditioned, as well as understanding (§§25–26; this is Kant's treatment of quantity in the case of the sublime). Because the experience of the sublime is one of frustration followed by satisfaction at the realization of the power of our own reason, Kant describes the quality of our feeling of the sublime as a mixed feeling, akin to the moral feeling of respect as he described it in the *Critique of Practical Reason,* in which an initial feeling of pain is followed by a feeling of pleasure all the more intense because of what goes before it (§27). Next, taking the place of a discussion of relation, Kant describes the experience of the dynamical sublime as one induced by the power, rather than mere magnitude, of the mighty forces of things such as towering seas and thundering waterfalls. Here the recognition that such forces could easily destroy our physical being—although, of course, we must be physically secure in order to survive this experience—leads us to recognize a mighty force of another kind within ourselves, namely the power of free will under the rule of practical reason, which cannot be deterred from its purpose by mere physical threats or blandishments (§28).

Finally, in a brief treatment of the intersubjective validity of the experience of the sublime as a treatment of its modality, Kant proposes that the experience of the sublime as well as that of the beautiful can be shared. However, it presupposes a level of moral development that the feeling of the beautiful does not require. Thus it depends, to some extent, on each person's efforts toward moral and aesthetic self-development.

In his treatment of the fine arts (§§43–54), Kant posits that genius is a gift of nature which, unlike Gerard's conception of genius, consists not in a single special faculty, but in the heightened ability of all of the cognitive capacities, which allows the genius to manifest unusual originality in the invention of content for works of art as well as the creation of form for the expression of that content (§46, 49). A genius for content is necessary for artistic success, because, in contrast to what he suggested earlier (§14), Kant now assumes that all art, even natural beauty (see §51), is the expression of aesthetic ideas. By this he seems to mean something like a central organizing theme or invention for a work that can make an idea of reason—typically, a moral idea—palpable to us by the wealth of concrete imagery and associations that it presents or suggests (§49). Aesthetic ideas link content, form, and matter in a way that expresses the freedom of the imagination of the artist, yet leaves room for the freedom of the imagination of the audience. As the philosopher of human autonomy par excellence, Kant is always suspicious of any kind of art that simply imposes the artist's intentions on an audience.

The first half of the third *Critique* concludes with a brief "Dialectic of Aesthetic Judgment," the most important section of which is the discussion of the beautiful as a symbol of the morally good (§59). The experience of beauty, argues Kant, because it is an experience of the freedom of the imagination, can be taken as a symbol of the morally good exercise of the freedom of the will. Even though the experience of freedom of the imagination is not governed by rules, in the way freedom of the will in its moral capacity must be, the former is also palpable in a way the latter never is, and thus gives us concrete affirmation of our own freedom rather than the abstract affirmation of it we get through morality. This idea has influenced poets and thinkers from Friedrich Schiller (*Letters on the Aesthetic Education of Mankind,* 1795) to Herbert Marcuse (*Eros and Civilization* [1955] and *The Aesthetic Dimension* [1978]).

The "Critique of the Teleological Power of Judgment" is briefer than the treatment of aesthetics. However, it too has a complex agenda as it tries to steer a path between the naive realism of proponents of the "argument from design" in British and German philosophy and theology and the radical skepticism of David Hume's *Dialogues Concerning Natural Religion* (1779; translated into German in 1781). Kant begins (§§62–63) with the premise that it would be arbitrary for us to see nature as a system in which some things or creatures naturally exist as a means to an end for others—we could just as easily be a mere means for the flourishing of plants as they can be means for our own ends. But because of the limits of human casual explanation, the experience of organisms forces upon us at least the idea that they are products of purposive design (§§64–66). Once we have arrived at this idea, it is only natural to think, at least in a subjective though regulative way, that not only individual organisms but nature as a whole must also be designed, and that, if all is designed, it must have an end or purpose (§§67–68). As he continues, Kant seems to back away slightly from the claim of the difficulty of understanding organisms, until he finally concedes, in a proto-Darwinian moment, that perhaps everything about organisms can be explained according to mechanical laws of nature except for the possibility of life itself (§§80–81). But the crucial part of Kant's argument comes in what he deceptively labels a mere "appendix" on the method of applying teleological judgment (especially §§82–84). Here he states that we only can conceive of nature as a non-arbitrary system if we think of something that has unconditional value as its end, and this can only be us as moral rather than merely natural beings (§84). However, in order to think of our moral development as the ultimate end of nature, we must think of the object of our morality as being realized *in* nature. Therefore, we must see not just the development of our capacity to formulate moral intentions, but also the complete object of morality, the systematic realization of human happiness, or what Kant calls the "highest good." In turn, this can only be accomplished if we conceive of nature as the product of an Author who writes the laws of both morality and nature (§§86–87). The third *Critique* thus concludes with a reiteration of the argument for the existence of God as a postulate of *practical* reason with which Kant concluded the first two critiques. None of this argumentation is intended to compete with the theoretical knowledge we gain from the natural sciences. Rather it serves only as a guiding light for our own moral efforts. Hence the two halves of the *Critique of the Power of Judgment* come together: the experience of beauty confirms in us the belief that the freedom of the will on which morality depends is possible, and the experience of apparent design in nature gives us the courage to believe that the moral efforts we can undertake because of our possession of a free will can be effective in nature. Kant's third *Critique* thus constitutes the culmination of the optimism of the European Enlightenment.

This third *Critique* has had an extraordinary influence both in Germany and beyond. The notion of the experience of beauty as an experience of the freedom of the imagination laid the foundation for the aesthetics of detachment from Schopenhauer to the theorists of "art for art's sake." It also inspired those who see the aesthetic experience as preparation for the active use of human freedom toward the improvement of society, from Schiller through Schelling to the philosophers of the Frankfurt School. Kant's conception of the experience of organisms as an experience of at least apparent purposiveness also left its mark on Goethe's notion of organic form, which, in turn, found its echo in John Dewey's *Art and Experience* (1935). As already mentioned, Kant's initial espousal of aesthetic formalism, even though he undercut it later in the work, influenced theorists of modern painting; his theory of the sublime, even if misunderstood, has been adopted by postmodernist literary theorists. The work continues to be the subject of intensive study by philosophers and literary theorists alike, and there is no reason to think that fascination with it will end any time soon.

See also 1730, 1792 (August 26), 1796–1797, 1828 (Winter), 1853, 1947

Bibliography: Citations of Kant's works are based on the "Academy" edition, *Kant's Gesammelte Schriften,* vol. 5: *Kritik der Urteilskraft,* ed. Wilhelm Windelband (Berlin: Preussische Akademie der Wissenschaften, 1908). ———, *Critique of the Power of Judgment,* trans. Paul Guyer and Eric Mathews (Cambridge, U.K.: Cambridge University Press, 2000). Paul Guyer, *Kant and the Claims of Taste,* 2nd ed. (Cambridge, U.K.: Cambridge University Press, 1997). ———, *Kant and the Experience of Freedom* (Cambridge, U.K.: Cambridge University Press, 1993). John H. Zammito, *The Genesis of Kant's Critique of Judgment* (Chicago: University of Chicago Press, 1992).

Paul Guyer

1791, September 30

Emanuel Schikaneder's *Die Zauberflöte,* with music by Wolfgang Amadé Mozart, premieres at the Theater auf der Wieden in Vienna

Beyond Language

Die Zauberflöte (The Magic Flute) was Mozart's only major Viennese operatic project not sponsored by the royal court and not produced for the Burgtheater. The Theater auf der Wieden, in existence since 1787 and directed by Emanuel Schikaneder since 1789, was a modern capitalist venture with a wealthy private backer. As one of several suburban venues that sprang up in the 1780s, it continued the Viennese tradition of popular entertainment with a frequently parodic relationship to the court theater. With its eclectic repertory of plays and operas in German, the theater cultivated a similarly eclectic audience (it could accommodate nearly one thousand spectators), including both commoners and aristocrats.

More than anything, it was this unusual proximity of high and low culture that determined the basic tone of *Die Zauberflöte.* The conjunction of the "Egyptian" mysteries of the Masonic rite with the "Hanswurst" clowning of the opera's most memorable character, Papageno—a conjunction epitomized in the overture, where the patter of the comic bass is treated with the learned fugal and contrapuntal seriousness of sacred music—was immediately noted. It has delighted and given offense in equal measure ever since. For the duration of the opera's run, Schikaneder's theater became the new Globe.

Prince Tamino, assisted by the bird-catcher Papageno, embarks on a mission to rescue Pamina, the daughter of the Queen of the Night and the girl he loves. Pamina has been abducted by Sarastro, "a powerful, evil demon," who is holding her captive in his castle. The mission founders when the would-be rescuers are discovered and arrested by Monostatos, a Moor who runs Sarastro's security service and who also lusts for Pamina. As it turns out, Sarastro is not an inhuman tyrant, but a rather benevolent ruler and a high priest in the temple of Wisdom. Unwilling to force Pamina to love him, he surrenders her to Tamino.

Had the story concluded right here at the end of Act 1, *Die Zauberflöte* would have repeated the plot of Mozart's earlier Singspiel *Die Entführung aus dem Serail* (1782; *The Abduction from the Seraglio*), where a mission of Belmonte and his servant Pedrillo to rescue his beloved Konstanze from slavery in the harem of Pasha Selim is at first thwarted, but ultimately ends well, thanks to the Pasha's magnanimous act of renunciation. But *Die Zauberflöte* does not end here. If Act 1 replays *Die Entführung,* Act 2 reworks Mozart's one great serious Italian opera, *Idomeneo* of 1781. In *Idomeneo,* a young prince, Idamante, and an enemy princess, Ilia, must prove their willingness to face death before they are found worthy of one another and he can succeed to the throne of his father. Act 2 of *Die Zauberflöte* enacts a similar drama of *Bildung* (education). Tamino and Pamina are not granted as gratuitous a happy end as the lovers in *Die Entführung.* Rather, like the protagonists of *Idomeneo,* they must undergo a series of trials to prove themselves worthy of marriage, initiation into Sarastro's brotherhood, and future leadership.

Critics have pointed to this break in the story as the opera's main problem: the wronged mother turns out to be evil, the tyrant turns out to be good. But the break is not the problem; rather, it is the point. *Die Zauberflöte* treats of a reversal of values brought about by the passing of the old regime, in which the young and powerless depended for their happiness on the mercy of the old and powerful. It is about the replacement of the old by a new order, in which the young achieve happiness through their own autonomous acts and choices; autonomy replaces mercy (Nagel). The audience is educated along with the characters.

But the opera is also about the transition from a world at war to a world at peace. Here too it resembles *Idomeneo,* where universal peace is reestablished through a final wedding. From Rousseau through Hegel and Marx, one of the great myths, or meta-narratives, of modernity tells about the world that was once whole, was then torn asunder so that it is now internally divided, and will be put together again in the future. *Die Zauberflöte* stages one version of this myth. When the Queen of the Night's husband, the owner of the "all-consuming circle of the sun," was alive, the world was whole. Moon and sun, male and female were united. On his deathbed, the husband had bequeathed the circle of the sun to Sarastro and his initiates and had ordered the Queen and their daughter to submit to the guidance of the wise men. But the Queen does not wish to submit; rather, she wants to destroy the brotherhood, wrest the circle of the sun from Sarastro, and rule alone. This world of conflict between Sarastro and the Queen, sun and moon, male and female, is to be made whole by the union of the young: Sarastro's disciple and the Queen's daughter.

In a story of *Bildung,* it is to be expected that confusion about values will gradually be replaced by increasing clarity. The problem of the opera, if it has one, lies elsewhere, not in a midstream reversal of values. How are we to understand the conclusion to the cosmic conflict between fundamental oppositions—female and male, darkness and light, nature and culture, passion and reason, superstition and truth, vice and virtue, vengeance and forgiveness, death and love? Does the conflict end with the total victory of day over night, as suggested by the final scene, where the defeated Queen is "hurled down into the eternal night" and Sarastro announces "the rays of sun drive the night away"? Or does it end with some form of reconciliation between the opposing principles, as suggested by the union of Pamina and Tamino? The overall logic of the plot, aiming at a dynastic marriage and the young taking over from the old, supports the latter reading. Yet given Sarastro's final apotheosis, doubts cannot be fully dispelled.

Tamino and Pamina make their way through the perilous elements of fire and water, protected by the sound of the magic flute that had been carved by Pamina's father from a "thousand-year-old oak," presumably the mythic tree of life. Music thus becomes the symbol of a harmonious reconciliation in which nature is transcended by culture. Using music's power to wrest new life from the clutches of death, Tamino is a latter-day Orpheus— though unlike his predecessor, he ultimately carries the day and his music is instrumental, not vocal (he is the Orpheus who does not sing). His success may be read as a sign of the political and cultural optimism that prevailed for a brief historical moment between 1789 and 1793, an optimism unthinkable two hundred years earlier, when Monteverdi's Orfeo first sang. It was an optimistic belief, born of the French Revolution, in the possibility of remaking the world so it would become "a realm of heaven, and mortals equal to gods" (the words that end Act 1 and recur at the beginning of the second finale). The novelty of this new Orpheus's music, in turn, has to do with another revolution, aesthetic rather than political, and occurring in Vienna, not Paris, and with Mozart, not Mirabeau, at its center.

A striking aspect of *Die Zauberflöte* is that the music actually heard by the participants—as opposed to that heard as music only by the audience—is purely instrumental: Tamino's flute, Papageno's glockenspiel and panpipe, the horns of the priests. The introduction of the magic instruments in the quintet of Act 1, however, is preceded by another instrument, the golden lock with which the bird-catcher's mouth is shut to keep him from chattering. The first three sections of the first finale repeat this sequence: first, the virtue of silence is extolled, then the instruments demonstrate their virtues, the sound of the flute taming wild beasts while the glockenspiel tames the slaves. The silencing of speech seems prerequisite to the emergence of musical magic. For the two centuries preceding the premiere of *Die Zauberflöte,* music was predominantly conceived of as a mimetic art, inextricably linked with language, and devoted to the representation of human passions. Music performed passionate human speech and amplified its persuasive, rhetorical power. This conception of music, which originated with the birth of opera, acquired the status of a foundational myth in 1607 with Monteverdi's *L'Orfeo,* whose protagonist's singing has persuasive force even over the powers of the underworld. By 1791, Haydn and Mozart had produced instrumental music of the highest aesthetic order and during the following quarter century, this new Viennese music had been couched in a new aesthetic theory by people like E. T. A. Hoffmann and Arthur Schopenhauer. For them, music, separated from language and hence abstract rather than mimetic, had the power to pierce the veil of phenomena and to reveal, as no other medium could, the noumenal realm beyond. Music's subject matter was no longer human passion, but the infinite totality that is the metaphysical ground of being. By intimating this totality, Tamino's flute protects him and Pamina from destruction by the phenomenal elements. In *Die Zauberflöte,* modern abstract music achieves its own foundational myth as the abstract, autonomous subject of modern politics finds its own medium in the new, abstract, autonomous art.

On November 6, 1791, after hearing the twenty-fourth performance of the opera, Count Karl von Zinzendorf noted in his diary: "The music and the stage-designs are pretty, the rest an incredible farce. A huge audience." This, in a nutshell, summarizes the reception of *Die Zauberflöte* from Mozart's day to our own: the libretto has frequently been the butt of scorn. Yet the most original minds of the age—Goethe, Beethoven, Hegel—disagreed. Hegel, in his lectures on aesthetics, argued that, since in opera "music is the chief thing, though its content is given to it by poetry," a good libretto should steer clear of trivial, worthless feelings, on the one hand, and of excessive profundity of thought, on the other, and provide the composer with "only a general foundation on which he can erect his building." In contrast to its critics, Hegel regarded *Die Zauberflöte* as one of the finest opera libretti. Schikaneder's dramaturgy emphasized the nonverbal; and the best indication of the music's powerful content is the final transformation of darkness into light. The real problem of this opera is that the spectacular and the auricular overwhelm the verbal, undermining, thereby, the explicit claims of the text to the primacy of the mind over the appetites, senses, and passions. Platonism is preached, but not practiced here.

However, if the opera enacts the transition from the dark minor to the bright major—whether in the C-minor/C-major trajectory of Act 1, or, more crucially, in the same tonal trajectory of the central trial scene of the second finale, where an archaic Bachian counterpoint yields to a modern homophonic chorus—this process presents allegorizing interpreters with an irresistible temptation. By 1794, three principal readings had emerged. In the French-occupied Rhineland, an anonymous critic described Schikaneder and Mozart as Jacobin demagogues in the service of the Revolution and the opera as an allegory of the liberation of the French people (Tamino) from royal despotism (the Queen) by means of wise legislation (Sarastro). Pamina, the daughter of despotism, is read as an allegory of Liberty. In Austria, Johann Valentin Eybel, alarmed by the events of the French Revolution, gave an anti-Jacobin reading: the philosophy of the Jacobins (the Queen) gives birth to the Republic (Pamina), who is abducted by divine Wisdom (Sarastro) until the night is driven away and the light of legitimacy is reestablished through the marriage of the Republic to a royal prince (Tamino). From Prussia, attached to legitimacy but not frightened by the Enlightenment, came the first outlines of a Masonic reading which by the second half of the 19th century won out over other allegorical interpretations. A review sent by Ludwig von Batzko from Königsberg to the Weimar *Journal des Luxus und der Moden* emphasizes the primordial struggle of light and darkness, good and evil, enlightenment and prej-

udice, and briefly suggests that these are Masonic themes. Indeed, Schikaneder's and Mozart's Masonic sympathies are well documented. By the 1860s,
liberals worshiping the enlightened reform regime of Emperor Joseph II in the
1780s saw in the opera the story of the emperor's struggles with the Church
for Masonic ideals. The flood of interpretations in terms of Masonic allegory
continues unabated to this day.

Diverse generic traditions went into the making of *Die Zauberflöte* and determined its unique flavor: the Baroque improvised Viennese popular theater,
the fairy-tales of Wieland, the dramatic fables of Gozzi, the amazing scenic
machinery of Baroque opera, and, of course, the Singspiel. These elements
soon separated, with the popular Viennese spoken comedy of Nestroy and the
German romantic opera of Weber going different ways. The artistic heirs of
Die Zauberflöte—Beethoven's *Fidelio,* Wagner's *Parsifal,* and Hofmannsthal's and
Strauss's *Die Frau ohne Schatten*—invariably chose to purge the sublime of the
comic.

That Beethoven considered this the greatest of Mozart's operas is confirmed not only in the *Fidelio* score, but also by that opera's plot. The descent
of Beethoven's heroine into an underground dungeon to liberate her imprisoned husband is reminiscent of the travails of Pamina and Tamino as they sur-
mount obstacles and finally emerge into the light. More importantly still, the
fundamental optimistic minor-to-major, darkness-to-light emancipation scenario of Mozart's opera is taken up by Beethoven in his fifth and ninth sym-
phonies and becomes the exemplary archetypal plot of Austro-German absolute music—until the pessimistic, valedictory symphonic finales of Brahms and
Mahler.

Most haunting is the opera's spectral presence in Goethe's oeuvre. Goethe's
production of *Die Zauberflöte* at Weimar, which premiered on January 16, 1794,
was the longest running of all performances he staged during his directorship
of the Court Theater there. Although Goethe abandoned his hope of completing a sequel, *Der Zauberflöte zweiter Teil,* in 1798, he thought well enough of
his fragmentary sketch to include it in his *Gesammelte Werke* of 1807–1808.
Traces of the fragment's substance and form are everywhere in Goethe's later
work, above all in *Faust II,* a magic opera in its own right. Goethe himself
commented on the similarity of the Helena act, in particular, and Mozart's opera (Eckermann, January 29, 1827). But the projected sequel was doomed
from the start. The only composer who might have brought it to life—the
ideal composer for *Faust,* as Goethe confided to Eckermann (February 12,
1829)—alas had passed away. The popular view of Mozart as the "eternal
child" may have entered into Goethe's decision to end the published fragment
with the singularly moving image of the child Genius, son of Tamino and
Pamina, escaping from his sarcophagus like a butterfly from its cocoon. Set free,
not by the sound of the flute, but by his parents' speech, the winged child, like
Ariel, melts into thin air. Thus the abortive sequel lamented the passing of
the artist whose presence was the necessary condition for its own coming into
being.

See also 1773, 1818, 1828 (Winter), 1831, 1853, 1876, 1911

Bibliography: Wolfgang Amadé Mozart, *Die Zauberflöte,* K620, ed. Gernot Gruber and Olfred Orel, *Neue Ausgabe sämtlicher Werke,* II:5/xix (Kassel: Bärenreiter, 1970). Emil Karl Blümml, "Ausdeutungen der 'Zauberflöte,'" *Mozart-Jahrbuch* 1 (1923), 109–146. Dieter Borchmeyer, *Goethe, Mozart und die Zauberflöte,* Veröffentlichung der Joachim Jungius-Gesellschaft der Wissenschaften Hamburg 76 (Göttingen: Vandenhoeck & Ruprecht, 1994). Peter Branscombe, *W. A. Mozart: "Die Zauberflöte,"* Cambridge Opera Handbook (Cambridge, U.K.: Cambridge University Press, 1991). Hans-Georg Gadamer, "Die Bildung zum Menschen: Der Zauberflöte anderer Teil," *Kleine Schriften,* vol. 2 (Tübingen: Mohr, 1967), 118–135. Johann Wolfgang Goethe, *Der Zauberflöte zweiter Teil: Fragment,* ed. Dieter Borchmeyer and Peter Huber, in *Sämtliche Werke* I.6 (Frankfurt am Main: Deutscher Klassiker Verlag, 1993), 221–249. Norbert Miller, "Die Erben von Zauberflöte und Glockenspiel: Peter von Winters 'Labyrinth' und das Märchentheater Emanuel Schikaneders," in Carl Dahlhaus and Norbert Miller, *Europäische Romantik in der Musik,* vol. 1 (Stuttgart-Weimar: Metzler, 1999), 497–538. Ivan Nagel, *Autonomy and Mercy: Reflections on Mozart's Operas,* trans. Marion Faber and Ivan Nagel (Cambridge, Mass.: Harvard University Press, 1991). Jean Starobinski, *1789: The Emblems of Reason,* trans. Barbara Bray (Cambridge, Mass.: MIT Press, 1988).

Karol Berger

✑ 1792
Salomon Maimon writes his *Lebensgeschichte*

Identity and Community

The figure of the *Ostjude,* the Jew from Eastern Europe, has long been a fixture in the German—including the German-Jewish—imagination. His geographic journey from east to west can never, by the light of this image, become a cultural journey. Whatever efforts he makes, he can never divest himself of his Eastern origin, he can never overcome his lack of *Bildung,* in the Western sense. A contributing factor to the formation of this image was the *Lebensgeschichte* (1792; *Autobiography*) of the 18th-century Jewish philosopher Salomon Maimon.

Maimon's autobiography is the tale of his circuitous journey from east to west, and as he tells it, from darkness to light. His depiction of Polish-controlled Lithuania is an inverted world of unreason as seen in an anecdote about his grandfather. As leaseholder of an estate with a bridge in bad repair, Maimon's grandfather suffered the wrath of any Polish nobleman who tumbled with his entourage into the swamp below the bridge. "My grandfather, therefore, did all within his power to guard against such happenings. For this purpose he stationed one of his people to keep watch at the bridge, so that, if any noble were passing and an accident of this sort should happen, the sentinel might bring word to the house as quickly as possible, and the whole family would thus have time to take refuge in the neighbouring wood" (8). To repair the bridge was not an option. Nor was an education in modern mathematics and philosophy for the young Salomon. His formal education was limited to the Talmud and Jewish law; knowledge of science, such as he was able to acquire, was only stolen scraps gleaned from his father's forbidden books or from textbooks brought back by travelers from the West. He had to decode these texts like ciphers, a task at which he succeeded by establishing correspondences between the Hebrew and the Latin alphabets. It was only years later, after he had educated himself in the speculative theosophy of Kabbalah and the Aristotelian rationalism of Maimonides, and after more than one failed attempt, that Maimon gained access not only to the West but also to its body of knowledge, at first in Berlin under the aegis of Mendelssohn, then—after acquiring a reputation as a freethinking libertine who has no intention of supporting himself—at the Gymnasium at Altona.

The autobiography ends with Maimon proudly recounting the beginning of his career as an author of philosophical works in German. Yet, by his own admission, he had mastered neither the German language nor German manners, which suggests that even he could not entirely overcome his origin. For Maimon himself says that the thoughts of "Jews newly arrived from Poland" are "for the most part confused, and [their] language is an unintelligible jargon" (224). If such a description were to come from a German, or even a German Jew, it would be regarded as a blatant expression of prejudice. But since the description came from the *Ostjude* himself, it could all too easily be accepted as a statement of fact. In the mid-19th century, Kuno Fischer, a historian of philosophy who appreciated Maimon's philosophical contribution, needed no justification for this remark about Maimon:

> [His] unusual sharp-wittedness certainly had the intention of giving his investigations the illuminating and penetrating force of a methodical presentation, but not the necessary breeding and cultivation. In accordance with his Talmudic manner, he preferred to write in a commenting and disputing fashion, without properly sifting and ordering the materials. The linguistic failures of the writing style are due to these defects. It is admirable that he learned to write German to the extent that he did; passages occur in his writings in which the thought breaks through with a truly flashing force and overcomes the language, even plays with it in surprising turns, but Maimon never became a German author.

Did it occur to Fischer that Moses Mendelssohn, generally acknowledged as exemplary in his organization and style, was also a native Yiddish speaker with a Talmudic education, although he was born only a few hundred miles west of Maimon? Or did he consider the possibility that Maimon's depiction of the *Ostjude* was at best an expression of self-loathing, at worst a stratagem designed to magnify his own achievements while excusing his faults?

It is suggestive to compare Maimon's autobiography with the first German book about Jewish life, *Der gantz judisch Glaub (The Entire Yiddish Faith)* by Anthonius Margaritha, first published in 1530. Written by a convert to Christianity, the book offers German-speaking Christians an informed view of the

Jewish liturgical year and life cycle, while orienting its account around conversion, the culmination of the author's own story. By 1792, to be sure, much had changed. But a preface by Maimon's friend, Karl Philipp Moritz, who initiated the autobiographical project, suggests an updated version of the Margaritha model. Moritz sees Maimon's story as one of individual enlightenment, despite tremendous odds: "This biography . . . will be attractive for anyone to whom it is not a matter of indifference how the power of thought can develop itself in a human mind, even under the most pressing circumstances, and how the genuine drive after science does not allow itself to be deterred through obstacles which appear insurmountable." But Moritz also sees "special value" in Maimon's story because it is the story of the enlightenment of a Jew—"an impartial and unprejudiced presentation of Judaism, of which one can indeed assert with reason that it is the first of its kind and thus deserves special attention at the present time when the cultivation and enlightenment [*Bildung und Aufklärung*] of the Jewish nation has become a particular object of reflection." Moritz's phrase "the cultivation and enlightenment of the Jewish nation" was open to several interpretations, depending on one's position in the debate to which he alludes. In one view, advocated not only by Christians but also by some Jews, the enlightenment of the Jews would amount to what Kant called "the euthanasia of Judaism." It would be, in effect, a conversion to the religion of reason. Among those who held this view were also some who thought the enlightenment of the Jews impossible, just as some in earlier generations had denied the possibility of a genuine conversion from Judaism to Christianity. Others thought enlightenment of the Jews was a real possibility, which was either to be promoted or, for those loyal to Judaism, to be resisted at all costs.

According to yet another viewpoint, an enlightened Jewish nation would practice an enlightened Judaism. Here one thinks especially of Mendelssohn's *Jerusalem,* another suggestive point of comparison for Maimon's autobiography. The distinguishing mark of Judaism from the natural religion of reason was for Mendelssohn not its beliefs, which were entirely rational, but a system of revealed law, eternally valid for the Jewish people. Unlike Maimon, Mendelssohn became a universally acknowledged master of the German language and manners, while maintaining an observant life within the Jewish community. He did not seek the role of public defender of Judaism. It was thrust upon him in 1769, when he was challenged by Johann Caspar Lavater either to convert to Christianity or to give his reasons for remaining a Jew. In part, the depiction of Judaism in *Jerusalem* is the culmination of Mendelssohn's public refusal to convert.

Where, in a space defined by Margaritha, Kant, and Mendelssohn, does Maimon's autobiography stand? If it has the structure of a conversion narrative, then it is the tale of a gradual transformation, without any vision on the road to Damascus and without resolution. But a transformation from what? To what? One climax of the story is Maimon's attempt, at a time of utter despair, to convert to Christianity. Unable to converse intelligibly in German, Maimon dictates a letter, which he then presents to a Lutheran pastor. It contains the following declaration:

> I am a native of Poland, belonging to the Jewish nation, destined by my educa-
> tion and studies to be a rabbi; but in the thickest darkness I have perceived
> some light. This induced me to search further after light and truth and to free
> myself completely from the darkness of superstition and ignorance . . . I have
> . . . resolved, in order to secure temporal as well as eternal happiness, which de-
> pends on the attainment of perfection, and in order to become useful to myself
> as well as others, to embrace the Christian religion. The Jewish religion, it is
> true, comes, in its articles of faith, nearer to reason than Christianity. But in
> practical use, the latter has an advantage over the former; and since mortality,
> which consists not in opinions but in actions, is the aim of all religion in gen-
> eral, clearly the latter comes nearer than the former to this aim. Moreover, I
> hold the mysteries of the Christian religion for that which they are, that is, alle-
> gorical representations of the truths that are most important for man. By this
> means, I make my faith harmonize with reason, but I cannot believe them liter-
> ally. I beg therefore most respectfully an answer to the question, whether after
> this confession, I am worthy of the Christian religion or not. If I am, I am pre-
> pared to carry my proposal into effect; but if not, I must give up all claim to a
> religion which enjoins me to lie, that is, to deliver a confession of faith which
> contradicts my reason.
>
> (254–255)

Is this a resolution to follow Margaritha by converting? Or to follow Mendelssohn by rejecting conversion in all but name? Given how difficult it is to provide an answer, it is no wonder that the pastor rejected Maimon as "a scabby
sheep, and unworthy of admission into the Christian fold" (126). Maimon's letter shows a clear preference for the Jewish faith over the Christian, while
evincing a general commitment to interpret religious mysteries allegorically.
Indeed, not only did Maimon adopt his surname out of respect for Maimonides, from whom he learned this method of interpretation, he also devoted one hundred and fifty pages of his autobiography to an exposition of
Maimonides' philosophy. If his autobiography has a mission beyond the desire
to contribute to the new discipline of empirical psychology, it is to convey the
central doctrines of Maimonides to a German-speaking audience.

Still, there is no doubt that Maimon's relationship to Judaism changes dramatically during the period covered by his autobiography. Before his meeting
with the pastor, he had already ceased to observe Jewish law, which he justified
through a radicalization of both Maimonides and Mendelssohn. Radicalizing
Maimonides' criticism of anthropomorphism, Maimon declines to lead grace
after meals on the grounds that it would be "impossible for me, without manifest aversion, to say prayers which I regard to be the result of an anthropomorphic system of theology" (246). Following Mendelssohn's account of Judaism
as a legal system, Maimon agrees that for Jews "who from family attachments
and interests profess the Jewish religion, to transgress its laws" is wrong, and

that no Jew can free himself from obligation to Jewish law by converting to Christianity, since Jesus "observed these laws himself and commanded his followers to observe them" (230). "But how," Maimon asks,

> if a Jew wishes to be no longer a *member of this theocratic state,* and goes over to the *heathen* religion, or to the *philosophical,* which is nothing more than pure, natural religion? How if, merely as a member of a *political state,* he submits to its laws, and demands from it his rights in return, without making any declaration whatever about his religion, since the state is reasonable enough not to require from him a declaration with which it has no concern? I do not believe Mendelssohn will maintain that even in this case a Jew is bound in conscience to observe the laws of his fathers' religion merely because it is the religion of his *fathers.*
>
> (230)

Thus Maimon assumes a new identity. In the first place, it is the identity of a philosopher. Yet, his identity remains in some sense Jewish, not only because of his Jewish origin and his Maimonidean version of natural religion, but also because the reasonable civil state does not yet exist. He cannot avoid being defined in relation to the Jewish community of which he no longer is a part. Responding to the pastor's rejection of his inquiry, Maimon articulates his heterodox version of Jewish identity by giving a new twist to a biblical phrase with a long history of Christian interpretation: "I must confess, Herr Pastor, that I am not qualified for Christianity. Whatever light I may receive, I shall always make it luminous with the light of reason. I shall never believe that I have fallen upon new truths, if it is impossible to see their connection with the truths already known to me. I must, therefore, remain what I am—a stiff-necked Jew" (257). To be stiff-necked, with regard not only to Christianity, but also to Judaism, is a long-standing Jewish tradition.

In addition to the theoretical problem of identity, Maimon needed to solve the practical problem of sustenance. In his account, "the majority of Polish Jews consists of scholars, that is, men devoted to an inactive and contemplative life," and a scholar who is fortunate enough to marry well "spends his whole life in learned leisure" (44). Rejecting the entreaties of German Jews to learn a trade, Maimon continued the custom of Eastern European Jewry of seeking financial support from Jewish benefactors. No doubt this became more difficult once he withdrew from the Jewish community, but, since he was not a Christian, a university position was out of the question. Three years after the publication of his autobiography, Maimon at last found a non-Jewish patron, Count Adolf von Kalckreuth, on whose Silesian estate he took up residence. It was there, in the early 19th century, that he drank himself to death. According to one report, he was buried outside the Jewish cemetery of Glogau. This seems appropriate. For Maimon was still defined by his withdrawal from the Jewish community. Even in 18th-century Germany, Western land of enlightenment, there existed as yet no community that he wished to join.

See also 1767, 1775, 1782, 1790

Bibliography: Kuno Fisher, *Fichtes Leben, Werke und Lehre. Geschichte der neuern Philosophie,* vol. 6 (Heidelberg: Carl Winter, 1869). R. Po-chia Hsia, *The Myth of Ritual Murder: Jews and Magic in Reformation Germany* (New Haven, Conn.: Yale University Press, 1988). Immanuel Kant, *The Conflict of the Faculties* [1798], trans. Mary J. Gregor and Robert Anchor, in Kant, *Religion and Rational Theology,* ed. Allen W. Wood and George di Giovanni (Cambridge, U.K.: Cambridge University Press, 1996). *Salomon Maimon's Lebensgeschichte: Von ihm selbst geschrieben und herausgegeben von K. P. Moritz* [Berlin, 1792]; trans. J. Clark Murray, *Solomon Maimon: An Autobiography* (London and Boston: Gardner, 1888; rept. Urbana and Chicago: University of Illinois Press, 2001). Moses Mendelssohn, *Jerusalem, or, On Religious Power and Judaism,* trans. Allan Arkush, with introduction and commentary by Alexander Altmann (Hanover, N.H.: University Press of New England, 1983). Karl Philipp Moritz, "Preface," in *Gnothi sauton oder Magazin zur Erfahrungsseelenkunde,* 10 vols., 1783–1793; rept., Anke Bennholdt-Thomsen and Alfredo Guzzoni, eds. (Lindau, Germany: Antiqua, 1979).

Paul Franks

ℒ *1792, August 26*

The French National Assembly bestows on "le sieur Giller, publiciste allemand," the honorary title of *Citoyen français*

An Aesthetic Revolution

Like many German intellectuals of his time, the poet Friedrich von Schiller (1759–1805) shared the ideals and hopes of the French Revolution. However, he shrank from the brutality of revolutionary measures and, by 1793, he was horrified by its bloody logic. The French Revolution shattered his optimistic view of history and changed his teleological belief in the perfectibility of humanity. A comparison of the praise he lavished on "our enlightened age" in his inaugural address of 1789 in Jena with his cultural criticism at the beginning of the *Aesthetic Education of Man* of 1795 reveals this change. Seven weeks before the outbreak of the French Revolution, Schiller presented to his students an idealized image of "our humanitarian age," culminating in the praise of the "productive middle class, the creator of our whole culture which anticipates a lasting happiness for humanity." When that same productive middle class took the first step in France to free itself from the oppressive Old Order and to extend its cultural influence into the political sphere, Schiller still insisted on the Enlightenment ideal of a "monarchy of reason," in which the happiness of the subjects will be reconciled with the rule of enlightened absolutism. Ironically, the official document of Schiller's honorary French citizenship reached him six years later, when he had long since changed his view on the French Revolution.

In France, however, the poet of *Die Räuber (The Robbers)* was viewed as a sympathizer of the French Revolution, even as a revolutionary. This may have been a productive misunderstanding. Schiller's robber fantasies certainly could be staged as a revolutionary drama—and as such it was performed in Paris in

1792. In writing the play, Schiller was not much concerned with a specific political situation, and only a few changes were necessary to transform Karl Moor's total rebellion against society into an action play for any revolution. Although the protagonist appears as a reluctant rebel, his actions as a robber are directed against all those who abuse their position of privilege in order to satisfy their lust for wealth and power. The play depicts the anarchic struggle of one righteous individual against an "ink-splashing age." Karl's revolt demonstrates that personal injury leads to frustration and only then to battle against social injustice. And yet, there are those famous lines, which transform a band of robbers into virtuous republicans: "Put me in front of an army of guys and I will make a republic out of Germany." It was this rebellious gesture and the moral pathos of the play generally that earned Schiller his honorary French citizenship.

Schiller's next three plays (a bourgeois tragedy, *Intrigue and Love;* a "republican tragedy," *Fiesco;* and a historical drama, *Don Carlos*) firmly established him as the "poet of freedom," if not of revolution. The audience in Mannheim's National Theater certainly understood these as contemporary plays and as an indictment of the existing political and social order. Schiller himself called them books that have to be burned by the authorities. Common to all of these early political dramas are idealistic noblemen who rebel against an established order. Their revolutionary activism and pathos of freedom shake the foundations of despotic absolutism, but in the end they are either defeated or forced to bow to the old order. These endings should warn us against reading these plays as anticipating the French Revolution. On closer examination, Schiller's early political dramas remain entangled in his contradictory views of enlightened despotism. This is most obvious in *Don Carlos* (1786).

The drama is famous for its centerpiece, Scene 10 in Act 3. Marquis Posa, the political idealist, pleads for "freedom of thought" before King Philipp II of Spain. Posa's famous line "Restitute humanity's lost dignity, sire, allow freedom of thought" became the encapsulated meaning of the play and proverbial independent of it. As is often the case with extractions like this, it renders the meaning neither of the play nor of the scene. Freedom of thought would be too modest an ideal for Posa, who has far more in mind, namely the political freedom of the Netherlands. He has to use prudence before the despot. Freedom of thought seems harmless compared to the republican liberty to which he aspires, which would be unspeakable under these circumstances. For Philipp, even Posa's cautious utterances are unheard of and constitute already a dangerous practice of freedom of thought. However, it is doubtful whether Philipp even listens to what Posa is saying, since he is otherwise preoccupied. As is evident from the preceding scene, Philipp desperately needs someone he can trust, a confidant who will put his jealous mind at ease. The end of this central scene stands in stark contrast to the beginning: it is the king's unhappy state of mind rather than Posa's ideas for political reform that has become the issue. Posa becomes Philipp's privy counsel, charged with the task of spying on the queen and on Don Carlos. The private has superseded the political.

Posa now has the power to advance his own political agenda, and with every step he takes, his scheme becomes clearer. He secretly conspires against the Spanish crown to gain liberty for the Netherlands and for Spain "the highest possible freedom for the individual under a flourishing state." Don Carlos, the crown prince, is the hope and instrument of his political will. In the end, when their dreams are shattered, the audience recognizes what they had been up against. The triumph of the Inquisition sheds a new light on the tragedy as a whole. In his "Letters on Don Carlos," Schiller states that he wanted to avenge prostituted humanity by exposing the power and infamy of the Inquisition: "The drama shows the confrontation between an absolute despot who is controlled by the Inquisition, and the ideal of a cosmopolitan republic in which tolerance and religious freedom rule."

How Posa establishes a connection between the rebellion in the Netherlands and his ideal of a "new state of freedom" seems at times revolutionary, but he is neither a Danton nor a Robespierre. What Schiller historicized in his play are the best ideas of the Enlightenment, provocative in his time and in Germany, yet still pre-Revolutionary. The play holds up a mirror to kings and princes who consider themselves enlightened without living up to the universal ideas of human freedom and dignity. What Schiller advocates is nothing less, but also no more, than political reform: religious tolerance even under a state church, freedom of thought as a precondition for a bourgeois public sphere, and the pursuit of happiness under enlightened absolutism. This is Schiller's utopia, an enlightened "new state" in which a constitutional monarchy guarantees freedom, justice, and happiness for its subjects.

One year later, in the introduction to *The History of the Secession of the United Netherlands from the Spanish Government,* Schiller goes even one step further by praising the "new republic" as an example of "what people dare to do for a just cause and what they can accomplish through unity." The insurrection is presented here as a model for oppressed people under similar circumstances, and he concludes that the happy success of this daring rebellion "will not be denied to us, if time is on our side and similar circumstances require such action from us." This was the closest Schiller ever came to legitimizing a revolution. When he republished the text in 1801, he was careful to omit these sentences. He now turned to aesthetic theory as a substitute for history, as he grappled with the political and social problems of his age.

Schiller's aesthetic turn occurred at the beginning of 1793, as evidenced in letters to his friend Christian Gottfried Körner, in which he expresses disgust with the execution of Louis XVI and mentions his aesthetic project. In a letter of February 8, 1793, he develops his idea about beauty for the first time, summing it up with the famous definition: "Beauty is nothing but freedom in appearance." What is so surprising about this original definition, despite its controversial deduction, is the fact that Schiller uses the moral and political concept of freedom to make it a part of his aesthetics. Since beauty is a subjective experience and freedom is projected onto the appearance of the beautiful object, liberty can only be an inner experience; or, as he states in the second letter of *On the Aesthetic Education of Man:* "If man is ever to solve the problem of politics in practice, he will have to approach it through aesthetics, because it is only through beauty that man makes his way to Freedom" (9). This, *in nuce,* is Schiller's response to the political and cultural crisis of his time, and sums up his proposal for the aesthetic education of humanity.

Schiller's epistolary essay, which is generally known as the "Aesthetic Letters," is more than just an ontology of beauty, as it is often interpreted; it can be read as the first political aesthetic, since it seeks a long-term aesthetic solution to a dangerous political situation. In a programmatic letter of July 13, 1793, to the Prince of Augustenburg, his Danish benefactor, Schiller draws a clear connection between politics and aesthetics, between his shattered hopes for the French Revolution and the need for an aesthetic education. Although he understands the French Revolution as an attempt to institute a government of reason, he doubts whether it has succeeded. Schiller already assumes by 1793 that the French Revolution has failed. Based on this assessment, he develops his cultural criticism and aesthetic theory, imbuing contemporary history with a utopian perspective. Since he rejects the violent overthrow of existing forms of government as well as any attempt at nursing feudal despotism back to health, he advocates aesthetic education as a third solution. By raising the ethical standard to the highest level, a gradual transition from absolutism to a state of reason would become possible. This seemingly peculiar interdependence of aesthetics and politics determined henceforth Schiller's aesthetic philosophy of history.

The central notion of the "Aesthetic Letters" is the concept of autonomous art, which opposes art to reality, in particular to political and social concerns. This notion is vulnerable to accusations of ideology, a reproach that has repeatedly been leveled against it. The argument runs as follows: The concept of autonomy justifies the withdrawal of art from reality, separating art from life, and compensates for what is lacking in society—freedom, equality, justice—without changing it. However, Schiller uses the new concept of art's autonomy quite differently. He compensates, so to speak, with a good conscience. In the context of his political and cultural criticism, autonomy has a critical function. The negation of the political and social reality requires the anticipation of a better world. The autonomy of art establishes freedom from external restraints and art projects onto the future what is not yet. The autonomy of art corresponds to Schiller's cultural criticism as his aesthetic education does to art's utopian function.

Since he sees the process of civilization as the cause of the deplorable cultural condition, Schiller has to search for means to overcome it. Anthropologically, the crisis is the result of antagonistic forces within human nature. In typical Kantian fashion, Schiller establishes a dualism between nature and freedom, sensuousness and reason, or in his own terms: material impulse and form impulse. The crisis of modern civilization came about through the alienation of reason from nature. The dominant form impulse is responsible for a condition in which repressive reason subjugates sensuousness in order to increase cultural productivity. The result is a rational culture in which reason dominates nature by exploiting outside nature and repressing inner nature. Alienated labor, specialization, and the loss of totality are consequences of the renunciation of sensuousness. Since the harmonious interaction of the two basic impulses has been lost in the process of civilization, a third force has to reconcile them by making sensuousness rational and reason sensuous. For Schiller, only the play impulse, whose object is beauty and whose goal is freedom, can have this function. He even goes so far as to promise that the play impulse will support not only the entire fabric of aesthetic art but also "the still more difficult art of living" (109). At this point, the revolutionary quality of Schiller's aesthetic education comes into focus. Since life under the auspices of the play impulse "loses its seriousness" and is freed "from the bonds of every purpose, every duty, every care" (109), life becomes a carefree existence without the constraint of want or the coercion of labor. It becomes that blissful state of mind which the Greeks "transferred to Olympus [but] was meant to be realized on earth" (ibid.). In the experience of art, humanity plays with its possibilities and playfully develops its full potential.

If art sets the individual free momentarily and if the play impulse is the liberating force for a new civilization, the question arises what an "aesthetic state" would look like. Schiller's answer at the conclusion of his lengthy essay is rather short and a bit cryptic: "In the Aesthetic State everybody is a free citizen, having equal rights with the noblest. [. . .] As a need, it exists in every finely tuned soul; as a realized fact, we are likely to find it, like the pure church and the pure republic, only in some few chosen circles" (219). This is certainly less than one would expect as a counterproposal to the French Revolution. It also seems to corroborate the argument of those who criticize the abstract and esoteric nature of the essay. But even here, more is left to discover than meets the untrained eye.

The "finely tuned soul" corresponds to the individualization and internalization of an aesthetic education. For Schiller makes it clear from the beginning that "all improvement in the political sphere has to proceed from the ennobling of character" (55). If one can speak of revolution at all, it is "a total revolution of the whole mode of sensuous perception" (205), which is to say, an aesthetic revolution. This revolution involves the abolition of the repressive controls civilization imposes on sensuousness. Art will be the venue for accomplishing this change of consciousness that will precede political change. As for the "few chosen circles," which have already achieved the conditions of the aesthetic state, the courts of Copenhagen and Weimar, the romantic literary circles or the Jewish salons in Berlin come to mind. The members of these circles are already free from want and need and beyond having to struggle for existence, and their lives foreshadow how "a future generation might experience in blissful indolence . . . and develop the free growth of its humanity" (43). These circles are the nucleus of a future aesthetic state in which the individual is led through beauty to freedom. Rather than being a social utopia, Schiller's aesthetic state is a utopian model of harmonious humanity, where the antagonistic forces of nature and freedom, sensuousness and reason, individual and state are in balance. "The Aesthetic State alone can make it real because it consummates the will of the whole through the nature of the individual," and its universal law is "to bestow freedom by means of freedom" (215).

Schiller's aesthetic education is an idealistic, peculiarly German, answer to the French Revolution. It replaces a political education with an aesthetic one, changing nothing but our perception of beauty. Nevertheless, this change is a radical change. Art becomes autonomous and its function becomes one of transforming humanity in order to make freedom possible. Schiller's criticism of the existing political order leads him to demand "freedom of thought," which aims at a bourgeois public sphere and ultimately at an enlightened constitutional monarchy. His cultural criticism and his aesthetic solution are truly utopian: Schiller's aesthetic utopia aims at the liberation of humanity from want and need, and a move toward a state of freedom beyond necessity. This ideal of humanity is something infinite, "which in the course of time we can approximate ever more closely, without ever being able to reach it" (95). It is a regulative idea that demands what is not yet but is to come. Art keeps this ideal alive, enlightens humanity's path, and strengthens the utopian impulse. The aesthetic illusion becomes pre-appearance that anticipates human freedom in the aesthetic sphere, where it becomes unassailable. The aesthetic experience allows, at least momentarily and through contemplation, for a sense of human completeness; it restitutes, strengthens, and motivates the individual; it anticipates future possibilities and opens new perspectives. This is far more than was ever expected of aesthetics.

See also 1796–1797, 1800, 1833, 1835

Bibliography: Friedrich von Schiller, Plays, Walter Hinderer, ed., Foreword by Gordon Craig; The German Library 15 (New York: Continuum, 1983). ———, On the Aesthetic Education of Man in a Series of Letters, ed. and trans. Elizabeth M. Wilkinson and L. A. Willoughby (Oxford, U.K.: Oxford University Press, 1967).

Klaus L. Berghahn

1796, April
August Wilhelm Schlegel calls for a poetic translation of Shakespeare's works

The "German" Shakespeare

August Wilhelm Schlegel (1767–1845) wanted to be remembered, among other things, as having been the "first who dared, on German soil, / To wrestle with Shakespeare's spirit," for having created "the model of Shakespeare's image" in Germany (Sämmtliche Werke, 1, 303). This wish has come true. The fame he achieved for his translations in blank verse of fourteen plays by William Shakespeare—published between 1797 and 1810—has virtually eclipsed his accomplishments as a poet, literary historian, critic, and one of the initiators of German Romanticism. While only specialists still peruse Schlegel's poetry and criticism, his Shakespeare translations—attempts at debunking them from the early 19th century on notwithstanding—continue to speak to German readers and audiences, as is evidenced by the plethora of current German Shakespeare editions using Schlegel's text. In order to grasp the historical significance of these translations, which Schlegel himself considered unprecedented—as daunting as Jacob wrestling with the angel of God—we must look not only at his take on Shakespeare but also at the crucial role Shakespeare played in the development of German literature and culture, particularly in the 18th century.

When Schlegel announced his intention to translate Shakespeare in verse in his essay "Etwas über William Shakespeare bey Gelegenheit Wilhelm Meisters" (Observations on William Shakespeare on the Occasion of Wilhelm Meister), published in the April 1796 issue of Friedrich Schiller's monthly *Die Horen,* the Elizabethan author had long been a much-discussed figure in Germany. Since he was first mentioned in German print in Daniel Georg Morhof's *Unterricht von der Teutschen Sprache und Poesie, deren Uhrsprung, Fortgang und Lehrsätzen* (1682; *Lessons on German Language and Poetry, Their Origin, Development, and Precepts*), Shakespeare had been presented as a major figure in the German variant of the *querelle des anciens et des modernes* (dispute of the ancients and the moderns). Repudiated by those, such as the critic Johann Christoph Gottsched, who looked to the precepts of French classicism and the ancients, especially Horace, in matters of aesthetics and taste, Shakespeare's works were viewed as exemplars of the modern and the new, of original genius, subversive of reason and decorum by those who endeavored to develop an anti-classicist aesthetic, predicated on spontaneous creativity, genius, and close attention to real life. Foremost among these were Johann Gottfried Herder, Jacob Michael Reinhold Lenz, and Johann Wolfgang Goethe. "Nature! Nature! nothing as natural as Shakespeare's characters," the young Goethe exclaimed in 1771 in a representative testimony to the fascination which Shakespeare exerted on the Sturm-und-Drang generation critical of Francophile Prussian absolutism.

It was, among other things, Shakespeare's perceived realism and sense of history, his scrutinizing portrayals of passion and its consequences, his characters' violation of decorum and social-linguistic codes—even the aristocrat Hamlet can be lewd and obscene talking to Ophelia—and, finally, his disregard in the construction of his plays for unity of time, place, and action that enthralled such aspiring anti-classicist authors and theater practitioners as Lenz, Goethe, and Schiller. *Hamlet,* in particular—owing to the escalating conflict between thought and action at the tragedy's center—rallied a generation already under the spell of Goethe's *The Sorrows of Young Werther.* It was a generation eager to act, yet restrained by the tight grip of a monarch who closely observed his subjects' endeavors and viewed any infraction of established aesthetic laws as a potential threat to the political order, as Frederick the Great's negative verdict on Goethe's *Götz von Berlichingen* documents. So powerful was Shakespeare's impact on German audiences that his tragedies are said to have made theatergoers lose consciousness, and—as at a performance of *Othello* in Hamburg in 1779—even to have caused several premature births. By the end of the 18th century, Shakespeare was so well established on the German scene that Schlegel felt justified in stating, in the above-mentioned essay, that "next to the English [Shakespeare] does not belong to any other people as intimately as to the Germans, because by no other people is he so much read, so deeply studied, and so warmly loved both in the original and in translation" (*Sprache*, 99). Echoing his brother's enthusiasm in a famous 1798 fragment, Friedrich Schlegel declared that Shakespeare's "universality is, as it were, the center of romantic art" (*Werke*, 55).

Surprisingly, Shakespeare's works had made their way among the Germans despite the absence of poetic translations that would have allowed them to resound fully in German—idiomatic differences permitting. With the exception of a limited group capable of understanding Shakespeare in the original, his plays had been read and performed, for the most part, in bowdlerized versions and stage adaptations based on a small number of available, yet, as Schlegel pointed out, insufficient German versions. Among them were Caspar Wilhelm von Borck's *Julius Caesar* (1741), the very first German Shakespeare translation (in alexandrines), and Christoph Martin Wieland's prose renditions of twenty-two plays (1762–1766), completed and emended (1775–1777) by Johann Joachim Eschenburg. When Schlegel called for a poetically faithful translation of Shakespeare's oeuvre, he embarked on an enterprise of extreme literary and cultural significance: giving an adequate German voice to that foreign poet who, unlike any other, had captivated the German imagination and who was considered the "greatest dramatic poet" (*Sprache*, 88). Such a translation, Schlegel contended with a nod to Wieland, Eschenburg, and Goethe—whose *Wilhelm Meister* relies on Wieland's prose version for his *Hamlet* production—"could be more faithful than the most faithful prose translation" (*Sprache*, 116).

Schlegel succeeded in making good on his intention only in part. Between 1797 and 1801, he translated—with the assistance of his wife, Caroline (1763–1809)—thirteen of Shakespeare's plays, including *A Midsummer Night's Dream*, *Romeo and Juliet*, *Julius Caesar*, *The Tempest*, *Hamlet*, and *The Merchant of Venice*. Because of a falling out with his publisher and the breakup of his marriage, Schlegel had to interrupt the project and abandon it for good after the publication, in 1810, of his version of *Richard III*. Not until 1833 was the project completed, under Ludwig Tieck's direction, by the latter's daughter Dorothea and Wolf Graf von Baudissin. The result of this cooperative enterprise—the so-called Schlegel-Tieck Shakespeare—would become the classical German Shakespeare, fully vindicating Schlegel's claim to having established the "model of Shakespeare's image" in Germany. It is indeed through Schlegel's wording that such memorable lines from Shakespeare as Hamlet's "Sein oder Nichtsein, das ist hier die Frage" ("To be or not to be: that is the question" [*Hamlet*, 3.1]), or Escalus's concluding "Denn niemals gab es ein so hartes Los / Als Juliens und ihres Romeos" ("For never was a story of more woe / Than this of Juliet and her Romeo" [*Romeo and Juliet*, 5.3]), to name only two instances, have become engraved in the minds of the literate German public.

Several factors contributed to the effectiveness and longevity of Schlegel's endeavor. To begin with, unlike Borck and Wieland, Schlegel did not have to start from scratch. Not only did he have the fruits of a century-long engagement with Shakespeare to reap, he also had substantial previous translations to draw on. By the mid-1790s, he had tried his hand at rendering *A Midsummer Night's Dream* in 1788–89 (together with Gottfried August Bürger) and *Hamlet* in 1793, and thus was able to benefit from past errors. Since his intended audience was well acquainted with Shakespeare through his predecessors' accessible and readable versions, Schlegel could presume to make hitherto unprecedented aesthetic demands adequate to the range of Shakespeare's semantic and prosodic artistry and sufficiently complex and appealing to sustain their force into the present. Schlegel was also helped by the fact that in the course of the 18th century, owing to the works of Gottsched, Lessing, Klopstock, Herder, Goethe, and others, and a growing output of translations in addition to the Shakespeare translations—Wieland's Horace (1782/1786) and Johann Heinrich Voss's (1751–1826) Homer (1781/1793) are particularly noteworthy—a sophisticated German idiom had evolved, supple and capacious enough to adapt and absorb the intricacies of foreign idioms and personal styles.

So central had the cultural-aesthetic significance of translation become that, upon reading Shakespeare in Schlegel's translation, Novalis wrote to him on November 30, 1797: "For us [Germans] translations have been opportunities to grow and expand . . . To translate is as good as to write poetry, as to create original works—and more difficult . . . In the end, all poetry is translation. I am convinced that the German Shakespeare is now better than the English" (Apel, 99). And in his 1801 novel *Godwi oder Das steinerne Bild der Mutter* (*Godwi, or The Stone Image of the Mother*), Clemens Brentano went so far as to suggest that "the romantic itself is a translation" (chap. 8). The Romantics' equation of poetry with translation went hand in hand with their conception of poetry as self-reflexive or, as Friedrich Schlegel put it, as both "poetry and poetry of poetry" (*Werke*, 53). Hence, poetic translation, essentially the poetry of poetry, and, in particular, the poetic translation of one of the greatest modern poets, Shakespeare, would necessarily allow for the creation of the highest poetry. All these factors—historical, cultural, and aesthetic-poetological—contributed to creating an immensely stimulating, productive milieu for Schlegel's project. Ultimately, however, it was his own ingenuity as a translator, his capacity to enlist the ideas and aesthetic-cultural achievements of his time for his own purposes as a poet's poet, that aligned and orchestrated these factors to culminate in his vision of Shakespeare.

Schlegel, whose ultimate aim was to make the reader forget that he "has a copy before him" (*Sprache*, 117), proceeded according to three fundamental principles:

1. In language in general and in poetry in particular, form and content are inseparable. This meant that Shakespeare's iambic pentameters must be viewed

as an organic component of the overall significance of his plays, that his poetry's "recurring rhythms" must be treated as the "pulse of its life" (112). Hence, the new translation must be in iambic pentameter, reverting to prose only where Shakespeare used it. Given Schlegel's professed objective of translating the complete Shakespeare, this meant that for the first time, Germans would be able to experience as close an approximation to Shakespeare's artistry as the German idiom would permit. The fact that by the end of the 18th century blank verse—originally, an import from Britain—had been well established in German letters played in Schlegel's favor.

2. To translate as faithfully as possible. In view of Shakespeare's status as a genius, his text had to be approached with utmost care and reverence. This meant that, notwithstanding linguistic infidelities necessitated by idiomatic differences and, more importantly, by the impossible demand of simultaneous prosodic and semantic faithfulness, Shakespeare's translator had to follow "step by step the letter of his meaning" (101). "Hard may the translator's fidelity be at times," Schlegel conceded, yet "he ought not to fear being reproached for the most liberal use of the entire range of our language" (116–117). And although he will "not always be able to give line for line," he will endeavor to "reclaim the space lost in one instance in another" (110).

3. To recreate the ease and agility of Shakespeare's "simple, strong, grand, and noble" style (115). The translations must "never . . . seem heavy or cumbersome" (117) but be put into the most artless, "immediate and natural language" (110). The translator "ought rather to skip a wayward little expression than succumb to [cumbersome] paraphrase" (ibid.).

Schlegel had set himself, of course, an impossible task: to translate as faithfully as possible and to create a text that would stand on the pillars of its indigenous merits. In its scope, intent, and comprehensiveness, the project was indeed unprecedented. And while Schlegel may not have managed to adhere to all his principles concurrently, at their best his translations—such as the following particularly self-reflexive exchange between Polonius and Gertrude (*Hamlet*, 2.2.96–110)—bear out Schiller's judgment, expressed in his letter to Schlegel of March 11, 1796, that "heaven ought to be grateful" (Blinn, 2:38):

Polonius: . . . hier zu erörtern,
Was Majestät ist, was Ergebenheit,
Warum Tag Tag; Nacht Nacht; die Zeit die Zeit:
Das hieße, Nacht und Tag und Zeit verschwenden.
Weil Kürze denn des Witzes Seele ist,
Weitschweifigkeit der Leib und äußre Zierat,
Fass' ich mich kurz. Eu'r edler Sohn ist toll,
Toll nenn' ich's: denn worin besteht die Tollheit,
Als daß man gar nichts anders ist als toll?
Doch das mag sein.
Königin: Mehr Inhalt, wen'ger Kunst!
Polonius: Auf Ehr', ich brauche nicht die mindste Kunst.
Toll ist er, das ist wahr; wahr ist's, 's ist schade;

Und schade, daß es wahr ist. Doch dies ist
'ne törichte Figur: sie fahre wohl,
Denn ich will ohne Kunst zu Werke gehn.

Polonius: To expostulate
What majesty should be, what duty is,
Why day is day, night night, and time is time,
Were nothing but to waste night, day, and time.
Therefore, since brevity is the soul of wit,
And tediousness the limbs and outward flourishes,
I will be brief. Your noble son is mad:
Mad call I it; for to define true madness,
What is't but to be nothing else but mad?
But let that go.
Queen: More matter, with less art.
Polonius: Madam, I swear I use no art at all.
That he is mad, 'tis true; 'tis true 'tis pity;
And pity 'tis 'tis true: a foolish figure;
But farewell it, for I will use no art.

See also 1735, 1773, 1774, 1778, 1784, 1792 (August 26), 1800 (January)

Bibliography: Friedmar Apel, *Sprachbewegung: Eine historisch-poetologische Untersuchung zum Problem des Übersetzens* (Heidelberg: Carl Winter, 1982). Hansjürgen Blinn, ed., *Shakespeare-Rezeption: Die Diskussion um Shakespeare in Deutschland,* vol. 1: *Ausgewählte Texte von 1741 bis 1788;* vol. 2: *Ausgewählte Texte von 1793 bis 1827* (Berlin: Erich Schmidt, 1982, 1988). August Wilhelm Schlegel, *Sämmtliche Werke,* ed. Eduard Bücking, 12 vols. (Leipzig: Weidmannsche Buchhandlung, 1846–47). ———, *Sprache und Poetik,* ed. Edgar Lohner (Stuttgart: Kohlhammer, 1962). Friedrich Schlegel, *Werke in einem Band,* ed. Wolfdietrich Rasch (Vienna: Hanser, 1971). William Shakespeare, *Sämtliche Werke,* Englisch-Deutsch, trans. August Wilhelm Schlegel et al., ed. L. L. Schücking, 12 vols. (Wiesbaden: Emil Vollmer, n.d.).

Michael Eskin

♌ *1796, June 10*

Jean Paul arrives in Weimar on foot from the town of Hof

An Alien Fallen from the Moon

On June 10, 1796, Jean Paul completed the journey on foot from his impoverished home in the town of Hof to the cultural mecca of Weimar. He had been invited for a brief stay by Charlotte von Kalb, an important supporter of artists within the social world centered at the court. His arrival, to say the least, was greatly anticipated by all. Jean Paul's second novel, *Hesperus,* had been published a year earlier and had taken the German literary world by storm, surpassing in both sales and public interest Goethe's *Wilhelm Meisters Lehrjahre* and Ludwig Tieck's *William Lovell,* which appeared at the same time.

Jean Paul the author was a household name; Jean Paul the person was a mystery. However, the anecdotes describing his reception resulted, in the words of Max Kommerell, in material for "a great unwritten comedy" rather than the happy ending to the story of a parvenu. Wieland, an admirer of his work and later a close friend, listened in bemused discomfort as Jean Paul dismissed the ancient Greeks as childish and of no importance for contemporary art. Goethe spun his dinner plate in annoyance as Jean Paul elaborated his theory of tragedy; and Schiller, upon making his acquaintance, delivered the lasting image of Jean Paul in Weimar: "Alien, like one who has fallen from the moon." As he arrived in Weimar, so he remains as a literary figure: an alien, an outsider, a writer *sui generis*.

The metaphorical road taken by Jean Paul (Johann Paul Friedrich Richter, 1763–1825) to Weimar was longer than the stretch he covered on foot. After the publication of an utterly unsuccessful collection of satirical writings, *Grönländische Prozesse* (1783; *Greenlandish Processes*) at the age of twenty, he wallowed for a decade in poverty and obscurity, determined to live from his literary output but reluctant to forego the obsolete genre of satire. After a sympathetic publisher encouraged him to gather his wealth of witty ideas into novel form, Jean Paul achieved his initial breakthrough when Karl Philipp Moritz responded in awe to the unsolicited manuscript of his first novel *Unsichtbare Loge* (1793; *The Invisible Lodge*). After wondering whether Wieland or Herder might be playing a prank, Moritz exclaimed that the work had surpassed Goethe and posed the unknown author a question that is still pertinent today: "Who are you?"

Jean Paul was a major literary force in his day, one who carved his own path by consciously distancing himself from both Classicism and Romanticism. While most of his contemporaries worked through the importance of ancient Greece, Jean Paul chose decidedly modern precursors: the British authors Swift, Sterne, Fielding, and Richardson. Although his literary production remains confined to prose, one cannot comfortably classify his six main works as novels. Riddled with postponed prefaces, multiple appendices, interruptions, satirical "extra-pages," affective outpourings, and comical cold showers, the genre of the novel was radically deformed under Jean Paul's pen. Like an organist improvising through every tone and register, Jean Paul submits his ever-present themes—God and death, the "I" and the body—to continuously modulating forms of expression, as if searching for the right phrasing or key. At the center of his literary world stands an isolated, abandoned character, in all his moods and modes, as he tries to address the world, other people, his own finitude, and the possibility of a "second world." The literary language oscillates—often in abrupt counterpoint fashion—between an abundance of obscure witty analogies (which today often leave the reader helpless) and moments of lyrical expressiveness that transcend the boundaries of poetry and prose. A novel by Jean Paul, therefore, is strenuous. Goethe complained of "brain cramps" while reading him. A reviewer compared his prose to a "collection of ruins." And even his admirers, among them the philosopher Friedrich Theodor Vischer, lamented the "horse's labor" required to plow through it. Jean Paul was fully aware of the alienating effect of his literary manner. In an appendix to *Biographische Belustigungen* (1796; *Biographical Enter-*

tainments), he even put his style on trial with himself acting as defendant, prosecutor, and judge, and ultimately condemns himself to refrain from such excesses. The sentence, however, was never carried out.

Given the difficult structure and language of a Jean Paul novel, Schiller was not entirely cynical when he described the popularity of *Hesperus* as "psychologically strange." Although *Hesperus* is one of the most affective works in German literature, with tears falling on nearly every page, the main story is framed by the proto-Godot structure of the narrator waiting on an island for a dog to swim to shore and deliver reports on the characters, which are embellished to make chapters, called "Dog-Dispatches." Hence, the subtitle: *45 Hundposttage (45 Dog-Dispatch-Days)*. The dog, needless to say, often arrives too late, leaving the narrator, one "Jean Paul," with nothing to do but kill time with digressions on any subject but the plot. While the story is secondary to the meandering musings of the narrator, *Hesperus* also unleashes an emotive-poetic power previously unprecedented in a prose piece. Herder, for example, was unable to work or concentrate for days after reading the novel. Jean Paul's mobilization of intense affect explodes the boundaries of the sentimental novel. The emotions are often those of abandonment, as if the character attempted to orient himself while tumbling into an abyss. Viktor, the protagonist, holds a pseudo-death sermon over a wax double of himself, which begins as a joke and ends "with a shudder of his I": "I! I! You abyss that runs back deep into the darkness within the mirror of thought—I! You mirror within a mirror—you shudder within a shudder!" (*SW*, 1, 939). And Emanuel, an Indian mystic and Viktor's teacher, is accompanied to his grave not by the soft wings of angels, but by the harsh silence of the heavens: "Silence is the language of the world of spirits, the starry heavens the bars of its language [*Sprachgitter*], but behind the bars of stars [*Sternengitter*] appeared neither a spirit nor god" (*SW*, 1, 1135). The poet Paul Celan, for one, recognized Jean Paul's enormous insight into transcendental loneliness.

Although he never matched the success of *Hesperus*, Jean Paul was the first German author to forgo an official position and to live entirely from his writing. His oeuvre, especially when one counts his unpublished aphorisms, notes, drafts, and excerpts, is massive: six voluminous novels, three idylls, a major aesthetic treatise, a book on pedagogy, political essays, and numerous shorter prose and theoretical pieces. His third novel, *Siebenkäs* (1797; *Seven Cheeses*), is perhaps his most readable today. Siebenkäs and Leibgeber are *Doppelgänger* (a word coined here by Jean Paul) who are such good friends and so identical in appearance that they decide to exchange names. Siebenkäs (who is Leibgeber) consequently loses his inheritance and, thereby, lays the first stone that will become the death bed of his new marriage. As an advocate for the impoverished, Siebenkäs cannot make ends meet and tries his hand at writing. His drive to write continually runs aground on his good but simple wife's drive to sweep and clean; each swish of the broom or swipe of the cloth destroys the overly sensitive writer's concentration. Even their attempt to work together by candlelight—he writes, she sews—regresses into a witty charade of her trimming the wick first too late, then too early. In the end, Job's dung heap is delivered to Siebenkäs's living room: "In the 12th century one still pointed to the deteriorated dung heap upon which Job had suffered. Our two easy chairs are this dung heap and can still be viewed" (*SW,* 2, 116). *Siebenkäs* presents Jean Paul at the height of his comic precision through which he slowly dismantles the semblance of domestic bliss with a painstaking humor that at once reveals and redeems the underlying misery. For Siebenkäs, there is only one escape: not death, but the next best thing—faking death. With Leibgeber's help, Siebenkäs dies leaving both him and his wife to move on to new lives and new loves. The critical impulse of Jean Paul's comic realism is, however, writ large at the novel's end: "The dream of life is dreamed on a bed that's too hard" (*SW,* 2, 575).

Inserted into *Siebenkäs* is Jean Paul's most famous and influential work: the monstrous dream vision "Die Rede des toten Christus" ("The Discourse of the Dead Christ"). A precursor to Dostoevsky's "The Grand Inquisitor" and Nietzsche's "The Mad Man," this short text describes a dream in which the unresurrected Christ announces to his followers that there is no God; he, a poor carpenter, has been duped like the rest. Deprived of a heavenly father, humanity is orphaned in a universe driven by chance. As the world collapses into chaos, the narrator awakens from the dream, relieved that in this life he can still worship God. Although Jean Paul delivers here one of the first of God's death certificates, he wrote this text in the spirit of Jacobi, Herder, and Hamann, his philosophical allies, and in the service of a Pietist-tinged furor to inspire such fear at the loss of God that renewed faith would necessarily result. The concluding affirmation of faith, however, is at best ambivalent: The subjective desire for a God fully usurps the question of his objective existence. Even if there is no God, one should believe so as to make this life bearable, a thought Jean Paul never surrendered. However, it was not as a religious-philosophical text that "The Discourse of the Dead Christ" left its mark: Through Madame de Staël's translation into French in 1811 (omitting the final awakening), its literary images and existential ideas came to exert a powerful influence on Gérard de Nerval, Victor Hugo, Honoré de Balzac, Jules Michelet, Charles Baudelaire, and Gustave Flaubert.

Jean Paul was never short on strange, humorous, or monstrous ideas for structuring his texts: he writes a story with footnotes that correspond to nothing in it (*Des Feldpredigers Schmelze Reise nach Flätz,* 1809); a doctor collects deformities in nature—six-fingered hands, eight-legged rabbits—and dreams of being born with a Siamese twin on his back (*Dr. Katzenbergers Badereise,* 1809). Even his fragmentary autobiography is presented by a "professor of the history of himself" (*Selberlebens-beschreibung,* 1819). Yet his wittiest idea is also his most widely read story: the idyll *Leben des vergnügten Schulmeisterlein Maria Wutz in Auenthal (The Life of the Cheerful Little Schoolmaster Maria Wutz in Auenthal),* included as an appendix to his first novel, *Unsichtbare Loge* of 1793. Eager to stay abreast of the rapidly advancing *Zeitgeist* but too poor to afford books, Wutz writes his own library, filling it with titles such as *Kant's Critique of Pure Reason* or *Goethe's The Sorrows of Young Werther.* Although Wutz studies his idiosyncratic library with the love of a philologist, his intellectual capacity does not quite match his literary-philosophical zeal. In writing his treatise on space and time, for example, he knows no better than to define them as "the inner *space* of a ship and that *time* of the month, which one calls menstruation" (*SW,* 1, 426). Wutz, it must be admitted, is a bit ridiculous. But this childlike fool possesses a will to happiness in the midst of misery that is expressed in the story's subtitle, *Eine Art Idylle (A Sort of Idyll).* In *Wutz* (and later *Quintus Fixlein* and *Das Leben Fibel*), Jean Paul fundamentally reforms the idyll genre. Although he defines the idyll as "complete happiness in limitation," the limitations (usually socioeconomic) are enormous, while the happiness is utterly subjective and bitterly fought for. One must tarry in the face of the quotidian and discover "microscopic amusements" where otherwise are none. Although the Biedermeier style took over where Jean Paul left off in his idylls, Nietzsche was only partially correct when he called Jean Paul "a curse in pajamas." The light Jean Paul casts on the everyday is not the petty bourgeois celebration of simplicity, but the first glow of redemption shed upon the triviality of the quotidian.

In the course of his career, the comic came to play an ever more central role in Jean Paul's writing. In his aesthetic treatise *Vorschule der Ästhetik* (1804; translated as *The Horn of Oberon*), Jean Paul became the first writer to place notions of the comic at the center of his aesthetic thought. Discussions of the beautiful and the sublime yield to lengthy explications of the ridiculous ("the infinitely small" and "the arch-enemy of the sublime"), wit ("the disguised priest who marries every couple"), and the cornerstone of Jean Paul's own theory and praxis: humor. Jean Paul's humorist is always, in part, a melancholic, one who goes through life's stages with "a tragic mask, at least in the hand" (*SW,* 5, 129). Humor is not simply an aesthetic category, but an entire worldview: "When man, as in ancient theology, looks down from the extramundane world onto the mundane, then it drifts by small and futile. When man measures out and links the infinite world with the small world, as humor does, then a laughter emerges, wherein both pain and grandeur abide" (*SW,* 5, 129). The perspective of humor is not one from the clouds looking down on the world and scorning its futility. Rather, the humorist has his feet firmly on the ground, he collects all the moments of finitude and uses them to measure the infinite distance to the infinite world. Failing miserably in his task, the humorist doubles over with sublime laughter that pains and uplifts, owing to the ridiculousness of the project. Humor adheres to what Jean Paul calls a *lex inversa;* it is the world viewed as a great carnival, in which "man's road to hell paves for him a road to heaven" (*SW,* 5, 129).

Together with Hölderlin and Kleist, Jean Paul belongs to a triumvirate of non-classifiable writers between Classicism and Romanticism. Yet whereas Hölderlin and Kleist were relatively unknown in their day and met critical acclaim only in the 20th century, Jean Paul was a literary phenomenon in his lifetime. And yet, apart from the fundamental critical work by Max Kommerell, Kurt Wölfel, and a few others, Jean Paul has not enjoyed the scholarly interest that has been showered on the other two. Since his death, Jean Paul has been read intensely by those readers who perhaps matter the most: other authors. Except for Goethe, perhaps no writer has had a greater influence on German literature than Jean Paul. Among his admirers are Gottfried Keller, Adalbert Stifter, Robert Walser, Hugo von Hofmannsthal, Oskar Loerke, Paul Celan, and Thomas Bernhard. But it was Stefan George who most profoundly delineated the significance of Jean Paul. In a eulogy from 1896, George reunited Jean Paul and Goethe, just as they had met a century earlier in Weimar. This encounter had, however, a different outcome. George undertook a radical revision of the German literary tradition, insisting upon two centers of gravity within it—one occupied by Goethe, the other by Jean Paul. Goethe, in sum, must yield half the pedestal to Jean Paul. If Goethe, ever the great observer, is the master of clarity, precision, and balanced construction, then Jean Paul, the dreamer, provides the object's aura, colors, hues, and tones. For the poet George, Goethe is the architect of the German language, Jean Paul its musician. In this second, figurative return to Weimar, Jean Paul no longer appears as "one who has fallen from the moon," but as "the most forgotten" German author.

See also 1773, 1782, 1792 (August 26), 1786, 1796-1797, 1806, 1882, 1897

Bibliography: Stefan George, "Jean Paul," in Tage und Taten (Berlin: Georg Bondi, 1927). Hugo von Hofmannsthal, "Blick auf Jean Paul," in Gesammelte Werke: Reden und Aufsätze I (Frankfurt am Main: Fischer, 1979). Timothy J. Casey, ed., Jean Paul: A Reader, trans. Erika Casey (Baltimore: Johns Hopkins University Press, 1992). Jean Paul, The Horn of Oberon: Jean Paul Richter's School for Aesthetics, trans. Margaret R. Hale (Detroit, Mich.: Wayne State University Press, 1973). ———, Sämtliche Werke [SW], ed. Nobert Miller et al. (Munich: Hanser, 1959–). Max Kommerell, Jean Paul (Frankfurt am Main: Klosterman, 1977). Kurt Wölfel, Jean Paul-Studien (Frankfurt am Main: Suhrkamp, 1989). R. R. Wuthenow, "Jean-Paul-Aufsätze," in Des Luftschiffers Gianozzo Seebuch und Über die natürliche Magie der Einbildungskraft (Frankfurt am Main: Insel, 1975).

Paul Fleming

🜔 1796–1797

A one-page description of German Idealism is jotted down by an unknown author

A New Program for the Aesthetic Education of Mankind?

When Franz Rosenzweig first published this single sheet of paper, written on both sides in Hegel's hand, in 1917, it created a small sensation in philosophical circles, and it has been the subject of hundreds of scholarly articles ever since. Rosenzweig gave the fragment the title "Das älteste Systemprogramm des deutschen Idealismus" (The Oldest System Program of German Idealism), maintaining that the text itself was a copy and its real author was not Hegel but Schelling. Rosenzweig's thesis was challenged by Wilhelm Böhm, who thought he detected Hölderlin's voice in the writing. The aesthetic passages in the second half of the *Systemprogramm,* in particular, he tried to show, expressed ideas only Hölderlin held at the time. Although Ludwig Strauß agreed with Böhm, he nevertheless tried to resuscitate the Schelling thesis one year later. While the passages in question, he contended, are clearly the result of Schelling's conversations with Hölderlin in the second half of 1795, they are not sufficient for establishing the latter's authorship.

In 1965, Otto Pöggeler gave the debate a new direction when he insisted that the text was not a copy at all but was composed by Hegel himself. Pöggeler's thesis was disseminated with authoritative force by the Hegel-Archive, of which he was the director. As such, it is now the most widely accepted version. Nevertheless, no real consensus exists and the *Systemprogramm* continues to appear in the standard editions of all three thinkers. In this conflict, only the date when the page was written can be stated with reasonable certainty, based on the paper's watermark and other criteria: the end of 1796 or early 1797, which is the time when Hegel joined his friend Hölderlin in Frankfurt.

The main reason for the difficulty of determining the authorship lies in the writing's rhetorical and programmatic, even agitatory, nature. The author states with supreme confidence what remains to be done in philosophy after Kant and promises to carry it out himself. Much of the writing sounds like slogans, encapsulating ideas not uncommon for the time. They could have been used (and indeed were used) by various writers in late-18th-century Germany. The author of the fragment concludes with the promise that he will present the public with something that can establish "universal freedom and equality of spirits" and provide a key to "the last, the greatest work of mankind." This, too, has contemporary programmatic parallels, most prominently in Schiller's *Letters on the Aesthetic Education of Man.*

Many commentators have attempted to establish the authorship of their favored thinker by citing from his published works phrases or words that correspond to key phrases or words in the *Systemprogramm.* Not surprisingly, this strategy has not met with much success. Too many of the passages can be matched with roughly similar passages in the writings of too many authors to be of help in establishing the authorship of the fragment with any degree of certainty. None of the passages, it seems, has a unique and sole occurrence in the works of only one of the three candidates.

A reasonable alternative strategy, therefore, is to take a closer look at those passages for which no matches can be found. Two passages, in particular, have no pendant in the works of Schelling, Hölderlin, or Hegel. Consequently commentators have glossed over these in relative silence.

The first of these passages is found in the opening paragraph of the fragment: "I would like to lend wings once again to our sluggish physics, advancing so laboriously by experiments. So if philosophy provides the ideas, experience the data, we can finally arrive at the physics on a grand scale that I expect of future ages. It does not appear that present-day physics can satisfy a creative spirit, such as ours is, or ought to be." The second passage, even more enigmatic than the first, occurs in the second half of the text: "Monotheism of reason and of the heart, polytheism of the imagination and of art, this is what we need!"

As long as we confine our view to the works of three possible authors of the *Systemprogramm,* these passages resist comprehension. The physics of the first passage is not at all identical with the speculative "Spinozism of physics" for which Schelling later became famous. For the second passage, there is not even the faintest echo in the works of any of the three. However, as soon as we broaden our horizon, we note that both passages are allusions to Goethe. The second one is a variant of one of Goethe's favorite sayings that has entered into his *Maximen und Reflexionen* and into a letter to F. Jacobi of January 6, 1813, for example. The first takes up Goethe's theory of physics and especially his critique of the use of isolated experiments in the investigation of nature, as formulated in his essay "The Experiment as Mediator between Object and Subject" (1792), but also in "Excerpt from 'Studies for a Physiology of Plants'" (1795), which apparently was a fruit of his discussions with Schiller. The two texts had not yet appeared in print when the *Systemprogramm* was composed— nor had the passage on monotheism. Whoever wrote the sentences of the *Systemprogramm* must have been in contact with Goethe and have had access to his thinking at the time.

Of the three candidates, only Hölderlin fits this criterion. In November 1795, when Schelling was still a student at the Tübingen *Stift* and Hegel worked as a private tutor in Switzerland, Hölderlin moved to Jena, where he lived close to Schiller and was an almost daily guest at his house. This also led to frequent encounters with Goethe. As he wrote to his friend Neuffer on April 28, 1795: "I still always drop by to see Schiller, where I now usually meet up with Goethe." Of the approximately eighteen weeks Hölderlin spent in Jena, Goethe was present during seven and a half weeks. And it was mostly scientific activities that brought him to Jena: anatomical and optical experiments, botanical observations, and, of course, visits to the new botanical garden. Another reason for Goethe's frequent visits to Jena was his friendship and collaboration with Schiller, which arose from their famous encounter outside a meeting of the Jena Society for Scientific Research in July 1794. On that occasion, Goethe had tried to sketch a symbolic plant to illustrate the metamorphosis of plants, but was met with Schiller's deep-seated skepticism: "This is not an observation from experience, but an idea," Schiller objected to Goethe's presentation. "Then I may rejoice that I have ideas without knowing it, and can even see them with my own eyes," Goethe replied with some annoyance. Even though on the face of it Goethe's *scientia intuitiva* and Schiller's strict Kantianism are difficult to reconcile, both men realized that the ground for fruitful joint endeavors might have been laid. Thus when rewriting his *Letters on Aesthetic Education* for publication, Schiller tried to make his thoughts more appealing to Goethe. This can be seen especially in the footnote to the thirteenth *Letter,* where Schiller gives a Goethean explanation for the "slow progress" of the natural sciences in terms of their propensity toward teleological judgments. Goethe did indeed have a well-known aversion toward teleological judgments in the sciences. But he saw the reason for the slow progress of physics elsewhere, namely, in its erroneous dependence on isolated experiments—a view he developed further in the essay "The Experiment as Mediator between Object and Subject."

By virtue of his presence in Jena, Hölderlin became a witness to the debates between Goethe and Schiller. If the passage in the *Systemprogramm* about the "sluggish physics, advancing so laboriously by experiments" that it needs to be lent wings could be attributed to Hölderlin, it would suddenly appear in a new light: namely, as his taking a stand in the debate, and as implicitly criticizing Schiller's explanation in the thirteenth *Letter* from Goethe's point of view. But why should Hölderlin take a stand on this issue at all? He was busy with his novel *Hyperion* and he had plans for a work to which he gave the title "Ideal einer Volkserziehung" (Ideal for a System of Popular Education), as he wrote to Hegel from Jena. When he was invited to contribute articles to Niethammer's new journal, he promised to compose "philosophical letters" on that topic, more precisely, *New Letters on the Aesthetic Education of Man*. Yet Hölderlin was not the only one who competed with Schiller concerning the education of man. Goethe published a series of novellas, *Unterhaltungen deutscher Ausgewanderter (Conversations of German Emigrants),* in Schiller's magazine *Horen* that contained an alternative to, and implicit criticism of, Schiller's educational ideal. Then there was Fichte, who developed in his lectures a theory that was incompatible with Schiller's. Before long, it led to the *Horenstreit* (Horen dispute), which resulted in Schiller's break with Fichte and a temporary estrangement of Fichte from Goethe. Hölderlin, who attended Fichte's lectures and was so close to all three of them that he must have been able to anticipate what was coming, left town shortly before the conflict erupted: "A flight," in his own words, "from people and books."

But now a hypothesis suggests itself that is worth exploring: Could it be that the *Systemprogramm* is a sketch of, or plan for, Hölderlin's *New Letters on the Aesthetic Education of Man?* And since its date coincides with Hegel's arrival in Frankfurt, perhaps occasioned by Hölderlin's wish to share his literary plans with the friend he had not seen in several years? If we consider this hypothesis seriously, a different strategy for reading the text suggests itself. Rather than searching for matching sentences in the works of the putative authors, it might be more fruitful to look for similar passages in the writings of the authors against whom Hölderlin set off his own position, and who provided the foil for his educational program: Schiller, Fichte, and Goethe. We already noticed references to Goethe and Schiller in two passages. What about the others?

Interestingly, all the key ideas in the first paragraph, up to the physics passage, vary or reiterate views Fichte expressed in his lectures while Hölderlin was in Jena, or to which Hölderlin had access in written form: all future problems in philosophy will fall under moral theory; the representation of the self is an idea; the world emerges with the I in a "creation out of nothing." All of these are theorems central to Fichte's theory of consciousness, which he developed in his lectures and which the author of the *Systemprogramm* endorses.

After the excursion into the Goethean theory of nature, he turns to another topic that found expression in Fichte's lectures (as well as in several other authors): namely, that humanity is an ideal, and that the state, as something mechanical, is a mere means to the realization of a truly human society, something that eventually must be overcome and abolished. The *Systemprogramm,* however, is peculiar in that, while it by no means advocates anarchy, it also does not advocate the Fichtean superiority of the moral over nature, according to which the physical realm is merely the sensuous material for the realization of our duty. On the contrary, the ideas of nature as well as those falling under the rubric *Menschenwerk* (human creation)—ideas of government and legislation as well as ideas of "a moral world" with its own legislation—are emphatically declared to be subsumed under a higher idea that unites them all. Incidentally, such subordination of all moral legislation to a still higher realm of "unwritten laws" is thematized and elaborated in a fragment by Hölderlin that dates from the same time as our text. This fragment had the earlier title "On Religion" but is now recognized as a draft for his essay *New Letters on the Aesthetic Education of Man.* In the *Systemprogramm,* the idea in which "truth and goodness" are said to be sisters is the idea of "beauty, taking the word in the higher Platonic sense."

Virtually all commentators on the *Systemprogramm* agree that the reflections on beauty "in the higher Platonic sense" are Hölderlin's in spirit. The same views lie at the heart of the Athenian speech in his novel *Hyperion* and inform most of his lyric compositions. Even before coming to Jena, Hölderlin had written to Neuffer that he planned to write an essay on "the aesthetic ideas," and that he wanted to base his reflections on a passage in Plato's *Phaedrus* (probably 250d–251a). The author of the *Systemprogramm* now conjoins the thought of a Platonic hierarchy of ideas, with beauty its supreme member, with the program of an education of mankind and with the goal of "universal freedom and equality" of all spirits: "Until we render the ideas aesthetic, that is, mythological, they are of no interest to the *people,* and conversely until mythology is rational, the philosopher must be ashamed of it."

The glorious and inspired concluding passages of the *Systemprogramm* that demand a new mythology, a mythology of reason as the last and greatest work of mankind, have often been claimed for Schelling and Hegel. After all, it was Hegel who expressed the need for a new mythology as early as 1793 (in the so-called Tübingen Fragment), and Schelling's interest in mythology can likewise be traced to his student days. However, this apparent ease of ascription to either one of the two philosophers requires that we take lightly the *Systemprogramm*'s striking qualification that the mythology of reason is not to be expected from a philosopher. It is not to be expected from a philosopher, because, as the author of the *Systemprogramm* states a few lines earlier, all philosophy must come to an end, as must history and the political state: "Poetry alone will survive all the other sciences and arts." Rather, "a higher spirit, sent from heaven, must found this new religion among us." Yet this new religion, paradoxically, is heralded in the same breath as the "the last, the greatest work of mankind." So if the author of the fragment plans to carry out the proposed project himself, he must be philosopher enough to challenge Schiller, Goethe, and Fichte on the requirements for an education of humanity. He must also think of himself as a poet, as a "spirit sent from heaven," as well as a member of mankind.

In whom are such attributes combined? Only in Hölderlin. Schelling and Hegel both regarded him as their philosophical equal at this time, and for a while he planned to lecture at the side of Fichte and Schiller at the University of Jena. Only Hölderlin can think of himself as a divine messenger: "Holy vessels are the poets" *(Buonaparte)*. The conviction that divine inspiration shapes the poet's work found a classical expression in Plato's *Phaedrus,* where poetry is described as a "divine gift," as an inspired "product of a madness that comes from the Gods" (244a, 245a). Hölderlin stands squarely in this tradition: "To grasp the Father's ray, no less, with our own two hands / And, wrapping in song the heavenly gift / To offer it to the people" *(Wie wenn am Feiertage . . .)*. Accordingly, it is in this "higher Platonic sense" that he sees his own vocation: "To serve the Highest" *(Dichterberuf)* and "seized by the power of jubilant madness" *(Brot und Wein),* to become a "teacher of mankind."

If this is so, we must read the *Systemprogramm* as Hölderlin's vision of his *New Letters on the Aesthetic Education of Man*—a work that, to our loss, had to remain a fragment.

See also 1786, 1790, 1792 (August 26), 1808, 1828 (Winter), 1913

Bibliography: Mythologie der Vernunft, ed. Christoph Jamme and Helmut Schneider (Frankfurt am Main: Suhrkamp, 1984. "The Oldest System Programme of German Idealism," trans. Taylor Carmen, *European Journal of Philosophy* 3/2 (1995): 172–174. Eckart Förster, "'To Lend Wings to Physics Once Again': Hölderlin and the Oldest System Programme of German Idealism," *European Journal of Philosophy* 3/2 (1995): 174–198.

Eckart Förster

✑ *1799, June*

Alexander von Humboldt and Aimé Bonpland embark on a research voyage to South America

Holistic Vision and Colonial Critique

Although he achieved international renown during his lifetime, Alexander von Humboldt (1769–1859) has since fallen into relative obscurity. From one perspective, this decline may be attributed to the fact that his research did not fit into a specific area of knowledge but included such fields as botany, chemistry, plant geography, physical geography, zoology, economics, and cultural and literary history, all of which have since become autonomous disciplines. Specialization had already begun in the first half of the 19th century, but in this early phase the individual disciplines could still be integrated under the heading of *Naturphilosophie* (natural philosophy).

There are deeper philosophical reasons for Humboldt's holistic views, how-

ever. Above all, we can understand his work as an attempt to offer an integrated view of man in the cosmos, formulated in a way that would undo
the dichotomies that had plagued science and philosophy since the ancient
Greeks. Humboldt indicates the encompassing character of his vision at the
very beginning of his magnum opus, *Kosmos* (1845–1862; *Cosmos*): "Beginning
with the depths of space and the regions of remotest nebulae, we will gradually
descend through the starry zone to which our solar system belongs, to our
own terrestrial spheroid, circled by air and ocean, there to direct our attention
to its form, temperature, and magnetic tension, and to consider the fullness of
organic life unfolding itself upon its surface beneath the vivifying influence of
light" (trans. Otte, 79–80). In a letter of July 5, 1799, written in La Coruña,
Humboldt makes a larger claim for his research trip than its more obvious goal
of taking astronomic measurements, observing fauna and flora, and collecting
fossils: his purpose, rather, is to discover the interrelation between animate and
inanimate nature and to establish the harmony in which they exist.

These principles underlie his two works of synthesis, *Ansichten der Natur*
(1807; *Views of Nature*) and *Kosmos.* His aim, as he formulates it in *Ansichten der
Natur,* is nothing less than to uncover "the influence of the physical on the
moral world, the mysterious reciprocity between the sensorial and the external
world . . . when it is viewed from a higher plane" (247). The mystery he wants
to solve is that of the mutual influence *(Ineinanderwirken)* of the knowable and
the sensorial worlds. The same idea reappears in a more exhaustive treatment
in the French preface to *Kosmos,* where he argues that the interaction between mind and nature opens up the creative powers of the human spectator.
Humboldt was so immersed in this romantic view that his holistic aims could
not be met by purely scientific exploration. In most of his works of synthesis,
Humboldt seeks to integrate scientific observation with an imaginative and
emotional response he wishes to spark in the reader. In other words, he argues
against Descartes's opposition between idea, taken as the correct representation
of the observed phenomena, and image, a representation that is compromised
by the interference of feelings. Yet his method was quite different from that of
Novalis, who, though himself a scientist, believed that mystic exploration transcended what he regarded as the poverty of science. Humboldt's holism may
owe something to Goethe, who emphasized man's sense of awe before the interrelated laws that govern nature. In placing scientific and sensory experience
under the aegis of a common aesthetic, Humboldt's holism was a utopian project. This may be the deeper reason why modern readers tend to neglect it.

Humboldt's education had provided an excellent preparation for his voyage to South America. He received scientific training at the University of
Göttingen and at the Freiburg Mining School, where he studied under Abraham Werner, the creator of a new historical geology. Humboldt also studied
under the botanists Christian Wilhelm Dohm and Carl Ludwig Willdenow. At
the same time, he acquired and learned how to handle geographic and astronomical instruments. He was deeply influenced by his personal acquaintance
with Georg Forster, who participated in Captain Cook's second exploration

voyage. In Forster's company, Humboldt went on a preparatory expedition through Germany, the Low Countries, France, and England. With this background and a quite substantial private fortune at his disposal, Humboldt decided to start his career as a *Forschungsreisender* (research traveler). In 1798 he was in Paris, where he associated with the French botanist Aimé Bonpland (1753–1858), who was to be his travel companion on the South American journey. Initially they sought out Bougainville, in order to join him on his research trip to the South Pole, and later Captain Baudin, who was preparing to circumnavigate the world. As both of these attempts failed, Humboldt and Bonpland decided to focus on the Spanish colonies in South America. From January to May, Humboldt was in Spain, where he performed preparatory barometric measurements. In March of the same year, thanks mainly to his acquaintance with the enlightened minister Mariano Luis de Urquijo, and after an audience with King Carlos IV of Spain and his consort, Maria Luisa, Humboldt was given a special passport that would allow him and Bonpland to conduct research freely in the New World. They also had the support of the Marquis of Iranda, Simón de Arragora, who persuaded the Madrid bankers Mendelssohn and Friedlander to underwrite the project.

In June 1799 Humboldt and Bonpland embarked on a corvette for the Canary Islands. On July 13 they sighted the South American coast; on the night of the 14th, they disembarked in Venezuela. There they began the research that was to take them first to Cuba, then back to Venezuela, Colombia, Ecuador, the viceroyalties of Peru and Nueva España (Mexico), and again Cuba, from where they proceeded to the United States and then to Europe, arriving at the port of Bordeaux in June 1804. Humboldt estimated his total expenses for the journey as more than one third of his personal estate.

In 1807, after settling in Paris, he began to write the first part of his and Bonpland's most inclusive travel report: *Relation historique du voyage aux regions equinoxiales du Nouveau Continent (Historical Narrative of the Voyage to the Equinoctial Regions of the New Continent)*. The first edition was published in three volumes (Paris, 1814–1825). This work was the most important part of the so-called *Corpus americanum,* which ranged from his 1807 work on the "geography of plants" through essays on politics in the New World to the 1834 *Geographical History of the New Continent*. These works were all written in French and published in Paris, but some, such as the political essay on "New Spain," were rapidly translated into German.

The South American reception of this enormous body of work was as laudatory as had been the international recognition of his works of synthesis, *Views of Nature* and, above all, *Cosmos*. Yet despite early praise of his lively descriptions and more recent assessments of Humboldt as a key figure in the history of Latin American culture, no systematic study of Humboldt's work has to date been attempted. The task would be enormous, given the extraordinary range of Humboldt's and Bonpland's research: their account of the different climates of the region they had studied, their measurements of the height of mountain chains, and Humboldt's critical observations about the regime imposed on the Indians by the religious missions and the political-economic strategies implemented by Spain, and his prognosis for the colonies' future political independence and economic and cultural potential. Humboldt argued against the view held by many European naturalists, travelers, and thinkers, who characterized the New World as marked by unhealthy lands, terrible vegetation, frail animal species, and inferior races. Buffon (1707–1788), De Pauw (1739–1799), Raynal (1713–1796), and above all Hegel (1770–1831) are some of the thinkers who viewed the new continent as structurally incapable of rivaling Europe. Hegel remarks in his *Enzyklopädie der philosophischen Wissenschaften* (1817; *Encyclopedia of Philosophy*) that the New World can only be a "booty for Europe." The Old World, in contrast, represents a perfect triad: torpid Africa, "the inarticulate spirit which has not awakened into consciousness"; Asia, "characterized by Bacchanalian extravagance and cometary eccentricity"; and Europe, which "forms the consciousness, the rational part, of the earth, the balance of rivers and valleys and mountains—whose center is Germany" (2: 350). Four years later, Hegel makes similar arguments in his *Vorlesungen über die Philosophie der Geschichte* (delivered starting in 1821, posthumously published; *Lectures on the Philosophy of History*).

In contrast to Hegel, Humboldt avoided terms that denigrated the new continent. And, against Hegel's linear Eurocentrism, he presented a more complex view of the American native cultures, arguing that it would be wrong to judge the civilizations of Mexico and Peru according to the same principles we use when speaking of ancient Greece and Rome. Unlike many of his contemporaries, Humboldt neither portrayed the New World as a promised land nor blamed the conquerors for having destroyed a new Greece. In fact, Humboldt was not trying to antagonize De Pauw or Hegel. Rather, he showed that empirical knowledge opposes a priori speculation.

In the *Historical Narrative,* Humboldt notes a difference between the old and the new forms of colonization. In the colonies of ancient times, "intellectual culture, modified by different forms of government, frequently brought on the envy of the metropolises. Through this happy competition, arts and letters achieved their heyday in Ionia, on the Greek mainland, and in Sicily." This lucky competition has not been repeated in the modern colonies, separated from their centers by great distances. The history of these colonies contains only "two notable events: their foundation and their break from the mother land" (II, 379). His understanding of the major difficulties faced by the new colonies prevents him from idealizing them. Having lived in Latin America during the time of the wars of independence, Humboldt realizes that one of the reasons the movement for independence was not unanimously supported by the population is that in each community a few privileged families preferred "to be deprived of certain rights rather than share them with others" and chose foreign domination "in place of authority administered by Americans belonging to an inferior caste" (IV, 168). In the same passage, he comments on the consequence of the predominance of rural over urban life. As the colonists spent most of their lives in the field, engaged in agricultural or mining activities, they lacked an effective community spirit and, although they had chosen an autonomous government that would allow them the "full freedom of commerce," they had as a matter of fact opted for "the idleness and the habits of a life of indolence" (ibid.). This indolence, furthermore, implied an absence of intellectual curiosity. In contrast with the traditions of North American colonization, literacy was not encouraged: "The number of persons aware of the necessity of reading is not very large, and this is true even in those Spanish colonies which show a higher level of civilization" (IV, 213–214). A metropolitan policy that placed no trust in the populace, Humboldt adds, was responsible for this state of affairs. As a result, ambition was limited among the colonial subjects: "One could say that they live not to enjoy their lives but only to aggrandize them" (IV, 215).

Thus, it would be a mistake to conclude that Humboldt's *Historical Narrative* is just a reply to arbitrary and abstract disparagement of South America. Although Humboldt was clearly enthusiastic about the possibilities of conducting wide-ranging research in the vast unexplored area, he also sympathized, albeit covertly, with the political cause of the Spanish colonies. This, however, does not make him a disseminator of the *leyenda negra* of Spain in Europe. The actual situation he faced was much more complex. Consider, for instance, the condition of the black slaves. Humboldt does not fail to recognize, on the one hand, the "mildness of the Spanish legislation, compared with the Black Code of most of the colonizers in both Indias" (III, 224). On the other hand, this relatively positive aspect does not alter the fact that "civil authority is powerless in everything that concerns domestic slavery" (225). Not even the governor's power is sufficient "to reform the abuses virtually inherent in the European colonization system" (226).

In addition to Humboldt's interests in physical research and the state of human society, he was also eager to investigate pre-Columbian history. By comparing what had happened in America with the great changes that had occurred in Central Asia, about which there was ample knowledge, he explained that in America economic factors were decisive: "The steppes, although more fertile than those in Asia, have remained without flocks, because meridional American prairies lack animals that furnish abundant milk" (VI, 71). Consequently, economics determined the politics of the great pre-Columbian empires, their customs, and the kind of monuments and works of art they left behind. Humboldt argued that pre-Columbian civilization was unlike Greek civilization for quite concrete reasons that, contrary to Hegel's interpretation, were not a sign of constitutional weakness and inferiority.

Humboldt's holism encompasses research in the fields of general geography (including the investigation of fauna and flora) and history (socioeconomic and political, contemporary, colonial, and pre-Columbian). For European readers, South America was a remote land, thick with imaginary associations and feelings accumulated mostly since the 18th century. Yet in the many thousands of pages of his travel report, Humboldt never once exploits a scene for its exotic character.

His political essays on the viceroyalty of New Spain and the island of Cuba take a similar approach. In his *Essai politique sur la Nouvelle Espagne (Political Essay on New Spain)*, Humboldt first concentrates on the topography. On the one hand, because of the cordilleras, only the coasts enjoy the warm climate necessary for the production of goods that compete with Caribbean production (sugar, indigo, cotton, and bananas); on the other hand, the region's huge metal deposits are found at lower altitudes than in Peru, which facilitates their exploitation. In addition, New Spain suffers a shortage of navigable rivers. All in all, however, Humboldt's evaluation is quite positive. If the viceroyalty's natural resources were well cultivated, it would be able to supply the world with all the tropical products needed (sugar, cochineal, cocoa, coffee, and so on), as well as timber and minerals, particularly iron and copper. The defects of colonial administration, however, discourage exploitation of these resources. Humboldt's criticism becomes emphatic when he describes the *encomienda* system, in force until the reign of Charles III (1759–1788), under which soldiers and men of letters who had stood out in the conquest submitted entire Indian tribes to forced labor. Though the system was later abolished, Indians were eventually placed under the permanent tutelage of landowners because legal rights were restricted to white men. Humboldt's vehement condemnation of this situation is expressed in a most polite tone. He points out that the decimation of the Aztec priests has led to ignorance on the part of the Indian populations about their own culture. Unable to avenge themselves on their conquerors, they frequently acted as agents of oppression against their own brothers. In an incisive synthesis, Humboldt characterized Mexico as rife with inequalities.

In short, for Humboldt, the problems that colonial Mexico faced would be easily solved if there were "a free and well-ruled people" (290). Expressing in the language of his own time his enlightened libertarian ideals and liberal political and economic positions, Humboldt concluded his work with the hope that his analyses would convince the authorities that the welfare of whites would be ensured on a long-term basis if equal freedom were also extended to the Indians, "this race that strong oppression has humiliated but not degraded."

See also 1647 (Olearius), 1784, 1789, 1800, 1828 (Winter), 1831

Bibliography: Alexander von Humboldt, *Kosmos: Entwurf einer physischen Weltbeschreibung*, 5 vols. (Stuttgart-Tübingen: J. C. Cotta, 1845–1862). ———, *Cosmos: A Sketch of the Physical Description of the Universe*, trans. E. C. Otte, 2 vols. (Baltimore and London: Johns Hopkins University Press, 1997). ———, *Ansichten der Natur* (1807; 3rd enlarged and improved edition, 1849).— ———, *Relation historique du voyage aux regions equinoxiales du Nouveau Continent, fait en 1799, 1800, 1801, 1802, 1803 et 1804* (Paris, 1814–1825). G. W. F. Hegel, *Enzyklopädie der philosophischen Wissenschaften im Grundrisse*, 3 vols. (1830; Frankfurt am Main: Suhrkamp, 1986). G. Brude-Firnau, "Alexander von Humboldt's Sociopolitical Intentions: Science and Politics," in *Traditions of Experiment from the Enlightenment to the Present: Essays in Honor of Peter Demetz*, ed. David Wellbery and Nancy Kaiser (Ann Arbor: University of Michigan Press, 1992), 45–62. Mary Louise Pratt, "Alexander von Humboldt and the Reinvention of America," in *Imperial Eyes: Travel Writing and Transculturation* (London and New York: Routledge, 1992), 111–143.

Luiz Costa Lima

𝒬 *1800*

Publication of "Hymns to the Night" establishes Novalis as the prophet of romantic supernaturalism

Intimations of Mortality

One can easily get the impression that Friedrich von Hardenberg (1772–1801), better known as Novalis, must have been the author of a prodigious body of work. How else to explain the prominence he is accorded in literary histories, the still growing mountain of scholarship devoted to every aspect of his writings, the important part he has played in stirring the imagination of writers from Edgar Allan Poe and Gérard de Nerval to Hugo von Hofmannsthal and Stefan George? Yet Novalis's noteworthy writings would comfortably find room in one sizable paperback (an English version of which has yet to be produced). His literary output proper would take up only about one-third of that volume, and most of that section would be filled by two unfinished novels: *Heinrich von Ofterdingen* (1802; *Henry of Ofterdingen*) and *Die Lehrlinge zu Sais* (1802; *The Novices at Sais*), which, though attractive to readers drawn to a florid image of Romanticism, precious and allegorical as they are, have tended to alienate many others. In the slender corpus that remains, one comes across well-crafted poems and beautiful devotional songs—nothing that might immortalize an author—until one reaches the poem known as "Hymnen an die Nacht" (1800; Hymns to the Night), a cycle of six prose poems interspersed with verses concerned with mortality and its transfiguration in religious illumination. It is only a small exaggeration to claim that Novalis's towering literary reputation rests primarily on these dozen pages.

This poetic cycle stands out so powerfully in form, linguistic sensibility, and conceptual depth that even its widely acknowledged historical position—as a milestone in German, indeed European, literature—is far surpassed by its palpable literary force. Unlike many of Novalis's other writings (and writings of the period in general), "Hymns" has retained much of its affective charge. It continues to captivate readers with the richly crafted profusion of its images; it continues to perplex; it cuts to the bone, refusing to be dismissed by the hand of history, which arranges its objects in orderly patterns while keeping them at bay. This poem does not permit the reader—even from a distance of more than two hundred years, across an ocean, and through another language—to flatter it with adjectives such as "important" or "exemplary," for what it has to say is something urgent. Though the urgency is clearly audible, the intense concentration of language and thought, while pushing the poem toward an imaginary core, radiates outward and leads us to a fresh understanding of Novalis's work as a whole. Because it is the only major literary text the poet brought to completion—the only work, in the term's strongest sense—it gives the measure of his poetic talent and invigorates the reception of the writings he was unable to complete before his untimely death at twenty-eight.

That death, scarcely half a year after "Hymns" first appeared in print, has consistently cast its shadow over its reception. And for good reason: since the anticipation of death is the poem's main concern, it is difficult not to read it as a proleptic—even prophetic—meditation on the poet's own death. Novalis had most likely already contracted tuberculosis when, in the summer of 1800, he published the poem in what turned out to be the last issue of *Athenäum,* a journal edited by his friends Friedrich and August Wilhelm Schlegel that was synonymous with early (or Jena) Romanticism. The thematic and temporal contiguity of Novalis's own decline and the motif of death in "Hymns" has not only encouraged a biographical reading of the poem, but also contributed to an alternative understanding of Romanticism. The romantic stock images— the happy Middle Ages, for example, or the blue flower of romantic longing, a motif from *Ofterdingen*—are not transfigured through the idealizing vision of the poetic genius but are twisted by a diseased mind. "The rosy glow in the poetry of Novalis," Heinrich Heine would observe a few decades later, "is the color not of health but of consumption" (*The Romantic School,* 77, translation modified). It is not only Novalis's death that suggests the mutual entanglement of biographical and poetic themes. If "Hymns" is suffused with premonition of the poet's mortality, so was his life. He witnessed the death of two of his six younger brothers, one by suicide. But the deepest traces, both emotional and poetic, were left by the death of his fiancée Sophie von Kühn, to which Novalis alludes directly in "Hymns." He had fallen in love with her when she was a child of twelve, and she died in March 1797 at age fifteen, also of tuberculosis. A few notes he made in his diary after visiting her grave reappear verbatim in the third hymn. The dead bride is so powerfully present in the poem that when the first hymn proclaims, "In dew drops I want to sink down and mix with the ashes" ("Hymns," 11), we cannot help imagining the lover grieving at the tomb of his beloved.

But the biographical evidence is ambiguous at best, and thus an uncertain guide to "Hymns." At the time the poem was composed, probably late 1799 through early 1800, Sophie, dead now for two and a half years, while not forgotten, had been replaced the year before he started writing. Novalis had announced his engagement to one Julie von Charpentier in December 1798. At the completion of the poem in early 1800, he was still in good health and his letters and diaries give no hint of an expected early death. On the contrary, that year abounded with vigorous activity. He completed the first part of *Ofterdingen* and embarked on the second, studied Goethe and the 16th-century mystic Jakob Böhme, conducted a geological survey in his capacity as mine inspector at the salt works in the Saxon town of Weissenfels, wrote poetry, continued his scientific studies, and found time to apply for a higher-level post to which he was appointed just three months before his death. By no means did the author of "Hymns to the Night" move inexorably toward a reunion with his dead lover as some biographers have intimated.

On one level of description, the large movement of the poem is clear enough: it takes the anguished voice of the lyric subject—"alone, as no one was alone before, driven by unspeakable fear"(17)—and dissolves this atomized fear of death into a longed-for embrace with Christ in death. Much as in Wordsworth's ode "Intimations of Immortality," here too the voice of the poem attempts to process the fact that "there hath passed away a glory from the earth." While the "Ode" mourns that loss by turning back to the pastoral glow of "recollections from early childhood" to "find / Strength in what remains behind," the two vectors along which the "Hymns" move—forward in time and down in space—inevitably intersect in the grave, "the earth's womb" (39). The poem's closing stanza reads:

> Down now to the sweet bride, on
> To Jesus, to the beloved—
> Comfort, the evening turns gray
> On those who love and grieve.
> A dream will break our fetters off,
> And sink us forever in our Father's lap. (43)

It is not difficult to recognize the mold of Christian mysticism: the heavily sexualized union with Christ leads to an oceanic feeling in which the subject—now a collective we in contrast to the earlier I—"feel[s] no chains" (33), melting into a love in which "there's no dividing left" (37). The full suspension of all distinctions—twice compared to opium-induced narcosis (11, 15)—can only happen under the cloak of darkness, for light, as we know from the opening verses of *Genesis,* is the first separation introduced by God into the uniform chaos before creation. Light not only sustains all life—as Novalis repeatedly states— but, more fundamental, it also constitutes the very condition under which any distinctions can be made. Thus the desire to put an end to all "dividing" requires a move "away from Light's kingdoms" (39), where no distinctions plague us, least of all the one between life and death.

Yet the linguistic means of expression Novalis employs do not always represent the lyric subject's genuine hunger for a mystical union with requisite certainty. In the stanza quoted above, the reader of the original German may wonder whether the lines "evening turns gray / On those who love and grieve" ("die Abenddämmerung graut / Den Liebenden, Betrübten") might also be rendered as "dusk terrifies / Those who love and grieve." The multiple meanings of *graut* reflect the psychological complexity of this scene, for is the total absence of distinctions—the fall into inanimate nature—not frightening even for those who hope to gain relief through it? And does the dream of the penultimate line that is meant to "break our fetters off" not announce a similar complication? The poem has been at pains to distinguish the "holy sleep" from its mere "shadow which, in that twilight before the true Night, you"—night—"throw over us" (15), for its argument demands sharp distinctions: light and dark; false night and true night; the shadow of sleep and "eternal slumber" (39); ultimately, the fear of death and the longing for it. Yet its imagery inevitably moves in the gray zone of ambiguity. Shadows and twilight require a mixture of light and dark, and sleep, even the eternal kind into which the subject falls in the last stanza, produces dreams that are attended by complications. "Is not every dream . . . a significant rent in the mysterious curtain that hangs a thousandfold about our inner life?" Henry, the voice of the poet, rhetorically asks in Novalis's fragmentary novel (*Ofterdingen*, 19).

This is not to say that the religious redemption the poem celebrates is entirely nullified by ambiguities and linguistic loose ends. The trajectory of the poem leads to the embrace of death—in both senses: embraced by death as well as embracing death—yet especially in its early parts the poem registers manifold hesitations, doubts, and deferrals. The ambivalence comes through at the very opening: while the title leads us to expect a paean to the night, its opposite, light, is praised: "What living person, gifted with any sense, does not love, more than all the wondrous appearances of spread-out space around him, the all-joyful Light" (11). Despite its form, this is not a question, but an assertion of truth, general and operative, from which the I of the poem does not exclude itself. If in the end darkness turns out to unfurl the even more marvelous inner spaces of religious love, the opening light has not been exposed as the false sheen on the world's surface. On the contrary, it is embedded in the very order of things: "As inner soul of life it is breathed by the vast world of restless stars, and swims dancing in its blue tide—the glittering, ever-peaceful stone breathes it, the sensuous, sucking plant, the wild and burning many-formed beast—but above all that glorious stranger"(11). What is striking here is not so much the idea that the illuminated world—stars, waters, plants, animals, humans—is a vast organism, steadily more animated as it gets nearer to us; this romantic theme is familiar enough, laid out in detail by the philosopher Friedrich Wilhelm Joseph Schelling, whom Novalis knew and admired. What strikes the reader is the animation not of things but of words: images such as "the sensuous, sucking plant" and "the wild and burning many-formed beast" are of such flagrant plasticity that we would not be surprised to encounter them in the poetry of a much later age, in Rainer Maria Rilke, for instance, or in T. S. Eliot. The intensity with which its glow is described prevents the light from being simply eclipsed by the night of the poem. Accordingly, when later on the lyric subject exults that "my secret heart stays true to the Night," he nonetheless vows, turning away from the dark and addressing the light: "I shall . . . celebrate the full splendor of your sheen, . . . gladly observe the meaningful motion of your mighty, luminous clock—fathom the symmetry of forces and the rules of the play of countless spaces and their times" (19). To be sure, light is associated here with the clockwork regularity of space and time posited by rational science, but the poem does not therefore shun it.

The tension between the unambiguous drive for a mystical union beyond all distinctions and the ambiguity of the poetic means giving expression to that drive is perhaps most palpable in the figure of the "glorious stranger," who early in the poem luxuriates in the glow of the light and who reappears in several of Novalis's other writings. On one level, "Hymns" can be read as a narrative of homecoming: "The wish for strange lands is gone away, / And now we seek our Father's house," the sixth hymn intones (39). That this house is indeed a home exerting a powerful pull of belonging, the poem proceeds to make explicit: "For we must go to our home [*Heimat*], / To know and see the holy time" (41). Yet the path along which the stranger seeks his home, the process by which the alien becomes familiar, does not, as Novalis himself recognized, map neatly onto the path of poetry, least of all of romantic poetry. A notebook entry from 1800 reads: "The art of *alienating* in a *pleasant* manner, of making an object strange but nevertheless familiar and attractive, that is romantic poetics" (*Schriften,* III: 685). The space between the alien and the familiar, where the familiar turns alien and the alien familiar, is the space of Romantic poetry. It makes an uncanny home, a place not of repose but of a ceaseless motion, crossing the boundary between the known and the unknown. Part of what makes the poem so haunting is that it gives voice to the wish to find a home for the glorious stranger, to cease its own movement, yet its success as poetry entails a failure at fulfilling the very wish it announces. In its most forceful passages, "Hymns" registers the resistance, inherent in poetic language, to the urge that gives rise to poetry in the first place.

See also 1600, 1786, 1796 (April), 1800 (January), 1824, 1922 (February)

Bibliography: Heinrich Heine, *The Romantic School and Other Essays,* ed. Jost Hermand and Robert C. Holub (New York: Continuum, 1985). Novalis, *Hymns to the Night,* trans. Dick Higgens, revised edition (New Paltz, N.Y.: McPherson & Co., 1984). ———, *Hymns to the Night and Other Selected Writings,* trans. Charles E. Passage (New York: Liberal Arts Press, 1960). ———, *Henry von Ofterdingen,* trans. Palmer Hilty (New York: Ungar, 1964). ———, *Schriften,* ed. Richard Samuel et al. (Stuttgart: Kohlhammer, 1977–). Simon Reynolds, ed., *Novalis and the Poets of Pessimism,* includes "Hymns to the Night," trans. James Thomson (Norwich, U.K.: Michael Russell, 1995). Citations from "Hymns to the Night" are from the Higgens translation, which has been modified with the help of the Thomson and Passage translations.

Michel Chaouli

♌ *1800, January*

Friedrich Schlegel completes *Das Gespräch über die Poesie*

The Emergence of Literary History and Criticism

In 1799, while Friedrich Schlegel (1772–1829) was still working on his novel *Lucinde*—a characteristically romantic attempt to wed narrative with a theory of the novel—he wrote his sister-in-law Caroline Schlegel (1763–1809) that he was editing a lecture on style in Goethe's earlier and later works and planned to integrate it into an encompassing essay on poetry. That essay is acknowledged today as a turning point in the history of literary criticism and theory. Completed in January 1800, it appeared the same year in the third volume of the journal *Athenäum* that Schlegel edited together with his brother August Wilhelm Schlegel (1767–1845). If the *Athenäum* is the central periodical of early Romanticism—often referred to as Jena Romanticism—then the *Gespräch über die Poesie (Dialogue on Poetry)* is the fullest statement of that movement's views on the significance of literature. The *Dialogue* dramatizes a discussion among two women, Amalia and Camilla, and five men, Lothario, Andrea, Ludoviko, Antonio, and Marcus. Their conversation frames four essays, each of which is presented to the group by one of the male participants. An introduction develops the theme of poetry in general, proclaiming the conjunction of poetry and nature while, with a typical paradoxical turn, defining the latter as an "unconscious poetry" (*KFSA* II, 285). In its precise characterizations, its theoretical ambition, its learnedness, and its wit, the *Dialogue* is certainly one of the richest and most intriguing achievements in the history of the German-language essay.

The dialogue form refers us to the *Symposium* of Plato, whom the *Dialogue* also praises for prefiguring the "transitions from poetry into philosophy and from philosophy into poetry" (304) that Schlegel himself advocated here and elsewhere. It also alludes to the ambience of romantic sociability as exemplified in the freewheeling intellectual interchanges characteristic of the salons of the day. This synthesis of classical form with its modern counterpart is an announced goal of Schlegel's poetics in the *Dialogue*. Scholars have often recognized individual figures from the Jena circle in Schlegel's text: August Wilhelm Schlegel, his wife, Caroline, Friedrich Schlegel, and his lover, Dorothea Veit, shared the same house in Jena, where Ludwig and Amalie Tieck, Friedrich von Hardenberg (Novalis), Friedrich Schleiermacher, and Friedrich Wilhelm Joseph von Schelling often visited. Yet the *Dialogue's* fictive personae cannot be simply associated with particular individuals. Rather, the *Dialogue* charts a model of romantic sociability as a self-reflection of society within society. For the Romantics, social differentiation is decisively decoupled from any assigned stratification and increasingly becomes an issue of education *(Bildung)*, such that sociability itself is seen as an aesthetic project. Schlegel's aesthetics of the social in the *Dialogue* contrasts different individual perspectives, thereby attesting to the condition of modernity with its dispersion and individualization. Yet at the same time, the poetic structure of the *Dialogue* endeavors to unite these diverse and contrasting perspectives, thereby linking the individual and the communal, the subjective and the objective in a new form of organization meant to recreate the relative closure of classical form (in social terms, of the Greek polis) under the condition of modern dispersion. The first and the fourth contributions to the *Dialogue,* Andrea's "Epochen der Dichtkunst" (Epochs of Poetry) and Marcus's "Versuch über den verschiedenen Styl in Goethes früheren und späteren Werken" (On Stylistic Differences in Goethe's Earlier and Later Writings), provide a historical frame for the second and third essays, the pivot of Schlegel's Romantic poetics, Ludoviko's "Rede über die Mythologie" (Speech on Mythology) and Antonio's "Brief über den Roman" (Letter on the Novel).

"Epochs of Poetry" documents Schlegel's declaration in the *Dialogue* that "the scholarly approach to art and literature has to be its history" (290). The essay sketches the development of literature from Greek antiquity to the late Middle Ages, a period that marks the beginning of "modern" literature for Schlegel and other Romantics, up to the epochal threshold of contemporary literature. Thus, the modern is promoted to a concept with which Romanticism reflects on and describes itself: it coincides with the romantic. Medieval poetry and even more so early Renaissance literature in Italy (Dante, Petrarca, Boccaccio, Ariosto, Guarini), Spain (Cervantes), and England (Shakespeare) vouch for the onset of the modern or the romantic. Whereas Shakespeare had already epitomized the violation of classicist rules and the emergence of the poetic genius for the Storm and Stress movement, and poets such as Ariosto and Guarini were widely read in the 18th century, Dante became more popular only with August Wilhelm Schlegel's partial translation of the *Divine Comedy,* and the significance of Cervantes's *Don Quixote* for the development of the modern novel was first recognized by Friedrich Schlegel and the Jena circle. Boccaccio was reappraised for the dialogical, conversational frame of his novellas (297), in which Schlegel saw the precursor of literary self-reflection, a position he elaborated at greater length in his critical essay *Nachricht von den poetischen Werken des Johannes Boccaccio* (1801; *Report on the Poetic Works of Giovanni Boccaccio*). This tradition, Andrea claims in his "Epochs of Literature," broke off in 1616 but was renewed in Germany with Winckelmann's historical appreciation of ancient art, with Goethe's literary innovations, and with tendencies which are the signature events of the Romantics' own project: a new coupling of philosophy and poetry, forms of translation that are literary themselves, modes of critique that have become scholarship; in short, the institution of literary criticism as Schlegel delineates it in and with his *Dialogue* (303).

In his "Speech on Mythology," Ludoviko reinterprets the late 18th-century project of a new mythology as a potential aesthetics that would revise the relationship between the individual and the general, the single work and its genre. His emphatic expectation of the "new dawn of a new poesy" (311) to be brought about by a new mythology at first seems surprising, given that the call for a new mythology was by no means novel: Herder had already objected to the Enlightenment's denunciation of mythology in his *Briefe über die neuere deutsche Litteratur* (1767; *Letters on Recent German Literature*) and reevaluated its poetic quality and "heuristic value" for a renewal of poetic imagination. In his essay *Literarischer Sansculottismus* (1795; *Literary Sansculottism*), Goethe had bemoaned the political disunion of Germany and its consequent deficit of a national literature, for which there was no "center point of social life and education," a complaint that seems to be echoed in Ludoviko's initial argument that contemporary poetry lacks the decisive "center point" that mythology furnished for the ancients (312). For Schlegel, mythology is to offer more than just an inventory of poetic images, as it did for Herder. In the *Dialogue,* the concept of a new mythology emerges as the basis of literary criticism and as the foundation of a theory of literary forms because of its bearing on the relationship between part and whole. Since Greek literature had mythology as its "center point," all individual works were interconnected and formed "one singular, indivisible, completed poem" (313).

Because modern, individualized literature lacks such a center, it has to recreate a structural equivalent to the function of ancient mythology with different techniques: it can but allegorically refer to—and constantly reflect on this referential process—what remains unrepresentable for it, namely the integrated whole of a politically ordered cosmos, or what Schlegel here calls the one Work. New mythology, Ludoviko suggests, is to be "the most contrived, the most artificial of all artworks because it is to encompass and include all other works" (312). A new mythology, in short, is an intellectual, self-reflexive endeavor that hinges on a self-implicating relationship between part and whole and relies on philosophy and the "dynamic paradoxes" of physics (322), whereas old mythologies expressed the "youthful imagination" (312) and sensual intuition with which the ancients grasped their natural and cultural environment. The new mythology is advertised as an "intriguing symmetry of contradictions," its task is to reflect a modern concept of order that accommodates complexity, and its method is one of "interrelatedness and constant transformation" (318). Moreover, Ludoviko's (written) "Speech on Mythology" reflects on its own medial status as spoken word and oral discourse—as *mythos* with its persuasive and performative function. The "Speech" thus pinpoints the intersection of different media around 1800, exemplified, for example, in the Romantics' renewed interest in oral discourses in an era of expanding publication, increased literacy, and much ado about the rage for reading.

The core of Schlegel's attempt to delineate a new critical theory of literary genres can be seen in the *Dialogue's* third contribution, Antonio's "Letter on the Novel." He does not understand the novel as an individual genre different from drama or the lyric. Rather, he "detests" the novel *(Roman)* as a single genre, but demands that all poetry be "romantic," and tautologically defines the novel as "a romantic book" ("Ein Roman ist ein romantisches Buch," 335). Schlegel's play on the semantic field *"Roman"* (novel) and *"romantisch"* (romantic) recalls the novel's more humble origins in popular culture, and alludes to "romantic" as the vernacular Romance languages (in opposition to Latin, the language of erudition), to the popular tradition of (epic) romances, and to the epochal concept used only after the mid-18th century to label medieval literature as the onset of modern Romanticism. Because it attests to modern disintegration and individuation, the novel paradoxically becomes the overarching form that can include all other genres and combine philosophical or critical discourse with poetic fiction, diegesis with mimesis, and thereby restore a functional equivalent to the lost totality of a representable world given in classic mythology. The novel's task is to "mix and link the most heterogeneous elements and all mythology," Schlegel had already stated in his *Literary Notebooks* (*KFSA* XVI, 354 no. 99), and in the *Dialogue* he has Antonio reiterate that the novel should be a "mixture of narrative, song, and other forms" (*KFSA* II, 336).

Novels that would constitute a "romantic book" in this emphatic sense, however, are yet to appear. Starting from a dispute he and Amalia had about enjoyable novels, Antonio charts the contemporary terrain of novelistic writing. He dismisses Fielding und Lafontaine (whom Amalia likes) as plot-oriented, didactic Enlightenment authors who cater only to passively receptive readers "killing their time," and appreciates Sterne, Diderot, and Jean Paul (whom Amalia dislikes) as authors who create narrative "grotesques" that Antonio counts among the few "romantic products of our unromantic age" (330). The term "arabesque," used interchangeably with "grotesque" to characterize the digressive narrative style of these authors, stands in for an ornamental, antimimetic representation in the face of interdicted or impossible representation.

Transferred onto the context of novelistic digression, arabesque is one of the concepts (in that sense similar to wit, irony, and parabasis) with which Schlegel captures the idea of representing the level of representation together with the object of representation, and of reflecting on this two-leveled process.

Digression and diegetic fragmentation in Sterne, Diderot and Jean Paul, however, still remain too much a matter of individual whim: of "naive" arabesque and "natural poetry" *(Naturpoesie)*. In contrast, the genuinely romantic novel would have to be a "poetry of artifice" *(Kunstpoesie)* and present "a sentimental plot in fantastic form" (333). The conceptual pair naive/sentimental may be a faint echo of Schiller's differentiation of those terms as the respective signature of ancient and modern literature in *Über Naive und Sentimentalische Dichtung* (1796; *On Naive and Sentimental Poetry*); Schiller, however, had still seen the novel as an "impure" medium. Schlegel appropriates the poetologically charged term "sentimental" and redefines it, taking care to differentiate its meaning from 18th-century sentimentalism. Characterized by "love" and "religion"—romantic concepts that target the idea of the bond, or, in more abstract terms, of pure relationality—the "sentimental" comes to stand for yet another mode of referring to an irrepresentable absolute or infinite. Supplemented by such a reference to the absolute both in form (the fantastic) and content (the sentimental), novelistic "whim" *(Willkür)* is no longer merely individual, as in Sterne or Jean Paul, but transcends individual subjectivity. "The novel," Schlegel had recorded in his *Literary Notebooks,* is "after all the unison of two absolutes, absolute individuality and absolute universality" (*KFSA* XVI, 121 no. 436). A blueprint for the combination of the infinite and the finite, the meta-genre of the self-reflexive romantic novel best tallies with the project of a "progressive universal poetry" (*KFSA* II, 182 no. 116). Were such novels in fact to emerge, Antonio states in the *Dialogue,* a theory of the novel "would have to be a novel itself" (337). A genre that includes other genres and discourses, the new romantic novel would even include its own critical theory. At the threshold of its emergence, the theory of the novel given in the *Dialogue* takes the form of a letter, a dialogical, communicative medium of written address; but then Schlegel saw the letter as "a form of the present" and as "particularly romantic"; he labeled "the novel itself a kind of letter" (*KFSA* XVIII, 494 no. 222).

In a final, shorter contribution "On stylistic differences in Goethe's earlier and later writings," Marcus appraises Goethe as the "founder and leading writer of a new poetry" (*KFSA* II, 382). He traces Goethe's literary development through three stages that roughly correspond to later literary-critical classifications into Storm and Stress, pre-classical, and classical phases. While he judges *Werther* (1774) to be "obsolete," he fully applauds the novel *Wilhelm Meisters Lehrjahre* (1795–96). Two years earlier, Schlegel had already published a critical essay *Über Goethes Meister* (1798) which emphasized the "irony hovering over the entire work" (137). Acclaiming Goethe's "universality" and ranking him as the equal of Cervantes and Shakespeare, the *Dialogue* again voices an earlier critical vote from the *Athenäum* fragments, where Goethe's "purely poetical" and "most complete poetry of poetry," Dante's "transcendental" poetry, and Shakespeare's "universal" poetry had been seen as the great triad of modernity (206 no. 247). Goethe thus stands in for a renewal of romantic poetry, as the first essay on the "Epochs of Literature" had already suggested. Moreover, he heralds the romantic configuration yet to come by presenting an "antique spirit in a modern guise" and bringing the classic and the romantic into harmony (346)—the highest aim of poetry, as Marcus concludes and the final discussion of the friends confirms. The essay "On stylistic differences in Goethe's earlier and later writings" reflects on its literary-critical statements as something that remain "necessarily incomplete" and fragmented (340), yet also integrates the threads of the earlier three contributions on the historical development from ancient to modern literature, on the necessary renewal of ancient mythology under the modern condition, and on the "progressive" character of the novel.

Oscillating between attempted integration and admitted fragmentation, Schlegel's romantic poetics does not end in an image of harmony or synthesis. Calling up the mythical strife between Marsyas and Apollo, the *Dialogue* closes with a modern statement in classic guise, as it were, a self-reflexive comment well aware of fiercely competing poetological perspectives. For a new romantic poetry and poetics to emerge, it has to change—sometimes violently change—the rules and the horizons of earlier interpretations and, to mark the event of its own emergence, reinterpret or recode the past as the precursor of present poetological ideals.

See also 1792 (August 26), 1796 (April), 1796 (June 10), 1800, 1804 (May 18), 1826, 1831

Bibliography: Friedrich Schlegel, *Gespräch über die Poesie,* in *Kritische Friedrich-Schlegel-Ausgabe [KFSA],* vol. II, ed. Ernst Behler (Paderborn: Schöningh, 1967), 284–351. *Dialogue on Poetry and Literary Aphorisms,* translated, introduced, and annotated by Ernst Behler and Roman Struc (University Park: Pennsylvania University Press, 1968).

Bianca Theisen

♫ 1804

Die Nachtwachen des Bonaventura is published anonymously in F. Dienemann's *Journal von neuen deutschen original Romanen*

The Night of Imagination

The night belongs to the privileged sectors explored by the Romantic imagination. Novalis's "Hymnen an die Nacht" (1800; Hymns to the Night) and E. T. A. Hoffmann's *Nachtstücke* (1817; *Night Pieces*), which includes the tale "Der Sandmann" (The Sandman), are well-known testimonies to this fascination. But perhaps the most radical exploration of the nocturnal imagination of this period is the novel *Die Nachtwachen des Bonaventura (The Night Watches of Bonaventura),* anonymously published in 1804, subsequently attributed to such major writers as Jean Paul and Hoffmann, and today generally held to be the work of a certain Ernst August Klingemann. Little is known of Klingemann's life, however, and his authorship of the book has never been fully confirmed. The novel consists of sixteen "vigils," in which a night watchman named Kreuzgang relates his nocturnal meanderings, ruminations, and visions. To read these reflections today is to encounter a dark and violent side of the imagination, the literary rendering of which must be considered among the most significant and provocative achievements of Romanticism.

One year after the publication of *Night Watches,* Hegel wrote a brief text entitled "The Night of the World," which is part of the manuscripts of his *Jenaer Realphilosophie.* Highlighting the negative power of the imagination, which is to say its proclivity toward dissolution rather than synthesis, he writes: "The human being is this night, this empty nothing . . . In phantasmagorical representations it is night all around; a bloody head suddenly shoots up, there another white ghastly apparition suddenly emerges, only to disappear again. One catches sight of this night when one looks another human being in the eye—and there gazes upon a night that becomes *awful"* (*Jenaer Realphilosophie,* 181). For Hegel, difference *(Entzweiung)*—in the dual sense of separation and strife—is the source of all philosophical desire, while attaining the Absolute is its ultimate aim. At the same time, Hegel is eager to designate this Absolute toward which all philosophical endeavor strives as a primordial state, as the night that exists prior to the light of day. In this sense, the goal of philosophy consists in reintegrating diurnal existence into nocturnal nothingness. This process produces a form of becoming in which difference, enmeshed with the Absolute, emerges as its manifestation. Hegel articulates here what was to become a common theme for many Romantic writers from Tieck and Hoffmann to Arnim and Brentano. The nocturnal power of the imagination was considered ideal for the performance of difference, where madness and self-expenditure give expression to the negative. Here the disruptive, decomposing aspects of mental processes dismember what the diurnal eye puts together, even if it assumes, at times, an ironic and even parodic tone.

Bonaventura's night watchman, Kreuzgang, uses the flights of fancy he embarks on during his nightly vigils to articulate the absolute void on which all imagination feeds. From the start, he draws an analogy between himself and the poet, whom he observes writing in a dimly lit garret from the street below. And yet although he concedes that they are both night watchmen, he sees himself as a "satirical Stentor," whose function it is to interrupt the "dreams of immortality" his brother in spirit composes "up in the air" and to denounce the cold rationality, clerical hypocrisy, and political censorship that have infected the world (Gillespie, 31). How Kreuzgang came to this position is quickly told. Left by his mother in a treasure chest on the cloistered walk of a church, he was raised by a shoemaker. In his youth, he writes political pamphlets, for which he is arrested. Because of the brilliance with which he defends himself, he is judged partially insane and transferred to an asylum. There he meets the young actress with whom he had performed in a production of *Hamlet* and for whom reality had unfortunately become poetry. In the seclusion of the asylum, he experiences the mad ecstasy of love until his Ophelia dies, giving birth to a stillborn child. Back among the sane, Kreuzgang becomes director of a puppet theater, but his play *Judith and Holofernes* is interrupted by a police raid and his puppets are confiscated, because of the revolutionary potential inherent in the public display of a beheading. Finally, he accepts the newly vacated post of night watchman, having discovered that, under the protection of darkness, he can give free rein to his wild and unseemly imaginings.

Beginning with the first vigil, the night emerges as a dangerous, but also fertile site where transgression, death, madness, and poetry are conjoined. Choosing for himself the hybrid role of Shakespearean fool and melancholy Hamlet feigning madness, Kreuzgang tears off the mechanical masks that, during the day, cloak the awful nothingness at the core of the world. His corrosive spirit turns the night into a scene where fallacy and hypocrisy are recognized as protective guises and where the distinction between terrible insight and feverish hallucination is blurred. Kreuzgang's nocturnal eye sees through the mask of religious faith behind which the devil fights for a dead man's soul. He discovers in the judge, who spends his nights signing death warrants, a mechanical puppet, and a cuckold to boot. Standing on the pedestal of the statue of Justice, Kreuzgang blows the horn that calls the guardian of paternal law to the scene of his wife's infidelity, a prank that reveals legality to be as fictitious as religious authority. Appropriating the Shakespearean figure of the world as stage, he insists that all appearances are nothing more than phantasmagoria, and all events are utterly contingent. He demonstrates that there is no integrated "I" behind the many masks people don and that the individual is ultimately alone in a state of absolute nothingness.

Posing as the one who sees through the fallaciousness of daytime laws and conventions, Kreuzgang, the wandering fool, views his madcap deeds as ethical acts. His wild performance of difference is meant to provoke and incite, to rile up his audience, because, as he claims, "otherwise nothing strikes home anymore and men on the whole have become so flabby and spiteful that they carry on in a downright mechanical fashion and commit their secret sins out of sheer indolence" (135). Through the corrosive bend of his nocturnal imagination, he demonstrates that "life is only the cap and bells which the Nothing has draped around to tinkle with and finally to tear up fiercely and hurl from itself" (141). Assuming the role of fool emerges as the only truthful attitude, since there is, finally, nothing substantial behind the masks that support the fiction of a consistent symbolic community. The act of removing the various masks can be seen as being in accordance with the Enlightenment spirit of seeking to awaken humanity to awareness of the emptiness at the very core of the social order. However, only the jester, the philosopher of the night, has the fortitude to endure gazing into the void. To all those committed to society's codes, any notion of worldly phenomena as mere phantasmagoria proves unbearable.

And yet, though Kreuzgang may be convinced that everything rational is absurd, his own delusion, which recognizes in nocturnal phantasmagoria the only reality available to human beings, appears to him "more rational than the reason deduced in systems" (157). In this sense, his performance of difference does not merely seek to place folly above wisdom, error above truth, or death above life. Rather, his insistence that all external appearances—including what appears to be an authentic sign of truth, the human skull—are masks subverts the very oppositions that sustain rational discourse. Stripped of all ontological meaning, pejorative terms such as *folly, error,* and *death* become the sole vocabulary capable of registering the Absolute in its worldly manifestation.

This "night of the self" which Bonaventura's watchman plays in his wanderings recalls the manner in which Western mythopoetics has allegorized the night since antiquity. The goddess Nyx, a great cosmogonic figure, was feared and respected even by Zeus. Hesiod describes how she is born of chaos and gives birth herself to the heavens and to the day, while the Orphic theogonies tell of her immense influence over creation. These hymns relate how Nyx lived in a cave and instructed the younger generations of gods in the task of world making. Her oracular powers assured her influence long after she had passed on her scepter to her son Uranus. Yet from the start, this divinity was conceived as an ambiguous progenitor. Not only are sleep, death, dream, and erotic ecstasy her children, pleasure, friendship, and sympathy are as much her offspring as are age, fate, strife, murder, anguish, sorrow, and revenge. Indeed, in his treatise on mythology *(Götterlehre)* of 1791, Karl Philipp Moritz conjectures that the mysterious darkness Nyx personifies gives allegorical shape to the fact that there is something of which even the gods are in awe, because it exceeds anything that can be described by opposing mortal and divine existence. She represents the unrepresentable entity that can only be thought of as outside and beyond the world of differentiation that began with the distinction between chaos and life. All that comes from this cryptic space, be it the force of contingency and fate or the force of imaginary corrosion, relates to night's two aspects: the primordial, the absolute negativity that recedes from the gaze of humans, and the nocturnal, the phantasmagoria that offer an externalized approximation of this abyss.

Yet the voyage into the night played through in *Night Watches of Bonaventura* is far removed from any mystic experience of the proximity of divinity, where self-expenditure is transformed into a moment of genuine self-recognition. In the phantasmagoric representations, which Kreuzgang presents in the course of his vigils, the nocturnal emerges as the monstrous underbelly of rational constructions. Indeed, the syntheses of the sensuous manifold and a primordial power of decomposition in *Night Watches* prove to be two aspects of the same disruptive power of the imagination. As Kreuzgang walks through the night, he mentally reenacts what Hegel calls the "night of the world," the violent dismemberment and dispersal of synthetic reality into spectral apparitions. But he does so by producing a plethora of synthetic reconstructions, performing the negative, disruptive aspects of the imagination at its utmost.

In the final vigil, Kreuzgang decides to turn the graveyard into the stage for his nocturnal theater, with death as its director. He finds himself in the company, not only of the poet who throughout the text serves as a spiritual brother of sorts, but also of a Gypsy woman, who claims to be his mother. Then, at the grave of an alchemist, he comes across his father's head of stone. Embracing both the "brown gypsy mother and the petrified father" in a "touching family scene," he listens to the story of his birth (Gillespie, 235). One Christmas Eve, the mother relates, the alchemist had decided to conjure up the devil. At the very moment the devil appeared, her son was born. Refusing the devil's offer to serve as the child's godfather, the mother, unwilling to place the infant into Christian hands, conveyed him instead to the treasure hunter, who raised him in his shoemaker's home. As the narrative continues, they force open the grave of Kreuzgang's father with the help of a fortune-teller and, to their surprise, discover that the old necromancer was still "lying there unscathed on the pillow" (Gillespie, 245). It is as if, stored in "death's subterranean museum," he had successfully defied Nothingness. Looking into his father's eyes, Kreuzgang catches sight of a night so awful that even the most authentic representation is inadequate to this manifestation of absolute negativity. When he touches his father's corpse, it crumbles into ashes, leaving a small pile of dust on the ground. As he casts a handful of this dust into the air, Kreuzgang concludes his tale by enacting the conundrum around which his entire journey into the night has revolved. What irrevocably remains is "Nothing!"

See also 1782, 1796 (June 10), 1800, 1818, 1828 (Winter)

Bibliography: Die Nachtwachen des Bonaventura / The Night Watches of Bonaventura, bilingual edition, ed. and trans. Gerald Gillespie, Edinburgh Bilingual Library 6 (Austin: University of Texas Press, 1971). August Klingemann, *Die Nachtwachen des Bonaventura,* with *Des Teufels Taschenbuch,* ed. Jost Schillemeit (Frankfurt am Main: Insel, 1974). Georg Wilhelm Friedrich Hegel, "Jenaer Realphilosophie," in *Frühe philosophische Systeme* (Frankfurt am Main: Ullstein, 1974). Karl Philipp Moritz, "Götterlehre oder mythologische Dichtungen der Alten," in *Reisen: Schriften zur Kunst und Mythologie,* vol. 2, ed. Horst Günther (Frankfurt am Main: Insel, 1981).

Elisabeth Bronfen

♌ *1804, May 18*

Napoleon Bonaparte is proclaimed Emperor Napoleon I

The Subject and Object of Mythology

Christa Wolf's novel *Kein Ort. Nirgends* (1979; *No Place on Earth*) imagines a meeting between Karoline von Günderrode (1780–1806) and Heinrich von Kleist (1777–1811). The fictional encounter of the two writers takes place at a small afternoon gathering on a country estate in June 1804. The counterpoint between their halting, charged dialogue and ominous private thoughts evokes the affinity of their literary biographies as misfits among their Romantic contemporaries. Wolf's title emphasizes this shared sense of historical and social misplacement of a literary vocation that cannot be lived freely and will end early for both authors in suicide within a few years. Besides reviving interest in Günderrode's writings, Wolf's novel also reproduced a curious pattern of reception. Her intensely imagined Günderrode-cum-Kleist joined the fictions put into print by writers of Günderrode's time. She inspired the title figure of Achim von Arnim's novella *Melück Maria Blainville, die Hausprophetin aus*

Arabien (1812; *Melück Maria Blainville, the House Prophet from Arabia*) and the epistolary novel *Die Günderode* (1840) by Bettina von Arnim. Her life may also have been the basis of the enigmatic figure of Ottilie in Goethe's *Die Wahlverwandtschaften* (1809; *Elective Affinities*). If Günderrode's persistent appeal as a literary *sujet* has until recently overshadowed critical attention to her own works, it has also lent her personal history a lingering aura of myth.

In the course of her brief literary career, Günderrode crafted her own identity as an author. Her first collection, *Gedichte und Phantasien* (1804; *Poems and Fantasies*), appeared under the masculine pseudonym Tian, as did her second collection, *Poetische Fragmente* (1805; *Poetic Fragments*), and other prose and dramatic works. A third collection, called *Melete,* withdrawn from print after Günderrode's death in 1806 and first published a full century later, was to appear under the name Ion. While the use of such pseudonyms was common at the time, in Günderrode's case it reflected defining complexities in her life and work: her own contested sense of gender, the striking androgyny of her heroic figures, and the age's tacit restriction of women writers to specific literary genres. The anonymous review that disclosed Günderrode's identity a month after the publication of *Gedichte und Phantasien* closed with the condescending advice to the poet not to sink further into the "depths of dark mysticism" but remain within the "sphere of inner feeling, of beautiful and tender depiction" proper to a woman (*SW* III: 62).

The reviewer's passing reference to "mysticism" was a reaction to the collection's eclectic imagery and form, its air of mytho-gothic fantasy, and fatalistic plots, all of which he attributed to the influence of the "fashionable poetry" of the Romantic school. The dismissive reduction missed entirely Günderrode's entrenched, yet idiosyncratic, position within the currents of turn-of-the-century culture, particularly as regards the sources of her "mysticism"—an almost exclusive recourse to myths and legends. Günderrode developed a poetic praxis that actualized her contemporaries' identification of poetry with myth, while construing, at the same time, the historical status of myth in a distinctive way.

Since the mid-18th century, the scholarly and antiquarian impulses that produced compendia of ancient mythologies coexisted with a new mode of anthropological examination of myths as originary language of the human imagination. J. G. Herder became an influential representative of both trends. His collections of *Volkslieder* and paramyths were conceived in the late 1760s in tandem with a series of historio-poetological writings that defined myth as the origin of poetry and promoted mythology as an inspiring inventory for modern poets. The double response to the poetic potential of myth was repeated by Karl Philipp Moritz, who edited a volume on Egyptian mythology and wrote a highly popular compendium of Greek and Roman myths, while offering in his novel *Andreas Hartknopf* (1786) an allegory of myth as the medium of poetic fantasy. An even closer adequation of poetry and myth accompanied the so-called syncretic tendency in Romanticism that sought to combine these various modes in the modern reception of myth. In *Gespräch über die*

Poesie (1800; *Dialogue on Poetry*), Friedrich Schlegel declared mythology and poetry to be "one and indivisible" and, given the central place they once held in ancient culture, capable of revolutionizing the social order and fusing all arts and sciences. Whatever its radical claims, the Romantics' "new" mythology did no more than shift the emphasis of a desire for continuity manifest in earlier mythographic discourses. Whereas Storm and Stress aesthetics hoped to recover in myth a valued authenticity for the poetic voice, and the ongoing work of lexica and folkloric collections aimed at maintaining the integrity of heterogeneous cultural traditions, the Romantics theorized a renewal of the cultural function of myth.

Günderrode's use of myths as a poetic source might be said to have combined features of the antiquarian and anthropological receptions of myth. Her wide-ranging attention to various mythological traditions gave her oeuvre an encyclopedic quality, which Clemens Brentano criticized as the "scholarly air" of her first collection (*SW* III: 63). Yet by proceeding with an anthropologist's reduction of historical variants to an original essence, Günderrode distilled from these variegated traditions one particular idea: the promise of immortalization, which became the tendentious focus in her adaptations of stories of gods, heroes, and lovers. With it she upheld the conventional view of poetry as preservation of heroic deeds in song. In Günderrode's poetic fictions, Ariadne is hurled toward death and transfigured into a divinity; an anxious Mohammed receives a prophetic vision that his deeds will live forever; the Celtic Darthula commends herself to a bard before she falls in battle; and the Scandinavian Mora's death is witnessed only by the bards who sing of it. If Günderrode's plots typically tend toward violent death and self-sacrifice, they do not linger there. "Death is a chemical process," one character authoritatively remarks, "a breakdown of energies, but no Destroyer" (*SW* I: 33). It is the passage through death, the relativization or transcendence of mortality, rather than a final end that Günderrode persistently imagines.

The recourse to traditional stories and the traditional view of poetry as an immortalizing record of heroic feats stands in contrast to a decidedly modern approach signaled in the title "Poems." It not only designates the poetic texts that make up more than half of the collection, it announces an experimental, lyrical style that dominates her dramatic and her prose pieces. As a result, the heroic scenarios, which the poet so obsessively rehearses, are rendered without the heroic forms of epic and tragedy. A fashionable title at the time for non-belletristic and literary publications alike, "fantasies" signified for Günderrode, as it did for Wilhelm Heinrich Wackenroder's *Phantasien über die Kunst* (1799; *Fantasies on Art*) and would for E. T. A. Hoffmann's own literary debut, *Phantasiestücke in Callots Manier* (1814–15; *Fantasy Pieces in Callot's Manner*), a collection of writings whose coherence was achieved not in formal terms but by the author's idiosyncratic standpoint. In Günderrode's case, idiosyncrasy rests largely on formal intervention, the parsing and shaping of received tales toward the idea of immortality. Her handling of myths is akin to the Romantic tendency toward fragmentation; the term "fragment" is attached to two texts in this collection and is the overall heading of the second collection. This technique produced a pattern of fractured mythologems gathered from eclectic traditions, Greek, Nordic, Egyptian, Persian, Indian, and others.

The idea of preservation in song, prominent in Günderrode's writings, also assumes a specific modern inflection through her adherence to a philosophical argument formulated in Novalis's writings and Schelling's philosophy of nature against the very idea of stasis. Drawing on their conceptual vocabulary of development, infinite self-realization, and necessary transitions, Günderrode casts poetic immortalization as a dynamic, historical process. In the philosophical-didactic texts in *Gedichte und Phantasien,* she takes up again the argument in favor of regarding the past as vitally continuous with the present and the future rather than as a received artifact entrusted to nostalgic moderns. Accordingly, the function of poetry is transformed from preservation alone to cultivation of a sense of historical continuum, quickened with the idea that this continuum itself is utopian in character. To be immortal—the entitlement or wish of so many Günderrode figures—is to be enchained in the infinite movement of history. Günderrode allegorized this premise in the drama *Immortalita* and embedded it in the poem "Des Wandrers Niederfahrt" (The Wanderer's Descent), an elliptical redaction of the epic journey to the underworld. She separates the hero's traditionally exceptional status for this descent, the suspension of his mortality, from any idea of transcendent immutability. Her wanderer's experience of immortality is explicitly formulated as a doctrine of perpetual "becoming" in the upper world, the sphere where human deeds unfold in historical time (*SW* I: 73). Günderrode's approach to myths links immortality with mutability, which she preserves in a kaleidoscopic, poetic arrangement. By regarding myths neither simply as artifacts of a past stage of human culture nor as the (Romantic) promise of a still unrealized future, her poetic works make a case for a role of myth in the present.

In the early 19th century, speculation that myth had entered into history received a more immediate sense. For Günderrode, and many of her contemporaries, Napoleon was both the incarnation of a heroic past and the herald of a political utopia. The writing of her two poems about Napoleon coincided with political events decisive in his career and for the popular imagination. The unpublished poem "Buonaparte in Ägypten" (Buonaparte in Egypt) was dated December 1799, occasioned by the coup of the Directory the previous month that had established Napoleon as first Consul of the French Republic. Extolling the general in hyperbolic terms common at the time, Günderrode elevated his victory in Italy in 1797 and the invasion of Egypt of 1798 and 1799 to a pattern of mythical grandeur:

Wer ruft der Vorwelt
Tage zurück? wer reiset Hüll' und Ketten vom Bilde
Jener Isis, die der Vergangenheit Räthsel
Dasteht, ein Denkmal vergessener Weisheit der Urwelt?
Buonaparte ist's, Italiens Eroberer,

Frankreichs Liebling, die Säule der würdigeren Freiheit
Rufet er der Vorzeit Begeisterung zurüke
Zeiget dem erschlaften Jahrhunderte römische Kraft.

Who calls to mind the ancient
Days? who tears veil and chain from the image
Of Isis, that enigma of the past, a monument
To the forgotten wisdom of prehistory?
It is Buonaparte, Italy's conqueror,
France's darling, recalling the enthusiasm of
Antiquity, the pillar of a worthier freedom,
Showing a flaccid century Roman strength.

(*SW* I: 369)

Napoleon is presented here as the hero of a monumental historical legacy, the savior of revolutionary and Roman-republican ideals, and the redeemer of Ancient Egypt's cultural legacy.

Günderrode's poetic alignment of Ancient Egypt, Republican Rome, and modern France had a material counterpart in Napoleon's revival of the imperial Augustan tradition of claiming architectural war spoils from Egypt. The lines hymning Napoleon's potency suggest an image—the ancient "pillar" shown to a "flaccid" modernity—that would come to be permanently associated with this military campaign. The erection on the Place de la Concorde of the obelisk from the Temple of Luxor, coveted by Napoleon's first mini-army of Egyptologists but obtained only three decades later by the post–Napoleonic government, became the defining monument to Napoleonic glories in war and science. Through his practical role of furthering Egyptology, of collecting and preserving cultural artifacts, Napoleon was akin to the folklorists and mythologists of his day. And in the cultivation of his own mythical status, he also seemed to meet the Romantic cry for revolutionizing the political and social order through a self-created mythology.

The nimbus of legend that began to surround Napoleon during the Near Eastern campaign, intensified by journalists in Europe, is reconsidered in Günderrode's second poem, the more obliquely titled "Der Franke in Ägypten" (The Frank in Egypt). This time Napoleon himself presents a *précis* of his accomplishments and records their insufficiency:

Ins Gewühl der Schlachten,
Warf ich durstig mich,
Aber Ruhm und Schlachten,
Ließen traurig mich:
Der Lorbeer der die Stirne schmückt,
Er ist's nicht immer der beglückt.
Da reichte mir die Wissenschaft die Hand,
Und folgsam gieng ich nun an ihrer Seite,
Ich stieg hinab in Pyramiden Nacht,
Ich mas des Möris See, des alten Memphis Größe . . .
Doch ach! die alte Sehnsucht ist erwacht,

Aufs neue fühl ich suchend ihre Macht,
Was geb ich ihr? Wohin soll ich mich stürzen?

Into the tumult of battle
Eagerly I threw myself,
Yet glory and battle
Brought melancholy:
Crowning laurel upon the brow
Does not always bring happiness.
Then science extended her hand,
And diligently I followed her,
I descended into the dusky pyramids,
I surveyed the Moris, and old Memphis's span . . .
And yet the old longing stirs
Again I feel its searching power,
How to appease it? what to pursue?

(SW I:81–82)

Military glory and scientific zeal leave a stubborn remainder of longing. Rather than moving through "the fabled land of Egypt" as its confident re-deemer-heir, Napoleon is hailed as a lost "stranger" by a maiden who herself turns out to be another displaced European. The poem portrays Napoleon as profoundly alienated from the heroic identity crafted in Günderrode's earlier "Buonaparte in Egypt." In its hesitation over his status, this later poem was as anticipatory of, as the earlier poem was responsive to, the popular perception of Napoleon. Included as the final text of *Gedichte und Phantasien,* the poem was published a month before Consul Bonaparte was declared emperor in May 1804. The exchange of republic for empire initiated a recasting of Napoleon from hero to tyrant. Among many disappointed admirers was Beethoven, who tore out the dedication to Napoleon from the score of his *Eroica* symphony. Caution, rather than disillusionment, sets the tone of Günderrode's poem. It expresses by equivocating what the other texts in *Gedichte und Phantasien* assume or grant: the promise of immortality. The feats that should secure his fame are disqualified and love is declared the new basis for Napoleon's claim to heroism. "Love must lead to the shadows of heroes," he declares, claiming the maiden whose voice then disappears from the poem (*SW* I: 84). Love here is not the ideal it typically represents in Günderrode's work, the experience of immortality within mortal limits and with a mystical, transcendent character it increasingly assumes in her later writings. Instead, Napoleon is simply consigned to a romance, and Napoleonic conquest is trivialized. Günderrode's implicit critique here of her own earlier mythologizing introduces a wariness into her writings, which, while still dramatizing immortalization and the transfiguration of historical person into mythical hero, never again makes direct reference to a contemporary figure or political development. The terms of her self-critique might be said also to extend somewhat ironically to the mythologizing of her own history. Critics and literary historians have tended to consign her life to a romance—her dramatic suicide over the dissolution of her relationship with Friedrich Creuzer, a married professor of classics in Heidelberg whose work would do much to establish the field of comparative mythology in the German academy of the early 19th century—and deny her recognition for her own literary achievement of linking poetic deeds with a continuous quest for immortality. As she wrote in an unpublished fragment that reads like a credo of her philosophical views and poetic ambitions: "Yet I work, through the influence I have on others, for the eternal" (*SW* I: 437).

See also 1782, 1784, 1800, 1800 (January), 1806, 1968

Bibliography: Hans Blumenberg, *Work on Myth,* trans. Robert M. Wallace (Cambridge, Mass., and London: MIT Press, 1985). Gerhart von Graevenitz, *Mythos* (Stuttgart: Metzler, 1987). Karoline von Günderrode, *Sämtliche Werke und ausgewählte Studien [SW],* 3 vols., ed. Walter Morgenthaler (Frankfurt am Main: Stroemfeld/Roter Stern, 1990). Friedrich Schlegel, *Schriften zur Literatur,* ed. Wolfdietrich Rasch (Munich: Deutscher Taschenbuch Verlag, 1972). Christa Wolf, *Kein Ort. Nirgends* (Munich: Luchterhand, 2000). ———, *No Place on Earth,* trans. Jan Van Heurck (New York: Farrar, Straus and Giroux, 1982).

Kelly Barry

1805, Summer

Goethe listens behind a curtain to Friedrich August Wolf lecturing at the University of Halle

Homer between Poets and Philologists

On June 5, 1794, Johann Heinrich Voss (1751–1826) visited Johann Gottfried Herder at his home in Weimar. They smoked pipes together in his study and then were called to tea with Wieland and Goethe and three other Weimar notables. The guests excitedly questioned Voss about his Homeric studies, especially about the geography of the *Odyssey.* Later Voss read aloud from his translation of that poem to enthusiastic applause. Since Friedrich August Wolf (1759–1824) had visited Herder a short time before, Goethe and the others pressed the latter concerning Wolf's theories about Homer, of which they had heard only vague but intriguing rumors. In the following winter, the Freitagsgesellschaft (Friday Society), a group of about a dozen Weimar intellectuals—those named above, as well as others including Schiller and Wilhelm von Humboldt (1767–1835)—met weekly at Goethe's house, where Goethe himself read aloud a book of Homer's *Iliad* in Voss's translation (published 1793) and all the participants argued passionately about the meaning and beauty of both the Greek and the German texts.

In the 1790s, Homer, and to a lesser extent the rest of Greek literature, of which he was thought to be both the source and the culmination, was the blazing center around which the varied constellations of German cultural life revolved. Among the older generation, Wieland continued in the vein of the gently satirical popular philosophy of his masterworks, *Geschichte des Agathon (The History of Agathon)* and *Die Abderiten (The Abderites),* by producing a series of entertaining and edifying novels set in an enlightened antiquity. Wilhelm

Heinse's (1746–1803) novel *Ardinghello* (1787; 2nd ed., 1794) depicted an ideal-ized, amorally aesthetic utopian community harking back to an ancient syn-thesis of art and nature, while Herder, in his *Ideen zur Philosophie der Geschichte der Menschheit* and *Briefe zur Beförderung der Humanität (Ideas on the Philosophy of the History of Mankind* and *Letters on the Promotion of Humanity),* gave a panoramic survey of the development of mankind in which Ancient Greece was the paradigm of unsurpassed humanism. Among the younger writers, Friedrich Schlegel endowed Greek literature with the kind of all-encompass-ing cultural and stylistic history that Winckelmann had supplied for ancient art, and laid the foundations not only for a more profound understanding of ancient literature but also for the theoretical understanding of modern, Ro-mantic poetry. Humboldt explored in a series of profoundly idealistic essays the originality and naturalness of ancient Greece as the foundation for all pos-sible humane political and historical action. Hölderlin developed a complex philosophical vision of the relation between antiquity and modernity in his early lyrics, hymns, odes, and elegies, his novel *Hyperion* (1797–1799), the frag-ments of his tragedy on Empedocles (1797–1800), and in his theoretical es-says. Karl Philipp Moritz (1756–1793) presented in his enormously popular *Götterlehre* (1791; *Treatise on Mythology*) a systematic but undemanding account of ancient myths as the free play of the creative imagination. Connecting all these figures, Goethe and Schiller devoted much of the decade to an intensive examination of classical antiquity and its living heritage in their poems, essays, and correspondence with one another. Viewed close up, all these writers differ from one another as widely in their projects as in their personalities; but seen from our distance, they all used, each in his own way, the Greeks in a sustained attempt to renew German culture.

Why the Greeks? The answer many contemporary Germans gave was a large part, if not all, of the story. The hopes initially inspired among many by the French Revolution for the progress of liberalism and humanity had been shattered by the Terror and foreign wars, which called into question modern man's ability to find orientation from within himself alone and, therefore, sug-gested the urgent need of finding other sources of moral refinement prior to any drastic political reform. Given the fact that the established religious order no longer seemed able to provide convincing answers—especially in denomi-nationally divided Germany—the Ancient Greeks became a welcome substi-tute—ideal, unsurpassed, dead. German fascination with Ancient Greek cul-ture is one small expression of the epoch-making process of secularization that furthered modernity and thereby ended the domination of classical antiquity over the West as the sole validation and reference point for later ages. The so-called tyranny of Greece over Germany was in fact part of the emancipation of Germany from Greece. But Greek culture could never have assumed this role without the contribution of two mediators in the preceding decades: Johann Joachim Winckelmann (1717–1768), who had made ancient art intelligible as the expression of a culture of political freedom, bodily beauty, and fine weather; and Voss, whose translation of the *Odyssey* (1781; *Homers Odüßee*) had made Homer, for the first time, not only a Greek or a Latin poet, but a German one.

Hence the unanimous enthusiasm for Voss's translation in Weimar among intellectuals of different generations and very different tastes. To understand what was at play, consider a passage from this translation, chosen almost, if not quite, at random, from the very beginning of Book 14 of the *Odyssey*. Odysseus, back in Ithaca, parts ways with Athena, who has explained to him the situation at his palace, and sets out to find Eumaeus, his faithful swineherd. The visit of the heroic king to his swineherd is a deliberate mixture of levels and genres. Homer is allowing Odysseus to work his way up very gradually from the lowest depths of his suffering and despair to the triumph that he will only achieve at the end of the epic. The meeting with the lowly Eumaeus is a very early step in this ascent; yet Homer takes care, at the same time, not to make Eumaeus too humble—he may be a swineherd, but he is after all a heroic swineherd, son of a king, loyal, prudent, dutiful, industrious, and honorable. Here is Voss's rendering:

> Aber Odüßeus ging den rauhen Pfad von dem Hafen
> Ueber die waldbewachsnen Gebirge, hin wo Athänä
> Ihm den treflichen Hirten bezeichnete, welcher am treusten
> Haushielt unter den Knechten des göttergleichen Odüßeus.
> Sitzend fand er ihn jezt an der Schwelle des Hauses, im Hofe,
> Welcher hoch, auf weitumschauenden Hügel, gebaut war,
> Schön und ringsumgehbar und groß. Ihn hatte der Sauhirt
> Selber den Schweinen erbaut, indeß sein König entfernt war,
> Ohne Pänelopeia, und ohne den alten Laertäs,
> Von gesammelten Steinen, und oben mit Dornen umflochten.

> But Odysseus went on the rough path from the harbor
> Over the forest-overgrown mountains, to where Athena
> Indicated for him the excellent shepherd, who most loyally
> Kept house among the slaves of godlike Odysseus.
> He found him now sitting on the threshold of the house, in the courtyard,
> Which was built high, on a hill looking far on all sides,
> Beautiful, and one could walk around it, and big. This the swineherd
> Himself had built for the pigs, while his king was distant,
> Without Penelope, and without old Laertes,
> From gathered stones, and on top with thorns interwoven.

Voss's language is elevated yet direct. His renderings are largely accurate and reveal intense study of the poem and of ancient and modern scholarship about it. But above all, his meter, German dactylic hexameters, provides an astonishingly viable equivalent in the modern language for Homer's Greek dactylic hexameters: the long, spacious lines provide ample room for polysyllabic epithets; the supple rhythms vary between slow and stately, rapid and excited; the varying number of syllables (anywhere from thirteen to seventeen) in each line gives the translator the freedom to find exactly one word, and not more nor less than one, for every important lexical item in the original.

But if the spirit of ancient poetry was to infuse German letters with genuine vitality, it was clearly not enough just to do good translations of Greek and Latin poems into German. The audience for new poems and novels set in the ancient world, however enthusiastic, was ultimately small. What most people wanted to see in books was themselves, but themselves ennobled by an aura of antiquity. This meant telling a story whose content was recognizably modern with a form that was in some way ancient. In this sense, the spirit of Weimar Classicism achieved its most perfect expression in Goethe's short epic poem *Hermann und Dorothea* (1797). Voss himself had pointed the way in *Luise: Ein ländliches Gedicht in drei Idyllen* (1783–1784; *Luise: A Country Poem in Three Idylls;* revised and republished in 1795). Goethe's poem retains the harmonious contrast between modern contents and ancient form characteristic of *Luise.* However, he exacerbates both the modern and the ancient features of Voss's idyll while sacrificing the triviality of its quotidian details in favor of a more general, abstract level of characterization. Its plot—the gradual maturation and emancipation of young, diffident Hermann from his rather boorish, bourgeois father; the conflict between old and young; misunderstandings and reconciliation; the triumph of love and the concluding betrothal—is typical stuff for comedy and romance. But Goethe set this bright story against the dark background of political turmoil and human disaster—the expulsion of the German inhabitants from the west bank of the Rhine by the Revolutionary French armies—and the catastrophic fire that destroyed the depicted German village a generation before. Here romance can indeed thrive, but only at the edge or in the shadow of tragedy, and the cheerily mindless vitality it inherits from its generic background is darkened, and steeled, by the contrast with death and suffering which it must, and just barely can, overcome.

Despite its popularity and critical success, Goethe's poem did not, as Wilhelm von Humboldt predicted, spawn a series of German verse epics. One of the reasons for the genre's short life had to do with the relocation of classical antiquity within the broader context of learning. At the very moment when the German Classic poets were attempting to appropriate Homer for their own literary and cultural purposes, the German Classics professors were beginning to claim him as their own philological and scholarly possession. The shadow of Friedrich August Wolf, professor at the University of Halle, floated, perhaps somewhat menacingly, over the tea party of those literary figures meeting at Herder's house in the summer of 1794. All these writers were eager to know more about his theories, but none of them could have imagined what their ultimate consequences would be.

The immediate scandal Wolf's *Prolegomena ad Homerum (Prolegomena to Homer)* produced when it appeared in 1795 derived from his demonstration that the internal inconsistencies of the Homeric epics and the external circumstances of Greek culture in the period of their composition combined to prove that Homer must have been illiterate and that he composed his poems orally, so that the transmitted written texts could not be his own work but must have been produced by later ages. Wolf's denial of Homer's authorship of our *Iliad* and *Odyssey* and his claim that these epics, far from being the consummate masterpieces centuries of aesthetic criticism had acclaimed them to be, were embarrassingly sloppy and self-contradictory caused a sensation. Goethe read the volume, written in an abstruse and convoluted Latin, as soon as it appeared, and immediately reported his disagreement in a letter to Schiller of May 17, 1795. He dismissed Wolf's criticisms as pedantic, picayune, and more subjective than they might at first seem. Yet when Goethe made Wolf's acquaintance later that same month, he became a close and lifelong friend of the often uncongenial professor and his initial skepticism about Wolf's theories eventually yielded to a more positive attitude.

This was due in part to a typically Goethean strategy of self-protective development and self-enhancement. In Wolf's demolition of the classic status of Homer, he saw an opportunity for himself, as a later and lesser poet, to write his own epic poems in the Homeric manner without having to fear competition from an overwhelming and unsurpassable rival. Alluding to the Homerids, the followers and venerators of Homer who, according to Wolf's theories, had been largely responsible for developing the poet's oral verse into the form we know today, Goethe wrote in an elegy about "Hermann and Dorothea": "For who would dare to struggle with gods? And who with the One? / But to be a Homerid, even only as the last one, is fine."

The ultimate importance of Wolf's *Prolegomena* did not reside in his claim about Homer's orality or in his criticism of the formal imperfections of the *Iliad* and *Odyssey*. There was ample precedent for both these views. Wolf's true originality lay in his discovery that the whole of ancient culture, from its earliest beginnings to Late Antiquity, had been involved in constructing the transmitted text of Homer, and in his recognition that consequently, to understand Homer, it was necessary to understand the entire development of ancient literary culture. No one who read Wolf closely could any longer take classical antiquity to be a timeless moment of consummate perfection, manifested in transcendent and almost divinely inspired masterpieces. Instead it was seen as having spread out and thickened into a vast series of varied and determinate cultural and political formations, each one of which had left its all too human fingerprints on the broken and heterogeneous artworks that have come down to us. To study Homer meant to study those formations, in all their specificity, variety, and endless details. This was no longer a job for dilettantes, for poets, for literati: it was hard, dusty work, and it was up to the classicists to get it done.

Wolf's *Prolegomena* is the birth cry of the profession of *Altertumswissenschaft*, classical studies, as it was institutionalized throughout Germany in the decades following the book's appearance. This trend ultimately caused Homer to be split off from the wider culture of literary amateurs and to be assigned to the narrower monopoly of the philologists in schools, universities, and academies.

In the 1790s, Homer could still be the object of lively debate at dinner parties and in informal societies which brought together intellectuals of different professions and taste but who shared not only a love for Greek poetry but above all a conviction that Homer was the common property of all mankind and that men could become fully human by being engaged in his writings. A decade later, things had changed. Goethe remained friends with Wolf and often met with him to discuss philological questions. He liked to maintain contact with scientists and scholars in the fields that interested him, keeping up-to-date with the latest discoveries and checking their reactions to his own views, proud when they agreed with him, and content to ignore them when they did not. In 1807 Wolf publicly dedicated to Goethe the first volume of the new journal *Museum der Alterthumswissenschaft (Museum of Classical Studies),* with which the institutionalization of the new field of scholarship was inaugurated. Yet one cannot help but sense that by this time the German intellectual world had started to be split into separate, competing enclaves: the Homer of the poets and the Homer of the professors was no longer the same.

In the summer of 1805, Goethe visited Wolf in Halle for some weeks. When he expressed a desire to hear the professor's lectures, Wolf's daughter showed him where he could listen to them, concealed behind a curtain. Why did Goethe hide himself? To protect Wolf's students from being distracted by the presence of the great poet? To prevent Wolf from being sidetracked by his friend? Or to shield the poet himself from too close a complicity in the scholarly presentation of ancient literature? In a poem entitled "Das verschleierte Bild zu Sais" (1795; The Veiled Statue at Sais), Schiller had created a powerful image for the inviolable limits set to man's desire for scientific knowledge: a youth dares, against the counsel of his elders and his conscience, to tear back the veil covering the statue of an Egyptian goddess and is punished by the withering of his vitality and an early death. Might not the curtain that hid Goethe have been preserving a free space for poetry against the claims to hegemony of a new, scientific scholarship?

See also 1768, 1782, 1784, 1786, 1808

Bibliography: Johann Wolfgang von Goethe, *Hermann und Dorothea,* ed. Keith Spalding (New York: St. Martin's Press, 1968). ———, *Hermann and Dorothea,* trans. Daniel Coogan (New York: Ungar, 1966). Johann Heinrich Voss, *Homers Werke,* 2 vols. (Stuttgart: Cotta, 1856). Friedrich August Wolf, *Prolegomena to Homer, 1795,* trans. Anthony Grafton, Glenn W. Most, and James E. G. Zetzel (Princeton, N.J.: Princeton University Press, 1985).

Glenn W. Most

᷒᷒ *1806*

Heinrich von Kleist despairs over Prussia's defeat at the hands of Napoleon

Die Hermannsschlacht *and the Concept of Guerrilla Warfare*

"We are the people subjugated by the Romans. The goal is to plunder all of Europe in order to enrich France," writes Heinrich von Kleist (1771–1811) in a letter to his sister Ulrike on October 24, 1806, ten days after Prussia's cata-strophic defeat in the battle of Jena and Auerstädt (*SWB* II, 771).

The comparison between Rome and Paris had, of course, already been made by such revolutionaries as Robespierre and Saint-Just, and that between Caesar and Napoleon by the latter himself, but in invoking the same historical precedent Kleist implies something else. Napoleon, who, after having named himself first consul of the Republic, had himself crowned emperor by Pope Pius VII, is simply a tyrant or, to translate Kleist's German phrase literally, a bloodthirsty villain. In addition, his conjuring up of the ancient Germans in their relation to the Roman Empire is a clear reference to the battle in the Teutoburg forest, which Hermann won over Quintilius Varus, thereby halting the Roman conquest of northwestern Europe. The victory was recorded by Tacitus and other Latin authors. A more recent German adaptation at the time was Friedrich Klopstock's drama *The Battle of Hermann* (1769), which, al-though imbued with a religiously flavored patriotism, avoided—unlike Kleist's later version of the drama, *Die Hermannsschlacht*—any allusions to the political situation within which it was written.

Napoleon's victory confirmed that the Prussian army, supposedly the best of its time, could be beaten. The mobile and fierce warfare of the French was simply more efficient. And the French emperor further diminished the Prus-sian military's power by insisting on a severe reduction of its size in the Treaty of Tilsit, which concluded the war and was ratified in 1807.

As elsewhere in Europe, the French incursion imported quite a few of France's new institutions and ideals to a country that had not experienced a revolution. In 1807, for instance, Prussia abolished all forms of bondage and serfdom, instituting instead a military draft for all male citizens of a certain age. It is important to note, however, that the administrators and government of-ficials who advocated and initiated such reforms did not belong to the group of those who favored alliance with Napoleon. They emulated the French in the name of a new Prussian nationalism. The people who sided with Napo-leon were conservative members of the nobility who were not nationalists but considered the newly crowned emperor as one of their own class. The ten-sions grew when the French authorities intercepted a letter that the Prussian minister Baron vom Stein had addressed to Count Sayn-Wittgenstein, urging him to help organize a popular uprising against Napoleon in Prussia and Aus-tria.

Stein was exiled, but Gerhard von Scharnhorst and August von Gneisenau, who were in the process of reorganizing the Prussian army, remained in charge. They were thrilled when only six weeks after their friend's dismissal, news of a popular uprising against Napoleon in another part of Europe reached Berlin. On May 2, 1808, exasperated by the way the emperor and his general Murat were bullying both their former king and their present king, the people of Ma-drid started a revolt, which soon spread all over Spain. Waged by poor peasants with flails, scythes, and bare hands, the tools of their trade, the war was a small one, as the Spanish word "guerrilla" indicates, but effective nonetheless. Goya's paintings and etchings bear witness to the brutality exerted on both sides. The first rebellion of its kind against a modern army, this fight has provided many uprisings since then with a name.

Gneisenau, who had had the opportunity to study guerrilla tactics in the American War of Independence, and his colleague Scharnhorst wrote several memoranda about methods for instigating the Prussian population to a similar revolt, but one that would not endanger the civil order of the state. King Frederick William III, however, remained extremely skeptical. Yet when he engaged Scharnhorst's disciple Carl von Clausewitz as tutor for his own son in 1811, the Crown Prince received lectures on "small war" tactics that anticipate core ideas of Clausewitz's book *On War* (1834). And when Napoleon's army was retreating from the Russian winter in disarray, the king finally gave in to his advisors and signed what Carl Schmitt later called the "Magna Carta of the guerrilla fighter" (47). The "Landsturmedikt" (Edict for the Formation of a Civil Militia), which took effect on April 21, 1813, summons every Prussian citizen regardless of age, sex, and social class to an irregular fight against Napoleon's troops and thus amounts to the abolishment of the civil order by the very authority that is in charge of guarding it. The resolution came too late: the battle of Leipzig was fought and won by regular soldiers.

Kleist's activities and whereabouts during that time are, as usual, only fragmentarily documented. On January 30, 1807, while on his way to Dresden with a group of friends, he was captured by the French authorities for reasons that remain unknown to this day, and taken as a prisoner of war to Fort Joux near Pontarlier. As Kleist himself notes in a letter, this was the prison where Toussaint L'Ouverture, the leader of the black uprising in San Domingo, to-day's Haiti, had died in 1803. (The rebellion was to provide the background for Kleist's novella "The Betrothal in San Domingo.") On his release, Kleist chose to stick to his original plan. Instead of going back to Prussia, he returned to Dresden, the capital of a state, Saxony, whose sovereign had just been promoted from elector to king by Napoleon because of his timely support.

Kleist's two years in Dresden, from 1807 to 1809, were a period of great productivity and hope. He completed three dramas, *Penthesilea, Käthchen of Heilbronn,* and *The Battle of Hermann,* several novellas, and various other texts. He also founded and co-edited a journal, *Phöbus,* with his friend Adam Müller. Another big money-making scheme, which turned out to be an illusion in the end, was to print German translations of the Code Napoléon and other French government publications. Talking of this particular project in a correspondence that at almost all times bears the marks of ever-present censorship, Kleist does not refrain from adding that, regarding his own position, no political conclusions should be drawn from such plans (*SWB* II, 793).

Like every male descendant of his family, which belonged to the oldest Prussian nobility, Heinrich von Kleist was predestined for a military career. He fought in the first coalition war against the French revolutionary army (1792–1797), and he quit the service when the second of these wars was under way (1798–1801). The reasons for this decision can be gleaned from a letter to his elderly friend Adolfine von Werdeck, a confidante of Queen Luise of Prussia: "If a young man courageously wants to take up arms against the enemy who is threatening his fatherland, he is told that his king is paying an army, which protects the state for money. —Hail to Arminius [i.e., Hermann] for finding a great moment. For what would be left for him to achieve today but to serve as second lieutenant in a Prussian regiment?" (November 1901; Kleist was a second lieutenant at the time of his resignation).

Seven years later, the heroic moment for a new Hermann appears to have arrived. Kleist writes his *Battle of Hermann,* which proves that despite his resignation from the Prussian army he has kept up with the latest developments in military theory and practice, perhaps through his comrades Rühle von Lilienstern and Heinrich von Pfuel or through his link to Gneisenau. His version of Hermann's battle adapts Gneisenau's theory of guerrilla warfare for the stage.

The play starts with a telling scene. Hermann and his wife, Thusnelda, have organized a hunting party, inviting friends and allies including the Roman legate Ventidius and the princes and sovereigns of various German tribes. As the curtain rises, the Germans are gathered together discussing politics. Two topics are on their minds: the Roman invasion of Germany, and petty quarrels amongst themselves. It appears that Rome is shrewdly taking advantage of the situation by pitting the various German principalities against each other, thus gaining more influence and ending up occupying all of the territory. The allusion to Napoleon's politics is obvious. The latest Roman coup attempts to exploit the rivalry between the two largest German states that still remain independent: Hermann's Cheruska, alias Prussia, and Marbod's Suevia, alias Austria.

The German princes at Hermann's party cannot understand how someone of their host's political standing could go off hunting in such times and how he could even think of a possible alliance with the Romans—two fundamental and symptomatic misunderstandings that the whole drama sets out to rectify. For both hunting skills and alliance with the enemy are essentials of guerrilla war. The first point is brought home immediately when Ventidius kills an aurochs (a wild ox), which, wounded by an arrow from Thusnelda's bow, attacks the archer. "You were doomed," the Roman boasts, whereupon one of the German princes asks: "Was she standing in the open field when discharging the arrow?" Told that she was positioned in the middle of the forest when it happened, the German hunter cannot but laugh: "An aurochs is not a cat, and, as far as I am concerned, it is not known to climb up to the tops of pines and oaks." The sense of this remark is lost on the foreign guests as well as on some of the Germans. The powerful, bulky aurochs is the regular Roman army, the forest is one of Germany's great military assets praised as such in Clausewitz's writings and Eichendorff's poems, and the nimble Thusnelda, whose femininity is crucial within this context, is the guerrilla fighter par excellence.

1808 was the year when the riflemen of the Prussian army were grouped into special ranger battalions. Equipped with the best light weapons technology of the day (precision rifles instead of guns), they were trained in the mobile and flexible tactics that had been developed by French troops in the revolutionary wars. For Kleist, each and every citizen, regardless of age, gender, or social rank, can be a ranger. Yet hunting techniques and skills provide guidelines not only for tactical maneuvers, but also for the principles of martial law. To the guerrilla fighter, the enemy is not a human being with inalienable rights even in the fog of war, but a game animal. The drama's final act concludes with a series of symptomatic scenes. Regular soldiers, whether enemies or traitors from Hermann's own ranks, are granted neither an honorable death in the form of a duel nor the status of a prisoner of war. All of them are finished off like animals in a slaughterhouse—one of them being bludgeoned, for instance, with a "club of double weight" (*SWB* I, 612).

Another point that Hermann's German peers are unable to grasp is his refusal to defend his territory and belongings; he simply seems to be giving in to the superpower. Here is Hermann's response: "By Wotan! Surrender! Are you crazy? All my belongings, goods and chattels, the totality of what used to be mine, which as a forfeited possession still is in my hands, all of that, my friends, shall I stake in order to relinquish it all, like King Porus, gloriously in death. Surrender! —By Mana, I plan to ignite a war, which, like a fire in a deadwood forest, shall spread all over Germany, blazing up in flames unto the sky!" This is the politics of scorched earth, which is so furious that Hermann advises his peers to send their wives and children out of the country before the battle starts. The only traditional political move Hermann deems necessary to make is to ally himself clandestinely with his rival Marbod. The highly personal pact is sealed with an offer to sacrifice the life of his two sons in case of betrayal. The boys and a dagger are the pledges attached to Hermann's letter.

The Spanish guerrilla war began as a spontaneous rebellion of the masses. The Prussian reformers dreamt of a similarly fierce uprising, but instigated and controlled from above. Thus Hermann's alliance with Rome (which refers, of course, to Prussia's less than voluntary pact with Napoleon) appears as a ruse of war, with three goals: to lure the Roman army into the German swamps and forests; to ensnare it between Hermann's troops in its rear and Marbod's forces in its front; and to trigger the hatred of the population against the invaders. Hermann takes care to publicize and exaggerate each and every crime the Roman troops commit against the populace. When a German virgin is killed by her own father because she was raped by a Roman soldier, Hermann orders her dead body cut up into as many pieces as there are German clans so that a portion of her flesh can be sent to each tribe as token of a general rebellion. The barbarous scheme replaces all diplomatic transactions with allies and peers. And when it turns out that the Roman soldiers behave with all too much discipline for his purposes, Hermann dresses a group of trustworthy Germans in Roman uniforms and has the country looted, sacked, and burnt down by his own men.

Hermann's first victory, however, is won on what we might call the home front. Although she is comfortable with the plan to finish off the Romans instead of fighting another German nation, his wife ventures to ask him for one favor: to spare Ventidius's life. The Roman legate, her link to the latest Roman (or, better, Parisian) fashion, has been romantically wooing her—on occasion even daring to snatch one of the blond locks right off her head. While true to her first love, Hermann, Thusnelda is nonetheless moved by the philanderer's attention. Hermann, who has had his own thoughts on Ventidius's maneuvers from the beginning, intercepts a letter from him to Livia, empress of Rome, which encloses the stolen curl together with an ominous explanation: it is a sample of the blond hair that would be shaved from Thusnelda's head after Rome's victory over Hermann and turned into a fashionable wig for the empress. The revelation of this plan turns the mild Thusnelda into a wild beast, which every woman in Kleist's oeuvre becomes when she finds herself betrayed. Penthesilea feasts on her dead lover's body; Thusnelda—having lured the traitor into the woods under the pretense of a rendezvous—has the deed done by a starving she-bear.

One last difference between regular and guerrilla troops should be mentioned: the Romans have their banners, the Germans have the choirs of their bards. Visual signals organize the divisions of an army in the field of battle. But "in the night of battle," poetry made in Germany, the country of poets and thinkers, is a much more efficient way to coordinate masses in the dark, and also to speak to the soul and the heart. Heinrich von Kleist's war songs are a good example.

Armed with such decisive weapons and having mobilized not just his army but each and every citizen, Hermann can afford to skip one of the most important parts of a supreme commander's job, the issuance of orders. There is no need for an order of battle or a plan of operations, because the rage and hatred of the population take over. The enemy will be not just beaten as in traditional wars, but annihilated.

When the German princes meet to celebrate their victory, Marbod offers the crown of Germany to his former rival, Hermann. Translated into the terms of the time: Franz II of Habsburg, who, on August 6, 1806, had abdicated the imperial crown and dissolved the centuries-old Holy Roman Empire of the German Nation after Napoleon beat Austria in the battle of Austerlitz and formed the so-called alliance of the Rhine, hands the crown to another German sovereign, King Frederick William III of Prussia. There remains but one thing—"for us, my brethren, or for our grand-children"—to do: to start the march on Rome itself (*SWB* I, 628).

After the battle of Aspern, Napoleon's first great defeat, on May 21–22, 1809, Kleist's hopes ran high. He even went to inspect the battlefield. But Napoleon turned the tables once again, beating the Austrians on July 5–6, 1809, in the battle of Wagram. There is no doubt that his growing domination of Europe was one of many reasons for the enigmatic double suicide of Heinrich von Kleist and Henriette Vogel on November 21, 1811.

The figure of the guerrilla fighter, however, also known as the terrorist, who confounds the distinction between friend and foe in a hall of mirrors, was to loom large not just over Germany's but indeed all the world's future.

See also 1203 (Summer), 1749, 1804 (May 18), 1835 (December 10), 1932

Bibliography: Heinrich von Kleist, *Sämtliche Werke und Briefe* [*SWB*], ed. Helmut Sembdner, 2 vols. (Darmstadt: Wissenschaftliche Buchgesellschaft, 1983). Carl Schmitt, *Theorie des Partisanen: Zwischenbemerkung zum Begriff des Politischen* (Berlin: Duncker & Humblot, 1963).

Wolf Kittler

♫ *1808*

Friedrich Hölderlin's poems *Der Rhein, Patmos,* and *Andenken* appear in the *Musenalmanach für das Jahr 1808*

Poetic Revolution

When the *Musenalmanach* for the year 1808, edited by Hölderlin's friend Leo von Seckendorf, appeared in the fall of 1807 with three of Hölderlin's major long poems, the author of these poems had almost vanished from the world and apparently took no notice of the publication. In September 1806, "le pauvre Holterling," as a witness, Countess Caroline of Hessen-Homburg, referred to him, was taken away from Homburg and brought to a psychiatric clinic in Tübingen. A few months later, in May 1807, he was transferred, presumably incurable, to the house of the carpenter Ernst Zimmer in Tübingen, where he remained until his death in 1843 in a room with a bay window, shaped like a little tower, overlooking the Neckar River.

While the poet thus seemed far removed from his own works and inaccessible to the world, the world, with few exceptions, also took little notice of them. The last work Hölderlin published himself, the translation of Sophocles' *Oedipus Tyrannos* and *Antigone* (1804), had provoked the literary elite of Weimar to laughter and mockery. Among those who were more positively inclined, nostalgic memories of the young, promising author of the novel *Hyperion* (1797/1799) and regrets over the tragic fate of the later Hölderlin tended to overshadow the attentiveness to the peculiar and specific style of his later poetry. Some aspects of this style were even considered to be signs of madness. Seckendorf felt compelled to change with "extreme care" certain passages in the poems edited by him, "in order to bring some sense into them."

To be sure, there were exceptions. One reviewer remarked the "truly original" tone of Hölderlin's poems, but added that they suffer from a "lack of clarity in their form of presentation." It was on the margins of the public literary world that Hölderlin's work lingered for a long time in a kind of limbo. Throughout the 19th century, the poet remained in the shadows, a curious ghost in the canon of German literature, occasionally noticed in a flash of recognition, as for example in a letter by the young Nietzsche. It was a hundred years after the *Musenalmanach* of 1808 that Hölderlin's work began to gain recognition for its uniqueness and that its effects began not only to echo through 20th-century European poetry but also to leave an indelible mark on philosophical thinkers from Benjamin and Heidegger to Blanchot. The reason for dwelling on the vicissitudes of Hölderlin's reception is that the historical contingencies of this case coincide with something at the core of Hölderlin's poetry and poetics.

The three poems published in the *Musenalmanach* of 1808 stand in an eccentric constellation with the majority of poetry written and published at the time. One of the more sensitive reviews that remarked on the originality of these poems also critically noted their "darkness," which the reviewer ascribed to the fact that the talented and elegiac author of *Hyperion* lived in that "foreign world" of the ancients and their language. The ease and elegance of his imagination were shattered "by the heavy word." The critical ear perceived something crucial in Hölderlin's poetry: its unusual diction, tone, and style.

A motif like the "Rhine" seemed to fit well enough into the perception of German Romanticism. The river was imbued with numerous imaginary and symbolic connotations from the political and national associations as *the* German river, popularly named "Father Rhine," to the legendary and magical evocations of its banks lined with old castles and ruins, and towering over it all the most magical of figures, the Loreley. Thematically, *Patmos* too might have corresponded to a certain religious-Christian strain in German Romanticism; and *Andenken,* the most consistently "lyrical" in tone, could certainly appeal to a romantic sensibility. Indeed such a quintessentially romantic poet as Brentano praised the beauty of these poems, or more precisely *manches Schöne,* many beautiful aspects in them. Symptomatically, the most resonant contemporary effect of a Hölderlin poem was produced by the first stanza of *Brot und Wein (Bread and Wine),* which Seckendorf had published in the previous *Musenalmanach* of 1807 as an isolated poem under the title "Die Nacht" (The Night). Apparently only isolated elements of Hölderlin's poetry could resonate with his contemporaries, as *schöne Stellen,* beautiful passages.

To hear only *schöne Stellen* means, of course, not to hear the composition, not to hear all those dimensions of the "beautiful passage" whose specific tone and meaning is part of a structure, nor the singularity of their position and relation to other passages. Hölderlin's poems are rigorously structured, even "calculated," compositions. *Der Rhein* and *Patmos,* for example, both consist of fifteen stanzas, of which each seems to play with the possibility of fifteen verses, but varying the number just slightly (*Der Rhein:* 15-16-14, 15-15-14, 15-16-14, 15-16-14, 15-15-12; *Patmos:* 15-15-15, 15-15-15, 15-15-15, 16-15-15, 15-15-15). Hölderlin evidently had a predilection for triadic compositions, in this case five times three. Other poems are even more rigorously composed in triadic formations. The elegy *Bread and Wine* consists of three times three stanzas, each consisting of eighteen verses or three times three distichs (a distich consisting of two verses; a dactylic hexameter alternating with a dactylic pentameter, the classical elegiac meter). Hölderlin scrupulously counted his verses and stanzas. In the case of *Bread and Wine,* the traces of this counting can still be seen on the manuscript in the form of the black dots left by the still wet pen with which the poet counted the lines.

This presumably mechanical type of composition goes against the grain of the concepts of poetry prevalent since the end of the 18th century, and seems at odds with the image of Hölderlin as the "visionary" poet. Yet Hölderlin is provocatively adamant about the mechanical (and not only technical) aspect of poetry. His translations of Sophocles are accompanied by remarks that have the character of a poetic manifesto against the dominant aesthetics of the time. The notes on Oedipus begin with a postulate that must have stunned Hölderlin's contemporaries: "It will be good, in order to secure a civil existence for the poets of our time . . . to elevate poetry to the *mechane* of the Ancients. . . . Modern poetry lacks above all schooling and craftsmanship, namely that the mode of its production can be calculated and taught, and, once it has been learned, its exercise can be reliably repeated." If one abstracts the peculiar diction of this passage (which, of course, is its essence), one might think that one was reading the poetry of Opitz or Gottsched, precisely the kind that was so vigorously and passionately rejected in the second half of the 18th century in the name of genuine expression, true feeling, and the inner, living beauty of poetry. Hölderlin's apparently anachronistic poetics is an implicit as well as explicit critique of the emerging dominant aesthetics of expression. His poetic theory and praxis put into question the concept of poetry as self-expression, and, more radically, they confront any aesthetics of expression with a poetics of presentation *(Darstellung).*

What seems at first glance an esoteric, playful, or even obsessive preoccupation with calculable laws of poetry, filling whole sheets of paper with tables of permutations of tones and their sequences, is in fact an attempt to formulate not only a philosophy of composition, but a philosophy, logic, and poetics of re-presentation. Two fundamental principles guide these poetics: (1) all poetic presentation *(Darstellung)* occurs in time and is, therefore, sequential; this is the basis for a poetics of alternating tones and representations *(Vorstellungen);* (2) no presentation is a simple, straightforward expression of a pre-given condition or being; thus there is not only a sequence of tones, but every manifest tone is the "artistic character" *(Kunstcharakter)* of a "basic tone" *(Grundton)* that cannot appear as such, but only in its opposite character. The basis for the tragic constellation, for example, is an underlying "basic tone" of original unity and intellectual intuition that can only be presented in the sequential tearing apart of all unity, in the tragic, painful dissemination of what was One. What Hölderlin describes as the tragic condition is the condition of all presentation. Hölderlin's vocabulary and its differentiation of a musical *Grundton,* and the figural artistic character of presentation foreshadows in a certain way Nietzsche's early aesthetics of a Dionysian, musical foundation of being and its Apollonian manifestation in defined forms and beauty.

Hölderlin's critique of aesthetic expression in the name of poetic presentation is accompanied by a poetic praxis that becomes all the more idiosyncratic in tone and diction as it turns away from any notion of poetry as individual self-expression. At the time of his last great poetic composition, Hölderlin was fully aware of his distance from current poetic productions. In a letter of December 1803 to his publisher, Friedrich Wilmans, he evokes the "still childlike culture" of his time, and he opposes the "tired flight" of love poetry to "the sublime and pure jubilation of songs about the fatherland" *(vaterländische Gesänge)*. The opposition metonymically names two poetic poles: poetry as private self-expression of feelings as opposed to public poetry about the historical condition of its time in its cultural and national specificity. *Vaterländische Gesänge* are not so much patriotic songs as they are poems aiming at the articulation and presentation of the entire symbolic and imaginary order of the epoch. "Patriotic" they are in the sense the French words *patrie* and *patriote* assumed after the French Revolution, when *patrie* referred above all to the revolutionary state, and *les patriotes* were the revolutionaries and Jacobins as opposed to the royalist aristocrats. The fact remains, of course, that it was still a revolution in the name of the father, the reinstatement of the patriarch by the fraternal horde. Thus, the word was appropriated in the 19th century by nationalists and by the National Socialists in the 20th century, together with part of Hölderlin's poetry.

Hölderlin wrote his assessment of contemporary culture in the year of the death of Klopstock (1724–1803), perhaps the most influential force in the transformation of German poetry in the 18th century. Klopstock's poetry was for Hölderlin the only exception to the "still childlike" culture with its "tired flight" of love poetry. In several ways, he even saw himself as Klopstock's heir. The master's experimentation with classical prosody laid the foundation for a new understanding of meter and rhythm in German poetry. He trained, so to speak, the German language for the foreign meter of Greek and Latin verses and ode forms of which Hölderlin became the unsurpassed master. With *Patmos,* one of the three poems published in the *Musenalmanach* of 1808, Hölderlin literally assumed Klopstock's mantle. Count Friedrich von Hessen-Homburg had asked Klopstock in 1802 to compose a major religious poem to counter what he feared was the undermining of religion and theology by the Enlightenment and modern philosophy. Klopstock declined, and Hölderlin, who heard of the request through his friend Sinclair, wrote a long poem, addressing and reflecting on the presumed author of the apocalypse on the island of Patmos. He sent the manuscript, dedicated to the count, to Sinclair, who delivered it on January 30, 1803, on the occasion of the count's birthday. According to Sinclair, the count reacted with gratitude and joy. No direct response from the count is documented.

For all its religious and Christian motifs, the poem was not likely to soothe the count's pious anxieties. The poet's voyage to the island of Patmos is as much a voyage to the apocalyptic visionary of Christianity as it is a voyage to Hölderlin's most symbolically charged landscape, that of the ancient Greeks and their oriental, Asian roots. And, more important, like many of Hölderlin's later poems, it is a poem about the highly precarious status of prophets, vision-aries, and poets.

Hölderlin has often been designated a "prophetic" and "visionary" poet. He himself refers to Klopstock's exceptional poetry as "prophetic." But, in ac-cord with Schlegel's historian as a "retrospective prophet," Hölderlin's pro-phetic voice is concerned less with things to come than with a scrupulous reading of past and present signs. *Patmos* ends with an admonition to poetry as good interpretation: "that the firm letter be cared for, and that what is be well interpreted" *(daß gepfleget werde / Der veste Buchstab, und bestehendes gut / Gedeutet;* vv. 224–26). In contrast to the late-18th-century rhetoric of the poet as creator and procreator, Hölderlin's poetry emphatically undermines all fan-tasies of "creative writing." His poet is a witness *(Zeuge)* rather than a creator or procreator *(Erzeuger)*.

The status of the witness is a precarious one. Much of Hölderlin's later po-etry addresses this danger. The figure of John, the author of the Apocalypse, is such a witness, just as Rousseau represents the figure of the modern prophet. Rousseau appears in the poem *Der Rhein* as well as in an ode, *Rousseau,* which is, oddly and symptomatically, the transformation of an ode to which he first gave the title *An die Deutschen (To the Germans).* What began as a historical-prophetic address to the Germans turns into a self-reflective meditation on the legitimacy and possibility of the poetic voice in the face of history. For Hölderlin, Rousseau is the modern paradigm of such a voice. There is always the question: what legitimates the poet's word, and if the poetic word does tes-tify to something true, if something true does happen in it, how will the wit-ness not be consumed by the fire of the true word? In the background is al-ways the frightening example of Semele, who wanted to experience the god in his true being, and was instantly incinerated by the encounter. Poetic pre-sentation *(Darstellung)* is as much a protective veiling of Being as it is its revela-tion.

Hölderlin's insistent return to the Greeks, to Greek forms, and the Greek gods cannot be reduced to a nostalgic mourning for a lost culture, although mourning is certainly a formative force of Hölderlin's poetic language. But it is above all an attempt at interpretation and a relentless reading of a historical constellation. What the French call *la querelle des anciens et des modernes* has been a constitutive element of the various cultural self-identifications in Europe since the Renaissance, whenever a national culture enters into a critical forma-tive phase. This happened in Germany in the 18th century. For Hölderlin, a modern cultural identity became possible only by a thorough working-through of this question. Working through means neither simple imitation nor simple rejection, but the elaboration of the historical difference. The more in-tensely Hölderlin immersed himself in Greek culture, the more clearly he en-visioned the modern difference.

Hölderlin's poetry does not talk about these issues. It presents them in a poetic language that is not *Gedankenlyrik* (poetry illustrating philosophical thoughts). Poetry, for Hölderlin, was a specific mode of thought, different from philosophy, but equal, perhaps even more powerful, in its own right. The poetics of alternating tones assumes another meaning here: poetic presentation moves in calculated sequences through the various modes of human representation: sentiments, reflections, intellectual intuition. Poetic thinking happens not in one of them, but in their constellation and sequence, above all in the caesuras, in the interruptions of the flow of representations.

Long before Nietzsche, Hölderlin read in the apparent serenity and clarity of Greek culture and its artistic presentations a darker, passionate, violent background, something he called "oriental" and which he transformed into the manifest style of his Sophocles translations. In doing this, he performed something that is at the core of memory and history: the effect of a *Nachträglichkeit*, the *après-coup*, the belatedness with which latent significances become effective in a most powerful way at a much later time. This was and still is the effect of Hölderlin's poetry in the 21st century.

See also 1730, 1748, 1796–1797, 1882, 1927

Bibliography: Friedrich Hölderlin, *Gedichte, English and German,* trans. Michael Hamburger (London: Routledge, 1966). ———, *Sämtliche Werke und Briefe,* 3 vols., ed. Michael Knaupp (Munich: Hanser, 1992). ———, *Sämtliche Werke: "Frankfurter Ausgabe"* (Frankfurt am Main and Basel: Roter Stern / Stroemfeld, 1975–).

Rainer Nägele

♌ 1815

Jacob and Wilhelm Grimm fashion their collection of German folktales for a family readership

Folklore and Cultural Identity

In 1944, when the Allies were locked in combat with German troops, W. H. Auden decreed the Grimms' *Fairy Tales* to be "among the few indispensable, common-property books upon which Western culture can be founded." Since they were first published in two volumes in 1812 and 1815, Jacob and Wilhelm Grimm's collection of German folktales had become "next to the Bible in importance." Along with Charles Perrault's *Tales of Mother Goose* (1697), they almost instantly became the authoritative source of fairy tales now disseminated across many Anglo-American and European cultures. Considered timeless in content and universal in appeal, the tales have found their way into a variety of international media, ranging from opera and ballet to film and advertising. Perpetually appropriated, adapted, revised, and rescripted, they are to this day a kind of cultural currency highly valued and widely accepted.

When Jacob (1785–1863) and Wilhelm (1786–1859) Grimm first came up with the idea to compile German folktales, they had in mind a scholarly project. What they wanted was to capture the "pure" voice of the German *Volk* and to preserve in print the oracular *Naturpoesie* of the common people. Priceless folkloric treasures could still be found circulating by way of mouth in towns and villages at that time, but, as they saw it, the advancing forces of industrialization and urbanization imperiled their survival and demanded immediate action.

Weighed down by a ponderous introduction and by extensive annotations, the first edition of Grimms' *Fairy Tales* had the look of a scholarly tome rather than of a book for a broad audience. It contained not only the classic fairy tales that we associate with the name "Grimm" but also jokes, legends, fables, anecdotes, and all manner of lore.

The 211 tales in the seventh and final edition of 1857 have come to constitute a cultural archive of German folklore, a repository of stories thought to mirror and model national identity. Many folklorists and literary historians remain heavily invested in perpetuating the notion that the Grimms' tales were rooted in a peasant culture and that they were spontaneously produced by raconteurs who tapped into the creative unconscious of the German *Volk*. In recent decades, however, scholarly investigations into the origin of the collection have challenged the notion that the Grimms' folktales are examples of unmediated *Volkspoesie* or *Naturpoesie*.

The Grimms relied on numerous sources, both oral and literary, in compiling their collection. Their annotations to the tales reveal the degree to which they raided various existing national collections and relied on literary sources and European analogues to construct the "definitive" folkloric version of a tale. While they may not have cast a wide net in their efforts to identify oral tales—"We were not able to make broad inquiries," they conceded in their introductory essay—they spent many years listening, taking notes, and drafting different versions of each tale. The vast majority of their informants were literate women from their own social class, but they also relied on tales told by "untutored" folk raconteurs. Dorothea Viehmann, the daughter of an innkeeper of French Huguenot descent and widow of a tailor, was, ironically, the star witness for the folkloric authenticity of the collection. While the Grimms were at pains to emphasize the "purity" of the language in their collection, they failed to acknowledge that the versions to which they were treated must have deviated sharply from what was told at harvest time or in the spinning room. The "stable core" to which they refer in their introduction may have been intact, but the manner in which the tales were told must have been considerably altered, moving in a register vastly different from the crude language, ribald humor, and earthy strokes of folk versions. Who would be surprised to learn that informants of any social class might want to impress the dignified brothers with their good breeding and polite diction?

To a great extent, the Grimms' scholarly ambitions and patriotic zeal guided the production of the first edition of the *Fairy Tales,* published during the Napoleonic War. But once the collection was in print, reviewers weighed in with critiques that took the brothers (Wilhelm in particular) back to the drawing board to revise, rescript, and redact. One critic denounced the collection as tainted by French and Italian influences. Another lamented the vast amounts of "pathetic" and "tasteless" material and urged parents to keep the volume out of the hands of their children. August Wilhelm Schlegel and Clemens Brentano were disheartened by the raw tone of the folktales and recommended a bit of artifice to make them more appealing.

In successive editions, Wilhelm Grimm fleshed out the texts to the point where they were often double their original length. He polished the prose so carefully that no one could accuse it of being rough-hewn. More important, the Grimms suddenly changed their view about the intended audience for the tales. What had originally been designed as documents for scholars gradually turned into bedtime reading for children. As early as 1815, Jacob wrote to his brother that they would have to "confer extensively about the new edition of the first part of the children's tales" and expressed high hopes for strong sales of the second, revised edition.

While Wilhelm Grimm's son claimed that children had taken possession of a book that was not theirs to begin with, Wilhelm clearly helped the process along by deleting "every phrase unsuitable for children." In practice, this meant removing virtually every reference to premarital pregnancy. In the first edition of the *Fairy Tales,* Rapunzel's daily romps up in the tower with the prince have weighty consequences: "Tell me, Godmother, why my clothes are so tight and why they don't fit me any longer," a mystified maiden asks the enchantress. In the second edition of the *Fairy Tales,* Rapunzel simply asks the enchantress why she is so much harder to pull up to the window than is the prince. "Hans Dumm," the story of a young man who has the power (and uses it) to impregnate women simply by wishing them to be with child, was eliminated from the second edition of the tales. "The Frog King, or Iron Heinrich," the first tale in the collection, no longer ends with the overjoyed couple retiring for the night on the princess's bed but with a prenuptial visit to the father-king.

The Grimms were intent on eliminating all residues of risqué humor in the tales they recorded, yet they had no reservations about preserving, and in some cases intensifying, the violence. Cinderella's stepsisters are spared from being blinded in the first recorded version of the story, but in the second edition of the *Fairy Tales,* doves peck out their eyes and a moral gloss is added to the story: "So both sisters were punished with blindness to the end of their days for being so wicked and false." Rumpelstiltskin beats a hasty retreat on a flying spoon at the end of some versions of his story, but the Grimms chose to show how he is so beside himself with rage that he tears himself in two. In successive editions of the *Fairy Tales,* the grisly particulars about the fate of Briar Rose's unsuccessful suitors become clearer. When they fail to scale the hedge surrounding the castle, "the briar bushes clung together as though they had hands so that the young princes were caught in them and died a pitiful death."

In 1823, Edgar Taylor published a translation of selected tales from the Grimms' collection under the title *German Popular Stories.* It was this edition, illustrated by George Cruikshank, that inspired the Grimms to prepare a so-called *Kleine Ausgabe,* or compact edition of the *Fairy Tales.* This collection of fifty tales, which appeared in time for Christmas in 1825, revealed that the new implied audience for the Grimms' collecting efforts was children. The original goal of producing a cultural archive of folklore gradually gave way to the desire to create an educational manual *(Erziehungsbuch).*

Today, adults and children read Grimms' *Fairy Tales* in nearly every shape and form: illustrated or annotated, bowdlerized or embellished, faithful to the original German or fractured, parodied or treated with reverence. Even more impressive, the Grimms' stories have come to be disseminated across a wide variety of media. Little Red Riding Hood is mobilized to sell rental cars and Johnny Walker Red Label; Disney's Snow White has sung on screen about the prince who will rescue her to several generations of children; "Fitcher's Bird" has been reprinted with photographs by Cindy Sherman; selected tales have been illustrated by Maurice Sendak; and Humperdinck's *Hansel and Gretel* is routinely performed in opera houses. The Grimms' stories have also served as the raw material for literary works ranging from Anne Sexton's poetic re-scriptings of fairy tales in a volume called *Transformations* to Margaret Atwood's *Robber Bridegroom* and Angela Carter's volume of short stories *The Bloody Chamber.*

The tales of the Brothers Grimm figure prominently in the cultural production of German-speaking countries, where they have functioned as text, pretext, and subtext in narratives for both children and adults. Readers can get their Grimm in scholarly form with annotations, in illustrated editions of single stories, in abridged anthologies, or in modern adaptation. They will encounter Grimms' fairy tales in the writings of Sigmund Freud, Ernst Bloch, and Walter Benjamin, who all understood the profound resonance of the stories and read them as culturally symptomatic texts. They will discover a profusion of intertextual references to the stories in the works of Bertolt Brecht, Alfred Döblin, and Günter Grass. The powerful afterlife of the *Fairy Tales* challenges readers to understand the social energy of the tales and their psychological hold on the popular and literary imagination.

In the course of the last two centuries, Grimms' *Fairy Tales* has surpassed all folkloric and literary competitors in attaining canonical status. Enshrined as the authentic source of German folklore, the collection has been integrated into the educational curriculum of most German lands and has come to figure as a national monument commemorating the depth and reach of the cultural imagination.

Not surprisingly, in the 1930s, the government of Nazi Germany fostered the cult of the Grimms' collection, endorsing its use as a *Hausbuch,* or domestic manual, for instilling a sense of racial pride in children. For many Nazi commentators, the protagonists of the tales were models of "folkish virtues" as they followed their racial instincts and demonstrated courage in the struggle to find a racially pure marriage partner. The *Arbeitsgemeinschaft für deutsche Volkskunde* (Central Committee for the Study of German Folklore) emphasized the importance of the Grimms' collection in building a sense of cultural kinship and forging a strong national identity. After World War II, the Allied occupation forces issued strong warnings about the sinister aspects of the stories—to little effect, for the collection never lost its popular appeal.

That the Grimms' *Fairy Tales* includes tale types that resemble the stories of many other cultures—for example, Little Red Riding Hood or Cinderella—suggests that fairy-tale plots enact psychodramas that transcend cultural specificity. In the preface to the first edition, the Grimms refer to a "stable narrative core" that remains intact despite regional variations. The events in the stories, they state, are so basic that many readers will have encountered them in real life. Oddly, those events include abandonment and the threat of murder: "Parents have no food left and, as a result, have to cast out their children, or a hard-hearted stepmother makes them suffer and would even like to see them die." It may be true that child abandonment and hostile stepmothers figured more prominently in the harsh social climate of past eras, but even in the Grimms' day, a stark contrast existed between the thematic preoccupations of fairy tales and contemporary social practices.

Psychologists have taken the view that fairy tales are far more symptomatic of inner realities than of historical fact. "In a fairy tale," Bruno Bettelheim has pointed out, "internal processes are externalized and become comprehensible as represented by the figures of the story and its events." Hoping to reclaim fairy tales for therapeutic purposes, Bettelheim argued that children need fairy tales in order to work through family conflicts and hostile feelings. Cultural historians have protested against what they see as a flattening of the tales and a disavowal of their cultural contingency. For Robert Darnton, Eugen Weber, and others, fairy tales offer windows into the mental world of earlier centuries; they reveal the social, economic, and personal stakes of everyday life in specific cultures.

In recent decades, feminist critics have entered the debate, siding with historians and equating fairy tales with old wives' tales, or an oral culture of anecdotes, gossip, family histories, and fantasies. Marina Warner sees in these stories a form of social regulation and negotiation on issues ranging from romance, courtship, and marriage to sibling rivalry and generational friction. In the 19th century, the tales of the predominantly female storytellers were appropriated by male compilers and transformed from elastic narratives able to accommodate new values and social mores into rigidly codified tales.

In many ways, the Grimms' collection gives us myth and cultural history in a single, compact package. By putting a familiar spin on conflicts that inspire the stories in the archive of our collective imagination, the tales are also culturally symptomatic, at times even eerily prescient. Stories in the Grimms' *Fairy Tales* may reflect fears that beset all of us—the dread of being abandoned, assaulted, or devoured—along with ubiquitous fantasies about romance and wealth, but they also show how certain anxieties and desires can take a local turn. The Grimms' version of an international tale type known as "The Three Gifts," for example, moves in a sinister mode. "The Jew in the Thornbush" glorifies a stalwart, guileless Teutonic lad and demonizes Jews as grasping, depraved monsters who deserve public humiliation and punishment.

The Grimms' *Fairy Tales* collection has become the object of study for scholars from a variety of disciplines. In recent years, critics have come to recognize the inherent power of these cultural stories; not only do they reflect psychic realities and lived experience, they have also shaped lives through their construction of cultural anxieties and desires. "Where else could I have gotten the idea, so early in life," Margaret Atwood writes of the Grimms' collection, "that words can change you?"

See also 1808, 1929 (October), 1936 (February 27), 1949

Bibliography: Jacob and Wilhelm Grimm, *Kinder- und Hausmärchen,* ed. Heinz Rölleke (Stuttgart: Reclam, 1980). ———, *The Complete Fairy Tales of the Brothers Grimm,* trans. Jack Zipes (New York: Bantam, 1987). W. H. Auden, "In Praise of the Brothers Grimm," *New York Times Book Review* (November 12, 1944), 28. Bruno Bettelheim, *The Uses of Enchantment: The Meaning and Importance of Fairy Tales* (New York: Knopf, 1976). Robert Darnton, "Peasants Tell Tales: The Meaning of Mother Goose," in *The Great Cat Massacre and Other Episodes in French Cultural History* (New York: Basic Books, 1984). Maria Tatar, *The Hard Facts of the Grimms' Fairy Tales* (Princeton, N.J.: Princeton University Press, 1987). Christa Kamenetsy, *The Brothers Grimm and Their Critics: Folktales and the Quest for Meaning* (Athens: Ohio University Press, 1992).

Maria Tatar

♫ 1818

Daniel Schmolling is executed for the murder of his fiancée

The Occult, the Fantastic, and the Limits of Rationality

In 1817 the tobacco-rolling apprentice Daniel Schmolling was found on the outskirts of Berlin next to his mortally wounded fiancée. He admitted stabbing her and was arrested and tried for murder. Although the killing was premeditated, there was no recognizable motive; only some mysterious urge that drove him to the deed. In the absence of a motive for the crime, Schmolling's lawyer requested the expert testimony of a psychiatrist, a certain Dr. Merzdorff. On the strength of the psychiatric evaluation that Schmolling had not been in control of his mental faculties at the time he committed the crime, the defense argued that the accused was not accountable for the murder, though he should be kept in police custody. The crime, according to Merzdorff, represented an outbreak of Schmolling's otherwise latent form of madness, neither physically nor mentally recognizable, which medical experts termed *amentia occulta*. The judge refused to accept the medical interpretation and found the accused guilty of murder.

The ruling was confirmed by the court of appeals. In his legal brief, the appellate court judge cited recent psychiatric literature, arguing that the medical defense of *amentia occulta* was scientifically unacceptable. The absence of a motive for a deed did not constitute sufficient evidence of the defendant's insanity.

Furthermore, philosophical reflection shows that ultimate insight into what motivates a person in his or her decisions and actions is hidden from that person. Hence the unavailability of a clear motive is not a criterion for distinguishing between the normal and the pathological. The appellate judge who set forth this opinion was E. T. A. Hoffmann (1776–1822).

A year later, Hoffmann published a story entitled "Das Fräulein von Scuderi" (Mademoiselle de Scudéri). Immediately translated, it triggered his tremendous fame in 19th-century France. The most lasting testimony to the reception of E. T. A. Hoffmann as a romantic artist and raconteur of the fantastic was Jacques Offenbach's popular opera *Les contes d'Hoffmann*, which had its world premiere in Paris on February 10, 1881.

"Mademoiselle de Scudéri" can be called a detective story, or even a tale about the origin of the detective story, as it situates the genre in the historical context of the creation of a police force in 17th-century France. The novelist Madeleine Scudéri, the spinsterly protagonist, becomes the ancestress of Miss Marple as she solves a string of puzzling jewelry thefts, for which even the most sophisticated efforts of the recently established police force had been employed to no avail. The crimes had been committed by the famous jeweler Cardillac, who, driven by some mysterious urge, follows his customers on their nightly visits to their lovers. He embraces and stabs them from behind and then robs them of the very jewelry he had created for them. To the extent that the jewelry is unique in beauty and style, Cardillac is not just a craftsman; he is an artist in the emphatic sense. Both his artistry and his obsession to murder his customers originate, as Hoffmann's narrative construction shows, in a transgressive desire passed on to him by his mother. When she was one month pregnant, Cardillac's mother was captivated by the jewelry of a courtier who had once been an admirer of hers. She sought him out, and as they secretly embraced, she suddenly found herself crushed to the floor by his falling weight, caught in the stiff arms of a dead man. It is this traumatic prenatal encounter that Cardillac is now driven to reenact; a trauma that not only makes him repeat the prenatal shock in his deadly embrace of his customers, but that also produces the creative urge that makes him an outstanding artist. This interpretation of the criminal jeweler as the embodiment of the dark romantic artist later found its expression in Paul Hindemith's opera *Cardillac* (1926).

To the extent that both the fictitious murderer and the guilty man in the murder case Hoffmann judged appear sane except for the irrational urge that drives them to commit a crime, Cardillac's obsession parallels Schmolling's *amentia occulta*. In both cases, we are confronted with the opacity of an action that defies rational explanation. In his story, Hoffmann accounts for the inaccessibility of this mysterious urge by means of a model of trauma and seduction: the jeweler's strongest desire is, in fact, the desire of another. It is a sexual desire, but to the extent that it is without a naturally predetermined aim or object, it is radically perverse. The narrative of Cardillac's traumatic encounter, positing a disruptive shock as the primal scene of seduction and sexualization, constitutes the only fantastic element in this otherwise quite rational detective story. Indeed, in many of Hoffmann's fantastic tales a traumatic encounter explains the opacity of desire and the limits of rationality and consciousness, a model that works with the latent but enduring effects of an overpowering childhood experience.

Two of Hoffmann's most famous fantastic tales, "The Sandman" and "Nutcracker and Mouse King," bear witness to the importance of this kind of shock and the repetition of its effects. In "Nutcracker" the seductive, unsettling tales and gifts with which the unmarried Uncle Drosselmeyer or his emissaries repeatedly shower the young Marie produce traumatic experiences for the child. In "The Sandman," it is the student and aspiring poet Nathanael who seeks and desires to encounter the sandman, despite the terror and shock the apparition in its many guises instills in him.

Unlike the sandman's sinister effect on Nathanael, which drives him finally into psychosis, attempted murder, and ultimately suicide, Drosselmeyer's avuncular commerce does not end in violent death or madness but merely in the girl's socialization. Especially in its sweetened and simplified ballet version, "The Nutcracker" could become an annual Christmas ritual celebrating the desire that animates bourgeois consumer culture. Based on the same musical score by Tchaikovsky, but situated in the 1970s, Mark Morris's ballet "The Hard Nut" comes much closer to Hoffmann's tale of violence and seduction than the classical ballet. Morris's choreography highlights the manipulative nature of the encounter between the child and Drosselmeyer, the mysterious, talented toy maker and storyteller.

"The Sandman," with its grim ending and sardonic coda, provoked Sir Walter Scott's condemnation of Hoffmann's "sick" fiction in the *Quarterly Review* (1827). In contrast to Scott, Sigmund Freud found in "The Sandman" a general model for the encounter with the limits of rationality. He argues in "Das Unheimliche" (1919; The Uncanny) that the aesthetics of the fantastic, which he terms "the uncanny," is based on the reader's confrontation with a crucial but repressed childhood trauma. In the case of "The Sandman," the uncanny feeling stems from Nathanael's being haunted by a traumatic childhood experience that ended in his father's horrible death, a frightful event that is echoed in Nathanael's fear of losing his own most essential organ, his eyes. For Freud, Nathanael's childhood trauma exemplifies the castration threat.

Hoffmann's stories establish a close connection between traumatic shock— a sexualizing event leading to either madness or death, or sometimes a normal adult life; and aesthetic sensation—such as the reader's reaction to a shocking story that is valued for its sheer intensity. What seems to be at stake in Hoffmann's work, aesthetically and poetically, is an extremely disruptive sensation that, nevertheless, has a tonic or "enlivening" effect of pleasurable unpleasure. Even the authorial narrator in "The Sandman" makes use of fire imagery to describe his own sensations as he switches from the initial epistolary presentation to a third-person narration, asking the reader not only to imagine, but actually to experience the same state of extreme excitement and pressure the narrator feels and wants to communicate. With this emphasis on the sheer intensity of sensation, the aesthetics of the fantastic transcends a representational model of literature. The goal of a work of art, or tale, is the effect it produces in and for its reader or audience. Consequently, the role, function, and nature of the artist must also be dramatically different, analogous to those fictional artists and artisans that populate Hoffmann's stories as powerful seducers, charlatans, and technicians of the imaginary. Ultimately, this new artist figure must be understood in the historical context of radically changing models of power and knowledge.

The case of Daniel Schmolling, which occasioned Hoffmann's lengthy legal exposition, is symptomatic of an emerging "struggle of the faculties." Suddenly medical expertise threatened to displace juridical authority in determining guilt. Julius Hitzig, Hoffmann's friend and first biographer, did not discuss the Schmolling case in his biography but published the entire case in his new journal on criminal law in an issue devoted to the insanity defense. He used Hoffmann as an example of a judge who does not pay enough attention to the medical experts and instead ventures into philosophical and psychiatric debates that exceed his legal competence. This clash between an older, exclusively juridical notion of guilt and the modern sciences of psychiatry, psychology, and pedagogy, which claim to understand, document, heal, and educate an individual, is also thoroughly elaborated and commented on in the conflict between the police and Mademoiselle de Scudéri.

The police arrest Cardillac's apprentice, Olivier Brusson, who is found bending over his stabbed master. All the evidence speaks against him. Only Scudéri is convinced of Brusson's innocence, because she witnessed Brusson's arrest and saw the wild grief of his beloved Madelon, Cardillac's daughter. Her conviction is based on sentimental intuition rather than factual knowledge. And indeed Brusson, who turns out to be her foster grandchild, confides exclusively to her virginal but maternal ear the terrible story of his discovery of Cardillac's secret nocturnal excursions. Brusson's confession confirms Scudéri's initial, intuitive belief in his innocence. From this angle, Scudéri looks like the humane source of comfort who argues in vain with the police officials as she attempts to rescue her foster grandchild from the threat of torture. But Brusson appears innocent only in the light of his intimate family history, his poor but honest background and upbringing, his affectionate love for the old lady, and his devotion to Madelon. Only through Scudéri's sentimental focalizing can this information about Brusson be made relevant enough to overshadow the fact that, in traditional legal terms, Brusson is not at all innocent, but actually, because of his silence, a guilty accomplice to the horrible jewelry murders.

As Scudéri lends a confessional ear to Brusson's true story, she assumes the role of understanding mother, a role that is key to the mid-18th-century culture of sensibility. Nevertheless, she cannot be reduced to bourgeois domesticity. Throughout the story, she is also portrayed as a devoted court lady, to whom the king can turn in a political crisis. When she finally approaches the king to plead Brusson's case, she stages her speech very carefully. In this last phase of the story, Scudéri appears as an artist and technician of the imaginary who manages not only to persuade the king through her powerful performance but also to usher in a new regime of power. The impact of her performance is described in the fire and life imagery that belongs to the fantastic tale's aesthetics of shock and seduction. The king is so overwhelmed by "the violence of the liveliest life that glowed in her speech" that he is barely able to grasp all she says when she suddenly throws herself at his feet, imploring him to pardon Brusson.

The manner in which the king pardons Brusson demonstrates that Scudéri's performance has seduced the king even to adopt a new style of power. When Brusson is finally released from prison, Madelon receives a generous dowry from the king so that she might marry her lover. "But then they should both leave Paris. This is my wish." The concluding detail, as well as the fact that the couple chooses to move to Geneva, the hometown of Brusson's father and of Rousseau, emphasizes the epochal transformation that is announced by the king's pardon. By reconstituting Brusson's innocence and by concerning himself with what would happen to his subject after he is released from prison, the king demonstrates the exercise of an entirely new style of power. It is a form of power that polices populations and monitors their everyday lives. Scudéri, the powerful performance artist, has accomplished this transformation through her seductive speech and through her artful display of Madelon.

In 1821, Hoffmann included "Mademoiselle de Scudéri" in his collection of tales *Die Serapions-Brüder (The Serapion Brothers),* which stands in the tradition of Boccaccio's *Decameron.* Introduced to the literature of German classicism by Wieland and Goethe, the framed novella cycle continued as a Romantic genre in works such as Ludwig Tieck's *Phantasus* (1811–1816). Serapion, who is adopted as the patron saint of the exclusively male group of friends in Hoffmann's framing narrative, is also the protagonist of the first story. He is a well-educated nobleman who abandons his diplomatic career in order to live out his life as a hermit in the woods, in imaginary identification with the martyr Saint Serapion. The so-called "principle of Serapion," the rule guiding the storytelling evenings, requires that whoever recounts a story must be as ardently convinced of his vision as Serapion. However, the intensity of the vision is not only a poetic and aesthetic principle; it is also a means of intoxication equivalent to alcoholic spirits, the hot punch (*Feuerzangenbowle*) the friends consume during their gatherings. This contextualizing frame enables us to discern a final historical aspect of the fantastic tale. In addition to its psychological and political dimensions, the tales produced according to Serapion's principle of visionary intensity provide an escape from a world increasingly felt to be monotonous, tedious, and routinized. The equivalent of a temporary intoxication, Hoffmann's art is situated in close proximity to entertainment and mass culture.

See also 1773, 1786, 1804, 1899

Bibliography: E. T. A. Hoffmann, *Sämtliche Werke in sechs Bänden,* ed. Wulf Segebrecht et al. (Frankfurt am Main: Deutscher Klassiker Verlag, 1992). *Selected Writings of E. T. A. Hoffmann,* ed. and trans. Leonard J. Kent and Elizabeth C. Knight, 2 vols. (Chicago: University of Chicago Press, 1969). Sigmund Freud, "The Uncanny," in *The Standard Edition of the Complete Psychological Works by Sigmund Freud,* trans. James Strachey, vol. 17, 218–52 (London: Hogarth Press and Institute of Psycho-Analysis, 1959). Neill Hertz, "Freud and the Sandman," in *Textual Strategies,* ed. Josué V. Harari, 296–321 (Ithaca: Cornell University Press, 1979). Friedrich Kittler, "Eine Detektivgeschichte der ersten Detektivgeschichte," in *Dichter—Mutter—Kind* (Munich: Fink, 1991), 197–218. Wulf Segebrecht, "E. T. A. Hoffmanns Auffassung vom Richteramt und vom Dichterberuf: Mit unbekannten Zeugnissen aus Hoffmanns juristischer Tätigkeit," *Jahrbuch der deutschen Schillergesellschaft* 11 (1967): 62–138. Dorothea von Mücke, *The Seduction of the Occult and the Rise of the Fantastic Tale* (Stanford: Stanford University Press, 2003).

Dorothea E. von Mücke

1824, October 2

Heinrich Heine ends his walk through the Harz Mountains with a visit to Goethe in Weimar

Heine's Versatility

Heinrich Heine's prose poem *Die Harzreise (The Harz Journey),* published in 1826, recounts a young law student and poet's walking trip through the Harz Mountains, an area adjacent to the famous university town of Göttingen where Heine had studied law. Along the way, the young man ambles through the forest, visits a mine, climbs Dr. Faustus's Blocksberg, and has various encounters with fellow students, local miners, and society people. The account alternates between social satire and present-tense descriptions of the natural surroundings: the dewy haze, the cool green moss, the murmuring brooks. Style and thematics dramatize the dichotomy between society and nature, convention and poetry, in true Romantic spirit. *The Harz Journey,* one of many journalistic works for which Heine is famous, makes up one segment of his popular *Reisebilder* (1824–1828; *Travel Pictures*), literary travelogues of visits to the Harz, the North Sea, and Italy. The narrative is interspersed with lyric poems that were excerpted and published in 1828 in *Buch der Lieder (Book of Songs),* Heine's best-known collection of Romantic lyric poems, many of which have been set to music.

Heine (1797–1856) was also an innovator of modern journalism and politically engaged writing. He was among the first on the Continent to develop the vocation of the belletristic journalist. After settling in Paris in 1831, Heine established himself as a cultural intermediary between the two sides of the Rhine. His lively, often humorous accounts from the Paris period combine autobiographical details and political reportage, satire and critique, opinions and personal gossip. His "subjective style," he says in *Lutetia* (1854), meets Horace's demand to both edify and entertain. His essay *Die Romantische Schule* (1836; *The Romantic School*) was intended to elucidate German literature for a French public and counteract what Heine saw as the errors in Madame de Staël's work on the same subject. It was first serialized in French and appeared only later in book form in German. In this oft-quoted text, Heine seemingly bids farewell to what he called the *Kunstperiode,* the epoch of autonomous high art he associated with the age of Goethe, and calls for a new, politically engaged, materialist literature in its place.

Nevertheless, Heine remains important as a lyric poet whose idiom epitomizes a very German sort of Romanticism. Fairies and water sprites abound in his verse, along with dream images, melancholia, and a folkish ballad style. Before World War II, high school students in the United States typically memorized poems like "Die Lorelei" in German class. This poem about the wiles of the siren of the Rhine was perceived as so quintessentially German that it was included in poetry anthologies of the Nazi era, though it was attributed to an "anonymous" poet. Heine's Romantic tendency resonates as late as 1851 in the very title *Romanzero,* his final volume of poetry. At the same time, Heine was hailed, or decried, as a leftist or even revolutionary writer with socialist leanings. He struggled with German censorship throughout his career; his works were banned with those of other writers of the "Young Germany" movement in the 1840s; Karl Marx counted him among his friends.

It was during this time that Heine wrote two remarkably original verse epics, "Atta Troll" and "Deutschland: Ein Wintermärchen" (Germany: A Winter's Tale), both testimonies to his poetic virtuosity. Both epics are critical of German politics and call for a new freedom with a focus on life here on earth. But despite the revolutionary tone of "A Winter's Tale," Heine never allied himself with any particular political party or position.

Heine is a multifaceted figure with shifting alliances whose writings cover a wide variety of genres. The only really stable thing in Heine's writing is its instability and its unreliability. His versatility is grounded not in the thematics of social dichotomies—German/Jew, German/French, journalism/poetry, law student/poet—but in the very rhetoric of subjectivity that the articulation of these opposites presupposes. His lyric subjectivity and his journalistic subjective style put in question the reliability of the "I" as much as they present it. Heine's struggle between a poetic world in which everything is animated and connected, and the divided world of conventions, prose, and desiccated historicism, can be seen as indicative of a struggle between coded rules of language, allied with the repetition of print, and subjective vocalization typical of lyric poetry, seeking to inscribe individuality and alteration into the solidity of printed matter. With the increase in printed material (300 percent in Germany and France between 1740 and 1800), the "I" becomes a mere device, a bit of script joined with other bits.

In *The Harz Journey,* Heine borrows, as so often, from other writers, repeats commonplaces and snippets of popular speech. This kind of writing erodes the authority of autobiography and counteracts the value of originality. Even when he uses autobiographical form, Heine deviates from his own story. For example, it is well known that Heine visited Goethe at the end of his walk through the Harz Mountains; but this encounter is strangely omitted from the poem. If *The Harz Journey* were indeed autobiographical, surely the meeting with Goethe would be an important episode. Its omission suggests perhaps an anxiety of influence and a cultural ambivalence characteristic of Heine in many ways.

This ambivalence is in part responsible for Heine's troubled reception; his name evokes a discomfort that Adorno called "die Wunde Heine" (the wound Heine). A depiction of Goethe is omitted from Heine's account along with any reference to Goethe's poem, "Harzreise im Winter" (1777). Instead of mentioning his visit to Goethe directly, the narrator tells of a meeting with a journeyman tailor who is "so thin that the stars could shimmer right through him, like Ossian's misty spirits" (2: 111). The popular character of the tailor is not derived from an actual experience in Heine's life; rather it is an imitation of the spirit figures from the already problematic text of Ossian. The journeyman misquotes a few lines from Goethe's *Egmont;* the narrator points out that "such corruption of the text is commonplace among the people." The journeyman also sings a ballad, "Lottchen bei dem Grabe ihres Werthers" (2: 111) (Lotte at the Grave of Her Werther), one of the many popular imitations of Goethe's *Sorrows of Young Werther.* Later, the narrator meets a society woman who asks if he has read *Werther.* The reference to these popularizations replaces any direct representation of Goethe, and is supposed to show how deeply Goethe has penetrated the spirit of the people. What makes *The Harz Journey* peculiarly historical is not its realistic or mimetic depiction of historical individuals or original experience. It is historical in the sense of what might be called a cut-and-paste job, meaning a compilation of hearsay and excerpts from other authors.

Even in his own time, Heine was criticized for this aspect of his writings and was often accused of plagiarism and outright lying. The problematic reversibility of report and expression, though, does not originate in a particular personality; it derives from the mechanical nature of language, palpable in rules of grammar and made emphatic in mass printing. In *The Harz Journey,* Heine denounces the empty autonomy of writing in the context of historical legal studies in Göttingen. In the opening lyric stanzas, the "I" proclaims his intention to set out and leave the "heartless" town behind and ascend the mountains to a place more alive and closer to nature. Even the dreams of Göttingen's legal scholars display the lifelessness of logical thinking, as the narrator recounts: "It was early when I left Göttingen, and the scholar ** surely lay in bed and dreamt as usual: he wanders around a beautiful garden; in its beds are growing a multitude of white slips of paper on which citations are written. They shine lovingly in the sunlight and he picks several of them here and there, and carefully transplants them into a new bed while the nightingale cheers his heart with all of its sweetest tones" (2: 105). The white slips of paper glimmer, just as the misty spirit from Ossian shines through the figure of the journeyman tailor. Heine's composition follows the same pattern of gathering and transplanting, marginalizing the figure of the nightingale, the poetic voice, which accompanies but does not encompass the process of composition. Heine's own writing partakes of the transplanting it critiques. By the same token, it reinscribes the impotence or blankness of the "I" it tries to animate. In the next paragraph, the narrator overhears two schoolboys saying: "'I want nothing more to do with Theodor, he is an idiot; yesterday he didn't even know the genitive form of *Mensa*.' As meaningless as these words sound, I am compelled to relate them, in fact, I'd like to have them written on the gate of the town as the city motto" (2: 105). The critique of the mechanical nature of grammar is itself grammatized, literalized into an imagined inscription.

This aspect of Heine's writing is perhaps what is most troubling; for critique through repetition and inscription asserts the power of writing and the letter, and leaves no figure of a psychological or emotive subject subtending the text. Grammar, a superindividual set of rules governing the possible production of discourse, presents a subject-position devoid of any particular reference. The display of this emptiness is the reason for the instability and anxiety connected with the name "Heine." The reversibility between empty and full, or death and life, structures the movement between the "two worlds" of *The Harz Journey*. As the empty position appears, anxiety arises around the plenitude of what replaces it. This movement appears clearly in the famous scene in the *The Harz Journey* in which the narrator dreams of the Göttingen law library. As he loses himself in reading old judicial dissertations, the clock strikes twelve and a gigantic Themis, sword and scales in hand, enters the room, accompanied by various members of the faculty. These juridical figures from the past continue to file in, each contributing to the deafening disputes. When Themis orders silence, the mayhem only increases: "The whole assembly howled as if gripped by a death-like fear, the ceiling creaked, the books came tumbling down from the shelves. In vain the old Münchhausen [first trustee of the university] stepped out of his frame to command quiet, the raging and shrieking became wilder and wilder" (2: 109–110). The lyric power of animation, the dream-force, animates even the driest of lawyers. The source of anxiety is not the dead letter, but its animation—here, of lifeless allegorical and historical figures. It is the narrator's absorption in his reading that brings about this reversal. Reading and writing transfer the semblance of life from one sign to another.

The reversibility of animation creates a haunting atmosphere and allows the author to undercut the Romantic idyll he describes. One episode in *The Harz Journey* recounts a visit to a mining community, a Romantic topos reminiscent of Novalis and E. T. A. Hoffmann. In his description of a homely scene, Heine makes explicit the connection between animation, the fusion of subjectivity with its surroundings, and the phantasm of originary or immediate experience. He describes the miners' life:

> As quietly restful as the life of the people seems, it is indeed an authentic and lively life. The ancient, trembling woman who sat across from the huge cupboard behind the oven has probably been sitting there for at least a quarter of a

century, and her thinking and feeling is surely innerly intertwined with all the corners of this oven and all the nooks and crannies of this cupboard. And cupboard and oven live, for a human being has poured a part of his soul into them. Only through this deeply intuitive life, this "immediacy," could the German fairy-tale come into being, whose peculiar characteristic is that not only animals and plants, but also objects that seem to be completely devoid of life speak and act.

(2: 118–119)

Heine equates this animated world with the "infinitely meaningful" life of childhood. "During that time," he writes, "everything is equally important to us, we hear everything, we see everything . . . whereas later we become more intentional, occupy ourselves more exclusively with particular things, laboriously exchange the clear gold of intuition for the paper money of book definitions, and gain in breadth of life what we lose in depth" (2: 119). Here is a romantic idealization of rural life, a poetic idyll in which all things are connected and communicative. The transitional metaphor of exchange, however, belies the viability of the original scene. If the immediate relation to the "thing itself" is like having "clear gold," its value still lies in exchange, for its value can only be recognized from the perspective of "paper money," of a representational token used in a relationship of commerce.

The narrator next visits a mint in the silver mines to see how money is made. One would expect here a spectacle of inherent value. Instead, the narrator addresses the newly minted coin and passes it on into a ceaseless system of exchange that can be likened to language itself. The direct address dramatizes the semiotic process:

> With a kind of strange and touching awe, I looked at the new-born blank thalers, took one in hand as it came off the coining stamp, and said to him: "Young thaler! What fates await you! How much good and how much evil will you give rise to! . . . how you will be loved and then cursed! How you will aid debauchery, procuring, lying and murdering! How you will wander restlessly through clean and dirty hands, for centuries, until finally, burdened with guilt and exhausted through sin, you will be gathered up with your forbears in the lap of Abraham, who will melt you down and purify you, and re-form you to a new and better being."
>
> (2: 115)

Direct address lends motion to its addressee; but the coin takes on only a semblance of life, a mutable identity and value as it passes from hand to hand. The poetic idiom which once hoped to call its addressee into being, to create animated figures that shine forth life and value on their own, is a blank coin, a mute token. We see instead the dual production process that stamps out the words and simultaneously tries to make sense of them. *The Harz Journey* juxtaposes two models of value: one opposing gold and paper money, inherent and exchange value; the other showing that all value is gained through endless, uncontrollable exchange. The relation between Heine's romanticism and his journalism can also be understood as an allegory of the instability of value thanks to which no "I" is finally identifiable. The subject of Heine's subjective style remains dispersed and differentiated; it is perhaps this quality that continues to open the "wound Heine."

See also 1774, 1828 (November), 1831, 1835 (December 10), 1828, 1947

Bibliography: Theodor W. Adorno, "Die Wunde Heine," *Noten zur Literatur* (Frankfurt am Main: Suhrkamp, 1981). ———, *Notes to Literature,* trans. Shierry Weber Nicholsen (New York: Columbia University Press, 1991). Susan Bernstein, *Virtuosity of the Nineteenth Century: Performing Music and Language in Heine, Liszt, and Baudelaire* (Stanford, Calif.: Stanford University Press, 1998). Roger F. Cook, *A Companion to the Works of Heinrich Heine* (Rochester, N.Y.: Camden House, 2002). Heinrich Heine, *Sämtliche Schriften,* 6 vols. (Munich: Hanser, 1975). Jost Hermand and Robert C. Holub, eds., *Poetry and Prose* (New York: Continuum, 1982). ———, eds., *The Romantic School and Other Essays* (New York: Continuum, 1985). Frederic Ewen, ed., *The Poetry of Heinrich Heine,* trans. Louis Untermeyer (New York: Citadel Press, 1969). Jeffrey L. Sammons, *Heinrich Heine: A Modern Biography* (Princeton, N.J.: Princeton University Press, 1979).

Susan Bernstein

♌ *1826, November 30*
Wilhelm Schadow assumes the directorship of the newly founded Academy of Art in Düsseldorf

Art between Muse and Marketplace

The star of the Düsseldorf Academy of Art rose seemingly overnight. When Wilhelm Schadow arrived in the town on the Rhine in November of 1826, its art academy was a struggling provincial school. Four years later, the first generation of Schadow's pupils had ascended to celebrity status on the German art scene. From then on, the academy was associated with the so-called *Düsseldorfer Malerschule* (Düsseldorf School of Painting). Its hallmark was a naturalistic idealism, a style that fused idealized *Formempfinden* (sense of form), passion for literary subject matter, and emulation of the old masters with painstaking observation of nature and emphasis on coloring.

By 1854, however, the picture looked less rosy, and Wilhelm von Schadow had more than one reason to take stock. Although he had just been ennobled, an honor bestowed for the first time on a Prussian artist, he loathed the way in which the climate of Düsseldorf's artistic world had changed. The academy had ceased to be the intimate circle of dedicated students over which Schadow kept watch as a paterfamilias. With the meteoric rise of the academy as one of Europe's leading places of art education, the number of students dramatically increased and with it vanished the harmonious unity of the early years. Not every student shared Schadow's lofty ideas about naturalist idealism or his insistence on the primacy of historic themes in painting and religious art. The resulting artistic disputes received added impetus from growing confessional conflict and political tensions.

In addition, the steep economic recession that settled over Prussia in the

1840s impoverished many Düsseldorf artists. Existential worries thus added fuel to the rivalries within an overpopulated artistic community. With the economic decline, the *Kunstvereine,* the art societies, too, began to stagnate. As figureheads for bourgeois patronage, these societies had played a key role in the blossoming of art and art markets in the 1830s and early 1840s. The Kunstverein der Rheinlände und Westfalen (Art Society of the Rhenish Lands and Westphalia), founded in 1829, had been instrumental in securing the success of the Düsseldorf Academy. In the absence of traditional patrons—court and church—the art societies had become a major source of support. As the market tightened, Schadow's influence on the decisions of the Kunstverein became a bone of contention and he himself became a hated target for those whose style or genre he had marginalized. A fierce battle over market share, exhibition space, and patronage replaced the idyllic Biedermeier atmosphere the Polish Count Athanasius Graf Raczynski had eulogized in the first volume of his *Geschichte der neueren deutschen Kunst* (1836; *A History of Recent German Art*). To make matters worse for Schadow, his health and eyesight were failing. And it was as such an "old invalid" that he wrote a remarkable autobiographical novella entitled *Der moderne Vasari* (1854; *The Modern Vasari*), which portrays the art world in the mid-19th century in all its complexity.

The publication of *The Modern Vasari* marked a time of cultural and political crisis. Writing afforded Schadow an opportunity to extol his concept of naturalist idealism, and to cast his account as the history of avant-garde art. Beyond theoretical questions of style and meaning, *The Modern Vasari* also called attention to the socioeconomic side of art production, portraying the situation of the arts around 1850 in the novella's fictive narrative, the frame story. The book illustrates the modernity of a man who was emphatically antimodernist, and thus, once more, confirms the notion of the century as an age marked by the simultaneity of the nonsimultaneous. Convinced that art and life form an inseparable bond, Schadow reflected on the role of academies and art societies, of art criticism and art history, of exhibitions and museums in the age of capitalism: "Though art is born in heaven, it is still produced on earth."

The spine of Schadow's novella is a series of chronologically arranged biographical sketches of those artists who, to his mind, carried forward the regeneration of German art. The biographies serve as starting points for discussion of the principles of the perfect artwork, thus theoretical issues outweigh biographical detail. Schadow sought to increase the reflective mode of his novella, to transform his reflections into "reflections of reflections," into a kind of *Universalpoesie* (universal poetry), by surrounding the biographical sketches with several layers of commentaries, from poems to fictive dialogues. These commentaries criticize, elaborate, and interpret the traditional history of modern art, as they develop a complex system of cross-references among each type of text—the latter being also self-referential. The novella resembles a *matreshki*, a Russian doll, with each text encapsulating another.

In particular, the performance of a play in chapter 2 increases the reflective mode of the novella, as it narrates nothing less than the history of art. Embedded in the fictive description of a royal visit, which occasioned the play's performance, this text within a text is itself an arabesque, a hybrid of recitation and *tableaux vivants* (living pictures). Surfacing abruptly, the play represents an inverted *mise en abyme,* a delayed beginning, as it allows the reader to examine Schadow's entire theoretical construction of the development of art from antiquity onward. The frame story thus breaks up the chronological structure of the biographical sketches, moves back and forth in time, and jumps around from place to place, and in so doing provides a running voiceover that interweaves past and present, history and theory, the paths of the dead with the problems of the living. The emphatically subjective nature of these commentaries serves to counterbalance the objective tone of the sketches.

Following the composition of Friedrich Schlegel's *Gespräch über die Poesie* (1800; *Dialogue on Poetry*), Schadow constructed his novella in the form of a dialogue. His main partner is the "old inspector," in homage to his close friend Karl Mosler, art historian and inspector of the Düsseldorf Academy. He and the old invalid represent the view of the established academicians, the generation of Romantics whose own rebellion against the art establishment had catapulted them to the pinnacle of power in the academy. The chorus of Mosler and the old invalid is supplemented by the voices of younger artists, Schadow's pupils, who have turned away from academic tradition and its normative values. They represent those who have forsaken the academic hierarchy of the arts—privileging historical and religious subject matter in painting—to pursue more lucrative branches of art, above all genre painting. This conflict between the older and the younger generation is a conflict of idealist notions of art; art as an intellectual, morally uplifting enterprise in juxtaposition with the reality of the marketplace thus forms the central theme of the novella.

As a counterweight to the theoretical discussions and intellectual pastime, the narrative introduces the heartwarming sentimental adventures and love affairs of two young art students, the genre painter Dolph and his friend Franz, a landscape painter. Their escapades transport the reader into the daily life of the academy, evoking a world of small-town coziness and Biedermeier snugness, fragile and slowly vanishing in the aftermath of the revolutionary uprising of 1848. Young girls read Amaranth von Redwitz, women hatch plots to secure happy marriages for the town's lovesick, while men eagerly chase after honorific titles. The bourgeoisie emulates the aristocracy, yearning for the attention of those of high birth. In the figures of Dolph and Franz, Schadow draws up a concise picture of the strategies for climbing the social ladder. These true-to-life ingredients bestow on *The Modern Vasari* the semblance of a roman à clef, although the author carefully avoids unmediated aliases and creates most of the characters from composite elements.

It would be a mistake, however, to assume that Schadow's nostalgia and adherence to Romantic ideals prevented him from embracing new technologies. The book itself is a testimony to the contrary; its design of an arabesque interplay of text and lavish illustrations marks it as the product of a new print culture. At the beginning of the century, new printing techniques, such as lithography and a refined version of the woodcut, had revolutionized the artistic possibilities of reproduction and transformed book illustration into an experimental field. The new type of woodcut made it possible to join text and illustration on the same page, printed together in one single step. The woodcut thus became the perfect medium for Schadow to realize his understanding of text as a poetic product that comprises both word and image. In addition, the fusion of text and image became a metaphor for Schadow's workshop ideal as it merged the different authorships of text, illustrations, and technical execution into one homogeneous whole.

The artist who designed the illustrations was Julius Hübner, Schadow's pupil and future brother-in-law. Hübner's vignettes at the beginning of each chapter embody the belief in the convertibility of the idea into different media. Depicting the play and action of cute, comical cherubs, often dressed in rococo garb, the vignettes prefigure the content of each chapter. While a modern reader might easily mistake the cherub motif for a lighthearted, purely decorative ornament, for contemporaries it signified an ironic trope, a topsy-turvy world of satire.

Yet it may well be that the contemporary reader of *The Modern Vasari* faced a greater problem in deciphering the vignettes' complex iconography—the source of their true wit and critical potential. Schadow comments extensively on the lack of a unified basis for cultural knowledge that would allow modern audiences to comprehend the allegorical artworks. With regard to Schinkel's frescoes in Berlin's Altes Museum, Schadow concludes that antiquity as a source for public imagery has been exhausted, but confesses that he does not have a convincing alternative, now that Christianity, too, had ceased to be the fabric of all experience. Schadow's wide-ranging activities to circulate art, virtually as much as physically—in exhibitions, articles, or plays, as prints, reproductions, or original artworks—also have to be understood as a form of memory work. The circulation of art aims to solidify a cultural code, to enhance a collective memory that enables producers and recipients to participate in the same system of signification. Schadow's understanding of the formation of self and artwork is profoundly historicist. For him, everything new is born out of an already existing text. He vehemently condemns the hubris of the modern genius who thinks of his work as *creatio ex nihilo*. Schadow demands immersion in the past, pursuit of an emulative concept of autonomy that will lead to true independence only through absorption and extension of the existing. The formation of the author's self occurs through memory work, at the end of which the historical text becomes a pretext for the self's own text.

The narrative describes the successful emulation of text into art and art into life. Art is the medium through which Dolph will gain the hand of his beloved Henriette, whose father wishes to betroth her to a respectable bureaucrat. Performing a living picture of "Tristan and Isolde," the two display their love mediated as play and their performance becomes the moment of catharsis that ensures the fulfillment of Dolph's desire.

It was not by chance that Schadow modeled his *Modern Vasari* on the famous *Lives of Artists* by the Renaissance painter Giorgio Vasari. Schadow discusses his model in detail; his description elucidates the process of emulation, reworking, and transformation, of succession and overcoming he considers necessary for all creative production. Analysis of *The Modern Vasari's* intertextuality can help us gain a better understanding of the way his paintings, too, work within and with texts. For Schadow emphasized the necessity for artists to study literature, history, and art history, which he regarded as essential sources for our collective memory. The fabric of existing texts, written or sung, drawn or painted, real or fictive, is the cloth we are made of.

At the very end of the novella, the old invalid concludes that there is still much to be done. And indeed, Schadow conceived of a second part to *The Modern Vasari* that was, however, never executed. Again, he saw his idealism sideswiped by the reality of the marketplace, as the lavish edition of his *Modern Vasari* proved too expensive for a broader audience. His art historical novella remained a fragment of a larger text. But then, what would better suit a romantic endeavor than to remain *infinito?*

See also 1800 (January), 1860

Bibliography: Wilhelm Schadow, "Gedanken über eine folgerichtige Ausbildung des Malers," *Berliner Kunstblatt* (1828): 264–273; reprinted in Athanasius Graf Raczynski, *Geschichte der neueren deutschen Kunst*, vol. 1 (Berlin, 1836), 319–330. ———, "Ueber den Einfluss des Christenthums auf die bildende Kunst" (Düsseldorf, 1842). ———, "Einige Worte über Kunstkritik," *Correspondenz-Blatt*, 1, 2 (February 1845): 17–20. ———, "Die Düsseldorfer Malerschule," *Correspondenz-Blatt*, 1, 6 (October 1845): 57–62. ———, *Der moderne Vasari* (Berlin, 1854). ———, "Was ist ein Kunstwerk?" (ca. 1860–1862), ed. Walter Jürgen Hofmann, *Jahreshefte der Kunstakademie Düsseldorf*, vol. 1 (1988). ———, "Zwei Parteien in der Kunstwelt: Idealisten und Materialisten" (ca. 1860–1862), ed. Heinrich Theissing, *Jahreshefte der Kunstakademie Düsseldorf*, vol. 3 (1990–91). ———, "Jugenderinnerungen," *Kölnische Zeitung* (August 28–September 17, 1891): 701–756.

Cordula Grewe

🖋 *1828, Winter*

Five years after construction of Karl Friedrich Schinkel's Altes Museum began, Georg Wilhelm Friedrich Hegel delivers his lectures on the philosophy of art at the University of Berlin for the last time

Hegel's End-of-Art Thesis

"Art, considered in its highest vocation, is and remains for us a thing of the past. Thereby it has lost for us genuine truth and life, and has rather been transferred into our *ideas* instead of maintaining its earlier necessity in reality and occupying its higher place" (*Aesthetics*, 10). This is the most forceful of Hegel's (1770–1831) many formulations of what might be called his End-of-Art Thesis. It appears near the beginning of the published version of his lectures on aesthetics, *Vorlesungen über die Aesthetik,* which he delivered for the fourth and final time in the winter semester of 1828, at the University of Berlin. The thesis is so intricately woven into the texture of Hegel's lectures, however, that it must be regarded as a central and indeed a structural feature of his philosophy of art, rather than a critical *obiter dictum* regarding the art of his time. And it addresses as much what other philosophers have said about art, as art itself.

Of course, art will go on being made. There will be art after the end of art. "Art can be used as a fleeting play, affording recreation and entertainment, decorating our surroundings, giving pleasantness to the externals of our life, and making other objects stand out by artistic adornment" (7). So understood, art will play a variety of roles in what Hegel terms the "objective spirit" of a society—the system of meanings and practices that constitute the form of life its members live. But Hegel was not speaking of art in terms of objective spirit when he advanced the End-of-Art Thesis. "The universal need for art . . . is man's rational need to lift the inner and outer world into his spiritual consciousness as an object in which he recognizes again his own self" (31). *This* is art's highest vocation, to which alone the End-of-Art Thesis is applicable. So the truth of the thesis is consistent with art, and even great art, continuing to be made. In the epilogue to his lecture, *Origin of the Work of Art* (1935–36), Martin Heidegger wrote: "The judgment that Hegel passes in these statements cannot be evaded by pointing out that since Hegel's lectures . . . we have seen many new art works and art movements arise. Hegel did not mean to deny this possibility. The question, however, remains: is art still an essential and necessary way in which truth that is decisive for our historical existence happens, or is art no longer of this character?" (700).

Heidegger implied, wrongly, that despite a century of artistic revolution, it was still too early to say whether the End-of-Art Thesis is true. He is wrong because the thesis makes no prediction about the future of art. Hegel's thesis is not so much about art as it is about our relationship to it. It is a thesis about human beings, whose progress in self-understanding means that we can never again relate to art as our predecessors did when it "afforded that satisfaction of spiritual needs which earlier ages and nations sought in it" (*Aesthetics*, 10). For us, art is merely an object of intellectual consideration—"and that not for the purpose of creating art again, but for knowing philosophically what art is" (11).

Indeed, aesthetic preoccupation with taste, as in Hume or in Kant, testifies precisely to the fact that the older relation to art has been superseded. "Taste is directed only to the external surface on which feelings play," Hegel wrote. "So-called 'good taste' takes fright at all the deeper effects of art and is silent when externalities and incidentals vanish" (34). Art is now an object for study and philosophical analysis, but it no longer satisfies, by itself alone, the deepest needs of the spirit. We have outgrown art, so to speak.

If there should be again a moment when art regains its earlier purpose, it would not be because of the kind of art that came about, but because we ourselves reverted to an earlier condition. If that were to happen, we would not be able to say of the art in question that it was "an essential and necessary way in which truth that is decisive for our historical existence happens." It is precisely the end of art when that question can be entertained. The moment it is entertained, the answer is clear. When art really does express the kind of truth in question, no one, in the spirit of cultural or artistic criticism, can wonder whether it does. We cannot undo the history of mind that has brought us to our present situation.

I have used the word Mind where Hegel employed the word *Geist* or Spirit. "Spirit" is not a word to which the spirit of the English language is especially hospitable, corrupted as the word has been by occult preoccupations and New Age metaphysics. Broadly speaking, the defining activity of Spirit is thinking. In this, Hegel is very close to Descartes, who attempted to prove that he was, essentially and necessarily, a thinking being—a *res cogitans*. Hegel differs from his predecessors in that he saw thinking as having a history. The various historical phases of art are phases of thought expressed as art. Art is "born of the spirit and reborn," he wrote—*aus dem Geiste geboren und wiedergeboren* (2). Hence art is through and through a product of thought, though limited by having to express its thoughts through sensuous means. The End-of-Art Thesis proclaims our liberation from having to find sensuous equivalents for the content of thought. Thinking has risen above and beyond what art is capable of. Art belongs to a less evolved mode of thinking than what the mind is capable of, not only ideally but actually, and this higher capability is found only in philosophy.

Hegel distinguishes three modes of thought, which he terms "subjective, objective, and absolute spirit." Subjective spirit corresponds to Descartes's *cogito*—to cognitive operations of the mind. *Objective* spirit, by contrast, is thought objectified, as it is, for example, in works of art, or in political institutions, moral codes, or forms of family life. It is from the perspective of objective spirit that any institutional theory of art becomes credible. The subjective mind of the artist is constrained by the objective structures of the art world. Art becomes a matter of absolute spirit when, whatever other roles it may play, it offers, like religion and philosophy, "one way of bringing to our minds and expressing the *Divine*, the deepest interests of mankind and the most comprehensive truths of the spirit" (7). It is as a superseded moment of absolute spirit that art has come to an end. Art will no doubt "intersperse with its pleasing forms everything from the war-paint of savages to the splendor of temples with all their riches of adornment" (3). But trammeled by its dependence on sensuous means, art is incapable of showing spirit to itself as spirit. Religion clearly failed to register this limitation, since it recruited art as a way of giving its ideas vivid and graphic expression: "The advent of art, in a religion still in the bonds of sensuous externality, shows that such religion is on the decline. At the very time it seems to give religion the supreme glorification, expression, and brilliancy, it has lifted religion over its limitation . . . Beautiful art, from its side, has thus performed the same service as philosophy: it has purified the spirit from its thralldom" (*Philosophy of Mind,* 296–297). But philosophy has lifted thought over art's ineradicable limitation. "Art no longer affords that satisfaction of spiritual needs which earlier ages and nations sought in it, and found in it alone, a satisfaction that, at least on the part of religion, was most intimately linked with art." Alas, "The beautiful days of Greek art, like the golden age of the later Middle Ages, are gone."

> The spirit of our world today, or more particularly, of our religion and the development of our reason, appears as beyond the stage at which art is the supreme mode of our knowledge of the Absolute. The peculiar nature of artistic production and of works of art no longer fills our highest need. We have got beyond venerating works of art as divine and worshiping them. The impression they make is of a more reflective kind, and what they arouse in us needs a higher touchstone and a different test. Thought and reflection have spread their wings above fine arts.

> (*Aesthetics*, 10)

It must be clear from this barest of outlines that the End-of-Art Thesis is systematically connected with the whole of Hegel's thought, and far more loosely connected with the actual history of art than may have been evident to his critics. He saw art as, so to speak, a staging area in the epic of self-knowledge. Having provided that transitional, but momentous, service, art may now lapse back into the entertainment and ornamentation so important for the enhancement of human life. The End-of-Art Thesis is the defining idea of Hegel's philosophy of art, and his philosophy of art is the heart of his entire philosophical system. He could not have based his philosophy of art on an empirical study of artistic practices, as an art historian or a psychologist of art would. For these empirical studies yield no clue to art as a phase of Absolute Spirit. These are the profound differences, then, between Hegel's End-of-Art Thesis and various formulations of the late 20th century, where it really served as a summary judgment on the present condition of art. It is not, in general, today enunciated as corollary to a great philosophical system like Hegel's, which brings the whole of Spirit into a tremendous whole. Philosophy in the late 20th century would hardly be regarded as affording "that satisfaction of needs which earlier nations sought in it." Its role in human thought is a question mark, and its recent history an agony of self-critique. More than this, the intellectual context in which the end of art is currently addressed is very different from that against which Hegel's thesis must be viewed.

As might be sensed from Hegel's constant exaltation of philosophy over art, his system of aesthetics had a polemical edge. To get a clearer sense of this, let us turn to the last section of Part One of *Lectures on Aesthetics*—"The End of the Romantic Form of Art," where the term "romantic" takes on a double meaning. It refers to one of the great stages art passed through, culminating in the Renaissance. This is romantic in the sense of narratives called romances. But it also describes certain philosophical attitudes that defined German romantic poetry and inflamed German poets.

Romanticism held art to be superior to philosophy. The End-of-Art Thesis translates into the end of Romanticism in this sense. It does so because Ro-

manticism's claim to superiority rested on the fact that, unlike mere philosophy, art presents its ideas in sensuous form. This was the defining position of
German Romanticism, which exalted art and artists within the larger scheme
of life. "It was proposed to hold that in art the real religion, the truth, and the
Absolute were to be found and that art towered above philosophy because it
was not abstract but contained the Idea in the real world as well and presented
it there to concrete contemplation and feeling" (628–629). Most of Hegel's au-
ditors in 1828 would have detected in these words one of Friedrich Schelling's
characteristic thoughts, which makes an invidious comparison between philosophy and art: "Philosophy *as* philosophy can never be universally valid. Absolute objectivity is given to art alone. If art is deprived of objectivity, one may
say, it ceases to be what it is and becomes philosophy; give objectivity to philosophy and it becomes art. Philosophy to be sure reaches the highest level, but
it brings only, as it were, a fragment of man to this point. Art brings *the whole
man,* as he is, to that point, namely to a knowledge of the highest of all, and in
this rests the eternal difference and the miracle of art" (*System of Transcendental
Idealism,* 374–375). Something of this sort, Hegel says, may very well have been
true at certain stages in the history of Spirit. Indeed, what Schelling was describing might be art "in its highest vocation." But at the present moment of
art—Hegel's moment—the relationship between philosophy and art is precisely opposite to Schelling's view.

Each of Hegel's three stages of art—symbolic, classical, and romantic—involves a different kind of relationship between the vehicle of art and its meaning. It is symbolic when there is, between the two, only an "affinity." It is classical when there is an "identity." It is romantic when some reference to spiritual
states is the best explanation of why the artwork appears as it does. The end of
art means the liberation of the artist from all such constraints. "Bondage to a
particular subject matter and a mode of portrayal . . . are for artists today something past, and art has, therefore, become a free instrument which the artist can
wield . . . in relationship to any material whatever" (*Aesthetics,* 605).

It is astonishing that Hegel should see the end of art in what is in effect a
total pluralism, though he could not have foreseen the kind of pluralism that
defines the art world today. "Today," he writes, "there is no material that stands
in and for itself above this relativity." Any material, shaped in any way, can be
art "only if it does not contradict the formal law of being simply beautiful and
capable of artistic treatment" (605). It would surprise Hegel that beauty is no
longer regarded as a "formal law of art." But the deep pluralism of art was
something he already understood. "Every form and every material is now at
the service and command of the artist whose talent and genius is explicitly
freed from the earlier limitation to one particular art-form" (606). The artist,
to paraphrase a stunning thought of Marx and Engels, can do symbolic art in
the morning, classical art at noon, romantic art in the afternoon—and the philosophy of art in the evening. The whole internal logic of the history of art
culminates in absolute artistic freedom.

But artists are no longer, in Hegel's philosophy, the great cultural heroes through reference to whom Romanticism defined itself. Their era in that capacity is irrevocably over. So the End-of-Art Thesis must be understood in terms of two opposing systems of German thought in the early 19th century, each of which deals in different ways with art and the intellect, and with the role of each in terms of human understanding. Hegel announced a new age of reason, in which thought is the substance of Spirit: "The sole thought which philosophy brings to the treatment of history is the simple concept of Reason: that Reason is the law of the world and that therefore, in world history, things have come about rationally" (*Reason in History*, 11).

Historically, however, the romanticist concept of art and the artistic genius proved irresistible, long after Hegel's philosophy of art withered into a dusty topic for historians of philosophy. The romanticist vision of art flourished in the works of Wagner and of Nietzsche, the Futurists and the Abstract Expressionists. It continued to exert a powerful attraction on Theodor Adorno and the Frankfurt School in the earlier part of the 20th century. Only in the later 20th century, through the realization in artistic practice of the freedom Hegel foresaw, did his philosophy of art once again move to the center of aesthetic discussion.

See also 1790, 1876, 1882, 1927, 1947

Bibliography: Hans Belting, *The End of the History of Art?* trans. Christopher S. Wood (Chicago: University of Chicago Press, 1987). Arthur C. Danto, *After the End of Art: Contemporary Art and the Pale of History* (Princeton, N.J.: Princeton University Press, 1997). Georg Wilhelm Friedrich Hegel, *Hegel's Aesthetics: Lectures on Fine Arts,* trans. T. M. Knox (Oxford, U.K.: Clarendon, 1975); citations in the text are from this translation. ———, *Hegel's Philosophy of Mind: Part Three of the Encyclopedia of Philosophical Science,* ed. J. N. Findlay. ———, *Reason in History: A General Introduction to the Philosophy of History,* trans. Robert S. Hartman (New York: Liberal Arts Press, 1953). Martin Heidegger, "The Origin of the Work of Art," trans. Albert Hofstadter, in Albert Hofstadter and Richard Kuhns, eds., *Philosophies of Art and Beauty: Selected Readings in Aesthetics from Plato to Heidegger* (New York: Modern Library, 1964). Friedrich Schelling, "System of Transcendental Idealism," in Hofstadter and Kuhns (1964).

Arthur C. Danto

♫ *1828, November*

Franz Schubert devotes the "last strokes of the pen" to proofreading the first edition of *Winterreise*

Schubert's Political Landscape

In Wilhelm Müller's (1794–1827) and Franz Schubert's (1797–1828) cycle of lieder *[Die] Winterreise,* a scorned lover assumes the poetic role of wanderer and embarks on an aimless journey through a cold, rough, inhospitable winter landscape, a disturbing, unsettling world where motives of nature are tuned as images of death. The continuous eighth-note repetition within the 2/4 pulse in Schubert's score of the first lied symbolically sets the pace, drawing the wanderer irresistibly into a movement he does not control, not its reason nor its direction, its measure, its timing: "Ich kann zu meinen Reisen nicht wählen mit der Zeit" ("I cannot choose the time for my journeys").

Unlike *Die schöne Müllerin,* a Müller-Schubert cycle that grew out of a bourgeois song-play with changing configurations of *dramatis personae, Winterreise* has no acting characters besides the one protagonist. The opening verse, "Fremd bin ich eingezogen, fremd zieh ich wieder aus" ("A stranger I came, a stranger I depart"), and its musical setting determine the tone and intention of the whole. In a subtle interplay of rhythm and pitch, Schubert accentuates the very first word, *fremd* (strange), against both the literary meter and the musical 2/4 meter, assigning it twice to an upbeat and to the highest note of the falling half-phrases, thus emphasizing at the very beginning the expression of estrangement as the iconic sign of this wandering. Twenty-four monologue stations testify to the persistent experience of isolation and alienation—there is no way out. The utterance of this innermost experience is itself immediately subject to reflection, corresponding to Hegel's definition of the lyrical: "In lyric [. . .] it is feeling and reflection which [. . .] draw the objectively existent world into themselves and live it through their own inner element, and only then, after the world has become something inward, is it grasped and expressed in words" (2: 1133).

This permanent self-reflexivity in a *monologue intérieur* creates different states of consciousness that define the chain of lieder as a lyrical circling-in-itself. "The eccentric architecture of that landscape, in which every point is equally close to the center, reveals itself to the wanderer, who circles through it without moving ahead [. . .], the first step is as close to death as the last one [. . .]. And Schubert's themes are wandering in the same manner as the miller boy or he whom his beloved jilted in wintertime. They don't know of history but of telescopic circumvention: any alteration in them is a changing of light" (Adorno, 25).

The definite article in Müller's title suggests singularity. Schubert's title excludes the definite article. The one, specific journey thus becomes "Winterreise" as a general human condition, a metaphor indicating the troubled relationship between—in the terminology of German idealism—the individual and the world. It seems that Wilhelm Müller conceived of *Die Winterreise* as allegorical diagnosis of his actual present. The practice of censorship would explain the encoding of the lyrical presentation. Indeed, Müller made many theoretical statements that point to his enlightened sense of political responsibility. They all suggest that his *Die Winterreise* was more than a private love story. That Schubert likewise understood his own *Winterreise* as an encoded parable of the sociopolitical conditions of Austria under the restrictive Metternich System, can only be inferred. Schubert was by no means apolitical; his circle of friends was spied upon by the secret police, and the affair surrounding his friend Johann Senn, who was imprisoned in 1820, has rightly been seen as one of the reasons for Schubert's resigned mood during the last years of his life.

Schubert's poem "Lament to the People!" of 1824 asserts, in its final stanza, the indisputably political role of art as a mode of governorship for better, that is, liberal, times:

> Only to you, O holy art, is it granted as yet
> To depict, in an image, the times of strength and action,
> To ease, a bit at least, the haunting pain,
> Which will never reconcile them with their destiny.

Applied to *Winterreise,* this model of thought renders the lieder cycle comprehensible as political parable, even if in concrete terms it does not depict "times of strength and action" but a time of resigned reflexivity. The erratic wanderer's journey through an impenetrable landscape, an incommensurable world governed by powerful, anonymous, impersonal institutions, represents the situation of the individual longing for freedom and self-realization within the repressive police state of the Metternich era. Here the sensitive individual, unable to realize a longing for freedom, turns to art. "Willst zu meinen Liedern Deine Leier drehn?" ("Will you turn your organ for my songs?") In light of Schubert's "Lament" poem, this call for aesthetic practice means that the ideas of freedom and self-determination in the work of art will be possible until the return of "times of strength and action." This is not an optimistic view of the world and society. Only through an ironic twist will Schubert's cycle culminate in the apotheosis of music making as secret metaphor for art as political memory and as projection into the future. Both, the protagonist and the musician are outcasts. And their first attempt at a metaphorical duo ends with a metrical disaster. The singer's irregular placement of 2/4, 1/4, and 2/4 measures on top of the pianist's normal 3/4 leaves the continuation in a state of complete ambiguity. Since the 1830s, these songs have been regarded as ciphers for sociopolitical conditions. It remains a remarkable fact that, far into the industrial age, preindustrial metaphors such as the landscape evoked in Schubert's musical motives continue to carry such force and persuasive power to illuminate the present.

It is no surprise that the 20th century, convulsed as it was by violent and exhausting wars, mirrored itself most realistically in *Winterreise.* About a century after Müller and Schubert, Thomas Mann reiterated the Lindenbaum verses with their subjunctive at the end of *Der Zauberberg* (1924): "Und seine Zweige rauschten als riefen sie mir zu" ("And its branches rustled as if they called to me"), in other words, calling Hans Castorp to death. Mann understood *Winterreise* as a commentary on the danger posed by the "world feast of death"—World War I—to the individual. After World War II, Peter Härtling, in *Der Wanderer* (1988), mirrors his wanderings through bombed-out Europe not only in the destiny of other Europeans hounded to death by the Nazis, but also in an attempt to interpret the experience of alienation: the first two lines of *Winterreise* serve as the book's epigraph. In the winter of 1977, Klaus Michael Grüber, together with the ensemble of the Berlin Schaubühne, staged a performance of Hölderlin's epistolary novel *Hyperion* in the Olympic Stadium of Berlin, a structure built with programmatic intent by the Nazis. Grüber gave the performance, which was understood as a critical diagnosis of contemporary issues, the title "Winterreise." This was also the code name for the federal police operation to capture members of the Red Army Faction (RAF) in the 1960s. Grüber's presentation, which features an interplay of fascist architecture, classical drama, and scenic action, outdoors in the middle of the winter, was meant as a critique of the cold political and social climate within the Federal Republic of Germany. "Winterreise" served as its metaphor.

As a poet, Müller followed the traditional concept of the lied of the *Goethezeit,* aspiring to a lyric that was singable, and aiming for popularity and simplicity. In our days, Stephen Sondheim has reiterated this principle in a brief but precise statement quoted in a *New York Times Magazine* article: "Once a line becomes poetry, it's not a lyric" (March 12, 2000). These lyrics are complemented by music with a similarly simple melody, and it is the singer who, "using the same melody for each stanza, has to highlight the various meanings of the single stanzas" (Goethe, 1801, quoted in Schwab, p. 69). The accompanying instrument is the piano, then on its way to becoming a staple in the bourgeois household. Under such premises, "through-composing" was considered "reprehensible"; where it was accepted in the realm of the lied, the genre was called "Ode" or "Gesang."

It is Schubert's historical achievement that he gave the genre a new orientation: the art song, a creation tied to the poetry of Goethe. Following other musical genres, the lied now also aimed at constituting a work, an artifact, a self-contained aesthetic entity. Compositional aspects of this development are the rescue of the melody from the middle norms of singability and simplicity; the individualization of this melody, in line with the form and structure of the poem itself; and the technical demands beyond the ability of the singing or playing amateur. Together with the emancipation of the melody, the strophic principle is broken up and through-composing raised to noble status. Decisive, however, is the growing importance of the piano in partnership with the voice: the piano, indeed, defines the compositional physiognomy of the art form lied, its design as a character piece, and demands a revaluation of the music relative to the text. Thus the lied becomes the analogue to the lyrical piano piece—here, Mendelssohn's "Songs without Words" form the bridge, not only in terminology. From now on both genres were to undergo a parallel development.

This is, in principle, the status of the Schubert lied. But as if it were a shadow of history, traces of its emancipation remain engraved in its very contours. Thrasybulos Georgiades saw its historical position as the transition from the convivial lied of the *Goethezeit* to the "lied as musical structure," in which the popular roots of the genre are actively effaced. In Schubert's lied, the singing still determines the genre. So the voice always defines the formal frame; despite its growing role in creating the artwork, the piano remains subordinate to the voice. Schubert's compositional process, with the notation of the voice as the first step, confirms this hierarchy. The preludes in most cases quote the melody that lies ahead, while the postludes corroborate what the voice has already spelled out. With this, Schubert's lieder preserve a popular element as central to the art song.

Joseph von Spaun's recollections of the first performance of *Winterreise* (most likely its first part only), in 1827, indicates what the lied meant to Schubert, his circle, and his time:

> For some time Schubert appeared melancholy and exhausted. When I asked him what was troubling him he would say only, "Soon you will hear and understand." One day he said to me: "Come over to Schober's today, and I will sing you a cycle of horrifying lieder. I am anxious to know what you will say about them. They have affected me more than any of my other lieder." So he sang the entire *Winterreise* through to us in a voice full of emotion. We were utterly dumbfounded by the mournful, gloomy tone of these lieder, and Schober said that only one, "Der Lindenbaum," had appealed to him. To this Schubert replied, "I like these lieder more than all the rest, and you will come to like them as well."

The lied is part of the social gathering and the cultivation of art in the bourgeois home; the social place of the genre is the private circle, or the semipublic soirée of privately organized musical societies (such as the Viennese Society of the Friends of Music), not yet the concert hall. Not until later in the 19th century did the lied, at first as a single work, enter the concert stage, in a program that would constitute more or less a pastiche. Concerts of lieder alone are known only from the second half of the century on, introduced on the initiative of great singers. Julius Stockhausen sang the first concert devoted exclusively to the entire cycle of Schubert's *Die Schöne Müllerin,* in 1856 in Vienna. Credit for the introduction of *Schubert-Abende* goes to the Viennese singer Gustav Walter, whose first such recital, devoted exclusively to Schubert, in 1876, was met with enthusiasm. Already in 1887, Hugo Wolf could write about an "epidemic" of lieder recitals in Vienna.

By its nature the lied is a small form, unable on its own to fulfill the demands of the new bourgeois theory of art. As a result, lieder, like the related lyrical piano pieces, were published as collections. By assembling single lieder into a *Reihe* (series) or a *Kranz* (ring), a *Zyklus* (cycle) or even *Kreis* (circle)— that is, groupings that are structured according to a leading principle—composers tried to assert the same dignity and relevance for the lied as were accorded genres with large dimensions, such as oratorio or symphony.

Fictive rendering of experience is part of the founding constellation of the modern lyric. "Horrifying lieder": the composer points at the distress, the tragic, within the cycle. Indeed, *Winterreise* was never absorbed into the traditional postulates of the lieder genre—social gathering, artistic entertainment, domestic music making. Rather, these lieder are characterized by elevated artistic demands, requiring an equivalent higher intensity of creative efforts on the part of the composer; but Schubert alludes equally to the lieder as intentional historical parables, an understanding that is unusual for this genre. It is also helpful to remember that parallel to the work on *Winterreise,* Schubert composed songs of serene joy, such as "Der Hirt auf dem Felsen" (The Shepherd on the Rock)—the importance of creative fiction for high art cannot be overestimated.

Schubert was keenly aware of the special position of *Winterreise,* not only within his own oeuvre, but within the genre as a whole. The complexity of its contextual, representational, and art-historical position demanded equally complex compositional means and measures. The beautiful naiveté of tone, character, and formal design of *Die schöne Müllerin* was not suitable for *Winterreise.* Here the strophic lied form recedes into the background; indeed, only three purely strophic songs appear, for specific modes of expression— "Frühlingstraum," with its internal structure of changes in tempo and character, is more a two-part lied than strophic—and there are four varied strophic lieder. These same songs, however, are characterized by an artificial game that is played with the strophic form itself, as in "Der Lindenbaum"; they show sudden structural breaks, changes of tempo, melodic extravaganzas, major-minor variants, and so on. In this way, the seemingly simple, strophic principle of repetition is used to achieve rather complex artistic formulations. Dominant in *Winterreise* are individual designs derived directly from the literary texts. We find a rich arsenal of different musical textures and characters (Budde, 81ff), models and formulas taken from the classical-romantic musical language and combined to form a compositionally coherent, expressive unit that reflects the poetic construction and meaning of the text. Thus we find an arioso juxtaposed with a recitative ("Frühlingstraum"); periodically structured melodies ("Gute Nacht") and melodic split-offs and divisions that become independent, fragmentary entities (the doubled consequent at the beginning of "Der Lindenbaum"); ornamentally whimsical melodic figurations for specific modes of expression—coloratura-like runs in the second half of "Wetterfahne," melodic excesses in "Irrlicht"; settings quasi for brass bands ("Das Wirtshaus," "Die Nebensonnen"); instrumental characters in general—the unisons in "Letzte Hoffnung," integrating the voice; chorale-like chord progressions with a leading upper voice ("Der Lindenbaum," beginning; "Im Dorfe," end). There is even the normal lied setting: a voice with a figuratively elaborated piano accompaniment ("Erstarrung"), to outline just a few. In most of *Winterreise,* the piano part is essentially helping to formulate specific characters. Besides the patterns of figurations typical for an accompanying piano ("Die Post"), structural themes from other musical spheres appear: tremoli that imitate orchestral techniques for the string section ("Einsamkeit") or similarly orchestral octave and double-octave runs ("Letzte Hoffnung"); from the vocal realm derive melodic lines in the piano that surpass the voice ("Der greise Kopf"), and so forth. Schubert's creative fantasy seems to have invested an unusually high degree of historical consciousness and awareness in the task of writing a work that pretends to represent the truth about the new society which, at the beginning of the 19th century, was so optimistically envisioned and only a quarter of a century later seemed to have no practical chance of becoming reality.

See also 1808, 1828 (Winter), 1831, 1943

Bibliography: Theodor W. Adorno, "Schubert" (written 1928), *Musikalische Schriften* 4, 18–33, ed. Rolf Tiedemann, *Gesammelte Schriften* 17 (Frankfurt am Main: Suhrkamp, 1997). Elmar Budde, *Schuberts Liederzyklen* (Munich: Beck, 2003). G. W. F. Hegel, *Aesthetics: Lectures on Fine Art,* trans. T. M. Knox (Oxford: Clarendon, 1975). Hans Joachim Kreutzer, "Wilhelm Müller: Der Artist in den Traditionen der Literatur," *Obertöne: Literatur und Musik* (Würzburg, 1994), 176–195. Heinrich W. Schwab, *Sangbarkeit, Popularität und Kunstlied: Studien zu Lied und Liedästhetik der mittleren Goethezeit 1770–1814* (Regensburg: Bosse, 1965). Susan Youens, *Retracing a Winter's Journey: Schubert's "Winterreise"* (Ithaca, N.Y.: Cornell University Press, 1991).

Reinhold Brinkmann

✌ *1831, July 21*

Goethe notes in his diary: "Conclusion of the main business"

Faust *and the Dialectic of Modernity*

When, on the cusp of his eighty-second year, Johann Wolfgang Goethe recorded in his diary that the "main business"—the term he employed to refer to his *Faust*—was finally finished, he marked the completion of a project begun nearly sixty years before. Can a dramatic-poetic work of such protracted genesis possibly possess formal and thematic unity? Only, one is tempted to answer, if the socio-cultural conditions and artistic conventions obtaining during its gradual composition were stable throughout. Then the texture of an author's experience, his formal preferences, his field of references, the order of his values, and his sense of vocation might remain constant even across such a long stretch of biographical time.

However, the period during which Goethe worked on his *Faust*—discontinuously, to be sure—was dense with transformation. Consider only such turning points of political history as the French Revolution, the Napoleonic Wars, and the collapse of the Holy Roman Empire of the German Nation, all of which immediately touched Goethe's life and deeply affected his thought. Consider the philosophical revolution inaugurated by Kant and carried out by his idealist successors, Fichte, Schelling, Schopenhauer, and Hegel, all of whom Goethe knew personally. Or consider the evolution of Goethe's own literary work from the sentimentalism of *Die Leiden des jungen Werthers* (1774; *The Sorrows of Young Werther*) and the Sturm und Drang of his early hymns, to the measured classicism of his dramas *Iphigenie auf Tauris* (1787; *Iphigenia in Tauris*) and *Torquato Tasso* (1790); from his Bildungsroman *Wilhelm Meisters Lehrjahre* (1795–1796; *Wilhelm Meister's Apprenticeship*) to the tragic, hermetic novel *Die Wahlverwandtschaften* (1809; *Elective Affinities*); from the palpable eroticism of *Römische Elegien* (1795; *Roman Elegies*) to the mysterious spirituality and parabolic intricacy of *West-östlicher Divan* (1819; *West-East Divan*). Nowhere is stability perceptible, everywhere there is accelerating change.

Consider further such formative experiences as the move to Weimar, where Goethe occupied a host of demanding official positions, his journey to

Italy, his friendship with Schiller, and his immersion in botany, animal physiology, and optics, fields in which Goethe made significant discoveries. Consider finally that, when he began his *Faust,* Goethe was an unknown author in an underdeveloped literary milieu and that, upon its completion, he was the foremost living exemplar of "world literary" culture, a concept he himself had invented. In short, when one reflects on all that intervened between Goethe's first engagement with the Faust legend and the accomplishment of the work some eight months before his death, on March 22, 1832, it is difficult to imagine how his *Faust* could hold together at all.

This suspicion is strengthened when one turns to the work itself. It consists of two parts, the first of which divides into the "scholar's tragedy"—Faust's despair at attaining pure knowledge, leading to his alliance with the devil Mephistopheles—and the "Gretchen Tragedy"—Faust's illicit and disastrous love affair with Margarete, called Gretchen. The second part is yet more disparate, consisting of five loosely connected acts, each of which takes place in a different sphere of experience. Act 1 shows Faust at the emperor's court, where he orchestrates entertainments, draws Helen of Troy from the abyss of the past, and participates in a bit of financial wizardry (the invention of paper money). Act 2 returns to the medieval study where the play began and where Wagner, Faust's former amanuensis, has succeeded in creating a homunculus, a sort of test-tube human spirit. The act concludes with an elaborate "Classical Walpurgis Night" in which Homunculus leads Faust on a tour of often obscure mythological scenes culminating in the conception of Helen. In Act 3, Faust finds himself in Ancient Greece, where, in the guise of a late-medieval lord, he is joined in love with the beautiful, but ghostly Helen only to see their offspring, Euphorion, fall from the cliffs to his death, at which point Helen too disappears. Act 4 is devoted to military exploits, with Faust and Mephistopheles introducing techniques of warfare that secure the victory of the emperor's forces. In Act 5, Faust appears as a colonial ruler who undertakes a vast project of engineering, both civil—building dikes to hold back the seas—and social— a utopian community of "free" individuals. All of this ends with the murder of the ancient couple Philemon and Baucis, for which Faust bears responsibility, and then Faust's own death, when, blinded by Care, he mistakes the sound of the gravediggers' grim labor for the realization of his engineering enterprise. There follows a coda of sorts in which Faust's "immortal part" is extricated from Mephistopheles' grasp and borne upward through a medieval hierarchy of souls toward the "eternal feminine."

Goethe once remarked that the Helen act (II, 3) extended from the defeat of Troy to the destruction of Missolonghi (where Lord Byron died in 1824), but the reach of the entire drama, especially if one takes the natural historical dimension into account, is literally incalculable. The "Prologue in Heaven" that precedes part I suggests a vision of the world as it was on the "first day" of creation and the ascent of Faust's postmortal self, with which the drama concludes, is directed toward an open future. The unities of place, time, and action, which, however tenuously, had contained Western drama since antiquity, are cast aside. *Faust* exceeds even the scope of Homeric and Vergilian epic, out-reaches even the cosmic vision of Dante. And it does so while drawing on the entire gamut of stylistic registers, from blank obscenity to mystical conceit, from ceremonious rhetoric to heart-rending lyricism, from learned allusion to ludic nonsense.

But if the usual criteria of literary unity fail us in our attempt to understand (a verb that doubtless claims too much) Goethe's *Faust,* perhaps we should look elsewhere for generic comparisons. A suggestive example is the genre of the encyclopedia, which, of course, achieved one of its pinnacles—the *Encyclopédie* of d'Alembert and Diderot—in Goethe's lifetime. The ambition of an encyclopedia is to chart not the world, not an action, but knowledge in all its manifestations. It is a meta-epistemic genre that collects, displays, and or-ders all that practical, scientific, aesthetic, psychological, social, and religious inquiry has achieved. Not that Goethe patterned his work on that of the encyclopedists. The point, rather, is that his *Faust* shares with their project the feature of redoubled or reflective learning; it is first and foremost a document of staggering erudition, which absorbs within its web of references treatises on magic and witchcraft, historical and art historical knowledge, political history, interpretation of myth, theological speculation, science, technical expertise, and much more. It interweaves the legend of Faust with the Book of Job and the Gospel of John. The section on Gretchen recapitulates the structure of bourgeois tragedy, with generous use of Shakespearean technique. In part II, ancient myth, Homeric epic, Attic tragedy, medieval love poetry, the operas of Monteverdi, renaissance pastoral, Calderon's plays, the courtly masque, and Dante's religious vision make their presence felt. The versification is a virtual catalogue of metrical and strophic forms from antiquity to Goethe's time. The protagonist, whom we first see with a book by Nostradamus on his desk, dis-appears from sight at the drama's end in a vision drawn from the Church Fa-ther Origen (by way of the 18th-century religious historian Gottfried Arnold). *Faust* is a book that interconnects many books in a vast and intricate semantic network. The space it charts is that of European cultural memory.

Helpful as it is in highlighting the meta-epistemic and, as it were, archival character of *Faust,* the encyclopedic paradigm is misleading insofar as it sug-gests a static order viewed from a single, quasi-omniscient perspective. *Faust,* by contrast, is sustained by a forward-moving drive epitomized in what can be called the drama's key word: *Streben* ("striving"). Faust's character consists in just this: that he incessantly reaches beyond the satisfactions of the present mo-ment, that each accomplishment is merely a platform for his next undertaking. Whereas dramatic characters are typically defined by the substantive goals they pursue, for Faust pursuit itself, regardless of goal, is primary. This feature en-ables us to see what is at stake in Goethe's drama. Aristotle had imagined that every being—including humankind—is endowed with a goal toward which its efforts are directed and the attainment of which is its unique perfection.

This concept of a universe of preordained "places," in which action realizes its purpose and thereby achieves rest and fulfillment, was carried over into the Christian Middle Ages. With modernity, however, the closed universe opens onto infinity. In Giovanni Pico della Mirandola's speech "On the Dignity of Man" (1486–87), the human being is defined as that creature for whom there is no predestined niche, but whose destiny it is freely to create his own office. In the anthropology of Thomas Hobbes (1588–1679), the Aristotelian principle of internal purpose (entelechy) is replaced by a principle of self-conservation and self-aggrandizement, which no particular end can satisfy. Desire and endeavor are not teleologically determined vectors, but modes of self-affirmation. The human being—such is the structure of its every activity—is its own end, and this end resides solely in the ongoing realization of its dynamic potential.

Viewed against this background, *Faust* is not merely a modern drama, but the drama of modernity, an exploration of how human life unfolds when it detaches itself from the ordinations of tradition and embarks on a project of energetic self-assertion and self-optimization. And for this reason *Faust* presents itself to us as a meta-epistemic document, for among the fields of appropriation opened up to the modern subject are those of past cultural achievements. An essential component of modernity is that it understands itself historically. Just because it is the drama of modernity, *Faust* is also a drama of cultural memory and historical consciousness. The unity of *Faust*—to return to our initial question—does not stem from plot or place, nor is it rooted in a single thematic domain. Rather, it derives from the structural dynamic that characterizes modern "striving" in the encyclopedic breadth of its expressions: love, history, politics, art, knowledge, religion, science, economics, and technology.

One of the crucial innovations of Goethe's rendering of the Faust story was to replace the pact between Faust and Mephistopheles with a wager, and a rather peculiar one at that. For Faust bets that no blandishment Mephistopheles might proffer—no pleasure, no glory, no possession, no achievement—could count as genuine fulfillment; that no moment of time could come to which Faust might say: "Tarry, you are so beautiful." It is a wager that the discrepancy between will and attainment is ineluctable, that experience, here and now, will never cause his striving to abate.

Since this wager sets the conditions on which Faust's salvation will be decided at the drama's end, it is not surprising that the passage in which it is formulated has gathered as much commentary as any in German literature. Here we must confine ourselves to two salient aspects. The first is that the wager formalizes what was described above as the structure of modern consciousness; what Faust bets on is his own unquenchable drive toward an ever enhanced optimization of his own resources. But the wager also makes clear on what playing field this striving is to be tested: the field of experience in time, of human finitude. Faust makes the wager, in other words, after realizing that immediate access to the Absolute—be it the harmonious order depicted in the sign of the macrocosm, be it the natural force embodied in the Earth Spirit—is foreclosed to him. The fraught alliance between Faust and Mephistopheles the wager institutes, and which holds constant throughout the play, expresses the fact that the open-endedness of modern striving can only be realized in a world of thoroughgoing conditionality. Mephistopheles is not a power extraneous to Faustian subjectivity; he is not an avoidable evil, and for this reason, in contradistinction to its predecessors, Goethe's *Faust* is finally not interpretable in moral terms. One must not forget the full title of the work: *Faust, a Tragedy.* The lethal pairing of Faust and Mephistopheles expresses the founding surmise of Goethe's drama: modernity realizes itself in accordance with a tragic dialectic; to set sail for the open seas of self-affirmation—and this voyage *is* modernity's destiny—is to founder, at tremendous cost, on the shoals of human finitude.

One of the deepest mysteries of Goethe's *Faust* is certainly the fact that Mephistopheles, as he himself notes, is a blatant anachronism. Why did Goethe elect to bring the devil—or one of his vicars—onto the stage in an age that boasted of having freed itself of such superstitions? Our parsing of the play as embodying the tragic dialectic of modernity suggests an answer to this question. The pairing of Faust and Mephistopheles expresses (at least) three features of the modern condition. Mephistopheles exhibits, first of all, the dependence of modern striving on instruments and mediations it does not fully control. Mephisto (as Faust calls him on one occasion) provides the enabling means for Faust's every project, from winning Gretchen's heart to the evacuation of Philemon and Baucis from their idyllic hut. Precisely these means, however, eventually overwhelm each enterprise with murderous consequences. Second, Mephisto embodies the fact that the Faustian drive toward optimization, however elevated its avowed intentions, is inextricably entwined with a violent, destructive tendency, which Goethe traces even to the core of Faust's erotic desire. And third, Mephistopheles' inveterate cynicism—a feature that earns him almost all the cutting, comic lines in the play—illustrates the duplicity of modern consciousness, the fact that it can always step outside of itself and see, even in its highest aspirations, baseness; in its deepest convictions, mendacity. Under the conditions of finitude, every love is also a seduction and betrayal, every creation implies destruction, every truth we aver is eventually belied.

Since the complete *Faust* became available, posthumously in 1832, readers have endeavored to sever Faust from Mephistopheles, to distinguish high ideals from evil machinations. But this betrays Goethe's basic insight in the play: the insight that, like Prometheus to his rock, we are fettered to our finitude. Our actions take place in a world we did not make and bear consequences we cannot foresee. Our every impulse is a monster of tenderness and aggression. Our every intention is susceptible to ironic reversal. And worst of all: the ineluctable necessity of this dual—or dialectical—structure affords us no exculpation.

There are deeper mysteries still. Part I, the disasters of which include heartless castigation, murder (of mother, brother, child), madness, and unspeakable horror, ends with a "voice from above" declaring Gretchen "redeemed." Part

II, the catastrophes of which culminate in the murder of the elderly couple Philemon and Baucis and the torching of their home, ends with a coda that traces the ascent of Faust's soul, guided finally by Gretchen's spirit, toward ever higher spheres. In other words, the concluding gestures of both parts—however relativized and uncertain they may be—seem to suspend tragic finality and to suggest the possibility of salvation. We may trace this gesture to Goethe's conviction that there is such a thing as the unassailable purity of love or that the drift of natural immanence is directed toward the good. But what Goethe ultimately believed, and whether he even had ultimate beliefs, remains forever inscrutable. As we close the greatest poetic masterpiece in the German language, we are left with the unresolved dissonance of hope and despair. No reader can say what this dissonance means in itself, but each reader must decide what it might mean for his or her own life, here and now.

See also 1596, 1774, 1786, 1790, 1792 (August 26), 1796–1797, 1828 (Winter), 1943

Bibliography: Johann Wolfgang von Goethe, *Faust,* ed. Albrecht Schöne, 4th rev. ed., 2 vols. (Frankfurt am Main: Deutscher Klassiker Verlag, 1999). ———, *Faust-Dichtungen,* ed. Ulrich Gaier, 3 vols. (Stuttgart: Reclam, 1999). ———, *Faust,* second edition, ed. Cyrus Hamlin, trans. Walter Arndt (New York and London: Norton, 2001).

David E. Wellbery

♌ 1833

Rahel Levin Varnhagen's three-volume collection of letters to her friends is published shortly after her death

Writing between Genres and Discourses

Even the title of this book, *Rahel: Ein Buch des Andenkens für ihre Freunde (Rahel: A Book of Commemoration for Her Friends),* raises questions. It begins with a proper name, but only with the given name, Rahel. It is meant to be a book for Rahel's friends, who shall remember her. Or is it they who will be remembered? It is indeed a very peculiar book: a collection of diary entries and letters, written between October 20, 1787, and February 23, 1833, in three extensive volumes, about eighteen hundred pages. To whom are these texts addressed? Flipping through the pages one encounters familiar names: Wilhelm von Humboldt and Friedrich Schlegel, Friedrich Gentz and Clemens Brentano, Hermann Graf Pückler-Muskau, Heinrich Heine, and Ludwig Börne. But Humboldt, Heine, Schlegel, and Börne, among the best known in the group, have only one letter each. Pückler comes off a little better: he has five. Gentz has eleven, and only Brentano seems to have been a major correspondent, the recipient of thirty-four letters. Other correspondents would only be familiar to specialists, while the bulk of the letters is written to people who have been totally forgotten. Everybody is to be found here, actresses and philosophers, acculturated Jewish women and unconventional countesses, young intellectuals and civil servants. The "friends" obviously represent a heterogeneous group of people whose memory survives exclusively in these letters. The only connection between them was this woman, with whom they all were acquainted.

But what is this woman, the writer of all these texts, to be called? Many of the letters are not signed at all; some are signed "R.," "R.L.," or "R.R.," others "Fr. V" or "F.V.," very few "Friederike Varnhagen." Almost never is the signature "Rahel." The preface to the book tells us nothing about the writer. The readers learn only that a book with the same title had been published previously, that copies had been distributed only to friends, that the recent reissue had been expanded from one to three volumes and was completed in Berlin in December 1833. A long introduction—fifty pages—untitled, but signed "K. A. Varnhagen von Ense" and dated "Berlin, im April 1833," reveals the identity of the woman who wrote the book: "Rahel Antonie Friederike Varnhagen von Ense, born Rahel Levin, later known under the family name of Robert."

The complex name marks a complex identity: Rahel Levin, the daughter of a Jewish merchant family, born 1771 in Berlin, where she died in 1833, has come down to posterity under the name of Rahel Varnhagen, a name she never bore. In order to marry Karl August Varnhagen, a Prussian diplomat and writer, in 1814, she had to convert to Christianity. For her baptism, she chose Antonie and Friederike as her given names, the latter in honor of King Friedrich II of Prussia, in whose realm she was born and brought up. The name Rahel had to disappear from her Christian identity; in Prussia, one could not be baptized with a Jewish name.

The book, however, emphasized exactly this suppressed name. Many readers even called it the *Buch Rahel (Book of Rachel),* giving it a biblical sound. And they all responded as "friends." For the first, private edition of 1833, of which only very few copies survive, this is no surprise. The book was addressed to "friends" because only they received a copy, as a list of recipients found among the Varnhagens' papers, now in the Biblioteka Jagiellonska in Krakow, clearly shows. But one year later, the expanded version entered the public sphere. With this, both halves of the title become almost unreadable. How are we to approach a book that neither is published anonymously nor bears the author's name? How are these texts to be read when the foreword states that they are addressed to readers who have become friends of Rahel's even after Friederike Varnhagen had passed away or will become friends of her in a vaguely circumscribed future? Varnhagen's introduction provides the reader with an explicit reading strategy: "This communication is only for friends. Whoever will receive them as an unknown or a stranger might read its content like a found letter not written to him but exactly therefore to be read discreetly and charitably" (I.3).

The reception history of the book shows that the readers almost exclusively followed this suggestion. *Rahel: Ein Buch des Andenkens für ihre Freunde* was understood as a kind of autobiography; editors often rearranged its letters and supplied information about the writer's life. The theoretical quality of this unusual book, however, has not yet been fully appreciated. In contrast to the notions of authorship that appeared in Europe around 1800, anchoring writing in the exceptional individual, here a heterogeneous group of people produced a composition together. Without addressees, without friends who answer her letters, no writing would be possible. And yet a break with established genres always carries its own risks. Authors who write books can be relatively confident that their work will be preserved in libraries. Those who write letters, however, are prey to all the vicissitudes of their dispersal. Sooner or later letters tend to get lost. A historical vulnerability is built into the form, and so Rahel Levin Varnhagen had to develop a strategy to prevent these writings from disappearing. Already in her early twenties, she collected and kept all the letters she received. Before she left for Paris in 1800, she asked a friend not only to tend to this collection, should she die, but also to try to retrieve from her various correspondents all the letters that she herself had written—a clear indication of how very seriously she took this particular form of writing and collecting.

Rahel Levin Varnhagen's new strategy forced her to confront another problem, since she wanted not only to preserve all this ephemeral material, but publish it as well. As early as 1812, she began a long series of epistolary publications in various journals, following two contradictory organizational principles. The first project is a dialogue in which she engaged with Karl August Varnhagen. The couple selected from their correspondence remarks about Goethe's work, and arranged them in a montage. Later publications exhibit a different structure: in these, only Rahel Levin Varnhagen is heard. The replies are not part of the printed dialogue.

The *Book of Commemoration* follows the latter structure. The timing of its initial publication—only a few weeks after Rahel's death—as well as the selection of letters presented, suggest that the Varnhagens had finished this book during Rahel's lifetime. Included are letters to friends who already had died or with whom the friendship had not survived. These letters, therefore, had already been returned to the Varnhagens. Dozens of letters to Varnhagen, preserved in the Varnhagen collection, show that he started to collect his wife's letters immediately after her death. Therefore he was able to finish the expanded version as early as December 1833. But he did not stop with this date. A beautiful third version of the *Book of Commemoration* has been discovered in Krakow: three thick volumes in quarto format, bound in pigskin. For this book, on which he continued to work at least through the 100th anniversary of Goethe's birth on August 28, 1849, Varnhagen used a copy of the 1834 edition, pasted every single page into a passe-partout to gain space for additions, and included transcriptions—handwritten, of course, on colored paper—of all the letters he had managed to get back from Rahel's correspondents. This manuscript, which was never published, contains more than fifteen hundred letters and diary entries, three times the size of the 1834 version. In 2003, the first edition of this book became available online; an electronic publication seems to be the only appropriate mode for a work in progress. All additions and previously unpublished letters are shown in different fonts, highlighting the manifold layers of its production. In the 21st century, publishing technology has at long last caught up to the complexity of the *Book of Commemoration*.

This book can be read as an archive of reflections on the changes that occurred around 1800, discussed not only by individuals involved in those transformations but also by those who—for various reasons—were relegated to the margins. The new institutions of modern bourgeois life and their discourses are challenged: bourgeois marriage and the discourse of love, authorship and the image of the genius, post-revolutionary politics and the denial of the achievements of the French Revolution, the modern university with its division into disciplines as well as its pattern of exclusion.

In March 1803, Rahel wrote in her diary: "Slavery, war, marriage!—and people are astonished and try to mend things." She thus connected several discrete phenomena nobody else had previously seen as related. In one of her earliest letters, she presents the impossibility of a happy marriage as metaphor for the way Christians and Jews live together in Germany.

When Wilhelm von Humboldt started to work on the guidelines for the modern university—to be founded in Berlin in 1810— Rahel understood this institutional innovation also as the end of a very special kind of intellectual productivity the two of them had developed together. In June 1809, she wrote to him: "What studies we might have completed with one another; what worlds of life we could have discovered: what accounts you could have gotten from me! You should be ashamed, you sedulous incompetent researcher!" (I.430).

As these quotes show, Rahel thought in a way that cannot be easily integrated into existing genre categories. Unlike many of her contemporaries, Henriette Herz, Dorothea Schlegel, Bettina von Arnim, and others, she was never drawn to writing narrative or poetry. Hers was a special kind of thinking that did not move within disciplinary boundaries and established fields of knowledge. "I do not have a stored up stock of thoughts [*aufgespeicherten Geistesvorrath*]," she once wrote. A special moment, a conversation, a book, or anything else might serve as the occasion for productivity.

It was not until the 1920s, the time of the Weimar Republic, that intellectual Jewish women recognized the *Book of Commemoration* as a major theoretical achievement. Margarete Susman's *Frauen der Romantik* (1929; *Women of the Romantic Era*) is one of the very few attempts to view these texts "as veins of gold in primordial rock, an entire, great system of thought." Inspired by her reading of Nietzsche, Susman perceived Rahel's book as a way of thinking that cannot be reduced to existing theories. Only a new way of thinking, such as Rahel's, can provide a genuine reflection of what it means to be Jewish in a Christian-dominated society. According to Susman, Rahel experienced being Jewish as the "fundamental tie of her life." Yet at the same time, Susman sees a "particular, basic Jewish force" at work here, the "power for joy to bloom even above the abyss [. . .] Chassidic mysticism calls it the Burning." The term "Jewish" marks here a kind of otherness with historical roots, which is likewise grounded in the collapse of metaphysics. In this reading, Rahel has left behind the archive of a conflict that modernity inevitably faces. She did it in such a radical way, says Susman, that the "form of her life and being are so strange to us that they are both unimaginable."

Hannah Arendt, however, who had almost finished her biography of Rahel Varnhagen when she fled Germany in 1933, came to a different conclusion. Relying on the extensive version still available in the Staatsbibliothek in Berlin before the manuscripts were relocated to the East, Arendt saw the book as a document of the failed attempt at assimilating into German culture, even before it really started. Arendt views Rahel's book in terms of highly restricted generic possibilities. Recast as biography and thus subject to chronology, the theoretical significance of Rahel's work is again effaced and with it the book on which Arendt based her reconstruction. She never pays tribute to the unpublished *Book of Commemoration* from which many of her quotes are drawn. Instead, she blames Varnhagen for having changed Rahel's letters in his transcriptions. Arendt never consulted Rahel's manuscripts and we, therefore, read here "Rahel Levin" as prepared for the future by her husband.

It was only in the 1980s that scholars gained access to the Varnhagen archive in Krakow. And only then did it become obvious that Rahel Levin's "work," which survived very close to the sites where the European Jews had been murdered in the 20th century, calls for publication. In 1997, the first of six volumes of a critical annotated edition of Rahel Levin Varnhagen's correspondence appeared. In contrast to the *Book of Commemoration,* this edition presents only exchanges of letters. It adheres to the dialogical structure of the archive in which the letters are grouped by correspondent. The edition concentrates on previously unpublished parts of Rahel Levin's work, namely the correspondences with women friends, with her family, and her diaries. It shows the difficult process of acculturation in Germany as well as the quality of a work written by a group. Both are aspects of the work's modernity. In the early 20th century, young intellectuals again came to realize that only collective intellectual production can provide adequate understanding of their time.

See also 1800 (January), 1824, 1942

Bibliography: Rahel: Ein Buch des Andenkens für ihre Freunde, ed. Karl August Varnhagen, 1 vol. (privately published, 1833); 3 vols. (Berlin: Duncker und Humblot, 1834). *Rahel-Bibliothek: Rahel Varnhagen, Gesammelte Werke,* ed. Konrad Feilchenfeldt et al., 10 vols. (Munich: Matthes und Seitz, 1983). *Edition Rahel Levin Varnhagen,* ed. Barbara Hahn and Ursula Isselstein, 6 vols. (Munich: Beck, 1997–). Margarete Susman, *Die Frauen der Romantik* (1929), ed. Barbara Hahn (Frankfurt am Main: Insel, 1996). Ursula Isselstein, *Der Text aus meinem Herzen: Studien zu Rahel Levin Varnhagen* (Turin, Italy: Tirrenia Stampatori, 1993). Hannah Arendt, *Rahel Varnhagen: The Life of a Jewess,* trans. Richard and Clara Winston, ed. Liliane Weissberg (Baltimore and London: Johns Hopkins University Press, 1997). Heidi Thomann Tewarson, *Rahel Varnhagen: The Life and Work of a German Jewish Intellectual* (Lincoln: University of Nebraska Press, 1998).

Barbara Hahn

♩ *1834*

The physiognomy of the year 1834 finds its reflection in a photograph of Franz Grillparzer and the premiere of his play *Der Traum ein Leben*

Viennese Biedermeier

Writing history, Walter Benjamin noted, is putting a face on numbered years. For the year 1834, we might find, as the literal realization of historical physiognomy, the face of a typical Viennese *Raunzer,* the unhappy, grouchy complainer who thrives on his unhappiness much too much to deal with its causes. As a metaphorical face, we might select the image of a laborious dream of action that turns into a nightmare of unwanted change and is replaced with resignation.

The literal physiognomy is represented by a photograph of Franz Grillparzer (1791–1872) and the metaphorical one in his play *Der Traum ein Leben (Dream, a Life),* which premiered at the Vienna Burgtheater on October 4, 1834. When Marie Ebner-Eschenbach commented on the significance of the photograph (taken shortly before Grillparzer's death), which shows the face of a very disgruntled, embittered old man, she did not realize that it was the face of a generation, that is, the image of a time whose dreams remained unrealized. She imagined the impressive forehead as surrounded by great ideas which an ill fate (the "Unstern" governing Grillparzer's life) had prevented from being realized, and she adds: "What this man has suffered is most movingly evidenced in the mouth, with its telling silence and clear traces of dogged pain and suppressed fury." The anguish of a tortured life that found refuge only in a dream is at the center of Grillparzer's—and many of his contemporaries'—creative process. The dream taking the place of a wanting life is the programmatic title of an entire period—notably in Austria, where Ludolf Wienbarg's concurrent *Ästhetische Feldzüge* (1834; *Aesthetic Campaigns*), dedicated to "young Germany" and thereby inspiring a movement famous for its literary activism, had little chance of gaining any ground.

Grillparzer's hypochondriacal pessimism, to which he admitted in a diary entry of September 1850, has to be viewed within the wider context of Viennese Biedermeier culture and politics. With its characteristic combination of severe political restrictions, quiet family circles, social glamour, and flight into the fantasy of music, dance, and theater, the Biedermeier has been both celebrated and denounced as the bourgeois period when a nostalgically constructed dream world, doomed from the start, was anxiously protected against the harsh realities of industrialization.

In spite of its widely commercialized reputation for bourgeois *Gemütlichkeit,* the era between the Vienna Congress in 1815 and the March revolution of 1848—often called the "Metternich Era" in reference to the chancellor (since 1821) of the German Confederation, Clemens Prince Metternich (1773–1859)—was a period of uneasy calm, much anxiety, and outright oppression. In historical accounts of this period, the Biedermeier paradigm of private bliss and acquiescence was repeatedly challenged by the concurrent *Vormärz* (pre-March period, that is, the era before March 1848) paradigm of public agony and critical defiance. Satisfaction with the peace of the status quo, based on what historians identified as Metternich's principle of *Beharrung* (persistence), was emphasized in the former paradigm, and discontent and unrest, based on the principle of *Bewegung* (movement), in the latter. Not surprisingly, the dominant political climate at different times favored the affirmative rather than the critical stance. After Biedermeier scholarship began to flourish in the early Nazi period, with its penchant for particularly "German" patterns of compliance, the Austrian *Anschluß* of 1938 and the horrors of World War II increased the need for a nostalgic escape into *Wiener* Biedermeier (which also was the title of a richly illustrated book with no fewer than five editions from 1941 to 1944). In the conservative postwar Adenauer era, it was invoked against its critics in Friedrich Sengle's monumental three-volume study, *Biedermeierzeit* (1971–1980). The view that grants the Biedermeier certain redeeming, if not redemptive, qualities seems to have triumphed over the critical positions that see in the *Vormärz* period a more realistic and progressive, though failing, response to the crisis of modernity.

Generally believed to be the fullest expression of Biedermeier values, Grillparzer's drama *Der Traum ein Leben* nevertheless reveals their dialectical implications. It stages an escape from discontent with inaction and tedium through a thrilling excursion into a fairy tale of action only to turn the exotic dream into a nightmare of intrigue and murder. In the end, the restless hero, Rustan, who in the dream is a tyrant usurping an abusing power, is happy to return to the tranquillity of his simple, unassuming life. Standing in for the audience, Rustan has learned his lesson, it seems, when he proclaims: "Eines nur ist Glück hienieden, / Eins, des Innern stiller Frieden / Und die schuldbefreite Brust!" (v. 2650 ff: One thing only is happiness on earth, / One thing only, a quiet inner peace / And a heart freed from guilt!). Obviously, the physiognomy of 1834 is a political nightmare, which serves to justify another escape, not activism, but what Germans, and Austrians, call *Innerlichkeit* (retreat into oneself), an uneasy peace of internalized conflict. The calm of Biedermeier complacency seems restored, the guilt of violence removed, and any doubt about the status quo forever dispelled.

Therefore, it is perhaps not surprising that in this case the censors did not intervene. But what appeased their ever-watchful eyes on the surface in fact undermined the very principles the drama seems to promote. Rustan is delivered from his dangerous dream of action only because he turns into an agent of the very oppression that has rendered his life inactive and miserable. By acting out —and with dramatic aplomb—the violence that is tearing at the social fabric, Rustan becomes the unwitting instrument in representing the unrepresentable: the reckless abuse of political power. While the place of action, Samarkand, seems remote from Vienna, the exotic locale barely hides the temporal, historical, and even political proximity of Vienna. What is dreamed up as a fairy tale turns out to be political reality; it is the cozy home that is the really exotic.

The king's daughter Gülnare falls in love with Rustan in his dream only because he is the namesake of another Rustan, the legendary hero of ancient Persian fairy tales. His powerful name is a faint reminder of the legendary romantic hero of the same name. But however mythically removed his name may seem, Grillparzer's Rustan shares it also with Napoleon's valet and bodyguard—a fact so widely known that Karl Immermann relates in his cultural memoir of 1839 that one of his aunts was called "Tante Rustan" because of her Bonapartist views. Grillparzer's drama *König Ottokars Glück und Ende* (*King Ottokar's Good Fortune and End;* completed in 1823 and not performed before 1825) was first banned by the censors because Ottokar's actions were an obvious, embarrassing reminder of Napoleon's marriage to the daughter of his former enemy, Emperor Francis II. One might assume that in the aftermath of Napoleon, the dramatic presence of Rustan, too, was well grounded in contemporary conflicts.

The fiction of temporal as well as spatial distance easily becomes transparent to indicate changes in the contemporary culture, thus rendering the literary text into a timely cultural document. Read as much horizontally in the context of its symbolic signification as vertically in its traditional historical patterns, Grillparzer's *Der Traum ein Leben* may offer some answers to a question suggested by Erich Auerbach in *Mimesis* (1946): "If German writers after 1840 did not produce any serious representation of contemporary social reality and historical movement, how can literary texts written in the mid-1830s, especially within Austrian literature with its pronounced resistance to social mobility and historical change, be expected to provide clues for a better understanding of such failing?" How can Grillparzer's drama of 1834, which was never central to a merely literary approach to his oeuvre, indicate in cultural terms the caesura usually connected with the July Revolution of 1830, Hegel's death in 1831, and Goethe's death in 1832, a caesura (with some lag time allowed for the less developed south) that would signify not only a new time but, more importantly, also a new sense of time with its frequent invocation of the zeitgeist? And how could this drama mark the halfway point between 1823, when Grillparzer presented his enthusiastic hymn on the Austrian *Sonderweg* (particularism) in *König Ottokars Glück und Ende,* and 1847, when he completed his moving portrait of an Austrian *Sonderling* (outsider) in *Der arme Spielmann (The Poor Minstrel)?*

Grillparzer confessed in his autobiography of 1853 *(Selbstbiographie)* that he always considered himself equal to the "classics" in German literature, Goethe and Schiller, but he was not a classicist. While some of his earlier plays, *Sappho* (1818), the trilogy *Das goldene Vließ* (1820; *The Golden Fleece*), and *Des Meeres und der Liebe Wellen* (1829; *The Waves of the Sea and of Love*), were based on characters and topics from Ancient Greece, Grillparzer cannot be claimed for

German classicism. In spite of an understandable effort, notably in the United
States, to use the "Austrian classicist" to balance and even challenge the cultural hegemony of Prussia and of Germany at the time of the Nazi regime,
Hofmannsthal's dictum of 1922 in his *Rede auf Grillparzer (Speech on Grill-*
parzer) still holds true: "The debate among his contemporaries, whether he is a
classicist or a romanticist, is of no relevance." Not only did Grillparzer resent
German idealism, he also did not share the classicists' emphasis on the timeless-
ness of the human condition. Unlike Goethe and Schiller, who were rooted in
the ideals of the German Enlightenment and tested by early Romanticism,
Grillparzer, born more than a generation later, came from a cultural background in which the Baroque, with its keen sense of the temporality of human
existence, seemed to veer directly into a melancholy variant of 19th-century
historicism.

Grillparzer is best known for dealing with, and sometimes glorifying, earlier periods of Austrian history, as in his dramas *König Ottokars Glück und Ende*
(1823), *Ein treuer Diener seines Herrn* (1826; *A Loyal Servant to His Master*),
Libussa (1847), and *Ein Bruderzwist im Hause Habsburg* (1848; *Fraternal Strife in*
the House of Habsburg). The particularly Austrian sense of history, as it was later
juxtaposed to the Prussian sense of abstraction in Hofmannsthal's renowned
typology, served Grillparzer already in the 1830s to define the anthropological
basis for what he tried to establish as genuinely Austrian literature. When
he posed the question, in a seminal case of 1837, "Worin unterscheiden sich
die österreichischen Dichter von den übrigen?" (How Do Austrian Writers
Differ from Others?), he named as points of distinction virtues of the Austrian
character, "Bescheidenheit, gesunder Menschenverstand, und wahres Gefühl"
(modesty, common sense, and true feeling), in implicit contrast to what he perceived as German immodesty, speculation, and rationality. Obviously developed for dramatic characterization, these qualities were first and most compel-
lingly embodied by a saint-like, yet plain character, Rudolf, who in *König*
Ottokars Glück und Ende is the first Habsburg to be elected German emperor
and thus, in Grillparzer's loving portrayal of a bourgeois emperor addressed as
"Herr Kaiser," the founding father of the Habsburg myth.

It is against the background of such moral genealogy of dynastic rule that
Rustan's transformation from tyrant into unassuming family man takes on special significance. His return to the simple virtues of the Austrian character is an
obvious plea directed as much to the powers-that-be in Vienna as to their
German counterpart. Embodying for the duration of a bad dream the very
forces that had victimized him, Rustan's dual character vacillates between the
vita contemplativa and the *vita activa,* between *Beharrung* und *Bewegung,* with the
balance of the status quo in danger of collapsing. Uncontrolled mobility now
lurks even on the Austrian horizon, threatening a sea change that would no
longer be just cultural.

No other word is invoked as often in *Der Traum ein Leben* as *Ruhe* (rest), so
much so that its implicit opposite, *Unruhe* (unrest), becomes the temporal foil

of the suppressed action. The threat of movement, mobility, and eventually unrest was to undermine the tranquility of the Biedermeier politically as well
when the revolutionaries of 1848 traveled easily from one capital to another
on the newly developed railway. Friedrich List, the champion of rail transportation, published the plan for the entire train system in March 1835, just a few
months after the premiere of *Der Traum ein Leben,* on the front page of a popular magazine. The projected system was stretched to include Thorn in the
east and Prague, Munich, and German Basel in the south. However, it excluded Vienna and Austria altogether, thus indicating that German unity
without Austria was already being implemented technically long before it was
advanced politically. But the more Austria appeared shielded from modernity
and untouched by the threat of change, the more critics of the status quo recognized and celebrated the cultural and political significance of this new tool
of *Bewegung.* In the poem *Sie wollen Freiheit, nun wohlan* (1842; *They Want Freedom—Well Then, Onward*), Grillparzer joined his colleagues Anastasius Grün
(*Poesie des Dampfes [Poetry of Steam],* 1837) and Karl Beck (*Die Eisenbahn [The
Railroad],* 1838), who placed their hopes in the railway as a vehicle of free
movement and, eventually, freedom itself. Friedrich List's vision of the railway
as a spiritual rather than technical innovation left no doubt about its revolutionary potential. This sentiment was invoked in a poem by Karl Beck in 1838:

> Rasend rauschen rings die Räder,
> Rollend grollend, stürmisch sausen's,
> Tief im innersten Geäder
> Kämpft der Zeitgeist, freiheitsbrausend.

> All around wheels roar racing,
> Rolling, growling they storm in haste,
> Deep inside its innermost veining
> The zeitgeist rages, freedom breathing.

Beck's iron serpent, the mythologized *Eisenschlange,* was bound to be a major
threat to the Biedermeier paradise. Unlike the dragons in the fairy tale and the
serpent Rustan is believed to have killed on his way to political power, the
monster of the zeitgeist could not be restrained so easily.

The fact that Rustan becomes a hero only by laying claim to an act he did
not commit indicates that true heroism belongs to the past and that the subject
as an agent of historical change needs to be redefined. While evoking the fairy
tales staged in Viennese theaters, from Mozart's *Zauberflöte* (1791) to Ferdinand
Raimund's *Der Alpenkönig und der Menschenfeind* (1828; The King of the Alps
and the Misanthrope), Grillparzer's seemingly romantic nightmare reveals a
new reality in which Rustan, in spite of the play's ostensible message, cannot
live happily ever after. After all, a scathing account of *Österreich wie es ist* (1828;
Austria as It Is) had been published by Karl Postl (better known under his
American pen-name Charles Sealsfield, 1793–1864), outside the reach of Austrian censors. The assertion that "Austria is closer to a crisis than any other
country" explains the need for the ever-present spies: "The broad network of

the secret police in Austria surpasses anything imaginable." Indeed, the police state reaches as far as Rustan's dream world:

In dem Inneren eurer Häuser
Lauern meine wachen Späher,
Was ihr noch so leis' gesprochen,
Reicht von fern bis an mein Ohr.

In the interior of your homes
Lurk my watchful spies;
Whatever you say no matter how softly,
Reaches my ears from afar.

If the "mouth with its telling silence," as Maria Ebner-Eschenbach remarked, is a striking feature of the physiognomy of 1834, Grillparzer has given that silence a dramatic voice. In the most compelling moment of the drama *Der Traum ein Leben,* the deaf-mute Kaleb regains the ability to speak only to voice one word, whereby he identifies the king as a murderer and brings down his reign of terror. However fictional, that single word was the most powerful outcry of the Viennese *Raunzer* and the most compelling indictment of the Biedermeier.

See also 1786, 1791, 1792 (August 26), 1826, 1835 (December 10), 1902

Bibliography: Franz Grillparzer, *Werke in sechs Bänden,* ed. Helmut Bachmeier (Frankfurt am Main: Deutscher Klassiker Verlag, 1986–). ———, *Plays on Classic Themes,* trans. Samuel Solomon (New York: Random House, 1969). Friedrich List, "Eisenbahnen," in *Staats-Lexikon oder Encyklopädie der Staatswissenschaften,* ed. C. v. Rotteck and C. Welcker, vol. 4 (Altona, 1837).

Hinrich C. Seeba

♫ 1835

Under constant threat of arrest and imprisonment, Georg Büchner composes his historical drama *Dantons Tod*

The Guillotine as Hero

Georg Büchner was born on October 17, 1813, in Goddelau near Darmstadt and died, at the age of twenty-three, on February 19, 1837, in Zurich, where he was a lecturer on the faculty of medicine. Despite his relatively small body of work—three dramas, *Dantons Tod* (1835; *Danton's Death*), *Leonce und Lena* (1838), and *Woyzeck* (1837), and the story "Lenz" (1839)—he is now considered one of the most important writers in 19th-century German literature, along with Heinrich Heine and Theodor Fontane. His literary fame emerged only posthumously. When Naturalism dispensed with the idealist notion that reality must be rendered poetic, Büchner's radical realism became firmly established as the prototype of literary modernity. The author has since been elevated into the ranks of Shakespeare and the young Goethe, and compared to the likes of Jakob Michael Reinhold Lenz, Christian Dietrich Grabbe, and even Bertolt Brecht and Heiner Müller. The reputation of this political, aesthetic, and literary extremist grew steadily in the 20th century, as indicated by the fact that the Büchner Prize, Germany's most coveted literary award, is named for him.

In his lifetime, Büchner remained an outsider who gained little recognition. He developed an interest in the history of the French Revolution at an early age and followed attentively the political and literary as well as the national and international events of the day. In the spring of 1834, the student revolutionary Georg Büchner became actively involved in the political turmoil of the Restoration. He founded the Giessen Society for Human Rights and wrote, with Ludwig Weidig, a pamphlet called "Der hessische Landbote" ("The Hessian Messenger"), a political tract addressing the economic misery of the people with a call for violent, revolutionary action: "Peace to the huts! War on the palaces!" (*Complete Works and Letters*, 41). In September of the same year, he returned to his hometown of Darmstadt and reorganized the Darmstadt group, while secretly preparing to liberate his friends, who had in the meantime been imprisoned. Over a five-week period in early 1835, under acute duress and in constant fear of arrest, he composed the historical drama *Dantons Tod (Danton's Death)*. To use a Benjaminian metaphor, this text is a "tiger's leap" into the past. It draws a line between the crisis of the present (1834–35) and the crisis in the aftermath of the French Revolution forty years earlier: the Jacobins' bloody reign of terror of 1794.

In *Danton's Death*, Büchner shows how political and economic instability, combined with the Jacobins' organizational ineptitude, conflicting ideologies, and political strategies, created a permanent state of emergency that led inexorably to their self-annihilation. The ideological strife between the two principal Jacobin factions—of Robespierre and Saint-Just, who represent a terrorist conception of virtue calling for the annihilation of all dissenters as counter-revolutionaries and traitors, and of Danton and his sympathizers, who advocate the end of the terror—culminates in a confrontation that ends with the arrest, judgment, and execution of Danton and his followers by the Revolutionary Tribunal. The battle between these two factions gives rise to a third bloc, headed by Committee of Public Safety members Bertrand Barère and Jean-Jacques Billaud-Varennes, two cynical, power-driven politicians, who plan the execution by guillotine of Robespierre and his followers.

The guillotine emerges in Büchner's play as the decisive historical agent and the only hero, as a historical panorama, spanning the period from the September Massacres of 1792 to July 1794, comes into focus. However, the actual time frame of the action is substantially more condensed, extending from the guillotining of the ultra-revolutionary Hébertists on March 24, 1794, to the guillotining of the moderate Dantonians on April 5, 1794, with the showdown between Robespierre and Danton and their followers forming the dramatic highpoint.

Büchner's dramatization uses the state of emergency and the collapse of all political, economic, legal, and moral constraints to demonstrate that historical events, though they may not be entirely anonymous processes to be fatalistically accepted, cannot be manipulated or controlled in the strict sense. History is characterized by paradox. It is stylized both as a natural, quantitative, repetitive process without beginning or end and as a willed, qualitative, and unique process with an origin and a goal. This paradox, which resists a conceptual solution, unfolds temporally in the play's movement. One only has to compare Danton's fatalistic statement in act 2, scene 5: "We are puppets; our strings are pulled by unknown forces, we ourselves are nothing, nothing!" with his urgent expression of irrepressible agency in the third act: "Men of my sort are invaluable in revolutions, on our brows hovers the spirit of liberty."

Büchner's paradoxical conception of history calls for a new approach to the construction of dramatic character. The model of historical individuality elaborated in Goethe's prototypical historical drama *Götz von Berlichingen* (1773) is no longer feasible. In its stead, Büchner has his dramatic figures perform merely scripted roles, but inserts, at the same time, moments of authenticity into their speeches. The most radical figure in the play is the flatly constructed character of Saint-Just. He understands universal history as a clearly decipherable text and positions himself as both a participant within the text of history and an observer outside it. Saint-Just thus is not only a character who interprets history, but also one who intervenes in it, correcting it with strokes of his pen: "Each comma is a sword stroke and each period a decapitated head" (3:6). Conceived as a grand historical tragedy, the bloody business of rejuvenating mankind is infused with connotations of sublimity. Through the merciless character of Saint-Just, Büchner exposes the murderous consequences of a philosophy of history, combined with an idealist aesthetics of the sublime, guiding political action during a state of emergency.

Robespierre, though more hesitant, nevertheless approves Saint-Just's plan to send the Dantonists to the guillotine. Extremely skillful as a purveyor of phantasms, he postures as teacher and political pastor, directing the people's desire for virtue toward his own person and exploiting their credulity as he styles himself a messiah. He "turn[s] the Revolution into a lecture hall for morality and the guillotine into a pulpit" (3:6). As a "military policeman of heaven" (1:6), he views the political system exclusively in terms of a moral code, dividing the virtuous from the non-virtuous and summarily executing the latter. His sole hesitation derives from the technical consideration that overuse of the lethal instrument could dull its capacity to intimidate the populace: "It's not good if the guillotine begins to laugh: the people will no longer fear it" (3:6).

By entering the fray of moral, political, legal, and aesthetic discourses that characterize the revolutionary situation, Robespierre claims a monopoly on interpretations and decisions. Here the play gets at the heart of the contradiction between an amoral system of self-preservation, with its politics of tactical measures, and a moralist conception that lays claim to universality and endeavors to subsume ethics, politics, law, and aesthetics under the rubric of virtue. The idealists Robespierre and Saint-Just coolly compose the list of victims, consent to shabby procedural manipulations, and carry out a politics of deceptive propaganda. The Revolution, describing itself as moral, virtuous, and sublime, gives birth to grotesque monsters, who commit murder and become so enmeshed in the machinery of the guillotine that they unintentionally prepare their own beheadings.

The politics of the guillotine pursued by the Jacobins and, in particular, by Robespierre and Saint-Just serves a variety of functions. To their minds, the guillotine is the site where the incorruptible sovereignty of the people is demonstrated in action. The guillotine also has an integrative function insofar as it produces moments of sublimity that unite Jacobins and the people in the phantasm of the people as a single healthy, virtuous body, defending itself against blood-sucking, hostile parasites. As a terrifying machine with the "instinct of a tiger" (4:2), the guillotine is an instrument for controlling the people's wrath: "The people are a Minotaur that must have a weekly supply of corpses if it is not to devour its leaders" (1:4). And most importantly, the guillotine distracts attention from the extreme economic misery, for which neither Robespierre, nor Danton, nor the people themselves have found a solution. In a gruesome parody of the Eucharist, it offers "heads instead of bread, blood instead of wine" (3:10), and in this it is even partially successful: "The children are crying, they're hungry. I have to let them look, so they'll be quiet" (4:7).

Unlike Robespierre and Saint-Just, the functionaries who endow the Revolution with meaning, Danton, the great rhetorician of the Revolution, withholds his participation in this ghastly game of duplicity. He suffers too greatly under what is called the "heterogeneity of purposes": "These days everything is worked in human flesh. That's the curse of our times. Now my body will be used up, too. One year ago I created the Revolutionary Tribunal. I ask God and mankind to forgive me for that; I wanted to prevent new September massacres, I hoped to save the innocent, but this gradual murder with its formalities is more horrible and just as inevitable" (3:3). Danton exhibits remarkably ambivalent traits. Having given up on the murderous project of completing the social revolution, he pursues, with great rhetorical force, a hedonism centered on individual pleasure. Yet his attempts at indulging are always linked to experiences of privation. He is bound to his wife, Julie, whom he loves "like the grave" (1:1), while he wallows, at the same time, in debauchery. He is a confirmed womanizer, who is, nonetheless, merely "making a mosaic" with his prostitutes (1:4).

Conscience, Danton says in his dialogue with Robespierre, is no more than "a mirror before which an ape torments itself" (1:6). And yet pangs of conscience caused by his complicity in the September Massacres repeatedly evoke in him a regressive desire to lose himself in Nothingness. During his imprisonment, Danton speaks in the language of paradox. He claims that "Nothingness is the world-god yet to be born" (4:5), but he is, nonetheless, aware that, as Something, he himself cannot cross over into that oblivion. "Nothingness has killed itself, Creation is its wound, we are its drops of blood, the world is the grave in which it rots" (3:7). As the future narrows and the guillotine approaches, this multifaceted role-player of the Revolution admits in a moment of authenticity: "Yes, it's so miserable to have to die" (4:3) and, "I'm leaving everything behind in terrible confusion. No one knows how to govern" (4:5).

The people, suffering in dire need and numbed by pleasure, are always presented in street scenes. Mercilessly exploited, they are in no way among the beneficiaries of the Revolution. The people are neither a class in itself (Marx) nor a sovereignty. Rather they are victims of deception, capable of only fleeting and partial insight. Only occasionally do they see through the parasitic play of the roguish Dantonists. No state could be formed with such a mob, which simply follows the impulse of the moment: "Kill anyone without a hole in his coat! Kill anyone who can read and write! Kill anyone who turns up his toes when he walks!" (1:2). Yet, like Danton and his adherents, the people have a sense of humor and wit. Robespierre and Saint-Just, by contrast, speak with a revolutionary pathos that produces a deeply serious and literal discourse of decisiveness devoid of all comedy, irony, parody, satire, and travesty, a discourse that approaches sublime kitsch.

Not a tragedy in the Aristotelian or Hegelian sense, this serious drama of terror is variously permeated by comic, cynical, satirical, and grotesque passages. Obscenities too play an important role in the discursive universe of this radically realistic and provocatively indecorous "piglet drama," as Karl Gutzkow called it. Büchner himself clearly stated his disavowal of all artistic idealizations: "The dramatic poet is in my eyes nothing but a writer of history. . . . His greatest task is to come as close as possible to history as it actually happens. . . . The poet is not a teacher of morality" (*Complete Works and Letters*, 276).

Büchner draws on a great variety of sources for this four-act prose drama, from the Bible and folklore to Shakespeare, Rousseau, Goethe, Hegel, Fichte, and Heine. Interspersed throughout are reflections on language and art, making this a highly self-referential text interwoven with a multitude of allusions. More than a sixth of the text consists of a series of quotations (from Mercier, Thiers, and others), which enhance the realistic effect. Space is privileged over time, as paradigmatically linked models are juxtaposed. However, there is no Archimedean point from which these paradigmatic series can be understood, and the play remains irreducibly labyrinthine and confusing. Not even the guillotine, the sole protagonist of the piece, fulfills this function. As a matter of fact, the guillotine is paradoxically constructed as both metaphor and metonymy. It is a metaphor insofar as, at the moment of beheading, sovereignty is shown in action; it is a metonymy because this moment cannot be stabilized, but rather always leads to additional moments, more beheadings.

Büchner organized the text in a highly complex interplay of *poiesis* and *mimesis* that leaves the audience with a variety of possible interpretations, one or the other of which has often been taken as the cornerstone of the play. While the play seems to suggest both a nihilistic worldview and an aesthetically inflected metaphysics of nature, it also takes a metahistorical, anthropological perspective that highlights experiences of love, pleasure, solidarity, and misery.

Yet this anthropological materialism is not dogmatically asserted; rather it is profoundly disturbed by a riddle that Danton, looking back on the September Massacres, formulates this way: "It must—it was this 'must.' Who will curse the hand on which the curse of 'must' has fallen? Who has spoken this 'must,' who? What is it in us that whores, lies, steals, and murders?" (2:5). This play provides no answer to these questions. In fact, Büchner had no solution to the enigma of necessity, the "must." It was just this riddle of an unknown force governing human life and action that gave Büchner, in early 1835, a time when he found himself in dire straits, the creative stimulus for a highly complex, pluralistic, and paradoxical literary text which, however, leaves the desire for meaning, a lesson, or a prescription unfulfilled.

Not surprisingly, the historical drama's uneasy, paradoxical concept of history, its denial of previously valid rules of conduct, and its radical realism without a hint of poeticized history was beyond the grasp of Büchner's contemporaries. Like his other, equally radical and challenging play, *Woyzeck,* based on the medical and forensic evidence of a murder case that had aroused early debates on the insanity defense, *Danton's Death* did not become a stage success until the post–World War I period of the Weimar Republic. Today it is recognized, along with Christian Dietrich Grabbe's *Napoleon oder die 100 Tage* (1829–30; *Napoleon or the 100 Days*), Peter Weiss's *Marat/Sade* (1964), and Heiner Müller's *Der Auftrag* (1978; *The Task*), as one of the most significant dramas on the French Revolution in the German language.

See also 1774, 1824, 1964, 1977

Bibliography: Georg Büchner, *Complete Works and Letters,* trans. Henry J. Schmidt, ed. Walter Hinderer and Henry J. Schmidt (New York: Continuum, 1986). ———, *Werke und Briefe,* ed. Karl Pörnbacher, Gerhard Schaub, Hans-Joachim Simm, and Edda Ziegler (Munich: Deutscher Taschenbuch Verlag, 1988). ———, *Dichtungen,* ed. Henri Poschmann (Frankfurt am Main: Deutscher Klassiker Verlag, 1992). Jutka Devenyi, "Consciousness and Structure in Danton's Death," *Journal of Dramatic Theory and Criticism* X, 1 (Fall 1995): 43–57. Laura Ginters, "Georg Büchner's *Dantons Tod:* History and Her Story on the Stage," *Modern Drama* 39 (1996): 650–667.

Harro Müller
Translated by A. Homan

♫ 1835, December 10
The Diet of the German Confederation bans the writings of Young Germany

Emancipation and Critique

On December 10, 1835, the Diet of the German Confederation decided to ban the writings of a group of writers labeled "Young Germany." Specifically mentioned in the edict were Heinrich Heine, Karl Gutzkow, Theodor Mundt, Ludolf Wienbarg, and Heinrich Laube. The members of the Diet acted in response to a heated and often vicious debate that had been fueled by Wolfgang Menzel, the influential editor of the literary supplement of the *Morgenblatt für gebildete Stände (Morning Journal for Educated Classes).* In a series of articles, published between September and October of that year, Menzel had suggested in highly polemical language that the works of the young generation, especially Gutzkow's novel *Wally, die Zweiflerin* (1835; *Wally, the Doubting Woman*), showed blatant disregard for common moral and religious standards. The German Diet, in particular the representatives of Prussia and Austria, insisted on measures to curb potential political unrest. Five years after the July Revolution of 1832 and only two years after a local upheaval in Frankfurt, they were greatly concerned about the possible impact of popular works of fiction on public opinion. This was in all likelihood the reason for including Heine, who lived in Paris by then and was not closely associated with the group of young writers who began publishing in the early 1830s. However, he and his fellow intellectual and publicist Ludwig Börne, who had become known during the 1820s as critics of Germany's post-Napoleonic restoration, served as models for the new generation. Heine and Börne continued their forceful literary and political intervention in the 1830s from Paris where they cultivated their connections with French literati. Börne's *Briefe aus Paris* (1832–1834; *Letters from Paris*) and Heine's *Französische Zustände* (1833; *French Conditions*) explicitly broadened the scope of the German debate and thereby—at least in the eyes of the German governments—induced instability. The ban issued by the German Diet, however, went beyond these typical measures. It stipulated that the members of Young Germany should be more strictly supervised because "their efforts are clearly designed to attack the Christian religion in the most insolent manner, to denigrate the existing social order, and to destroy discipline and morality through fictional works that are accessible to readers of all classes."

The goal of the edict was a general suppression of subversive literature. Although the envoys of the states at the Diet were by no means unanimous in their assessment of the potential danger from the Young Germans, their decision was seen as a sharp turn in the attitude of the German governments, not only by the writers themselves but also by public opinion and later historians. While the actual measures pronounced in the edict primarily reinforced the strict enforcement of existing laws, the literary and political impact became very noticeable, especially since one member of the group, Gutzkow, faced criminal charges and received a prison sentence for his literary activities. Even for Heine, who lived in exile and could therefore not be brought to trial, the situation became serious and he had reason to fear that his writings, published by Hoffmann and Campe in Hamburg, might be banned. The edict made a special point of reminding the authorities of the free city of Hamburg to supervise Heine's publisher. As a result, Heine saw himself forced to plead with the Diet to lift the restrictions. Still, for him this was no more than a tactical move in his ongoing confrontation with the political authorities in Germany. For the younger writers who resided in Germany, however, the edict significantly changed their outlook. A process of de-politicization set in that took the sting out of their writings. While the journals they had founded or attempted to launch before December 1835 deliberately transcended the boundaries of the established literary public sphere, their later endeavors avoided conflict by returning to a more traditional type of literature. For strategic reasons they even distanced themselves from the goals of the early 1830s which had aimed to transform the public sphere into a place for emancipatory discussions.

It is interesting to note that Menzel and other conservative and nationalist authors who defended the status quo rarely focused on the political issues that were part of the Young German agenda. Instead, their invective raised religious and moral objections, charging that novels such as Gutzkow's *Wally* or Mundt's *Madonna* (1835) were written under the influence of dangerous foreign ideas subversive of public morality and trust. The publicist and critic Ernst Schlesier summarized the "doctrines" *(Grundlehren)* of Young Germany under four headings: first, questioning of spiritual authority in general; second, attack on law and state because their authorities are seen as arbitrary; third, critique of the institution of marriage as a negative restriction; and fourth, attack on knowledge in general because it supposedly causes unhappiness. The last point may be an allusion to the Young German embrace of the Saint-Simonian notion of sensual happiness. The author later refers explicitly to the "epicurean sensualism, which consumes spirit and body at the same time, which poisons the organism of life and tears it out of its braces and joints, which ridicules morality and religion as well as state and church, which mocks order and moral senses, modesty and law as well as the physical and intellectual interests of the peoples and the governments." Menzel attacked his former collaborator Gutzkow in similar terms and described him as a fundamentally immoral writer, whose *Wally* is "full of sickly, pathological, studied lasciviousness." For Menzel, Gutzkow was the exemplary case of a young writer who violated the foundations of religion in order to develop his own dubious moral views. This logic is typical of the opponents of Young Germany. Invoking religion increases the stakes of the debate.

In their polemical responses to Menzel's attack, both Börne and Heine exposed his strategy as the abnegation of a former radical liberal who had sold out to the state for personal gain. Indeed, Menzel's language paralleled that of the Prussian censor, who described *Wally* as a work that "tries to attract attention through the most insolent insults, the most repugnant diatribes against the founder of Christianity, and through unrestrained mockery of any religious belief." In other words, by 1835 Menzel's liberalism and nationalism coincided with the defense of the political status quo—a logical but unexpected conclusion of his personal development, which began when he was a radical *Burschenschaftler* (fraternity brother).

Later critics have occasionally argued that the writers mentioned in the edict of 1835 had actually little in common and that it was only through the intervention of the state that they were recognized as a group. Indeed, as it turned out, they were mostly concerned with their own professional survival and demonstrated little interest in the fate of their fellow writers. Still, while the Young Germans did not have an explicit program, there was arguably something like a project, although it lacked full clarity and precise definition.

The state censors, who feared the influence of the young writers on a wider audience, clearly misjudged their actual impact. However, the censors did recognize their intention, that is, a radical revision of the concept of literature, of its production, its thematic concerns, and its dissemination. The aim was, as Wienbarg put it, to democratize literature. The Young Germans aimed at decreasing the distance between the established idea of high culture and the broad reading public. For this reason, they distanced themselves, sometimes even polemically, from the Romantics and followed Heine's verdict that the "Age of Art" *(Kunstperiode)* of Goethe and his generation had come to an end because the concept of aesthetic autonomy had lost its value and function.

The young writers liked to see themselves as radically modern and future oriented. What the historian Reinhart Koselleck observed as a hallmark of the late 18th century, namely a sense of temporal acceleration, is heightened in the writings of Gutzkow, Laube, Mundt, and Wienbarg. Literature was to be completely contemporaneous with the actual present. Hence Wienbarg's dictum: "Become engaged. Focus your efforts on life." This postulate stresses the need for a close correlation of social life and literary production, concern with contemporary issues and preference for language that reflects the dynamic process of the present. This shift would also undermine the value of traditional poetic forms. While the young Heinrich Heine still thought of himself as a poet, Theodor Mundt proclaimed the "emancipation of prose." To be sure, the prose style that Mundt and his cohorts favored was as removed from the cumbersome rhetoric of 18th-century scholarly prose as it was from the refined measure of Goethean prose. As the opponents of Young Germany correctly observed, the new style was indebted to Börne and, in particular, to Heine. What attracted them to Heine's prose was its wit and elegance, but also its polemical force. In Heine's prose they found a medium for effective public intervention. Moreover, Börne's and Heine's prose could serve as prime examples of an expanded definition of literature, a conception that would no longer support exclusive notions of individual inferiority. The writer thus stepped into a new arena where he took up novel and distinct functions. Among other things, he combined the roles of poet and journalist.

For this reason, journals became crucial for the self-understanding of the Young Germans. Heine's dictum that journals were the fortresses of the modern writer applied even more to writers like Gutzkow, Laube, and Mundt. For their project, journals were indispensable. Through their journals, they defined a new form of literary communication in which philosophical conceptions, aesthetic proposals, and political postulates ideally received equal importance. Most of these journals, however, were short-lived and failed to reach the broad audience their founders had in mind. As the dramatist and revolutionary Georg Büchner correctly pointed out to Gutzkow, the complex style of these journals was unsuited for the masses. Not surprisingly, the radical Young Hegelians of the 1840s criticized the project of the Young Germans as an extension of older forms of "salon literature" *(Salonliteratur),* which was closer to the Romantics in its radical subjectivism than to the political issues of the day. The

critic and historian Robert Prutz noted: "In the case of Young Germany, political partisanship erodes to the level of the literary clique, freedom becomes arbitrary, and the philosophical system turns into a one-sided, exclusive school."

By placing Young Germany within the history of literary movements from Storm and Stress to Romanticism, Prutz grasped the Young Germans' impetus to create a new, more accessible kind of literature, but he failed to acknowledge what set the Young Germans qualitatively apart, especially with regard to their ideo-political propensity. The terms that most saliently describe their undertaking are emancipation and critique. While the call for emancipation was articulated in several thematic concerns—opposition to traditional forms of religion and morality and re-evaluation of the sensual nature of life—the idea of critique transcended thematic considerations. It applied to the Young Germans reading their age as a critical period—influenced by the doctrines of the French Saint-Simonians—as distinguished from an organic one. But it also carried forward notions of early Romanticism and refers to the character of literature itself. Not a mimetic but a critical impetus should define and shape literary production. Hence the boundary between fictional texts and philosophical writings becomes rather fluid and more established forms of narrative as well as orthodox modes of literary criticism break down. In both instances, a strong notion of subjective freedom, which also played a central role in the writings of Heine, determined the concept of critique. It contained, at least implicitly, subversive political elements, which made the state authorities uneasy. Along these lines, Mundt had argued as early as 1830—only a few weeks after the outbreak of the Revolution in Paris—that the aristocratic period of literature was over and would be followed by a more republican system of literature. In 1834, Wienbarg proclaimed in *Ästhetische Feldzüge (Aesthetic Campaigns)*: "Poets and writers of aesthetic prose do not exclusively, as they did before, serve the Muses, rather, they also serve the fatherland, as they are allied with all powerful tendencies of our time."

While it is true that the members of Young Germany began to revise their program of critique as early as the spring and summer of 1835, that is, before the edict of the German Diet, the impact of the impending, and then actual, repression left its mark on their self-perception. A stronger emphasis on the creative and aesthetic aspect of writing can be noted after 1835, partly in response to the demonstrated power of the censors and to possible sanctions by the state, such as jail terms, but also partly in response to the internal dynamics of the original project. The concept of critique was considered exhausted by 1835. Thus the period between 1835 and 1840 is characterized by a shift toward more conventional literary and aesthetic concerns. Journals such as the *Jahrbuch der Literatur (Yearbook of Literature)* and *Deutsches Literaturblatt (German Literary Journal)* presented themselves to their readers as loci for literary discussions—at the expense of social and political issues. More importantly, they no longer claimed to be part of a movement. Instead, they stressed their non-partisanship. Laube and Mundt, in particular, began to distance themselves from their Young German past and their former allies. Mundt even declared himself in favor of "measure and beauty" as lasting aesthetic norms.

This radical turn was clearly designed to hide the author's iconoclastic political past, for his novel *Madonna* had received the critical attention of the Prussian Superior Board of Censorship *(Oberzensurkollegium)* for its allegedly immoral and politically dangerous character. Laube, who had been imprisoned in 1834, also reinvented himself as a connoisseur and friend of the beautiful to please the state authorities. With the exception of Heine, who never gave up the fight against the crippling apparatus of state censorship, the members of the group either dropped or adjusted their projects in order to survive. As it turned out, they were more vulnerable than the previous generation of writers for two reasons. First, their goal of revising the literary public sphere from the ground up also implied a new definition of the role of the writer. The poet turned into a public intellectual. However, the political conditions in Germany were not ripe for such a concept, since in the majority of the German states constitutional rights were not guaranteed. Moreover, in terms of their social background, these writers were underprivileged and, therefore, economically vulnerable. They owed their social status almost exclusively to their academic training and their uncommon agility in the literary market. To procure an economic subsistence, they became small, though highly competitive, literary entrepreneurs who would rather adjust than fold. Yet this survival no longer took place under the rubric of Young Germany.

Although the professional careers of authors like Gutzkow, Laube, and Mundt were by no means limited to the years between 1830 and 1835, their success as a group was to a large extent cut short by the edict of the German Diet. The successful intervention of the state clearly demonstrated the relatively weak position of professional writers in Germany who attempted to reshape their role in the public sphere. Ultimately, they were insufficiently prepared for a serious clash with state authority because they did not fully realize that their aim to broaden and democratize the concept of literature would be regarded as subversive and was subject to prosecution. They counted on a general notion that German society was in need of modernization, but failed to grasp that the German governments, while partly in favor of such modernization, were determined to control this process. This determination slowed, at least for a number of years, the emergence of an institution of literature in which public issues could be articulated and freely discussed. While the 1840s witnessed a more successful recurrence of this struggle by politicized writers, such as Ferdinand Freiligrath and Georg Herwegh, after 1849 the tension between state and professional writers decreased because a separate political public sphere was carved out, thereby releasing the artist from the task of expounding specific political issues.

See also 1786, 1800 (January), 1824, 1835, 1848, 1986

Bibliography: Helga Brandes, *Die Zeitschriften des Jungen Deutschland: Eine Untersuchung zur literarisch-publizistischen Öffentlichkeit* (Opladen: Westdeutscher Verlag, 1991). Alfred Estermann, ed., *Politische Avantgarde 1830–1840: Eine Dokumentation zum "Jungen Deutschland,"* 2 vols. (Frankfurt am Main: Athenäum, 1972). Jost Hermand, ed., *Das Junge Deutschland: Eine Dokumentation* (Stuttgart: Reclam, 1966). H. H. Houben, *Jungdeutscher Sturm und Drang: Ergebnisse und Studien* (Leipzig: Brockhaus, 1911). Helmut Koopmann, *Das Junge Deutschland: Eine Einführung* (Darmstadt: Wissenschaftliche Buchgesellschaft, 1993). Hartmut Steinecke, *Literaturkritik des Jungen Deutschland: Entwicklungen—Tendenzen—Texte* (Berlin: Schmidt, 1982).

Peter Uwe Hohendahl

🔖 1837, August 4
Annette von Droste-Hülshoff writes to a friend about her interest in reconstructing an unsolved crime

Crimes of Probability

Even as a child, Annette von Droste-Hülshoff (1797–1848) was captivated by the story about the unsolved murder of a local Jewish tradesman in 1760 which circulated in her grandparents' household in Westphalia. Her interest in this story deepened when, in 1818, her uncle published "Geschichte eines Algierer-Sklaven" (Story of an Algerian Slave), which he presented as a documentary account of this mysterious historical incident. Almost twenty-five years later and after reading and rereading her uncle's account, Droste-Hülshoff transformed the historical case into what was to become one of the most widely read and most often interpreted novellas of the 19th century. The final version of *Die Judenbuche* (1842; *The Jew's Beech Tree*) was the result of numerous drafts and revisions that bespeak the author's deep, perduring fascination with the enigmatic link between a murder, the flight of the suspect, and his suicide after a twenty-eight-year absence from the scene. Although the root of this fascination may have been a typical childhood taste for crime and suspense, Droste-Hülshoff's sensibility developed it into a profound examination of universal questions of morality and religious belief. What began in her childhood as a circumstantial interest in a tale about crime and punishment and subsequently turned into a critical examination of the truth value of her uncle's published account culminated in a highly complex work of literature, which, at its core, examines the uncertain relationship between truth and fiction, law and order, justice and the validity of judgments.

The unsolved murder case serves Droste-Hülshoff as the starting point for her inquiry into the attainment of truth and justice in a society that is depicted as corrupt and morally bankrupt. In *The Jew's Beech Tree,* the author portrays her own immediate socio-historical environment. Longstanding legal conflicts between the landed gentry (to which Droste and her family belonged) and the rural population regarding property rights to the surrounding forests have turned this provincial Westphalian backwater into a community torn by strife. The property conflicts play out within unreliable, ineffective judicial institutions, and the villagers are often driven to acts of violence and revenge. In this environment, both the foresters, whose task it is to protect the legal rights of the landed gentry against lawless poaching on the lord's forests, and the Jews, who are excluded from any civic rights, become the targets of a common law aggression against outsiders. The disputed forest, symbol of the harsh socio-economic divisions in the region, becomes the stage for a series of suspicious deaths.

Without any indication of cause of death, the corpse of Hermann Mergel, the impoverished father of the story's protagonist, Friedrich, is found in the woods. Within an interval of several years, the slain bodies of the forester Brandis and of the Jewish trader Aaron are discovered. The series of deaths concludes twenty-nine years later with the apparent suicide by hanging of a person who could be either Friedrich or his double Johannes. Although Friedrich is considered the main suspect in the murder of Brandis and Aaron, he can never be proven guilty beyond a reasonable doubt due to unconvincing and contradictory evidence. Instead of resolving the mystery by presenting a truth attained through careful investigation and the coherent reconstruction of events, *The Jew's Beech Tree* testifies to the unattainability of such a truth. In the Brandis case, the hearings lead to neither trial nor verdict. In the death of Aaron, Friedrich's flight and suicide stand in for a legally attained confession of guilt and its punishment. In the end, the case is left open and the issue of whether Friedrich is the perpetrator of the crimes or the victim of circumstantial evidence remains unresolved.

Indeed, the unresolved question about truth complicates the generic alignment of *The Jew's Beech Tree* with the crime genre—an alignment that Droste-Hülshoff herself initiated when she gave an early draft of the novella the title *Friedrich Mergel, eine Criminalgeschichte des 18. Jahrhunderts (Friedrich Mergel, An 18th-Century Crime Story)*. Critics have also pointed to striking similarities with the collection of famous criminal cases by François Gayot de Pitaval (1734–1743; *Causes célèbres et intéressantes*) and Friedrich Schiller's novella *Der Verbrecher aus verlorener Ehre (The Criminal Due to Lost Honor)*. The ambiguous story of *The Jew's Beech Tree* and its context, however, suggest that the question of genre here might be more complex.

The years 1840 to 1842 mark a period of unprecedented creativity in Droste-Hülshoff's life. It was then that she achieved an independent literary voice after years of self-imposed personal restrictions due to her status as a woman of noble birth and a still uncertain style. Her lyrical production suddenly exhibits determination and her own stylistic signature. With the completion of the cycle of religious poetry *Das Geistliche Jahr (The Spiritual Year)* and the composition of her finest ballads as well as experiments with verse novellas, Droste-Hülshoff seemed to have found both the form and content that define her most famous works.

Driven by a fundamental and painful crisis of faith, Droste-Hülshoff ponders in these works existential conditions of humanity and their interdependence with social, political, and economic circumstances. In her view, moral and ethical value systems are necessarily undermined when they are no longer secured by a strong faith in a God-given order but depend instead on arbitrary social structures and venal human passions. The problem of moral contingency—of the local, social, and cultural determinants of morality—informs Droste-Hülshoff's entire literary work at the time *The Jew's Beech Tree* is published. By turning to the tradition of the crime genre for the manifest plot of her famous novella, she employs one more literary venue to explore the basic question of how to achieve justice and truth when they are no longer guaranteed by a strong faith and are obscured by deception and vengefulness.

Droste-Hülshoff originally planned to integrate the crime story into a larger work devoted to the unique customs and character of the people of Westphalia. Upon the urging of a friend, however, her fictional account was published under the now familiar title *Die Judenbuche,* which was chosen by the publisher, not Droste-Hülshoff. Her original title, *Ein Sittengemälde aus dem gebirgichten Westphalen (A Portrait of Moral Life in Mountainous Westphalia),* still serves as subtitle and refers to the former ethnographic project. Parts of the incomplete Westphalia project were published posthumously as *Bei uns zu Lande auf dem Lande (At Home with Us, in Land and Countryside).* By setting her novella in a Westphalia that originally had been part of a sociocultural study, Droste-Hülshoff is able to investigate the hermeneutic question of truth in three areas: of the crime, her cultural home, and her own text.

The Jew's Beech Tree denies its readers an easy understanding of its subject matter. The moment this work received critical attention—especially after it was included in the influential *Deutscher Novellenschatz* (1876; *Treasury of German Novellas*), edited by Paul Heyse and Hermann Kurz—the multitude of possible interpretations became obvious. A broad consensus about the novella's proper generic home has never been reached: the novella can be considered neither an example of a *Dorfgeschichte* (village tale), the main representative of the mid-19th century novella, nor of the early realist or Biedermeier novella. Its uncanny, obscure features do not permit such easy categorization. Too multilayered a text and too opaque a narrative, *The Jew's Beech Tree* continually disappoints the critic's wish for unequivocal interpretive solutions. Because of its disquieting open-endedness, contemporary scholarship has expressed discontent with interpretations that read this novella exclusively as either an allegory of religion and metaphysics, justice and punishment, or as an allegory of socialization and individuation. Instead, recent scholarship has focused on the obscurity of the narrative and the ambiguous structure of the plot, the hermeneutic obstacle central to both the theme of the text and its poetics.

When the lord of the manor receives a letter from the chief presiding judge of a nearby town stating Friedrich Mergel's probable innocence, it is not only the lord who obtains the unexpected news but the reader, almost surreptitiously, is notified of the motto that informs the entire narrative and motivates its enigmatic structure. By slipping the sentence "Le vrai n'est pas toujours vraisemblable" (The true is not always true-seeming) from *L'Art Poétique (The Art of Poetry)* by Nicolas Despréaux Boileau (1636–1711) into this letter, Droste-Hülshoff articulates an epistemological problem that her text in endless variations deems unsolvable, namely, to draw a definite distinction between the true and the probable.

The mystery of a murder case affords Droste-Hülshoff occasion for reflecting on a fundamentally shaken confidence in the basic components of our belief system. In her view, the mystery of indecipherable clues, combined with the senseless brutality of murder, confront us with the limits of our rational understanding and access to the world. When the ethical sphere of law and punishment is no longer governed by universal criteria of truth but is circumscribed by merely probable signs instead, then the world, as Droste-Hülshoff sees it, necessarily loses all firm contours and takes on ghostly appearances.

Thus the world of *The Jew's Beech Tree* dissolves into inconclusive clues, hints, and allusions unable to support fixed identities or guaranteed meaning. The tapestry of characters is populated by phantoms and doubles whose insubstantial being is aptly called "Niemand" (nobody); the rules of causality and motive are constantly upset by the eruption of superstition and the illogic of resemblances and correspondences. Examples can be found in the incomprehensible exchanges between Friedrich and Brandis, or Friedrich and his mother, which, rather than helping to explain the subsequent murders, confuse the reader with their non sequiturs and leave wide open the question of Friedrich's possible motive, the plausibility of his involvement in Brandis's killing, or Brandis's role in the illegal raiding of the forest.

Droste-Hülshoff's narrative technique forces the reader into the role of a detective. It is characterized by a conspicuous withholding or disguising of crucial information. Thus it remains unclear whether the mysterious family ties between Friedrich, his double Johannes, and his uncle Simon—whose striking resemblance also with Johannes suggests a father-son connection—indicate their complicity in the crimes against the forest. Equally unclear are the circumstances of Johannes'/Friedrich's release from Turkish bondage after twenty-eight years and the utterly confounding information about the time and place of the murderous incidents. The task of combining clues based on missing information grows even more difficult when Droste-Hülshoff emphasizes the significance of singular objects as telling pieces of evidence. Thus, the lord first reads Johannes Niemand's possession of silver buttons as sentimental memorabilia obtained from Friedrich, only to interpret their meaning later as evidence identifying Johannes as Friedrich. Both interpretations could be either false or valid. Sometimes designated "Indizienstil" (a circumstantial style as in the legal term "circumstantial evidence"), Droste-Hülshoff's narrative draws the reader into the vortex of a semiotic labyrinth that permanently leads astray and distracts judgment by attaching probable significance to any object or person, thus declaring true significance null and void. Without the guidance of a narrator, the reader is asked to rank the evidence and evaluate characters who feign documentary authority or authentic speech.

In Droste-Hülshoff's case, it remains unclear whether the lack of reliable criteria for truthful communication precipitates a crisis of faith or whether the crisis of faith causes her to question all truth statements. Either scenario would undermine her faith in the words of common language and in religion as the word of God. Framing the narrative are a poetic prologue that appeals to the Christian notion of mercy and the translation of a Hebrew inscription serving as an epilogue that warns of retribution for violent acts against the Jewish community. Rather than initiating a religious discussion of mercy versus revenge, the frequent citations from both the New and the Old Testament provide the author with the religio-historical documentation that allows her to invoke the biblical tradition of inscriptions in their "judicial, funereal, and testamentary" function (Kilcher/Kremer, 251). The Bible in this case serves as the paradigm of a book that inscribes the semiotic correspondences between the letter and the law (the text constantly plays on the linguistic similarity of the German word for book and beech tree, *Buch* and *Buche*). Drawing on the Judaic tradition of endowing inscriptions with magical forces, Droste-Hülshoff connects the motifs of murder with the judicial power of the word as the ultimate guarantor of ethical and moral order.

Thus the Hebrew inscription hewn into the symbolic beech tree avenges Aaron's death. However, neither the original inscription nor the translation Droste-Hülshoff provides at the end of the text unequivocally reestablishes a decipherable world. All the deaths in this story are linked to either an oral or written tradition: death welcomes Hermann Mergel into the community of ghosts and superstition; Brandis's murder awaits its resolution in the form of archived judicial documents; and Aaron is memorialized within a vengeful inscription. No letter, word, or inscription remains for Friedrich/Niemand; his identity is made legible by a scar that has survived bodily decomposition. Like all the readers of and in this text, however, the interpreter of this scar, and of Friedrich's buttons, the lord of the manor, has shown his unreliable powers of deciphering by believing in inconclusive clues. The German philosopher Ernst Bloch aptly called these "clues ex machina."

See also 1792 (August 26), 1848 (October 11), 1867, 1876

Bibliography: Annette von Droste-Hülshoff, *Historisch-Kritische Ausgabe: Werke, Briefwechsel,* ed. Winfried Woesler (Tübingen: Max Niemeyer, 1978). Jeffrey Sammons, ed., *German Novellas of Realism* (New York: Continuum, 1989). Ernst Ribbat, ed., *Dialoge mit der Droste: Kolloquium zum 200. Geburtstag von Annette von Droste-Hülshoff* (Paderborn, Munich, Vienna, Zurich: Schöningh, 1998). Andreas Kilcher and Detlef Kremer, "Romantische Korrespondenzen und jüdische Schriftmagie in Drostes Judenbuche," in Ernst Ribbat and Winfried Freund, *Annette von Droste-Hülshoff* (Munich, 1998). *Annette von Droste-Hülshoff: Die Judenbuche,* with commentary by Christian Begemann (Frankfurt am Main: Suhrkamp, 1999). Barbara Beuys, *Blamieren mag ich mich nicht: Das Leben der Annette von Droste-Hülshoff* (Munich: Piper, 1999).

Anette Schwarz

1848, February

Karl Marx and Friedrich Engels write *The Manifesto of the Communist Party* weeks before the outbreak of Europe-wide revolutions

The Reinvention of a Genre

Since its publication in 1848, *The Manifesto of the Communist Party* has achieved a degree of efficacy rivaled perhaps only by the Bible and the Qur'an. In his preface to the English edition of 1888, Friedrich Engels could boast that the *Manifesto* had become "the most international production of all Socialist literature, the common platform acknowledged by millions of workingmen from Siberia to California" (*Manifesto*, 135–136). From the time of its original appearance, it went through roughly 544 editions and was translated into thirty-five languages; after 1917, an explosion of new editions and translations propelled the *Manifesto* to the status of a global bestseller.

The *Manifesto*'s fame and notoriety have not always assured close attention to its particular argument and style. Even though the *Manifesto* demands the violent overthrow of existing bourgeois capitalism, it may come as a surprise to some how positively Marx and Engels speak about both the bourgeoisie and the capitalist system. They celebrate capitalism as a genuinely revolutionary force that did away with inherited privilege and national self-interest. Through capitalism, Marx says in his famous formula, "all that is solid melts into air" (92), a slogan that has been used to define the mood of modernity more generally. Modernity connects goods, people, and ideas around the world, bringing about what we now call globalization. However, even though Marx and Engels accord recognition to the achievements of the bourgeoisie, they also make clear that they see these achievements as a double-edged sword. Capitalism did away with outmoded privilege, but its need for workers willing to labor for minimal wages has created unprecedented misery and two inequitable classes: the capitalist bourgeois class and the industrial proletariat. While traditional artisans, protected by their guilds, the authors explain, owned the tools of their trade, industrialization puts these tools in the hands of factory owners and robs the workers of every last shred of independence. There always was a class of the poor and disenfranchised, but capitalism created a new condition of dependence and a new class: the industrial proletariat.

What distinguishes the *Manifesto* from other texts that merely bemoan the lot of the urban poor or hope for a return to more natural modes of production is a lack of nostalgia for preindustrial times. Early 19th-century reformers and socialists, such as Saint-Simon and Charles Fourier, dreamt up worlds without exploitation, and occasionally they set up small enclaves to keep the revolutionary forces of capitalism at bay. Marx and Engels label these predecessors "utopian socialists" and dedicate the last third of the *Manifesto* to dismissing what they see as their fantasies. What the two authors share with these utopians and with the growing fictional literature depicting the misery of the proletariat is their compassion for the exploited. But, they insist, a better world cannot be created by rolling back bourgeois capitalism, but only by directing its revolutionary potential toward a different end. Industrialization cannot and should not be undone; rather it should be seized and developed further for the good of all people.

It is the ambiguous—Marx would say "dialectical"—role of capitalism that determines the unique form of the *Manifesto*. Texts labeled "manifesto" had been issued before, going all the way back to the radical wing of the Puritan revolution in 17th-century England. But then the term "manifesto" was exchangeable with open letter, declaration, petition, and the like, all of which meant to make public and manifest the will of a dissenting collective. At the same time, "manifesto" was also used to refer to declarations of kings, heads of state, or the Church. It was only with the manifesto of Marx and Engels that this form became a distinct genre with a set of specific components, in particular, its combination of historical argument, economic analysis, and revolutionary agitation. The *Manifesto* presents a sweeping history of modes of production from the practices in tribal societies to those under feudal land-ownership and the medieval guilds, and their culmination in the modern factory system. This history presents itself as detached and scientific, based on a single principle, namely the changing ways in which human beings produce their livelihood, the manner in which they transform the world through their labor. But at the same time, it is history written from the perspective of the present and based on the premise of the polarization of bourgeoisie and proletariat. Indeed, the manifesto begins with the sentence: "The history of all hitherto existing society is the history of class struggles" (89). Marx and Engels do not write history for history's sake. History is a point of departure for something else: active intervention. For only through such intervention can the achievements of capitalism be retained and transformed into communism.

The *Manifesto* thus adds something to history; it becomes a tool for change, a weapon in the class struggle. "Working Men of All Countries, Unite!" (125) is the final, resounding slogan with which the *Manifesto* reveals that it wants not history but action, that the history it tells has one purpose only: the creation of a different future. In his *Theses on Feuerbach,* written just before the *Manifesto,* Marx had urged philosophers not merely to interpret the world, but to change it. The *Manifesto* contributes to this change by raising the consciousness of the proletarian workers, uniting them, and rousing them to action. The *Manifesto* becomes a genre that aims to employ philosophy and history to instigate political change.

The urgency, the sense of imminent action and revolutionary overhaul that permeates the *Manifesto,* is not only a result of the authors' analysis of capitalism and its transformation into communism. It is also a response to the rumblings of revolution being felt throughout Europe in 1848. After the two great revolutions of the late-18th century, the American and the French, the revolutions of 1848 played a pivotal role in shaping revolutionary thought for generations to come. In Germany, Richard Wagner was banished for his revolutionary writings and found refuge in Paris, where another writer and dreamer of a new social order, Heinrich Heine, had settled more than a decade earlier to escape the repressive conditions in Germany. More common, however, was a reaction to and critique of the revolutionary politics of these violent days, as manifested in Friedrich Hebbel's antirevolutionary plays, for example the drama *Agnes Bernauer* (1851). A more passive reaction to the revolution led to widespread retreat into the home or into nature, producing the escapist literature of Adalbert Stifter and other mid-century writers who concocted worlds untouched by the forces of modernization.

German literature and French utopian socialism are not the only components that make up the context within which the *Manifesto* is situated. Marx's prior writings, such as *The German Ideology* (1846), draw heavily on the idealist philosophy of G. W. F. Hegel and his critic Ludwig Feuerbach. And in their attempts to formulate an economic critique of capitalism, Marx and Engels were indebted to British economists, such as David Ricardo. From these various strands, they created a text that blended abstract philosophical thought, economic analysis, and socialist ideals.

The intellectual and literary horizon of the *Manifesto* thus extends far beyond the various traditions of German thought and literature. In fact, the *Manifesto* lauds as one of the achievements of capitalism the erosion of "one-sided" national literatures and the creation of one single "world literature" (93). The term had been coined a few decades earlier by Goethe, who thought of it as the exchange and translation of the various national literatures. Marx and Engels, however, had something more radical in mind, a literature conceived as translated on the world market, a literature whose language of origin and place of production are secondary, and whose real aim is attaining the status of world literature. The *Manifesto* itself must be seen as a prime example of such a new form of world literature, to be translated, as the preamble demands, into many languages while belonging to none.

The authors' aspiration toward some kind of world literature, however, was due not merely to immodesty on their part, but to the fact that they themselves lived in tenuous exile. The *Manifesto* was conceived and written at a time when the authors moved frequently from place to place, between Paris, London, Manchester, Brussels, and Germany. Marx had already been forced to renounce his Prussian citizenship and was soon to be banished from Paris as well. The text is sprinkled with a whole series of exile tropes, beginning with the anxiety that communism may turn out to be a mere specter without a proper home or place and culminating in the claim, "The workingmen have no country" (109). This "countrylessness" of the proletariat, the authors acknowledge, is not yet fully achieved, due to the arbitrary division of Europe into nations. This, however, is what the *Manifesto* claims theoretically and seeks to achieve practically in its final appeal to proletarians of "all countries" to unite. The *Manifesto* bears the mark of its authors' displacement but seeks to turn this displacement into a denationalized world literature and world revolution.

Equally central, in this regard, is the actual place of the *Manifesto*'s publication, first as a pamphlet of twenty-three pages and then in serialized form in the London German-language newspaper *Deutsch-Londoner Zeitung,* where it was printed between March and July of 1848. The publication in London was in line with the privileged geopolitical position accorded to England in Marx and Engels's understanding of capitalism. Due to the conviction that industrialization should not be undone but rather accelerated and redirected, it was from this advanced place that the authors sought to spearhead the revolutionary transformation of capitalism into communism.

This transformation, however, took much longer than Marx and Engels had hoped. The backlash against the failed revolutions of 1848 led to decades of political reaction. Parliaments were dissolved, liberties abolished, repressive regimes installed, and the *Manifesto*'s hopes for an immediate revolutionary overhaul were forced into hibernation. Even at the founding of the Working Men's International Association in 1864, Marx downplayed the significance of the *Manifesto* in order to forge alliances with anarchists and other socialists who did not subscribe to his program. It was only after his death in 1883 that, in the late eighties and nineties, the *Manifesto* began its triumphant rise to world prominence, bolstered then by the rapidly growing German Social Democratic Party (SPD). The most important events in the history of the *Manifesto,* however, were the Russian Revolutions in 1917—the more moderate February Revolution followed in October by the Bolshevik Revolution. For the first time, a great European power was demolished by a revolution inspired by the *Manifesto.* If the *Manifesto* thus became a real political force almost overnight and further accelerated the rate of its translations and editions throughout the world, it also came under greater criticism. Contrary to the authors' expectation, the revolution did not take place in a highly industrialized country, such as England, but in relatively backward Russia. This pattern continued throughout the 20th century, when communism merged with various anticolonial struggles. Nonetheless, the October Revolution, in particular, inspired other revolutionary movements to return to the *Manifesto,* for example the short-lived Spartakus group in Germany (1918). In the *Spartakus Manifesto,* Rosa Luxemburg urges a return to the *Manifesto* as a foundational document and even dismisses the omissions and mistakes Marx and Engels had admitted to in their various prefaces. After almost seventy years of relative insignificance, the *Manifesto* finally came into its own.

Marx and Engels left not only the legacy of communism, but also the legacy of a literary form they created to articulate communism: the genre of the manifesto. However, the manifesto did not remain a political venue alone; it soon became the preferred form of artistic movements as well. In the early 20th century, in the hands of such writers as the former socialist Filippo Tommaso Marinetti, the manifesto moved from politics to art, where hundreds and thousands of manifestos launched an almost unending string of "-isms," including Futurism, Surrealism, Dadaism, Vorticism, Purism, Estridentism, and so on. Some of these movements, like the Berlin Dadaists, the Surrealists, and the Situationists, were closely allied to revolutionary socialism, but others, such as British Vorticism, were not. Still, the two types of manifesto, the socialist manifesto and the art manifesto, intersected again and again, most notably when Leon Trotsky and André Breton, the most prominent writers of socialist and art manifestos respectively, collaborated in the "Manifesto for a Free Revolutionary Art" (1938) or when Guy Debord, the leader of the Situationists and an important intellectual force behind the May 1968 revolt in France, demanded a new version of the Marx and Engels *Manifesto*.

How *The Communist Manifesto* can and should be adapted to changing historical conditions is a question that has not been laid to rest after the break-up of the Soviet Union in 1989. Since then, it has gained new prominence as a theoretical and prophetic text about globalization. At the same time, critics of neoliberal globalization—what is wrongly labeled the antiglobalization movement—have returned to it as a text that, rather than being opposed to globalization, seeks to change its direction and character. In the 21st century, the *Manifesto* continues to stimulate critical analysis and to inspire protest; it still cautions against looking back to putatively better times and exhorts the reader to look forward and work toward changing the course of history. The year 1848 marks the date of the *Manifesto's* first publication, and it is in many ways tied to this date. Unlike many other texts, however, it resists being relegated to the museum of literary history and demands to be read as a text for the present and for the future.

See also 1828 (Winter), 1831, 1835 (December 10), 1848 (October 11), 1876, 1916

Bibliography: Louis Althusser, *For Marx,* trans. Ben Brewster (London: Verso, 1979). Marshall Berman, *All That Is Solid Melts into Air: The Experience of Modernity* (New York: Penguin, 1988). Mary Ann Caws, ed., *Manifesto: A Century of Isms* (Lincoln: University of Nebraska Press, 2001). Robert V. Daniels, ed. and trans., *A Documentary History of Communism and the World: From Revolution to Collapse* (Hanover, N.H.: University Press of New England, 1994). Dirk J. Struik, ed., *Birth of the Communist Manifesto, with Full Text of the* Manifesto, *All Prefaces by Marx & Engels, Early Drafts by Engels, and Other Supplementary Material,* annotated and with an introduction (New York: International Publishers, 1971). Robert C. Tucker, ed., *The Marx-Engels Reader* (New York: Norton, 1978).

Martin Puchner

♫ *1848, September 12*

Switzerland ratifies the national constitution, establishing a representative federated government

Marginality and Melancholia

With the peacefully accomplished act of federation, Switzerland emerged as one of the few long-term winners from the maelstrom of the revolutions of 1848. Protected by its political neutrality as well as its commitment to civil self-defense, Switzerland went on to become, in the course of the 19th century, a globally recognized icon of internal stability and smooth financial and industrial modernization. The Helvetian success story reinforced the tendency to view the material blessings conferred by cantonal federalism as a providential transfiguration.

In a story that culminates in an idyllic description of a national folk festival, Switzerland's most celebrated 19th-century novelist hymned the Swiss version of "E Pluribus Unum" in "Das Fähnlein der Sieben Aufrechten" (The Little Banner of the Seven Upright): "This multiplicity within unity, may God preserve it for us, that is the true school of friendship, for only when political solidarity has come to consist of the personal friendship of an entire people has the highest goal been reached!" Interestingly, the author of this encomium, Gottfried Keller (1819–1890), departed from his homeland almost exactly a month after the ratification of its federal constitution to spend the next six years in Heidelberg and Berlin, courtesy of a stipend awarded him by his home town of Zurich. Until then, Keller had been known among his compatriots chiefly as an articulate but underemployed political lyricist and agitator and a vehement voice in the municipal debates leading up to the events of 1848. In spite of his sometimes rabid patriotism, Keller, as well as Zurich's city fathers, felt that his creative development would best be furthered beyond the borders. They were right. In Heidelberg, Keller settled down to the drawn-out composition of his autobiographic, eight-hundred-page masterpiece, *Der grüne Heinrich (Green Henry)*, a novel written in the wake of constitutional consolidation that explores the constitution of the Swiss subject.

Although the bulk of Keller's work remains untranslated, he is probably the best-known Swiss author of his century; and yet, the narrative that established his reputation as a Swiss writer was composed during years abroad. Likewise typical of the ambivalences in Keller's life and work is the fact that he worked hard to secure this reputation, even as he became increasingly exasperated with his country's swift adaptation to capitalist modernity. In his later years, he took to referring, rather dismissively, to the "local Swiss affairs" on which his earlier writings had focused. Nonetheless, Keller is most lastingly identified with those earlier works—"early" here being a relative designation, given that the author was a late bloomer as well as a pathological procrastinator and reviser, who could spend decades conferring final form on his compositions. His most widely read works, besides *Green Henry*, finally published in 1855 and then in a revised second edition in 1880, include *Die Leute von Seldwyla (The People of Seldwyla)*, a collection of novellas composed between 1856 and 1874; the *Züricher Novellen (Zurich Novellas)*, written 1860–1877 and published 1876–1877; and the popular *Sieben Legenden* (1872; *Seven Legends*).

Keller's mastery of the novella form places him squarely within the tradition of one of the key prose genres of 19th-century German literature. *Green Henry*, however, although often referred to as a *Bildungsroman*, actually calls the entire lived experience and ideology of *Bildung* so strongly into question that it might better be characterized as an anti-*Bildungsroman*. Keller's magnum opus also draws on the traditions of the spiritual autobiography and Rousseau's *Confessions*. Its closest relative, within German, may well be Karl

Philipp Moritz's *Anton Reiser,* another brutally bleak, self-flagellating, autobio-graphically colored account of a failed artist.

It needs to be specified that Keller's Switzerland meant German-speaking Switzerland. Keller never pretended to speak for French, Italian, or Rhaeto-Romanic Switzerland. Indeed, one could get through most of his collected works without being alerted to the existence of regions like Valais, Ticino, or the Engadine. Keller's Switzerland means above all Zurich, where the author was born as the son of a trained, diligently self-improving woodworker, who died when the child was four, and was raised, along with the one of his five siblings who survived infancy, in modest middle-class circumstances by his mother. Keller was able to attend an elite municipal academy until, at the age of fourteen, he was singled out and expelled for being the ringleader of a stu-dent insurrection. This penalty had a devastating effect on his family's aspira-tions to middle-class respectability as well as on his own sense of personal identity and communal legitimacy. During the years of enforced, homebound idleness that followed, Keller took up watercolor painting and sketching as comforting distractions. Having then set his sights on becoming a landscape painter, he struggled through two ill-starred apprenticeships and two unsuc-cessful years in Munich before debt forced him to return home. *Green Henry* essentially recapitulates this history. At the age of thirty-two, after his return from the seven-year sojourn in Germany that subsidized the composition of *Henry,* Keller belatedly acquired lasting economic and social respectability by accepting the politically influential position of Zurich Council Secretary. He spent six-sevenths of his life in the city of his birth, rarely leaving its environs in his later years, never marrying, and sharing a house most of that time with the sister he wrote out of his autobiographical masterpiece, and the mother he killed off in it.

And yet, in spite of his strong attachment to his native soil, Keller's work displays an extremely complex, critical relationship to the German literary cult of *Heimat* (homeland). For instance, a crucial episode in *Green Henry* centers on the traditional carnival reenactment, in the village where the adolescent Heinrich was sent after his academic disgrace to live with relatives, of the Wil-helm Tell saga, an episode in the Swiss struggle for self-determination that had acquired mythical salience. In a fashion typical of Keller's historical irony, he has the villagers center their bucolic celebration around a schoolbook edition of the text of (the non-Swiss) Schiller's drama *Wilhelm Tell*. Here and else-where Keller emphasizes that the folk tradition and culture he is propagating were in the process of being reinvented as a national heritage, and that litera-ture played a crucial, not always noble, role in the retooling of the civic image to satisfy current agendas. The Zurich novellas, devoted to the compilation and subsequent fate of the Manesse Codex, a collection of medieval minne songs that are themselves sophisticated transcriptions of circulating folk material, comprise Keller's most extended and light-hearted meditation on this theme.

Keller also shows acute awareness of how literature constructs social reality by infiltrating psychic reality. Hadlaub, the young scribe of the Manesse Codex, learns to love romantically by copying love songs. Heinrich's textual internalization has less felicitous consequences. He may describe his relatives' rustic Tell pageant with the cheerily supercilious connoisseurship of a visiting city kid and budding aesthete, but years later, during the most wretched days of Heinrich's ill-starred Munich sojourn, as he dreams of flying back to Zurich on a golden horse, laden with the riches that would guarantee the prodigal son a forgiving reception, he hears a "hard voice" thunder: "Is there no one who will knock this disgrace to his country *[Landverderber]* out of the air?" Thereupon a "fat Wilhelm Tell, who had been sitting hidden in the top of a linden tree," magically appears and turns his bow and arrow on "the new Icarus," who plummets out of the sky and into a shaken wakefulness (III, 717).

The incident, however amusing, reveals just how oppressed Heinrich is by what he views as a fatal failure to live up to the standards the ridiculous, implacable archer embodies in the Swiss mind. And indeed, Heinrich's story documents, to a great extent, his almost predestined inability to fill the shoes of various ancestral incarnations of Swiss manhood and competency. In Heinrich's case, however, it is a matter of filling a coat rather than shoes: he acquires his moniker "Green Henry" because, throughout his youth, his penny-pinching mother clothes him in suits she refashioned from his dead father's green military reserve uniforms. Eventually, Heinrich chooses to wear only green, turning what was a stigma into the flaunted badge of personal originality, communal marginality, and affinity with nature.

As the title of one of Keller's best-loved tales puts it: "Kleider Machen Leute" (Clothes Make the Man). For Heinrich, green symbolizes the painful double bind that shapes his tormented subjectivity. In his case, the badge of his originality also signifies the straitjacket of the familial, national, and cultural past that inhabits him just as much as he inhabits it. The weight of the paternal heritage incorporates ideals that, when not lived up to, recoil upon the subject in the form of lacerating self-condemnation. As a result of this misfit between himself and his national *habitus,* Heinrich, like some of Keller's other memorable characters, grapples not only with paralyzing inhibition, but also with an abject sense of bad conscience.

For Heinrich, *Bildung,* the concept of aesthetic and educational self-cultivation, initially appears to offer a way out of this torment. *Bildung* holds out an illusion of artistic self-fabrication that responds to what Keller calls "the sickness of wanting to be something other than one is" (*Zurich Novellas,* "Der Narr auf Manegg," V, 130). In Heinrich's case it functions as an alibi for the haphazard, autodidactic enthusiasm of a socially disenfranchised youth. Contrary to its promise, *Bildung* only produces more "half-heartedness" and more bad conscience in Heinrich, who ultimately ends up regarding himself as a lousy artist as well as a failed son and citizen. In Munich, the anticipated flowering of his talent fails signally to take place. Instead of becoming a master of his medium, he remains a raw lump of disorganized material. Unable to afford art school, he hangs out in the vicinity of the city's art academies and sneaks into university lectures. And yet, although he lives in debt and near starvation and is compelled to unload his paintings and possessions on a second-hand art dealer, he is still mortifyingly unable to tear himself away from the city that represents the dream of freedom from the demands of his austere homeland.

The experience of mortification, in the sense of being lethally stuck, occurs frequently in Keller's oeuvre. The state of paralysis that threatens to render his protagonists emotionally and economically dysfunctional signifies not just personal humiliation and social marginalization but, somehow, the specter of petrified suspension that haunts modern subjectivity. This fear of being rendered inanimate feeds Keller's fascination with the motif of being buried alive. "Thoughts of One Buried Alive" is in fact the title of an early poem cycle. And two of Keller's most memorable characters, the abused foster child Meretlein, whose encapsulated story prefaces Heinrich's main narrative, and the executed boy Dietgen, in the Seldwyla novella of the same name, literally rise from the dead to wreak at least a well-deserved moment of terror on their persecutors.

The most striking revenant in Keller's oeuvre is Heinrich himself, who undergoes a resurrection between the first and the second revised edition of the novel. In the first version, Heinrich is only able to tell his own story in the first half of the work; in the second half, a third-person narrator pops up to recount how the protagonist, who has encouraged his mother to mortgage the house in order to pay off his debts and support another wasted interval in Munich, then compounds his dereliction by neglecting to write to his mother and delaying his return. He finally gets back to Zurich just in time for his mother's funeral. Devastated with shame, he follows her into the grave shortly thereafter.

The novel's second version commutes the death sentence, but just barely. Heinrich, arriving back just in time to witness his unconscious mother's demise, survives to devote himself to the duties of a solitary civil servant, "which however were incapable of casting any light on the shadows that filled my desolated soul . . . because everything that I perceived took on the shade of dusk . . . Occasionally, and ever more audibly, the wish no longer to exist stirred within me" (III, 849–850). This is not life so much as the afterlife of melancholia, defined by Freud as "interminable mourning for an ungrievable loss." While alive, the mother was a colorless figure, the source of unappeasable expectations and insufficient funds. And yet her death transforms Heinrich into an empty husk filled with a contrition that can only be relieved in public service.

The omnipresence of death in *Green Henry* makes the novel a regular festival of funerary motifs. Heinrich's opening description of his ancestral village segues into a detailed consideration of the town's picturesque cemetery, "the earth which literally consists of the disintegrated limbs of passed-on generations; it is impossible that there is a piece of earth less than ten feet deep that hasn't at one time made its way through a human organism" (III, 313). This sense of the morbid weight of the collective past suffuses the entire novel. The death of Heinrich's father is the template for his experience of an existence replete with inflicted absences: "My father died so early that I never even got to hear him recount anything about *his* father" (III, 15). The deaths and funerals of Heinrich's paternal grandmother, his first love Anna, and his mother mark the phases of his life. It is his internalization of these losses that, far more powerfully than his haphazard *Bildung,* finally organizes his melancholic subjectivity and the narrative that traces its genesis. Toward the end, Heinrich briefly recounts how, after years of suicidal dreariness, he is recalled to life and confidence by the reappearance of Judith, a lost love from the village. Although their unexpected reunification unleashes mutual rapture, they both reaffirm the desire to "renounce the crown of matrimony, in order to remain all the more surely in possession of the happiness that now fills our souls!" (III, 860). And indeed, they remain true to this pledge for twenty years, until Judith dies.

This conclusion underlines *Green Henry's* almost uncanny similarities to Charles Dickens's *Great Expectations* (1860–1861), another novel that opens with a narrator who is a fatherless boy contemplating the family cemetery. Like Green Henry, Dickens's Pip, whose name also marks him as the carrier of an organically charged developmental drive, pays for the agonizing failure to live up to the great expectations instilled in him with not just blasted social and professional aspirations, but also the renunciation of his beloved. However, Pip, unlike Heinrich, is the victim of a real deception, and is likewise given concrete opportunities to redeem himself for his blind self-absorption through real acts of compassion toward his misguided elders, Magwitch and Miss Havisham. Moreover, the deliberately ambiguous wording of the revised conclusion Dickens appended to the novel (another similarity to Keller's work) suggests at least the glimmer of a possibility that Pip will be belatedly reunited with his old love after all. *Great Expectations'* final concession, however weak, to the pull of the happy ending emphasizes, by contrast, just how radically absolute *Green Henry's* commitment to the value of relinquishment remains. In the psychic economy installed in and by means of this narrative, loved ones are retained, paradoxically, through willed renunciation, in a securely atemporal, immaterial afterlife. The last sentence of the novel fades out on the narrator's image of himself "once more wandering the green paths of memory" as he peruses the account of his life, which he had composed for Judith and received back following her death. Green Henry has finally, belatedly, identified his medium. It is not the visual image but the word that furnishes the most dependable access to the storehouse of mental images that anchor his affective universe. Language, assuming concrete form in the manuscript of what is presumably the novel *Green Henry* itself, comes to occupy the place of loss and enforced renunciation.

The term *Entsagung* (renunciation) is central to the Poetic Realism with which Keller, like most of his generation of German fiction writers, is identified. The poetics of *Entsagung* encourages the sensitive individual beset by the limitations and obligations attendant to active participation in modern life to seek out a saving refuge in the transcendent realm of the imagination. In the broadest sense, Keller's autobiographical masterpiece may be said to follow this compensatory strategy. But few if any works of his contemporaries make the price exacted by this melancholic syndrome so devastatingly clear. Heinrich's narrative ends as an extended necrology; the green paths of memory he traces out may just as well have been the graveyard with which he began.

See also 1782, 1792 (August 26), 1848 (October 11), 1860, 1867

Bibliography: Gottfried Keller, *Sämtliche Werke,* 7 vols., ed. Thomas Bönig, Gerhard Kaiser, Kai Kauffmann, Dominik Müller, and Peter Villwock (Frankfurt am Main: Deutscher Klassiker Verlag, 1985). ———, *Green Henry,* trans. A. M. Holt (New York: Grove, 1960). Gerhard Kaiser, *Gottfried Keller: Das gedichtete Leben* (Frankfurt am Main: Insel Verlag, 1981). Sigmund Freud, "Mourning and Melancholia," in the *Standard Edition of the Complete Works of Sigmund Freud,* vol. 14, trans. and ed. James Strachey (London: Hogarth Press, 1953–1974).

Chris Cullens

☾ 1848, October 11

Disturbed by reports from Vienna about the revolution he had initially supported, Adalbert Stifter takes up permanent residence in provincial Linz

Tales of a Collector

Published in the wake of the failed revolution of 1848, Stifter's (1805–1868) second collection of narratives, *Bunte Steine* (1853; *Many-Colored Stones*), programmatically exempts itself from the world of historical upheaval and turns to "harmless things," such as the common stones found in the collection's titles: fool's gold, granite, limestone, rock crystal, tourmaline, and bergmilch. While Stifter's earlier collection *Studien* (1844; *Studies*) still resorted to Romantic motifs and bore traces of the author's admiration for Jean Paul, *Many-Colored Stones* initiated a new poetic strategy, which eventually led to the disjointed repetitiveness of his late prose and established his fame as the most boring German-language writer. Friedrich Hebbel, his contemporary and, in many respects, adversary, promised the crown of Poland to anyone who could actually make it through Stifter's last novel, *Witiko* (1864), in which essentially nothing happens in the course of 900 pages. Narrative prose and dialogue are reduced to stylized rituals devoid of any affective inflection.

In contradistinction to *Witiko* and the late novellas, Stifter's narratives in *Many-Colored Stones,* written and rewritten between 1845 and 1853, still maintain sufficient plot structure to keep a reader's attention. Many of the stories center on enigmatic characters—for example, the nameless child with the abnormally big head in "Tourmaline" or the impoverished pastor in "Limestone," who has a mysterious attachment to expensive white underwear. While some of the lengthy and overly detailed landscape descriptions already suggest the eventual disintegration of Stifter's prose into sheer linguistic components, these narratives are probably Stifter's most readable and have, therefore, acquired canonical status in German schools alongside Keller's *Die Leute von Seldwyla (The People of Seldwyla)* and Annette von Droste-Hülshoff's *Judenbuche (The Jew's Beech).*

Stifter's stones (and stories) lack the fascination the telluric realm exerted on the Romantic imagination; their appeal is banal and superficial, "because they did not lose color and life as quickly as plants" (13). But Stifter's determination to distance himself from Romanticism brings him no closer to the programmatic Realism of his time. Its proponents, such as Wilhelm Raabe or Theodor Fontane, prescribed literature's task as the transfiguration of banal life into essential life. But Stifter hoped to find direct access to the essential in the banal; in fact, he sought to identify the banal as the essential. This tenet corresponds to the ideal of literature as a natural process rather than a rhetorical or aesthetic strategy, as was the case for many Realists, who sought to elevate prosaic life through aesthetic refinement. For Stifter, the goal of literature was not the poetic transfiguration of the world but the gathering up of its things, convinced, as he was, that any rock is already precious and valuable or will reveal itself as such one day. Banal objects are thus regularly endowed with the allure of future significance. Writing amounts to excavating, collecting, and ordering the world of things in such a way that, ideally, nothing is left out or lost.

The only concept of nature that could sustain this project is the early Enlightenment notion of physicotheology, the belief in natural history as the ordered unfolding of a meaningful universe. While Stifter's contemporaries wrestled with the fact that the older religious faith in nature as God's open book had become incompatible with modern scientific views, Stifter maintained that nature spoke for itself and would eventually reveal its laws—if only one looked properly. A few years before Darwin's theory of evolution in *On the Origin of Species* (1859) established the notion of nature as an open-ended process, Stifter returned to the superseded model of natural history in the hope that it would allow the divergent realms of nature and history, religion, and language to exist on one plane. The enormous efforts required by this restorative project prove how deeply Stifter in fact registered the disintegration he sought to overcome or at least to slow down.

Despite his aversion to abrupt changes, such occurrences are not entirely absent from Stifter's texts. Even the modern paradigm of dynamic, contingent evolution asserts itself in recurrent catastrophes that unpredictably, yet regularly, shake up his slow-motion world: the plague in "Granite," hailstorms, blizzards, floods, and fires in other stories. These ruptures in the continuum seem to be a prerequisite for narratives that set out to prove that exceptions, contingencies, or even revolutions are eventually absorbed by the power of endurance and persistence. Yet, by a logic similar to the psychoanalytic notion of repression, what Stifter sought to exclude returns to haunt his narrative.

In didactic fashion, "Granite" introduces its young protagonist to the modalities of representation that need to be followed if objects such as common stones are to disclose their significance. In the course of a walk from one village to another, a grandfather teaches his grandchild how to look. The peripatetic exercise is also a mnemotechnic operation; as the grandfather explains and recalls the history of natural sites such as the Power Beech, the Behring Spring, or the Triple Pine, he retrieves and transmits their history. Each inspected natural site is embedded in a historical narrative, and natural objects, in turn, record each narrated historical event: "Memory is preserved in a number of things" (38). Narrative for Stifter consists in the collection of things and their ritualistic recollection: "Remember that it was your grandfather who first showed you this" (36). This mode of recalling and transmitting communal life by showing and telling is subsequently contrasted with another model of representation enclosed as a narrative within the frame-narrative. The grandfather relates the story of a family long ago that tried to escape the ravages of the plague by retreating into the high forests. The failure of their attempt to escape the collective fate is sealed by their desire for a private, artificial system of signification. When the agreed-upon smoke signals announcing the end of the epidemic finally appear, almost the entire family in the forest has perished. In a strange reversal of Adam and Eve's expulsion from Eden, the sole survivors, a young boy and a girl, find their way back to civilization only because of the boy's ability to read the signs of nature. But the pointed opposition of natural signs and artificial signs had already collapsed in the narrative's frame. Nature does not speak for itself; this is the pedagogical point of the grandfatherly initiation of the child into the communal and familial fabric. Nature requires narrative as supplement, just as narratives need to be substantiated and verified by visual evidence. Vision seems indeed the privileged paradigm of this writer who, like Goethe, wanted above all to be a painter. What Stifter tried to bring into view is the virtually invisible, that which is overlooked and underestimated in its inconspicuousness.

The most concise summary of Stifter's poetic credo can be found in his notion of "das sanfte Gesetz" (gentle law), set forth in the brief preface to *Many-Colored Stones,* in which Stifter not only defends himself against the charge of dealing with trivialities—"beetles and buttercups," as Hebbel put it—but also professes his confidence in the powers of constancy and persistence. Responding to the charge that his prose tends to neutralize the differences between nature and history, banality and sublimity, the significant and the insignificant, Stifter writes: "The flow of the air, the rippling of the water, the growth of grain, the waves of the sea, the greening of the earth [. . .] I consider these great; the splendidly rising storm, the lightning that splits houses, the tempest that drives the surf, the fire-spewing mountain [. . .] I consider [. . .] them smaller because they are only effects of much higher laws" (6). Stifter's appeal to the higher laws produces a radical nondifferentiation between human actions and natural development: "As it is in external nature, so it is in the internal nature of the human race. A whole life full of justice, simplicity, efficacy, mastering oneself [. . .] I consider great" (7–8). In effect, this gentle law demands of humans the behavioral characteristics of stones.

The "gentle law" makes extraordinary demands on a writer who, after all, cannot show or tell but has to write. Stifter's language seeks to perform mimicry of its objects and wishes to divert any attention from itself. Virtually devoid of metaphors, Stifter's prose abstains from psychological motivations and other interpretive interventions to such a degree that it accrues an emotional flatness and two-dimensionality that seems to have found expression in the uniform landscapes for which his narratives are famous. Typically, Stifter feels compelled not only to describe the object in question but also to describe the rules governing its description and thus to describe describing. As critics of descriptive prose from Lessing to Lukács have pointed out, such a procedure can only undermine coherence. The peculiar effects of excessive descriptions were not lost on modern writers. Arno Schmidt, for example, aptly characterized Stifter's paradoxical attempts at linguistic self-suppression as exercises in "self-fossilization."

Whereas many different authors—Nietzsche and Kafka, Thomas Mann, Hofmannsthal, and Peter Handke among them—have been drawn to the mixture of petrification and atrophy characteristic of Stifter's texts, they have been equally fascinated (or repelled) by the pervasive impression of a paralyzing quietude. According to Walter Benjamin, the absence of language's acoustic dimension conceals the fundamental ethical problematic of Stifter's oeuvre: "Language as it is spoken by Stifter's protagonists is ostentatious. It is only the exhibition of emotions and thoughts in moot space." Martin Heidegger argued conversely that Stifter's ostentatious gestures point out the very phenomenology of pointing and signification. That 20th-century and contemporary authors should be attracted to precisely those features of his prose that irritated Stifter's contemporaries is due not only to changing tastes but also to an enduring fascination with the paradoxical poetical goal Stifter set for himself: to write in such a way as to make stones speak—and to make them speak as if they spoke for themselves.

While the relations between the stones in the titles and the actual narratives are tenuous and sometimes enigmatic—"tourmaline is a dark stone, and what is being told here is very dark" (122)—the introduction insists on their poetological relevance as collectibles. Just as children collect and sort worthless objects, Stifter writes with characteristic understatement: "I too have put together a collection of little games and gimmicks for young people, so that they may delight in it" (14). In the last sentence of the preface, Stifter explicitly likens stone collecting to story writing: "Because there is an infinite number of stones, I cannot anticipate how large this collection will eventually become" (15). However, these stone-stories often result in collecting another type of small and "harmless things" (12), the very children populating *Many-Colored Stones*.

Following a literary fashion at the time, Stifter packaged his collection as children's stories. Hoping to capitalize on the Christmas sales of 1852, he subtitled *Many-Colored Stones* "A Holiday Gift," but his typically protracted revisions delayed publication into 1853. Yet they deserve to be called children's stories not only because their protagonists are mostly children but also because several stories depict an educational process. As pedagogical tales, however, they bear little resemblance to the idealized notion of *Bildung* developed in the Goethe era and whose own version the professional pedagogue Stifter unfolds in excruciating detail in his novel *Indian Summer* (1857; *Nachsommer*). But nei-

ther do the portrayed children qualify unambiguously as instances of romanticized wild children. Even though some, such as "the brown girl" at the center
of the color-coded *tableau vivant* of "Fool's Gold," recall an archaic figure such
as Goethe's Mignon, the children generally seem to share more features with
the desolate Kaspar Hauser, the abandoned youth whose case and story occupied Stifter's contemporaries. The phantasm of children's innocence is regularly undercut by the fact that the children enter their stories as traumatized
and often awkward disfigured or estranged outsiders. In "Tourmaline," for example, Stifter leaves little doubt about the pathological features of the nameless
child who emerges from the basement of a Viennese suburb. Set on Christmas
Eve, "Rock Crystal" stages a nativity scene based not on the birth of Christ
but on the children becoming natives in the village where they had previously
lived as strangers. The peculiar pastor in "Limestone" is also essentially a child
who failed to grow up and finds his place in the community of children only
after his death. None of these "buds of humanity," as Stifter calls children in his
preface, ever blossoms. They die or disappear, or their stories end when they
reach puberty.

Stifter's narratives, which seek so desperately to enforce the laws of nature
and the laws of language, seem drawn to children because "they do not revolutionize" and because they presumably have a more immediate relationship to
the world of objects. But the collection of "wild children" in *Many-Colored
Stones* can also be understood as a test case for demonstrating the problematic
consequences that any identification of the world of language with the world
of objects harbors. Nowhere is this more evident than in "Tourmaline," where
the affinities between Stifter's own prose and the strange writing habits of the
anonymous child protagonist are most manifest. This girl, who does not know
how to distinguish between a sign and what it signifies, has been anticipating
her father's death in writing but fails to recognize his death when it actually
occurs. Ignorant of the gap between doing and saying, she "blindly believes the
words of others" (156). Of her writings the narrator says: "Her mode of expression was clear and succinct, the composition of sentences was good and
correct, and the words themselves were elevated, though without meaning"
(165). On the surface "Tourmaline" suggests that romantic excesses are responsible for the child's pitiful state: her father expelled his wife upon discovering that she was having an affair with a famous actor. However, the girl's father too was, like Stifter as a child and as a writer, a collector of things. His
apartment was plastered with portraits of famous people. The girl's mental and
physical peculiarities—the abnormally large head and her proclivity for theat-
rically reciting famous literary passages she fails to understand—quite literally
point back to her father's obsession with famous heads.

As excluded others whose reintegration into the community either fails or
remains dubious, Stifter's literary children bear witness to what his desire for a
total collection seeks to suppress: the fact that the claustrophilic logic of enclosure organizing any collection depends on exclusion in the first place. Perhaps
the other side of seeking to identify language and nature is the terrifying pros-

pect of no longer being able to distinguish between things and word-things, reality and literature, stones and people. This terror may be said to have found its bodily expression in the strange children of Stifter's last collection.

See also 1796 (June 10), 1837, 1848 (September 12), 1876, 1895, 1979 (Handke)

Bibliography: Adalbert Stifter, *Werke und Briefe: Historisch-Kritische Gesamtausgabe,* ed. Alfred Doppler and Wolfgang Frühwald (Stuttgart, Berlin, Mainz: Kohlhammer, 1978–; cited as HKG). ———*Limestone and Other Stories,* trans. and ed. David Luke (New York: Harcourt, Brace, 1968). Jeffrey L. Sammons, ed., *German Novellas of Realism I* (New York: Continuum, 1989). Eric Blackall, *Adalbert Stifter: A Critical Study* (Cambridge, U.K.: Cambridge University Press, 1948). Christian Begemann, *Die Welt der Zeichen: Stifter-Lektüren* (Stuttgart and Weimar: Niemeyer, 1995). Eric Downing, *Double Exposures: Repetition and Realism in Nineteenth Century German Prose* (Stanford, Calif.: Stanford University Press, 2000).

Eva Geulen

ᚿ *1853*

An article published in George Eliot's *Westminster Review* brings belated fame to the philosopher Arthur Schopenhauer

Aesthetic Salvation

When the British drama critic John Oxenford published his essay "Iconoclasm in German Philosophy" in the highly visible *Westminster Review,* its subject, Arthur Schopenhauer (1788–1860), had dwelled in obscurity for decades. Apart from a warm personal remark from Goethe and the briefest of reviews by Jean Paul, his masterpiece, *Die Welt als Wille und Vorstellung* (1819; *The World as Will and Representation,* hereafter *WWR*), had met with no audible echo in the post-Napoleonic intellectual world. Subsequent publications—*On the Will in Nature* (1836), *The Two Fundamental Problems of Ethics* (1841), the second volume of *WWR* (1844), two thick collections of *Parerga and Paralipomena* (1851)—did little to alter this, despite the award of a prize to him by the Norwegian Academy of Sciences. Though embittering, the lack of recognition at least afforded the pallid consolation of confirming one of Schopenhauer's firmest convictions. Works of genius, he believed, can only be recognized for what they are once the passage of time has consigned their contemporaries to oblivion. The silence surrounding his achievement, then, was an occasion, not for despair, but for patience. After the early disappointment of his academic ambitions (almost no students attended his lectures at the University of Berlin), Schopenhauer retired to Frankfurt, where he lived on an inheritance from his merchant father. However, he knew not to squander the time and freedom this unintended stipend afforded him. He assiduously perfected his command of languages, ancient and modern, followed literary trends, and registered scientific discoveries with keen interest. Each day he practiced the flute for an hour, carefully perused the *Times* of London, and undertook a bracing constitutional with his poodle. A meticulously observed regimen of study and writing enabled him to pursue the ramifications of the system he had outlined in *WWR*.

Thus, when the wave of admiration initiated by Oxenford's still highly readable *compte rendu* finally reached him, Schopenhauer had acquired such solid confidence in his achievement that his tardy fame seemed to him a matter of bemusement.

It is useful to chart briefly the literary and artistic dimension of that fame. Certainly its most effective amplifier was Richard Wagner, who became acquainted with Schopenhauer's work in the 1850s during his exile in Switzerland. From *WWR,* which contains, as Georg Simmel later put it, the "most profound interpretation of music" ever conceived, the composer drew the metaphysical legitimation of his ambitious aesthetic program. Another early admirer was the playwright Friedrich Hebbel, who, during a visit to Schopenhauer's apartment, offered his services as literary herald of the philosopher's fame. In 1862, the Romanian critic Titu Maiorescu declared Schopenhauer the "man of the century" and supervised the translation of his works into his native language, thereby laying the foundation upon which, nearly a century later, the Romanian-French writer E. M. Cioran would erect his brilliant pessimistic constructions. Schopenhauer became an indispensable resource for many of the most important realist writers across Europe. When Tolstoy's neighbor, the poet and translator Afanasii Fet, brought Schopenhauer's thought to the novelist's attention in the spring of 1869, he spent the following months studying and translating the philosopher's works. Without the "sustained ecstasy" of that summer, as Tolstoy described it, *Anna Karenina* would never have been achieved. Turgenev was deeply influenced by reading Schopenhauer, as were Germany's most significant realists, Wilhelm Raabe and Theodor Fontane. In France, Guy de Maupassant made creative fictional use of the philosopher's speculations on spectral apparitions, and Schopenhauer is even a character in his uncanny tale *Auprès d'un mort* (Beside Schopenhauer's Corpse). Nor was Schopenhauer's influence limited to Europe. Herman Melville, to name a distinguished American example, drew on the philosopher's metaphysical views in shaping the powerful vision of his later works.

Schopenhauer's thought likewise proved formative for a remarkable range of modernist writers. Joris-Karl Huysmann's decadent novel-manifesto *A rebours* (1884; *Against Nature*), for example, owed much of its scandalous effect to citations culled from a French edition of Schopenhauer's apothegms. In the same year, Emile Zola published his anti-Schopenhauerian novel *La joie de vivre (The Joy of Life),* which, not unlike Nietzsche's writings of the 1880s, sought to overcome pessimism through the affirmation of vital existence. Perhaps the most significant Francophone case of inventive reception was that of Marcel Proust, who was first introduced to Schopenhauer's philosophy in 1894 and whose multivolume *À la recherche du temps perdu* (1913–1927; *Remembrance of Things Past*) incorporates, as Samuel Beckett later demonstrated in an incisive essay, crucial Schopenhauerian themes. The Symbolist movement, whether in Belgium (Maeterlinck), Russia (Belyi), or Austria (Hofmannsthal), cannot be understood apart from its Schopenhauerian inspiration. In England, Joseph Conrad, Thomas Hardy, and Ford Maddox Ford were among the writers who adapted the philosopher's ideas to their works. Brazil's greatest novelist, Machado de Assis, transformed Schopenhauer's pessimism into a remarkably supple instrument of narrative exploration, and a generation later the Argentinian Jorge Luis Borges elaborated Schopenhauer's thoughts on time and eternity in his alembicated metafictions. Among the major German-language novelists of the 20th century, Thomas Mann was perhaps most deeply affected by his engagement with Schopenhauer. Indeed, his novels *Buddenbrooks* (1901) and *Der Zauberberg* (1924; *The Magic Mountain*), to mention only the two most prominent examples, are composed according to Schopenhauerian categories. But if Mann is the most devoted disciple among modern novelists, he by no means stands alone. Suffice it to mention Heimito von Doderer and Thomas Bernhard, whose works are imbued with Schopenhauerian themes.

Scanning the delta of influence that fans out from Schopenhauer's work, one can identify three sources of its prodigious literary fecundity. One is the very thought that most clearly marks Schopenhauer's innovation vis-à-vis the philosophical tradition. He is the first philosopher to conceive of being as sheer enigma. As Clément Rosset phrased it, he is the premier philosopher of the absurd. Such is the implication of the metaphysical thesis announced in the title of Schopenhauer's masterpiece. To claim that the inner nature of the world is Will is to render the world at once unknowable (we only know in the mode of representation) and pointless (there is no reason for the world's existence).

It is not surprising that this doctrine should fall on deaf ears in the years immediately following the publication of *WWR*. The 1820s were the decade of Hegel's triumph. The students at the University of Berlin who flocked to *his* lectures were taught that Spirit had finally reached the point in its history when the identity of the rational and the real was thoroughly understood and expressed. In the 1830s and 1840s thinkers such as Ludwig Feuerbach, Karl Marx, and Søren Kierkegaard chipped away at Hegel's system, often with conceptual chisels—most prominently, the "dialectic"—forged by Hegel himself. During the same period, the complexity of positive knowledge began to explode the confines of philosophical synthesis. Accelerating industrialization transformed traditional patterns of economic and social life, and political disasters, such as the failed revolutions of 1848, demolished the belief in the inevitability of historical progress. By 1853, the year Oxenford's article appeared in the *Westminster Review,* traditional confidence in reason had been sufficiently shaken for Schopenhauer's absurdist vision to gain plausibility. For Schopenhauer's modernist admirers, it would become compelling.

At the beginning of the second book of *WWR,* Schopenhauer accounts for his philosophical originality this way: "We can already see that the essence of things is never to be grasped *from the outside:* however one might seek to know it, one never gains anything more than images and names. In this, one is like a person who walks about a castle searching in vain for an entrance and occasionally sketching the facade. And yet this is the path that all philosophers prior to me have taken" (*Sämtliche Werke*, I, 156). The point is not that previous philosophers have failed to use the right method for knowing the essence of things, but that they have tried to know that essence at all. Knowledge merely explicates one representation through reference to another, replaces images with other images, words with other words. The knowable world is an artifact of the brain, which begins its work by transforming impulses into objects arrayed in space and time. Patterns of cause and effect and paths of inference ramify this basic representational structure, but bring it no closer to an adequate apprehension of the real. As knowers, we trade in a currency that will never be converted into the gold of things in themselves. However, it is not merely the content of the view expressed here that accounts for Schopenhauer's influence on modernist literature; the crucial matter is that he was able to dramatize the enigmatic character of being in richly suggestive figurations. The cited passage is a case in point. In the course of his intense study of Schopenhauer's work in 1916–1917, Franz Kafka found in the simile of the impenetrable fortress the organizing trope of his novel *Das Schloß* (published 1926; *The Castle*). Like Schopenhauer's knower, Kafka's protagonist, the surveyor K., never gains access to the power that obscurely reigns over his existence. Such are the filiations of literary history that an image invented around 1817 to illustrate an epistemological argument can become a novelistic emblem of interpretive despair almost exactly a century later.

The second reason for Schopenhauer's influence in the late 19th and throughout the 20th century is that his philosophy stripped mankind of the last remnants of its godlike status. Among the anecdotes documenting Schopenhauer's eccentricity, one of the most telling has it that, when his poodle misbehaved, he expressed his irritation by calling the dog "human." Apocryphal or not, the story encapsulates the central tendency of Schopenhauer's anthropology. In his view, the human being is, like all animals, principally concerned with maintaining its existence and prolonging the life of the species. To be sure, humans are distinguished from their fellow creatures by their capacity to reason, but this is hardly an ennobling qualification. Far from affording insight into the way things are or reflecting our divine heritage, reason is merely our ability to extricate ourselves from immediate experience through the use of language and concepts and to establish thereby an orientational framework that embraces past and future events. Reason expands the playing field, but remains nonetheless an instrument in the service of self-perpetuation; it complicates but by no means elevates the character of animal life. On the contrary, the advent of reason discloses dimensions of risk and perfidy unknown to the speechless species. The rational animal is unique among the creatures for its cunning and mendacity, for the burden of guilt it inevitably bears, for the fear of death that shadows its every experience. From this point of view, to call a dog "human" has the force of a reprimand.

This disillusioned assessment of our anthropological specificity highlights an important intellectual tradition that flows into, and is, in turn, transformed by Schopenhauer's thought. The view of human action as proceeding from (dissimulated) self-interest had been elaborated with great acumen by such 17th-century moralists as La Rochefoucauld in France and Balthasar Gracián in Spain. Schopenhauer knew and admired their work. He brilliantly translated Gracián's *Hand-Oracle* and attained stunning mastery of the moralists' preferred literary form, the aphorism, but he also recast the moralist idea of pervasive egotism in metaphysical terms that profoundly influenced modernist conceptions. In particular, Schopenhauer argued that the ubiquitous conflicts arising from the pursuit of self-interest express the unappeasable strife at the core of our very being. Having no object, the metaphysical Will can assert itself only by turning on itself; its every affirmation is at once a negation; its forms are pitted against one another in unremitting antagonism. To be, on this account, is to be avaricious. Human beings are individuated centers of relentless craving, acting out the metaphysical drama of the Will's autophagy. The title John Oxenford chose for his path-breaking essay could hardly have been more apt. Schopenhauer was fiercely iconoclastic in the sense that his doctrine of the rapacious desire at the heart of human affairs exposes all eudaemonistic and irenic ideals as either disingenuous or deluded. His transformation of the moralist tradition thus disclosed fields of inquiry whose convolutions such modern iconoclasts as Nietzsche, Freud, and Horkheimer—all avid readers of Schopenhauer—would subsequently chart.

The picture of life Schopenhauer paints, then, is among the bleakest in the history of the West. We are cast into an opaque, pointless existence; our efforts to know the world press it into forms and categories without purchase on reality; our social life is rife with deception, manipulation, and cruelty; the satisfactions we strive for inevitably prove disappointing. The inescapable accompaniments of each individual's brief sojourn on earth are want, anxiety, and regret. One of Schopenhauer's remarkable achievements is his ability to infuse this pessimistic litany with the surprise of insight. A virtuoso of the negative, he conveyed his doleful message in exquisitely balanced paragraphs, replete with keen observation, lively erudition, and wit. He sensed, as Flaubert and Kafka would, that even the worst of all possible worlds doesn't exempt its denizens from the obligation to write well. On the contrary, under such conditions stylistic perfection becomes a singular source of gratification. This brings us to the third reason for Schopenhauer's prodigious literary influence, the extravagant significance he attributed to aesthetic experience.

In Schopenhauer's account, to view the world aesthetically is to become detached from all particulars of individual identity and to assume the disinterested standpoint of a "pure subject of representation." The anxieties and desires that normally preoccupy us fall away and we become impersonal onlookers whose only purpose is to reflect the configurations of things. Aesthetic contemplation offers a unique vehicle of redemption from the unrelenting suffering that is life. Indeed, one of the features that made Schopenhauer's description of the aesthetic attitude so compelling is the echo of accounts of the mystical *visio beatifica*. In his redaction, however, the "loss of self" and "union with God," implied by the notion of beatific vision, are transformed into thoroughly secular phenomena and the salvation they make available perdures but a moment. For it is not God with whom the contemplating subject merges, but the metaphysical Will in one of its archetypal forms. In contrast to all our quotidian or scientific endeavors to know the nature of the world, aesthetic experience has genuine metaphysical content, revealing the timeless patterns the empirical world only imperfectly reproduces. And this metaphysical insight achieves its highest form in the art that eschews representation altogether. Music, says Schopenhauer, is the supreme art because, rather than presenting an archetype of the Will's objectification, it makes the Will itself intuitively accessible, revealing the world's dynamic, dissonant essence. It is understandable that a composer with an exalted sense of his artistic mission, such as Wagner, would find this view congenial.

An honest assessment of Schopenhauer has to conclude that his philosophical significance has diminished since its heyday initiated by Oxenford's essay in 1853. In contradistinction to both his revered master Kant and his despised contemporary Hegel, he is no longer a serious interlocutor for today's philosophers. This withering of interest on the part of the philosophical guild should not, however, obscure Schopenhauer's immense cultural achievement. His writings infused major intellectual and spiritual traditions with new semantic energy and his vision of life remains unrivaled as an expression of the bleaker aspects of human experience. His prose is unquestionably one of the finest stylistic achievements in the German language. Modern music, art, and literature are imbued with his influence and our collective sense of human psychology is indebted to his insights. But perhaps the most culturally important aspect of Schopenhauer's work is the qualities of character it evinces, among the most salient of which are resoluteness in the pursuit of an intellectual project, unstinting candor, contempt for fashionable cant, and compassion for all forms of creaturely anguish. In Schopenhauer's writings, these characteristics congeal into one of the most forceful and memorable personae in all of philosophical literature. This persona, much more than the theses he propounded, make Schopenhauer's work, as Nietzsche recognized, an irreplaceable educational resource.

See also 1790, 1828 (Winter), 1882, 1902, 1912 (June), 1914, 1947, 1989 (February)

Bibliography: Arthur Schopenhauer, *Sämtliche Werke,* ed. Wolfgang Freiherr von Löhneysen, 5 vols. (Frankfurt am Main: Suhrkamp, 1986). ———, *The World as Will and Representation,* trans. E. F. J. Payne, 2 vols. (New York: Dover Books, 1969). Bryan Magee, *The Philosophy of Schopenhauer,* 2nd ed. (Oxford, U.K.: Clarendon Press, 1997). John Oxenford, "Iconoclasm in German Philosophy," *The Westminster Review,* n.s. 3 (1853): 388–407. Georg Simmel, *Schopenhauer and Nietzsche,* trans. Helmut Loiskandl, Deena Weinstein, and Michael Weinstein (Amherst: University of Massachusetts Press, 1986).

David E. Wellbery

ℒ 1855

Ferdinand Kürnberger presents a novelistic critique of America

German-American Literary Relations

Dr. Moorfeld, the idealistic protagonist of Ferdinand Kürnberger's novel *Der Amerika-Müde: Amerikanisches Kulturbild* (1855; *The Man Who Was Weary of America: An American Cultural Portrait*), is a keen observer of the American scene in what he considers all its damning detail. When he enters the house of his New York host, Staunton, he notices numerous features of the interior, from statues and the absence of a library to wallpapers, curtains, and furniture. His account of the fabric covering the couch is representative: the "powerful orange color pattern" resembles nothing so much as a forest fire, he claims, reacting "with more than a smile that no aesthetic hesitation tempered the insinuation to sit down on fiery flames" (37). Ludicrously satirical descriptions of this kind have characterized many German-language America books since Kürnberger's. For example, the weary narrator of Max Frisch's *Montauk* (1976) notes that a "jauchefarbener Spannteppich" (manure-colored wall-to-wall carpet) brightens up his Long Island motel room. Kürnberger's detail of the flaming sofa is kept alive in *Der Amerika-Müde,* suggesting the hero's somewhat excessive America-fatigue, his weariness of the aesthetically impossible, politically disappointing, religiously hypocritical, economically ruthless, and generally ridiculous hell Kürnberger sees in the New World (typically assuming a non-American reader's consent). The Bible—tellingly, the only book in the Staunton household—is ostentatiously displayed on a round table in front of the "forest-fiery sofa." Fittingly, the American *Urwald* (primeval forest) that Moorfeld searches for turns out to be literally a district gutted by fire, and in the end he barely escapes an apocalyptic anti-German riot in New York that culminates in the conflagration of the German-American neighborhood of *Kleindeutschland.* While new immigrants are arriving with the chanting praise song of free America, "Vivat das freie Amerika" (the novel's ironic last line), the reader and Moorfeld know better: going back to Europe constitutes an exodus from the "pillar of cloud" of the burning *Kleindeutschland.*

Along with its elaborate fire symbolism, the novel goes into countless details that make America appear hellish: terrible cooking by women who don't care to cook or the boorishness of mixing champagne and brandy in the same glass; the disgusting presence of spittoons in a government office building and the complete absence of hygiene on a steamboat where a single towel serves all; the repetitive, square, checkerboard-like grid in the layout of Philadelphia, and the ridiculous origin of the song "Yankee Doodle." Bad taste rules in the world of American arts and scandalous financial speculations permeate all areas of life. Children act as if they had complete superiority over their own parents, and the educational system is a travesty. Black slavery and inhuman treatment of Indians round off the picture of a world in which God's commandments are simply meaningless. In *Der Amerika-Müde,* the New World is worse than the Old in every way; even the windows open only halfway in America.

The thin plot serves as an excuse to include not only the narrator's observations, but also lengthy discussions and letters full of miscellaneous cultural snippets. The Austrian writer Kürnberger (1821–1879) had a remarkable flair for scathing descriptions. Although the novel has not been translated into English, it still holds interest for readers across the ideological spectrum. Some might be intrigued by the 1848 revolutionary backdrop of some of Kürnberger's assessments and by his general anticapitalist and occasionally explicit socialist pronouncements, others might find congenial the claim that internally homogeneous European nation-states display spiritual and aesthetic superiority over the vulgar decadence of the heterogeneous United States.

It is telling that Max Weber, in his book *The Protestant Ethic and the Spirit of Capitalism* (1904–1905), drew on and partly adopted Kürnberger's satirical portrait of Benjamin Franklin to launch his own critique (Fluck). Thus Kürnberger's schoolmaster Mr. Mockingbird introduces Franklin's "Advice to a Young Tradesman" with the comment: "The conversion of human existence into shillings and pounds only deserves our pardon because of the invention of the lightning rod. Without it, this would be the doctrine . . . : They make tallow out of cattle and money out of men" (33). Weber cites this passage in his discussion of Franklin. Contemporary readers may not only be impressed with Kürnberger's Marxian and quite systemic critique of the way in which capitalism makes deception and humbug normative (Steinlein). They might also be surprised by Kürnberger's observation of the state penitentiary in Pennsylvania, which anticipates Michel Foucault's famous critique of the panopticon: "To be sure, it's a miracle of human intelligence. One single guard has five hundred cells under surveillance! That character sits like a spider in its sack: from him the whole terrible building fans out; no cell window looks into another one, and yet he can look into all of them!" (326). After speaking with some miserable prisoners who relive the horrors of their lives in their lonely cells, Moorfeld concludes that while European censors merely murder thoughts, American prisons surrender prisoners to their own thoughts, making their haunting fantasies the breeding ground of insanity. "May the abyss devour the Pennsylvanian system," is Moorfeld's ultimate response to this comparison.

Within the code of the book, the United States simply has no culture, and this very richly developed aspect of the novel presumably accounted for its appeal to a conservative Eurocentric readership. Moorfeld's first aesthetic pleasure ("Kunstgenuß") after his arrival in America is representative: in a coffeehouse where he stops to have ice cream, a black band is playing "a strangely cut-up rhythm, the beat of which was somewhat obscure and, moreover, handled rather independently by each artist!" (20). Jolted by the music's sudden shifts from sharp to flat, Moorfeld tears the fiddle away from the first violinist and demonstrates the "correct" way to play the figure. Although the players respond politely, they do not change their style, but play the piece at the same point with the same "barbarism" as before. For Moorfeld and his author, polyrhythms and blues notes are mistakes and flaws that need to be corrected. The opposite side of the same coin is the American treatment of European genius. This is illustrated by the fate of Mozart's librettist Lorenzo Da Ponte, whose death in America in 1838 Kürnberger, in a stroke of poetic license, links to the mob riot in New York. Beauty and America are incompatible in innumerable ways.

For Kürnberger, the heterogeneous nature of the United States cannot provide a basis for culture or beauty. At best, the Americans are an incomplete people ("ein unfertiges Volk"); at worst, they are hopeless barbarians who will never acquire a sense of art or of other higher ideals. Moorfeld's friend and, later, antagonist Benthal specifically deplores ethnic heterogeneity in the newly expanded Union and doubts that the Puritan in Boston and the Frenchman in New Orleans, the palm country of Florida and the ice blocks in Maine and Vermont, could have anything in common. When, as in the case of Texas, a new star joins the Stars and Stripes, what looks like an increase in national power merely accelerates its ultimate demise. Kürnberger not only anticipates a civil war between North and South, but also prophesies one between Atlantic and Pacific America.

Kürnberger's observations of the New World had considerable influence on other writers, but oddly enough, they are not based on personal experience. Kürnberger never went to America, and all his descriptive details were either borrowed or invented. His novel was a response to Heinrich Heine's term *europamüde* (weary of Europe) as popularized by Ernst Willkomm's novel *Die Europa-Müden* (1838; see Robertson). Kürnberger based his novel on idealized accounts of the poet Nikolaus Lenau's (1802–1850) brief and disappointing settlement in America in 1832–1833; and he shares with Lenau the motif of the impoverished natural scene of the New World. This was a theme that 18th-century European intellectuals from de Pauw to Buffon had circulated and Jefferson attempted to counter in his *Notes on the State of Virginia* (1787).

Columbus reported in a 1493 letter to Luis de Santangel that the (European) nightingale and other birds of a thousand kind were singing when he landed on Hispaniola. Many later observers of America were hesitant to project such European sounds onto the New World; and it became a meaningful fact that America was a continent without nightingales. For Lenau, this was a serious and symbolic shortcoming, for was not the absence of the beloved European singing bird symptomatic of the general depravity of the New World, where aesthetics has been sacrificed to economics? Just a few days after landing in America, Lenau wrote in a letter home: "The nightingale is right not to visit these scoundrels. I see a deep and serious significance in the fact that America has no nightingale. It seems like a poetic curse. It would take the voice of Niagara to preach these villains that there are higher gods than those coined in the mint" (Robertson, 22–23).

The land of the dollar was simply not a home for nightingales; and

Kürnberger's choice to give the Franklinesque teacher the name "Mocking-bird" is, of course, a sarcastic comment on this fact. The only time the word nightingale appears in the novel is in a French song, in which the line "Nous entendrons le rossignol chanter" (We shall hear the nightingale sing) strikes Moorfeld as a direct satire on his actual walk through the American forest. With Kürnberger's characteristic excess, he represents the American *Urwald* as an eerily silent forest without any birds, butterflies, or animal sounds, and in which European trees exist only "pseudonymously," so that even such a cele-brated season as autumn appears to him more vulgar and less appealing in the northeastern American than in the European forest.

Kürnberger's extreme Americophobia responds to a countervailing trend of Americophilia in German writing about the new nation. It is only natural that writers who actually went to America were likely to be more ambivalent than Kürnberger. Friedrich Gerstäcker's novel *Nach Amerika* (1855; *Toward America*), for example, pokes fun at the no-nightingale theme when during the landing in New Orleans "the full, mourning tone of a nightingale could be heard clear as a bell—a bird brought across the Atlantic by emigrants" (Durzak, 146). Perhaps even more complex was the negotiation of German lit-erature and American themes for those who decided to stay in the United States or who were American-born German-Americans. (Nearly seven mil-lion Germans emigrated to the United States between 1820 and 1970, and over twenty-five million Americans claim German descent.) At least twenty-five thousand titles were published in German in the United States, and many books were produced in English and other languages. These works, now col-lecting dust on the shelves of archives, await new readers.

The mid-19th century generated numerous German-American novels, several of which followed the format of Eugène Sue's *Mystères de Paris* (1842; *Mysteries of Paris*). One of the first was the anonymous *Geheimnisse von Philadel-phia* (1850; *Secrets of Philadelphia*), of which only the beginning chapters have survived, including lively interracial scenes in a black-German bar and a re-markable account of conspicuous consumption and the illusions it generates in Philadelphia society.

In *Cincinnati, oder Geheimnisse des Westens* (1854–1855; *Cincinnati, or The Se-crets of the West*), Emil Klauprecht develops a sensationalist plot, one part of which is set in the free colored Hotel Dumas, decorated inside with portraits of Toussaint L'Ouverture and (a Germanized) *Friedrich* Douglass, and scenes of the freeing of the slaves in the West Indies, of Cinqué's rebellion on the *Amistad,* and from *Othello.*

Ludwig von Reizenstein's *Die Geheimnisse von New-Orleans (The Secrets of New Orleans)* may well be the most lurid of the German-American "myster-ies." After its long serialization in the *Louisiana Staats-Zeitung* in 1854 and 1855, its publication in book form was suppressed. In addition to an interracial love comedy plot, the novel also contains a remarkably candid chapter enti-tled "Lesbische Liebe" (Lesbian Love). The love dialogue between a German Creole woman and another woman who has left her husband is highly eroticized and unlike anything in English-language American fiction of the time. The binational location may have made Reizenstein bolder than most other writers of the 1850s.

One of the most distinguished novels of manners in the German-American tradition is Reinhold Solger's *Anton in Amerika* (1862), which purports to be a sequel to Gustav Freytag's *Soll und Haben* (though Solger's novel is not anti-Semitic). Tracing a similar trajectory to Kürnberger's *Amerika-Müde*—from New York, to the West, and returning to New York—*Anton in Amerika* takes readers into many different social worlds. It is a good example of a Balzaquian eye observing the New World. So is Caspar Stürenberg's *Klein-Deutschland: Bilder aus dem New Yorker Alltagsleben* (1885; *Little Germany: Pictures from Everyday Life in New York*), set in a tenement whose multilingual inhabitants give it a combined quality "of Noah's ark and the tower of Babel" (3).

The theme of language mixing runs through many of these novels. Kürnberger saw code switching as "Kauderwelsch" (gobbledygook), criticizing it sharply in a letter from Moorfeld to Benthal about Pennsylvania Dutch. Citing some particularly egregious examples in which speakers carelessly mix English and German, Moorfeld asks: "Can one imagine a poet in this tongue? Yet a nationality that is unable to produce poets is like a tree that does not bloom. It is dead. That is the case with the Pennsylvania Dutch" (343). Klauprecht takes a more positive view of the linguistic melting pot, enriching his novel with numerous examples of Americanized German that re-create the intensity of language interaction in Cincinnati. A master of "Germerican" was the comic poet Kurt Stein ("K.M.S."), whose hilarious spoofs of canonical German literature in volumes with titles like *Gemixte Pickles* are responses to the demands for linguistic purity and the worship of *Kultur* that had been promulgated by Kürnberger but were becoming obsolete by the late 19th century.

Because German-American literature does not exist in the kind of cultural isolation for which *Der Amerika-Müde* yearned, but implies in its very hyphenate adjective that it is part of an interaction, some works may have a unique ability to record manners ironically, while others achieve a prophetic quality in foreshadowing thematic concerns such as same-sex love or green politics and linguistic aspects of the transnational period that have all but replaced the nationalist era in which "German America" may have had something unnatural, oxymoronic, or merely comic about it, as it had for Kürnberger. Perhaps the tree of German America bloomed after all.

See also 1799, 1824, 1912 (September), 1953 (March 26)

Bibliography: Ferdinand Kürnberger, *Der Amerikamüde: Amerikanisches Kulturbild* (repr. Frankfurt: Insel, 1986). Marc Shell and Werner Sollors, eds., *The Multilingual Anthology of American Literature: A Reader of Original Texts with English Translations* (New York: New York University Press, 2000). K.M.S., *Die Allerschönste Lengevitch: Die Schönste Lengevitch mit Gemixte Pickles und Limberger Lyrics zusammen downgeboilt, und plenty geseasont mit Additions von Neugehatchter Nonsense* (New York: Crown, 1953). Manfred Durzak, "Nach Amerika: Gerstäckers Widerlegung der Lenau-Legende," in Sigrid Bauschinger, Horst Denkler, and Wilfried Malsch, eds., *Amerika in der deutschen Literatur: Neue Welt—Amerika—USA* (Stuttgart: Reclam, 1975), 135–153.

Winfried Fluck, "The Man Who Became Weary of America: Ferdinand Kürnberger's novel *Der Amerika-Müde* (1855)," in Werner Sollors, ed., *The German-American Tradition* (forthcoming). Harold Jantz, "Amerika im deutschen Dichten und Denken," in Wolfgang Stammler, ed., *Deutsche Philologie im Aufriss,* 2nd ed. (Berlin: Erich Schmidt Verlag, 1962), 310–371. Ritchie Robertson, "German Idealists and American Rowdies: Ferdinand Kürnberger's Novel *Der Amerika-Müde,*" in Ritchie Robertson and Edward Timms, eds., *Gender and Politics in Austrian Fiction* (Edinburgh: Edinburgh University Press, 1996), 17–35. Rüdiger Steinlein, "Ferdinand Kürnbergers *Der Amerika-Müde:* Ein 'amerikanisches Kulturbild' als Entwurf einer negativen Utopie," in Bauschinger et al., 154–177.

Werner Sollors

᠅ 1860

Jacob Burckhardt essays the Italian Renaissance

A Model for Cultural History

Jacob Burckhardt's *Die Cultur der Renaissance in Italien: Ein Versuch (The Civilization of the Renaissance in Italy: An Essay)* was as good as dead on its arrival in the public sphere in September 1860. The publisher Schweighauser had published Burckhardt's *Cicerone,* which became *the* guide to Italian art for cultivated Germans, in 1855, and had paid very well for it. Though Burckhardt warned his friend not to do so, he printed 750 copies of his author's new book-length essay—only to have hundreds of them still on his hands, tied up in bales in his storehouse, as late as January 1862. Hardly any reviews appeared at first, and Burckhardt himself became so conscious of the book's faults that he even stopped sending copies to his German friends.

The book, moreover, represented only a fragment of what Burckhardt (1818–1897) had originally planned to write. A disciple and friend of the pioneering German art historian Franz Kugler, he hoped to produce a comprehensive study of the civilization of the Renaissance as it expressed itself in art and architecture as well as in political institutions and social life. Gradually, however, the materials he collected became so immense, and his belief in the autonomy of art so firm, that he decided to exclude the arts and confine himself to a general essay on the culture of Renaissance Italy. Even that proved hard to complete. Excited by the Florentine bookseller Vespasiano da Bisticci's lives of his contemporaries, which he read soon after their publication in 1839, Burckhardt made excerpts from many of the individual and collective biographies that the fame-besotted Italians of the Renaissance had produced in such abundance. He worked through chronicles and treatises, diplomatic reports and books of jokes, perusing them all with the same slightly obsessive Swiss precision. Soon he found himself, as he would again and again in later life, enmeshed like Laocoön in sheaves of notes. "Yesterday," he wrote to the poet Paul Heyse on 14 August 1858, "I cut up 700 little slips, with quotations from Vasari alone, which I had written down in a book, and rearranged them to be glued up again, organized by topics. From other authors I have some 1,000 more quarto pages of excerpts on art and 2,000 on culture. How much of all this will

I really be able to work through?" Only capitalists with completely free time could carry out an operation on this scale, "but they don't do things like that."

Yet even as Burckhardt made fun of his obsessive working habits and the ensuing fragmentation of his materials, his thoughts about the Renaissance crystallized. A set of notes from summer 1858 show that he had decided to organize his work not as a narrative, the form brilliantly employed by his teacher of history, Leopold von Ranke, but as a topical essay on "politics, war, papacy (fame and individualism), antiquity, discovery of the world, discovery of the human being." He would reveal "the human being of the Renaissance" by examining "individualism, fame, versatility, passion, the highest things," and even "the relation to Islam." In winter 1858–59, Burckhardt still tried to fuse these general categories with a detailed treatment of Renaissance art in his immensely popular lectures in the Basel Museum. But the book that emerged from Schweighauser's presses avoided detailed critical treatment of the arts in favor of calling a lost world back to life. Burckhardt began by confessing that no two writers would reconstruct a given culture in the same way. But he went on to offer a vivid and cogent reconstruction of Italian Renaissance culture, couched in a concise and often epigrammatic form and adorned with brilliantly colored anecdotes that made for compulsive reading.

The Renaissance, for Burckhardt, emerged from the crucible of Italian politics in the later Middle Ages. After the popes and the emperors exhausted one another in the struggles that followed the Investiture Controversy, he argued, the Italian states found themselves *de facto* independent. A couple of republics and a great many despots took the opportunity offered by this power vacuum to create states of a new kind—states which Burckhardt described as "works of art," since they rested not on historical precedents but on conscious planning. In the political world that these men brought into being, violence became both common and terrifyingly uninhibited. The despots who survived—as well as the rivals they forced into exile, and even the lesser citizens who retired from the public stage of communal life as tyranny took hold—developed personalities of a new kind. In their search for fame, the only permanent memorial they could hope for in a world in flux, they created a new culture—one that consisted not only in new forms of literature and art, but also in new forms of behavior and ritual, clothing and furniture.

"Every period of civilization," Burckhardt stated in one of his most pregnant and influential aphorisms, "which forms a complete and consistent whole not only manifests itself in political life, in religion, art, and science, but also sets its characteristic stamp on social life." The men and women who created the new civilization of the Renaissance did this more effectively than most. Medieval people, inextricably caught in the sticky web of long-established social orders, had regarded themselves only as members of groups and had glimpsed the outer world only through a sort of veil, "woven of faith, illusion, and childish prepossession, through which the world and history were seen clad in strange hues." Renaissance people, by contrast, lived on their own resources. They saw the world objectively and examined themselves subjectively. And they exercised these new capacities again and again. They developed a new passion for and a new scientific way of understanding nature, wrote vivid and penetrating autobiographies, created new kinds of festival and social life, and even ventured to put men and women on the same social and cultural footing. Since the fifteenth century, scholars had defined the Renaissance as the period in which scholars, artists, and finally all educated men and women had set themselves to master the classical in art and literature. Burckhardt, an expert historian of Italian art and architecture, of course recognized the pervasive importance of the classics. But he insisted that the monuments and texts played a new role only because the Italians' situation enabled them to interpret them in a new way. Secular, passionate only about this world, obsessed with honor and fame, the Italians, as Burckhardt boldly stated more than once, were the first moderns: "Benvenuto [Cellini] is the sort of person who can do anything and venture anything, and who measures himself by his own personal standard. Like it or not, this figure visibly embodies the modern human being."

The Civilization of the Renaissance in Italy was the work of an anti-Hegelian who claimed that he had no talent at all for philosophy. But it embodied a Hegelian philosophy of culture nonetheless, in its drive to show how every segment of Renaissance culture formed one facet of the great jewel that was Italian Renaissance culture—or one more creation of the same period *Geist*. Nonetheless, the book was anything but dry or general. Burckhardt's chapters began with bold statements about the coherence of the lost world he called back to life. Colorful brief stories, vividly described in the present tense by a writer who portrayed himself as a kind of guide, or Cicerone, to the past, drove each general point home. Though Burckhardt's general theses were clear, in the body of his work he preferred allusion to clear statement and irony to literalism. Everything stimulated, nothing satisfied the reader. Even when, in one of the most breathtakingly memorable passages in the book, Burckhardt used the life and work of Leon Battista Alberti to exemplify the new phenomenon of the "universal human being," he calmly remarked that Leonardo exemplified it still more clearly—and broke off his treatment there. At once the three-dimensional recreation of a culture and a series of deliberately fragmentary essays, Burckhardt's *Civilization of the Renaissance in Italy* burned and fascinated and irritated its readers at one and the same time.

Though sales were slow at first, and reviews were scarce, the book gradually gained recognition as the model for a new kind of history. Just as Burckhardt had brought his teacher Kugler's works up to date, so younger scholars added material to and eliminated it from his pointed, artistically balanced essay, until it became a massive, heavily footnoted study. Even as Burckhardt gradually lost faith in his vision of Renaissance individualism, moreover, it became a central topic of historical scholarship and debate. Some young scholars adopted—or adapted—it, notably his Basel colleague, the young classical philologist Friedrich Nietzsche. Others, especially medievalists, attacked it, tracing the roots of modern subjectivity and objectivity into the thought of Saint Francis and even more unlikely places. Every discussion of the problem of the

Middle Ages or the origins of modernity had to begin with a ritual reference, positive or negative, to Burckhardt's *Renaissance*.

Burckhardt's vision of the Renaissance struck home outside as well as inside the universities. Every bourgeois family had an illustrated copy of Burckhardt's book in its glass-fronted bookcase. And every newly rich entrepreneur or banker who could manage it built a Renaissance villa in the suburbs in which to pursue a modern version of the life of art that Burckhardt had so eloquently evoked. Sgraffito facades and rusticated windows flanked the tramlines in wealthy suburbs like Grünewald, outside Berlin. The creator not just of the scholarly study of the Renaissance, but of the larger phenomenon of "Renaissanceismus," Burckhardt enjoyed a fame and impact unusual for any historian—even in history's own century, when the discipline provided the ideological underpinnings for nationalism and empire, and royalty, aristocrats, and patricians competed in their zeal to fill Germany's cities and forests with mock-traditional hunting lodges, town halls, and universities. Yet he also found eager readers in more subversive quarters. Sigmund Freud, who read and partly transcribed the introductory passage on method in the published version of Burckhardt's cultural history of Greece, drew on it to describe "gleichschwebende Aufmerksamkeit," the analytic way of listening, with equal attention, to everything that a patient said, however silly or implausible it might seem.

No one was better qualified than Burckhardt to become one of the dominant historians of the age. Born in 1818 to a modest branch of a patrician family, deeply rooted in the culture of the old Swiss city-state of Basel, he studied history and art history at the new Prussian universities of Berlin and Bonn in the 1840s. The young Burckhardt learned to use the tools of his scholarly trade from those who did the most to forge them, like Kugler and Ranke, whose famous seminar he attended, and whose approval of his scholarship he cherished to the end of his life. In the German universities, he experienced the excitement and inspiration that come from joining an intellectual revolution just as its wave crests. Burckhardt's work bore the impress of his formation to the end of his long life. When he argued in his *Griechische Kulturgeschichte (History of Greek Culture)* that the Greeks had not been the happy sunlit beings described so influentially by Winckelmann and others, he echoed what he had heard in the classroom of the great philologist and historian August Böckh. Kugler, his beloved teacher of art history, showed him how to study such "antiquarian" subjects as the development of costume, furniture, and architecture—and suggested that even the history of art should itself eventually form part of a larger history of culture.

But Burckhardt's sensitivity to history was also sharpened by the larger conditions in which he grew up. He came of age in a Europe still shaken by the French Revolution, the conquests of Napoleon, and the transformation of Prussia and other older monarchies. Like Marx, he always knew that history could shatter institutions and assumptions that seemed as solid as granite. Like Marx, too, Burckhardt directly witnessed some of the revolutionary violence of the 1840s—in his case, the mass demonstrations and civil wars that shook his native Switzerland. But unlike Marx, Burckhardt was inspired by present history to look to the past with love and to the future with foreboding. Always conservative by inclination, he became an impassioned defender of what he called "old Europe." Burckhardt saw the independent city-state of Basel, with its narrow elite of silk-ribbon-makers and its scholarly and scientific dynasties, as something more than an inherited home. It was a particular kind of state and civilization, one that could serve as an alternative to the new empire that took shape in Germany in the late 1860s. He regarded his duties as a Basel professor as overwhelmingly important, and genuinely preferred teaching many subjects, sixteen or eighteen hours a week, to the students at his tiny university, to the better-paid, research-centered life of a German ordinarius at Berlin, where he was offered, but declined, the position as Ranke's successor. Though many German scholars and publishers urged him to publish his work on the history of Greece, Burckhardt consistently refused to do so, or even to leave Basel to lecture, and left much of the revision of his lectures to be done after his death.

History provided the focus for Burckhardt's mental life from his youth until his death in 1897. More like his teacher Ranke than most of his fellow students, he refused to specialize in a place or a period. Burckhardt's essay on the Italian Renaissance set a research agenda for historians and art historians throughout Europe. In his lectures on the cultural history of the Greeks, the great work of his last years, he was still opening trails that later scholars would spend generations surveying, clearing, and paving. Burckhardt gripped his hearers—and posthumously shocked his readers—by his emphasis on the fundamentally agonistic quality of Greek society and civilization, its acceptance of permanent struggle for mastery as the natural condition of men and cities. He made the institutions and character of the Greek *polis* or city-state the fundamental subject of Greek history. Though some of the *viri eruditissimi,* irritated by Burckhardt's failure to cite (their own) recent scholarship, condemned his book as dead on arrival, many others found it inspiring. Burckhardt's work did as much as that of any other thinker or scholar—including Nietzsche—to inspire the rebellion against historicism in which so many younger German classical scholars and ancient historians participated, down to the 1920s. The scholars of the Weimar age of *Geistesgeschichte* (history of spirit) looked back to Burckhardt as he had looked back to Ranke: as their *Altvater.* Students and readers alike were particularly fascinated by the general reflections on history that reached print after his death, in which he expressed his fears for the survival of Europe and articulated a model for understanding history through the interplay of three forces, the state, religion—and culture.

Of all the great historians of the nineteenth-century German world, of all the high masters of historicism, only Burckhardt still finds readers outside Germany and outside the world of professional scholarship. Only Burckhardt still helps both to define the agendas of professional historical research and to fix students' first, indelible impressions of Ancient Greece, the Roman Empire in

Late Antiquity, and the Italian Renaissance. His ambiguities—did he aestheticize state power or fear it? did his Renaissance mark the birth of "old Europe" or of its dissolution?—continue to provoke sharp debate. For all its deep roots in a particular time and place, for all its errors and lacunae, his work has proved uniquely resistant to history.

See also 1768, 1784, 1805, 1826, 1882, 1899

Bibliography: Felix Gilbert, *History: Politics or Culture? Reflections on Ranke and Burckhardt* (Princeton: Princeton University Press, 1990). Maurizio Ghelardi, *La scoperta del Rinascimento: L'"Eta di Raffaello" di Jacob Burckhardt* (Turin: Einaudi, 1991). Lionel Gossman, *Basel in the Age of Burckhardt: A Study in Unseasonable Ideas* (Chicago and London: University of Chicago Press, 2000). John Hinde, *Jacob Burckhardt and the Crisis of Modernity* (Montreal, Kingston, London, and Ithaca: McGill-Queen's University Press, 2000). Werner Kaegi, *Jacob Burckhardt: Eine Biographie*, 7 vols. (Basel and Stuttgart: Schwabe, 1947–82). Arnaldo Momigliano, "Introduction to the Greek Cultural History of Jacob Burckhardt," in *Studies on Modern Scholarship*, ed. G. W. Bowersock (Berkeley, Los Angeles, and London: University of California Press, 1994), 44–53. David Norbrook, "The Life and Death of a Renaissance Man," *Raritan* 8 (1985): 89–110. Karl Weintraub, *Visions of Culture: Voltaire, Guizot, Burckhardt, Lamprecht, Huizinga, Ortega y Gasset* (Chicago and London: University of Chicago Press, 1966).

Anthony Grafton

♍ *1865, Summer*

Wilhelm Busch publishes *Max und Moritz,* a forerunner of the comics, which would become one of Germany's most popular books

Unruly Children

Charles Foster Kane, the cinematic version of the newspaper tycoon William Randolph Hearst, died uttering the word "Rosebud," the symbol of the childhood his sudden wealth had deprived him of. The real Hearst might well have died exclaiming "Max und Moritz," names that connote a less romantically tinged image of childhood than that evoked in Kane's last word. Wilhelm Busch's masterpiece was the model for *The Katzenjammer Kids,* which debuted in 1897 in the *American Humorist,* the Sunday supplement that boosted sales of Hearst's *New York Journal.* Reports conflict on whether Hearst first encountered *Max und Moritz* during a childhood stay in Germany or later through an American translation. Rudolf Dirks, a German-American whom Hearst hired to draw the miscreant "Katzies," peppered his characters' speech with a corresponding patois (recall: "Ve haf vays") that contributed to their popularity. Given this line of influence, Busch's pictorial stories may be described as an important forerunner of the newspaper comic strips that attract their Sunday readership to this day.

Wilhelm Busch (1832–1908) aspired to being a painter and a poet but was never more successful than when he combined visual and verbal art. Hailing from the North German village of Wiedensahl, to which he returned in the self-chosen seclusion of his later years, Busch joined the throng of aspiring artists drawn to Munich. His characterization of the city as "famous for its art and beer" illumines something of his early experiences there. Although he enrolled at the Royal Academy of Arts in 1854, his energies were funneled more directly toward the activities of a young artists' club, whose members ate, drank, and made merry by caricaturing each other. Kasper Braun, a guest at the club, invited Busch to become a regular contributor to the satirical weekly paper *Fliegende Blätter (Loose Leaves)* in 1858 and to *Münchner Bilderbogen (Munich Picture Strips)* in 1859. The illustrations he provided to texts and jokes by others afforded him financial independence for the first time. Out of this caricature work, he developed sequential *Bildergeschichten* or pictorial stories. The earliest were without text, but Busch soon began adding his own verses, usually rhymed couplets. He regarded his pictorial stories as harmless diversions and sources of income, but, for better or worse, Busch owes his fame and popularity to precisely these works of visual-verbal art.

After a false start with *Bilderpossen* (1864; *Antics in Pictures*), his first book in this genre, Busch found his voice with *Max und Moritz: Eine Bubengeschichte in sieben Streichen* (1865; *Max and Moritz: A Juvenile Story in Seven Pranks),* which Kasper Braun had the foresight to publish in book format. Those *Bilderpossen* that included text typically paired two lines with an image in such a way that the verses faithfully explained the pictures. One might leave out either images or text and still understand the story. In *Max und Moritz* such symmetry was abandoned. The punch line of the tale derives not only from the humorous-grotesque images and the witty, laconic verse, but from the ironic discrepancy between picture and word. This tension on the level of form corresponds to a tension within the narrated world, in which the tranquility of self-satisfied, middle-class adults is explosively disturbed by two mischievous children. In the end, the pranksters are killed and peace is restored, but it is a peace overshadowed by the violence required for its enforcement.

Busch's drawings often silently complicate the explicit message of the text. For example, the very first image ironically counters the statement about "wicked" children it accompanies. It is by no means clear from the smiling faces of Max and Moritz that these children are wicked at all and, if wicked they are, then their countenances make that condition seem rather appealing. Furthermore, that the prologue and conclusion, where the ostensible moral is pronounced, are without illustration suggests that Busch had reservations about the values he apparently advocates and thus consigned the moral to oblivion. In his verses, Busch occasionally assumes the standpoint of social order but subverts that very standpoint through his images. Generally he shies away from overtly decrying the status quo; he obviously preferred to express his misgivings about 19th-century bourgeois society skeptically and indirectly. Nonetheless, the images and verses of *Max und Moritz* together represent an unspoken critique of a mechanized, hierarchical world, the violent order which Busch's unruly children repeatedly provoke and thereby expose.

Max und Moritz has been translated more than 190 times into fifty-one lan-

„Ach!" — spricht er — „die größte Freud'
Ist doch die Zufriedenheit!"

Rums! Da geht die Pfeife los
Mit Getöse, schrecklich groß.
Kaffeetopf und Wasserglas,
Tabaksdose, Dintenfaß,
Ofen, Tisch und Sorgensitz —
Alles fliegt im Pulverblitz.

guages, as well as into fifty-one German dialects, and has inspired countless retellings in poetic, dramatic, musical, and filmic form. A school (!) in Germany and a restaurant in Brooklyn have been named after the mischievous pair; the first rockets Wernher von Braun successfully launched were called Max and Moritz; among sundry items, one can even purchase Max and Moritz salt-and-pepper shakers. The immense popularity of these figures is indisputable and even today one has no difficulty finding a German who can recite several Busch verses by heart. Indeed, one of the hallmarks of the work is its insistent trochaic tetrameter, which impresses its monotonous rhythm on the reader's, or listener's, memory much like the mechanical "Rickeracke! Rickeracke!" of the mill in the seventh and final prank. No wonder it has been imitated in commercial jingles.

In order to understand the *Max und Moritz* phenomenon, one should consider the depiction of children in early 19th-century German texts: imperfect, yet perfectible beings in need of enlightened guidance; sweet, innocent beings who occasion in us nostalgia for our own lost carefree days; and redeemers of the human race. Adalbert Stifter's innocents in "Bergkristall" (Rock Crystal), one of his *Bunte Steine* stories (1853; *Many-Colored Stones*), bring harmony to the adult community by uniting two towns in search of their greatest treasure, their children. Friedrich Fröbel, inventor of the kindergarten, regarded children not only as plants requiring the tender care of adults but also as ideal representatives of all human possibility. The children of lexica, such as the Grimms' dictionary or Brockhaus's encyclopedia, are more soberly characterized, but a sentimental-romantic current is evident there as well. Children are defined as beings that lack intellect and reason, much as they were defined in previous centuries. But they also are reputed to possess positive traits that adults lack, such as goodness and honesty. In the 19th century, the cult of childhood was at its height.

Then Heinrich Hoffmann (1809–1894) came along. The children of his deceptively titled *Lustige Bilder und drollige Geschichten* (1844; *Amusing Antics and Funny Stories*), later titled simply *Der Struwwelpeter (Slovenly Peter)*, seem to be cut from the same mold as are Max and Moritz. Hoffmann's children ignore the well-intended advice of adults and suffer the consequences. The punishment of childish infractions is usually meted out either by objects, as when a girl playing with matches burns to death, or by animals, as when a boy torments his dog and gets bitten. In two cases, adults punish the children. One of these is surprisingly gruesome, given the tenor of the rest of Hoffmann's collection: a tailor cuts off the thumbs of a child who obstinately insists on suck-

---

Page 27 from *Max und Moritz*, showing Lämpel lighting his pipe and the subsequent explosion. The legend to the top panel can be translated as "'Ah!'—he says—'the greatest pleasure: / Satisfaction, joyous leisure!'"; to the bottom panel, "Bam! The pipe now detonates / With noise quite awful to relate. / Water glass and coffee pot, / Tobacco-box and inkwell (splot!) / Table, stove, and comfy chair— / All scatter in the powder's flare." (Department of Printing and Graphic Arts, Houghton Library, Harvard College Library)

ing them. This makes for a rather memorable drawing. Hoffmann was the first to depict such negative child protagonists in a period—the *Biedermeier*—that otherwise upheld images of good, well-behaved children as models to follow. Hoffmann's children are all strong-willed and none of them mend their ways. None convert and become good children—they would rather die first. Hoffmann effectively punctured a dominant idea of childhood and helped make Busch possible.

At first glance, *Slovenly Peter* and *Max and Moritz* seem of a piece. In both pictorial stories, children are at odds with adults and the depiction of punishment is often grotesque. However, the adult world in Hoffmann is present only as a foil for displaying the unrepentant stubbornness of several children. In Busch, by contrast, the collision of child and adult worlds is much more dynamic, since Max and Moritz are not merely strong-willed malcontents but devious tricksters. The conflicts Hoffmann's children experience derive from what one might now regard as normal childish behavior: curiosity regarding fire, refusal to eat soup, rocking one's chair at the dinner table. But Busch's children are more than childish: they sabotage their elders for the sake of sabotage. Playing pranks is a source of absolute delight to them. In fact, unlike Hoffmann's children before and the Katzenjammer Kids after, Max and Moritz are never depicted crying or in distress. Never. They smile throughout the entire work, even in death.

Another significant distinction is the fact that the advice and admonitions of Busch's adults are anything but enlightened and well intended. Busch describes a society whose adult inhabitants are concerned above all with securing a calm, cozy, and contented existence. And yet these adults are by no means gentle souls; they are willing to grind troublemaking children through a mill in order to keep the peace. How does one become this sort of peace-loving adult? Some children in Busch's oeuvre are not ground into feed, but conform, thus presumably becoming adults who will re-enforce the social order. In *Plisch und Plum* (1882; *Plisch and Plum*), Paul and Peter, the child owners of the canine title characters, beat their pets until they obediently do tricks, just as their father had thrashed the boys themselves until they learned to be good. Before the beatings, the children and the dogs were anarchic troublemakers, not due to a wicked or stubborn nature, but due to an exuberance for life and to youthful energy. Such exuberance is diminished by corporal punishment, which effects an initiation into the social order and a normalization of one's desires. Paul and Peter come to value order and discipline, and their former wild, free play becomes tame and regimented. In works such as *Plisch und Plum*, Busch shows both the method and the costs of socialization in the culture of 19th-century Prussia.

Many of Busch's children—along with animals, such as *Hans Huckebein der Unglücksrabe* (1867; *Hans Huckebein, Raven of Misfortune*) or *Fipps der Affe* (1879; *Fipps the Monkey*)—do not conform. Like Till Eulenspiegel, they move from one merry prank to the next, until they are killed. Unlike Eulenspiegel, who tended to play pranks only on those who wronged him first, Max and Moritz need no such justification. They are motivated, in part, by hunger. Three of their seven pranks, along with the final prank played on them, concern eating or being eaten. Yet, they are hardly malnourished; this is no German *Les miserables*. The children are driven by sheer impulse; they disregard anything that stands in the way of their will. Tellingly, their parents are completely absent; there are no figures who hold any authority over them. Max and Moritz represent pure drive, free of social constraints.

In the society Busch depicts, all seem to enjoy themselves and their positions, except when a prank is being played on them. Max and Moritz are having a ball tormenting animals, stealing food, setting a booby trap for the village tailor and teacher, placing bugs in their uncle's bed, and sabotaging a farmer's work. In turn, those adults whom Max and Moritz have not incapacitated take great satisfaction in curtailing the troublemakers: baking them in dough, trapping them in sacks, and finally executing them with cruel and unusual punishment. The farmer and miller clearly savor grinding the troublemakers into bird feed with mocking smiles. There's a sadistic strain in Busch's world, in which both children and adults derive enjoyment from harming others. One difference is that the adults' punishment—or should we call it a retributive prank?—reduces chaos, while the children's pranks increase it. Some have suggested that Max and Moritz express the Schopenhauerian Will, and Busch certainly found Schopenhauer's jaundiced assessment of human affairs congenial with his own worldview. From this perspective, the other characters—the adults— illustrate the Will held in check by socialization, the Will compromised.

Busch describes and depicts a rigid social order, and one must read and view carefully to comprehend this. In the first prank, Max and Moritz tie pieces of bread to strings in order to catch three hens and a rooster and cause them to choke to death. The drawings stylize the rooster as a drill sergeant mustering his troop of hens, who dutifully stand at attention. The hens then march in lockstep toward the bread as the rooster counts time. Even after they are all entangled in a tree branch and die, they hang in an impossible harmonious order. Although the chickens are certainly not an allegory of the Prussian army, Busch uses animals to illustrate a militaristic society. This is equally true of the June bugs that Max and Moritz collect from a tree and place in their uncle's bed. As he sleeps, the bugs march out single file until he awakens and stamps them to death. The final images of this prank show the uncle smiling mockingly, pointing at the carnage, and enjoying his status as victor. He then returns to bed, snoring, having won peace again. Of course, smashing bugs to protect one's nap does not seem especially barbaric, and even the punishment meted out to Max and Moritz evokes a sort of poetic justice. But in both cases, the violence of the punishers exceeds reasonable force and involves obvious pleasure. This hardly speaks favorably for a civilization that condones such treatment of juvenile tricksters.

Not that Busch regarded children as naturally good. Unlike Jean-Jacques Rousseau's Émile, who instinctively feels sympathy with suffering animals and humans, Max and Moritz demonstrate only self-assertive instincts. But it may be that Busch regarded children as naturally active and, in the context of a rigid social order, as disruptive. The opening lines of the text—"Oh, how often we must hear / Or read of wicked children!!"—lament not so much that wicked children abound as that such complaints about wicked children are so common. Busch's view of children would be romantic only in one sense: his children are honest; they are what they are, active and selfish. The adults too are selfish, but they mask it. Adults are distinguished from children primarily through their hypocrisy, through their attempts to deceive others and themselves about the true nature of their enjoyments and motivations. A comparison of all the characters' smiles demonstrates this point nicely. The children throw their heads back and their arms out, laughing and smiling openly and widely when a prank succeeds, while the adults snicker, half-concealing their smiles with their hands, as they play a final prank on the children. In the world Busch depicts, adults strive to maintain the peace and above all to protect their afternoon snooze within a regimented, but in no way ideal or just, society. Society is a bastion against disturbance, of which Max and Moritz, with their irrepressible will-to-pranks, provide an inexhaustible source.

The moral of Busch's tale seems to be: what goes around comes around. The pretense of a loftier conclusion is undermined when Busch puts an empty claim in the mouth of "good" Uncle Fritz, who opines: "Yes, that [being deliberately ground in a mill] comes from dumb pranks." In another tale, Diogenes summarizes with kindred banality: "Yes, yes, that [two children being crushed to death] comes from that [rolling his barrel down a hill]." Such an assessment of cause and effect has, of course, been a part of popular cartoons ever since, from Tom and Jerry to the Road Runner and Coyote to Itchy and Scratchy. American culture is no less a stranger than German culture to *Schadenfreude,* joy in the suffering of others. Perhaps the smiles most worthy of interpretation are those of Busch's readers, be they children or adults.

See also 1500 (Eulenspiegel), 1848 (September 12), 1848 (October 11), 1853, 1899

Bibliography: Wilhelm Busch, *Max and Moritz: With Many More Mischief-Makers More or Less Human or Approximately Animal,* ed. H. Arthur Klein (New York: Dover, 1962). ———, *Max und Moritz/Max and Moritz,* ed. Robert Godwin-Jones, Virginia Commonwealth University, February 1999 (*www.fln.vcu.edu/mm/mmmenu.html*). Dieter P. Lotze, *Wilhelm Busch* (Boston: Twayne, 1979).

Anthony Krupp

♫ 1867

In the year of Baudelaire's death, Eduard Mörike releases the fourth and definitive edition of his own collected poems

Intimations of Mortality

First published in 1838, Mörike's *Gedichte (Poems)* appeared in revised form in 1847, again in 1856, and once more in 1867, growing incrementally from

143 to 226 poems. The slight compass of Mörike's production is surprising given his generally high standing within the pantheon of German poets, due in part to the wide range of genres in which he excelled. Matching his poignant lyricism and acute ear for popular registers was his dexterity with the sonnet and, especially, various classical meters. Forms derived from antiquity came to predominate as the years progressed—a trend consistent with the nature of Mörike's poetry overall, in which images frequently crystallize around sudden impressions and chance encounters. His epigrams represent a particular expression of an aesthetics that concentrates perception on the momentary and the minute, but so too do those many unassuming poems that first appeared as inscriptions accompanying gifts or as entries in albums. Occasional poems are not marginal to an oeuvre whose variety mirrors that of *The Greek Anthology,* with its ekphrases, epitaphs, dedications, love poems, and so forth. Mörike (1804–1875) arranged his editions so that ballads, sonnets, epigrams, elegies, odes, and other genres occur in clusters, giving his *Gedichte* the taxonomic feel of an anthology, in which poems borrow their status from the found objects they often describe.

One serendipitous find places Mörike himself at the center of curiosity, enfolding classical learning into a milieu as content as it is closed. Entitled "Schul-Schmäcklein" (1838; "School-Wit"), the poem evokes schoolboys sizing up a new master. Deeming him praiseworthy, they agree to leave him unruffled, but they add that one can tell from the verse he writes that he knows Latin—and uses snuff. The clear self-irony attests to an uncertain vocation. Disinclined toward the pastoral career for which he was trained, Mörike, some of whose poems pay explicit homage to Roman forebears, sought solace in the prospect of a secular post, where Latin and tobacco alike are vague reminders of stifled desires. Mörike was once disciplined for smoking while a student at the Tübingen Evangelical *Stift,* the seminary where, on the eve of the French Revolution, Hölderlin, Hegel, and Schelling had become friends. By the time Mörike began his studies in 1822, post-revolutionary ferment had yielded to the political quiescence and concomitant shortening of vision for which the Biedermeier is the familiar synonym. Mörike's timeline corresponds closely to that of Carl Spitzweg (1808–1885), the Munich painter known for his humane caricatures of bookworms, cactus collectors, Sunday strollers, and other insouciant denizens of a small world whose myopia is made concrete by the almost opaque eyeglasses worn by many of these figures. The caricature *Schmetterlingsfänger* (1840; *Butterfly Catcher*), its net-wielding subject peering through heavy lenses at a colorful specimen, makes light of the hunt and projects a pacified existence conveyed elsewhere by sentries caught yawning, or even knitting, while songbirds nest in the muzzles of dormant cannons (see *Peace on the Home Front,* 1840/45).

Transformed by industrious birds into quasi-natural objects, these cannons, their barrels brimming with bits of grass and straw, are variations on the "verdant ruin," which in the bucolic tradition signified the rejuvenation of art through a beneficent nature. A favored genre of the Enlightenment, the idyll

Carl Spitzweg, *The Butterfly Catcher*, ca. 1840. (Museum Wiesbaden)

held a renewed appeal at a time when the middle-class interior offered refuge from the world at large, and when an almost programmatic short-sightedness found expression in the collector's focus on minutiae. The idyll is suited to a domestic compromise in which happiness itself is scaled down and passions are diverted onto things. In Mörike's "Wald-Idylle" (1829; Forest-Idyll), the speaker, reading fairy tales from the Brothers Grimm under a tree, longs inwardly for the peasant girl next door. A "tanned wench," she is the vital opposite of Snow White, who is preserved in a crystal casket like a porcelain miniature. This contrast between suspended animation and exposure to the elements recurs in another of Mörike's idylls, "Der alte Turmhahn"

(1852; The Old Weathercock). Initially subtitled "Still-Life," it is the story of a rooster-shaped weathervane that is brought indoors after spending more than a century affixed to the steeple of a village church. From his new, cozier perch on the rectory stove, the bronze figure contentedly watches the parson composing his weekly sermon. Salvage and salvation thus converge in an interior domain where happiness is constituted by carefully assembled material things—old books, a fine walnut desk, writing implements, even cacti. This contentment is completed when a spider hangs its web on the weatherworn metal bird, yet another ruin both naturalized and domesticated by time.

"The Old Weathercock" is set in the village of Cleversulzbach, the quiet venue where Mörike had his first parsonage. A reluctant purveyor of the Word, he likely relished this image of retirement and of someone other than himself performing the duties of pastor. This snug tranquility conceals a deeper turbulence, however, which is sublimated through the studied artifice of the idyll itself and through objects gilded by the light of the rising sun. When the bird, which narrates its own story, recalls how it endured "one-hundred-and-thirteen years" of seasonal extremes, it echoes the martyrdom off-handedly expressed in the opening line of "Peregrina V" (1829): "Love, they say, stands lashed to a pole." This is one in a cycle of poems about love and betrayal, in which the innocence of the beloved translates into all-embracing amorality—an unbridled Eros that erodes the boundaries of the social world, which relegates passion to the outside. Peregrina's glowing cheeks recall the robust sensuality of the young peasant woman in "Forest-Idyll." The latter appears with a jug of cool milk for her woodcutter-father and embodies the voluptuousness that tradition often ascribes to women who serve refreshment. Peregrina's real-life inspiration, a foundling of fascinating beauty and mysterious background named Maria Meyer, was working as a barmaid when Mörike met her in 1823. While the details of their involvement are obscure, it is clear that Mörike's intense passion strained the limits of sanity and left him, in a word, a poet. Peregrina personifies temptation, and with it the dark ambiguity that imbues the drink she proffers: "With a smile you hand me death in the cup [*Kelch*] of sins" ("Peregrina I").

The extended cup is central to a body of work in which, repeatedly, heady drafts and unguent vapors combine in a distillate of proto-Symbolist evocation. Other guises of the forbidden fruit include—in "Forest-Idyll"—the apple that poisons Snow White, itself the product of a devious alchemy. *Kelch,* as both "calyx" and "chalice," supplies a figure that governs the shift from the natural to the artificial. The tempestuous Peregrina, her hair strung with wildflowers, has her own snow-white counterpart in the marble vessel found in Mörike's most famous poem, "Auf eine Lampe" (1846; To a Lamp). Reminiscent of various examples from *The Greek Anthology,* and comparable to certain of Rilke's "thing-poems," these lines describe a lamp that hangs from the ceiling of a room, its "almost forgotten" pleasures captured in the friezelike imagery on the object itself:

On your white marble shell, whose rim
An ivy wreath weaves round with golden-green brass,
A flock of children dance merrily their rondo.

The idyll is present here in the concentrated form of the bas-relief, that is, as
form only. The lamp mimics the goblet, "ivy-encrusted with clusters of gold,"
for which Theocritus's shepherds compete. Yet, the object of Mörike's poem,
as well as its tone, is funereal. Though "still in place" ("Noch unverrückt"),
it is in place *of* something else. Literally suspended, it substitutes for a beauty
less abiding but more alive. In this respect, "To a Lamp" contrasts with
"Versuchung" (1844; Temptation), in which the delicate shape of a woman's
arm, while sculptural, offsets the lifeless pallor of the marble lamp: "How I
thirst / At the shimmering white of her curved arm!"

An epigram, "Temptation," describes a woman preparing a dessert, apparently for children, her "more fragrant lips" superseding the sweetened blend of
fruit and wine. Smell fosters the association between the object of erotic desire
and the "silver chalice," which is assured of becoming her substitute. In "To a
Lamp," the tenuous chains by which the marble bowl is suspended identify the
object as being contiguous with distant pleasures. Paradigmatic for "Temptation" is an earlier epigram, "Vicia faba minor" (1837), in which a flower's scent
unexpectedly restores the signifying chain, triggering memories of temptations past:

Spare me this perfume: bewitching, it reminds me
    Of the curls that once ensnared my senses.
Away with this blossom! black and white, it tells me
    That the seductress, oh! paid dearly with her life.

"Vicia faba minor" and "Temptation" straddle the period when Mörike was
hard at work on an anthology of Greek and Latin verse, *Classische Blumenlese*
(1840; *Classical Bouquet*). Yet his supple control of classical meters is anything
but the pedantry suggested by the self-ironical "Schul-Schmäcklein," mentioned earlier. On the contrary, the epigram provided Mörike with a vehicle
for condensed articulation, and for organizing perceptions around concrete
things or fleeting impressions. In the twin distichs of the exquisite "Auf dem
Krankenbette" (1837; On the Sickbed), for example, hope figures as a sudden
flash of sunlight, which the wing of a passing bird deflects into a shadow-filled
room.

There is another dimension to "Vicia faba minor," however. While the title
may invoke classical exemplars, it also smacks of basic gardener's Latin (likewise
"Datura suaveolens," 1837). One can well imagine the subject, botanical guide
in hand, identifying this particular species of vetch *(vicia)*. A similar taxonomic interest is registered in the lyrical "Auf eine Christblume" (1841; To a
Christmas Rose), which is addressed to a winter-blooming flower, "cousin to
the lily" ("Lilienverwandte"), found in the snow by a wooden gravesite. In a

letter to his friend Hartlaub, Mörike quotes a description from a certain Pastor Müller's *Gartenbüchlein (Little Garden Book)*, expressing wonder at this flower's unusual fondness for cold. The setting—a wintry grove with a frozen pond and a deer grazing nearby—summons the "cold pastoral" of Keats's Grecian urn to which Mörike's lamp bears a close resemblance. And much as a "gentle spirit of solemnity" encompasses the lamp, so a butterfly's "delicate spirit," drawn by the subtle fragrance, circles unseen around the vernal blossom.

Doubling the already rarefied sensuousness of the flower's scent, the butterfly exhibits qualities that readily endear it to the Biedermeier sensibility—delicacy, elusiveness, ephemerality, and a natural, though tentative, proximity to other cherished objects. "Im Weinberg" (1838; In the Vineyard) describes a butterfly, wings of a luminous blue, lighting on a Bible's gilded spine as on a flower. "Peregrina II" invokes the wings of a butterfly ("Schmetterlingsgefieder") to suggest the feathery softness of a lover's eyelashes. "Im Park" (1847; In the Park) compares the young foliage of a chestnut tree to the moist wings of a freshly pupated "papillon." The apparent ubiquity of the butterfly in these, and other, examples reflects, beyond a general fascination with entomological detail, a penchant for collecting. Metonym for an abandoned desire, of which it remains a tenuous and fragile reminder, the butterfly—collector's object par excellence—guides a displacement that makes of "life-long passion" an oxymoron. Spitzweg's *Schmetterlingsfänger,* which gently ridicules the popularity of butterfly collecting, follows on the heels of such voluminous, life-consuming studies as Oxenheimer and Treitschke's *Die Schmetterlinge von Europa* (1807–1835) and Hübner's *Europäische Schmetterlinge* (1805–1841). Vladimir Nabokov, an accomplished lepidopterist as well as novelist, noted the stubbornly aesthetic bent of German butterfly specialists, who over the course of the 19th century resisted dissection and microscopy as means of categorization, favoring instead the "philately-like side of entomology." Although postage stamps had yet to be introduced, it is interesting to consider the eventual appeal of this new collector's item, which in its variety and coloration seems almost an extension of the natural world.

Anthologies partake of this same obsession with collecting. The Grimm brothers characterized the tales they gathered as rare natural specimens worth preserving, and so they appear in Mörike's "Forest-Idyll," merging with the sights and sounds of the woodland setting. The idyllic "Bilder aus Bebenhausen" (1863; Pictures from Bebenhausen), one of Mörike's last poems, presents itself as a collection, consisting as it does of eleven vignettes, each one a picture. The subject, a member of a drawing party who has strayed from his group, explores a deserted monastery and its surroundings, resting afterward under trees at the forest's edge. Here, in the heat of mid-afternoon, the fading din of church bells melts with the hum of bees, which envelops the contented speaker in the acoustical equivalent of sunshine. Collectors in their own right, the bees figure an artisanal industry that connects them to the well-wrought object. Theocritus's ivy-wood cup, offered in reward for a "delectable song," is coated with sweet wax, the *melos* that bees produce. "Sweetest Sappho," the addressee of another poem from the same year, is the source of a gift, a hairnet teeming with tiny golden bees (1863; Erinna to Sappho).

The hairnet's precious fabric *(Geweb')* foregrounds a workmanship also present in the net *(Netz)* spun by the spider in "The Old Weathercock." Like the delicate chains suspending the lamp, these tissues suggest the intricacy with which material things and human experiences are intertwined. Scent is a less tangible yet more powerfully affective filament. The poet Erinna, who is fated to die at nineteen, glimpses death in the mirror while parting her hair with a scented comb. This artifact recalls the story of Snow White, who succumbs to a poisoned comb (poison and perfume being fruits of a common art), and indeed it is the sudden, sickly pallor of her cheeks that leaves Erinna staring dizzily into a terrifying, night-like chasm, that is, "in die nachtschaurige Kluft schwindelnd hinab [staunend]." As much as any moment in Mörike's work, this image identifies what the idyll wards off. The scene that Erinna's premonition disturbs is patently bucolic: golden sunlight suffusing her garden draws her from her bed. Sunlight reflecting off the hairnet on her dressing table is also what retrieves her from the brink of despair, and she resolves to make an offering of Sappho's gift to Demeter in the hope of gaining a little more time. It seems a modest exchange, but one commensurate with a sensibility that, in the face of death, or even just waning creativity, finds comfort in the inner life of things.

See also 1786, 1800 (Novalis), 1808, 1815, 1834, 1837, 1848 (October 11), 1910, 1922 (February)

Bibliography: Christopher Middleton, Introduction to Friedrich Hölderlin and Eduard Mörike, *Selected Poems,* trans. Christopher Middleton (Chicago: University of Chicago Press, 1972), xxviii–xxix. Eduard Mörike, *Sämtliche Werke,* vol. I, ed. Jost Perfahl (Munich: Winkler, 1976). Vladimir Nabokov, *Novels and Memoirs 1941–1951* (New York: The Library of America, 1996), 462. Helmut Schneider, "Dingwelt und Arkadien: Mörike's 'Idylle vom Bodensee' und sein Anschluß an die bukolische Gattungstradition," *Zeitschrift für deutsche Philologie* 97 (1978): 24–51. Gerhard Storz, *Eduard Mörike* (Stuttgart: Klett, 1967), 297–299, 349–350. Peter von Matt, *Liebesverrat: Die Treulosen in der Literatur* (Munich: Hanser, 1989), 169–209. Theocritus, *Idylls and Epigrams,* trans. Daryl Hine (New York: Atheneum, 1982), 3–4. Siegfried Wichmann, *Carl Spitzweg* (Herrsching: Schuler Verlagsgesellschaft, 1985), 156, 432.

Kenneth S. Calhoon

𝄞 1876, August 17

The world premiere of Wagner's *Ring* cycle at the opening of the Festspielhaus in Bayreuth comes to an end

Wanting Art

Late in the evening of August 17, 1876, the world premiere of the tetralogy *The Ring of the Nibelung* came to an end at the new Festspielhaus (festival house) in Bayreuth. Each time the curtain had fallen on one of the preceding works in the cycle, *Das Rheingold* (August 13), *Die Walküre* (August 14), and

Siegfried (August 16), Richard Wagner (1813—1883), the composer, had re-fused to appear on stage despite frenzied applause, so overwhelmed was he by his sense of the futility of the entire enterprise. Now, after the final curtain had fallen on *Götterdämmerung,* and after one half hour of delirious applause, the Master finally appeared on stage, surrounded by the cast. "You have seen what we can do," he said to the audience, "now it's up to you to want [nun ist es an Ihnen, zu wollen]. And if you want, then we shall have an art." It was a typically Wagnerian pronouncement, at once sententious and hermetic. The audience, so the report goes, was perplexed, the artists were offended. If art is merely *in potentia,* then where does that leave Bach, Haydn, Mozart, and Beethoven? Let alone that evening's—or the preceding week's—achievement?

"To want" is a key verb in the Wagnerian lexicon. Not just because it appears frequently in his voluminous writings, but also because of its polemical shading, distinguishing a natural need from an artificial desire. In Wagner's mind, a true artist—say, an artist of the future, one who could not tolerate the degradation of art in the contemporary world—would naturally want to do away with a cosmopolitan culture of operatic artifice and display (understood as quintessentially French) and replace it with a natural community committed to music-dramatic absorption (understood as quintessentially German). In Wagner's view, this natural community could hardly exist in the contemporary world. It did, once, in Ancient Greece. But for the artist of the future to address himself to such an audience, the community—of artists, artworks, and the art-loving, art-sustaining public—would have to be reborn. But how? It could not be resurrected artificially. Artifice was a hallmark of the very culture of cosmo-politanism so abhorred by the true artist. The new community would have to generate itself. And it would generate itself in the process of aesthetic contem-plation, out of a double recognition that the spectacle and diversion it *thought* it wanted was not worth wanting and that the true artwork it really wanted was just beyond its grasp, was, well, wanting.

How would the community-to-be arrive at such an insight? It would need to be triply transported—linguistically, aesthetically, and physically. First, it had to be removed from what Wagner, in one of his most inspired and insidi-ous formulations, termed "the hubbub of our official-state-business language-intercourse" ("unseres staatsgeschäftlichen Sprachverkehres"; *Gesammelte Schriften und Dichtungen,* 4:128). And the community-to-be had to be removed from the aesthetic correlative of that official-state-business language-inter-course, the culture of operatic spectacle, which Wagner loathed for its grandil-oquent display of superficial effects without causes. With this double removal comes the prospect of a salutary absorption, both social and aesthetic. The community would materialize out of an apprehension of aesthetic form, the emanation in the real world of a natural, unified aesthetic expression—for ex-ample, the artwork in its totality *(Gesamtkunstwerk)*—that would replace an ar-tificial, senseless hodgepodge of spectacular effects (for example, opera). As al-ways where Wagner is concerned, the stakes are extraordinarily high: not only will a profound, uniquely German, art replace French and Italian confections (propagated, in part, by Jews), but this German art will reassume the legacy of Attic tragedy. In important respects, then, the artwork of the future is conceived as an artwork of the past—and an artwork of elsewhere. The artwork of the future would have to be presented at some remove from cosmopolitan culture, enabling it to take root in a soil more conducive to its cultivation. And as that artwork takes root, so will the non- (indeed, the anti-) cosmopolitan aesthetic community that is its proper audience. That, at least, was the theory.

As is typical of Wagner, the theory is keenly responsive to political realities. Originally, the composer had planned to present his tetralogy at a court opera house in Munich. It was to be built by Gottfried Semper, the famed Berlin architect, according to Wagner's specifications and under the sponsorship of his patron and protector, Bavaria's King Ludwig II. But intense resistance to the project at the Bavarian court and in the press scuttled the plan. In Wagner's mind, of course, that resistance was symptomatic of a much larger problem: the Germans were being manipulated by false guardians of art. That is, German art—its theaters and opera houses, in particular—had been commandeered by a Judaified, Francophilic clique. As a result, the pure, natural German sense of art had been corrupted. Rather than reflecting the will of the people, it reflected the self-interest of that clique. In 1873, three years prior to the premiere of the *Ring*, Wagner writes: "Whoever has had serious dealing with the German theater in the hope of meeting some power of discrimination, some support by an energetic expression of will *[energische Willensmeinung]* on the part of public taste, must have perceived at once that his efforts were totally fruitless and could only stir up strife against himself" (*GSuD*, 9: 313; *Prose Works*, V: 311). In Wagner's mind, the aesthetic revolution had to come from below, from the public rather than the artist. It was up to them to muster that "energetic expression of will." But since the public in the metropolis was in thrall to those false guardians, it was "totally fruitless" to expect such an expression from them. What to do? If he couldn't bring German art to the people, he would bring the people to German art. Thus, Wagner shifted his sights to the provincial town of Bayreuth in northeastern Bavaria. More than in Gertrude Stein's Oakland, in Wagner's Bayreuth, there was indisputably no there there. This was part of the point: there would be Wagner there and not much else. Indeed, when the festival first opened, this became a real problem. As Tchaikovsky reported in a dispatch from Bayreuth, the few restaurants in town were utterly overwhelmed by the throngs attending the festival. "Throughout the duration of the [first] Festival, food forms the chief interest of the public; the artistic representations take a secondary place. Cutlets, baked potatoes, omelets—all are discussed much more eagerly than Wagner's music."

In Wagner's mind, the idea of a new stage festival was tied to the idea of a new stage. Shortly after settling on Bayreuth as the locale for the new festival, Wagner decided to build a Festspielhaus, a new kind of German theater for a new kind of German artwork and a new kind of German public. By shifting from Munich to Bayreuth, Wagner claimed, he was escaping one totality—a nefarious one, utterly opposed to his, and King Ludwig's, plans, and by extension, to German art—in order to cultivate another, a sacred totality that wholly supported his plans and German art. This totality would not be the mere recipient of his Artwork of the Future; it would educe its production: "If a totality *[eine Gesamtheit]* once sets itself against the high-minded intentions of a sole mighty ruler [that is, King Ludwig], I found that I could turn to another totality *[eine andere Gesamtheit]* with a work [that is, *The Ring*] which blossomed under the shelter of this mighty one—a totality to whom, *by its own will,* I could entrust the realization of the work's performance" (*GSuD:* 9: 314; *PW,* V: 312; trans. modified, emphasis added). In other words, the other totality would *want* the total work of art; and by being wanted, the new German art would be born.

It is hard to overstate the difference between the Festspielhaus and the standard opera house of the day. In German opera houses, as in Paris and Milan—Wagner liked to point to the French and the Italians—the lights in the auditorium were never dimmed, thus facilitating the manifold distractions and diversions among and between the patrons during the course of a performance. In Wagner's Festspielhaus, the auditorium was completely dark. In German opera houses, as in Paris and Milan, the perimeter of the auditorium was ringed with boxes, separating the spectators by class and multiplying the spectacles, since the aristocrats in the boxes competed with the lavish display on stage. In Wagner's Festspielhaus, the perimeter of the auditorium was ringed with walls and doors. The auditorium was designed to create a unified community utterly absorbed by the events on stage. The seats were wooden, not plush; the rows were raked to afford each spectator unimpeded sight of the stage and uninterrupted by aisles that might afford easy entrance and exit but would divide the community. The orchestra was housed below the stage, eliminating the pit and rendering the conductor and the musicians invisible. The focus was to be on the total work of art: an utterly absorbing artwork presented to a community constituted in its utter absorption.

Not just any artwork would do. Wagner's messianic sense of departure and disdain was registered in the generic labeling of the project. Instead of an opera, Wagner was preparing "A Stage Festival Play to be Performed over Three Days and a Preliminary Evening" ("Ein Bühnenfestspiel aufzuführen in drei Tagen und einem Vorabend"). The differences between Wagner's work and standard opera were obvious and overwhelming. They encompassed unprecedented aesthetic aspirations and compositional procedures—for example, its insistence on through-composition in lieu of the conventional alternation of spoken and sung materials—as well as unprecedented practical demands on the singers, musicians, and audience—the initial performances of the *Ring* cycle totaled fourteen hours. But perhaps most significantly, Wagner's festival presented the Nibelungen saga in operatic form.

Since its rediscovery in the mid-18th century, the medieval epic *Nibelungenlied* had become ideologically charged and had repeatedly been invoked as Germany's *Iliad*. In the process, it served to suture a variety of deeply felt national wounds. As hopes for a unified Germany were dashed after the Napoleonic wars, several early romantic writers, including August Wilhelm Schlegel, turned to the *Nibelungenlied* as a work that consolidated Germany's "inner" identity. From that point onward, the epic was revisited and reworked in a host of forms—in painting, poetry, ballet, sculpture, literature, and drama. One of the most famous treatments was Friedrich Hebbel's tripartite dramatic adaptation of the medieval epic. Another celebrated adaptation is Fritz Lang's and Thea von Harbou's massive two-part film *Die Nibelungen,* released with great fanfare in Berlin in the mid-1920s. Like so many of the Nibelungen adaptations prepared in the 19th century and the first half of the 20th, both the drama and the film were inflected as programmatically nationalistic. The Lang–von Harbou film was dedicated to the German *Volk,* and Hebbel, in a famous letter, disavowed any credit for his adaptation, deflecting it instead onto the "great song of the German nation."

Given the longstanding association of this material with German nationalism, and given Wagner's longstanding preference for Germanic subjects and his concomitant, duly chauvinistic concerns regarding the preponderance of foreign works on Germany's opera stages, it is not surprising to find him working on an adaptation of the Nibelungen material. But Wagner's aspirations, like his aesthetics, were not conventionally nationalistic. In the end, *The Ring* encompasses several other works, including the Old Norse *Thidreks Saga,* the Icelandic *Poetic Edda, Völsungen Saga,* and the *Prose Edda.*

The Ring, like so many of Wagner's works, renders many of the composer's social and aesthetic preoccupations in relatively transparent, allegorical form. As George Bernard Shaw, among others, has noted, the tetralogy juxtaposes malevolence, artifice, and greed against purity, nature, and selflessness. For instance, in the first scene of Act I of *Siegfried,* the eponymous hero recognizes that his self-interested guardian and pseudo-father Mime is hoarding the fragments of Siegmund's—that is, Siegfried's true father's—shattered sword. With growing astonishment and characteristic impetuousness, Siegfried demands that Mime forge the fragments of Siegmund's sword right then and there: "Today, I swear it, I want that sword; I shall have it today!" It is a striking moment, not just for its encapsulation of Siegfried's intemperate, naïve abandon, but also as a pithy dramatization of Wagner's concept of want: the natural hero, long misled by the malevolent Mime, arrives naturally at the recognition of what he truly wants—in this case, the reconstitution of his proper, natural heritage that will enable him to abandon his false guardian and his unnatural home.

In important ways, Wagner imagined himself as a Siegfried amidst an operatic culture of Mimes, but the composer's exit from that culture was hardly as stormy or sudden as Siegfried's. The first performance at Bayreuth was more than a quarter century in the making, dating back to 1848, when Wagner prepared the first prose sketch of the work. Before the composition of *Götterdämmerung* was concluded in 1874, Wagner spent more than three years searching for a cast of suitable singer-actors. Needless to say, in Wagner's eyes, such singers were as much wanting as they were wanted for a true German art. In similar fashion, he put together a festival orchestra from among exceptional instrumentalists at German opera orchestras. Rehearsals for the first festival took two full summers. The first round of rehearsals at Wahnfried, Wagner's Bayreuth residence, commenced on July 1, 1875; the second began the following May.

It is hard to say which was the more onerous undertaking, preparing the *Ring* or building the Festspielhaus. Both projects took place at the same time and, of course, Wagner supervised both. The complications were staggering. When the second summer of rehearsals began in May, there were still no seats in the auditorium. The bills were mounting so that by the conclusion of the First Festival, the deficit stood at 148,000 marks. The steam machines proved unusually obstreperous, the singers were often surly, and, in Wagner's eyes, their acting was almost always sub-par. The instrumentalists were uneven and the conductor Hans Richter's tempi were unpredictable. The list went on and on. Most important, Wagner kept changing his mind about what he wanted the singers to do. The frustration and confusion of composer and singer-actors were understandable: Wagner was launching a revolution in operatic staging. Rather than positioning the principals front and center so that they could sing directly to the audience, Wagner demanded that they interact with one another, responding to the orchestra for psychological as well as musical cues. In place of grand gestures and stock tableaus, Wagner wanted organic, natural expression—and he wanted his singer-actors to want that too. During those summers of 1875 and 1876, it was hard for the singers and the composer to know precisely what this entailed.

As rehearsals during that second summer progressed, it became clear that the festival would be a major cultural event, attracting an array of dignitaries—including Kaiser Wilhelm, Grand Duke Vladimir of Russia, the emperor of Brazil, and various German kings, grand dukes, princes, and princesses—a battery of critics from around the world, as well as a host of Europe's most prestigious composers—including Tchaikovsky, Edvard Grieg, Anton Bruckner, Franz Liszt, and Camille Saint-Saëns.

However, for Wagner the festival succeeded for all the wrong reasons: the dramatic enactment was unsatisfying and the crowd hardly seemed to notice. Indeed, as Tchaikovsky had noted, the crowd seemed more absorbed by the scene outside the festival than that on the stage of the Festspielhaus. There was no palpable sense of a community that had formed in anticipation of the festival. German art, it would appear, was still wanting. And the dispirited Wagner wanted his audience to know, if only so they might learn to want something else entirely—something like Bayreuth as it should be; something, that is, that Wagner wanted and, more important, that he wanted them to want as well.

See also 930, ca. 1200, 1210, 1791, 1853, 1882, 1911, 1928

Bibliography: Bernard Shaw, *The Perfect Wagnerite: A Commentary on the Ring of the Niblungs* (rpt. New York: Dover, 1967). Stewart Spencer et al., eds., *Wagner's Ring of the Nibelung: A Companion* (New York: Thames and Hudson, 1993). Frederic Spotts, *Bayreuth: A History of the Wagner Festival* (New Haven, Conn.: Yale University Press, 1994). Wolfgang Storch, ed., *Die Nibelungen: Bilder von Liebe, Verrat, und Untergang* (Munich: Prestel, 1987). Richard Wagner, "A Communication to My Friends," in *Richard Wagner's Prose Works,* trans. W. Ashton Ellis (London: K. Paul, Trench, Trübner, 1895; rpt. Lincoln: University of Nebraska Press, 1993) 1: 267–392.

————, "Final Report on the Fates and Circumstances That Attended the Execution of the Stage-Festival Play *Der Ring des Nibelungen* Down to the Founding of Wagner Societies," in *Richard Wagner's Prose Works* V: 307–319.

David J. Levin

✑ 1882, August 26

Friedrich Nietzsche announces his achievement of newfound health

Nietzsche and Modernity

The language in Nietzsche's work is frequently apocalyptic, sometimes strident, bordering on hysteria, and always figurative, elliptical and elusive. Its status as literature, culture criticism, armchair anthropology, or philosophy, therefore, is always at issue. But a new sort of assessment and prophecy emerges with the 1882 publication of *Die fröhliche Wissenschaft* (*The Gay Science* [FW]), the book that contains the images and formulations so famously identified with Nietzsche's name, many for the first time, like nihilism (§346) or "Übermensch" (overman), first mentioned in §143. In §125, we hear the "mad man" *(der tolle Mensch)* announcing that God is dead, and that we have killed him. And we learn for the first time of the strange image that seems a figurative embodiment of Nietzsche's best hope for some sort of reorientation, some recovery or convalescence from the illness caused by such a death and such a failure of desire, a reorientation and attitude supposedly provoked by the thought experiment about "the eternal return of the same" (§341).

The publication of the book also marks a personal transformation. Or so says Nietzsche (1844–1900). The back cover of the 1882 edition (there will be another in 1887 with a new Preface and a Part V) proclaims, "This book marks the conclusion of a series of writings by Friedrich Nietzsche, whose common goal is to erect a new image and ideal of the free spirit." The books grouped in this period do not include *Die Geburt der Tragödie aus dem Geist der Musik* (1872; *The Birth of Tragedy Out of the Spirit of Music* [GT]), and the four essays collectively published as *Unzeitgemäße Betrachtungen* (1876; *Untimely Meditations* [UB]). They coincide roughly with the onset of illnesses serious enough to keep Nietzsche from teaching (1876), his disillusionment with Wagner, an intellectual break with Schopenhauer, his final resignation from the university (1879), and the beginning of his nomadic, ever more solitary life. The books he cites as belonging to that period are *Menschliches, Allzumenschliches (Human, All Too Human), Der Wanderer und sein Schatten* (*The Wanderer and His Shadow;* later published as part of the former), *Morgenröte: Gedanken über die moralischen Vorurtheile* (*Dawn: Thoughts about the Prejudices of Morality),* and *The Gay Science.* The claim he makes about this new period is quite striking, and directly confronts a question persistently raised by the Nietzsche reception—the nature of and basis for affirmation. Nietzsche implies that his earlier deflationary attacks on the autonomy of normative life, his "psychologizing" exposure of human, often "immoral," origins had left him psychically ill, caught in a spiritual "winter." With *The Gay Science,* he "triumphs" over winter, returns to health and especially to "hope." His "nausea" is now over. He has overcome any tragic pessimism, or even nihilism, and can proclaim the birth of a creature at least as strange as a "musical Socrates": a "gay science."

Nietzsche does not abandon his psychological critique of Christian moralism, the "French" attention to the low origins of the high, and the hope for "free spirits," all so prominent in these works. But his themes become more comprehensive. After *The Gay Science,* he begins to write the three books most responsible for his reputation, books that mark the beginning of a kind of avant-garde, modernist philosophy, often more influential outside the academy than within: *Also sprach Zarathustra* (*Thus Spoke Zarathustra* [ASZ]), *Jenseits von Gut und Böse* (*Beyond Good and Evil* [JGB]), and *Zur Genealogie der Moral* (*The Genealogy of Morals* [ZGM]). The problem of the "free spirit" apparently now requires answers to much larger questions and cannot by itself be the chief or primary question, and the solution to the problem of the possibility of such a free spirit is announced as a "gay science."

A gay or joyous science is not supposed to make us feel better, happier, and it cannot possibly be a matter just of a more cheerful focus, as if a Nietzschean "look on the bright side of things" is being proposed. A different sort of claim to knowledge is announced, still psychological and genealogical, and still about hidden origins and historical fate, but somehow not from what the *Genealogy* will call the perspective of "old, cold, and tedious frogs, creeping around men and into men as if in their own proper element, that is, in a swamp." The problem Nietzsche poses, and so the task for these new genealogists, in order to remain "brave, proud, and magnanimous animals" even in the face of what they discover about motivation and meaning, is this: "To *know* how to keep their hearts as well as their suffering *in bounds* [ihr Herz wie ihren Schmerz im Zaum zu halten wissen]" (ZGM, 258). How does one do that? What sort of knowledge is this?

The answer seems to some extent connected to the historical resonance of the title, *la gaya scienza* of 12th-century Provençal lyric poetry. What then does such a free spirit *know?* Perhaps, as Nietzsche explains, that which one would have to know to write such lyrics, or "love as passion—which is our European specialty," an "invention" that "must be credited to the Provençal knight-poets, those magnificent and inventive human beings of the 'gai saber' to whom Europe owes so many things and almost owes itself" (JGB, §260). The gay science then is carnal knowledge; not so much knowledge of what love is, as how to love and live well, not technically or strategically, but in a way that "does justice" to the requirements of love and life. And the problem of its possibility leads Nietzsche to his largest question: the objective side of the problem of desire; in other words, what might be "lovable" as a prospect or a possible way of life in the modern world, or how there might be "ideals" worth striving for, worth the sacrifice and pain.

The "master question" that emerges with *The Gay Science* and the mature work of the eighties (1883–1888) may have little to do with the problem of being, the epistemology of perspectivism, or the metaphysics of the will to power. *Zarathustra* begins with Zarathustra's mysterious reasons for "going down" among men—"I love man" and "I bring men a gift" (ASZ, 13). *Good and Evil* opens with the startling supposition that truth is a woman and philosophers are clumsy lovers (JGB, 11). And *Genealogy* begins with a strangely affirmative quotation from Matthew's gospel about the "treasure" being where the "heart" is (ZGM, 247). Merely replacing reliance on moral objectivity or the supposedly self-imposed law of freedom in Kant and the post-Kantians with some strong "creative" will to power would look out of place in the context suggested by the various openings in Nietzsche's masterworks. That is, one cannot will to desire, any more than one can talk someone into desiring.

But whatever the troubadours knew, and so whatever Nietzsche seeks to rediscover, it now comes with a considerable amount of intellectual and moral tension, the burden of our "intellectual conscience" or intensely critical self-consciousness, which Nietzsche frequently acknowledges. Such a possibility suggests a combination of what he calls "light-heartedness" (cheerfulness, *Heiterkeit,* §343) and a certain "heaviness" or *gravitas* (§341). Such paradoxical formulations are found throughout Nietzsche's writings. What is needed is a tragic pessimism as an aesthetic justification of existence, a pessimism of strength, or a "musical Socrates," or the ability to "dream" without first having to "sleep" (FW, §59).

The Gay Science sends us looking not so much for the will to power or a Heracleitean metaphysics in the later Nietzsche, but for the link between possible value now and desire, for the conditions necessary to fulfill the needs of late modernity, a still "self-overcoming" desire. But it also leads to what Nietzsche knew would complicate mere reliance on the satisfaction of desire alone. For desire is polymorphous and essentially historical; there is no natural hierarchy of the desirable. If the death of God means the death of confidence in matching desire with the intrinsically desirable, and if, in anxiety, we want what everyone else wants ("herd society"), resistance to such leveling must be made with an intellectual conscience, as Nietzsche stresses emphatically at the beginning of *The Gay Science* (§2). We cannot pretend to reanimate a polytheistic tragic culture; we cannot pretend that strength of purpose alone, merely willing that humans be more than human, as well as all too human, suffices. And we cannot naively invoke any longer a Socratic or Enlightenment view of the absolute value of truth. Yet "not in itself *absolutely* valuable" does not mean "*not* valuable." In other words, we also cannot concede that various desires and satisfactions are simply equivalent or radically incommensurable, that there can be no order of rank because there cannot be an absolute or objective one. As Nietzsche recognized in Plato, especially *The Republic,* a deep tension remains between eros and its satisfactions—often private, incommensurable with those of others, always just one's own, partial—and justice, the older word for intellectual conscience, wanting what is fit or meet to want, what impartially would be desirable. How to measure and assess this counterclaim of intellectual conscience, in the right way, is what Nietzsche meant by "knowing how to keep one's heart as well as one's suffering in bounds." Without that tension, there is no dissatisfaction or self-overcoming; only the easily satisfied "last men" who have invented happiness and who blink.

While all of Nietzsche's paradoxical formulations derive from this basic tension, many also promise some sort of resolution: an actual "artist's metaphysics," a "musical Socrates," a "cheerful pessimism," a tragedy that is also a parody—in a phrase, a "gay science." But the more detailed and explicit discussions in the texts still only point to and promise a resolution rather than offer it. In *The Birth of Tragedy,* the nature of Aeschylus's Prometheus is at the same time "Apollonian and Dionysian," and can be expressed in a conceptual formula that recalls the theme just introduced: "All that exists is just and unjust and equally justified in both" (GT §9). The promise, in *Untimely Meditations,* that history can be employed for life is stated explicitly and carefully in the language of justice, as it must be, lest this appeal to life turn out to be a call for the ideological use of history, even for wishful thinking. "No one has a greater claim to our veneration," Nietzsche insists, "than he who possesses the drive to and strength for justice" (UB, II, 286). But, again, this cannot mean that the "historical sense" should reign "without restraint" *(ungebändigt)*. While just in itself, this would be unjust to life and its demands, and too violent for the "mood of pious illusion" necessary for life, especially since "it is only in love, only when shaded by the illusions produced by love, that is to say, in the unconditional faith in right and perfection, that man is creative" (UB, II, 295–297).

The goal of doing justice to "love's illusions"—and so an injustice—as well as to our intellectual conscience, or to justice, is suggested in *The Gay Science* elliptically and elusively. What is needed now is a way to "incorporate or embody knowledge" *(das Wissen sich einzuverleiben)* and to make it instinctive (FW §11). Or, we have gambled on finding the answer to a difficult question: "To what extent can truth endure incorporation *[Einverleibung]?*—that is the question, that is the experiment" (FW §110).

This is not an entirely new question. It evinces deep connections with the problem of moral motivation and harmony, important in German philosophy since the first reactions to Kant (as in Schiller's aesthetic education and Hegel's critique of "positivity"). Nietzsche returns self-consciously to the Socratic understanding of philosophy as fundamentally erotic, where philosophic wisdom satisfies a lack without which the satisfaction of any other desire is incomplete and unsatisfying. But he is not sanguine about our modern resources for facing the issue, and more often than not a gay, or life-affirming, stance, given all we have gone through, looks ever more dubious. Being incapable of such incorporation is a frequent characterization of what we cannot do with what we take to be true. We know Nietzsche's claim that this incapacity has to do with a failure of desire, and so with his claim about the conditions for and nature of human desire itself. This all is said to mean that we moderns do not have a culture (or a "gay science"). Our culture is not a living thing; we are walking encyclopedias; the whole of modern culture looks like a book titled "handbook of subjective culture for outward barbarians" (UB, II, 74).

One last echo from the original meaning of *la gaya scienza* might indicate a remedy. We cannot really believe that some naturalist rendering of poetic seduction is possible. It is possible to say that there is some sort of biological drive behind our efforts to reproduce, for example, and even behind the creation of social rules for that process, but it is not possible to imagine such a language of need and drive employed in an address to another, as a practical proposal to another. And yet all of this does not mean that we require some sort of idealized distortion of such a nature in order to be able to bear each other's claims on one another. Here the language of appearance and reality breaks down in a way that Nietzsche clearly signals as a model for what he means by, hopes for, a *gaya scienza,* where that breakdown is taken to heart.

This way of putting it makes clear that Nietzsche also imagined that the experiment of so addressing each other might fail and fail catastrophically. An attachment to life and to each other might just require the kind of illusion that we have now also rendered impossible. If so, then the most sweeping expression for what is now needed will turn out to be as impossible as it sounds: the appearance and language of philosophers, now that there really no longer is such a thing as philosophy.

See also 1150, 1853, 1876, 1905, 1912 (June), 1929 (Autumn)

Bibliography: Friedrich Nietzsche, *Sämtliche Werke: Kritische Studienausgabe,* ed. Giorgio Colli and Mazzino Montinari (Berlin: de Gruyter, 1988). ———, *Beyond Good and Evil,* trans. Walter Kaufmann (New York: Harper and Row, 1966). ———, *The Birth of Tragedy,* trans. F. Goffing (New York: Doubleday, 1956). ———, *On the Genealogy of Morals,* trans. Walter Kaufmann and R. J. Hollingdale (New York: Vintage, 1969). ———, *The Gay Science,* trans. Walter Kaufmann (New York: Vintage, 1974). ———, *Thus Spoke Zarathustra,* trans. Walter Kaufmann (New York: Viking, 1966). Jürgen Habermas, *Philosophischer Diskurs der Moderne* (Frankfurt am Main: Suhrkamp, 1985). Martin Heidegger, *Nietzsche,* 2 vols. (Pfullingen: Neske, 1961).

Robert B. Pippin

℞ *1888, June*

Wilhelm II becomes emperor of Germany and revives its colonial aspirations; six months later, Wilhelm Raabe begins his anti-imperialist novel *Stopfkuchen*

Germany's Heart of Darkness

"Once more on board!" To a late 19th-century reader, these opening words of Wilhelm Raabe's *Stopfkuchen: Eine See- und Mordgeschichte* (1890; *Plumcake: A Tale of Murder and the Sea,* trans. as *Tubby Schaumann*) would have been more than just an indication that the narrator is writing his story during a sea voyage. In 1888, when Raabe (1831–1910) began writing the novel, these words would have borne the breath of a new era, marked by the twenty-nine-year-old emperor's enthusiasm for everything maritime. A grandson of Queen Victoria, Kaiser Wilhelm II was determined to build a German fleet that would challenge the British Empire's hegemony on the seas. By the time *Stopfkuchen* was completed, in late 1890, the words "once more on board!" would have acquired yet another connotation. For now, as a popular cartoon expressed it, the "pilot" Bismarck, who had been largely opposed to German imperial expansion, had been "dropped from the German ship" and Wilhelm II had announced a "new course" for the imperial vessel. Among other plans for change, Wilhelm II decided to become more aggressive in acquiring and developing German overseas colonies in order to obtain raw materials for German industry as well as territories for the increasing numbers of German workers who wished to emigrate. Under Wilhelm II, the colonies, hitherto run by independent mercantile companies, came under the protection of the imperial government and their function was reconceived as part of Germany's bid for world power.

To enlist his readers' sympathies for a book that was an unsparing attack on German imperialism, Raabe tells the story from the perspective of a German citizen. This figure, known only as Eduard, had settled in British South Africa, married a Dutch woman, and is raising a family there when he returns to Germany on a brief visit. Eduard employs the thirty days of his return voyage from Germany to the Cape of Good Hope to set down an account of his stay in the fatherland, including a lengthy inset story told by his stay-at-home friend Heinrich Schaumann. Immersed in writing, Eduard scarcely notices the course the voyage is taking, though for the reader the alternation of calm and stormy weather creates an often-amusing critical counterpoint to his narration.

Indeed, while the novel's subtitle leads the reader to expect a tale of murder on the high seas, the main action of *Stopfkuchen* takes place at home rather than abroad. In a humorous inversion, what German promulgators of colonialism called their country's need for a "place in the sun" is rewritten in Eduard's narration to apply to the homeland itself, which to his mind is "a sun-illumined dot among the most lovely green." We hear next to nothing about Eduard's life in "hottest Africa" except for the lion skin on his living room floor and a satiric portrait by Spitzweg of German bourgeois life on the wall. Thus, although both Eduard's visit to Germany and his friend Heinrich Schaumann's long inset narrative seem to have little to do with colonialism, a constant undercurrent of ideological conflict with German colonial aspirations runs through the entire book.

The major portion of the novel is composed of the long, rambling narrative told by his old friend. Heinrich's story revolves around a murder of which his father-in-law had been suspected. It becomes quickly clear that Heinrich has long since discovered the real perpetrator's identity, but has withheld this information for some time, even from his wife, who longs for her father's exoneration. On the surface a ruminative man given to smoking his pipe in an idyllic outdoor setting, Heinrich is, in fact, intent on attacking the comfortable provincial existence he himself seems to embody as well as the worldly superi-

The German Empire, 1871

ority his friend Eduard represents in his eyes. Heinrich's ever-expanding harangue rivals his rotund figure. His nickname, Stopfkuchen (literally, stuffed cake), is derived from a delicious morsel made from leftover bits of pastry filled with leftover butter, sugar, and raisins. His garrulous, digressive narrative sends his listeners constantly off in search of plums in the pudding.

Despite his apparently contemplative nature, an aggressive streak in his character is suggested symbolically by the fact that his farmhouse had originally been constructed as a fortress by Saxons during the Seven Years' War. Throughout his childhood, he dreams of "taking the Red Fortress by storm"; and he finally does so by marrying the owner's daughter, Valentine Quakatz. By the time of Eduard's visit, Valentine (also called Tine or Tinchen) has become a sedate, somewhat portly matron; in her youth, however, she was a scrawny creature who behaved like a wildcat, furiously defending her father against rumors that he murdered a cattle dealer named Kienbaum.

Despite the apparent contrast between Heinrich the stay-at-home and Eduard the adventurer, the two have much in common. Heinrich's acquisition of the red fortress finds its equivalent in Eduard's establishment of what is ironically called a "knightly estate" in South Africa. Both men have become farmers. Heinrich leases part of his land to the sugar-beet industry, thus creating competition for the sugar-cane production of the colonies. He greets Eduard by offering him a cup of coffee (a colonial product) with plenty of sugar. At the beginning of the novel, Eduard insists that he is "still among the educated" even if he has not quite mastered the latest Prussian spelling reform. As a former ship's doctor, he has a special interest in geography and travel writing and still recalls much of what he learned in school. Heinrich is equally knowledgeable, punctuating his narrative with literary allusions and references to history, geography, and paleontology.

Raabe's decision to use Eduard as the lens through which Heinrich, Valentine, and the other characters are seen has important consequences. Eduard diverges markedly from the rational or sensible narrators of German Realism, such as the schoolteacher in Theodor Storm's *Der Schimmelreiter* (1888; *The Rider on a White Horse*). It is not by coincidence that Eduard records his story on board a ship, standing, as he puts it, "no longer on the firm ground of the fatherland, but on my sea legs once more, on the moving planks of the great waves of the ocean." The irony here, as so often in *Stopfkuchen,* cuts both ways, against Eduard's narrative competence and against the seemingly solid fundaments of the fatherland. Next to Joseph Conrad, Raabe was one of the first writers to grasp the effect of colonialist ideology on narrative technique and strategies of representation.

In several of his novels prior to *Stopfkuchen,* Raabe experimented with variants on the peripheral narrator. Here, in the short novel he regarded as his masterpiece, he creates a brilliant juxtaposition of three narrators. Eduard's narrative frames Heinrich's story about the murder of Kienbaum, and at the center of the novel, Tinchen tells the story of Heinrich's courtship and the early years of their marriage in her own words. The three narratives do not form neat

Chinese boxes, however. They constantly intrude on each other, interrupting the flow. The major part of the novel is taken up by two conversations. The first takes place at Heinrich's house, the "Red Fortress"; the second, at the village inn, the "Golden Arm." Raabe introduces this dialogic tool not only to hold the reader's attention during Heinrich's extravagantly digressive narration, but also to keep the various points of view in constant interaction with one other. By juggling the narratives, the author prevents the three main characters' perspectives from becoming discrete blocks. But he also keeps the reader invested in the story and he infuses it with subtle irony in which nothing is ever merely black or white. As the characters respond to each other, interrupt each other, even ventriloquize each other, reductive polarities and stereotypical opinions are put into question.

The heart of darkness in Raabe's curiously decentered colonial narrative is the death of Friedrich Kienbaum. Heinrich reveals the solution to the mystery for the first time at the village pub, ostensibly to Eduard alone, but in fact also to the barmaid, who he knows will spread the news rapidly. Tinchen, who is not present at the pub, has to wait for Heinrich to return home before she hears that her father was not a murderer after all. To Eduard's great dismay, his childhood idol, the postman Störzer, turns out to be the guilty party. While Störzer's guilt is mitigated somewhat by the fact that the killing was an accident, it is nonetheless exacerbated by the fact that Störzer never came forward to take the blame. Significantly, the murderer is a figure with a professional interest in the connections between Germany and foreign countries. Although Störzer has not actually traveled to other countries, he is indirectly connected with German expansionism by the very fact that he carries communications between Germany and overseas.

The scene in which Heinrich recounts how he extracted Störzer's confession is at once hard-hitting and humane. Heinrich refrains from revealing the truth until old Störzer has died; but by delaying, he does an injustice to Tinchen and her innocent father, both of whom are bearing the burden of a guilt that has not been proven. Similarly, Heinrich's revelation of the true perpetrator on the eve of Störzer's funeral isolates the postman's family from the townspeople, who refuse to join in the obsequies. The reason for Heinrich's otherwise inexplicable decision to reveal the identity of the murderer at this point seems to come from a desire to teach Eduard a lesson. Eduard is indeed profoundly shocked by the story, but it is not clear to what extent he understands its deeper meaning, in particular, its application to his own situation. Heinrich's frequent hints about the guilt of those who colonize other parts of the world seem to fall on deaf ears. Eduard's boyhood readings of travel writings by François Levaillant had led him to place African natives on the same level as exotic animals—he speaks of "Le Vaillant's Africa and his Hottentots, giraffes, lions, and elephants"—and even as an adult, he describes black Africans as "an exotic, heathen pack of niggers." Heinrich's ironic jabs fail to jolt Eduard out of his prejudiced thinking.

Eduard generally tends to avoid difficult issues. Characteristically, when his ship passes the mountains of Angra Pequena, he refuses to go on deck to look at this landmark, since he has seen it before. The German reader of 1890 would be well aware, however, that these mountains were the first German colonial acquisition (in 1884). The novel insists repeatedly on Eduard's casual acceptance of German colonialism, as represented symbolically in this scene. Raabe also works hard to break down the dualism of home and abroad. The mutual interdependence between the two spheres is made evident by the constant superimposition of different locations and time frames and the confusing use of pronouns that transcend geography and temporality by seeming to refer to one thing or person when they actually refer to another. Finally, the apparent opposition of isolationism and expansionist interests, represented metaphorically by the eloquent names of the "Red Fortress" and the "Golden Arm," is undermined by the way in which the thread of Heinrich's yarn remains virtually unbroken by the shift from one location to the other.

Raabe's development of what, in hindsight, can be seen as a proto-modernist narrative technique, derived in part from his engagement with the issue of German imperialism. The breakdown of traditional narration is directly linked to the characters' attempt to grasp the old world and the new at once, holding fast to traditional knowledge while assimilating information that contradicts it. One metaphor for this dislocation is Heinrich's position as a distinguished member of modern scientific societies on the basis of his having reassembled the fossilized mammoth bones he found on his property. Another metaphor is the postman Störzer, whose passion is geography and whose colleagues calculate that he has walked five times around the globe without ever having left home. The complex nature of an expanding world where interconnections can only be understood through a prodigious leap of the imagination is precisely what makes traditional storytelling impossible. The involvement of familiar people and places with overseas events that seem remote and almost unintelligible is a recurrent theme in the novel.

Despite his subtle delineation of the problems of self and other in the imperial age, Raabe's personal politics were not progressive. He saw himself as a liberal; he admired Bismarck, and had a low opinion of the parliamentary system. He harbored a certain nostalgia for what he regarded as a better, more humane past, and he was not always able to rise above 19th-century stereotypes of women and Jews (the latter an issue that has led to heated controversy in recent criticism). Still, his intuitive understanding of human psychology allowed him to approach German imperialist expansion with a more nuanced sensibility than many of his contemporaries. Even his earlier novel, *Abu Telfan oder Die Heimkehr vom Mondgebirge* (1868; *Abu Telfan or The Return from the Moon Mountains*), another tale of a man who returns to Germany from Africa, does not endorse the idealized myths of settler existence promulgated to promote Germany's acquisition of overseas territories in the mid-1880s. *Stopfkuchen* subverts colonial mythmaking more aggressively, notably through its ironic relation to the colonial propaganda disseminated in the last decades of the 19th century in picture books and adventure tales for schoolboys. Perhaps most significantly, the novel, for all its references to natural history, does not subscribe to the kind of Social Darwinism that was used by some proponents of German colonialism, such as the explorer Carl Peters, to justify the subjugation of native peoples by Europeans. Finally, unwilling to lay blame one-sidedly—even Heinrich is called a "torturer"—Raabe suggests that idealistic German citizens were themselves inevitably tarnished by the brush of imperialist expansion. What is often regarded as an acquiescent position characteristic of German realism is, in Raabe as in his contemporary Fontane, essentially a recognition that there can be no simplistic solutions to the private individual's attempt to escape the powerful tug of larger national enterprises.

See also 1478, 1557, 1804, 1867, 1895

Bibliography: Wilhelm Raabe, *Sämtliche Werke,* ed. Karl Hoppe, vol. 18 (2nd rev. ed., Göttingen: Vandenhoek & Ruprecht, 1969). ———, *Novels,* ed. Volkmar Sander, foreword by Joel Agee (New York: Continuum, 1983). Jeffrey L. Sammons, *Wilhelm Raabe: The Fiction of the Alternative Community* (Princeton, N.J.: Princeton University Press, 1987). Philip J. Brewster, "Onkel Ketschwayo in Neuteutoburg: Zeitgeschichtliche Anspielungen in Raabes *Stopfkuchen,*" *Jahrbuch der Raabe-Gesellschaft* (Braunschweig: Waisenhaus-Buchdruckerei und Verlag, 1983), 96–118. Hubert Ohl, "Eduards Heimkehr oder Le Vaillant und das Riesenfaultier: Zu Raabes *Stopfkuchen,*" in Hermann Helmers, ed., *Raabe in neuer Sicht* (Stuttgart: Metzler, 1968), 247–278.

Judith Ryan

♫ 1895

In the autumn of his years, Theodor Fontane publishes *Effi Briest* to lasting acclaim

Apparitions of Time

In 1898, the year of Theodor Fontane's death (b. 1819), an essay by Friedrich Engels, himself dead three years, surfaced in which he condemned English empiricism and explained the Anglo-American fascination for the paranormal as a reaction to the stifling influence of speculative thought. Henry James's *The Turn of the Screw* appeared that same year. Meanwhile, Freud's inquiries into the origins of hysteria were widening into a more complex theory on the power of the dead to influence the living (as exemplified by the ghost of Hamlet's father). *Effi Briest,* which Fontane, alluding to the 19th-century vogue of spirit rapping, claimed to have written "almost psychographically," adds to a repertoire already teeming with phantasms. The young Effi, neglected by the ambitious bureaucrat she has recently married, grows uneasy in his house, said to be haunted by the spirit of a Chinese servant whom the previous owner, a seafarer, had brought home to the provincial Baltic town of Kessin. At a time when European artists and designers sought inspiration in Chinese and, particularly, Japanese forms of representation, the Chinese ghost introduces an incipient modernist intuition into a novel whose full characterizations make it a crowning, though belated, achievement of German realism. As early as 1853, Fontane attributed the flowering of literary realism to a more general weariness with speculative trends—a weariness aptly expressed in *Effi Briest* by the refrain with which Effi's father habitually forecloses discussions that verge on the metaphysical: "Das ist ein weites Feld" ("That is a vast field").

A fitting motto for a man whose fortunes rise and fall with the price of grain, von Briest's words form the novel's closing sentence, circumscribing the unremittingly palpable grave marker—Effi's—that has supplanted a sundial in her parents' garden. It was within view of this spot that Effi, at seventeen, became engaged to Geert von Innstetten, a thirty-eight-year-old protégé of Bismark who twenty years earlier had courted Effi's mother. Effi leaves the family home at Hohen-Cremmen, bucolic but within shopping distance of Berlin, for remote Kessin, whose heavy, sea-swept skies accentuate an oppressive social milieu. The birth of a daughter, Annie, interrupts a routine otherwise enlivened only by soirées hosted by the endearingly stilted aesthete Gieshübler. Lonely, bored, and feeling manipulated by her husband's patronizing stratagems—he appears to nourish her fear of the ghost in order to keep her in check—Effi is seduced by an acquaintance of Innstetten's, a Major Crampas, said to be a Don Juan. The affair greatly agitates Effi, who is relieved when Innstetten is transferred to Berlin, where life settles into a more contented course. Then, six years later, Innstetten discovers a hidden cache of letters from Crampas, which Effi has inexplicably saved. Driven by the same inflexibility that drove Effi wayward in the first place, Innstetten kills Crampas in a duel, summarily banishing Effi and removing Annie entirely from her care. Effi's parents support her financially but, mindful of their own reputations, insist that she remain in Berlin, where she perseveres for three years in modest circumstances. Embittered by a failed attempt to reestablish ties with Annie, Effi shows signs of consumption, prompting her physician, the kindly Rummschüttel, to urge her parents to reclaim her. At their invitation, she returns to Hohen-Cremmen, living out her last year in a kind of melancholy peace, comforted by her surroundings, even learning to paint. Effi, once admonished by her mother for being a "daughter of the air," finally succumbs to an affliction of the lungs.

Effi's grave, centered in a setting painstakingly described in the novel's opening paragraph, is inversely symmetrical with that of the Chinese servant, who lies buried by the dunes outside Kessin. Effi's headstone holds firm amidst the wind-strewn autumn leaves, the ultimate bulwark against her own inclination toward distraction. This predisposition, to which her mother's gentle admonition refers, is projected by the ghost, who is manifest as nothing more than fresh air. The rustling that disturbs Effi's sleep shortly after her marriage is dismissed as the blowing of curtains in a room whose stuffiness compels the housekeeper to leave a window open. Stifled from the start, Effi gradually succumbs to what the narrator identifies as a susceptibility to the currents and vapors of the night ("Nachtluft und Nebel"). When Rummschüttel extols the view from the rear window of Effi's Berlin apartment, he evokes the very atmosphere to which she falls victim: trains coming and going, disappearing behind stands of trees, white smoke filtering sunlight.

The image is reminiscent of the dozens of views of the Gare Saint-Lazare by Claude Monet (1877), in which panting locomotives are the source of atmospheric effect. Steam engines epitomize a modernity defined by increasing impermanence, the aesthetic counterpart of which is Impressionism, in which objects appear inseparable from the intangible space surrounding them. Impressionism seemed close at hand when Marx and Engels observed in *The Communist Manifesto* about the effects of modernization that "everything solid melts into air [*verdampft*]." The aristocratic-agrarian order, embodied by Effi's father, is implicated in this dissolution, which a generation of painters raised to a scientific technique, soon to be confirmed by a new conception of the physical world that equated matter with energy. In 1893, as Fontane was finishing the main draft of *Effi Briest,* Monet completed a series of some thirty paintings of haystacks, each exploring the object from the same vantage point but at different times of the day and under varying seasonal conditions. These *meules* appear dense or diaphanous depending on the hour and the air. In a word, Monet painted the effect of time, which is precisely what Innstetten resists by challenging the suggestion that Effi's affair might be subject to a statute of limitations *(Verjährung):* "I would never have thought that *time,* purely as time, could have such an effect [*könne so wirken*]." The effect of time is apparent in Crampas's letters, however. They are yellow with age after only six years. Innstetten examines them by the light of a lamp whose green shade is fitted with transparent photographs of Effi—mementos of an evening's diversion in Kessin. Innstetten slowly rotates the lamp, pondering the images one by one. His adherence to principles he believes constant wavers in the face of a medium sensitive to momentary impressions. In 1848—Marx and Engels were heralding the "specter" *(Gespenst)* of communism—Balzac described in *Cousin Pons* the new process of photography as a means of culling specters from the atmosphere; daguerreotypy he likened to the kind of divination "spurned . . . by those who cleave to solid, visible forms." Spirit photography was among the occult practices Engels assailed when he ventured that empiricism, by thwarting speculation, left society vulnerable to superstition. The advent of photography did not bolster realism but helped erode the materialist predilections to which, as Fontane argued, realism owed its reign. Even in the service of empiricism, photography attenuated the tangible, visible world. By fostering a clearer insight into the anatomy of appearances, it revealed the perceived world as a composite.

While Monet and his contemporaries were learning to see objects differently in light of photography, they were also discovering a kindred sensibility in Japanese woodcuts, which reveled in an aesthetic of the transient effect. The works of Hokusai and Hiroshige, in particular, became widely popular in Europe during the latter half of the 19th century, their influence extending into fashion and the decorative arts. *Japonisme* makes an early appearance in *Effi Briest* when Effi, prior to her marriage to Innstetten, scandalizes her mother by proposing that their conjugal bed be decorated with Japanese motifs. There is also a tiny illustration, "cut out of a picture book," showing a Chinese figure in brightly colored traditional dress. Innstetten's diffident housekeeper, Johanna, had pasted it to the arm of a chair, as if to keep Effi's mind on the ghost. The picture follows Effi to Berlin tucked inside Johanna's *portemonnaie*—an emblem of the avenues of trade that had brought the Chinese servant to Kessin. Of particular interest, however, is a uniquely lyrical moment, in which modernization and Eastern tradition are paired with the rhythm and economy of a Japanese *tanka*: "Schneelandschaft mit Telegraphenstangen, auf deren Draht geduckt ein Vögelchen saß" ("Snowy landscape with telegraph poles, on whose cable a bird sat bowed"). This line, which describes a postcard Effi receives on the eve of her affair, recalls her mother's cautionary characterization and portrays Effi—ephemeral, ineffable—with what in the Japanese pictorial canon is the very image of transiency: a perched bird.

Two decades later, Ezra Pound, in the spirit of the haiku, conjured an image to fix the "apparition" of faces glimpsed in a crowded Paris Metro station in *Personae*: "Petals on a wet, black bough." Images disburdened of syntax are compatible with the technique of montage, itself consistent with the accelerated perception of the metropolis, in which apparitions flare up momentarily and chance encounters are the rule. It is in a streetcar in downtown Berlin that Effi unexpectedly spies her own daughter, whom she has not been permitted to see for several years. With its telegraph poles, the picture postcard exemplifies an emerging image repertoire suffused with modernity. The remarkable line with which the narrator verbally reproduces the card's visual shorthand accords with the abbreviation dictated by haiku and telegram alike. The impersonality of the latter contrasts with Gieshübler's archaic calligraphy, not to mention the vaguely familiar handwriting that draws Innstetten's eye to Crampas's letters. In both cases, the specific character of the writing corresponds to a physical defect, Gieshübler being a hunchback, and Crampas's left arm having been shattered in an earlier duel. Their letters, like their bodies, exhibit stigmata that are antithetical to an impersonal, bureaucratic order, of which the telegraph is both instrument and expression, and in which individuality as such is stigmatized. The postcard poignantly summarizes Effi's isolation within this world; oblivious to the wintry landscape, the telegraph conveys Innstetten's indifference—his devotion to principle and matching lack of tenderness, which has made Effi uneasy from the start. The ghost, who appears while Innstetten is away overnight, personifies both her anxiety and his absence. Appropriately, Effi's bedroom is provided with an electrical connection that enables her—with telegraphic economy—to summon Johanna after hearing footsteps: "She rang three times in rapid succession, so that I immediately thought it meant something."

Kafka would later describe telegraphy in a letter to Milena as a "trafficking with ghosts" *(Verkehr mit Gespenstern),* evoking the disembodiment imposed (and guaranteed) by this medium. Kafka, who was himself variously stigmatized, likely found solace in the inherent anonymity of the telegraphic message, which in any case corresponds to a democratic ideal. In Fontane's last novel, *Der Stechlin* (written 1895–96), telegraphy is the explicit synonym of modernization: Dubslav von Stechlin, aging and likable denizen of a waning aristocracy, complains that the telegraph has undermined traditional courtesies and neutralized the distinctions that define his social world. Yet he concedes the grandeur of a technology whose effects are indeed far-reaching: "In the end it's a great thing . . . this electrical current, tap, tap, tap, and if we wanted . . . we could inform the emperor of China that we were gathered here and thinking of him." Dubslav, for whom one revolution nowadays is much like the next, yields to forms of modernization that, *pace* Marx and Engels in *The Communist Manifesto,* were eroding national boundaries and creating "from the numerous national and local literatures . . . a world literature." In this respect, Effi's move to the German capital constitutes a retreat from the spirit of modernity, of which Kessin is the peculiar, peripheral locus.

Kessin is a liminal space, where the dissolution of borders creates a sense of unhomeliness: Effi in fact uses the word *unheimlich,* typically translated as "uncanny," to describe Innstetten's house, which is not only haunted but also replete with the previous owner's maritime souvenirs. This quality applies to the many mercurial figures who populate Kessin, most notably *Alonso* Gieshübler: his hybrid nomenclature (a clue to Thomas Mann's admiration for *Effi Briest*) offends an avowed sense of regional identity ("If you come from Friesack, you can't have a name like Raoul"; *Der Stechlin*). A younger Fontane, embracing the regionalism of his fellow northerner Theodor Storm, acclaimed a literature born of a "love for the spot [*Fleck*] that bore us" (*SW,* vol. 21/1, 32). Yet for all its local color, Kessin is a museum of dislocated souls, the Chinese ghost being only the most extreme example. Even Innstetten comes to see his hard-wrought mobility as the enemy of a contentment that depends on being situated "where one belongs"; happiness itself is an effect of time that dissolves into "the shimmering appearance of things" (*SW,* vol. 7, 418). In the end, the ultimate impermanence is marked by the continuity of place. Recalled by telegram to the spot that bore her, Effi is buried behind the manor house her family has owned since the reign of Georg Wilhelm (1595–1640). *Effi Briest,* the novel's title, recurs as the lapidary inscription on Effi's headstone, leaving her parents to contemplate a world grown insubstantial.

See also 1834, 1848 (February), 1899, 1912 (September)

Bibliography: Honoré de Balzac, *Cousin Pons,* trans. Herbert J. Hunt (London: Penguin, 1987). Friedrich Engels, "Natural Science and the Spirit World," in *The Dialectic of Nature,* ed. and trans. Clemens Dutt (New York: International Publishers, 1940), 297–310. Theodor Fontane, *Sämtliche Werke,* vol. 7 *(Frau Jenny Treibel, Effi Briest),* vol. 8 *(Der Stechlin),* vol. 21/1 *(Literarische Essays und Studien),* ed. Edgar Gross, Kurt Schreinert, Charlotte Jolles, et al. (Munich: Nymphenburger Verlagsbuchhandlung, 1959ff). Wolfgang Hädecke, *Theodor Fontane* (Munich: Hanser, 1998). Franz Kafka, *Briefe an Milena,* ed. Jürgen Born and Michael Müller (Frankfurt am Main: Fischer, 1983). Karl Marx and Friedrich Engels, *The Communist Manifesto* (New York: Pathfinder, 1987). Ezra Pound, *Personae: The Shorter Poems,* ed. Lea Baechler and A. Walton Litz (New York: New Directions, 1990). John Zilcosky, "The Traffic of Writing: Technologies of 'Verkehr' in Franz Kafka's *Briefe an Milena,*" *German Life and Letters,* 52 (1999): 365ff.

Kenneth S. Calhoon

ℒ 1897

The publication of *Das Jahr der Seele* revives traditional artisan bookmaking

Stefan George and Symbolism

In 1889, a young man from the Rhineland, who had grown up speaking both French and German and whose name, Etienne George, was pronounced as it would be in France, went to Paris for the first time. Even though he had already written several verses and dramas, at age twenty-one, he had never met a poet of any note before. Within weeks he became a regular at Stéphane Mallarmé's famed Tuesday Evenings in the Rue de Rome and everything in Etienne George's life changed.

Mallarmé, who was then at the zenith of his fame as the supreme representative of symbolism, taught George (1868–1933) not just a new way of making poetry, but also how to be a poet. Mallarmé's conventicles were attended by major literary and cultural figures of the day. It was a diverse, cosmopolitan group, mirroring the international composition of the symbolist movement itself. All regarded Mallarmé as the supreme Master, the consummate artist who spoke of Poetry as if it were a holy sacrament and he, the Poet, an anointed priest performing rites before faithful acolytes.

It has been often said—and many symbolists said it themselves—that their conception of poetry was designed to combat what they perceived as the corrupt movement in literature known as naturalism. But symbolism's real opponent, if it must be framed in adversarial terms, was not naturalism at all, or solely, but a predominant strain within the traditional view and practice of Western art as a whole. In the course of two and a half millennia, there was never any serious question that art's business was to capture the shapes, colors, sounds, even the movements that surround us and to render them in recognizable form. For the symbolists, however, art had a much greater and more difficult task to fulfill. Objects become symbols of otherwise hidden realities, visible tokens for what cannot really be represented. Thus, even when speaking of the natural world, a symbolist is always talking of something else. The phrase Mallarmé used to describe the effect of a symbol, the "mood" he said it renders, means literally "state of soul" *(état d'âme)*. The words of a poem act as a conduit, leading through an inexplicable alignment to a sort of spiritual attunement to the poet's vision and, ultimately, to an encounter with what was variously called the "Idea," the "Infinite," or the "Absolute." And it was the poet, and the poet alone, who supplied the medium enabling this encounter to occur.

George took Mallarmé's concept of poetry and the poet to heart and made it his own. He was especially drawn to the notion that the poet possesses supreme authority and that the poem is an instrument for exercising unrestricted power over the world. Almost everything in his later development—his haughty, aristocratic bearing, his exclusive elitism, his disdain for the modern, bourgeois world, and his need to be at the center of a circle of admirers and eventually disciples—finds some parallel in this first encounter in Paris. Over the next several years, George wrote a series of books—all privately published in small editions of one to two hundred copies—in which he elaborated his own version of the symbolist creed. When he published his first book, *Hymnen* (1890; *Hymns*), one of the first people he sent it to was Mallarmé, who recognized its affinity to his own endeavors. It was also in homage to the French master that his German disciple had published the *Hymns* under the name he would henceforth use: Stefan George.

In his next three books, George elaborated on the insights he had gained in the *Hymns*. In 1891, he published *Pilgerfahrten (Pilgrimages)*, followed the next year by *Algabal*, loosely based on the life of the decadent Roman emperor Heliogabalus. In 1892, he also founded a literary journal, *Die Blätter für die Kunst (Pages for Art)*, modeled after similar French ventures and intended to showcase the "new art." In 1895, he published another book of poetry with the ungainly title *Die Bücher der Hirten und Preisgedichte, Der Sagen und Sänge und der Hängenden Gärten (The Books of Eclogues and Eulogies, of Legends and Songs, and of the Hanging Gardens)*.

His fifth book, *Das Jahr der Seele* (1897; *The Year of the Soul*) marks a departure from his previous work in several ways. It was the first of several books George was to produce together with Melchior Lechter, a painter and graphic designer who was inspired by William Morris and his Kelmscott Press to revive artisan traditions of bookmaking and to repudiate modern, mass-produced merchandise. As the first result of this collaboration, *The Year of the Soul* was described as "indisputably one of the most beautiful books that has appeared in Germany in recent times" (Grautoff 104).

Everything about the book's physical aspect bespoke the resolve to recapture the imagined virtues of a distant past. The exquisite workmanship and choice materials, as well as the woodcut image adorning the title page depicting a winged angel in a long, trailing gown and seated in front of a pipe organ, the blue and red capital initials suggestive of a medieval manuscript, and, finally, the small print run of only 206 copies, all contributed to the impression that *The Year of the Soul* breathed the spirit of a different and implicitly better age.

Next to *Algabal*, *The Year of the Soul* is the most tightly organized and thematically unified work George had yet produced. It is also his most intensely personal, most lyrically plangent work. To this day, it remains his most popular cycle of poetry, the one thought to be most accessible, most available to an emotional response because it seems to be such an open expression of the poet's own emotions, of his own soulful experience. A kind of melancholy wash appears to have been spread over the interior landscape of the poet's soul, giving everything a slightly faded, somewhat elegiac cast, mournful, sometimes even morose. Heightening the sense that the poet is speaking from the depth of his soul, that we have been made privy to the intimate colloquy of the poet with himself, the preface affirms and denies its autobiographical relevance. In response to questions about whether "identifying certain people or places" would aid the understanding of individual poems, George advises it would be

Title page of *Das Jahr der Seele,* design by Melchior Lechter. (Houghton Library, Harvard College Library)

"unwise" to look for "the human or natural original" in all of poetry, including his own. "It has experienced such a transformation through art," he explains, "that it has become insignificant for the creator himself and any knowledge of it for others would confuse rather than enlighten." We are told that where names do occur—actually none do, only initials—they are meant only as a "tribute" or "gift" to those so honored. Most important, the preface concludes, is to remember that "seldom are I and you so completely the same soul as in this book" (*Werke* 4: 7).

It is true that familiarity with the particulars of George's life is not crucial to understanding the poems; the story they tell, while not exactly unambiguous, is comprehensible on even a fairly general plane. But never before had he inscribed so much of himself, and in such an unconcealed manner, into his work. For the first time, George places his poetic persona in the middle of his own world—many of the poems take place along a river that can only be the Rhine and within a natural setting that likewise evokes the hills and valleys around his native Bingen—and he choreographs a complex shadow dance with figures that are recognizable, if faint, distillates of various people he knew—and some of whom he loved.

The book is divided into three main parts. The first is the most dramatic and easiest to grasp. It tells of a failed liaison that is soon followed by a more fulfilling one. This part also consists of three segments and, in adherence to the governing temporal motif of the collection—the "year" is marked out by the consecutive passing of the seasons—they are grouped in seasonal clusters: "After the Harvest," "Pilgrims in the Snow," and "Victory of Summer." George exploits the common symbolic values of autumn and winter to convey a sense of growing darkness and cold, of exhausted life and the approach of slumber and death. But the object of this symbolic death is the poet's attachment to a woman, or perhaps it is more accurate to say to Woman in general. Even though the relationship is not particularly warm, the poet says to the female companion in the autumnal first sequence, "I will learn gentle tender words for you" (*Werke* 4: 14), as if it cost him no small effort to do so. Their conversation is subdued, tempered, almost hushed, and often punctuated by long silences. Sitting on a bench, each lost "in dreams," they "only gaze and listen when in pauses / The ripe fruit thumps down on the ground" (*Werke* 4: 15).

It is a beautiful image, to be sure, but not one that conveys much passion. Rather the opposite is implied—a spent flame, waning light, dissipating heat. Finally, the poet says he has put into words what they both already know, and he writes her a letter and watches from a distance as she reads it:

> Next to a high and withered flower
> You unfolded it · I stand apart and think . . .
> It was the white sheet that fell from your hand
> The brightest color upon the pallid surface (*Werke* 4: 21)

It is difficult to read these lines without being reminded of George's tentative approaches toward a young woman he knew by the name of Ida Coblenz and the end to their epistolary relationship in 1896. He originally wanted to dedicate the book to her but changed the dedication to his sister when Ida Coblenz disappointed him. But the frame of reference here is much wider, having less to do with a single person, and more with her entire gender. The first section ends with the poet, having bid his female companion farewell, saying, "I feel that no sooner has time separated us / Then you will no longer inhabit my dream" (*Werke* 4: 22). George was not just saying goodbye to Ida Coblenz; he was saying that, henceforth, women would no longer find a place in his world.

The second section, "Pilgrims in the Snow," underscores this break. In one poem the image of the flower—frequently a symbol of sexuality in George's work—is used to express the finality of the event. A flower on his window ledge he had long faithfully tended is wilting and has become hateful to his sight:

> To eradicate from my mind the memory
> Of its earlier blossoming fortunes
> I choose sharp tools and I snip
> The pale flower with the diseased heart. (*Werke* 4: 31)

Capping this break, and leading into the triumphant "Victory of Summer," the poet constructs a "pyre," which he says he builds for his "memories" and "for you," and lights it. Walking away from the flames, he climbs into a boat and sees that "Yonder on the shore a brother / Waves and swings the happy banner" (*Werke* 4: 33). It is with this "brother" that the poet celebrates the exuberant summer solstice.

The happiness that eluded the poet earlier now appears within reach. "The air stirs as if moved by new things," an arousal that heralds "a new adventure" (*Werke* 4: 36). In the poems that follow, the poet indulges in descriptions of his companion and their "adventures," and for the first time in George's work the beloved is no longer hidden behind the neutral pronoun "you," but receives a definite sex. Moreover, George becomes as explicit about the nature of the relationship between the two lovers as he has ever been before:

> Are you still reminded of the beautiful image of him
> He who boldly grabbed the roses on cliffs' edge ·
> He who forgot the day in hot pursuit ·
> He who supped the full nectar from umbels? (*Werke* 4: 40)

The last word—"umbel"—is strange in German, too. *Umbelliferae* are a class of flowering plant whose individual stalk rises from the same point or bulb, as in the case of geraniums, milkweed, onions, or, most suggestively, leeks. Likewise, the word he uses for "nectar" is equally abstruse—*Seim*—and bears a strong similarity to the word in German commonly used for both "seed" and "semen," namely *Same*. The phallic connotations of the last line, although still well camouflaged, mark a startling departure from his earlier reticence to call things by their name.

George's new directness was related to his increased desire to play an active role in the world and not merely dominate it in and through language. In one of the poems from "Victory of Summer," the poet reminds himself as much as his lover to take joy in the here-and-now, hoping "that this sweet life may satisfy us · That we live here as thankful guests!" (Werke 4: 38). Similarly, in a syntactically complicated strophe, the poetic voice envisions a time when the ideal and the actual will coincide. But until that day arrives, he says, one should not condemn the desire to flee into history and the imagination as a way of experiencing, or at least of anticipating, love. From this point on, George would strive to merge the ideal and the real.

Yet eventually the summer ends, as all summers must, and the poet again finds himself lonely and bereft of the plenitude he has just extolled. Except for tributes to his friends in the middle section, a dark, somber mood dominates the rest of the book, thematically enunciated by the title of the concluding part, "Sorrowful Dances." One poem will suffice to illustrate the pall cast over the last few pages of *The Year of the Soul*. The image of a cold hearth, filled only with the charred remnants of a now extinguished fire, gives the poem an almost funereal resonance:

> You stepped up to the hearth
> Where all embers have died ·
> The only light on the earth
> Was the moon's cadaveric color.
>
> You dipped your pallid fingers
> Deep into the ashes
> Searching feeling groping—
> That there may be a glow again! (*Werke* 4: 118)

The image of dead or dying embers illuminated by wan, crepuscular light is, at the turn of the century, so common as to risk being hackneyed. Nations, entire cultures, even the whole world seemed bathed in a kind of twilight glow, spent of all vitality, exhausted, and emitting an audible death-rattle. This was how George saw the Wilhelminian Empire at the fin de siècle: outwardly vigorous and hale, but inwardly corrupt, worm-eaten, and irreversibly moribund. Yet the poem is resigned, not jubilant, and there is no indication that the extinction is desired; quite the opposite. The poet's dreams mingle with the ashes; his hope to rekindle the flame, an expression of his wish to relive the heady days of summer, is now no more than the dead gray residue running through his fingers—or the black ink flowing from his pen. The poem, and indeed all of *The Year of the Soul,* does not just bid farewell to a past overcome; it eulogizes, and renounces, the poet's ambitions to challenge the world with the creation of a poetic realm, of fashioning, like an alchemist, an alternative universe out of the chimerical stuff of language alone. From now on, poetry would continue to play a crucial role in the construction of George's realm, but increasingly as a means, not as an end in itself. In the new century, until his death in 1933, he depended more and more on his group of followers, his "Circle," to embody his will and to place his stamp on the world.

See also 1796 (June 10), 1902, 1912 (July–October)

Bibliography: Stefan George, *Gesamt-Ausgabe der Werke,* 18 vols. (Berlin: Georg Bondi, 1927–1934). Robert Boehringer, *Mein Bild von Stefan George* (Düsseldorf and Munich: Helmut Küpper, 1968). Otto Grautoff, *Die Entwicklung der modernen Buchkunst in Deutschland,* 2nd ed. (Leipzig: Hermann Seemann, 1902).

Robert E. Norton

1899, August 6

In a letter to his friend Fliess, Sigmund Freud describes the reader's path through *Die Traumdeutung*

The Dream as Symbolic Form

In *Die Traumdeutung* (1900; *The Interpretation of Dreams*) Sigmund Freud (1856–1939) assigns an unwonted theoretical value to the dream, conceiving of it as "a window, to cast a glance into the interior of the mind." The dream is not only the detritus of the phenomenal world; it is an exemplary phenomenon that throws light on the hybrid, contested nature of all of mental life. In its bizarre way, the dream's first kinship is with conspicuously abnormal mental products spawned by the tension between antithetical psychic forces. This is consistent with the neuroses and other occluded manifestations of the Unconscious, such as hysterical symptoms, obsessive ideas, phobias, and parapraxes. But as the manifestation of clashing psychic forces, the dream also represents all elements of normal mental life. All notions and feelings and moods—whether judged normal or abnormal on pragmatic or conventional grounds—represent a play of forces aiming to discharge and to inhibit, since gratification, as well as the less than pleasurable thrust toward gratification, of repressed unconscious wishes imperils the well-being of the psyche. Indeed, "the degree of our psychical normality" is "indicated by the measure of such suppression."

Mental life—this is Freud's main contribution—is the product of the oppositional character of psychic agencies: behind the dream, as behind every mental act, lies the clash of psychical systems: the Unconscious, the Preconscious, and surface perception or consciousness. Their struggle for predominance is complex, and in each case has a history. The hybrid entity that arises from their collision immediately enters into a new relation with the systemic forces that produce it. The dream, for example, represents an overcoming of the resistance of the Preconscious to the gratification of unconscious wishes and can prompt resistance in the patient to its interpretation; and that resistance can, in turn, become the motor of another dream.

The extreme detail and theoretical inclusiveness of Freud's analysis in a work that went through eight editions justifies his claim to having unified the main currents of all previous dream theories. Freud's chief contribution was to minimize the role of impressions of actual experience—by "the remains of the day"—as well as somatic stimuli and to make them entirely serviceable to the Unconscious bent on gratifying an infantile, usually sexual, desire. This is the "unsuspected psychic resource" whose key function the reader is alerted to from the start and whose discovery will resolve the enigma of the dream. It will not do, says Freud with a glance at the prevailing climate of materialist psychiatry, to reject psychic causes simply on grounds that they are only psychic. To assume such causes when the evidence suggests them is not to fall captive to dreaded metaphysics. The dream is intelligible according to the rhetoric of a scientific psychology that includes the concept of the Unconscious. The psychic is not the metaphysical.

The latent content of every dream is the unconscious wish. Freud generates a profusion of metaphors to describe this mechanism—the dream as a safety-valve, fireworks, a capitalist venture. The latter is of greatest current interest: "To put it [this matter of wish fulfillment] in the form of a comparison: the daytime thought might possibly play the part of *entrepreneur* for the dream; but the entrepreneur who has the idea, as we say, and the will to translate it into action, still cannot do anything without capital; he needs a *capitalist* to take on the expenses, and the capitalist in this case, who contributes the psychical expenditure for the dream, is always and unfailingly, whatever the daytime thought might be, *a wish from the Unconscious.*" Typical of Freud's discursive style is to complicate and relativize such conceits. He promptly adds:

> On other occasions the capitalist is himself the entrepreneur; in dreams, indeed, that is the more usual case. An unconscious wish has been aroused by the day's work, and it now creates the dream. All the other situations possible in the economic circumstances I have just suggested as an example also have their parallels in the procedure of the dream; the entrepreneur is in a position to contribute a small amount of capital himself; several entrepreneurs might turn to the same capitalist; several capitalists might club together and provide what the entrepreneurs require. Likewise, there are also dreams that are supported by more than one wish.

This insatiable explanatory habit accounts for the innumerable contradictions and rhetorical tensions within the text. Every mental entity—the manifest content of the dream, the latent content of the dream, every posited agency or process, the censor, or the secondary process—requires additional analysis in light of the traces of the foster forces it bears and the struggle between retention and discharge in which it is caught up. For example, in a discussion in the course of which the main charge of the dream work is continually associated with the Unconscious, Freud declares at the close that the preconscious inhibiting system "emits its own energy charges." Such a claim requires a fresh account of the relationship of drive to energy. It is also amusing to learn that the Preconscious acts "to prevent a certain development of unpleasure" by "strangling" unconscious excitations.

The inspiration for *The Interpretation of Dreams,* according to the Preface to the third English edition (1931), came to Freud as a gift of insight of the sort "that falls to one's lot but once in a lifetime." Dating the reception of the gift is not easy. The recent publication of Freud's *Project of a Psychology,* conceived around 1895, reveals that the *Interpretation* accumulates several key ideas that Freud harbored for most of the last decade of the 19th century, including the thesis of the dream as wish fulfillment with a regressive thrust. Here, Goethe's image in *Poetry and Truth* for the composition of his novel *The Sorrows of Young Werther* is apposite for Freud's text, all seven hundred pages of it: "The whole crystallized from all sides and became a solid mass the way the slightest jolt will immediately turn a vessel of water at the freezing point to solid ice."

The Interpretation of Dreams has abundant drama, a factor captured in Freud's description of his book in a letter of August 6, 1899, to his confidant Wilhelm Fliess. Freud describes the opening chapters: "The whole is structured like the phantasy of a walk. First the dark wood of the authorities (who cannot see the trees)—without a prospect, full of meandering paths. Then a concealed defile, through which I lead the reader—my model-dream [the "Irma dream"] with its oddities, details, indiscretions, bad jokes—and then suddenly the heights and the prospect onto the demand: 'Where would you like to go now?'" But where one would like to go is not necessarily where one is taken. The later portions of *The Interpretation* read as at least two different books, marked by the variable texture of the narrative. The middle is leavened by the description and analysis of a great many novella-like dreams; the last third is dense, jargon-freighted, meandering. Freud himself confessed to the inadequacy of his expository powers for the task at hand, which is to provide a scientific account of the enigma of dream formation and at the same time discover, by means of the theoretical reconstruction of the dream, nothing less than "how the psychical apparatus is constructed."

The enigma of the dream, and the chief spur to its interpretation, lies in the dissimulative, mask-like relation of the manifest content to the latent desiderative content that uses it. This relation forms the core symbolic structure of the dream: the interpreter strives to render the manifest content transparent to its underlying thoughts and wishes, where "the layering of the meanings of dreams, one on top of the other, is one of the trickiest but also most richly revealing problems of the interpretation of dreams." Under theoretical scrutiny, certain particular and also typical dreams yield the main principles structuring the dream work: "condensation" [*Verdichtung*] aims to fuse into a polysemous, multivalent unity a variety of latent motifs; "displacement" *(Verschiebung)* brings about a shift of psychical intensity in the manifest dream onto a seemingly innocuous element. The operation of both principles arises from the attempt to satisfy the "censor," and indeed the dreamer is, as a rule, witty and inventive enough to accomplish this. Other dreams under analysis give rise to other rules, including a third principle, "regard for representability" (*Rücksicht auf Darstellbarkeit*), where "a colorless and abstract expression of the dream-thought is exchanged for a pictorial and concrete one," a process that contributes to the famous rebus character of the dream. The fourth principle, "secondary revision" *(die sekundäre Bearbeitung),* describes the work of the mind near wakefulness of sorting out the nascent dream to meet expectable standards of coherence and narrative logic.

Much of Freud's own "explanation" of the workings of the dream, as suggested in the metaphors cited above, is itself rhetorical and only symbolic of the pure science for which he strives. The reader, who often figures implicitly as the authority whose assent is sought, feels like the captain of a ship in distress at sea. To be involved in the rhetorical interpretation of entities that are themselves symbolic, composite, and representative— the dream, the hysterical symptom, the parapraxis—is to be caught in a continual vertiginous motion. It becomes impossible to distinguish the subjective treatment from the subject matter. Not unlike the dream itself, Freud's analysis places great weight on the "pictorial and concrete" resources of its diction, which may appear at one moment to apply to the thing to be interpreted, and at another to the rhetoric of the interpretation, which lies close to the heart of the interpreter. For example, the dream as a composite of interests arising from the Unconscious and the Preconscious necessarily introduces an element of anxiety which, for Freud, is "soldered" onto the unconscious wish. But, as he remarks, the anxiety that is perceived to adhere to the anxiety dream—a point that seems to threaten the postulate that every dream is a wish fulfillment—can be due to the anxiety out of which the dreamer comes to give an account of his dream. Freud's answer to the damaging objection to the wish fulfillment thesis is given with such noticeable hesitation and reluctance that the reader will register a certain anxiety adhering to the explanatory process itself. His earlier claim that patients report anxiety dreams in order to vex their analyst, whom they regard as invested in the principle of wish fulfillment, and in this way gratify their sadistic desires, only heightens the impression of his own discursive anxiety.

The exigency of symbolic explanation arises from the impossibility of identifying the referent directly. "The Unconscious is the true reality of the psyche, *its inner nature just as unknown to us as the reality of the external world, and just as imperfectly revealed by the data of consciousness as the external world is by the information received from our sensory organs.*" And so, at every step of the way, the argument has to be advanced by means of rapid exchanges between the authority of the author and the credulity of the reader if a paralyzing skepticism is to be subdued. (Skepticism is the exact name of the philosophical position that the demurrer above, in italic, invokes.) It is up to Freud's rhetorical power to evoke the valiant, truth-besotted researcher and explorer, who "if Heaven I cannot bend, then Hell I will arouse." (Freud took this motto for the *Interpretation of Dreams* from the seventh book of Virgil's *Aeneid.*) Still, the reader will want to know what principle governed the selection of figures, since they are not literal, inescapable features of the object; they provoke his desire to grasp the author's authority as arising from an authorial intention. In Freud's case, beginning with the announced exigency of reproducing his *own* dreams, the author's presence is nearly overwhelming. The reader is confronted with an individual psyche that claims to be typical, yet can be grasped only through a psychology that is at that very moment being elaborated.

Later critics of *Interpretation* have tended to give up on its science and have read it through the prism of the figures that inform its diction (though this approach is certainly at odds with Freud's intention). At the level of its sample dreams and its extended rhetorical analogues, *Interpretation* can be seen as autobiographical and has properly been described as "semi-disguised." Reinterpreting Freud's interpretations of his dreams to uncover significant omissions, distortions, displacements, and the like, became a cottage industry, especially in the 1970s among students of the neo-Freudian analyst Jacques Lacan. In Lacan's proselytizing spirit, the *Interpretation of Dreams* itself shaped a new French, and subsequently American, way of reading texts that persists to the present. Freud's work has in some sense become a handbook of innovative hermeneutics that takes literarily inflected, often seemingly absurd, dream texts as "scripture." How can such an interpretation do its work, what are its tools and procedures? Each of the fundamental principles of the dream work offers a way of guiding hermeneutic attention. "Condensation" translates to "metaphor" in the text, or figures based on resemblance; "displacement" translates to "metonymy," or meanings evoked through an association of ideas on lines of cause and effect, part and whole. The regard for representability can provoke a heightened critical attention to the image under the aspect of prosopopoeia, giving a figure or face to a hypothetical entity, as to the self in autobiography, whereas secondary elaboration is a plain token of the will to coherent narrative. The technique of attending to inconspicuous, unemphasized moments; the alertness to polysemy, ambiguity, and overdetermination; the awareness that signifieds can masquerade as signifiers, verbal elements as pictures, and literal meanings as slang figures, and the reverse; readiness to suspect affirmations as masked negations; the high premium placed on the form of the presentation, answering to Freud's attentiveness to the manner in which the dreamer gives an account of his dream (where does he hesitate, where does he claim vagueness?), all have their place in recent criticism. Finally, the entire *Interpretation of Dreams* has held a particular appeal among literary theorists as a heterogenous, oscillatory text in its own right that invites deconstruction. From this perspective, it is seen as a theory of the dream text that draws unconsciously on all rhetorical resources of the dream itself.

Interpretation can be read as a source book unrivaled for its richness of detail of the internalized social life of upper-middle-class Vienna at the turn of the 20th century. Carl Schorske, in his monumental *Fin-de-Siècle Vienna: Politics and Culture,* sees Freud constructing a psychoanalytical empire half-conscious of his exclusion from the real empire building of anti-Semitic imperial Austria. *The Interpretation of Dreams* thus became a foundational text for what is currently called cultural studies. To judge from the variety of perspectives in which *The Interpretation of Dreams* has been and can be read, it may well survive the therapeutic component of psychoanalysis itself, as witness the variety of symposia held on the hundredth anniversary of its first publication and coinciding with a time of rampant criticism of Freud's science.

See also 1774, 1902, 1918

Bibliography: Sigmund Freud, *The Interpretation of Dreams,* trans. Joyce Crick, Introduction by Ritchie Robertson (Oxford, U.K.: Oxford University Press, 2000). Harold Bloom, ed. *Sigmund Freud's The Interpretation of Dreams: Modern Critical Interpretations* (New York: Chelsea House Publishers, 1987). Mikkel Borch-Jacobsen, "Do Freud's Fibs Matter?" *London Review of Books* 22, 13 (6 July 2000): 4–5. Colin McGinn, "Freud under Analysis," *New York Review of Books* (June 2000): 20–24. Carl E. Schorske, *Fin-de-Siècle Vienna: Politics and Culture* (New York: Knopf, 1980). Samuel Weber, *The Legend of Freud* (Minneapolis: University of Minnesota Press, 1982).

Stanley Corngold

1902, October 18–19

Hugo von Hofmannsthal's fictional letter "Ein Brief" appears in two parts in the Berlin newspaper *Der Tag*

The Limits of Language

Cast in masterful prose, Hugo von Hofmannsthal's text "Ein Brief" (A Letter) describes a loss of language that must have astounded readers familiar with the work of the brilliant young Austrian writer. The *Chandos Letter,* as it became known, initiates modern literature's fascination with the need to speak without being able to say anything meaningful. The protagonists of Samuel Beckett's *Endgame* and Peter Handke's *Kaspar* are heirs to the figure Chandos, whom Hofmannsthal invented as his alter ego. Dated August 1603, this epistolary confession is addressed to the English philosopher and statesman Francis Bacon (1561–1626) and articulates the troubled relationship between language and experience characteristic of much experimental 20th-century European writing. At the center of the *Letter,* Hofmannsthal, the magical wordsmith of *fin-de-siècle* Vienna, has Chandos disclose the loss of his ability to render a unitary state of the world in words: "For me everything disintegrated into parts, those parts again into parts; no longer would anything let itself be encompassed by one idea. Single words floated round me; they congealed into eyes which stared at me and into which I was forced to stare back—whirlpools which gave me vertigo and, reeling incessantly, led into the void" (134–135).

This admission is all the more startling, considering the ease with which both the imaginary Chandos and the poet Hofmannsthal once conjured up dreamlike images with words. "In those days," Chandos sums up the physical intensity he felt at the center of life, "I, in a state of continuous intoxication, conceived the whole of existence as one great unit" (132). Reflecting on his earlier writing, the urbane, gentlemanly aristocrat Chandos, age twenty-six, takes on the traits of his author, who at that age had obtained a second doctorate in literature from the University of Vienna. Hofmannsthal, the scion of a well-to-do Viennese family with a passionate love for the arts, is twenty-eight at the time *A Letter* is published. Like the composite figure Chandos, he is married and the father of a daughter. He lives contentedly in a small Rococo country house outside the Habsburg capital, which remains his residence until his death in 1929. Whereas Chandos forswears "words" (136) and with this any attempt to return to his poetic calling, Hofmannsthal continued his successful writing career as dramatist and commentator on the writings of English, French, and German authors from the Renaissance to his own day. From 1908 on, he collaborated with Richard Strauss on several operas. The high point of this collaboration is undoubtedly *Der Rosenkavalier* (1911), in which music and words combine to recreate, in the Rococo Vienna of Empress Maria Theresia, the psychologically fine-tuned sensations of social interplay between classes that still characterized Vienna as Habsburg rule began to wane. In the year 1920, Hofmannsthal, Strauss, and the theater producer Max Reinhardt founded the Salzburg Festival, where one of the centerpieces to this day is either Hofmannsthal's play *Jedermann (Everyman)* or *Das Salzburger grosse Welttheater (The Salzburg Great World Stage)*. As in the case of *Everyman,* which is based on the English morality play, the writer reworked already existing texts from world literature, culminating in the unfinished *Der Turm* (1927; *The Tower*), an attempt to recast the Spanish dramatist Calderón's *Life Is a Dream*. Hofmannsthal worked for more than twenty-five years on this tragedy in which he investigates the relationship of politics and the psyche through the decline and fall of the Habsburg Empire. The central psychological conflict in *The Tower* is oedipal, between father and son, but whereas Calderon questions the limits of early 17th-century rationalism and sides with justice and grace, Hofmannsthal seeks to strike a balance between the rule of law, necessary for the coherence of a multiethnic, diverse society, represented by the father-king, and the creative energy and empathy of the son, the poet-prince.

The theme of the relation between the poet and the state, alluded to in the figures of Chandos and Bacon, who occupied prominent positions during the reign of Elizabeth I and the Stuarts, received numerous treatments in European literature, not the least in Goethe's play *Torquato Tasso*. Exposing the fissure between divine, true art and mundane, vulgar life, the theme is a favorite subject among *l'art pour l'art* (art-for-art's sake) French and Belgian Symbolist poets. The Irish poets Oscar Wilde (1854–1900) and W. B. Yeats (1865–1939) and the Belgian poet Maurice Maeterlinck (1862–1949) belong to this modernist movement, as did Rainer Maria Rilke and the German high priest of aestheticism, Stefan George (1868–1933). Hofmannsthal's early impressionist lyrical poetry, published under the pseudonym Loris while he was still in high school, shows intense involvement with the vibrations of the "inner self" (*Prosa II*, 130) that was characteristic of much of Symbolist writing. Poems like "Lebenslied," together with some short verse plays, notably *Der Tod des Tizian (The Death of Titian)* and *Der Tor und der Tod (Death and the Fool),* embrace the metaphorically enclosed realm of heightened aesthetic sensibility that attracted George's attention. For members of Jung Wien (Young Vienna), a loosely connected avant-garde literary group, to which belonged the influential critic Hermann Bahr (1863–1934) and the dramatist Arthur Schnitzler (1862–1931), Hofmannsthal's lyrical genius was path-breaking.

To the dismay of his admirers, the *Chandos Letter* breaks with aestheticism, "the form of which one can no longer say that it organizes subject matter, for it penetrates it, dissolves it, creating at once both dream and reality, an interplay of eternal forces, something as marvelous as music or algebra" (131). He abandoned poetry; Chandos describes the renunciation as a fall from "a state of inflated arrogance" into "despondency and feebleness," a state where he has "lost completely the ability to think or to speak of anything coherently" (133). This admission is all the more astonishing coming from an author who had believed so fervently in the power of the word, only to abandon its world-creating function to simply "bear witness," as the prince says in *The Tower:* "I was there, although no one knew me."

Hofmannsthal was always aware of what T. S. Eliot later called the "dissociation of sensibility," that is, the moment when, in the age of Bacon, literary language split from communicational or vehicular language, and high culture was severed from society. Chandos thus draws a distinction between exigent vehicular language that is insufficient to "penetrate into the core of things" (130), and a radiant poetic language of being which talks out of objects "with tongues" (131). His description of the inability to express thought adequately by means of speech, for which Freud had coined the term "aphasia" in 1891, is not, therefore, merely a critique of poetic language and the aesthetic attitude of Young Vienna. Rather, *A Letter* veils the crisis of *fin-de-siècle* Vienna, a crisis consisting for Hofmannsthal in the consciously felt experience of "coming after" and being heir to a sophisticated European cultural tradition, which, however, is no longer able to project satisfying utopias. Chandos, comparing himself to the Roman orator Crassus, recognizes a mirrored self-image, "reflected across the abyss of centuries" (139). Such introspection and the baggage of history add to Hofmannsthal's unease about all communicative ability in and through language, because, as he says elsewhere: "Words have placed themselves before things, words take away all life from human beings, and when we open our mouths there are already ten thousand dead speaking with us."

The crisis that permeated *fin-de-siècle* Vienna, the watershed from the 19th to the 20th century—comparable to the crisis of post–Elizabethan England when Bacon proclaimed that knowledge is power—arose from the disintegration of an old order and the fermentation of new thoughts. The centrality of the intelligentsia in Vienna belied the fact that its exponents like Hofmannsthal, Sigmund Freud, Ernst Mach, Ludwig Wittgenstein, Hermann Broch, and the composer Arnold Schoenberg belonged to a class that, though economically mostly well off, was socially and politically functionless under Vienna's anti-Semitic mayor, Karl Lueger. Hofmannsthal points out, furthermore, that this was an age that witnessed the transformation of a pre-industrial organic community into an industrial mass society. Modern society and culture seemed to Hofmannsthal "hopelessly pluralistic, lacking in cohesion or direction." Chandos credits neither religious ideas nor worldly ideas with providing unitary structures. Rather, the nature of our epoch, Hofmannsthal wrote in 1905, "is multiplicity and indeterminacy. It can rest only on *das Gleitende* [the moving, the slipping, the sliding], and is aware that what other generations believed to be firm is in fact *das Gleitende*."

The notion of instability and flux pervades Chandos's letter, as he is haunted by microscopic lucidity and experiences reality as a mosaic of integral structures that defy description. The *Letter* ushers in the revolt of literature against language, comparable to, but perhaps more radical than, Gustav Klimt's concurrent revolt in art and Arnold Schoenberg's in music. This revolt is directed against the pathological condition, the "serious illness" of mind (129), to which Chandos alludes, which has plagued a rationalist age, centered on the idea of a unitary self in control of the subject. Freud, in *Studies on Hysteria* (1895), dispelled these ideas by positing the laws of the unconscious for understanding the human psyche. The unconscious operates through a series of associations where different trains of elements form veritable networks, with nodal points at the intersection of several lines. While Schnitzler articulated the life of emotions through the ambivalence he saw between old morality and new psychological reality, Hofmannsthal, in the *Chandos Letter,* applies language and its ability to relate to things with semi-surgical precision.

Bacon and the empirical procedure he was the first to advocate hover as a sign of historical memory over the *Letter,* as do his reflections on poetry and the theater extolled in *The Advancement of Learning* of 1605. However, the split self presented by Chandos's initial question about the continuity of personhood echoes the critique of a unitary self, voiced by the physicist Ernst Mach (1838–1916) as well as Freud's psychoanalytical observation. In *Analyse der Empfindungen* (1885; *Analysis of Sensations*), Mach declares the *I* (ego) to be *unrettbar* (unsalvageable). The Cartesian unitary self is nothing but a practical entity for the purpose of preliminary observation. As a mere function of the empirically given, the ego is variable. According to Mach, the "thing, body, matter are nothing but a relation between elements." Consequently, the ego, as far as it is scientifically cognizable, is reduced to a bundle of changing sensations. No fundamental difference exists between the psychic and the physical world, and there are, furthermore, no isolated acts of sensing, feeling, willing, and thinking. Chandos's distaste for philosophical concepts rendered in the words "spirit, soul, or body" (133), together with his strong objection to a language of "judgment" that these terms inevitably entail, chimes with Mach's insight. Moreover, sensations are the determining force that animates Chandos's existence. No matter how lowly or sublime are the sources of sensation, "an immense sympathy, a flowing over into these creatures, or a feeling that an aura of life and death, dream and wakefulness, had flowed into them—but whence?" (137). The reciprocity of sensation in the form of "celestial shudders" derives from the miracle of perceiving an object like the shrubbery as such (137). The "flood of divine sensation" (136), which "words seem too poor to describe" (136), vouchsafes the "never-ending interplay" of things in the world and guarantees meaning by way of a mystical union between self and others: "Indeed, something entirely unnamed, even barely nameable which, at such moments, reveals itself to me, filling like a vessel any casual object of my daily surroundings with an overflowing flood of higher life" (135). At "the moment of epiphany," as James Joyce later called the experience of unity between the ego and the objects in the world as such—Hofmannsthal calls it "revelation"—words can never represent the fullness of being. "Words desert me" (135), Chandos proclaims; and in a posthumous fragment, Hofmannsthal attests to the limits of language so distinctively and meticulously outlined in the *Chandos Letter:* "That which is most profound in experience defies words, I always felt that words divide human beings instead of connecting them."

By demonstrating the fissure between language and experience, the *Chandos Letter* conjoins the critique of language that characterizes Viennese thought at the *fin de siècle*. First voiced by Fritz Mauthner (1849–1923), the philosopher and cofounder of the Freie Bühne Theater in Berlin, the critique of language inaugurates the linguistic turn in the 20th century, a turn from speculative philosophy and metaphysics toward a definition of philosophy as linguistic or conceptual analysis, which dominated philosophy for nearly a century. Ludwig Wittgenstein (1889–1951) is its most prominent and influential representative. However, Mauthner's *Beiträge zu einer Kritik der Sprache* (1901–1902; *Contributions to a Critique of Language*), albeit somewhat obscure, is closest to Hofmannsthal's lifelong concern with the failure of language. Mauthner reacted with enthusiasm to the publication of the *Chandos Letter* and, convinced of having found a soul mate, approached Hofmannsthal. Although Hofmannsthal was familiar with Mauthner's not very well-known work by 1901, the poet emphasized the similarity in their thoughts rather than admitting any influence, and kept at a distance. Nevertheless, Hofmannsthal shares with both Mauthner and Nietzsche the assumption that words are but a series of metaphors. Language users believing that language renders a unitary "truth" merely forget the historical conventionality of language arising from its "metaphoricity." Language is a construct that deludes us to infer unity between word and world, when that unity is nothing but interpretation. Similarly, our belief in the ability to communicate truly with other human beings in verbal language is but an illusion. Mauthner, like Karl Krauss, one of the fiercest critics of the Viennese cultural vacuity and linguistic sloppiness in his day, held that all language use is ideological. Thus he searched for an originary pure language, a search in which Hofmannsthal did not participate.

His position is closer to his fellow Viennese Wittgenstein, who argues in *Tractatus Logico-philosophicus,* completed by 1918 but published only in 1921, that philosophy is a battle against the bewitchment of our intelligence by means of language. That "about which we cannot speak must remain silent" because, according to Wittgenstein, a philosophy that aims at the logical clarification of thoughts has no room for metaphysical and ethical statements. Such statements do not constitute meaningful assertions. Although the unspeakable does exist, it will only "show" itself. This is the revelation Hofmannsthal seeks when he maintains, with Mauthner, that thought is essentially fluid, beyond linguistic utterances and superior to them. What is required, Chandos contends, is a condition that allows us "to think with the heart" (138), and hence complement the rational, logical investigations of the philosopher with an analysis of feeling.

Wittgenstein distinguishes between descriptions and experiences of the world. The *Chandos Letter* provides an analytical description of the experience of Wittgenstein's claim that language is the limit of our world. Only the epiphany of "a kind of feverish thinking, but thinking in a medium more immediate, more liquid, more glowing than words," a thinking that "too, forms whirlpools, but of a sort that does not seem to lead, as the whirlpools of language, into the abyss" will transport us into the self and thus into "peace" (140).

It is at the limits of language, the frontier where identities tremble and pass into something else, into the open and the void. The epiphany lays bare an experience of the pure pulse of being, but it also alters cognition. Hofmannsthal thus turns to an exploration of the ethical in language which he feels lyrical poetry cannot articulate adequately. With the *Chandos Letter,* the author begins to concentrate on work for the stage. Admitting the "spiritual foundation" derived from Mauthner's psychology of language as regards "the fluid ego," Hofmannsthal decides that changing expositions of the modern self can best be rendered in dramatic form. For the writer sees the task of the poet in the modern world where, in the words of Yeats, "things fall apart, the centre cannot hold," as one of having to knot together disparate elements. Analogous to Freud's dream work and Mach's research into sensations, the dramatist Hofmannsthal gathers the elements of a disintegrating world into a world of relations among them by revealing the hidden forms in which the parts of life are bound to each other. Mindful of the oscillating quality and ultimately untenable demand of language to speak truth by which to create unity, Hofmannsthal's plays, like the conversational piece *Der Schwierige* (1921; *The Difficult One*), depend largely on gesture. Language reconfigured as gesture interrupts the flow of talk and opens a different kind of space where, caught up in the living flux of things, human beings glimpse the momentary possibility of togetherness. Converging on the nodal point of the various concerns with the limits of verbal expressivity that pervade the crisis of language, Hofmannsthal asks, in the voice of *Der Schwierige,* for ways in which a speaker can act, if speaking always already constitutes a form of cognition of the futility of action. "How does the lonely self get to a point where it can tie *[verknüpfen]* itself into society?" How can a variable self "be insolubly bound to society?" In short, Hofmannsthal, like Wittgenstein, recognizes language as an ultimately ethical problem, which leads him to posit the question of the relationship between language and community.

See also 1897, 1899, 1910, 1911, 1929 (Autumn), 1953 (April)

Bibliography: Hugo von Hofmannsthal, *Selected Prose,* trans. Mary Hottinger and Tania and James Stern, intro. Hermann Broch. Bollingen Series XXXIII (New York: Pantheon Books,

1952). ———, *Gesammelte Werke in Einzelausgaben,* ed. Herbert Steiner (Frankfurt am Main: Fischer Verlag, 1951). Allan Janik and Stephen Toulmin, *Wittgenstein's Vienna* (New York: Simon and Schuster, 1973). William M. Johnston, *The Austrian Mind: An Intellectual and Social History 1848–1938* (Berkeley: University of California Press, 1972). Carl E. Schorske, *Fin-de-Siècle Vienna: Politics and Culture* (New York: Vintage, 1981). Stefan H. Schultz, "Hofmannsthal and Bacon: The Sources of the Chandos Letter," in *Comparative Literature,* XIII (Winter 1961): 1–15. George Steiner, "Silence and the Poet," in *Language and Silence: Essays 1958–1966* (Harmondsworth, U.K.: Penguin, 1969), 57–76.

Reingard Nethersole

♫ *1905*

Frank Wedekind is tried on charges of purveying obscene materials

Eroticism and the Femme Fatale

Bertolt Brecht once proclaimed that Frank Wedekind's greatest work was his personality. Most critics cast their votes in favor of the "Monstertragödie" (both a "monster tragedy" and a "tragedy of monsters") that was split in two and published under the titles *Erdgeist* (1895; *Earth Spirit*) and *Die Büchse der Pandora* (1904; *Pandora's Box*). While Wedekind was writing the first draft of what is known as the Lulu plays, he was fully aware of the work's potential shock effect. By abandoning the conventions of bourgeois theater and investing the play's representational energy in the seductive allure and destructive effect of a prostitute, Wedekind courted outrage, controversy, and even legal action. He was threatened several times with litigation and stood trial, with his publisher, in 1905, on charges of disseminating obscene materials. Wedekind first engaged in a spirited critique of the oppressive moral codes of bourgeois society in his play *Frühlings Erwachen* (1891; *Spring's Awakening*), showing how sexual repression breeds and deepens cultural anxieties, erotic perversions, and economic exploitation. Deeply influenced by Nietzsche and by 19th-century *Lebensphilosophie,* or vitalism, Wedekind's plays and essays were seen as endorsing the emancipation of the flesh and celebrating the pleasures and perils of sensuality.

Wedekind is difficult to align with any particular literary or theatrical movement and he can, therefore, be seen as something of a cultural iconoclast who lived up to the democratic sympathies reflected in his full name, Benjamin Franklin Wedekind. Unlike his father, who engaged in political polemics to undermine the authority of the Kaiser, Frank Wedekind mobilized satire to unmask the hypocrisy of bourgeois society and attack its oppressive institutions. For him, political freedom was useless in a culture that preached constant self-denial and promoted submission to authoritarian rule.

Breaking with classical theatrical conventions, Wedekind practiced a stylistic radicalism that led directly to the formal innovations of Expressionism and the epic theater of Bertolt Brecht. Conflating the tragic with the grotesque, blending high pathos with low comedy, creating characters who embody abstract principles and are devoid of psychological depth, stringing together epi-

sodes rather than mapping developmental trajectories, and drawing attention
to staging practices through self-conscious theatricality, Wedekind promoted a
spirit of experimentation that was to define modernist theater and direct its
creative efforts.

Lulu is Wedekind's most memorable dramatic creation. The Dadaist Richard Huelsenbeck saw her as a German incarnation of the *femme fatale,* a figure
that had become an icon of dreadful beauty in 19th-century literary and visual
culture. In the poetry of Charles Baudelaire, the prose of Théophile Gautier,
and in paintings by Dante Gabriel Rossetti, Edward Burne-Jones, and Gustave
Moreau, the *femme fatale* is a figure symptomatic of a crisis of masculinity at a
time of rapid social and cultural change. In his novel *A rebours* (1884; *Against
Nature*), J.-K. Huysmans, the French apostle of decadence, captures the strange
mix of anxiety and desire aroused by the *femme fatale.* She is, in his words,
framed as the "symbolic incarnation of undying Lust, the Goddess of immortal
Hysteria, the accursed Beauty exalted above all other beauties . . . , the monstrous Beast, indifferent, irresponsible, insensible, poisoning—like Helen of ancient myth—everything that approaches her."

The *femme fatale* harbors a threat that is not always transparent or predictable. Linked with discourses on sexuality, urbanization, technology, and modernity and associated with stylistic periods from the turn of the century—
decadence, symbolism, and art nouveau—the figure was reinvented in different cultural climates and received its generic label only in the early part of the
20th century. Biblical antecedents include Eve, Lilith, Jezebel, Delilah, Judith,
and Salomé, while classical precursors include Helen of Troy, Circe, Medusa,
Medea, and the Sirens. A figure of excess, the *femme fatale* serves as the site of
meditations on femininity, evil, beauty, sexuality, sterility, and death. Although
she can be seen as the carrier of power, she seems curiously deprived of agency,
for her aura of terror derives from fears linked to loss of control and the threat
of dissolution.

In the prologue to *Erdgeist,* Wedekind constructs Lulu as a creature of car-
nality and deceit, a literary successor to the figure of Lilith, whom Goethe had
resurrected for the temptation of Faust. She is introduced as "a true animal, a
wild, beautiful animal," and described as a snake that breeds evil, attracts, seduces, and poisons. The supreme danger of woman lies in her ability to mask
murderous intentions with a dazzling, attractive appearance. This essentialist
view of woman and her true nature is countered by Wedekind's other play,
which presents Lulu as an aggregate of cultural citations, a figure affiliated with
the biblical Eve and the mythical Pandora. That Lulu is fashioned from cultural
citations becomes even more evident in the play's many transparent references
to Goethe's *Faust* and Nietzsche's *Jenseits von Gut und Böse* (1886; *Beyond Good
and Evil*).

As the symbol of cultural fears and fantasies about women, Lulu adheres to
the conventional script for the *femme fatale.* Emptied of all personal, individualized passions and deprived of a social identity, she is characterized by a pathological lack of affect and uncertain parentage—even her name changes with

her interlocutors. She thus is the product of multiple mythical, biblical, and literary antecedents that combine to make her "the supreme incarnation of woman." She is described as an "angel of death" who leaves a trail of corpses in her wake. Yet Lulu also parodies and undermines the script for the *femme fatale* through her overly compliant, excessive enactment of the roles assigned to women in a patriarchal society. For this reason, critics have been divided in their views about the play, some condemning it for its re-inscription of socially repressive norms, others praising it for its emancipatory potential.

Lulu is invested with a subversive power that threatens the ego boundaries of the masculine subject as well as the stability of the entire social order. In one production, Lulu was referred to as a "rabble-rousing proletarian" whose transgressive spirit incites men to riotous living and social rebellion. By putting an end to Lulu's disruptive reign, Jack the Ripper becomes a kind of folk hero whose knife carries out what Karl Kraus called a "deed of liberation." That the original monster-tragedy comprising the two Lulu plays was prefaced with the dedication "To the Avenger" suggests that Wedekind saw Jack's deed as a form of social management rather than as a criminal act. In this context, it is worth noting that Wedekind himself played Jack the Ripper in the Viennese production of *Pandora's Box*.

While Lulu may be seen as destructive female sexuality incarnate, she may also be aligned, in a positive sense, with the spirit of instinct, flesh, and desire, that is, as a perfect embodiment of the pleasure principle, stifled and suppressed by bourgeois morality. The bourgeois subject, as Wedekind points out in an essay on Eros, continually defines itself through prohibitions and taboos. In constructing its identity against what is perceived as dirty, repulsive, crude, or corrupting, this subject produces a powerful form of transgressive desire that ceaselessly undoes the work of civilization.

For Wedekind, the phobic exclusion of sexuality from polite culture intensifies and perverts sexual desire. Yet erotic liberation promises more than it can deliver, for Lulu's nomadic sexuality ends in tragedy. The rhetoric of sexual emancipation, as Wedekind points out, is often deeply enmeshed with the repressive discourses from which it seeks to free itself. In his play *Die Zensur* (1908; *Censorship*), the playwright Buridan embraces a course of action to bring sexuality out of hiding, but this too turns out to be little more than a self-serving effort to master the threat of female sexuality through art and social control. Similarly, Wedekind's *Spring's Awakening* mounts a critique of Wilhelmine Germany, attacking its rigid educational system and its repressive family structures, but the hedonistic vitalism endorsed by the Masked Man at the end offers no real solution to the social problems the play exposes.

The iconic status of Wedekind's Lulu becomes evident in the powerful afterlife of *Earth Spirit* and *Pandora's Box*. Although the *femme fatale* had, in general, proliferated as an immobile and silent figure—much like the Sphinx she so often resembles— she was also endowed with a humanizing moral voice. Bizet's Carmen, Puccini's Turandot, Wagner's Venus, and Strauss's Salomé can all be seen as operatic precursors of Alban Berg's Lulu. Berg, who set Georg Büchner's *Woyzeck* to music (*Wozzeck,* 1925) and died while still at work on *Lulu,* was attracted by the idea of a controversial literary work as the vehicle for the revolutionary twelve-tone method with which he was experimenting. Transforming the figure of Alwa from playwright to composer, but retaining the full carnal details of the play's intrigues, Berg produced a richly textured drama that marked a radical departure from the elevated tone of operatic tradition.

Lulu also made her appearance in the cinematic culture of Weimar Germany, where she took her place with other vamps of the 1920s and 1930s, most notably Maria in Fritz Lang's *Metropolis* and Lola Lola in Joseph von Sternberg's *Der blaue Engel (The Blue Angel).* Lola Lola, based on the character Rosa Fröhlich in Heinrich Mann's novel *Professor Unrat* (1905), was also inspired by Wedekind's Lulu. The actresses who portrayed vamps on stage, on screen, and in real life—Marlene Dietrich, Pola Negri, and Theda Bara—owed much to Louise Brooks's impersonation of the Lulu figure in Georg Wilhelm Pabst's 1928 film *Pandora's Box.*

Though Pabst's film was not a commercial success, it came to occupy a central position in the iconography of feminine evil and fed into discourses on sexual cynicism in Weimar Germany. Like Wedekind, Pabst placed the socially marginal figure of the prostitute at center stage, fetishizing the figure of Lulu to show the lure and fascination of the stylized cinematic image. Pabst put into play figures of sexual transgression ranging from incest, sado-masochism, and lesbianism to prostitution, repressed homosexuality, and androgyny in a film that charts the relationship between what Siegfried Kracauer termed "social disintegration and sexual excesses." Thomas Elsaesser has argued that Pabst's *Büchse der Pandora* reflects more on the sensuality of its own medium than on the sexual climate of Weimar Germany and that the latter is merely a pretext for dwelling on the former. "The achievement of Pabst's film," he writes, "is to have presented sexuality *in* the cinema as the sexuality *of* the cinema, and to have merely used as his starting point the crisis in self-understanding of male and female sexuality that characterized his own period" (Elsaesser, 9).

Lulu's evolution from sexually empowered *femme fatale* to abject victim of male sexual violence runs parallel with a historical shift in representational practices from the turn of the century to the Weimar period. If artists and writers of the 1890s produced images of sexually predatory women, dwelling on their monstrous sensuality, their modernist counterparts seemed far more invested in showing women as victims of predatory male sexuality. In 1918, the artist George Grosz had himself photographed as Jack the Ripper, hiding behind a mirror with knife drawn, ready to assault a woman who is admiring her image. Grosz's photograph was taken at a time when the battle between the sexes in prewar Europe had reached its highest pitch. The First World War, with its unmanning horrors, intensified sexual conflicts and anxieties from the prewar era and produced a groundswell of sexual anger directed against women, who had cheered men on as they marched off to war, then had, presumably just as cheerfully, replaced them in the workplace.

While many of the artists, writers, and filmmakers of Weimar Germany may never have seen a trench or inhaled mustard gas, they were all implicated in the psychic fall-out of the war years: the sense of resentment directed against victors and noncombatants, a crisis of subjectivity occasioned by military defeat, and an acute sense of the body's vulnerability to fragmentation, mutilation, and dismemberment. During the war years and in the period following the armistice, the ravaging effects of war on the male body were put on display on the canvases of George Grosz and Otto Dix, in novels by Ludwig Renn and Erich Maria Remarque, and in combat memoirs by Ernst Toller and Ernst von Salomon. In the same era, sexual murder *(Lustmord)* came to figure prominently in Germany's artistic and literary production. Whether we look at the disemboweled prostitutes painted by Dix or read about the violent assaults on women in Döblin's novel *Berlin Alexanderplatz* (1929), it becomes clear that the representational energy once bestowed on producing what Bram Dijkstra calls "idols of perversity" was reinvested in morbid images of bodily fragmentation and dissolution.

Wedekind's Lulu plays have a kind of prescience in their presentation of woman as seductive temptress and as debased victim, as a cipher for male fears of being engulfed, and as a sign of the need to eradicate the threat of female sexuality. For Klaus Theweleit, these two conflicting images of women, joined in Wedekind's Lulu but generally separated in cultural production, are symptomatic of disturbances in the collective male psyche of prewar and postwar Germany.

Wedekind's valorization of Eros led to heightened understanding of the role of gender and sexuality not only in art but also in the culture of everyday life. After Wedekind, it became impossible to ignore sexual politics encoded in public discourses, aesthetic images, or political events. Even war, hitherto seen as a political conflict or framed as generational conflict, figured as part of a larger sexual struggle or battle of the sexes. In crafting a tragedy of monsters and a monster tragedy, Wedekind was able to disclose phobic anxieties and desires that would lead to a broader understanding of what was at stake in cultural conflicts, large and small.

See also 1831, 1882, 1928, 1929

Bibliography: Frank Wedekind, *Werke,* ed. Erhard Weidl (Munich: Winkler, 1990). ———, *Lulu: A Sex Tragedy,* trans. Charlotte Beck (London: Heinemann Educational, 1971). Virginia Allen, *The Femme Fatale: Erotic Icon* (Troy, N.Y.: Whitston, 1983). Thomas Elsaesser, "Lulu and the Meter Man: Pabst's *Pandora's Box* (1929)" in *German Film and Literature,* ed. Eric Rentschler (New York: Methuen, 1986), 40–59. Peter Jelavich, *Munich and Theatrical Modernism: Politics, Playwriting, and Performance, 1890–1914* (Cambridge, Mass.: Harvard University Press, 1985). Elizabeth Boa, *The Sexual Circus: Wedekind's Theatre of Subversion* (Oxford, U.K.: Basil Blackwell, 1987). Ward B. Lewis, *The Ironic Dissident: Frank Wedekind in the View of His Critics* (Columbia, S.C.: Camden House, 1997).

Maria Tatar

℥ 1906

Raphael Friedeberg is expelled from the German Social Democratic Party and joins the *Lebensreform* movement

An Alpine Vegetarian Utopia

In the early years of the 20th century the German social democrat Raphael Friedeberg launched a critique of the traditional definition of socialism as endorsed by the German Social Democratic Party (SDP) under the leadership of Karl Kautsky. In effect, Friedeberg's argument constituted a two-pronged challenge to traditional Marxist politics: first, by denouncing the parliamentarism of both the SPD and the Second International and calling for a political strategy based on the trade unions and the idea of the General Strike; and second, by defending anarchism, atheism, internationalism, antimilitarism, and direct action. These proposed political strategies stood in sharp contrast to the position taken by the SDP. In the ensuing quarrel with Kautsky, Friedeberg moved toward what he called an "anarcho-socialist" position. In particular, he criticized Marx's 1859 *Critique of Political Economy,* questioning the thesis that history was driven solely by economic factors. The stage was now set for both Friedeberg's expulsion from the Social Democratic Party, which took place in 1906, and for his defiant turn toward Kropotkin, rather than Marx, as the primary theorist of socialism.

Friedeberg had first visited the small Ticino town of Ascona in 1904 because of ill health, including a heart condition. According to Hans Manfred Bock and Florian Tennstedt, to whose writings on Friedeberg I am greatly indebted, it was probably Erich Mühsam who suggested a visit to Ascona. Following his expulsion from the SPD, Friedeberg returned there in 1906, still suffering from poor health. During his convalescence he renewed his acquaintance with Mühsam and generally integrated himself into the community of social rebels and misfits who had created at Ascona a utopian community dedicated to vegetarianism, bohemianism, naturism, theosophy, spirituality, nude sunbathing, the arts, especially music and dance, and a general program of *Lebensreform.* Ascona had become a new version of Schwabing, the bohemian quarter of Munich, an autonomous community that could pursue its anarcho-naturist agenda without harassment from civil or state authorities.

It may seem surprising at first that a small village in the Swiss mountains should play such a significant role in the development of German culture—or perhaps one should say counterculture. However, the Ticino had attracted exiled politicians, artists, and intellectuals as early as the 1860s, when the anarchist leader Mikhail Bakunin arrived in Locarno. By the end of the 1890s, Ascona first showed signs of becoming the center of a self-conscious counterculture. In 1900 a small group of Tolstoyans, vegetarians, and nature lovers could be found living in the hills above the village. During the same year, a small group of young people, who subsequently became the core of the Ascona counterculture community, met in Munich. These were Henri Oedenkoven from

Belgium, Ida Hofmann from Montenegro, the Austrian Karl Gräser, as well as Hofmann's sister, Jenny, Gräser's younger brother, Gusto, Ferdinand Bruser, another Austrian, and Lotte Hattemer, from Berlin. Most of them were firmly settled in Ascona by 1904.

The group's members had many different interests and talents, but all were eager to establish a community where they would be undisturbed in the pursuit of their interests, however eccentric they might seem to outsiders. At the Munich meeting, it was decided to divide the group into pairs to reconnoiter Switzerland for a suitable site. It was the Gräser brothers who eventually stumbled upon Ascona. Oedenkoven bought three and a half hectares of land on a hill overlooking the village, renaming it Monte Verità or Berg der Wahrheit (Mountain of Truth), and set about building a nature-cure sanatorium, followed by an art school and a workshop to make reform clothing. Although the commercial implications of these countercultural projects immediately caused a split among members—the Gräser brothers departed in protest—the sanatorium was completed in 1902. Its regimen included vegetarian meals, radical politics, sunbathing, airbathing, earth cures, water cures, discussions of theosophy and sexual radicalism, as well as recitals of Wagner's music. In due course, Hermann Hesse submerged his body in the earth of Ascona and Jacques Dalcroze, founder of eurhythmics, submitted to an eight-day fast.

The Gräser brothers eventually returned, Gusto to live in a cave and Karl in a wooden house constructed without metal parts, together with Jenny Hofmann, who wore clothes with buttons made from date pits. Also in 1902, the Asconans made a pilgrimage to Milan to meet Annie Besant, the theosophist, and Jenny's sister Ida published a feminist pamphlet, attacking the institution of marriage, patriarchal religion, and conventional education, while recommending Buddhism and the natural life, followed by her pamphlet, *Vegetarismus! Vegetabilismus!,* to promote vegetarianism as the gateway to feminism, pacifism, animal rights, and reform dress, among other radical goals. Two years later, in 1904, anarchism returned to Ascona in the person of Raphael Friedeberg, who turned Ascona into a center for itinerant anarchists, many of them political exiles.

In 1904, Friedeberg insisted that Erich Mühsam and Johannes Nohl must join him in Ascona. Since Mühsam and Nohl were both wanted by the German police at the time, they readily accepted the invitation. By 1906, Ascona was well known in the widening circle of *Lebensreform* supporters. This was the year in which Hermann Hesse came to visit Monte Verità. Also among the visitors was Otto Gross, an eccentric disciple of Freud, Kropotkin, and Stirner, who sought to link psychoanalysis with sexual radicalism and anarchism with antimoralism. As Martin Green has chronicled in detail, Gross's world overlapped not only with Ascona but also with that of Carl Jung, who became his analyst, and that of Max Weber, through his relationship with the von Richthofen sisters—Frieda, who subsequently married D. H. Lawrence, and Else, who married Weber's protégé Edgar Jaffe. Max Weber himself visited Ascona in the spring of 1914. Gross eventually fled Ascona, wanted by the police for questioning following the suicide of his lover Lotte Hattemer, one of the founders of the Monte Verità community. This strange, sinister man also exerted an intriguing influence on Franz Kafka, who met Gross in Prague, talked with him throughout his train journey back to Vienna, and met with him again subsequently at Max Brod's house.

As Hartmut Binder has pointed out, Kafka wrote *The Trial* during the year in which Otto Gross was arrested and imprisoned on the insistence of his father, a law professor, whose lectures Kafka had sat through week after week while he was at university. Max Brod, who was less susceptible to the counterculture than Kafka, was to write a novel, *Das grosse Wagnis* (1919; *The Great Venture*), featuring Dr. Askonas, the crazed leader of a dissident mountain community. Among other Asconians who influenced now-famous writers was Gusto Gräser. Hermann Hesse, who had surely read and was influenced by his German translation of the *Tao Tě Ching,* supported him when he got into trouble for his pacifist views and writings at the outbreak of war in 1914. At this time, Gräser left Ascona to spread the message of pacifism within Germany itself. Arrested, deported to Budapest, and put under psychiatric observation, he was eventually sentenced to six months in a military jail when he refused to swear allegiance to the flag. After the war, Gräser returned briefly to Ascona before leaving again for Munich, where he found that his old anarchist views no longer commanded respect in the new revolutionary climate, even though Erich Mühsam had been a major figure in the 1918 uprising and Edgar Jaffe had been appointed minister of commerce of the Bavarian Soviet Republic.

While later historians dubbed Ascona a "suburb of Schwabing," its political ethos was neither militant nor administrative enough to leave a lasting mark on events. Monte Verità remained an experiment in utopianism rather than a model for revolutionary politics. During the war years, Monte Verità became a refuge for dissidents and other fugitives from Germany. After his release from jail in 1924, the revolutionary playwright Ernst Toller came to Ascona, where he wrote his *Schwalbenbuch* (1924; *The Swallow-Book*). He returned again in 1933, following his expulsion from Germany by the Nazis. From the world of performance came the dancer and choreographer Rudolf Laban, who assembled around himself a dance troupe through which, with the help of his partners and protégées Suzanne Perrotet and Mary Wigman, he was to transform modern dance profoundly. It is worth noting that Isadora Duncan had visited Ascona in 1913; yet Wigman seems to have wished to distance herself from Duncan's legacy. After seeing Sophie Taeuber dance at the Dadaist Cabaret Voltaire in Zurich in 1917, Wigman adapted Dadaist ideas to her own dance practice.

Laban arrived in Ascona from Munich, where he had attracted the attention of the poet, dance critic, and theorist Hans Brandenburg, a protégé of Eugen Diederichs, the founder (in 1906) of the German Youth Movement, which was given to sun worship and neopaganism. Diederichs had also supported Gusto Gräser's follower Friedrich Muck-Lamberty, who led a strange pilgrimage of the long-haired and sandal-clad through Germany in 1920, singing and dancing and preaching. Diederichs and his circle represented another aspect of the nascent counterculture, one that was markedly more *völkisch,* that is, German national, in spirit. However, Diederichs supported not only Brandenburg, Laban, and Muck-Lamberty, but also Carl Gustav Jung, whose relationship with Ascona was quite close, although he settled in the canton of Zurich. It is interesting to note that even Max Weber was impressed by the spiritual feeling of Diederichs's German Youth Movement. Under Diederichs's influence, Ascona imbibed a strong dose of *völkisch* neo-paganism that flew in the face of the internationalist, libertarian roots of the community's founders.

Laban, in particular, revered the sun and showed interest in alchemy, numerology, magic, and other such beliefs. He also became interested in Ordo Templis Orientalis, a kind of countercultural freemasonry, established in Ascona by Theodor Reuss. His successor as master was the notorious magician Aleister Crowley. Another such group, which attracted the attention of Laban's lover Suzanne Perrotet, was the Mazdaznaan cult, founded in Switzerland by Otto Hanisch, also known as Ottoman Zar-Adusht Ha'nish. The Mazdaznaan movement preached vegetarianism, sun worship, and other doctrines freely adapted from Zoroastrian scriptures. In the 1920s, the Mazdaznaan movement still retained a residual influence on the ideas of visual artists associated with the Bauhaus. Laban, Wigman, and their group combined the dance aesthetic of Dalcroze with a Dionysian attachment to Nietzschean, cultic, and *völkisch* ideas: the ideas of creativity emerging from the landscape, of dance as invocation to the sun, of free love and corporeal thought, of service to the goddess with the seven stars on her brow. Laban's and Wigman's dance movement led, at first, to success and then, with a shift in the policy of the Nazi regime in 1936, to disenchantment and exile.

The Asconan legacy in dance was thus transferred from Germany to England and America, where the libertarianism and radicalism of Schwabing and the Dadaist Cabaret Voltaire in Zurich, a venue where many of the Laban dancers had once performed, finally overcame the conservative legacy of Diederichs and Brandenburg. Among the many other artists who had gathered in Ascona were not only Hans Arp and Sophie Taeuber but also Marianne von Werefkin and Alexei von Jawlensky, who arrived from Zurich on Easter 1918. Others were Otto Niemeyer and the Dutch painter Otto van Rees. In 1916, Hugo Ball, the founder of Dada, wrote to Tristan Tzara that he had found in Ascona "a multitude of stupid idiots who want to live in a state of nature, wandering around in sandals and Roman tunics." He was particularly incensed by the absence of books and newspapers. The painter El Lissitzky and his wife, Sophie Lissitzky-Küppers, visited Ascona in 1924 and noted disapprovingly that it was full of bizarre characters and strange sects.

Through Dada, Ascona intersected with the world of Emil Szittya and Blaise Cendrars, whose novel *Moravagine,* Green argues, was based on the case of Otto Gross. Cendrars, along with Hesse and Kafka, was among the writers who carried the Asconan message into the hall of fame of European literature. In 1920, the golden age of Monte Verità finally reached its end when Oedenkoven and Hofmann sold Monte Verità and departed. They eventually settled in Brazil, where they founded yet another sanatorium on the model of Monte Verità, once again putting on their sandals and tunics and a band around their shoulder-length hair, as Martin Green describes them in his book *The von Richthofen Sisters*. That same year, the Laban dancers also left Ascona. Remnants of the radical counterculture remained, but the extraordinary experiment had effectively run its course. Little of the golden days of utopian experiment survives, although the baths, sunk into the lawn for nude sun-bathing, are still there and visitors can still imagine they can hear the faint echoes of Ascona's unique contribution to 20th-century art and culture as they wander across the lawns and clamber, panting, up the slopes of Monte Verità.

The community of anarchists, vegetarians, nudists, and terpsichoreans gathered at Ascona in the first decade of the 20th century did not cause any great tremors in the history of European culture as a whole. It would be more accurate to say that the Asconan counterculture was the first in a cycle of countercultures that arose and faded away in decade after decade throughout the 20th century. These countercultures were not intellectual movements but lifestyle movements, attempts to break free from what were perceived as conservative strictures on individual freedom and experimentation. It is easy to see analogies between Ascona and the hippie communities of the 1960s, although few, if any, of the latter had any awareness of this distant predecessor. In this sense, the story of Ascona is just one chapter in the story of bohemianism, entangled, as it often was, with doctrines of free love, natural diets, and artistic self-expression. Looked at another way, we can see Ascona as a kind of detour on the long road of bohemianism, a stopover somehow combining Munich with Zurich—Expressionism and Dadaism, but also anarchism and pacifism.

The story of Ascona is of a kind of utopian attempt to bring into reality desires and aspirations mainstream society would inevitably suppress. The Asconan utopia lasted longer than most and it collapsed, not because its foundations were badly constructed, but because, in the end, it was too cut off from the rest of society to produce a real sense of fulfillment. It was too involved with beliefs and not enough with hard thinking. It failed, but it also set in motion ideas that would surface again and again in fresh configurations. While it lasted, it could properly be called a success, and it is for this reason that it can still inspire hope as well as scorn.

See also 1914, 1916, 1923, 1927 (June)

Bibliography: Martin Green, *Otto Gross, Freudian Psychoanalyst, 1877–1920: Literature and Ideas* (Lewiston, N.Y.: E. Meller Press, 1999). ———, *Mountain of Truth: The Counterculture Begins: Ascona 1900–1920* (Hanover, N.H.: University Press of New England, 1986). ———, *The von Richthofen Sisters* (New York: Basic Books, 1974). Harald Szeeman et al., *Monte Verità* (Locarno: Armando Dadò Electrice [1978?]). Susan A. Manning, *Ecstasy and the Demon* (Berkeley: University of California Press, 1993).

Peter Wollen

✑ *1910, January 27*

Rilke finishes dictating his novel *Die Aufzeichnungen des Malte Laurids Brigge* to a secretary at his publisher's house in Leipzig

Urban Experience and the Modernist Dream of a New Language

Rainer Maria Rilke's (1875–1926) *Malte* occupies a singular position in the history of modernist prose. Begun in Paris at a time of a pivotal crisis of the poet's creative imagination and finished, with some difficulty, far from Paris, Rilke's only novel is fundamentally concerned with poetic language, vision, and imagination. It tells the story of Malte, a twenty-eight-year-old Danish aristocrat whose artistic aspirations bring him to Paris, where he begins to record his life crisis, experiences, and memories in a series of diary-like notations. However, Rilke soon abandons, especially in the second part, the fictional convention of telling the story of an individual bound by defined space and chronological time. Fictional plot gives way to a series of literary and historical reflections. Read in light of this second part, even the first, a more direct narrative of Malte's traumatic reactions to city life, appears less like a novel and more like a concatenation of narrative fragments primarily controlled not by a storyline, but by a consciousness and subjectivity in crisis.

Thus it makes sense that Rilke should draw on the convention of the diary form. But here, too, the suggestion of a sequential fictional diary is abandoned as soon as it is introduced. There is only one conventional diary heading, the one on the first page, "September 11, rue Toullier." After that, the reader's expectation of a consistent progression in time and space is again undermined. The informed reader of Rilke will soon begin to wonder to what extent the figure of Malte serves as a screen for the poet himself—Rilke in Paris, his own life crisis as a poet, his sense of alienation and estranged perception, of ego loss or ego dispersal—all displaced and rewritten as the life crisis of a fictional figure. And, indeed, key passages are lifted almost verbatim from the poet's correspondence, not even rewritten, but simply copied into the text.

And yet, *Malte* is not simply a veiled autobiography either. The German title *Aufzeichnungen* gives a hint. "Notebooks" is an imprecise rendering. It weakens the tentative sense of "Aufzeichnung" as written notation, disjointed jottings; it loses its visual connotation as drawing *(Zeichnung)* or sketch; and it loses its documentary sense as a recording. Subjective and objective dimensions are merged in this very word, just as the usual separation of the written from the visual is suggestively overcome. Dispersal and fragmentation of text and subject alike are assumed. The micro-organization of the text into seventy-one distinct sections of varying length and weight corresponds to this sense of Aufzeichnungen at the level of form, just as Malte's key project in Paris, learning how to see, confirms it in the register of subjective consciousness and sensuous perception.

The literary result is a text that remains elusive both in content and in form.

But as soon as one focuses on the dispersed nature of these Aufzeichnungen, rather than searching for some unifying principle of composition, such as the *Bildungsroman* or the *Künstlerroman,* a key inspiration for Rilke's extraordinary prose emerges. It is Baudelaire's *Petits Poèmes en prose* (1869), also known by the earlier title *Le Spleen de Paris.* Baudelaire's seminal attempt, after the completion of *Les Fleurs du mal,* to write a form of poetic prose that captures the movements of the psyche is creatively continued in Rilke's *Malte.* At a key point in his reflections on writing, Malte copies a passage of Baudelaire's "A une heure du matin" (53), which articulates the writer's despair at not being able to produce poetic verse. Indeed, *Malte* as a whole can be read through the Baudelairean veil as an attempt to write the city in a new way, to create a poetic prose adequate to the confusing and disorienting experience of the modern metropolis, an experience that requires another, not yet known, mode of poetic expression beyond verse, meter, and rhyme, but also beyond fictional plot.

But the comparison with Baudelaire does pose a problem. In contrast to Baudelaire, Rilke is rarely seen as a poet of the city, and rightly so. We picture Rilke in the isolated North German artist colony of Worpswede; we remember the recluse on the Adriatic in Duino or at Muzot, the castle in the Alps, places that gave rise to the high ambition of his late poetry, the *Duino Elegies* and the *Sonnets to Orpheus.* In the poems of his Paris period, it is never the street, the bustle of people, the energy of urban movement that provide the material for the *Dinggedichte* of the *Neue Lieder.*

Paradoxically it was Rilke's anti-urban sensibility that gave rise to the figure of Malte, who may represent one of the most persuasive poetic embodiments of Georg Simmel's metropolitan type of individuality, and who projects Simmel's intensification of nervous stimulation in the extreme. But while subjective and objective culture do fall apart in Malte's experiences and perceptions, he is Simmel's metropolitan individual only with a significant traumatic twist. In Simmel, as in Walter Benjamin later on, the metropolitan type develops a protective organ that shields him from the onslaught of images and impressions. Malte, however, completely lacks this Freudian protection against stimuli *(Reizschutz)* that would either neutralize the shock experiences of modern urban life or strike poetic sparks out of the urban experience, as did Baudelaire.

The main problem Malte faces in his encounter with Paris, as a city of poverty, misery, and death, is his inability to protect himself against the onrush of stimuli and shocks. He is totally permeable to the outside world. Everything he sees and hears seems to go right through him, even to annihilate him. This inability to fend off the aggressions of the outside world is narratively linked to Malte's childhood on his family's estate, which he remembers with great intensity—and with an overwhelming sense of loss and disorientation—during his stay in Paris.

Here Rilke draws on a theme typical of the 19th-century novel, the move of the protagonist from country to city. But the paradigm is significantly re-written. It is not the innocence and naiveté of pre-urban life that give way to alienation and disillusionment in the city. Memories of Malte's childhood past and urban present are uncannily intertwined in his psyche, with one exacer-bating the other. The narrative suggests a fundamental affinity between the haunting psychic aspects of Malte's early childhood experience and his disrup-tive, fragmented perceptions of the modern city. Rilke probes a dimension of perception and experience not found in the reflections of either Simmel or Benjamin. Malte, the solitary foreigner in Paris, never becomes a man of the crowd. He is neither flaneur nor dandy, both of which would require some identification with metropolitan life, which Malte lacks. Issues of exchange, commodification, and consumerism, so prominent in Simmel and Benjamin, are all but absent from Rilke's urban world. And Benjamin's concern with the impact of modern media and information culture on the structure of experi-ence appears in Rilke at best as part of a vague, fairly unoriginal critique of the superficiality of modern civilization against which he posits his modernist writing.

At the same time, the novel can be read as a paradigm of the city affecting and radicalizing basic structures of perceptual experience in a way not imag-ined by Simmel, Benjamin, or Freud. Malte's inability to gird himself with an armor against the onslaught of urban shocks and stimuli, it turns out, is grounded in early childhood perceptions. Rather than parrying the shocks of metropolitan modernity and transforming them into verse—an image Benjamin took from Baudelaire's poem "Le Soleil"—Malte remains defense-less. The shocks penetrate him down to the deepest layers of unconscious memory traces, which hurl themselves into the quarry of childhood memo-ries, breaking loose large chunks that then rise to the surface and merge gro-tesquely with his view of city life.

In the first half of the story, Malte reproduces fragment upon fragment of his past, fragments that lack the explanatory intervention of the analyst or the interpretive framing of a narrative voice. The modernist narrative with its tor-tured subjectivity, its experimental ruptures and discontinuities, emerges out of the constellation of a childhood trauma of the fragmented body and the shat-tering and unavoidably fragmentary experience of the metropolis. The ab-sence of an adequate *Reizschutz,* resulting from Malte's insufficiently devel-oped ego structure, determines the course and structure of the narrative.

It is particularly the haunting imagery of the body that couples childhood trauma with the threatening encounters with figures and events in the city. The narrative is littered with descriptions of body fragments that take on a life of their own and disrupt the imaginary unity of the body surface. Clearly, these are not oedipal anxieties of loss in the sense of Freudian castration anxiety. Rather they are anxieties of excess, of overflowing, of volatile boundaries be-tween the inner and the outer world, carrying a ubiquitous threat of invasion of the self. However, these experiences of excess are not to be misread as exu-berant expansions of self, as a Deleuzean dynamic of liberated flows of desire in a schizoid body, nor do they represent the pleasurable symbiotic merger of self and other as in Freud's "oceanic feeling." Rilke's persistent use of the imagery of disease and filth, aggression and death points in a different direction.

The paradox is that these visions of bodily excess carry with them a phantasmagoria of loss and death, a voiding of all sense of self. Malte describes himself as a nothing that begins to think, a blank piece of paper waiting to be written on. The voiding of the self appears as a precondition for the new mode of writing the text itself aspires to. But this condition for writing is indissolubly linked to the visual, to Malte's project of learning to see in a novel way. This new vision takes shape in the famous passage in which Malte describes his horrifying, almost hallucinatory view of the residual inside wall of a demolished house, now the outside wall of the adjacent building. The rust-spotted open channels of toilet pipes, the residue of moldy paint, and pieces of wallpaper still sticking to the walls of bedrooms at various heights are nauseating traces of a decayed, ghostly interior. This interior has now become the exterior, a visual, spatial urban void captured with images of bodily decay, of digestion, filth, and disease. Malte is terrified and runs (45–48).

The dissolution of boundaries here obliterates all differentiation between the animate and the inanimate, between body and things, the perceiving subject and built urban space in both its real and phantasmagoric manifestation. However, this experience of terror, which would be enough to overwhelm any oversensitive, but deep-down authentic subject, cannot be attributed to the city alone. No, the terror, as Malte writes, is already at home inside of him.

Even if Malte initially hopes to find some relief from the city by remembering his non-urban childhood, it soon turns out that his childhood itself is packed with similarly horrifying, uncanny experiences. If Malte's loneliness in Paris makes him want to escape into the past, the past provides no relief. His childhood traumas resurface with a vengeance, but the reader never quite knows whether the city triggers childhood memories or whether these memories structure and shape Malte's city experience in the first place.

Malte's uncanny experiences have been variously explained in Freudian oedipal, Kleinian pre-oedipal, Lacanian, and Winnicottian terms, but the text eludes such approaches which, by focusing on Malte/Rilke's familial relations, usually ignore the dynamic links between childhood anxieties and city experience. They also pay scant attention to Malte's fearful identification with fragile objects, his fear of going to pieces, which not only marks key experiences of the child and of the young adult, but energizes and shapes his writing project. In a key passage that weaves together shattering objects with the fragmented body, Malte conjures up an image of apocalypse in writing and language that might bring all his pains to an end:

> For the time being, I can still write all this down, can still say it. But the day will come when my hand will be distant, and if I tell it to write, it will write words that are not mine. The time of that other interpretation will dawn, when not one word shall be left upon another, and every meaning will dissolve like a

cloud and fall down like rain. [. . .] this time, I will be written. I am the impression that will transform itself. It would take so little for me to understand all this and assent to it. Just one step, and my misery would turn into bliss. But I can't take that step; I have fallen and I can't pick myself up because I've gone to pieces.

(52f.; translation corrected)

See also 1899, 1902, 1922 (February), 1929 (October), 1936 (February)

Bibliography: Rainer Maria Rilke, The Notebooks of Malte Laurids Brigge, trans. Stephen Mitchell (New York: Vintage, 1985). Andreas Huyssen, "Paris/Childhood: The Fragmented Body in Rilke's Notebooks of Malte Laurids Brigge," in Andreas Huyssen and David Bathrick, eds., Modernity and the Text: Revisions of German Modernism (New York: Columbia University Press, 1989), 113–141. David Kleinbard, The Beginning of Terror: A Psychological Study of Rainer Maria Rilke's Life and Work (New York: New York University Press, 1993). Friedrich Kittler, Discourse Networks 1800/1900 (Stanford, Calif.: Stanford University Press, 1990), 315–336. Walter Sokel, "The Devolution of the Self in The Notebooks of Malte Laurids Brigge," in Frank Baron, Ernst S. Dick, and Warren R. Maurer, eds., Rilke: The Alchemy of Alienation (Lawrence: Regents Press of Kansas, 1980).

Andreas Huyssen

♫ 1911, January 25

Der Rosenkavalier, keystone of the twenty-year collaboration of Hugo von Hofmannsthal and Richard Strauss, premieres in Dresden

The Agency of the Past

The first operatic collaboration between the Austrian poet and playwright Hugo von Hofmannsthal (1874–1929) and the Munich-born composer Richard Strauss (1864–1949), Der Rosenkavalier ("The Cavalier of the Rose," or perhaps better, "Messenger of the Rose"), remained their greatest popular success. Both libretto and score are undoubtedly among the richest and most finely crafted of any up to that time (or since), bearing comparison to the collaboration of Mozart and Lorenzo Da Ponte in Le nozze di Figaro (1786) and Giuseppe Verdi and Arrigo Boito in Falstaff (1893), as well as to Richard Wagner's opera Die Meistersinger von Nürnberg (1868). Indeed, significant traces of all three of these celebrated operatic comedies can be found in Der Rosenkavalier. Critics preoccupied with revolutionary modernist aesthetics in the early decades of the 20th century, particularly in Hofmannsthal's Vienna, have often been skeptical, if not outright hostile, toward a work so deeply steeped in the past. What was initially termed the "regressive" appearance of Der Rosenkavalier was exacerbated by the consciously avant-garde profile of the pair of one-act operas Strauss had composed just before, Salome (1905), based on a translation of Oscar Wilde's one-act play, and Elektra (1909), for which Strauss abridged Hofmannsthal's drama of 1904. But as that modernist legacy has become more fully subsumed into history, we can perhaps better appreciate the distinctive counterpoint of historical milieus evoked by the opera's text and music, ranging from a late-Baroque Vienna to that of J. N. Nestroy and Josef Lanner in the 1830s and 1840s, of Johann Strauss Jr. and Johannes Brahms in the 1880s, even up to that of the painter Gustav Klimt and the "Secession" and of Sigmund Freud, Gustav Mahler, and Arnold Schoenberg.

Midway through the composition of *Elektra,* Strauss and Hofmannsthal began discussing ideas for a comic opera drawn on the memoirs of Casanova, an interest Hofmannsthal had initiated in his comedy *Der Abenteurer und die Sängerin* (1898; *The Adventurer and the Singer*) and was now developing in a second play, *Christinas Heimreise* (1910; *Christina's Voyage Home*). Neither play was ever adapted for music, however. Instead, within two weeks of the premiere of *Elektra,* Hofmannsthal announced a plan for a neo-Rococo comedy he had drawn up with the help of Count Harry Kessler on the basis of characters and situations from Molière, Louvet de Couvray, and Beaumarchais. "I have spent three quiet afternoons here," he wrote from Weimar on February 11, 1909, "drafting the full and entirely original scenario for an opera, full of burlesque situations and characters, with lively action . . . It contains two big parts, one for a baritone [a role Hofmannsthal later changed to a soprano] and another for a graceful girl dressed up as a man, à la [Geraldine] Farrar or Mary Garden. Period: the old Vienna under Empress Maria Theresia." Calling this scenario "entirely original," despite its nearly complete reliance on literary "found objects," is wholly characteristic of Hofmannsthal. For him, the originality lay in his manner of reviving and to some extent reinventing the literary past.

The *Rosenkavalier* libretto is the most deeply rooted in literary history of all Hofmannsthal wrote for Strauss. The elaborately layered historical texture was well suited to the temperaments of librettist and composer alike, however different they often seemed to be in other respects. For much of his career, Hofmannsthal worked best when adapting texts from the European literary canon. Strauss, too, was a synthesizer of sorts, having traced a stylistic trajectory from Mendelssohn and Schumann to the brink of atonality and Expressionism. Furthermore, he was deeply versed in the symphonic and operatic repertoire of the Classical and Romantic eras through his extensive conducting career. The prescient postmodern aura of the *Rosenkavalier* score was a result of the composer's decision to cut loose from the imperative of material, technical progress that drove his younger Viennese colleagues (the Schoenberg school) and, like Hofmannsthal himself, to cultivate in new ways a whole spectrum of inherited traditions.

The principal characters of *Der Rosenkavalier* have multiple literary and musical precursors. Molière's *Monsieur de Porceaugnac* (1669) was the starting-point: the bumptious, uncouth gentleman from the countryside who comes to town to woo a younger, wealthy bride, but whose presumption is finally foiled by the girl and her younger suitor. Molière's porcine leading role is transformed to a bovine one in the figure originally intended as the title character of Hofmannsthal's piece, Baron Ochs ("ox") auf Lerchenau. Ultimately, though, Ochs's truest spiritual avatar is Shakespeare's Falstaff (by way of

Verdi's): a fat, jovial, sensualist cavalier whose impecunious circumstances in no way undermine his self-esteem, and whose willingness to delude himself belies, at times, a more fundamental worldly wisdom.

By casting the young "messenger of the rose," Octavian, as a mezzo-soprano trouser-role, Hofmannsthal and Strauss introduced a conscious allusion to Cherubino in Mozart's *The Marriage of Figaro.* As in this operatic version of the Beaumarchais comedy, circumstances contrive to disguise the cross-dressed mezzo as a girl, ironically bringing the travesty game full circle. The older woman to whom the adolescent boy is first attracted, the *Feldmarschallin* or field-marshal's wife (familiarly, the Marschallin), begins as an analogue to the Countess in *Figaro,* neglected by her husband and wistful for days gone by. Ultimately, however, she descends from the Marquise in Couvray's *Aventures du Chevalier de Faublas* (1781), an experienced noblewoman who introduces a cross-dressing adolescent to the secrets of love. In yielding Octavian to a younger spouse, with pensive resignation, the Marschallin also resembles Wagner's Hans Sachs, who does the same for Eva in *Die Meistersinger.*

The nouveau-riche father of the bride, Herr von Faninal, has many precedents in 17th- and 18th-century comedy, starting with the gullible paterfamilias figures of Molière's comedies, *Le Bourgeois Gentilhomme* and *Les Fourberies de Scapin.* The crux of the opera's plot, and one of its few original elements, is Octavian's mission to present the young Sophie von Faninal with a ceremonial silver rose on behalf of her official suitor, Baron Ochs. But even here, the motif of love's messenger becoming love's object has its own venerable comic pedigree, for example Viola/Cesario in Shakespeare's *Twelfth Night,* where cross-dressing figures even more centrally.

Hofmannsthal fleshed out the ambience of late-Baroque Vienna using a wide range of period sources. The second scene of the opera's first act, in which the Marschallin receives a motley crew of vendors, servants, and solicitors while Baron Ochs discusses the dowry of his intended bride with a notary, is closely modeled on details from William Hogarth's picture "The Countess's Morning Levée" from his series entitled "Marriage à la mode" (1745). Details borrowed from Hogarth include the lady at her vanity table, an attendant hairdresser, an African pageboy and a smaller boy in Moorish costume, a singer accompanied by flute, and a humble female petitioner. The faintly archaic, socially calibrated tone of the libretto reflects Hofmannsthal's intimate knowledge of Austrian history and literature generally as well as his study of the Viennese court diaries of Prince Johann Josef Khevenhüller from the 1740s. From these and other contemporary sources, he drew many other details, names, social functions, etiquette, décor, and incidental period references. He took particular pride in the historically and socially multi-layered dialect he had constructed in his libretto. In a coyly titled "Unwritten Afterword" to the opera, published in *Der Merkur* in March 1911, Hofmannsthal defended himself against charges of having constructed the "picture of a past epoch" in any laborious, documentary sense: "The language is to be found in no book, though it remains in the air, for more of the past is preserved in the present than one suspects." The continuing agency of the past—political, social, literary, and personal—within the present was, indeed, an article of faith underlying much of Hofmannsthal's oeuvre.

Richard Strauss's musical score presents an even more elaborate kaleidoscope of idioms, high and low, past and present. Heard across Hofmannsthal's characters, their language, and the fastidious neo-Rococo of Alfred Roller's original sets and costumes, even Strauss's distinctively modern refinements take on a period air. The complex, overlapping rhythms and dissonant layering of the woodwind birdcalls that announce the morning after Octavian's and the Marschallin's night of lovemaking in the first scene, for example, are much closer in technique to Stravinsky's *Rite of Spring* than to the stylized pastoral effects of 18th-century music. In context, however, they convey a feeling of delicately crafted artifice, mediating between a Rococo world of musical clocks or mechanical birds and a modern mode of realistic, even scientific observation. Strauss realizes this languid bedroom scene, reminiscent of paintings by Boucher or Fragonard, with a "technological" sophistication grounded in the age of photography and recording.

The music of the opera's opening scene as a whole "records," as it were, the history of Austro-German opera, from Christoph Willibald Gluck to Wagner and beyond, while subjecting its models to parody and critique. The orchestral prelude, for example, is an invisible scene of frenzied Wagnerian lovemaking. Contrasting masculine and feminine motives embrace, urging each other on through mounting harmonic sequences until the ensemble of whooping French horns signals, graphically and almost comically, a somewhat premature climax—appropriate to the enthusiastic amorous novice Octavian, though amusingly at odds with the romantic dignity of the Wagnerian model. In this detail, Strauss was able to score a small victory against the censorship that initially plagued Hofmannsthal's libertine libretto, while also anticipating a more explicit Wagnerian parody in the ensuing dialogue. Alluding to the metaphysical colloquy of Tristan and Isolde at the center of Wagner's eponymous music drama, Octavian broods over language as a barrier to transcending the isolated subject: "What means this 'you' and 'I'? They are mere words; and yet, there is something in them, dizzying, tugging, yearning, and pressing, something languishing and smoldering." Then the exalted Wagnerian tone of both text and music modulates abruptly to the language of the nursery, the Marschallin addressing him as her "sweet little boy" ("Du bist mein Bub, du bist mein Schatz"). Like Tristan, Octavian longs for the night and curses the daylight, but his solution is simply to pull the blinds, with cartoonish assistance from the orchestra. A moment later, the two are drinking hot chocolate from small porcelain cups, accompanied by a Rococo minuet of calculated preciosity: now the would-be Wagnerian hero is reduced to a Dresden-china figurine, underscoring the inherently epicene character of the mezzo-soprano impersonating an adolescent 18th-century nobleman.

When Octavian disguises himself as a chambermaid to elude the Marschallin's visitor, Baron Ochs, the music adopts a Viennese waltz idiom of more recent vintage. The immediate and lasting popularity of *Der Rosen-kavalier* is due in large part to Strauss's liberal deployment of the sentimental-lyrical waltz style throughout the score. Apparently it had been Hof-mannsthal's idea to introduce "an old-fashioned Viennese waltz, sweet and yet saucy," which should "pervade the whole of the last act," as he put it in a letter to Strauss of April 24, 1909. Strauss extended this concept to a whole series of waltz tunes, variously woven through the entire opera, to characterize Octavian's disguise, Ochs himself, and the popular "spirit" of Vienna, gener-ally. The anachronism of the late-19th-century waltz style suffusing Hof-mannsthal's portrayal of Theresian Vienna is an appropriate signature to the work as a whole. Relating to the prototype of the composer's universally pop-ular namesake (Johann Strauss Jr.) as homage and parody at once, the *Rosen-kavalier* waltzes mingle with ersatz Rococo—the "minuet" and Italian tenor aria of Act 1—neo-Wagnerian passion, and avant-garde descriptive effects. The result is a musical parallel to that interpenetration of past and present Hofmannsthal had sought to achieve, in more recondite form, in his earlier poetry and plays.

Consciousness of time, of history at the personal level, is the special attri-bute of the Marschallin. Her brief moment of self-reflection toward the end of Act 1 stands out because it is the first and only time any character is alone on stage during this otherwise busy act. Strauss matches this exceptional situation with the lightest scoring of any passage in the opera, allowing the Marschallin's reflections on the paradoxes of outer change and inner continuity of subjective consciousness to emerge clearly as text. The exposed condition of her words is emblematic of an unguarded revelation of the inner self. As such, it could be seen as a tribute to the historical aesthetic of the opera aria, a formalized ges-ture of reflection and self-presentation. In her other great moment, the trio crowning the final scene of the opera, the Marschallin is again reflecting by herself, but now in the presence of the newly formed couple, Octavian and Sophie. This, too, is a typically operatic moment, a contemplative ensemble in which the characters conduct aria-like internal monologues, but here, the har-monic intertwining of the three soprano lines manifests their mutual presence and the social bonds they are in the process of negotiating.

Count Harry Kessler commemorated his friend in a diary entry of July 19, 1929, several days after Hofmannsthal's sudden death from stroke. "With Hofmannsthal a whole chapter of German culture has been carried to the grave." He was "one of the last great baroque poets, belonging to that same tree whose finest fruits were Shakespeare and Cervantes." Kessler defines this transhistorical baroque aesthetic as "the grafting of genuine feeling upon con-sciously artificial matter."

This account of Hofmannsthal's "baroque" sensibility applies to much of his oeuvre, from the Renaissance settings of the early verse dramas to the prin-cipal work of his later years, *Der Turm* (1925; *The Tower*), the product of a life-long preoccupation with Calderón's *Life Is a Dream*. Above all, it applies to the work Kessler himself helped to create, *Der Rosenkavalier.* In this reading, the baroque qualities of the work are not so much found in its re-creation of a mid-18th-century ambience as in the attitudes behind it, the ways in which the libretto and music celebrate their own artificiality. Delight in artifice, in literary masks and conventions, also constitutes an important ingredient of the opera's actual modernity, especially when overlaid with distinctly contemporary concern for subjectivity and historical awareness.

The central scene of the opera, Octavian's "presentation of the rose" to Sophie, is emblematic of this studied artificiality, and of the work's simultaneous commitment to the baroque and the modern. Strauss's setting of the presentation scene is tonally grounded, but in the unusual, one might even say "artificial-seeming" key of F-sharp major. The vocal lines cleave closely to this tonic key, timidly and decorously, while the orchestra suggests the shimmering hues of the silver rose and the quasi-exotic preciousness of the setting with cascades of apparently unrelated triads sounded by flutes, celesta, harps, and high, muted violins. Like much of the score, the scene evokes a decorative, quasifamiliar past with complex, even slightly disorienting modern means.

For much of the 20th century, critics dismissed *Der Rosenkavalier* as a nostalgic confection, pandering to a hedonistic, essentially philistine late-bourgeois public. Certainly there is a strong valedictory strain to the piece, a farewell of sorts to an operatic tradition spanning two centuries and now entering its twilight phase. Nonetheless, the polished artifice of its surfaces, the linguistic self-consciousness, the formal play with literary and musical conventions, the element of subjectivity accorded to comic masks and dramatic tropes all permit *Der Rosenkavalier* to claim its place in a modernist genealogy. At the same time, in espousing uninhibitedly pluralistic values in place of contemporary ideological imperatives of progress, this collaborative venture turned out to be more genuinely forward-looking than anyone might have predicted.

See also 1791, 1876, 1902, 1928, 2001

Bibliography: Hugo von Hofmannsthal, *Sämtliche Werke,* vol. 23 (*Operndichtungen* I), ed. Dirk O. Hoffmann and Willi Schuh (Frankfurt am Main: Fischer, 1986). Willi Schuh, ed., *Hugo von Hofmannsthal, Richard Strauss: Der Rosenkavalier—Fassungen, Filmszenarium, Briefe* (Frankfurt am Main: Fischer, 1971). Richard Strauss, *Der Rosenkavalier,* orchestral score (Berlin and Paris: Adolf Fürstner, 1910; rept. New York: Dover, 1987). *A Working Friendship: The Correspondence between Richard Strauss and Hugo von Hofmannsthal,* trans. Hanns Hammelmann and Ewald Osers (New York: Random House, 1961). Hermann Broch, *Hugo von Hofmannsthal and His Time: The European Imagination 1860–1920,* ed. and trans. Michael P. Steinberg (Chicago and London: University of Chicago Press, 1984). Bryan Gilliam, ed., *Richard Strauss and His World* (Princeton, N.J.: Princeton University Press, 1993). Alan Jefferson, *Richard Strauss: Der Rosenkavalier,* Cambridge Opera Handbook (Cambridge, U.K.: Cambridge University Press, 1985). William Mann, *Richard Strauss: A Critical Study of the Operas* (London: Cassell, 1964). Mathias Mayer, *Hugo von Hofmannsthal* (Stuttgart and Weimar: J. B. Metzler, 1993).

Thomas S. Grey

1912, March

Gottfried Benn completes his studies in dermatology and shocks the public with a volume of poetry on medical themes

Provocation and Parataxis

A drunken corpse on a table with an aster wedged between its teeth. A nest of young rats in the stomach cavity of a drowned girl. An undertaker pulling a gold tooth from the mouth of a prostitute and heading off to a dance. A woman lying on a pillow of dark blood, her throat slit open with a knife. These images dominate the first four poems of Gottfried Benn's (1886–1956) five-poem cycle *Morgue*. "Requiem" concludes the series with an inversion of Christian motifs. Throughout, the poet's attention and rhetoric are trained on human body parts and surrounding images, the flower, the rats. *Morgue* was published together with four other poems in March 1912, and the first edition of five hundred copies sold out in eight days. One poem evokes macabre images of sick and screaming whores, prisoners, and outcasts. "Mann und Frau gehn durch die Krebsbaracke" (Man and Woman Walk through the Cancer Ward) contains grotesque portrayals of the cancer ward:

> Hier diese Reihe sind zerfallene Schöße
> und diese Reihe ist zerfallene Brust.
> Bett stinkt bei Bett. Die Schwestern wechseln stündlich.
> . . . . .
> Nahrung wird wenig noch verzehrt. Die Rücken
> sind wund. Du siehst die Fliegen. Manchmal
> wäscht die Schwester. Wie man Bänke wäscht.

> Here these rows are decaying wombs
> and this row is decaying breast.
> Bed stinks beside bed. The nurses change shifts hourly.
> . . . . .
> Little food is taken. The backs
> have wounds. You see the flies. Sometimes
> the nurse washes them. As one washes a bench. (1:16)

The use of synecdoche and metaphor underscores the depersonalization.

These provocative images shocked the bourgeois audience of the day and were rejected by all but the most avant-garde as scandalous and disgusting. One critic lamented: "Ugh! What an unbridled imagination, devoid of any intellectual decency, is there exposed; what disgusting delight in the abysmally ugly, what malicious pleasure in bringing to light things that cannot be changed" (quoted in Hohendahl, 26). Another warns: "Anyone who intends to read these . . . poems should prepare a stiff drink. A very stiff drink!!!" (quoted in Hohendahl, 91). Here the decay of the body is presented without any sense of nobility or transcendence. More brutal and grotesque than Baroque portrayals of decay and without contrasting images of transcendence, the poems are a cold, irreverent challenge to human dignity. For Benn no longer the summit of creation, the human being is shown with bodily functions, including decay and dissolution, stench and obliteration. The death of a girl makes possible the "beautiful youth" of the rats that live off her body (1:11). The second section of "Der Arzt" (1917; "The Doctor") opens with the unsettling line "Die Krone der Schöpfung, das Schwein, der Mensch" ("The pinnacle of creation, the swine, man"; 1:14). Humanity is reduced to biology, the dissolution of the body, decay, death.

Even the choice of themes was unconventional in art, especially poetry. The images are revolting and overwhelming. The message is despair over the inability to counter decay with transcendence of any kind. Benn undermines not only the notion of humanity as the pinnacle of creation, but the concept of human life as having any higher meaning whatsoever. The form too is unusual. Benn, a practicing physician in his mid-twenties, mixes the language of science and dissection with the vocabulary of the everyday and the rhetoric of religion and poetry. The form is for the most part unrhymed free verse. The very first poem, "Kleine Aster" ("Little Aster"), underscores the disjunction between title and content. The thoracic cavity of the corpse becomes the stunning image of a vase for the beautiful flower. The body is dissolved into parts, including the brain, which is bereft of any greater significance. The poetic self does not reach out to nature or another self; he coldly dissects the body parts. The images are often paratactic, unrelated. When they are not grotesque, they border on the ironic, as in the poem "Requiem": "Den Schädel auf. Die Brust entzwei" ("The skull open. The breast in two"; 1:13). What remains intact is only the artistic craft of the poems themselves; everything else seems bereft of higher meaning.

Benn's foray into the unusual and grotesque can be seen as part of the wider movement of literary Expressionism, which spanned the decade from 1910 to 1920. The historical presuppositions of Benn's poetics and the development of Expressionism are manifold. In Germany the Industrial Revolution started late but made quick strides. In 1871, when Germany became a unified country, nearly two-thirds of the population lived in rural areas; by 1925 nearly two-thirds lived in urban areas. Berlin, where Benn lived during those years, grew from 1 million in 1880 to 2 million in 1910 and to more than 4 million in 1920. The crowded German cities of the early 20th century were turbulent and imposing, noisy and problem-ridden, vibrant and dynamic places.

From 1871 until the outbreak of the First World War, Germany enjoyed unprecedented political stability. Most of the Expressionist authors were born in this era between 1885 and 1895. Benn was born in 1886. After Bismarck had united Germany, an entire generation of Germans did not experience war. Traditional societal values remained intact, including the elevation of order, authority, and obedience. Life was stable, in the eyes of some, sterile. Many greeted the war as a release from the banality of life.

Germany's intellectual world was changing as rapidly as were its cities and industry. At the end of the 19th century, Friedrich Nietzsche had sealed for the

Expressionist generation the idea that transcendent values were a fiction, a human invention for the purpose of imposing power on others. Values did not correspond to any intrinsic truths; they were fictions, empty of higher meaning. Nietzsche's pronouncements precipitated a crisis of consciousness, with no clear orientation to fill the vacuum left by lost values.

Though specifically German, the Expressionists were influenced by a wide range of international figures: Walt Whitman, Charles Baudelaire, Stéphane Mallarmé, Arthur Rimbaud, and Filippo Tommaso Marinetti, to name only the poets. Marinetti visited Berlin one month after the publication of *Morgue,* and a translation of one of his Futurist manifestoes was published there that spring. Abstraction and distortion in art, along with the elevation of anxiety as a theme, culminating in the influential works of the Norwegian painter Edvard Munch, were also part of this general intellectual current and were represented in Germany by two major groupings of Expressionist artists, "Die Brücke" ("The Bridge") in Dresden and later Berlin, with Ernst Ludwig Kirchner and Karl Schmidt-Rottluff, among others, and "Der Blaue Reiter" ("The Blue Rider") in Munich with Wassily Kandinsky and Franz Marc, among others.

Literary Expressionism, unlike Futurism, was not a conscious grouping of authors, but a loose set of writers who published in some of the same journals and whose writings had a variety of common themes and features. The two most prominent Expressionist journals were both published in Berlin, *Der Sturm (The Storm),* beginning in 1910, and *Die Aktion (Action),* beginning in 1911. The foremost lyrical theme was no longer nature, but urban life, which led to its own genre designation, *Großstadtlyrik* (big city poetry). Poets drew on smells, sounds, modes of transportation, commerce, technology, and the bustle of city life for poetic themes. The city was portrayed as both daemonic and dynamic. As in painting, so in poetry, the modern metropolis was feared and criticized, but was no less a source of fascination. City life alienates and poisons; it is impersonal and materialistic, yet also vibrant and multifarious. Georg Heym's "Der Gott der Stadt" (1910; "The God of the City") inverts the traditional rhetoric: the church steeples are transformed into the black factory chimneys, and the city is an insatiable deity or demon to whom millions pray and from which they blindly seek their salvation. Related to the theme of the metropolis is technology. While technology seems to carry on a life of its own, the individual becomes increasingly an object, without life or soul.

A loss of higher meaning and purpose is also prominent. Heym writes in "Mitte des Winters" (published posthumously, 1922; "The Middle of Winter"): "Weglos ist jedes Leben. Und verworren / ein jeder Pfad" (Pathless is every life. And confused / Each and every path). Life is spatially and temporally disjointed. Neither past nor future has any significance. This crisis stems in part from the disenchantment with the increasing rationalization of society. The desire of the intellect to be free isolates and perverts the vital instincts. In his early works, Benn expresses a desire for loss of the self, a giving over to the subrational and the primitive, and a yearning to abandon the overly cerebral:

"Den Ich-Zerfall, den süßen, tiefersehnten" ("The disintegration of self, sweet and deeply longed-for" ("Kokain," 1917; "Cocain"). Suicide becomes a major motif, as in Albert Ehrenstein's "Der Selbstmörder" (1917; "Suicide"):

> Ich grüße den Tod
> Denn Sein ist Gefängnis,
> Im Hirn haust Qual,
> das Auge verengt Welt,
> und schlecht ist Geschlecht,
> es vermehrt sich.
>
> I welcome death.
> For being is a prison,
> Agony lives in the brain,
> The eye constricts the world
> And the species is specious,
> It multiplies.

The flight from consciousness is also central to Benn's early prose works. His Rönne stories, for example, "Gehirne" (1914; "Brains"), relate the anguish of the brain surgeon Rönne. Characterized by discontinuity, much like Benn's poetry, the stories depict dismemberment of reality along with the dissolution of the coherent self.

The sense of dissolution is collective, not simply individual, and it is related to the crisis of transcendence. "Es ist ein Weinen in der Welt / Als ob der liebe Gott gestorben wär" ("There is a weeping in the world, / As if the good Lord had died") writes Else Lasker-Schüler in "Weltende" ("End of the World") as early as 1905. The sense of collective crisis involves attacks on bourgeois sterility, hypocrisy, and narrowness, partly motivated by the common theme of the son's revolt against the father, but it reaches its pinnacle in the wide range of Expressionist poems with truly apocalyptic themes. The first great anthology of Expressionist poetry, *Menschheitsdämmerung* (1920; *The Dawn of Humanity*), edited by Kurt Pinthus, opens with Jakob van Hoddis's "Weltende" (1911; "End of the World"), an eight-line poem, with disjointed images evoking disaster.

The Expressionist does not see progress in the currency of society: materialism, militarism, or nationalism. And yet some Expressionists spoke of regeneration and transformation. The messianic rhetoric of revitalization is not universal and was foreign to Benn and Expressionists like van Hoddis, Alfred Lichtenstein, and Georg Trakl. Benn's poems had religious layers and employed religious language, but they tended to empty religion of its higher meaning, as in "Man and Woman Walk through the Cancer Ward," where the image of a rosary is used for the soft cancerous nodules in the dying woman's breast. Trakl, too, often inverted religious symbols in dark and opaque poems more characterized by despair and decay than by hope and transcendence.

Pinthus's anthology emphasizes the messianic strain and contains the following sections: "Collapse and Cry," "Awakening of the Heart," "Exhortation and Indignation," and "Love of Human Beings." The title of the anthology, *Menschheitsdämmerung,* can mean dawn or dusk and so captures the ambiguity of transition and the movement's circling around pessimism and optimism. These works contain an appeal to renewal, the refrain of the new human being, an exclamatory call to fraternity, spirit, humanity, heart, and soul in the face of a bestial existence. At times a political program is evoked, as in Johannes R. Becher's "Der Sozialist" (1916; "The Socialist"). Much of the messianic rhetoric is abstract, as in Ernst Stadler's "Der Spruch" (1914; "The Maxim"), Karl Otten's "Die jungen Dichter" (1918; "The Young Poets"), or Franz Werfel's *Der Weltfreund* (1911; *Friend of the World*). Often the emphasis on brotherhood and ecstasy becomes bombastic, hollow, and stale. For Benn the pathos of "the new human being" was "the last fever of lying out of a mouth already swollen from discharge" (3:125). The Expressionists were clearly better at diagnosing evil and shocking people than in painting a path to salvation, even if this impulse is irrepressible and surfaces in some respects, if highly subdued and much later, in Benn's elevation of artistic form as a manifestation of the absolute, a position he assumed after briefly embracing, then abandoning, National Socialism.

Not all Expressionist poetry was as stylistically innovative as Benn's, but several tendencies are visible. Common to all is the nonmimetic, nonrepresentational character. Even Benn's cancer wards are hardly realistic. The artists express their concept of the world without seeking to represent objective reality. More specifically, Expressionist poetry makes frequent use of parataxis. Images are juxtaposed with a certain degree of randomness and without any overarching sense of grammatical relation or causality. This is especially evident in works such as Trakl's "Im Winter" (1910; "In Winter") and "Trübsinn" (1912; "Melancholy"), van Hoddis's "Weltende" (1911; "End of the World"), Max Hermann-Neisse's "Nacht im Stadtpark" (1914; "Night in the City Park"), and Lichtenstein's "Die Dämmerung" (1910/11; "Twilight") and "Der Morgen" (1913; "Morning"). We find the structure in *Morgue and Other Poems* as well, especially in "Requiem" and "Man and Woman Walk through the Cancer Ward." In addition, the language tends to be bold, intense, shocking, as might befit the depiction of decay and crisis, apocalypse and war. Highly charged and enthusiastic rhetoric, even when it ends with an allusion to destruction, is evident, for example, in Stadler's "Fahrt über die Kölner Rheinbrücke bei Nacht" (1913; "Ride Across the Cologne Rhine Bridge at Night"). Expressionist poetry has little of the subtle refinement and sensitive delicacy of turn-of-the-century Impressionism. The language is also very heterogeneous. Benn is the most pronounced example here, employing a montage style that links clinical language, everyday language, religion, and poetry. Expressionist lyric is a mix of tone as well as of diction: the serious and comical seem to combine in works such as van Hoddis's "End of the World," Benn's "Nachtcafé" (1912; "Night Cafe"), or Lichtenstein's "Twilight."

Finally, some Expressionist poetry was highly concentrated. Here the best example is August Stramm, who was influenced by Marinetti's Futurist manifestoes, which recognize the world as a disjointed array of information and events, brought to life by newspapers, cinema, telephones, airplanes, phonographs. Such a world calls for new forms—above all, collage. Adjectives and adverbs must disappear, so too must finite verbs and punctuation. The well-formed sentence is abandoned, replaced by a telegram-like style, with frequent use of compound nouns, phonetic spelling, and onomatopoeia to convey the continuity and rush of life, and a variety of typographical accents for emphasis. Stramm took these precepts further than most, with his paratactic linking of nouns and transcendence of conventional syntax. But aspects of the so-called telegram style are also evident in the early Benn. Paradoxically, in their efforts to convey the pace of reality and its vitality, such works remain, despite their innovative form, highly, if abstractly, mimetic.

Although Expressionists transformed our sense of poetry and had a very good sense of the ills of society and the consequences of the abandonment of metaphysics, their abstract answers were of little help to those seeking positive guidance. Many artists, disillusioned by the shortcomings of the movement, turned to a new sobriety, which was more concrete, more social, and more cynical. One of the few poets who outlived Expressionism as an active artist, Benn enjoyed a revival after World War II with works that turned much more to a classical elevation of pure form. Despite the distance in time, many of the Expressionist problems are still our own: loss of orientation resulting from the crises of Christianity and metaphysics; the search for appropriate and innovative modes of expression; the role of the ugly within aesthetics; and the new responsibilities of art in an age of technology.

See also 1882, 1910, 1921, 1929 (October), 1999

Bibliography: Gottfried Benn, Prose, Essays, Poems, ed. Volkmar Sander (New York: Continuum, 1987). ———, Sämtliche Werke. Stuttgarter Ausgabe, 7 vols., ed. Gerhard Schuster (Stuttgart: Klett-Cotta, 1986–). Roy F. Allen, German Expressionist Poetry (Boston: Twayne, 1979). Peter Hohendahl, ed., Benn—Wirkung wider Willen (Frankfurt am Main: Athenäum, 1971). Kurt Pinthus, ed., Menschheitsdämmerung: Dawn of Humanity: A Document of Expressionism with Biographies and Bibliographies, trans. and intro. Joanna M. Ratych, Ralph Ley, and Robert C. Conard (Columbia, S.C.: Camden House, 1994). Walter H. Sokel, The Writer in Extremis: Expressionism in Twentieth-Century Literature (Stanford, Calif.: Stanford University Press, 1959). Silvio Vietta, ed., Lyrik des Expressionismus, 3rd ed. (Tübingen: Niemeyer, 1990). John Willett, Expressionism (New York: McGraw-Hill, 1970).

Mark W. Roche

♫ 1912, June

Thomas Mann completes his novella Der Tod in Venedig after a year of writing

The Lasciviousness of Ruin

Many Junes after Thomas Mann (1875–1955) finished his most famous story, the newspaper USA Today (June 7, 1999) reported that the Publishing Triangle, "a group of 250 gay men and lesbians who work in publishing," was about to release a list of what they called the "100 Best Lesbian and Gay Novels." *Der Tod in Venedig (Death in Venice)* would be at the top of the list, the number one "gay novel" of all time. Dorothy Allison, a prominent lesbian author and one of the judges who created the list, was quoted calling Mann's story "an aesthetic and ethical struggle useful to me and my community."

Allison's carefully chosen words offer much to consider, particularly now that *Death in Venice* has become the foremost example of a genre, gay literature, that did not and could not openly exist in the Europe of 1912. When she speaks of "my community," she might refer primarily to gays and lesbians, but perhaps also to other writers and artists, and indeed perhaps to an even broader group of men and women involved in aesthetic and ethical struggle. Allison seems to suggest that Thomas Mann wrote a story centered on artistic and moral issues that could be useful both to remarkable individuals like Allison (and Mann himself) and to the community of which such individuals are a part, whatever we choose the word "community" to mean.

We can be certain that Mann did not imagine the community he wished to address in the summer of 1912 as anything like the members of the Publishing Triangle. Much as such a group might have interested him, nothing of the kind was imaginable at the beginning of the 20th century in a society that displayed official and relentless hostility to the practice of homosexuality. The memory of the trial and imprisonment of Oscar Wilde in the mid-1890s was still fresh in the minds of Europeans of the 1910s, and even hints of homosexuality could create large-scale public scandal. Mann was acutely aware that there was no visible gay community to which he could turn for public support of the kind offered by the Publishing Triangle nearly a century later, and he knew that he would have to be extremely careful in presenting his material to a potentially hostile audience. When he mentions beginning work on *Death in Venice* to Philipp Witkop in a letter (July 18, 1911), he is careful to stress the high moral tone of his project: "I am in the midst of a work: a really strange thing that I brought back with me from Venice, a novella, serious and pure in tone, concerning a case of pederasty in an aging artist. You say, 'Hum, hum!' but it is quite respectable." Mann's insistence that his material is "quite respectable" in spite of its treatment of homoeroticism is instructive. One of the most important features of the homosexual attraction felt by Mann's protagonist, Gustav Aschenbach, for the Polish boy he sees on the beach is that it is *not* respectable. It is dangerous, improper, impermissible, and ultimately fatal. When Aschenbach goes so far as to whisper the words "I love you," not to Tadzio himself but to the empty darkness, Mann's narrator describes it as "impossible under these conditions, absurd, reviled, ridiculous" (*Death in Venice*, 44). Mann can claim that his fiction is respectable precisely because it presents Aschenbach's passion as completely out of bounds. He appears to have understood from the outset that his story could succeed in 1912 not by embracing homosexuality as a lifestyle but by placing it in a context where its impropriety is beyond question. Mann's astounding achievement is to have made this absolutely impermissible homoerotic feeling interesting, understandable, and mov-

ing not only to a potential audience of gay readers but to the average heterosexual, possibly even homophobic, European. At the very moment when the
narrator confesses that Aschenbach's "I love you" is absolutely impossible, he
also affirms that it is "holy and venerable even under these conditions" (44).
That the community of readers, including those indifferent or hostile to gays,
has regularly assented to this affirmation is testimony to Mann's skill at turning
what seems at first eccentric and "queer" to the very center of his audience's
concern.

In a world that finds a list of "100 Best Lesbian and Gay Novels" not only
appropriate but even worthy of featured treatment in a mass-market newspaper like *USA Today*, it is particularly important to remember how different our
world is from the world of 1912, when issues of a far different sort were at the
center of attention. That world is not only the one in which Mann himself
lived, it is the one in which he explicitly sets his story. The tale opens on "a
spring afternoon in 19—, a year that for months glowered threateningly over
our continent" (3). The mysterious 19— could be any year in the still young
20th century, but Mann's audience would certainly recognize it as 1911, a year
marked by diplomatic crises. The blank left in the date, a typical touch of
Mannean irony, in fact withholds little or no significant information, but it
does set a tone of apparent editorial tact appropriate for a story dealing with
scandalous events. Thus the very mention of "19—" at the commencement of
the narrative insists that what is to come will be both threatening and sensational, a story fitting the circumstances of a continent on the brink of the most
ruinous war anyone had ever experienced.

Oddly enough, the moment of crisis in which Mann's story is set and in
which it first appeared in print marks one of the high points in the history of
German letters. Not only did *Death in Venice* appear in print in the fall of 1912,
during those same months Franz Kafka composed "The Metamorphosis," another investigation into the psychology of ruin. Today these two stories are by
far the most widely read works of German literature, even more firmly seated
in the European canon now than Goethe's *Faust*. For a large number of educated non-Germans, these fruits of autumn 1912 represent everything they
will ever know about a rich German literary tradition. The highest artistic success thus comes on the brink of political and cultural collapse.

As surprising and strange as this circumstance may be, it is worth pondering
as more than an odd coincidence or evidence of worldwide educational decline. For the author of *Buddenbrooks*, a novel that equates artistic success with
the onset of ruin, there would be nothing at all surprising in the apparent paradox of the success-in-failure of German culture in 1912. He had been pondering such issues throughout his career. And thus when Mann writes in the
opening lines of *Death in Venice* about a glowering threat hanging over Europe,
we can be sure that he is deliberately putting his story of individual ruin in the
context of a much larger ruin that is about to befall all of Europe, a ruin that
was as palpable in Kafka's Prague as in Mann's Munich.

How important this sense of ruin is to *Death in Venice* should be apparent from the title, which after all does not allude to "Romance in Venice" or even "Lust in Venice" but to a disastrous and in many ways humiliating collapse. The focus of attention right from the start is on decline, fall, and dissolution. In many ways the English word "dissolution" perfectly captures Mann's intended fusion of lasciviousness and ruin. Aschenbach's experience in Venice is a relentless process of dissolution in which the protagonist, as he becomes more and more dissolute, comes closer and closer to dissolving into formlessness. Mann makes this fusion concrete in the figure of the sea, a place clearly identified in the story both as the scene of sensuous abandon and as the elemental "ground of all being" to which the soul returns in death. The setting in Venice, a city completely dominated by water, affords the opportunity for numerous variations on this theme. Canals, fountains, and the great lagoon that separates the city from the barrier island of the Lido all provide locations for important events in the tale. The entire city is a "sunken queen" on the verge of dissolving in the waters that surround and nurture it.

But again and again, it is the sea itself that dominates the story and its protagonist. The narrator stresses Aschenbach's love of "the beach scene, this view of a carefree society engaged in purely sensual enjoyment on the edge of the watery element," and he even hyperbolically alludes to "the nakedness sanctioned by the bold and easy freedom of the place" (25). It seems unlikely that, aside from little children, anyone on that beach was actually naked, but Mann's language pushes the sexuality of the situation right to the edge, scattering on the sands before the reader's eye a crowd of rhetorically nude bodies. The sea itself begins to take on the seductive qualities of the beach society: "A silky white sheen lay on the Pontos, its broad stretches undulating languidly" (34).

The story also makes clear that this sensuality is morally suspect. Aschenbach "loved the sea from the depth of his being" because as an artist, he harbored "an affinity for the undivided, the immeasurable, the eternal, the void. It was a forbidden affinity, directly contrary to his calling, and seductive precisely for that reason" (26). There are thus two sorts of seduction inherent in Aschenbach's sojourn on the seashore, one physical, the other spiritual. The physical seduction (the naked flesh and the "bold and easy freedom" found on the beach) is powerful, but no more so than the spiritual seduction represented by the ocean's formless immensity. The "watery element" seems to call on the artist to let go of his art, to release himself from the discipline of form, to abandon the laborious quest for artistic perfection in exchange for the perfection of absolute release into nothingness.

From its opening paragraphs, the story emphasizes Aschenbach's struggle to keep formal control both of his artistic material and of his own physical and mental self. The mechanism of the plot is set in motion at a moment of loss of artistic control in which Aschenbach fails to master the difficulties of his "dangerous" morning's work, "which just now required particular discretion, caution, penetration, and precision of will" (3). As the story progresses and Aschenbach finds himself attracted to the "perfectly beautiful" Polish boy he sees on the Lido, an attraction he himself feels is far out of bounds, he is once again in need of discretion, caution, and precision of will. But he can no more master his surging emotions than he could master his recalcitrant material, and he lets himself dissolve instead in the waters of his Venetian adventure.

That Aschenbach, the dignified, respected model of discipline and restraint, should permit himself to develop a crush on one so young is bad enough, but it is catastrophically worse that this youthful beloved should be a boy. And the story requires this ultimate catastrophe. It would not do for the hero's ruin to be partial, as indeed it might seem if the plot hinged on an older man's infatuation with a young girl. Mann claimed at one point that he first conceived the story as a retelling of Goethe's love for Ulrike von Levetzow, "the love of the seventy-year-old for that little girl" (94). But that would not nearly have been a dissolute enough love for Mann's purpose, not nearly impermissible enough. Mann had far better material at hand in his own experience—for he had himself become fascinated with a Polish boy he saw on the beach in Venice in 1911—and in his vivid personal understanding of both the attractions and the dangers of homosexual love. No one knew better than Mann the cost of living a life of renunciation and severe discipline, and no one knew better than he what it would cost if he were to let that discipline slip. What we would call today a "gay lifestyle" was never a real option for a man of Thomas Mann's ambitions living in his time and place.

Mann cared deeply about his career, and in particular he cared about his stature in the community. In 1911, at the age of thirty-six, he aspired to, but had not yet attained, the level of public esteem he ascribed to his character Aschenbach. A writer known to practice homosexuality would simply not be granted such esteem by Europeans of the early 20th century, no matter how excellent his work. In a very real sense, then, what happens to Mann's hero in the story is exactly what Mann feared might happen to him if he ever let himself go: Mann's relation to this aspect of his story is not unlike that of Goethe toward suicide in *The Sorrows of Young Werther*. Mann was clearly determined that such a thing should never take place in real life, and as far as we know it never did.

This is not to say that Mann rejected or regretted his own homosexuality or that *Death in Venice* is intended as a cautionary tale against pederasty. On the contrary, the existence of homoerotic feelings is one of the fundamental assumptions on which the fiction is built. It has been argued that homosexuality "should be assumed in Mann's works, given its importance both in late 19th-century Germany and in his personal life" (Reed, *Death in Venice*, 219), and there is substantial evidence both here and in Mann's other stories to support this claim. It is equally clear, however, that Mann felt renunciation was necessary for him. His attraction to men, he claimed in a late diary entry, evoked in him "only a renunciation, specifically a not-to-be-determined, wishful-impossible one" (quoted in Reed, *Death in Venice*, 217). Everything we know about Mann's life suggests that, at the time he wrote *Death in Venice* and for the rest of his life thereafter, he steadfastly persisted in this renunciation.

Aschenbach, however, is unable and/or unwilling to renounce his passion for the beautiful Tadzio, and this inability to maintain his long-held habits of self-discipline leads to his contracting a fatal case of cholera. Mann's readers, straight or gay, are made to understand, through the deftness of Mann's prose, both the great strength of Aschenbach's artistic will and the even greater strength of his overwhelming need to let go, to ride the wave of passion, to relax in the cushions of a gondola and float onward in pursuit of love. Aschenbach succumbs in his aesthetic and ethical struggle, but he does so in a process so carefully and sensitively described that the reader feels a deep sense of kinship with him. He becomes part of our community, and his story is useful to us.

See also 1831, 1882, 1912 (September), 1943

Bibliography: Thomas Mann, *Death in Venice: A New Translation, Backgrounds and Contexts, Criticism,* ed. and trans. Clayton Koelb (New York: Norton, 1994). ———, *Gesammelte Werke,* vol. 8: *Erzählungen, Fiorenza, Dichtungen* (Frankfurt am Main: Fischer, 1960–1974). T. J. Reed, *Death in Venice: Making and Unmaking a Master* (New York: Twayne, 1994).

Clayton Koelb

♫ 1912, July–October

Carl Einstein publishes a radically experimental short novel in serial form in the expressionist journal *Die Aktion*

An Optics of Fragmentation

Bebuquin oder Die Dilettanten des Wunders (1912; *Bebuquin, or Dilettantes of the Miracle*) was Carl Einstein's (1885–1940) earliest published literary work and remains his sole contribution to the German literary canon. Although he was bitterly disappointed by its reception, several notable contemporaries did hail it as a literary milestone. And yet Einstein, only twenty-four when he finished *Bebuquin,* never again produced a literary text that approached its impact; it was as a writer on art that he achieved the greater fame.

Literature and art criticism were not conflicting vocations for Einstein; rather they functioned as two discursive modes through which he addressed the philosophical issues central to his thinking. The protagonist seeks to remake himself and the world by changing his perception of it, and this is also the focal point of Einstein's art theory and criticism. "Through vision we change human beings and the world," he wrote in 1931 (*Die Kunst des 20. Jahrhunderts,* 92). Consistent with this theoretical position, the visual imagery of *Bebuquin,* generally treated summarily in the literature on the novel, is as crucial to its meaning as are its often abstruse dialogue and bizarre narrative.

Einstein's short novel is the product of a particular moment in the nagging cultural crisis of modernity. Nietzsche had first articulated its principal themes—the death of God, the loss of myth and of a unified culture, the epistemological crisis of faith in the objectivity of science and reason, the resulting nihilism and fragmentation of modern experience. Like Nietzsche,

Einstein offers at once a diagnosis of the modern malaise and a searing expression of longing for a cure.

The narrative argument of *Bebuquin* is contained in its subtitle, "Dilettantes of the Miracle": the dilettante and the miracle are for Einstein incompatible. The dilettante, who lives for the moment, cultivates his individuality and subjectivity, pursues pleasure, and is unwilling to subordinate himself to any collective purpose, is the embodiment of modern fragmentation and formlessness. The miracle—a miracle because it must transcend reason, science, and logic—is a compelling collective myth, an instrumental fiction with the force of law, capable of restoring to human life and to work a unifying form and purpose.

Paradoxically, *Bebuquin* brilliantly exemplifies, on many levels, the cultural malaise that is its subject and that its protagonists long to overcome, not least in its assertive—and dilettantish—metaliterary self-reflexivity. "What bad material I am for a novel," laments Bebuquin in chapter 2, "since I will never do anything, I revolve within myself; I would gladly say something clever about action, if only I knew what it is" (*Bebuquin,* 8). Even Bebuquin's name, as Dirk Heißerer has proposed, is self-reflexive, a compound of "book" (French, *bouquin*) with "Beb," a contraction of *Bébé* that Einstein used elsewhere in referring to the character, his alter ego (Heißerer, 113–114). In short, Bebuquin is named after the book about himself. Such devices recur throughout, as in Bebuquin's prayer in chapter 12: "Lord, grant me a miracle, we have been seeking it since chapter one" (34). And yet this narcissistic self-reflection becomes symptomatic of the futility of that quest.

The transcendence of the self as a precondition of the miracle is drastically signified in the novel by death. The three major characters—Bebuquin, Euphemia, and Nebukadnezar Böhm, dilettantes all—are in search of a miracle, and each has a characteristic encounter with death. Euphemia, in a circus trapeze act, resolves, "for formal reasons," to break her neck, but suffers a failure of nerve. "Morally ruined," she repairs to the Cloister of the Free Miracle of Blood, taking the easy, anachronistic path of religion (27, 32). Böhm dies in chapter 1 but, irredeemably a dilettante and hence resistant to self-surrender and the fixity of death, continues to inhabit the narrative in wildly varying scales and shapes, until he is buried under bizarre conditions in the penultimate chapter. Only Bebuquin, though initially anxious to preserve and cultivate his individuality, grows weary of his dilettantish existence and resolves to liquidate it. In the desperate hope of achieving transformation, and perhaps a miracle, he wills and achieves his own death, and the "book of Beb" ends abruptly.

Einstein wrote to the art dealer Daniel-Henry Kahnweiler in 1923 that he wanted to tell a "story precisely of sensations, with experiences brought into the foreground, of which so-called things are at best a symptom." This certainly fits the textual world of *Bebuquin* (*Carl Einstein–Daniel-Henry Kahnweiler: Correspondence,* 140). Those experiences are of deranged senses, of persons and objects with blurred or fluid identities, at times even of seemingly disembodied speech. When Einstein published the first four chapters of the work in 1907 under the title "Herr Giorgio Bebuquin" (the mixture of languages, resisting identity, itself an example of dilettantism), he omitted all quotation marks from the dialogue. In the completed nineteen-chapter version, he may originally have had the same intention, for he added quotation marks—often carelessly and inconsistently—by hand to the typescript, leaving the impression that it was only an afterthought or a late concession to his publisher. Even with these insertions, it is unclear in numerous passages who is speaking, or whether we are reading a monologue, dialogue, or interjections of the narrator. Subsequent editors have tried to minimize the confusion, but the evidence suggests that Einstein, in defiance of novelistic convention, wished precisely to cultivate such ambiguity.

Paralleling this treatment of speech is the relentlessly destabilizing opticality of the novel's visual ambience. Persons and objects are continually distorted, fragmented, and transfigured by a rich array of light sources—arc light, gaslight, oil lamps, headlights, sunlight, moonlight, and reflections, exemplifying the period's fascination with the rapidly evolving technology of electric light and its transfiguration of the urban landscape. Furthermore, the often fantastic visual details in *Bebuquin* occur within the sparsest intimations of spaces, turning these luminous fragments into the visual milieu of *Bebuquin* and the sensory experience of its characters. Einstein eschewed description, and these images are trenchantly metaphorical: "The lights hung from the ceiling in clumps, bursting the walls into shreds." An automobile has "two horribly blinding headlights, which ripped open white pits of light in the glistening asphalt, where shadows of the last strollers flickered in the rainwater." "Bebuquin strode stiffly into the foggy night. The reflections of the arc lights stormed through the tree branches and swam like broad opalescent fishes on the wet ground" (13, 22, 44). In each of these passages, the optical transfiguration wrought by light destroys tactile forms and surfaces and produces hallucinatory effects. In rare instances where contained spaces figure in the text, they are dissolved by light, shadow, and color: "The night slowly took on color, the little white room became opalescent like old stone, blazing shadows traversed the walls, a small white cloud stood before the window, a burning sunbeam shone through it. Bebuquin's body vanished into the shadow, only his head, amidst the waves of twilight color, gazed at the sinking cloud" (35). The opticality extends even to some of the characters. Böhm has a reflective silver-plated skull inlaid with precious stones. Bebuquin characterizes himself as "a mirror, a motionless puddle glistening from gaslight, who mirrors" (4).

In two instances the purely optical images of mirrors determine events with dire consequences. Pandemonium breaks out when a crowd of circus spectators comes under the spell of a distorting mirror-faced column. Unable to turn their gaze from it, taking its strange, disturbing reflections for reality, they panic. Frantically contorting their bodies in an attempt to reconcile them with the mirror image, many are driven to madness or suicide. In another bizarre incident, the narcissistic Böhm becomes distracted by an overhanging mirror as he attempts to engage in sex with Euphemia. "In the finely faceted jewel plates of his head, he saw how her breasts fractured into multifarious strange forms and gleamed in shapes such as no reality had ever given him." Dazzled by these polymorphous reflections, Böhm collapses, "and his body nearly burst in the battle between two realities . . . Now groping his half forgotten body, he could no longer comprehend it; it writhed in pain, for it no longer matched what he saw" (5–6). As a result of this disjunction between his haptic body and his optical body, Böhm dies. And yet he lives on as a purely optical being, walking through walls, gliding over treetops, lounging in the cognac; he has no stable form, no physical identity; he remains the formless dilettante, even in death.

For both Böhm and the circus-goers, fleeting optical sensations are so powerful that they overwhelm and short-circuit established networks of visual memory and cognition. This is precisely the kind of experience, albeit in less drastic form, that certain critics attributed at the time to Impressionist painting. While most critics writing on Impressionism focused on aesthetic issues, some German critics perceived in this art an unsettling character. Hermann Bahr (1863–1934) saw in Impressionism not merely an innovative painting technique but, more profoundly, a radically subversive way of perceiving and experiencing the world. Undermining faith in the truth of appearances, it took from "pious people their comfortable, solid, secure world to hurl them out into the dizziness of churning transformations." This view of Impressionism as a reflection of epistemological uncertainty was an interpretation mediated through the writings of Nietzsche and the philosopher and physicist Ernst Mach (1838–1916).

As noted, numerous commentators have seen in *Bebuquin* a literary response to Cubism, the art movement of which Einstein became a major champion around the time of the novel's publication. But as he notes on the first page, he wrote *Bebuquin* between 1906 and 1909, when Cubism was as yet unknown to him and its works had not been exhibited in Germany. However, Einstein certainly was familiar with Impressionism. Although associated primarily with the period from the 1860s to 1880s in France, it became a factor in the German art world only in the 1890s. When Einstein began work on *Bebuquin,* it was still seen as the dominant art form of the early 20th century, a view he himself shared as late as 1910.

Most scholarship on *Bebuquin* emphasizes its considerable literary debt to French Symbolism: Einstein dedicated it to André Gide, some of whose early work was influenced by that movement. Yet for Einstein a close affinity existed between Impressionism and Symbolism. In a 1913 essay, "Über Paul Claudel," he designated Stéphane Mallarmé an Impressionist. Later, Einstein elaborated the point: both Mallarmé and the Impressionists shattered the stable identities of familiar forms; both exalted the vivid fugitive image over a synthetic whole. In a Mallarmé poem, "Signs rationally alien to one another are united, and biologically differentiated functions are hallucinatorily wed" (*Die Kunst des 20. Jahrhunderts,* 45 and 47). This applies equally to the imagery in *Bebuquin.*

In viewing Symbolism and Impressionism as expressions of the same sensibility, Einstein shared the views of Bahr and the art historian Richard Hamann. In *Impressionismus in Leben und Kunst (Impressionism in Life and Art),* Hamann elevated Impressionism to a *Weltanschauung,* a zeitgeist suffusing the whole of European culture since the 1880s. Pervaded by "a boundless individualism and egotism," the impressionist ethos resisted wholeness and synthesis. The impressionist artist, poet, or composer was a delicate seismograph, set vibrating by every fugitive sensation or experience; his response was essentially passive, reactive. Isolating the fugitive optic stimulus from the storehouse of visual memory, Impressionism valued richness of sensation over order. The "destruction of form, the bent and broken, the dissolved and disturbed had supplanted the beauty of form" (*Impressionism in Life and Art,* 50, 155, 158, 192).

The visual milieu of *Bebuquin,* a mélange of fugitive distortions and destructions of impressionist vision, is one with the culture of dilettantism it critiques. Einstein's way of equating the text's optics and its narrative substance is wholly consistent with the theory of art he was then developing. Art for him was not primarily an aesthetic phenomenon but a medium of cognition. Following the theorist Conrad Fiedler, Einstein believed that art determined how we see, and how we see constitutes our reality. "The subject matter of art," he wrote in 1915 in the essay "Totalität," "is not objects, but configured vision," and vision in *Bebuquin* is configured by Impressionism (*Werke,* 215).

The distinctive optics of that world can be perceived most clearly in a rearview mirror, as it were—in Einstein's early critical responses to Cubism from around the time of *Bebuquin*'s publication. What he emphasized in Cubism were the qualities conspicuously absent from the visual imagery of his novel—vigorous plasticity of form and intense awareness of space, qualities, he believed, that were shared by the art of great collective cultures of the past.

If *Bebuquin* is not a cubist work—whatever that might be—it manifests a longing, however tentatively articulated, for the qualities Cubism seemed to promise when Einstein discovered it in 1912. Bebuquin's resolve to die, not by his own hand but by a sheer act of will, is in effect what Einstein called, in an unpublished manuscript of 1910, "the will to form." Lying on his deathbed, Bebuquin stares intensely at the ceiling as he attempts to bore a hole into it. It is as if he were striving, in a reach toward transformation, to reintegrate the optic with the haptic by pressing his passive senses toward agency, as if to make his death a *spatial* passage. On the last night of his life, while asleep, Bebuquin's hands grope upward; later, intermittently parting his eyelids, he stretches fingers and toes outward. Then he awakens for the last time and speaks. The text reads: "He gazed coolly and said / Out" (50). This word, at once the last of Bebuquin the character and of *Bebuquin* the book, implies not only closure but movement out of the self-reflexive text—by the same protagonist who had earlier declared "I shall never do anything, I revolve within myself." Significantly, although the book ends with the death of its main character, Einstein originally titled it a *Vorspiel,* a "prelude."

In his brief afterword to the novel's first edition, Franz Blei characterized

Bebuquin as "a book whose greatest value, given the current state of our culture, is that it can find no reader, at least none that I could 'introduce.'" His gleefully condescending hyperbole proved prophetic: although a second edition of the novel was published in 1917, there was not another until 1963. Only since then has it been more or less continuously in print in German. Yet even today *Bebuquin* remains one of the most hermetic texts in early 20th-century German prose, admired by specialists, analyzed by scholars, yet resistant to the embrace of a broader public.

See also 1882, 1897, 1902, 1912 (March)

Bibliography: Christoph Braun, *Carl Einstein: Zwischen Ästhetik und Anarchismus: Zu Leben und Werk eines expressionistischen Schriftstellers* (Munich: Iudicium, 1987). Carl Einstein, *Bebuquin*, 2nd. rev. ed., ed. Erich Kleinschmidt (Stuttgart: Reclam, 1995). ———, *Die Kunst des 20. Jahrhunderts,* ed. Uwe Fleckner and Thomas W. Gaehtgens (Berlin: Fannei & Walz, 1996). ———, *Werke, Band I: 1907–1918,* ed. Hermann Haarmann and Klaus Siebenhaar (Berlin: Fannei & Walz, 1994). Dirk Heißerer, *Negative Dichtung: Zum Verfahren der literarischen Dekomposition bei Carl Einstein* (Munich: Iudicium, 1992). Klaus H. Kiefer, *Diskurswandel im Werke Carl Einsteins: Ein Beitrag zur Theorie und Geschichte der europäischen Avantgarde* (Tübingen: Niemeyer, 1994). Thomas Krämer, *Carl Einsteins "Bebuquin": Romantheorie und Textkonstitution* (Würzburg: Königshausen & Neumann, 1991). David Pan, *Primitive Renaissance: Rethinking German Expressionism* (Lincoln: University of Nebraska Press, 2001). Reto Sorg, *Aus den "Gärten der Zeichen": Zu Carl Einsteins* Bebuquin (Munich: Fink, 1998).

Charles W. Haxthausen

🖋 *1912, September*

The collapsing Austro-Russian détente provides a key metaphor for Kafka's story "Das Urteil"

Kafka's Narrative Breakthrough

Numerous impulses came together to create what Franz Kafka (1883–1924) himself saw as a remarkable creative breakthrough: his composition of "Das Urteil" (The Judgment) in the course of the night of September 22 to 23, 1912, from ten in the evening to six in the morning. He described the experience in his diary as a "complete opening of body and soul." "Das Urteil" appeared in 1913 in a literary magazine edited by his friend Max Brod and produced by a distinguished publishing house, the Kurt Wolff Verlag. Together with his longer story, "Die Verwandlung" (1915; The Metamorphosis), "Das Urteil" remains the most frequently read and discussed of Kafka's short fictions.

Kafka was already known in Prague literary circles for his prose pieces that enacted, while often also parodying, turn-of-the-century decadence. Yet, some common thematic concerns aside, "Das Urteil" is strikingly different from these texts. Neo-Romantic lassitude and ennui give way to a more energetic, intense mode of expression, and poetic meditation is replaced by a new sensibility for the grotesque. In these respects, "Das Urteil" shows a kinship with the Expressionist movement, which represented inner, psychological struggles by means of exaggerated verbal and gestural effects. As in Expressionism, central to "Das Urteil" is a conflict between father and son that threatens to constrain the freedom and extinguish the higher aspirations of the younger generation.

Kafka's own relationship to his father, made famous by the posthumously published "Letter to His Father" (written in 1919), was an important element in the making of "Das Urteil." During 1911 and 1912, Franz's lack of interest in business provoked escalating conflicts with the elder Kafka. Depressed by these altercations and struggling to find time for his writing, Kafka repeatedly entertained thoughts of suicide. Despite these troubles, he succeeded in completing the manuscript of his first volume of prose texts, *Betrachtung* (1912; *Meditation*), which he delivered to his friend Max Brod on August 13, 1912. That same evening, he met his future fiancée for the first time. In the following month, he began writing "Das Urteil."

Beyond its autobiographical origins, however, the story should be seen against the backdrop of a historical period fraught with tensions among several European nations. The year 1912 had repeatedly been punctuated by warlike rumblings and even trial mobilizations. In particular, relations between Russia and the Austro-Hungarian Empire, which had begun to break down in 1908 over the annexation of Bosnia and Herzegovina, became increasingly strained. Cooperation between St. Petersburg and Vienna was intermittent throughout 1912. The Austrian Emperor Franz Josef, furthermore, was 82 years old, and although he continued to assert authority, he suffered repeated periods of illness and was frequently unable to attend ministerial councils.

Though Kafka is often portrayed as an alienated outsider, this political turbulence was by no means lost on him. Indeed, he was an active member of coffee house groups during 1911–12, where political as well as literary topics were discussed; he read numerous newspapers and attended public lectures on matters of social and economic import; and he was involved in several "anarchist" (actually socialist) meetings and demonstrations. In October 1912, he commented in a letter on events in the First Balkan War that posed a threat to the Austrian position. Contemporary readers of "Das Urteil" would have been well aware of the problematic relations among Germany, Russia, and Austro-Hungary during this period. The motifs of betrayal, the writing of "false letters," the encryption of Georg's engagement in his letters to his friend in Russia by means of continued references to someone else's engagement—all these elements are amusing adaptations of the difficult political atmosphere of 1912 to the family scenario of the story's plot.

Several other aspects of the narrative depend on the reader's awareness of the fragility of Austro-Russian relations during the years leading up to World War I. The apparent contradiction between the father's question, "Do you really have this friend in Russia?" and his claim to have been in secret contact with the friend in Russia all this time is an allusion to diplomatic relations between Russia and the Austro-Hungarian Empire. Georg reminds his father that the friend had been accustomed to tell "incredible stories about the Russian Revolution [of 1905]" on some of his earlier visits home. For the past three years, the friend has had to stay in Russia, but Georg is unwilling to be-lieve the friend's claim that he is unable to leave because of the uncertain polit-ical situation there. At the beginning of the story, Georg pictures his friend as having no real connection with his countrymen in Russia, but no genuine friendships with Russians either. All of this Georg ascribes to social ineptitude on the friend's part; he seems oblivious of actual political crises within Russia and between Russia and its European neighbors.

To summarize the complex connections between "Das Urteil" and the real world, we can say that multiple strands of personal and world history "broke through" into the narrative in a quite extraordinary way. It is important to un-derstand, however, that the story is not "about" Kafka's feelings of inadequacy, his difficult relation to his father, his ambivalence about his engagement, or his unwillingness to be a businessman at the expense of his literary energies. Nor is it "about" the Expressionist generation, the problems of Jews in a Western-ized culture, the tensions between Austria and Russia, or the looming world war. Rather, these elements form the metaphorical structure that subtends "Das Urteil." Bringing together these many ingredients into a coherent narra-tive was one element in Kafka's creative breakthrough.

Concurrently with political and personal issues, a cultural event also con-tributed to "Das Urteil": the arrival of a Yiddish theater group that performed in Prague between October 1911 and January 1912 and that captured Kafka's admiration. Several impulses from Yiddish drama, notably its exaggerated use of gesture, are incorporated into "Das Urteil." The father's sudden emergence from beneath the bedclothes, for example, derives from one of the plays Kafka saw at the Yiddish theater. Indeed, Georg accuses his father of being an actor or "comedian." The final scene, in which Georg swings over the railings of the bridge before falling to his death, shares much of this theatricality. Yet both of these moments also have distinctly Expressionist aspects as well.

Kafka's father was scornful of his son's passion for the Yiddish theater group and virulently criticized its principal actor, Yitzhak Löwy, and the Eastern Jewish culture he represented. Several readers have seen Yitzhak Löwy as a partial model for the friend in Russia. Georg's repeated fantasy of his friend's having yellow skin, though overtly attributed to incipient illness, suggests a link between the friend in Russia and the world of Eastern Judaism. Georg's representation of his friend accords with an orientalist view common at the time, in which Russia, East Asia, and Eastern Jewry are more or less unre-flectively conflated. In this way, the unreliable Austro-Russian détente can be seen as mapped onto an equally unstable relationship between unassimilated Jews and Western European culture.

Other aspects of the culture of the time also make their way into the story. In his diary entry of September 23, Kafka notes that while composing "Das Urteil" he had been thinking about Freud. It is not clear exactly which of Freud's works Kafka had read by 1912. Certainly, two of the journals he read, *Pan* and *Die Neue Rundschau,* published numerous articles about Freudian the-ory between 1910 and 1912. Further, Kafka read and discussed the competing psychological theories of Franz Brentano and Sigmund Freud in Bertha Fanta's Prague salon during 1911 and 1912. It is fair to assume that Kafka knew about psychoanalytic views on sexuality, repression, and the family romance. Certainly such motifs as the competitive interaction between Georg and his father; the father's criticism of what he sees as his son's fiancée's flirtatious behavior and his suggestion that Georg violated the memory of his mother by getting engaged; Georg's distress about his father's unwashed underwear; and his desire to please his parents despite his father's final condemnation of him all fit into the mold of Freud's Oedipus complex. Similarly, Georg's procrastination about telling his friend in Russia of his engagement, his unwillingness to invite the friend to his wedding, and his attempt to put his father to bed and cover him up with blankets all suggest that repression and its effects lie at the heart of "Das Urteil." Kafka probably also knew Freud's theories about jokes and puns ("Der Witz und seine Beziehung zum Unbewußten" [Jokes and Their Relation to the Unconscious] had appeared in 1905). Part of the story's narrative wit turns on wordplay involving the idiom "to have someone in one's pocket." Georg, attempting to gain the upper hand over his father, is taken aback when the latter claims not only to be in cahoots with the absent friend in Russia but also to have Georg's customers "in his pocket." "He has pockets even in his nightshirt!" thinks Georg, in his literal-minded way.

Critics generally agree that the "friend in Russia" is Georg's alter ego, a self-projection that has split off from the self who writes the crucial letter about his engagement. Desiring to free himself from the constraints of bourgeois existence (including sexuality and marriage), Georg imagines another self who is a perennial bachelor. This self is represented by the friend in Russia. How does this psychoanalytic reading tie in with the larger thematic concern of home and abroad articulated in the story? One witty moment is Georg's announcement to his father that he has sent news of his engagement "to Petersburg." His father mistakes Georg's meaning; although Georg finds this surprising, no contemporary reader of the story would have done so. In 1912, reporting something "to Petersburg" would have meant sending a diplomatic message via the ambassador stationed in that city. One can imagine listeners chuckling as Kafka read this part of the story aloud.

The most significant breakthrough in "Das Urteil" was Kafka's development of the limited third-person narration that was to be characteristic of many of his most famous texts, including his novels, *Der Verschollene (Amerika: The Man Who Disappeared), Der Proceß (The Trial),* and *Das Schloß (The Castle),* and the major part of his story "Die Verwandlung." Unlike omniscient third-person narration, the limited mode restricts itself to the perceptual field of the protagonist, allowing us access to the character's experiences from within while at the same time providing a measure of distance that enables us also to criticize his understanding.

In his diary entry for September 23, Kafka links "Das Urteil" with a text of his own from the previous year. This possibly unfinished story, "Die städtische Welt" (The Urban World), is an account of a dispute between father and son.

A comparison of "Die städtische Welt" and "Das Urteil" shows very clearly the difference between narrating events from the outside and narrating them from a position close to that of the protagonist. Composed in Kafka's diaries on February 11, 1911, "Die städtische Welt" depicts a student who comes into conflict with his father because of his inability to complete his dissertation. In "Die städtische Welt," both father and son are shown from the outside. By contrast, "Das Urteil" is narrated through the filter of its protagonist's highly ambivalent feelings. In "Die städtische Welt," Oscar's father moves between table and window, is seated or standing, silent or giving vent to accusations by turn; but he never actually seems to change size, as does Georg's father in "Das Urteil." A comparison of the two narratives shows how dramatically the shift to limited third-person presentation opens up possibilities for psychological exploration of the central figure.

Like many literary texts of its time, "Das Urteil" probes the relation between fantasy and reality. Not by chance, the narrative is configured around a complex set of images involving reading and writing. The story opens with Georg sitting at his desk after finishing his letter to the friend in Russia: but writing unleashes fantasy, as Georg's eye shifts from the real scene outside his window to an imagined scenario. The relationship between Georg and his friend is now entirely epistolary. But so is his father's relationship to the friend. Even the father's description of the friend in Russia as "so yellow he's fit to be thrown away" makes the friend sound like one of the old newspapers the father has been pretending to read. Like Prague German, commonly known as "paper German" because of its estrangement from the richer and more vital usage of the German-speaking lands, the friend in Russia is virtually a paper person. This notion that the friend subsists more firmly in writing than in reality permits a multiple pun involving concepts of representation. When Georg's father claims that he has been the "representative" here at home of the friend exiled abroad, the immediate reference is to the business use of this word. The play with "Petersburg" suggests, at the same time, an ambassadorial meaning.

But above all, "Das Urteil" is about the ways in which written language, whether personal correspondence or creative literature, represents reality. Like most of Kafka's writings and those of his modernist contemporaries, "Das Urteil" is a highly self-reflexive text. Kafka was well aware of this aspect of his story. He also saw it as a product of multiple intertextual connections. In the diary entry whose reference to Freud has been cited most often by critics, Kafka notes that he was thinking of many other texts as well while he wrote "Das Urteil": of Max Brod's novel *Arnold Beer*, of the novels of Jakob Wassermann, of Franz Werfel's story "Die Riesin: Ein Augenblick der Seele" (The Giantess: A Moment of the Soul), as well as of his own earlier piece, "Die städtische Welt." While these connections are too sketchily indicated in the diary passage to yield firm conclusions, a common thread in all these texts is a concern with the problem of the creative personality in an alienating modern world.

In this sense, "Das Urteil" is a key text for the study of modernism. It initiates a form that has become the very essence of the "Kafkaesque." This effect is due not only to the presentation of a classic psychological double-bind, but also to the fundamentally polysemantic metaphorical structures of the text. Above all, its modernism expresses itself in the puzzling nature of the story, which requires readers to work through its internal contradictions and pull together its apparently disparate levels of allusion. Objecting, as most readers do, to Georg's passive acceptance of his father's "death sentence" involves us in reading against the grain. The very process of reading "Das Urteil" teaches its readers to do what Georg himself does not: to understand words metaphorically rather than literally.

See also 1899, 1912 (March), 1912 (July), 1914, 1921

Bibliography: Franz Kafka, *Ein Landarzt und andere Drucke zu Lebzeiten* (= *Gesammelte Werke in zwölf Bänden,* vol. 1), ed. Hans-Gerd Koch (Frankfurt: Fischer, 1994). ———, *The Complete Stories,* ed. Nahum N. Glatzer (New York: Schocken, 1971). Mark Anderson, ed., *Reading Kafka: Prague, Politics, and the Fin de Siècle* (New York: Schocken, 1989). Evelyn Beck, *Kafka and the Yiddish Theatre: Its Impact on His Work* (Madison: University of Wisconsin Press, 1971). Stanley Corngold, *Franz Kafka: The Necessity of Form* (Ithaca and London: Cornell University Press, 1988). Richard Gray, ed., *Approaches to Teaching Kafka's Short Fiction* (New York: Modern Language Association of America, 1995). Roy Pascal, *Kafka's Narrators: A Study of His Stories and Sketches* (Cambridge, U.K.: Cambridge University Press, 1982). Ritchie Robertson, *Kafka: Judaism, Politics, and Literature* (Oxford: Clarendon Press, 1985). Walter Sokel, *The Writer in Extremis: Expressionism in Twentieth-Century German Literature* (Stanford: Stanford University Press, 1959).

Judith Ryan

1913, October

Franz Rosenzweig renounces his decision to convert to Christianity

The New Thinking

In the introduction to his magnum opus *Der Stern der Erlösung* (1921; *The Star of Redemption*), Franz Rosenzweig (1886–1929) depicted the horrors of the trenches of World War I as the traumatic experience precipitating the final collapse of a moribund cultural tradition in Europe. Reversing Schiller's call to "throw off the fear of things earthly" in the poem "Das Ideal und das Leben" (The Ideal and Life), Rosenzweig revokes the humanist tradition exemplified by the poet with these words: "All cognition of the All originates in death, in the fear of death. Philosophy takes it upon itself to throw off the fear of things earthly, to rob death of its poisonous sting, and Hades of its pestilential breath" (*Star,* 3). Rosenzweig's own philosophical project, by contrast, was to develop a "new thinking" grounded in the experience of human finitude. In the last year of his life, by then fully paralyzed by the amyotrophic lateral sclerosis he had first contracted in 1921, Rosenzweig read an account of the famous debate between Ernst Cassirer and Martin Heidegger in Davos, Switzerland. He saw this debate as ultimately a struggle between the old and the new thinking. He clearly saw Heidegger's position as akin to his own: "For what else is it when Heidegger, against Cassirer, gives philosophy the task of revealing to man, 'the specifically finite being,' his own 'nothingness in all freedom,' and of calling him back 'to the harshness of destiny, from the lazy aspect of a man who only utilizes the works of the spirit'?" (*Philosophical and Theological Writings*, 150–151). This represents, of course, a radical critique of the ideology of cultural edification and self-perfection associated with the idea of *Bildung* that had so powerfully informed German-Jewish life in the post-Enlightenment era. Indeed, Rosenzweig's entire career as a thinker and cultural figure can be understood as an effort to elaborate a new logic of the "remnant" or "remainder" capable of accounting for the radically finite character of the self. And that logic would, in turn, demand a new conception of community and social engagement. The philosophical and theological rigor with which Rosenzweig elaborated this logic distinguishes his project from numerous other efforts to develop a post-*Bildung* conceptual framework for politics and ethics in the wake of World War I. Among the others who had distinguished themselves in this effort were the German-Jewish intellectuals Ernst Bloch, Gershom Scholem, and Walter Benjamin.

In a sense, Rosenzweig's thought of the remainder begins with renouncing his intended conversion to Christianity. As a young man, he had been a member of a group of historians and philosophers—many like himself students of Friedrich Meinecke—dedicated to bringing about a cultural renewal on the basis of a new appropriation of German Idealism and, more generally, the legacy of 1800. Several of the Jewish members of this circle, among them Rosenzweig's cousins, Hans and Rudolf Ehrenberg, had converted to Christianity, and by 1913 he had resolved to do the same. Because he wanted to convert in the fashion of the original Christians, that is, as a Jew, he immersed himself in Jewish learning first. In the course of these preparations, he underwent a radical change of heart galvanized by a Yom Kippur service he attended in a small, orthodox synagogue in Berlin in October 1913. A few days after this experience, he wrote to his cousin Rudolf Ehrenberg: *"I will remain a Jew"* (Glatzer, *Franz Rosenzweig,* 28).

In the *Star,* Rosenzweig later invoked the prophetic notion of the "remnant of Israel" to suggest a link between the logic of the remainder and of being a Jew: "But Judaism, and it alone in all the world, maintains itself by subtraction, by contraction, by the formation of ever new remnants" (*Star,* 404–405). Rosenzweig sees Judaism as a response to the singularity of human existence. What ultimately makes a human life irreplaceable is not this or that positive attribute, but the utter alterity of death that installs in life a dense core of existential loneliness, and this is, in some sense, who we are. To count as singular, one has to be supernumerary, to persist beyond the logic of parts and wholes, beyond cultural systems of exchange. Death endows existence with what Rosenzweig calls an "indigestible actuality" outside of the cognitively mastered world (*Star,* 11). What he terms the "meta-ethical self" signifies the part that is not part of a whole, an excess out of joint with respect to the generality of any classification or identification.

Once this paradoxical dimension of the meta-ethical self is understood, the contours of Rosenzweig's thinking come into view. What persists in the meta-ethical self is the radical distinctness of the human dimension or realm of being from divine or worldly being. Rosenzweig saw in this the *Gärstoff* (leaven) that thwarts every effort to bind the three realms of being one to the other. He writes in *Philosophical and Theological Writings* that during the three epochs of European philosophy—cosmological antiquity, the theological Middle Ages, and anthropological modernity—these efforts assumed characteristic forms: (1) the essence of the human and divine is located in cosmic phenomena or material forces; (2) the human and worldly are seen as so many attributes or emanations of divinity; (3) God and cosmos are conceived as projections of subjectivity. Once the dimension of the meta-ethical self is understood, all efforts at reduction break down and a new way of thinking emerges, one whose object is not the ultimate essence of God, world, or man, but the modes of relation that obtain among them. *The Star of Redemption* undertakes to think of those relations in terms of the Judeo-Christian concepts of Creation (the relation of God and world), Revelation (the relation of God and man), and Redemption (the relation of man and world).

One way of illuminating the thought revolution Rosenzweig endeavored to bring about is to regard the two modes of thought as distinctive approaches to enigma. In his book *Understanding the Sick and the Healthy: A View of World, Man, and God*—although written to make the *Star* more accessible, he never published it himself—Rosenzweig states that the problem in traditional philosophy (the "old thinking") is that all experiences of enigma are met with the question: What is it really? The radical reorientation in thinking he proposes involves a shift from the epistemological problem of the enigma of the other to the existential, ethical, and ultimately political encounter with the enigma in the other. As he puts it in *The Sick and the Healthy,* the error of the old thinking is the inability to let go of experiences of wonder in the face of the enigmas arising in daily life. The philosopher is unable to wait for life itself to bring the solutions to his marveling, to integrate his wonder into the very fabric of living. With regard to the enigma of sexual difference, for example, Rosenzweig writes that its normal solution is found in the experience of love: "Woman is aroused by man and man submits to woman. But even as they marvel at each other, the solution and dissolution of their wonder is at hand—the love which has befallen them. They are no longer a wonder to each other; *they are in the very heart of wonder*" (*Sick and Healthy,* 40). Every human "coupling," claims Rosenzweig, copes—really, practically—with the enigma of sexual difference. The philosopher, by contrast, is unable to wait for such solutions. "He does not permit his wonder, stored as it is, to be released into the flow of life. He steps outside the continuity of life and consequently the continuity of thought is broken. And there he begins stubbornly to reflect" (40).

This withdrawal from the continuity of life marks the advent of all metaphysical thinking, thinking that aspires to knowledge of the essence of things. None of this would be of any consequence were it not for the fact that metaphysical thinking is not limited to professional philosophers. "But as it happens," Rosenzweig writes, "any man can trip over himself and find himself following the trail of philosophy. No man is so healthy as to be immune from an attack of this disease" (42). The lure of metaphysical thinking doesn't befall everyday life from the outside; everyday life itself is by its very nature susceptible to this withdrawal from, this fantasmatic defense against, our being in the midst or flow of life. Rosenzweig undoubtedly felt that in modernity such defense mechanisms had assumed the status of the norm.

One of the remarkable features of the *Star* bears on the linguistic, indeed the literary, thought upon which its arrangement rests. The relations among the three regions of being, whose irreducibility has been established, can be realized only in the context of a linguistic practice correlated with a specific horizon of temporality. This view has much in common with, and is perhaps in part indebted to, Friedrich Hölderlin's doctrine of the modulation of tones in poetic speech. Creation, revelation, and redemption form a sequence (*Reihe*) in which an epic tonality gives way to lyrical address and then, finally, to a dramatic mode of enunciation. As Rosenzweig puts it with reference to the structure of the *Star*:

> And now this great world poem is retold in three tenses. However, it is really narrated in the first book alone, the book of the past. In the present, the narration gives way to immediate exchange of speech because what is present, whether human beings or God, cannot be spoken of in the third person; they can only be listened to and addressed. And in the book of the future, the language of the chorus governs, for the future seizes the individual only where and when it can say *We*.
>
> (*Philosophical and Theological Writings,* 125)

Worldly being as creation (or *creature*) is thus sustained by narrative speech in the past indicative (as in Genesis 1). The full experience of presentness, as the always unprecedented intensity of the now, is revealed in the imperative urgency of a lover's address—exemplified in the Song of Songs, which Rosenzweig considered the key document of revelation. The experience of the future as passionately anticipated is sustained by liturgical practices of praise and thanksgiving—as in the exhortative Psalm 115.

It was this messianic understanding of the dimension of futurity that led Rosenzweig to a radical critique of historicism. (The messianic critique of historicism is better known from the work of Walter Benjamin, on whom Rosenzweig had an enormous influence.) Without a supplementary orientation toward the Kingdom—at least that is Rosenzweig's wager—the historical imagination remains stuck in a narrow and rigid conception of what is, at any given moment, possible in human life and society. The future without such anticipation, without this "wish to bring about the Messiah before his time," or the temptation to "coerce the kingdom of God into being" is no real future. It is only "something that drags itself everlastingly along the long, long trail of time" (*Star,* 227).

Rosenzweig's entire thinking might be encapsulated in the idea that human beings are oriented in the world not only by the norms of the social reality into which they are born, but also by the intervention of "truth-events"—to borrow a term from Alain Badiou—that gather a subject from that which is left over and is unable to be taken into this shared space of reasons. That which is foreclosed from the symbolic, from the space of social reality in which individuals assume their identity can, Rosenzweig suggests, return in the demand for radical transformation of that reality, a demand authorized by the eventful revelation of one's singularity. Singularity is the possibility of more life that opens at the points where the identities in which we have invested ourselves break down under a pressure immanent in identity formation itself. Paradoxically, it is from such fractured events that the subject is able to elaborate forms of fidelity to that very unbinding. The liturgical practices of the two communities of faith that shaped the Western tradition provide to Rosenzweig's mind the primary form of this paradoxical fidelity. They hold out the possibility of not forgetting, of ever renewing, the eventful emergence of one's singularity beyond the attributes of socially sanctioned identity. The proper field of such fidelity is not the mystical cultivation of contact with the divine, but the very social reality that produced it as its remainder. The special position of Judaism and Christianity, writes Rosenzweig in the *Star,* "consists precisely in this: that even if they have become religion, they find in themselves the impulses to free themselves from their religiosity in order to find their way back to the open field of actuality" (*Philosophical and Theological Writings,* 130).

It perhaps makes good sense, then, that Rosenzweig abandoned a promising academic career and dedicated himself, after completing the *Star,* to a unique project in Jewish adult education. Founded in Frankfurt in 1920, the Free Jewish *Lehrhaus* (house of teaching) was an institution designed to offer a radically new model of *Bildung* to acculturated Jews, one that would allow for a certain dissimilation after more than a century of efforts to assimilate into the wider society. This would be "a new sort of learning," one for which "he is the most apt who brings with him the maximum of what is alien" (Glatzer, *Rosenzweig,* 231). In a long, passionate letter to Friedrich Meinecke, Rosenzweig explained why he left the university. "The one thing I wish to make clear," he wrote, "is that scholarship [*Wissenschaft*] no longer holds the center of my attention, and that my life has fallen under the rule of a dark drive of which I'm aware that I merely name by calling it my Judaism." One of the effects of this rule was, as Rosenzweig put it, that he was now more firmly rooted in the earth than he had been when he wrote his dissertation, "Hegel and the State," under Meinecke's supervision. This rootedness was an enhanced capacity to find value in the mundane details of everyday life: "The small, at times exceedingly small, thing called [by Goethe] demand of the day [*Forderung des Tages*] which is made upon me in my position at Frankfurt, I mean the nerve-wracking, picayune, and at the same time very necessary struggles with people and conditions, has now become the real core of my existence and I love this form of existence despite the inevitable annoyance that goes with it" (Glatzer, *Rosenzweig,* 96–97).

One should, no doubt, hear in the phrase "Forderung des Tages" something far more resonant than Rosenzweig appears to be saying in the narrow context of this letter. One should think, above all, of his otherwise confusing oscillation in his discussion of the neighbor in the *Star,* between the use of the masculine and the neuter forms *der Nächste/das Nächste:* he who is most proximate, what is most proximate or nearest at hand. In the *Star* it is clear that Rosenzweig means not simply spatial proximity but a specific "manifestation of urgency"—to use a locution from Benjamin—at a moment of danger. These are moments when the fantasmatic organization we have (unconsciously) given to what was precluded from our social reality becomes insupportable. What is most proximate, *das Nächste,* is thus not only the one nearest me or even the one whose distress calls out to me but also the very situation of distress in which I now find *myself* implicated. The "nearest thing" is, thus, not simply the other in need but also the very barrier—a barrier sustained by the work of fantasy—that keeps me separated from him or her. And as Rosenzweig suggests in the final words of the *Star,* each time we work through such a barrier, each time we respond to such a demand of the day, we enter more fully, more profoundly, into the midst of life *(ins Leben).*

See also 1792 (August 26), 1808, 1828 (Winter), 1831, 1902, 1927, 1936 (February), 1946–1947

Bibliography: Nahum Glatzer, ed., *Franz Rosenzweig: His Life and Thought* (Indianapolis, Ind.: Hackett, 1998). Martin Heidegger, *Kant und das Problem der Metaphysik* (Frankfurt am Main: Vittorio Klostermann, 1973). Franz Rosenzweig, *The Star of Redemption,* trans. William W. Hallo (Notre Dame, Ind.: University of Notre Dame Press, 1985). ———, *Understanding the Sick and the Healthy: A View of World, Man, and God,* trans. Nahum Glatzer (Cambridge, Mass.: Harvard University Press, 1999). ———, *Philosophical and Theological Writings,* trans. and ed. Paul W. Franks and Michael L. Morgan (Indianapolis, Ind.: Hackett, 2000). Eric L. Santner, *On the Psychotheology of Everyday Life: Reflections on Freud and Rosenzweig* (Chicago and London: University of Chicago Press, 2001).

Eric L. Santner

᪥ *1914, July*

Franz Kafka transposes the guilt of an unredeemed literary promise into his novel *Der Proceß*

Ecstatic Release from Personality

Franz Kafka (1883–1924) was born into a German-speaking Jewish family in Prague, the capital of a Czech-dominated province of the Austro-Hungarian Empire. He attended the German National Altstädter Gymnasium, studied law at the German Charles University, and worked for thirteen years at the partly state-run Workers' Accident Insurance Institute. He lived out his secretly tormented life within a radius of a few miles from the Old Town center, held captive by the city he called the "little mother with claws." The tension of these inner identity conflicts in isolation from the "din of the world" is reflected in the main characters of his three novels, all unfinished and unpublished in his lifetime: *Der Verschollene* (1912–1914, publ. 1927; *Amerika,* better, *The Boy Who Was Never Heard from Again*); *Der Proceß* (1914–1915, publ. 1925; *The Trial*); and *Das Schloß* (1922, publ. 1926; *The Castle*). While he took great interest in the politics, history, and public culture of his place and time, he transposed the polemical complex into a private, recondite, dreamlike fictional work.

Although he rose to the position of senior legal secretary at the company where he worked, Kafka was, by his own account, a token Jew among Germans and, after 1918, a token German among Czechs. The "world of the office" shapes the spaces within which Josef K., the central character of *The Trial,* encounters the court officials who have him arrested for an unnamed crime. Other parts of the urban landscape Josef K. traverses on his quest, such as attics and lower-middle-class tenements, were familiar to Kafka from his erotically charged city walks and from visits to the homes of insurance clients. But office work and urban distractions also drained his energy and threatened to leave nothing over for what chiefly mattered to him: literature.

Kafka funneled his preoccupation with guilt and guiltless ecstasy after 1900 into his writings. When he wrote well, he knew ecstatic moods of extraordinary intensity. He wrote in his *Diaries* about the composition in 1912 of his breakthrough story "Das Urteil" (The Judgment): "Only *in this way* can writing be done, only with such coherence, with such a complete opening up of the body and the soul." "The Judgment," which, like *The Trial,* ends with a death sentence carried out at the behest of an inexplicably powerful anonymous authority, allowed Kafka to realize a portion of his "creative abilities," "mysterious powers which are of ultimate significance to me." Here, in the literary field, he noted in his *Diaries,* "I experienced states . . . in which I completely dwelt in every idea, . . . and not only felt myself at my boundary, but at the boundary of the human in general." However, when he began writing "In der Strafkolonie" (In the Penal Colony) in late 1914, he noted about the abject prisoner awaiting execution, "He seems to have forgotten his own judgment [to wit, Kafka's story 'The Judgment']"! Since Kafka's "happiness, abilities, and every possibility of being useful in any way" had always been in the literary field, to forget such things would be to provoke at least his moral death.

On the face of it, the fate of Josef K., a high-ranking bank official, has little in common with the fate of the modern writer. Yet, other *Diary* entries decidedly prefigure the analogy between Kafka the writer and the feckless Josef K. in their common relation to a third entity, the higher court. In 1910, Kafka wrote: "How do I excuse my not yet having written anything today? In no way [*mit nichts*]. . . . I have continually an invocation in my ear: 'Were you to come, invisible judgment [*Gericht*]!'" Between 1910 and 1914 the court's claim sounded ever more decisive. In 1913 Kafka describes himself to his fiancée, Felice Bauer, as a man "chained to invisible literature by invisible chains [who] . . . screams when approached because, so he claims, someone is touching those chains." This image sponsors a scene in *The Trial,* in which an accused man in the law offices screams when Josef K. touches his arm "quite gently." The usher explains: "Most defendants are so sensitive." "Chained" to their guilt, which gives them a sensitive surface, they are like Kafka, "chained" to literature, an inexhaustible source of guilt as a higher promise only intermittently redeemed.

The Trial also alludes to Kafka's personal struggle as a writer by suggesting that the verdict against Josef K. is a judgment, not on the unexplained accusation with which he is confronted at the outset, but on the way in which he conducts his case. As the Chaplain explains in the Cathedral scene, "The proceedings gradually merge into the judgment." In a letter to Felice, Kafka wrote: "I have never been the sort of person who carries something out at all costs. . . . What I have written was written in a lukewarm bath." In the matter of its erotic character, too, there may be no great difference in the way Kafka the writer and Josef K. the bank officer conduct their cases. The Chaplain charges Josef K., "You seek too much outside help, . . . particularly from women." This remark could refer to K.'s sexual dalliances with the student's lover, following the First Interrogation, and with Leni in the chambers of Lawyer Huld ("Grace"). It also refers especially to his hopes aimed at a woman of somewhat more elevated social standing, the petty bourgeois Fräulein Bürstner (whom he has nonetheless sexually molested). As K. is half-dragged, half-escorted to his death in the closing chapter, he glimpses her figure ahead of him, and for an instant she seems to evoke, if only inadvertently, a moment of insight into "the futility of resistance." Perhaps he has learned a little at the end, when he discards his impulse to keep Fräulein Bürstner steadily in view ("he could do without her now"), or perhaps he simply drops her out of apathy.

What, one might ask, does K.'s sex-besotted manner of conducting his trial have to do with Kafka as a writer? One should not underestimate the autoeroticism of the writing intensity for Kafka. This deeply private, not so innocent, game stands opposed in his mind to married sex, and yet it is not sex; better, it is that sex which is not-sex, or may not seem to be the ascetic delight to which Kafka gives the dubious names "dilettantism" and "mania for pleasure," and which for him lacks all redemptive qualities. In 1920, he wrote the summary aphorism about a person he calls "He":

> All that he does seems to him, it is true, extraordinarily new, but also, because of the incredible spate of new things, extraordinarily dilettantish, indeed scarcely tolerable, incapable of becoming history, breaking short the chain of the generations, cutting off for the first time at its most profound source the music of the world, which before him could at least be divined. Sometimes in his arrogance, he has more anxiety for the world than for himself.

The pleasure of writing here appears equivalent neither to the ecstatic loss of self in writing nor to the sexual act of maintaining "the chain of generations." Mere perverse delight in writing recurs throughout Kafka's work. In a famous letter to Max Brod (July 5, 1922), he links his *Schriftstellersein* (being a writer) to

Genußsucht, or a mania for pleasure, and damns it as "devil's work." Kafka writes for the complex pleasure writing gives—the pleasure of writing is the sex of the ascetic and hence part of an economy of guilt. So it may not be surprising that when he began his work on *The Trial,* in late July 1914, just before the outbreak of the world war, he should profess, "I am hardly moved by all the misery and more determined than ever. . . . I will write in spite of everything, absolutely; it is my fight for self-preservation." Since the idea of self-preservation includes the pleasure of the individual subject, especially under such circumstances, it will provoke a heightened sense of guilt. Without positing an efflux of the guilt attaching to the very project of writing *The Trial,* it would be difficult to understand Josef K.'s readiness, by and large, to acknowledge a trial that lacks any civil-legal justification. The conflict between the pleasure of writing and married sex had become especially acute for Kafka at that time. The onset of composition was dictated by twin catastrophes: The break-up of his engagement with Felice Bauer took place at the Hotel Askanischer Hof in Berlin on July 23, which he called "the court of justice in the hotel." On July 28, Austria declared war on Serbia. In a mood of jubilation, possibly in anticipation of his own explosive destruction, Kafka wanted to enlist but was rejected. Owing to the general mobilization, he had to move out of his parents' apartment and, as he put it, "receive the reward of living alone," adding, "but it is hardly a reward; living alone results only in punishment."

In fact, in late 1914, Kafka was able to work on *The Trial* for several months with good progress. His determination to provide this novel with an ending showed itself in an extraordinary compositional maneuver. Feeling that he would never be able to bring his previous novel, *Der Verschollene,* to a close, this time he wrote the first chapter, "The Arrest," together with the final chapter, "The End," and, moreover, left a coded marker in the novel of what he had done. Here is a sign of what Malcolm Pasley has described as "the parallel process run through by fictional events and the acts of writing that produced them." It is worth noting that the German word for "trial," which Kafka spells "Proceß," means precisely this in English: process. Thus a specific connection exists between Josef K.'s trial and Kafka's own "trial" of writing this novel. These two processes, or trials, act and react together and in some instances actually seem to fuse. For example: "On the way to his execution, K. urges himself to stay calm and analytical," adding: "Do I want to show now that even a yearlong trial could teach me nothing? . . . Shall they say of me that at the beginning of my trial I wanted to end it, and now, at its end, I want to begin it again?" This reflection is remarkable considering that Kafka intended to end writing *The Trial* at the very beginning (of his writing it); and now, having reached the end, he wanted to begin again. Writing these lines, Kafka was in the very process of ending his own *Proceß* at its inception—in order to take up where he had left off with Josef K.'s arrest. A difference in valence within the symmetry of Josef K. and Kafka opens up, however: what Josef K. in no way wants to be said about him, Kafka wants, above all, to be said on his account.

This difference is a measure of the varying consciousness of their predicament. Kafka wrote *The Trial* precisely because, unlike Josef K., he was unable to declare himself innocent.

It can be said, then, that Kafka began his project with defiant expectancy, but, as his mood darkened, a punishable guilt for the entire process set in, which he expressed in a specific invidious comparison between this process and that of the time of his literary breakthrough in 1912. On August 15, 1914, he notes: "Today I am not so completely protected by and absorbed by my work as I was two years ago [that is, during the period of the main composition of *Der Verschollene,* "Das Urteil," and "Die Verwandlung"]; nevertheless, I have a direction, my regular, empty, insane bachelor's life has a justification." Writing *The Trial* becomes more and more an act of establishing the author's superiority over his hypocrite brother Josef K., which, however, appears to become harder and harder to do. Yet it is clear that if Kafka does not succeed in finishing off Josef K. in a coherent manner, it is he himself who will be finished.

Thereafter there are few happy diary entries during the process of writing *The Trial.* By the beginning of the following year, the project had run aground. However, what was at stake for Kafka throughout the writing of *The Trial* was something beyond alleviating his empirical miseries. He seeks justification—redemption into the (greater) freedom that perhaps awaits him, as he states—which depends entirely on his continuing to write while still condemning Josef K. The tension created by these goals and the author's lack of sympathy for the central character places this novel in an unusual position within Kafka's oeuvre. Kafka's decision to compose the scene of Josef K.'s brutal execution at the very outset may derive from his need to make sure he would be punished. Later on, he seems unable to justify this action. His callousness can be understood as a reflex of the intensity of his desire to annihilate his own empirical ego as the bearer of a life situation he could not endure—that of the writer who does not write or does not write well enough. At the same time, as a writer, as a warrant of the ecstatic promise of self-annihilation, he means to survive. Hence, nothing in Kafka is linear, and nothing he does or writes is without a touch of subterfuge, as he was the first to concede. Even Josef K.'s condemnation in advance is arranged along ingenious rhetorical lines that cast doubt on its validity.

In its first manuscript version, the opening sentence of *The Trial* reads: "Someone must have slandered Josef K., for one morning, without having done anything truly wrong, he was *captured*" (emphasis added). Later Kafka crossed out the word "captured" and replaced it with the more obviously legal term "arrested." The shift into legal language supplies the inner design for the novel, which Kafka elaborated further as he wrote. The design may be understood as Josef K.'s attempt to come to terms with his sense of guilt by insufficient—indeed, by childish—means.

Josef K. presumes that he will be brought to trial by a duly constituted civil court, which, even in the absence of specific charges, will exonerate him. But he merely repeats Kafka's authorial leap into a seeming legality and thus takes the bait that will lead to his death, for it becomes increasingly evident that no ordinary legal means exist for his rescue. It is Kafka as author who made the leap ahead of K. when he replaced "captured" with "arrested": the author is guilty of this evasive leap of thought before his puppet is. The manuscript inscribes the impulse to flee an existential drama for a legal one as the very move that Josef K. will be punished for making. Josef K. acts at odds with the truth of his situation, but in forcing him to do so, Kafka does not obviously distance his character from himself. By making K. misunderstand his situation and only hinting at its truth, Kafka makes sure that the truth exists essentially as something K. will never grasp.

If this truth has been shown to be an efflux of the guilt that originated in Kafka's *Schriftstellersein,* does this establish Kafka's superiority over his victim in the novel? Or have we finally returned to a guilt whose ultimate origin compels it to remain an enigma? Josef K.'s death by stabbing is especially harrowing to witness, since it is impossible to know whether it is deserved or not. Perhaps it is this very impossibility that sustains *The Trial* as an indispensable work of literary consciousness.

See also 1899, 1906, 1912 (June), 1929 (Autumn)

Bibliography: Franz Kafka, *Der Process,* ed. Malcolm Pasley (Frankfurt am Main: Fischer, 1990). ———, *Der Process,* ed. Roland Reuß (Frankfurt am Main: Stroemfeld/Roter Stern, 1998). ———, *The Trial,* trans. Breon Mitchell (New York: Schocken, 1998). Stanley Corngold, "*The Trial* / 'In the Penal Colony': The Rigors of Writing," in *Franz Kafka: The Necessity of Form* (Ithaca, N.Y.: Cornell University Press, 1988), 228–249. Heinz Politzer, *Franz Kafka: Parable and Paradox* (Ithaca, N.Y.: Cornell University Press, 1962), 163–217. Ritchie Robertson, "The Intricate Ways of Guilt: *Der Prozeß* (1914)," in *Kafka: Judaism, Politics, and Literature* (Oxford, U.K.: Clarendon, 1985), 87–130.

Stanley Corngold

1916, February 5
Cabaret Voltaire opens in Zurich

"The Jingling Carnival Goes Right Out Into the Street"

Like many German artists, the dramatist-poet Hugo Ball and the singer-poet Emmy Hennings left their country for Zurich because of the First World War. Lacking any other way to make a living, they opened a nightclub where they could exploit Ball's ability to play the piano and Hennings's repertoire of café tunes. They found a bar at 1 Spiegelgasse, a twisting street in the older part of town. Having already made common cause with the Alsatian poet and sculptor Hans Arp, they placed notices in the local papers, inviting "young artists" to "give musical performances and readings at the daily meetings," or to offer "suggestions and contributions of all kinds" for an intended "center for artistic entertainment."

The result of this genteel entreaty was an explosion. The core group that made up the company of Cabaret Voltaire—completed by two Romanians, the painter Marcel Janco, and the poet and dramatist Tristan Tzara, who appeared the first night, and the German poet and medical student Richard Huelsenbeck, who arrived a week or two later—immediately launched into increasingly bizarre and unstable performances. The small bar was packed every night. People from all parts of Europe climbed out of the audience to recite poems and sing obscene songs. Boundaries collapsed between art forms—poetry, drama, music, dance—and between works seriously offered to the audience and performances, provoking fights with the crowd. A cloud of art-as-redemption was first ignored, then satirized, and then attacked head-on. A hailstorm of art-as-destruction—of all illusions, and first the illusion that any form of art, or idea of culture, could be superior to ordinary life—came down as noise music and sound poetry, violent gestures and outlandish costumes. Though failing to destroy the cloud of redemption, that storm made the audience, and history, forget the cloud was there. Within two months, as Ball wrote in his journal on March 2, the cabaret had become "a race with the expectations of the audience."

Of the countless attempts by historians, critics, and participants to fix the meaning of what took place at the Cabaret Voltaire—events that by April took the name "dada," found in a dictionary, meaning yes and no, hello and goodbye, father and hobby-horse, shampoo and scum—this was the most profound. By placing artist and audience on the same plane of moral authority and aesthetic will, the phrase contained a complete critique of Kultur—of German culture as a god and all Germans as its exemplars, made in its image.

As Huelsenbeck would never cease to brag as the century moved on, when Hitler denounced Dada in *Mein Kampf,* and then at the 1934 Nuremberg speech filmed in *Triumph of the Will,* he was embracing the very sense of culture that Dada had already damned—heroic Kultur as at once the creator and tribune of the national soul. As Huelsenbeck explained in Berlin after the war, it was the cauldron of the Cabaret Voltaire that had for the first time truly asked the question, "What is German culture? (Answer: Shit)." Kultur was "the idea of a nation" as a "cultural association of *psychopaths*" who "march off with a volume of Goethe in their knapsacks to skewer Frenchmen and Russians on their bayonets." It was an idea Theodor Adorno echoed after the Second World War when he stated, "To write poetry after Auschwitz is barbaric." The implication was that poetry should have prevented Auschwitz, should have made mankind too good for such an atrocity, and having failed to do so, had travestied itself. It was this church of culture that Dada sought to destroy or, rather, dispel—because Dada understood Kultur *as* a spell—in favor of the charnel house of what Ball, Tzara, Arp, Janco, and Huelsenbeck, each arguing with himself more than with the others, would call "life" or "time."

The dadaists watched—they watched themselves, as if standing outside their own, previous identities—as an evening of Russian folk songs gave way to a French-German-English poem chanted, screamed, danced, and whispered by Tzara, Janco, and Huelsenbeck, as Ball's performance of Bach, Brahms, and "It's a Long, Long Way to Tipperary" turned into six-way lewd dancing. In such storied works as Ball's "Karawane" or Huelsenbeck's "Negro poems," the very words of poetry were turned blank and void, with sounds freed from argument and set loose in the room as pure signifiers, or anti-signifiers. On April 11, 1916, following disagreements among the Dada six over the formal establishment of a society, an international exhibition, and a literary anthology, Ball ecstatically reported from the cabaret that "the jingling carnival goes right out into the street." They came to understand that the purpose of the nightly performances was not art, not literature. In Ball's more rational formulation, the race with the audience was a search "for the specific rhythm and the buried face of this age . . . for the possibility of its being stirred, its awakening. Art is only an occasion for that, a method." Or, as Arp put it, "For the dadaist, life is the meaning of art." "Madness and murder were rampant when Dada in the year 1916 rose out of the primordial depths of Zurich," he wrote in 1948. "Dada wanted to frighten mankind out of its pitiful impotence."

"Whoever has made the most of his time has lived for all times," Huelsenbeck said in 1920, as if to suggest that by pursuing Dada to the fullest—"Dada came over the dadaists without their knowing it," he said elsewhere that same year: "In the hands of the gentlemen in Zurich, Dada grew into a creature that stood head and shoulders above all present," but "despite the most impassioned efforts, no one had yet found out what Dada was"—the dadaists were sacrificing themselves to history, for the sake of those to come. It was a suggestion Huelsenbeck immediately reversed, as if Dada itself could bring about what he had called for in one of his favorite Cabaret Voltaire poems, "The End of the World." "The time is Dada-ripe," he wrote in 1920. "With Dada it will ascend, and with Dada it will vanish." The Cabaret Voltaire was "a laboratory," one critic wrote decades later, merely skating over the surface of Arp's Frankensteinian "Automatic Drawing, 1916": "The law of chance, which contains all other laws, and is as incomprehensible for us as the primal origins of life, can only be experienced by yielding oneself to the subconscious. I maintain that he who observes this law will create pure life."

In the race between the dadaists and their audience, between their performances and time, time and the audience outstripped performance. In 1958 Huelsenbeck was a Manhattan psychoanalyst. He sat in his office at 88 Central Park West and looked out on the park, "mild and green": "And yet at night, women are raped there, and anyone out for a breath of air will be mugged by gangsters. That's what dada is—a movement with inner danger. When you approach it, it's like a purring cat. You'd like to caress it and draw sparks from its fur. But if you try, then the sparks turn into nuclear catastrophes. *In 1916, dada was what is occurring now in the heart of the man in the street.* Then only a very few of us felt it; now everybody feels it on his back."

The Cabaret Voltaire lasted less than six months. In that time it became a legend—a legend ambitiously exported to Paris by Tzara and to Berlin by Huelsenbeck. Soon enough "dada" would be the magic watchword "the gentlemen in Zurich" knew it could be, seized on by artists' groups in New York and all over Europe. For the rest of the century, in unlikely places around the world—in nightclubs in London, in the streets in Zurich—people would claim the word, or the legacy, as they tried to live out the Dada idea.

The idea was that in a single place, in a single moment of time, it was possible to utter words or make gestures that would negate all the shibboleths and pieties, all the received truths and unquestioned propositions, of one's own place and time. "Adopt symmetries and rhythms instead of principles," as Ball wrote on March 12, 1916, fashioning a manifesto without the title. "Oppose word systems and acts of state by transforming them into a phrase or a brushstroke": transforming them *into* a phrase or a brushstroke, not the utilitarian *by* a phrase or a brushstroke, because through any such actions, word systems and acts of state might be redecorated, but they would remain word systems and acts of state.

In the cabaret, the gestures included such acts as Huelsenbeck pounding on an oversized drum, rolling it across the stage, sitting on it, then kicking it, then examining it as if the sounds issuing from it had an unquestioned effect and no apparent cause; the whole company appearing in grotesque masks contrived by Janco, the faces of the six torn to pieces as if by grenades and patched up again; Ball encasing himself in a multicolored cardboard costume, designed by Janco, his hands wrapped in claws, his arms in enormous flapping wings, on his head a striped toque two feet high, and chanting blank sounds with such conviction the crowd leaned forward to catch their meaning ("like a magical bishop," Ball said, but he looked just as much like a magical beetle—transformed into, not transformed by). The words included suggestive songs by the French cabaret composer Aristide Bruant, poetry by Apollinaire, and Ball's declaiming "The Prophet's Ascent" from his unfinished novel *Tenderenda the Fantasist,* an allegory of a savior as con man as entertainer. "Verily, nothing is as it seems," the prophet says; soon he is "dazzled by the bluster of his own words." He flaps his arms and flies—but the crowd in the city below, gathered to greet "a new God," responds only with contempt. The prophet gives in to their calls for his greatest hit, the one trick he's known for. He produces "the magnifier," a giant mirror, holds it up to the jeering rabble, and then vanishes as the shards of the magic glass "sliced through the houses, sliced through the people, the cattle . . . all the unbelievers, so that the count of the gelded mounted from day to day." "The Spiegelgasse was a mirror without a reflection of ourselves," Huelsenbeck wrote on December 26, 1965, on the fiftieth anniversary of the Cabaret Voltaire. Is this what he meant? Did the people in the cabaret—the drunken students and the curious tourists, the artists and the philosophers—understand that this was as full a statement as any the dadaists could make about what they were and what they wanted? Did it matter? The Cabaret Voltaire was a nightclub; bills had to be paid, broken glass had to be replaced, something better, stranger, louder had to be found for the next night, or the place would have to close.

Even though the race between artists and their audiences became more frantic as the century moved on, the idea of such a race proved to be infinitely exportable. With or without the Dada name, it excluded no one. "We never promised anybody anything," Huelsenbeck wrote in 1957. Dada, he said, "developed out of nothing into something, but even in somethingness, it never lost the feeling of nothingness." This was the smell of the laboratory, the spell of negation, the faith that oppression, power, orthodoxy, even guns and tanks could be erased as one covered over a brushstroke or crossed out a phrase. It was a promise that erased itself, in its self-parody, its ridiculousness, its megalomania, its shell-game. If they believe this, they'll believe anything, one can hear Ball saying to himself when on Bastille Day 1916, in the Waag Hall in Zurich, at the first and last Dada concert in Zurich, he issued his "Dada Manifesto": "How does one achieve eternal bliss? By saying dada. How does one become famous? By saying dada. With a noble gesture and delicate propriety. Till one goes crazy. Till one loses consciousness . . . Dada world war without end, dada revolution without beginning." *If they believe this they'll believe anything, but am I sure I don't believe it?*

In 2002, Swiss Life, the insurance concern that then owned 1 Spiegelgasse, announced its intention to convert the disco on the ground floor into shops. Sixty young people, dressed in the most respectable or disreputable costumes, occupied the space. They painted their faces white, or put on masks, or, for a photographer, held black strips over their eyes, precisely as one would hold up a disposable camera, but without hiding their grins. "Dada ist global," ran a headline in the Zurich *Tages-Anzeiger.* "Ist Dada auch lokal?"

Whether Dada is local or not in Zurich today, it was global in Zurich in 1916. It was the presence on stage and in the audience of people from different nations, and the speech of many nations as it came from those on stage to the audience or from the audience to those on stage, that helped demystify German Kultur and German literature in the Cabaret Voltaire. The sound poems, the poems in three languages simultaneously, took the demystification further. It was a serious intellectual experiment. "We have now driven the plasticity of the word to the point where it can scarcely be equaled. We have achieved this at the expense of the rational, logically constructed sentence," Ball wrote on June 18, 1916. "You may laugh; language will one day reward us for our zeal . . . We have loaded the word with strengths and energies that helped us rediscover the evangelical concept of 'the word' (logos) as a magical complex image."

As literature Dada did not exist. No argument can be made for a transformative effect of the Cabaret Voltaire on German literature. Rather, Dada as an event, as an experiment, the Cabaret Voltaire as a laboratory, as a nightclub that opened and closed, remained, and remains today, as doubt. Then and now, Dada asks, Is this great novel in truth a hoax? Is the speech given by the Nobel laureate, the prime minister, the reclusive poet accepting an honorary degree, fully as void as virtuous people cannot allow themselves to suspect it might be? Forcefully, uproariously in 1916, perhaps altogether silently in most of the years that followed, Dada is the question, the rebuke, the dunce cap lying in wait for

any celebrated artist or politician, any irrefutable proposition or historical necessity foolish enough to expose itself to its Dada double, which can reappear
in any place at any time. Arp, 1948: "Despite the war, it was a lovely era which
we will always remember as idyllic when the next world war comes and we are
changed into hamburger and scattered to the four corners of the world."

See also 1906, 1912 (March)

Bibliography: Jean (Hans) Arp, *Jours Effeuillés,* ed. Marcel Jean (Paris: Gallimard, 1966); English
edition, *Arp on Arp,* trans. Joachim Neugroschel (New York: Viking, 1972). Hugo Ball, *Die Flucht
aus der Zeit* (Munich: Duncker and Humblot, 1927); English edition, *Flight out of Time,* ed.
John Elderfield, trans. Ann Raimes (Berkeley: University of California Press, 1996). ———,
Tenderenda the Fantasist (1914–1920), trans. Malcolm Green, in *Blago Bung Blago Bung Bosso
Fataka!* ed. Malcolm Green (London: Atlas Press, 1995). Richard Huelsenbeck, *En avant Dada*
(Hanover: Paul Steegemann Verlag, 1920); trans. Ralph Manheim, in *The Dada Painters and Poets*
(1951), 2nd ed. (Cambridge, Mass.: Harvard University Press, 1989). ———, ed., *Dada Almanach*
(Berlin: Erich Reiss Verlag, 1920; facsimile edition, New York: Something Else Press, 1966).
———, *Memoirs of a Dada Drummer,* ed. Hans J. Kleinschmidt, trans. Joachim Neugroschel
(Berkeley: University of California Press, 1991); includes *Mit Witz, Licht und Grütze: Auf den
Spuren des Dadaismus* (Wiesbaden: Limes Verlag, 1957). "Dada ist global. Ist Dada auch lokal?"
Tages-Anzeiger (Zurich), March 16, 2002.

Greil Marcus

1918, November

During the final days of the First World War, Karl Kraus's epilogue, "Die letzte
Nacht," to his not yet published antiwar drama *Die letzten Tage der Menschheit* is
rushed into print

War and the Press

Even careful readers of Karl Kraus's (1874–1936) satirical journal *Die Fackel
(The Torch),* in which many of the documents that undergo dramatization in
The Last Days of Mankind first appeared, must have been surprised by the way
the tragedy was initially published. A series of four special issues opened unexpectedly with a photograph of Kaiser Wilhelm II standing in a wintry landscape juxtaposed with the epilogue's title, "The Last Night." The use of this
image as the frontispiece, traditionally reserved for a portrait of the author, suggests the emperor's and, indeed, Germany's responsibility for the catastrophic
conclusion of the war. Given Wilhelm's abdication in early November 1918
and precipitate flight to Holland, this combination of frontispiece and title
page evoked the iconography of a "Wanted" poster. And the closing line—"I
did not want this to happen"—returns to the German emperor, who had
made this remark in 1915 after witnessing heavy casualties on the Western
front. By having not Wilhelm but the "Voice of God" speak these words, the
sentiment is stripped of its ameliorative historical context and becomes an expression of eschatological uncertainty.

Kraus's prompt, aggressive response in 1918 contrasts starkly with his restraint at the outbreak of the war. Unlike some greater, and many lesser, writers who rushed to literary arms, Kraus did not react in print at all. He suspended publication of *Die Fackel* for almost six months before breaking his silence in December 1914 with an issue comprising in its entirety the essay "In These Great Times," in which he painstakingly deconstructed the widely held notion that the war would bring spiritual and intellectual renewal. In subsequent wartime issues, Kraus refined the satirical method he had developed of criticizing the press by glossing extensive quotations from articles and advertisements in daily newspapers and other journalistic venues. Although he had once coined the aphorism "Satires the censor understands should be banned," he occasionally had to leave embarrassing blank spaces as traces of censorship in *Die Fackel*. These unaccustomed setbacks and the access he subsequently gained to material too sensitive to publish under martial law must have been prime considerations in his decision to express his condemnation of the war in dramatic form.

The "monstrous drama," as Kraus himself called it, allowed the satirist to document the horrendous events that took place in four years of war and to transform them in an expressionist manner. Following the publication of the so-called Act Edition between November 1918 and August 1919, Kraus made extensive revisions between 1920 and 1921. No longer bound by censorship, and responding to postwar revelations, he reworked a handful of scenes and added almost fifty more. The play first appeared in book form in 1922, and it was reissued in a final, minimally revised edition in 1926.

Despite the drama's apocalyptic title, the opening scene of the prologue begins with an incident firmly grounded in historical reality. A newsboy shouts out headlines about the event that precipitated the war, the assassination of Archduke Franz Ferdinand in Sarajevo on June 28, 1914. Each first scene in the following five acts begins almost identically, with some variation on "Extra, extra, read all about it!" The dramatic treatment of this acoustic detail culminates in Act V, Scene 53, with corybants and maenads parading through the streets while headlines become unintelligible screams and the formulaic "Extra!" decomposes dadaistically into eerie babbling: "xtra!-tra!-ra!"

Even if this discordant leitmotif of the press's ubiquity did not reverberate throughout the play, it would be impossible to overlook the centrality of newspapers and their readers. The Patriot and the Subscriber, characters who engage periodically in what might be called chauvinistic monologues in two parts, the Oldest Subscriber, and his intimate associate Old Biach all figure prominently as consumers of journalism. What they subscribe to—in the broadest sense of the term—is the *Neue Freie Presse (New Free Press)*, the "prayer book of cultured people everywhere," a journalistic encomium cited approvingly by Old Biach himself. Economically liberal and politically conservative, this widely respected Viennese daily wielded enormous power behind the scenes in the Austro-Hungarian Empire. By having characters refer to Moritz Benedikt, the editor-in-chief and owner, reverentially and exclusively as "He" and "Him," as if they were observing the prohibition against uttering the divine name, Kraus deftly satirizes the blind devotion of the newspaper's readers and their uncritical acceptance of its editor's political opinions. Old Biach, in particular, fiercely insists on parroting Benedikt's point of view, and his speeches gradually disintegrate into phrases cobbled together from lead articles. Eventually, in Act V, Scene 9, Biach collapses and dies, choking on Benedikt's trademark fillers, including one trifle that Cleopatra's nose was one of her best features.

Such darkly comic, even farcical characterizations of the consumers of the press give way in the presentation of one of its most formidable producers, Moritz Benedikt himself, first to satirical precision and then to polemical exaggeration. In keeping with Benedikt's own strategy of operating in the background, Kraus has him appear in the drama only twice. The warmongering editor is presented initially as a disembodied voice in Act I, Scene 28, where he is contrasted with another, more benevolent Benedict, who has appeared in the previous scene. First, the "praying Benedict," Pope Benedict XV, who led a peace initiative during the war, beseeches God to reconcile the warring nations. Then, "the dictating Benedict" is given a speech consisting of an excerpt from an actual editorial, in which he describes with obvious glee how marine fauna in the Adriatic are getting fat off the corpses of Italian sailors. In keeping with the implicit contrast between Christian and Jew in this linked pair of scenes, the Lord of the Hyenas, the central character in the epilogue, appears with the exact looks and dress of Moritz Benedikt in a rare photograph Kraus had published in *Die Fackel* in 1911. In verse that parodies the songs of redemption at the end of Goethe's *Faust II,* the Lord of the Hyenas celebrates the triumph of evil that has forced the Son of Man to make way for himself, the Antichrist.

Casting Moritz Benedikt as a Jewish Antichrist is only one of many anti-Semitic moments in the drama that have impeded its reception since 1945. Most Kraus scholars have been as reluctant to deal with this central issue as other literary historians have been eager to belittle or dismiss his satirical achievement because of it. Both abridged English translations of the play have avoided the problem entirely by not including the incriminating scenes and passages. Kraus himself had second thoughts, and one obvious change between the "Act Edition" of 1918–1919 and the "Book Edition" of 1922 is the increased exposure of the *Reichspost,* a newspaper with close ties to the ascendant Christian Social Party. Its two "Admirers" not only recite loyalist pieties about the Habsburgs in their sleep; they also indicate their intention, in Act IV, Scene 1, to use the next offensive as a pretext for "taking care of" the Jews.

It is important to emphasize that the most prominent representative of the press—she appears almost a dozen times in all five acts—is Alice Schalek, a real-life correspondent for the *Neue Freie Presse,* who happened to be Jewish but is not so identified in the play. She was, however, the only female reporter the Austro-Hungarian high command allowed to visit the front lines. In an act of reverse feminism, Kraus depicts her as a scavenging newshound roaming the edge of the battlefields in search of human-interest stories. Like all journalists in the play, she is presented not as a rounded character but as a mouthpiece of her own sensationalistic articles, which are recited verbatim. That she walks and talks only adds to the irony that informs Kraus's transformation of the documents at his disposal.

The emphasis on the journalists and on the way in which their ideologically corrupt texts empty the imagination and preclude critical perception could give the impression that the drama avoids a direct confrontation with the violence and brutality of war. In fact, Kraus does not shrink from depicting such occurrences and does so sometimes with unsettling directness. In Act III, Scene 44, an Austrian lieutenant in South Tyrol shoots a waitress for refusing to serve him more wine. In Act IV, Scene 34, set in a Vienna police station, an inspector and a patrolman brutally interrogate a prostitute, whom they deride as a "syphilitic whore." Act V, Scene 14, depicts the battlefield of Saarburg in Belgium, where a German officer peremptorily executes a wounded prisoner of war when a common soldier hesitates to carry out his order.

When Kraus first published a scene from *The Last Days of Mankind* in *Die Fackel* in 1915, he called the work-in-progress a "tragedy" but also gave it an unlikely genre designation, "Ein Angsttraum" (A Nightmare). This terminological ambiguity undoubtedly reflected his ongoing search for a dramatic form capable of capturing surrealistic aspects of the war that had become apparent even in the hinterland. The eventual subtitle, "A Tragedy in Five Acts with Prologue and Epilogue," seems like dramatic traditionalism by comparison. But the substance of the play strains at this framework even in the much more carefully structured, revised edition of 1922, where the number of scenes jumps in uneven increments from thirty in the first act to fifty-five in the fifth. The "Act Edition" also contains photographic frontispieces—including images of nurses posing in gas masks and a grisly execution scene—for all seven parts of the drama, a startling innovation that suggests both experimental verve and compositional perplexity. Kraus evidently sought to suggest meanings in the visual narrative beyond the ability of the text's verbal montages to convey.

Even as the revisions in the "Book Edition" rendered the drama less documentary and more visionary, Kraus went to great lengths to ensure that the dramatic action at least overlapped with the actual historical progress of the war. The first scenes of the prologue and the five acts can be linked quite precisely to specific months in each year between 1914 and 1918. The last scene of the fifth act takes place against the background of the final Austro-Hungarian defeat in October 1918 on the Piave River in northern Italy. However, the chronology within the acts is not straightforward. Many scenes, despite characters from real life and allusions to historical fact, cannot be precisely dated. But it seems that even such apparent confusion was calculated. As early as 1897, Kraus's review of Gerhart Hauptmann's naturalist comedy *The Beaver Coat* lavished praise on a play constructed on similarly unconventional principles. Not only does *The Last Days of Mankind* dispense with a conventional plot; it also forgoes "an actual conclusion" and presents alternate, contradictory endings.

Two of these tentative conclusions, the final scene of the fifth act and the finale of the epilogue, highlight one of the drama's most important innovations: Kraus's way of confronting technological modernity with the most experimental modernist medium of the era, film. In the epilogue, the provocation takes the form of parody. Just before alien powers "from above" provide a real apocalypse by raining destruction on the warring nations of earth, a chorus of *Kino-Operateure,* or cameramen, appear, petulantly demanding better lighting for their feature film *Doomsday.* By contrast, the last scene of the fifth act ends with a series of "apparitions" projected onto a monumental patriotic painting that has been transformed into a giant screen. Here, a kind of ideal critical cinema undoes journalistic propaganda and patriotic photo reportage by representing the horrors and atrocities of the war realistically and without theatrical mediation.

The final monologue of the Grumbler, a figure through which Kraus boldly integrated his own authorial persona into the text, has also rightly been understood as another possible ending of the drama. The Grumbler—the term ironically embraces a common local criticism of Kraus's habitual negativity—appears more often in the play than any other character and periodically engages in dialogues with a companion called the Optimist, who represents a rational as opposed to a critical attitude toward the war. These exchanges are initially cast as intellectual conversations that comment on and interpret the unfolding events. By the fifth act, which contains twice as many of these dialogues as the first, it is clear that they also function as epic interruptions that provide heuristic relief from increasingly disorienting changes of location and from the chaotic welter of patriotic and chauvinistic discourses.

In one of his most scathing attacks on "Prussian ideology," the Grumbler castigates those Germans who think that the adjective *deutsch* has a comparative and a superlative form. Even more provocative, he concludes his own participation in the drama by invoking Shakespeare, the national poet of the hated British Empire. Horatio's words at the end of *Hamlet* referring to "carnal, bloody, and unnatural acts" and "casual slaughters" serve the Grumbler's satirical reconstruction of a global catastrophe misrepresented by the media. The defiant pathos of such appropriations portrays the Grumbler as a heroic intellectual figure. And yet he too ultimately relinquishes the last word to the nonsensical final syllable of the newsboys' shouts that hauntingly reappear at the end of his summation. By equating this "fundamental sound of the times" with the "echo of his bloody insanity," he points to his own inescapable complicity in the war. Kraus's monstrous drama remains as ambiguous as it is bold and scathing.

See also 1831, 1912 (September), 1916, 1922 (February), 1928, 1981, 1983

Bibliography: Karl Kraus, *The Last Days of Mankind: A Tragedy in Five Acts,* abridged and edited by Frederick Ungar, trans. Alexander Gode and Sue Ellen Wright (New York: Frederick Ungar Publishing, 1974). ———, *The Last Days of Mankind,* selections arranged and translated by Max Knight and Joseph Fabry, in *In These Great Times: A Karl Kraus Reader,* ed. Harry Zohn (Montreal: Engendra Press, 1976), 157–258. ———, *Die letzten Tage der Menschheit: Tragödie in fünf Akten mit Vorspiel und Epilog,* ed. Christian Wagenknecht; *Schriften,* vol. 10 (Frankfurt am Main:

Suhrkamp, 1986). ———, *Die letzten Tage der Menschheit,* "Akt-Edition," rept. of the 1918–1919 edition (Frankfurt am Main: Zweitausendeins, 1976). ———, *Die letzten Tage der Menschheit,* "Stage Version," ed. Eckart Früh (Frankfurt am Main: Suhrkamp, 1992). Edward Timms, *Karl Kraus, Apocalyptic Satirist: Culture and Catastrophe in Habsburg Vienna* (New Haven, Conn.: Yale University Press, 1986). Leo A. Lensing, "Moving Pictures: Photographs and Photographic Meaning in Karl Kraus's *The Last Days of Humanity,*" in Anna K. Kuhn and Barbara D. Wright, eds., *Playing for Stakes: German-Language Drama in Social Context* (Oxford, U.K., and Providence, R.I.: Berg, 1994), 75–100.

Leo A. Lensing

♫ *1921, April*

A German film introduces Americans to a new aesthetic

Cinema and Expressionism

On Sunday, April 3, 1921, just over a year after its Berlin premiere, Robert Wiene's provocative film *Das Cabinet des Dr. Caligari (The Cabinet of Dr. Caligari)* opened at the Capitol, one of the largest movie palaces in New York. Attracting a record audience of twenty thousand on the first day, this foreign motion picture became a fiercely debated cultural event, doing for cinema what the Armory Show did for American painting in 1913, when an innocent America was first exposed to the European avant-garde. *Caligari's* success was all the more remarkable because the film hailed from Germany, the hated enemy of the Great War, barely three years past. It also violated every rule and convention of Hollywood. The film's visual shock effects and nonlinear narrative constituted an autonomous film reality all but unknown to American cinema, accustomed to realism and romance. *Caligari's* fusion of madness and malevolence, psychoanalysis and deception was deeply disquieting, and remains so to this day.

American audiences were sharply divided over this latest import from their former adversary, coming on the heels of Ernst Lubitsch's equally successful costume drama *Madame Dubarry* (1919; *Passion*). *Caligari* confirmed fears that artistically ambitious films made in Germany might challenge Hollywood's world dominance. It is not known whether *Caligari* was produced for export, but the characters' non-German names—Jane, Alan, Franzis, Caligari, Cesare—clearly obscured the country of origin and allowed American advertisers to claim it came from Europe, even if word soon got out about its precise provenance. While some critics wanted to ban *The Cabinet of Dr. Caligari* and other decadent German films altogether, others praised it as one of the most artistic films ever made. *Exceptional Photoplays,* an independent trade paper of the American film industry, remarked in 1921 that, compared to *Caligari,* American films looked as if they were made for "a group of defective adults at the nine-year old level." In that view, German cinema was a model for an innovative, "literary" filmmaking deemed unsuitable for the American mass market. Hollywood's film industry, aided by the press, responded to the foreign invasion by drawing a sharp line between the two national cinemas. The *New*

York Times claimed on May 21, 1921, that Germany's Expressionist films are "too gruesome for the American public," the actresses are "not young and beautiful enough," and the themes are generally "gloomy." Expressionist cinema was said to be artistic but unwatchable—a label that still clings to films from Germany.

In 1920s America, the term "Expressionist," at first interchangeably used with "Cubist" or "Futurist," was mostly associated with German art. It served as a catch-all for a modernist style typified by twisted perspectives, jagged lines, fragmented spaces, and a focus on extreme psychological states. In Germany, "Expressionism" meant a heterogeneous movement that began in 1905 with painters of "Die Brücke" and ended in 1927 with Fritz Lang's film *Metropolis*. The urge for abstraction and, simultaneously, the desire for radically subjective articulation touched all media, from painting, poetry, prose, and drama to architecture, stagecraft, and, finally in the postwar period, cinema. Although the anticipation and experience of the First World War provided the secret center for most of Expressionist art and literature, it was the avant-garde cinema of the 1920s that appears most haunted by the trauma of mass death and defeat. The loss of two million young German men in combat (of a total of nine million casualties) in four years reverberated throughout the Weimar period and found oblique expression in images of murder and violence; in scenes of hysteria and madness; in fantasies of invasion and assault.

The Cabinet of Dr. Caligari tells the story of a mysterious psychiatrist who is engaged in a study to see whether a person under his hypnotic control can be manipulated to murder, a proposition reminiscent of generals who sent soldiers to the front on a mission to kill. The film begins with the classical scenario of storytelling. Visibly tormented by traumatic memories, a young man, Franzis, begins his talking cure: "I will tell you." He addresses an older man, sitting next to him with a vacant stare. The foreground is partially obscured by dead tree branches. Despite the eerie setting, the scene resembles a psychoanalytic session in which the patient revisits a traumatic experience that is part lived, part imagined. As Franzis recovers his past, his companion assumes the role of listener and surrogate analyst, acting as the audience for the narrative that unfolds.

Caligari's intertwined stories are told in flashbacks, an ideal narrative trope to convey the enactment of repressed memory. Franzis's master flashback gives rise to further flashbacks, creating a Chinese-box effect of stories within stories. When Franzis reaches the end of his tale, he and his companion get up and enter the courtyard of an insane asylum, where they are both inmates. Only at this point do we realize that we have witnessed the crazed story of a mental patient. We feel shocked and betrayed. When Franzis sees Dr. Caligari, he assaults him: "You all believe I am mad. That is not true. It is the director who is mad," whereupon he is put back in a straitjacket and transported to a cell—the very cell that Dr. Caligari had occupied in what must have been Franzis's fevered dream. Who is mad and who is not? What is real and what is fantasized? The film leaves these questions tantalizingly open.

Dr. Caligari's alter ego is a traveling showman who exhibits a somnambulist patient, Cesare, as a freak in a fairground sideshow. We see Dr. Caligari ushering onlookers into his "cabinet," a large tent with seats arranged in parallel rows and a small stage. This cabinet alludes to a time when shady entrepreneurs traveled from fair to fair to exhibit films as new technical gimmicks. Franzis and Alan join the crowd in the cabinet where Cesare is introduced as a clairvoyant. When Alan asks the question that in the trenches had been on every soldier's mind, "How long do I have to live?" Cesare replies: "Till dawn." Sent by Caligari, Cesare later stabs Alan as he is sleeping. The plot revolves around Franzis's attempts to identify the murderer of his friend. Is it Cesare or Caligari? But maybe this entire scenario was merely a figment of Franzis's hysterical imagination, a movie within a movie?

Caligari enacts the disorienting experience of a traumatic event on the visual as well as narrative level. Different from all naturalistic depictions of life in and out of the trenches—as illustrated in the film *All Quiet on the Western Front* of 1930—Wiene's film rejects all semblance of realism. This anti-mimetic stance was itself political because all too often realism had been misused for war propaganda. Cinema had indeed become the handmaiden of the military when, in 1917, General Erich Ludendorff founded the UFA film studios to produce films that portrayed Germany in a positive light. *Caligari*'s radical otherness implied a critique of the uses of film for deceptive or naive representation. Just as Dada destroyed the syntax and semantics of what it considered to be the language of war and oppression, so did the contemporaneous *Caligari* challenge the existing grammar of cinema. It mocked perspective, undermined expectations, decomposed and shattered forms, shapes, and straight lines. Shorn of naturalistic detail, artificial, ghostly and silent, the film still projects an image of a mortified world that is at once elemental and liminal.

Caligari's stark visual style is indebted to the set designs of Expressionist theater. Stage directors like Max Reinhardt, Jürgen Fehling, and Leopold Jessner had experimented with abstraction, using cubes, pillars, and crudely painted canvases to bring out the essence of a play. Stunning lighting effects isolated the characters, sliced spaces, and deformed objects. Psychology and realism were banned in order to focus on the gist of character or story, further expressed by histrionic acting, stylized sets, and operatic choreography. A total studio production, *Caligari* presented an unreal, visibly constructed world without open spaces or streets. The high, inward-leaning walls seem to close in on the figures, and the narrow paths they walk look like trenches. The feeling of constriction in this film is also emphasized by the camera: it rarely uses long shots and almost never pans or tracks—all of which would imply a sense of freedom to move about. Instead, the camera tends to alternate between medium shots in order to advance the story, and abrupt close-ups that produce a shock effect. The film's dynamic thus derives less from a moving camera than from mise-en-scène and intrusive editing that underscores a narrative centered on control, fear, and paranoia.

The film's disregard for temporal linearity blurs distinctions between past and present, delusion and experience, dream and consciousness. A detective story at its core—who is the murderer in our midst?—*Caligari* conceals as it reveals, deceives as it uncovers, represses as it remembers. If the enigma of this film is the true identity of the mysterious, murderous Dr. Caligari, it is never resolved. In the mind of the narrator, his patient, the war psychiatrist doubles as a charlatan and mad scientist reminiscent of the famous French psychiatrist Jean-Martin Charcot. Wearing a top hat, Dr. Caligari even looks like known caricatures of Charcot. The film abounds in *Doppelgänger* effects. The narrator himself appears as a character in the narrative, Cesare is replaced by a life-size puppet, and Dr. Caligari is given a split personality. When it dawns on the audience toward the end of the film that the narrator himself might be hallucinating, the roles are suddenly reversed: in the last scene the doctor declares that he finally understands Franzis's "mania" and knows now how to cure it. In 1920, retelling the traumatic past was diagnosed as mania and madness.

Janus-faced, the figure of Caligari embodies two types of war psychiatry operative in World War I: one that sent shell-shocked patients back to the front and all too often to their deaths, and another, based on psychoanalysis, that attempted to cure the patient by slowly uncovering the cause of trauma. Franzis's narrative, his own "film," delusional as it may be, revisits the war by unmasking the psychiatrist as a murderer. In an act of transference, he projects his own insanity onto his doctor, who may, according to the logic of the film, be insane himself.

An emphatically modernist text, *The Cabinet of Dr. Caligari* has provoked myriad readings, most of which engage with Siegfried Kracauer's influential psycho-political history of Weimar cinema, *From Caligari to Hitler* (1947). Written in exile, this study tried to understand Germany's turn toward National Socialism by analyzing Weimar film fantasies as prefiguring the Nazi regime. Do these films' troubled protagonists embody national traits and propensities that led to Hitler? The question itself is part of a larger post-1945 reeducation debate that has centered on how to make Germans understand themselves and their past in order to keep another Nazi "mania" from occurring.

Wiene's film marks a bold beginning of Weimar Germany's coming to terms with the wounds of the lost war. It sought to preserve a memory of the war experience that ran counter to the official, harmonizing commemoration practices that began in 1920. In the spirit of George Grosz, Otto Dix, and the Berlin Dadaists who painted a scathing picture of the German bourgeoisie in 1919–1920, *Caligari* was an equally aggressive and grotesque indictment of bureaucracy and the medical establishment. The film was still in the theaters when the First International Dada exhibition opened in Berlin in May 1920.

Later Expressionist films are no less preoccupied with evocations of submission, betrayal, and sudden death. F. W. Murnau's *Nosferatu—eine Symphonie des Grauens* (1922; *Nosferatu—A Symphony of Horror*) translates the mass killing of the Great War into a story about a life-destroying vampire from the East who brings the plague to Germany. Fritz Lang's two-part *Nibelungen* (1924) stages the murder and revenge of Siegfried and ends with fire and a bloodbath, while his *Metropolis* (1927) culminates in an apocalyptic flood—another metaphor for war—to cleanse the world of what many denigrated as soulless modernity. Lang's films were studio productions and as such underscored the war's eradication of nature and the transformation of entire regions into desolate no-man's-land. Stripped of all contingencies and ambiguities in the life-and-death situation of the front and reduced to its bare essentials, the world became simple and abstract. The experience of this war demanded a new aesthetics, and German Expressionist cinema delivered it.

Drawing on painting and stagecraft, *Caligari* emphasized mise-en-scène to highlight invisible processes of the subconscious, dreams and hallucinations, trauma and insanity. Despite its un-American pessimism and darkness, or maybe precisely because of it, German Expressionism, as epitomized by *Caligari,* had a major impact on American horror films of the 1930s and the film noir cycle of the 1940s and 1950s. In fact, Hollywood genre films would be unthinkable without Weimar German prototypes. *Caligari* inspired psychological horror movies; *Nosferatu* pioneered the vampire film; and Lang's *M* transformed thrillers into studies of pathological behavior. When a large part of the Berlin film industry left Nazi Germany for Hollywood in 1933, it brought with it the German school of Expressionist filmmaking. There was a remarkable affinity to film noir, not in the least because the menacing and sinister mood of these films once more reacted to a trauma, that of World War II and genocide. Fritz Lang's *Scarlet Street* and *The Big Heat,* Billy Wilder's *Sunset Boulevard* and *Double Indemnity,* Robert Siodmak's *The Killers* and *Criss Cross,* Edgar G. Ulmer's *Detour,* and dozens more films made by German exiles used Expressionist techniques to tell stories about murder and mayhem, about fear, hatred, and guilt. These techniques consisted of intricate storytelling devices (flashbacks, embedded stories, unreliable narrators), striking visuals (stark black-and-white contrasts, symbolic lighting effects, exaggerated camera angles, distorted sets), and heavy metaphorical use of objects and gestures. The aesthetics of Expressionist cinema is elegantly summarized by the silent film maxim: When nobody speaks, everything speaks. *Caligarisme,* as the French call Expressionist cinema's stylistic legacy, has survived mainly in popular culture, energizing the crime and horror genre and often giving these formulaic films an experimental edge.

In 2002, Robert Wilson, the American avant-garde artist, wrote and directed *Doktor Caligari,* a theater play based on the film of more than eighty years ago. The export of 1921 has come back as an American import. Presented as homage to the visual power of silent cinema, and *Caligari* in particular, Wilson's production at the Deutsches Theater in Berlin confirmed the cult status of this first modernist art film. *The Cabinet of Dr. Caligari* has become part of global culture—freely circulating across continents and various media, used by film schools everywhere as the quintessence of German Expressionism, and now recycled as a postmodern performance piece.

See also 1899, 1912 (March), 1912 (September), 1923, 1936 (February)

Bibliography: Mike Budd, *The Cabinet of Dr. Caligari: Texts, Contexts, Histories* (New Brunswick, N.J.: Rutgers University Press, 1990). Lotte H. Eisner, *The Haunted Screen: Expressionism in the German Cinema and the Influence of Max Reinhardt* (Berkeley: University of California Press, 1969). Anton Kaes, *Expressionismus in Amerika: Rezeption und Innovation* (Tübingen: Niemeyer, 1975). Siegfried Kracauer, *From Caligari to Hitler: A Psychological History of the German Film* (Princeton, N.J.: Princeton University Press, 1947; repr. 2004). David Robinson, *Das Cabinet des Dr. Caligari,* BFI Film Classics (London: British Film Institute, 1997). Robert Wiene et al., *Das Cabinet des Dr. Caligari: Drehbuch von Carl Mayer und Hans Janowitz zu Robert Wienes Film von 1919/20,* Filmtext (Munich: edition text + kritik, 1995).

Anton Kaes

♌ *1922, February*

Overcoming a prolonged writing block, Rilke completes his *Duineser Elegien*

Modernism and Mourning

It is not easy to account for the charismatic appeal of Rilke's *Duineser Elegien* (1923; *Duino Elegies*). It would seem that this cycle of ten poems can be understood only by readers steeped in Rilke's private vocabulary and in the hermetic traditions on which he drew. Nonetheless, both German and English speakers (as well as of the many other languages into which the *Duineser Elegien* have been translated) never cease to be captivated by the sense of a personal voice speaking directly to the reader's innermost anguish the poems create. Other readers find the cycle stylistically precious, heavy-handed, even embarrassing. At once the last gasp of symbolism and the record of a crucial phase of modernism, the *Duineser Elegien* deserve to be read from a new contextualizing perspective. The cycle's long gestational process over a period of ten years can be attributed in part to Rilke's fragile psyche; but it can also be traced to a combination of historical factors: World War I, the German economic crisis, technological modernization, and the dissolution of traditional concepts of art and craftsmanship.

The immediate impetus for the *Elegien* was a psychological crisis Rilke underwent while writing the novel *Die Aufzeichnungen des Malte Laurids Brigge* (1910; *The Notebooks of Malte Laurids Brigge*), the fictional diary of a young poet terrified by the fragmentation and chaos of modern urban life. When he had completed the novel, Rilke succumbed to a severe depression. A trip to North Africa the following year turned into a deeply disturbing experience that only exacerbated his despair. Throughout his years of crisis, Rilke refused to undergo psychoanalysis: his writing, he believed, was itself a therapeutic practice, "a kind of self-treatment." Oddly enough, his friend Lou Andreas-Salomé, who was trained in Freudian analysis, supported his avoidance of psychotherapy.

Rilke began the *Elegien* in 1912 during a solitary sojourn at Castle Duino, the cliff-top northern Italian residence of Princess Marie von Thurn und Taxis. From the outset, Rilke conceived of these elegies as a sequence of ten long poems, but his 1912 visit to Duino produced only the first two, along with fragmentary beginnings of several others. A decade later, when the entire cycle had taken shape at long last, Rilke dedicated it to the princess in whose castle it had begun and whose patronage had helped him so generously during its gestation.

Seeing himself as a latecomer in a tradition already largely exhausted, the speaker of the elegies is obsessed with the transitory nature of life and the frequently untimely nature of death. The intervention of World War I and the ravages of modern warfare gave new relevance to the cycle's concern with those who die young. This theme was doubtless what later made the *Elegien* so popular among German soldiers in World War II and German-speaking students in the early postwar period. In this respect, the *Duineser Elegien* recaptured some of the effects of Rilke's early prose poem about a young 17th-century knight, *Die Weise von Liebe und Tod des Cornets Christoph Rilke* (1899, revised version 1904; *The Lay of the Love and Death of Cornet Christoph Rilke*), which, somewhat to its author's dismay, had become extremely popular during World War I. The success of both poems derived in great measure from Rilke's ability to convey wartime psychology from the inside.

During the war years, Rilke wrote relatively little. His "Fünf Gesänge" (1914; Five Cantos), composed in the first few days of the war and published as part of a collection of poems by various hands written in response to the war, lead the reader from a renewed sense of invigoration to a vehement attack on the pain and suffering of war. The "Fünf Gesänge" stand in stark contrast to the war fervor expressed in the rest of the anthology. In late November 1915, Rilke returned to work on the *Duineser Elegien,* writing the entire fourth elegy in a spurt of creative energy just two days before he was to report for military service.

The theme of death recurs throughout the cycle in various guises: the motif of the early dead, the figure of the hero, allusions to Attic urns and Egyptian grave monuments. Although the poems meditate at length on the intimate relation between life and death, they are not war poems in an ordinary sense. Rilke's works had long manifested a preoccupation with death, from early short stories like "Die Turnstunde" (1902; The Gym Lesson) through poems of his middle period like "Orpheus.Eurydike.Hermes" (1907; Orpheus; Eurydice; Hermes) and "Hetärengräber" (1907; Graves of the Heterae) to the lengthy passages about modern, impersonal death in the sterile atmosphere of public hospitals in *Malte Laurids Brigge.* The three disastrous weeks Rilke spent at military training camp in 1915 and his subsequent assignment (until mid-1916) at the Austrian military archives to turn horrifying battle reports into eulogies for dead heroes exacerbated his concerns about death in the modern world.

The tenth elegy, begun in 1912 but not completed until 1922, follows a youth, recently dead, on his journey into the "landscape of the Laments." Marked by ruined monuments, temples, and even a sphinxlike tombstone, this terrain mirrors the Egypt Rilke had seen on his 1911 voyage down the Nile.

The "Laments" figure as an ancient race in a landscape where everything seems to speak through the silent medium of hieroglyphs. A young "Lament" leads the dead youth into the foothills, from where he must climb alone into the "mountains of primal suffering." In the final lines of the elegy, the speaker turns back to the familiar world of the living, maintaining that we must learn a radically new way of thinking if we are to draw comfort from our mental confrontation with death.

Parallel with these meditations runs a sustained critique of modernity. Repeatedly, the world of antiquity is contrasted with the present day. Greek urns depict "love and departure" in gestures at once incredibly delicate and consolingly permanent. In the biblical days of Tobias, angels appeared as if they were mere fellow travelers, familiar and far from frightening; the fate of heroes was predestined in their mothers' wombs; crafted objects were simple, useful, and tangible. Modern life is seen as intrinsically transitory, vanishing, crumbling away, resisting efforts to preserve the few precious things that remain. We struggle to find a strip of "fruitful land between river and rock"; we are estranged from genuine feeling; technology has replaced religion. Recurrent images of houses, buildings, and monuments illustrate the contrast between the solidity of ancient edifices and the insubstantiality of modern structures. Even the classical elegiac meters employed in the cycle (with the exception of the fourth and the seventh elegies) seem to have crumbled, and few lines fully actualize the traditional verse form.

Modern consumerism and, above all, the economic crisis of the early twenties are vividly present in the tenth elegy. Here the present-day world figures as an amusement fair on the unsightly fringes of town. Show booths and sideshows vie for the visitor's attention; but "adults can view most specifically how money reproduces, anatomically, not for enjoyment alone: the genital organ of money, everything, the whole procedure—that's instructive and fruitful." Lovers embracing in the grass and dogs engaged in what comes naturally are by no means regarded with the same kind of horrified prurience as vulgarly copulating, ever proliferating money. This pecuniary metaphor, itself part of Rilke's extravagant figurative style, takes on a dark, threatening undertone if read against the backdrop of the German inflation of 1921 to 1923, when sights of consumers wheeling in their money by the barrowload were not uncommon. Rilke himself was particularly sensitive to the eroding power of inflation, dependent as he was on the exchange rates between the German and Swiss currencies. The territorial changes that resulted from the war made Rilke temporarily stateless: his publisher was located in Germany, but the only country that would accept him as a resident (and even that only after much difficulty) was Switzerland. Against this backdrop, the fifth elegy's reference to "eternally valid good luck coins" can only be read ironically. For readers in 1922, when this elegy was composed, the idea of coins that did not lose their value would have seemed preposterous. Linguistically and thematically, the money metaphors in the *Elegien* are closely related to Georg Simmel's account of the modern culture of money as a "thoroughgoing relativity of values."

Linked with this critique of consumerism and materialism is a deep fear of abstraction. Again and again the elegies wrestle with what they present as modern estrangement from concrete, tangible reality. The rope maker in Rome and the potter on the Nile, representatives of ancient craftsmanship that is increasingly dying out, create functional objects with their own hands. The modern world, by contrast, is powered by electricity, the invisible form of which seems a direct expression of the modern epoch: "The spirit of the times creates vast powerhouses, faceless as the pulse of tension which it derives from all things."

Akin to invisible electricity, the monuments of modern times are ideas. Like many modernist works, the *Duineser Elegien* explore the possibility of returning to primal forms of existence. Where the expressionist Gottfried Benn, in his 1913 poem "Gesänge" (Cantos), longs to revert to life as "a little clump of slime in a warm bog," the speaker in Rilke's elegies envies migratory birds, always in touch with the powers of nature. He longs to share the full-circle vision of insects, and envisages the bliss of tiny winged creatures that remain forever, as it were, in a womb of air.

Drawing on ideas of his friend, the philosopher, aesthete, and mystic Rudolf Kassner, Rilke structures the *Elegien* as an argument against atavistic thinking. In the precarious atmosphere of the months preceding the outbreak of the world war, Rilke repeatedly invoked Kassner's notion of a new turning. By the time he came to write the seventh, eighth, and the major portion of the ninth elegies in February 1922, he had redefined his concept of the reversal he was aiming for. He understood it now in a twofold sense: first, as a shift away from the divine to the earthly; and second, as a transformation of concrete reality into the invisible medium of poetic ideas. In other poems of his late period, he calls this medium *Weltinnenraum* (inner cosmic space), the transposition of the vast external world into an interior, imaginary realm.

With this gesture, Rilke distanced himself from the kind of modernism represented by abstract art. No matter how impenetrable Rilke's late poetry may be, it insists on preserving "the recognized shape" of the things it represents. The speaker of the elegies raises questions about the concept of abstraction. One of the most striking images in the *Duineser Elegien* is the evocation of the angels at the beginning of the second elegy as mirrors deflecting their own radiance back to themselves. Is self-sufficiency, independence from context, a necessary feature of art? If so, how can it draw into itself the kind of personal or more generally human experience the elegies seek to articulate?

The fifth elegy probes this question further in the image of acrobats inspired by Picasso's painting *Les Saltimbanques* (*The Street Performers;* 1905). In this central elegy of the sequence, written in 1922 after the tenth elegy was completed, the acrobats become figures for the simultaneous transience and permanence of art. Their constantly re-created human pyramid is seen as both nature and culture: a tree subject to the changing seasons and a miraculous tower contrasting with the flimsy constructions of modern architecture. In an amusing allusion to Eichendorff's famous poem "Mondnacht" (Moonlit

Night), the street performers' threadbare carpet is "laid on like a bandage, as if the suburban heaven had hurt the earth there." Art, at its most accomplished, is presented in the fifth elegy as a potential consolation for transience and loss, and yet it is clear that this is an ideal that can never quite be attained.

If the *Duineser Elegien* are in a very real sense a poetic record of the disturbing second decade of the 20th century, what accounts for their enduring popularity? Perhaps it is the personal struggle they convey, often through a private vocabulary, disturbing leaps in logic, unmediated shifts between prosaic and elevated language. The discrepancies arising from the poem's gestation over a ten-year period seem to correspond in some profound way to the mind's most intimate flights. The reader seems to witness a deeply troubled consciousness as it wrestles with a conundrum neither it nor we can fully comprehend.

Pieced together in a moment of creative exhilaration in February 1922, the *Duineser Elegien* lack the coherence of a consistent whole. Their fragmentary nature, only barely pasted over at several important junctures, is testimony to their genesis at a stage when writing no longer pours forth seamlessly, as Rilke had experienced during the single stormy night in 1899 when he composed his *Cornet*. The *Duineser Elegien* are an expression of the same restorative modernism present in T. S. Eliot's *The Wasteland*, published in the year when Rilke completed his work. Though in different ways, both poems wrestle with the problem of fragmentation in modern civilization. They examine central issues concerning poetry in the modern period. Whose voice speaks when the modern poet takes up his pen, they ask, and how does this voice relate to the most basic questions of human existence and belief?

By addressing such larger issues, the *Duineser Elegien* may be seen as a self-help manual. Certainly, Rilke employed the meditative framework as a way of coming to terms with his own depression, anxiety, and repeated writing blocks. Many readers of the *Duineser Elegien* have seen in the cycle a key to understanding their own psychological perplexities. In this respect, these elegies resemble another famous work of 1922, James Joyce's *Ulysses,* once ironically described by Leslie Fiedler as "a guide to salvation through the mode of art, a kind of secular scripture." Rilke often received letters from readers longing for words of wisdom from the famous poet. "What letters! There are so many people who expect I don't know quite what of me—help, advice, from *me,* who find myself so helpless in the face of the most pressing needs of life!" Fear of personal helplessness and creative impotence are interwoven in the elegies with deep anxieties about modern existence and the imminence of disaster.

In the final analysis, the *Duineser Elegien* have no solution for any of these problems; they reflect them in a sweeping meditation that moves from despair to a poignant though fragile consolation. The uncertainty of its conclusion is, perhaps, also part of the cycle's appeal to later readers: the *Duineser Elegien* do not send out a completely articulated message, but come to a halt at a precarious resting place. Even where they seem to interpret the world for us, they continue to call out for further decoding of its mysterious hieroglyphic language.

See also 1808, 1910, 1912 (March), 1918

Bibliography: Rainer Maria Rilke, *Duino Elegies and The Sonnets to Orpheus,* trans. A. Poulin, Jr. (Boston: Houghton Mifflin, 1977). ———, *Duino Elegies,* the German text, with an English translation by J. B. Leishman and Stephen Spender (New York: Norton, 1939). ———, *Sämtliche Werke,* ed. Ernst Zinn (Frankfurt am Main: Insel, 1955), vol. 1 *(Gedichte: Erster Teil).* Ralph Freedman, *Life of a Poet: Rainer Maria Rilke* (New York: Farrar, Straus & Giroux, 1996). Judith Ryan, *Rilke, Modernism and Poetic Tradition* (Cambridge and New York: Cambridge University Press, 1999).

Judith Ryan

℞ *1922, July 23*

Walther Rathenau is assassinated near his home

Lion Feuchtwanger's Jud Süss

The assassination in 1922 of Walther Rathenau, the first Jewish foreign minister of Germany, and Lion Feuchtwanger's (1884–1958) interest in the fate of Joseph Süss Oppenheimer, the court Jew at the Duchy of Württemberg who had been strung up in a cage and hanged before a jeering crowd two centuries earlier, have more than mere symbolic value in common. A staunch advocate of historical fiction that brings figures of the past into a living relationship with the present, Feuchtwanger, himself a Jew, had long seen Rathenau as both exemplar and theorist of the modern Jew who could mediate between the "white-skinned, technology-obsessed West" and the "contemplative, ego-denying Orient." "What I wanted to do," he remarked in 1929, "was to map out the path of a white-skinned man, the path leading from the narrow European notion of power through the Egyptian notion of immortality to the Asian notion of denial of the will and practical activity. My decision to have a Jew go down this path occurred because the turning of the White Man toward Oriental values expressed itself with particular clarity in the being and destiny of the Jews" ("Über Jud Süss," 390). Six years later, he was more explicit about the connection: "Years ago I wanted to map out the path of a man from action to inaction, from activity to contemplation, from a European to an Indian worldview. It was tempting to represent this idea by using a figure from the present: Walter Rathenau. I tried but failed. I moved the material back two centuries and attempted to portray the path of the Jew Süss Oppenheimer: I came closer to my goal" ("Vom Sinn und Unsinn des historischen Romans," 511).

Feuchtwanger was not the only novelist inspired by Rathenau's career and character. In *Der Mann ohne Eigenschaften (The Man without Qualities),* Robert Musil draws a rather satirical portrait of him in the figure of Arnheim, the polyglot millionaire who mixes corporate efficiency with Eastern mysticism. Nor was Feuchtwanger the first writer drawn to the story of "the Jew Süss," the spectacular rise and fall of the 18th-century court Jew who emerged from obscure circumstances to become chief financial advisor to Duke Karl Alexander of Württemberg in 1733 and one of the wealthiest, most powerful men in Germany. His execution a scant five years later triggered a flood of publications that quickly transformed him into a legendary figure. Süss's opulent lifestyle as a familiar of the duke's inner circle, his numerous sexual liaisons, and finally his sudden fall from favor, trial, and execution provided an ideal morality tale for Germans and Jews. Later, in the modern period of Jewish emancipation, numerous fictional and historical accounts of his life served as a parable for the dangers and limits of assimilation, from Wilhelm Hauff's romantic and openly anti-Jewish novella of 1827 to Theodor Griesinger's similarly oriented *Swabian Family Chronicles* of 1860; from Marcus Lehmann's idealized biography of 1872—one year after Jews were granted full emancipation in the new Reich—to Feuchtwanger's own ambiguous fictionalization in his play *Jud Süss: Schauspiel in drei Akten* (1917; *Jud Süss: Drama in Three Acts*) and novel *Jud Süss* (written 1920–1922, published 1925). The most notorious treatment remains Veit Harlan's 1940 Terra film—based on the Hauff novella, and not, as often assumed, on Feuchtwanger's novel—which portrays Süss as an unmitigated scoundrel whose execution frees Stuttgart from the "plague" of Jewish influence. Goebbels felt so strongly about the film's ideological value that he ordered it shown to all German soldiers leaving for the Eastern front.

Taking Manfred Zimmermann's 1874 biography as historical guide, Feuchtwanger sought to portray Süss within a complex web of social, religious, and political forces in pre-modern Germany, focusing on the period between Süss's encounter with Karl Alexander in 1732 and his execution six years later. But the novelist's interest in this period was not merely antiquarian. Feuchtwanger understood Süss as a modern Jew who anticipated the fundamental generational shift that took place in the last quarter of the 19th century from tradition to bourgeois assimilation—a shift that often asserted itself in ostentatious flaunting of new wealth and status. In the novel, traditional Jewry is embodied by Isaak Landauer, who wears traditional garb, speaks a faulty, Yiddish-inflected German, and wields his considerable economic and political power from the sidelines. In Landauer's eyes, Süss is vulgar and preening, "puffed up like a peacock" and unaware of "the delicate pleasure of wielding power in secret" (17). Süss for his part is deeply embarrassed by Landauer's "greasy sidelocks, his soiled caftan, his guttural laugh" (18).

Süss's fashionable clothing signifies his willingness to enter into a relationship with German society that far exceeds the economic connections maintained by Jewish financiers like Landauer. Though he refuses to convert, he abandons traditional garb, dietary restrictions, and religious observance, and frequents the highest levels of Christian society. The bulk of the novel is, in fact, dedicated to the strangely intimate tie that develops between Süss and the duke. Feuchtwanger takes as historical fact the story that Süss procured for Alexander, then regent of Serbia, a cabbalistic prophecy that he would accede to the throne of Württemberg. When this comes true, the duke sees in Süss the supernatural agent of his destiny and makes him his closest financial and political advisor, symbolically "baptizing" him in a humiliating scene by having his

730 / Lion Feuchtwanger's Jud Süss

dirty bath water dumped on the elegant Süss. No friend of the Jews, Alexander resents his advisor's influence but is incapable of doing without him. By the same token, Süss's fortunes rise and fall with the duke's protection. He becomes a kind of second self to the duke, capable of intuiting his innermost thoughts and wishes, profiting materially but at the expense of his own identity and self-worth. German and Jew are linked in an uncanny symbiosis which Feuchtwanger, invoking the cabbalistic notion of metempsychosis, depicts as an organic merging of two souls within the same body: "Something surged from one to the other, throbbed this way and that without a word said . . . They shared a single life, the Jew silently responded by deeds to the unspoken questions and demands of Karl Alexander; it seemed as if he exhaled the air that the duke inhaled; they were parts of one single body, indissolubly linked" (354).

Yet perhaps the most strikingly modern aspect of Süss's Jewishness concerns the "Oriental values" that Feuchtwanger saw in Süss's refusal to convert when he was facing the gallows, although conversion might have saved his life. "I saw how he let himself fall. I understood his fortune and his fall as one and the same. His path was an allegory for all our [modern] development, the path from Europe to Asia, Nietzsche to Buddha" ("Über Jud Süss," 390). Here too we recognize Feuchtwanger's concern with his own era at the expense of historical verisimilitude. Like many German-speaking Jews of his generation, he saw in a mystical, non-Orthodox notion of "Eastern" Judaism—popularized especially by Martin Buber's lectures on the essence of Judaism and his translations of Chassidic tales—a source of nondogmatic spiritual renewal. In the novel, this kernel of Eastern Judaism is embodied by Süss's uncle, the miracle Rabbi Gabriel, who prophesies Alexander's accession to the crown, and by Süss's daughter Naemi, who lives in a secluded forest retreat in a white cube house that the neighboring German community perceives as "oriental." So long as Süss's symbiotic relation with the duke is in effect, he keeps this part of his life secret, or *verkapselt,* repressed. But it is this core of Jewish spirituality that, in the end, magically transforms him into a figure of biblical grandeur and nobility. Power and money reside with the duke at court; but truth resides in Rabbi Gabriel, the prophetic, magical personage (straight out of Buber's tales of the Baal Shem Tov) whose very physiognomy is marked by his divine election: "Three furrows, sharp, deep, short, almost vertically above his nose, were cut into his forehead; and they formed the holy letter, the *shin,* the initial of God's name, Shaddai" (41). If Gabriel functions as Süss's religious conscience, Naemi's task is to lead her father back to his lost Jewish soul (Kinkel, 60).

The novel's plot issues directly from the tension between Süss's competing relationships with the duke and his daughter. In his role as procurer of money, luxury goods, and women for the duke, Süss winds up sacrificing the virgin daughter of the prelate Weissensee, Sibylle Magdalene, who is raped by the duke and forced to become his mistress. When Weissensee learns that Süss also has a daughter, he plots revenge by leading the duke to her retreat, where she dies trying to escape his drunken advances. Aggrieved but morally culpable,

Süss seeks to avenge Naemi's death by a complicated plot that results in the duke's death. But grief over his lost daughter has opened the "capsule" of his Jewish spirituality, and, with his worldly self symbolically executed in the death of the duke, Süss lets himself fall into the hands of his enemies. In prison, shortly before his execution, this immolation of his personal will results in a "great, fulfilling gift": the magical reappearance of his daughter.

Süss's return to Judaism in the novel's final pages constitutes its dramatic high point and is marked stylistically by a shift from its dominant mode of expressionist fragmentation and hyperbole to a measured, deliberately archaic, biblical tone. Isaak Landauer leads a group of prominent Jews who try to save Süss's life, and when this fails, they say a moving prayer to the dead while Süss himself cries out his faith in the "one and only God of Israel, Yahve, Adonai" before the assembled populace. Finally, simple Jewish peddlers remove his corpse from its ignominious perch, transport it to Fürth under cover, and give him a proper burial. Rabbi Gabriel himself closes Süss's eyes and watches over the corpse, under whose head lies "a small clump of earth from the land of Zion."

Süss's "Jewish" spirituality is of a bizarre sort, however. It does not consist in a return to the sacred books, nor does it consist in concrete actions on behalf of the Jewish community. (His intervention in the Ravensberger blood libel charge to save an innocent Jew occurs only because of external pressure, not because of an awakening religious conscience.) The crux of Süss's spirituality consists in what Feuchtwanger termed the special "destiny of the Jews" to represent the "White Man's turn to Oriental values."

Here is where present and past, modern assimilated Jew and court Jew, intersect. Feuchtwanger's unorthodox thinking was influenced by Walther Rathenau's 1913 study *Zur Mechanik des Geistes oder vom Reich der Seele (The Mechanization of the Spirit, or the Realm of the Soul),* in which the future foreign minister describes the true end of man as an Oriental "soul birth," a state of inner peace achieved by "abnegation and contemplation." Rathenau's description of the *Zweckmensch,* the goal-driven individual, corresponds to Feuchtwanger's expressionist portrait of Süss as the cold businessman intent on accumulating ever larger quantities of money, power, and experience. But Rathenau's account of a "soul birth" corresponds to Süss's "breaking of the capsule" and spiritual growth in prison, expressed in his renunciation of all material comfort, his physiognomic transformation, and the magical return of Naemi. Süss thus serves as the foil for the modern Jewish financier and intellectual, both of whom, owing to their historical and ethnic situation between East and West, achieve a symbiosis of the striving Western man of intellect with the contemplative, Eastern soul.

Five years after the publication of *Jud Süss,* Feuchtwanger made explicit this Hegelian conception of the "historical process of the Jews." Given ancient Judea's geographic position, he claimed, the ancient Jews absorbed the teachings of three regions: "The East taught them to renounce; the West taught them to become; the Middle East to be." "Oriental" nations and "peoples of color" have historically possessed a superior religious, social, and psychological sense, he affirms, whereas the "white-skinned," "barbaric" peoples of the West concentrated their energy on "technological progress, the invention of machines" (473). In the modern age of travel and global commerce, however, the world resembles a grand hotel in which a central authority must provide for all guests equally. The Jews, he claims, are uniquely suited for the role of cultural mediators. Cosmopolitan and anti-nationalist by virtue of their historical experience, they are also a highly literary people dedicated to the Book, and can thus provide the world with its "cultural memory." With these far-reaching pronouncements—the veracity of which is not at issue here—Feuchtwanger not only supplies the theoretical framework for an understanding of Joseph Süss Oppenheimer, he also alludes to the political role of his own novel *Jud Süss* in the market-driven, technology-obsessed realm of world capitalism. In this context, his historical fiction serves as the cultural memory of modernity, the Jewish teaching of "being" against the German, "Faustian," world of action, technological progress, and "striving."

Whether it was this audacious, indeed revolutionary, message that was responsible for the novel's immediate and enormous popular success or whether the public merely enjoyed a racy, well-told story set in a historic locale is hard to determine. Reluctantly published by a small press after the major publishing houses had turned it down, *Jud Süss* went through five impressions of 39,000 copies within the year, sold over 200,000 copies in German, and was translated into seventeen languages by 1931. The novel established Feuchtwanger's reputation as a major author in Germany and abroad and made him a wealthy man. It also ensured him continued income and a degree of independence during his years of exile from 1933 until his death in California in 1958. But surely, part of the success of Feuchtwanger's novel was due to its disquieting topic at a time when much of Europe—and particularly Germany and Austria—was still deeply divided about the place of Jews in predominantly Christian societies. Astute readers of the novel can easily recognize in the portrayal of 18th-century Württemberg a foil for modern, capitalist Germany. They might also catch the veiled references to blood-libel trials, the Dreyfus affair, and the Bavarian *Sondergerichte* (special courts) that resisted Prussian authority at the end of World War I. Numerous Jewish readers felt uncomfortable with Feuchtwanger's unvarnished portrait of Süss's unscrupulous business tactics and social climbing: "No swastika-bearing author could have bettered" the author of *Jud Süss,* complained a reviewer for the newspaper of assimilated German Jews in 1925 (cit. Barbara von der Lühe, 41). And when the Nazis came to power, it was only a matter of time before another version of Süss's life—in Veit Harlan's film—would gain prominence.

When Feuchtwanger was writing his novel in the early years of the Weimar Republic, he could not have known how closely Süss's manner of death would resemble the fate of the Jews in Germany under Hitler—a violent, nationalist turn that he himself would chronicle in best-selling novels such as *Erfolg: Drei Jahre Geschichte einer Provinz* (1930; *Success: Three Years of Provincial History*), *Die*

Geschwister Oppenheim (1933; *The Oppenheim Siblings*), and *Exil* (1940). But the assassination of Walter Rathenau on July 23, 1922, even as Feuchtwanger was writing the conclusion to his novel, provided deadly confirmation of his intuition. The sound of those bullets haunts his novel even today.

See also 1515–1517, 1594, 1792, 1882, 1913, 1929 (Autumn)

Bibliography: Lion Feuchtwanger, *Jud Süss* (Berlin: Aufbau Taschenbuch Verlag, 1991).
———, "Über Jud Süss" and "Vom Sinn und Unsinn des historischen Romans," in *Centum Opuscula: Eine Auswahl,* ed. Wolfgang Berndt (Rudolstadt: Greifenverlag, 1956). F. Knilli and Siegfried Zielinski, "Lion Feuchtwangers *Jud Süss* und die gleichnamigen Filme von Lothar Mendes (1934) und Veit Harlan (1940)," *Text + Kritik* 79–80 (1983): 99–121. John Spalek and Sandra H. Hawrylchak, *Lion Feuchtwanger: A Bibliographic Handbook,* vol. 1 (Munich: K. G. Saur, 1998). Barbara von der Lühe, "Lion Feuchtwangers Roman *Jud Süss* und die Entwicklung des jüdischen Selbstbewußtseins in Deutschland," in *Lion Feuchtwanger: Werk und Wirkung* (Bonn: Bouvier, 1984). Manfred Zimmermann, *Josef Süss Oppenheimer, ein Finanzmann des achtzehnten Jahrhunderts* (Stuttgart: 1874).

Mark M. Anderson

᪐ *1923, Spring*
Walter Gropius appoints László Moholy-Nagy master of the preliminary course, heralding changes in the mission of the Bauhaus

Photography, Typography, and the Modernization of Reading

"It is not the person ignorant of writing but the one ignorant of photography who will be the illiterate of the future" ("Fotografie ist Lichtgestaltung," 1928; "Photography Is Creation with Light," 77). Within months of the publication of this prognostication by László Moholy-Nagy (1895–1946), the literary critic and philosopher Walter Benjamin cited it to express his own faith in photography as a source of knowledge. In a review of Karl Blossfeldt's book *Urformen der Kunst: Photographische Pflanzenbilder* (1928; *Originary Forms of Art: Photographic Images of Plants*), Benjamin considers how the new photography, of which Moholy was a pioneer, affects human perception and changes the nature of our knowledge of the world. According to Benjamin, to look at photographs, such as Moholy's or Blossfeldt's, is to behold a "geyser of new image-worlds" that "hisses up at points in our existence where we would least have thought them possible" ("Neues von Blumen," 1928; "News about Flowers," 156). Benjamin's sense that the image-worlds of photography were penetrating contemporary life in unprecedented and unexpected ways represents a central preoccupation of both popular and philosophical thought in Germany in the 1920s. From X-rays to illustrated papers to cinema, the "mediality" of photography was seen as transforming human perception of the concrete existence of things. Moholy's photographic book *Malerei, Photographie, Film* (1925; *Painting, Photography, Film*) is a document of that transformation, and a call for its radical expansion.

Published in 1925 as the eighth volume of a projected fifty in the series

Bauhausbücher (Bauhaus Books) and reprinted in a revised edition in 1927, *Painting, Photography, Film* is a primer in photographic literacy, a compendium of techniques for the production of new image-worlds. The book's stated aim is "simply to classify, in terms of the use of media, those optical creations which exist today" (*Malerei,* 5–6; *Painting,* 9). Logically, aesthetic judgment should play no part in that classification, but Moholy's assessment of contemporary visual media is hardly disinterested. Indeed as the opening line of the 1925 edition announces, the book is an "apologia for photography" (5). Its premise holds that photography, especially in its cinematic forms, is without equal as a medium of representation in the historical situation of modernity. Moreover, as Moholy understands it, photography has an unparalleled capacity to reshape perception and, thereby, to transform human experience.

Simply put, the logic of *Painting, Photography, Film* is this: every age ought to find its forms of representation in media appropriate to that age; if contemporary life has been revolutionized by new technologies, then it becomes the task of visual media to transform optical perception accordingly; as scientific experiments using stop-motion, microscopic, and telescopic images demonstrate, photography succeeds in effecting such a transformation. It *"makes visible existences which cannot be perceived or taken in by our optical instrument, the eye"*; through photographs *"we see the world with entirely different eyes"* (*Painting,* 28–29). For Moholy, the camera is a technological prosthesis that revolutionizes human vision, and photographs materialize new ways of seeing.

Emblematic of a shift in the orientation of the Bauhaus that took place four years after its establishment as a state school of art and architecture in Weimar in 1919, *Painting, Photography, Film* is an experimental book designed with an eye to a mass audience accustomed to reading photographically illustrated newspapers and watching motion pictures. The original curriculum of the Bauhaus unified instruction in the fine and applied arts with the aim of training artists and craftspeople to create the architecture of the future as a *Gesamtkunstwerk* (total work of art). In the summer of 1923, the architect Walter Gropius, founding director of the Bauhaus, announced fundamental changes in the school's program: its workshops would strive to integrate the visual arts and industrial technology, for example by producing prototypes for mass production. Moholy had joined the Bauhaus faculty in the spring of 1923 as master of the *Vorkurs* (preliminary course) and metal workshop. His appointment was soon associated with the changes Gropius sought to implement. The series of Bauhaus Books the two began to plan in late 1923 exemplified the school's changed ambitions. "Our goal," wrote Moholy in a letter to the Russian constructivist Aleksandr Rodchenko, "is to give a summary of all that is contemporary." Originally planned for publication in brochure form, the Bauhaus series was to include volumes not only on art, architecture, and design, but also on politics, religion, science, literature, and economics. The final item on a list of prospective subjects was, simply, "Utopia" (*Moholy-Nagy,* 392–393).

Though no official instruction in photography was offered at the Bauhaus until 1929, a year after Moholy resigned from the faculty, photographic practices assumed an important place in its everyday work following the school's move to the small industrial town of Dessau in 1925. Photographs of Gropius's landmark main Bauhaus building by Moholy and other faculty members quickly became icons of modernism. Others, taken by Moholy's wife, Lucia Moholy, reproduced the principles of Bauhaus design in images of architecture, furniture, and housewares through which it was publicized. Photography was crucial to Moholy's own art by 1923 and soon played a role in both his pedagogy and his engagement with technology.

Hungarian by birth, Moholy began his career as a painter in Budapest in 1918 and joined the circle of avant-garde artists around the journal *Ma (Today)*. He was a supporter of the Hungarian revolution and, though not a member of the communist party, he, like many of his fellow artists and intellectuals, left Budapest for Vienna following the fall of the soviets and the onset of the counterrevolutionary white terror. From Vienna he moved to Berlin, where he settled in January 1920. There Moholy quickly established friendships with Hannah Höch and Raoul Hausmann, key figures in Berlin Dada's pioneering experiments in photomontage, as well as Kurt Schwitters, with whom he briefly shared a Berlin studio, and the Dutch artist Theo van Doesburg, editor of the journal *De Stijl*, in which Moholy's first writings on photography appeared in 1922. Through Schwitters, himself both an artist and a designer of innovative advertising and typography, Moholy came to know the Russian artist El Lissitzky, who arrived in Berlin in 1921. Lissitzky's work during his Berlin period included the publication of two books, the Russian avant-garde poet Vladimir Mayakovsky's *For the Voice* (1922) and his own *Of Two Squares* (1923). The latter's experimental typography anticipates Moholy's work as editor and designer of the Bauhaus books. Alongside his enthusiastic reception of Dada photomontage, Moholy's exposure to Lissitzky's work, and to the news Lissitzky brought of the Constructivist movement in the Soviet Union, had a decisive impact on his art.

Moholy's first experiments in photography date to 1922, when he began to make cameraless photographs or "photograms" in collaboration with Lucia Moholy. In the same year, he also produced a series of paintings known as *Telefonbilder (Telephone Pictures)*, presaging the enthusiasm for standardized production and technological media that would mark his Bauhaus work. Although he designed the *Telephone Pictures* using mechanical drawing tools, graph paper, and a commercial color chart for the porcelain enamel of which they were made, he did not paint them himself. Their actual production took place in a factory that manufactured enamel signs, and to which—according to Moholy's later descriptions—he transmitted instructions by telephone, allowing technicians to reproduce his designs, first in pencil on graph paper and then, on a larger scale, in enamel on steel supports. For Moholy, the experiment amounted to the invention of a new pictorial medium intended to transform both the production and the reception of art. According to the model of the *Telephone Pictures*, a painter would generate a medial transmission of a pictorial composition, a factory would produce a painting, and a buyer, using the painting's standardized title, would repeat the painter's medial work by ordering art over the phone. Moholy commissioned several telephone pictures himself, though he probably did so in person at the factory. Those works were included in his 1924 exhibition at Berlin's renowned Sturm Gallery, but the experiment never engaged the participation of potential buyers.

Moholy's attempt to modernize the making and viewing of art by using technologies of industrial production involved a larger utopian aim of finding a mass audience for art. Though unrealized in the *Telephone Pictures* project, this aim was reconceived at the Bauhaus both in Moholy's supervision of students designing prototypes for industrial production and in the development of the Bauhaus Books. Moholy wrote two and collaborated on one of the books, while designing all but three of fourteen volumes published between 1925 and 1931.

Paradigmatically, the language of industry comes to the fore in an introductory note to the first edition of *Malerei, Photographie, Film,* where the book is described as having been "assembled" rather than written (4). Like Russian Constructivism—but importantly removed from the historical context of the early Soviet Union to that of the Weimar Republic—Moholy's idea of the photographic book as a new form of communication imagined a mass audience that would be transformed by the experience of visual media derived from modern industrial technologies and determined by modernist design principles. The book was thus conceived as both a defense of photography and an exemplary realization of its possibilities. One measure of the success of Moholy's enterprise is the number of widely distributed photographic books that appeared in its wake. From Blossfeldt's *Originary Forms of Art* to Franz Roh and Jan Tschichold's *Foto-Auge: 76 Fotos der Zeit* (1929; *Photo-Eye: 76 Photos of the Age*), from Albert Renger-Patzsch's *Die Welt ist schön* (1928; *The World Is Beautiful*) to Werner Gräff's *Es kommt der neue Fotograf!* (1929; *Here Comes the New Photographer!*), a range of titles published in Germany in the second half of the 1920s established the new genre that *Painting, Photography, Film* had initiated.

Moholy was a prominent advocate and prolific practitioner of what came to be called the "New Typography." In a 1925 essay, he argues that despite the possibilities offered by modern technology, book design has changed remarkably little since Gutenberg, and he calls for typographical reform of pages whose "monotonous gray" enervates readers ("Zeitgemässe Typographie— Ziele, Praxis, Kritik," 1925; "Contemporary Typography—Aims, Practice, Criticism," 294). *Painting, Photography, Film* employs a variety of typographical elements to enliven its pages and thereby its readers: arrows direct the eye into and out of blocks of text as bullets call attention to individual lines of type; dense black horizontal and vertical bars intersect with paragraphs set in a standard serif font beneath bold sans-serif headings; key words and phrases suddenly appear in sans-serif boldface among lines of regular type. Moholy's construction of *Painting, Photography, Film* demonstrates his belief that "typographical communication" should develop "specific forms" that are "determined psycho-physically and by content" ("Contemporary Typography," 295). "Every age," he writes, "has its own optical disposition. Our age: that of the film, the electric-light advertisement, the simultaneity of sensorily perceptible events" (*Painting*, 39). The book sets out to reproduce the effects of film and advertising through an experimental interaction of photography and typography designed at once to represent and generate the sensory simultaneity characteristic of early 20th-century modernity, especially the experience of metropolitan life.

Drawn mostly from published sources, the illustrations that comprise the second part of *Painting, Photography, Film* extend the claims of Moholy's written defense of photography—they make his case visually supplemented by compact, matter-of-fact captions that stand apart from the unwieldy polemic of the text. Moholy expanded the captions for the revised edition, the only version to appear in translation. In addition to dozens of photographic images borrowed from popular and scientific books and periodicals, *Painting, Photography, Film* features photographs by Renger-Patzsch, Man Ray, and others, as well as reproductions of Moholy's own work—photograms, photographs, photomontages, an oil painting, and two experiments in the new medium he called "typophoto." As Moholy envisioned it, typophoto is a model for a "new visual literature" based on the integration of photomechanical printing techniques and modernist typographical experiments, a literature that will at once demand and produce "literacy of photography."

The fourteen-page typophoto called "The Dynamic of the Metropolis" replaced the horizontal linearity of the conventionally typeset page with the simultaneity of words and photographs juxtaposed in irregular grids, thereby transposing the cinematic metaphors of Moholy's text into pages to be read as if they were frames of film projected on an upright surface. A final double-page spread sums up Moholy's efforts to compel readers "simultaneously to comprehend and to participate in the optical events" his book represents (*Painting*, 23–24). Intended to enact the modernization of reading as a dynamic, corporeal activity, the page design juxtaposes images that variously thematize photography's capacity to reproduce bodily experiences of the simultaneity of perception. A rider bounces along on an elephant's back as the beast charges forward, nearly bursting the picture's border; a skier on a run down a mountain skids through two frames of a film-strip, his path marked by shadowy tracks and snowy bursts of light; a circus artist's body, balancing poles, and the high-wire resemble the composition of a Constructivist sculpture stretched across the surface of a photograph; and, in an X-ray on the opposite page, the transparent corpse of a bird "swims through the water, very slowly," as though photography could bring the dead back to life. Paratactic lists naming individual frames, subjects, and techniques likewise thematize the operations of both cinema and typophoto itself. Finally, two lines of vertical type repeat the command with which the book's last chapter of text concludes: "READ THE WHOLE THING THROUGH QUICKLY ONCE MORE" (*Painting*, 129).

The last word of *Painting, Photography, Film* is "END," but rather than being marked with a full stop, the end of this book, presented typophotographically as the end of a film, opens with a colon onto the future, which is to say, it opens onto the next reading. For Moholy, this reading, embodied and participatory, is bound to be cinematic: "Photography will lead in the near future to a replacement of literature by film" (1923; "The New Typography," 75). He thus conceives the new literacy of photography as the expertise of the moviegoer, an expertise his reader is made to share. In the context of Moholy's and Gropius's utopian project to offer a mass audience "a summary of all that is contemporary," the photographic book served as a technology for the construction of an embodied, collective reading public that modernism, in the end, never produced.

See also 1916, 1921, 1936 (February)

Bibliography: Walter Benjamin, "Neues von Blumen" (1928), in Benjamin, *Gesammelte Schriften,* vol. 3, ed. Rolf Tiedemann and Hermann Schweppenhäuser (Frankfurt am Main: Suhrkamp Verlag, 1991), 151–153, trans. Michael W. Jennings as "News about Flowers," in Benjamin, *Selected Writings, vol. 2: 1927–1934,* ed. Michael W. Jennings, Howard Eiland, and Gary Smith (Cambridge, Mass.: Harvard University Press, 1999), 155–157. Eleanor M. Hight, *Picturing Modernism: Moholy-Nagy and Photography in Weimar Germany* (Cambridge, Mass.: MIT Press, 1995). László Moholy-Nagy, "Fotografie ist Lichtgestaltung," *Bauhaus* 2, 1 (1928): 2–9, reprinted in Andreas Haus, *Moholy-Nagy: Fotos und Fotogramme* (Munich: Schirmer, 1978), 75–78, trans. Mátyás Esterházy as "Photography is Creation with Light," in Krisztina Passuth, *Moholy-Nagy* (London: Thames and Hudson, 1985), 302–305. László Moholy-Nagy, *Malerei, Photographie, Film* (Munich: Albert Langen, 1925). ———, *Malerei, Fotografie, Film,* 2nd rev. ed. (Munich: Albert Langen, 1927), trans. Janet Seligman as *Painting, Photography, Film* (Cambridge, Mass.: MIT Press, 1969). ———, "Zeitgemässe Typographie—Ziele, Praxis, Kritik," *Gutenberg-Festschrift* (Mainz: Gutenberg Gesellschaft, 1925), trans. Mátyás Esterházy as "Contemporary Typography—Aims, Practice, Criticism," in Passuth, *Moholy-Nagy,* 293–295. ———, "Die neue Typographie," in *Staatliches Bauhaus zu Weimar, 1919–1923,* ed. K. Nierendorf (Weimar and Munich: Bauhausverlag, 1923), 141, trans. Sibyl Moholy-Nagy as "The New Typography," in *Moholy-Nagy: An Anthology,* ed. Richard Kostelanetz (New York: Da Capo Press, 1970), 75–76.

Brigid Doherty

♩ *1924, October*

Arthur Schnitzler's novella "Fräulein Else" is published in *Die Neue Rundschau*

Modernism and Hysteria

Arthur Schnitzler's novella "Fräulein Else" reads like a classic case history in hysteria. Indeed when, at the end of the narrative, the protagonist faints after having exposed her naked body to a group of hotel guests while they were having their after-dinner coffee in the music room, her cousin Paul, a gynecologist, explicitly calls this scandalous performance a hysteric attack. Though Schnitzler (1862–1931) wrote and published this story some three decades later, the fact that the strange event it describes takes place on September 3, 1896, indicates a link to the ground-breaking *Studies in Hysteria* published by Sigmund Freud and Josef Breuer in 1895. Like Freud's young women patients whose stories inspired the discovery of the workings of the unconscious, Schnitzler's heroine comes from an assimilated Viennese Jewish family and suffers from a variety of psychic disturbances—excessive daydreaming, unsatisfied sexual desire that culminates in histrionic exhibitionism, and an exaggerated sense of vulnerability leading to a suicide attempt—all of which articulate a precarious social position. Though privileged enough not to have to work, yet not wealthy enough to imagine for herself a future without financial constrictions, she is—like several of Breuer's and Freud's patients—a bride, waiting to exchange her financial and emotional dependence on her father for a state of dependence on a husband. In ancient Greece, hysteria was regarded as a malady due to a desiccated, displaced uterus wandering through the body in search of nourishment and causing pain where it momentarily attaches itself. In modern times, Freud's perception of the human mind as a psychic apparatus is an analogous metaphor. Like the displaced uterus, his young, educated, unmarried female patients were foreign bodies, floating from one place of leisure to the next without fully belonging anywhere. Afflicted by a *tedium vitae* and barred from any creative outlet for their talents, these highly intelligent young women had an acute sense of their inability to support themselves and a concomitant awareness of being utterly dependent on the plans their families had for them. Their minds wandered endlessly in search of psychic nourishment. When fixated on one spot—in Else's case, on the complex ambivalence connected with her ravishing beauty—such peregrinations of the mind could also lead to disturbed behavior.

Schnitzler has recourse to Freud's postulate that the hysteric will choose her fantasy life and the hallucinations it entails over material reality as he relates the stories his nineteen-year-old heroine devises both to explore what the future holds for her and to clarify her discontent with her own family—notably their effort to cling to a lifestyle of leisure her father cannot afford. In the late afternoon of this fateful early autumn day, Else, who is vacationing with her wealthy aunt at a spa in San Martino di Castrozza, is called away from a tennis match with her cousin Paul by the delivery of an express letter from her mother. As she reads of her father's impending bankruptcy owing to embezzlement and misappropriation of his trustees' funds, along with her mother's prediction that an arrest is imminent, Else's daydreams of unfulfilled sexual desires and expectations for the future begin to unravel. Her mother's plea that she approach the art dealer Dorsday, who also resides at San Martino, and ask him for a loan of 30,000 Gulden triggers an acute sense of vulnerability. Fully cognizant that her mother is banking on her daughter's seductive charms to counterbalance her husband's fiscal irresponsibility, Else sees herself as the pawn in a high-stakes game among men, which is shameful to her and yet also flatters her vanity. When Dorsday names his conditions for his agreement—namely to be permitted to spend a quarter of an hour gazing at her naked body—Else has a fit of hysteria. In her mind, a simple, albeit clandestinely obscene transaction is exaggerated into a life-and-death predicament. Her histrionic excess obliquely gives voice to the fact that the protective fictions that have so far surrounded her—her fantasy that her beauty will procure her happiness, her father's fantasy that the borrowed money will solve his financial woes, Dorsday's fantasy that viewing Else's naked beauty will satisfy his desire for her—gloss over an inescapable, irrepressible sense of something being awry, an intimation of how erroneous is the belief that happiness can be fully achieved and that conflicts can be successfully resolved. Indeed, as Else deliberates whether to speak with Dorsday or not, and then whether she would be able to meet his conditions, she plays through four fantasy scenarios, each of which counterbalances her sense of shame at being asked to prostitute herself with a sense of exaggerated self-importance. In the first scenario, she is cast as her father's savior. The second involves two mirror inversions of a guilt scenario, in which the first part plays through the fantasy that, were she to decline Dorsday's request, she would be responsible for her father's demise, while the second part plays through an accusation launched at her family that they will be responsible for her own demise. Finally, when the act of exposing her body becomes inextricably enmeshed in her mind with its destruction (be it in the sense of losing her moral innocence or in the sense of suicide as the outcome of this act), her thoughts wander to a fourth variation. This final scenario revolves around the idea that, once she has committed this act concomitant with self-destruction, her family will rise to save her.

As the stories she tells herself to make sense of her situation unfold, Else is not only aware that each role she fashions for herself is a pretense, protecting her from the devastating recognition of her own insignificance. She is also, more importantly perhaps, forced to face the emotional impasse she finds herself in. Lacking the skills for any type of employment and having beauty as her only asset, she sees unresolved questions about her own sexual desire inevitably turn into issues of economic exchange. Cognizant that her worth lies in her being a desirable object to the masculine gaze, she speculates about her future by speculating with her beautiful body. Schnitzler's decision to present the narrative as one long internal monologue interspersed with dialogue allows the heroine to give voice not only to her daydreams but also to her assessment of these, so that from the start she views the very performance of feminine charm she also enacts with a critical eye. Else sees her power in holding the male gaze enraptured with her beauty, even while she realizes that going along will disempower her because it reduces her to the object of both her father's clandestine bargaining and her admirers' clandestine voyeurism. Indeed Dorsday, whom she finds unappealing, simply makes explicit what mars the feminine role ascribed to her, namely that insofar as her erotic desire is inextricably entwined with financial transactions, she is in complicity with the very cultural forces that weaken and injure her. She complies with this erotic commodification, pleased that Dorsday wishes to see her naked, since she is aware of her beauty—only to experience shame after having articulated this exhibitionist desire, to accuse herself of being common, and to declare this desire to be a form of self-debasement.

While the aunt calls her niece's scandalous self-display in the music room a pathological expression of sexual frustration and plans to have her institutionalized once they have returned to Vienna, Else's fit of hysteria is, so Schnitzler seems to suggest, an expression of Else's psychic ambivalence about the manner in which late 19th-century Viennese culture calls upon its daughters to turn themselves into objects of masculine desire yet denounces the impropriety of such behavior. Her scandalous deportment exposes the obscene kernel subtending the bourgeois family—whereby parents use their children to preserve their own pleasure—by enacting a clandestine affair in public and turning the hotel lounge into her stage for performing to excess the part she has been assigned in the pact between her father and a potential suitor. While Dorsday's desire to gaze at her naked beauty in private (in his room or in a clearing in the woods) implies a secret bond of mutual subjection, exposing herself not just to him but to all the guests present in the music room seems the only way to broadcast her complaint about what proves to be an insoluble dilemma.

As Freud stated in his early case histories, hysteria can be read as the attempt on the part of the afflicted woman to speak with the body where symbolic language fails. In the case of Schnitzler's Else, presenting her naked body to the public bespeaks the psychic impasse that torments the daughter. She knows that she has to comply with her father's wish, even though she knows it will do no good, since he will never really recover from his financial misfortunes. Similarly, as she knows that whatever form of romantic exchange she submits herself to will always be humiliating because the demands sexuality makes fuse empowerment with vulnerability.

As in the fragmentary case history of Dora, whom Freud treated around the turn of the century, Else's acute sense of abandonment reaches a breaking point because the father, upon whose authority she depends, proves fallible in many ways— in his role as lawyer and trustee as well as in his role as protector of his daughter. Even though he insists that everything can still be saved, Else knows, as she repeatedly notes, this is not the case. Her theatrical protest seeks to disclose the fallibility of paternal authority as such, which exploits filial devotion to cover up its own ineptitude. The naked body of the daughter, lying unconscious in the center of a hotel lounge, stands for the brutal price extracted for upholding the fiction of the inviolability of the bourgeois family. It refers to the inconsistencies at the heart of any symbolic institution such as the family. Yet, while the hysteric points out the fallibility of her interpellator, she fully believes in his power and authority. In fact, she must trust in the paternal law, given that her fantasy world is premised on the assurance that happiness is possible. However, those moments when the inconsistency of symbolic reality leaks through in the form of obscene traces of paternal illegality, as in the clandestine pact between her father and Dorsday, make her question the legitimacy of paternal actions that involve her as a subject. In other words, Else protests the very symbolic institution that also determines her self-definition. She demonstrates that the language of hysteria is one that refuses the refusal of knowledge about discursive impasses and inconsistencies inherent in paternal authority.

As Juliet Mitchell has noted, a hysteric can be seen as a creative artist of sorts, telling tales and fabricating stories about psychic reality, seduction and fantasy, helping Freud ground a theory of subjectivity on the question of who tells the story and to whom it is told. Hysteria thus is not only a symptom of traumatic experience which troubles the psychic apparatus and keeps it on the move. Nor is it merely an articulation of what remains after symbolic interpellation, which is to say what will not be assimilated by it. Rather the language of hysteria insists that something must be spoken even while, insofar as these utterances of discontent are voiced as narratives, the fantasy scenes produced are interminable. One of the most enervating aspects of hysteria is, after all, that it defies closure. As Freud so painfully learned in his struggle to find a solution to this psychosomatic discontent for which no organic lesions can be found, the afflicted subject keeps producing new symptoms, exchanging one disturbance for another, once a proposed interpretation promises a cure.

Early in Schnitzler's novella, Else asks herself why in the stories she keeps telling herself she continues to speculate on her condition, given that she is not writing her memoirs. Yet, in the course of the internal monologue that begins with her leaving a tennis match and ends with her lying on her hotel bed after having taken a large dose of Veronal in the hope of killing herself, she makes up all kinds of stories about herself based on the sentimental fiction she reads. Even before she has opened her mother's letter, she imagines how, were she suddenly to fall from the window sill, journalists would speculate she had killed herself owing to an unhappy romance, only to refute such a conjecture by denying that what keeps her thoughts restlessly moving from one fantasy scenario to another has nothing to do with an unhappy romance.

Something bothers her, yet this troubling sense of something not being right has no clear name. It can only be designated as what it is not. Therefore, she must speak to herself and play through a wide range of ambivalent, contradictory narratives that keep circling around images of her death. The only solution she can find for the gnawing sense that each scenario she creates is only a protective fiction against the corrosive force at the heart of all self-fashioning is to materialize this fragility in the form of her beautiful exposed corpse. Following her meeting with Dorsday, and before she has decided how to respond to his proposal, Else falls asleep on a bench in the woods behind the hotel. In a hallucinatory dream, she enacts her sense that the art dealer's wish to see her naked beauty transforms her into a living corpse. She imagines not only how she will look dead and how others will respond to this tragic event but also that she will continue to live on after her own demise, her revivified corpse walking away from the graveyard where she is about to be buried. This impossible scenario—to enjoy death and to continue living—is what her hysteric self-exposure in the music room ultimately aims at.

Schnitzler's narrative leaves open whether the dosage of poison she swallows is actually sufficient or whether her suicide attempt is yet another form of the hysteric's complaint, ultimately refusing closure. The narrative moves seamlessly from the delirious Else laughing hysterically after having discarded the only piece of clothing she was wearing, to the way her mind registers what is happening to her after she has fainted. Her thoughts once again begin to wander freely, while her body is quickly covered with her coat and carried to her hotel room. She is in more places than one—unconscious and conscious, mute and speaking, feeling utterly incapacitated and giving voice to it. This is another form of hysteric exhibition, though one only the reader is privy to. Something keeps driving her fantasy and with it the story. Having failed to attract the attention of those watching over her unconscious body to what she has done, Else finally gives in to the fantasy that she is flying and dreaming. The last words are truncated. Her narrative voice remains unhooked.

See also 1899, 1912 (June), 1921, 1989

Bibliography: Arthur Schnitzler, *Fräulein Else,* trans. Robert A. Simon (New York: AMS Press, 1925). ———, *Das erzählerische Werk,* vol. 5 (Frankfurt am Main: Insel, 1961). Sigmund Freud, *Studies on Hysteria* (1893–1895), *Standard Edition,* vol. 2 (London: Hogarth Press, 1955). ———, "Fragments of an Analysis of a Case of Hysteria (1905)," *Standard Edition,* vol. 7 (London: Hogarth Press, 1953). Juliet Mitchell, *Women: The Longest Revolution: Essays in Feminism, Literature, and Psychoanalysis* (London: Penguin, 1984).

Elisabeth Bronfen

1927
Martin Heidegger's *Sein und Zeit* "strikes like lightning"

The Limits of Historicism

Hurriedly put together and incomplete at that, it was rushed into print and soon afterward abandoned by its author. Nevertheless, *Sein und Zeit (Being and Time)* is one of the masterpieces of 20th-century philosophy. We must thank the faculty of the University of Marburg for its appearance. Martin Heidegger (1889–1976) had been teaching at Marburg for a few years when a regular professorship became available. He was a captivating lecturer but at the age of thirty-eight he had published as yet almost nothing. When the opportunity arose, he was, therefore, urged to get something into print. Instead of putting together his notes for a study of Aristotle on which he had been working steadily, Heidegger compiled some writings of a different, more ambitious kind. In 1927 the text appeared in Edmund Husserl's *Jahrbuch für Philosophie und phänomenologische Forschung (Yearbook for Philosophy and Phenomenological Research),* a solid 437 pages, confidently entitled *Being and Time: First Half.*

But the work was not enough to satisfy Heidegger's opponents, and he did not get the position. However, when his mentor Husserl retired soon afterward from his position at Freiburg University, Heidegger was named his successor. In the meantime, *Being and Time* had made him instantly famous. According to one reviewer it was like lightning striking the sky of German philosophy.

Many readers still regard it as his greatest achievement, even though he went on to lecture, write, and publish for another forty years.

At first glance, *Being and Time* looks like a traditional philosophical treatise. In both form and content it lays claim to being *wissenschaftlich* (scientific), that is, systematic, scholarly, and professional. Heidegger was never to repeat this stylistic experiment. His preferred mode of writing later on was the essay, or the talk written up as an essay, or the lecture course written up as a book—and this because he no longer believed in the kind of philosophy that demanded systematic, scholarly, professional treatment.

Though conservative in appearance, *Being and Time* was in effect a revolutionary treatise. It was most hostile to the idea that the rise of empirical science had reduced the task of philosophy to understanding, analyzing, and justifying the methods by which knowledge is attained. In contraposition to this neo-Kantian and positivist conception of philosophy as theory of knowledge or as logic of the sciences, Heidegger declared it to be "universal phenomenological ontology" (38).

In this respect, he followed Husserl, who also had sought to renew philosophy by attending descriptively to things in themselves and specifically to the facts of consciousness. But *Being and Time* applied the phenomenological method in a manner alien to Husserl. For one thing, it gave priority to man's practical dealing with the world over his theoretical understanding. Heidegger insisted that "the kind of dealing which is closest to us is . . . that kind of concern which manipulates things and puts them to use" (67). And where Husserl had sought to construct the world out of pure consciousness, on the Cartesian model, Heidegger assumed from the start that we exist in the world as embodied beings. What distinguished him most from Husserl, however, was that his phenomenological ontology was intended to raise, above all, "the question of the meaning of Being." This famously dark question was, on Heidegger's account, "both the most basic and the most concrete" (9).

Although the question of Being was to be the central concern of his whole career, it was hardly what drew readers to *Being and Time.* Even philosophers had difficulty focusing on it when reading the book. Although the question of being was highlighted in the introduction, it took a backseat in the subsequent discussion. He had left the question to be considered further in the second half of the book in conjunction with "a phenomenological destruction of the history of ontology" addressing Kant, Descartes, and Aristotle (39). In the end, he never wrote that volume, instead changing his course from phenomenology to a history of Being.

The early readers of *Being and Time,* for the most part, became fixated not on the question of Being but on the road Heidegger proposed to travel in its pursuit. At the very outset, he asked the question how anything could be said about the nature of Being. And to this he gave the surprising answer: "We ourselves are the entities to be analyzed" (1). For *Dasein,* as Heidegger calls the human condition, has a quite peculiar character. It "is an entity which does not just occur among other entities. Rather it is ontically distinguished by the fact that, in its very being, that being is an issue for itself" (12). We therefore can find access to Being itself by considering what it is to be human. *Dasein* is, so to say, the royal road to *Sein* (Being).

The first, published half of *Being and Time* accordingly offers an analysis of Dasein as a means for finding the answer to the question what Sein itself is. Pursuing this route, Heidegger was keen to distance himself from "philosophical anthropology"—that burgeoning philosophical movement of the 1920s. His "analytic of Dasein is not aimed at laying an ontological basis for anthropology" (200). Insofar as it helps "to make such an anthropology possible, or to lay its ontological foundations," it "will provide only some of the 'pieces,' even though they are by no means inessential ones" (17). This is important because Heidegger has been criticized unfairly for his silence on such essential human features as sex and gender. His own concern was instead with two basic characteristics of Dasein: first, "The 'essence' of Dasein lies in its existence"; and, Dasein "is in each case mine" (42). The first characteristic implies that Dasein has no predetermined essence; the second that it must choose itself. As such, Dasein is capable of being in one of two states. "Because Dasein is in each case essentially its own possibility, it *can,* in its very being, 'choose' itself and win itself; it can also lose itself and never win itself; or only 'seem' to do so" (42). Dasein is accordingly either authentic *(eigentlich)* or inauthentic *(uneigentlich).*

In either of these two forms, it is inherently a being in the world and as such a being with others. Each individual Dasein is also always dependent on other Dasein, and from this comes its initial inauthenticity. "Dasein as everyday being with one another stands in *subjection* to others. In itself it *is* not; its Being has been taken away by the Others" (126). In this dependence, Dasein is leveled down by an anonymous, public "One" that supplies it with norms, rules, and concepts. As a result, "everyone is the other and no one is himself" (128). The condition of inauthenticity is marked by idle talk, empty curiosity, ambiguity, and "fallenness"—the state in which Dasein "drifts along toward an alienation in which its ownmost potentiality for being is hidden from it" (178).

Anxiety drives Dasein from this state into a condition of authenticity. "Anxiety makes manifest in Dasein its being toward its ownmost potentiality for being—that is, its being free for the freedom of choosing itself and taking hold of itself. Anxiety brings Dasein face to face with its being free for . . . the authenticity of its being as a possibility which it always is" (188). Dasein is concerned with the world and this concern or care is, indeed, the being of Dasein. The precise character of this care is determined by the fact that we are always running forward toward death. "Death is Dasein's *ownmost* possibility. Being towards this possibility discloses to Dasein its ownmost potentiality for being, in which its very being is at issue" (263).

No short summary can give an adequate picture of the richness of Heidegger's analyses of the inauthentic and authentic conditions of human Dasein. His vivid descriptions employ a suggestive mixture of religious, philo-

sophical, and everyday terms. There are evident allusions to Kierkegaard's opposition of sinfulness and salvation and to Kant's distinction of heteronomous
and autonomous forms of consciousness. We have to look far to find a philosophical writer who can speak with such intensity of the fallenness of the human condition, of anxiety and death, of care, guilt, and the call of conscience,
and who can do so without sliding into religious stereotypes or trite psychologizing.

The richness and complexity of Heidegger's argumentation inevitably has
given rise to misinterpretations. Most prominent among them is the belief that
he is proposing an "ethics of authenticity." Sartre praised him on that account
as an existentialist, while others have berated him on the same grounds as an
elitist. Against this charge, Heidegger himself emphasizes repeatedly that his
distinction between authentic and inauthentic is meant ontologically rather
than evaluatively, that he seeks to characterize two different modes of being,
and that he is concerned with these only to the extent that they bear on the
question of Being.

The misunderstandings are due to a failure to focus properly on Heidegger's own analytical concerns, which are intended to show, above all, that authentic human Dasein is characterized by a specific kind of orientation in
time. This temporality "gets experienced in a phenomenally primordial way in
Dasein's authentic being as a whole" (304). According to Heidegger, the temporality of Dasein is not captured in standard philosophical, scientific, or everyday conceptions of time because it must be understood as "the primordial
condition for the possibility of care" (372). Dasein's being is care and this care
manifests itself as a "toward-oneself," "backward to," and "letting oneself encounter" (328f.). Dasein's practical concerns are always most immediately directed toward the future. "The primary phenomenon of primordial and authentic temporality is the future" (329). But Dasein can direct itself to the
future only insofar as it has been something and only as something "concerned with what is factually ready to hand in the environment." Future, past,
and present belong together in the structure of care and as such constitute its
"ecstatic" temporality. These considerations lead Heidegger to his most challenging conclusion: because in facing the future authentically we are always
confronting death, because all care is, indeed, a being toward death, primordial,
authentic time must itself be finite.

It is this finitude that constitutes human Dasein as historical. "Authentic
being toward death—that is to say, the finitude of temporality—is the hidden
basis of Dasein's historicality" (386). Birth and death are the two outer limits
between which each individual Dasein operates. "Factical Dasein exists as
born; and, as born, it is already dying, in the sense of being toward death . . . As
care, Dasein *is* the 'between'" (374). Thrown into the world, Dasein faces a
"there" (*Da*) in which it discovers for itself "current factical possibilities of authentic existing" (383). These constitute an inheritance that Dasein, as thrown,
is bound to take over, either in the form of surrender or in that of a creative rejoinder. Faced with its inheritance, Dasein is brought "into the simplicity of its

fate" in which it discovers itself to be part of a community, a people, and most specifically, a generation. "Dasein's fateful destiny in and with its 'generation' constitutes the full, authentic reality of Dasein" (385f.).

Heidegger's reflections on authentic and primordial temporality and on Dasein's historicality are unusually dense and show signs of the rush to get his book into print. But the overall intent of his thought is not in doubt. The temporality and historicality of human Dasein are meant to give us decisive clues for the overarching question of the meaning of Being. Against the entire Western philosophical and religious tradition that always believed that the fullest reality is eternal and unchanging presence—whether in the form of Platonic ideas, or as divine existence, or under the imprint of necessary truth—Heidegger meant to say that Being itself is inherently temporal and historical.

We are left with two questions concerning this profoundly challenging thought. The first is what it implies, the second how it is grounded. Heidegger's claim that Being itself is historical seems to boil down to this in *Being and Time:* since Being is to be understood as the Being of beings, that is, of whatever is, Being itself must possess the ontological characteristic of beings. Heidegger already granted that Dasein, as one kind of being, is historical. But the conclusion of *Being and Time* takes a step further by saying that even tools and other human artifacts as well as the things of nature present before us must be conceived historically. It also says that all conditions of Dasein, all its moods, states of mind, as well as its cognitive states, must be thought of in historical terms. Heidegger writes: "If Dasein's being is in principle historical, then every factical science is always manifestly in the grip of this happening" (392). Even the discipline of history must be thought of historically. Finally, he agrees with Wilhelm Dilthey that "there is, therefore, no real philosophizing which is not historical" (402).

Historicism is a persuasive doctrine for all kinds of reasons quite apart from those advanced in *Being and Time.* But it is also difficult to maintain, and this is clearly illustrated in Heidegger's attempt to think it through to its most radical consequences. For it is not at all obvious that we can succeed in a radical historicizing of everything. Can one really fully historicize the standpoint from which to make such a radical claim? Heidegger seems to have realized the problem by the end of the published part of his book. He came to see then that he had reached his radically historicist conclusion by postulating that Dasein has invariant and necessary characteristics that can be examined in a systematic, nonhistorical fashion. But this is in conflict with the conclusion reached. If that objection holds—and Heidegger never came to doubt it—the constructions of *Being and Time* must be misguided and its project incapable of being completed as planned. Heidegger finishes his text accordingly with some open questions: "How is this mode of temporalizing temporality to be interpreted? Is there a way that leads from primordial time to the meaning of Being? Does time itself manifest itself as the horizon of Being?" (437). And to these questions there is no obvious answer to be provided in the terms of *Being and Time.*

Heidegger's book has found both ardent admirers and bitter enemies. The former have often surrendered themselves too easily to the magic of Heidegger's language and imagination. The latter have often been too sweeping in their condemnation of Heidegger's ideas as instances of metaphysical nonsense, or too polemical in mindlessly ascribing Heidegger's later political mistakes to the ideas of *Being and Time,* or too pedantic in their rehearsal of particular errors in argumentation. The attractiveness of *Being and Time* lies ultimately in Heidegger's burning commitment to an utterly independent philosophical thinking. To both the camp followers and the critics one wants to say: "Go ahead! Try to do better."

See also 1790, 1808, 1820 (Winter), 1946, 1979

Bibliography: Martin Heidegger, *Sein und Zeit: Erste Hälfte,* in *Jahrbuch für Philosophie und phänomenologische Forschung,* vol. 8, 1927; published separately as *Sein und Zeit* (Tübingen: Niemeyer, 11th ed., 1967); *Being and Time,* trans. J. Macquarrie and Edward Robinson (New York: Harper & Row, 1962). (The translation gives the page numbering of the German text that is here cited.)

Hans Sluga

1927, March

Walter Benjamin and Franz Hessel's German translation of Marcel Proust's *A l'ombre des jeunes filles en fleurs* is published

The Task of the Flâneur

In an announcement in Suhrkamp's 1957 catalogue of the final volume of Eva Rechel-Martens's complete translation of *A la recherche du temps perdu (Auf der Suche nach der verlorenen Zeit),* Theodor Adorno suggested that Proust's novel could at last perform a crucial role for German literature. Less as a model for imitation, the *Recherche* should serve as the standard by which writers measure their own work. German prose, Adorno claimed, ought to be perceived as pre- or post-Proust. This work would become a dividing line, a threshold, a means of self-definition and renewal for a literary tradition that had been utterly devalued in Nazi Germany.

What Adorno may have had in mind was an encounter with Proust, dating from well before the war and on a much more private level, at a critical point in the intellectual career of his friend Walter Benjamin (1892–1940). Begun in the wake of a failed attempt to qualify for a professorial appointment and a sociopolitical "awakening," between the end of a marriage and the start of a new, overwhelming love affair, Benjamin's work of translating Proust's *Recherche* came at a point of transition in his own career. A major reorientation in Benjamin's thinking occurred at this time. And while the shift expresses a fresh and firm commitment to Marxism, there are many reasons to regard the turn as representing a deep and lasting engagement with the methodology, style, and image of Marcel Proust, France's great narrator of awakenings.

The changes that coincided with and qualified Benjamin's turn to Proust are especially evident in his professional writings. As he himself described it to Gershom Scholem, this period of "exaltation" was founded primarily on a resolution to move away from his hitherto hermetic approach to writing toward a more open, expository style, disclosing "the actual and political elements of [his] ideas" (*Correspondence*, 257). Like many of those writing within the context of social, economic, and moral devastation that characterized the Weimar Republic, Benjamin renounced literary esotericism and adopted a clearly stated political position. Earlier reflections on the inexpressible qualities of language gradually yielded to avowals of communicability. Theoretical issues receded before concrete presentations of the material at hand. Abstraction of any sort he rejected.

An interesting consequence of these choices was Benjamin's rekindled interest in collaboration. The first piece along those lines was an urban portrait of Naples, which Benjamin wrote with Asja Lacis. This remarkable woman, a citizen of Latvia and longstanding member of the Soviet Communist Party, was intensely active in Moscow's avant-garde and had worked closely with Brecht's experimental theater in Munich. In the summer of 1924, during a stay on the island of Capri with her companion Bernhard Reich, she entirely captivated Benjamin, who had come there alone to write his book on the German baroque as the prerequisite for his application for a post at the University of Frankfurt. As Lacis recounts in her memoirs, Benjamin often referred to Proust, spontaneously and passionately translating passages out loud for her. And indeed, the "Naples" essay, with its stunning attention to details and gestures, the theatricality of city-life, and the "porous" intermingling of private and public spaces, arguably owes much to Proustian style.

If Benjamin's *vita nuova* began that summer on Capri, it was in the following year that the new directions were definitively affirmed. By spring, he had returned to Berlin, prepared to submit his book on the German baroque mourning play. He expected that this work would secure for him the teaching post at Frankfurt. The committee, however, found his work unacceptable and warned Benjamin that, should he pursue his application, he would certainly be turned down. With no further prospects for an academic position, Benjamin was compelled to make his way as a freelance literary writer. Fortunately, almost directly after the withdrawal of his book on the mourning play, he was contracted by the publisher Die Schmiede to translate the second, fourth, and fifth volumes of Proust's *Recherche*. This offer came through the personal mediation of Rudolf Schottlaender, a distant relative, whose translation of the first volume appeared by year's end. His chances for a professorship demolished, Benjamin eagerly returned to the "task of the translator," as he had done some years before when he translated Baudelaire's *Tableaux parisiens* and, more recently, the prose poem sequence *Anabase* by Saint-John Perse. The latter job had been offered to Rilke before being passed along to Benjamin on Hofmannsthal's recommendation; and although it evidently posed some linguistic difficulties, none equaled the problems of Proust's novel, which called for an entire reformulation of Benjamin's translation theory and practice.

Die Schmiede, established in Berlin in 1921, had enjoyed rapid success as a publisher of expressionist and post-expressionist literature. With a sound reputation for good compensation and fair treatment of authors, it had attracted an outstanding roster of writers, many of whom came from the house of the noted publisher Kurt Wolff. Among them were Gottfried Benn, Franz Kafka, Heinrich Mann, Ernst Weiß, Willy Haas, and Georg Kaiser. In 1922, the year of Proust's death, Die Schmiede's director, Julius Salter, had purchased the German rights to the entire *Recherche* from Gallimard at an unprecedented price and, anticipating the appearance of the remaining volumes in France, planned to publish the complete set in German translation. From its inception, however, despite its grand ambition, the project was destined to falter, due both to some misguided decisions and to circumstances beyond anyone's control.

In the first place, the choice of Schottlaender for the volume was problematic. The twenty-six-year-old classical philologist had neither the professional credentials of a Romanist nor the experience of a worldly *homme de lettres.* The obvious choice would have been Ernst Robert Curtius, professor of Romance Languages at Heidelberg, who had introduced Proust to Germany in 1922 with a highly influential essay devoted to the author. Even though Curtius expressed interest in translating Proust, Salter turned down his offer, presumably for financial reasons. Curtius's revenge came in the form of a scathing review of Schottlaender's work. Printed in the Berlin journal *Die Literarische Welt,* the piece listed error upon error and thereby gave rise to an entire chain of critical reviews nearly unanimous in their denunciation of the Proust debut. Hermann Hesse was one of the few who, in an article for the *Berliner Tageblatt,* recognized the translation's merits. It was clear, however, that Die Schmiede could not continue to employ Schottlaender for this project. Nor, upon closer scrutiny, could it accept the work of Walther Petry, who had edited the press's "Classics of Erotic Literature" and just submitted his manuscript translation of *Le côté de Guermantes.* Instead Salter offered Benjamin, in the early months of 1926, the responsibility for putting out a complete Proust translation in collaboration with his fellow Berliner and friend Franz Hessel.

Hessel was no stranger to French literature or to exhausting projects. His novel *Pariser Romanze* (1920; *Paris Romance*), with its rich evocation of his days in Paris before the war, first brought his name to prominence, winning the attention of Rilke, Hofmannsthal, and Rudolf Borchardt. The book barely conceals the story of his marriage to Helen Grund and their intimate relationship with Henri-Pierre Roché, whose own account of the ménage à trois, *Jules et Jim* (1953), was to become the basis for the François Truffaut film. Life of the Belle Époque, viewed through the bohemian lens of the artists and writers of Montparnasse and the Café du Dôme, prepared Hessel well for the Proust project. Moreover, as one of the principal readers for Rowohlt Verlag, he had recently coordinated the complete German edition of Balzac's *Comédie humaine,* which ultimately appeared in forty-four volumes. While he organized this massive undertaking, Hessel became part of the Berlin circle around Siegfried Kracauer, Ernst Bloch, and Ernst Weiß, and thereby came to know

Benjamin, whom he immediately hired to join the Balzac team with an offer to translate *Ursule Mirouët*.

Besides collaborating with him on Proust, Hessel also became a critical and highly influential figure in Benjamin's career. On his recommendation, Ernst Rowohlt published Benjamin's study of the baroque mourning play as well as his quasi-surrealist collection of aphoristic observations and images, *Einbahnstraße* (1928; *One-Way Street*). After a stay together in Paris in the spring of 1926, the two embarked on yet another collaboration, an essay on the arcades of Paris, which was originally slated for the Berlin journal *Der Querschnitt*. Although this piece never made it into print, it constitutes the foundational text for the project that occupied Benjamin for the remainder of his life, the so-called *Passagen-Werk (Arcades Project)*.

What Hessel contributed to Benjamin's intellectual profile—and this is partly what makes the encounter with Proust such a decisive turning point— was a new way of experiencing the modern city. Hessel had a passion for strolling along the streets, straying through various neighborhoods and quarters, getting lost by resisting the need to "find one's way." In a word, Hessel was a *flâneur*, one who had mastered "the difficult art of taking a walk." This approach to modern experience provided Hessel with a narrative means to portray the Paris of yesteryear as well as contemporary life in his native city, particularly in *Spazieren in Berlin* (1929; *Strolling in Berlin*). The pedestrian method, with its deliberate cultivation of disorientation, inspired Benjamin's own *recherches,* both dating from 1932, *Berliner Chronik (Berlin Chronicle)* and *Berliner Kindheit um Neunzehnhundert (Berlin Childhood around 1900)*. In short, with Hessel, Benjamin uncovered the flânerie quality of Proust's "fan of memory," which "never comes to the end of its segments"; he participated in the novelist's insatiability, where "remembrance progresses from small to smallest details, from the smallest to the infinitesimal" (*Berlin Chronicle, Selected Writings,* 2:597).

Benjamin's encounter with Proust represented in condensed form the new mode of seeing inspired by his friendships with Hessel and Asja Lacis. In this vision, the cityscape infiltrates the space formerly reserved for language. Henceforth these two foci of Benjamin's thought operated in a dialectical relation, pulling toward some ground of reconciliation, however vague. As he would express it to Max Rychner, Benjamin was convinced there was "a bridge to the way dialectical materialism looks at things from the perspective of [one's] specific stance to the philosophy of language, strained and problematic as that bridge may be" (*Correspondence,* 372).

The problem is essentially one of finding a suitable critical methodology for investigating urban space by means of a philosophy of language. The tension between an awareness of language as fragmentary and of experience as *flânerie* is articulated in much of Benjamin's correspondence from the time when he was working on the Proust translation. Early in the project, in the cold autumn of 1925, Benjamin describes the conditions of his work in Riga, where he had gone to complete *Sodom und Gomorrah* and to reunite with his beloved "Bolshevik" Asja Lacis. Typically, Benjamin frames his activity within the town's brutal melancholy, which "with great force can seize whoever has walked across the Roman streets." Here, he continues, he toils day and night, attending to the "infinite brittleness in the details," which makes him "think of Chinese porcelain that has to be packed carefully for shipment to Germany" (*Briefe*, 3:93). What remains of Benjamin's earlier meditations on linguistic philosophy is an intense awareness of the fragility of language. His formulation recalls, for example, the well-known image from his essay "The Task of the Translator," which recognizes both the translation and the original "as fragments of a greater language, just as fragments are part of a vessel" (*Selected Writings*, 1:260). The metaphor of fragile porcelain also points to the image of the mosaic, whose "majesty in fragmentation" serves as an illustration of philosophical contemplation in Benjamin's study of baroque drama, where "truth-content is only to be grasped through immersion in the most minute details of subject-matter" (*Origin of German Drama*, 28). The modification that working on Proust brings is that now this intensive reflection on the fragmentary quality of language coincides with a preoccupation with strolling through the city—walking "across the Roman streets." Accordingly, while living in Paris with the Hessels, Benjamin writes to a friend about his daily regimen: he begins working on Proust immediately upon getting out of bed, before washing, dressing, or breakfast, then spends the afternoons sauntering through the city (*Briefe*, 3:420–421).

In a sentence that Benjamin and Hessel never touched, Proust writes, "The function and the task of a writer are those of a translator" (*Le temps retrouvé*, 3:926). Along similar lines, the perambulatory gaze of the *flâneur* transforms the city into a foreign text awaiting translation. The disorientation is but an index of the reader's inexhaustible curiosity, passively fighting against the rapidity of modern transportation. It is literally a method—a "way" or "path"—whose critical force is perfectly analogous to the "retarding elements" that Leo Spitzer recognized in Proust's style. In his own essay "Zum Bilde Prousts" (1929; "The Image of Proust"), Benjamin refers to the inversion of Penelope's apotropaic project of infinite delay, unraveling by day what has been woven at night, disdaining the teleology of memory in favor of the detailed arabesques of aimless amnesia. Here, Benjamin's elaboration of Proustian recollection, which is "much closer to forgetting than what is usually called memory" (*Selected Writings*, 2:238), corresponds to what he once characterized in a letter to Scholem as the near illegibility of his translation (*Correspondence*, 289).

Committed as it is to the literalness espoused in the essay on translation, Benjamin's rendering of the twists and turns of Proust's syntax mimic the experience of losing one's way. The principal difference, then, between the *Recherche* and the *Arcades Project* is a simple matter of focus, but this distinction is also the critical line that keeps the two thinkers apart. The inwardly spiraling recollection from Proust's cork-lined room translates into the flashes of "profane illumination" before the marketplace. The claustrophile finds his precise echo in the agoraphile.

Despite growing financial difficulties, Julius Salter published Benjamin and Hessel's *Im Schatten der jungen Mädchen* in the early spring of 1927. Given the scandal associated with the Schottlaender translation, the critical attention to the new volume was significant and, on the whole, quite positive. Regardless, Die Schmiede was irrevocably on its way to bankruptcy and within a year it sold the Proust rights to the Munich publisher Reinhard Piper. Piper was eager to retain Benjamin and Hessel to produce a complete edition of the *Recherche,* but both authors had already begun to move to other projects. As early as September 1926, only a year after Benjamin had demonstrated great fervor for the project, he confided to Scholem his need to move on. "Unproductive involvement with a writer who so splendidly pursues goals that are similar to my own, at least former, goals occasionally induces something like symptoms of intestinal poisoning in me" (*Correspondence,* 305). The ecstasy of inspiration was sliding into fear of contamination. As for Piper, caught in the turmoil of high inflation, plans for the translation started to fall apart. Tedious negotiations led to general disinterest, until the project died slowly and quietly. *Die Herzogin von Guermantes*—a title that Benjamin and Hessel would not approve—did appear in 1930, but the German reading public was already moving in other, less open directions. The manuscript of *Sodom und Gomorrah,* portions of which Benjamin had enthusiastically recited to Lacis as she directed her illegal communist theater in Riga, has to this day never been discovered.

See also 1910, 1929 (Autumn), 1936 (February)

Bibliography: Walter Benjamin, *Selected Writings: Volume 1, 1913–1926,* ed. Marcus Bullock and Michael Jennings (Cambridge, Mass.: Harvard University Press, 1996). ———, *Selected Writings: Volume 2, 1927–1934,* ed. Michael Jennings, Howard Eiland, and Gary Smith (Cambridge, Mass.: Harvard University Press, 1999). ———, *Gesammelte Briefe,* 6 vols., ed. Christoph Gödde and Henri Lonitz (Frankfurt am Main: Suhrkamp, 1995–). Momme Brodersen, *Walter Benjamin: A Biography,* trans. Malcolm R. Green and Ingrida Ligers (London and New York: Verso, 1997).

John T. Hamilton

1927, June

On the cusp of his fiftieth birthday, Hermann Hesse publishes *Der Steppenwolf*

The Lesson of the Magic Theater

Relegated to the fringes of the German literary canon in his lifetime, the writings of Hermann Hesse (1877–1962) achieved widespread recognition only after his death, and then primarily outside the German-language sphere. Colin Wilson's analysis *The Outsider* (1956) led the Beat Generation to take up Hesse as if he were one of their own. Hesse's greatest promulgator, however, was the Harvard psychologist Timothy Leary, who regarded his writings as an example of Buddhist-style interiority and the value of psychedelic experience. Staging performances based on the Magic Theater episode in Hesse's novel *Der Steppenwolf* (1927; *Steppenwolf*) during 1965 and 1966 in New York and at his summer camp in Millbrook, Leary encouraged his audience to take a trip with the novel's protagonist, Harry Haller, metaphorically entering his bloodstream and participating with him in his strange experiences. By initiating a North American Hesse boom, Leary enabled young Americans of the 1960s to identify with an alienated character who could serve as a model for anti-establishment rebellion. Later, opponents of the Vietnam War found that Hesse's critique of militarism, as figured in one of the lessons Harry Haller learns in the Magic Theater, resonated with their own views. From America, this image of Hesse spread to the German student revolution of 1968. Asian readers, who had long been impressed by Hesse's push beyond Western culture and his incorporation of Eastern metaphysics and utopianism into his writings, became devoted fans of his novels *Demian* (1919) and *Siddhartha* (1922). Despite a relative lull in critical reception of Hesse's works in the later decades of the 20th century, a revival of interest now seems likely. The first fully annotated edition of Hesse's collected works, including his correspondence and political writings, is currently in preparation. Exhibitions and conferences in Berlin, London, and Hesse's hometown of Calw in Baden-Württemberg celebrated the 125th anniversary of the author's birth in 2002; and in the same year a new Hermann Hesse museum opened in Seoul, South Korea, with more than twenty-five hundred artifacts.

Although younger readers tend to be especially drawn to *Der Steppenwolf,* the work was in fact a product of the author's maturity. In arranging for the novel to appear in time for his fiftieth birthday, Hesse was not indulging in a mere conceit. Centered on a character who too was soon to turn fifty—and who was initially planning to commit suicide at this point—the novel in many ways takes stock of Hesse's own life. One contemporary reviewer deemed it "an exhausting confession at which all criticism can only fall silent" (Hsia, 263). Other critics compared the novel unfavorably to *Der Zauberberg* (1924; *The Magic Mountain*), which Thomas Mann had published in time for his own fiftieth birthday celebrations. It is perhaps unfair to compare Hesse's *Steppenwolf* to the philosophically ambitious *Zauberberg;* still, both novels attempt to present a critical portrait of contemporary society and to reconceive the role of the writer in the modern world.

Der Steppenwolf was first and foremost an indictment of modern bourgeois life. Its deep ambiguities are a product of the crisis of modernity during the Weimar Republic. The novel's protagonist, an aestheticized outsider, attempts to break out of the rigid strictures of a lifestyle he finds oppressive and to cut through unreflecting obeisance to cultural traditions he himself understands in more sophisticated terms. Torn between desire to belong to the domestic sphere and distaste for the forms it has taken, the protagonist sees himself divided between a human and a wolflike self. The excesses with which he experiments as he tries to resolve his inner dichotomy and the sexual explicitness of their portrayal left contemporary readers embarrassed and bewildered. They were also disturbed by the novel's critique of modern industrialism, a source of national pride for many Germans of the time.

During the First World War, Hesse had already gained a reputation as a critic of modern militarism. Until 1917, when he was officially asked to desist, he was a prolific contributor of antiwar essays to newspapers and journals. In the postwar period, he continued to come under attack for his pacifist stance. Later, the Nazi regime declared his writings "unerwünschte Literatur" (undesirable literature) and, although he had now become a Swiss citizen, prohibited him from reprinting old works or publishing new ones during the period 1939–1945. In this respect, the regime bore out Hesse's suspicion of the Prussian Academy of the Arts when he resigned from his position as a foreign member of the creative writing section in 1931, declaring that in the event of another war, he believed its members would "deceive the people by order of the government about every vital issue." Hesse's receipt of the first Nobel Prize for literature awarded after the Second World War in 1946 marked a turning point in his career. In the same year, he also received the Frankfurt Goethe Prize. The two awards spoke to Hesse's lifelong antimilitarism and his emphasis on a "world-citizenry" modeled on that advocated by Goethe. Pilloried throughout much of his life, Hesse now became the best-selling 20th-century German author worldwide.

Hesse's appeal stems from his protagonists' quests for an identity that rejects the reified modern industrial (and now postmodern, postindustrial) age of late capitalism. His heroes wish to escape what Max Weber once termed the "iron cage"—the instrumentalization of the world and of the self. Hesse's most famous outsider figure, Harry Haller, a writer and self-styled "wolf of the steppes," chooses not to become part of the "never-ceasing machinery" that controls people's lives. He is appalled by the jingoistic professor who invites him to dinner, as well as by his landlady's narrow-minded businessman-nephew, who writes a preface for the confessional text that Haller leaves behind when he departs the town unannounced (*Steppenwolf,* 4; 78). By rejecting these aspects of the modern world, Haller adopts an aesthetic code of inwardness. His hero worship of Goethe and Mozart is symbolic of his obsession with *Kultur*—the high culture of literature, classical music and poetry, including his own. His elevation of these creative modes is as intense as his neo-Romantic, Nietzschean rejection of modern *Zivilisation* —a philistine, commodity-oriented attitude. Popularized by the cultural pessimism of Oswald Spengler's *Der Untergang des Abendlandes* (1918–1922; *The Decline of the West*), the dichotomy of *Kultur* versus *Zivilisation* challenged long-held ideals deriving from the Enlightenment. Originally, the German goal of self-cultivation *(Bildung)* followed a path of humanistic integration, embracing culture and civilization, self and world. But Germany's belated industrialization at the end of the 19th century made it difficult for individuals to take this course. Haller's self-obsession is not entirely of his own making; it stems from the sociological conditions of modernity. Yet his rejection of Weimar Germany's technological and commercial progressivism, particularly its more militaristic applications, leaves him with few alternatives.

In the course of the story, Haller discovers a new path to self-development. In the surroundings of the modern city, beneficial experiences of diversity, deviance, and otherness can be found for the introverted individual. In developing this idea, Hesse turned to Freud, whose works he later admitted made a stronger impact on him than those of Jung, despite his own former experience as a patient of a Jungian psychoanalyst (Richards, 113). By maintaining exposure to the world, Freud suggests, we can encounter an alterity that also lies potentially within us. Haller overcomes his death wish during his nightly forays into the old quarter of the city (a fictional amalgam of Basel and Zurich). These excursions spark in him a seemingly uncharacteristic curiosity about modern mass culture's spectacular commodity consumption. The Magic Theater's vulgar flashing electric sign that first beckons Haller is a correlative of this new interest. He is then initiated into contemporary dancing, uninhibited sex, jazz music, and drug-induced visions by Hermine, her friend Maria, and the musician Pablo.

The uncannily recurring invitations to enter the mysterious Magic Theater—emanating from the city's bestial unconscious, so to speak—summon Haller to emerge from his frozen immobility as narcissist. The "Treatise on the Steppenwolf," an inset text that analyzes Haller from an external perspective, helps him to see that he has become untouchable and disconnected. After decades of striving for independence and a life free from bourgeois morals, he is now "incapable of relationship" (47). The treatise, however, has made him a reader of his own self, able to recognize his weaknesses. Haller now admits that his advocacy of pacifism conveniently kept him from the fate of others in the trenches of the Great War; he understands that his private investment income makes him a member of the bourgeoisie; and he feels ill at ease with such radically alternative lifestyles as Hermine and Pablo lead.

Most dangerous for Haller's chances of ever "healing" himself—a word Hesse himself later applied to the protagonist's trajectory in a foreword to a 1961 edition of the novel—is the fact that the urban domain with which he is to connect is itself so damaged. While his earlier turn away from the material world had led him to espouse the ideals of aesthetic modernism, it also left a void that needed to be filled. It is at the Magic Theater that Haller is able to act out his narcissistic identity on an imaginary level and to gain a symbolic glimpse into aspects of the world with which he was previously unwilling to become engaged.

Haller's entry into the Magic Theater finally occurs at a masked ball to which Hermine has invited him. The novel's famous culminating scene is marked by a series of narcissistic doublings that lead to a surreal orgy. Hermine starts off the doubling effect when she appears at the ball dressed as a handsome youth, the image of Haller's childhood friend Hermann. Her name is, of course, already the female version of Hermann (not coincidentally also the first name of Hesse himself); and now Hermine assumes the role of her masculine other. As in their previous encounters, she functions primarily as Harry Haller's *anima,* in the Jungian sense. From his own Jungian analysis, Hesse was familiar with this concept, expressed in Jung's writings by such formulations as "a meeting with oneself is, at first, the meeting with one's own shadow" (*Ar-*

chetypes, 20–21). During Haller's initial meeting with Hermine, the young woman advises him that her role would be "a kind of looking glass" for him; and he, in turn, confirmed that her face was a "magic mirror" (108). As Jung put it, "Whoever goes to himself risks a confrontation with himself. The mirror does not flatter, it faithfully shows whatever looks into it" (*Archetypes,* 20). Hermine's ability to alternate sexual identities as she pleases (not only does she attract Haller's desire, but she also gives him her lover, Maria) facilitates her role in opening up repressed areas of Haller's sexual identity: in desiring her, he can engage both his heterosexual and homosexual longings.

Pablo leads them both from the dance floor into the Magic Theater, where he gives them hallucinogens. Taking over from Hermine as Haller's double, Pablo plays several initiator roles for the protagonist: he teaches Haller "to play chess with the little figures" (217), and substitutes for him in the field of sexual conquest, making love with Hermine in his stead. The Magic Theater leads Haller beyond the dualistic "wolf" posture that the treatise had already criticized. In the theater, Harry Haller is in effect cured of his "mirror stage," as Lacan might have put it, precisely by the use of mirrors. Holding up a pocket mirror, Pablo makes Harry not only double in number, but legion. Only when Pablo throws the little mirror away does the Steppenwolf image fade, allowing the "multitudinous Harrys" to appear in a gigantic wall mirror. Harry Haller finally understands that countless possibilities lie within him, all and any of which can be discovered by means of the Magic Theater.

Every doorway that Harry enters in the Magic Theater's virtual reality can lead him either to blissful composition or violent decomposition of the self. Calling this process a *Figurenspiel* (game of figures), Pablo asks to play with "a few dozen" pieces of Harry's "personality broken up." This division of the self into pieces reaches a crisis when Haller enters into a world at war with its own machines and enthusiastically involves himself in a mass shooting of people driving by in automobiles. In this savage parody of what happens when humankind assumes the machine-perspective as an absolute, Haller and a friend shoot passing cars over the cliff, justifying their actions by citing a pacifist wish to rid the world of machines and capitalists in one fell swoop. As one of their dying victims points out, however, they themselves are using guns to achieve this aim. The atrocity of this scene articulates Hesse's own fears about the technologized modernity that exploded into being during the First World War, when human beings were used as pawns in a drawn-out, machine-driven conflict.

Another destructive scene involves the alternation of aggression and self-disgust, metaphorically encapsulated in the image of the Steppenwolf. While in the Magic Theater, Harry observes a reversal of roles in which a wolf becomes a trainer who teaches a human being to eat live animals. This scene holds up a mirror to Harry's own former desire to tear human society apart and live without regard for conventional morals. In the Magic Theater, woman is also portrayed as a commodity that can be destroyed at will: when a jealous Harry discovers the lovers Pablo and Hermine as they lie asleep and naked, he stabs her to death. Fortunately, this turns out to occur only on the level of the theater's imagined reality. In the final episodes of the novel, Pablo revives Hermine as a diminutive sex object and puts her in his pocket as a "toy figure" (217). Hermine's "death" and her shrinking into a doll are a part of a stage set, the purpose of which is to reveal to Harry Haller the advantages of mutable identity. The culmination of the scenes in the Magic Theater is reached with Haller's final insight that "all the hundred thousand pieces of life's game were in my pocket" (217). Haller now recognizes Pablo as a "clever architect" (193) who can reset the pieces of the soul to play different personality games and create an individual's world afresh in new settings. At the close of the novel, Haller comes to understand that this is what he must now learn to do for himself.

How might this conclusion be evaluated? Certainly, the Magic Theater functions to open up the closed circuits of Harry Haller's mind—though, to be sure, only under the influence of drugs. Yet the reader is not given any sense of how the protagonist will negotiate his new understanding of engagement with the world. Perhaps one important motif is that of outwardly oriented play. Another is the idea of meeting external change with inner flexibility. Haller's recognition that the self can best become engaged with the world by marshaling its protean possibilities is perhaps the ultimate lesson of the Magic Theater.

See also 1791, 1882, 1899, 1906, 1918, 1937

Bibliography: Sigmund Freud, "On the Uncanny," *Collected Papers,* vol. 4 (New York: Basic Books, 1959). C. G. Jung, *The Archetypes and the Collective Unconscious,* trans. R. F. C. Hull (Princeton, N.J.: Princeton University Press, 1969). Hermann Hesse, *Der Steppenwolf* (Frankfurt am Main: Suhrkamp Verlag, 1997); *Steppenwolf,* trans. Basil Creighton, Joseph Mileck, and Horst Frenz (New York: Henry Holt, 1963). Adrian Hsia, ed., *Hermann Hesse im Spiegel der zeitgenössischen Kritik* (Bern and Munich: Francke, 1975). Timothy Leary and Ralph Metzner, "Hermann Hesse: Poet of the Interior Journey," *The Psychedelic Review* 1.2 (1963): 167–182. David G. Richards, *Exploring the Divided Self: Hermann Hesse's* Steppenwolf *and Its Critics* (Columbia, S.C.: Camden House, 1996).

Janet Ward

⚲ *1928, August 31*

Kurt Weill and Bertolt Brecht's *Die Dreigroschenoper* premieres at the Theater am Schiffbauerdamm in Berlin

The Urform *of Opera*

"I'm not exactly asking for an opera here," says Macheath, the antihero of the Weimar Republic's theatrical smash-hit *Die Dreigroschenoper (The Threepenny Opera).* The occasion for the comment is a wedding reception, held in an illegally occupied stable. The wedding (by no means his first) is that of Macheath himself, a dashing, notorious criminal known as Mack the Knife. Given his dangerous lifestyle, several widows will presumably survive him, among them Polly, whom he has just married, and Lucy, daughter of his old friend Tiger Brown, London's chief of police. Along with his excessive fondness for the bourgeois institution of marriage, Macheath displays nouveau riche pretensions to taste. When his men supply stolen furnishings, he claims to know the difference between Chippendale and Louis Quatorze. Later, under arrest and awaiting execution, though ultimately pardoned, he requests his favorite food: asparagus. Why does he receive a pardon? "So at least in opera," concludes his father-in-law and arch-rival Peachum, "you can see for once how mercy comes before justice." Neither Macheath nor his creators ask for an opera, but a connection to high culture is part of his, and the piece's, style.

If *Die Dreigroschenoper* is an opera, it is an opera with significant material and institutional differences. The premiere took place on August 31, 1928, in a small theater (Berlin's Theater am Schiffbauerdamm), not at an opera house. Playing to a broader audience than traditional opera, the first production also drew on a wide spectrum of performers from various theatrical backgrounds. No one in the cast was a professional opera singer. The instrumentalists, drawn from the world of dance bands, remained in full view on the stage as visual property—opera turned inside out, as it were. Yet thanks to these differences, Kurt Weill (1900–1950) and Bertolt Brecht (1898–1956), each in his way, managed to say something about the genre. "It presented us with the opportunity," as Weill remarked at the time, "to make 'opera' the subject matter for an evening in the theater." *Die Dreigroschenoper* is art about art.

The work begins, like many an 18th-century piece for the operatic stage, with an overture. While the musical idiom is recognizably related to baroque music, it is defamiliarized by linear counterpoint, bold modern harmonies, and an unusual instrumental line-up. Both texture and timbre impart a 1920s flavor, with two saxophones, two trumpets, a trombone, a banjo, timpani, and a harmonium. Underscoring the generic ambiguity, the playbill described *Die Dreigroschenoper* as a "play with music"; but it also informed the audience that they had come to watch an adaptation of an early 18th-century piece, *The Beggar's Opera,* presented "in a prologue and eight scenes after the English of John Gay." Brecht received credit not as author but as adaptor; his assistant Elisabeth Hauptmann provided the translation.

The idea of updating a theatrical classic informed the work from the beginning. Alerted to the huge success of Sir Nigel Playfair's revival of Gay's *Beggar's Opera* at the Lyric Theatre in Hammersmith, London—a production that opened on June 5, 1920, and ran for a record-breaking 1,463 performances over a three-year period—Brecht had Elisabeth Hauptmann prepare a working translation of the piece in the winter of 1927–28. The project soon took off when Brecht met the young impresario Ernst Josef Aufricht, who was in search of a play for his new company at Schiffbauerdamm.

Between its inception in early 1928 and its first performance on August 31, eight or so months later, the hybrid opera-cum-play with music underwent numerous and substantial reworkings, especially during the chaotic final month of rehearsal under the direction of Erich Engel. Apart from Gay's text, Brecht also used "interpolated ballads" by François Villon and Rudyard

Unpublished sketch by Caspar Neher, stage and costume designer for the first production of Brecht's *Dreigroschenoper.* (Max Reinhardt Archive, Bartle Library, SUNY Binghamton)

Kipling, as the playbill indicated. Given such frank borrowing, it might seem ironic, if not downright perverse, that Brecht should later have become embroiled in a plagiarism suit. When he was charged, by the critic Alfred Kerr, with having failed to credit the German translator of the Villon poems, K. L. Ammer, Brecht responded with an immortal line about his "fundamental laxity in matters of intellectual property."

When it came to contracts, Brecht was not at all lax about what he thought was his own intellectual property. But here he was making a statement about his aesthetic, his way of doing creative—as opposed to financial—business. A key concept is that of "montage." *Die Dreigroschenoper* juxtaposes its separate and separated elements almost in the manner of a film: the musical numbers; the spoken dialogue; the actors who speak and sing, with separate lighting *(Songlicht)* for the latter; the stage property, including the performing instrumentalists and the prescribed placards narrating the plot. The elements themselves are drawn from diverse sources, some acknowledged, some not.

The principal, openly acknowledged, source is Gay's play itself; then there are the Villon ballads. Kipling was also a declared source, although "Polly's Lied," based on Kipling's "Mary, Pity Women," was cut for the premiere. Throwing in a few more names would scarcely have detracted from the piece's originality: on the contrary, if anything, it would probably have enhanced it. In a work of radical montage, the roll call of elements forms part of the work. This was an era of creative recycling of earlier, classical art, the era known as neoclassicism. In music, the label principally applied to Stravinsky, which greatly irked his rival Schönberg. But Satie, Picasso, and Cocteau, brought together for the 1917 ballet *Parade,* had been influential too. The Brecht-Weill piece, itself heavily indebted to Stravinsky (as Weill readily conceded), fit right into this trend. Also symptomatic of the revivalist tendency were contemporaneous stagings of other classics—Shakespeare in particular in the spoken theater (in 1928, Berlin saw a modern-dress staging of *Macbeth,* for example), and Handel at the opera.

Weill's score, his second collaboration with Brecht, retains just one of the airs arranged by Pepusch for *The Beggar's Opera:* Peachum's "Morning Hymn." Initially this number was to follow the overture, as it does in Gay's work, but the last-minute insertion of the "Moritat von Mackie Messer" (Ballad of Mack the Knife) disturbed the neoclassical parallel. A high-low stylistic mix drawing on baroque idioms, traditional and popular song, opera and operetta, even (at the end) a Lutheran chorale, and colored throughout by the sonorities and idioms of the modern dance band, the music made a decisive contribution to the work's multilayered effects. A classic it was, albeit a provocatively refashioned one.

The desired effect was created not merely by the use of familiar and stylistically diverse means. Critical here is the way the elements are juxtaposed—surrealistically and ironically. Even where Weill comes close to reproducing the real thing, the text usually provides a jarring counterpoint. The "Pimp's Ballad," a tango written in the wake of the 1926 craze for this dance form, was Weill's own favorite example: "The charm of the piece," he wrote, "rests precisely in the fact that a rather risqué text . . . is set to music in a gentle, pleasant way." This mode of juxtaposition is not dissimilar to Gay's own practice of setting new ribald texts to well-known ditties associated with familiar, more innocent texts.

Weill's work is hard to pin down in terms of genre because genre is one of its topics. Yet this facet of the piece has not endured uniformly. One reason is obvious: Brecht turned his work into a classic by publishing a revised version of the libretto in the 1931 collected edition of his works *(Versuche)*, thus changing the complexion and purpose of the piece. Although he now referred to it as "an experiment in epic theater," he removed all references to Gay and many musical allusions, as well as much of the stage business—the very elements that convey the work's neoclassical playfulness. He also rewrote much of the dialogue to sharpen the political message, thereby becoming the work's first anachronistic interpreter or "misreader." In addition, to bridge the gap between the initial form and reception and his own changing conception of the function of theater, he published a set of notes to accompany this reprint. Drawing on Brecht's notes and his new, ideologically sharpened material, exegetes have often insisted on a political significance the work never possessed, even in its later version. Such readers even claimed that the initial reception was a misunderstanding on the part of the audience.

The distance Brecht placed between himself and the work's original incarnation at its 1928 production is nowhere more succinct or blatant than in the self-interview of 1933, first published in 1994:

> What in your opinion created the success of the "Dreigroschenoper?"
> I'm afraid it was everything that didn't matter to me: the romantic plot, the love story, the musical elements. When the "Dreigroschenoper" was a success, it was turned into a film. They put into the film everything I had satirized in the play: the romanticism, the sentimentality etc., and omitted the satire. The success was even greater.
> And what did matter to you?
> The critique of society. I had tried to show that the mind-set and emotional life of street robbers is immensely similar to the mind-set and emotional life of respectable citizens.
>
> *(Journale 1, 299)*

Brecht presents here a dichotomized view of the work: the sentimental, romanticized one he claims to have been the reason for its success versus the subversive, critical one he claims to have intended and which he had attempted to restore with his revision. The critical aspect of the original production, however, emerged from the self-conscious manipulation of artistic practices: it was not primarily directed against the Weimar Republic. Brecht's stark oppositions of sentimentality and critique are not so much mutually exclusive alternatives as they are two sides of the same "threepenny" coin.

Common to Weill's and Stravinsky's art is their opposition to Wagnerian music drama. The invocation of classicism in connection with their music always implies a negation of Wagner's romantic aesthetics, as it did in the work of Weill's teacher Ferruccio Busoni. Interviewed in 1929 by an Austrian journalist, Weill defined *Die Dreigroschenoper* as "the most consistent reaction to Wagner." Montage breaks up the seamless flow, the endless melodies of Wagner's music. But Weill's anti-romanticism entailed much more than that, as a brief article entitled "Romanticism in Music" published in Polish in 1928 makes clear:

> That which characterizes recent music, namely, the simplification of the means of expression, the avoidance of affective overload, the forging of a clear musical language—all this is unromantic in a certain measure; it is only necessary to attach the great human idea to those artistic achievements, and there will arise a modern classical art, which will be in the most complete opposition to romantic art. Modern times abound in great, all-embracing ideas, which are able to find artistic expression solely in classical form.

There are two sides to Weill's classicism: the type of language used and the presumed attitude of the audience. Both derive from Busoni's precepts about composition in general and opera in particular. The question of "classical form" is a tricky one, and in this connection Weill can be seen to depart from his teacher. Form in Busoni arises from unswerving commitment to an ideal of absolute music—an ideal so absolute that any notated score amounts to a necessarily imperfect transcription of a Platonic form of the work, what Busoni, using the language of German idealism, refers to as *Urmusik*. Form in Weill invariably has a dramatic significance, often an ironic one, such as in the "Pimp's Ballad" tango. In the same essay in which he describes opera as the theme of *Die Dreigroschenoper,* Weill states that he was trying with this work to produce the *Urform* of opera. This term, although revealing Weill's grounding in German idealism, is far from Busoni's *Urmusik*. It refers to the idea (admittedly also shared by Busoni) that musical theater has inherent laws and hence limitations. Weill's classical approach was to work within those limitations, making the work's narrative structure an eminently musical one, as was even more emphatically the case in his subsequent opera, *Aufstieg und Fall der Stadt Mahagonny (The Rise and Fall of the City of Mahagonny).* Used in a modern context, traditional means also serve an ironic purpose. The Third Three Penny finale, with its chorus, recitative, and happy ending, is at once the formal reality of 18th-century *opera seria* and, in its dramatic artificiality, a surreal reworking of it. On yet another level, it is a true indication of social corruption and injustice.

The instrumentation, the work's "sonic image" *(Klangbild),* as Weill would later refer to it, formed an essential ingredient of his surrealism. When the piece was performed on off-Broadway in the 1950s, Marc Blitzstein and Leonard Bernstein made changes to the score, such as the addition of a bass clarinet in the "Ballade von der sexuellen Hörigkeit" (Ballad of Sexual Dependency)—a number that, incidentally, had been cut from the premiere production. These changes in instrumentation were entered directly into Weill's autograph score and subsequently transmitted as "authentic" in the full score published by Universal Edition in 1972. The timbre of the bass clarinet is quite foreign to the sonic image of the original, which had created a tension or counterpoint between dance-band sonorities of the time and the other musical contexts invoked by the piece, notably the expressive sweetness of Weill's melodic invention.

If the sonic image is not preserved, what then? For one thing, we lose something essential about the way the composer imposes his personal stamp on the arrangement of the John Gay classic. But in becoming itself a classic, Weill's work has frequently been robbed of its authorial originality. The enduring nature of the piece became evident soon after the premiere, when Berlin, quickly followed by much of Europe, succumbed to intense doses of "Threepenny fever."

Several evergreen songs detached themselves from the work in a variety of arrangements, including Weill's own *Kleine Dreigroschenmusik*. Weill and Brecht became involved—though not as involved as they would have liked—in the production of the movie version that was directed by G. W. Pabst. A celebrated lawsuit ensued, putting on trial the matter of intellectual property in the incipient stage of the mechanical reproduction of art.

What had begun as a light-hearted, occasional adaptation of a theatrical classic eventually acquired much wider significance. For better and for worse, *Die Dreigroschenoper* became an enduringly resonant, multifaceted sign of the times. The Nazis, whose reading of the piece lacked any sense of irony, declared it the epitome of degenerate art, and accorded it pride of place in their 1938 exhibition of "Degenerate Music." After the war, partly because of its previously banned status, its cultural capital as emblem of the Golden Twenties only increased. For years, both before and after unification, it has maintained its status as Germany's most frequently performed theatrical work.

See also 1876, 1911, 1937, 1949

Bibliography: Kurt Weill, *Die Dreigroschenoper,* Kurt Weill Edition, I/5, ed. Stephen Hinton and Edward Harsh (Miami, Fla.: European American Music, 2000). ———, *Journale 1, Große Kommentierte Berliner und Frankfurter Ausgabe,* vol. 26 (Frankfurt am Main: Suhrkamp, 1994). ———, *Musik und musikalisches Theater: Gesammelte Schriften,* ed. Stephen Hinton and Jürgen Schebera (Mainz: Schott, 2000). Steve Giles, *Bertolt Brecht and Critical Theory: Marxism, Modernity, and the Threepenny Lawsuit* (Bern, Switzerland: Peter Lang, 1998). Werner Hecht, *Brechts "Dreigroschenoper"* (Frankfurt am Main: Suhrkamp, 1985). Stephen Hinton, ed., *Kurt Weill: The Threepenny Opera,* Cambridge Opera Handbooks (Cambridge, U.K.: Cambridge University Press, 1990). Dieter Wöhrle, *Bertolt Brecht: "Die Dreigroschenoper"* (Frankfurt am Main: Moritz Diesterweg, 1996).

Stephen Hinton

♄ *1929, October*

Alfred Döblin's *Berlin Alexanderplatz* puts flesh on the bones of Georg Simmel's metropolis

Narration and the City

In his essay of 1903, "Die Großstädte und das Geistesleben" (The Metropolis and Mental Life), the sociologist Georg Simmel ratified the metropolis as the locus of modernism in contrast to the "preachers of the most extreme individualism," Nietzsche and Ruskin (422). While acknowledging the negative aspects of metropolitan life they abhorred—the cash nexus, numeric calculation, pitiless objectivity, and personal reserve bordering on aversion to one's fellow man—Simmel asserted that the metropolis also "grants to the individual a kind and an amount of personal freedom which has no analogy whatsoever under other conditions" (416). The seeming anonymity of the city dweller amidst the urban mass not only sets him free, but elicits a much greater degree of individuation than one finds in small-town life—"the particularity and incomparability, which ultimately every human being possesses, [is] somehow expressed in the working-out of a way of life" (420). In the end, Simmel says, it is fruitless to oppose the cities; they are unalterably the location of modern life, where the tension between leveling egalitarianism and defensive individuality is greatest. In the metropolis, "the currents of life, whether their individual phenomena touch us sympathetically or antipathetically, entirely transcend the sphere for which the judge's attitude is appropriate" (423).

Twenty-one years later, the Berlin public health service doctor and novelist Alfred Döblin (1878–1957) reached the same conclusion: "One cannot reject or even evaluate the cities themselves, the foci of the social instinct. One can only confirm the existence of such forces of nature and their manifestations." In his essay "Der Geist des naturalistischen Zeitalters" (1924; "The Spirit of the Naturalistic Age"), Döblin rejects as specious the distinction between superficial, Western, democratic "civilization" and profound Germanic "culture" promulgated by Thomas Mann in *Betrachtungen eines Unpolitischen* (1918; *Observations of an Apolitical Man*). Like Simmel, he posits a spirituality for urban man that embraces, rather than fears, scientific and technical progress.

It is hardly surprising that Döblin should share with Simmel, his senior by twenty years, the conviction of a mentality and spirituality specific to the city. They were both Berliners (Döblin moved there from Stettin when he was ten). Both belonged to the German-Jewish intelligentsia that flowered at the turn of the century, in Berlin and Vienna particularly. In the first third of the 20th century, no city embodied the new spirit better than Berlin. This had much to do with its newness among the world's great cities and its phenomenal growth between 1871 and 1918 as the capital of an aggressively expansionist empire. After Germany's defeat in the First World War, the city became the focus of the political struggle for Germany's future and, at the same time, a place of unbridled experimentation in the arts and in unconventional ways of life.

Few works embody Berlin's modernist confluence of the political, the urban, and the avant-garde as successfully as Döblin's *Berlin Alexanderplatz*. It is the culmination of his effort to create a prose epic equal in its modernism to the paintings and poems of Futurism and Expressionism, the experimental theater of Brecht, and films such as Lang's *Metropolis* (1926) and Ruttmann's documentary *Berlin, Symphonie einer Großstadt* (1927; *Berlin, the Symphony of a Big City*). In 1929, his experiments with narrative voice, montage, and filmic style merged with his intimate knowledge of Berlin's East End to produce his masterpiece.

Even today *Berlin Alexanderplatz* has the look of a radically modern work. Although some aspects of it had been anticipated in the author's previous work and by contemporaries like James Joyce and John Dos Passos (the German translations of both *Ulysses* and *Manhattan Transfer* appeared in 1927), the novel's development was *sui generis.* Its critical and popular success prompted Döblin to return to contemporary Berlin from the exotic, historical, science-fiction, and mythical settings of his previous epic works *Die drei Sprünge des Wang-lun* (1915; *The Three Leaps of Wang-lun*), *Wallenstein* (1920), *Berge, Meere und Giganten* (1924; *Mountains, Seas, and Giants*), and *Manas* (1927). *Berlin Alexanderplatz* is, in every sense of the word, a contemporary novel: its primary narrative tense is the present, its plot takes place at the time of writing in 1927 and 1928, its core language is 1920s *Berlinerisch.*

The novel's complete title—*Berlin Alexanderplatz: The Story of Franz Biberkopf*—suggests the tension between the collective and the individual that is the novel's primary problematic. This is precisely the tension Simmel found at its most acute in the city: "The deepest problems of modern life derive from the claim of the individual to preserve the autonomy and individuality of his existence in the face of overwhelming social forces, of historical heritage, of external culture, and of the [technology] of life" (409). In *Berlin Alexanderplatz,* Simmel's "individual" takes concrete form as the erstwhile furniture mover, ex-convict, street vendor, burglar, and pimp Franz Biberkopf. One of the most remarkable things about the novel is Döblin's choice of central character. He rejects the assumption of bourgeois realism that only the middle and upper classes have interior lives of sufficient interest for a novel. From his earliest surviving literary work "Modern" (1896), through the naturalistic story "Von der himmlischen Gnade" (1914; On Divine Grace) and the reportage "Die beiden Freundinnen und ihr Giftmord" (1924; The Two Women Friends and Their Murder by Poisoning), Döblin is intent on exploring the lives of the Berlin proletariat, taking their humanity, however degraded, as a given. These are, after all, the people amongst whom he grew up and practiced medicine, like that other great physician-writer and celebrator of the ordinary and the urban, William Carlos Williams. At the same time, Döblin explores his own ambiguous sexuality and troubled attitudes toward women in the prostitute figures who recur obsessively in many of these works and constitute the only female figures in *Berlin Alexanderplatz.*

In the essay "Der Bau des epischen Werkes" (1929; The Structure of the Epic Work), published in the same year as the novel, Döblin explicates his conception of the epic work of art. He mocks the novel of bourgeois realism and takes Homer, Dante, and Cervantes as his models. He rejects well-crafted plot, Flaubertian narrative self-effacement, and the bourgeois hero in favor of open-ended parataxis, active narrative intrusion, and exemplary figures. In the novel, the narrator in his street-balladeer persona repeatedly insists on Biberkopf's exemplary uniqueness: "But this is no ordinary man, this Franz Biberkopf. I did not call him here for sport, but to share his hard, true, and enlightening existence" (49).

But in what sense can Biberkopf be regarded as exemplary? He is not a typical proletarian, as contemporary Marxist critics of the novel hastened to point out. Nor can he be understood as a "deutscher Michel," the average "German Mike," a good-natured, passive, obedient servant of the great and powerful. He comes closest to a typical 1920s petit bourgeois, attracted to Nazi rhetoric of law and order after being ruined by the economic disasters of the preceding decade. Early in the novel, he peddles racist papers: "He is not against the Jews, but he is for law and order" (97). Yet this too appears ultimately tangential to the core of Biberkopf's status as exemplary hero, especially in light of his positive and emblematic encounter with the two Jews in the first book of the novel.

Although Simmel seems to have an educated bourgeois in mind in his 1903 essay, Biberkopf can be understood as a textbook example of the personal freedom the sociologist identified as characteristic of city dwellers, liberated from traditional ties to family, soil, religion, or community. Beyond his military service and incarceration for the murder of his girlfriend Ida, we learn next to nothing about Biberkopf's past—or that of any other character in the novel, for that matter. The novel has spatial breadth rather than temporal depth. When he is released from Tegel Prison at the beginning of the novel, he experiences this freedom only as radical, terrifying isolation: "The punishment begins," declares the novel's second paragraph and first sentence in the present, its predominant narrative tense (4). He is immediately assaulted by the chaos of sensory impressions that Simmel identifies as the central psychological fact of city life—"the intensification of nervous stimulation which results from the swift and uninterrupted change of outer and inner stimuli" (410):

> Crowds, what a swarm of people! How they hustle and bustle! My brain needs oiling, it's probably dried up. What was all this? Shoe stores, hat stores, incandescent lamps, saloons. People got to have shoes to run around so much; didn't we have a cobbler's shop out there, let's bear that in mind! Hundreds of polished window-panes, let 'em blaze away, are they going to make you afraid or something, why, you can smash 'em up, can't you, what's the matter with 'em, they're polished clean, that's all. The pavement on Rosenthaler Platz was being torn up; he walked on the wooden planks along with the others. Just go ahead and mix in with people, then everything's going to clear up, and you won't notice anything, you fool. (5)

Döblin's montage brilliantly fleshes out Simmel's "uninterrupted succession of outward and inward impressions." Here, where the chaotic jumble presses in on the stunned Biberkopf, internal quotations mark the transitions from anxiety ("Crowds, what a swarm of people!") to defensiveness ("let's bear that in mind!") to aggression ("you can smash 'em up") to self-reproach ("you fool").

The entire novel unfolds from this initial situation; Franz Biberkopf, the individual man, struggles to come to terms with Berlin, the collective space in which he lives. Three mishaps of increasing ferocity—betrayal by a colleague, loss of an arm during a burglary, and finally the murder of his girlfriend Mieze—force him to acknowledge that he can neither stick to his original resolution to remain "decent" nor bull his way through on his own. He conceives of his life in heroic terms, mustering his courage early in the novel by singing "The Watch on the Rhine" and summoning military metaphors after losing his arm: "I won't go to smash. Forward, march!" (301). He is both boastful and self-pitying. The narrator-monteur, however, by inserting parallel stories chosen at random from the lives of the Berlin masses, is at pains to relativize Biberkopf's individual fate. "We shouldn't brag about our fate," says one of these figures, "I'm an enemy of Destiny, I'm not a Greek, I'm a Berliner" (60). The narrator's denial of tragic heroism to his central character reaches a climax at the end of the second book in an extended ironic comparison of Biberkopf and Orestes. While Aeschylus's hero is hounded by the Furies for his matricide, Biberkopf feels no remorse after having served his four-year sentence. His murder of Ida in a jealous rage is reduced to Newtonian formulas and medical jargon typical of the "unmerciful matter-of-factness" (411–412) that for Simmel characterizes the modern city.

Döblin's aim is not to abolish the humanity of ancient tragedy in favor of this matter-of-factness or objectivity (the German is *Sachlichkeit* and Simmel's phrase could also be translated as "pitiless objectivity"). He only agrees with Simmel that it is no longer possible to have one and ignore the other, and scientific objectivity always tends to relativize emotion and instinct. The city, Simmel said, is the place of unending struggle between the tendency to reduce all aspects of life to measurable quantities and the tendency of the individual to assert his uniqueness. This struggle informs the centrally important extended description of the slaughterhouse in the fourth book, a description that cannot but seem eerily premonitory to post-Holocaust readers. It is introduced just as Franz is recovering from a drunken funk after having been betrayed by his colleague Lüders. Were it not for its title, a *memento mori* from Ecclesiastes ("For it happens alike with Man and Beast; as the Beast dies, so Man dies, too"— 172), the slaughterhouse chapter would seem yet another example of the bureaucratic prose and statistics Döblin loves to paste into the text as the official voice of the city: "The slaughterhouse in Berlin . . . [covers] an expanse of 47.88 hectares, equal to 118.31 acres. Not counting the structures behind Landsberger Allee, 27,083,492 marks were sunk into this construction, of which sum the cattle-yards cost 7,682,844 marks, and the slaughter-house 19,410,648 marks" (172–173). The narrator goes on to describe the administrative and personnel structure of the slaughterhouse as well as to quote a scale of fees. The language of annual reports, however, soon gives way to a description of the animals being driven to slaughter ("death tribunals for the animals") in explicit contrast to the "peaceful streets nearby . . . in which people are strolling about" (174). By the end of the chapter, the narrative focuses on single acts of killing that are described in clinical detail and are simultaneously drenched in anthropomorphism. A steer yields to the butcher "as if it agreed and was willing, after having seen everything and understood that this is its fate" (180).

Thus begins the theme of sacrifice and acceptance of death's hegemony that dominates the second half of the novel. It is carried forward not by the discarded *Oresteia* material, but by two biblical parallels: the stories of Job (whose first appearance in the novel follows immediately after the slaughter-house passage) and of Abraham and Isaac. As the novel reaches its conclusion, this theme culminates in Biberkopf's acceptance of his responsibility for the deaths of Ida and Mieze during a symbolic death and rebirth—on the objective level, a catatonic state induced by his wrongful arrest for Mieze's murder (the doctors' discussion of the case in the locked ward of Buch Psychiatric Hospital recalls Döblin's own stint there as a young *Assistenzarzt*).

There is a suggestion that, in his new job as an assistant gatekeeper in a medium-sized factory, Biberkopf realizes his dependence on others and the need for solidarity with the downtrodden masses: "One is stronger than I. If there are two of us, it grows harder to be stronger than I. If there are ten of us, it's harder still. And if there are a thousand of us and a million, then it's very hard, indeed" (633). But this passage echoes Ecclesiastes 4: 9–12, not Karl Marx. He watches warily as unidentified groups march past "with flags and music and singing." Are they Nazis? Communists? Socialists? Whom will Biberkopf join? Döblin leaves these questions maddeningly open.

Berlin Alexanderplatz is ultimately neither a call to partisan action nor an analysis of the political crisis of the ailing Weimar Republic. Its greatness lies in the particularity and universal sympathy with which it spreads out the teeming life of the metropolis as a counterweight to the headlong fall of its central character. Alfred Döblin, the practicing psychiatrist who said that he would sooner give up writing than medicine, was profoundly acquainted with the deformations of character brought about by poverty, war, and exploitation. By coupling the structural principle of montage with the Berlin dialect that suffuses the language of both the characters and, increasingly, the narrative voice itself, he shows those deformations without judging them. Early in the novel, Biberkopf encounters an *Ostjude* (eastern Jew) who helps him regain his equilibrium by telling him stories, an emblem of narrative as healing. "But the most important thing about a man are his eyes and his feet," the Jew tells him. "You've got to be able to see the world and go to it" (25).

See also 1910, 1912 (March), 1929 (Autumn)

Bibliography: Alfred Döblin, *Alexanderplatz Berlin: The Story of Franz Biberkopf,* trans. Eugene Jolas (New York: Frederick Ungar, 1976). ———, *Berlin Alexanderplatz: Die Geschichte vom Franz Biberkopf* (Zurich and Düsseldorf: Walter, 1996). ———, "Der Geist des naturalistischen Zeitalters" and "Der Bau des epischen Werkes," in *Aufsätze zur Literatur* (Olten and Freiburg im Breisgau: Walter, 1963), 62–83, 102–132. Georg Simmel, "Die Großstädte und das Geistesleben," in *Jahrbuch der Gehe-Stiftung,* vol. 9 (Dresden, 1903). ———, "The Metropolis and Mental

Life," in Kurt Wolff, ed. and trans., *The Sociology of Georg Simmel* (New York: Free Press, 1950), 409–424.

David Dollenmayer

ℜ 1929, Autumn

A year before the first volume of his novel *Der Mann ohne Eigenschaften* appears, Robert Musil is awarded the Gerhart Hauptmann Prize

A Modernist Thought-Experiment

The publication, in 1930, of the first volume of Robert Musil's great "thought-experiment," *Der Mann ohne Eigenschaften* (1930–1978; *The Man without Qualities*), was a pivotal event at a time that was overshadowed by the past and the future. The novel took a long look back to the year 1913 and the old Austro-Hungarian Empire, even as it augured the coming of the Nazi regime in 1933 and the Second World War.

The Austrian writer Musil (1880–1942) began work on his novel, an ambitious narrative experiment, in 1924. He died in exile in Switzerland during the Second World War, still laboring on his unfinished novel. The narrative begins in August 1913 and sets out to cover the period of one year, but even after several thousand pages and eighteen years of writing on Musil's part, the end of that year, August 1914, is never reached.

Although based on intimate knowledge of the period and society it presents, *Der Mann ohne Eigenschaften* is not a historical novel per se. It is not a bitter-sweet nostalgic valedictory to the old Austro-Hungarian Empire, as is, for example, Joseph Roth's *Radetzkymarsch* (1932; *Radetzky March*). Its major thrust is moral. A writer with a broad view, Musil took the multicultural, multiethnic, multilingual, and politically paralyzed Austro-Hungarian Empire in its final days as representative of modern Europe and modern values generally. Austria in the novel becomes "Kakania," a humorous name derived from the abbreviation that preceded government offices and departments, "k.u.k." ("königlich und kaiserlich"; royal and imperial).

In sphere after sphere, old Austria and pre-war Europe evinced a bankruptcy of values. Musil called this world a realm of "Seinesgleichen" or "pseudoreality" and aimed at nothing less than lighting the way toward a new morality as guidance for the future. While the narrative never overtly bursts out of the frame of that one fateful year, Musil unobtrusively interweaves it with political and social implications that would become evident only later. The events that took place in Europe during the years when he was writing the novel—the aftermath of World War I, the rise of Nazism, and the outbreak of the Second World War—give the author a special angle of vision on the period between August 1913 and August 1914. The result is a novel that maintains its vitality and immediacy through identification of problems of values that Western culture has not been able to solve.

Nietzsche's claim that the world could be grasped only as an aesthetic phenomenon underlies all the great encyclopedic novels of the 20th century. Foremost among these are those of Marcel Proust, Thomas Mann, James Joyce, and Hermann Broch. All these writers integrated an aesthetic outlook with problems posed by new discoveries in science and philosophy, particularly cognition, memory, psychology, quantum physics, and relativity, so that art becomes knowledge. However, theirs is an aesthetic that, at bottom, looks back to and is essentially defined in terms of 19th-century notions of beauty and art. Musil's aesthetic, by contrast, is forward-directed and *Der Mann ohne Eigenschaften* is a work geared toward the 20th century. Rather than waxing nostalgic over lost values and notions from the Classical and Romantic periods, Musil embraces the exhilarating prospect of new aesthetic possibilities.

Unlike Proust, Joyce, and Mann, Musil did not have a literary formation. In common with his Austrian contemporary Broch, he was a trained scientist before he turned to literature. However, in the course of a long career of writing fiction, he forged a style unlike any other in German literature, a style that combines scientific precision with an expressive soul. It is witty, brilliant, metaphorically and psychologically incisive, with an acute ear for the way individuals think and speak. It is a style that compels readers to become actively engaged in the dilemmas the characters confront. Musil's readers cannot remain passive spectators looking at his world from the outside, as is often the case with Joyce and Thomas Mann, and to some extent with Proust.

Musil approached the writing of *Der Mann ohne Eigenschaften* from four major positions: as a scientist, he mobilized his training as a positivist, relativist, behaviorist, and mathematician; as a moralist, he wished to establish values for the right life; as a writer, he was concerned with the imaginative, idealistic transformation of reality; and as a mystic, he had an interest in transcending teleological categories in an *unio mystica*.

Ulrich, the main character in the novel, is a member of the Austrian upper bourgeoisie. At the age of thirty-two, he decides to take a year off—he calls it a "vacation from life"—in order to try to make sense of himself and the world he lives in. A utopian thinker of a questioning, Nietzschean bent, Ulrich has tried out and rejected several of the professions with which society stifles the intellectually curious. He withdraws from his previous attempts to gain purchase on society as a military officer, an engineer, and a mathematician. His aim is to find a way to construct a new and vital morality that does not operate on the terms society sets and that would accommodate the scientifically determined age of the 20th century. In this era of infinite possibilities, all false or "pseudo-real" selves would be replaced by true, reconceived identities.

Although Ulrich has, in fact, plenty of qualities, he rejects those the world insists on imposing. His refusal to conform to social expectations is the sense in which he is a "man without qualities." Ulrich is financially and intellectually independent, so, unhindered by any care for mundane necessities, he is free to think his way out of a decaying world toward a more genuine life. Yet Ulrich's attempt fails. He is often distracted and his ideas for a new society fall on deaf ears. Ultimately he withdraws from the world, together with his sister Agathe, who is his complementary female self. In the later parts of the novel, the siblings engage in long discussions about the possibility of attaining, even if only intermittently, a state of "daybright mysticism," in which the mystic remains part of the rational world. Musil terms this intermittent transcendence "the other condition."

The character Ulrich is not in a position to fill the broad social and historical canvas the author has in mind. To provide this perspective, Musil introduces a narrator who, looking over Ulrich's shoulder, is his complementary partner on one side, just as Agathe is on the other. It is the narrator who skewers, in essays of brilliant and witty satire, the pretensions of the frozen political and social structure of the Austrian Empire. The first part of the novel revolves around what is called the *Parallelaktion,* or Collateral Campaign, in which representatives of the crumbling old order hatch plans for upstaging the forthcoming jubilee of the Prussian emperor Wilhelm II with a jubilee of the Austrian emperor Franz Josef. These plans, presented with scathing satire, turn out to be an empty exercise in nationalism that cannot help but be ineffectual. The reader knows, furthermore, that the two emperors, whose subjects are competing in 1914 to arrange the most brilliant of anniversary festivities, will soon be allies in a devastating war.

Among the memorable characters is the Prussian industrialist Dr. Paul Arnheim—modeled on Walther Rathenau, the German-Jewish industrialist who was foreign minister in the early Weimar Republic. He strays into the Collateral Campaign and becomes a key participant despite his outsider status. Arnheim is a proponent of an artificial integration of "coal prices and soul" and believes he has found the new type of morality Ulrich is seeking. But Arnheim's convictions are eventually revealed to be reductive and philosophically unsophisticated.

Other characters in *Der Mann ohne Eigenschaften,* such as the bank director Leo Fischl, the prophet Meingast, and the proto-Nazi Hans Sepp, enlarge the scope of the portrayal of pre–World War I Austrian society. Only vaguely aware of the impending national and European crisis, the characters live their lives in what seems to them an eternally fixed, untroubled present. Only the narrator has a more farsighted perspective. "All lines lead to war," Musil wrote in a note about the novel. The characters of *Der Mann ohne Eigenschaften* would be dumbfounded if they knew that the end of their world was close at hand—in fact, just months away.

Although Ulrich and Agathe gradually disengage themselves from this society, *Der Mann ohne Eigenschaften* is not a pessimistic work. On the contrary, its energy is propelled forward by a sense of great urgency and hope in spite of the looming catastrophe. Ulrich longs to find a way and to develop a language that will reconcile science with mysticism, precision with soul, and will serve as a bridge to a new kind of utopian society. While this goal is never achieved in the novel, the author repeatedly synthesizes these opposites in brilliant language and style.

The great tension in *Der Mann ohne Eigenschaften* arises from a persistent, unresolved struggle between epistemology (How can the self know the world?) and introspection (How can we know the self?). The conflict formed perhaps the ultimate resistance to the completion of the novel. Musil, a trained behavioral psychologist, mathematician, and engineer who was also widely read in philosophy, refuses to place Ulrich above the fray. Yet Ulrich withdraws, at least partially, from everyday life in order to gain reflective distance. In the first glimpse we have of him, Ulrich is standing at the window in his study with a stopwatch. As he watches the traffic go by, he tries to measure the fluid dynamics of pedestrian and motor traffic in the street below. His aim is to "know" them. To borrow an image from William James, this is a procedure not unlike turning on the light to see what darkness looks like. Ulrich remains a committed epistemologist, but who is this self trying to know the world by means of a stopwatch? He has no family name, no face. Along with other psychologists of his time (though not Freud and his followers, whose views Musil disliked), Ernst Mach had dethroned the self as the organizing center that "knows" the world. Musil, who wrote his doctoral dissertation on Mach, believed with Mach that what we call the self is a mere bundle of perceptions and sensations that change with every moment. According to this view, sensation and perception are primarily physiological responses to external stimuli rather than operations of thinking. "The self is unsalvageable," Mach had declared; there is no truth, only an ever-changing continuum of functional relationships that are different in every situation.

Ulrich's basic conviction is that what makes the world work is a sense of possibility, of unrealized potential. Reality awakens a sense of the various alternatives that might become reality in a given situation: what causes one alternative to happen while others do not is a matter of accident or contingency. While this follows logically from Mach's position, it presents problems for Ulrich. On what fixed basis, from what fixed vantage point in the empirical world can he establish the new, enduring moral values he so earnestly seeks? Within a fluid reality, is there a way—as Musil puts it at one point—of formulating values so that even people who don't go to church on Sunday will know what to do?

Philosophically, Musil's multifaceted essayistic technique enables him to introduce subjectivity without an "I," the subjectivity of the anonymous outside narrator. The pseudo-selves of the society depicted in the novel are exposed as such by this unanchored narrator. Even Ulrich finds that he has to bracket his "self" as he goes about the paradoxical task of finding the right kind of life.

Consciousness and rational thought, for Musil, are grounded in feeling; if they were not, they would be cold and sterile. Like perceptions and sensations, feelings are unstable and fleeting; they are hard to catch and to subject to analysis. Musil's first novel, *Die Verwirrungen des Zöglings Törleß* (1906; *Young Törless*), explores this problem among adolescents in the more restricted setting of a boarding school. In *Der Mann ohne Eigenschaften,* Ulrich confides to his diary that emotions "must always arise anew if they are to endure, and even in doing this, they become different emotions. An anger that lasted five days would no longer be anger but a mental disorder" (1229). Language, specifically the language of the essay, seems to be the only device that can capture the fusion of consciousness and feeling. The essayistic narrator of *Der Mann ohne Eigenschaften* rejects the principle of "the law of narrative order" that has typically defined the genre of the novel and that also, according to Musil, defines people's everyday understanding of their own lives.

Musil's characters are complex composites, people with virtues and foibles, sensible ideas and foolish illusions. His intricate portrayal of female figures— Diotima, Bonadea, Clarisse, and Agathe—is an extraordinary achievement. With the exception of three people—Ulrich himself, the insane sex-murderer Moosbrugger, and the unhinged Nietzsche-devotee Clarisse—all characters are firmly convinced of the solid reality of the world they move in. Even those with whom Ulrich, and presumably Musil himself, is at greatest odds, such as Arnheim and the pedant Lindner, are credible personalities who have strongly held, if misguided, convictions. The narrator at once satirizes and embraces his characters, leaving the reader to puzzle over these apparent contradictions.

A major factor in this mode of presentation is Musil's intense interest in states of consciousness that determine the individual's relation to a world as experienced through sensation and perception. At one point, Musil even depicts the world as perceived through the eyes of the two horses drawing Count Leinsdorf's carriage. Considerable space is devoted to the consciousness of the mentally disturbed, notably of Moosbrugger, but also of Clarisse. The reader is admitted to the world as these alienated characters experience it, rather than through the lens of society as exemplified by the judicial and medical systems in which they are entangled. The instability of these fictional characters is subtly connected to the mysterious disease of the time. For Musil, "ordinary" and "insane" states of consciousness (to name just two) are alternate ways of knowing the world. His representation of an entire gamut of such states lays the groundwork for his formulation of mysticism, an "ecstatic" state in relation to ordinary consciousness.

Aside from its sheer brilliance, *Der Mann ohne Eigenschaften* is marked by an openness that assures its continuing freshness and fascination. This "thought-experiment" analyzes a society and a way of thinking that are on the verge of extinction and explores ways of replacing them with something that is truer, more ideal, and more humane, while still remaining open to every possibility. For this reason, Ulrich must fail in his search for closure, and the novel itself cannot attain this goal. Utopia is a projection into the future: it is not something that can be realized within everyday reality and remains an ever-to-be imagined reality of tomorrow.

See also 1882, 1902, 1922 (July), 1927 (March), 1928, 1929 (October)

Bibliography: Robert Musil, *Der Mann ohne Eigenschaften,* in *Gesammelte Werke in neun Bänden,* ed. Adolf Frisé, vols. 1–5 (Reinbek bei Hamburg: Rowohlt, 1978). ———, *The Man without Qualities,* 2 vols., ed. Burton Pike, trans. Sophie Wilkins and Burton Pike (New York: Knopf, 1995; rept., Vintage, 1996). ———, *Tagebücher,* ed. Adolf Frisé, 2 vols. (Reinbek bei Hamburg: Rowohlt, 1976). ———, *Diaries 1899–1941,* ed. Mark Mirsky, trans. Philip Payne (New York: Basic Books, 1999). ———, *Precision and Soul: Essays and Addresses,* ed. and trans. Burton Pike and David S. Luft (Chicago: University of Chicago Press, 1990). David S. Luft, *Robert Musil and the Crisis of European Culture, 1880–1942* (Berkeley: University of California Press, 1980).

Burton Pike

෴ *1931, January*

Chancellor Brüning convenes a commission of experts to discuss the deepening economic crisis

Irmgard Keun and the "New Woman"

In the midst of severe economic troubles and an unemployment rate of well over 4 million, accompanied by Nazi gains at the polls, Irmgard Keun brings a glimmer of hope for independence and self-reliance to her generation of women. As indicated by its subtitle, the novel *Gilgi—eine von uns (Gilgi— One of Us)* speaks to a readership that might derive strength from Gilgi's transformation from an *Uhrwerkmädchen* (clockwork girl) to a young woman who, after a series of setbacks, asserts her independence and gains self-understanding. While the subtitle suggests a collective experience of the profound tension between traditional femininity and modernity, the body and technology, it also proposes solidarity among women, one that Gilgi's friend Olga sees growing. Gilgi's optimism is expressed as: "You—you—you and I: we will make it."

When Irmgard Keun (1905–1982) wrote *Gilgi—eine von uns* in 1931 at the age of twenty-six, the modern woman had been on the stage in Weimar Germany for nearly a decade. By the early 1930s, she had become a social fixture and a visible part of the cityscape and the popular imagination. Pulp novels, popular magazines, film, and the fashion industry, not to mention the labor market, had shaped and secured her existence. Generally between the ages of eighteen and twenty-five (Gilgi is twenty-one), modern women could be seen among the masses of white-collar workers streaming out of offices and department stores where they worked as secretaries, stenographers, typists, or salesgirls. By the mid-1920s, the number of female white-collar workers had reached 1.5 million, three times that of 1907. Owing to new employment opportunities, technological innovation, and mass media, this generation of women stood at the vortex of social change. In spite of obstacles in the years of economic crisis and political instability, the new woman remained an icon of a hotly disputed modernity. While she symbolized the trend toward modernization, progress, Americanism, and the democratic ambitions of the Weimar Republic—"America forever," the narrator in *Gilgi* chimes, "Germany wants to see you"—she was also looked upon as an affront to middle-class morality, an aberration of femininity, and a contributor to the nation's demise. These discourses, vying to define what a woman's existence should be, provide the underlying theme for Keun's caricature of the modern girl and her reflection on young women's experiences of modernity.

Keun belonged to a generation of women writers who embraced modernity but recognized its limitations. While she shows great sympathy for her character Gilgi, who mobilizes all her assets—looks and clerical skills—to succeed, she also shows that she has no illusions about the course available to young women. Keun presumably drew on her own experiences and insights as a stenographer when she wrote her first novel, *Gilgi*. Much too precocious and brazen for her parents' taste, Keun was put to work at the age of sixteen as a clerk-typist in the office of her father's petroleum refinery in Cologne against her mother's wish that she attend an elite trade school or a girls' school. She did, however, take a break and attended a drama school for a while, returning to work for her father as a typist in 1929 and to write her novel. Her protagonist, Gilgi, a typist in Cologne, who is goal-oriented, exceptionally disciplined, unsentimental, sexually emancipated, and independent, fits the image of the thoroughly rationalized modern girl. Her early morning exercises and cold showers—a reference to the popular *Körperkultur* (physical culture) movement—her office work, the jobs that earn her an additional income, and the evening English, Spanish, and French language courses to improve her marketability, all fit neatly into her scheme to get ahead. Keun wryly represents Gilgi's work ethic and her naïve pleasure in time management, which reflect the principles promulgated by Frederick W. Taylor, who called for the rationalization and mechanization of the workplace as a means to increase mass production. Gilgi's life is "taylorized"; she is a hard-nosed competitor in a failing capitalist market, and she is as much a part of the machinery of modernity as the machine—the typewriter—is a part of her.

Keun's young woman thrives on personal achievement. In contrast to more typical portrayals featuring female white-collar workers either as dreaming of marrying the boss to secure their future or as victimized office workers, Gilgi skirts her employer's sexual advances and adeptly manages the workplace. Well aware of Christa Anita Brück's representation of sexual harassment in *Schicksal hinter Schreibmaschinen* (1930), Keun's narrator comments, "The main thing to understand is how to dodge them [men]. Forget the great tragedies of insults as in *Fate behind Typewriters*." Gilgi avoids the customary retrogressive narrative twists in her celebration of the power of the individual and rejection of cultural pessimism. Her confidence must have seemed a breath of fresh air to the masses of female white-collar workers whose jobs were severely affected by the Depression and who faced the pressures of growing protest against female employment in times of economic crisis.

Any reader in 1931 would have been acutely aware of the dire economic need facing Keun's characters. Several minor characters are laid off, or compete for low-paying jobs, or become eligible for the paltry emergency relief *(Krisenversorgung)* once unemployment benefits run out. When she loses her job, Gilgi collects 13 marks a month in unemployment benefits. The character Martin Bruck, a penniless writer who becomes Gilgi's lover, describes the pervasive impact of the Depression on Cologne during a walk through Ehrenstrasse and Breitenstrasse: "Pale, worn-out women with dirty children in tow, the run-down unemployed attempt to feed themselves on the warm smell of bakeries . . . A sad city. A sad country. Every opened mouth takes in the bad mood and despondency in the air. Tired eyes, unhappy faces" (97–98).

Gilgi is often referred to as a *Zeitroman*—a critical novel on contemporary society. The rapid scene changes and fragmented style of writing replicate the pulse of city life that cultural critics of the time saw as endemic to modern life. The snapshots of the economic situation, the repertoire of popular hits Gilgi sings, the magazine *(UHU)* and books (Erich Maria Remarque and Jack London) Gilgi reads, her clothes and appearance—pageboy hairstyle, slender legs, small breasts, boyishly slim hips, and "masculinized" female body—conform to the mandates of mass culture and fashion. Her performance falls within the orbit of *Neue Sachlichkeit* (New Objectivity), a term that describes a cultural attitude as well as an aesthetic trend. The New Objectivity grew out of a profound affirmation of technological rationalization in industry and a celebration of what was fondly referred to as "Americanism" as it emerged during a period of economic prosperity. Civilization was associated with the pleasures of consumption, with a transformed social space, and new freedoms. The arts duplicated a distanced, cold gaze in their recording of reality that became indicative of a way of life. Much like Gilgi, the new generation as a whole harbored an aversion toward the emotional fervor of Expressionism and toward the sentimentality of 19th-century melodrama and romance. Keun embraces aspects of the New Objectivity reflected in her representation of Gilgi and in her own prose, but she also criticizes its narrow scope and suppression of emotion. The artist Olga gently admonishes Gilgi for being heartless, and her socialist friend Pit calls her superficial, which curiously anticipates the left's critique of Gilgi as an indifferent white-collar worker. The process of maturation, however, counters the robotic life she leads, her single-mindedness, and her lack of compassion, while it speaks with urgency to modern woman's survival.

The family, as it appears in Keun's work, is a failing institution. None of the families presented promise a vital or hopeful image of family life: the unhappy upper-class Kreil, Gilgi's biological mother, is entangled in a litany of betrayals; Gilgi's poverty-stricken friends, Hans and Herta, are driven to suicide; Gilgi's friend Pit, a poor, leftist student, has severed ties with his bourgeois father; Gilgi's boss delights in extramarital affairs; and the petit-bourgeois Kron family, Gilgi's adoptive parents, is archaic and lackluster. Gilgi leaves the parental realm because of a conflict in values: "I can't stay here and allow myself to be treated like a faux-pas, to be graciously pardoned when in fact there's nothing to pardon" (110). With her departure, she writes herself out of the bourgeois dramas of previous centuries—Lessing's *Emilia Galotti,* Schiller's *Kabale und Liebe*—with impunity. By the same token, she interrupts the continuity of her own biography as someone who was considered a product of moral indiscretion.

More threatening to the identity of the modern woman than the adverse economic situation is the narrative of romance. Gilgi falls in love with Martin Bruck, an aesthete twenty-two years her senior, who draws her under his spell.

This love affair requires a traditional femininity that flies in the face of the goals of Gilgi the modern woman. The new, objective Gilgi, who once described love as a breakdown in the mechanism *(eine Betriebsstörung),* readily surrenders agency. She gives up her job, her language classes, and betrays her *Angestellten* (employee) existence of "street, dust, and daily life." All that remains of Gilgi's previous rewarding life are her two index fingers. She despondently reflects: "I don't belong to myself anymore. Someone else has turned me into the person I see in the mirror. I can't be proud of it" (134–135). She describes the conflict within herself as two halves that no longer fit together. The language becomes most dramatic when Martin appears, evoking, as he does, the memory of melodramatic romances that must have been familiar to 20th-century readers of pulp fiction. Upon first meeting Martin, Gilgi is struck by his power of attraction: "What is keeping her here? Her arms lie on the marble table as if frozen to it. She knows so many men, but Martin is different. Why does she like him? As if it were easy to find the right answer" (74). Keun's perspective on female experience was unique for the time. Kadidja Wedekind, one of Keun's contemporaries, applauds the novel's astute thematization of what she perceived as women's greatest dilemma. In Wedekind's words, the novel stages "the conflict of the modern woman who stands between work and the great love of her life."

Keun's novel appeared in the year when the volatile issue of abortion reached its climax with the arrest of both Else Kienle and Friedrich Wolf, physicians who were accused of violating Paragraph 218 of the penal code, which criminalized abortions. An estimated 1 million abortions were performed in 1931. In "The Kienle Case," Else Kienle, apart from detailing the circumstances surrounding her arrest, demands a more profound understanding of the economic despair that drives women to terminate pregnancies. In the novel, the situation of Gilgi's friend Herta brings home the despair families with children experience in times of national economic crisis. Similar to Dr. Kienle's commendation of women who recognize their responsibilities toward a child, Gilgi, who is pregnant by then, deems it immoral to have children for whom one cannot care. She speaks out against the notion of biology as destiny and subscribes to a morality that results in a new attitude toward abortion and toward children born out of wedlock. Gilgi tells Pit: "There are so many marriages in which fathers and mothers quarrel all the time—a child then is much better off having only a mother. If the child is healthy and if I can feed it, then it really doesn't make a difference. What can I say, Pit, I am just terribly immoral. I just don't get it—where other people have morals, I have a gap. I just don't understand why a child born out of wedlock should be considered immoral" (256–257).

The economic situation becomes most apparent when an old classmate, Hans, appears at Gilgi's door selling floor polish. He recounts his tumultuous employment history, which is destroying his family. The novel gains in complexity with the introduction of Hans and his wife, Herta, whose lives represent the dire circumstances able-bodied young couples face toward the end of the Weimar period. Coming from someone who was once gainfully employed as a secretary and is now impoverished, strapped with two children and expecting a third, Herta's advice to remain independent is particularly telling. The novel offers no way out for people like Hans and Herta, who end up committing suicide by gas inhalation. Their tragedy spurs Gilgi's resolve to start anew.

Keun's anti-illusionist representation tests both the conservative and liberal view of the family—the repository of social idealism—as the panacea for women and resists the belief held by both the left and the right in the Weimar period that a woman's true place is in the home. At the end of the novel, Gilgi weathers the circumstances that threaten to strike at the foundations of her modern identity: her love affair with Martin and her pregnancy. She recognizes that her position as the new woman cannot be reconciled with love or traditional gender arrangements. Economic independence is the prerequisite for the development of a self-reliant individuality—an ethos of the modern age. Before departing for Berlin (where Keun took her manuscript for publication), Gilgi comes to realize, "To be a person means to be a person for yourself, and to be a woman, and a worker and everything, to be everything." *Gilgi,* the modern woman's *Bildungsroman,* tracks an awakening, and the young Gilgi, on a turbulent road to self-recognition, became a beacon of change. Yet Keun's keen understanding of her age, so fraught with uncertainty, does not allow for a blind celebration of modernity. The novel ends with the image of a single orange left on the train track that is squashed by the very train that takes Gilgi to Berlin; do modernity and progress thus win out over nature? Like the future of the modern woman, the ending remains open.

With an advance of 400 marks (the monthly salary of three secretaries), Keun's first novel launched her career as a writer. *Gilgi—eine von uns* was a phenomenal success. The book underwent six printings, and more than 30,000 copies were sold in the first year, with a film adaptation, starring Brigitte Helm, in preparation. The social democratic newspaper *Vorwärts* serialized the novel, and Keun's picture appeared in almost every newspaper. Her own success, however, was short-lived. The Nazis condemned her work as "asphalt literature" that represented anti-German tendencies and was an offense to middle-class morality. Keun was blacklisted and the dreams of a self-made modern woman were destroyed.

See also 1670, 1765, 1848 (February), 1924, 1937, 1963

Bibliography: Irmgard Keun, *Gilgi—eine von uns* (Hildesheim: Claassen Verlag, 1993). Katharina von Ankum, ed., *Women in the Metropolis: Gender and Modernity in Weimar Germany* (Berkeley: University of California Press, 1997). Else Kienle, "The Kienle Case," in Anton Kaes, Martin Jay, and Edward Dimendberg, eds., *The Weimar Republic Sourcebook* (Berkeley: University of California Press, 1994), 213–216. Gabriele Kreis, *"Was man glaubt, gibt es": Das Leben der Irmgard Keun* (Zurich: Arche, 1991).

Barbara Kosta

✥ *1932*

Carl Schmitt asks what it means to be political

Politics, Technology, and History

Carl Schmitt (1888–1985) was at the height of his career in 1932 when he published *The Concept of the Political (Der Begriff des Politischen)*. As the author of such works as *Politische Romantik* (1919; *Political Romanticism*), *Die Diktatur* (1921; *The Dictatorship*), and *Politische Theologie* (1922; *Political Theology*), he was already recognized as an exceptionally brilliant, if controversial political and legal philosopher and *The Concept of the Political* could only confirm these earlier assessments. Thus, Ernst Jünger gave the essay his "highest praise," Martin Heidegger recognized it as "a most significant proposal," and Leo Strauss made it the starting point for his own reflections on politics.

Soon after its publication, Schmitt's life was to take a turn that until today interferes with a proper estimate of the essay's unique contribution to political thought. Having struggled, in the waning days of the Weimar Republic, to keep the Nazis out of power, Schmitt surprisingly joined them in the spring of 1933 and, for his own opportunistic reasons, accepted appointment to a professorship in Berlin and to various political offices. It is impossible now to read his work without this shift of allegiance in mind. However, neither Schmitt nor his essay has ever completely disappeared from the intellectual scene and today they are more visible than at any time since 1932. This is not surprising, since *The Concept of the Political* is as timely and thought-provoking today as it was then.

The essay's most original thought is neatly packaged into its title, which expresses Schmitt's conviction that the traditional understanding of politics could no longer be taken for granted and that the most fundamental task for political philosophy was therefore the clarification of the concept of the political. Since antiquity, politics had been conceived as that which pertains to the business of the polis or the state. This had been an adequate definition as long as the institutions had a solid foundation, but Schmitt thought that this was no longer the case. Modern individualism and global capitalism, class conflict and revolutionary turmoil had undermined the traditional political order in recent centuries; the erosion seemed no doubt particularly obvious in late Weimar Germany. The situation, Schmitt thought, demanded reflection on what politics means or can mean and why it is or should be important. His most remarkable achievement is to have made this apparently elementary point urgent and important.

His second original idea is that it should be possible to characterize the concept of the political without having to draw on extra-political notions. He writes, "the political has its own criteria which express themselves in a characteristic way" (25–26). This means that the fundamental notions of politics must be explicable without reference to moral, aesthetic, economic, or any other evaluative terms. The claim is to be understood as being first and foremost methodological in character. It certainly does not mean that ethics and economics have no relevance to politics, but the relation is for Schmitt a historical and not a conceptual one. Schmitt distances himself in this way on the one hand from those thinkers (like Plato) who seek to reduce political notions to moral ones, and on the other hand from theorists (like Karl Marx and many liberal and capitalist authors) who conceive politics in economic terms.

Schmitt offers us his own account of "the essence of the political" in the famously succinct and suggestive formula: "The specific political distinction to which political actions and motives can be reduced is that between friend and enemy" (26). Like all aphoristic formulations this proposition can take on many different senses and thus its author's intentions are easily misunderstood. It is inviting to read it now as reflecting the historical circumstances of Schmitt's own time. Germany's confrontation with the Allies in the First World War (to which the essay's dedication draws attention) and the bitter conflict between the political parties during the Weimar years might make this particular reading of Schmitt's formulations appealing.

But his conception of politics has deeper historical roots. Schmitt himself refers us to Thomas Hobbes, "truly a powerful and systematic political thinker," as one of his inspirations (65). Like Hobbes, he assumes conflict to be natural and endemic to the human condition. He agrees with Hobbes that political order and the decisive power of a sovereign are required to contain the ever-present potential for conflict. In addition, one notices the influence of Schmitt's Catholicism on his language. Following Augustinian theology he assumes "man to be by nature evil and not good," a "dangerous" and "risky" being (58). All genuine political theories, he believes, in fact "presuppose man to be evil, i.e., by no means an unproblematic but a dangerous and dynamic being" (61).

The *possibility* of war is, on this model, an essential ingredient of politics. Indeed, "war as the most extreme political means discloses the possibility which underlies every political idea" (35). But this conclusion is intended to favor "neither . . . war nor militarism, neither imperialism nor pacifism" (33). Yet the thesis has strong implications. Schmitt concludes from it that a completely pacified globe "would be a world without the distinction of friend and enemy and hence a world without politics" (35). Such considerations play a defining role in Schmitt's critique of liberalism, which has attracted both conservative and radical readers. He holds that liberalism's unrelenting critique of the political "has changed all political conceptions in a peculiar and systematic fashion" (69). Liberalism "evades or ignores state or politics and moves instead in a typical always recurring polarity of two heterogeneous spheres, namely ethics and economics, intellect and trade, education and property" (70). Though it claims to be able to bypass political conflict, liberalism ends up bedeviling the enemy in ever sharpened confrontations as morally evil and, hence, as worthy of extermination. War is abolished in favor of an imperialism that annihilates whole populations by such "peaceful" economic means as "terminating credit, embargoing raw materials, destroying currencies," by "economic sanctions and severance of the food supply" (78).

To counteract the dangerous dynamic in human nature, Schmitt asserts that we must not and cannot shy away from political mechanisms. Only these can impose order on the chaos of our natural affections and hostilities. Politics is more than a practical exigency for creating a clear, sharply defined, and delimited distinction of friend and enemy: it is a way of defining ourselves as historical beings. This observation leads Schmitt to a further important claim about the concept of the political, one which takes him considerably beyond Hobbes. He insists that the concept of the political is a strictly historical concept and that it is therefore impossible to give it an exhaustive formal and ahistorical definition.

The point is elaborated in a lecture entitled "The Age of Neutralizations and Depoliticizations," which Schmitt added to the 1932 edition of the essay; the English translation omits it even though it is essential to understanding Schmitt's conception of politics. Speaking from a broad perspective on the history of modernity, Schmitt reminds us that the center of Western thought has migrated through a number of different domains from the 16th to the 20th century: "There are four great, simple, epochal steps. They correspond to the four centuries and move from the theological to the metaphysical, from there to the humanistically moral and finally to the economic" (*BP*, 80). These transformations, he believes, bear directly on the concept of the political since "the decisive themes of confrontation in the friend–enemy grouping are also determined by the decisive domain" (86). Whereas, for instance, in the 16th century friend–enemy groupings were generally determined by religious disagreements, in the 19th century their defining characteristic became the conflict of economic interests. Different domains become politicized or depoliticized over time depending on whether they are central to the culture as a whole and whether their internal disagreements and struggles define the decisive friend–enemy distinction.

These reflections provide Schmitt with the tools for a critique of his own age. He argues that after the neutralization of theology, metaphysics, and ethics, the state too became neutral in the 19th century, introducing the possibility of politics itself losing its central place in Western culture. Threatening to replace it are technology and faith in technological solutions: "Compared to theological, metaphysical, moral, and even economic questions, the purely technological problems have something satisfyingly objective about them; these problems have convincing solutions and it is understandable that one should have sought to escape into technology from the confused problems in all other spheres" (*BP*, 89f).

But if technology can solve our problems efficiently and objectively, politics will no longer constitute the decisive struggle over the central domain of the culture. Schmitt is deeply convinced that we are in danger of losing an essential feature of our humanity, our capacity to distinguish ourselves existentially and historically. He remains certain, however, that faith in technology is ultimately bound to fail. Technology is, in any case, only an instrument in the human struggle: "Precisely because it serves everybody, it is not neutral. No single human and intellectual decision is determined by the immanence of technology, least that to be neutral. Every kind of culture, every nation, and every religion, every war and every peace can use technology as a weapon" (*BP*, 90). We can be sure then that technology will not provide an escape from politics, even though it is likely to transform its reality in as yet unforeseen ways.

These thoughts were to have a considerable impact on Heidegger's later critique of technological thinking. They were also very much in tune with Ernst Jünger's treatise on the worker. In the context of Schmitt's own thought these ideas are particularly enlightening because they illustrate his thesis of the historically specific character of the concept of the political. In addition, they provide an answer to the question of why the concept of the political is now the most pressing issue in political philosophy—for as technology and technological thinking become dominant, we find ourselves forced to rethink what it can mean to be political and to be human. While the concept of the political is at stake in every historical moment, it seems that the advances of technology have forced us to make its examination the pivotal project in political philosophy now.

Despite his anxiety over the health of politics and the state, Schmitt remains, in the end, confident of their survival. "State and politics cannot be exterminated" is his hopeful conclusion in 1932 (79). Political friend-enemy groupings have always led to the creation of states, with their clear separation of those who belong from those who do not, and it is, indeed, definitive of the state as an organized political entity that it "decides for itself the friend-enemy distinction" (29f). On this understanding politics concerns, in the first instance, the relations between whole states—though Schmitt allows that we can speak derivatively of politics wherever there is some sort of antagonistic moment, "even where awareness of the extreme case has been entirely lost" (30).

His model of politics remains, nevertheless, the system of early modern European states. "For the classical European state succeeded in something quite improbable," he wrote in a new preface to his essay in 1963, "to create internal peace, to exclude enmity as a legal concept, to abolish the feud, an institution of medieval law, to make an end to the confessional wars of the sixteenth and seventeenth century, which on both sides were conducted as particularly just wars, and to procure quiet, security, and order inside its territory" (*BP*, 10). By the 1940s Schmitt's confidence in the future of the state was becoming fragile, as he began to think about the emergence of global sea-based empires. By the 1960s he was sure that the time of the nation-state had passed. Where he had previously been a philosopher of the state, he now turned into a genuine philosopher of the political, who could see politics embodied in many places, in the emergence of new supra-national powers as well as in the realities of guerrilla warfare.

In a postscript to the 1932 edition of *The Concept of the Political* Schmitt offers an assessment of his achievement: "What I have said here about the 'concept of the political' is meant to provide a theoretical framework for an uncharted problem. The individual propositions are intended as points of departure for a material discussion; they are meant to assist scholarly examinations and exercises since [only] these are suited for the consideration of such a difficult subject-matter" (*BP,* 96). In other words, he did not believe to have closed the book on the question how the concept of the political was to be analyzed.

That is important to keep in mind as one considers what is attractive or problematic in Schmitt's treatise. It also helps us to put Schmitt's own troubled history into perspective. He did not see himself as a detached political thinker. He aimed to reflect objectively on the political facts but realistically denied having a superior standpoint. He insisted rather that "all political concepts, images, and terms have a polemical meaning." Political terms are incomprehensible if one does not know who is to be "affected, combated, or negated" by them (31f). The "existential" boundary between political friends and enemies could be constructed only in a political struggle; it "can be decided neither by a previously determined general norm nor by the judgment of a disinterested and therefore neutral party" (27). And in this conviction we can see a further and final characteristic of the concept of the political as he understood it, one which again separates him from Hobbes. It was that our understanding of this concept is itself political in nature and that therefore political thought, too, has a political character. Thus there can be for Schmitt no objective political science, but only an engaged political philosophizing.

It should be obvious that Schmitt means these remarks to apply also to his own thought: he can surely not demand from us that we share his political judgments. He may, nevertheless, still matter to us for his uncanny ability to give voice to his political moment. And that moment is in a broader sense still our own, for, in thinking about politics, we are still confronted with the question of technology: the ever growing web of machinery, the constantly expanding corporate and bureaucratic power, the ever more efficient administration of human needs, and the still dominant faith in technocratic solutions. Technology has already transformed political reality (for example, through globalization), and information technology is likely to accelerate that development. For that reason, we still face the question what politics can mean to us today. But was Schmitt right in defining politics, and thereby humanity, agonistically in terms of decisive friend-enemy groupings? Was he thinking too locally or too traditionally? What other terms have we available? What is the place of conflict in politics and in human life? Though we are right in distrusting his political judgment, Schmitt's essay on *The Concept of the Political* raises questions that still prove helpful today in confronting these issues. In reading him we can watch him precariously balancing on his conceptual tightrope—along which we too are forced to walk. We can only hope to learn from his falls.

See also 1927, 1936 (February), 1939

Bibliography: Carl Schmitt, *Der Begriff des Politischen: Text von 1932 mit einem Vorwort und drei Corollarien [BP]* (Berlin: Duncker & Humblot, 1963). ———, *The Concept of the Political,* trans. George Schwab (Chicago: University of Chicago Press, 1996). ——— "The Age of Neutraliza- tions and Depoliticizations," trans. J. McCormick, *Telos* 92 (1993). Heinrich Meier, *Carl Schmitt, Leo Strauss und "Der Begriff des Politischen"* (Stuttgart: Metzler, 1988). Hans Sluga, "'Conflict Is the Father of All Things': Heidegger's Polemical Conception of Politics," in *A Companion to Heidegger's Introduction to Metaphysics,* ed. Richard Polt and Gregory Fried (New Haven, Conn.: Yale University Press, 2001).

Hans Sluga

♌ *1935, March*

The filmed chronicle of the 1934 Nazi Party Congress presents a brave new world to the German public

Hitler's Imagined Community

Leni Riefenstahl's film *Triumph des Willens* (1935; *Triumph of the Will*), a cel- luloid account of the 1934 Nazi Party Congress, remains the most influential artifact of the Third Reich and arguably the most-quoted film ever made. The production constitutes Nazi Germany's ultimate self-advertisement, the sancti- fication of its leader and his new order by an army of cinematographers and technicians. Despite Nazism's legacy of murder and destruction, the film con- tinues to exercise a strong effect on viewers.

To portray, as the trade paper *Kinematograph* put it, "the authentic face of the new Germany," Riefenstahl claims she did nothing more than bear witness. "Not a single scene is staged. Everything is genuine. It is history, pure history." This was, of course, hardly the case. The director carefully choreographed what she filmed and painstakingly refined what her cameras recorded, let- ting two priorities guide her: "The first is the skeleton, the construction, the architecture. The second is a sense of rhythm." The Nazi Party "Congress of Unity and Strength" took place in Nuremberg from September 4 to 10, 1934. Riefenstahl's filmic endeavor—which runs a little under two hours—trans- formed the seven days of the congress into a three-and-a-half-day drama of epic dimensions. By juggling chronology, Riefenstahl condensed the more than 130,000 meters of exposed film to the 3,109 that remain in the final cut. She animated speakers and mobilized events to make them appear far more striking and compelling than their real-life counterparts.

Riefenstahl (1902–2003) had been a dancer before her rise to stardom in the twenties in Arnold Fanck's popular mountain films. Her directorial debut, *Das blaue Licht* (1932; *The Blue Light*), so impressed Hitler that he enlisted her to direct a film version of the 1933 party convention, which appeared as *Sieg des Glaubens (Victory of Faith)*. The result, claims Riefenstahl, was unsatisfactory. Because she had not been able to gain sufficient coverage and control over the placement of cameras, the resulting footage seemed to her wooden and uninspiring. She eschewed the static and tedious quality of newsreels and conventional documentaries and vowed to craft a film driven by an artistic idea and a dramatic structure. With Hitler's unconditional support and generous funding from the party, she made certain in 1934 that nothing would be left to chance. The enterprising and ambitious thirty-two-year-old director assembled a team of 120—cinematographers, technicians, photographers, and assistants, among them some of Germany's most talented film artists.

The modernist Walter Ruttmann served as a model in matters of editing. His urban opus, *Berlin, Sinfonie einer Großstadt* (1927; *Berlin, the Symphony of a Big City*), reconfigured diverse views from a day in the life of a metropolis into what he called "optical music." Riefenstahl spent five months selecting from eighty hours of footage what was visually most striking and graphically arresting, forging images and sounds into a dynamic synthesis of action, drama, and celebration interspersed with certain recurrent motifs and rhythmic principles: the German eagle, the party swastika, flags, flames, fire, and smoke. A concerted play of alternation generates unceasing stimulation and excitement as the camera moves from day to night, from dusk to dawn, from formal to informal gatherings, from dramatic to serene panoramas, from aerial views to the streets of Nuremberg, from everyday activities to passionate speeches and solemn ceremonies. Complementing and augmenting these images is Herbert Windt's score with its shifting registers between strident and subdued, blending Wagnerian flourishes, German folk tunes, military anthems, and party standards. Riefenstahl's aim was for a total effect, a sense that her cameras surrounded the event, a compelling whole pieced together by her editing, a ceaseless procession of sights and sounds that corresponded to the dynamic movement of the party.

The grandiose production enacted the party's desire to legitimize the Hitler regime and consolidate Nazi power with an appeal to the masses. In fact, Riefenstahl's film gave rise to reproductions as gala openings of the film's screening throughout Germany sought to recreate the spirit and spectacle of Nuremberg by featuring local party dignitaries. Riefenstahl's film projected German strength and greatness in keeping with the designs of the Nazi Party and the visions of its leader. As the reviewer of the magazine *Film-Kurier* put it at the time, "Germany has assembled before Hitler, for Hitler, in Hitler." His presence occupies one-third of the running time and his speeches constitute one-fifth of the sound and two-thirds of the dialogue. During moments when he is absent from the screen, tension arises where he might have gone and when he might reappear. His look invigorates his people; he mesmerizes women and children, he seems to sway buildings and statues, he even catches the attention of a house cat. Repeatedly Hitler's body seems to project a luminous aura through a halo surrounding his head and a ray of light emanating from his hand. Unlike *Sieg des Glaubens,* in which Hitler shared the stage with Ernst Röhm, the head of the SA whom he had murdered in June 1934, he is now the film's unrivaled star.

This performance had been in the making for more than a decade. Between 1919 and 1923, Hitler rarely allowed himself to be photographed. Wanted by the police in various German states, he had good reason to remain incognito. It was only in late 1923 that he allowed Heinrich Hoffmann to take pictures of him. The photographer placed the politician in theatrical poses redolent of silent cinema techniques accentuating certain body parts, especially hands and eyes, to intimate curative power and artistic strength. As his popularity rose in the late 1920s, Hitler liked to style himself, in the fashion of Stefan George, as a secret emperor who promulgates the idea of a spiritual Reich. He also modeled himself on Emperor Wilhelm II, who had been the first German media star. The leader-to-be's appeal was a function of an image, but not just an image. Until 1928 audiences were mesmerized by Hitler's voice, but often underwhelmed by his modest and unkempt stage presence. The Hoffmann portraits of 1928–29 were an essential part of humanizing the ruffian veteran and endowing his face with suggestive magnetism. His voice resonated so strongly among the masses because he cast himself as the spokesman of the common soldier, the defender of a generation of idealistic Germans who, so he claimed, had been betrayed and forsaken. With the coming of radio, this voice was raised to a higher power. With the arrival of sound film, the reproduced voice and refined image would find their ideal medium.

After the seizure of power, Joseph Goebbels, minister of propaganda and public enlightenment, engaged cinema as a key instrument for political persuasion. However, *Triumph of the Will* remained the first and only Nazi film that offered extensive and sustained close-ups of Hitler. "Never before have we seen the face of our Führer so near," exclaimed a German critic in 1935, "never before have we been able to study his features so carefully, never before could we read so much in his eyes." Goebbels, honoring the work at the annual National Film Prize ceremony, shared the sentiment: "Anyone who has seen and experienced the Führer's face in *Triumph of the Will* will never forget it; it will follow him in his everyday actions and in his dreams; it will ignite a glowing flame in the depths of his soul." Hitler became the only modern politician to assume the leading role in a feature-length film.

In orchestrating his own political legend, Hitler played a poet-priest, a messianic leader, whose idealized dream of refashioning Germany in his vision had, by dint of his will, become real. Nazism relied on the rhetoric of aesthetics to promote its political cause. "The statesman is also an artist," Goebbels submits in his autobiographical novel of 1929, *Michael:* "For him, the people represent nothing but what the stone represents for the sculptor . . . Politics is the plastic art of the state, just as painting is the plastic art of color . . . To form a people out of the masses, and a state out of the people, this has always been the deepest sense of true politics." Under fascism, Walter Benjamin observed in 1936, political relations take on aesthetic shapes.

Among the formal emphases in Riefenstahl's film, the most prominent surely is the precisely aligned rows of soldiers, often seen from a great distance in bird's-eye vistas. The perfectly ordered lines of hundreds and thousands of followers recall the staged masses in the Expressionist dramas of Ernst Toller and Georg Kaiser. They also bring to mind Siegfried Kracauer's essay on the "mass ornament" (1927; "Ornament der Masse") and his comments on a troupe of precision dancers, the Tiller Girls, whose performances featured "an immense number of parallel lines, the goal being to train the broadest mass of people in order to create a pattern of undreamed-of dimensions." The mass ornaments of Nuremberg mean to dazzle and enthrall the viewer with their "extreme perspectives of extreme uniformity" (Karsten Witte).

Riefenstahl had learned from the crowd scenes of Fritz Lang's *Metropolis* and Sergei Eisenstein's *Battleship Potemkin* as well as from Busby Berkeley's kaleidoscopic swirls of bodies in motion. Party propagandists insisted nonetheless that there was something culturally singular about Riefenstahl's monumentalism. The massed minions at Nuremberg become a privileged formation in a cinematic spectacle, performed before rows of audiences sitting in cinemas who in their own right constitute mass ornaments. The Nazis took the mythical potential of an abstract shape, infused it with a collective meaning, and enlisted it in the creation of an imagined community, a *Volksgemeinschaft* (national community).

This imagined community was also imaginary. Despite Riefenstahl's claims to verisimilitude, her film shows little regard for reality or history, yet it presents itself as the definitive version of the rally. The party maintained sole ownership and exclusive rights over all representations of the proceedings, strictly forbidding the screening of materials taken by any other cameras, be they silent or sound films, in 35mm or 16mm, until November 30, 1935. Repeated reference is made to the German past, especially to World War I. In a famous sequence, Hitler, Himmler of the SS, and Lutze of the SA, plus a faceless cast of thousands, honor the fallen soldiers of the lost world war. The commemoration of the war dead is ceremonial in tone, subdued in choreography, impressive in scale. The song "Ich hatt' einen Kameraden" (I Once Had a Comrade), written by the poet Ludwig Uhland in 1809, is heard. Looking at this manifestation, the audience gains a sense of completed events, self-evident and beyond question. Individual shots provide images of plenitude yet remain uncluttered. Every movement in each frame is controlled; not for a second does anything seem uncertain or unexpected.

As Hitler laid claim to the German past to possess the present, he effected crucial changes in the scope and shape of the film. Among other things, he squelched a lengthy prologue, assigned to Walter Ruttmann, about the Nazi Party's long struggle, since it was hardly possible to review this history without acknowledging the importance of Ernst Röhm and the SA. For this reason, the tribute to the war dead functioned as a crucial act of damage control in covering up a serious rift. It was a replay, though revised, of a similar tribute from *Sieg des Glaubens* showing Hitler and Röhm marching side by side. In 1934, Hitler and his deputies assume the mantle of protectors of their dead comrades' legacy. The Führer talks of a "dark shadow" over the movement in an oblique reference to the June massacre without mentioning Röhm's name.

Even in the final years of her life, the controversial filmmaker continued to spark debate among four main schools of thought. A critical approach, along the lines of Susan Sontag, castigates Riefenstahl for her collaboration with the Nazis, for her enthusiastic glorification of Hitler and his new order. A redemptive persuasion, sympathetic to the director's claims of political innocence, holds that the film is a consummate work of art that provides an objective record of the rally. A third school would have us distinguish between the bad politics of the Nazi Party and the aesthetic virtues of a cinematic hallmark. A fourth reading praises Riefenstahl for having crafted a spectacular fantasy of emotional agitation and erotic abandon. And, to be sure, her shots of erect bodies submitting to a mighty leader have exercised a considerable allure and influence on modern visual culture. From her rediscovery in the 1970s until her death in 2003, at the age of 101, Riefenstahl remained a vital and highly visible personality, hobnobbing with Andy Warhol, Mick Jagger, and David Bowie, quoted with respect and fondness by George Lucas, Roxy Music, and Rammstein, acclaimed by cineasts in Telluride and art buffs in Japan, photographed by Helmut Newton wearing the latest Versace fashions, and featured in a blockbuster biopic by Jodie Foster.

There is something both persistent and insistent about our own mass media's obsession with Riefenstahl and her iconography. Many observers have expressed concern that recycled Nazi images trivialize our sense of the historical past. Worse yet, critics complain, such mediated memories often uncritically reproduce and, in fact, even willfully celebrate the seductive appeal of fascist aesthetics. Take, for instance, the opening of the video *Michael Jackson: History 2,* where the regalia and uniforms of the Nuremberg rally become the trappings for a rock star's narcissistic self-promotion. The celebrity presents himself as a Führer amidst a sea of lights and mass ornaments, adored by throngs of enthralled admirers. Like many photographers, filmmakers, musicians, and commercial artists, Jackson poaches Riefenstahl's powerful images and images of power. Such appropriations possess equal measures of play, irony, and blitheness, but little sense that they might be problematic or irresponsible in light of the memories of destruction and suffering that cling to these historical artifacts.

"One of the principal tasks of film is to transmit to posterity a true picture of the past," observed the prominent Nazi director Wolfgang Liebeneiner in 1943. "Seen in this light, all the films that we are making today will be one day truly 'historical.'" *Triumph of the Will* provides a flattering self-image of an omnipotent dictator and a proud nation, a hagiographical portrait in the guise of a documentary record. Working on the cutting edge of cinematic modernism, Riefenstahl made use of advanced technological tools of sight and sound in ways that left indelible marks on the subsequent history of the mass media. Many of her innovations anticipated things that we now take for granted, be they sound bites, simulations, or political conventions staged for television cameras. The mass ornaments of Nuremberg, the building blocks of Hitler's imagined community, find their expression in Super Bowl halftimes and Olympic opening ceremonies. They also serve as prototypes for demonstrations of political consensus in times of crisis. In the mediated brave new world, current events do not simply take place; they are often scripted and staged and always synthesized. An elaborate technical apparatus, from lights, cameras, sound recorders, editing bays, and special effects to projectors, screens, and monitors, determines what we see of the world and how we experience history. For all that separates us from Hitler and the Nazis, *Triumph of the Will* retains a poignant, disturbing prescience.

See also 1897, 1936 (February), 1936 (May), 1937

Bibliography: Richard Meran Barsam, *Filmguide to* Triumph of the Will (Bloomington: Indiana University Press, 1975). Oksana Bulgakowa et al., *Leni Riefenstahl* (Berlin: Henschel Verlag, 1999). Klaus Kanzog, "Der Dokumentarfilm als politischer Katechismus: Bemerkungen zu Leni Riefenstahls *Triumph des Willens*," in Manfred Hattendorf, ed., *Perspektiven des Dokumentarfilms* (Munich: Schaudig & Ledig, 1995), 57–84. Lutz Kinkel, *Die Scheinwerferin: Leni Riefenstahl und das "Dritte Reich"* (Hamburg: Europa Verlag, 2002). Martin Loiperdinger, *Der Parteitagsfilm "Triumph des Willens" von Leni Riefenstahl: Rituale der Mobilmachung* (Opladen: Leske and Budrich, 1987). Steve Neale, "*Triumph of the Will:* Notes on Documentary and Spectacle," *Screen* 20, 1 (Spring 1979): 63–86. Leni Riefenstahl, *A Memoir* (New York: St. Martin's, 1992). ———, *Hinter den Kulissen des Reichsparteitag-Films* (Munich: Eher, 1935). Rainer Rother, *Leni Riefenstahl: Die Verführung des Talents* (Berlin: Henschel, 2000). Susan Sontag, "Fascinating Fascism," in *Under the Sign of Saturn* (New York: Vintage, 1981), 71–105.

Eric Rentschler

℞ 1936, February 27

Walter Benjamin sends Theodor W. Adorno the second of four versions of his theses on the development of art in the contemporary world

The Machine Takes Command

In his cover letter to Theodor Adorno, postmarked in Paris, we sense Benjamin's excitement. He knows he has written something very important, filled with prophetic power, and, precisely because of that, his lines betray more anxiety than usual in his letters to his dear friend. In late 1935, he had told his friends about a "programmatic" piece he was writing, a spin-off from his work *The Arcades Project,* which would reveal the "hidden structural character" of art in the modern world. What he was now sending to Adorno was the second version of the essay "The Work of Art in the Age of Its Technological Reproducibility"; it was cut and translated into French because Max Horkheimer preferred not to have the essay appear in German in the *Zeitschrift für Sozialforschung.* The French version of the essay was the only one published in Benjamin's lifetime. This essay—doomed to remain forever a work in progress—did not appear in German until 1955 in a third version, which Benjamin had prepared in response to Adorno's scathing criticism of the second. This third version is the one Hannah Arendt included in her 1968 collection of Benjamin's essays, *Illuminations.*

Benjamin's letter to Adorno betrays a certain edginess. Perhaps Horkheimer's response to his previews of the text has already rattled him. Like any author, he is eager to hear from his editors, his paymasters, and soulmates. He is most worried that Adorno will not appreciate the essay's odd mixture of "circumspection and caution in the destructive approach." Indeed, Adorno found Benjamin's relentlessness repellent, and any close reader of the text has to sympathize with Adorno. Benjamin fires off a barrage of intellectual ammunition. He literally assaults the reader with constant references to ballistics, highlighting his view of a close association between military and artistic technology. It is as if the text were a testing ground, far from the comfortable study of the genial French essayist Michel de Montaigne. As he moves from thesis to thesis, Benjamin constantly reframes what he just stated, the way Eisenstein reframes his subjects in the film *Potemkin,* leading the reader again and again to the issue of mechanical reproduction, albeit from different perspectives.

In "The Work of Art in the Age of Its Technological Reproducibility," Walter Benjamin shreds the fabric of the most cherished beliefs about art. Central to his theory is the notion that cinematic art is created, not by divine inspiration, but by a hybrid of human and machine. Thus the 1936 version of the essay provoked strong reactions from critics, disturbed by the fact that Benjamin puts the machine into the place thought to be occupied by human beings. His assertion that the mechanical component accounts best for the artwork's aesthetic qualities was seen as bordering on heresy. Design, as Benjamin sees it here, is practically without mind and such mind as remains is brought into a ghastly union with the mechanical.

Had he stated that machines commandeered the work of art, it would have been terrifying enough. But at least it would have conformed to the humanist nightmare of an abject modern world. In that account of things, industrialization brought about human mechanization—a view perhaps most forcefully expressed in such expressionist works as Georg Kaiser's plays *Gas I and II* (1918 and 1920 respectively) and Fritz Lang's film *Metropolis* (1927). But Benjamin did not say this. He set forth a much more challenging idea, dangerous because it negated all possibility for self-pity.

In Benjamin's time the radical left and right all over Europe saw art as a tool to push a political agenda. In Germany, the cultural movement that began in 1919, when avant-garde artists believed their work would advance a political revolution, had faded by the early 1930s. The Nazis, who came to power in 1933, espoused a state-controlled aesthetic nationalism. Benjamin proposed a third position, one that rejected the totalizing systems of the extreme right and left. Many artists and critics in the 1930s abandoned art for politics; Benjamin, by contrast, tried to find a way of attending to the demands of art and the demands of politics without compromising either. His artwork theses thus constitute a profound effort to work out that relationship at a time when only a few writers, like Lewis Mumford and James Joyce, were reflecting upon the aesthetic consequences of mechanical reproducibility.

Monumentalizing views of art tend to deny the material and the technical aspects of art production and reception. In his essay, Benjamin focuses not on the morality or the politics of art in any transcendent sense but on art making and its implications for the reception of a work. Rather than seeking unity, as criticism had traditionally done, he searches for disunity, like a detective looking for what is missing at a crime scene. Conventional bias toward unity, Benjamin argues, has blinkered observers of the arts and only by shattering this tradition and, in so doing, shattering the artwork will it be possible to reveal the multiple fragments from which it has been assembled in us.

Much of the scholarship on Benjamin's artwork essay consists of obsessive attempts to force his pragmatic notion of tradition—and the aura that ennobles artworks in the tradition—into a neat definition. While defining aura is nearly irresistible, it is also ultimately frustrating. The reason for this is that aura changes as time goes on. The process of sacralizing art is not a singular activity, but one performed by many minds and over a period of time.

Benjamin focused on the technical aspect of the artwork because he believed that the mechanical would lead to the heart of the matter. Attending to the concrete aspects of making an artwork, that is, film, was Benjamin's way of confronting responses from both his friends and his enemies to violent attacks on the arts. Leftist writers, like Bertolt Brecht and Theodor Adorno, often decried art as a mere tool of right-wing politics, while Stalinists and Nazis alike condemned art for not being enough of a tool of state interests.

To Benjamin's mind, film was a particularly compelling medium since it seems to present reality without human intervention. Film makes the art form transparent, or, as Benjamin formulates it, "the equipment-free aspect of reality has become the height of artifice; the sight of immediate reality has become the 'blue flower' in the land of technology" (SW 4:263). As we watch, we are led to ignore the function of the machine, but it is there, "an insensitive and invulnerable eye," as Ernst Jünger put it in 1934. The illusion of organic perfection that was the goal of German Romanticism—symbolized by the quest for the blue flower in Novalis's *Heinrich von Ofterdingen* (1802)—has been replaced by an immediacy achieved, ironically, by total artifice. Film is perceived as seamless, but in fact it is nothing but seams, having been assembled from vast numbers of shots that have been edited and re-edited, cut and chopped and then sutured together. Benjamin defines traditional art as a work that seduces by means of its aura, in other words, by the fact that it is hung up in museums and framed and guarded. The beauty of cinema, in Benjamin's utopian conception, lies in the fact that it does not lull the viewer into complaisance as the aura effect does, but invades our whole sensibility. Film makes salient the gesture, and the appeal of gesture—a slice of life, the minimal body movement, emphasized in so many films of the 1930s—attracts attention and draws the viewer directly into the scene on the screen. In the past, an artwork found its home in tradition; now, it finds its home in our bodies, according to Benjamin.

Within the contemporary culture of the cinema, Benjamin found forces strong enough to make a breach in the wall of tradition. But writing, too, was one in a series of mediating artifacts or machines from cave painting to printing press to cinema. Such mediating artifacts are never mere means, never transparent relays. Wherever they occur, as in writing or cinematography, they are among many structural elements that combine to perform a task. Human beings learn to use artifacts to do work that cannot be done by either them or machines alone. Popular and mass art is never the product of a human being working alone.

The first step for any new theory consists in stripping mythical significance from artworks. In contrast to those who would make life whole through art, Benjamin emphasized cultural practices that reveal how art can never join what life has sundered. Film, he says, gives us "manifold parts being assembled according to a new law" (SW 4:264). After first establishing his opposition to mythic views of art, Benjamin proceeds to develop a positive vision of what cinema does. As he shifts some of the contents of the human mental and sensory apparatus into the work of art, he clears the way for the reception of new challenges. Language has been the dominant system of symbolic, communicative action, but language is just one "dedicated system" among others. As Merlin Donald explains, it is "symbolic thought [in general that] is primary; it is the driving force" and it subsumes language along with visual representation (Donald, 255).

Fixated on a notion of authenticity as the key criterion for quality in artworks, many intellectuals of Benjamin's time decried the turn to mass culture. But Benjamin's friend Siegfried Kracauer recognized, as did Benjamin himself, that there was no point in shying away from engagement with developments in mass culture. As Kracauer wrote, "Self-pitying complaints about this turn to mass taste are belated [. . .] This is a petit bourgeois approach."

Benjamin's analysis of cinema strongly criticized the misconception, as he saw it, that it presents nature unmediated, a notion held dear by some of its admirers. Any understanding of human cognition—Benjamin's main concern was with what he called human apperception—requires the acknowledgment that humans are deeply embedded in the things through which they see, feel, and think about the world. Traditional works of art and traditional technologies, such as printing, exist safely outside the body. The peculiar aspect of the camera and of cinema is the way they dissolve the border between human and machine. Benjamin sees an entire network of agents—some human and some not—engaged in the production of the artwork. The sovereign self of traditional art theory with its ritualized account is thus scrapped as Benjamin, in the manner of a mechanic, erects a new account of art from the ground up.

Benjamin sees the advent of the camera as the harbinger of a whole set of changes in the realms of artistic creativity and society. Large numbers of people become conscious of themselves as agents in a process of mutual recognition triggered by the fact that now—thanks to mass reproduction and dissemination of the artwork—millions of people are able to respond to a single artwork. "The masses are a matrix from which all customary behavior is today emerging newborn" (SW 3:119).

Photography makes it possible for the human eye to take over from the hand, an advantage because the eye is much faster than the hand. Within photography, a certain negativity is at work, a "destructive, cathartic aspect." In the practice of the arts, it makes salient the idea of human sense perception. Benjamin invokes Kant and Hegel and like them he emphasizes the historical variability of "the organization of perception." The camera has no respect for performance as "an integral whole." It proceeds in an experimental way, testing each element in isolation as it goes along. The machine, the mediating artifact, links realms previously held separate. The machine makes possible an amalgamation that the mind, guided by tradition, may not be able to contemplate without disgust. Such minds crave purity and attempt to keep subjectivity and objectivity separate.

Benjamin writes exultantly, "The cameraman and machine are now one," adding, "we hardly know what really goes on between hand and metal." Film is the monstrous progeny at the center of the labyrinth that is Benjamin's text. The boldness of his position is made clear by his closest allies' energetic disparagement of his work. The correspondence of Benjamin and Adorno records the latter's attempt to coax his friend into taking the easier route. Decrying Benjamin's analysis of modern culture as nothing more than "wide-eyed presentation of mere facts" without any attempt to integrate these details into an account of "the total social process," Adorno provokes a defensive response. Benjamin repeatedly justifies his position and tries to free himself from his friend's efforts to dominate his project.

In a letter to Florens Christian Rang, Benjamin described his aim as a search for understanding 20th-century civilization in terms of the emergence of long-term forces of nature. In *The Arcades Project,* he writes: "One can characterize the problem of the form of the new art straight on: when and how will the worlds of form which, without our assistance, have arisen in mechanics, in film, in machine construction, in the new physics, etc., and which have overpowered us, make it clear for us what in them is nature?" Although the interplay between human beings and artworks, as he sees it, will no doubt continue, its form has changed profoundly.

Benjamin's careful attention to the agency of the machine in the creation of an artwork leads him to notice two crucial and symmetrical facets of human interaction with the machine. On the one hand, the machine guides human visuality to a degree that causes the human subject to take on aspects of the apparatus. On the other hand, the machine's agency turns human beings into mere props for the machine to pick up and inscribe. This shocking realization renders incoherent the old subject-object dichotomy. The new machine not only amplifies human cognitive abilities, it also transforms and reconstructs social relations. When the camera breaks up the continuity of human action into isolated gestures, making central what the conscious mind thinks is marginal, it pulls in its viewers, shocked to see their lives are woven of quasi-automatic, unconscious responses, quirks and twitches, that have a life of their own. Benjamin's intention is not to document the end of human agency but to claim that the forces of mechanical reproduction that seem so destructive of traditional humanist (and religious) values turn out, when properly understood, to be the vehicles of a far-reaching emancipation at once political, economic, and artistic.

Benjamin's theses are utopian and redemptive. His goal was grand. He sought to lay the groundwork for a future aesthetic. In the hope that film producers would rise to the challenge of the ideals he expounded in his philosophical essay, he dared to sound like Pollyanna in a land of cyborgs.

See also 1913, 1927 (March), 1935, 1937, 1940

Bibliography: Walter Benjamin, "The Work of Art in the Age of Its Technological Reproducibility," 2nd and 3rd versions, ed. Howard Eiland and Michael W. Jennings, trans. Edmund Jephcott and Harry Zohn, *Selected Writings* [SW] (Cambridge, Mass.: Harvard University Press, 2002 and 2003), vol. 3, 101–133, and vol. 4, 251–283. Merlin Donald, *Origins of the Modern Mind: Three Stages in the Evolution of Culture and Cognition* (Cambridge, Mass.: Harvard University Press, 1991). Miriam Hansen, "Of Mice and Ducks: Benjamin and Adorno on Disney," *South Atlantic Quarterly* 92.1 (Winter 1993): 27–61. Ernst Jünger, "On Pain," in *Photography in the Modern Era*, ed. Christopher Phillips (New York: Aperture, 1989), 207–210. Lewis Mumford, *Technics and Civilization* (New York: Harcourt, Brace, 1934).

Lindsay Waters

𝒬 *1936, May 1*

German Registry Offices begin systematic distribution of Hitler's *Mein Kampf* to all newlywed couples

Germans Reading Hitler

In late April 1936, newspapers across Germany reported on new procedures for recognizing and registering marriages. Beginning on 1 May, newlywed couples would receive from the local registry office a copy of Adolf Hitler's *Mein Kampf* (1925; *My Struggle*). Officials handed out thousands of copies of the 8-mark *Volksausgabe* (people's edition) every working day until the end of World War II nine years later in spring 1945. The directive from the Interior Ministry was part of a broader effort to insure that every German family would eventually possess the Führer's basic work. All this was part of the Nazis' effort to create a new aural and visual space in which Germans would be connected to the regime and encouraged to assume social and racial identities as so-called Aryans in the "thousand-year" Reich. In addition to distributing *Mein Kampf*, loudspeakers were installed on street corners and in other public places so the German people could hear important speeches and announcements. The availability of an inexpensive radio set, the *Volksempfänger* (people's receiver), afforded the opportunity to tune in to speeches by Hitler, Goebbels, and other party functionaries. Within just a few months of the Nazi seizure of power in January 1933, slogans, flags, speeches, and marches announced the new imperative to revolutionize and racialize the German way of life. By 1945, 10 million copies of *Mein Kampf* were in circulation; most families in the German Reich owned the book.

Nazis referred to *Mein Kampf* as the bible of the German people, but that claim calls into question how popular the book really was and how closely readers studied it. True, in 1933 Germans bought nearly one-and-a-half million copies, but in the eight years before the seizure of power, they had acquired only eighty thousand copies, and this despite the fact that 1.5 million Germans had at one point been party members and that 13.7 million voted for the Nazi Party. By the time of the July 1932 elections, the vast majority of party members did not own *Mein Kampf.* Indeed, few party leaders bothered to read the book, although some pulled out choice phrases to embellish their speeches. Even recruits to the SS, the elite ideological guard of the Third Reich, found *Mein Kampf* tough going. "It turns out," wrote one SS officer in June 1936, more than three years after the seizure of power, that selections of Hitler's *Mein Kampf* which had been read out loud in evening propaganda sessions were "not completely understood" by the men; "it is necessary to clarify them with personal lectures." Much of it is "very arduously written," concluded another training instructor tactfully ("Dienstleistungen," Bundesarchiv). After 1936, most Germans probably did own a copy and shelved it next to the classic works of Goethe and Schiller in that typical middle-class piece of furniture, the *Bücherschrank* (bookcase), not least so that they could be sure that neighbors or the postman, who came to collect fees for the radio, would see it, but they did not read it. And at the end of the war, millions of copies that had not been destroyed in air raids were burned. It would appear that *Mein Kampf* was kept and discarded opportunistically.

Mein Kampf was not widely read except as part of grammar school assignments, beginning in Prussia in 1934, and as part of the syllabus for ideological education, as was the case with the SS. However, the role *Mein Kampf* played in German life did not end there. It is useful to go back to the weddings. In the first place, the Führer's autobiography was given only to German couples, a designation which in 1936 meant something quite specific: Germans who had proven their racial identity as Aryans. According to instructions that applied to all registry offices, in compliance with the Nuremberg racial laws of September 1935, people in Nazi Germany belonged officially to one of four groups: Germans, Jews, *Mischlinge* first degree, and *Mischlinge* second degree. The laws regulating the marriage of *Halbjuden* (half Jews) and others were complicated, but they clearly forbade marriages between Germans and Jews. Thus the presentation of *Mein Kampf* culminated in a state ceremony that had been organized according to the racial fantasies outlined in *Mein Kampf.* Its distribution also served as a racial marker, dividing insiders from outsiders: Jews were not supposed to read or even touch the book. Prior to getting married and receiving *Mein Kampf,* German couples had to prove that they were "German." Beginning in 1936, prospective husbands and wives needed to document their Aryan racial status with notarized birth-, marriage-, and death certificates for each of their four grandparents and gather them in a folder called an *Ahnenpass,* a kind of genealogical passport. In contrast to a travel passport, there was no standard format for the proof of racial purity. In this effort to archive the racial self, Germans were required to assemble and bind the papers themselves. Prospective newlyweds also had to certify their genetic health, which often meant a visit to the local public health office and the acquisition of more documents. In addition to handing out *Mein Kampf,* the registry office provided couples with pamphlets on procreating good racial stock. Finally, German newlyweds received a coupon for a one-month trial subscription to a newspaper, preferably the Nazi daily, *Völkischer Beobachter. Mein Kampf* was thus one item in a broad effort to push Germans to document and comport themselves as Aryans. The emphasis was on becoming properly German. Whether or not Germans read *Mein Kampf,* they reenacted Hitler's own struggle to realize his racial self and in doing so became more recognizable as Aryans in Hitler's eyes and in their own. When in the final weeks of the war, Germans began to burn or otherwise destroy their copies of *Mein Kampf* and the other required items in their racial archives, they faced a not altogether simple task. Ordinary Germans were not necessarily criminals, but they were not silent bystanders either, since life in the Third Reich meant working to attain racial standing. *Mein Kampf* was not a lone volume in the *Bücherschrank* but a metonym for German life in the racial world of the Third Reich.

    Mein Kampf is the single most authoritative statement of Hitler's worldview. Initially published in two volumes, the first, more autobiographical volume, subtitled "Eine Abrechnung" (A Reckoning), appearing in 1925, followed two years later by a programmatic statement of Nazi Party philosophy and tactics, subtitled "Die nationalsozialistische Bewegung" (The National Socialist Movement). An authoritative single-volume "people's edition" came out in 1930. *Mein Kampf* makes very clear that Hitler saw himself as the appointed leader, the Führer, of German renewal. That the thirty-six-year-old Hitler worked in an autobiographical genre indicates the personal, messianic role he was ready to assume. With the publication of *Mein Kampf,* Hitler became the undisputed leader of the Nazi movement, which had won a small but dedicated cadre of true believers in the mid-1920s and attained its first success at the polls in 1930. Moreover, Hitler's personal ruminations about his service and Germany's conduct in World War I, which dominate the first volume, allowed him to introduce the themes that are then presented more thematically in the second: his determination to acquire living space in Eastern Europe, his resolve to make Aryans out of Germans and to rid Germany of its Jews, and his belief that a resurgent Germany needed to defeat both France and Russia. In retrospect, Winston Churchill confessed that "there was no book which deserved more careful study from the rulers, political and military, of the Allied powers" (cited in Caspar, 3). Again and again, Hitler emphasized that Germany's interest did not lie in the restoration of the prewar status quo, but in the assumption of her biological destiny as a great power. For this reason, *Mein Kampf* should be considered a revolutionary tract.

    Since the book was poorly written and badly organized, it acquired an increasingly elaborate index which allowed readers not only to find Hitler's particular view on a particular subject but also the system to Hitler's thinking. The subheadings in the entry for "*Bürgertum*" (citizenry or bourgeoisie), for example, reveal at a glance the ideological space between left and right that the Nazi Party sought to occupy:

> Bourgeoisie: bourgeois class parties; party program; failure in the Revolution; gatherings; the end of its mission; lack of energy; lack of national pride; insufficient national feeling; hurrah patriotism; social sins; petty bourgeoisie and artisans; pacifism; neglects politics for economics; failure in the Revolution; acquiescence to the Revolution; failure to educate about the Peace Treaties; and Bismarck; and Jewry; and racial purity.

All the elements of Hitler's program are on display here: mobilizing national energy, building a people's community on the basis of race not class, and fighting the lost world war over again. As important as specific pronouncements in *Mein Kampf* were, and they often determined Nazi legislation, it was the tone and syntax of the writing that contributed more decisively to the Nazification of everyday life: the venomous, pitiless brutality of its phrases, the stark, encompassing racial choices with which Germans were confronted, and the emphasis on incorporation into and mobilization of the racial whole. "Words can be like tiny doses of arsenic," observed Victor Klemperer about Nazi language: "They are swallowed unnoticed, appear to have no effect, and then after a little time the toxic reaction sets in after all" (Klemperer, 15–16).

Mein Kampf exposes a world in which battle readiness is the paramount injunction and permanent state of being. *Mein Kampf* propounds the necessity of a relentless struggle, or *Kampf,* and every individual's absolute dedication to the great task ahead. Throughout the book, nouns build a vision of a new racial world, adjectives betray the urgency and strain of the Aryan project, and verbs insist on the possibility of remaking Germany in this way.

Hitler wrote *Mein Kampf* in the summer and fall of 1924 while imprisoned in Landsberg Fortress for his part in the failed November 1923 "Beerhall Putsch." However, it was not so much the leisure of incarceration than the experience of the trial that preceded it that compelled him to write his story. Until 1924, Hitler did not conceive of himself as the destined leader of national revolution. Indeed, the putsch revealed the extent to which he still thought in terms of alliances with more established right-wing figures, such as Gustav Ritter von Kahr, the general state commissar of Bavaria, and especially Erich von Ludendorff, hero of the world war. In the trial that followed, media attention first focused on Ludendorff, but he spoke tersely, seeking to distance himself from the putsch. It became increasingly clear that the celebrated commander, who appeared every day in court wearing full-dress military uniform, did not represent the new Germany. Hitler, by contrast, wore civilian clothes, greeted well wishers, and trumpeted his intention to destroy the Weimar system. It was this populist bearing that earned Hitler newspaper headlines across Germany. Thanks to the trial, his name became a household word. But more decisively, the trial revealed to Hitler and his sympathizers the inadequacy of Germany's traditional elites, the importance of winning over the public, and the benefits of populist politics. Paradoxically, these were lessons of democracy.

The single-mindedness of *Mein Kampf* should not mislead readers into thinking that the text was unique, however. In its audacity, *Mein Kampf* colludes with an array of redemptive political tracts in the 1920s. Premised on the acknowledgment of total destruction in the present, these tracts used the catastrophe they outlined to authorize complete renovation and reshaping in the future. Ernst Jünger, Moeller van den Bruck, Carl Schmitt, and many others conjured up fearsome dangers at home and abroad in promoting their restless redesign. At an abstract level, on the right and the left, Weimar culture was characterized by the deep impression of the demands of the new world that the world war had left behind. "Right after the end of the Great War," wrote Hermann Hesse in 1932, "our country was full of healers, prophets, and disciples, and echoed with the forebodings of catastrophe and hope for the arrival of a third Reich" (quoted in Hass, 163).

Mein Kampf rehearsed, without setting in motion, the vast political mobilization that had occurred in Germany after the November Revolution in 1918. It authorized a brutal, highly chauvinistic, yet grassroots political activism that produced countless versions of *Mein Kampf*. Members of the Nazi Party as well as the patriotic association *Stahlhelm* frequently worked in an autobiographical genre, describing their personal entry into politics and conversion experiences in their speeches, sketching out the reasons "why I became a National Socialist," thus reproducing Hitler's own literary self-presentation in *Mein Kampf*. In many ways, this practice was a continuation of the nationalized gestures of writing and publishing and otherwise circulating letters from the front during the war. Future party members remembered themselves as ravenous readers, fascinated with history already in school, as Hitler had reported about himself in *Mein Kampf*, and later browsing newspapers until they finally picked up a Nazi edition, or attended political meetings until they found themselves in agreement with this or that Nazi orator. "Having thrown aside the Marxist idea long ago, I thought and thought," recalled one miner who, upon reading Hitler in 1928–29, felt that his "words went right to my marrow" (Fritzsche, 171). Another future member of the Nazi Party, a teacher from Vorsfelde, had two books on his desk in the 1920s: "Adolf Hitler's *Mein Kampf* and Karl Marx. *Jawohl* Karl Marx! . . . Learning, reading, comparing" (Fritzsche, 172). Eventually, the teacher admitted, "Karl Marx disappeared" from his desk; Hitler did not.

The image of books on a desk should draw our attention to the extent to which popular history was consumed and produced in countless versions throughout the 1920s. Ernst von Salomon, for one, described his reading frenzy after World War I: "For a time I was fascinated by political economy . . . my pockets were full of brochures and charts . . . then I turned to religion," and later to "literature," so that on his shelf "Rathenau and Nietzsche, Stendhal, and Dostoevsky, Langbehn and Marx were jumbled together" (Salomon, 208, 214–215). This historical context reveals the limits of an autobiographical focus only on Hitler or his writings; many other Germans were on the same journey in the 1920s and 1930s. The handout of *Mein Kampf* at the registry office in 1936 was, therefore, neither completely surprising nor entirely unwelcome.

See also 1932, 1935, 1937, 1939, 1946/1947

Bibliography: Adolf Hitler, *Mein Kampf* (Munich: Franz Eher Nachfolger, 1930); *Mein Kampf,* trans. Ralph Manheim (Boston: Houghton Mifflin, 1971). Reichsministerium des Innern, "Dienstleistungen für die Standesbeamten und ihre Aufsichtsbehörden," Bundesarchiv Berlin-Lichterfelde, R 1501/127452, and reports in the Rasse- und Siedlungshauptamt of the SS, NS 2/131. C. Caspar, "*Mein Kampf*—A Best Seller," *Jewish Social Studies* 20 (January 1958). Peter Fritzsche, "On Being the Subjects of History: Nazis as Twentieth-Century Revolutionaries," in Igal Halfin, ed., *Language and Revolution: The Making of Modern Political Identities* (London: Cass, 2002), 161–184. Ulrike Hass, *Militante Pastorale: Zur Literatur der antimodernen Bewegungen im frühen 20. Jahrhundert* (Munich: Fink, 1993). Victor Klemperer, *The Language of the Third Reich: LTI, Lingua Tertii Imperii: A Philologist's Notebook,* trans. Martin Brady (Somerset, N.J.: Athlone, 2000 [1957]). Werner Maser, *Adolf Hitlers* Mein Kampf: *Geschichte, Auszüge, Kommentare* (Esslingen: Bechtle, 1981). Ernst von Salomon, *Die Geächteten* (Berlin: Bertelsmann, 1930). Barbara Zehnpfennig, *Hitlers* Mein Kampf: *Eine Interpretation* (Munich: Fink, 2000).

Peter Fritzsche

℞ *1937, June 30*

Josef Goebbels orders the selection of modern German artworks for an exhibition of "Entartete Kunst" in Munich

Spectacle of Denigration

After their accession to power in January 1933, the Nazis' campaign against modern culture was not content with eradicating it but often involved demonstrations of contempt and vilification. For literature, this was exemplified by a series of public bonfires that "consigned to the flames," to use the incantation ritually repeated by the book-burners, the works of banned and "undesirable" authors. For the visual arts, the medium took the form of traditional exhibitions, none more notorious than the display of "Entartete Kunst" (Degenerate Art) mounted in Munich in 1937, from where it traveled to a dozen cities in Germany and Austria over the following three years.

About 650 paintings, sculptures, drawings, prints, and books were culled for this purpose in less than three weeks from some thirty-two public collections by a commission working under direct orders from propaganda minister Josef Goebbels. This exhibit was intended to contrast with a concurrent display of official art in the Grosse Deutsche Kunstausstellung (Great German Art Exhibition), which Hitler himself had opened the previous day. Such high-level sponsorship and instructive juxtaposition gained for this exhibition exemplary status as the quintessential instance of the Nazis' virulent attack on modernism in the visual arts. Moreover, the fact that some two million visitors attended the exhibit in Munich—five times as many as saw the Grosse Deutsche Kunstausstellung—underscored the epochal importance of "Degenerate Art."

Significant works by virtually all leading artists of the time, including Max Beckmann, Otto Dix, Ernst Ludwig Kirchner, Erich Heckel, Wassily Kandinsky, and more than one hundred others, were gathered under the defamatory but resonant rubric "degenerate" and subjected to curatorial abuse in a disdainful installation with mocking texts and misleading labels. At least some of the rooms had specific themes. The first was devoted to the rubric "Insolent Mockery of the Divine," the second contained only works by Jewish artists, the third had images of women and was called "An Insult to German Womanhood," military subjects were titled "Deliberate Sabotage of National Defense," and so on. Some rooms were devoid of disparaging wall texts, others combined random groupings of disparate works. While the hanging of some works showed surprising sensitivity and imagination, every wall was crowded, often to jarring effect. The works of art were subjected to a museological show trial, one that seems to sum up the Nazis' barbaric cultural policy of relentless hostility toward avant-garde or experimental art in all media and across all genres.

From another perspective, the representative status may seem unwarranted or unearned. How can such an exhibit, restricted to works owned by municipal and state institutions and gathered, arranged, and installed in less than three weeks, carry this interpretive weight? The haphazardness and arbitrariness of these two circumstances—the exclusive focus on publicly owned works of art and the hastily executed organization—bear some exploration for the light they can shed on Nazi cultural policy toward the visual arts, and, by extension and contrast, to the other arts.

While on one level it may have been simply convenient for Goebbels's commission to requisition works from public institutions over which the government had some authority, the actual presentation of the works makes it clear that it was precisely the public ownership of these works that was one of the main targets of the entire undertaking. The label for each object not only gave the artist's name and the title of the work but also registered the institution that had purchased it and, most significantly, often specified the price paid. So, for example, the visitor could learn that the Stuttgart museum had paid 3,000 marks for Beckmann's 1917 *Self-Portrait* in 1924, that the Berlin National Gallery laid out 25,000 marks for Emil Nolde's *Christ and the Adulteress* in 1929, or that the Hanover Provincial Museum spent 1,000,000 Reichsmark (a provocatively high figure, explained by the inflation of the early 1920s) for a painting by Heckel in 1923. The point was driven home by labels below many works announcing "Paid with the tax money of the working German people." A key element in the propaganda tactics of the "degenerate art" exhibition was to reinforce popular resentment at the strangeness and incomprehensibility of much modernist art by playing on popular resentment over alleged misuse of public money.

The close association of money and visual art in Nazi cultural policy was consistent and extended beyond the acquisition of "degenerate" art to its disposal. As Goebbels noted in his diary in the spring of 1938: "Paintings from the degenerate art action will now be offered on the international art market. In doing so we hope at least to make some money from this garbage." "This garbage" encompassed some sixteen thousand works of art by fourteen hundred artists gathered both in the initial 1937 sweep of German museums for the exhibition and a campaign of confiscation later that summer. Through an auction of 125 outstanding paintings and sculptures in Switzerland in 1939 and through sales and exchanges with a select group of local dealers with access to foreign currency, the Nazis were able to dispose of a remarkable number of these works. While the dispersal through sale has had the unintended beneficial effect of creating enhanced international appreciation for the achievements of modern German art, the policy put at risk works deemed of little or no commercial value. And that risk was realized in March 1939 when some five thousand of these works were, to the best of our current knowledge, destroyed in a bonfire held in the courtyard of Berlin's main fire station. Although this conflagration was, in the end, not staged as a public spectacle, one of the organizers had hoped that this would be "a symbolic propaganda action" at which he "would be happy to deliver a suitably caustic funeral oration." Given the Nazi regime's commitment to state control and exploitation of the arts, it is appropriate that the confrontation with the visual art it despised should be so marked by attention to the public dimension: the earlier acquisition and display of modernist art by state museums and its potential to serve the new state as both propaganda tool and money maker.

If the fact that works were impounded only from public institutions offers a window onto the financial and institutional dimension of the "degenerate art" exhibition, the speed and efficiency of its implementation are also telling. It may be tempting to see indifference and casualness in the remarkably short period between the order to impound works and the opening of the display, amounting to an expression of the organizers' contempt. However, this rapidity is surely more plausibly accounted for if seen as based on confident knowledge of what to choose and how to denigrate it, a knowledge based on at least four years of experience in organizing such exhibitions to display cultural policy. That cultural policy, in turn, had extensive roots in antimodernist ideologies going back to at least the late 19th century, as exemplified in Max Nordau's "Entartung" (1893; Degeneration), a pseudoscientific treatise attacking many aspects of modern civilization and the arts.

The "degenerate art" exhibition was the culmination of a series of art exhibitions mounted in various, predominantly provincial, towns throughout Germany since the Nazis had come to power. The titles of just some of these exhibitions from 1933 alone give a clear taste of their polemical and propagandistic intent: "Images of Cultural Bolshevism" (Mannheim), "Government Art 1918–1933" (Karlsruhe), "Chamber of Horrors" (Nuremberg), "Art That Did Not Issue from Our Soul" (Chemnitz), "November Spirit: Art in the Service of Subversion" (Stuttgart), and even one called "Degenerate Art," this last organized in Dresden and sent on a very successful tour over a three-year period.

There had been some uncertainty in the early years of the Nazi dictatorship over policy toward modern art, with one faction of the party, initially supported by Goebbels, advocating endorsement of the Expressionists as essentially Nordic artists in tune with the Germanic soul and appropriate for the new Reich. Another faction, led by Alfred Rosenberg, championed a popular (*völkisch*) agenda in the arts. This indecisiveness was effectively resolved by Hitler's 1934 speech at Nuremberg warning against the dangers of the avant-garde and an excessively retrograde German art, thereby emphatically committing the regime to the support of art that celebrated a beautiful, heroic ideal of German identity in styles derived at some remove from Classical Antiquity and 19th-century Realism. The works shown in the 1937 "Grosse Deutsche Kunstausstellung" demonstrated this aesthetic.

Just as Nazis used the juxtaposition of the two 1937 exhibitions to make clear the programmatic distinctions between what was acceptable and unacceptable art, so too did they use tendentious juxtapositions to illustrate the supposed characteristics of "degenerate art" itself. The booklet issued to accompany the exhibition described the nine thematic sections, and then went on to four pages with illustrations comparing specific works by modernist artists to works made by the mentally ill. Other such publications asserted parallels between modernist art and work by amateurs and by tribal, and therefore primitive, peoples. The Nazi worldview had no trouble extending this associative chain to "Jewish Bolshevism," although only 6 of the 112 artists in the exhibition were actually Jewish and probably even fewer had Bolshevik allegiances.

The Nazis not only manipulated the general public's latent resentment of public funding of modern art, but also mounted an effective campaign against that art, in part because an element of truth could be found somewhere in most Nazi accusations: some avant-garde artists were politically subversive, internationalist, antimilitarist; some did appeal to abstracted ideas of the "primitive," the outsider, the insane; some did indeed mock traditional middle-class values. All of this reinforced the Nazis' contention that this art was the product of sick minds and a sick society. Not only was the art degenerate, that is, so degraded that it no longer even belonged to the category of art properly speaking—a status reflected in the quotation marks around the word "art" in the title of the published exhibition guide—but the artists too were implicitly "degenerate," that is, not fully human.

To keep the body politic healthy, these alien presences had to be purged. Just as the offending works of art had to be removed from circulation, so too did their creators. Nazi cultural policy had initiated that effort remarkably quickly after January 1933. The combined effect of the Professional Civil Service Restoration Act of April 1933 and pressure on the venerable Prussian Academy of Arts in Berlin ensured the quick removal of Weimar cultural luminaries from public positions. Museum directors were removed from their posts and artists were dismissed from teaching positions. Two leading members of the academy, Heinrich Mann and Käthe Kollwitz, were forced to resign after publishing an appeal to unify leftist party candidates in opposition to Nazism in February 1933; several more members, among them Alfred Döblin, Thomas Mann, and Ricarda Huch, resigned rather than accept the Nazification policies of Gottfried Benn, the newly elected successor to Heinrich Mann as head of the academy's literary section. Many more "undesirable" members were duly expelled.

The subsequent fate of such figures varied widely. Some emigrated and others chose to remain in Germany and submit to what was called inner emigration. Beckmann, having lost his teaching position in Frankfurt, continued to paint in Berlin until he left for Amsterdam immediately upon hearing the broadcast of Hitler's speech at the opening of the Grosse Deutsche Kunstausstellung in Munich. He was represented by ten paintings and as many prints in the "degenerate art" exhibition. Even an artist like Nolde, whose sympathies for Nazi policy extended as far as joining an affiliated party and signing a call for loyalty to Hitler in 1934, as well as defending the suitability of his art to the new regime's ideology, eventually experienced repression after early indications of official acceptance: a work ban, confiscation of more than one thousand works in the "degenerate art" campaign, revocation of academy membership. The complexities of this example are multiplied by the fact that it was the experience of Nolde's paintings during a visit to the "degenerate art" exhibition in Munich that immediately prompted Bernhard Sprengel to secretly start collecting the artist's work and become one of Nolde's most loyal and passionate collectors, both during and after the Nazi years.

The uncertainties and ambiguities in the case of a figure such as Nolde—which resonated in German literary culture as late as 1968 when Siegfried Lenz in his novel *Deutschstunde* modeled the ambivalent character of the painter Nansen on the artist—have certainly highlighted contradictions and disparities in Nazi cultural policy, which should not be presented or perceived as monolithically consistent. The "degenerate art" exhibition itself was not free of inconsistencies. For example, works by the sculptor Rudolf Belling appeared in both of the parallel exhibitions. Consider also the decision to remove a painting by Franz Marc but to leave four others on view, following a letter from the German Officers' Federation complaining about inclusion in the exhibition of works by a man who had earned the Iron Cross and given his life for his country in the First World War. However, such apparent lapses in logic do not substantially invalidate the brutal uniformity with which the contributions of modernist art and artists were effectively occluded in Germany. After some hesitation in the first year and a tactical easing of restrictions in 1936 when the world's attention was focused on Germany as the host country for both the Winter and Summer Olympic Games, Nazi Germany embarked with the "degenerate art" exhibition of 1937 on a definitive and decisive public purge of the visual arts avant-garde.

See also 1912 (March), 1935, 1936 (May), 1939

Bibliography: Peter Adam, *Art of the Third Reich* (New York: Harry N. Abrams, 1992). Stephanie Barron et al., *"Degenerate Art": The Fate of the Avant-Garde in Nazi Germany* (New York: Abrams, 1991). ———, *Exiles + Emigrés: The Flight of European Artists from Hitler* (Los Angeles: New York: Abrams, 1997). Jonathan Petropoulos, *Art as Politics in the Third Reich* (Chapel Hill:

University of North Carolina Press, 1996). ————, *The Faustian Bargain: The Art World in Nazi Germany* (Oxford and New York: Oxford University Press, 2000).

Peter Nisbet

᭒ *1939, September*

Germany invades Poland and Ernst Jünger completes *Auf den Marmorklippen* as he is called to active duty

The Problem of "Inner Emigration"

Ernst Jünger's novel *Auf den Marmorklippen* (*On the Marble Cliffs*) was published in 1939 just as the Second World War was breaking out. Since the story's antihero is characterized as a dangerous, violent, eccentric warrior who plunges a peaceful island civilization into an apocalyptic war, the novel has often been regarded both as remarkably prescient and as a statement of literary opposition to the Nazi regime. The ambiguous plot, the novel's place in Jünger's oeuvre, and its reception render such a view too simplistic.

The first question is why this novel was allowed to be published at all after Josef Goebbels's propaganda ministry had stymied every voice of opposition or pushed it underground since 1933. Several factors about Jünger (1895–1998) must be taken into account: his status as a larger-than-life hero of the Great War; the course of his political allegiances, including a break with political activism after 1934; and the evolution of his thinking in the 1930s.

Jünger first became a public figure in 1918, when Emperor Wilhelm II personally bestowed on him the highest medal of the German army, the Pour le Mérite, for acts of great bravery and for suffering multiple injuries at the head of a *Sturmtruppe* (advance unit) on the Western Front. Urged on by his father, Jünger collected the notes jotted down throughout the war and published them in a memoir, *In Stahlgewittern* (*In Storms of Steel*). This book was published first in 1922 and then in six different, heavily revised versions in the course of the 1920s and 1930s. Hitler admired the book, which he regarded as the most eloquent expression of the front generation's experience in battle. In 1925 he sent Jünger a copy of *Mein Kampf* and Jünger responded with an enthusiastically dedicated copy of *In Storms of Steel*. A planned meeting between them never materialized and Jünger had no further personal communication with the leader of the party.

Neither did Jünger come into contact with Goebbels in the early 1930s when he lived in Berlin on his veteran's pension, supplemented by income he gained as a writer, art critic, and journalist. Goebbels tried to enlist Jünger as a party activist, but was greatly disappointed when his overtures were rebuffed. Although Jünger continued to be active in right-wing politics until the fall of 1933, his was an independent voice advocating an alliance of workers and soldiers along the anticapitalist, corporatist lines envisioned by Kurt von Streicher, the Catholic trade unions, Nazi labor groups, and the aristocratic officer class. Jünger's famous treatise, *Der Arbeiter* (1932; *The Worker*), was no doubt the most cogent expression of a conservative "revolution from the right." After 1934, Jünger withdrew from politics into what has often been called inner emigration. The term refers to a strategy developed by intellectuals during the Nazi regime who later claimed they had opposed the system but chose to hide their discontent by turning to nonpolitical pursuits or launching subtle critiques that could be read between the lines of seemingly innocuous texts. After the war, and even today, the extent to which the inner emigrants were really opposing the regime is a matter of great controversy. A good example is the debate over Martin Heidegger's Nietzsche lectures of the mid-1930s, which supposedly contain sharp criticism of biological racism and signal the philosopher's turning away from Nazism. Immediately after the war, Thomas Mann accused the inner emigrants of being treasonous fellow travelers whose various cultural activities accomplished nothing but grant some respectability to the regime. The reception of *On the Marble Cliffs* revolves around a similar question: how should we interpret the fact that Jünger kept publishing, even nonpolitical texts such as his travelogues, during the Nazi regime?

For Thomas Mann, Jünger's position directly revealed the problem with inner emigration. Although we now know that Mann hesitated to leave Germany and did so on the insistence of his daughter Erika, he recognized early on the ineffectiveness of working to change the system from within. In 1943 Mann specifically pointed to the contradiction in Jünger's actions. Having contributed to the rise of Nazism through his "saber rattling," Mann asserted, Jünger retreated into seclusion when he found the results to be unpleasant. In a letter to the writer Harry Stochower, Mann states, "Jünger now expresses his contempt for the torturers and their thugs, but he himself flayed a few skins and wallowed with pleasure in inhumanity" (*Briefwechsel*, 289–290). Jünger's response to Mann's criticism was indicative of the bitterness of those intellectuals who felt they had no choice but to stay in Germany and do what was possible to maintain some cultural standards even as German culture was being subverted by primitive *völkisch* nationalism and racism. When asked about the most famous German writer in Californian exile, Jünger told a French journalist: "Thomas Mann just packed up and left. An emigrant cannot understand. He didn't share the tragedy of his people. How could he hope to find an echo among the people after that?" (Mann, *Briefwechsel*, 289–290).

On the surface, Jünger's *On the Marble Cliffs* is a story about two brothers living on a subtropical island who become involved in a violent struggle against a powerful war lord, the Chief Ranger, an evil genius who suddenly disrupts the quiet life of a marina community. Embedded in a mosaic of philosophical and botanical observations is a narrative of almost orgiastic violence. The novel can be read as a statement of opposition to the Nazi regime inasmuch as the situation in Germany bears some similarity to the power struggle between the aristocracy and the church on one side and the Chief Ranger and his armed thugs on the other. The Chief Ranger commands a paramilitary group known as the "Mauretanier" (Mauritanians), an army of ruffians whose warrior camaraderie and vigilante mentality resemble the Freikorps associations (veterans' leagues) of the Weimar period. The brothers come into contact with the forces of opposition, including a priest, Father Lampros, and two warriors, Prince Sunmyras and a fanatical subaltern named Braquemart, who attempt to assassinate the Chief Ranger, but are caught and tortured to death. Sunmyras may personify the aristocratic resistance to Hitler, and his plans to kill the Chief Ranger presciently end in failure. The climax of the story is an apocalyptic battle described in the language of deadly fascist kitsch: giant knife-collared dogs and great poisonous snakes join the fray. Some figures might almost have stepped out of a comic book, like the old Belovar, whose ears are hung with golden rings and his head wrapped in a red bandana. He fights with medieval weapons as he joins in battle with the two brothers. The Chief Ranger finally engulfs the entire island in flames, his men murdering and plundering in an orgy of violence. The two brothers escape at the last moment in a ship filled with fleeing inhabitants and return home to their father's house in a mythical place called Alta Plana somewhere to the north of the island with the marble cliffs.

The entire story can be read as a dark fairy tale, or as a gothic horror story. The very first lines of the book immerse the reader in a macabre, ghostly remembrance of things irretrievably past: "How irrevocably beyond recall (are moments of happiness). We are more mercilessly separated from them than from any other distance. In the afterglow the images stand out even more enticingly. We think of them as we do of the body of a dead lover who lies deep in the earth and who appears to us like a desert mirage, in an enhanced and more spiritual splendor." Nostalgia is cast here as the memory of a dead body. The contrast could not be sharper between the first image of remembrance of happy things past and the second image of a ghostly corpse come to haunt us. In Jünger's fascist style, death, love, and memory are intertwined without seeming incongruous because the author camouflages the language of violence in nature metaphors—the desert mirage, the deep earth. The link between the fascist style and the gothic novel has been overlooked in the critical literature about *On the Marble Cliffs,* but the sense of impending horror brought on by the increasingly violent incursions of the Chief Ranger and the ossuary extravagance of a site of torture called Köppelsbleek fit perfectly into the tortuous mood that is a hallmark of the gothic tale.

The characters in the novel only vaguely mirror actual Nazi leaders. The Chief Ranger is an earthy, violent man with insatiable carnal appetites, hardly consonant with the hypochondriacal, petit-bourgeois Adolf Hitler. And although Goebbels felt he was satirized in Braquemart, his unceasing devotion to Hitler contradicts the image of the fictional rebel. It took the Nazi censors several months to recognize the book's subversive undertones; Goebbels became furious and eventually had the book taken out of print. Even when the work was no longer available in the book trade, it continued to be publicly discussed. In occupied Belgium and France, reviews passed the military censor even as late as the summer of 1942. After the war, a circle of Jünger's personal friends in France, many associated with such right-wing journals as *La Table*

Ronde, Rivarol, Figaro, La Patrie, Renaissance, and *La Nation Française,* propagated an image of the German writer as the most vigorous voice for a revival of European culture, against godless communism as well as Western secularism and materialism. German treatments of the novel often regarded it as a rare example of nonconformity among the books published with the imprimatur of the Third Reich. It is not enough, however, to remain on the surface of the text as a story of opposition.

Earlier works by Jünger, such as *Das abenteuerliche Herz* (1928/1939; *The Adventurous Heart*) and the techno-utopian *Der Arbeiter* contain ideas that are in certain respects akin to fascism. Their style, however, is avant-garde, futuristic, disruptive, and subversive—qualities of what scholars have called fascist modernism. The unlikely pairing of the two terms denotes an aestheticization of politics that was hostile to certain aspects of modernity—for example, the drive for equality—yet sought to channel the energy of the modern into an alternative utopia. By contrast, *On the Marble Cliffs* has none of this eruptive energy; it is elegiac and nostalgic. At most one could argue that the style reflects some aspects of literary Expressionism. Goebbels, in fact, first championed a version of a so-called Nordic Expressionism in his struggle over the future of German art. He may even have initially supported the publication of the novel because of his distaste for vulgar *völkisch* art and literature.

One cannot ignore the testimony of the novel's contemporary readers. Many read it as a prediction of a bad end for National Socialism, though some of the soldiers' interpretations are ambiguous. One wrote, "When we could steal away a moment from the horror of the bombs flying overhead and read a few pages of *On the Marble Cliffs,* suddenly we knew what we were experiencing" *(Vorwärts).* Another wrote that the soldiers took it up as gospel. But if it was a gospel, what did it proclaim? Most soldiers who read it during the war recognized the allegorical significance of the tale as some kind of commentary on the regime that had sent them into battle. Heinrich Böll, who disliked the mysticism and symbolism in what he considered Jünger's antiquated German, nevertheless felt constrained to acknowledge the personal courage of the author of *On the Marble Cliffs,* a book that he felt deserved a place in the resistance to Nazism. Jünger himself never revealed his own thoughts, but expressed his distaste for the regime by not conforming to its expectations. It must be remembered that readers in Nazi Germany had been starved of political literature that did not slavishly echo fascist language. *On the Marble Cliffs* might have appeared more oppositional than it really was simply because readers were desperate for a narrative that refused to conform to the unquestioning triumphalism of party literature. It is unlikely that the book would have gone through so many printings in the first two years of the war had the censors detected an obvious oppositional stance. However, once the Gestapo learned that the book was perceived as unorthodox, it was quickly censored in 1942.

Jünger himself saw *On the Marble Cliffs* as an "unfinished" novel that might have influenced historical events, but was also a product of history. He perceived a kind of metaphysical interaction beyond time that resisted contemporary events. It would be simplistic to read the novel as an allegory of National Socialism. Much more pertinent is its aestheticization of fascism, its transformation of fascist ideology into a conquest of the imaginary that ultimately failed to become reality. The moment of flight that ends *On the Marble Cliffs* can be followed recursively as an instinctive response in many of Jünger's literary works. At the historical juncture when German intellectuals had to decide for or against working within Nazi state ideology, the message of futility and escape at the close of *On the Marble Cliffs* is homologous to the strategy of the inner emigration. The narrator and his brother return to the mythological north, that is, to the imaginative locus of their original fascination with, and then intellectual abandonment of, fascist politics. In the same way, the conservative revolutionaries opposed the reality of the existing regime by deferring the fascist utopia into the future or the subjunctive. When they finally abandoned it altogether, a new opponent, the liberal-democratic order of the Federal Republic, was firmly in power, and that reality called forth different tactics of opposition and sometimes also new paths of inner emigration.

See also 1937, 1940, 1943

Bibliography: Ernst Jünger, *Auf den Marmorklippen* (Hamburg: Hanseatische Verlagsanstalt, 1939, 1941); *On the Marble Cliffs, a Novel,* trans. Stuart Hood (London: New Directions, 1947). Marcus Paul Bullock, *The Violent Eye: Ernst Jünger's Visions and Revisions on the European Right* (Detroit, Mich.: Wayne State University Press, 1992). Jeffrey Herf, *Reactionary Modernism: Technology, Culture, and Politics in Weimar and the Third Reich* (Cambridge, U.K.: Cambridge University Press, 1984). Thomas Mann, *Briefwechsel* (Frankfurt am Main: Fischer, 1963). Egon Mayr, "Zweideutig, ästhetisch und verkannt," *Vorwärts* (March 27, 1975). Elliot Y. Neaman, *A Dubious Past: Ernst Jünger and the Politics of Literature after Nazism* (Berkeley: University of California Press, 1999). Thomas R. Nevin, *Ernst Jünger and Germany: Into the Abyss, 1914–1945* (Durham, N.C.: Duke University Press, 1996). Jonathan Petropoulos, *Art as Politics in the Third Reich* (Chapel Hill: University of North Carolina Press, 1996).

Elliot Y. Neaman

1940, Summer

Marseille becomes the gathering place for thousands of refugees from Nazi-occupied Europe seeking overseas visas

Crisis and Transition

In the summer of 1940, fugitives from parts of Europe invaded by Nazi Germany found temporary refuge in unoccupied southern France as they desperately awaited visas that would permit them to continue their flight to overseas countries. In the years since 1933, when a first wave of writers opposed to Nazism had left Europe from countries as various as the Scandinavian nations, Russia, Switzerland, France, and Portugal, the mechanisms and modalities of escape had changed. At that time, Klaus Mann had written from Le Lavandou, in the South of France, on behalf of those first exiles to Gottfried Benn asking why he had not withdrawn from the Prussian Academy of Arts, as had several other writers, including his own uncle, Heinrich Mann. Benn responded sharply, accusing the exiles of spending time at "bathing resorts" in the South of France instead of putting their talents to use in building the new German state. While this was certainly a blow below the belt, it is also true that Klaus Mann and his famous father, Thomas Mann, had a somewhat easier time leaving Europe than those authors who were attempting to leave from southern France in 1940, after the Nazis had occupied the northern part of the country.

Some of those refugees who were congregating in Marseille in 1940 despaired of escaping and took their own lives. Others made frantic efforts to obtain the papers that would help them escape. In this group was also the author Anna Seghers (1900–1983), who ultimately left Europe, with the help of the League of American Writers. Ensconced at a table in a café in Pamiers, near Marseille, Seghers began work on a short novel, *Transit,* which encapsulates the predicament of the refugees caught in a nightmarish world of bureaucratic procedure. *Transit*'s compact and focused form distinguished it from the other two most significant literary accounts of the exile experience, Klaus Mann's *Vulkan: Roman unter Emigranten* (1939; *Vulcan: Novel among Emigrants*) and Lion Feuchtwanger's *Exil* (1940; *Exile*), both of which are panoramic in scope and aim to present a realistic critique of the period. Unlike Seghers's novel, Mann's and Feuchtwanger's are set in Paris, where a preponderance of exiles lived between 1933 and 1940.

The plight of the exiles in Marseille is vividly captured in a comment by *Transit*'s narrator, a German worker of about thirty. Sitting in a harbor-side pizzeria in the spring of 1941, he recalls for an unnamed listener the anxious mood of the refugees: "At that time, everybody had just one wish—to sail; and just one fear—to be left behind. Anywhere—as long as it took you away from this shattered country, this shattered life, this star! People listened to you avidly as long as you told them about ships that had been captured or had never arrived, and visas that had been bought or forged, and countries that were issuing transit permits" (155). But even those who did procure visas were often trapped: ships rarely set out from the harbor towns of southwestern Europe in 1940 and 1941. Because of its proximity to Lisbon, the Portuguese capital, Marseille was one of the last escape hatches. To reach the Portuguese port city, a refugee needed an official permit to leave France and a transit visa allowing travel through Spain and Portugal. Marseille, the city on which Seghers's protagonist, traveling under the assumed name of Seidler, gazes one morning in early autumn of 1940, appears to him not as a place of transit, but as the goal of his flight. When he first sees the shimmering blue Mediterranean, he experiences a rare moment of happiness prompted by the mere fact that he was alive. Although he prefers to present himself as a drifter or "maverick," rather than as a refugee or exile, he has, in fact, escaped from a concentration camp where he was interned after hitting a uniformed Nazi in a street brawl. For him, Marseille is a point of repose and respite. The real Marseille, in the fall of 1940, was a city in which a maverick such as Seidler might well gain the sense that he had arrived at a safe haven. It was a romantic, dirty, hard-edged city, the "Casablanca of the northern shore" (Marino, 104). Hitler had called it an "asylum for the international underworld." However, it was far from being a safe haven for the refugees from Hitler's Reich. On June 22, 1940, Marshal Pétain signed an armistice with Nazi Germany. Pétain's regime, headquartered in Vichy, agreed to deliver to the Germans on demand any of the thousands of resisters to Nazism who were residing, hiding, or held in camps in the unoccupied part of France. Anna Seghers ranked high on the Gestapo's wanted list.

Born Netty Reiling into an upper-middle-class Jewish family, Seghers had joined the Association of Proletarian Writers in 1928 and soon thereafter the Communist Party. That year she was awarded the prestigious Kleist Prize for emerging writers for her stories "Grubetsch" and "Der Aufstand der Fischer von Santa Barbara" (1928; The Revolt of the Fishermen), among others. In numerous essays and speeches, she had declared her opposition to the Nazis. When it became clear that she could not stay in Germany, she fled to France with her husband and two small children, living until summer 1940 in Bellevue, a suburb of Paris. Here she wrote several novels, notably *Das siebte Kreuz,* (1942; *The Seventh Cross*), which the American Book of the Month Club selected for October 1942. In May 1940, when the German army invaded France, Anna Seghers's husband, along with other German or Austrian male refugees, was sent to the French internment camp at Le Vernet. Seghers and her children managed to flee to unoccupied France in September 1940.

Seghers's personal experiences confirmed her determination to use her writing as a tool in the fight against Nazism. In her exile writings, she developed a view of politically committed art that stands in distinct opposition to the theories of her Hungarian friend and discussion partner Georg Lukács. In the late thirties, debates on realism and on political art among exiles in Paris and Moscow had been conducted primarily through the Russian exile journal *Das Wort,* as well as in personal communications. Charged exchanges between Georg Lukács, Bertolt Brecht, Hanns Eisler, and Ernst Bloch challenged Seghers's position on literature and politics. In two letters to Lukács, she questioned his insistence on a dogmatically defined concept of realism that was based on the traditional literary canon and on an allegedly scientific conception of reality. She pleaded instead for an open-ended realism informed by national histories and indigenous cultural traditions. In this regard, Seghers's exile writings show a closer affinity with leftist writers such as Ernst Bloch, Walter Benjamin, and Bertolt Brecht than with Georg Lukács. In these writers' view engaged art should not be constrained to conform to a narrow realist mandate; rather it should remain open to formal experimentation and free from prescriptive aesthetic theories. In accord with this belief, the protagonists of Seghers's fictions—most of them working-class men and women—come to perceive a striking analogy between political freedom and the spontaneity of aesthetic imagination.

Alongside her creative experimentation, Seghers also returned, at first sight paradoxically, to traditional aspects of literature such as storytelling, an aspect of narrative generally held to be missing in modernist texts. Walter Benjamin was the first to recognize the political significance of Seghers's narrative accounts of contemporary history. In his review of *Die Rettung* (1937; *The Rescue*), a novel about the economic crisis in a German mining town around 1930 and the gravitation of working-class people toward National Socialism, Benjamin emphasized Seghers's return to an earlier narrative tradition: the chronicle or almanac. He stressed the significance of Seghers's formal experimentation, especially the dissolution of a major plot into multiple stories, told not from the perspective of an omniscient narrator but from that of common people. Inspired by Benjamin's reading of her novel, their conversations about the relationship between literature and history, and his essay "Der Erzähler" (1936; The Storyteller), Seghers continued her literary experiments. In particular, she aimed to enlist her readers to gain critical insight into contemporary history and to envision a future Europe liberated from Nazi dictatorship.

In "The Storyteller," ostensibly a study of the 19th-century Russian writer Nikolai Leskov, Benjamin traces the development of storytelling from earlier times to modern times, where it seems to have disappeared. Regretting the loss of this age-old craft, Benjamin argues that stories are sites of wisdom from which vital impulses are communicated to the body politic. Convinced that the diminished role of the storyteller as human counselor was related to the loss of the ability to transmit experience, Benjamin writes during his exile in France: "If today 'having counsel' is beginning to have an old-fashioned ring, this is because the communicability of experience is decreasing . . . After all, counsel is less an answer to a question than a proposal concerning the continuation of a story just unfolding. To seek this counsel one would first have to tell the story . . . counsel woven into the fabric of real life is wisdom" (Benjamin, 86–87). He attributed the dissolution of story and storytelling to the rise of the bourgeois novel and the development of modern mass media. "The birthplace of the novel is the solitary individual," he writes, one "who is no longer able to express himself by giving examples of his most important concerns, is himself un-counseled and cannot counsel others" (86–87). To give counsel is precisely the function that Seghers sought to restore to her prose fiction, an aim explicitly stated in such novels as *Das siebte Kreuz, Transit,* and in her short story "Der Ausflug der toten Mädchen" (1946; Excursion of the Dead Girls).

In *Transit* (1944), reflections drawn from Seghers's discussions with Benjamin in the late 1930s are woven into dialogical narrative form. Seghers gives her storyteller a listener-companion, a configuration of the exiled author's readers. Looking especially to a readership in a future, liberated Germany, Seghers chronicles contemporary events and experiences that Nazi propaganda kept from the German people. She was particularly concerned about the country's youth. "A no-man's land was to be established between the generations," Seghers's narrator warns in *Das siebte Kreuz (The Seventh Cross),* which "old experiences would not be able to traverse" (140). Like all her exile writings, *Transit* attempts to reclaim that "no-man's land" and to settle it with storytellers to inform future generations about what really happened under the dictatorship and thus help build a new society after the defeat of Nazi Germany. In a key passage, the narrator of *Transit* articulates this more practical role when he states that he would want to be an "inventor, but not on paper" (17). Although he initially privileges participation in the actual struggles of the times over the act of writing about them, Seidler does come to understand that narratives, too, are modes of intervention in daily affairs. Reading a novella about mass executions in Spain by Franquist troops in 1937, which had caused its author to be refused an entrance visa, Seidler is stunned that the written word should be deemed so dangerous as to be "stopped at the borders" (145).

Seghers reiterates in all of her exile writings her conviction that storytelling constitutes vital cultural work. In *Transit*, Seidler's accidental discovery of manuscript pages and other materials in a suitcase belonging to a dead writer named Weidel sets off a process in which he becomes a storyteller in his own right. As his gift for storytelling unfolds, he becomes a brother, so to speak, of Odysseus the exile and spinner of tales, a figure akin to the heroes of legends and fairy tales—as well as of rebel prophets of antiquity (*Fehervary*, 170). In these configurations, Seidler transcends his immediate situation. His dual role of exiled working-class protagonist and first-person narrator is given expression in a key passage near the end of *Transit*. Ensconced at the Mont Vertoux, one of his favorite harbor pubs, he listens, initially with feigned annoyance, to the usual "many-tongued babble . . . about boats that would never sail, boats that had arrived or had been wrecked or captured." In a sudden change of mood, however, he regards the chatter around him as "age-old harbor gossip, yet ever new: Phoenician, Greek, Cretan, Jewish, Etruscan, Roman" (304). At this point, Seghers grants him a unique moment of historical insight, one that closely resembles Benjamin's concept of "das Jetzt der Erkennbarkeit" (the now of perception), as he concludes: "It was then that I contemplated things seriously for the first time—past and future, each other's equal in impenetrability, and the state which consular language calls transitory but is commonly known as the present. The net result of my thought was a dim conception—if a dim conception can be called a result—of my own inviolability" (304).

Already in her earlier work, *The Seventh Cross*, Seghers, informed by Jewish mysticism, had insisted that there is something "unassailable and inviolable" at the core of every human being (338). In Franz Kafka's aphorisms, she found a formulation that encapsulates this idea: "Man cannot live without a permanent trust in something indestructible in himself, though both the indestructible element and the trust may remain permanently hidden from him" (43). For Seghers and her narrator-protagonist, this belief is the spark that animates stories oral or written. Near the end of *Transit*, a fellow exile insists that the dead writer Weidel, although he may have been defeated in his struggle against historical circumstances, would continue to live in his stories, which "can wait, ten years, a hundred years" (307). Seghers went on to create a masterful configuration of this credo in the story "Der Ausflug der toten Mädchen," written during her Mexican exile (1943–1946). *Transit* hesitates between closure and openness: its protagonist-narrator journeys in the company of the dead man whose legacy he perpetuates by telling his stories and by shaping the experience of exile into art. The novel's ambiguous ending, akin to the blank page at the end of Weidel's unfinished manuscript, is a powerful expression of an age of "crisis and transition."

For Seghers, exile in France and Mexico proved a transition as well. After returning to Germany (more precisely, to the Soviet-occupied zone of Berlin) in 1947, she plunged into political activity. In the German Democratic Republic (GDR), which was established in 1949, she was president of the German Writers' Union from 1952 to 1978 and rapidly became a literary icon. Nonetheless, her panoramic retrospective on the Nazi period, *Die Toten bleiben jung* (1949; *The Dead Stay Young*), begun during her Mexican period and thus before Socialist Realism became the accepted East German dogma, caused enormous controversy when it appeared in the GDR. Seghers continued to write essays and fiction until her death in 1983. It is fair to say, however, that her exile period was the crucible for some of her most enduring works.

See also 1936 (February), 1943, 1949 (October), 1949 (Brecht)

Bibliography: Anna Seghers, *Transit,* ed. Silvia Schlenstedt (Berlin: Aufbau Verlag, 2001); *Transit,* trans. James A. Galston (Boston: Little, Brown and Company, 1944). ———, *Das siebte Kreuz: Roman aus Hitlerdeutschland,* ed. Bernhard Spies (Berlin: Aufbau Verlag, 2000); *The Seventh Cross,* ed. James A. Galston (Boston: Little, Brown and Company, 1942). Walter Benjamin, "The Storyteller: Reflections on the Works of Nikolai Leskov," in *Illuminations,* trans. Harry Zohn, ed. Hannah Arendt (New York: Schocken Books, 1969), 83–109. Helen Fehervary, *Anna Seghers: The Mythic Dimension* (Ann Arbor: University of Michigan Press, 2001). Gertraud Gutzmann, "Bei Gelegenheit der Transit-Lektüre," in *Faschismuskritik und Deutschlandbild im Exilroman,* ed. Christian Fritsch and Lutz Winckler (Berlin: Argument-Verlag, 1981), 178–190. Andy Marino, *A Quiet American: The Secret War of Varian Fry* (New York: St. Martin's Press, 1999). Christiane Zehl Romero, *Anna Seghers: Eine Biographie 1900–1947* (Berlin: Aufbau, 2000). Alexander Stephan, *Anna Seghers im Exil: Essays, Texte, Dokumente* (Bonn: Bouvier, 1993).

Gertraud Gutzmann

Ꝓ *1942–43, Winter*

News of the Nazi death camps changes Hannah Arendt's vision for her planned book on modern anti-Semitism

Origins of Totalitarianism

Hannah Arendt was forty-five years old when *The Origins of Totalitarianism* was published in 1951, after going through many more revisions than any of her other books. An account of the book's progress from gestation, birth, and development to the critical debates that are still going on more than twenty-five years after the author's death in 1975 would yield a vivid political history of the first half of the 20th century as understood in the second half. Intellectuals and political actors, indeed all who wish to understand the period of the world wars, have had to come to terms with this monumental book.

Hannah Arendt envisaged, reframed, reorganized, and expanded the book many times in the years 1941 to 1949. The project was informed by her experience as a refugee from Nazi Germany first in France for nearly a decade, and then in New York. Arendt's husband, Heinrich Bluecher, a former communist from Berlin and self-taught military historian, brought his passion and perspective to the book, as did their émigré circle with ties to Marxism, German Zionism, *Existenzphilosophie* (existentialism), and the pre-war German cultural life that they all knew was gone forever.

Arendt first conceived of the book as she was writing a series of articles in 1941 for the German-language New York newspaper *Aufbau*, in which she advocated the formation of a Jewish army as part of the Allied military force. Her initial plan was to show how the Jews were drawn into the center of European politics and to point a way for them to think and act politically in response. She began reading widely to try to set modern anti-Semitism in the broader context of European overseas and continental imperialism. This new form of anti-Semitism was one promulgated by political parties and fueled by racism. In the winter of 1942–43, however, she was propelled to a starker, deeper vision. As news of the Nazi death camps reached America, her book became her response to the incredible fact that "killing factories" were operating day and night all over Nazi-controlled Eastern Europe. Twenty years later, she looked back on the moment in an interview:

> At first [early in 1943] we did not believe it . . . because it was militarily unnecessary and uncalled for . . . A half a year later, when it was proven to us, we finally believed it. Before that, one would say to oneself so, we all have enemies. That's quite natural. Why should a people have no enemies? But this was different. This was as though the abyss had opened. Because one always had the hope that everything else might someday be rectified, politically—that everything might be put right again. This couldn't be. This should never have been allowed to happen . . . none of us could reconcile ourselves to it.

As she read reports, memoirs of survivors, and documents from the Nuremberg Trial, Hannah Arendt came to see in the death camps a key factor of what she had called "race imperialism." She first developed this idea in a manuscript entitled "The Elements of Shame: Antisemitism—Imperialism—Racism." Building on these initial attempts, she shifted the book's focus toward the shame of the camps, in which, for no political purpose, people were totally dominated, terrorized, deprived of their rights and their "right to have rights," of their capacity to act, and finally of their completely devalued lives.

Eventually, Hannah Arendt gathered everything she had written between 1943 and 1946 into the first two parts, "Antisemitism" and "Imperialism," of the book, which she retitled *The Origins of Totalitarianism*. From there she set out to write a new third part: "Totalitarianism." In this final section, she argues that the Nazi camps defined an unprecedented form of government that was not a deformation of tyranny or an extreme of authoritarian dictatorship, but a single party brought by a political movement into absolute power expressed in an institution of total terror. At the same time, through reading materials from the Soviet Union available in the West, including an anonymous memoir titled *The Dark Side of the Moon*, Arendt came to grasp that the Stalinist regime, too, was defined by totalitarian institutions of terror, purges, and labor camps. "The really essential things—which I have to put together with Russia," she wrote to her former teacher and friend Karl Jaspers in September 1947, "are just now becoming clear to me."

When *The Origins of Totalitarianism* appeared in 1951, an anticommunist campaign, presided over by Senator Joseph McCarthy, was sweeping American politics. The McCarthy era, as the period is now called, colored the third part of *The Origins of Totalitarianism* and several essays she wrote in the years before and just after its publication. It intensified Arendt's search for a new understanding of totalitarianism, which she articulated in a call to action guided by what she called "a new political principle," "a new law on earth." She claimed that politics—in the sense of citizens speaking and acting in a world, a public space, variously allowed by different forms of government and secured by their laws—appears only under certain historical conditions. By the same token, it can also disappear. Totalitarianism, she argued, is the disappearance of politics: a form of government that destroys politics, methodically eliminates speaking and acting human beings, and attacks the very humanity, first of a specific group, and then of any group at all. In this way, it made people superfluous as human beings. Such is totalitarianism's "radical evil."

In diverse ways, this essential thought of Arendt's reverberated through the reviews and discussions that greeted her book in 1951, in America and in Europe. But most of her respondents were trapped in ways of thinking that she had struggled to transcend. They were impervious to her urgent message: "An insight into the nature of totalitarian rule, directed by our fear of the concentration camp, might serve to devaluate all outmoded political shadings from left to right, and, beside and above them, to introduce the most essential political criterion for judging the events of our time: will it lead to totalitarian rule or will it not?"

On the American and European right, Arendt's analysis was welcomed because it could be interpreted as implying that to be anticommunist was to be antitotalitarian. Opposition to not just the Soviet Union but also Marxist ideology took on the moral righteousness of opposition to Nazi Germany and Nazi ideology. Arendt realized very soon after the publication of her book that the mainstays of anticommunism in America were people who had been communists—"the ex-communists." These intellectuals' rigid mode of thinking remained unchanged in their new allegiance. In terms of their fundamental dispositions, the anticommunists were ideologues who could change causes without dislocation and whose dictate was, simply, that the end justifies the means. Victory for democracy over totalitarianism, they held, justified any means for promoting democracy—including totalitarian means.

On the American and European left, communists and socialists objected to two aspects of Arendt's theory: her disregard of their idea that a fascist regime is the very opposite of a Marxist revolution, and of their argument that the Soviet Union under Stalin was a betrayal of Marxism and Marxism's concern with social justice. This perspective made it virtually impossible for readers on the left to appreciate Arendt's attention to the elements of totalitarianism and the antipolitical processes by which these elements had crystallized and might again crystallize. The idea that Hannah Arendt was a voice of the American cold war was particularly intense in France, where, in 1951, anti-Americanism was widespread (fueled by fear of the Marshall Plan as an assault upon French sovereignty). Although often cited in French political debates, *The Origins of Totalitarianism* was not translated into French until after 1968. Not until the change in the French intellectual climate initiated by the generation of 1968 did scholarship on Hannah Arendt begin to proliferate, giving rise to a scholarly French edition of *Origins* that contained all prefaces and additions.

The reception of Hannah Arendt's book in Germany was especially complex, in part because the Nazi past remained, in the familiar phrase, "unmastered." In addition, Arendt's commitment to a "comity of nations"—by which she meant a federation of European states—presented a challenge to unreformed German nationalists of all kinds. Initially, however, her work was enthusiastically received by a small group of intellectuals around the journal *Die Wandlung (Transformation),* directed by Karl Jaspers, Dolf Sternberger, Werner Kraus, and Alfred Weber. As a European rather than a German journal, *Die Wandlung* was closer to being beyond "all outmoded political shadings from left to right" than any publication in postwar Germany. The journal not only published the essays Hannah Arendt wrote while she was composing *The Origins of Totalitarianism* but also issued them as a collection under the title *Sechs Essays (Six Essays)* through Springer Verlag in 1948.

Arendt's association with *Die Wandlung* came about through Karl Jaspers, who had survived the war, along with his Jewish wife, Gertrude, in Heidelberg. Their correspondence, beginning in 1945, which was eventually published after both had died, is also a rich commentary on *The Origins of Totalitarianism.* In her letters to Jaspers, Arendt passed judgment on every major political event in America and in Europe, using as her yardstick the question "will it lead to totalitarian rule or not?"

A visit to Germany in 1949 marked the first of many reunions with Jaspers. Arendt had undertaken this trip on behalf of Jewish Cultural Reconstruction, an organization dedicated to preserving Jewish texts and artifacts that had been looted by the Nazis. Her impressions of Germany were recorded in an article called "The Aftermath of Nazi Rule," published in *Commentary* in 1950—an article that can be read as an addendum to *The Origins of Totalitarianism.* Nazism had been worse than a tyranny for the Germans, she noted, because totalitarianism "kills the roots" of a people's political, social, and personal life. Not until 1952 did she express optimism that the German people's roots would ever regenerate. At this point, German voters made what she saw at first as a halting start at repudiating the Nazi past. By abandoning their "primitive nationalism," they committed themselves to a vision of a future Europe, betokened by Konrad Adenauer's support for the proposed European Defense Community (EDC). But Arendt soon came to distrust this vote, and indeed Adenauer himself, whose advocacy of a "Christian Europe" and restoration of the national army she viewed as a re-Nazification. When she finally found a German publisher for *Origins* and translated it into her native language in 1953, she dejectedly expected that her views on Nazi and Soviet totalitarianism would be distorted and exploited by the Adenauer majority, just as they were by the American anticommunists—and she was right.

When Arendt was revising and updating *Origins* once more for a 1958 edition, she moved her "Concluding Remarks," in which she had expressed her hope for a "comity of nations" dedicated to securing "the right to have rights," into the second and third parts. Instead of the original conclusion, she ended the volume with an essay called "Ideology and Terror." Here, she justified in greater detail her claim that Stalin's Soviet Union was a form of totalitarianism. She also added an epilogue focused on the 1956 Hungarian Revolution. In this addition, she explored the Soviet Union after Stalin and praised an institution that arose in Hungary and was diametrically opposed to concentration or labor camps: revolutionary councils. These revisions to *Origins* heralded Arendt's shift through the late 1950s and into the 1960s toward an exploration of revolutionary traditions in Europe and America. For the student movement of the late 1960s in America and Europe, she was the author of *On Revolution* and *On Violence*. The 1960s brought another revision to *The Origins of Totalitarianism* as well.

When Arendt went to Jerusalem in 1961 to witness the trial of Adolf Eichmann, her response to this event brought a new dimension to her thinking. Her most controversial book, *Eichmann in Jerusalem: A Report on the Banality of Evil*, became, in effect, part of the unfolding story of *The Origins of Totalitarianism*, especially its discussion of "radical evil." Arendt was aware that by locating radical evil in the lack of military or political purpose that characterized the Nazi genocide, she had not addressed the question of motivation; that she had looked at Nazi ideology but not at any individual Nazi—not even Hitler—as a purposeful person or a thinker. From observing Eichmann, she concluded that he was not someone who thought or judged, but only someone who thoughtlessly obeyed his Führer's will and exemplified the moral environment in which he lived. This conclusion, along with her reflections on how the Nazis in their ruthlessness had manipulated the Jewish Councils, made Arendt's report the center of an international controversy. In Germany, this controversy spilled into a furor over Rolf Hochhuth's play *Der Stellvertreter* (1963; *The Deputy*), which questions the motives of Pope Pius XII's silence when he learned of the killing of the Jews. It was *Eichmann in Jerusalem* that became, in Germany, the primer for the generation of 1968 as it tried to break with the generation of the Nazi fathers.

By the end of the 1960s, the possibility that totalitarianism—in the mid-century form she had analyzed—would recur was no longer Arendt's galvanizing fear or her sole criterion for political judgment. *Origins* became a book that could be reissued as three books, each encompassing one of the three parts of the original, *Antisemitism, Imperialism, Totalitarianism*, each with a new preface describing the political realities of the late-1960s world. The *Totalitarianism* preface could discuss the "detotalitarianizing" of the Soviet Union, its return to political purposes, national interests, and a late 20th-century form of continental imperialism—a match for the late 20th-century form of overseas economic imperialism being practiced by America.

In the five years before her death, Hannah Arendt worked on the posthumously published three-volume *The Life of the Mind,* which contains her last commentary on *The Origins of Totalitarianism.* This is a reflection on Adolf Eichmann's thoughtlessness, the banality of the evildoer. While watching the man at the trial, a question "imposed itself" on her—one that she could no more get away from than she could from her awareness of his role in the murder of the Jews : "Could the activity of thinking as such, the habit of examining whatever comes to pass or to attract attention, regardless of results and specific content, could this activity be among the conditions that make men abstain from evil-doing, or even actually 'condition' them against it?"

See also 1932, 1946, 1967, 2001

Bibliography: Hannah Arendt, *The Origins of Totalitarianism* (New York: Harcourt, 1951; after 1973, editions of this work contain all of Arendt's prefaces and additions). Hannah Arendt and Karl Jaspers, *Correspondence: 1926–1969* (New York: Harcourt, 1992). Margaret Canovan, *Hannah Arendt: A Reinterpretation of Her Political Thought* (New York: Cambridge University Press, 1992). Jerome Kohn, ed., *Hannah Arendt's Published and Unpublished Essays from 1941–1951* (in preparation). Elisabeth Young-Bruehl, *Hannah Arendt: For Love of the World* (New Haven, Conn.: Yale University Press, 1982).

Elisabeth Young-Bruehl

ᳵ 1943, May 23

Five months after Roosevelt and Churchill agree to demand Germany's unconditional surrender, Thomas Mann begins his novel *Doctor Faustus*

A Musical Prefiguration of History

Thomas Mann's ties to his native Germany were irreparably broken in April 1933 when the celebrated writer was denounced by an alliance of musicians, academics, and political figures—among them composers Hans Pfitzner and Richard Strauss—for allegedly having besmirched "the memory of the great German Master, Richard Wagner," in a speech on the occasion of the fiftieth anniversary of Wagner's death. This painful experience drastically affected Mann's conception of German music, particularly in view of the fact that the events surrounding the Wagner anniversary coincided with the appointment of Adolf Hitler to the chancellorship. Shocked and intimidated by what he took to be a calculated act of "national excommunication," Mann decided not to return to Germany from a series of lecture engagements abroad, and to settle for the time being in Switzerland. For the next three years, he avoided an open break with the Nazi regime even though he had been an implacable foe of the Hitler movement prior to 1933. Forced to take a stand in February 1936, Mann declared his solidarity with the "other Germany," the

Germany of the exiles, and in countless articles and speeches, he initiated what amounted to a personal war against Nazi Germany.

In the United States, where Mann lived from 1938 until 1952, he soon emerged as one of the most articulate critics of Hitler and his regime. Long before the attack on Pearl Harbor in December 1941, Mann had sought to convince a reluctant American public of the necessity of waging war against Germany. Once America had joined the battle, he was haunted by the specter of a possible soft peace and a political compromise that might leave the Nazi regime in place. Throughout, he advocated the complete, unconditional eradication of the Nazi evil from German culture, no matter what toll it might take.

With the fortunes of war turning against Germany in 1942–43, Mann began to ponder the end of the Third Reich. Having completed *Joseph and His Brothers* early in 1943, he took up the project that had preoccupied him intermittently throughout the Hitler years: a "book concerning Germanism," which would probe and interrogate the very culture that harbored a Hitler. This proved a task infinitely more delicate and painful than the propaganda work he contributed to the Allied cause. In fact, he considered the time he spent crusading against Nazism "a morally good era." Hitler had "the great merit of producing a simplification of emotions." *Doctor Faustus,* however, posed questions of responsibility and guilt with endless ambiguities, taxing Mann's abilities as chronicler to an unprecedented degree. A characteristically ambitious novel, *Doctor Faustus* was the first attempt in German literature to reckon with the German past in light of recent events. As such, even now, the work remains unsurpassed not only in terms of literary sophistication but also in depth and sharpness of vision.

Mann began writing on May 23, 1943—the date on which his fictitious narrator, Serenus Zeitblom, begins the biography of his recently deceased friend, the composer Adrian Leverkühn. Zeitblom is an early retiree from his position at a gymnasium, where he taught Classics. Both his sons are Nazis, whom he has reason to fear. As a witness to the unraveling of the Third Reich from within, he interweaves his biographical account with wide-ranging, increasingly self-critical reflections on the course of the war and on the vexing relationship between Leverkühn and Germany itself.

When Mann embarked on the novel, many details in the life of Leverkühn were yet to be determined, just as Germany's ultimate defeat was still two years away. The conception of Leverkühn received a renewed impetus in July 1943 when Mann met the philosopher and composer Theodor W. Adorno, who had been a pupil of Alban Berg. Mann read the manuscript of Adorno's treatise on the music of the so-called Second Viennese School of Arnold Schoenberg and his followers, *Zur Philosophie der neuen Musik (On the Philosophy of Modern Music)*. In due course, he gave his new "privy councilor" the first thirty chapters of the book and asked him for advice and counsel. Adorno's most important contribution was the invention and description of the culminating compositions of Leverkühn's last phase. Work on *Doctor Faustus* had to be interrupted in April of 1946, after chapter 33, when Mann had to undergo surgery for life-threatening lung cancer. After his recuperation, he completed the novel without further delay. Unexpectedly, Mann and Adorno clashed over the novel's ending. Adorno insisted on unmitigated "negativity," while Mann favored a more conciliatory outlook. Rather pointedly, he gave the final note of Leverkühn's last composition to a "high G on the cello"—a transparent cipher of grace *(Gnade)*.

Doctor Faustus was first published in Switzerland in October 1947. The following year it was published in the United States and in Germany. Its critical reception in the English-speaking world was mixed. In Germany, the novel met mostly with hostility since it was seen as a wholesale indictment of German culture and seemed to support the notion of collective guilt. Equally disturbing was the perceived suggestion that Germany had taken the road to barbarism not in spite of its worship of music, but because of it. In the country of his birth, Mann's *Doctor Faustus* remains his most controversial work.

Much of the intellectual scope and narrative sophistication of the novel can be gleaned from the elaborate frame of paratexts, which offer clues to its complexity and help us put the book in context. Its very title establishes a link to the Faust myth, which had been given two contradictory treatments in German literature. On the surface, Mann's novel evokes the original 16th-century chapbook, in which the hero's eventual fate is eternal damnation. Like the 16th-century Doctor Faustus, on whom he is modeled, Leverkühn enters into a pact with the devil when he deliberately contracts syphilis in exchange for twenty-four years of inspired creativity. Leverkühn too clings to his belief in the possibility of grace; his crowning work, the symphonic cantata *The Lamentation of Doctor Faustus,* is constructed on a twelve-tone row set to Faustus's last words: "For I die as both a wicked and a good Christian." On a deeper level, Mann's novel also evokes Goethe's momentous revision of the myth in which Faust is granted redemption. This line of signification is anchored in the implied identity of Esmeralda, the woman from whom Leverkühn contracts the disease, and Madame Tolna, the behind-the-scenes benefactor and promoter of his career. Esmeralda's love, like Gretchen's, may be read as an intimation of eventual grace. This covert web of allusions lies beyond the narrator's horizon and has to be assembled from the novel's pervasive subtext on the theme of grace. With the novel's title alone, Mann generates a measure of equivocation that permeates the entire narrative.

In a companion piece to *Doctor Faustus,* his Library of Congress address "Germany and the Germans," Mann puts his finger on what he calls a "grave error" in the Faust myth: "If Faust is to be representative of the German soul [. . .] he should have been a musician." In the novel's subtitle, its second paratext, this error is corrected, for this Faust book is "The Life of the German Composer Adrian Leverkühn as Told by a Friend." It took Mann some time to settle on this particular formula for his reconceptualization of Faust as a musical genius. Its crucial elements are the words "des deutschen Tonsetzers." The term *Tonsetzer*—German for composer—harks back to the *Tonkünstler Joseph Berglinger,* Wilhelm Heinrich Wackenroder's seminal novella of 1796 about the tragic fate of a musician; it also alludes to Mann's contemporary Hans Pfitzner, who for ideological reasons preferred the usage "Tonsetzer" and "Tonkunst." Above all, however, the term "deutscher Tonsetzer" signals the basic conviction proclaimed by Wagner and Nietzsche, and reaffirmed by Mann, that music was "the most German of the arts" and that music—"German" music—held the key to an understanding of German culture. Hence the striking premise of capturing the seeds of what Friedrich Meineke called the "German catastrophe" in the life and work of a German composer.

Of the introductory paratexts, the nine-line epigraph in Italian, from Dante's *Inferno* (Canto 2), is perhaps the most surprising element in what is an emphatically German book. As he is about to give us his version of the Faust story, thereby entering an inferno of his own, Mann invokes Dante and his descent into hell—a gesture later echoed by Leverkühn in his musical settings of passages from Dante. The epigraph also underscores the role of compassion *(pietate)* and of memory *(mente).* Mann seeks to guard against undue compassion for an inferno he deems well deserved and to trust the accuracy of his memory of what he has seen and experienced. The epigraph also hints at the profoundly confessional character of *Doctor Faustus,* into which Mann has woven several familiar motifs from the tortured history of his own ambiguous sexuality.

Two additional paratexts complete the book. The six-page epilogue, which provides a transition from the fictitious world of Leverkühn and Zeitblom to the postwar reality of their creator, has three parts. The longer middle part summarizes Leverkühn's life from his mental breakdown to his burial. Many details of this narrative recall the fate of Friedrich Nietzsche, one of the models for the character of Leverkühn, including the date of his death, August 25. This account is preceded by a remarkably self-conscious reflection in which Mann, through Zeitblom, remarks on the uncertain future of his manuscript. There is no chance now (1945), he writes, to have it published in Germany. He hopes that the manuscript will be taken to the United States, where much of European culture has survived the "orgies" of the "monster-state," but despairs of the translatability of the "all too radically German passages." This proved to be highly prescient. The first English translation was very problematical, and English readers had to wait until 1997 for the more satisfactory version by John E. Woods. Zeitblom adds—and here the identities of narrator and author become blurred—that Germany has grown "utterly alien" to him. He hopes that his loyalty to Leverkühn and to what he stands for will make up for "having fled in horror from my country's guilt." The epilogue concludes, ambiguously, with a brief prayer for mercy and grace for "my friend, my fatherland."

Mann added a brief author's note to the slightly shortened 1951 printing of the novel. This was occasioned by the bizarre charge of plagiarism by Arnold Schoenberg, who, before actually reading the book, objected to the alleged characterization of his twelve-tone technique as the work of the devil. To appease the irate composer, Mann explicitly stated what should have been obvious, that the method of composition presented in chapter 22 and ascribed to an "entirely fictitious musician" is "in truth the intellectual property of [. . .] Arnold Schoenberg." As unessential as this note may appear today, it testifies to the profoundly controversial character of Mann's indictment of German culture.

Most critics who reject the novel proceed from the assumption that Mann intended to draw a kind of symbolic equivalence between Leverkühn and Germany. But *Doctor Faustus* cannot be read as an allegory of Hitler and Nazi Germany. The book is a hybrid—part fictional biography, part historical novel. It reconstructs in vivid detail, and with magisterial authority, the cultural climate of Leverkühn's Germany, meanwhile suggesting that it prefigured much of what was to come. But what precisely is being prefigured here? The clearest indication is found in chapter 25, the spiritual core of the book, where the motivation for Leverkühn's Faustian pact is laid open. The inner voice Leverkühn thinks is the devil promises what he desires most: "You will lead, you will set the march for the future." In other words, Leverkühn will achieve and exert hegemony. Eerily, this echoes Schoenberg's famous pronouncement that his invention of the dodecaphonic method of composition would ensure the dominance of German music for another hundred years.

By striving for musical leadership and hegemony, Leverkühn betrays and corrupts his cosmopolitan heritage. By the time Mann came to write *Doctor Faustus,* he had realized that the widespread, deceptively nonpolitical discourse of the universality of German music harbored a nationalist, potentially aggressive mentality that induced many Germans to believe that the perceived hegemony of German music justified, and legitimized, Germany's push for political hegemony—for the proverbial "place in the sun." Leverkühn is determined to eliminate from the musical work any and all elements that cannot be considered thematic. His Schoenbergian ideal of a strict style requires a rigorous organization of the musical material, prefiguring excesses of organization and control of a much more concrete and sinister sort.

This implication is made explicit in another companion piece to the novel, *The War and the Future* (1943), in which Mann observed, "the monstrous German attempt at world domination . . . is nothing but a distorted and unfortunate expression of that universalism innate in the German character." In its older, purer form—music, for instance—German universalism had "won the sympathy and admiration of the world." It was the desire for power and world domination that "corrupted this universalism and turned it into evil." Mann is hopeful, however, that "German universalism will again find a way to its old place of honor" and contribute to the "spiritual enrichment of the world." In other words, what happened in Germany—and what Leverkühn's music prefigures—cannot be attributed to an evil strain endemic to German culture; rather, it resulted from a process of perversion of something good and benign—a process that is assumed to be reversible.

Today it seems that it is precisely Mann's comprehensive critique of German culture—the depth of his unsparing, self-critical insights—that will assure this book a lasting place in German literature. On closer inspection, however, Mann's insights reveal some notable instances of blindness, the most serious of which is that nowhere in the novel do we hear of anti-Semitism. The Munich of the proto-fascist era does not appear to harbor any anti-Semites. German musical life—contrary to all evidence—shows no trace of discrimination against Jews. Furthermore, the figure of the impresario Saul Fitelberg strikes many as a caricature of a certain Jewish impresario, and in Dr. Chaim Breisacher we are even treated to the questionable phenomenon of a Jewish fascist. In a novel that is meant to illuminate Germany's path into *Anti-Humanität,* Mann's insensitivity to this aspect of the problem constitutes an undeniable flaw, one that has to taint the considerable greatness we attribute to the book.

Despite this reservation, Thomas Mann's *Doctor Faustus* stands out for its vivid representation of musical life in Germany in the first quarter of the 20th century, for its unmatched verbal re-creations of music, and above all for its profoundly probing interrogation of the fateful nexus between culture and politics.

See also 1596, 1831, 1876, 1882, 1912 (June), 1947

Bibliography: Thomas Mann, *Doctor Faustus,* trans. John E. Woods (New York: Knopf, 1997). ———, *The Story of a Novel: The Genesis of Doctor Faustus,* trans. Richard and Clara Winston (New York: Knopf, 1961). ———, *Addresses Delivered at the Library of Congress, 1942–1949* (Washington, D.C.: Library of Congress, 1963). Gunilla Bergsten, *Thomas Mann's* Doctor Faustus: *Sources and Structure of the Novel,* trans. Krishna Winston (Chicago: University of Chicago Press, 1969). Patrick Carnegy, *Faust as Musician: A Study of Thomas Mann's Novel* Doctor Faustus (New York: New Directions, 1973). John F. Fetzer, *Changing Perceptions of Thomas Mann's* Doctor Faustus: *Criticism 1947–1992* (Columbia, S.C.: Camden House, 1996). Herbert Lehnert and Peter C. Pfeiffer, eds., *Thomas Mann's* Doctor Faustus: *A Novel at the Margin of Modernism* (Columbia, S.C.: Camden House, 1991). Hans Rudolf Vaget, "Amazing Grace: Thomas Mann, Adorno, and the Faust Myth," in Reinhold Grimm and Jost Hermand, eds., *Our Faust: Roots and Ramifications of a Modern German Myth* (Madison: University of Wisconsin Press, 1987), 169–189.

Hans Rudolf Vaget

♩ 1946, April
Karl Jaspers's essay "On German Guilt" is published

Guilt and Atonement

In 1945, having suffered its second military defeat in less than thirty years, Germany was not only physically devastated but spiritually depleted as well. The enormous loss of life, territory, and economic prosperity was accompanied by moral questioning and reprobation. Although Germany had been compelled after World War I to assume responsibility for the outbreak of hostilities in August 1914, and was made to pay draconian reparations to the victors, the aftermath of Hitler's war brought with it a more troubling confrontation with guilt. Shortly after the unconditional surrender to the Allies in May 1945, it became evident that the legacy of National Socialism involved more than just the militarism and totalitarianism that made it anathema to liberal societies. Gradually, as reports from concentration and extermination camps were publicized, the world became aware of the full scale of the atrocities committed by the German nation. Although the Nazi government perpetrated many criminal acts against its own citizens in the period from 1933 to 1945 and against other peoples during the Second World War, and although under Nazi rule many religious, ethnic and political groups—the Sinti and Roma, the mentally ill, homosexuals, Jehovah's Witnesses, eastern Europeans, communists, and socialists—were severely persecuted, the German genocide of the Jewish people occupies a special place in history. The enormity of the crime—close to six million Jews were murdered—the systematic nature of this annihilation, and the recognition that these acts of mass murder were planned and carried out by a nation formerly considered among the most civilized on earth are factors that make what came to be known as the Holocaust remarkable and almost unfathomable. In the immediate postwar years, guilt was not an abstract concept, and while the Allies were in a position to decide how to deal with the most abhorrent Nazi criminals, the Germans were left to themselves to confront the appalling crimes undertaken in their name.

Almost alone among his countrymen, the philosopher Karl Jaspers faced the question of German guilt openly in his essay "Die Schuldfrage" (The Question of German Guilt). It became the single most important intellectual contribution to coming to grips with the Nazi crimes for the first half-century following World War II, and a foundational document for the official public stance toward the ignominies of the Nazi regime. Jaspers first dealt with the question in a series of lectures, delivered at the University of Heidelberg during the winter semester of 1945–46. The students present are reported to have treated his presentation with disdain and derision. However, when "Die Schuldfrage" was published by Lambert Schneider Verlag at the end of the term, it became a major event and was widely read and appreciated by German intellectuals. Its tone was sometimes professorial, unemotional, and aloof; Jaspers's plea for reasoned argument at a time when the horrors of the war were being revealed to an incredulous public might be taken for insensitivity. But readers also sensed Jaspers's serious engagement with issues both philosophical and practical, and his recognition of the stakes involved in suggesting propositions to deal with a highly delicate situation.

The treatise tackled two of Jaspers's major concerns in the aftermath of the war: higher education and moral philosophy. As universities in Germany began to reopen, Jaspers asked how students would relate to their professors after a period in which learning and education had been made the instrument of the state. Although he addresses this matter directly in the preface to the 1946 edition, in the essay itself his primary focus is on issues of German responsibility, German national character, German identity, and on guilt and atonement for the crimes committed by the Nazis in the name of the German people. Jaspers saw the possibility of a new beginning for Germany as a truly democratic nation adhering to Western values, but only if an intellectual elite were to reflect on its moral obligations, establish open lines of communication, and assume responsibility for genuine leadership.

From his previous career path, Jaspers may seem to have been ill suited for the task he took upon himself. Born in 1883, he attended the universities of Göttingen and Heidelberg; at the latter institution he soon found his way into a circle that included Max Weber, who exerted an enormous influence on him, especially on his political thought. Graduating with a degree in psychology, Jaspers was first appointed professor of psychiatry, before he switched to a position in philosophy, first at Heidelberg, and after the war at Basel. All of Jaspers's writings prior to 1933 were in the fields of psychology or philosophy. During the Weimar era, he became widely known, along with his colleague Martin Heidegger (1889–1976), as one of the founders of existentialism. Although he published a book entitled *Die geistige Situation der Zeit* (The Spiritual Situation of Our Times) in 1931, he later admitted that at the time of writing, he was completely oblivious of National Socialism and was astounded later by that party's electoral success. Indeed, an indication of Jaspers's political naiveté is his publication in 1932 of a book on Max Weber in a series called *Schriften an die Nation (Writings to the Nation),* which included books by right-wing luminaries like Oswald Spengler, Wilhelm Frick, Ernst Krieck, and Josef Goebbels. After the Nazi accession to power, however, his political education was rapid. Married to a Jewish woman and repelled by the vulgarity of the new regime, Jaspers refused to align himself with Nazi ideology, and in 1937 he was removed from his professorship. After the war he moved to Switzerland and taught at Basel, but he continued to exert an enormous influence on German affairs through his writings and his cooperation with the Allies. Jaspers was most dismayed by the way higher education had capitulated to the Nazis, and particularly disappointed in friends like Heidegger, who abandoned him and apparently supported the criminal regime.

Part of his personal attempt to come to terms with the past was his publication of "Die Schuldfrage." But this essay is also a response to several postwar exigencies. In suggesting ways to approach the topic of guilt and atonement, Jaspers was competing with the beginnings of a process he was witnessing firsthand and that was called denazification. This term referred to the Allies' method of dealing with the enormous number of Germans implicated by membership in the Nazi Party or related organizations, or by nonmilitary activities during the war. Its goal was to remove dangerous elements from positions of authority. Administered first by the occupying powers, denazification, like many other policies, differed widely from one occupation zone to another. In the Soviet sphere of influence, for example, a much more severe policy was initially instituted. Former Nazis were dismissed from the civil service, in part to secure a foothold for Communist Party functionaries. In the West, the American zone was initially prepared to act most vigorously to eradicate Nazi influences, but even here the will and ability to perform this enormous task soon waned. By March 1946, denazification had been turned over to the Germans themselves, in whose hands it gradually degenerated into a farce. The questionnaires Germans were asked to complete to determine their degree of guilt became objects of ridicule—as evidenced in the satirical novel by Ernst von Salomon (1902–1972), *Der Fragebogen* (1951; *The Questionnaire*)—and with the advent of the cold war, the Allies rapidly turned their attention to new geo-political concerns. As a result, a vast number of Germans who had been enthusiastic party members and supporters of Hitler eventually received pardons or outright acquittals for all crimes.

Perhaps more important for Jaspers's essay was the Allies' policy toward the upper echelon of the party, the military, and industry. It was decided that these members of the Nazi elite would be criminally prosecuted before an Allied tribunal, and the first and most celebrated trial took place in Nuremberg from October of 1945 until October of 1946. The preparations for and the beginning of the Nuremberg trials thus coincided with the composition of Jaspers's lectures on German guilt. Standing trial were twenty-four prominent Nazis accused of crimes either as individuals or as leaders of various criminal organizations—the cabinet, the leadership of the party, the SS, the secret service, the Gestapo, the SA, the General Staff, and the Supreme Command of the Armed Forces. The defendants were tried for crimes against peace and against humanity, for war crimes and for conspiracy to commit these offenses. Thousands of pieces of evidence were introduced by the prosecution and the defense; 240 witnesses were called; and 300,000 affidavits were considered. The twenty-two defendants who remained in October of 1946—Robert Ley committed suicide and Gustav Krupp von Bohlen und Halbach was not able to stand trial because of his mental and physical condition—were given a variety of sentences from prison terms to capital punishment. Three of the accused were acquitted. Hermann Göring, one of the eleven condemned to death, avoided punishment by committing suicide the evening before his scheduled execution. More rigorous and successful than denazification, the Nuremberg trials also served an exemplary function and demonstrated to the native population and to the world that the rule of law had returned to German soil. Indeed, Jaspers's text, which was completed before the end of the first trial (there were eleven in all), is a German defense of the trials' legitimacy, a legitimacy that many Germans called into question on technical and substantive grounds. In arguing that the Nuremberg trials were not simply instances of victors' justice, and that actions for which there were no statutes at the time were still offenses that could be legitimately prosecuted, Jaspers sanctioned the Allied undertaking.

But Jaspers also challenged an opinion prevalent in certain circles among the Allied powers that would hold all Germans equally accountable for the Nazi crimes. Toward the end of the war and immediately thereafter, the Allies focused a great deal of attention on the question of what to do with Germany when hostilities ceased. The answer depended to a large extent on how one evaluated German guilt. Some believed that the German people were funda-

mentally innocent of wrongdoing and that they had been possessed temporarily by an evil cohort of political leaders. In this view only Hitler and his
henchmen bore true guilt; the contention was that a fundamentally evil regime had either duped, mesmerized, or intimidated the general population
into cooperating. Others explained Nazism as a logical outgrowth of German
developments, tracing the origins of the Third Reich back to the Franco-
Prussian War, yet others to failed attempts at democratic revolution, or even to
the Reformation and Martin Luther. This view not only tends to exculpate
Germans as victims of their unfortunate historical circumstances but also
erases differences among the citizenry, negating the possibility of individual
and moral choice.

However, some politicians and writers advocated a collective guilt thesis
whereby all Germans bore the guilt for National Socialism and its crimes. The
reasons for this guilt varied from the highly questionable thesis of a particular German character to the claim that the German psyche had undergone an
unusual formation. A weakened form of this thesis has been advanced by psy-
choanalytically inclined writers from Wilhelm Reich, in *Mass Psychology of
Fascism* (1929), to Klaus Theweleit in *Male Fantasies* (1977), who have identified a common denominator or psychic etiology in the mentality of Germans
or a particular group of Germans. A primary aim of Jaspers's essay "Die
Schuldfrage" was to discredit faulty arguments about German guilt, especially
the idea of collective guilt. Jaspers also wished to counteract plans by some
Allied factions favoring the complete de-industrialization of Germany.

In his deliberations, Jaspers relied heavily on more moderate opinions,
in particular those of Hannah Arendt (1906–1975) and Dwight MacDonald
(1906–1982), the only two authors cited in the essay. Arendt, whose thesis on
totalitarianism was to become a cornerstone of Western political thought in
the 1950s and whose report on the Eichmann trial of 1961 in Jerusalem gained
notoriety for its "banality-of-evil" thesis, contended in 1945 that guilt cannot
be fairly determined by an outside agency. The reasons people had for joining
the Nazi Party, for carrying out actions and orders, and for not attempting to
oppose even the most horrific crimes of the regime were too various and too
subtle for a definitive determination of guilt. Writing shortly before the end of
the war, Arendt predicted that there would be relatively few war criminals—at
least in the sense of those who were both responsible and guilty. Many would
be responsible without any proof of guilt; and many guilty without being responsible. What interested Arendt more was a phenomenon she dealt with
later in her book on the Eichmann trial: evil in the guise of bureaucracy and as
an outgrowth of modernity. In her own essay on German guilt, she presents
Himmler as the typical bourgeois paterfamilias seeking to provide a secure future for his family. Under him were men acting without passion, simply following orders, fearing the bread lines; these men were neither evil nor insane,
as were Hitler and some of his cohorts, but ordinary citizens caught up in the
mechanisms of modern society. In "The Responsibilities of Peoples," Mac-
Donald is even more radical than Arendt with respect to German guilt. He

maintains that the most heinous crimes, although they were unique, were carried out against the will and without the knowledge of the German people. Comparing the persecution of African-Americans in southern states with Nazi atrocities, MacDonald argues that "whereas anti-Negro violence in America is a real 'folk' activity, carried on against the State with its police (which, of course, wink at it); in Germany it is the reverse: pogroms are carried out by the State and the forces of 'law and order' against the folkways."

Jaspers could not be quite so exculpatory about his country or compatriots, but he did suggest categories that mitigated the guilt and responsibility of most Germans for the crimes committed in their names. Only criminal guilt, he asserted, could be tried before a court of law and punished. All other forms of guilt had different adjudicative authorities and consequences. Political guilt was most appropriately determined by the victors; the appropriate punishment was loss of sovereignty; the Third Reich can thus be found guilty in a political sense because of the actions of the state. But Jaspers went on to argue that this guilt holds no direct consequence for individuals. In the case of individuals not responsible in any criminal sense, Jaspers develops the categories "moral guilt" and "metaphysical guilt." One's conscience and one's God, respectively, are the authorities that determine these classes of guilt. The notion of collective guilt was at cross purposes with Jaspers's categories: the German state could be held liable for its actions by the victorious Allies, but the guilt of Germans must be ascertained individually, either in a criminal court for actual criminal violations, or through introspection in the case of noncriminal actions. Jaspers must have recognized that the application of his four categories of guilt would produce only a small number of criminally guilty, and that the vast majority of the population would to a large extent be exonerated. He also took into account the possibility that people might approach the moral and metaphysical categories in a cynical spirit. But he sincerely believed that only by engaging in moral cleansing and spiritual renewal could Germany lift its pariah status and enter once more the community of civilized nations.

"Die Schuldfrage" was the most influential postwar intellectual response to Nazism and the Holocaust. Because it readily admitted the criminal activity of the fascist regime, yet exonerated most of the German people from direct responsibility, and because it relied on a moralistic rhetoric that involved humility, contrition, and atonement, it functioned well throughout the postwar period as a framework for German retrospection on the Nazi past. It set the tone for the official political culture of the Federal Republic, establishing a moral consensus for confronting Germany's troubled legacy. From discussions of reparations and commemorations of the "night of broken glass" *(Kristallnacht)* to relations with Israel and Willy Brandt's kneeling gesture at the Warsaw ghetto monument, West Germany adhered to a high ethical path that resonates with Jaspers's ideas. Jaspers himself, however, was not satisfied with the impact his essay had in the immediate postwar era or in the ensuing two decades.

It is a curious and sobering fact of intellectual life in West Germany that this essay stands virtually alone. Except for a few official proclamations from the churches and occasional remarks by politicians, there was no intellectual response to the questions concerning German guilt and responsibility, even as the extent of German atrocities became widely known. There was no general discourse, no public sphere for the issues Jaspers raised: in an interview with Rudolf Augstein, editor of the magazine *Der Spiegel,* in 1965, Jaspers lamented that his essay had found no echo among German intellectuals. And in 1967, two years before his death, Jaspers judged that the spiritual reversal he had deemed necessary if Germany was to redress its grave transgressions had not occurred. Although the reception of "Die Schuldfrage" did not satisfy its author's expectations and inspired scant public response, it was nonetheless the most influential document in postwar Germany's attempt to confront its troubled past.

See also 1927, 1942–43, 1986

Bibliography: Karl Jaspers, *The Question of German Guilt,* trans. E. B. Ashton (New York: Dial Press, 1947). Anson Rabinbach, "The German as Pariah: Karl Jaspers's *The Question of German Guilt," In the Shadow of Catastrophe: German Intellectuals between Apocalypse and Enlightenment* (Berkeley: University of California Press, 1997), 129–165, 240–246. Renato Rosa, ed., *Karl Jaspers Erneuerung der Universität: Reden und Schriften 1945/46* (Heidelberg: Lambert Schneider, 1986). Dwight MacDonald, "The Responsibility of Peoples," *Politics* (1945). Hannah Arendt, "German Guilt," *Jewish Frontiers* (1945).

Robert C. Holub

ᎧᏱ 1946/1947

A novel and a book of jottings document life and language during the Nazi regime

Intellectuals under Hitler

In the fall of 1946, Werner Krauss (1900–1976), professor of Romance languages at the University of Marburg, published a novel with the coded title *PLN: Die Passionen der halykonischen Seele (PLN: The Passions of a Halycon Soul).* Authorized by the American military government, the book appeared from the distinguished Frankfurt publishing house Vittorio Klostermann. The acronym PLN stands for "PostLeitNummer," the postal code introduced by the Nazis in 1944 to control postal service under conditions of "total war." "Halycon" is a mutation of the word "halcyon," derived from the myth of Alcyone, daughter of the wind god Aeolos. Mourning for her shipwrecked husband Ceyx, she threw herself into the sea, but the gods took pity on the couple and transformed them into ice birds. The two birds spent fourteen days in a protected, windless space created by Aeolos. Metaphorically, the phrase "halcyon days" means a respite during which storms cannot occur. In German literature and philosophy, from Wieland to Nietzsche, the concept of the halcyon had come to stand for a posture of contemplation untouched by the rough winds of politics. In Krauss's usage, the reversal of letters in the deformed word "halycon" is intended as an ironic critique of a tradition of inwardness that permitted German intellectuals to be seduced by Nazism.

PLN was produced in a print run of five thousand copies at a price of 7.50 Reichsmarks each; not all copies were sold. Two years later, the novel was republished by the Potsdam press Rütten & Löning, in the Soviet Occupied Zone, licensed by the Soviet military administration in Germany. In the preface, the author describes the circumstances that had motivated the "seismographic accuracy" of his novel. He had begun writing in 1943 while in detention in Plötzensee and completed it in military prison in Lehrter Straße 61, Berlin. A young fellow prisoner, Alfred Kothe, had smuggled the book out at serious risk to his own life. Although the "novelistic cloak" originated in Krauss's need to conceal what he was writing, the "ciphers and hieroglyphs" corresponded, he believed, to a deeper truth about society under Nazism. The novel, a mixture of parody, detective story, and practically every register of social satire, is among the best of the few literary testimonies to what Krauss called inner Germany. The term was derived from Stefan George's phrase "secret Germany," which described the conservative German elite following World War I and was used during the Third Reich by Ernst Kantorowicz to refer to intellectuals who were neither Nazis nor members of the resistance.

The tragicomic hero of *PLN* is the Imperial Postmaster of Greater Halycon, Alois Schnipfmeister, whose actions are modeled on Krauss's involvement in the Berlin antifascist resistance group Red Orchestra, led by Harro Schulze-Boysen and Arvid and Mildred Harnack. Schnipfmeister's intellectual opposite is Critilo, a character from *El Criticón* (1651), an allegorical novel by Baltasar Gracián, to whom Krauss had devoted a scholarly book, *Graciáns Lebenslehre* (1947; *Gracián's Life Wisdom*). A dialogue in *PLN* between Schnipfmeister and Critilo makes clear that the two seemingly opposite figures represent, in effect, the two sides of the author himself.

The acronym PLN makes the novel a quasi-biography of the postal institution and its totalizing perversion of communication under Nazism. In an unpublished essay of 1946 titled "Betrachtungen und Erfahrungen über die deutsche Opposition" (Reflections on and Experiences of the German Opposition), Krauss describes the posture of German inwardness in terms relevant to his novel: "All these people had the puzzling ability to absorb the crassest contradictions [. . .] Most educated Germans had constructed a kind of repression mechanism that enabled them to endure without protest the worst sorts of attacks and atrocities."

Yet Krauss's diagnosis of the "halcyon days" assumed a certain distance from Nazi modes of thought that did not yet exist in the immediate postwar period. Krauss himself was surprised by the reaction to his book. Writing to his friend Samson B. Knoll, chief interrogator at the Information Control Detachment Marburg of the U.S. Army, he notes, "Most people read *PLN* with increasing puzzlement. When I wrote it, I had no idea, of course, that a postwar attack on 'inner Germany' would be seen as such a cruel blow" (December 15, 1946). In

Krauss's view, this reaction showed that many Germans still clung to the tradition of inwardness and continued to repress memories of the Nazi period.

In 1947, from the Berlin publishing house Der Aufbau in the Soviet Occupied Zone, another book with an acronymic title appeared: Victor Klemperer's *LTI: Notizbuch eines Philologen (LTI: A Philologist's Notebook)*. LTI stands for Lingua Tertii Imperii—language of the Third Reich. Like Krauss, Klemperer (1881–1960) was a professor of Romance languages and a student of Karl Vossler, founder of the anti-positivist school of "idealistische Neuphilologie" (Idealist New Philology). The two scholars took very different paths, however: the Hispanist Krauss, influenced by Marxism and Erich Auerbach, conceived of literary studies as a historical task, whereas Klemperer saw his own work on 18th- and 19th-century French literature as an account of leading poetic figures. Nonetheless, the two entered into dialogue after the war as witnesses and record-keepers of "inner Germany." In his notebook, Klemperer observes the similarity of their two books in the laconic note "Duplicity: PLN-LTI" (May 15, 1947, St. 1, 375); and in a letter to Krauss he writes, "Strange coincidence in the similarity of titles: *PLN-LTI,* though neither of us knew about the other. But the idea was in the air" (March 15, 1948).

They first met in person in Berlin on July 6, 1946, on the eve of a conference of the Kulturbund zur demokratischen Erneuerung Deutschlands (Cultural League for the Democratic Renewal of Germany), a Russian initiative started the previous year. Both spoke at the conference. In a thumbnail sketch in his diary, Klemperer describes their meeting. It took place in the dining room of the Hotel Adlon, at that time a partial ruin: "Here I introduced myself to Werner Krauss, the most important acquaintance—actually the only new one—I made on this trip. In his mid-forties, slender, tall, with a bold and bushy mane of dark blond hair, more like an artist than a scholar [. . .], a member of the Communist Party and a cultural revolutionary" (St. 1, 272). A photo in the weekly *Sonntag,* accompanying a report on the conference (July 14, 1946), showed the two scholars in conversation. Later, Klemperer wrote two reviews of *PLN* (1948 and 1950), analyzing it as a "coded history of the times" and a "compendium and parody of the Hitler idiom" that complemented his own notebook *LTI.* Under the title "Philologie unterm Fallbeil" (1950; Philology under the Ax), Krauss emphasized the affinity between the two books and their attempt to define the spirit of the times by focusing on language: "The excess of abbreviations with their organic smartness, their advertising potential, and their religious seduction, their secret society airs were a quite particular characteristic of Nazi language." In February 1947, Krauss augmented Klemperer's critique of Nazi language with a perspective from below in his essay "Die Flucht ins Argot: Betrachtungen über den Zustand unserer Sprache" (The Flight into Slang: Reflections on the Condition of Our Language), which appeared in the Freiburg journal *Die Gegenwart (The Present).* The essay examined what he called the "language of World War II"—the speech patterns used in concentration camps and in military units. Describing these two idioms as reactions to official modes of speech and thought, Krauss argued that the Nazis' alleged total transformation of society had in actuality been merely superficial. Unlike the effects of the French and the Russian revolutions, "Nationalism and Fascism, which did not believe in principles, could not possess any real language" (WKW 8, 114).

Both *PLN* and *LTI* document a phase of amnesia in the early years of German postwar history, characterized by relative silence about the atrocities of the Nazi period. Although only a small number of readers perceived the importance of *LTI* at the time of its first appearance, Klemperer's book was frequently reprinted in the 1960s in both East and West Germany. Starting in 1995 with the publication of his diaries, from which Klemperer had mined *LTI*, the work received renewed attention and fresh consideration. *PLN*, by contrast, has remained relatively occluded, despite the publication of two annotated re-editions in East and West Germany, in 1980 and 1985 respectively. Unlike *LTI*, *PLN* was never translated into English. Herbert Marcuse, a friend of Krauss, attempted to interest Viking Press, in New York, in bringing out a translation, but without success.

LTI, which Klemperer often called—in an allusion to Voltaire—his *Dictionnaire philosophique de l'Hitlérisme*, analyzes in thirty-six entries the manipulative rhetoric of the Nazis and their institutions. The entries are gathered together under a motto drawn from Franz Rosenzweig: "Sprache ist mehr als Blut" (language is more than blood). Klemperer's linguistic examples differ significantly from those collected in a series of articles by Dolf Sternberger that appeared between 1945 and 1948 in the Heidelberg periodical *Die Wandlung (The Transformation)* under the title *Aus dem Wörterbuch eines Unmenschen (From the Dictionary of a Monster;* published in book form in 1957). The difference was in Klemperer's perspective as a Jewish observer who was still connected to everyday life rather than segregated from it, as were concentration camp prisoners. The documentary precision with which Klemperer notes ways of speaking and thinking among different segments as well as on the radio and in newspapers gives his jottings the character of a collective journal.

Klemperer comments on a wide range of usages. The word "gleichschalten," for example, a word from electro-technology meaning to synchronize and, by extension, to bring into line, was a key term in Nazi parlance, characteristic of the attempt to disguise the fascist order as progressive and ultramodern. Similarly, "liquidieren" (to liquidate), the Nazi word for killing people they found undesirable, was derived from the new language of commerce. Other terms, such as "aufnorden" (to make something appear more Nordic), were expressions of Nazi ideology and its emphasis on racist geopolitics. Klemperer noted, too, the positive spin the Nazis gave the adverb "blindlings" (blindly), which he calls a "typical pillar" of Third Reich language, used to describe the ideal attitude with which Germans should follow the Führer.

Klemperer, who had begun to keep detailed diaries in 1918, continued this habit after the demise of the Third Reich, registering with philological precision what he called LQI, Lingua Quartii Imperii—the language of the GDR. Part of the interest of the diaries for their German readers is the way they embed the Hitler period into a larger narrative. In contradistinction to Klemperer's diaries from before and after, however, his diaries from the Nazi period are characterized by the way in which they use writing as a mode of survival and a search for individual identity. Klemperer saw himself excluded on the ground of race and, at the same time, placed outside the reach of law because of his marriage to an Aryan woman. His early intimations of anti-Semitism, which led to his conversion to Protestantism in 1919, were confirmed in 1933, when he saw himself, "a Christian and a nationalist, between all the stools" on account of his Jewish heritage (L1, 187). His diaries become a balancing rod "without which I would have fallen a hundred times" (*LTI,* 1). He describes his writing strategy as a recollection of a game he had played in childhood in which paper soldiers were cut out, pasted on cardboard, and assembled into whatever formations one wished. His collection of locutions from the Third Reich was similar to the collection of "paper soldiers" (Z1, 621), a record of intellectual resistance to Nazi modes of thought.

Klemperer's diaries are at once a chronicle and an autobiography. The author, who had been a passionate moviegoer in his youth, becomes an observer both of the times and himself. His diaries are unique in that he discusses the problem of Nazi and German anti-Semitism as a burning question of cultural identity for a German and an assimilated Jew who has been declared an enemy of his country. He also records other people's struggles to come to grips with this issue. He notes, for example, a conversation between an SA officer and a Jewish doctor he overheard while engaged in forced labor in 1943. Though tenaciously nationalist, the SA man denies the existence of a Jewish race and the notion of pervasive anti-Semitism among the German people. The Jewish doctor counters that anti-Semitism is ineradicably intertwined with things German. In an ironic twist, Klemperer confesses that he "goes a long way" with the views of the SA man. In another passage, he comments: "Actually, I feel more shame than fear. I always felt myself to be truly German" (Z1, 15).

In a 1995 speech on the occasion of the posthumous award to Victor Klemperer of the Geschwister Scholl Prize of the City of Munich, Martin Walser described Klemperer's struggle for his German identity as a "trust in culture that remained indestructible in spite of all he had suffered" (Walser, 16). Walser's reading, however, neglects the question of German participation in applying the Nazi racial laws, a question that troubled Klemperer himself from 1935 on. In his novel *Verteidigung einer Kindheit* (1991; *Defense of a Childhood*), Walser had made use of Klemperer's diaries even before their publication. At the same time as he memorialized Klemperer, however, Walser also shaped the German reception of the diaries by articulating a sense of victimhood for the older generation. Walser was rightly criticized for this position. Klemperer's diaries, far from documenting a continuity of German cultural identity, are in fact an unvarnished and painful report on the self-destruction of "inner Germany" when it submitted to totalitarian power.

The publication of Klemperer's diaries in 1995 was greeted around the world as a cultural and literary event. They were the subject of two television

programs, and an American film is in preparation. Upon Klemperer's death in
1960, Werner Krauss praised his colleague's "gift for style, penetrating interpretive skill, and ability to create the large historical synthesis." Krauss was
speaking about Klemperer's scholarly studies, but the same eloquent style and
analytical skills are evident in his diaries. Krauss and Klemperer, two German
specialists in Romance languages who crossed—in different ways—the borders between scholarship and literature, were convinced that the days of "inner
Germany" had come to an end. Their works remain as warnings should any
attempt be made to revive it.

See also 1897, 1913

Bibliography: Victor Klemperer, *LTI: Notizbuch eines Philologen* (Leipzig: Reclam, 1987); *The
Language of the Third Reich: LTI—Lingua Tertii Imperii: A Philologist's Notebook* (London and New
Brunswick, N.J.: Athlone Press, 2000). ———, *Ich will Zeugnis ablegen bis zum letzten: Tagebücher
1933–1945,* 2 vols. (Berlin: Aufbau Verlag, 1995); *I Will Bear Witness: A Diary of the Nazi Years
1933–1941* (New York: Random House, 1998–1999), 2 vols. Werner Krauss, *Das wissenschaftliche
Werk,* vols. 1–3, ed. Manfred Naumann (Berlin and Weimar: Aufbau Verlag, 1984–1989); vols. 4–
8 (Berlin and New York: de Gruyter, 1994–1997). ———, *Briefe 1922 bis 1976,* ed. Peter Jehle
with Elisabeth Fillmann and Volker Springborn (Frankfurt am Main: Vittorio Klostermann,
2002). ———, *PLN: Die Passionen der halykonischen Seele* (Frankfurt am Main: Vittorio
Klostermann, 1946). Stuart Taberner, "'Wie schön wäre Deutschland, wenn man sich noch als
Deutscher fühlen könnte': Martin Walser's Reception of Victor Klemperer's *Tagebücher 1933–
1945* in *Das Prinzip Genauigkeit* and *Verteidigung der Kindheit,*" *Deutsche Vierteljahrsschrift für
Literaturwissenschaft und Geistesgeschichte* 73 (1999): 710–732. Martin Walser, *Das Prinzip
Genauigkeit: Laudatio auf Victor Klemperer* (Frankfurt am Main: Suhrkamp, 1996).

Karlheinz Barck

♩ *1947*

Max Horkheimer and Theodor Adorno's *Dialectic of Enlightenment* is published

Snatching Defeat from the Jaws of Victory

When contrasted with the generally euphoric postwar celebration of the
enlightened, democratic values that had prevailed over the irrationalism and
inhumanity of fascism, the twin presuppositions of Horkheimer and Adorno's
1947 study, *Dialectic of Enlightenment,* are particularly sobering. The authors argue that "enlightenment is as totalitarian as any system" and "the fully enlightened earth radiates disaster triumphant." Had the work been written even one
or two years earlier, its central premise—the critique of both fascism and advanced consumer capitalism as twin forms of totalitarianism—would scarcely
have been thinkable. Just what, the book seems to ask, has been won, after all?

To substantiate their argument, Horkheimer and Adorno expand the concept of Enlightenment—generally identified with the political, cultural, and
scientific thought characteristic of bourgeois culture since the 18th century—
to mean any thought that seeks to systematically order and control the human
environment. The authors begin by analyzing the "instrumental" nature of
Enlightenment rationality in the historically limited sense and go on to trace a

continuous line from "mimetic," "mythic," and "metaphysical" modes of behavior all the way back to the pre-Socratic philosophers in ancient Greece.
Enlightenment, they argue, has served at each stage to debunk any human relationship to the world that is not one of simple mastery and control. It is a radical skepticism that finally undercuts even its own claims to validity.

In a subsequent anthropological excursus on Odysseus, they read the mythical narrative as humankind's emergence into modern subjectivity. The archetype of the bourgeois subject is Odysseus, who escapes the blinded Cyclops by
answering, when challenged, that he is "Udeis"—no one. Such facile self-
abnegation, according to Horkheimer and Adorno, is the very precondition of
bourgeois subjectivity. This same notion of self-assertion through self-abnegation is then followed through in chapters on the Marquis de Sade and on anti-
Semitism. The systematic nature of Sade's pleasure seeking, they argue, allows
the Sadean subject to "master" his pleasure through a mastery of the system.
Such dispassionate passions—characteristic also of Kant's emphasis on "disinterest" as the key to aesthetic experience—allow the subject to become a subject through subjection to the rigors of an objective rationality. In such instances, the systematic demands of reason themselves become irrational. The
authors' analysis of anti-Semitism likewise relies on a logic of self-abnegation
linked to mimesis. Anti-Semites, they argue, "cannot stand the Jews yet imitate
them." The Jews represent the anti-Semites' "own self-portrait" in their longing "for total possession and unlimited power at any price." The aggressive affect of the persecutors is projected onto the victims as something that must
first be externalized and then punished. But in punishing, anti-Semites act out
the very aggression they punish in the other. More interestingly, though,
Horkheimer and Adorno identify in anti-Semitism a quasi-utopian moment.
As "moments of biological prehistory"—as a race, that is, a group that can be
entirely reduced to its racial characteristics—the Jews represent a moment of
longed-for, unmediated self-identity. As representatives of "happiness without
power," the Jews represent that which the anti-Semites—following the logic of
a self-abnegating reason—have left behind.

Dialectic of Enlightenment is most famous—or infamous—in the English-
speaking world for its consideration of the "culture industry," a term the
authors coined to describe the homogenized—and homogenizing—culture
emerging from Hollywood and rendered global by new means of mass distribution. The concept of the culture industry is central to the work's reformulation of the question of ideology. Rather than being a set of ideas imposed by
the prevailing powers to reinforce that power—the authors' model of authoritarian society—in a totalitarian order, ideology functions to assure social acquiescence at a level that predates rational choice. The subject of the culture
industry conforms not because he fears the consequences of nonconformity,
but because the possibility of nonconformity has been foreclosed by the cultural values that inform his social interactions and political choices.

Owing to their relentless critique of a culture they see as infantilizing,
Horkheimer and Adorno have often been misrepresented as cultural conserva-

tives patrolling the borders of high and low culture. Certainly, Adorno's own *Aesthetic Theory* is a textbook example of high modernist cultural theory. To polarize high and low culture in this way, however, is to misunderstand completely the operation of the dialectic within this sweeping critique of Enlightenment. The authors of *Dialectic of Enlightenment* foresee and challenge the hegemony of American consumer culture in the postwar era without ever—and this too is often forgotten—opposing it in an undialectical way to some putatively superior (and presumably European) culture. They walk a tightrope between mere relativism—that is, the assumption that high and low, real and consumer cultures are just equivalent commodities appealing to different culture consumers—and mandarin elitism. Again and again, Horkheimer and Adorno insist that contemporary popular culture unmasks the unacknowledged barbarism upon which Western culture has always been predicated. As such—that is, as a gesture of demystification—popular culture has much in common with the work of Enlightenment whose values it otherwise seems to flaunt.

The curious publication history of *Dialectic of Enlightenment* tells much about its significance for postwar intellectual life in both Germany and the English-speaking world. Written by the two Frankfurt School exiles in America over the period of 1941 to 1944, the work was published in 1947 by a Dutch publishing house. It was republished in 1969/70, after years of being passed around in bootleg copies by a new postwar generation of politically motivated students of culture.

On the face of it, it is a typical exile story. Two highly cultured intellectuals shoehorn themselves into Los Angeles, where a mass culture they deplore holds sway, a collaborative retreat into a friendship that Adorno would characterize in another exile work, *Minima Moralia,* as "the narrowest private sphere, that of the intellectual in emigration." The work's subsequent circulation within a public sphere continues to bear the marks of exile—secrecy and marginality, the intimate passage of ideas from one friend to another outside regular channels of institutionalized intellectual life.

But there is another way to look at this history, another way to read this work. The displacements that mark a work of exile are at one and the same time emblematic of a global cultural network whose emergence the work itself analyzes. *Dialectic of Enlightenment*—no less than that other seminal work of exile culture, Erich Auerbach's *Mimesis*—is as much an event in Anglo-American cultural history as in German intellectual life. It is perhaps significant that Auerbach's organizing category of "mimesis" is also a central concern in this work. Whereas Auerbach reconstructs a history of mimesis as narrative of a humanist cultural project, for Horkheimer and Adorno the term is considerably more problematic as it connotes a conformist tendency to adaptive, acquiescent behavior. Like Auerbach, Horkheimer and Adorno assign Homer's *Odyssey* a privileged position, but give it a very different reading. With its episodic movement from the land of the lotus eaters, to the fooling of the Cyclops, the encounter with the enchantress Circe, and finally the return home, the *Odys-*

sey now becomes an allegory of humankind's growing instrumental control over, and alienation from, the natural world.

By an irony of history, a work that testifies to a cultural misconnection—the failure of the European émigré to feel at home in America—in fact is now perhaps the foremost piece of German cultural criticism that has become de rigueur reading in American university classrooms. The famous analysis of the "Culture Industry" has become a grounding text of cultural studies in the American academy, though its argument is generally caricatured as an elitist rejection of mass culture.

Written at a time when an Allied victory over the Axis Powers was by no means assured—though for the authors "the end of the Nazi terror was within sight"—the work was finally published at the time of postwar reconstruction in Germany. Yet, as the authors note, "the book as published contains no important alterations of the text written during the war." Even in the preface to the new edition of 1969, the authors note, "We have been far more sparing with alterations to the text than is usual with new editions of works published decades before. We did not want to retouch what we had written." In a work that presumes, as the authors state, again in the 1969 preface, that the core of truth is historical, rather than an unchanging constant to be set against the movement of history, such editorial reticence is remarkable indeed. It is as if a certain historical moment and a certain intimate space were exempt from the dialectic at the work's core. The critique of a totalized, and potentially totalitarian, culture arrogates to itself a curiously totalizing validity.

The belated reception of *Dialectic of Enlightenment* both in Germany and the United States needs to be understood in terms of cold war cultural politics. From the perspective of the liberal center, the critique of mass entertainment flew in the face of attempts to democratize the experience of culture. Adorno and Horkheimer explicitly reject both attempts to make "high" culture more accessible and attempts to render "low" culture more serious and prestigious. From the point of view of the left, meanwhile, any form of the totalitarianism thesis was problematic, even if, in this case, it was fascism and capitalism rather than fascism and communism that were being linked. The work's ad hoc and less than rigorous usage of Marxist terminology and the move beyond materialist determinism were also clearly anathema to Marxist orthodoxy. From the perspective of the political right and cultural conservatives, however, the analysis was still clearly structured along the lines of a Marxist critique, rendering the supposed "elitism" of the work's cultural stance effectively unusable.

One reason why *Dialectic of Enlightenment* nevertheless found such broad, if belated, resonance in the United States was that the authors jettisoned traditional categories of Marxist analysis. From the earliest Marxist writings of Georg Lukács—particularly his work *History and Class Consciousness*—the Western Marxist tradition to which the Frankfurt School belongs placed its emphasis on the centrality of the commodity form and the phenomenon of fetishism as a broader social phenomenon. However, it was precisely the potential uncoupling of a structure of fetishism from the actual circulation of commodities that allowed Horkheimer and Adorno, in *Dialectic of Enlightenment,* to posit language itself as the bearer of an alienated and instrumental relation to the natural and social world. Any critique of capitalism, therefore, is submerged in a broader epistemological critique, according to which "it [is] possible to trace the notion of enlightenment as progressive thought back to the beginning of traditional history." Challenging "historians who date the notion of the burgher only from the end of medieval feudalism," Horkheimer and Adorno reach back to Greek mythology and even aboriginal myth to demonstrate the operation of enlightenment thought. Thus, the radical nature of the analysis potentially allows for a blurring of the political thrust of the critique.

The essence of the so-called dialectic of enlightenment is encapsulated in the authors' opening declaration: "We are wholly convinced—and therein lies our *petitio principii*—that social freedom is inseparable from enlightened thought. Nevertheless, we believe that we have just as clearly recognized that the notion of this very way of thinking, no less than the actual historic forms—the social institutions—with which it is interwoven, already contains the seed of the reversal universally apparent today."

The specific social forms produced by this dialectic need to be understood as marking a threshold from the class society of classical Marxist analysis to a new technocratic social order, while "the growth of economic productivity furnishes the conditions for a world of greater social justice; on the other hand, it allows the technical apparatus and the social groups which administer it a disproportionate superiority to the rest of the population."

The authors' move away from the class analyses of Marxism in this work toward the critique of instrumental reason that would dominate subsequent writings by the Frankfurt School should, therefore, be understood not simply as a methodological shift, but as a response to what they perceive as a historical rupture in the formation of class in the age of postindustrial technologies. The central dialectic, too, works itself through this category of subjectivity. Even though the traditional bourgeois subject is the only perspective from which Horkheimer and Adorno can envision rational political critique and praxis, it is itself the most radical form of the totalitarian structure through which human relationships with the natural and social worlds—and thereby their own human potential—have become purely instrumental and manipulative.

The authors also take aim at existentialist cheapening of Marx's analysis of alienation and the canonization of ego-psychology that was becoming the trend in the United States. As cultural buzzword, the liberal critique of "alienation" goes hand in hand with the phenomenon of "fragmentation." In such a presentation, our alienated relation to the social and cultural norms would be reflected in a fragmented psychical life and in the forms of modernist art and literature. Rather than being a structured and formal response to social existence, fragmented forms of modern art are reduced to mere forms of expression. According to Horkheimer and Adorno, the social presupposition of such an argument—that modern society lacks the cohesion of earlier, putatively "organic" communities—is not only false but self-serving: "The sociological theory that the loss of objectively established religion, the dissolution of the last remnants of precapitalism, together with technological and social differentiation or specialization, have led to cultural chaos is disproved every day."

Popularization as cultural critique of what Adorno would elsewhere call the "jargon of authenticity" serves precisely to mask the reality of global capitalism. It calls for "totality" and an end to alienation through "authentic" experience, when it is, in fact, totality—in the form of the capitalist marketplace—that needs to be resisted. In the aesthetic realm, the fragment is not an expressive moment of a supposedly fragmented psyche, but a utopian critical moment from which totality might be resisted. The fragmentation of the exile experience—its editorial exemption from the historical dialectic and its identification with a private sphere that both Horkheimer and Adorno already know to be obsolete—is symptomatic of the utopian impulse that remains at the heart of so thoroughly pessimistic a work.

While many of the strategic moves beyond classical Marxist analysis in *Dialectic of Enlightenment* are responses to concrete historical developments in social formations, the political program those moves produce is, it must be conceded, eviscerated: "True revolutionary practice depends on the intransigence of theory in the face of the insensibility with which society allows thought to ossify." In retrospect, for example, the book's fragmented analysis of anti-Semitism—a theoretical counterpart to the empirical work members of the Frankfurt School were conducting in the United States at that time into the thought-processes of the "authoritarian personality"—while provocative, certainly seems too little, too late.

After their return to West Germany, Adorno and Horkheimer repeatedly insisted on this "intransigence of theory" in opposition to radical elements in the student movement of the 1960s who occasionally cited the analysis of *Dialectic of Enlightenment* as their impetus to an unmediated program of political action. It might be argued that the utopian political projects of the 1960s became terroristic only when—in the 1970s—theoretical intransigence itself hardened into an undialectical ideological arrogance in the hands of a new generation. The disabling dialectic of this work is, perhaps, that its critique of totality is itself as totalizing—and ahistorical—as the repressive rationality it opposes.

See also 1848 (February), 1944, 1967, 1977

Bibliography: Theodor Adorno, *Minima Moralia: Reflections from Damaged Life* (London: Verso, 1978). Andrew Arato and Eike Gebhardt, eds., *The Essential Frankfurt School Reader* (New York: Continuum, 1982). Jay Bernstein, *The Frankfurt School: Critical Assessments* (London: Routledge, 1989). Peter Uwe Hohendahl, *Prismatic Thought: Theodor W. Adorno* (Lincoln: University of Nebraska Press, 1995). Martin Jay, *The Dialectical Imagination: A History of the Frankfurt School and the Institute of Social Research 1923–1959* (Berkeley: University of California Press, 1973). Gillian Rose, *The Melancholy Science: An Introduction to the Thought of Theodor W. Adorno* (London: Macmillan, 1979).

Andrew Hewitt

♫ 1949

Brecht stages *Mutter Courage* in Berlin as a model for his concept of epic theater

History, Evidence, Gesture

On November 5, 1947, Bertolt Brecht (1898–1956) arrived in Zurich from his American exile. He had left the United States on November 1, after being interrogated by the House Committee on Un-American Activities on October 30, 1947. He spent the first November days in Paris, where he met Anna Seghers, who had recently returned from exile in Mexico. In Paris, he saw a staging of André Gide's theater version of Kafka's *The Trial* in Jean-Louis Barrault's Théâtre de Marigny ("a confused presentation, instead of a presentation of confusion," in Brecht's judgment). Zurich was the first way station on Brecht's gradual return to the stage in Germany.

In March 1933, Zurich had also been one of the early way stations on Brecht's long road into exile, "changing countries more often than shoes," as one of his poems puts it. But it was not for nostalgic reasons that Brecht first went to Zurich. The city theater of Zurich had become a refuge for many German actors and directors who had fled the Nazis or were expelled by them. Thus, the Zürcher Schauspielhaus was one of the foremost German-language theaters in the 1940s. It was also the only stage that presented Brecht's plays in German during that time. It was in Zurich that *Mutter Courage* was first staged in April 1941 under the direction of Leopold Lindtberg, with stage sets by Teo Otto. Brecht found these sets so congenial to his vision of the epic theater that he used them again for his model staging of the play in 1949 at the Deutsches Theater in Berlin.

Mutter Courage und ihre Kinder (Mother Courage and Her Children), set during the Thirty Years' War that ravaged Germany and large parts of Europe in the 17th century, was a commentary on war and its devastation. Brecht wrote the first version in the fall of 1939, at the beginning of World War II; when it was first staged in Zurich in 1941, the war was about to become a global war. In 1949, Brecht's first staging in Germany marked a moment when the cold war had entered its most intense phase, politically and symbolically represented by the founding of two separate German states later that year.

At the end of 1945, Brecht had written to his publisher Peter Suhrkamp that *Mutter Courage* might be the most apt of his recent plays to begin the revival of the German theater. His letter makes it clear that he was concerned less with the thematic than with the theatrical aspect. For Brecht political theater implied new forms of production, presentation, and reception rather than political themes. Thus the reconstruction of the German theater would have to take up the struggle for a different form of theater than had been central to Brecht's efforts in the twenties and early thirties: "You know that I found it necessary already before Hitler to intervene in the productions of my plays because of their experimental character."

Brecht's 1949 staging of the play in Berlin was an immediate success, but it also unleashed a controversy. Much more was obviously at stake concerning the form of this theater than mere content. Few critics quarreled with the political message as they understood it. However, heated debates ensued about a theater that called itself epic and seemed to put into question the dramatic mission of theater per se. This debate was a resumption of the Expressionism debate which raged primarily in the exile journal *Das Wort* in 1937 and 1938. It also set the stage for the continuing debates about cultural politics in the German Democratic Republic (GDR) in the 1950s and '60s.

The reactions provoked by Brecht's staging of *Mutter Courage* in 1949 revealed the Expressionism debate to be, in essence, a modernism debate about a style and mode of presentation that undermined conventional notions of representation and mimesis. The Expressionism debate began with an essay by Klaus Mann, son of Thomas Mann, about the poet Gottfried Benn and his support for the Nazis. Klaus Mann's essay "Gottfried Benn: Die Geschichte einer Verirrung" (Gottfried Benn: The Story of an Aberration) suggests that Benn's was the individual aberration of a great poet and intellectual. Responding with an essay of his own, Bernhard Ziegler, who under the pseudonym of Alfred Kurella became one of the leading ideologues of socialist realism in East Germany, made a counterclaim. Benn's association with the Nazis, he said, was not an individual aberration, but the symptomatic unveiling of the true spirit of Expressionism as a dehumanizing, disfiguring, artistic decadence that inevitably had to lead to fascism. Ziegler's essay coined the terms of the debate. Georg Lukács summarized them in a concluding essay, entitled "Es geht um den Realismus" (What Is at Stake Is Realism). He opposed his concept of realism, a mode of representation that mirrors the world in familiar anthropomorphic forms, to a formalism that disfigures the familiar and repeats the alienation of the modern world in the decadent products of many modern artists.

Brecht did not enter the controversy at the time, but he followed it attentively and wrote ironic commentaries in his journal. It was clear that his concept of epic theater with its *Verfremdung,* the defamiliarization of the familiar forms and images through which we represent the world to ourselves, was diametrically opposed to Lukács's aesthetics. After he staged *Mutter Courage,* Brecht could no longer avoid entering the ideological and aesthetic debate that the style of the performance provoked. The critic Fritz Erpenbeck, a former editor of *Das Wort* and close ally of Lukács, made a distinction between the great poet and playwright Brecht and Brecht the theoretician of the epic theater. Erpenbeck's plea for a healthy drama attacked Brecht in such ominously fascist terminology as "volksfremde Dekadenz" (decadence foreign to the people).

What, then, is behind the seemingly formalist opposition of an epic theater versus a dramatic theater? Why did Brecht call for an epic theater already in the early twenties? And why did his opponents ferociously defend the dramatic theater? Pitting the epic against the dramatic had a long tradition in

German aesthetics. Brecht became aware of it in 1947 and 1948 when he read (ironically, inspired by an essay of Lukács) the correspondence of Goethe and Schiller, in which epic versus dramatic was a major topic. Brecht quotes one of Schiller's differentiations in the preface to the model book of *Antigone:* "The dramatic action moves in front of me, whereas I move around the epic action that seems to stand still" (BF 25, 75). Schiller concludes that the relationship of the subject to the epic action is freer than its relationship to the dramatic action, where "I am chained to the sensual presence and my imagination loses all freedom." Brecht found in Schiller's formulations a surprising confirmation of his own concept of epic theater as a means of distancing the audience from the action on stage.

The extent to which the opposition of epic and dramatic occupied minds already in the late 18th and early 19th century is evident from both Hegel's aesthetics and a letter from Hölderlin to his friend Böhlendorff in 1801, in which he links modern drama to "epic treatment." There is no indication that Brecht knew Hölderlin's letter, and it is most likely he had not read it when he coined the term "epic theater" in the 1920s. This makes it all the more significant that these two very different poets arrived at the same conclusion that modern theater had to move toward an epic treatment.

Brecht's notion of epic theater derived independently from his increasing awareness, as playwright and director, that the representation of the modern world on stage required a radical rethinking of the actors' position within the dramatic action and of their relation to the audience. From a Marxist point of view, Brecht found himself faced with a paradox: for Brecht the Marxist, history was the product of human action rather than the result of some dark fate; at the same time, the complexity of production relations in the industrial world could not be represented through the actions of individuals.

For Hegel, the essence of the dramatic consisted in what he called an "intensive totality," that is, the representation of constitutive, conflictual elements of a historical period in one, concentrated intersubjective conflict. Hegel saw the conflict between Antigone and Kreon in Sophocles' tragedy as the representation of an epochal conflict between two equally valid concepts of law, producing a new historical era. The eponymous central figure of *Antigone,* the play Brecht used as his first stage experiment in Switzerland after returning from exile, is no more exemplary than *Mutter Courage* as an agent of history. Both characters stand in an oblique, mediated relation to the events. They are not the controlling agents, and yet, through their actions, they are active participants in a complex web of relations.

The presentation of the mediation that both separates and links individual subjects and the events and actions of their world poses a technical problem for the playwright. It can be called the problem of evidence. Classical aesthetics, especially classical drama, requires the representation of general conditions in individual cases and actions. This presupposes a certain immediacy between the individual's perception and the general condition. The human condition can become evident in a single individual case.

As a playwright of the scientific age, Brecht wanted to move away from what he considered metaphysical mystifications and write plays appropriate for the contemporary state of knowledge. Modern science places a high value on evidence, and so does Brecht. There is a scene in his play *Galileo Galilei* (first performed in English in New York in 1947 with Charles Laughton in the title role) where Galileo invites the court of Florence to look at the moons of Jupiter through his telescope. But when the theologian and the mathematician arrive, they first want to debate the principle of whether such moons can exist. Galileo repeatedly counters their objection with the simple invitation: Why don't you just look? The power of evidence, it would seem, reduces the pompous theoreticians to ridiculous fools. The critic Erpenbeck's response to the staging of *Mutter Courage* put him unwittingly in the company of the two learned fools when he insisted that the specific performance and its success were not important; what was needed was a discussion of general principles of the drama.

And yet, the need to treat drama in an epic way is based on a fundamental distrust of immediate evidence. Brecht once said: "A photograph of the Krupp factories does not reveal the laws and mechanisms of capitalist society." It is not a metaphysical question of a world of appearances covering a true world of essence, but rather of a world of highly mediated appearances that are the only evidence we have. But each appearance is insufficient insofar as each depends on its relation to all the others. It is not enough to keep one's eyes open, although, as Brecht remarks, it is better than rolling one's eyes in poetic ecstasy.

The problem of evidence in modern aesthetics and poetics highlights a paradigmatic difference between a tradition of bourgeois aesthetics, dominant since the end of the 18th century and still championed by Lukács, and the major thrust of modern poetics, represented, in part, by Brecht's concept of the epic theater. It is not by chance that this difference is paradigmatically articulated in terms of optical instruments. In his major late work on aesthetics, Lukács illustrates the difference between what he calls "anthropomorphic" aesthetic representation versus "desanthropomorphizing," unaesthetic, and decadent forms with the example of optical aids: glasses are a permissible aid, because they correct and restore natural vision; microscopes and telescopes are necessary scientific instruments, but not aesthetic, because they go beyond the field of natural, anthropomorphic perception. As if in anticipation of Lukács's argument, Brecht wrote in 1937: "Whereas the 'inner eye' does not need any microscopes or telescopes, the external eye needs both. The experience of other people is dispensable for the visionary. Experimentation is not a habit of visionaries." But experimentation is and should be a habit for the modern playwright, who, according to Brecht, is not a visionary, but a conductor of experiments.

From these premises certain technical consequences follow. Because the immediate evidence is not sufficient, epic theater must introduce artificial means that uncover the invisible. This technique implies a shift away from the classical and romantic concept of the symbol as an immediate, sensual representation of the general in the individual. This shift moves the epic theater closer to the structure of baroque allegory and emblems. Not only does the setting of *Mutter Courage* in the 17th century have a thematic dimension because of the Thirty Years' War and its almost mythical status in the history of German ideology, but the age of the Baroque also points at a shift in the modes of representation. Walter Benjamin's book *The Origin of the German Mourning-Play* reveals the seemingly obscure and almost forgotten theatrical productions of the German Baroque as paradigms of a radical differentiation between modern theater and ancient tragedy. Brecht refers to the same constellation when he emphasizes the links of his epic theater with the Elizabethan stage.

Brecht's subtitle defining *Mutter Courage* as a "chronicle" *(Eine Chronik aus dem dreißigjährigen Krieg)* was particularly annoying to some critics. Brecht defended himself by linking his concept of the chronicle with the Elizabethan genre of the history play. Formally, Brecht's chronicle does not present History (with a capital *H*) in one unified action as an intersubjective conflict. Rather it presents history as a series, or a constellation, of relatively independent scenes through which the central character moves like the picaresque hero of the early European novel. The model for Mutter Courage is the heroine of *Die Landstörzerin Courasche,* a German picaresque novel by the baroque writer Grimmelshausen. The picaresque form also has its modern correspondences. Some of Strindberg's plays, for example, are arranged as series of "stations." The form is obviously not ideologically fixed, but is a determined undermining of a certain tradition of bourgeois drama, centered on the notion of a unified historical subject whose actions can be understood through psychological motivation.

In his battle against the psychological drama, Brecht finds himself closely allied with Walter Benjamin as well as with the French surrealist writer Antonin Artaud. Artaud's theater and theory have often been seen as irrational and ritual as opposed to Brecht's rational and political theater. However, despite these differences, both Brecht and Artaud were in search of a theater that transcended the dominant European tradition of psychologizing drama. Each found exemplary models in the East Asian theater: Artaud in Balinese theater, Brecht in Chinese theater—which he came to know firsthand through the performances of a Chinese troupe in Moscow and Berlin—and Japanese Noh theater. Noh theater was one of the models for his *Lehrstücke* (instructive pieces), the most radical avant-garde form of Brechtian theater.

Like Artaud, Brecht found in East Asian theater the element central to his own concept of theater: the gestural body replacing the psychological character as constitutive figure and force. The gestural body implies the externalization of dramatic and psychological interiority; yet it is not a return to a fiction of a natural body. The theatrical and gestural body is artistic and artificial, its movements and gestures highly stylized and even ritualized. Theater, says Brecht, should be "spiritual, ceremonial, ritual." It is constituted through a body that speaks, but its language and grammar are gestural, not verbal. The gestures that speak are not the expressions of an individual, but choreographic responses to other gestures in a topographical space where the identity of the figures is determined by their position in a field of forces. This language and grammar of Brecht's theater still remains to be deciphered and read—and perhaps still to be performed in a theater to come.

See also 1670 (Grimmelshausen), 1792, 1808, 1828 (Winter), 1848 (February), 1928, 1936 (February 27), 1940, 1967

Bibliography: Bertolt Brecht, Gesammelte Werke (Frankfurt am Main: Suhrkamp, 1967). ———, Große kommentierte Berliner und Frankfurter Ausgabe (Berlin: Aufbau, and Frankfurt am Main: Suhrkamp, 1989). Klaus-Detlef Müller, ed., Brechts Mutter Courage und ihre Kinder (Frankfurt am Main: Suhrkamp, 1982).

Rainer Nägele

1949, October 7
The German Democratic Republic is founded

Socialist Realism as Heroic Antifascism

The year 1949, when the German Democratic Republic was founded, was also the year when several landmark works by communist writers appeared. Anna Seghers published an epic novel on German history covering the period from 1918 to 1944, Die Toten bleiben jung (The Dead Stay Young); Willi Bredel published the second volume of a trilogy, Verwandte und Bekannte (Relatives and Acquaintances), that starts with the Paris Commune in 1871 and ends with the construction of a new Germany in 1948; and Stephan Hermlin published his reportage "Hier liegen die Gesetzgeber" (Here Lie the Lawmakers) and the story "Zeit der Gemeinsamkeit" (The Time of Communality), both dealing with the Warsaw Ghetto uprising and Daniel Rapoport's monument commemorating the uprising. These texts were part and parcel of the construction of East Germany's discourse on antifascism, a discourse that gave prominence to the Communist Party's resistance to National Socialism and presented the GDR as the legitimate heir of this resistance.

Die Toten bleiben jung and Verwandte und Bekannte, which focus on the heroic struggle and death of (communist) fathers and sons, eventually became the new state's foundational novels, while Hermlin's narrative about the Jewish communist resistance, presented in equally glorifying terms, ultimately receded into the background. The GDR's official discourse aimed to erase the memory of the Nazis' Jewish victims. In 1949, however, the terms of official discourse were not yet firmly settled. Shocking, often personal memories of the Nazi genocide still haunted the party's Jewish members, returning at this time from exile or from the Nazi camps. For literature and film in the GDR, the memory of what is now called the Holocaust and its victims remained a contested topic, despite the communist government's many attempts to silence that memory.

Seghers, Bredel, and Hermlin, who were active members of the German Communist Party (KPD) before 1933, had recently returned from exile. Both

Bredel (1901–1964) and Seghers (the pseudonym of Netty Reiling, later Netty Radvanyi, 1900–1983) had joined the KPD in the 1920s, and left Germany in 1933; they were also members of the KPD's Union of Proletarian Revolutionary Writers (BPRS). Hermlin (the pseudonym of Rudolf Leder, 1915–1998), like Seghers from a Jewish family, joined the youth organization of the Communist Party in 1931, and left Germany in 1936. While Bredel returned from Moscow to Berlin in 1945, Seghers came from Mexico to Germany in 1947; Hermlin returned from Switzerland to West Germany in 1945 and moved to the Soviet-occupied sector of Berlin in 1947.

The formation of the GDR in October 1949 took place in the landscape of the cold war. With the Berlin blockade in 1947–48 by the Soviets, a period of political and cultural openness, including cooperation across the borders of the Eastern and Western zones, had come to an abrupt end. The establishment of two German states in the fall of 1949 was an after-effect of this first cold war confrontation which reached its climax in the 1950s, when Stalinism came to permeate the political culture of the East and opposition to communism came to characterize the West. In the eastern part of Germany, that is, the Soviet zone, the leadership of the Sozialistische Einheitspartei Deutschlands (SED; Socialist Unity Party of Germany, which had resulted from a merger in 1946 of the Communist and Social Democratic parties) had already taken decisive steps toward abandoning its immediate postwar program of an "antifascist democratic state" in favor of a Soviet-style society with the SED as the leading party. This transition affected not only the politics of East Germany but its culture as well.

In the realm of politics, the transition involved abandoning the idea of a "special German path to socialism" initially advocated by the SED. Its founding manifesto of June 11, 1945, declared that its goal was not a "Soviet Germany," but an antifascist, democratic government with all rights and liberties of a parliamentary democracy. This idea was soon abandoned, however, and in 1952, Walter Ulbricht triumphantly announced the construction of socialism on German soil. The cold war and the presence of a Soviet occupying force guaranteed the dominance of the Moscow exiles over the so-called Western exiles. The exiles returning from France, the United States, and Mexico had supported the original postwar program of democratic antifascism; many of them were eventually excluded from the party in the purges of the 1950s. Nonetheless, the conflict between Eastern and Western exiles continued to resurface throughout the 1950s and '60s.

The communist government's stance toward the victims of the Holocaust played a central role in these conflicts. From the beginning, the SED leadership tried to silence party members who emphasized Nazi anti-Semitism and its catastrophic effects. This repression culminated in the mid-1950s in the trial of Paul Merker, a party member who raised the issue of reparations for Hitler's Jewish victims (Herf, 91ff, 106–161). The history of the "Day of the Victims of Fascism," celebrated every year on the second Sunday in September, demonstrates most clearly the SED's ambivalence toward its Jewish members

(Bodemann, 101). In the 1980s, the SED began to institute more public commemorations in response to both West Germany's increasing commemorative activities and the growing interest in the Shoah (the Hebrew term for the genocide) among GDR intellectuals.

In the realm of cultural politics, the tensions caused by the gradual formation of a separate communist state surfaced in discussions of socialist realism versus Western modernism. The Kulturbund, founded in 1945 in all occupied zones by Johannes R. Becher, another Moscow exile, had been associated with the project of "democratic antifascism." Becher's organization, which attempted to assemble the broadest possible spectrum of authors and public intellectuals—Gerhart Hauptmann, who had initially welcomed the Nazis, agreed to chair the organization—did not survive in the atmosphere of the cold war. In 1951, the SED leadership joined Shdanov's infamous campaign against Western formalism and published a manifesto entitled "Against Formalism and Western Decadence." "Socialist realism" or realism *tout court* was defined ex negativo in opposition to "modernism," while Western modernism was defined in opposition to realism—on both sides of the divide.

This reductionist dichotomy dominated scholarship in East and West Germany alike. Yet the cold war paradigm obscures the complexity of actual cultural production in the GDR. No public figure embodied the contradictions that marked the SED's cultural politics and cultural production in the GDR more strikingly than Anna Seghers, who was elected president of the GDR's Writers' Union in 1952. In this public function, Seghers represented the GDR as a German Jew who had returned to the "better Germany" as a committed communist writer with a bourgeois background and as an author steeped in both European elite and proletarian culture. Seghers published not only a series of monumental novels about the new socialist society in the East, but also literary works deeply indebted to European modernism.

Between the second half of the 1940s and the late 1950s, an official discourse of heroic antifascism gradually emerged in the GDR. Literature played a crucial part in the elaboration of this discourse through narratives that provided the foundation for its symbolic politics and helped to construct a new order of values and beliefs. Deploying the metaphor of paternity, the communists developed a master narrative revolving around the antifascist father. Bredel's *Verwandte und Bekannte* and Seghers's *Die Toten bleiben jung* both contain such heroic father figures. These novels depict the resistance to Hitler's regime as the political legacy of communist fathers to their communist sons. The father figures are characterized by heroic masculinity in their courageous fight against Nazism, and their eventual tragic deaths. Starting with the serialization of novels in the very first newspapers published in 1945, such literature was widely disseminated and made obligatory reading in schools. Seghers's and Bredel's novels, for instance, narrate the pre-history of the GDR by constructing the antifascist father's sublime body as a site of identification (Hell, 32–34). Unheroic and peripheral are the Nazis' Jewish victims.

The SED leadership's efforts to silence discussions about the Holocaust intersected with the ideological commitment of Jewish communists, like Seghers and Hermlin, to a reductive Marxist interpretation. In this view, Nazi anti-Semitism was merely an attempt to find scapegoats on whom to blame the crisis of capitalism. Anti-Semitism became an issue of secondary importance and the story of Holocaust victims was relegated to the margins. In *Die Toten bleiben jung,* Seghers includes only a few Jewish figures among the many characters in a vast panorama of German society between the two world wars, and in all cases, they represent different versions of the scapegoat thesis.

Similarly, Bredel portrays Jewish prisoners in his trilogy as victims in need of protection from their communist cellmates, and the excessively heroic masculinity of his communist figures contrasts sharply with his portrayal of meek Jews. Bruno Apitz's bestseller *Nackt unter Wölfen* (1958; *Naked among Wolves*), about communist inmates in Buchenwald who save a Jewish boy, also rests on this dichotomous structure contrasting heroic communists and unheroic victims.

In reality, however, the story of East German foundational narrative is not quite so clear-cut in all phases. In stark contrast to the marginalization of the Holocaust in her epic historical novel, Seghers organizes two of her earlier stories, "Ausflug der toten Mädchen" and "Post ins Gelobte Land" ("Excursion of the Dead Girls" and "Mail to the Promised Land," both written in 1943–44 and published in 1946 in New York), around the loss of the Jewish mother. Here, the traumatic evocation of loss unsettles the antifascist story and coexists uneasily with it. In the case of Seghers, Hermlin, and other Jewish communists, the repression from above encountered a repression from within that was the result of their own traumatic experiences. This combination of political and psychic repression produced a particularly conflicted body of literature about the past.

A comparison between Otto Gotsche's novel *Die Fahne von Kriwoj Rog* (1959; *The Flag of Kriwoj Rog*) and Stefan Hermlin's short story "Hier liegen die Gesetzgeber" elucidates the difference between the official Stalinist antifascist line, and the Jewish exiles' presentation of the German past during a period when the official antifascist discourse was not yet set in stone. In Gotsche's novel, antifascism takes the form of a story exclusively focused on the communist resistance and its heroes. In "Hier liegen die Gesetzgeber" and "Zeit der Gemeinsamkeit," Hermlin projects the heroic narrative of strong antifascist fighters and weak Jewish victims onto the story of the Warsaw Ghetto uprising.

Gotsche, a long-time party member who had been active in the communist resistance inside Nazi Germany, a celebrated working-class author, and one of the GDR's most orthodox cultural functionaries, was commissioned to write *Die Fahne von Kriwoj Rog* in 1957 to celebrate the fortieth anniversary of the Bolshevik revolution. The first excerpts of the novel appeared in 1959 with an introduction by Christa Wolf in *Neue deutsche Literatur (New German Literature).* This novel tells the story of a Mansfeld miners' family who hide a flag from the Nazis that had been given to the miners by their Soviet comrades. In several extremely brutal scenes, the novel describes an antifascist father's heroic suffering at the hands of the Gestapo and his refusal to give up the flag even under the most excruciating torture. Nowhere does Gotsche's novel even allude to the Shoah, to anti-Semitism, or to the Nazis' Jewish victims. Rather, it asserts that the victims of National Socialism, and its opponents, were all German communists.

Hermlin's "Hier liegen die Gesetzgeber" comes to a similar conclusion about the Nazi past. Yet, in building his argument, Hermlin engages the memory of Jewish suffering, framing the Warsaw Ghetto uprising of April 1943 as the fearless revolt of young Jewish communists and left-wing Zionists. According to the narrator, the Warsaw monument's inscription "To the Jewish People—Its Heroes and Martyrs" marks it as both a monument of mourning and a message from the dead to the living. This message is a call to communist reconstruction of postwar Europe. "Hier liegen die Gesetzgeber" thus established a communist Jewish legacy. The narrator remarks that the insurgents remembered "an old tradition of their very old people: its heroism." In doing so, "Hier liegen die Gesetzgeber" celebrates a heroic version of Jewish history. The other side of this heroic resistance is passivity. As he walks around the monument, the narrator juxtaposes passive religious and active political Jews. The bas-relief on the reverse side of the monument, depicting "the line of people . . . walking toward their death," represents the supposed passivity of the religious Jews; the "last defenders of the ghetto" on the front panel, grouped around their young leader, "his beautiful face, ready for death, turned toward the enemy" (99), represent Jewish resistance.

The narrator of "Hier liegen die Gesetzgeber" is suspended between his desire to participate in the act of reconstruction and his desire to mourn the dead, and, ultimately, to become one of them. Melancholia, the "illness of mourning" (Torok, 107), finds expression in the topography of emptiness that permeates the text. The square around the monument, the narrator observes, is empty, "a monstrous, dead terrain" (101). A similar tension characterizes "Zeit der Gemeinsamkeit." While the frame employs a narrator reflecting on his visit to the ruined site of the former ghetto, the inset story revolves around the rebellion's young leader. The clash between the elegiac frame and the story's dramatic tale is strikingly raw.

This formal disparity springs from tensions produced in the encounter between the exiles' discourse on antifascism and the traumatic reality of the Shoah. In the immediate postwar years, there was room for a discourse on antifascism that tried to come to terms with the reality of the Shoah, albeit in a rather problematic and conflicted way. As the Nazis' Jewish victims disappeared from official memory in the 1950s, the voices that mourned them also fell silent. In the context of heroic antifascism, the memory of the victims of Nazi genocide proved to be most intractable. The tensions that arose from this conflict opened ruptures in even the most orthodox texts of this period. Far from constituting "closed" realist narratives, the heroic antifascism of Socialist Realism inevitably took a modern shape.

See also 1940, 1968, 1976

Bibliography: Bruno Apitz, *Nackt unter Wölfen* (Halle: Mitteldeutscher Verlag, 1958). Willi Bredel, *Verwandte und Bekannte* (Dortmund: Weltkreis Verlag, 1981). Otto Gotsche, *Die Fahne von Kriwoj Rog* (Halle: Mitteldeutscher Verlag, 1959). Julia Hell, *Post-Fascist Fantasies: History, Psychoanalysis, and East German Literature* (Durham, N.C.: Duke University Press, 1997). Jeffrey Herf, *Divided Memory: The Nazi Past in the Two Germanys* (Cambridge, Mass.: Harvard University Press, 1997). Stephan Hermlin, "Hier liegen die Gesetzgeber," in *Stephan Hermlin: Äußerungen 1944–1982,* ed. Ulrich Dietzel (Berlin: Aufbau-Verlag, 1983), 99–104. ———, "Zeit der Gemeinsamkeit," in *Erzählungen* (Berlin: Aufbau-Verlag, 1970), 135–204. Anna Seghers, *Der Ausflug der toten Mädchen: Erzählungen* (Darmstadt and Neuwied: Luchterhand Verlag, 1989). ———, "Post ins gelobte Land," in *Erzählungen (I): Auswahl, 1926–1946* (Darmstadt and Neuwied: Luchterhand Verlag, 1977). ———, *Die Toten bleiben jung* (Darmstadt and Neuwied: Luchterhand Verlag, 1981). Maria Torok, "The Illness of Mourning and the Fantasy of the Exquisite Corpse," in Nicolas Abraham and Maria Torok, *The Shell and the Kernel,* vol. 1 (Chicago: University of Chicago Press, 1994), ed. and trans. Nicolas T. Rand, 107–124. James Young, *The Texture of Memory: Holocaust Memorials and Meaning* (New Haven, Conn.: Yale University Press, 1993).

Julia Hell

1952, Spring

Heinrich Böll makes a plea for "rubble literature," then documents its decline

Making History Visible

In the spring of 1952, at the ninetieth session of the "Wednesday Discussion" series founded by the bookseller Gerhard Ludwig, Heinrich Böll (1917–1985) addressed audiences in the third-class waiting hall of the Cologne central train station. His speech, "Bekenntnis zur Trümmerliteratur" (Declaration of Loyalty to Rubble Literature), laid claim to the critical designation of "rubble literature" and defended its emphasis on everyday existence in the aftermath of the Second World War. Rejecting the approach of the "blind-man's-bluff" writer who "looks inward" to "construct a world for himself," Böll insisted that the contemporary author must confront his real surroundings and record them truthfully. This perspective entailed a vision that could see even those things that had not yet "surfaced in the optical realm"—what Böll, in a later essay on fellow rubble author Wolfgang Borchert, dubbed a writer's "X-ray gaze." Only thus could literature contribute to the necessary healing process of a wounded postwar Germany. As Böll reflected, the nation's destruction was not simply external. The writer's work must bring to light its internal ravages, laying bare the social and cultural impact of Nazism and the war. History had to be made visible.

The location of the literary gathering was particularly appropriate to Böll's message. The waiting hall served as a way station for the kind of ordinary people who populate his writings. An audience of passersby in 1952 would have easily recalled earlier encounters with trains overflowing with returning soldiers and refugees—the very scenes that the authors of rubble literature assiduously recorded. Böll himself had captured these images in two previous postwar novels, *Der Zug war pünktlich* (1949; *The Train Was On Time*) and *Wo warst du, Adam?* (1951; *And Where Were You, Adam?*). As the primary mode of transportation in postwar Germany, the train—and thus the railroad station—served not only as a real means of relocation, but also as a symbolic marker of the nation's movement away from the past and into a new, albeit unclear, future. The site of the Wednesday Discussions suggested that literature too had to move along the path to national recovery.

By 1952, however, the social and political landscape already looked very different than it had in 1945, and the arts were changing accordingly. The vast majority of former soldiers had returned, the currency reform of 1948 had deepened the division between the two Germanys, and a building boom now supplanted the painstaking process of clearing away debris. The most marked development took place in the Federal Republic, where the "economic miracle" gave rise to a flourishing consumerism. As the physical traces of the war dissipated, many writers turned from the gritty realism of earlier postwar cultural production toward a more overtly aestheticized style less informed by political urgency than by literary tradition. Unlike Böll, these authors believed that Germany's new circumstances required a new art, aimed at a bright conception of the future rather than a dark view of the past.

In 1954, two years after paying homage to rubble literature, Böll published a novel that recorded this moment of transition, *Haus ohne Hüter* (published as *Tomorrow and Yesterday,* but meaning literally "a house without a guardian"). Written in the spare style for which Böll had become famous with short stories like "Wanderer, kommst du nach Spa . . ." (1950; Traveler, If You Come to Spa . . .), the novel bears many of the hallmarks of his previous rubble works, from its preoccupation with morally ambiguous cityscapes to the fate of returning soldiers, but it also marks a shift in Böll's writing. It is a coming-of-age story of two fatherless boys from different economic circumstances: Heinrich Brielach, whose mother scrapes together a living with help from a series of "uncles" (boyfriends); and Martin Bach, whose wealthy mother prefers to live in the past, nursing the memory of her fallen husband, the celebrated poet Raimund Bach. The story explores perspectives that largely had been absent from Böll's earlier writings, through attention to the home front, experiences of women and children, and the lives of Germany's upper classes. It also served as a platform for Böll to intervene in the heated debates about the future of German art, particularly cinema. As a self-styled cultural critic, Böll took a strong interest in the development of German film, and he published several reviews in 1952. Böll's concern with cinematic structure influenced *Haus ohne Hüter,* and its episodic arrangement and flashback structure evokes the experimental film of the time. He also had cinematic aspirations for the text, and, although no film was ever made, in 1954 an association of film distribution companies awarded Böll the top prize for a treatment he submitted that was based on the novel.

There were compelling reasons for Böll's interest in cinema. Television had yet to make inroads in the Federal Republic, and 1954 was a peak year for moviegoing, with an estimated 5,640 theaters in operation serving some 50 million viewers. Developers were once again building movie houses for mass audiences, some seating as many as 2,800. Although Hollywood had dominated the West German film scene since the end of the war, the native *Heimat* film genre—generally set in the countryside and focusing on a romantic conflict mirroring urban-rural tensions—began to offer serious competition. Yet despite the commercial success of German cinema in the 1950s, many cultural critics from the left perceived it as being in crisis. In dire tones, they argued that postwar cinema had failed to live up to its early promise and was now an utter failure—the result of emphasis on entertainment and box office returns instead of cultural enlightenment. In 1950, the writer Wolfdietrich Schnurre published the contentious pamphlet "Rettung des deutschen Films: Eine Streitschrift" (Rescue of German Cinema: A Polemic), in which he offered a "symptomatology" of a German film industry whose decline in quality was becoming increasingly "catastrophic." He accused German filmmakers of recasting "the misery of our times as a pathetic reconstruction drama," and criticized their tendency to "adopt the stereotypes of Nazi cinema, as though nothing had changed since then." Only by embracing realism, he argued, could German cinema contribute to a new culture of freedom and truthfulness.

In *Haus ohne Hüter*, Böll reenacts the tension between the immense popularity of contemporary German film and critics' assessment of it as an artistic failure. He aligns himself with Schnurre in expressing concern that the Nazi aesthetics were being perpetuated in postwar art. At the same time, Böll acknowledges the importance of cinema as the most significant public space of its age for the articulation of collective desires and fears—the place where Germans might come to terms with the past. He suggests that films help forge a national narrative, but expresses skepticism about the contributions of current cinema, which he criticizes for its investment in a systematic erasure of the past.

Böll most thoroughly develops the complex relationship of German cinema to the past through the figure of Nella Bach (mother of protagonist Martin Bach). Nella sees the world as a film, assigning meaning to her experiences according to cinematic conventions. The memories of her married life and the war are gray, fragmentary, and appear "authentic" and historical, evoking the visual and narrative motifs of early rubble films and Italian neo-Realism. Her later life, by contrast, she perceives as scripted and artificial, like the B-movie characters her many suitors seem to resemble, or the colorful, commercial travel films that increasingly overwhelm her vision and blot out the past.

Nella's first extensive film memory unfolds following a chance encounter at a gathering of literati with the man who caused her husband's death. A former lieutenant, Gäseler now works as a literary critic. Nella, wishing to escape the present and revisit the past, retreats to the ice cream parlor where she and Rai once spent many hours. As she ducks into a dark street, she leaves the "realm of bright lights" and heads for that space where she can "patch together the film, the strips that had become dreams, to thread them on the teeth of the crankshaft." The film that frames Nella's recollection of life before widowhood is dark, colored by the tension of historical as well as personal events. As she screens the past, Nella remembers not only the early moments of her relationship with Rai, but also the persecution of leftists and the Jews, the struggle for many to emigrate, and the general atmosphere of nationalism. Her film exemplifies Böll's ideal of a visible history, in which personal and public remembrance are intertwined. Böll suggests that film can provide a form of popular memory.

Nella's film fantasy continues until the celluloid negative abruptly snaps and she is jolted back to her postwar surroundings. The relationship between the present and the past appears tense, strained like the taut negative and liable to rupture at any point. Memory, like this reel that Nella repeatedly reviews, provides a fragile and imperfect record of the past, and sustains only a fleeting connection. Böll suggests that historically engaged cinema is imperiled. Nella's memory-film does not have infinite access to history, and can provide only a partial record. It cannot convey the story of the life she lost—that film, she later explains, is gathering dust on the floor in some archive. At the same time, Nella's fragmented narrative parallels the structure of the novel, providing a possible, if problematic, model for a literary practice of critical vision.

Böll sets Nella's stark film recollections against the Agfa-colored world of the *Heimat* film. When her son Martin attends a movie with the melodramatic title *Captives of the Heart,* he must first watch a series of advertisements. The narrative emphasizes the presentation's commercial nature and suggests that the film also sells a worldview. The main feature unfolds in a bucolic setting, and traces the development and resolution of a love triangle between a hunter (dressed entirely in green), his girlfriend, and a mysterious villain. Martin, bored with the familiar and sanitized story, falls asleep halfway through the picture, awaking only for the final moments. The film concludes as the happy couple—now both clad in green—reunite in a wedding chapel to the sound of twittering birds. The neat narrative closure of the film contrasts sharply with the ruptured storytelling exemplified by Nella's screen memory, while the ahistorical setting recalls the insular fantasy world of the "blind-man's-bluff" style that Böll criticized in his earlier essay. Unlike this verdant fiction, which Böll derides, Nella's film attempts both to record the central issues of her time and to engage them directly and critically.

If Nella's screen memories engage with recent national history, the literary world she encounters is more interested in creating tales of a new Germany. Former Nazis make up the scholarly circle studying her husband's writing, and they discuss the future of German lyric poetry while avoiding or glossing over the past—a practice that Nella condemns as creating "culture from cadavers." As she muses, her husband's work makes an appealing subject for any political age, because he symbolizes "a youth senselessly sacrificed, or, if one shifts the lens a bit, . . . a youth meaningfully sacrificed." Böll decries the critics' readiness to rework the past to suit the postwar period. He implicates visual representation in his attack, borrowing the image of the lens and making explicit the connection between his criticism of contemporary cinema and the politics of postwar literature. Nella's film-memory, however fragile, provides a bulwark against the systematic forgetting or "rewriting" taking place in the surrounding culture. Her private film acts as a stay against the encouragement of the outside world to move on and leave the past behind.

When Nella finally prepares to confront Rai's killer, she again experiences the encounter in cinematic terms. But now the film is second-rate, peopled with bad actors in a flat landscape—the very sort of film that Böll's contemporaries were attacking. Nella agrees to accompany Gäseler to his debut lecture, "What Can We Expect from Lyric Poetry Today?" Driving through picturesque landscapes, Nella is overwhelmed by the image of a film "without darkness, . . . without atmosphere." Nella tries without success to summon her anger, as she realizes that the man who once loomed so large in her imagination has a profile suitable only for an "advertisement." As the banal narrative continues, Nella finds herself unable to access her older screen memories. Her defense crumbles, and faced with the dull, commodified reality that Gäseler represents, she begins to lose her hold on the past. The gray, grainy film of Nella's former life gives way to the insipid and blanched-out screen narratives of the present. Cinema, Böll seems to imply, contributes to the culture of forgetting.

Film requires cover of darkness to be seen, and in a similar fashion, the more Nella is exposed to the light, the more she loses her ability to summon her memories of the past. Böll exposes the danger inherent in the seemingly innocuous commercial cinema of the 1950s, suggesting that it reduces historical specificity to a series of rote narratives and stock characters. Although he pans the film of the era for its lack of political engagement, he also uncovers a politics behind its project. For Böll, West German cinema of the 1950s threatens to crowd out the memory of the war with bland travel-brochure images, touting the glories of the reconstruction while obscuring Germany's troubled history. The memory of that past, he suggests, may soon be relegated to the archives, lost to sight.

At a moment when critics of film argued that movies might be improved if more writers participated in the filmmaking process, Böll offered up a cinematic novel. He suggests that the critical traditions of the cinema might, paradoxically, be kept alive in literature. At stake is the sustaining of a national narrative that addresses and accepts responsibility for the past. Nella's shadow-filled memories of the war represent a counterfilm and a rejection of the prevailing 1950s cinematic aesthetic, and prefigure the work of the New German Cinema in the 1960s and 70s, which attempted to bring the national past back to light.

Böll remained a politically engaged author until his death in 1985, and maintained an avid interest in the intersections of literature, politics, and the visual arts. In his later work, he repeatedly returned to the central themes of *Haus ohne Hüter,* writing about the German relationship to the past, the cultural significance of visual media, the disintegration of the traditional family, and the reconstruction of the nation. In his 1959 "family novel" *Billard um halb zehn (Billiards at Half-past Nine),* for example, architecture replaces cinema as the central metaphor for the concrete traces of Germany's past. Throughout his career, Böll stayed true to the project set forth in his first essay on rubble literature, addressing multiple levels of signification in an effort to represent the full complexity of a historical moment. Only thus could history become visible and the German past emerge as an object for serious reflection, only thus could the nation's deepest wounds begin to heal. In 1972, in recognition of this lifelong effort, Heinrich Böll was awarded the Nobel Prize for Literature, "for his writing which through its combination of a broad perspective on his time and a sensitive skill in characterization has contributed to a renewal of German literature."

See also 1946 (April), 1952 (Autumn), 1953 (March), 1984

Bibliography: Heinrich Böll, *Romane und Erzählungen,* ed. Bernd Balzer (Cologne: Kiepenheuer & Witsch, 1987). ———, *Schriften und Reden* (Munich: Deutscher Taschenbuch Verlag, 1985). ———, *Tomorrow and Yesterday* (New York: Criterion Books, 1957). Viktor Böll and Markus Schäfer, *Fortschreibung: Bibliographie zum Werk Heinrich Bölls* (Cologne: Kiepenheuer & Witsch, 1997). Heide Fehrenbach, *Cinema in Democratizing Germany: Reconstructing National Identity after Hitler* (Chapel Hill: University of North Carolina Press, 1995). Wolfgang Schivelbusch, *In a Cold Crater: Culture and Intellectual Life in Berlin, 1945–1948,* trans. Kelly Barry (Berkeley: University of California Press, 1998). Wolfdietrich Schnurre, *Rettung des deutschen Films: Eine Streitschrift* (Stuttgart: Deutsche Verlags-Anstalt, 1950).

Jennifer M. Kapczynski

1952, Autumn
Mohn und Gedächtnis, Paul Celan's first authorized collection of poetry, is published

Poetry after Auschwitz

Paul Celan's *Mohn und Gedächtnis (Poppy and Recollection),* published in autumn 1952 in Stuttgart by Deutsche Verlags-Anstalt, is the first collection of poems for which their author took official responsibility. An earlier collection, *Der Sand aus den Urnen (Sand from the Urns),* published in Vienna in 1948, was taken out of circulation almost immediately at Celan's request, presumably because of numerous printer's errors. A more important reason, however, was no doubt that the poems of his youth in the volume no longer satisfied him. Paul Celan, then twenty-eight years old, had recently left Vienna, after a six-month stay, for Paris, where he lived until 1970 when he ended his life by throwing himself into the Seine River. Upon his arrival in Paris, he wrote to distant relatives in Israel: "Nothing in the world can make a poet stop writing poetry, even if he is Jewish and the language of his poems is German."

Paul Celan, whose real name was Paul Antschel, was born in 1920 in Czernowitz, capital of the Bukovina, a border province of the Austro-Hungarian Empire until 1919 when it became part of Rumania with the Treaty of St. Germain. The language of the Jews in the Bukovina was German, and Ger-

man culture was what Paul Antschel breathed throughout his childhood and
adolescence. His first poems, written between 1938 and 1944 and gathered
in the first part of *Der Sand aus den Urnen,* show the influence of Baudelaire
and the French symbolists as well as German poets of the early 20th century,
such as Stefan George and above all Rilke. In 1940, the Red Army invaded
Czernowitz; a year later it was forced to retreat before victorious German
troops. A ghetto was set up in the Jewish quarter of the city, and the Germans' Rumanian allies began to deport the Jewish population to camps in
Transniestria, between the Dniester and Bug rivers. Paul Antschel's parents
were among those deported in July 1942. They were murdered in the winter
of the same year. Paul was sent to a Rumanian work camp where he spent a
year and a half, until February 1944, excavating stones and building roads—
hence, no doubt, the recurrence in his works of the theme of stone and the
metaphor of digging. The murder of his parents and, beyond his own personal
tragedy, the extermination of the Jews during World War II, serve as the traumatic background of his poetic oeuvre as a whole.

Paul Antschel returned to Czernowitz in February 1944, then again occupied by Soviet troops. He settled in Bucharest in April 1945, where he wrote a
series of poems employing the symbolist themes of nostalgia and exoticism,
yet influenced by surrealist techniques of unlikely associations of images and
sudden ruptures of tone. Celan's decision to include some of these poems in
the first part of *Mohn und Gedächtnis* was probably intended to contrast another series of poems, also composed in Bucharest, in which he evoked the
concentration camps for the first time, his mother's death, and the wound
within him that would never heal. It was also in Bucharest that the famous
"Todesfuge" (Death Fugue) was published in Rumanian translation in 1947; it
had been written in 1944 or 1945, and was now signed with the poet's new
name: Paul Celan.

Among the texts Celan wrote in Vienna, a group of poems marked by a
completely new style stand out. They are a series of love poems in which the
poet addresses a woman directly, thus inaugurating the dialogic form that came
to distinguish his entire oeuvre. In these love poems, Celan also renounced
post-symbolist rhetoric and the conventional imagery that had characterized
the poems of his youth. Instead he adopted a direct evocation of situations and
emotions anchored in reality. Critics have long wondered whether these poems correspond to actual experiences or whether they are a revival, in a new
poetic language, of a traditional theme in European lyricism. Only in 1997 did
the poet and literary critic Christine Koschel discover, in the Celan archives in
Marbach, Germany, the copy of *Mohn und Gedächtnis* Celan had given in 1952
to his friend the Austrian poet Ingeborg Bachmann; twenty-two poems (these
very love poems) were accompanied by the handwritten dedication "f.D."
(meaning "für Dich"—"for you"). Thus the mystery concerning the level of
reality of these poems, as well as the identity of their addressee, was resolved. It
had been known that Paul Celan had met Ingeborg Bachmann, who was then
twenty-two, shortly after he arrived in Vienna, and that they had a passionate

relationship. When Celan left Vienna for Paris, their contact remained unbroken, and Bachmann even visited Celan in Paris in 1950. The two poets continued to correspond until 1961. Even after that, Bachmann, who had in the meantime become one of the most famous poets writing in German, persisted in evoking, in both her fiction and theoretical texts, the figure of Paul Celan and her fascination with him.

Only with the discovery of the coded presence of Ingeborg Bachmann in the love poems of *Mohn und Gedächtnis* did the dominant theme of this work become clear: the tension between the opposing poles of memory and forgetting. To be sure, this duality appears in the book's very title, but for most readers it spoke of a traditional literary topos, that of the poet who, like Orpheus, must first descend into the kingdom of the dead to draw the past from the shadows where it lies buried. Moreover, the extreme musicality of the language, the richness of images, and the harmonious integration of diverse elements of poetic discourse—beyond the deliberate dissonances and carefully calculated ruptures of tone—give the poems of *Mohn and Gedächtnis* a melodious charm that has long masked the tragedy and sadness expressed in them. The two inspirations alternating throughout the collection—a poetics of memory, suffering, and sadness, and a poetics of love, appeasement, and hope—seek reconciliation, but, in the end, their divergence seems impossible to bridge. While the first love poems, dating from the Vienna period, speak of an internal liberation and the promise of a new life, as at the end of "Erinnerung an Frankreich" (Memory of France)—"Wir waren tot und konnten atmen" (We were dead and were able to breathe)—the last poem in the collection, "Zähle die Mandeln" (Count the Almonds), closes with the disenchanted appeal of the poetic subject to the woman he addresses: "Mach mich bitter. / Zähle mich zu den Mandeln" (Make me bitter. / Count me among the almonds).

This ambivalence of joy and sorrow, of forgetting and memory no doubt crystallized in Paul Celan's and Ingeborg Bachmann's love affair: "Wir lieben einander wie Mohn und Gedächtnis" (We love each other like poppy and recollection), proclaims the central verse of the poem "Corona." Beyond the vertigo of amorous feelings, dialogue between the Jewish poet who miraculously escaped extermination and the young Austrian woman who had grown up in a country dominated by Nazi ideology could only have been difficult, tense, and fraught with misunderstandings. Yet this ambiguity itself also reflects Paul Celan's internal split, as he was torn between desire to relearn how to live and the marks, still fresh within him, left by the personal and collective catastrophe he had experienced. In reality, the very question at the heart of *Mohn und Gedächtnis* was played out in the relationship between the two poets: is it still possible to write poetry after Auschwitz? This question, posed by Theodor W. Adorno in an essay published three years after *Mohn und Gedächtnis,* had for Celan but one answer: there was no other solution for him but to continue writing. Six years after publication of his book, in his "Bremen Prize Speech," Celan explained why the German language, although profoundly corrupted by the Nazi regime's use of it, had remained his medium of self-expression:

> Reachable, near and not lost, there remained amid the losses this one thing: language. It, the language, remained, not lost, yes in spite of everything. But it had to pass through its own answerlessness, pass through frightful muting, pass through the thousand darknesses of deathbringing speech. It passed through and gave back no words for that which happened; yet it passed through this happening. Passed through and could come to light again, 'enriched' by all this.

Celan's poetic work bears witness to an endless process of calling the German language into question—worked, decomposed, mined from within—to make it able to express "its own answerlessness," its "frightful muting," "the thousand darknesses of deathbringing speech." In *Mohn und Gedächtnis,* however, this process had not yet begun; its poetic language is still traditional, marked by the search for a new harmony that, beyond the influence of post-Symbolism and Surrealism, tends toward the creation of a form of "modern beauty." Indeed, the brilliance of its poetic language is what won *Mohn und Gedächtnis* instant success with German critics, who believed they discerned in these poems the desire of a Jewish poet and survivor to transcend mourning and suffering and somehow sublimate past horrors with the magic of poetry. Thus the critic Hans Egon Holthusen interpreted "Todesfuge" as "a flight beyond the chambers of history and their horrors . . . to ascend toward the ether of pure poetry." Reception in Germany of *Mohn und Gedächtnis,* and particularly of "Todesfuge," was characterized until the 1960s by the tendency, voiced by critics who had lived during the Nazi regime, to propose an aestheticizing reading of Celan's poetry, not wishing to acknowledge its continual reference to external reality, and especially to the reality of history.

The collection *Mohn und Gedächtnis,* which numbers fifty-six poems, is divided into four parts: the first takes the title of Celan's first book, *Der Sand aus den Urnen (Sand from the Urns),* and contains twenty-three poems from that first collection with two new poems, "Chanson einer Dame im Schatten" (Chanson of a Lady in the Shade) and "Spät und Tief" (Late and Deep). The second part consists entirely of the poem "Todesfuge"; its prominence in the structure of the collection proves just how important this poem was for Celan. The third part, entitled "Gegenlicht" (Counterlight), comprises seventeen poems, one of which, "Auf Reisen" (On a Journey), is taken from *Der Sand aus den Urnen;* the others were probably composed in Paris, as were the thirteen poems of the last section, entitled "Halme der Nacht" (Stalks of Night).

Three distinct thematic units can be discerned in this collection. The earliest poems, dating from the Bucharest period and some from Vienna and contained in the first part, still evoke, in the style of Stefan George, scenes of an ancient warring civilization with the conventional accessories: lances, swords, banquets, amphorae, standards, and banners. A second thematic group are the love poems, the earliest of which date from Vienna, the others from Paris with the recurrent motifs of night, sleep, a mirror, a window, a door, eyes, hair, a rose, wine. Other love poems refer directly to nature—to trees and flowers, water and fire, the sun and stars. One of the central themes in these poems is time, as, for example, in the last section of "Corona." Contrasting with these love poems are the poems that evoke the memory of extermination, such as "Der Reisekamerad" (The Travelling Companion), "Totenhemd" (Shroud), or "Espenbaum" (Aspen Tree):

> ASPEN TREE, your leaves glance white into the dark.
> My mother's hair was never white.
>
> Dandelion, so green is the Ukraine.
> My yellow-haired mother did not come home.
>
> Rain cloud, above the well do you hover?
> My quiet mother weeps for everyone.
>
> Round star, you wind the golden loop.
> My mother's heart was ripped by lead.
>
> Oaken door, who lifted you off your hinges?
> My gentle mother cannot return.

But the central poem in this group is "Todesfuge." With its contrapuntal construction, its gripping opening, and the obsessive repetition of the metaphor of "black milk," with the evocation of the "grave in the breezes" the prisoners must dig, and its terrible phrase "Der Tod ist ein Meister aus Deutschland" (Death is a master from Germany), "Todesfuge" succeeded in accomplishing the impossible: to represent, through the medium of poetic language, what might have seemed absolutely beyond representation. Celan, however, irritated by the aestheticizing reading of his poems in Germany, stepped back more and more from this text, to the point of taking up the same theme in an infinitely more complex poetic form in "Engführung" (Stretto, or Straitening), published in 1959. "Todesfuge" has nevertheless remained, for generations of readers, the most poignant expression of the reality of the Holocaust in 20th-century literature.

After *Mohn und Gedächtnis,* the theme of the murder of the Jews became increasingly important in Celan's work. In *Sprachgitter* (1959; *Speech Grille*), the two poems that frame the collection—"Stimmen" (Voices) and "Engführung"—invoke in a coded manner, as is often the case in Celan's writing, the experience of the Shoah. This is equally true of "Gespräch im Gebirg" (Conversation in the Mountains), written in the same year. In *Die Niemandsrose* (1963; *The No-One's-Rose*), however, the Holocaust experience appears in the foreground and is much more explicit. Poems like "Es war Erde in ihnen" (There Was Earth in Them), "Die Schleuse" (The Sluice), "Chymisch" (Alchemical), "Eine Gauner- und Ganovenweise" (A Lay of Rogues and Thieves), "Radix, Matrix," "Mandorla," "Benedicta," and "Hüttenfenster" (Tabernacle Window) exemplify this development. Even in later poems, such as "Singbarer Rest" (Singable Remainder), "Fadensonnen" (Thread-Suns), or

"Die nachzustotternde Welt" (World to Be Imitated by Stuttering), the incurable wound of the Holocaust experience still haunts the texts.

See also 1808, 1897, 1922 (February), 1947, 1963, 2001

Bibliography: Paul Celan, *Gesammelte Werke in fünf Bänden,* ed. Beda Allemann and Stefan Reichert, with Rudolf Bücher (Frankfurt am Main: Suhrkamp, 1983). ————, *Poems,* trans. Michael Hamburger (New York: Persea Books, 1980). Bernhard von Böschenstein and Sigrid Weigel, eds., *Ingeborg Bachmann und Paul Celan: Poetische Korrespondenzen* (Frankfurt am Main: Suhrkamp Verlag, 1997). Adrian del Caro, *The Early Poetry of Paul Celan* (Baton Rouge: Louisiana State University, 1997). Wolfgang Emmerich, *Paul Celan* (Reinbek bei Hamburg: Rowohlt, 1999). John Felstiner, *Paul Celan, Poet, Survivor, Jew* (New Haven, Conn.: Yale University Press, 1995).

Stéphane Moses

1953, March 26

The Bayerische Rundfunk broadcasts Max Frisch's radio play *Herr Biedermann und die Brandstifter*

Coming to Terms with the Past

Against the backdrop of what was called the West German *Wirtschaftswunder* (economic miracle), Bavarian Radio broadcast a play by a Swiss writer that was to resonate for some time to come. Max Frisch's *Herr Biedermann und die Brandstifter (Mr. Biedermann and the Arsonists)* achieved in an especially telling way what came to be called *Vergangenheitsbewältigung* (coming to terms with the past). It is important to realize that, although the Federal Republic had been established four years before the broadcast of the Frisch radio play, the state of war had officially been lifted only two years earlier, and the occupation statute was removed only the year before. The economic miracle and a consciousness of being haunted by the Nazi past coexisted in an uneasy tension. Frisch's (1911–1991) play, therefore, should be viewed together with a cluster of other radio plays by such authors as Günter Eich, Walter Jens, and Ingeborg Bachmann that probed such questions as how National Socialism had come about, what its implications were for the postwar period, and what might be the best means to come to grips with it culturally.

Two major points need to be highlighted in connection with this wave of socially critical productions. First, the radio plays of the years 1947 to 1968 are a special inflection of Marshall McLuhan's dictum the "medium is the message." In these works, the message is not the medium, but the repudiation of the medium, radio. In addition, they repudiate an essential part of the history of the radio play in the Weimar period that preceded the Nazi regime. For not only had radio played a crucial role in Nazi propaganda, but in the Weimar Republic it had also served as a medium for avant-garde experimentation. In trying to avoid the negative associations thus adhering to the medium, Frisch and his contemporaries in fact (re-)established what one might call the negative aesthetics of radio, which, in effect, implied a continuation of the Nazis' condemnation of the Weimar avant-garde tradition. Second, the postwar writers' deployment of the radio play placed technology and literary text from the outset in an adversarial relationship, which continues to define debates about literature and the media in Germany to this day. The acoustic characteristics of *Biedermann*—its use of fading and suppression of sound—have important implications for radio as a means in the process of coming to terms with the past.

Frisch's play investigates the moral conditions of a specific social group, the middle class, whose passivity in the face of clear signs that democracy was being undermined in the final years of the Weimar Republic made possible in the first instance—in Frisch's view—the seizure of power by the Nazis in 1933. In the play, Herr Biedermann rejects the increasingly obvious reality of his situation, the fact that the people camped out in his attic are arsonists intent on burning down the entire town of Seldwyla. Gasoline cans in the attic and the proclamation by the uninvited guests, Eisenring and Schmitz, "we are arsonists," does nothing to alert Biedermann to what is going on. Thus he becomes an accomplice, even helping to measure out the fuse and providing the matches. At no point does Biedermann admit his role in the crime. However, the play is not a psychological study of an individual alone, but of a whole social class. Frisch's critique begins with the name of the main figure: the word "Biedermann," originally meaning a man of honor, is today used only ironically to designate an uncultivated or even simple-minded person. In Frisch's play, Herr Biedermann is an average middle-class person, head of a small business, homeowner, husband, and employer of a household maid. His humanistic faith in the "good in every man" superficially justifies his passivity in dealing with the arsonists. The fictitious town of Seldwyla, known from Gottfried Keller's novellas as an idyllic location in Switzerland, represents the Weimar Republic. Since German listeners know that Seldwyla is fictitious, though it is meant to designate the historical reality of the Weimar Republic, they are placed in a position similar to Biedermann's, who turns a blind eye to the possible consequences of the presence of arsonists in his house. The listeners become part of the cast as they are forced to interact with Biedermann's account of the strange happenings in Seldwyla.

The play's action alternates throughout between two levels of time. The first level is that of the narrator, set in the fictional real time of the broadcast on March 23, 1953. The narrator, introducing himself as the "author," interviews Herr Biedermann about the conflagration of Seldwyla. The second level is an imaginary representation of Biedermann's account of the events. The play consists of eleven "announcements" and ten "scenes." In announcement 7, for instance, Biedermann tells—in the fictitious studio—how he spent the evening of the day he discovered the gasoline cans in his attic. The "author" interrupts Biedermann after a few words, demanding that the story be presented in dramatic rather than narrative form. A gong sounds, and the presentation shifts to a scenic rendering of the past. The two levels seem separated by some sort of acoustic pane of glass. The "scenes" in the play are actually flashbacks of Biedermann's memory.

This structure highlights an essential feature of 1950s radio plays. The radio audience listens to an interior rather than an exterior world. The model for the radio play of this period is not the live broadcast but a mode of self-interrogation conducted by a thinking mind.

This concept of inner space, where all action is internalized action, implies a particular choice of technical means. From this perspective, the "author's" announcements in Frisch's play replace cuts as a way of linking the individual scenes. Transitions between scenes and announcements are effected either by pauses or by fade-outs. The play has six fade-outs and one fade-in, but no cuts. In radio plays, cutting and fading are opposites: they characterize different styles and have different meanings. While the cut exhibits the materiality of the medium, the fade-out or fade-in disguises it by creating imaginary depth. Cutting suggests that something is withdrawn from the experience of the subject, while fading creates the effect of switching between two separate continuums. Sound is used here not as sound itself, but as a sign of an imaginary consciousness.

This strategy is a major element in German radio plays of the 1950s and 1960s. Coming to grips with the past figures in these works as a process of creating an imaginary inner space by repudiating the materiality of the acoustic signifier. Historians of the radio play that emerged during the remarkable boom this form experienced in postwar Germany take account of this central feature in various ways. External conditions—the destruction of most theaters and cinemas in the air raids of World War II—doubtless provided a partial reason for the 500 plays that were broadcast annually, and the 160 that appeared in print between 1945 and 1960. Significantly, West Germany led all other European countries in this prolific production. But radio plays were also an instrument for mobilizing the imagination of the audience, who would thus engage in the process of coming to terms with the Nazi past. Plays from the 1950s that were written especially for radio emphasized an aesthetics of the acoustic in which language itself stood at the very center. This type of play has aptly been termed by Margret Bloom "Hörspiel der Innerlichkeit" (radio play of inwardness), and in the work of such authors as Günter Eich it even became a hermetic text based on a highly problematic worship of the word.

Reduction of sound effects constitutes another essential feature of the postwar radio play. *Herr Biedermann und die Brandstifter* is a characteristic example. With the exception of the last announcement, noises are reduced to a small set of key sounds: doors opening, steps coming and going, the telephone ringing, water running, the sound of the wooden attic ladder being put in place. In the radio production of Ingeborg Bachmann's play *Zikaden (Cicadas),* we find a similar reduction in sound effects. The director of this version, Gert Westphal, ignored Bachmann's stage direction calling for the character Stefano to "whistle, whimper, call, and cry out"—the only direction in the entire play that calls for sounds other than words. The only acceptable sounds were those that had already acquired symbolic force. Indeed, some critics regard this reduction in sound effects as virtual proof of the literary quality of these plays. In the radio plays of inwardness, it was as if radio, as medium, had to be made to disappear. This demotion of sound is characteristically accompanied by a celebration of silence, of the telling pause, that grips the audience's imagination.

Frisch's *Biedermann* play shows the way in which the listener's imagination was mobilized. In announcement 7, the "inner stage" turns into a court scene in which the "author" questions, defends, and judges both himself and his alter ego. In this respect, *Herr Biedermann und die Brandstifter* can be understood as a gloss on Kant's chapter about conscience in the second part of the *Metaphysik der Sitten* (1797; *Metaphysics of Morals*). Kant's concept of conscience is already oriented toward drama, and the "inner stage" of the radio play can be regarded as an extension of Kant's concept of the *inneren Gerichtshof* (inner court). Exaggerating slightly, one could say that it is bad conscience that motivates inwardness to unfold in the first place and produces a form of art based on inner self-interrogation.

Yet many of these innovations in the radio play were not quite as new as they seemed. In fact, the type of radio play some theorists advocated after World War II recurred, in effect, to an aesthetic of radio developed in Nazi Germany in a decisive break with the avant-garde radio art of the Weimar period. *In 1932, Richard Kolb had published a book called Horoskop des Hörspiels (Horoscope of the Radio Play).* Kolb had been a member of the Nazi Party from the beginning, and legend had it that during the suppression of the Munich Putsch in 1923, he stood in front of Hitler to protect him from being shot. On April 19, 1933, he became director of the Bayerische Rundfunk (Bavarian Radio). Josef Goebbels owed many ideas to him, notably the conception of radio as a propaganda tool. Kolb's theory of the radio play centered on the idea of the word as a creative force which, liberated from the exterior world, would trigger an "image of the absolute" in the listener. According to this theory, radio and listener melt into "one single organism" to form an "acoustic unit," the instrument with which the National Socialists imposed their ideological synchronization on an entire population. Between 1933 and 1940, Günter Eich, whose language-centered radio plays dominated the scene after 1945, wrote several plays for radio, and he no doubt absorbed many of Kolb's ideas about the creative force of the word. In particular, Eich's postwar texts for radio betray a continuation, in some sense, of Kolb's doctrine that the action and the characters of radio plays are not in front of the listeners, but inside their heads.

The fact that the radio play became a literary genre after the war is a historical effect of a politically motivated attitude toward the relationship between art and media technology. Early plays, such as Hans Flesch's *Zauberei auf dem Sender* (1924; *Magic at the Radio Station*), set inside a radio station, and Ernst Johannsen's *Brigadevermittlung* (1929; *Brigade Communication*), which consists entirely of telephone calls, had already introduced a level of self-reflexivity to the radio drama similar to Richard Hughes's *Comedy of Danger,* which was broadcast in German translation in 1924. Orson Welles's *War of the Worlds* (1938) provided another brilliant example of a radio production reflecting on its own medium. In works of this type, the boundaries between radio play, simulated live report, or actual live report are fluid and cannot be drawn with precision.

There is, however, yet another type of German radio play that reemerged only after 1968. This is not derived from literature at all, but from film. In this type of production, the cut is paramount as in film. In the early 1930s, experiments were made with the use of film as a material for editing sound. An example is Walter Ruttmann's "radio film" *Wochenende* (1930; *Weekend*)which uses the Triergon or light sound process as its medium. The type of radio Kolb propagated so successfully severed the radio play from its connection with film and turned it into a literary subgenre.

The configuration of the relationship between literature and (media) technology in postwar Germany as oppositional is the result of a successful coming to terms with the past. Kolb's negation of the sound experiments that were central to Weimar radio art had a lasting influence on the radio play after 1945. The postwar preference for fading over cutting as a technique of shifting between scenes and levels is just one example of this tendency. Frisch's *Herr Biedermann und die Brandstifter* exemplifies this repudiation of cutting and, with it, of modernist approaches to radio as a medium. As late as 1963, the historian of radio drama Heinz Schwitzke described fade-in and fade-out as state-of-the-art techniques, even though the introduction of magnetic tape had facilitated cutting as a compositional strategy.

Rejection of the kinds of experimentation that characterized Weimar radio art persisted in the German radio plays until relatively recently. It was only with the Neues Hörspiel (New Radio Play) developed by Ernst Jandl and Friedericke Mayröcker in the 1960s that the sound poetry of an earlier avant-garde was reactivated. The phase of the word-centered radio play in the postwar era came to an end with Max Bense and Ludwig Harig's *Der Monolog der Terry Jo* (1968; *The Monologue of Terry Jo*), the prelude to several experimental works for radio, among them Paul Pörtner's *Schallspielstudien* (1970; *Sound Play Studies*). Nevertheless, owing to the carry-over of Kolb's doctrine of the "creative word" into the 1950s, its valorization of the "inner stage," and the individual probing of conscience within this imaginary framework, the notion of the radio play as part of literary history remains tied to a problematic legacy.

See also 1848 (September 12), 1935, 1962, 1963

Bibliography: Max Frisch, *Herr Biedermann und die Brandstifter,* in *Dreizehn Europäische Hörspiele,* selected by Hansjörg Schmitthenner (Munich, 1962). Max Frisch, *The Firebugs: A Morality without a Moral: A Play,* trans. Michael Bullock (New York: Hill and Wang, 1962, rpt. 1982); this is the stage version, not the radio play discussed in this entry. Margret Bloom, *Die westdeutsche Nachkriegszeit im literarischen Original-Hörspiel* (Frankfurt am Main, 1985). Martyn A. Bond, "Some Reflections on Postwar Hörspiele," *New German Studies* 4 (1976): 91–100. Mark E. Cory, "Soundplay: The Polyphonous Tradition of German Radio Art," in Douglas Kahn and Gregory Whitehead, eds., *Wireless Imagination: Sound, Radio, and the Avant-Garde* (Cambridge, Mass., 1992), 331–371. Gerhard Prager, "Das Hörspiel und die Zeichen der Zeit," in Prager, ed., *Kreidestriche ins Ungewisse: Zwölf deutsche Hörspiele nach 1945* (Darmstadt, 1960), 415–429. August Soppe, *Der Streit um das Hörspiel 1924/25: Entstehungsbedingungen eines Genres* (Berlin, 1978).

Renate Usmiani, "The Invisible Theater: The Rise of Radio Drama in Germany after 1945," *Modern Drama* 13 (1970/71): 259–269.

Bernhard Siegert

♫ 1953, April

Wittgenstein's long-awaited second work, *Philosophical Investigations,* is published

A Ladder Turns into a Fly-bottle

In the spring of 1953, the publication of Wittgenstein's second book was eagerly awaited throughout the philosophical world. There may never have been a philosophical work whose appearance was met with greater anticipation, especially in England, and nowhere more so than in Cambridge, where Wittgenstein lived, taught, and worked for most of the years of the work's gestation and composition. Various preparatory notebooks, studies, and drafts had been circulating since the mid-1930s, often clandestinely, in philosophy departments of the United States and the British Isles. The entire Anglophone philosophical community, aware of the impending arrival of *Philosophical Investigations,* knows that it has been in preparation for twenty-fours years, knows that Wittgenstein worked on it ceaselessly for twenty-two of those years (that is, ever since his return to philosophy in 1929, following a decade-long hiatus after the completion of his first book), and knows that for the last two of those years, since the philosopher's death, his translator and editors have labored tirelessly to bring the work out as soon as humanly possible. The initial publication is a bilingual German-English edition.

The task of translation itself is a formidable one. No one is more conscious than the translator—Wittgenstein's student, later a famous philosopher in her own right, Elizabeth Anscombe—of the attention the philosopher lavished on every line of his original German text. Some of the conditions under which the work came into being are themselves already the stuff of legend, such as the author's various abrupt departures, sometimes for months at a time, to isolated locations in Norway, Ireland, and elsewhere, to be alone with his thoughts, in places where he could, without the distracting presence of other people, be free to fashion and refashion each of the sentences that were to make up this book—the book that was to be his life's work.

The author's only previous work, *Tractatus Logico-Philosophicus,* is itself a philosophical classic that had given rise to an entire tradition of thought—a tradition that one knows somehow to be a central target of criticism in the later work. Though the influence of that early work had remained strong, by 1953, the unpublished later work managed to exercise a formidable underground influence, despite the absence of any formal publication or definitive expression thereof sanctioned by the author.

At one point, late in *Philosophical Investigations,* we come upon the following remark: "If a lion could talk, we could not understand him." It seemed to some that this remark might serve nicely as a motto for the subsequent reception of the work: The lion spoke, and indeed we could not understand him. Countless interpretations now abound. The later Wittgenstein is said to be a pragmatist, a realist, an antirealist, a foundationalist, an antifoundationalist, a deconstructionist, a cultural materialist, a relativist, an idealist, a solipsist, an empiricist, a critic of relativism, idealism, solipsism, and empiricism, and so on. There is no consensus regarding a proper understanding of this work. One dimension of this problem pertains to the form of the work—its "peculiar literary character." To what extent should it be taken into account in any attempt to reach such an understanding?

One need only glance at *Philosophical Investigations* to be struck by its idiosyncratic form. Those who have attempted to characterize it tend to resort to terms familiar from literary analysis—as aphoristic, fragmentary, modernist, deconstructive, ironic, and so on. The prose styles of various other authors, such as Gotthold Ephraim Lessing, Georg Christoph Lichtenberg, Karl Kraus, Otto Weininger, Oswald Spengler, or Franz Kafka, are invariably invoked for comparison and cited as ostensible influences. However, this approach fails to do justice to the peculiar combination of patience and passion, philosophical meticulousness and ethical fervor that pervades Wittgenstein's work. Karl Kraus, one of Wittgenstein's favorite authors, offers a useful point of departure for discussion of the literary dimension of Wittgenstein's prose: "There are authors in whose work form matches content not merely as clothes do the body but as the soul does the body."

To many of his expositors, Wittgenstein, like Socrates or Pythagoras, seems to call for the sort of treatment that adduces anecdotes and biographical details in an attempt to come to grips with his work. This tendency is due not so much to the way Wittgenstein lived, which indeed caused anecdotes about him to proliferate, but more to the fact that the authors of such accounts take the anecdotes and details in question to illuminate something about Wittgenstein *qua* philosopher. These expositors feel in part encouraged by remarks scattered throughout the philosopher's writings: "You cannot write anything about yourself that is more truthful than you yourself are." "Nothing is so difficult as not deceiving oneself." "If anyone is *unwilling* to descend into himself . . . he will remain superficial in his writing." "Working in philosophy . . . is really more a working on oneself." "That man will be revolutionary who can revolutionize himself." Such remarks—when one comes upon them in the middle of a broader philosophical investigation—may strike one as extraneous. They appear to testify to an ethical struggle accompanying the philosophical one. Many such remarks also attest to the fact that Wittgenstein himself took the relation between these struggles to be internal rather than merely external. By choosing this particular form, Wittgenstein sought to engender such a struggle in his readers as well, that is, to enact, and enable the reader to enact a progression of philosophical experiences that are the way stations along the road to philosophical clarity.

Here is an important parallel between Wittgenstein's early and later work: Both works set out to deepen the reader's philosophical perplexity as an essential precondition for achieving the sort of clarity to which they wish to lead. Wittgenstein wanted his earlier book, the *Tractatus,* bound together in a single volume with *Philosophical Investigations.* In the Preface to *Philosophical Investigations,* he justifies this idea, stating, "The latter could be seen in the right light only against the background of my old way of thinking." To understand why the later work took the form it did, we need to understand what Wittgenstein sought to retain and what he sought to reject of his earlier conception of philosophy.

What the two apparently discrepant halves of this volume, as originally intended, have in common is their unusual forms. Everything the author says about each one, in the prefaces and elsewhere, suggests that this peculiarity of form is not merely a matter of style—an outer layer of literary ornamentation of which the work can (and perhaps should) be divested without violence to its philosophical content. Commenting on *Tractatus*—but the point applies equally to the *Investigations*—Wittgenstein remarks in a letter to the Austrian publisher Ludwig von Ficker: "The work is strictly philosophical and at the same time literary."

Wittgenstein held Ficker, the editor of the influential Austrian literary periodical *Der Brenner,* in high regard as a discerning publisher of literary works. Knowing that he shared with Ficker an admiration for such writers as Kraus, Rainer Maria Rilke, and Georg Trakl, Wittgenstein suggested that his own work, despite its initial appearance as a mere treatise on logic, had much in common with the writing of these authors. In the same letter, Wittgenstein highlighted the reasons why Ficker should publish the *Tractatus* in a periodical devoted chiefly to literary texts.

Gottlob Frege, the father of modern mathematical logic and the philosopher whom Wittgenstein most admired and whose writings more than any other influenced his early work, was alarmed by Wittgenstein's emphasis on the literary aspect of his work. Responding to Wittgenstein's comments on form in the Preface to the *Tractatus,* Frege wrote: "The pleasure one is to have in reading your book can, therefore, not have its ground in the . . . content, but only in the form. . . . In this way the book becomes really more of an artistic than a scientific *[wissenschaftliche]* achievement; that which is said in it takes second place to how it is said." Frege intended this as an objection, but Wittgenstein did not regard it as such. For Wittgenstein, form and content were intimately related in a fully realized work of philosophy. He remained true to this view as shown in his attitude toward his later work: "Philosophie dürfte man eigentlich nur dichten" (Philosophy should be written only as literature).

Nevertheless, commentators on Wittgenstein's work still generally adopt an exegetical procedure that implicitly regards the form of the work as merely an optional decorative feature. In other words, their expository practice appears to presuppose that there is no great difficulty in prying the philosophical jewels loose from their setting. When such exegetes claim that Wittgenstein makes his points indirectly rather than directly, or that he communicates his meaning by attempting to say what he cannot say, they construe the absence of what is said to be due to an obstacle that prevents the author from expressing what he wants to be able to express. They seldom fail to pay homage to the remarkable style of both works. But to be fully entitled to the claim that Wittgenstein is a great writer, one must be able to make out how his finely crafted work serves—rather than frustrates—his philosophical ends.

Throughout his life, Wittgenstein selected works of poetry and literature—not to mention the Grimms' fairy tales and Hollywood westerns—as instances of ethical reflection. He regarded these works as exemplary achievements of both literary craft and ethical thought, as if each of these forms presupposed the other. Tolstoy's story "How Much Land Does a Man Need?" is a literary work that Wittgenstein held in particular esteem on these grounds, even though it contains virtually no overt ethical theorizing. In contrast, it was precisely those among Tolstoy's literary works that most extensively indulge in ethical remarks, such as his novel *Resurrection,* which Wittgenstein deplored most. Wittgenstein saw the ethical as contained in what is uttered or written without ever being itself that which is uttered or written. If we try to pry it loose from its life setting, it will get lost.

What is the form of the *Tractatus*? Here is Wittgenstein's description in the work itself: "My propositions serve as elucidations in the following way: anyone who understands me eventually recognizes them as nonsensical, when he has used them—as steps—to climb out through them, on them, over them. (He must, so to speak, throw away the ladder after he has climbed up it.)" The book takes the form of a ladder—a ladder we are to ascend and then throw away. This revelation comes at the conclusion of the work—in its penultimate section—and thus comprises a part of the book that Wittgenstein enjoins Ficker to read as an instance of a moment when the ethical point of the text receives comparatively immediate expression. Here, at the end of his book, Wittgenstein does not speak of the reader coming to understand the sentences contained in it; rather he speaks of the reader coming to understand him, the author of the book. We are told that the author's propositions serve as elucidations by our coming to recognize them as nonsensical. Wittgenstein does not ask his reader to grasp the thoughts which his nonsensical propositions seek to convey. One does not reach the end by arriving at the last page, but by arriving at a certain point in an activity—the point when the elucidation has served its purpose and the illusion of sense is exploded from within. The sign that we have understood the author of the work is that we can throw away the ladder on which we have ascended. This is to say, we have finished the work, and the work is finished with us, when we are able to throw away the sentences in the body of the work—sentences about "the limits of language" and the supposedly ineffable things that lie beyond them. What we need to do is allow ourselves, and our relation to our desires, to be transformed through engagement with Wittgenstein's work.

In *Philosophical Investigations,* Wittgenstein makes a similar point. Just as he emphasized that the *Tractatus* was not a "Lehrbuch" (a presentation of philosophical doctrine), he remarks in *Investigations:* "My aim is: to teach you to pass from a piece of disguised nonsense to something that is patent nonsense." This is a crucial moment of continuity in his conception of philosophical authorship as he passes from his early to his later work. It is this conception of philosophical method, as a means for effecting a transition from latent to undisguised emptiness, that is a common source of the widely different forms of the two halves of Wittgenstein's envisioned volume.

The methodological assumption underlying this conception of authorship is nicely summarized in a remark found in a 1931 manuscript by Wittgenstein: "In philosophy we are deceived by an illusion. But this—an illusion—is also something, and I must at some time place it completely and clearly before my eyes, before I can say it is only an illusion." In *Investigations,* however, he no longer seeks to place the illusion clearly before the reader's eyes by presenting him with a ladder to ascend and then throw away. Now the trope of the ladder gives way to that of the fly-bottle: "What is your aim in philosophy? To show the fly the way out of the fly-bottle." Wittgenstein comes to regard his earlier self as possessed by a false sense of freedom from philosophical bewitchment, while remaining trapped in the fly-bottle of philosophy. His primary designation, both early and late, for those debilitating forms of reflection that enslave our ability for thought and hold us intellectually captive to forms of nonsense that we mistake for sense, is "metaphysics." His primary designation for those liberating forms of reflection that enable us to overcome such forms of enslavement is "philosophy." Armed with this terminology, we can put his central later criticism of his early work as follows: His early work sought to practice a method of philosophy that had metaphysical thinking built into its very conception of philosophical method.

The more he scrutinized his earlier work, the more such moments of metaphysical insistence—moments in which a philosophical requirement is laid down—came to light. It is important to realize that, at the time when he was writing the *Tractatus,* Wittgenstein would not have regarded these metaphysical commitments as metaphysical. Hence the following thought dominates his later methods of philosophy: "The decisive moment in the [philosophical] conjuring trick [is] the very one that we thought quite innocent." Much of his later writing seeks to pinpoint the occurrence of each of these moments in his earlier writing. The earlier Wittgenstein was concerned with clarifying propositions and adopting and applying a perspicuous form of notation that would avoid "the fundamental confusions of which the whole of philosophy is full" by furnishing an absolutely clear way of expressing thoughts. To the later Wittgenstein, the very hankering for such a mode of expression appears in itself the expression of the metaphysical spirit par excellence. This profound break with his earlier thought is, nevertheless, folded into a fundamental continuity of his philosophy. Early and late, Wittgenstein sought to find a way of doing philosophy without advancing philosophical theses, which would, nevertheless, enable the reader to pass from a state of philosophical perplexity to a state of complete clarity in which philosophical problems are completely

erased. Yet, later he came to realize that his earlier method of clarification embodied an entire metaphysics of language, which illustrated that the most crucial moments in "the philosophical conjuring trick" are those that are apt to
appear as most innocent.

It turned out to be much more difficult to avoid laying down requirements
in philosophy than his earlier self had imagined. Hence, an approach to philosophical problems entirely different from his early work needed to be developed. Most of all, the later work required a different form of writing—one that
would mirror the reader's own philosophical temptation in a such a way as to
move from the trivially true to the merely apparently deep, from the ordinary
expression of thought to metaphysical assertion, from sense to nonsense, from
language at work to language on holiday.

See also 1815, 1902, 1910, 1918, 1963

Bibliography: Ludwig Wittgenstein, *Tractatus Logico-Philosophicus,* bilingual edition, trans. C. K.
Ogden (London: Routledge & Kegan Paul, 1922). ———, *Philosophical Investigations,* bilingual
edition, ed. G. E. M. Anscombe and R. Rhees, trans. G. E. M. Anscombe (Oxford, U.K.:
Blackwell, 1972). ———, *Culture and Value,* bilingual edition, ed. G. H. von Wright, trans. Peter
Winch (Oxford, U.K.: Blackwell, 1980). ———, *Briefe an Ludwig von Ficker,* ed. G. H. von
Wright (Salzburg: Otto Müller, 1969). Stanley Cavell, "Declining Decline: Wittgenstein as a
Philosopher of Culture," in *This New Yet Unapproachable America* (Albuquerque, N.M.: Living
Batch Press, 1989). Cora Diamond, *The Realistic Spirit* (Cambridge, Mass.: MIT Press, 1991).
Norman Malcolm, *Ludwig Wittgenstein: A Memoir,* 2nd ed. (Oxford, U.K.: Oxford University
Press, 1984). Ray Monk, *Ludwig Wittgenstein: The Duty of Genius* (New York: Free Press, 1990).

James Conant

♌ 1958

Günter Grass wins the Group 47 Prize for two chapters from his novel in progress, *Die Blechtrommel*

Politics and Literature

Fourteen years had passed since the defeat and collapse of the Nazi regime
when Günter Grass's novel *Die Blechtrommel (The Tin Drum)* appeared to
spectacular success in 1959. But the past still cast a dark shadow over German
life and politics. In the West, the conservative government of Konrad
Adenauer had provided the country with continuity and political stability
since the founding of the Federal Republic in 1949; yet, the chancellor was
frequently criticized by the right as well as the left. Some of his appointments
to political office often struck observers as influenced by a desire to rehabilitate former Nazis, and his decision to yield to the pressure of the Western
Powers and rearm the country was regarded by the Socialists, the university
community, and some of the churches as opening the door to a return of the
militarism that had played such a baleful role in German history, while also
making all prospects for the reunification of the country more difficult. The
currency reform of 1948 had sparked a remarkable economic recovery, but one

of the principal effects of this *Wirtschaftswunder* (economic miracle) was to blunt the memory of the past and encourage people to turn a blind eye to the activities of neo-Nazi elements and the National Democratic Party, which gained considerable strength in the 1960s. Finally, the now aged chancellor's refusal to yield to those in his party who wished him to retire in favor of a more vigorous leader spread an air of disenchantment over the country; new ideas and initiatives were postponed, and government authority suffered in consequence. Grass's novel was informed by all of these circumstances and tendencies.

Born in the Free State of Danzig in 1927, Grass witnessed the growth of National Socialism in the city after 1935 and its takeover by Germany in 1939. He served in the German army in 1944–1945, and after war's end he worked as a stonemason before studying art in Düsseldorf and becoming a practicing artist. In politics, he was a committed Social Democrat from an early age and took an active interest in the issues of the day. In the years 1954 to 1955, he played a prominent role in agitations against rearmament, a position to which he held after he became one of Germany's most famous novelists. From the beginning, he was critical of those writers who had remained silent in face of the worst Nazi outrages, as he was of those ordinary Germans who accepted anything that was described as a matter of civic duty. In January 1967, in a speech to young people in Gelsenkirchen, he recalled the words of the governor of Berlin after Prussia's defeat by Napoleon's army at Jena in 1806, "The king has lost a battle; calm is the foremost civic duty" ("Der König hat eine Bataille verloren, Ruhe ist die erste Bürgerpflicht"). Germany, he said, would never become a democracy unless its citizens abandoned their propensity for order and adopted disquiet and agitation *(Unruhe)* as their primary obligation on important issues that affected the well-being of their society. By natural inclination, Grass tended to be a disturber of the peace.

When he became a practicing artist, Grass understandably turned to Group 47, a loose association of writers who believed that social activism was a legitimate part of their calling and were generally critical of the values of their time. Fritz Raddatz tells us that in the early years of his connection with this group, Grass was so impecunious that he had to sell his drawings and lithographs to other members so he could pay for travel expenses to the meetings. He also produced self-illustrated volumes of comic verse and several short plays that aroused attention for their brutal explicitness of language and the absurdity of their themes. But he was primarily interested in writing a contemporary novel. After several failed drafts and an unfinished verse epic about a bricklayer who becomes alienated by the affluent society and chains himself to a pillar, whence he issues manifestos like a modern stylite, Grass finally succeeded. At a meeting of Group 47 in Großholzleute in 1958, Grass read two chapters of the almost finished *Blechtrommel* and was awarded the highly coveted Group 47 Prize. Publication by Luchterhand followed one year later.

Hans Magnus Enzensberger has called *Die Blechtrommel* "a *Wilhelm Meister* drummed out on tin." This is apt, since Grass's theme is essentially that of growth, on three different levels: its leading character, whose physical growth is halted in 1927, when he is three years old, and does not resume until 1945; Nazism in Danzig; and democracy in western Germany during the occupation years and the first years of the Federal Republic, a development that is viewed with some skepticism.

Grass's approach is that of the *Schelmenroman,* the picaresque novel that describes the fantastic adventures of a hero with extraordinary gifts. During most of *Blechtrommel,* Oskar Matzerath, the son of a German grocer (although he suspects that his real father may be Jan Bronsky, an official in the Polish post office), looks and behaves like a child of three. His constant companion is a tin drum, which serves as his means of communication with the outside world and also as an instrument for awakening memories. His voice is capable of breaking glass from a great distance and with formidable accuracy, a gift he uses in self-defense and as an anarchic weapon against authority. Since he is unable to adjust to a regular school routine, his formal education is limited to what he gleans from a collection of loose pages torn from Goethe's *Die Wahlverwandtschaften (Elective Affinities)* and an illustrated, highly pornographic book about Rasputin. This combination endows his reflections on life with critical rationality as well as an unconquerable prurience. Thus armed, and with a proclivity for finding himself in situations of historical significance and violent issue, Oskar witnesses and recalls the tragic events of Danzig under Nazi rule.

In the early postwar period, German novelists who dealt with Nazism found it difficult to do so without resort to a highly metaphysical and symbolic approach. This was true of Elisabeth Langgässer (*Das unerlöschliche Siegel,* 1946; and *Märkische Argonautenfahrt,* 1950) as well as Hermann Kasack (*Die Stadt hinter dem Strom,* 1947), whose books were often moving but lacked immediacy or any urgent sense of the way in which German society had been corrupted by the Nazis. This was true also of Thomas Mann, who, perhaps because he spent most of the years of the Hitler dictatorship in the United States, chose in his great novel *Doktor Faustus* (1947) to demonize the movement, with the result that, as Michael Hamburger put it, he "paid a paradoxical tribute to its perverse appeal." The writers of Group 47, by contrast, were resolved to dissolve this nimbus of mystery and fate and to present Nazism in its everyday dress. Grass was certainly the most effective in doing this. *Die Blechtrommel* contains nothing that is either heroic or diabolical about the Nazis. They are bogus strongmen, whose banal rituals and mindless brutality would have been intolerable had the German middle class been able to distinguish between the trappings and the responsibilities of power and had they not been so deferential to the shouted commands of those in uniform.

Representative of these compliant masses is Oskar's father, who is portrayed proudly piecing together his uniform, first the cap, "which he liked to wear even in fine weather with the 'storm strap' in place, scraping his skin," then the brown shirt, and finally "the shit-brown riding britches and high boots." In this array, he attends the Sunday demonstrations of the party on the Maiwiese (the same demonstration whose martial order Oskar disrupts by inspired beating of his drum in three-quarter time). The older Matzerath, Oskar tells us, was uncompromising about his attendance at these events even in the worst of weather and refused to carry an umbrella while in uniform. "Duty is duty, and schnaps is schnaps!" he said.

It was the incorrigible romanticism and the hidden resentments of people like Matzerath that made them responsive to the appeals of Nazism. And it was their confused conviction that duty has its own imperatives regardless of its object that transformed them into brutes who could convince themselves that they were doing something admirable and noble when they are—as in *Blechtrommel*—breaking up a Jewish toy-merchant's shop and defecating on his rugs or ordering the machine gunning of a group of nuns on an outing at the beach.

The Nazis were sustained, moreover, by a collective stupidity that was ready to believe in the patently impossible. In an eloquent passage that reveals his creator's anger at the established churches for encouraging this foolish faith, Oskar says:

> An entire credulous nation believed, there's faith for you, in Santa Claus. But Santa Claus was really the gasman. I believe—such is my faith—that it smells of walnuts and almonds. But it smelled of gas. . . . Credulous souls . . . believed in the only-saving gas company which symbolizes destiny with its rising and falling gas meters and staged an Advent at bargain prices. Many to be sure believed in the Christmas this Advent seemed to announce, but the sole survivors of these strenuous holidays were those for whom no almonds or walnuts were left—although everyone had supposed there would be plenty for all.

Oskar's life and adventures as an adolescent are set against a historically accurate, and sometimes remarkably circumstantial, account of the rise and fall of National Socialism in Danzig. He witnesses the first agitations of the movement, the growth of anti-Semitism and its violent eruption in November 1938, the Nazi assault on the Polish post office which ended with the conquest of the city and touched off the war against Poland, the impact of the Second World War on the populace, and the Russian bombardment and occupation. Oskar's involvement in these events is often accidental and generally accompanied by the death of people close to him, for which he bears varying degrees of responsibility. Sigismund Markus, the supplier of his drums, dies in his shop on *Reichskristallnacht;* Oskar's Polish uncle, who is probably his real father, doing him a service, becomes involved against his will in the defense of the Polish post office and is shot by the Nazis after its surrender; during Oskar's visit to the Atlantic Wall, his diminutive sweetheart is killed by a bomb at the beginning of the Allied invasion when she goes to get a cup of coffee that he has refused to fetch; a youth gang called the Dusters, of which he becomes the leader during the disintegration of Nazi Danzig, is betrayed to the police, and all of its members, except for Oskar, are condemned to death; and his German father is shot by the Russians as he tries to swallow his Nazi badge and chokes because

Oskar has left its clasp undone when he handed it to him. After this last debacle, Oskar, as if driven by a compelling desire to lead a normal existence, begins
to grow again and moves with the remaining members of his family to the
West.

He works for a time as a stonemason (as Grass did himself), and later as an
artist's model and a jazz musician. However, his erotic adventures, which are as
complicated in his new existence as they were in the old, lead to his being
charged with murder and placed in an institution. On the eve of his thirtieth
birthday, he is proved innocent of the charge and released. Now of almost normal size, he is free to plan a new career. As he looks to the future, however, he
is seized by nameless foreboding and memories of sins committed in the past.

> Always somewhere behind me, the Black Witch.
> Now ahead of me, too, facing me, Black.
> Black words, black coat, black money.
> But if children sing, they sing no longer:
> Where's the Witch, black as pitch?
> Here's the black, wicked Witch.
> Ha! ha! ha!

Oskar, like his creator, is doubtful about the stability of Western society. Too
many of its citizens complain about how much healthier German society
would have been, how gloriously the arts and sciences would have flourished,
if only there had been no currency reform and everyday existence had remained what it was in the worst days of the occupation. This tendency, which
Oskar calls the "romanticism of lost opportunities," does not prevent them
from indulging in the worst excesses of an affluent society, becoming self-
absorbed and insensitive to the needs of others. For a time, Oskar is a musician
at the Onion Cellar, a nightclub where the customers pay exorbitant sums for
the right to cut up onions so they can weep again and give vent to their pent-
up feelings of guilt. Even worse is the uncertainty many people feel about the
legitimacy of the new order and the incompleteness of their mental liberation
from the old. On a midnight excursion, Oskar and a friend become involved
with two ominous-looking types in green hats, who are dragging a third man
between them and, on being challenged, confess that they are seeking a quiet
place where they can kill him. They produce an official order of execution
dated October 1939 as justification. Nothing that Oskar and his friend say
about the peace settlement and the new government can dissuade them; one
of the green hats points out that their arguments are without juridical foundation, since the peace treaty was never signed or even drawn up. "I vote for
Adenauer just the same as you do," one of them says. "But this execution order
is still valid; we've consulted the highest authorities. We are simply doing our
duty and the best thing you can do is to run along."

The reception of *Die Blechtrommel* was remarkable for the extremes of
opinion it elicited. Praise of the vitality of Grass's style, his extraordinary poetic
gifts, and the genius of his power of invention predominated, but many critics

seemed worried about his burlesque attacks on organized religion, his de-romanticized treatment of relations between the sexes and the exuberant detail with which he described them, and the savage, often sadistic, inventiveness of his prose when he was writing about things that had been held sacred by the pre-war generation.

Grass might have responded to those who decried the bluntness of his language that they were rather missing the point and forgetting the fateful role language played in creating National Socialism, propagating its doctrines, and concealing its crimes. In his novel *Hundejahre (Dog Years),* Grass launched a devastating attack on the bureaucrats, soldiers, philosophers (particularly Martin Heidegger and his followers), professors, and churchmen who manipulated and corrupted the German tongue during the Nazi period. He held the conviction that the German language had to be purged of this debasement to make it worthy of serving the new German democracy. The prose of *Die Blechtrommel,* its frankness, its explicitness, its outrageous humor, and its insistence on calling a spade a spade, marks the beginning of Grass's important contribution to the cleansing process.

See also 1500 (Eulenspiegel), 1638, 1670 (Grimmelshausen), 1831, 1943, 1946/1947, 1967

Bibliography: Günter Grass, Die Blechtrommel (Darmstadt and Neuwied: Hermann Luchterhand Verlag, 1959); The Tin Drum, trans. Ralph Manheim (New York: Random House, 1961). John Reddick, The "Danzig Trilogy" of Günter Grass (New York: Harcourt Brace Jovanovich, 1974). Hans Magnus Enzensberger, "Wilhelm Meister, auf Blech getrommelt," in Von Buch zu Buch: Günter Grass in der Kritik, ed. Gert Loschütz (Neuwied and Berlin: Luchterhand, 1965), 8–12. Michael Minden, "A Post-Realist Aesthetic: Günter Grass, 'Die Blechtrommel,'" in The German Novel in the Twentieth Century: Beyond Realism, ed. David Midgley (Edinburgh: Edinburgh University Press, 1993), 149–163. Patrick O'Neill, ed., Critical Essays on Günter Grass (Boston: G. K. Hall, 1987). Hans Dieter Zimmermann, "Günter Grass: Die Blechtrommel (1959)," in Deutsche Romane des zwanzigsten Jahrhunderts, ed. Paul Michael Lützeler (Königstein/Ts.: Athenäum, 1983), 324–339.

Gordon A. Craig

♫ 1962, February

Friedrich Dürrenmatt's *Die Physiker* abolishes tragedy at the height of the cold war

From a Tragedy of Physics to a Physics of Tragedy

For a brief shining moment in the early 1960s, Swiss playwrights dominated the German stage. Friedrich Dürrenmatt's *Die Physiker* (1962; *The Physicists*), first performed in Zurich on February 20, 1962, was the most successful play of the season, and Max Frisch's *Andorra* (1961) was a close second. The main reason for the enthusiastic reception of Dürrenmatt's play was, no doubt, its topicality. Between its conception in 1959 and the end of its first season, the United States and the Soviet Union almost went to war over Cuba, an American spy plane was shot down over Russian territory, the Berlin Wall was erected, France tested its first atom bomb, and Switzerland held a referendum on whether or not to acquire nuclear weapons. Clearly, *Die Physiker* was a play under the bomb, and audiences reacted accordingly. It also benefited from a marked change in literary taste. The postwar preference in German theater for modern classics that had been banned under the Nazis, followed by a brief predilection for the theater of the absurd, was winding down, and the reign of politically committed documentary theater was about to commence. Dürrenmatt's play appeared to bridge the gap. A comedy that piles up corpses, a police drama that turns into a paranoid display of paradoxical twists of logic and grotesque sexual-atomic slapstick, a satire that, in violation of ancient rules, precedes rather than follows the tragedy, it catered to audiences familiar with theater of the absurd. Its focus on the ethics and effects of modern science also pointed toward more politically engaged plays, such as Heinar Kipphardt's *In der Sache J. Robert Oppenheimer* (1964; *In the Matter of J. Robert Oppenheimer*). The interesting question, however, is not why the play received such a warm welcome but what underlying qualities enabled it to become one of Dürrenmatt's (1921–1990) critically most acclaimed and financially most rewarding ventures, second only to the perennially popular *Der Besuch der alten Dame* (1956; *The Visit*).

The main source of inspiration was Robert Jungk's *Heller als tausend Sonnen* (1956; *Brighter than a Thousand Suns*), a best-selling history of nuclear physics that focused on the scientists rather than the science. By retracing the gradual decline of physics into politics, Jungk provided Dürrenmatt with a background narrative that took the shape of an elegy, a chronicle of the avoidable loss of atomic innocence. It was avoidable because Jungk endorsed Werner Heisenberg's belief that in the summer of 1939 twelve people—that is, an exclusive group of top researchers including Heisenberg himself—"might still have been able, by coming to mutual agreement, to prevent the construction of atom bombs" (*Thousand Suns,* 81). But mutual distrust, opportunism, political expediency, and the takeover by the war machine conspired to turn the international scientific fraternity into—to quote Bertolt Brecht's *Galileo Galilei*— "a race of inventive dwarfs who can be hired for any purpose" (*Life of Galileo,* 109). Brecht said much the same, though he moved the pivotal year of disgrace back to 1633, when Galileo was summoned to appear before the Inquisition. Toward the end of the play, Galileo argues that a more defiant posture on his part could have resulted in a Hippocratic oath for scientists, a vow to use their knowledge exclusively for the common good. Now, however, the gap between social and scientific progress had become so pronounced that the scientists' "cry of triumph at some new achievement will be echoed by a universal cry of horror" (*Life of Galileo,* 109).

Such sentiments are absent from *Die Physiker.* No alliance of socially enlightened scientists can predetermine how their work will be used. The isolation of the physicists at Les Cerisiers—the name pays homage to Anton Chekhov's equally ineffective landed gentry secluded in its cherry orchards— stands for the inability of the gifted few to influence a constitutionally mindless world that cares little for their motives and aspirations and that treats the results of their labor "as a pimp treats a whore" (*Physicists*, 22). Dürrenmatt's "21 Points to *The Physicists*" spells out the futility of individual action: "Every attempt by an individual to resolve for himself what is the concern of everyone is doomed to fail" (*Plays and Essays*, 156). Since the effect of physics is of concern to all, no individual scientist, not even Heisenberg's group of twelve, can take care of these matters. "What concerns everyone can only be resolved by everyone" (ibid.). At first glance this may sound like a Brechtian appeal to the masses, but it actually presupposes what the play clearly rules out: a collective action that will cut through the walls of Les Cerisiers.

Neither does *Die Physiker* allow for withdrawal into the privacy or innocence of so-called pure research. "Everything that can be thought"—the megalomaniacal Mathilde von Zahnd informs her inmates—"is thought at some time or other. Now or in the future" (*Physicists*, 89). There is no exclusive ownership of ideas, no genius that guarantees a monopoly of insight; rather, there is a kind of statistical distribution that prescribes, for instance, that during the 1930s some members of a loose group of interchangeable individuals focusing their experiments on the atomic nucleus will achieve nuclear fission and some will not. The question, then, is not: who had the idea first? But: which agency is the first to get its hand on it and make it work? Furthermore, the play emphasizes the simple fact—too simple, indeed, for many philosophical discussions—that an idea becomes a social event not when it is publicized or put to use but when it is stored. Cassandra can speak the truth only under the condition that nobody will believe her; Möbius will write the truth only under the condition that, locked up in his self-imposed exile, nobody can read him. But that condition is never met: everything Möbius writes and then destroys, the mad doctor possesses in duplicate. Mechanical reproduction is the basis for Möbius's concluding insight that "what was once thought can never be unthought" (*Physicists*, 92). In Dürrenmatt's paranoid universe, there is no space that cannot be observed. Even the ivory towers that claim to observe the world are themselves closely scrutinized; and if, as in the case of Les Cerisiers, there is no outside agency looking in (in the play, the police fails to do so), the institution is bound to have its own internal observers.

These issues have made *Die Physiker* part of a group of German plays—ranging from Brecht's *Galileo* and Kipphardt's *Oppenheimer* to Carl Zuckmayer's *Das kalte Licht* (1955; *The Cold Light*)—that attempt to spell out the social, political, and ethical implications of the paradox best expressed by Kipphardt's Oppenheimer: "We, the physicists, find that we have never before been of such consequence, and that we have never before been so completely helpless" (*Oppenheimer*, 106). Most of the plays build on each other but advocate very different points of view of what scientists did, could have done, or should do. *Die Physiker*, for instance, has been labeled a direct revocation of Brecht's *Galileo*. This highly exploitable mixture of ethics and didactics, especially potent in the sequence Brecht-Dürrenmatt-Kipphardt, is a schoolmaster's dream and has done its share to earn *Die Physiker* that most indisputable mark of canonization: a guaranteed presence in German high school exams. Yet, what ultimately makes it such a compelling text is that underneath the "tragedy of physics" there lurks what may be called a "physics of tragedy."

Die Physiker strictly adheres to the Aristotelian unities of time, place, and action. "The action takes place among madmen and therefore requires a classical framework to keep it in shape" (*Physicists*, 10). This might be dismissed as one of Dürrenmatt's sarcastic asides were it not for his explanation, in his essay on "Problems of the Theater," of how these unities came about. "Greek tragedy was possible only because it did not have to invent its historical background; it already possessed one. The spectators knew the myths with which each drama dealt" (*Plays and Essays*, 236). Greek audiences were thoroughly familiar with the stories and could therefore concentrate on how they were presented and playwrights were able to perform all the feats of condensation and abbreviation, including the strict adherence to the three unities, that were later codified as poetological prescriptions. In *Die Physiker*, however, the audience knows nothing, and most of what it learns in the course of the play turns out to be wrong. Möbius may be a modern Oedipus who, knowing the danger that he poses to others, tries to avoid his fate only to end up where he should not, but the background of the story is constantly reinvented as characters and institutions keep changing their identity. Nonetheless, despite the conspicuous absence of a common framework that gave rise to tragedy, *Die Physiker* retains, indeed foregrounds in highly self-conscious fashion, that very form. Why did Dürrenmatt choose to do this?

Tragedy always required more than mere familiarity with staged events. There had to be a degree of identification that would allow dramatized events to represent the world in such a way that solutions found onstage would influence subsequent behavior offstage. By identifying with Oedipus, we learn to avoid his fate. This, however, requires a comprehensible, tangible story of hubris, guilt, and responsibility: a clearly identifiable subject has to commit clearly identifiable transgressions that result in clearly identifiable consequences, which, in turn, will (or will not) be realized, maybe even regretted by the perpetrator. Dürrenmatt, however, declares that all this no longer exists: "Tragedy presupposes guilt, despair, moderation, lucidity, vision, a sense of responsibility. In the Punch-and-Judy show of our century, in this backsliding of the white race, there are neither guilty nor responsible individuals any more. No one could do anything about it, and no one wanted to. Indeed, things happen without anyone in particular being responsible for them. Everything is dragged along and everyone gets caught somewhere in the sweep of events" (*Plays and Essays*, 254).

This passage may be mimicking the self-exculpatory rhetoric common in post–Nazi Germany, but the diagnosis is also linked to both the history and the content of modern physics. In essence, it distills the story told in Jungk's *Heller als tausend Sonnen* of how the road to Hiroshima was paved with good intentions. From the innocent days of early atomic research to the advent of the hydrogen bomb, the participants are caught up, dragged along, swept away; and try as they may to control events and predetermine the outcome of their actions, things keep happening that nobody ever wanted to happen. "Thus, the sum of a thousand individual acts of an intensely conscientious character led eventually to an act of collective abandonment of conscience, horrifying in its magnitude" (*Thousand Suns,* 209). To other writers, the modern scientist appears to be one of the last figures capable of representing the tragic: here, so it seems, is a tangible structure of hubris and nemesis, here are great men succumbing to ambitious dreams, only to be felled by powers they thought they could control.

In Dürrenmatt, the exact opposite applies: the story of modern science—with its erosion of responsibility, manipulation of intentions, and blindness for future consequences—defies the very basis for tragedy and calls instead for comedic and grotesque forms of representation which alone can do justice to the essential fuzziness of physics and politics. Guilt arising from tragic failure can, if at all, exist only "as a personal achievement, as a religious act" (*Plays and Essays,* 255). At the end of the play, Möbius/Oedipus is free to retire into his personal realization that he was unable to protect the world from his actions, but that is a purely private matter and altogether irrelevant, considering the fact that the mad Mathilde von Zahnd is about to conquer the world. The very foundation of tragedy—that the fate and the eloquent self-realization of the hero have some impact on the world—is abolished.

Finally, it is important to realize that *Die Physiker* also links the obsolescence of the tragic to the content of modern physics. While the play has little to say about any particular theory, it does appear that the relationship between play and society is similar to that between modern scientific models, especially within the realm of microphysics and reality. "The state has lost its physical reality, and just as physics can now cope with the world only in mathematical formulas, so the state can only be expressed in statistics" (*Plays and Essays,* 253). After all, tragedy had always been a somewhat Newtonian business: it presupposed a certain proportionality of cause and effect as well as a discernible clash of distinct and stable bodies with more or less predictable results, not a fuzzy, chaotic world in which microscopic causes may have unpredictable macroscopic effects and in which the appearance of particles depends on the ways in which they are observed. No wonder, then, that a world devoid of stable, clearly definable elementary particles should find its aesthetic correlative in dramatic constructs that are equally devoid of stable, clearly definable subjects. In *Die Physiker,* with its grotesque plot twists and constant surprises, the action on stage is as paradoxical and unpredictable as events in the physical and political world. If the physical structure of the world has changed so dramatically, how can the physics of tragedy remain the same? "A drama about physicists must be paradoxical" (*Plays and Essays,* 156).

This, then, is the beautiful paradox of the play: *Die Physiker* represents the fact that the political and physical worlds can no longer be represented; but it is precisely this paradoxical endeavor that compels Dürrenmatt to adhere strictly to a bygone aesthetic form. The play does not represent society in any conventional fashion since that would contradict the basic diagnosis of unrepresentability, which takes its cue from the formal apparatus of modern physics. Just as with the increasingly complex mathematical formulas of microphysics, the dramatic form of *Die Physiker* is so perfect because its referential function is so tenuous. But there is still an understanding that this procedure in itself will be able to tell the audience something about the world, that is, fulfill some representative function with limited political import. Not enough to rally the audience to challenge or change the world, because that would presuppose an understanding of how an essentially fuzzy world works and how it can be influenced with predictable results, but enough to give up old illusions of taking charge. "Drama," Dürrenmatt concludes "21 Points about *The Physicists*," "can dupe the spectator into exposing himself to reality but cannot compel him to withstand it or even master it" (*Plays and Essays*, 156).

See also 1949, 1953 (March 26), 1964

Bibliography: Friedrich Dürrenmatt, *Die Physiker: Eine Komödie in zwei Akten,* vol. 7 of 37 vols. (Zurich: Diogenes, 1998); *The Physicists,* trans. James Kirkup (New York: Grove, 1964). ———, *Plays and Essays,* ed. Volkmar Sander (New York: Continuum, 1982). Bertolt Brecht, *Life of Galileo,* trans. John Willet (London: Methuen, 1986). Robert Jungk, *Brighter than a Thousand Suns,* trans. James Cleugh (New York: Harcourt Brace Jovanovich, 1958). Heinar Kipphardt, *In the Matter of J. Robert Oppenheimer,* trans. Ruth Speirs (London: Methuen, 1967).

Geoffrey Winthrop-Young

ᒼ 1963

Ingeborg Bachmann begins writing her cycle of novels *Todesarten* against the backdrop of the Auschwitz trials

Love as Fascism

Thirty years after her untimely death, Ingeborg Bachmann (1926–1973) remains an enigmatic figure. Her life and writings are a contested legacy in postwar German literature. Championed by an older generation of writers and critics in the early 1950s, Bachmann first became known as a poet. Two collections of formally accomplished, passionate, yet austere and biting verse—*Die gestundete Zeit* (1953; *Mortgaged Time*) and *Anrufung des großen Bären* (1956; *Invocation of the Great Bear*)—made the young Austrian from Klagenfurt a media star in Germany and an instant classic for the literary establishment, a worthy heir, she was called, to Rilke, Mörike, and Hölderlin. For many of her readers, Bachmann never surpassed her early triumphs, and her turn to prose in the 1960s was seen as a betrayal of her poetic vocation and a descent into popular, even trivial literature. A more recent generation of readers, however, has interpreted this turn as Bachmann's epoch-making rejection of a patriarchal, classically oriented literary tradition. The novels and unfinished fragments collectively known as *Todesarten* (variously rendered as "Ways of Dying," "Death Styles," or "Manners of Death"), which Bachmann herself characterized as "a new manner of writing" conceived in response to "new experiences of suffering" (*Interviews*, 139), have attained almost cult status as the beginning of a new aesthetic that redefines the relationship between literature, writing, and women.

Bachmann's turn from poetry to prose—in many ways comparable to the young Hugo von Hofmannsthal's turn from lyric poetry to more socially engaged forms of drama, opera libretto, and essay—is mapped out conceptually in four lectures Bachmann gave at the University of Frankfurt in 1959–60 on the subject of "Problems of Contemporary Literature" *(Dichtung)*. A graduate in philosophy from the University of Vienna, Bachmann had already written important journalistic essays on Wittgenstein, Musil, Kafka, Proust, and other 20th-century thinkers and writers. But the Frankfurt lectures, inspired by the early, proto-structuralist work of Roland Barthes as well as the critical theories of Theodor Adorno and Walter Benjamin, offer a sustained interrogation of the problem of the modern literary self. Whether analyzing the status of the lyrical "I" or the novelist's "negotiation" of proper names, Bachmann repeatedly returns to the modernist "crisis of language" particularly evident in the Habsburg turn-of-the-century tradition she felt at home with as well as in a broad range of European writings. Many of the themes and formal aspects of *Todesarten*—the denial of a proper name to the protagonist in *Malina;* the use of musical notation; unstable or "hysterical" narrating voices; the incestuous brother-sister relationship; the search for a utopian "other realm"—can also be found in the writings of Kafka, Hofmannsthal, Musil, Beckett, and Faulkner, whom she discusses in these lectures.

And yet the Frankfurt lectures surprise by omission. Given the focus in *Todesarten* on female suffering and the Nazi past, these subjects occupy at best a marginal position in what seems to be a critical elaboration of Bachmann's own formal aesthetic development. Two events that took place a few years after the lectures and that Bachmann imaginatively linked, seem to have served as catalysts for the decisive shift. The much-publicized Auschwitz trials of Nazi officials in the years 1963 to 1965 led Bachmann to read extensively in the medical and legal literature on the Holocaust. The deterioration of her relationship with the Swiss writer Max Frisch in 1962–63 resulted in her hospitalization for depression and caused a dependence on alcohol and medication that would continue for the rest of her life (and directly contribute to her death). "The virus of crime [cannot] simply have disappeared from our world twenty years ago," she declared around 1965 in an introduction to a narrative that would become a central text in *Todesarten,* "just because murder is no longer praised, desired, decorated with medals, and promoted" (*Der Fall Franza,* 3–4). The "virus" has gone underground, become more refined and "subtle," and has thus entered the domain of the writer, who now becomes a kind of criminal-medical investigator. In the increasingly charged political atmosphere of the mid-1960s, Bachmann insists that writing helps break down the walls of silence, complicity, and taboo upon which Germany's postwar identity had been constructed. The stormy demise of Bachmann's relationship with Frisch should not be discounted as a mere biographical sensation, for nothing in her previous work approaches the vehemence and negativity with which she depicts the "fatality" of gender relations in *Todesarten*. Traumatized by what she felt was Frisch's systematic attempt to destroy her emotionally and his exploitation of their love in *Mein Name sei Gantenbein* (1964; *Let My Name Be Gantenbein*), Bachmann responded with the story of a woman's psychic destruction by her husband in *Der Fall Franza* (begun 1963, first published 1978; *The Book of Franza*), and an almost clinical description of a famous woman writer's progressive loss of voice and identity in *Malina* (1971), the two principal narratives in the *Todesarten* cycle. To be sure, references to the "severe laws of love" and to Nazi war crimes are not absent in Bachmann's poetry, radio plays, and first collection of stories, *Das dreißigste Jahr* (1961; *The Thirtieth Year*); but the way she merges both the tone and the polemic of these two themes—identifying "fascism" as the "first element in the relationship between a man and a woman" (*Interviews*, 144)—distinguish *Todesarten* from all her other writings and subsequently proves to be a key factor in the feminist reception of the "new" or "other" Bachmann.

Bachmann's relationship with Frisch had begun in 1958 and came to a difficult end early in 1963. She suffered a nervous breakdown and was hospitalized in Zurich for a while. Subsequently, she accepted an invitation from the Ford Foundation to live in Berlin where, from the spring of 1963 until November 1965, she led an isolated, even secretive existence. In this Berlin period, she began work on a book about a journey "through an illness" and the "Egyptian darkness," to which she refers in a letter of August 28, 1963, to her publisher as "Todesarten." Later she called it *The Book of Franza, The Franza Case,* or simply *Franza*. This novel begins with the mysterious disappearance of Franza Ranner from a mental institution outside Vienna, where her husband, the Viennese psychiatrist Leopold Jordan, had placed her and turned her into a clinical "case" for sadistic psychological experiments. Narrated largely from the point of view of her brother Martin, who sets out to find her and eventually undertakes a trip with her to Egypt, the novel describes Franza's futile efforts to escape the influence of her husband and recover her lost childhood self. The two key events of the story, the "journey through illness" and the "journey through Egyptian darkness," take place on several symbolic levels. The protagonist's travels correspond to an actual journey at the time of the official opening of the Aswan High Dam in 1964, for which it was necessary to flood an entire inhabited region with a history stretching back to pharaonic times. It is also a metaphorical journey through the psychic wounds inflicted on Franza by Leo Jordan, who is depicted as the "refined" peacetime equivalent of Nazi doctors who tortured concentration camp inmates. All his wives—three including Franza—have mysteriously "disappeared," victims of his cold clinical rage. Although Jordan never actually appears in the novel—his ghostliness making his psychological presence even more uncanny—Franza can never escape his deadly reach. On her journey to Egypt, she visits a doctor in whom she recognizes a former Nazi doctor and war criminal in hiding: the "Bluebeard" monsters are everywhere. Bachmann thus equates National Socialism and the "personal fascism" in the relations between man and woman.

This original, yet controversial way of intertwining the personal and the historical is somewhat reminiscent of Sylvia Plath's poem "Daddy," which is based on a similar linkage. Leo Jordan, the "vulture of the century," personifies both types of evil—Nazi inhumanity and Western patriarchal oppression—just as Franza explicitly identifies with all manner of victims during her trip to the East: Jews under the Nazis, a bound woman, the natives of Papua, and the ancient Egyptian Queen Hatshepsut.

Bachmann never completed her "Franza" novel, a version of which was first published posthumously in 1978 in the four-volume edition of her collected works. Nor did she continue two other related novels begun in the mid-1960s—*Requiem für Fanny Goldmann* and an untitled narrative about a woman named Eka Rottwitz—which also remained fragments and were published after her death. Instead, she turned to another project, *Malina,* which she came to feel was the necessary introduction or "overture" to the entire *Todesarten* cycle, and which she now conceived as a large-scale portrait of postwar Austrian society much like Joseph Roth's Habsburg novels and stories with their interwoven plots and characters. *Malina* bears little formal resemblance to Roth's essentially realist narratives, however. It is also stylistically more innovative than the other *Todesarten* texts. Unlike *The Franza Case,* which uses a third-person narrator closely allied with the brother's perspective, *Malina* adopts the unstable point of view of an unnamed woman writer whose voice alternates between anxious stammering and utopian lyricism, biting social commentary and metaphysical despair. The novel begins more like a play, with a cast of characters and a distinct place and time of action. But musical quotations from Schoenberg's *Pierrot Lunaire* and Beethoven's late string quartets, as well as musically orchestrated dialogue fragments, transform the text into a "word opera" reminiscent of Francis Poulenc's tense monodrama *La Voix humaine* (1959) or—closer to Bachmann's Austrian tradition—of Arthur Schnitzler's stream-of-consciousness novella "Fräulein Else," which also uses musical notation at the emotional high point of the narrative. Organized into three sections associated with the three men in her life—her lover Ivan, her male housemate Malina, and a ghoulish "third man" who functions as symbolic father and Nazi—the text traces the narrator's initial happiness in love, her betrayal, and the progressive silencing of her voice. In counterpoint to this grim narrative are the utopian voices of fairytale and lyrical verse ("The Princess of Kagran"), in part quoting poems by Paul Celan, with whom she had an earlier decisive personal relationship. The haunting, thriller-like conclusion to *Malina* recounts the female narrator's disappearance into a crack in the kitchen wall in her apartment, while the shadowy Malina looks on in impassive silence. "It was murder"— the novel's final sentence affirms the destruction not so much of a person as of a voice, the subtle shift from the first to the third person marking the passage from this "overture" to the actual "ways of [female] dying" that will be depicted in the *Todesarten* novels proper.

Like *The Franza Case,* which it introduces, *Malina* operates on several symbolic levels. First, the locale is the Vienna of "today," a largely recognizable postwar Vienna in which the narrator, Ivan, and Malina lead conventional bourgeois lives. Second, the narrator lives in what she calls her "Ungargassenland" ("the land of Hungarian Lane"), an intensely imagined cultural landscape encompassing such diverse texts as the poems of Paul Celan, the music of Schoenberg, and the dream theories of Freud and Jung, all woven into the story. Finally, the narrative works on a psycho-mythical level in which all three characters represent functions of the narrator's psyche. The reader's journey through the story thus corresponds to the narrator's descent into the psychic and archetypal hell of nightmare, trauma fantasies, and the collective unconscious. In the nightmare middle section, "The Third Man," a symbolic father, who cuts out his daughter's tongue and presides over an entire cemetery of "murdered daughters," is depicted as a concentration camp commandant who kills his victims with poison gas. Freudian depth psychology and Nazi inhumanity merge with the *film noir* atmosphere of postwar Vienna so brilliantly captured in Orson Welles's *The Third Man*.

One of the key, if perplexing, aspects of Bachmann's weaving together of these various levels concerns the relation between the female narrator and the relatively marginal character who gives the novel its name. "Malina"—a female name in Slavic languages, and of feminine grammatical aspect for anyone as familiar with Italian as Bachmann was—is also a near anagram of "anima," the Latin word for soul or psyche, and a crucial term in Jungian psychology. The character Malina functions as the female subject's rational *Doppelgänger*, the shadow who presumably will allow her identity and voice to continue beyond her murder as an actual character in the *Todesarten* cycle. Bachmann raised this issue of gender in an interview, admitting that one of her oldest memories was that she could narrate "only from a masculine position." In writing *Malina*, however, "it was as if I had found my own person, that is, had not denied this feminine "I" and still placed emphasis on the masculine "I" (*Interviews*, 99–100). Bachmann's death prevented her from reworking the narratives begun before *Malina*, and although she experimented with using the figure Malina as both a character in and a narrator of the other *Todesarten* stories, the cycle itself remains formally heterogeneous and fragmented. Rather than using a unified narrative voice that is both feminine and masculine, *Todesarten* speaks with a plurality of voices whose gender remains mixed and sometimes uncertain.

The five stories collected in *Simultan* (1972; *Three Paths to the Lake*), which Bachmann originally titled "Viennese Women," are sometimes considered part of the *Todesarten* cycle not only because of their focus on female experience but also because of occasional textual overlaps and the reappearance of a few characters in marginal roles. But whereas *Todesarten* insists on the tragic, ineluctable "war" between men and women, the stories in *Simultan* seek to restore lightness and charm to love relationships. Bachmann herself, writing these stories on the side during her work on the *Todesarten* narratives, considered them a diversion from and correction to her work on the darker cycle.

The problems and controversies raised by *Todesarten* continue to resonate today for Bachmann's readers. Against the formal perfection of her poetry, the easy fluency of her cultural journalism, or the measured autonomy of her short stories, the broken narratives of her novel cycle stand out as provocative and exceptional "failures"—not only because they are fragmented and unfinished, but also because they are in a deep sense unfinishable, caught up in the conundrums of narrating female subjectivity from within a patriarchal language and culture. But precisely this apparent failure is instructive, calling to mind similar examples of literary vision that foundered on the contradictions and injustices of society: Georg Büchner's unfinished drama *Woyzeck,* Kafka's three unfinished novels, and Celan's literary and personal response to the Shoah. The broken lives and unfinished writings of these authors are the "exceptional failures" against which Bachmann measured her own existence; they should also help us measure the achievement of *Todesarten.*

See also 1902, 1910, 1924, 1947, 1952 (Autumn), 1953 (March 26), 1953 (April)

Bibliography: Ingeborg Bachmann, *Werke,* 4 vols., ed. Christine Koschel, Inge von Weidenbaum, and Clemens Muenster (Munich and Zurich: Piper, 1978). ———, *"Todesarten"-Projekt: Kritische Ausgabe,* 5 vols., ed. Monika Albrecht and Dirk Göttsche (Munich and Zurich: Piper, 1995). ———, *Wir müssen wahre Sätze finden: Gespräche und Interviews [Interviews],* ed. Christine Koschel and Inge von Weidenbaum (Munich and Zurich: Piper, 1983). ———, *Malina,* trans. Philip Boehm, ed. Mark M. Anderson (New York: Holmes and Meier, 1990). ———, *The Book of Franza and Requiem for Fanny Goldmann,* trans. Peter Filkins (Evanston, Ill.: Northwestern University Press, 1999). Hans Höller, *Ingeborg Bachmann* (Reinbek bei Hamburg: Rowohlt, 1999). Sara Lennox, "The Feminist Reception of Ingeborg Bachmann," *Women in German Yearbook 8* (1993): 73–111. Sigrid Weigel, *Ingeborg Bachmann: Hinterlassenschaft unter Wahrung des Briefgeheimnisses* (Vienna: Zsolnoy, 1999).

Mark M. Anderson

1964, April 29

Peter Weiss's play *Marat / Sade* premieres in Berlin at a time of radical politics and the politicization of art

Dramaturgies of Liberation

In 1967 the German newspaper *Die Zeit* carried an article entitled "Die Verfolgung und Ermordung der Strafjustiz durch die Herren Teufel und Langhans" (The Persecution and Assassination of Penal Justice by Messrs. Teufel and Langhans), prompted by the antics, both in the streets and in court, of Fritz Teufel and Rainer Langhans, the two most prominent members of the self-styled Kommune I. This most notorious of the radical student communes that sprang up in Berlin in the 1960s gained enormous publicity by staging spectacular political happenings. The group's provocations, for which its members were hauled into court, went as far as distributing leaflets inciting arson in department stores to give the populace "an authentic Vietnam feeling." It was, therefore, wholly apposite that, in seeking to characterize the communards' subversive, theatrical spirit, *Die Zeit* should invoke the title of a play that had first been performed some three years earlier, *Die Verfolgung und Ermordung*

Jean Paul Marats dargestellt durch die Schauspielgruppe des Hospizes zu Charenton unter Anleitung des Herrn de Sade (1964; *The Persecution and Assassination of Jean Paul Marat as Performed by the Inmates of the Asylum of Charenton under the Direction of the Marquis de Sade*). Peter Weiss's *Marat/Sade* is at once a sustained debate on the politics of revolution and an artistic happening, both an attempt at political intervention and an exercise in total theater that owes as much to the shock excess of Antonin Artaud's theater of cruelty as it does to the rationalist dialectic of the dramaturgy of Bertolt Brecht.

The setting of Weiss's play is the bathhouse at the Charenton asylum on July 13, 1808, the fifteenth anniversary of the assassination of French revolutionary Jean Paul Marat. To commemorate this event, and as a form of therapy, the inmates perform a drama that is both written and produced by the Marquis de Sade, who has been interned there since 1803. Sade's play remains fairly faithful to the historical facts surrounding the assassination: it shows Charlotte Corday, a young woman who, distressed by the bloodshed of the Revolution under the Jacobins, resolves to murder Marat and goes to his house three times before gaining entry. Sade exploits this position as an onstage spectator throughout the action, to conduct an imaginary dialogue about the Revolution with his imaginary protagonist Marat. It is this philosophical debate, rather than the inner or the outer play, that constitutes the centerpiece of Weiss's drama.

Weiss later commented that what interested him in this fictional intellectual confrontation was "the conflict between an individualism carried to extreme lengths and the idea of a political and social upheaval." Moreover, his object of identification—initially, at any rate—had been Sade, in whom he recognized "a very modern figure." Like "the modern advocates of a third approach," among whom Weiss, albeit to his own displeasure, counted himself in 1964, Sade "falls between two stools," despising the corruption of the old social order but balking at the violent measures of the radical reformers ("Author's Note on the Historical Background to the Play," *Marat/Sade*, p. 113). Thus, in his dialogue with Marat, Sade concedes that "at first I saw in the revolution a chance / for a tremendous outburst of revenge / an orgy greater than all my dreams." However, this initial enthusiasm gives way to disillusionment as the revolution turns into dictatorship and leads "to the withering of the individual man / and a slow merging into uniformity / to the death of choice / to self denial / to deadly weakness / in a state / which has no contact with individuals / but which is impregnable" (*Marat/Sade*, scene 20). Sade reacts by withdrawing from the world into a cult of individualism bordering on solipsism—"I believe only in myself" (scene 18)—and takes refuge either in the fictional world of his imagination or in the private sphere of sexual gratification. His stance is one of detachment from where he can "watch what happens / without joining in / observing / noting down my observations" (scene 20), with the best he can hope for being "some light on our eternal doubt" (scene 33).

The choice of Marat, in preference to other Jacobin extremists such as

Robespierre or Saint-Just, to play the part of Sade's antagonist was no doubt influenced by the fact that he too was a writer. In contrast to Sade, however, Marat did not use writing to escape reality but to change it: "When I wrote / I always wrote with action in mind / kept sight of the fact / that writing was just a preparation" (scene 28). As such, Marat embodies the Marxian principle, elaborated in the eleventh "Thesis on Feuerbach," on the unity of theory and practice—an ideological affinity recognized by Friedrich Engels when, in an article in 1884, he praised Marat as a precursor of revolutionary socialism. In Sade's play within Weiss's play, this historic status is alluded to in the four singers' lament that Marat is a century ahead of his time; in their musical history —delivered in the "Interruptus" before Corday wields the fatal dagger—in which Marat learns to what extent his ideals have been betrayed in the fifteen years following his demise; and in the drama's final tableau, a reconstruction of Jacques-Louis David's famous portrait of the writer-revolutionary, pen and paper in hand, working actively for the cause until the moment of his death.

Weiss's fictional clash of philosophies prefigured actual ideological debates during the second half of the 1960s in which Marat's and Sade's arguments were configured in numerous variations: collectivism versus individualism, political versus personal liberation, Marxian class theory versus Reichian social psychology, sectarian dogmatism versus anti-authoritarian spontaneism, and so on. Ironically, Weiss himself reenacted the dispute when he became embroiled in an ideological spat with Hans Magnus Enzensberger over Vietnam. With Marat-like certainty, Weiss castigated the poet for his political indecisiveness and was duly rebuked in a tone redolent of his own creation, the fictional Sade: "I'm no idealist. I prefer arguments to confessions, doubts to emotions. I hate revolutionary chatter and I don't need ideologies free of contradictions. In cases of doubt reality is what decides" (*Kursbuch* 6, 1966, 165–176). Beyond these unwitting parallels, however, Weiss intended his play to connect with West German reality in a very specific fashion. Principally by means of what Ernst Schuhmacher termed "the stereometric view," Weiss brought to bear on history the threefold encapsulation of time, place, and action. Thus the modern public of 1964 doubles as the Parisian audience which Coulmier, the director of Charenton, invites to the asylum on July 13, 1808, to watch Sade's dramatization of the historical events of 1793. Although the outer play is virtually coextensive with the inner one, the focus on 1793 is continually disrupted: with the exception of the inmate in the role of Marat, the actors in Sade's play frequently forget they are playing a part and revert to their real situation at Charenton so that the audience can never be entirely sure whether they are hearing words scripted by Sade or spontaneous utterances spoken out of character by the patients. Coulmier repeatedly interrupts the performance to protest that Sade reinstated lines censored for suggesting affinities between Marat's time and Napoleon's, whereby he merely points up the parallels. Both Marat and Sade are given to anachronistic statements constructing analogies with the 20th century, in particular with Nazism, that are clearly addressed to the contemporary audience. Thus Marat can predict that wars "whose weapons rapidly developed / by servile scientists / will become more and more deadly / until they can with a flick of a finger / tear a million of you to pieces" (scene 23), while Sade counters with the chilling assertion that "Nature herself would watch unmoved / if we destroyed the entire human race" for "haven't we experimented in our laboratories / before applying the final solution" (scene 12). This stereometry of time yields a series of interacting sequences: the years 1789—the storming of the Bastille, the emblematic revolutionary moment presaging the overthrow of the *ancien régime;* and 1945—the defeat of Germany and end of National Socialism—both of which gave rise to hopes for a new social order. Four years later in each case, the new era received constitutional expression, in the Jacobin Constitution of June 1793 and the German *Grundgesetz* of May 1949. Yet the hopes expressed in these formulations, when viewed from a vantage point fifteen years removed (1808 and 1964 respectively), seem to have come to naught following a period of political and economic restoration.

This schematic reading of the text is given an additional inflection by the ending. Although Weiss subsequently insisted that any production of his play in which Marat does not emerge as the moral victor should be deemed to have failed (*Materialien,* 101), certain aspects of the drama militate against this conclusion, most notably its "prismatic structure" (Peter Brook) and the fact that this particular Marat is, in any case, a theatrical construct of Sade's. Moreover, within their personal dialogue, the playwright even allows himself the privilege of uttering the final word, albeit the paradoxical one of "for me the last word can never be spoken / I am left with a question that is always open" (scene 33). In fact, Coulmier attempts to have the last word as he once again seeks to reassure his Parisian audience that things have changed since Marat's time and "we have no oppressors, no violent crimes" (scene 33). Of course, the modern audience recognizes the hypocrisy of these remarks, not least because it reads in Weiss's program notes that "not only the mentally ill were interned in Charenton, but also people who were unwelcome in Napoleonic society for political reasons" (*Verfolgung und Ermordung Marats,* p. 9). Nor are Coulmier's efforts at conciliation any more successful in the context of 1808. Incited by the passions unleashed by Sade's play, the inmates enact an insurrection of their own, forming a belligerent column that, in a frenzy of shouting and stamping, marches on the audience before Coulmier in desperation orders the curtain lowered. While this ending is far from unambiguous in political terms, in some productions the inmates' revolt has been played variously as presaging counterrevolution. Coulmier's muscular attendants brutally quell the rebellion and anarchy. The lunatics take over the asylum— personal liberation in Sade's sense. By not sticking to the script, the patients assert themselves as individuals. The column of inmates, comprising mostly political internees, marches in disciplined formation not on the audience but on their immediate oppressor, Coulmier. What remains constant is the catalytic power of art. It is Sade's play that serves as a form of psychic release and triggers the revolt, an outcome the playwright celebrates with a triumphant laugh.

In its central concerns—as a discourse on historical change and the role of writers in effecting it—*Marat/Sade* stands firmly at the beginning of a period when West German literature underwent marked politicization. Prompted by the multifaceted agenda of protest fashioned by the anti-authoritarian student movement and the APO—a loose alliance of extra-parliamentary forces forged in opposition to the formation of the Grand Coalition—and, in particular, its plans to introduce the Emergency Laws, writers were increasingly drawn to the notion that the primary function of literature was to be an instrument of social and political change. Symptomatic of that trend was the documentary drama of the 1960s inaugurated by Rolf Hochhuth's controversial play about papal responsibility for the Holocaust, *Der Stellvertreter* (1963; *The Deputy*). Weiss was a prominent figure of both documentary and politically committed drama. While he may have conceived the ideological collision at the heart of *Marat/Sade* as a form of interior monologue expressive of his own inner conflict, he very quickly resolved his dilemma and in a series of personal statements and interviews—most notably the article "10 Arbeitspunkte eines Autors in der geteilten Welt" (1965; "Ten Working Propositions of an Author in the Divided World")—he declared his allegiance to socialism and a literature of political commitment.

Weiss's next play, *Die Ermittlung* (1965; *The Investigation*), based on the transcripts of the Auschwitz trials held in Frankfurt between 1963 and 1965, represents documentary drama in what is arguably its purest, most rigorous form. Although *Marat/Sade* was not without some basis in historical fact—the Marquis de Sade did indeed write and direct plays while he was interned at Charenton from 1803 until his death in 1814, and Weiss drew directly on Marat's writings for his statements in the play—the playwright's concern with authenticity in *The Investigation* was such that he could claim not to have invented anything since what was to be presented on stage "can contain nothing but the facts as they came to be expressed in words during the course of the trial" (*The Investigation*, 10).

While it would be difficult to imagine two plays by the same author (let alone consecutive ones) that are more different, *The Investigation*, nevertheless, reveals two principles of construction fundamental to *Marat/Sade*. First, the technique of interlocking time levels is once again employed for the purpose of underlining the continuity between the past and present, both in terms of attitudes and values and the restoration of a capitalist system which, as Weiss insists in the introduction to *The Investigation*, "conferred guilt on those many others who never appeared before this court" (10). Secondly, despite the austere mode of production Weiss sought to impose on *The Investigation*—he was adamant that no attempt be made to reconstruct the courtroom nor any concessions to naturalism that might deflect attention from the spoken text—he nevertheless insisted that the success of documentary theater as a political forum was ultimately dependent on artistic considerations: "Only by making full use of the range of artistic techniques available can the documentary dramatist hope to achieve maximum effect in his confrontation with reality. Only in this way can theatre become a means to influence public opinion" (*Rapporte 2, 96*). In *Marat/Sade,* the myriad theatrical devices deployed, including song, dance, acrobatics, and mime, helped generate a collage of styles that fused Brecht's technique of alienation with Artaud's notion of theater as immediate, violent subjective experience. In *The Investigation,* Brecht's influence is once again apparent in the use of distancing effects but this time, as already indicated by the play's subtitle "An Oratorio in 11 Cantos" and Weiss's recourse to blank verse, wedded to a structure redolent of Dante's *Inferno.*

Just as in a later documentary drama *Viet Nam Diskurs* (1968; *Discourse on Vietnam*), Weiss echoed another central concern of the German student movement, namely its critique of the United States' involvement in Vietnam, so with his stark interrogation of the Nazi past, the playwright sustained the anti-authoritarian students' indictment of their parents' generation for compliance with fascism. Moreover, as realized in the closing moments of Peter Brook's famous production of *Marat/Sade,* Weiss's play set up an additional confrontation that might now be seen as an exquisite metaphor for the relationship between the two generations. Amid the pandemonium of the inmates' riot, the stage manager, in modern dress, suddenly emerges and blows a whistle that freezes the action and seemingly brings the performance to an end, as the actors turn to face the audience. Partly with a sense of relief, the latter start to clap, only to rapidly give way to apprehension and discomfort as the actors mock this applause by indulging in slow, ironic clapping and derisory, menacing gestures. Just as Weiss and Brook unsettle the audience with a political experience that is not framed within the conventional rules of fourth-wall staging, so the student movement sought to storm the political stage, showing neither respect for the traditions of established politics nor concern for the consternation and outrage some of its methods caused. Of course, Weiss's published version of the ending—in which the patients' insurrection is forcibly put down by Coulmier's henchmen—might also be said to have had its parallel in reality as the ever-more clamorous and violent protests of the student movement met with the stern, countermanding government measures and the students' most inspirational leader, Rudi Dutschke, fell victim, like Marat before him, to a deranged assassin.

See also 1835, 1848 (February), 1949, 1962, 1967

Bibliography: Peter Weiss, *Die Verfolgung und Ermordung Jean Paul Marats dargestellt durch die Schauspielgruppe des Hospizes zu Charenton unter Anleitung des Herrn de Sade* (Frankfurt am Main: Suhrkamp, 1964; rev. ed., 1965); *The Persecution and Assassination of Jean Paul Marat as Performed by the Inmates of the Asylum of Charenton under the Direction of the Marquis de Sade,* trans. Geoffrey Skelton, adapt. Adrian Mitchell (London: Calder and Boyars, 1966). ———, *Die Ermittlung* (Frankfurt am Main: Suhrkamp, 1965); *The Investigation,* trans. Jon Swan (London: Calder and Boyars, 1966). ———, "Notizen zum dokumentarischen Theater," in *Rapporte 2* (Frankfurt am Main: Suhrkamp, 1971), 91–105. Karlheinz Braun, ed., *Materialien zu Peter Weiss'* Marat/Sade (Frankfurt am Main: Suhrkamp, 1967).

Rob Burns

1967, June 2
A police shooting sets off the student revolt

Transformations of the Literary Institution

The shooting of the student Benno Ohnesorg during a demonstration against the Berlin visit of the Shah of Iran on June 2, 1967, brought about a dramatic historical and cultural sea change in West Germany. This shooting was the spark that transformed the Berlin-centered student demonstrations into a national protest movement. As Botho Strauss (b. 1944) observed in his essay "Versuch, ästhetische und politische Ereignisse zusammenzudenken" (1970; Attempt to Think Aesthetic and Political Events as One), it marked the end of the postwar period, the end, that is, of the postwar social consensus built around the economic miracle of reconstruction, growth, and rising prosperity, identified with the politics of the Christian Democratic Party. It also marked the end of the critical consensus about the role of the writer and the function of literature in postwar German society. The negative examples of the political instrumentalization of literature in Nazi Germany and in the German Democratic Republic had rendered all ideological commitments suspect and had strengthened the determination to protect the writer's autonomy by drawing a clear line between literature and politics. By challenging this separation, the student movement called into question the self-perception of the "oppositional intelligentsia," as Hans Magnus Enzensberger called them, and provoked the rapid disintegration in 1967–68 of Group 47, a body of writers that had been the moral-critical authority and representative voice in West German literature for twenty years. Given this new situation, Strauss asked, how can we think of aesthetic and political events as being one: a question directed to the aestheticization of politics in the student movement and to a corresponding politicization of literature, which looked back to the pre-Nazi period of the Weimar Republic for its models.

The German student movement formed part of the international student protests that spread during the second half of the 1960s from the United States to Western Europe (Germany, France, and Italy), South America, and the Pacific Rim countries (Japan, Australia). The common mobilizing factor of the revolt was the war in Vietnam. The year 1968, however, has come to stand historically for much more than demonstrations, sit-ins, and open confrontations. The protests manifested in dramatic form the emergence of a new kind of politics: the displacement of class conflict by generational conflict, driven by the rapid expansion of universities in Western societies and more generally by the spread of youth cultures. The student movements signaled a shift from the old class politics of industrial society, based on economic interests, to a new political agenda, based on, what Inglehardt called post-materialist values, which, in turn, found effective expression in the social movements of the 1970s, most notably the environmental and feminist movements.

In West Germany, the motivating force behind the protest movement, centered in Berlin, was the growing dissatisfaction, frustration, and anger aroused by domestic political developments. The Grand Coalition composed of the two main political parties, the Christian Democratic Party (CDU) and the Social Democratic Party of Germany (SPD), formed after the 1966 elections, appeared to confirm the failure of the postwar goal of democratizing society. The restoration of old authoritarian structures and attitudes under Konrad Adenauer, together with the economic miracle of the 1950s and 1960s, which had integrated the working classes into capitalist society, confronted the student activists, as they saw it, with a system that had discredited the politics of democratic reform and neutralized the possibility of open political struggle. It was this view of a system without alternatives that brought about a break between the old and the new left and led to a new conception of action directed toward cultural as opposed to political revolution. Confronted with a perceived closure of the social system and negative experiences with authoritarian socialization, the student activists focused on the self-liberating, self-transforming potential of collective action in the form of acts of symbolic protest, provocation, and violence.

The Surrealist inspiration of the May '68 revolt in Paris, epitomized by the wall slogan "All power to the imagination," has been widely recognized. That the Surrealist connection also played a key role in Germany is not as well known, despite the fact that the leading figures of the Berlin movement— Rudi Dutschke, Bernd Rabehl, Fritz Teufel, and Rainer Langhans—all came out of the anarchist-Surrealist group Subversive Action and its successor, the Commune I, both of which were offshoots of the Situationist International, which saw itself as the true inheritor of the Surrealist revolution. The Situationists defined themselves as professional cultural revolutionaries, dedicated to reviving the avant-garde program of reuniting art and life. Provocative actions aimed at preparing the ground for revolt through the creation of situations that exposed the rules of the social game to ridicule. Subversive action was thus credited with the power to revolutionize consciousness and liberate the creativity of poetry and drama. In the words of the theoretician of the Situationist revolt Guy Debord: "In the spectacle, reality appears and the spectacle is real." The reality of the spectacle, both for the participants and for the media, appeared in the theater of street demonstrations as well as at the trial of Teufel and Langhans in the wake of June 1967 during which the legal system was reduced to a farce.

The theory and practice of symbolic action posed a direct challenge to writers on their own ground. While the cultural revolution sought a symbolic politics that would blur the boundaries between art and political action, the process of self-liberation accorded a leading role to the imagination by mobilizing subjective needs and emotions. The contrast became all the more acute as both sides invoked rival versions of Critical Theory: the students, that of Herbert Marcuse, the guru of the Berkeley revolt, exponent of the Great Refusal and of a politics of liberation; the writers, that of Theodor Adorno, who designated authentic art as the means of uncompromising resistance to administered society. Marcuse and Adorno held in common the view that the hegemony of capitalist consumer society creates a false consciousness and alienates individuals from their true needs. They differed sharply, however, on the possibility of breaking out of the one-dimensional repressive system. The West German student movement embodied the activist critique and rejection of postwar literature and its moral-critical impulse, legitimated by Adorno's distinction between aesthetic and political engagement, a distinction strongly defended by Günter Grass against the student radicals in *Aus dem Tagebuch einer Schnecke* (1971; *From the Diary of a Snail*).

Hans Magnus Enzensberger, a leading member of Group 47, whose adept balancing act between poetic autonomy and social criticism had established him in the 1960s as a model Adorno-style intellectual, was quick to articulate in self-critical, though overstated, fashion the failure of the literary opposition. In the essay "Berliner Gemeinplätze 1" (1968; Berlin Commonplaces 1), he drew up the balance sheet of postwar literature. The left intellectuals had to admit that after twenty years of Group 47, manifestos, and declarations, they had nothing to show for their efforts other than that their literary production was, in the deepest sense, politically unproductive. Like Botho Strauss, Enzensberger stressed the end of a literary-historical epoch: "This intelligentsia was tied to the historical trauma of 1945, tied to specifically German complexes and phenomena, from collective guilt to the Wall." Both Strauss and Enzensberger posed the question of thinking literary and political events as one under the impact of the complex atmosphere that characterized the student revolt. A heady combination of carnival spirit and Marxist slogans, anarchy and discipline made itself felt from the months after the shooting of Ohnesorg until the radicalization of the revolt following the attempted assassination of Rudi Dutschke on Easter Sunday 1968. Enzensberger's call for revamping the function of literature as a medium of ideological critique and political instruction was one of the answers proposed (if not necessarily practiced) by writers in response to the new situation created by the protest movement. Not only had the modernist model of autonomous literature lost its legitimacy, the institution of literature itself, and its rules, were suddenly open to question. Since theater had the greatest affinity with the street theater of the demonstrations, while at the same time presenting the most visible embodiment of the literary institution, it is not surprising that it should reemerge as a public-political forum where rethinking of the relation between aesthetics and politics could take place. Neither is it surprising that the polarization of positions appeared most clearly in relation to the theater nor that the opposing positions should define themselves in relation to the dominating figure of Brecht and his version of revolution in the theater.

Peter Handke (b. 1942) openly embraced the Situationist logic of carnival revolt in his essay "Strassentheater oder Theatertheater" (1968; Street Theater or Theater-Theater). He advocated avant-gardism as a liberating force from the straitjacket of institutions. He hailed Fritz Teufel and his Commune as the true successors to Brecht. Unlike Brecht's theater company, the Berlin Ensem-

ble, with its presentation of contradictions resolvable on stage, the Commune
understood that, as social institution, theater cannot be used as an instrument
for societal change. The theatricalization of reality practiced by the Commune
enacted a form of "terroristic" provocation which complemented Handke's
own, earlier "terroristic" provocation of the reality of the theatrical institution
in his play *Publikumsbeschimpfung* (1966; *Offending the Audience*). The changes in
society Handke envisaged are aesthetic rather than political: the convergence
of everyday life and art in a common space.

The opposite pole to Handke's avant-gardist prescription for exploding the
limits of the theater as institution was Peter Weiss's break with the Surrealist
inspiration of his production up to his play *Marat/Sade* (1964) and commitment to a direct politicization of the theater. His 1968 manifesto "Notizen
zum dokumentarischen Theater" (Notes on Documentary Theater), written
appropriately for a "Brecht-Dialogue" in East Berlin, represents the most determined and single-minded attempt to recover the social function of art by
carrying the political impulse of the '68 movement into the theater. In his documentary plays, including *Viet Nam Diskurs* (1967; *Discourse on Vietnam*), Weiss
sought to go beyond the Brechtian didactic play and abandoned dramatic
parables in favor of a critical selection and montage of authentic materials.
Through its analytical concentration on the essential, that is, the exemplary
presentation of conflicts in terms of groups, forces, and tendencies, the documentary theater was to assume the role of a public tribunal in the service of
militant political enlightenment. According to Weiss, the theater would regain
its place in public life by involving the audience in a rational process of judgment that eschews all forms of emotional manipulation. But to do this, the
documentary drama would have to turn its back on the commercial institution
and find a new audience and a new sphere of activity in schools and factories.

Although Weiss places reason in opposition to emotion and insists on
the difference between political action and artistic production—his Marxist
critique of aesthetic avant-gardism—his conception of documentary theater
shares with Handke's street theater the desire to escape "theater-theater" by recovering a social function for art beyond the confines of the bourgeois institution of art. But can art, can literature still lay claim to such a liberating role?
Both Peter Schneider (b. 1940) and Enzensberger answer in the negative, but
from opposite positions. Taking his cue from the events of May 1968, Schneider argues in his essay "Die Phantasie im Spätkapitalismus" (1969; The Imagination in Late Capitalism) that the cultural revolution must begin by freeing
the imagination from its cooptation by the culture industry, which transformed
the once progressive-utopian function of art into the regressive protection of
reality from the pleasure principle: "Cultural revolution is the conquest of reality by imagination. Art in late capitalism is the conquest of imagination by
capital." Wishes and fantasies must break out from their imprisonment within
art and become political action. However, Enzensberger is skeptical of the
dreams of cultural revolution. In his famous verdict on literature in contemporary society, "Gemeinplätze, die Neueste Literatur betreffend" (1968; Com-

monplaces concerning the Latest Literature), he points to the inescapable domination of the reality principle. If there is any truth in the proclamations of the death of literature, it lies in the subordination of artistic production to the laws of the market. Given this subordination, we must abandon the illusion, underlying the self-understanding of the literary opposition, that there is a necessary correlation between progressive art and progressive politics. In other words, there are objective reasons why literature is not revolutionary and why literary works can no longer claim an essential social function. Enzensberger thus negates the possibility of thinking art and politics as one by pointing to the collapse of the presumed correspondence between formal-literary and social-political innovation and to the end of the avant-garde in the culture industry.

If we follow Enzensberger, the outcome of the student challenge to the literary institution was primarily negative. It signaled the collapse of the modernist idea of aesthetic opposition and the end of the avant-gardist dream of cultural revolution. More positively, "1968" can be understood in retrospect not as a failed cultural revolution but as an ongoing process of cultural modernization, evident in a new concept of both the political and the aesthetic. The politics of the social movements that came out of the student revolt of the 1960s had major transforming effects on Western societies in the sphere of gender relations and in the environmental critique of industrial society. The aesthetic surplus value that Schneider discerned in collective symbolic action found its practical realization—with and against the culture industry—in the aestheticization of daily life, the proliferation of alternative subcultures, and the individualization of lifestyles. The literary-historical consequences, however, seem to have been more ambivalent. The end of modernist aesthetics, leading to the postmodernist dismantling of cultural hierarchies, confirmed rather than contested the hegemony of the market. But it also led to new developments in literary theory and literary sociology, including the study of popular literature and mass media. If the '68 and post-'68 literary generations no longer share the same sense of the public role of the writer as did the postwar generation, this may well indicate that the older idea of literary society is giving way to that of a media society with a corresponding marginalization of the literary public sphere—a development, we might note, delayed in the German Democratic Republic until the fall of the Wall.

See also 1942–43, 1947, 1958, 1964

Bibliography: Peter Bürger, *Theory of the Avant-Garde* (Minneapolis: University of Minnesota Press, 1984). Guy Debord, *Society of the Spectacle* (Detroit: Black and Red, 1983). Hans Magnus Enzensberger, "Commonplaces on the Newest Literature," in *Critical Essays* (New York: Continuum, 1982), 35–45. Günter Grass, *From the Diary of a Snail,* trans. Ralph Manheim (New York: Harcourt Brace Jovanovich, 1973). Peter Handke, "Offending the Audience," in Handke, *Kaspar and Other Plays* (New York: Farrar, Straus and Giroux, 1969). ———, "Strassentheater und Theatertheater," *Theater heute* 4 (April 1968): 6–7. Martin Hubert, *Politisierung der Literatur— Ästhetisierung der Politik: Eine Studie zur literaturgeschichtlichen Bedeutung der 68er Bewegung in der Bundesrepublik Deutschland* (Frankfurt am Main: Lang, 1992). Ronald Inglehart, *The Silent Revolution* (Princeton, N.J.: Princeton University Press, 1977). Herbert Marcuse, *An Essay on Liberation* (London: Allen Lane, 1969). Peter Schneider, "Die Phantasie im Spätkapitalismus und die

Kulturrevolution," *Kursbuch* 16 (March 1969): 1–37. Botho Strauss, "Versuch, ästhetische und politische Ereignisse zusammenzudenken—neues Theater 1967–70," *Theater heute* 11 (November 1970): 61–68. Peter Weiss, *Discourse on Vietnam* (London: Calder and Boyars, 1970). ———, "Notizen zum dokumentarischen Theater," *Theater heute* 3 (March 1968): 32–34.

David Roberts

ℚ *1968, August 21*
Socialism with a human face dies in the streets of Prague

Utopian Hopes and Traces of the Past

The brutal repression of the uprising against the communist regime in Czechoslovakia, known as the Prague Spring, in August 1968 had strong repercussions in the German Democratic Republic (GDR) as well. The East German writer Wolfgang Hilbig still vividly recalled in 1995 the ominous atmosphere of that summer and the feeling of stagnation that followed in its wake (*Die Einübung der Aussenspur*, 134–135). Heiner Müller's agonized reflections on the role of critical intellectuals in the East, *Hamletmaschine* (1977; *Hamlet Machine*), condensed the Czech, East German (1953), and Hungarian (1956) uprisings into a dark history, the "petrification of hope" under communism (56). Yet no writer mourned the Prague Spring more passionately than Uwe Johnson, who structured his work *Jahrestage* (1970–1983; *Anniversaries*) around this event. Beginning in August 1967, the novel ends abruptly on August 20, 1968, the day of the invasion and one day before Gesine, the novel's protagonist, is scheduled to arrive in Prague. Gesine's cautious enthusiasm for Alexander Dubcek's new "socialism with a human face" is haunted throughout by the melancholic knowledge of its catastrophic end.

In contrast to Heiner Müller or Uwe Johnson, Christa Wolf (b. 1929) never made 1968 the explicit subject of any of her books. As a cultural and political event, 1968 represents a curious lacuna in her work. Yet her second novel, *Nachdenken über Christa T.* (1969; *The Quest for Christa T.*), testifies to an intriguing moment of nonsynchronicity and deferral in the GDR's political and cultural history. In East Germany, the Prague Spring and its violent repression were ultimately experienced as a ghostly repetition of the infamous Eleventh Plenary Session of the East German Socialist Unity Party (SED) and its radically antidemocratic measures in 1965. Christa T., who, like Johnson's Gesine, comes to embody the utopian hopes for a different socialism, dies long before Gesine vanishes in Prague.

Nachdenken über Christa T. is deeply implicated in the cultural imaginary of 1968 in both East and West. While 1968 stands for a resurgence of the hope for democratic socialism on both sides of the wall, in the West, the year 1968 also crystallized around the memory of the Nazi past, producing once more a wave of intense, often highly problematic, memory work, which then spilled across the border. On both sides of the wall, renewed interest in the prehistory of the two German states also entailed an often autobiographical inquiry into individual psycho-social prehistories, and produced strikingly similar fantasies and identifications in the literature of non-Jewish German writers. With *Nachdenken über Christa T.,* Wolf tells the story of a double death. When Christa T. dies, the hope for democratic socialism dies with her. But the GDR's antifascist subject, this "new woman" who confidently believed herself cut off from the Nazi past, dies as well.

Nachdenken über Christa T. emerged in the shadows of the cold war. None of Christa Wolf's books has a publication history more complicated than *Nachdenken über Christa T.,* with the exception perhaps of *Was bleibt* (1990; *What Remains*). *Was bleibt* put an end to the West's romance with Christa Wolf that had begun with the publication of *Nachdenken über Christa T.* The earlier book tells the story of two women growing up in Nazi Germany. After losing contact during the war, they meet again as students in the newly founded GDR. Deeply shaken by Christa T.'s sudden death, the narrator reconstructs her friend's life. What emerges is the cautious portrayal of an outsider convinced that her country had abandoned socialism's utopian project of overcoming alienation. Christa T.'s personality is captured vividly in a scene of her blowing into a rolled up newspaper and lifting her voice to the sky in an exuberant shout. The novel, which ends with her death in 1963, tells a deeply melancholy story about the loss of the utopian values embodied by Christa T., a loss, the narrator insists, of concern not only to her, but to every single one of her readers.

It was Marcel Reich-Ranicki's enthusiastic review in *Die Zeit* that initiated the canonization of Christa Wolf in the West. According to Reich-Ranicki, Wolf's novel proved that she had learned her lessons from Western modernism. The book's message was clear: "Christa T. dies of leukemia, but the cause of her suffering is the German Democratic Republic" (*Dokumentation,* 105). Moreover, Wolf's story about a disillusioned generation that withdraws into the countryside represents a defiant gesture aimed at the universe of an older generation and its "iron-clad belief system." Wolf's gesture, Reich-Ranicki concluded, is "threatening rather than resigned" (*Dokumentation,* 106).

This enthusiastic review from the other side of the wall proved almost fatal for the author. It was a typical cold war event where the GDR's cultural functionaries anxiously reacted to any Western interpretation, reducing the complexities of both text and review in the process. Overlooking Reich-Ranicki's brief but consequential aside—"threatening rather than resigned"—which indicates that he knew perfectly well that Wolf's book was not simply a resigned farewell to East German socialism, GDR cadres soon began to pressure Wolf into responding publicly to Western reviews. Arguing that the novel's "ideological ambiguity" made Western readings of resignation and death possible, they urged her to clarify her intended message (*Dokumentation,* 113). The cold war needed clear statements, unequivocal texts.

But this cold war event was only the very last stumbling block on a torturous road to publication. Wolf began writing in the wake of the Eleventh Plenary Session, an East German cultural event that ended a short period of relatively open debates about politics and culture after the wall was erected in

1961. This "thaw" period came to an abrupt halt in 1965: books were taken out of printing presses, films stopped in the middle of production, writers and singers were prevented from appearing in public. After Wolf finished the manuscript of *Christa T.* in 1967, she added a chapter at the prompting of her editor and in the hope that this would make the book more palatable to the censor. In the spring of 1968, excerpts were published in the prestigious literary journal *Sinn und Form*. In the fall of 1968, however, the SED's central committee intervened, probably in response to Wolf's refusal to publicly support the invasion of Prague. As a result, only a few copies of the book were printed. At the writers' conference in May 1969, speaker after speaker criticized the work, pointing to its positive reception in the West. East German readers had to wait until 1973 for a more complete edition.

What exactly did Wolf's critics react to? *Nachdenken über Christa T.* is a complex text that tells many different stories. In the narrow political sense, it articulates the desire for a different socialism based on a heterodox version of Marxism; it also tells the story of a young woman's coming-to-consciousness; and finally, it introduces the topic of postfascist subjectivity. All these stories are embedded in a generational discourse about German history revolving around the conflict between the GDR's founding generation of antifascist fighters and their sons and daughters, whereby *Nachdenken* was tied to the paternal narrative of East German antifascism.

From its vantage point of the early 1960s, *Nachdenken* chronicles the awakening from the Stalinist fifties. Wolf's portrait of this era, which celebrated collectivity and dismissed "bourgeois individualism," is rather bleak. Reflecting on her generation's need to be "unassailable" by allowing no doubts to arise (*Quest,* 50–51), the narrator also remembers that only Christa T. seemed unaffected by states of rapture and the emotional excesses of political rituals. Suspicious of this new mood, Christa T. starts to think about the true meaning of change. More importantly, she begins to write. Her first story, entitled "Kind am Abend" (Child in the Evening), narrates the moment when a child thinks "I" for the first time (22). In a pivotal scene set on New Year's Eve 1961, Christa T. provokes her friends with the statement that genuine change means constant movement. She abhors things that are "fixed" (167). She herself comes to represent this transgressive desire for perpetual transformation, not unlike many other young women protagonists who were suddenly appearing in the literature and films of the early 1960s. Yet by the end of Wolf's novel, this figure, invested with the reformist energies of the early 1960s, has disappeared. The loss of the utopia Christa T. embodied is a deliberate challenge to the reader.

Femininity as the site of utopia is part of the heterodox Marxist tradition on which Wolf's novel draws. While the novel's political stance is linked to the idea of permanent revolution, its broader philosophical discourse draws on the romantic revolutionary utopianism of Ernst Bloch. The emphasis on process, the longing to transcend limits, but, above all, the position from which the present is criticized, all point to that "romantic sensibility" ("Romanticism as a

Feminist Vision," 108). Wolf's *Zivilisationskritik* (critique of civilization) is not limited to East Germany's petrified reality but aims at modernity itself as a "disenchanted" world, ruled by abstract rationality and the dissolution of social bonds. In *Kassandra* (1981; *Cassandra*) and especially in the lectures that accompany the story, Wolf reformulates this philosophical approach in more explicitly feminist terms, drawing on Horkheimer's and Adorno's critique of instrumental rationality. *Nachdenken,* however, the story about a young woman who is trying to combine marriage, children, and her desire to write, contains only traces of a feminist story.

The very act of writing is the central concern of chapter 19, the one she added after the novel's completion. The chapter oscillates strangely between dream and memory. It is in this atmosphere of uncertain boundaries that the narrator suddenly grasps Christa T.'s secret: her desire to write. And she makes another crucial discovery, a loose page with a single sentence: "The Big Hope or, The Difficulty of Saying 'I'" (169). Although this page soon disappears, Christa T.'s paradigmatic sentence eventually enters the narrator's own discourse. Reflecting on her friend's habit of writing in the third person, the narrator appropriates Christa T.'s sentence about the difficulty of writing in the first person by inserting it into her own text at the end of the chapter. In this chapter Wolf cautiously explores the relationship between narrator and subject. She questions the neat division between "I" and "she," between narrator and character, introducing some of the core themes and structures of her poetics of "subjective authenticity."

Should we read this relationship between narrator and character as an act of transference through which Wolf evades censorship by having the narrator contain Christa T.'s oppositional meanings? This is one reading, but others are possible once we take into account the multiple meanings encapsulated in Christa T. There is, for instance, the issue of continuity between past and present. When the narrator connects Christa T.'s thwarted desire to say "I" to her rebellious trumpet call "eighteen years ago" (169), she takes up once more the topic of postfascist subjectivity. Christa T., she told her readers earlier, belonged to a generation that slowly came to realize the futility of all efforts to enact a radical break with the Nazi past. Worse still, she starts to doubt that old and new can ever be neatly divided. Wolf calls this a "secret knowledge" and the narrator, it turns out, shares this secret: "How does one cut oneself away from oneself?" the latter asks (27). The "secret of the third person"—the act of writing not "I" but "she," which is the gesture of Christa T., but also that of Christa Wolf—seems linked to this secret knowledge about the continuing presence of the past.

The story Christa T. did not write confirms this suspicion, since its few remaining pages indicate that Christa T. set out to explore the traces of past events within herself. This is a prominent theme of Wolf's autobiographical novel *Kindheitsmuster* (1976; *Patterns of Childhood*) and her enormously influential essay on her new poetics, "Lesen und Schreiben" (1968; *Reading and*

Writing). In *Kindheitsmuster*, Wolf traces the emergence of a "victorious sub-ject" and its "victorious state," trying to recapture what this antifascist state and, consequently, the antifascist subject repressed, silenced, and denied. She thus completes a train of thought that began with Christa T.

Yet preoccupation with the past and different styles of writing with which to capture its traces does not exhaust the meaning of Christa T.'s "secret." One way of approaching this question would be to ask why Christa T. dies. *Kein Ort. Nirgends* (1979; *No Place on Earth*) and *Kassandra* shed some light on this problem. These novels too deal with the presence of the fascist past, and both contain fantasies of death and dying generated by that past. Written in the af-termath of the expulsion of Wolf Biermann from East Germany, *Kein Ort. Nirgends* imagines a meeting between the 19th-century writers Heinrich von Kleist and Karoline von Günderrode. The novel's opening lines evoke at once the narrator's crisis-ridden East German present and the deadly Nazi past. Fur-ther on, Wolf adds yet another layer to this dense historical palimpsest about the deadly continuities of German history, deliberately evoking the memory of Ulrike Meinhof, another German outsider overwhelmed by her postfascist fantasies. In this novel, German history drives intellectuals to their death. Simi-larly, Wolf's *Kassandra* announces her story from the outset as one that leads to her death. With *Nachdenken über Christa T.*, Wolf initiated a process of writing about the past that seems to entail the death of her protagonists, which seems to be the true, the deadly secret of Wolf's novel. It is not a deliberately per-formed "death of utopia" so much as a death in response to a reemerging past, a symptomatic and, therefore, systematic response tied to the emergence of a new way of writing. Wolf's third novel thus simultaneously submits "real exist-ing socialism" to a trenchant melancholic critique and embarks on an inquiry into the pre-history of the feminine postfascist subject. In *Leibhaftig* (2002; *Liv-ing Image*), meaning "living image" or "incarnate," Wolf returns once more to the issue of East German intellectuals' complicity with the dictatorship. Thirty-four years after *Nachdenken über Christa T.*, Wolf interweaves the story of a female protagonist's life-threatening disease with that of the GDR's de-cline. Toward the end, her protagonist rediscovers a new project, a reason not to die: "To follow the trace of pain" (*Leibhaftig*, 184). Linked to the loss of hope, her suffering is as excruciating as her utopian vision was immense. Is Wolf pro-posing to rewrite her novel about the death of utopia?

See also 1949 (October 7), 1976, 1977, 1983 (October 5–25)

Bibliography: Christa Wolf, *Nachdenken über Christa T.* (Hamburg and Zurich: Luchterhand Verlag, 1991 [1969]). ———, *The Quest for Christa T.,* trans. Christopher Middleton (New York: Farrar, Straus, and Giroux, 1970). ———, "Reading and Writing" in Alexander Stephan, ed., *The Author's Dimension: Selected Essays,* intro. Grace Paley, trans. Jan Van Heurck (New York: Farrar, Straus, and Giroux, 1993), 20–48. ———, *Leibhaftig* (Hamburg: Luchterhand, 2002). Angela Drescher, ed., *Dokumentation zu Christa Wolf* Nachdenken über Christa T. (Hamburg: Luchterhand, 1991). Uta Grundmann, Klaus Michael, and Susanna Seufert, eds., *Die Einübung der Aussenspur: Die andere Kultur in Leipzig 1971–1990* (Leipzig: THOM Verlag, 1996). Robert

Sayre and Michael Löwy, "Romanticism as a Feminist Vision: The Quest for Christa Wolf," *New German Critique* 64 (Winter 1995): 105–134.

Julia Hell

1976, November

Wolf Biermann's expulsion from the German Democratic Republic calls forth protests on both sides of the Wall

The Politics of Poetry

On November 16, 1976, the East German poet and balladeer Wolf Biermann (b. 1936) was stripped of his citizenship and refused reentry into his country on his return from a concert tour in West Germany. Biermann, it was asserted, was guilty of a "crude violation of his duties as a citizen of the German Democratic Republic" when he performed at a nationally televised concert in Cologne. In an unprecedented action the following day, twelve leading East German writers and one sculptor—Sarah Kirsch, Christa Wolf, Volker Braun, Franz Fühmann, Stephan Hermlin, Stefan Heym, Günter Kunert, Heiner Müller, Rolf Schneider, Gerhard Wolf, Jurek Becker, Erich Arendt, and Fritz Cremer—signed a petition, made available immediately to media in the East and West, requesting the government to rescind its decision. "Wolf Biermann was not, nor is he, a comfortable poet," the statement read, "and that is something he shares with many poets of the past. Our socialist state, mindful of what Marx said in *Eighteenth Brumaire* to the effect that the proletarian revolution never ceases to criticize itself, should be able to tolerate such discomfort in calm reflection" (*Opposition in the GDR,* 139).

From the very beginnings of his career as an artist-performer, Wolf Biermann was a provocateur. His unexpected appearance at a reading of the works of younger poets, organized by the writer Stephan Hermlin at the Academy of Arts in December 1962, initiated an unusually lively, candid discussion with the audience, which earned Hermlin a dismissal from the academy and Biermann a six-month performance ban and expulsion from the Communist Party. But as was often the case, the end result of Biermann's provocation was not entirely negative. The controversial evening proved a catalyst for a *Lyrik-Welle* (poetry wave) in which budding young artists like Volker Braun, Sarah Kirsch, and Rainer Kirsch gave public poetry readings in major East German cities. The lyric genre had suddenly emerged as a legitimate medium of political engagement. Nevertheless, although Biermann continued his public appearances in East and West Germany after the ban was lifted, his repeated criticisms of political inequities, together with his spectacularly successful concert and cabaret performances on both sides of the Wall soon resulted in a permanent *Berufsverbot* (proscription from practicing his profession) in 1965.

The silencing of Biermann was accompanied by numerous minor sanctions against other writers as part of the Party's crackdown on artists at the Eleventh Plenary Session of the SED (Socialist Unity Party of Germany) in December

1965. This was a clear indication of the limits of what would be tolerated. At one level, there was profound irony in the choice of Biermann as a cultural test case. The son of a Jewish Communist who had fought in the resistance movement against Nazism and perished in the extermination camps, Biermann chose to emigrate from Hamburg in West Germany to East Berlin in 1953 at the age of sixteen. He became a committed socialist and applied for membership in the Party at the age of twenty-six with the intent of devoting his life's work as an artist to the building of what was officially referred to as "the first socialist state on German soil." Seen in this light, Biermann appeared to be little different from any number of writers of his generation who saw in Marxism-Leninism and its socialist implementation a means to overcome the tainted past of an older generation. Like many of his contemporaries, Biermann saw in an alliance with working people and an emphasis on political engagement a way toward creating a qualitatively new culture.

Where Biermann overstepped the line, however, was neither in a lack of loyalty to official cultural policy nor in his at times stinging poetic barbs aimed at the sclerotic bureaucracy in the GDR. Such criticisms, while often frowned upon and even censored, were familiar themes of the industrial literature emerging in the late 1950s and early 1960s inaugurated by the Party in 1959 under the aegis of the so-called Bitterfeld Movement. Brigitte Reimann's *Ankunft im Alltag* (1961; *Arrival in the Everyday World*), Karl-Heinz Jakobs's *Die Beschreibung eines Sommers* (1961; *Description of a Summer*), Christa Wolf's *Der geteilte Himmel* (1963; *The Divided Heaven*), and Ernst Neutsch's *Spur der Steine* (1964; *Trace of the Stones*) are examples of works that, because they affirmed the socialist project as a whole, were permitted a certain license to depict everyday societal imperfections.

Biermann's transgression, however, was his access to modern media and his powerful connections to the cultural industry of West Germany. He not only wrote poems and set them to music, he performed them before ever-growing live audiences. An even greater threat to the power structure in the East was the distribution in 1965 of both a collection of his poems entitled *Die Drahtharfe* (1965; *The Wire Harp*), published by the West Berlin Wagenbach Verlag, and a recording made by Philips (against the express wishes of GDR officials) of an evening of song with the actor Wolfgang Neuss called "Wolf Biermann (Ost) bei Wolfgang Neuss (West)," performed in front of eight hundred fans at the Gesellschaftshaus am Zoo in West Berlin.

As was obvious in the Biermann petition of 1976, which was interspersed with references to Marx and proletarian self-criticism, even the most dissident writers who sought to modify or transform this system of thought for their own poetic needs chose to articulate their resistance within the framework of Marxism. For example, although Heiner Müller repudiated the naive historical progressivism of so many literary works, he did not abandon the Marxist historical dialectic in his own writings. His play *Die Umsiedlerin* (1961; *The Resettler*) tells of a history brought to a standstill by the devastating conditions of post–World War II Germany: "So it looked, this new age of ours: naked, as the newborn always are, wet / with mother's blood—covered with shit as well" (*Die Umsiedlerin*, 50). The work seems to suggest an almost total lack of hope. Yet, it is out of such negativity, not through enlightened leadership from above, that an inchoate energy emerges from the contradictions and even failures of postwar land reform that will set the course of things in motion again.

Given this bleary, uncertain depiction of history, it is no wonder that the premiere production of *Die Umsiedlerin*, put on by a student group at the School of Economics in East Berlin in the fall of 1961, was banned after one performance. Müller was expelled from the Writers' Union and a twelve-year prohibition was imposed on the performance of his plays. His candid portrayal of the anarchic conditions of early collectivization simply could not be tolerated a scant few months after the building of the Wall on August 13 of the same year.

If *Die Umsiedlerin* was banned above all because of its failure to adhere to the ideological tenets of a proper historical perspective, it was primarily on aesthetic grounds that Christa Wolf's *Nachdenken über Christa T.* (1969; *The Quest for Christa T.*) ran into trouble with the censors. Wolf's second novel was less a narrative than an at times tortured "reflection" (the literal translation of *Nachdenken*) on the life of a seemingly ordinary woman. But that was exactly the point. Christa T. was ordinary precisely because of her refusal (or inability) to conform to the categories and norms of a social system in which the anomalous individual must perforce remain invisible. The nameless narrator's "quest" for Christa T. increasingly reflects—and reflects upon—the conceptual inadequacies of those who claim to define and comprehend. The complicated textual rendering of this self-reflective process—the unmediated flashbacks and leaps into the future, the constant shifts in perspective—is itself an expression of a dilemma as well as the hoped-for means of overcoming it.

Christa T.'s modernist style was the reason for the "danger of ideological disorientation" attributed to it by those who sought to stop its publication. After a series of unsuccessful attempts to force Wolf into revising her manuscript, permission to publish was granted in May 1968, only to be rescinded in December because of the political uncertainties created by the Prague uprising in August of that year. The eventual token publication of eight hundred copies in spring of the following year was a mere symbolic gesture to match the book's simultaneous appearance in the West. Only in 1972 did a second edition provide a reasonable number of copies for the reading public in East Germany. The controversy led to Wolf's demotion from a central position in the Party's literary establishment—as late as 1965 she was still a candidate for the Central Committee—to celebrity dissident.

The policies of intimidation, censorship, banishment, expulsion, and perennial rehabilitation affected the career patterns of almost all major East German writers. This is not to say that there weren't periods of political relaxation or even a general liberalization of individual policies over the years. The gradual move away from the rigid norms of socialist realism, dominant in the 1950s, and toward aesthetic experimentalism in all the arts clearly meant an expansion of what was artistically permissible. Similarly, the recurrent, almost cyclical periods of political thaw in East Germany—in 1956, 1962, 1971, 1982, 1988—also led to ever more persistent demands for freedom of speech and self-expression. But what did not change was the just as predictable reassertion of control from above in response to almost any act of perceived artistic transgression. Hence, while increasing allowances granted to individuals indicated greater tolerance toward what could be expressed and the aesthetic form of its articulation, the deeper structures of decision making remained firmly in the hands of the ruling few. The result of this "war by proxy," as Heiner Müller once called it, was a growing sense among many writers of being infantilized, along with an equally strong determination to rid themselves of the state of dependency. The events of November 1976 offered just such an opportunity.

What distinguished the petition protesting the expulsion of Biermann from earlier attempts by writers to gain more freedom of expression was the signers' willingness to go directly to the Western press and circumvent the system of Party control and manipulation. This was at once an unprecedented act of self-initiation and a powerful statement about a collective desire for freedom of speech. However, more significant than the specific content of the statement, which many found to be almost placating in tone, was the decision by a group of writers to place themselves definitely outside the mechanisms of official control, and thereby on a collision course with the authorities. The response of the Party was harsh and unequivocal. Within days several signers had been pressured into publicly distancing themselves from the use made of their petition in Western media, thus destroying the solidarity of the group itself. In addition, three were expelled from the Party and the rest received varying sanctions ranging from censure to expulsion from other Party organizations.

Seen in this light, the link to Biermann becomes both real and highly symbolic. For what Biermann's contest with the authorities highlighted was the potential of the mass media and the importance of performance as a means to undermine the aegis of power and coercion. From his very first show at the Academy of the Arts, his appearances before ever-larger audiences, often accompanied or followed by some form of media enhancement, took on the aura of rock concerts. It should be mentioned at this point that shortly before his trip to Cologne, Biermann was permitted his one and only public appearance since the ban had been imposed in 1965 in East Germany. More than a thousand young people turned out to hear him sing in a church in the small town of Prenzlau. In retrospect, the highly public nature of this event was no doubt one more determining factor in the decision to expel him.

The most significant long-term repercussion of the Biermann expulsion in 1976 was the exodus from the country of numerous creative artists and intellectuals, many of whom had come of age in the GDR and were committed members of the cultural establishment. Writers such as Karl-Heinz Jakobs, Sarah Kirsch, Günter Kunert, and Jurek Becker, to name a few who permanently left East Germany at that time, had not only been shaped significantly by their active participation in the evolving literary life of the 1960s and 1970s, but had themselves helped define and expand its cultural boundaries during what now must be seen as its formative years. The loss of such writers constituted the exiling of the GDR's own political and cultural identity in an irremediable way. Moreover, the continued flight of young, disillusioned writers to the West throughout the 1980s makes clear that relations between the Party and writers had been irrevocably damaged and that, beginning with Biermann, the regime itself employed emigration policies as a form of social control.

In assessing the Biermann effect within the context of cultural policies in the GDR, a pathology emerges that takes us to the pulse of political culture in that society. Central in this regard is the extraordinary power attributed to the individual poetic voice as both a means to enhance the legitimacy of the newly minted proletarian order and as a perceived potential to subvert and destabilize that very same system. Wolf Biermann inhabited both positions. His initial success as a folk singer in the 1960s brought comparisons with Bertolt Brecht and the great tradition of the political *Volkslied* (folk song). However, his charisma with verse and guitar—his biting wit and performing joie de vivre—soon called forth the full measure of punitive censure by the state authorities. We now know from the Stasi (State Security) files that no fewer than seventy state security agents were assigned to report on him prior to his ouster in 1976. What was the danger of this poet? Why was poetry a threat in the first place?

In the early 1960s, it was above all the realm of lyric poetry that provided a medium for articulating controversial attitudes and presented the most significant challenge to official cultural policy. Beyond its function as a forum for public discussion, it was the values and subject matter specifically associated with the lyric genre (individualism, subjectivity, nature, love) that challenged the entrenched norms of a socialist society driven by the imperative of modernization at any cost. But even more threatening than the content of the poems was their tendency to communicate an attitude at the very level of their form: in this case the inevitable refusal of the poetic "I" to be ideologically responsible. Biermann's effusions were simply too unpredictable, too profaning, and, in some cases, downright crude.

But as much as Biermann evinced the power of the poet as activist in the GDR, it was his own fate as the absent presence, first in inner emigration and then in exile, that was a lingering reminder of what ultimately could never be said or sung in that country. Like Hamlet's father's ghost, "doomed for a certain time to walk the night," the specter of Biermann and Biermannism continued to haunt East German socialism as both the promise of a world that might perchance be better and the implied threat that there were those who were prepared to bring it about.

See also 1928, 1949 (October 7), 1968, 1977, 1989 (November 9), 1999

Bibliography: Wolf Biermann, *The Wire Harp*, trans. Eric Bentley (New York: Harcourt, Brace & World, 1968). Heiner Müller, *Die Umsiedlerin* (Berlin: Rotbuch, 1975). Christa Wolf, *The Quest for Christa T.*, trans. Christopher Middleton (New York: Farrar, Straus & Giroux, 1972);

Nachdenken über Christa T. (Halle: Mitteldeutscher Verlag, 1968). Roger Woods, *Opposition in the GDR under Honecker, 1971–1985* (New York: St. Martin's Press, 1986).

David Bathrick

☡ 1977, October

Red Army Faction terrorists commit suicide in prison

Intellectuals and the Failed Revolution

In the fall of 1977, citizens of West Germany were stunned by a series of terrorist acts. On September 5, the Red Army Faction (RAF), dedicated to destroying what it saw as an imperialist and fascist state and seeking the release of imprisoned RAF leaders Andreas Baader and Gudrun Ensslin, kidnapped industrialist Hanns-Martin Schleyer, president of the Federation of German Industries and former SS officer, and killed his guards and driver. On October 13, following protracted negotiations between the RAF and the German federal government, Palestinian terrorists acting in solidarity with the RAF hijacked a Lufthansa plane, taking ninety-one hostages. Five days later, an elite German commando unit launched a spectacular assault on the aircraft parked on the ground in Mogadishu, Somalia, killing the hijackers and securing the release of the hostages. The next morning, Baader and Ensslin, along with a third RAF member, Jan-Carl Raspe, were found dead in their high-security cells in Stammheim prison; the official cause of death in all three cases was suicide.

These events marked the demise of the first and most compelling generation of West German terrorists to emerge out of the student protests of the late 1960s; never again would the RAF—or any West German terrorist group—hold the attention and the imagination of West German intellectuals as it did in the times of Baader, Ensslin, and the brilliant political essayist who had preceded them into death, Ulrike Meinhof.

It was Meinhof above all—the studious intellectual who had moved from Protestant pacifism and a bourgeois marriage to a terrorist life underground—who fascinated East German playwright Heiner Müller (1929–1995) and who would appear as a mythical vision in his *Die Hamletmaschine* (1977; *Hamlet Machine*). In East Germany, 1977 was a time of increased political repression of writers. A liberalizing change in cultural politics had been announced in 1971 by the new First Secretary, Erich Honecker, who proclaimed, in a famous formulation, that there could be "no taboos" when literary writers proceeded from the firm basis of socialism. Writers subsequently enjoyed greater creative and political license, as evidenced by the publication or performance of previously discredited works, among them Ulrich Plenzdorf's *Die neuen Leiden des jungen W.* (1972; *The New Sufferings of Young W.*). But the expulsion of the songwriter/singer Wolf Biermann in 1976 signaled a return to more restrictive times. Müller, whose works were once again performed after a hiatus of more than a decade—criticism of his *Die Umsiedlerin* (1961; *The Resettler*) had led to his expulsion from the Writers' Association and a production ban on his plays until the mid-1970s—was one of the first to sign a document protesting the action against Biermann. Yet soon afterward he withdrew his signature under state pressure, with the understanding that his retraction would not be made public. A writer who had always been forthright in both his support for and critique of state politics, Müller evidently capitulated, choosing to retain the various privileges he had secured. Foremost among these was the privilege of travel to the West. Müller's extended visit to the United States in 1975 resulted in an explosive expansion of his interest from East German issues to anti-colonialism, avant-garde theater forms, and poststructuralist theory. The intellectual's defining moment of ethical failure—for which Bertolt Brecht's own choices and dramatic protagonists offer a relevant paradigm—reemerges in the breathtaking work Müller would compose in 1977.

Müller began writing *Hamletmaschine* in Bulgaria, where he lived across from Sofia's largest heating plant, which had been renamed after de-Stalinization in honor of Traitscho Kostoff, a government secretary who was executed in the early 1950s. For the Shakespeare translator Müller, *Hamlet* was the play most about Germany and most about himself. Müller contemplated a variant in which Hamlet, the son of a high party functionary who died under veiled circumstances, must come to terms with his own life under socialism. The result was a dense nine-page text on the ideals, aspirations, and counter-revolutionary actions of German intellectuals, and on the causes and consequences of a failed revolution—a self-vivisection of the critical German intellectual and the privilege that marked him in a repressive state. Composed of myriad remnants of texts and motifs from literature and history ranging from e.e. cummings's *The Enormous Room* (1922), T. S. Eliot's "Ash-Wednesday" (1930), and Jean-Paul Sartre's preface to Frantz Fanon's *Les damnés de la terre* (1961; *The Wretched of the Earth*), to the murders of Rosa Luxemburg and Karl Liebknecht in 1919, the Hungarian uprising of 1956, and the Charles Manson clan's slaying of actress Sharon Tate in 1969, *Hamletmaschine* is Müller's most widely recognized work.

Girded throughout by Marxist philosophy, postmodernist thought, and poststructuralist theory, and defying conventions of theatrical and dramaturgical practice, the play made its author an international star in the late 1970s and 1980s. It became the work of choice by Heiner Müller among Western intellectual and avant-garde theater artists, including most notably Robert Wilson, who directed the play at New York University in 1986. In stark contrast to its favorable reception in the West, the play was excoriated for its nihilism in the author's own country and could be published (1989) and produced (1990) in East Germany only as the state collapsed.

The phantasmagoric action of the play offers an immediate and deliberate challenge to traditional political and dramatic sensibilities. Any attempt at linear summary falls irresistibly into fragmentary form: Hamlet describes his father's funeral, during which he shreds the corpse and feeds it to the masses; following appearances by the Ghost, Horatio, Ophelia, and Polonius, Hamlet rapes his mother. Ophelia destroys the room that was her prison and walks into the street, covered in blood. She reappears among dead philosophers and a gallery of dead women as a whore with Claudius. Hamlet, wishing to be a woman and dressed in Ophelia's clothes, dances with Horatio until they freeze in an embrace beneath a Madonna with breast cancer. The Hamlet actor sheds his role on both sides of a civil uprising and retreats home into his flesh and excrement; suddenly, he steps into his father's armor and splits the heads of the naked women Marx, Lenin, and Mao. Ophelia sits in a wheelchair, wrapped in bandages, among the corpses and wreckage of the deep sea and proclaims hatred, contempt, death, and revolution in the name of the victims of the world. Yet beneath the seeming discontinuity of these images, the play's structure is intricately precise. With the first and fourth scenes devoted to Hamlet, the second and fifth scenes devoted to Ophelia, and the two figures meeting in a truncated dialogue in the third scene, the play presents in formal terms the chiastic confrontation of two character lines defined by vastly different experiences of history. At the work's core lie disturbing narratives of German history, German drama, and German revolution that launch a devastating critique of Germany's intellectuals.

The longer Hamlet scenes display a range of literary forms, from narration in past and present tenses to lyrical free verse, and employ a sophisticated repertoire of quotations—notably from Shakespeare, T. S. Eliot, and Müller himself—which continually disrupt the thematic, syntactic, and orthographic flow of the text. In this manner, dramaticality itself—the very possibility of drama—is posed as a problem. Müller's masterful challenge to the institutions of theater and of dramatic writing—his rendering of Shakespeare's most famous and, for Germans, historically most meaningful drama in this discontinuous, flayed manner—was scandalous within a tradition of theatrical performance and dramatic writing defined by the rationalist ideals of Lessing's dramaturgy and Hegel's aesthetics. Indeed, since the time of the Enlightenment, drama in Germany has been the privileged genre for serious national and philosophical discussion. To this normative model of bourgeois drama, one in which the teleology of progress unfolds through the medium of rational dialogue, Müller's Hamlet responds in the opening scene with an irreverent "BLABLA."

More is at stake here than just dramatic form; the model of bourgeois drama is deeply anchored in the humanistic ideals of the bourgeois Enlightenment. Müller's greatest attack—a more apt term might be "dissection" given the painstaking analytical rigor of the exercise—on Enlightenment ideals came in *Leben Gundlings Friedrich von Preußen Lessings Schlaf Traum Schrei* (1976; *Gundling's Life Frederick of Prussia Lessing's Sleep Dream Scream*), which immediately preceded *Hamletmaschine*. There, in scene after scene, Müller rehearsed the dialectic of self-denial, even to the point of self-execution, of Enlightenment subjects who are trained to serve an authoritarian ideal, a higher moral principle embodied by the father, while rebellious figures, representing the forces of youth, sexuality, and nature, are incarcerated in a Prussian insane asylum. Hamlet, the paradigmatic German intellectual, understands the dialectic of enlightened reason turning into tyranny, and he rebels: he wishes for a world without mothers, for the nonarrival of the new morning—for the disruption of historical "progress" that is nothing but continual destruction. The vision of a radical break with dramatic and historical tradition is Hamlet's moment of insight: "SHALL I / AS IS THE CUSTOM STICK A PIECE OF IRON INTO / THE NEAREST FLESH OR THE SECOND BEST," he asks pointedly (scene 1). Hamlet explicitly wishes to reject the family tradition, the historical continuum, the literary model, that requires him to murder in the name of a paternalistic authority. Thus when Hamlet rapes his mother at the end of the first scene, or finally climbs into the king's armor and murders Marx, Lenin, and Mao at the end of the fourth scene, he signals his tragic capitulation to the demands of the father—to models of drama and history founded on ideals of authority, teleology, and the dictates of institutionalized reason. In short, Müller's Hamlet illustrates the immensely consequential failure of the intellectual who betrays his revolutionary insight in order to perform the task required of him by the state: the guilty, privileged Hamlet emerges as a counterrevolutionary.

Shakespeare's Ophelia, the lover of a prince who finds her only salvation in insanity and suicide, represents the prototypical victim in the drama of the state-aligned intellectual. Müller's Ophelia, significantly, lives on as a mythical vision in her undersea world, proclaiming revenge and violence. While Hamlet's role is, literally, that of the subject who fulfills his role, Ophelia is defined by her categorical rejection of dramatic convention and historical continuity. She appears first as tradition would have her as the victimized, suicidal figure, "The one the river didn't keep. The woman dangling from the rope. The woman with her arteries cut open" (scene 2). A further reference to a woman with her head in the gas stove is autobiographical, alluding to the suicide of Müller's wife, the writer Inge Müller (1925–1966). Yet this Ophelia, unlike the failed Hamlet, rejects the prescribed model in uncompromising fashion: she smashes the furniture and destroys the room, the "battlefield that was my home," and enters the streets soaked in blood. The force of dramatic and political authority is brought to bear on the rebellious woman in the final scene when Ophelia, proclaiming revolutionary violence, is wrapped in bandages by men in white coats. Yet, despite being immobilized and silenced for the moment by institutional servants, Müller's Ophelia promises a radical rejection of the bourgeois male intellectual tradition which Hamlet, compromised by the privilege of his class, gender, race, and culture, is compelled to defend.

For his creation of Ophelia, Müller drew on the writings of Frantz Fanon, on the Greek myth of Electra, and—most importantly—on two significant women in 20th-century German politics. When Ophelia destroys her bourgeois domestic prison, the site of her subjugation by her male lover, she reenacts Ulrike Meinhof's vandalism of her own home in a wealthy Hamburg suburb in 1969 after a thwarted attempt to occupy the editorial office of her ex-husband's journal, *konkret*. The cultural organ of the radicalized West German intellectuals in the 1960s, *konkret* had turned to selling sex and scandal in order to increase its circulation. Meinhof's rejection of her ex-husband's editorial practices, coupled with their divorce and her increasing embrace of violence as a tactical means of protest, demonstrated her growing distance from the norms of bourgeois legality. A year later Meinhof aided in the escape of Andreas Baader from police custody and leaped, much like Ophelia, from her home into the streets and into a terrorist underground that would culminate in the formation of the Red Army Faction.

Equally portentous as a source for Müller's Ophelia is the Spartacist leader Rosa Luxemburg, who, along with Karl Liebknecht, was murdered in January 1919 in Berlin and whose body was thrown into the Landwehr Canal where it remained for four months before being recovered. Müller's Hamlet, notably, crawls like a "BLOATED BLOODHOUND" into his father's armor to kill the women Marx, Lenin, and Mao (scene 4); "bloodhound" was the term used by Social Democrat Gustav Noske to describe his own actions in organizing the military counterrevolution that put down the Spartacus uprising. Luxemburg's submerged body is evoked by the undersea Ophelia, who speaks in the name of the world's victims. The women—Spartacist revolutionaries, political terrorists, and undersea furies—are united by recognition of the importance of revolutionary action. This represents a vision of drama and history in direct opposition to the affirmative, teleological ideals enacted by the prince Hamlet, whose purpose, whether intentional or not, is to take his ordained place as father and king. The consequences, in Müller's view, are profound: the deaths of Luxemburg and Liebknecht represent for him the decapitation of the Communist Party in Germany, which led directly to the rise of fascism, world war, the division of Germany, the dependence of the East on the Soviet Union, and, ultimately, the failure of socialism in East Germany.

The revolutionary images of Müller's play, not surprisingly, met with mixed responses. Some critics see in Ophelia, and the third world victims she represents, the development of an aesthetic and political alternative to hegemonic European traditions; others see only empty or romantic utopianism, the wishful fantasy of a helpless and guilty author/Hamlet. It is clear, however, that Müller remained committed in his attempt to engage the voices of the oppressed—those for whom Ophelia first speaks "in the heart of darkness" and "under the sun of torture" (scene five). The vengeful Ophelia reappears in the words and images of the black slave Sasportas in Müller's *Der Auftrag* (1979; *The Task*), the barbarian Medea of *Verkommenes Ufer Medeamaterial Landschaft mit Argonauten* (1982; *Despoiled Shore Medea Material Landscape with Argonauts*), and, most violent and powerful of all, the African Aaron of *Anatomie Titus Fall von Rom Ein Shakespearekommentar* (1984; *Anatomy Titus Fall of Rome: A Shakespeare Commentary*) who, as the director of his own play, destroys the general Titus Andronicus, his family of sons, and the imperialist Roman state. Though immobilized and inchoate in *Hamletmaschine,* Ophelia becomes the forerunner of a line of increasingly complex dramatic agents and of increasingly violent acts of vengeance against the white European traditions represented by the mythical colonialist Greeks (Jason), the Roman Empire, the French Revolution, and the German Enlightenment. At a conference of Shakespeare scholars in 1988, Müller spoke of Hamlet as a failure whose crime was that he did not work on "difference." *Hamletmaschine*—at once the painful, self-reflective dissection of this failure in Germany, and the provocative vision of difference—was Müller's genial response.

See also 1767, 1796 (April), 1848, 1946, 1947, 1967, 1976

Bibliography: Jonathan Kalb, *The Theater of Heiner Müller* (New York: Limelight Editions, 2001). Heiner Müller, *Die Hamletmaschine,* in Müller, *Mauser* (Berlin: Rotbuch, 1978). ———, *Hamletmachine and Other Texts for the Stage,* ed. and trans. Carl Weber (New York: Performing Arts Journal Publications, 1984). ———, *A Heiner Müller Reader,* ed. and trans. Carl Weber (Baltimore: Johns Hopkins University Press, 2001). Arlene Akiko Teraoka, *The Silence of Entropy or Universal Discourse: The Postmodernist Poetics of Heiner Müller* (New York: Peter Lang, 1985).

Arlene A. Teraoka

♌ 1979

Güney Dal's first novel attracts little attention when published in German translation

Migrants and Muses

Where does one national culture end and another begin? The scope of public reaction to the American miniseries *Holocaust,* which aired on West German television in January 1979, suggests that some 20th-century histories and media know no national bounds, perhaps even that German history is the stuff of which much of world culture is made. In marked contrast, postwar demographics involving migrant labor from countries such as Italy, Greece, Spain, and especially Turkey have stirred little imaginative interest outside the social sciences. When the West German government and industry began recruiting Turkish workers in 1961, no one could have predicted that the growth of a diverse Turkish population in the Federal Republic would make these resident foreigners the largest minority in Germany at the end of the 20th century, or that German citizenship law would be profoundly liberalized in 1999 as a result of their presence. The byways of their influence on German culture are far more difficult to trace.

Compared with the seismic response to *Holocaust,* nary a whisper was heard when the translation of a minor Turkish novel appeared under the melodramatic title *Wenn Ali die Glocken läuten hört* (1979; *When Ali Hears the Bells Toll*). No one noticed that the tectonic plates of German and Turkish culture were quietly shifting. Bucking the usual constraints of time and place, Güney Dal (b. 1944) had made his Turkish literary debut from Berlin with a tale of mutinous Turkish laborers in the clutches of Western capitalism. Born on the cusp of the hot and cold wars that were to divide Germany and Berlin so famously into capitalist and communist halves, Dal was raised in the Westernized Republic of Turkey, where he studied French literature at Istanbul University before emigrating to West Berlin in 1972. Sporadic stints in industry and journalism preceded his literary success as a self-styled "chronicler of emigration." Yet, almost in spite of itself, the text that launched his career stymies any predictable account of capitalist exploitation or nationalist xenophobia.

One of three winning entries in a competition sponsored by an Istanbul publisher, the manuscript that became *İş Sürgünleri* (1976; *Exiles of Labor*) differs from the German translation in more than name. While *Sürgünleri* immediately confronts readers with everyday German animosity toward the country's "guest workers," *Ali* opens with friendly banter between the Turkish sociology student of the German title and his German girlfriend. The German novel also deviates from its Turkish version by casting one of Ali's compatriots at the American-owned plant in Cologne in dry, informational terms. If Schevket invites reader identification in *Sürgünleri,* in *Ali* he serves as a mere conduit to explain the wildcat strike called by Turkish ringleaders.

Both publications indulge in schematic renditions of unfair labor practices, the workers' growing indignation, and the well-orchestrated efforts of international capital, plant management, and local police to squash any revolt from below. This dominant plot exemplifies the international solidarity of the oppressed working class and a Turkish capacity for dignified leadership in a duplicitous world dismissive of Islamic peoples. Beyond this, the "strangely foreign creatures" who dare to strike are "a fragment of living memory" for postwar Germans lulled into passivity, an uncanny double of Germany's own working-class past, the one committed to fighting the fascist foe (92). East and West teeter in a delicate balance of competing master narratives. Dal presents a familiar agonizing tale of labor and capital, which held Germany divided and much of the 20th century in its grip. But he also depicts beleaguered workers as modern nationals, heirs to the Ottoman Empire humiliated by the European forces that prevailed in World War I. Yet the bells of the German title derive from a poetic lament by Mehmet Âkif Ersoy (1873–1936), who decried the sound of church bells ringing in the ears of Muslims when victorious Europeans occupied the imperial capital. The labor crisis resounds with a distinct echo of past conflicts of civilization similar to those evident in the West at the close of the millennium.

The contrast between the ineluctable course of the main story and an aberrant sidebar is electrifying. While strike-related events serve an ideological agenda in a style akin to socialist realism, the atypical ordeal of a Turkish worker in Berlin is narrated with psychological realism bordering on the surreal. In the character Kadir Derya, the author paints a powerful portrait of a man brought so low by the world's mocking cruelties that self-mutilation and death beckon as his only recourse. Understanding is kept at bay for character and readers alike as the ill-fated Kurdish migrant descends into despair and disaster. As he unwraps heavy clothing used for disguise in the blistering summer heat, he sees his body transformed in the mirror. Is an angry spirit punishing him by making his breasts swell? Are these distended appendages a figment of his imagination? Is he the unwitting subject of medical experiments? When he enters his workplace, the laboratory is likened to a labyrinth and Kadir to a somnambulist. His enemy is an invisible barrier, a glass door so clean that Kadir feels only battering blows from a faceless master. Feeding test animals and cleaning their cages, Kadir is grateful for the kindness of his German supervisor, who freely dispenses pills whenever the inarticulate foreigner signals stomach pain. By the time we learn that the lab manager has been frivolously treating the janitor's ulcers with estrogen, a desperate Kadir has sliced off the offending protrusions. "Suddenly there opened before him a huge, dark pit. Kadir found nothing to hold on to and fell inside" (152).

Like the hapless custodian, readers are left with "nothing to hold on to," a loss of all bearings that lends the text cultural significance. Kadir's story might be said to reinforce the ideological thrust of the manly mutiny in Cologne. Yet the estranged intensity of mutant anguish in Berlin is so compelling as to unsettle all stories that can be easily told. This transfigured Turk is not simply "unmanned" by systemic German indignities. Perceptual confusion about his symbolic transformation acts as a trigger for a broader sense of epochal disorientation. At the end of the 1970s, neither Germans nor Turks could accurately foretell who would be altered most by their encounters in Germany and how. The stereotypical chronicle of emigration one is tempted to associate with Dal implodes with *Ali*.

Out of step with national literary histories, this stylistic hybrid is an orphan text with many relatives. Năzim Hikmet (1902–1963) wrote much of his politically inspired poetry in Turkish prisons and Soviet exile. Ali cites this muse of Turkish leftists and intellectuals to bring home certain points. One of Năzim Hikmet's fellow prisoners wrote "Grev" (1954; Strike), a story Dal may have had in mind when he composed his radically different account of labor unrest. For Orhan Kemal (1914–1970) realistic dialogue and elliptical prose convey class conflict as a clash of feudal attitudes and bad manners. Dramatic potential accrues to the national government, whose ideal role is to mediate justly between the legitimate rights of both labor and capital. Europe is conjured as a civilized cipher of social balance, one without credibility a decade or so later for Turks migrating to Germany. Most of Turkey's "Germany literature," which portrays hard times suffered by the nation's human exports to Germany, appeared in the first decade of this exodus. Germany's own "guest worker literature," mostly poems and short prose in German by a broadly international coterie of fledgling authors, did not emerge until around 1980.

The year 1961 brought more than the Berlin wall and Turkish migrants to the German landscape. In one heavily industrialized area, the Union of Miners helped in the founding of Group 61 to promote realistic fiction about German lives and labors under the sign of advanced technology. The group's most prominent representative, Max von der Grün (b. 1928), included a Turk in a documentary of "guest worker portraits" years later titled *Leben im gelobten Land* (1975; *Life in the Promised Land*), a pale fraternal twin to John Berger's *Seventh Man* of the same year, a hauntingly poetic reportage written for English readers about migrant workers throughout Europe. Group 61 projects generally did not coincide with those of guest workers and other foreigners. It was not until 1985 that the German public was shaken when Günter Wallraff (b. 1942), a maverick investigative reporter known for bold undercover stunts, published an exposé of injustices he allegedly incurred while posing as a Turkish laborer named Ali. *Ganz unten (Lowest of the Low)* enjoyed the kind of bestseller status Dal's own *Ali* never approached.

Kadir's tormented interiority recalls the "New Subjectivity" of the 1970s, with which West German literature responded to political disappointments and theoretical abstractions surrounding the upheavals of 1968. Peter Schneider (b. 1940), a vocal activist in the international student movement, which in Germany targeted capitalist imperialism, German fascism, and bourgeois literature for damning critique, shattered the literary taboos of his antiauthoritarian generation with *Lenz* (1973), a fictionalized tale of an alienated intellectual's personal renewal. A more radical example of New Subjectivity is the anguished autobiography of Bernward Vesper (1938–1971), whose father was a Nazi poet and whose lover was a leftist terrorist. No renewal comes from his hallucinogenically induced "trip" (1977; *Die Reise*) into a private German hell with public ramifications.

If the travails of Dal's striking Turks can be likened to the political path of Schneider's Lenz, Kadir's descent into despair is closer in kind to a solipsistic hallucinatory sojourn. Yet, the intensely subjective focus of the autobiographical *Reise* connotes Vesper's fury over a postwar legacy of fascism and authoritarianism. Such defiance is wholly foreign to Kadir. While he succumbs to a mutation he cannot grasp, his seemingly marginal story resists any easy fit into the frame narrative.

The same might be said of Dal's place in German literary history. Kadir resembles most closely an odd blend of two famous characters in European literature—Gregor Samsa and Hamlet. The chronicle of a metamorphosis penned by Franz Kafka (1883–1924) in 1912 *(Die Verwandlung)* renders a nondescript clerk unforgettable when he awakens one morning to find he has turned into an offensive insect. Comprehension eludes the transfigured Kadir—just as it eluded his predecessor Gregor Samsa—as he crawls to his demise. Minus all princely attributes, Kadir agonizes over his secret quandary: "To be, or not to be" (*Ali*, 31). Hamlet's Shakespearean soliloquy on the shocks "that flesh is heir to" is eerily apt for the stumbling Kadir. The migrant's conceptual frame of reference has not kept pace with his changeling flesh, however, and this leads him to pose a misleading question. For his metamorphosis yields, not Hamlet's choice, but the condition of being and not being at the same time.

Kadir is emblematic of migrant authors who have contributed to German literature steadily since the 1970s. Whether their manuscripts are written originally in German or published only in German translation, literary critics have been slow to recognize these works as part of a changing literary landscape in and of Germany. One exception is Libuše Moníková (1945–1998), who left Prague for West Germany in 1971 after Soviet troops had brutally crushed the liberal reform movement known as the Prague Spring of 1968. Beholden to the high modernist styles of European masterpieces, her finely wrought novels, written in German by a formally trained literary scholar, have reaped broad acclaim.

Writers from many other countries have been less warmly welcomed into the German literary fold. Among those with Turkish backgrounds, Dal is not the best known, though the novels he continues to write have found an increasingly appreciative readership in both countries (with the Turkish original and its German translation sometimes appearing simultaneously). The literary success of Emine Sevgi Özdamar (b. 1946), who came to Germany as a guest worker in 1965 before she embarked on a theater career that straddled the two Berlins, paved the way for the recognition now accorded a younger generation. The coveted Ingeborg Bachmann Prize for literature was first bestowed on a Turkish-born artist in 1991 in celebration of Özdamar's novelistic talents. *Das Leben ist eine Karawanserai* (1992; *Life Is a Caravanserai*) sparked critical enthusiasm for its way of combining magical realism and whimsical word play to recount a young girl's peregrinations through Turkey before she joins other women guest workers bound for Germany. The exacting styles of writers such as Zafer Şenocak (b. 1961), a naturalized German citizen born in Ankara, and Yoko Tawada (b. 1960), a Hamburg resident who has garnered many laurels in Germany and her native Japan, plumb the mysteries of language in ways that hark back to the muse of the great German and Jewish poet from Rumania, Paul Celan (1920–1970). For their prose, poetry, and essays, Şenocak, Tawada, and others have won prizes established by the Bosch Foundation in 1985 for literature written in German by authors who first acquired language in a foreign tongue. The Adelbert von Chamisso Prize, for example, is named after a French aristocrat (1781–1838) who found Prussian refuge from the French Revolution and later bequeathed to German literature the enduring romantic tale of Peter Schlemihl, the man who parts with his shadow.

Dal's novels have more in common with those composed by the first recipient of the Chamisso Prize. Since the late 1950s, Aras Ören (b. 1939) has been active in theater, film, and literary circles in Istanbul and Germany. A permanent move to West Berlin for personal reasons in 1969 led to a long-standing editorial position with a major television company. A poetic trilogy that took a predominantly Turkish neighborhood in Berlin as its locus drew sustained attention to this new voice on the German scene. The three books, *Was will Niyazi in der Naunynstraße: Ein Poem* (1973; *What's Niyazi Doing in Naunyn Street: A Poem*), *Der kurze Traum aus Kagithane: Ein Poem* (1974; *The Brief Dream from Kagithane: A Poem*), and *Die Fremde ist auch ein Haus: Berlin-Poem* (1980; *A Foreign Land Is a House Too: Berlin Poem*), were first written in Turkish and subsequently published in German translation. As it is for Dal, Turkish remains the literary language of the prolific Ören, which sets these two writers apart from younger writers whose works need not be translated to reach a German audience. At the same time, Ören's primary readership has arguably been in Germany, where he is and is not a German author.

Also in common with Dal, especially his later novels, Ören fuses the theme of migrant labor in German society with meta-fictional reflections on modern narrative. A series of novels that took Ören from the 1980s well into the next decade conjures up the muse of Marcel Proust, the French modernist so famously in search of the past (1913–1927; *A la recherche du temps perdu*, or *Remembrance of Things Past*). Ören's quest is for the elusive present, shared by Germans and Turks in often surprising ways. When one of his migrant storytellers confesses to being "a nobody" (1988; *Eine verspätete Abrechnung*, 267; *A Belated Settling of Accounts*), we might be reminded of downtrodden Kadir. But here and elsewhere, Ören has the transformative adventures of Homer's epic Greek hero in mind. The cunning Odysseus rescues himself and his crew from the raging Cyclops by blinding him and then declaring that "No One" has inflicted the egregious wound. To be and not to be, that is the precariously consequential condition under which Turks and other migrant authors venture into the still uncharted no-man's-land of a transnational German literature for the present—and a future sure to bring more mutant marvels yet.

See also 1967, 1977, 2000

Bibliography: Güney Dal, *İş Sürgünleri* (Istanbul: Milliyet Yayınları, 1976). ———, *Wenn Ali die Glocken läuten hört,* trans. Brigitte Schreiber-Grabitz (Berlin: Edition der 2, 1979). Orhan Kemal, *Grev: Hikâyeler* (Istanbul: OK Yayınları, 1968). Russell A. Berman, Azade Seyhan, and Arlene A. Teraoka, eds., *New German Critique: Special Issue on Minorities in German Culture,* 46 (1989). Aras Ören, *Eine verspätete Abrechnung oder Der Aufstieg der Gündoğdus,* trans. Zafer Şenocak and Eva Hund (Frankfurt am Main: Dağyeli, 1988). Emine Sevgi Özdamar, *Life Is a Caravanserai: Has Two Doors, I Came in One, I Went out the Other,* trans. Luise von Flotow (London: Middlesex University, 1999). Zafer Şenocak, *Atlas of a Tropical Germany: Essays,* trans. and ed. Leslie A. Adelson (Lincoln: University of Nebraska, 2000). Sargut Şölçün, *Sein und Nichtsein: Zur Literatur in der multikulturellen Gesellschaft* (Bielefeld: Aisthesis, 1992). David Horrocks and Eva Kolinsky, eds., *Turkish Culture in German Society Today* (Providence, R.I.: Berghahn, 1996).

Leslie A. Adelson

ℒ *1979*
Peter Handke sets out on a narrative journey toward a poetics of space and time, presence and history

The Enigma of Arrival

With *Langsame Heimkehr* (1979; *Slow Homecoming*) Peter Handke (b. 1942) sets out on a journey that defines the writing process itself as a journey homeward, as a turnabout, comparable to Heidegger's *Kehre,* through which literature becomes the place and space of uncovering and recovering, being at home in the world. "Slow Homecoming" refers to the title story *(The Long Way Around)* and to the tetralogy it introduces: *Die Lehre der Sainte-Victoire* (1980; *The Lesson of Mont Sainte-Victoire*), *Kindergeschichte* (1981; *Child Story*), and the dramatic poem *Über die Dörfer* (1981; *Walk about the Villages*).

The tetralogy opens a new and still ongoing period in Handke's work. At first sight, it seems the very antithesis of his iconoclastic debut in the 1960s, dramatized by his challenge at the 1967 meeting of the Group 47 in Princeton to the ruling consensus in postwar West German literature. By rejecting political commitment, he sought, as he put it in *Gewicht der Welt* (1975; *The Weight of the World*), to break the spell of a didactic concept of literature in order to clear the way for his own mythical counter-conception, in sharp distinction not only to the highly charged politicized atmosphere of the 1960s but also to the "new subjectivity" of the erstwhile revolutionaries in the 1970s.

The programmatic turn of the late seventies points in fact to an underlying continuity, already articulated in Handke's anti-manifesto of 1966, "Literature Is Romantic," which takes up Sartre's distinction between poetry and engagement in order to deconstruct it. The opposition is illusory, since all literature, including engaged literature, is essentially unrealistic, that is to say, romantic. Handke insists that the writer's concerns are necessarily formal—not, however, in the sense of Hofmannsthal's dictum that form takes care of content, but rather in terms of the tension between the to-be-formed, and the pre-formed, the "universal pictures" that reduce the world to worldviews. This struggle against the realism of received worldviews has remained a key to Handke's preoccupation with the forms that constitute, both negatively and positively, self and world.

The impact of Handke's early work is due above all to his brilliant demonstrations of the mechanisms of the pre-formed: the terroristic production of the subject in and through language in the play *Kaspar* (1967), the foregrounding of the generative function of narrative schemas in the novel *Der Hausierer* (1967; *The Door-to-Door Salesman*), which describes and exemplifies the rules for generating detective stories. The reader is confronted with the program that produces the text—a highly conscious didactic exercise in the estrangement of narrative illusion. This deconstructive interrogation of generic forms prepared the way for explorations of the connections between form and experience in the 1970s, the moments of true feeling that transmute the alien world of signs into authentic signs of the world. Handke's romanticism thus possesses a double dimension. From the beginning, the priority of a self-thematizing writing means that form precedes subjectivity. The figures are constructed anti-psychologically as functions of the true subject of investigation—the preforming and then the transforming powers of form, through which the other, the mythical possibilities of writing are to be realized. The protagonist now becomes the transparent medium of an opening to the world, of the clearing of a space of experience before and beyond the subject-object split of the modern "age of world pictures" (Heidegger).

From the vantage point of *Slow Homecoming* Handke's trajectory can be seen, in retrospect, as a journey from Wittgenstein to Heidegger, from the rules of the literary game toward a phenomenological recovery of the co-presence, the co-herence, the co-constitution of self and world. In other words, the journey toward a self-authorizing poetics that, by taking homecoming as its theme, makes his work since the tetralogy a work in progress, a series of fresh departures in quest of what V. S. Naipaul has called the enigma of arrival. Indeed, it is the enigma of literature itself, waiting to be unfolded in the progression from the *rules* of the game to the self-authorizing *law* of the writing process. Beyond the demonstration that the real is an effect of literary convention lies the search for the real presence of the text.

The identity of the way and the goal, inherent in the idea of homecoming, is nicely captured in the English title, *The Long Way Around*. This short novel traces the way-stations—Alaska, California, New York—of the geologist Sorger's return to Europe. They are stations on a return that has yet to begin. His author tells him: "In the night plane to Europe it was as though you, my dear Sorger, were taking your 'first real journey,' the journey on which, as it is said, a man learns 'what his own style is'" (186). The end, which announces a new beginning, expresses the circularity of a narrative in which the authorial voice and its alter ego merge. Sorger becomes the "no one" of a narrative odyssey, whose absorption into the text is mirrored in his reading of his own treatise on space. As he reads in his hotel room in New York he sees himself disappearing into the scriptural topography of the earth. His "sleep of metamorphoses" symbolizes the enigma of dis-appearance, the enigma of the transformation of the visible into the invisible, of the world into the second presence of words, in like manner, *simili modo,* it seems to Sorger, to the transubstantiation of the bread and wine in the Mass.

Sorger, however, has yet to "touch home." Handke's search for the native ground of his writing, for his own personal style, follows Sorger's search for his own personal space, capable of canceling the "feelings of disgust and the sorrow of parting between him and the world" (130). Sorger thought that he had gained this sense of belonging through his science, through the study of the earth's forms, which has become for him a religious discipline of observation and description. The expansive sense of self and world, called forth by the "primordial forms" of the Alaskan wilderness, suddenly abandons him in California, plunging him into despair, from which he is rescued by a spontaneous gesture of neighborly warmth. The shared experience of the intimate sphere of family life points the way to his "second return to the Western world" in New York, where the lost sense of oneness with the "holy" space of nature yields to a new intimation of a shared human history. Space and time coalesce in an epiphany of the present moment, which reveals to Sorger the credo of his newfound faith: "I have learned . . . that history is not a mere sequence of evils . . . but has also, from time immemorial, been a peace-fostering *form,* that can be perpetuated by anyone (including me) . . . I believe in this moment; in writing it down, *I make it my law*" (114–115).

It is not surprising that Handke speaks of *The Long Way Around* as a philosophical story, which attempts to narrate the drama of space and time, or that he regards his philosophical excursion as clumsy and stumbling. Sorger is a transparent device, the empty space of a narrative in quest of a more than private myth of homecoming, which arises from the immemorial, ever renewed mystery of our being-in-the-world to find its focus in the vision of a possible human history, waiting to be reclaimed from the dark night of the 20th century. To recover this other world history, its "gentle law" (Stifter), its peaceful forms, and to give it a home in writing: this is the law Handke makes his own and the reason why he turns to Cézanne in the second part of the tetralogy: "At first Cézanne painted horror pictures, such as his *Temptation of St. Anthony*. But in the course of time, this sole problem became the *réalisation* of pure earthly innocence: an apple, a rock, a human face. His reality became the form he achieved, the form that . . . transmits an existence in peace. Art is concerned with nothing else" (147). Handke can therefore call Cézanne "the teacher of mankind in the here and now." We enter the kingdom of art, the realm of forms through the eternal moment of the here and now, the moment, experienced by Handke in 1971, "in which my usual self became something more than merely invisible, namely, *a writer*" (175): the moment announced at the end of *The Long Way Around*. Now it is the authorial I, the writer, who stands before the paintings of Cézanne, before Cézanne's mountain on "The Philosopher's Plateau" to ponder, in the wake of Rilke, Heidegger, and Merleau-Ponty, the lesson of Mont Sainte-Victoire. Like painting, writing creates "constructions and harmonies parallel to nature." It too celebrates the contemplation of nature, refracted through the patient eye of the geologist and the painter. When Sorger asks how space is to be narrated, he finds the answer in terms of the presence of the observer, the moment here and now of our shared journey through time, brought to presence in the act of writing and of reading. Handke's myth of the writer thus embraces the invisible church, the "never-to-be-defined nation" of his readers, from whom he draws the justification of his calling: the solidarity of "our common form of existence."

But how is this common form to be realized? How is the lesson of Sainte-Victoire to be transformed into the truth of storytelling, a truth "perceptible only as a gentle something in the transitions between sentences?" Handke finds the clue in a recurrent feature of Cézanne's paintings of the mountain, a fault line between two rock strata, indiscernible to the naked eye. This invisible point discloses "the structure of all these things within myself": "the whole mountain stood still in a yellow glow, as though turned to glass, yet did not, as another mountain would have done, cut off my homecoming" (198). Handke defines the truth of his writing as an art of transition: the transition, which both divides and brings together, is his formula for the articulation of the relation between the visible and the invisible, between the world and the word, that is, the relation of identity and difference central to the romantic theme of homecoming. The mystic moments of identity, of "real presence," are accordingly counterbalanced by the awareness of the writer as a master forger, staging the play of presence and absence. The enigma of arrival cannot be presented naively, it takes the form of poetological, indeed philosophical, reflection on the originary powers of writing. In *Child Story*, the child becomes the image of the pure potentiality of beginning, of the promise of poetry itself: "The same possibilities were reborn with every new consciousness, and the eyes of the children in a crowd—just look at them!—transmitted the eternal spirit" (273). *Walk about the Villages* ends with this gospel of renewal and rebirth in Nova's speech, whose declamatory pathos sits uneasily with the subtle and ironic self-reflexivity of the tetralogy.

With his turn toward an originary sense of space and time, presence and history, Handke makes good his claim that literature is romantic, but in the process he reinstates Sartre's opposition of poetry and engagement. The journey from the primordial spaces of the wilderness back to Europe is, at the same time, the quest for a poetic existence in writing, which will give form and significance to everyday life, far from the immediate issues of the day, the affairs of state, and media publicity. It is not, however, a program that commands ready assent in Germany, where suspicion toward an incriminated romantic tradition runs deep. Can the utopian vision of an existence in peace be rescued so easily from the dark night of the 20th century? Handke's radical distinction between the order of the state and the peaceful realm of art cannot fail to provoke the charge of escapism, of a flight into a re-enchantment of the world, carried by a poetic will to harmony that mystifies the role of the writer.

However unfair this criticism may be, it cannot be denied that there is a certain price to be paid for the disengagement from what Handke calls in his 1996 book on the ethnic wars in Yugoslavia "our imprisonment in the chatter of history and actuality." The very attempt to separate literature and ideology runs the danger of reverting into a blind ideologization of poetic vision in the face of a recalcitrant reality. Confronted by the horrors of genocidal conflict in Bosnia, Handke's quest for "justice for Serbia" refuses the notion of a calamitous fatality of history. Instead, it opposes the "evil facts" with the reconciling powers of "the poetic," the binding and comprehending truth of a more fruitful present. In pointing to the falling snow, to children at play, the writer appeals to the art of distraction, to art as the essential distraction. If this gulf between vision and reality has been the productive impulse of his work since *The Long Way Around,* it at the same time underlines the fragility of his poetics of homecoming.

See also 1848 (October 11), 1910, 1922 (February), 1927, 1953 (April), 1967

Bibliography: Peter Handke, *Langsame Heimkehr* (Frankfurt am Main: Suhrkamp, 1979). ———, *Die Lehre der Sainte-Victoire* (Frankfurt am Main: Suhrkamp, 1980). ———, *Kindergeschichte* (Frankfurt am Main: Suhrkamp, 1981). ———, *Slow Homecoming,* comprising *The Long Way Around, The Lesson of Mont Sainte-Victoire,* and *Child Story,* trans. Ralph Manheim (New York: Farrar, Straus and Giroux, 1985). ———, *Über die Dörfer: Ein dramatisches Gedicht* (Frankfurt am Main: Suhrkamp, 1981). ———, *Walk about the Villages: A Dramatic Poem,* trans. Michael Roloff (Riverside, Calif.: Ariadne Press, 1996). ———, *A Journey to the Rivers: Justice for Serbia,* trans. Scott Abbott (New York: Viking, 1997). Richard Firda, *Peter Handke* (New York: Twayne, 1993).

David Roberts

♩ *1981, December 10*

The Nobel Committee awards the prize for literature to Elias Canetti, making special mention of his autobiography

The Homecoming of a "Good European"

When the recipient of the Nobel Prize for literature was announced in 1981, many critics were at a loss to describe Elias Canetti. He had ties to many cultures, and each of these cultures was eager to claim him. Canetti is one of our finest writers, said the Germans; he thinks of himself as Viennese, said the Austrians; he is one of us by birth, said the Bulgarians; he spent the happiest years of his life in Zurich, said the Swiss; his heritage is Spanish, said the Madrileños; he has lived among us for forty years, said the English. For the winner of a prize usually tied to national identity, Canetti was strangely difficult to classify.

In his Nobel acceptance speech, Canetti acknowledged the multivalent nature of his life and work. He expressed thanks first and foremost not to particular individuals but to three cities: Vienna, London, and Zurich—the cities he considered most important in his development. There could hardly be a gesture more evocative of his cosmopolitan sensibility, or of the impulse toward universality that characterizes his work. Canetti is the avatar of Nietzsche's "good European," who is *heimatlos* (without a homeland) in an "honorable" sense; who is culturally and racially "manifold," and is heir to—has an obligation toward—the vast, ancient legacy of the European mind and spirit (Nietzsche, *The Gay Science,* section 377). Indeed, Canetti is *heimatlos* in this sense because he is *heimatreich:* rich in homelands.

In his autobiography, described by the Nobel committee as constituting a "peak" in his writings, Canetti explores his multifarious makeup and the sense in which he is "obligated" to the European cultural tradition. *Die gerettete Zunge* (1977; *The Tongue Set Free*) deals with his boyhood, his schooling, his early reading. *Die Fackel im Ohr* (1980; *The Torch in My Ear*—the allusion is to Karl Kraus's satirical Viennese magazine, *Die Fackel*) tells of his years in Vienna and Berlin up to 1931, and of his beginnings as a writer. The last volume, *Das Augenspiel* (1985; *The Play of the Eyes*), which did not appear until after the Nobel award, describes the Vienna of his late twenties and early thirties, before his emigration to England in 1938. He would live in London until his death in 1994.

The first volume of the triptych, Canetti's account of his childhood up to 1921, when he turned sixteen, is something of an inventory of his cultural and linguistic parts. It is, among other things, his effort to "embed my ideas in their place of origin" (*Secret Heart of the Clock,* s.v. "1977," 30). Significantly, the volume is again subdivided by city. The author's maturation process is described as a series of geographic displacements, expulsions, and expansions, largely on urban terrain. Every autobiography can be thought of as a homecoming—a revisiting and reintegrating of what time has dispersed, by an individual who has been exiled from the past. In Canetti's case, autobiography is the tale of "*ein* Heimkehrer in *viele* Länder"—"*one* repatriate returning to *many* countries" (*Secret Heart,* s.v. "1982," 103).

In fact, Canetti's Sephardic ancestors emigrated in the 1490s from Spain to Bulgaria via Italy, where they altered the spelling of their name, Cañete. His first mother tongues were Bulgarian and Ladino, a language descended from late 15th-century Spanish and spoken by Sephardic Jews. Later in his childhood, as he moved with his family to Manchester, Lausanne, Zurich, and Vienna, he acquired English, French, Latin, High German, Swiss German, and Viennese dialect.

In *Die gerettete Zunge,* Canetti describes Rustschuk, where he was born in 1905, as a town on the lower Danube that yearns to be a big city and that looks to Vienna as the epitome of the urban. Although it is small, it has the cultural and linguistic variety of a microcosm—the local population comprises Bulgarians, Greeks, Armenians, Albanians, Rumanians, Circassians, Russians, Sephardic Jews, Gypsies—and young Elias accepts this as the norm. To some extent, the boy identifies with Rustschuk: both he and the town strive to become cosmopolitan. Yet Canetti also comes to see the world, via the city, as a place of disjunction and alienation, a vast realm of displaced persons.

In 1911, the Canettis settle in England. After his father's sudden death—the first great trauma in the boy's life—Mathilde Canetti takes Elias and his two younger brothers to Lausanne and Vienna, then sends him to a boarding school in Zurich. With each successive move, his inner "storehouse" becomes more variegated. Following the French philosopher Michel de Montaigne, he reconceives the notion of self: "I as space, not as position" (*Secret Heart,* s.v. "1978," 54). He absorbs tirelessly, indiscriminately. Within the characteristic structural paradigm of autobiography—its doubling of the "I" into narrating self and narrated self, and the gradual convergence of the two—Canetti the seventy-two-year-old observes Elias the six-year-old and understands what the boy does not. The goal is "to create ever more space within the self—space for knowledge . . . space for people," he writes in "Der Beruf des Dichters" ("The Writer's Profession," *The Conscience of Words,* 243)—in effect, to build a city within the self.

Young Elias gradually incorporates a mass of voices and subjectivities. During his early years in Vienna (1913–1916), his mother reads Shakespeare with him and transmits to him her love of the theater. "Since the age of ten, I've felt as if I consisted of many characters," says Canetti more than once in his memoirs. His affinity for drama and the dramatic method is explicit: plays are his favorite medium, he says, and despite the success of his work in other genres, he thinks of himself as a dramatist before anything else.

The many characters in *Die gerettete Zunge* are sometimes round and sometimes flat, depending on whether the perceiving eye is that of the mature writer or of the young boy; the two perspectives are skillfully interwoven. Little Elias inhabits a world that displays many characteristics of fables or fairy tales, and which Canetti renders in a rhetorical mode appropriate to myth. *Die gerettete Zunge* is in this respect stylistically distinct from the later volumes of the triptych. For Elias, life is a flow of largely indistinguishable days punctuated by sudden, dazzling, inexplicable events. Individuals are sketched with exaggerated contours, reduced to a few salient traits, and named accordingly—"the Ogre," "the Wolf," "the Beard." By aestheticizing his memories, by turning them into myths and icons, Canetti endows the remembered past with an aura of certainty, a "reservoir of unquestionability" ("The Writer's Profession," 244). This enables him to avoid interrogating the tenuous, unstable process of memory. The narrative becomes an autonomous entity whose origins are lost, like those of myth. "I am not convinced that one should plague, pester, and pressure memory. . . . I bow to memory ["Ich verneige mich vor der Erinnerung"], to every person's memory. I want to leave memory intact" (*Torch in My Ear,* 308). Canetti's recollections assume an age-old form, yet they seem vivid and new: the child's perspective becomes a trope for freshness of vision. Mythic rhetoric is a device for rendering Elias's experience of the world—his sense of time, of powerlessness, of contingency. But it is also a means for Canetti to impose order on the welter of voices, characters, images, stories, and settings that constitute the recollected past.

Canetti's relation to his mother tongues is one of the most extensively examined issues in his work. Critics often say that he freely chose German as his artistic medium from the array of languages available to him, but to a large extent the decision was predetermined. In *Die gerettete Zunge,* Elias first encounters German as an instrument of exclusion: during his boyhood in Rustschuk, German is his parents' private dialect, the language of their courtship and of their student days in Vienna, the language they speak when they do not want Elias to understand. The lesson he learns from this is that it is a mistake to assume language is always a means of communication; it can just as often be a barrier to understanding. But far from being something odious, for the boy German belongs to a world of magical sounds, to an enchanted and privileged space. Several years later, after his father's death, Mathilde Canetti teaches her young son German in order to recreate the intimate linguistic community she has lost. The harsh methods she uses, bullying and humiliating him into learning the language in just a few months, increase his attachment to it. His admission to the privileged realm at the cost of such pain virtually assures that German will acquire primacy over his other mother tongues and will become the medium of his art. He is, as he says, "in thrall" to German (*Secret Heart,* s.v. "1980").

There is yet another binding element, according to Canetti: he writes in German because he is a Jew. Deliberately abstaining from the systematic degradation of German during the 1930s and 1940s, he is determined to help keep German "pure" during the years of its greatest political and ideological defilement. As a writer on the periphery, he sees himself fulfilling the essential role of conservator. For him, the goal is not just *eine gerettete Zunge* but *eine gerettete Sprache*—the redemption not only of individual expression, but of the language as a whole.

Thus, German becomes the very word-stuff of Canetti's life narrative, taking over even his early Bulgarian and Ladino memories (see his essay "Word-Attacks"). In *Die gerettete Zunge,* we see the boy Elias making his way into the German language through a series of other tongues. Every language boundary crossed means a new space entered, a new territory annexed.

Each acquired tongue brings transformations of the self, and Canetti comes to value metamorphosis as a power that opposes death. The writer, he says, is the "keeper of metamorphoses" (*Hüter der Verwandlungen;* "The Writer's Profession," 244). As such, the writer should preserve the ancient transformative myths (*Gilgamesh,* the *Odyssey*), use metamorphosis as a weapon against stagnation and decay, and show how metamorphosis can be an empathic medium, a way of understanding the other by becoming the other. Odysseus—risk taker, fiction maker, self-transformer—becomes Canetti's most important model.

Canetti's faith in the power of words, for both good and evil, is evident throughout his memoirs. From the famous opening passage of *Die gerettete Zunge,* in which an unknown man repeatedly threatens to cut off the boy's tongue (a passage that resonates in complex ways with *A Thousand and One Nights*), to the last paragraphs of *Das Augenspiel,* in which the death of the tyrannical Mathilde sets the son free to develop as an artist, the autobiography is a chronicle of increasing mastery over language and the finding of a personal voice. An essential step is the internalization of many voices, not just through reading but also through listening—a skill Canetti greatly valued. The constant danger is that one will close one's ears to others and allow one's "linguistic shape" to ossify. Canetti terms this rigid linguistic persona an "akustische Maske" (acoustic mask)—an individual's idiosyncratic and repetitive mode of expression, as unique as a fingerprint. In the plays *Die Hochzeit* (1932; *The Wedding*) and *Die Komödie der Eitelkeit* (1933; *The Comedy of Vanity*), and in the novel *Die Blendung* (1935; *Auto-da-Fé*), he presents such acoustic masks in all their repellent stridency. Characters express themselves with limited vocabulary and narrow tonal range; their utterances verge on the inarticulate, the bestial *(das Tierische)*. In these linguistic shapes, people seem pitiable as well as brutal—at once victims and perpetrators of a failure of language.

Canetti's preoccupation with linguistic hardening is a concomitant of his belief that individual time should be seen in the context of historical time, that each person unites ontogeny and phylogeny. The past of the species is immanent in the present of the individual; our most ordinary gestures betray us as primitives in the midst of our modern lives. This perspective informs the book he spent thirty years researching and writing: *Masse und Macht* (1960; *Crowds and Power*), a study of crowd phenomena of all types, from religious congregations and revolutionary mobs to armies, sperm, and the invisible legions of our deceased ancestors. Our challenge is to overcome the allure of the atavistic, to resist the easy security of limits, to develop beyond infantile egotism and the satisfactions of acquiring and incorporating, to integrate in a productive way the multitudes of which the self consists.

A necessary stage in this development, according to Canetti, is learning to make use of the internal wealth one has amassed. In *The Torch in My Ear,* he refers to the "monstrous character" of a creature that is intent only on consuming and absorbing—Canetti describes his younger self, for example, as "gulping" knowledge. One must eventually learn, in turn, to emit knowledge, and in Elias's case this means going beyond voracious reading to become a writer. *Das Strahlende,* "the radiant," is one of the key value terms in Canetti's work. Knowledge that does not radiate is sterile, closed in on itself—like that of Peter Kien, the prodigiously learned scholar in *Die Blendung* (literally "The

Blinding"), who spends his time amid his vast collection of books. Kien, who at the end of the novel deliberately goes up in flames with his priceless library, represents "the ignitability of the world" (*Torch in My Ear*, 371)—a world whose inhabitants are becoming ever more fearful, closed off, and solipsistic. Knowledge that does not radiate is liable to self-destruct.

In *Die gerettete Zunge,* Canetti the elderly writer is aware of the pitfalls of ivory-tower hermeticism, but young Elias is not. The boy encounters two versions of paradise: a tranquil valley in the Alps that offers a simple, isolated, almost medieval way of life—epitomized for Elias in its archaic, melodious dialect—and the luminous, apparently boundless city of Zurich, which both frightens and attracts him. In the end, it is his despotic, yet brilliant *(strahlende)* mother who steers him toward the city—toward risk, mutability, and heterogeneity. Canetti comes to feel that in the 20th century the writer-intellectual should cultivate the broadest possible range of experience. He must, as Nietzsche foresaw, be manifold, hybrid, and ecumenical in his thought, and must strive to produce works of comparable heterogeneity and breadth. According to Canetti, the novel of the future—an art form that we can only dimly envision—will be neither an essence nor a representative fragment, but a plenitude that mirrors the "richness and danger of the world."

See also 1882, 1918, 1952 (Autumn), 2001

Bibliography: Elias Canetti, *Die gerettete Zunge: Geschichte einer Jugend* (Munich: Hanser, 1977). ———, *Die Fackel im Ohr: Lebensgeschichte 1921–1931* (Munich: Hanser, 1980). ———, *Das Augenspiel: Lebensgeschichte 1931–1937* (Munich: Hanser, 1985). ———, *Auto-da-Fé,* trans. C. V. Wedgwood (New York: Continuum, 1947; rpt. New York: Farrar, Straus and Giroux, 1984). ———, *Crowds and Power,* trans. Carol Stewart (London: Gollancz, 1962; rpt. New York: Farrar, Straus, and Giroux, 1984). ———, *The Human Province* [Notebooks, 1942–1972], trans. Joachim Neugroschel (New York: Seabury, 1978). ———, *Earwitness: Fifty Characters,* trans. Joachim Neugroschel (New York: Seabury, 1979). ———, *The Conscience of Words,* trans. Joachim Neugroschel (New York: Seabury, 1979). ———, *The Tongue Set Free,* trans. Joachim Neugroschel (New York: Farrar, Straus, and Giroux, 1979). ———, *The Torch in My Ear,* trans. Joachim Neugroschel (New York: Farrar, Straus, and Giroux, 1982). ———, *The Play of the Eyes,* trans. Ralph Manheim (New York: Farrar, Straus, and Giroux, 1986). ———, *The Secret Heart of the Clock: Notes, Aphorisms, Fragments, 1973–1985,* trans. Joel Agee (New York: Farrar, Straus and Giroux, 1989). ———, *Notes from Hampstead: The Writer's Notes, 1954–1971,* trans. John Hargraves (New York: Farrar, Straus, and Giroux, 1998).

Maria Louise Ascher

♫ 1983

Elfriede Jelinek's novel *Die Klavierspielerin* shocks the literary world

Critique of Violence

Like its protagonist, Erika Kohut, who bursts onto the scene with the force of a whirlwind, Elfriede Jelinek's novel *Die Klavierspielerin* (1983; *The Piano Teacher,* 1988) took the literary world by storm. Powerful, poignant, and transgressive, this instant classic horrified and fascinated the critical establishment. Much like her Austrian compatriot Thomas Bernhard, whose controversial play *Heldenplatz* (1988) confronted his country with complicity in the Nazi murder of the Jews, Jelinek (b. 1946) shattered numerous literary and cultural taboos. The novel's graphically detailed accounts of a piano teacher's sexual perversions trampled the conventions of literary prose and redefined the codes and norms of literature, above all, feminist literature. *Die Klavierspielerin* is at once a novel and a manifesto.

By the late 1970s and early 1980s, the women's movement in Austria and Germany had created a new genre of women's literature *(Frauenliteratur)*. Like their radical counterparts in France, who espoused what was termed "feminine writing" *(écriture féminine),* German women writers, such as Verena Stefan, author of the widely read book *Häutungen* (1975; *Shedding*), called for the literary production of a new female body, feminist culture, and sensuality. Their aim was to create a utopian counterspace within a predominantly patriarchal society. The discovery of this new sensuality and sexuality meant a return to the (pre-Oedipal) mother-daughter bond, which, they said, Freudian analysts of femininity had neglected or suppressed. Jelinek's *Die Klavierspielerin,* however, hardly fits into this new feminist mold since it is anything but a celebration of feminine awakening. The story told rather resembles a psychoanalytic case history of perversion and mental breakdown as it depicts the torments and narcissistic aggressive outbursts of the pianist Erika Kohut, whose last name alludes to the American psychiatrist Heinz Kohut, known for his studies of narcissism.

Jelinek's biting, sarcastic narrative spans several days in the life of a thirty-eight-year-old woman, whose daily routines and rituals revolve around giving piano lessons, compulsive shopping, and voyeuristic outings to Vienna's red-light district, her only respite from the pathological family ties that bind her. Erika still lives with her overbearing mother, her father is safely confined to an asylum, and the mother-daughter pair functions as a "double monster," a figure Jelinek had already used in the play *Krankheit oder moderne Frauen* (1984; *Illness, or Modern Women*). The domineering female parent, "unanimously recognized as Mother by the State and by the Family," is "inquisitor and executioner in one." Erika is unable to give up this primary love object, which keeps her fixated on a variety of perverse behaviors: voyeurism, fetishism, sadomasochism, and genital self-mutilation. She is incapable of a meaningful or mature sexual relationship. When she tries to coax her student Walter Klemmer into a sadomasochistic sexual engagement, the affair ends in lesbian incest, rape, and self-mutilation. Overwhelmed with despair, Erika ends up plunging a knife into her shoulder. Rather than depicting a utopian feminist alternative, Jelinek applies the scalpel of her writing style to dissecting the violent nature of the patriarchal system. Critics of *Die Klavierspielerin* have been most at ease when they read the story as a Freudian case study, an approach apparently supported by the author's pronouncements that she intended to amend psychoanalytic conventions. Jelinek's graphic descriptions of Erika's perversions and sexual deviancy thus seem to follow Freud's vow that he would "call a spade a spade" during his analysis of Dora. But classifying *Die Klavierspielerin* as a psychiatric case study in literary guise does only partial justice to the novel's complexity. Insofar as the novel can be seen as an attempt at psychoanalytic "working through" *(Durcharbeiten),* the labor it performs takes place not at the level of character, but at that of ideology critique. As it opposes the violence of an aesthetic convention that lulls readers into complacency, the narrative—though generally considered to be Jelinek's most realistic work—undermines the empathetic model of realist tradition. In fact this novel is the opposite of a *Bildungsroman.* It shows Erika, a piano teacher, violating the pedagogical contract by seducing her student and instructing him in an altogether different sphere, that of sex. The sadomasochistic relationship Erika tries to set up with Klemmer serves her need to pass her own frustrations along to him. When Klemmer, for his part, wants to break out of this entanglement, he resorts to violence, a situation Erika is ill suited to handle.

By the same token, the novel undermines the tradition of the *Künstlerroman.* Erika, the anti-hero, is not an accomplished artist or virtuoso, but a piano teacher who has exchanged high art for the repetitiveness of technical craft. Furthermore, her work as a piano player (the German title highlights this side of her profession) means that she must play pieces others—frequently men—have written, rather than composing music herself. Much as she did in her play *Clara S. Musikalische Tragödie* (1984; *Clara S. Musical Tragedy),* Jelinek asks indirectly how women can be recognized as viable artists in a male-dominated world. Exploring the cultural etiology of women's inequality, she takes issue with Freud's assertion that women are incapable of artistic production because of an incapacity—as he regards it—to sublimate their sexual desires. Similarly, she opposes a traditional view in which intellectual pursuits devalue women as potential "objects of exchange" in the marriage market.

Die Klavierspielerin does not embrace sexual violence, or transgression, for its own sake. Its primary aim is to dismantle conventional representations of femininity and to probe familiar myths. The author's critique of contemporary ideology often involves the painful exercise of drawing on aesthetic and cultural conventions in order to question and countermand them. Modern myths about human nature, the concept of "feminine nature," and the constraining ways in which the female body has traditionally been viewed are among her targets. In this way, *Die Klavierspielerin* continues along a path Jelinek embarked on in her early, more openly materialist period. In her experimental "pop novel" *wir sind lockvögel baby!* (1970), for example, she employed collage and montage techniques to debunk the myths promulgated in the media. At that time, she was influenced by Roland Barthes's *Mythologies,* which sought to expose the seeming "naturalization" of cultural meanings. Following Michel Foucault's investigation into the history of sexuality and its cultural construction, *Die Klavierspielerin* suggests that Erika's aberrations are the outcome of the ways in which the female body has historically been disciplined. The story of Erika's perversions thus illustrates the negative consequences of suppressed female sexuality, while endorsing a postmodern conception of corporeal subjectivity as fragmented.

To do this novel full justice, the reader must be willing to suspend expectations about pleasurable reading. What is required is not consumption, but rigorous analysis of the text. This means adopting a "double gaze" that simultaneously perceives the novel's surface violence and abstracts from it a critique of the system from which this violence emanates. In many ways, the novel's representational, or empirical, level functions as an allegory of the construction and misconstruction of female sexuality. The shocking scenes of violent self-penetration are to be understood allegorically as attempts at "self-analysis" or "self-dissection." As Jelinek puts it in a short text called "Limits of Shame? The Everyday Violence of Female Hygiene" (1984), "This image of a woman who is penetrated literally by all kinds of kitchen utensils, is her own attempt to demystify her own body." It is an act of "necessary narcissism" in which Erika simultaneously performs a disturbing analysis of her own body and defies the boundaries set by men in their construction of the female body as a locus of "helplessness" and "shame." In an interview with the analyst Adolf-Ernst Meyer on Erika's self-mutilation, Jelinek explains that her protagonist's real act of transgression consists of her usurping the typically male role of voyeur, thereby contesting the notion that only men have the right to engage in "critical dissection."

Two themes run throughout *Die Klavierspielerin:* gender oppression and the suppression of women's rights. Jelinek's concern in all her works is to lay bare the covert violence in everyday gender relations. If her method is psychoanalytic, it is so only in the sense that she reveals the sublimated violence in everyday gender relations. Using a technique of "desublimation," she uncovers the affects that drive her characters and that override what are commonly thought of as rational moral decisions. These affective drives include rage, lust, and greed, as indicated by the titles of her novels *Lust* (1989) and *Gier: Ein Unterhaltungsroman* (2000; *Greed: Light Reading*). Jelinek views moments of extreme violence, such as sexual crimes, pornography, and murder, as "safety valves" through which underlying power structures come to the surface. This guides her interest in the extreme and what it tells about the internal logic of the normal and the norm, which she, in turn, parodies even as she demystifies oppression in societal relations. As a result, Jelinek's work is often marked by a sexual pessimism in which oppressive sexual relations are symptomatic of the "return of the same" in history. In this novel, as in her other works, Jelinek throws reality, albeit in exaggerated form, into her reader's face. Her aim is to counter society's violence by means of a deconstructive writing style that dissects the power dynamics at work in discourse. She does not shy away from reproducing pornographic speech, albeit in distorted fashion, and unleashing her technical arsenal, which includes not only satire and parody but also the gothic and macabre.

Jelinek is concerned both with universal themes, such as the suppression of women's rights, and with more local issues, such as Austria's Nazi past and a pervasive nostalgia for a "purified" *Heimat* (homeland), expressed in some of Austria's ultra-conservative media and the rightist Austrian Freedom Party (FPÖ). In the 1990s, Jelinek turned more explicitly to problems of political violence, cultural xenophobia, and narratives of exclusion. In *Wolken. Heim* (1990; *Clouds. Home*), Jelinek links the philosophical tradition of German idealism to xenophobic tendencies in German and Austrian cults of *Heimat*. In parallel with the gradual rise to prominence of the rightist Austrian Freedom Party (FPÖ), the themes of nationalistic violence and the persistence of Nazi elements acquire increasing predominance in her work. Already thematized in earlier dramas, such as *Burgtheater* (1984), her pursuit of remnants of the Nazi past in contemporary politics culminated in the play *Das Lebewohl* (2000; *The Farewell*), a fictional monologue by the FPÖ's former leader Jörg Haider. Critique of Austrian nationalism also permeates *Die Klavierspielerin,* though in a more subtle form. Jelinek lifts the veil of hypocrisy from Austria's high culture and uncovers the country's provincialism and cultural recidivism. The stage directions for her play *Totenauberg* (1991), about Martin Heidegger and Hannah Arendt, call for the use of a projection screen displaying, among other images, Jewish victims being collected for transportation and quasi-idyllic snow-capped mountaintops. As a backdrop to the characters' speech, these cinematic scenes of violence, nature, and skiing expose the aesthetic illusion *(Schein)* and inner contradictions of the words of the "old man" (Heidegger), leaving no doubt about his complicity in genocide. A later play, *Ein Sportstück* (1998; *A Sporting Piece*), pursues this reasoning even further. The spectacular production of the play at Vienna's Burgtheater, as directed by the late Einar Schleef, realized particularly well the author's intention: to unravel the pernicious connections between the mediatized mass spectacle of sport, militarism, and Nazi body politics.

To make the contrast between truth and illusion dialectically palpable, Jelinek often creates a counterpoint of discrepant stylistic styles, interspersing high cultural discourse with pornographic vulgarity or mundane trivialities. In the play *Das Lebewohl,* the bathos of Haider's discourse is overlaid with sublime language from Aeschylus's *Oresteia;* in her novel *Lust* (1989), fragments of Hölderlin's elevated poetic diction enter into uneasy dialogue with pornographic speech. Jelinek's play *Stecken, Stab und Stangl: Eine Handarbeit* (1996; *Stick, Staff, and Stangl: Something Handmade*), written in response to a brutal murder in 1995 of four young Roma, is a particularly complex example of this technique. The scandalmongering excerpts from Austria's tabloid *Die Kronenzeitung* are interwoven with Heidegger's glorification of "being-toward-death," fragments from Paul Celan's poetry, and horrendous statements by the commandant of the Nazi extermination camp of Treblinka, Franz Stangl.

In *Die Klavierspielerin,* Jelinek, herself a graduate of the Vienna music conservatory, juxtaposes her country's venerable musical tradition with Erika Kohut's tawdry behavior and her dubious explorations in the red-light district.

The musical theme of this novel serves to target the ossified mentality behind Vienna's cherished self-image as "the city of music." As Erika ascends the scale of musical ability, her accomplishments are contrasted with "Mozart's tormented spirit, moaning and choking." At the end of the novel, as Erika reaches the nadir of her sexual experiences, not much seems left of Austria's lofty cultural heritage.

As a virtuoso of the word, Jelinek has received the most prestigious German and Austrian literary awards, among them the Georg Büchner Prize (1998) and the Heinrich Heine Prize (2002), as well as the Nobel Prize in Literature (2004). In the tradition of language experimentation such as that of the Jewish-Austrian writer Karl Kraus, she distorts linguistic forms in order to reveal their hidden implications. Over the years, her style has become less narrative and more musical, marked by contrapuntal juxtapositions, thematic leitmotifs, and experimental sound patterns. Recognizing the intertextual, palimpsest-like nature of writing, she demonstrates how all language ultimately consists of repetition and variation, quotation and interpretation of previous texts. Seemingly driven by a compulsion to associate, she developed a style punctuated by elaborate metatheses, anagrams, near-rhymes, and alliterations. Quite the opposite of the playful excess it may seem at first glance, this style aims to unmask the ideological character of language and release an underlying truth.

Not averse to self-analysis, Jelinek once ironically characterized herself as a *Schreibtischtäterin* (perpetrator from the desk), whose writing is an attempt to ban and contain what she is striving to overcome. Designed as a way of subduing and subjugating the cultural forces that threaten to overwhelm the female subject and, in particular, the female writer, her strategy of feminine empowerment turns writing itself into an interminable process, one that must be deployed repeatedly and vigilantly. Her acclaimed novel *Die Klavierspielerin* is a striking expression of this idea, a work that established its author as an original and subversive voice among the politically engaged writers of the postwar generation.

See also 1899, 1918, 1924, 1927 (Heidegger), 1942–43, 1963, 1984, 1989 (February)

Bibliography: Elfriede Jelinek, *Die Klavierspielerin* (Reinbek bei Hamburg: Rowohlt, 1983); *The Piano Teacher,* trans. Joachim Neugroschel (New York: Weidenfeld and Nicolson, 1988). Christa Gürtler, *Gegen den schönen Schein: Texte zu Elfriede Jelinek* (Frankfurt am Main: Verlag Neue Kritik, 1990). Beatrice Hanssen, "Limits of Feminist Representation: Elfriede Jelinek's Language of Violence," in *Critique of Violence: Between Poststructuralism and Critical Theory* (London and New York: Routledge, 2000), 210–231. Marlies Janz, *Elfriede Jelinek* (Stuttgart: Metzler, 1995). *La Pianiste* (2001; *The Piano Teacher*), a film by the Austrian director Michael Haneke.

Beatrice Hanssen

♫ *1983, October 5–25*

Uwe Johnson undertakes his last public book tour

Anniversaries and the Revival of Storytelling

Uwe Johnson (1934–1984) made his name with novels in a tradition of multiply fractured narration initiated by Rilke in his *Aufzeichnungen des Malte Laurids Brigge* (1910), whose narrator despairs over the impossibility of straightforward storytelling in the modern age. The very titles of Johnson's *Mutmaßungen über Jakob* (1959; *Speculations about Jakob*) and *Das Dritte Buch über Achim* (1961; *The Third Book about Achim*) suggest that continuous and unambiguous narration is no longer possible. However, Johnson's motivation for his narrative experimentation differs from Rilke's. Underlying his complex technique was the fear that the cultures of the two German states may have been growing apart, even to the point where the use of language was not always mutually intelligible. The hidden positive in this development, however, was a corrective to the Nazi view that "blood and soil" determine national identity. Even Johnson's relatively more straightforward third novel, *Zwei Ansichten* (1965; *Two Views*), is based on the idea that cultural and intellectual factors are the essential determinants of identity.

Johnson's major literary achievement is a work that breaks with the avant-garde puzzle technique of his first two novels and tells a story in the fullest sense of the word. The four-volume *Jahrestage* (1970, 1971, 1973, and 1983; *Anniversaries*) shows no fear of the theoretical anachronism posed by enjoyment of epic narrative. As a result, it allows attitudes, emotions, and categories to emerge that, in the context of the hectic business of literary production and consumption, seem as inappropriate to our age as storytelling itself. To get through the 1891 pages of *Jahrestage* requires what the writer Max Frisch calls a "Homeric memory." Johnson's tetralogy flies in the face of Walter Benjamin's famous essay "The Story-Teller," which argues that the art of telling stories has fallen into disuse because it presupposes "the ability to exchange experiences." Modern warfare, inflation, technology, and struggles against political oppression tend to countermand the kind of exchange that underlies the act of storytelling. Johnson's *Jahrestage* traces such ways in which reliable narration is disrupted and dissolved by modern secular powers. But the tetralogy also fights— patiently and serenely—against the contemporary loss of experience. It does so by taking on the paradoxical task of making this loss palpable, even against the backdrop of New York City and all its multiplicity. In Rilke's novel, the urban environment is a major reason for the dissociation experienced by the protagonist; in *Jahrestage,* by contrast, the protagonist's problematic relation to family and national history is more important.

The basic narrative scheme of *Jahrestage* is transparent enough, and yet it lends itself to subtle fracturing and mirroring. It chronicles the days of a single year one by one in unbroken sequence—beginning with August 21, 1967, and ending with August 20, 1968—in the everyday life of the protagonist, Gesine

Cresspahl. She was born on the third day of the third month in 1933, in the rural village of Jerichow in Mecklenburg, an area that later became part of the German Democratic Republic. After June 17, 1953, the day of the uprising against the communist regime in East Germany, Gesine breaks off her studies of English language and literature at the university, and goes to West Berlin to train as a simultaneous interpreter. When she becomes pregnant, she takes a job at a bank. Her child Marie, born in 1957, was fathered by the train dispatcher Jakob Abs, whose death while crossing the railroad tracks forms the central mystery of *Mutmaßungen über Jakob.* Gesine Cresspahl then moves with Marie to New York, where she again finds work in a bank. In daily conversations with her daughter, now ten years old, Gesine gives a vivid picture of her life in New York, but summons up recollections of her father, Heinrich Cresspahl, and her early years in Mecklenburg under the Nazi regime and during the postwar era. As she thus braids a narrative of past and present, the *New York Times* enters the scene, in the role of the parodic modern equivalent of a Greek chorus. The newspaper's daily communications, sometimes quoted at length, sometimes paraphrased, interrupt Gesine's memory monologues and her dialogues with her daughter.

The author's narrative strategy highlights an underlying triadic structure. Not only was Gesine Cresspahl born on the third day of the third month in the thirty-third year of the 20th century in a country that called itself the Third Reich, three generations (Heinrich, Gesine, and Marie), three geographic spaces (Jerichow, in eastern Germany; West Germany; and New York), and three narrative points of view—first person, omniscient narrator, and pseudo-chronicle quotations from the *New York Times*—give the novel its shape. Johnson is not interested in a clean separation between the different points of view. First-person narration is used just as much by the narrator as by the characters. The novel also breaks with the traditional distinction between author and narrator: "Who's telling this story, Gesine. We both are. Surely that's obvious, Johnson" (1: 256). This playful inclusion of the author as if he, too, were a character in the novel was later picked up by Günter Grass in his novel *Ein weites Feld* (1995; *Too Far Afield*).

Clearly, the narrative mode of *Jahrestage* serves the needs of its larger intentions. At stake is totality: Johnson takes care that not even the slightest detail is lost. The author aspires to nothing less than an epic equivalent of the theological concept of the restitution of the whole—*apokatastasis panthon,* as the early Christian philosopher Origen termed it. He thus works toward recovering everything, all that has been vanquished, forgotten, set aside, and degraded. And nothing—not the softest lapping of the waves on a Mecklenburg beach, not a shred of flotsam, nor an unuttered remark—is too small to be included in the epic attempt of restoring wholeness to the world. For Johnson, all epochs of history have equally unmediated access to God. The historical Jericho, which an archeologist friend of Gesine is helping to excavate (2: 833), is no more connected to God than the Mecklenburg town of Jerichow. Both the biblical city and the place of Gesine's childhood have been so badly destroyed that only memory can salvage them. The narrator knows that the attempt to restore them is destined to fail, and that the struggle for restitution, therefore, is equivalent to an act of mourning. Mourned here is what Hegel called the "fury of disappearance," a psychological process that privileges memory.

Johnson's tetralogy has much in common with the monumental novels of the modernist period. Like Musil's *Der Mann ohne Eigenschaften* (1930–1932; *The Man without Qualities*), it explores the relation between private experience and its political context. The two strands are not presented as parallel, however, but as intricately intertwined. Like Proust's *A la Recherche du temps perdu* (1913–1927; *In Search of Lost Time*), *Jahrestage* attempts to recover past experience that seems to have vanished from consciousness (Neumann, 297). Whereas Proust's protagonist is a thinly disguised version of the author, *Jahrestage* bears a more complex relationship to autobiography. Both the Mecklenburg and the New York episodes are permeated by the author's experience (Johnson lived in New York for two years) in much the same way as the novels of Thomas Mann. As it digs deeper than its chronicle format might have us expect, the novel extracts sedimented layers of everyday life similar to James Joyce's *Ulysses* (1922). In contrast to Joyce's novel, however, *Jahrestage* does not mythologize its material; rather it shapes it into rhythmic patterns. Whereas Joyce compresses the entire complex extent of world history into an everyday microcosm of twenty-four hours, Johnson divides the weight of the world, as it were, and spreads it out over 366 days. This expansion technique permits repeated mirroring of daily rhythms in yearly rhythms, as well as in the rhythms of entire lifetimes. It allows for a consciousness of repetitive structures whose greatest appeal derives from the slightest of deviations.

Altogether, Johnson retrieves the insignificant and the trifling for today's literature, which seemed to have become so devoted to the sensational. Not the exception or the unheard-of event, but the modest experiences of every day are granted epic dignity in *Jahrestage*. In precision of detail, the novel resembles the works of Theodor Fontane and Thomas Mann. One of the finest miniatures in the entire narrative is Gesine Cresspahl's memory of German lessons given by a student teacher to her high-school class. The young pedagogue, Herr Weserich, had written his dissertation on Fontane's short novel *Schach von Wuthenow* (1882), and he wants his pupils to study this text with unconstrained exactitude. No place name, no name of a person, no foreign word, no colloquial expression, no special feature in the chapter titles, no finesse on the part of the narrator, and no hidden riddle escapes this teacher's attentiveness and love of detail. Gesine claims that she learned how to "read German" from him (4: 1707). Johnson himself learned how to write from a similar model of close reading. In his last series of public readings from his works, he read this episode to audience after audience. It highlights an analytic technique devoted to an imperative of exactitude.

The episode about the demands Gesine's teacher made on his students is preceded by a passage about the excessive heat during that July in Germany. "That Tuesday—we could have done without half of it. But don't wish your life away" (4: 1694). The last sentence is a hidden allusion to a scene in another novel by Fontane, *Irrungen, Wirrungen* (1888), in which the heroine's longing to join the twinkling stars in the night sky is met by her lover's reminder, "You mustn't wish your life away." Gesine, too, is not allowed to wish her life away. She opts for a curious ontological modesty. When a friend suggests that she "enjoy life for what it offers," she pretends to do so, and is taken by surprise when she actually takes pleasure in walking with her daughter to Riverside Park: "And I thought it was enough to be alive" (4: 1881–1882). Nothing is more remote from Gesine than the imperative happiness of the "American way of life." All the same, she has an aura of serenity whose mild glow is refracted by a silent trace of sorrow, born of the memory of what has vanished. Her serenity is based in an experience of existence that understands life as the most threatened of gifts. Her deeply religious mother had been obsessed with the idea of original sin and preoccupied with thoughts of death, and Gesine had grown up in the shadow of her mother's gloomy disposition.

Yet Johnson rejects the notion that this disposition toward death is of ontological origin. Instead, he draws emphatic attention to its political genealogy by contrasting Gesine Cresspahl's paternal and maternal forebears. Whereas her reticent but decisive father, Heinrich Cresspahl, came from a family of social democrats who wanted to see social acceptance of the ingrained bourgeois idea of the just life, her mother came from a family of German nationalists, later National Socialists, who were unable to dispense with a fascist aesthetic of heroism and death worship. Lisbeth Cresspahl wants to erase the guilt of her family's devotion to fascism, but she only succeeds in perpetuating it. After an early suicide attempt by drowning fails, she ends her life in the other element, fire. And before she does so, she tries to drown her five-year-old daughter Gesine so that she will be "safe," "far from guilt and becoming guilty" (2: 618).

Gesine's fear of passing on this guilt ensures that she thinks of herself as her "father's daughter" (2: 619). Daughter of her father, she recounts her genealogy to Marie, daughter of a mother, in long sequences where the work of mourning operates free from all repression. This mother-daughter relationship could not be less removed from posturing and sentimentality. The two of them are aware that existence cannot succeed as an everyday process if it does not possess a past as much as a present. To be sure, this hope is deployed by a figure living in a time without hope in both a biographical and a political sense.

Lack of hope is the point of convergence for three basic political sets of events during the year 1968. Gesine Cresspahl's consciousness registers them with remarkable, indeed overwhelming, sobriety. The Vietnam War, the impending Soviet intervention in Prague, and the empty gestures of the Student Movement enter into a constellation that clouds the hope for a liberated life. Hans Magnus Enzensberger's belief in the possibility of political engagement in those years, a belief that Johnson criticizes paradigmatically in his novel's entry for leap-year day, February 29, 1968 (2: 794–803), is revealed as naiveté about the way history functions. In his Frankfurt lectures on poetics, Johnson characterized his fictional character's remoteness from hope as a lack of joyful anticipation. Gesine, to whom he attributes a life of her own that holds sway even over the narrator, gradually loses her ability to look toward the future and turns increasingly to the past "in an attempt to discover how those preceding circumstances in her life were bound together by something other than mere succession" (*Begleitumstände,* 414).

Gesine Cresspahl repeatedly finds the other element, the one that ties her life's situations together into something beyond mere concatenation. This element is the metamorphosis of existence for which a very basic style of life is sufficient. The insight that this life contains not one but many stories whose strands can come together all the same leads the novel to conclude with a restrained celebration of the ever-metamorphosing human existence. Marie tells the story of a day on the Danish coast with her mother and an old friend, Herr Kliefoth: "As we walked along the beach, we got into the water. Shingle rattled about our ankles. We held each other by the hand: a child; a man on his way to the place where the dead are; and she, the child that I was" (4: 1891). A double metamorphosis: long waves that come in at a slant onto the beach of the fishing village Jerichow turn into the surf pounding the East Coast of the United States. The metamorphosis of locations in a non-synchronous life that persists in discovering elements of the biblical and the Mecklenburg Jericho(w) in the postmodern city of New York is joined by a metamorphosis of existence itself. Finite existence, in the face of inevitable dissociation, is held together by the power of memory and a joyful anticipation of the future that can also consist in joy over others and for others. Memory and anticipation, for their part, are bound together by the power of narration, which sets experience free and makes it possible for us to succeed in possessing ourselves without fear.

See also 1895, 1910, 1929 (Autumn), 1967, 1968

Bibliography: Uwe Johnson, *Jahrestage,* vols. 1–4 (Frankfurt am Main: Suhrkamp, 1988); *Anniversaries,* vol. 1 (contains vol. 1 and part of vol. 2 of the German original), trans. Leila Vennewitz (New York: Harcourt Brace Jovanovich, 1975); vol. 2 (contains the rest of vol. 2 and all of vols. 3 and 4), trans. Leila Vennewitz and Walter Arndt (New York: Harcourt Brace Jovanovich, 1987). ———, *Begleitumstände: Frankfurter Vorlesungen* (Frankfurt am Main: Suhrkamp, 1980). Ulrich Fries, *Uwe Johnsons Jahrestage: Erzählstruktur und Politische Subjektivität* (Göttingen: Vandenhoek & Ruprecht, 1990). Sara Lennox, "History in Uwe Johnson's *Jahrestage,*" *Germanic Review* 64 (1989): 31–41. Bernd Neumann, *Utopie und Mimesis: Zum Verhältnis von Ästhetik, Gesellschaftsphilosophie und Politik in den Romanen Uwe Johnsons* (Kronberg: Athenäum, 1978).

Jochen Hörisch

♫ 1984, September

The epic cinematic journey *Heimat* makes its debut on West German television

Homeland and Holocaust

When Edgar Reitz's fifteen-and-a-half-hour opus *Heimat* aired on West German television (ARD) during the fall of 1984, it took on the dimension of a national epic. "A Yearning for Heimat," proclaimed *Der Spiegel* in a cover story about the film's enthusiastic public reception. Indeed, more than 25 million viewers saw at least one episode. The chronicle of the family Simon and the fictional village of Schabbach traces much of the course of German experience in the 20th century. Rather than writing history large, the narrative limits its focus to everyday life in the Hunsrück region, a rural corner of western Germany between the Rhein, Mosel, and Nahe valleys. The film's eleven installments span the years 1919 to 1982, from World War I and the German defeat, to the rise of National Socialism and radical modernization during the Nazi regime, the impact of World War II, Allied occupation and postwar reconstruction, the new prosperity in the 1950s, the political changes and economic challenges of an increasingly global world, and ultimately to the transformation of the homeland into a virtual space.

The film is the work of Edgar Reitz, who was a signatory of the famous Oberhausen Manifesto (1962), in which twenty-six angry young film directors promised to bring about the birth of a new German cinema. Reitz and his cohorts spoke out against the medium's abuse under Hitler as well as what they saw as its moribund state in the postwar period. They assailed the established film industry for its deference to reactionary politics and commercial priorities, its lack of personal vision, formal sophistication, and experimental incentive. The pioneers of what would become the New German Cinema (NGC) denounced West Germany's willingness to suppress the Nazi past, to fall in with the dictates of Allied foreign policy, and to become a cold war bastion.

During the mid- to late 1970s, the NGC gained widespread notoriety, success at foreign film festivals, and circulation in international art houses. Its productions came to serve as models for an alternative cinema that defied the cultural mainstream. The central figures of the NGC were deeply suspicious of the entertainment industry and fashioned their works as acts of resistance. Rainer Werner Fassbinder stretched generic conventions to reveal the falseness and emptiness of Hollywood illusions. Werner Herzog probed borderline situations, exotic realms, and extreme subjectivities to produce images never seen on film. Wim Wenders's road movies showed restless young Germans living fugitive lives between stations, eternally in transit and for that reason at home nowhere. Alexander Kluge promoted a cinema that does not guide and overwhelm people, but rather offers heterogeneous collections of materials for spectators to create films in their own minds. NGC members fostered a counter public sphere, more extensive and inclusive than the closed world of the dominant media. Among the things they provided were alternative images of sex and gender roles, feminist narratives, omnibus films measuring the state of contemporary Germany, avant-garde challenges to ways of seeing, anti-establishment militant pamphlets, and documentaries of marginalized groups and minority perspectives. Despite a lack of financial success, NGC cultivated support systems—public subsidies and cooperative arrangements with television—that ensured a continuing base for production. Having gained stature and self-assurance, the NGC sought to renew German film history and reinvent Germany.

Reitz was an ardent advocate of an *Autorenkino,* a German cinema of auteurs, and as such he positioned himself as an agent of historical memory based on the belief that "film has much in common with our ability to remember." He attacked the American television series *Holocaust,* whose four parts appeared on West German television early in 1979 to seismic public response. The narrative featured two historical destinies: the Weiss family, assimilated Jews with a strong allegiance to German culture, who are persecuted and most of whose members perish in the death camps; the Dorf family are opportunists who profit from Hitler's rise to power and eventually become complicit in Nazi crimes. Sympathizing with the victims of violence, German audiences identified with the Jews as Jews. For the first time, it was said, a feature film about the Holocaust had managed to catalyze profound reflection in the Federal Republic about this repressed chapter of the past. Reitz strongly disagreed. He assailed the Hollywood mini-series for its false perspectives and schematic contrivances, its deference to soap opera aesthetics and its expropriation of Germany's past. Applying the rules of show business to German memory meant for Reitz a profound loss of experience and language. "With *Holocaust,*" he lamented, "the Americans have taken away our history."

Heimat would become Reitz's answer to *Holocaust*—a showdown with an American television series and a reckoning with German history. It was a product of Reitz's biography, his youth in the Hunsrück, as well as his collaboration over five years with scriptwriter Peter Steinbach and people from the region. *Heimat* consummated NGC's longstanding dream of a collective national epic and realized Reitz's radical desire to pursue "memory work" *(Erinnerungsarbeit)* that would challenge the dominant historiography, to reawaken immediate experience with sensual images that retain "the actual living substance of history." The film, with its elaborate cast—32 professional actors, 159 amateurs, and 3,863 extras—most of them speaking in the local dialect, followed the fate of a family over three generations. Mathias, a blacksmith and farmer, and his wife, Maria, are the parents of Eduard, Pauline, and Paul. The film's opening sequence shows the latter's return from the battlefields of World War I. He marries Maria Wiegand, but, increasingly restless and disaffected, he leaves Schabbach and settles in America. Katharina and Maria Simon are the abiding embodiments of *Heimat,* matriarchs associated with a timeless sanctity, emotional warmth, and an ahistorical realm of production and nurture. The death of Maria and the collapse of the family conclude the extensive saga of disintegration. A journey in time, the narrative depicts the vanishing of a tradition and a domestic space, a process attended by an acute blend of melancholy and disenchantment. In the closing passage, the Simon house becomes a historical monument maintained by an American foundation.

There was something bold about Reitz's conscious evocation of *Heimat,* a conflicted notion that brought to mind romantic vistas of rural splendor and pastoral bliss, but also recalled Nazi territorial aggression, glorification of native blood and soil, and persecution of all those deemed trespassers. As a distinctly German experience, the word *Heimat* conjures up an imaginary space of unity and succor, a shelter against modernity and the shock and fragmentation brought about by fundamental shifts in time and space. To make a film about *Heimat,* the director also had to reckon with the legacy of the *Heimatfilm,* a persistent genre in German film history, especially in the postwar era of the 1950s.

When the Oberhausen activists revolted against the German film establishment, they particularly had in mind the forces that had produced *Heimatfilme,* of which no fewer than three hundred appeared between 1947 and 1960. Makeshift domiciles for a nation in need of psychological and material shelter, these sentimental tales displayed a reassuring world of intact communities and unspoiled landscapes. In the early 1970s, the NGC had taken exception to this legacy in a series of *Anti-Heimatfilme,* which depicted the narrowness and inequity of provincial life and in which the picture postcard idylls of a previous era were replaced by less upbeat views of poverty-stricken peasants, tormented outsiders, and ruthless authorities.

Reitz's film vacillated between picturesque and ironic perspectives, at once extolling the homeland and dramatizing how its provincialism can catalyze a desire for wider experience. Each installment begins with an introduction by Glasisch Karl, an eccentric figure from the village, who reviews piles of photographs, images that quote and complement scenes from previous episodes and in that sense function as mediated memories. In contrast to the transparent narratives of generic convention, Reitz's epic foregrounds its own workings, as a collection of images, as a gathering of stories, and as a film that refers to other films (including the sights and sounds from both classical and critical *Heimatfilme*). It also reflects on the history of the media; we see how radios, cameras, and sound recorders gradually enter the everyday. These tools open up the world and at the same time undermine the intimacy of families and diminish the immediacy of reality. In bringing things closer, the media distance people from lived experience and spur the wish to transcend local horizons. Paul Simon is fascinated with technology and finds life in Schabbach increasingly stifling. One day he marches out of town and off into the distance; years later, after the war, he reappears as a wealthy American industrialist. Reitz's *Heimat* illustrates the toll modernity and modernization take on an extended family and a rural landscape. And yet, in this account, homeland and modernity are not placed in simple opposition to each other. Rather they become inextricably bound, even if the *Heimat* resists the changes of modern times—urbanization, tempo, abstraction, alienation. For all its formal complexity, self-reflexivity, and ironic sophistication, Reitz's film at times recalls traditional *Heimatfilme.* It sustains a marked polarity between the homeland and the rest of the world, vesting positive energies in the native soil and viewing sources of disturbance—be they National Socialism or American consumer culture—as intrusions and maintains an emotional tie to a pre-modern community.

Amid widespread concern in the 1970s about the atrophying of the countryside—acid rain and dying forests—and predictions of ecological catastrophes, environmentalists and citizen initiatives had cultivated a new relation to the homeland. While the film was in production, masses of activists throughout Germany were protesting against nuclear power and the danger posed by mounting cold war tensions and the introduction of NATO missiles. In the wake of these threats, a new sense of *Heimat* took shape. Germans embraced concepts once taboo, like nation and homeland, without the customary sense of uncertainty and shame.

According to dissenting voices in a chorus of international enthusiasts, the NGC's pinnacle also marked its aporia. *Heimat* responded to *Holocaust,* it was argued, by repressing the Holocaust. It presented a cozy, generally uncritical identification with the denizens of Schabbach and portrayed at length the upbeat side of National Socialism, the pride, the prosperity, and the well-being. Although one-third of its running time occurs during the Nazi period, the film shows next to no Nazi violence and nothing of the persecution of the Jews. Even if the film provided an alternative perspective, its idiosyncratic view became implicated in a larger debate about German history. The mideighties, to be sure, occasioned much soul searching as Germany observed various anniversaries: fifty years since Hitler's rise to power in 1933, forty years since the plot of July 20, 1944, and the German surrender on May 8, 1945, which was commemorated by Chancellor Kohl and President Reagan in a controversial ceremony at the military cemetery in Bitburg. The German public continued to grapple with the place of National Socialism in their collective self-understanding. A vehement *Historikerstreit,* a debate among leading historians, brought matters to a head. Reputable scholars reevaluated Nazi crimes and sought to justify them (even if monstrous and misguided) as defensive reactions to real threats. Seen in the context of other historical instances of mass murder, Nazi terror and genocide lost their unprecedented status. By removing from the murder of the Jews the stigma of singularity, one could hope to rethink German history and to refurbish national identity.

Viewed within the constellations of the *Historikerstreit* and Bitburg, NGC's most celebrated revisitings of the Nazi period—from Hans-Jürgen Syberberg's *Hitler, ein Film aus Deutschland (Our Hitler),* Helma Sanders-Brahms's *Deutschland, bleiche Mutter (Germany, Pale Mother),* and Fassbinder's *Lili Marleen,* to Reitz's *Heimat*—resonated in unexpected ways, evincing undeniable traces of revisionist rhetoric. In its most highly acclaimed historical narratives, modern Germany was presented as a country of victims and martyrs, of innocent and impotent bystanders. Repeatedly, the nation was allegorized as a violated or a vulnerable female body: as in *Heimat,* women were recruited as the stand-ins for a beleaguered homeland. These retro-scenarios systematically overlooked Jewish suffering and underplayed the killing machine. Since the late 1970s, the NGC had been engaged by the German Foreign Office and was presented in Goethe Institutes throughout the world as a valuable cultural ambassador. Nonetheless, in the minds of some commentators, this important counter-cinema, for all its formal power, historical urgency, and subjective volition, had now become complicit with revisionist forces.

Heimat elicited a profusion of historical period pieces that explore the Nazi past and its legacy within provincial localities and lush landscapes. Christian Wagner's vividly photographed and widely praised *Wallers letzter Gang* (1988; *Waller's Last Walk*), like *Heimat,* alternates between black-and-white and color footage, fixes on snapshots and albums, and exhibits atmospheric images of rural stretches. As an old railroad inspector makes his way down the tracks for the last time, he recollects a half-century of his life and, in the process, retraces German history. In Joseph Vilsmaier's *Herbstmilch* (1988; *Autumn Milk*), the viewer is led through the space of a woman's memory, while witnessing the change of seasons and the enduring strength of peasant life from 1938 to 1944. Michael Verhoeven's *Das schreckliche Mädchen* (1989; *The Nasty Girl*) is the exception in these revisionist tableaux. The high school girl Sonja scrutinizes the recent past of her birthplace Pfilzingen for an essay competition about "My Hometown under National Socialism." Instead of unearthing tales of courageous resisters, the intrepid researcher comes upon many skeletons in the city's closet and causes an uproar among church and municipal leaders.

Filmic representations of the Holocaust remained rarities in the Federal Republic until the late 1990s. Peter Lilienthal's *David* (1979) tells the story of a Jewish boy living underground in wartime Berlin. Michael Hoffmann and Harry Raymon's *Regentropfen* (1981; *Raindrops*) follows a Jewish family from a small Hunsrück village who were forced to abandon their home and small business and seek refuge abroad. The film's muted black-and-white images and low-key dramaturgy offers perspectives that made the lacunae of *Heimat* quite apparent—at least for the very few people who saw it. Didi Danquart's *Viehjud Levi* (2000; *Jew-Boy Levi*) likewise concentrates on the life of a Jew caught between the political fronts in a country on the move. Like *Heimat,* it views history from below, but differently. It elaborates the tribulations of Levi, a wandering peddler whose return to a Black Forest hamlet coincides with the arrival of a Nazi engineer and his brutal minions. In Reitz's retrospective reading of the 1930s and 1940s, Hunsrück Jews were present in passing verbal references but visually absent. Danquart's social drama fills in the blanks of *Heimat* and shows a fuller, far less idealized picture of the homeland.

Is it possible in postwar Germany to say *Heimat* and not speak of the Holocaust? Edgar Reitz's response to this dilemma was both impassioned and equivocal. He did not, he maintained, set out to idealize the homeland. His aim was to use it as a site of German memories. To be sure, Reitz painstakingly disclosed the Nazis' use of technology as a driving force in their destruction of pre-modern ways of life. He also showed how many Germans prospered under Hitler and at what price. Without question, he made clear that the Heimat, while for many a source of comfort, can also be inhospitable, cruel, and oppressive. The film, in fact, is at its strongest during the opening episode when the village is seen from the returned veteran Paul's increasingly distanced and disaffected perspective. This critical view all but disappears during the Nazi-era passages, which have little to say or show about German acts of violence and the true victims of history. If he had included the Holocaust in his epic, Reitz noted, the film would "have taken a different turn." Which is to say, as Gertrud Koch retorted, "in order to tell the myth of *Heimat,* the trauma of Auschwitz has to be bracketed from German history." A consummate act of memory work and the culmination of NGC's grand project, *Heimat* demonstrated the forgetfulness that can lie in remembering.

See also 1921, 1935, 1952 (Spring), 1986

Bibliography: Celia Applegate, *A Nation of Provincials: The German Idea of Heimat* (Berkeley: University of California Press, 1990). Peter Blickle, *Heimat: A Critical Theory of the German Idea of Homeland* (Rochester, N.Y.: Camden House, 2002). Elizabeth Boa and Rachel Palfreyman, *Heimat: A German Dream* (New York: Oxford University Press, 2000). Anton Kaes, *From Hitler to Heimat: The Return of History as Film* (Cambridge, Mass.: Harvard University Press, 1989). David Morley and Kevin Robins, "No Place Like Heimat: Images of Home(land) in European Culture," *New Formations* 12 (Winter 1990): 1–24. *New German Critique,* "Special Issue on Heimat," 36 (Fall 1985). Rachel Palfreyman, *Edgar Reitz's Heimat: Histories, Traditions, Fictions* (Frankfurt am Main: Peter Lang, 2000). Edgar Reitz, *Liebe zum Kino: Utopien und Gedanken zum Autorenfilm 1962–1983* (Cologne: Verlag Köln, 1984). Edgar Reitz and Peter Steinbach, *Heimat: Eine deutsche Chronik* (Nördlingen: Greno, 1988). Eric Santner, *Stranded Objects: Mourning, Memory, and Film in Postwar Germany* (Ithaca, N.Y.: Cornell University Press, 1990).

Eric Rentschler

♫ 1986, Summer

Jürgen Habermas chastises conservative historians for their attempts to "normalize" the German past

Democracy and Discourse

The postwar cultural history of the Federal Republic of Germany can be understood as a struggle with the German past. Since the publication of Karl Jaspers's *The Question of German Guilt* in 1946, the official attitude among German intellectuals was one of penitence and contrition with regard to the atrocities perpetrated by Germany during World War II. However, the intelligentsia remained by and large silent on the mass murder of the Jews, later called the Holocaust, in the immediate postwar period. Even in the early years after the war, there were voices who expressed a desire, mostly in private, for an end to Germany's special status and a more normal, sanitized approach to German history. It was only with the rise of the student movement in the late 1960s that a more politicized German citizenry confronted the Nazi crimes with abhorrence and shame.

With the election in 1982 of a coalition government presided over by the conservative Christian Democrat Helmut Kohl, revisionists seemed to believe that their day had come to effect a change in the long-held consensus concerning the Nazi past and set the stage for a confrontation with the liberal cultural elite. On July 11, 1986, the philosopher Jürgen Habermas took up the challenge. In an essay that inaugurated the controversy, "A Kind of Settling of

Damages," Habermas alleged that a conservative conspiracy was afoot that sought to reinterpret the legacy of German fascism and the Holocaust. He singled out for criticism three historians whose work he believed distorted the historical and political events of the past. Implicit in the writings of these conservative historians, he alleged, was the demand that the Federal Republic acquire its self-confidence as a member of the Western alliance by salvaging an acceptable past.

Habermas begins his observations on recent historiography with Michael Stürmer, a historian formerly at the University of Erlangen who was then a speechwriter for Kohl and director of a conservative think tank, the Ebenhausen Foundation for Science and Policy. According to Habermas, Stürmer had suggested in recent essays that the German government should not be content with being an administrative agency, but should, like a religion, give meaning and identity to its citizenry by furthering patriotism and a sense of national belonging. Stürmer is also said to have proposed that the government attempt to mold historical consciousness on the basis that "whoever fills the memories, coins the concepts, and interprets the past will win the future." A conservative historiography, therefore, was in Stürmer's opinion both morally legitimate and politically necessary. What Habermas found abhorrent about these views was the way history was being made the instrument of politics. Stürmer's remarks, he concludes in his essay, countenance a right-wing historiography that will work in consonance with the recently elected coalition government to construct a new national consciousness.

Indeed, Stürmer's agenda seemed to have found its way into the writings of the academic historian Andreas Hillgruber. A professor at the University of Cologne who worked extensively on diplomacy and foreign affairs, Hillgruber published in early 1986 two essays dealing with World War II in a short book entitled *Two Kinds of Demise: The Shattering of the German Reich and the End of European Jewry*. The very formulation appeared suspect to Habermas. The word "shattering" presupposes an act of aggression and an agent performing the aggressive act. An "end," by contrast, comes about of its own accord. The two accounts, left unconnected by the author, confirmed the bias of the title. In the first essay, Hillgruber explores the reasons why the soldiers on the Eastern front fought so desperately at the end of the war. He portrays the physical suffering of the civilian population at the hands of the invading Red Army and provides a detailed psychological portrait of the German soldier fighting to enable innocent victims of war to escape the clutches of Soviet revenge. The second essay is dry and factual; occurrences are narrated in a detached tone. There is no attempt to empathize with the fate of individual Jews. Indeed, the focus is on "Jewry," a collective noun that was evidently selected to parallel "Reich." The discrepancy in style and sympathies thus appears to underscore the infelicitous title. What disturbed Habermas most about Hillgruber's book was the historian's sympathy with the plight of the German soldier on the Eastern front, combined with a disregard for the larger issues of justice. Historians should not neglect the soldiers' subjective perspective but they must recognize it as a limited viewpoint invalidated by subsequent events. Habermas contended that Hillgruber eschewed what would be a normal, hermeneutic perspective on the important moral questions of the war. By proceeding in this fashion, he provided an acceptable German past, populated by well-meaning, courageous soldiers who are unfortunately fighting for an evil regime, but against an equally nefarious enemy.

The third person whose works incurred Habermas's criticism was not a historian by training. Ernst Nolte, a student of Martin Heidegger, is a philosopher by trade, although he is best known for his studies in the history of political ideas. His phenomenological approach to political history in *Der Faschismus in seiner Epoche* (1963; *Three Faces of Fascism*) was well received in Germany and abroad, and his work since then has centered on issues surrounding 20th-century German history. Nolte, more than any other intellectual besides Habermas, was responsible for the outbreak of what came to be known as the *Historikerstreit* ("historians' dispute"). Nolte fired the opening salvo with his article "The Past That Will Not Go Away" in the *Frankfurter Allgemeine Zeitung* of June 6, 1986. He states that this essay was originally scheduled to be read at the "Römerberg Conversations" in Frankfurt (a yearly forum devoted to discussion of important issues), but that he had been disinvited for unknown reasons and was thus compelled to publicize his thoughts in the newspaper instead. Since Habermas was a member of the board of the organization sponsoring the talks, and since the historians Hans and Wolfgang Mommsen, whose views on National Socialism are more in line with those of Habermas than with those of Nolte, held talks on the same topic on which Nolte was supposed to speak, there was at least some suggestion that Habermas, directly or indirectly, had something to do with the perceived snub. Habermas, who concedes he was privy to the correspondence between Nolte and the organizers, asserts that the essay was published in the newspaper under a "hypocritical pretext."

Much of Nolte's essay is devoted to a provocative discussion of the taboos surrounding National Socialism. Among the more controversial aspects of the article is his challenge to the uniqueness of the Holocaust. Using illustrations of other mass murders in the 20th century, he argues that the murder of the Jews was far from being an original undertaking and was in fact the German response to the same sort of social crises that gave rise to the Gulag. He suggests that it was an "Asiatic deed"—like the Turkish massacre of Armenians—committed to assure that Germany would not fall victim to a similar "Asiatic deed." Habermas saw Nolte's argument against the unique nature of the Holocaust as in line with the agenda Stürmer posed for historians interested in shaping present and future German identity. By relativizing the responsibility for the destruction of European Jewry, Nolte put into question the concept of moral responsibility that had become an accepted part of German consciousness since the end of World War II. By presenting the Soviet Union in its Stalinist phase as the ultimate model for the genocide, he fostered postwar Germany's connection with NATO and its cold war policies. The memory of the murdered Jews is sacrificed for the sake of a national history that is both purified, in the relative sense of not being any worse than other national histories, and characterized as steadfastly anticommunist.

Habermas's vehement critique of the three historians was prompted by his perception that they were part of a mounting effort to alter the political culture of the Federal Republic. Just one year prior to the historians' dispute, the Kohl government had attempted to stage a revision of the past by inviting President Ronald Reagan to participate in a commemorative ceremony at the military cemetery at Bitburg. This plan backfired, however, when it was revealed that forty-nine members of the Waffen SS were interred there. Some of these had participated in the massacre of civilians at Oradour-sur-Glane, France, in June of 1942, while others may have even served in concentration camps. Although the Kohl government was eventually discredited, Habermas argued that it endeavored to shift public sentiment away from the implicit moral consensus on the Nazi regime and its crimes. In an essay entitled "Defusing the Past," Habermas claims that President Reagan's appearance at Bitburg was part of a bargain: the gesture of reconciliation as compensation for the recent agreement to allow missiles to be stationed on German soil. But in striking this bargain, Reagan allowed himself to be made a pawn in an internal German dispute over politics and history. When the Kohl government failed in this effort, other forces had to be mobilized for the task of recasting the past. For Habermas the work of the conservative historians was a second ideological wave following the debacle at Bitburg.

Habermas's intervention in 1986, as well as his remarks about Bitburg in 1985, were consistent with his political practice and the theoretical principles he has held throughout his career. The monograph that established his prominence among West German intellectuals, *The Structural Transformation of the Public Sphere* (1962), dealt with the rise and fall of public discourse. Here he had argued that the public sphere was becoming increasingly deformed in the 20th century. His subsequent works can be seen as either contributions to a theory of unconstrained, reflective discourse or as strategic interventions that engage in critical debate with important theories or tendencies. He had allied himself with Theodor Adorno in a campaign against positivism and empirical reductionism in the social sciences, but a few years later, he also spoke out against impulses in the student movement that would have eliminated debate and free speech. His accusation of "leftist fascism" among student leaders was consistent with his opposition to nonreflective, noncritical thought. In the late 1960s, Habermas criticized the hermeneutics of Hans-Georg Gadamer and the social theory of Niklas Luhmann. Although Gadamer and Luhmann held antithetical positions on science and interpretation, Habermas detected in both the kind of exclusion of critique and reflection he deemed necessary for maintaining discourse and democracy. In a critique of poststructuralism in the 1980s, Habermas warned against abandoning enlightenment principles and suggested that the project of modernity can be completed through a turn to intersubjective forms of rationality.

In over four decades of intellectual life, Habermas has been a staunch advocate of open debate and has contributed to it himself. To a certain extent, he has assumed the role of public conscience in Germany, especially with regard to Nazi crimes. His intervention in 1986 was thus consistent with his previous theory and practice. Yet, not even Habermas could have predicted the virulent response his critique would unleash. The debate went on for more than a year, yielding scores of essays and more than a half-dozen books as historians and other scholars crossed swords over the meaning of fascism, the Holocaust, and historiography. Unfortunately most of the subsequent controversy focused on issues that were tangential at best to Habermas's concerns. Whether the Holocaust was unique or not and how best to write the history of Nazi Germany are important matters, but Habermas's main point was that the introduction of scholarly discussions into the public realm ran the danger of turning historiography into an instrument for political ends.

In particular, Habermas objected to the exploitation of history to further national identity. The conservative historians were only significant inasmuch as they contributed to a political agenda aimed at forming a national consensus around "conventional" identity. Habermas charged that what Stürmer desired and what Hillgruber and Nolte promoted was a nonreflective consciousness that affirmed Germanness while excluding perspectives critical of nationhood. The implication was that a conservative political program can survive best when it is not subjected to the scrutiny of a critique based on universal values, such as those operative in Jaspers's seminal reflections in 1946. The perceived attempt to reinstitute a conventional morality—in the sense of an ethnically or culturally determined morality—strikes at the very core of Habermas's political thought and explains the caustic, vehement nature of his engagement.

To counter the historians' implicit program, Habermas put forth the notions of "constitutional patriotism" and "postconventional identity." Both terms are based on a reflective, critical appeal to universal values of justice and morality rather than to conventions or traditions of ethnic or cultural identity. Though eventually championed by Habermas's supporters, these notions may be too subtle and academic for political practice. Indeed, although by most accounts Habermas and his liberal supporters could claim victory in the historians' debate, subsequent events raised new questions about the status of their arguments. The sudden, unexpected dismantling of the Berlin wall in November of 1989 and the rapid movement toward German unity brought with it a surprising recrudescence of nationalist sentiments. In the areas of the defunct German Democratic Republic, the drive for unification with the West was fueled in part by the prospects of acquiring economic security, while in the Federal Republic many conservatives, sensing the culmination of their nationalist ambitions, were delighted that unification was so readily achieved. Both perspectives seemed to require a sacrifice of universalist values, as embodied in the theory of socialism or in the founding ethics of the West. Habermas, of course, also entered the debates surrounding unification, and predictably argued for a new constitution and an emphasis on the crimes against humanity during the Nazi era.

Instead, the two Germanys became a single entity by implementation of a section in the Basic Law of the Federal Republic that allowed for the simple absorption of the Eastern states. These events altered the political ideology in both areas. In retrospect, the historians' debate was less a continuation of controversies over the meaning of World War II and the Holocaust than an anticipation of the inevitable change in public discourse on the German past. The moral and later political consensus of the initial postwar decades was questioned for the first time publicly and repeatedly in a call for "normalcy." In this sense Habermas's essay in 1986 was not simply a rallying cry for the liberal camp, but a resolute attempt to defend the universalist foundations of the old Federal Republic.

See also 1942–43, 1946, 1967, 1984, 1989 (November 9)

Bibliography: Jürgen Habermas, *Eine Art Schadensabwicklung* (Frankfurt a.M.: Suhrkamp, 1987). ———, *The New Conservatism,* trans. Shierry Weber Nicholsen (Cambridge, Mass.: MIT Press, 1989). ———, *The Structural Transformation of the Public Sphere: An Inquiry into a Category of Bourgeois Society,* trans. Frederick Lawrence (Cambridge, Mass.: MIT Press, 1989). ———, *The Theory of Communicative Action,* 2 vols., trans. Thomas McCarthy (Boston: Beacon Press, 1984, 1987). Rudolf Augstein et al., *Historikerstreit: Die Dokumentation der Kontroverse um die Einzigartigkiet der nationalsozialistischen Judenvernichtung* (Munich: Piper, 1987). Robert C. Holub, *Jürgen Habermas: Critic in the Public Sphere* (London: Routledge, 1991).

Robert C. Holub

℞ *1989, February*

Thomas Bernhard's will prohibits all performance, publication, and recitation of his work in Austria

Remembrance as Provocation

In his narratives, novels, and dramas, Thomas Bernhard (1931–1989) railed relentlessly against his native Austria and everything Austrian. What he saw as his country's repression of its historical past, its Nazi and Catholic state of mind, the petty pride it took in its cultural heritage, its filthiness, sloppiness, and "alpine half-wittedness," all were targets of his invective. He was, in turn, attacked for befouling his own nest and decried as a cantankerous scandal seeker and troublemaker, a mischievous, eccentric misanthrope. His work *Holzfällen: Eine Erregung* (1984; *Cutting Timber: An Irritation*), for instance, was briefly banned by court order, when Gerhard Lampersberg, who had mentored Bernhard in the 1950s, recognized himself in one of the novel's figures and filed suit. When Bernhard died on February 12, 1989, he left a will that resembled his literary works in its provocation of his native land: "I emphatically stress that I do not want to have any dealings with the Austrian state," his testament declares. Consequently, the will forbade publication and performance of his works in Austria. Bernhard, however, did not invent the literary scandal of which his will is but the last instance. Rather, he took up what can be seen as a legacy characteristic of the Austrian literary tradition. One need only think of Arthur Schnitzler, who upset the public with his open portrayal of erotic fantasies at the beginning of the 20th century, or the members of the Vienna Group who scandalized conservative postwar society with eccentric language games and literary experiments in the early fifties. Like many of his literary works, Bernhard's last will seems to have triggered, paradoxically, an almost inevitable disregard for its problematic decrees. Ten years after Bernhard's death, the stipulations of the will have been circumvented through the establishment of a foundation (generously funded by the Austrian state), new performances of Bernhard's plays may be staged in Austria again, and his writing is now accessible for research.

Auslöschung: Ein Zerfall (1986; *Extinction: A Novel*) has often been regarded as Bernhard's literary legacy and the high point, thematically and formally, of his prose. The narrative was written between 1981 and 1986, immediately following the publication of his five-volume autobiography, which appeared between 1975 and 1981. *Auslöschung,* in turn, is structured as a (fictive) process of autobiographical remembrance, but also programmatically styles itself as an "anti-autobiography." The chief narrator, Franz-Josef Murau, takes up a project similar to one that had preoccupied his uncle and attempts to record everything that Wolfsegg, the family estate, has meant and still means to him. In doing so, Murau seeks to efface *(auslöschen)* the estate and its problematic legacy. The title, *Auslöschung,* hints at the effacement of an individual, a literary, and a historical inheritance. The narrative's plot is minimal—a characteristic of Bernhard's form-oriented writing, which often displays a musical structure reminiscent of twelve-tone music. Franz-Josef Murau has just returned to Rome after his sister's wedding in Wolfsegg, when he receives a telegram informing him about his parents' and his brother's death in an automobile accident. He returns to Wolfsegg for the funeral and donates his entire inheritance to the Jewish community in Vienna. The time of narration spans three days, divided into two parts: one, corresponding to the time in Rome after the narrator hears of the fatal accident, is entitled "The Telegram"; two consecutive days in Wolfsegg, including the preparations for the funeral and the funeral itself, comprise the narrative's second part, entitled "The Testament." The narrated time, however, is highly fractured by Murau's perspective and his interior monologue, ranging from his childhood reminiscences and extending over several generations of his family and the role Wolfsegg played during the Nazi era. The narrator's first name, Franz-Josef (the name of many rulers of the old Austrian-Hungarian Empire), marks him as the successor to a tradition and history whose continuity the narrative both reestablishes and effaces.

The violation of a testament, the decline of a burdensome inheritance, and its subsequent liquidation or donation is a theme that runs through Bernhard's narratives from the early 1960s to the 1980s. The heroes of his prose texts inherit sinister estates with vast, unproductive properties and gloomy castles and other edifices, charged with the trauma of an individual and historical past. They find themselves faced with a "Herkunftskomplex" (*Auslöschung*, 201), a descent complex, as Bernhard calls it. Intellectual émigrés who have left the stifling atmosphere of their home country for Stanford, Cambridge, Oxford, Madrid, or Rome are brought back to Austria by a bequest that forces them to confront again what they believed they had left behind. The oppressive estate in *Verstörung* (1967; *Gargoyles*) drives its owners to suicide or madness; Prince Saurau perceives life at Hochgobernitz as imprisonment and leaves his property to rot and decay. In *Ungenach* (1968), the single heir to one of the largest estates in Austria rids himself of the unwanted inheritance by donating it to family friends and employees whose lives are marked by isolation, misfortune, or failure. The character Roithamer in *Korrektur* (1975; *Correction*), who has fled the family estate Altensam for an intellectual life in England but is repeatedly drawn back to it, tries, but fails, to counteract its destructive effect by constructing a cone-shaped edifice for his sister, and ends, like so many of Bernhard's heroes, in suicide. The plot draws loosely on the biography of Ludwig Wittgenstein, who gave away his huge inheritance. In the narrative fragment *Der Italiener* (1965; *The Italian*), later rewritten as a film script (1971), a young heir returns to Wolfsegg after his father, no longer able to bear the estate's historical burden, has committed suicide. During the Nazi era, Germans shot Polish soldiers hidden in the estate's gazebo; their mass grave is still on the grounds, and the young heir has never been able to escape the memory of their screams. With the narrative of this lingering trauma, the young heir shatters an Italian friend's trust in an ultimately rational world history. In response, the Italian recommends the "Abschaffung" (abolition) of the estate.

The almost baroque conjunction of theatricality and death in the earlier narrative fragment *Der Italiener*—the prince's body is laid out in state amid masks and costumes in the gazebo where a theater production was to be staged, but which had also been the site of a traumatic historical past—recurs in Bernhard's later texts, most markedly perhaps in *Verstörung*. The film script *Der Italiener* of 1971 clearly served as the basis for *Auslöschung*. In *Auslöschung*, Murau not only reverts to the term "Abschaffung" when he declares that he has "abolished" and "effaced" Wolfsegg and everything Wolfsegg entails for him. The use of the word transposes the film script's directions for the camera shots into the narrator's interior monologue. In *Der Italiener,* the gaze of the camera is doubled by the lens of a surveyor and his assistants who are observing the position of the camera, as the camera, in turn, observes their position. Similarly, in *Auslöschung,* Murau's observations are doubled through his present perspective on his past views of Wolfsegg. Murau may vilify film as an instrument of brainwashing and stultification, yet in *Auslöschung* photography and cinema serve as the matrix from which the narrative process of remembrance unfolds.

Reversing the historical constellation in *Der Italiener,* where Wolfsegg's owners were themselves traumatized and victimized by a National Socialism ascribed only to the Germans, *Auslöschung* paints a different picture of

Wolfsegg as representative of Austria's past. Murau's parents were not only eager collaborators, they were also hiding Nazi functionaries at the end of the war in the so-called children's villa where theater performances were staged, analoguous to the gazebo where Polish soldiers were hidden in *Der Italiener.* For Murau, Wolfsegg even qualifies as a "stronghold of National Socialism, at the same time a stronghold of Catholicism" (*Auslöschung,* 196). Bernhard had already exposed what he saw as a peculiarly Austrian association between National Socialism and Catholicism in his autobiographical writings, especially in *Die Ursache* (1975; *Gathering Evidence*), as well as in plays like *Der Theatermacher* (1984; *The Theater Maker*) and even more so in *Heldenplatz* (1988; *Heroes' Square*). *Heldenplatz,* which focused on the resurgence of anti-Semitism in Vienna, was published the same year that Austria scheduled a *Gedenkjahr,* a year of remembrance for the victims of the Nazi era, and Kurt Waldheim, accused of an active Nazi past, was elected president. The play scandalized Austria. *Auslöschung* points to a dual historical reference, dovetailing Austria's past and present: Murau was born in 1934, the year Austro-Fascism, an authoritarian form of government backed by political Catholicism, established itself, and the novel, apparently finished as early as 1981–82, was published in 1986, the year of extensive discussions in Waldheim's election campaign.

In taking such a decisive stance against repression of a historical past that was all too often glossed over as victimization by Germany rather than active involvement in Nazism, Bernhard was in line with a trend characteristic of Austrian literature after 1945. In *Moos auf den Steinen* (1956; *Moss on the Stones*), Gerhard Fritsch explored the possibility of donating a historically charged estate to be used as a refugee home or a cultural center. In *Sonne und Mond,* "a historical novel from the present" (1962), Albert Paris von Gütersloh had one of his heirs employ a burdensome bequest only to destroy or efface his own line. Like these writers, Bernard rejects the idea of an "inherited" past that is an overtaxing burden. The repression and recurrence of a traumatic and destructive past also run as an undercurrent through the works of Ingeborg Bachmann and Paul Celan, two authors who appear as literary figures in Bernhard's *Auslöschung.* In Bachmann's *Malina* (1971), the brutalizing aspects of war and its crimes subliminally continue as "a dark history" in the structure of gender relations, or as a "history within the *I,*" as Bachmann phrased it in her Frankfurt lectures on poetics. Bernhard's "bohemian poem" in *Auslöschung* makes reference to one of Bachmann's poems, "Böhmen liegt am Meer" (Bohemia lies by the sea), while the configuration of a literary and philosophical discussion conducted in the mountains is reminiscent of Celan's prose text *Gespräch im Gebirg (Conversation in the Mountains).* Through these real-life intellectuals and writers, as well as the fictional characters of Murau's uncle and his student Gambetti, *Auslöschung* outlines the possibility—always fragile and vulnerable—of a counterworld to the Wolfsegg complex. The group's discussion of Maria's poems and Schopenhauer's philosophy, for instance, is violently interrupted by the outburst of an enraged innkeeper who slanders the group as "riff-raff" who should be "wiped out."

The semantic field covered by the word "Auslöschung"—it spans a range of meaning from the stronger "eradication," "liquidation," "wiping out," and "exterminating" to the weaker "effacement" and "obliteration"—indicates the complexity of Murau's intent to do away with everything that Wolfsegg stands for. *Auslöschung* does not simply continue the Austrian literary tradition of remembering a repressed historical past, as it may seem at first glance. While the word "Auslöschung" in the title is highly charged with semantics of eradication by the Nazi regime, the protagonist now engages in his own act of eradication: Murau's project is thoroughly affected by what it opposes. The novel *Auslöschung,* thus, takes its narrative principle yet one step further—and beyond the literary tradition of remembrance, which it recollects—by effacing its own narrative gesture of effacement. By exterminating Wolfsegg, Murau observes, he eradicates himself. The narrator's self-effacement is accomplished quite literally when Murau's death is reported at the end by a second narrator, who appears only at the very margins (a frequent narrative ruse in Bernhard's novels). The narrator's self-obliteration—a maneuver one might be tempted to label "postmodern"—manifests itself on different narrative levels. It is prefigured in the fact that the uncle has destroyed his anti-autobiography, a project the narrator then takes up and continues. The narrator, in turn, has only the title "Auslöschung" as a project that seems to remain only a plan. And the second narrator, who would have been able to elaborate on the terms and conditions of Murau's end, limits his minimal narrative to an obituary of the utmost brevity: "(born 1934 in Wolfsegg, died 1983 in Rome)."

Minimalist plots and a technique of recondensation that collapses narrative sequences onto a novel's title, or reduces them to what the author calls irritation words, are characteristic of Bernhard's narrative style. His irritation words are reminiscent of a technique with which the members of the Vienna Group—H. C. Artmann, Gerhard Rühm, Konrad Bayer, Oswald Wiener— had experimented in the early fifties: the isolation of concepts and the individuation of words severed from their semantic context and set off against the white space of the page in one-word tableaux or constellations. The long, breathless narratives Bernhard spawns cannot obscure this significant influence on his writing. Yet the Vienna Group's interest in anti-narratives and its concern with decontextualizing and desemanticizing ready-made linguistic material had carried formalist reduction too far. In order to avoid the deadlocks of linguistic formalization, subsequent authors—including Peter Handke and Elfriede Jelinek—tried to reembed some of the Vienna Group's innovations in the literary tradition. Thus the peculiar citational technique with which Thomas Bernhard renews traditional interior monologue—a technique that can be seen as the hallmark of his prose—also severs preformed linguistic and literary units from their original contexts, while no longer positioning them in a vacuum of signification.

In *Auslöschung,* the recombination of formalist reduction with literary tradition is highlighted through an excess of intertextual references. The character Murau calls himself a "literarischer Realitätenvermittler," a "literary real estate agent" but also a "mediator of literary realities." He assigns Jean Paul's *Siebenkäs,* Kafka's *Proceß,* Hermann Broch's *Esch oder die Anarchie,* Robert Musil's *Portugiesin,* Thomas Bernhard's *Amras,* and Goethe's *Wahlverwandtschaften* (among other literary works) to his student Gambetti and mentions, in addition, Schopenhauer's *Die Welt als Wille und Vorstellung* and Kierkegaard's *Krankheit zum Tode.* But even as it is preserved, this literary "real estate" undergoes an obliteration similar to the effacement of Wolfsegg. While seemingly embedding itself within a literary tradition, the novel cuts itself off from this tradition by reducing it to a mere list of relatively few titles. The novel's subtitle, *Ein Zerfall,* means "decay" or "disintegration"; it is placed where one might have expected a genre specification such as "a novel" (as the English translation indeed subtitles the book). *Auslöschung: Ein Zerfall* thus again points to itself: the 650-page account chronicling the eradication of a historical and literary tradition is, in a way, but its own title.

See also 1924, 1952 (Autumn), 1963, 1983

Bibliography: Ingeborg Bachmann, *Frankfurter Vorlesungen: Probleme zeitgenössischer Dichtung* (Munich: Piper, 1995). Thomas Bernhard, "Der Italiener," in *Insel-Almanach auf das Jahr 1965* (Frankfurt am Main: Insel, 1964), 83–93. ———, *Der Italiener: Ein Film* (Frankfurt am Main: Suhrkamp 1989). ———, *Auslöschung: Ein Zerfall* (Frankfurt am Main: Suhrkamp, 1988); *Extinction: A Novel,* trans. David McLintock (New York: Knopf, 1995). Oswald Wiener, "Das literarische Cabaret der Wiener Gruppe," in Gerhard Rühm, ed., *Die Wiener Gruppe* (Reinbek bei Hamburg: Rowohlt, 1967), 401–418. Gitta Honegger, *Thomas Bernhard: The Making of an Austrian* (New Haven, Conn.: Yale University Press, 2001).

Bianca Theisen

1989, November 9
The breach of the Berlin wall initiates a new architecture of commemoration

A Republic of Voids

The wall that had divided East and West Germany for twenty-eight years started to crumble in late autumn of 1989. With it came down the best-known architectural symbol of Berlin since its sudden appearance on August 12, 1961, in the midst of an escalating cold war. Stretching for 97 miles, of which 27 ran through the city of Berlin, it was painted drab blue on the eastern side and covered with a rainbow of graffiti on the western, and ominous warnings that doubled as political allegories—"You are leaving the American sector." Constructed by the GDR at the height of the cold war to keep its citizens from escaping to the West, it marked a de facto border between the capitalist and communist systems.

Used as an urban message board, the longest in any city before or since, it featured a motley blend of rhetorical modes—denunciations, calls to action, testaments, poems and puns, nostalgic or utopian longings, ironic musings—until an ebullient crowd began pulverizing it with hammers and chisels on the eve of November 9, 1989. The demolition of the wall heralded the first of

Present-day Germany. Dotted line indicates the former border between East and West

many architectural and political transformations Berlin would undergo in the course of its becoming the capital of a reunified Germany.

The presence of the wall had sensitized Berliners to how public space shapes the character of a city, just as its disappearance challenged them to advance conflicting conceptions of the new monuments and buildings that would be adequate to the task of marking a hopeful beginning and remembering the suffering of the victims of the Nazi Holocaust and of the East German state. More than in most cities, architecture in Berlin reveals the past traumas whose traces are still lodged in the spaces of everyday life. This allegorical dimension to its architectural and urban palimpsests, the impossibility of parsing history and representation, marked the two major commemorative projects that coincidentally, but significantly, originated in 1989. The highly public aesthetic and political negotiation of the contested domain of historical memory suggests a more profound engagement with the German past as a defining trait of the Berlin Republic.

On June 23 of that year, the architect Daniel Libeskind won the competition for the "Extension of the Berlin Museum with the Jewish Museum Department." Sponsored by the Berlin Senate, it entailed constructing an extension to the Berlin Museum housed in the Kollegienhaus, a 1735 Baroque building constructed for the Prussian chamber court whose interior was destroyed during the war. Trained as a concert pianist but equally well versed in literature, modern music, philosophy, and the visual arts, Libeskind, who was born in 1946 in Poland to a Jewish family that had been decimated in the Nazi Holocaust, submitted a bold design in exquisitely rendered presentation drawings.

Libeskind conspicuously rejected the idea of a museum as a neutral container and articulated the profound curatorial dilemma faced by the museum and conveyed in the competition's awkward official title. Should the collection of Jewish materials be exhibited in an autonomous museum and thereby replicate the strategy of cultural exclusion practiced by the Nazis? Or should it be displayed with the holdings of the Berlin Museum and incur the risk of excluding or minimizing the history of persecution and extermination that transformed its contents into museological objects? Pursuing an "integrationist" agenda, the museum conceived of its mission as reciprocally illuminating Judaism and Jewish culture and the history of Berlin. Housed in a separate museum attached to the Berlin Museum, the Jewish Museum Department would preserve and exhibit records and documents related to Jewish cultural traditions, the history of the Jewish community, its evisceration from the German body social by the Nazis, and the contributions of the Berlin Jews to the development of the city.

Libeskind gave his design scheme the title "Between the Lines" and developed it as the culmination of multiple engagements with Berlin and its prominent Jewish and gentile cultural figures. Locating the addresses of Heinrich von Kleist, Rahel Varnhagen, Heinrich Heine, Mies van der Rohe, Arnold Schoenberg, and Walter Benjamin on a city map, he connected these points into a system of intertwining triangles and generated the shape of the building that resembles a fractured Star of David. Schoenberg's opera *Moses and Aaron* fascinated Libeskind for two divergent reasons: the composer could start but not complete it in Berlin, and Moses was unable to express the revelation of God, in which he saw a powerful evocation of the limits of representation. As he consulted the *Gedenkbuch* (memorial book) of Berliners deported and murdered during the Holocaust, Libeskind was further sensitized to the palpable absences that permeated the postwar history of the city. He designed a continuous sequence of sixty sections in the museum's zigzag footprint to parallel the "stations of the star" outlined by Walter Benjamin's apocalyptic vision of Berlin in *Einbahnstrasse* (1924; *One-Way Street*). As it replicates Benjamin's abrupt transitions in sharp angles, dramatic thresholds, and foreboding deadends, Libeskind's construction is more closely derived from literature than architectural designs generally are.

The structure's most provocative and original aspect, the voids that run throughout the building fragmenting the exhibition areas into jagged, irregular spaces, have a stunning impact on the visitor. As he sought to represent the

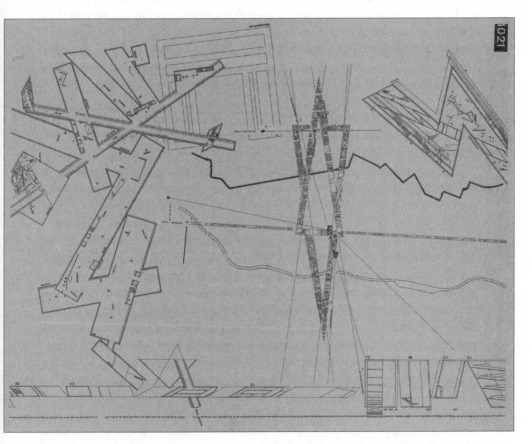

Plan for the Jewish Museum in Berlin by Daniel Libeskind, showing the Star of David created by mapping the addresses of prominent Jewish residents. (Studio Daniel Libeskind)

invisibility of the once vital Jewish presence in Berlin, which today is only discernible by reading "between the lines," Libeskind incorporated the empty, inaccessible spaces of absence, discontinuity, and reflection into the very shape of the building. In this way, he breaks with traditional museum architecture, which generally seeks to consolidate the cultural heritage. The voids in Libeskind's design evoke the absence of Jewish intellectual and cultural figures in contemporary Berlin as well as the "broken backbone" of the society from which the Holocaust issued.

If the voids stand for physical interference with chronology by displaying Jewish cultural objects in a destabilizing context and forestalling any unmediated continuities between their history and the German present, the interior plan of the museum fulfills a similar aim. Enabling the visitor to traverse its spaces as "open narratives," the entrance is more than thirty feet below the existing museum. This placement is meant to evoke the deep foundational affinity between German and Jewish culture and presents three possible itineraries, conceived as different historical modalities of this relationship. An "axis of continuity" suggests the present and the future and leads through the Kollegienhaus to the main exhibition areas. A second axis leads to the walled E. T. A. Hoffmann Garden, symbolizing exile and emigration and named after the writer who was for a time a judge in a nearby building. Its forty-nine columns planted with oak trees and stationed in a disorienting sunken floor are meant to evoke the year of Israel's independence, 1948, with an additional column containing soil from Jerusalem to represent Berlin. The third axis leads to the Holocaust Tower, a prisonlike structure accessible via a heavy metal door and illuminated by a distant window. Paul Celan's imagery of spatial passage is evoked by the courtyard named for the poet; its spreading mosaic is based on a drawing by his widow, Gisèle Celan-Lestrange.

At once suggesting the traditional Jewish prohibition against graven images, the voids in Libeskind's museum engage a rich legacy of literature, philosophy, and the arts. Jacques Derrida's theory of deferral of signification and Paul Klee's apocalyptic paintings of Berlin are but two of the references that commentators have noted. In its recourse to history, symbolism, and narrative, the building approaches the postmodernism espoused by Robert Venturi and Denise Scott-Brown. Yet its diagonally elongated windows, extensive use of unfinished concrete, and exterior cladding in zinc (a favorite material of the master Berlin architect Friedrich Schinkel) exude the confidence of an elegant high-tech modernism. Regardless of its ultimate genealogy or optimal categorization, the Jewish Museum struck an immediate chord with visitors whose enthusiastic patronage after the official opening on September 9, 2001, soon reached the highest attendance of any museum in Germany.

If Libeskind's museum explores historical memory through a unique architectural aesthetic, the fractious debates around the construction of a Holocaust memorial in Berlin introduced the problem of remembrance to the public arena of local and national politics. On November 7, 1989, the television journalist Lea Rosh, inspired by her visit to the Israeli Holocaust memorial, Yad

Vashem, established the "Supporters of the Construction of a Monument to the Murdered Jews of Europe" (Förderkreis zur Errichtung eines Denkmals für die ermordeten Juden Europas) to lobby politicians and gather public support for an earlier popular initiative associated with the Social Democratic Party. Its members included Daimler-Benz executive Edward Reuter, writer Siegfried Lenz, conductor Kurt Masur, and historian Eberhard Jäckel. Rosh was initially in favor of situating the monument on the former location of Albert Speer's chancellery, and rejected a proposal to build it on the "Topography of Terror," the former Gestapo headquarters complex, where Swiss architect Peter Zumthor later built a museum.

In October 1993, the Ministerial Gardens, a five-acre plot of land south of the Reichstag, the Brandenburg Gate, and Pariserplatz and close to the Potsdamerplatz and Berlin's main park, the Tiergarten, was made available by the federal government. Equally close to the sites of Hitler's bunker and chancellery, this central placement alongside the former "death strip" of the wall exploited the city's historically charged topography for the activation of collective memory. By means of a conspicuous public intervention in the urban landscape, it proposed the commemoration of the death of millions of Jews as the obligation of every German citizen and the permanent responsibility of the newly unified German state.

Proponents noted the absence of any monument or memorial where the German state publicly acknowledges its role in annihilating European Jewry, one-third of the total world Jewish population. The 1992 opening of a museum at the Wannsee villa, where the high-ranking SS officers and civil servants had convened in January 1942 to coordinate logistics for the Final Solution, underscored the central role the city of Berlin had played in this process as the center of power of the Nazi regime. Yet its location on the outskirts of the city minimized its public prominence. Similarly, Helmut Kohl's 1993 dedication of Schinkel's Neue Wache, an 1818 Prussian guard house on Unter den Linden, as a memorial to all victims of war and tyranny, struck Ignatz Bubis, the leader of Germany's Jewish community, as unsatisfactory because of its universalist grouping of Jewish victims with German perpetrators and the Christian symbolism conveyed by the pietà-like form of the interior sculpture by Käthe Kollwitz.

Disagreement over the proposed ends and means intensified. Romani Rose, leader of the Roma community, assailed that group's exclusion from a monument to the murdered Jews and attacked the alleged creation of an "apartheid" system that designated "first and second class" victims. The Berlin Building Senate agreed to construct a Roma memorial in front of the Reichstag. Julius Schoeps warned that the monument proposed by Rosh and her supporters had the potential of inadvertently stigmatizing Jews as "born victims." His fellow historian Reinhart Koselleck underscored the paradox of the German state commemorating Jewish suffering without the active involvement of the world Jewish community, a situation he claimed would officially "hierarchize" victims and more likely evoke the perpetrators and their crime. These issues were reflected in a fundamental terminological ambiguity. Was the project to be a *Denkmal* (monument serving as a remembrance) or a *Mahnmal* (monument serving as an admonishment) with its connotations of loss, warning, and admonition to avoid repeating the past?

In May 1994, 528 designs were submitted in open competition, followed by a public colloquium. On March 16, 1995, the jury composed of members of the "Supporters of the Monument" and government officials awarded first prize to the design of the Berlin architect Christine Jackob-Marks for a 20,000-square meter tilted concrete base on which the names of 4.5 million Holocaust victims were to be engraved. Its awkward monumentality displeased almost everyone, from Bubis to Daniel Cohn-Bendit, a European representative of the Green Party. Nazi hunter Simon Wiesenthal deflated its pretensions to historical completeness by noting that the names of many victims remain unknown. By June, Kohl had vetoed the project. Two years of political wrangling resulted in a second competition, whose jury and advisory committee included the distinguished architect Josef Paul Kleihues and the American Holocaust scholar James Young. In January 1998, the field was narrowed to four entries, with a design by architect Peter Eisenman and sculptor Richard Serra (who soon withdrew from the project) emerging as Kohl's favorite.

Their proposal to construct an undulating field of 4,200 unmarked concrete pillars, from one and a half to ten feet in height, refrained from any explicit symbolism, and Eisenman emphasized his desire for a monument that could not be photographed, just negotiated on foot by each individual visitor. As with Libeskind's museum, the design conceived of the Holocaust as an irreparable breach in German history that would be suggested by "an urban void" in the middle of Berlin. Its rejection of narrative or visual representation was even more strident than that of the Jewish Museum; its refusal to signify in the manner of a conventional monument was to evoke the Holocaust through an uncanny spatial and temporal experience. Eisenman spoke of his hatred of Steven Spielberg's film *Schindler's List,* which epitomized the "sentimental kitsch" his conception opposed.

Kohl requested modifications in the design to include parking for buses and sites for wreath laying and official visits. When he was replaced in office by the Social Democrat Gerhard Schroeder, the new Senator for Cultural Affairs, Michael Naumann, opposed what he regarded as the "Albert Speer monumentality" of Eisenman's design and proposed that Spielberg be invited to display his video archive of Holocaust survivors' narratives. Naumann and Eisenman eventually agreed on further changes in the design, including a reduction to 2,700 stelae and the inclusion of a "house of memory" that would contain an educational facility. On June 25, 1999, the Bundestag approved its construction by a vote of 314 to 209, with 14 abstentions. Ground breaking commenced on October 30, 2001.

The underlying stakes of the Holocaust memorial debate were revealed with particular clarity on October 11, 1998, when the writer Martin Walser, in his Frankfurt Peace Prize acceptance speech, attacked Eisenman's design as an instance of the pervasive "instrumentalization of our shame for contemporary purposes" in public life and criticized the invocation of Auschwitz as a "means of intimidation." Ignaz Bubis denounced his remarks as "intellectual arson" congenial to extreme rightists, while social theorist Jan-Philipp Reemtsma perceived in them a veiled attack against the efforts of victims of the Nazi forced labor system to obtain compensation from German corporations. By directing attention to the culture of commemoration, long a cornerstone of the Federal Republic of Germany, Walser and his critics revealed the ongoing contentions surrounding the Holocaust.

Architectural controversies in Berlin continue to make the newspaper headlines in the twenty-first century. After more than a decade of debate in the press, the German parliament voted on July 4, 2002, by a margin of 384 to 133 in favor of reconstructing the Royal Hohenzollern Palace. Its demolition by the East Germans on September 7, 1950, epitomizes for many West Germans the callous tastelessness they see as the legacy of the GDR. The kind of activities the new palace would house remained as vague as the source of the estimated 700 million Euros needed for its realization. Proponents laud the palace's connection to national tradition and the historical urban context that the faithful reconstruction of its baroque facade would create. Was the decision, which horrified both Libeskind and Eisenman, an implicit repudiation of architectural experimentation? Or was it a belated act of vengeance against the GDR regime that had gleefully torn down the aristocratic classical building to make way for an unsightly (but popular) Palace of the Republic? Once again, architecture provides a contentious focal point in contemporary Germany for the politics of remembrance and national identity.

See also 1952 (Autumn), 1984

Bibliography: Das Holocaust-Mahnmal: Dokumentation einer Debatte, ed. Michael S. Cullen (Zurich: Pendo, 1999). Andreas Huyssen, Present Pasts: Urban Palimpsests and the Politics of Memory (Stanford, Calif.: Stanford University Press, 2003). Brian Ladd, The Ghosts of Berlin: Confronting German History in the Urban Landscape (Chicago: University of Chicago Press, 1997). Daniel Libeskind, Jewish Museum Berlin (Amsterdam: G + B Arts International, 1999). James E. Young, At Memory's Edge: After-Images of the Holocaust in Contemporary Art and Architecture (New Haven, Conn.: Yale University Press, 2000).

                                                                    Edward Dimendberg

℞ 1999

The 250th anniversary of Goethe's birth is commemorated worldwide

The Skull beneath the Skin

In March 1999, the *Frankfurter Allgemeine Zeitung* ran a somewhat sensationalist article about an action the restoration department of the National

Museum in Weimar had undertaken in 1970. Noting that Goethe's body had begun to decay badly in its less than airtight coffin, the conservators decided to macerate—or cleanse—the bones before replacing them in a more protective sarcophagus. In so doing, they did exactly what Goethe himself had done with Schiller's skull and several bones after he had identified them—or persuaded himself that he had identified them—among a heap of bones in the crypt of the Weimar treasury, where they had been temporarily placed after Schiller's death in 1805.

Several days after the appearance of the article and its subsequent dissemination via television, the poet Durs Grünbein (b. 1962) wrote in the same paper, "if there is anything disturbing about the 'Goethe maceration,' it is the tireless work of digging by means of which an aura is thus undermined." Yet however seriously Goethe's reputation had been damaged by attacks on his "legendary status" in the aftermath of the 1968 student revolution in the year 1999, the 250th anniversary of the great writer's birth was celebrated around the world. The Goethe-Institut alone listed over 120 commemorative events in Europe, Africa, the Middle East, Asia, and Australia.

Critical debate about Grünbein's writing, especially since his receipt of the Büchner Prize in 1995, has tended to focus on what both his supporters and his detractors regard as the Benn heritage. Although Grünbein did not formally study medicine, he positions his work in the tradition of 20th-century writers who were also physicians by profession: Gottfried Benn, Alfred Döblin, and Ernst Weiss. He traces his integration of science and poetry to such earlier writers as Flaubert and Balzac as well. Yet clearly Grünbein's own poems and essays are also motivated by an ambition to rival Goethe. In a 1998 interview, Grünbein paid homage to Goethe by describing him as "the last universal genius in Germany—if we think of his [work on] morphology, his theory of colors, his [studies of] anatomy, and so forth." From this perspective, *Nach den Satiren (In the Manner of the Satires)* can be seen as a covert contribution to the celebratory activities of the Goethe anniversary.

Grünbein's earlier poetry, notably his volume *Schädelbasislektion* (1991; *Lesson from the Base of the Skull*), had already invited comparison with Goethe. Indeed, Grünbein's reflections on the human cranium can be seen as a continuation of Goethe's poetic and osteological obsession with Schiller's skull. Goethe's poem "Im ernsten Beinhaus . . ." (1826; In the solemn burial vault . . .) is as much a point of reference for Grünbein's *Schädelbasislektion* as are Goethe's anatomical studies, notably his discovery of the intermaxillary bone in the human jaw. Unlike Goethe, however, Grünbein does not undertake scientific studies himself: instead, he relies on scientific information that has filtered into the public imagination. In *Schädelbasislektion,* he develops a complex metaphor involving the brain stem and the cranial sutures. The brain stem, an important focus of modern medical research, consists of what remains of the fetal nervous system after other parts have differentiated to become the adult brain and spinal cord. The cranial sutures are the fusions that normally take place between what, in the fetus, were eight separate skull bones. In Grünbein's poetry, the cranial sutures stand for the "wall in the head," those traces of the division between former West and East Germany that persist in the psyches of German citizens even after the unification of the two countries in 1991.

The brain-stem metaphor represents subconscious attachments to the former East Germany and a more primitive way of life. Dresden, Grünbein's hometown, is the focus of these attachments. Playing on the similarity between the words "Lektion" (lesson) and "Läsion" (lesion), Grünbein proposes a connection between the trauma induced by the Allied bombing of Dresden during World War II and the trauma some psychologists impute to the physical experience of birth. He sees Dresden as the image of a "wound" in German cultural consciousness that should not be covered over. Rather than accepting a merger in which East Germany is simply assimilated into the Western culture of the Federal Republic, Grünbein suggests in *Schädelbasislektion* that something of the former German Democratic Republic should be retained, much as the brain contains the primitive brain stem within its mature structure. In making this suggestion, Grünbein consciously joins the debate initiated by Christa Wolf's novel *Was bleibt* (*What Remains,* 1990), about the problem of continuity and rupture after the reunification of the two German states. Eastern Germany's communist period has come to an end, but this historical break raises urgent questions about how and if post-unification culture should record both the memory of its oppressions and the sometimes flourishing literature born of the attempt to grapple with these oppressions.

Nach den Satiren is a meditation on this question of "what remains" after the fall of the Berlin Wall. A gently humorous five-line poem titled "Physiognomischer Rest" (Physiognomic Remains) filters this debate through an allusion to Goethe. Looking at himself in the mirror and focusing on his jaw (thus suggesting Goethe's anatomical investigations), the speaker of Grünbein's poem contrasts his present unshaven state with a future state in which his jaw will be no more than a white curve of bone. Goethe's conviction that he had picked Schiller's skull out of a pile of bones in a crypt is suggested by the opening lines, in which the speaker imagines someone finding his own skull after his death "among other bones." Grünbein's ironic approach to what remains of the human body also applies to the literary tradition.

In a note to *Nach den Satiren,* Grünbein explains how he understands the word "satire," in Latin originally a kind of poem recited after a banquet (the Latin *lanx satura* means "full plate"). "After the satires: that meant once everything had been said and chewed over, the way home, the hang-over, the time for intellectual play and digestion." The word "nach" in the title of Grünbein's volume has a dual meaning of "subsequent" and "in the manner of": in other words, it is both a work postdating the Classical satires and an imitation of the satiric mode developed by Juvenal. The poems attempt to register a bitter awakening on the part of East Germans after the first excitement of German reunification has worn off. Expecting to enjoy the economic prosperity or "full plate" of the Federal Republic, former East Germans are disappointed to find that their lives are still difficult and that they are not always fully accepted by their new fellow citizens. Traces of the East German past remain engraved, as it were, on the faces and in the minds of those who experienced it. Grünbein visualizes these traces with a metaphor that has haunted his poetry from its inception: an X-ray image of his own skull, fractured in a childhood accident. The X-ray film remains as a reminder of the accident, but Grünbein notes that even its clear image of the break in his skull has been preserved at the expense of the "more human" parts of his head, most particularly his eyes. Modern technology has reduced his cranium to a rudimentary form in which "the first face and the last" are seen as identical. Radiography achieves an effect not dissimilar to the maceration of Schiller's and Goethe's bones: the boy's flesh appears to have been "entirely removed" from his skull.

Grünbein's self-styling as the Goethe of his day stands in stark contrast to that of a poet from the previous generation, Rolf Dieter Brinkmann (1940–1975), a writer marked by the student movement of 1967–68. Using Goethe's *Italian Journey* of 1786–1788 as a point of reference, Brinkmann creates in *Rom, Blicke* (1979; *Rome, Views*) a personal record of a three-month stay in Rome during winter 1972–73. A chaotic collage of letters, jottings, and postcards, *Rom, Blicke* sets itself up as the antithesis of Goethe's poetic account of his sexual and creative rebirth in Rome. The rambling notebook's deliberate rejection of aesthetic form contrasts strikingly with Goethe's decision to render his Italian experience in classical meters and through allusions to famous writers from Roman antiquity. Brinkmann suspects that Goethe's poetic reawakening was a calculated and artificial experience, shaped by an explicit desire to rework the classical heritage in terms appropriate to the late 18th century. By contrast, the Rome Brinkmann experiences seems like nothing more than the "ruins of western history," deceptively inflated by the expectations with which German tradition has endowed it. Brinkmann's response to Rome is clearly defined by the sensibility of a person who grew up among the ruins of German cities and for whom the mere idea of "ruins" is charged with negative emotions.

In *Nach den Satiren*, Grünbein reverses Brinkmann's critique of Goethe while at the same time continuing and elaborating Brinkmann's thesis that modern culture falls short of its celebrated antecedents. Mimicking Juvenal's satires of his own society in a series of poems set in ancient Rome—poems with such titles as "A Questionable Guest at Emperor Nerva's Table," "Report on the Murder of Heliogabal by His Bodyguard," and "Hadrian Has Criticized a Poet"—Grünbein suggests that contemporary society is no less corrupt than that described by Juvenal.

Nach den Satiren is full of references to poetic predecessors, who remain beneath the surface of the poems like bones beneath the skin. When the speaker of the title poem claims that the body bears a "neuralgic refrain in the bones of the spine," he alludes to Goethe's *Römische Elegien* (1795; *Roman Elegies*), well known in the German tradition for the image of a lover tapping out the meter of his poem on the backbone of his sleeping beloved. Occasional lines in meters reminiscent of Goethe's elegies emerge in *Nach den Satiren,* sometimes with amusing effects. The title poem opens with a lengthy description of a walk home that suggests Friedrich Hölderlin's famous "Brod und Wein" (1800; Bread and Wine), a long poem in elegiac verse. But whereas the speaker of Hölderlin's poem is returning home after a full day's work, the speaker of Grünbein's poem sequence is wandering slowly homeward after a night of partying. Several images, such as that of the still closed post office, also recall Rilke's *Duineser Elegien* (1922; *Duino Elegies*), as does the loose adaptation of elegiac meters. Grünbein's speaker draws attention to his adaptation of traditional metrics by remarking that he is roaming through the city "auf freiem Fuß" (at liberty—literally, "on a free foot").

In a series of essays that are among the most interesting of his works, Grünbein had already begun to establish an image of himself as a successor to a lineage of poets and scientists whose work explores the nature of the creative impulse. In one of these essays, "Galilei vermißt Dantes Hölle" (1996; Galileo Surveys Dante's Hell), Grünbein asks whether poetic creativity can be scientifically quantified. He describes Galileo's interest in mapping out the underworld and reproduces diagrams of labyrinthine structures that Galileo believed represented the complicated layering of Dante's conception of hell. He argues that Galileo sees Dante's hell as an analog of the human ear, with its inner structure that recalls the labyrinth of the mythical scientist and creator Dedalus.

Grünbein's writing is a continual attempt to trace the origin of creativity to trauma, and thus to accord to poetry a privileged witness to suffering. Far from gratuitously exploiting medical terminology or harking back nostalgically to the willfully difficult language of classical modernism (as critics have accused him of doing), Grünbein uses ideas drawn from contemporary science to support his view that poetry has an important function to perform in Germany today. He sees poetry as a means for registering and understanding rupture and continuity since the fall of the Berlin Wall. "Think from the edge of the wounds," he exhorts the reader in his volume *Falten und Fallen* (1994; the title can be rendered as "Folds and Traps" or as "Folding and Falling"). As an East German who was born in the 1960s and had emigrated to West Germany six years before unification, Grünbein was poised to become the poetic spokesperson of the newly combined state and of the younger generation that would largely determine its course. In the debate about the double burden of past histories—the Nazi crimes against humanity and the oppressive regime of the communist GDR—Grünbein aimed to give poetry a special role in preventing the complete erasure of either of these German pasts.

Unlike those members of his generation who would prefer to move beyond reflection on the Holocaust, Grünbein returns to the theme of Nazi guilt again and again. His essays from the early 1990s on natural history museums, dioramas, and most pertinently on the Berlin "Museum of Deformations" (an anatomical collection that originated in the 18th century at the time of Frederick the Great as an institute of veterinary medicine, destroyed by fire in 1948), record what he terms the "Golden Age of Horror." His 1991 series of poems on Pavlov's experiments on dogs links Nazi medicine with Soviet science. Throughout his work, he remains alert to inherited structures of authority and subordination. Indirectly recalling Adorno's 1949 statement that "it would be barbaric to write poetry after Auschwitz," Grünbein tells us that for a long time he avoided thinking of his work as poetry, calling his writings simply "Versuche" (experiments). In this sense, he joins a long line of German-speaking poets who have grappled with the problem of how to respond to the guilt incurred during the Nazi regime. By combining reflection on Nazism with more personal reflections on the history of the German Democratic Republic, he configures himself as a true representative of the second postwar generation.

Memory, for Grünbein, is like "an archive that has collapsed under the weight of its murderous files, the documents of notorious inhumanity" (*Galilei,* 30). The contemporary German mind is not fully capable of pulling the disparate pieces of information together or unifying them through poetic vision. Grünbein conceives poetry as something like an anthropological glimpse into a lyric past structured like the primitive brain stem. Lyric texts, he claims, are a record of mental short circuits that take us on a broken journey backward in time. Their palimpsestic nature—their way of writing over the traces of earlier texts—grants us an experience akin to the visual effects of radiography. Like an X-ray image of the skull beneath the skin, poetry for Grünbein enables us to recover traces of the past in the present. In the title poem of *Nach den Satiren,* Grünbein alludes to the skull of a young Nazi soldier that was unearthed fifty years after the end of the war in the course of construction work at the Potsdamer Platz in Berlin. In an endnote, he tells us that work ceased at the site until the unknown soldier's remains had been formally laid to rest (*Nach den Satiren,* 222). In the ruined and still only partially reconstructed cityscape of the modern German capital, skulls actual and metaphorical are never far beneath the surface. Grünbein's poetry is constantly engaged in the unsettling task of unearthing them.

See also 1786, 1912 (March), 1922 (February), 1989 (November 9)

Bibliography: Rolf Dieter Brinkmann, *Rom, Blicke* (Reinbek: Rowohlt, 1979; 2nd. ed., 1997). Stephen Brockmann, *Literature and German Reunification* (Cambridge: Cambridge University Press, 1999). Durs Grünbein, *Schädelbasislektion* (Frankfurt am Main: Suhrkamp, 1991). ———, *Galilei vermißt Dantes Hölle und bleibt an den Maßen hängen: Aufsätze 1989–1995* (Frankfurt am Main: Suhrkamp, 1996). ———, *Nach den Satiren* (Frankfurt am Main: Suhrkamp, 1999). Wolfgang Heidenreich, ed., *Durs Grünbein: Texte, Dokumente, Materialen* (Baden-Baden: Elster, 1998). Karen Leeder, *Breaking Boundaries: A New Generation of Poets in the GDR* (Oxford: Clarendon, 1994). Albrecht Schöne, *Schillers Schädel* (Munich: Beck, 2002).

Judith Ryan

❧ *2000*

Reform of German citizenship law goes into effect, an art festival presents work by "foreigners among us," and a carnival of cultures in Berlin celebrates diversity

Spectacles of Multiculturalism

On May 12, 2000, Johannes Rau, the president of the Federal Republic of Germany, delivered a speech titled "Without Fear and Illusions: Living Together in Germany" at the Haus der Kulturen der Welt (House of World Cultures) in Berlin. The president's appeal for integration and repudiation of xenophobia emphasized that immigration was an economic necessity and an enrichment for German society, not a burden. Rau mentioned cross-fertilization in music and the arts as well as culinary pleasures: "The immigrants brought their recipes with them, their specialties, their spices and their drinks. Who can imagine our streets now without pizza and doner kebabs? . . . Germany is now one of the most colorful and open countries in the world. We have become more relaxed, richer in experience, and more tolerant."

Despite good intentions, however, the president reverted to "us" versus "them," polarities he had set out to dissolve. He proceeded to point out the challenges of coexistence: "Life together becomes difficult when old-established Germans no longer feel at home, when they feel like foreigners in their own country. It is one thing to enjoy multicultural radio programs in air-conditioned cars. It is another to sit on the underground and be surrounded by people whose language one cannot understand."

Protectionist concerns about immigration and the integrity of national culture had been on the agenda in Germany before. In March 2000, the government's proposal to give "green cards" to twenty-five thousand South Asian computer scientists provoked short-lived slogans such as "Kinder statt Inder" ("Children not Indians") or "Ausbildung statt Einwanderung" ("Education not Immigration"). Eventually, even the conservative CDU (Christian Democratic Union) party had to admit that Germany had become a country of immigration—a fact that had long been denied. If immigrants were an economic necessity, policies regulating immigration had to be put in place. In November 2000, Friedrich Merz, the general secretary of the CDU, coined the controversial concept of a German *Leitkultur,* a "leading" or "guiding" mainstream culture to which all immigrants were expected to adapt—a phrase that triggered another round of national public debate. About 9 percent (7.5 million) of Germany's resident population in 2000 was "foreign" (although not necessarily foreign born), that is, did not hold a German passport, a figure considerably higher than in other European countries, owing to a citizenship law that made it difficult for immigrants to become citizens. In Berlin, this figure was even higher. Thirteen percent of the city's population (17.4 percent in former West Berlin) were non-German, of which people of Turkish extraction formed the largest minority. Since the fall of the wall in 1989, questions of national unification, linked to anxieties about immigration and racism vis-à-vis ghetto-ization, have become contested issues. Meanwhile, the reformed citizenship law that went into effect in January 2000 has made it easier for immigrants to become German.

While political participation and representation as well as economic and social equality for immigrant populations remain goals yet to be realized, cele-brations of diversity and hybridity have become fashionable in the cultural realm. In 1989, representatives of the Goethe Institute who were keen to move beyond "exporting German culture" founded the Haus der Kulturen der Welt. Their aim was to foster reciprocity in cultural exchanges and to display cul-tures of the world at the new center in Berlin. From April to July 2000, the Haus der Kulturen der Welt, now funded by the Ministry of Foreign Affairs, presented an exhibition entitled "Heimat Kunst" under the aegis of President Johannes Rau. Alongside the exhibition, a touring festival displayed creative work by writers, artists, and filmmakers of immigrant background. The orga-nizers of the exhibition emphasized the gap between "Heimat" and "Kunst" in the title, suggesting that "home" might be found in "art" rather than in a nation or territory. Whether this subtle dislocation of historically charged con-cepts, like Heimat and Heimatkunst, was grasped by all visitors remains open. Critics of the festival pointed out that once again creative work by "foreign-ers" had been singled out and presented separately from that of "indigenous" artists in an act of positive valorization of difference, which nonetheless im-plied ghettoization. The series "Heimat Film," for example, did not include any classics of the *Heimat* film genre, nor did the contemporary work of "pure" Germans feature in the exhibition. Hito Steyerl, a video artist whose docu-mentary about Potsdam Square in Berlin, *The Empty Center,* was shown at the exhibition, argued that cultural institutions embraced artists of foreign back-ground as an enrichment of national culture and dispatched them as ambassa-dors to help Germany compete on a global market of consumable diversity.

The literary program within the "Heimat Kunst" festival avoided ethnic identification by featuring Emine Sevgi Özdamar in tandem with Doris Dörrie, Yoko Tawada with Marcel Beyer, José F. A. Oliver with Stephan Krawczyk, Zafer Senocak with Doron Rabinovici, and Herta Müller, as well as two roundtable discussions on the reception of German literature at home and abroad. The title "Deutschland neu lesen" ("Rereading Germany") was in-spired by "Reinventing Britain," a project by the British Council to rethink diversity in Great Britain with manifestos written by Homi K. Bhabha and Stuart Hall. This adaptation of the title suggests that the rhetoric of multicul-turalism and diversity is increasingly motivated by transnational dialogues and competitions. Any analysis of the construction and enactment of national and ethnic identities will, therefore, have to take into account the institutional frameworks and platforms that enable immigrants and minorities to formulate their claims and identity positions.

Another spectacle of multiculturalism, the Karneval der Kulturen (Carnival of Cultures), was produced in Berlin in June 2000. An annual street parade and fair that took place on the Pentecost weekend, this carnival of cultures stages in the streets of Kreuzberg a colorful spectacle of music, dance, and costumes from around the world. *Caipirinha* is everybody's favorite drink and can be bought at every corner. In line with this tropicalization of Berlin, the group Afoxe Loni, dressed in white and yellow costumes characteristic of Bahia, opens the parade with a street cleansing ritual involving water, firecrackers, and flowers to the accompaniment of a persistent drumbeat. Annet Szabo, one of the organizers, describes this performance as an Afro-Brazilian ritual known as *candomble*. An exotic ritual is thus transposed and recoded in the urban space, an invented tradition enacted at the head of a parade of cultures. A sense of enactment is also conveyed during the live transmission of the event on the local television channel. The reporters explain that not all of the performers in these traditional costumes are Brazilian—some Germans and Turks, too, have joined in the dress parade and are dancing along.

The carnival has become an exemplary platform for staging diversity. Berlin itself does not have a local carnival or *Fastnacht* tradition as do Catholic areas in southern Germany. This is an imported festival, inspired by London's Notting Hill Carnival or the West Indian Parade in Brooklyn, which Berliners have been quick to adopt. Within five years, the carnival has grown into one of the major popular street festivals of the new capital (along with Christopher Street Day and the Love Parade). In 2000, some 600,000 spectators lined the parade that featured 120 groups with 4,000 actors from more than 70 countries. Performances ranged from samba to voodoo, from belly dancing to masked pantomimes, and music using instruments from steel drums to hi-tech sound systems.

Unlike the Notting Hill Carnival with its Caribbean roots, the Berlin Carnival of Cultures did not grow out of one specific community, but was initiated by a cultural institution. The first Carnival of Cultures in 1996 attracted 55,000 spectators. The festival is organized by Werkstatt der Kulturen, a cultural center in the working-class district Neukölln that is funded by the Commissioner for Foreigners' Affairs of the Berlin Senate. In contrast to the more centrally located Haus der Kulturen der Welt, which displays the work of high-profile international artists, Werkstatt caters to a more local, community-based constituency.

In 1998, the carnival parade proceeded through the area around Kottbusser Tor, a predominantly Turkish part of Kreuzberg. Many Turkish residents of the district watched peacefully from their windows, and shop owners sold cold drinks or slices of melon on the sidewalk; but members of the Turkish community felt no need to display themselves on a float as an ethnic group in national costume. In the ensuing debate, the organizers who criticized Turkish residents for refusing to participate in the show, were told that carnival was not a Turkish tradition.

Two years later in 2000, however, the Turkish residents of Berlin seemed to have learned their lesson and gave a convincing performance of real Turkishness. The belly dance studio Karayilan presented a sultan surrounded by his harem—with German and Turkish dancers. Despite this enactment of a perfect Orientalist fantasy, the sparse visibility of the Turkish community in the multicultural spectacle remained a topic of discussion. When asked by a reporter about Turkish participation in that year's carnival, the organizer commented that there were, of course, some Turkish and Kurdish groups performing, as well as various multiethnic groups, including Turkish youngsters, playing hip hop and dj music. Nonetheless, she felt compelled to point out that, as Muslims, Turks could not embrace the carnival as do people from countries with a carnival tradition, owing to its open erotic connotations. Meanwhile, a Turkish paper reported with pride that "our Sultan Abdullah" with his harem had participated in the carnival.

Amid all the merriment, another television reporter interviewed Sanem Kleff, a representative from the Gewerkschaft für Erziehung und Wissenschaften (Union for Education and Sciences), who made a lengthy statement on the problems of integration and bilingual education at Berlin schools. With regard to the carnival, she concluded that the event had grown too big for her taste and that it did not reflect the real composition of Berlin: "One could get the impression that Berlin is populated by Brazilians!" The discourses surrounding the event are full of contradictions. On the one hand, syncretic mixing is emphasized (Germans and Turks can dress up as Brazilians), on the other hand, national and ethnic labels still serve as primary signposts of identification. The pleasures of transethnic cross-dressing are all too easily caught up in entrapments of identity, defined in ethnoculturalist and religious terms.

The organizers explain the reasons for staging a Carnival of Cultures on their web site: "As a city with the highest number of foreigners in Germany (ca. 440,000), Berlin plays the role of an 'integration studio.' Fears of foreign infiltration can only be alleviated by a cultural praxis of diversity, by integration—not assimilation—and peaceful coexistence, established with mutual respect and tolerance. Berlin must understand its international character as an opportunity and actively construct its role as mediator between the various mentalities." Clearly, the carnival is launched with higher claims than presenting just a fun festival. It forms part of a range of endeavors, showcasing the new Berlin as an open, cosmopolitan world city. Questions of the status of immigrant groups within the cultural fabric of Germany's capital and their contribution to it are linked to questions of self-presentation on a world stage.

Promotional material aimed at tourists employs a similar discourse. On a website of festival listings titled "Das Neue Berlin" (The New Berlin), we find the following short description: "The cultures of Africa, Asia, and Latin America in their traditional and modern forms encounter various European traditional cultures and subcultures—a creative process of production and learning for all contributors. For the past five years, the Carnival of Cultures has been a festival for all generations and social groups, open for new trends and styles. The audience, the actors and the organizers celebrate the diverse cultures that are at home in Berlin."

The inclusive gesture, encompassing all citizens of Berlin, attempts a synthesis between the traditional and the modern, but nonetheless revolves around the notion of separate cultures and contrasts between Europe versus its others—Africa, Asia, Latin America. It is cultures that are on display here. But what is really shown? Are these performances of ethnic pride? Of national pride? Demonstrations of unity in diversity? Does this carnival open up spaces of utopian liberation (in a Bakhtinian sense) in which hierarchies and binaries are momentarily unsettled?

The festival in 2000 engendered various forms of participation and commentary that challenged categories of identity politics. Like the carnival itself, the live transmission of the event by Radio Multikulti and the local television station SFB 4 had become increasingly professionalized. The voice-over commentary, rather overpowering and patronizing at times, gave explanations of the performances, making the spectacle accessible to the audience at home. As one reporter confused Mali and Bali, toying with an inflatable globe, the audience learned to perceive the whole world as carnival. Prominent politicians as well as random spectators and performers were interviewed, all joining in a celebration of tolerant, peaceful coexistence across a broad spectrum of ethnicities and age groups in the city. In this display of diversity, regional Germans from the Baltic to Bavaria also displayed their difference in the new Berlin. Traditional carnivals, such as Cologne's, too, have undergone increasing "Sambafication" over the years. The global circulation and appropriation of foreign food, music, and rituals also affect the core of old established indigenous traditions.

It would be too easy to dismiss the Carnival of Cultures version of multiculturalism as an institutionally staged ethnographic spectacle. What surfaces in these performances and surrounding debates are the paradoxes in discourses about having to have one's own culture. Rather than presenting a unified picture, the carnival shows culture as "a site of contestation and negotiation," in line with the UNESCO *World Culture Report 2000,* which suggests replacing metaphors of the "melting pot" and the "mosaic" with the idea of a "rainbow river." Cultural performances are enabled by institutional frameworks, but they cannot simply be reduced to top-down policy. Actors situate themselves in structures created by policy and participate in public parades in complicated, dynamic ways. Performers from a Neukölln youth club called Fusion chose to present themselves as masked hybrid fantasy creatures, which have nothing to do with ethnic identity, but are imaginative creations of modern urban folklore beyond a display of national or ethnic pride.

Meanwhile, for others, this carnivalist fusion does not go far enough in talking back against benevolent paternalism. The transethnic youth movement "Kanak Atak" countered the rhetoric of diversity as enrichment with a rhetoric of its own against multiculturalist incorporation. As Feridun Zaimoglu wrote in his polemical preface to *Kanak Sprak,* his collection of "voices from the margins of society" that was published in 1998 and captured a new, self-conscious voice in postmigrant youth culture: "A new form of fashionable appropriation: multiculturalism. Here, the Kanaki features as a glittering exhibit

in the great zoo of ethnicities, available for participant observation and astonished gawking. Expert 'speakers for the Turks' design colorful brochures to accompany guided tours through the Multikulti Zoo, where the Kebab Preserve
is positioned next to the Peruvian Music Pavilion."

See also 1979, 1984

Bibliography: Heimat Kunst, catalogue of an exhibition, April 7–July 2, 2000 (Berlin: Haus der
Kulturen der Welt, 2000). Gisela Welz, Inszenierungen kultureller Vielfalt: Frankfurt am Main und
New York City (Berlin: Akademie Verlag, 1996). Johannes Rau, "Without Fear and Illusions: Living Together in Germany," Internationale Politik: Transatlantic Edition 1:2 (Spring 2001). Feridun
Zaimoglu, Kanak Sprak: Misstöne vom Rande der Gesellschaft (Hamburg: Rotbuch, 1998); translation of preface in Deniz Göktürk and Anton Kaes, eds., Multicultural Germany: A Sourcebook
(forthcoming). German Council on Foreign Relations, www.dgap.org. "Das neue Berlin,"
www.berlin.de. "Why a Carnival of Cultures?" trans. Tes Skogmo, www.karneval-berlin.de. Haus der
Kulturen der Welt, www.hkw.de. UNESCO, World Culture Report 2000.

Deniz Göktürk

♌ 2001, December 15
W. G. Sebald dies in a car accident in Norfolk, England

Gray Zones of Remembrance

W. G. Sebald's last novel, Austerlitz, had just been published in English translation to enthusiastic acclaim when news of his untimely death shocked the
world of letters. In fact, this expatriate German writer's works had met with
great acclaim in the 1990s in England and the United States more than in his
home country, where, despite several awards, he remained an outsider to the
literary scene.

Sebald's fame rested on his subtle, intense exploration of the phenomenology of forgetting and remembering, a quality mostly absent in the writings of
other postwar German authors, whose works he saw marred by a "carefully
administered deficit of experience." Toward this end, he created a unique style
of memory narrative, located at the breaking point between documentary and
fiction and energized by what he called elsewhere "the monstrosities in the
background of my own life" (Luftkrieg und Literatur, 82).

An early admirer of the German-Jewish writers Peter Weiss, Paul Celan,
and Jean Améry, Sebald was also inspired by Alexander Kluge's deliberately
jarring mixture of documentary narrative, fiction, and photography, a technique he employed in almost all his texts to great effect. Both in Die Aus-
gewanderten (1992; The Emigrants) and in Austerlitz, Sebald writes about Jewish Grenzgänger (literally, border crossers), refugees and survivors, exiles and
emigrés, who live at the threshold of a foreign culture after having been dis-
possessed. As a German born in Bavaria in 1944, he researches their past, lends
them his voice, and listens to their stories, at times almost merging with them,
but never oblivious to his own status as a descendant of the perpetrators.

The sparse storyline of Austerlitz is quickly told, even if no retelling can do justice to the novel's complex temporal loops between past and present, its spatial crisscrossing of Europe, its multiple poetic correspondences, literary allusions, and mysterious mirrorings. A nameless narrator, whose sketchy life history closely resembles that of Sebald, tells us about his various travels from England to Antwerp, Brussels, and Liège, where time and again he somehow runs into Jacques Austerlitz, a strange but compelling character whose detailed narrations and reflections he writes down and reports to the reader. Austerlitz and the narrator first speak French, later English, which implicitly makes the German original itself a translation. And translation in the broadest sense emerges as central to Sebald's literary project: translation as the liminal space between past and present, between document and fiction, between human history and natural history, between the dead and the living.

Austerlitz is obsessed with an extensive project of architectural history—Benjaminian in scope—in which he explores the affinities between monumental 19th-century train stations, military fortresses, working-class housing projects, prisons, insane asylums, and court buildings—all representing the monumental architecture of an imperialist age as pure will to power and domination. Especially the Brussels Palace of Justice with its "walled-in voids" stands as an example of the "sanctioned violence" (29) perpetrated by colonialist Belgium in the Congo, a theme present already in Sebald's reflections on Roger Casement and Joseph Conrad in *Die Ringe des Saturn* (1992; *The Rings of Saturn*). But it is only the narrator who follows Austerlitz's thoughts from Belgian colonialism to Nazi Germany and its ideology of monumental architecture as ruin when he visits the fortress of Breendonck outside Antwerp, which was built before World War I and then used by the Nazis as a receiving and penal camp until 1944. This powerful beginning of a book that only marginally resembles the traditional novel rewrites Hannah Arendt's argument about the affinity between European colonialism in Africa and the Nazi regime, but it remains rather aloof at this stage from any human interest the reader might take in the two fictional characters.

Only slowly does it dawn on the reader that Austerlitz's obsessive architectural investigations are an avoidance strategy—avoidance of his own personal history and genealogy, a substitute for a life not lived. The narrator and Austerlitz first meet in 1967 in the *Salle des pas perdus,* the waiting room in Antwerp's Central Station, but soon lose contact for several decades only to meet again, by coincidence, in the bar of London's Liverpool Station in late 1996. Austerlitz is now retired from his London teaching position, has shipwrecked with his research project, and has suffered through a major language and identity crisis—itself a rewriting of Hugo von Hofmannsthal's famous *Chandos Letter* of 1902, a key document of Austrian modernism. After his nervous breakdown in 1992, Austerlitz finally began to listen to the voices of his own repressed past. On his travels to Prague, he learns from his former *Kinderfräulein* (nanny), Vera, that he grew up in Prague the child of Jewish parents, that he was sent to England on a *Kindertransport* in 1939 at four and a half, and that his mother, Agata, was first interned in Theresienstadt and then sent to a death camp in 1944, while his father tried to establish a home for the family in Paris, before all traces of him vanished in a French holding camp near the Pyrenees.

Liverpool Station is where Austerlitz first arrived in 1939. And this is where he reencounters, as if by magic, the narrator, to whom he now tells the story of his journey into his own past. We first hear about Austerlitz's childhood in Wales as Dafydd Elias, the adopted child of a Calvinist fire-and-brimstone preacher, and his morose, timid wife. We learn of his school years at Stower Grange and the only happy times of his adolescence during summer vacations at his friend Gerald's house, Andromeda Lodge, on the coast of Wales. We feel the shock when, at age fifteen, his headmaster reveals his real name to him, confronting him with an unknown past. We hear about his architecture studies in Paris in the late 1950s and about the death of that one and only friend Gerald in a plane crash in the Alps in the late 1960s, an event that led to "a withdrawal into myself which became increasingly morbid and intractable with the passage of time" (117).

As the reader is spellbound by the hallucinatory descent of Austerlitz into his past, rendered in a seamless flow of complex hypotactical sentences, curiously flat in tone, but emotionally loaded, the question imposes itself: what is documentary here and what is fiction? Since the narrator hardly makes an effort to distinguish himself from Sebald, the reader is tempted to take Austerlitz as a "real" character as well. Sebald told Maya Jaggi of the *Guardian* (September 22, 2001) that *Austerlitz* was a composite of two and a half biographies. One is the story of Susie Bechhofer, a Munich exile whose *Kindertransport* story and childhood in a preacher's household Sebald learned about from a British documentary program on Channel 4. The other is the story of a colleague of Sebald's, an eccentric historian of architecture, who delved into his past after early retirement and whose childhood photo looks at us intensely from the cover. But who then is the half figure? Unless there are parts of yet other biographies folded into the Austerlitz figure, we may consider that half as a piece of the author himself. Indeed, Sebald said in another interview that there is a lot of himself in Austerlitz. Some critics have been troubled by the notion that a piece of the German writer, however mediated through the narrator, should have entered into the make-up of the Jewish protagonist. To them, it suggests some notion of a German-Jewish symbiosis that should be anathema after the Shoah. But Austerlitz as a composite is a thoroughly fictional figure who should not be judged by such moralizing considerations. They miss the nature of Sebald's literary project, which is to compensate for an undeniable German deficit of memory and experience by practicing a kind of narrative mimesis of the victims of Nazism. Such mimesis requires a gray zone of identification and transference that allows for a reciprocal mimetic approximation without blurring the distinction between German narrator and Jewish protagonist. Austerlitz emerges from that gray zone with the narrator as his alter ego and only listener.

Of course, one cannot read *Austerlitz* as a realistic novel, even though it produces the effect of the real more powerfully than many historical studies. The Jewish name Austerlitz itself is already so overdetermined as to suggest historical and spatial dimensions that make Austerlitz a deeply allegorical figure: Austerlitz the battle site of Napoleon's victory over Austria; Austerlitz the name of the train station in Paris dedicated to that memory of French glory; Les Galéries d'Austerlitz as the wasteland near the station that served the Nazis as a storage depot for confiscated Jewish property during the occupation, the very site on which President Mitterrand's *grand projet* of the new Bibliothèque Nationale was to be built several decades later. Then, in a very different mode, Austerlitz is also the original family name of Fred Astaire. Jarring as it may seem, the name also bears a linguistic proximity to Auschwitz, an implication reinforced during Austerlitz's first visit to the Auschowitz Springs of Marienbad in 1972, an encounter that inexplicably seems to freeze him emotionally at the time. Only later does he realize that he had been subject to the return of an unconscious childhood memory of Marienbad, and to the knowledge of Auschwitz, where his mother may have perished. And here we have another gray zone that haunts Sebald's imagination—the gray zone between the living and the dead that is the zone of traumatic memory itself, that one wants to see and not see, to feel and not feel. Haunted memory work is what constitutes the bond between the narrator and Austerlitz.

The mimetic intimacy at work between the narrator and Austerlitz finds its culmination at the end when Austerlitz hands the narrator the keys to his London house and commends his whole collection of photographs to him before vanishing from the novel in search of the lost traces of his father. And it is as if Austerlitz has also bequeathed the forgotten Ashkenazi cemetery behind his London house to the narrator, who thus becomes something of a guardian of memory—Austerlitz's memory *as* the historical memory of his people. This is indeed the core of Sebald's writing project. It is not that he appropriates a Jewish identity—far from it. As a German of the postwar generation, he accepts his responsibility to remember while fully acknowledging the difficulty of such remembering across an abyss of violence and pain. Sebald remembers not as an objective historian of the real, but as a writer of fiction which, in its mediated form and periscopic strategies of telling, renders the stories told by others: Austerlitz to the narrator, Vera to Austerlitz, Agata to Vera, and ultimately the narrator to the reader. This echo chamber of voices conjures up all the vicissitudes and fragilities of forgetting and remembering in ways not attainable by historiography. Narrator and protagonist are bound by their blockage of traumatic historical memory, their pathological reluctance to engage with the past. Sebald's greatest achievement is his way of describing how this reluctance, this cloud of deliberate unknowing, is partially overcome by Austerlitz and the German narrator in their encounters over the decades, and how they face the outer limits of the knowable in their lives.

What makes this deeply inconsolable text such a pleasure to read is that processes of memory and experiences of space and time are dissected with consummate poetic skill and imagination. The narration itself puts time into slow motion and stops time entirely in moments of panic and horror or, alternately, in the much less frequent moments of a transcendent lightness of being. It immerses itself in the fluidity of hallucination, delves into a submerged optical unconscious in its extended explorations of the visual world, which, paradoxically, seems to grow ever darker the more light falls on the repressed past. Remembrance and forgetting are narrated and pictured in such a way as to open up a phenomenology of visual space, supported by the black-and-white photographs that leave the reader with memorable and powerful after-images: the vast, empty cupolas of the grand train stations, the village submerged in the reservoir, the gaze at the world through the silk veil in Alphonso's strange glasses, and his disquisitions on the life of moths, the pigeon returning home with a broken wing, the white cockatoos of Andromeda lodge, the haunting doorways of Terezin, the dystopian architecture of the new Bibliothèque Nationale, and always the threat of a loss of vision, of macular degeneration, of an entropy of color, a voiding of the world.

Memory indeed often resembles blurred vision. It produces after-images, hallucinations, partially conscious dream images in muted colors. For the post-Auschwitz generations, images and photos have become relics of a past that can only be approximated but never fully known in its experiential reality. The intensity of memories recovered in Sebald's narrative becomes so strong that a new kind of mimetic intimacy is created, an intimacy between Austerlitz and a reader willing to follow the narrator into the gray zone of Sebald's disconsolate vision of the world.

Sebald does not aestheticize pain as some critics have claimed. His carefully crafted language, close in salient ways to that of such 19th-century writers as Adalbert Stifter, and held to be mannerist by some, offers the possibility of imagining unimaginable pain. Its seeming restfulness and long syntactic breath makes the mimetic approximation of historical trauma possible for the reader. What emerges in the end is a vision of the world as ruin, as inverted and false as it appears at the very beginning of the novel in the description of Antwerp's Nocturama and its animals of the night who will go to sleep when the lights are switched on. The narrator remembers their "strikingly large eyes," comparing them to "the fixed, inquiring gaze found in certain painters and philosophers who seek to penetrate the darkness which surrounds us purely by means of looking and thinking" (4). While trying to remember his visit to Breendonck, the narrator laments that "the darkness does not lift but becomes yet heavier as I think how little we can hold in mind, how everything is constantly lapsing into oblivion with every extinguished life, how the world is, as it were, draining itself, in that the history of countless places and objects which themselves have no power of memory is never heard, never described or passed on" (24).

That which has now lapsed into oblivion and darkness as a result of Sebald's untimely death is the story of his own father—the German soldier in Poland in 1939, in France toward the end of the war—the story of the perpetrator as the great untold in Sebald's oeuvre. There are indications that he was about to turn to this task—coincidentally at the same age when Austerlitz first began to engage his family past. It is as if in death Sebald merged one last time with his protagonist. Just as Austerlitz disappears on the last pages of the novel to search for his father, Sebald has vanished from the world. And gone with him are the memories of *his* father, a narrative only he could have written. In that sense, *Austerlitz* truly stands as W. G. Sebald's death mask—the mask of another text that will never be written.

See also 1848 (October), 1902, 1911, 1927 (March), 1942–43, 1989 (February)

Bibliography: W. G. Sebald, *Austerlitz* (Munich: Hanser, 2001); *Austerlitz,* trans. Anthea Bell (New York: Random House, 2001). ———, *Luftkrieg und Literatur* (Munich: Hanser, 1999). ———, "Mit einem kleinen Strandspaten Abschied von Deutschland nehmen," interview, *Süddeutsche Zeitung* (December 22, 2001). J. J. Long and Anne Whitehead, eds., *W. G. Sebald: A Critical Companion* (Edinburgh: Edinburgh University Press, 2004). Mark R. McCullogh, *Understanding W. G. Sebald* (Columbia: University of South Carolina Press, 2004). Amir Eshel, "Against the Power of Time: The Poetics of Suspension in W. G. Sebald's *Austerlitz*," *New German Critique* 88 (Winter 2003): 71–96.

Andreas Huyssen

 Contributors

Tracy Adams, Department of French, University of Auckland

Leslie A. Adelson, Department of German Studies, Cornell University

Mark M. Anderson, Department of Germanic Languages and Literatures, Columbia University

Theodore M. Andersson, Department of German Studies, Stanford University

Marion Aptroot, Institut für Jüdische Studien, Heinrich-Heine-Universität, Düsseldorf

Maria Louise Ascher, Harvard University Press

Karlheinz Barck, Zentrum für Literaturforschung, Berlin

Kelly Barry, Department of Germanic Languages and Literatures, Columbia University

David Bathrick, Department of Theatre, Film, and Dance/Center for Theatre Arts, Cornell University

Thomas Bein, Institut für Germanistische und Allgemeine Literaturwissenschaft, Aachen

Frederick Beiser, Department of Philosophy, Syracuse University

Karol Berger, Department of Music, Stanford University

Klaus L. Berghahn, Department of German, University of Wisconsin, Madison

Susan Bernstein, Department of Comparative Literature, Brown University

Elio Brancaforte, Department of Germanic and Slavic Studies, Tulane University

Reinhold Brinkmann, Department of Music, Harvard University

Elisabeth Bronfen, Englisches Seminar, Universität Zürich

Rob Burns, Department of German Studies, University of Warwick

Kenneth S. Calhoon, Departments of German and Comparative Literature, University of Oregon

Rüdiger Campe, Department of German, Johns Hopkins University

Michel Chaouli, Department of Germanic Studies, Indiana University, Bloomington

Carol J. Clover, Departments of Scandinavian and Rhetoric, University of California, Berkeley

James Conant, Department of Philosophy, University of Chicago

Stanley Corngold, Department of German, Princeton University

Luiz Costa Lima, Department of Literary Studies, Universidade do Estado do Rio de Janeiro

Gordon A. Craig, Department of History, Stanford University

Chris Cullens, Independent Scholar, San Francisco, California

Arthur C. Danto, Department of Philosophy, Columbia University

Lorraine Daston, Max Planck Institute for the History of Science, Berlin

Jeremy Dauber, Department of Germanic Languages and Literatures, Columbia University

Edward Dimendberg, Department of Film and Media Studies and Program in Visual Studies, University of California, Irvine

Brigid Doherty, Departments of German and Art & Archaeology, Princeton University

David Dollenmayer, Department of Humanities and Arts, Worcester Polytechnic Institute

Michael Eskin, Department of Germanic Languages and Literatures, Columbia University

Karen S. Feldman, Departments of German and Rhetoric, University of California, Berkeley

Paul Fleming, Department of German, New York University

Eckart Förster, Philosophy Department, Johns Hopkins University

Paul Franks, Department of Philosophy, University of Toronto

Lisa Freinkel, Department of English and Program in Comparative Literature, University of Oregon

Udo Friedrich, Institut für Deutsche Philologie, Ernst-Moritz-Arndt-Universität Greifswald

Peter Fritzsche, Department of History, University of Illinois at Urbana-Champaign

Andreas Gailus, Department of German, Scandinavian, and Dutch, University of Minnesota

Marisa Galvez, Department of Comparative Literature, Stanford University

Eva Geulen, Department of Germanic Languages and Literatures, New York University

Peter Gilgen, Department of German, Cornell University

Deniz Göktürk, Department of German, University of California, Berkeley

Anthony Grafton, Department of History, Princeton University

Cordula Grewe, Department of Art History and Archeology, Columbia University

Thomas S. Grey, Department of Music, Stanford University

Max Grosse, Romanisches Seminar, Universität Tübingen

Hans Ulrich Gumbrecht, Department of Comparative Literature, Stanford University

Fritz Gutbrodt, Englisches Seminar, Universität Zürich

Gertraud Gutzmann, Department of German Studies, Smith College

Paul Guyer, Department of Philosophy, University of Pennsylvania

Klaus Haberkamm, Institut für deutsche Philologie II, Westfälische Wilhelms-Universität Münster

Barbara Hahn, College of Arts and Sciences, Vanderbilt University

John T. Hamilton, Departments of Germanic Languages and Literatures and Comparative Literature, Harvard University

Beatrice Hanssen, Germanic and Slavic Languages, University of Georgia, Athens

Wolfgang Haubrichs, Fachrichtung 4.1 Germanistik, Universität des Saarlandes

Anselm Haverkamp, Department of English, New York University

Charles W. Haxthausen, Graduate Program in the History of Art, Williams College

Julia Hell, Department of Germanic Languages and Literatures, University of Michigan

Andrew Hewitt, Department of Germanic Languages, University of California, Los Angeles

Walter Hinderer, Department of German, Princeton University

Stephen Hinton, Department of Music, Stanford University

Wernfried Hofmeister, Institut für Germanistik, Karl-Franzensuniversität Graz

Peter Uwe Hohendahl, Institute for German Cultural Studies, Cornell University

Amy M. Hollywood, The Divinity School, The University of Chicago

Robert C. Holub, Department of German, University of California, Berkeley

Jochen Hörisch, Seminar für Deutsche Philologie, Universität Mannheim

Isabel V. Hull, Department of History, Cornell University

Andreas Huyssen, Department of Germanic Languages and Literatures, Columbia University

Carol Jacobs, Department of Germanic Languages and Literatures, Yale University

C. Stephen Jaeger, Departments of Germanic Language and Literature and Comparative and World Literature, University of Illinois at Urbana-Champaign

Johannes Janota, Philologisch-Historische Fakultät, Universität Augsburg

Anton Kaes, Departments of German and Rhetoric & Film Studies, University of California, Berkeley

Jennifer M. Kapczynski, Department of Germanic Languages and Literatures, Washington University in St. Louis

Dieter Kartschoke, Institut für Germanistik, Freie Universität Berlin

Christian Kiening, Deutsches Seminar, Universität Zürich

Wolf Kittler, Department of Germanic, Slavic, and Semitic Studies, University of California, Santa Barbara; Department of German, Cornell University

Clayton Koelb, Department of Germanic Languages, University of North Carolina, Chapel Hill

Joseph Leo Koerner, Department of History of Art, University College London

Barbara Kosta, Department of German Studies, University of Arizona

Anthony Krupp, Department of Foreign Languages and Literatures, University of Miami

Joachim Küpper, Romanisches Seminar der Freien Universität Berlins

Niklaus Largier, Department of German, University of California, Berkeley

Leo A. Lensing, Department of German Studies, Wesleyan University

David J. Levin, Department of Germanic Studies, University of Chicago

Suzanne L. Marchand, Department of History, Louisiana State University, Baton Rouge

Greil Marcus, Independent Scholar, Berkeley, California

Karl Maurer, Romanische Philologie und Allgemeine Literaturwissenschaft, Ruhr Universität Bochum

Doris McGonagill, Department of Germanic Languages and Literatures, Harvard University

Gert Melville, Institute für Geschichte, Technische Universität Dresden

Stéphane Moses, Center for German-Jewish Culture and Literary History, The Hebrew University of Jerusalem

Glenn W. Most, Scuola Normale Superiore di Pisa; Committee on Social Thought, University of Chicago

Dorothea E. von Mücke, Department of Germanic Languages and Literatures, Columbia University

Harro Müller, Department of Germanic Languages and Literatures, Columbia University

Jan-Dirk Müller, Institut für deutsche Philologie, Universität München

Stephan Müller, Institut für Deutsche Philologie, Universität München

Helmut Müller-Sievers, Department of German, Northwestern University

Rainer Nägele, Department of German, Johns Hopkins University

Elliot Y. Neaman, Department of History, University of San Francisco

Reingard Nethersole, Graduate School for the Humanities and Social Sciences, University of the Witwatersrand, Johannesburg, South Africa

Stephen G. Nichols, Department of Romance Languages & Literatures, Johns Hopkins University

Peter Nisbet, Busch-Reisinger Museum, Harvard University

Robert E. Norton, Department of German and Russian Languages and Literatures, University of Notre Dame

Paul Oppenheimer, Department of English, City College, New York

Burton Pike, Department of Comparative Literature, CUNY Graduate Center

Robert B. Pippin, Committee on Social Thought, Department of Philosophy, University of Chicago

Debra N. Prager, Commitee on Degrees in History and Literature, Harvard University

Martin Puchner, Department of English, Cornell University

Helmut Puff, Departments of History and Germanic Languages and Literatures, University of Michigan

Eric Rentschler, Department of Germanic Languages and Literatures, Harvard University

David Roberts, School of Languages, Cultures and Linguistics, Monash University

Orrin W. Robinson, Department of German Studies, Stanford University

Mark W. Roche, Department of German and Russian Languages and Literatures, University of Notre Dame

Judith Ryan, Department of Germanic Languages and Literatures and Department of Comparative Literature, Harvard University

Eric L. Santner, Department of Germanic Studies, University of Chicago

Haun Saussy, Department of Comparative Literature, Yale University

Richard Erich Schade, Department of German Studies, University of Cincinnati

Jeffrey T. Schnapp, Department of Comparative Literature, Stanford University

J. B. Schneewind, Department of Philosophy, Johns Hopkins University

Helmut J. Schneider, Germanistisches Seminar der Universität Bonn

Jochen Schulte-Sasse, Departments of Cultural Studies and Comparative Literature and German, Scandinavian, and Dutch, University of Minnesota

James A. Schultz, Department of Germanic Languages, University of California, Los Angeles

Anette Schwarz, Department of German Studies, Cornell University

Hinrich C. Seeba, Department of German, University of California, Berkeley

Bernhard Siegert, Geschichte und Theorie der Kulturtechniken, Universität Weimar

Eckehard Simon, Department of Germanic Languages and Literatures, Harvard University

Hans Sluga, Department of Philosophy, University of California, Berkeley

Emery Snyder, Independent Scholar, New York

Werner Sollors, Department of English and American Language and Literature, Harvard University

James A. Steintrager, Department of English and Comparative Literature, University of California, Irvine

Peter Strohschneider, Institut für Deutsche Philologie, Ludwig-Maximilians-Universität München

Maria Tatar, Department of Germanic Languages and Literatures, Harvard University

Arlene A. Teraoka, Department of German, Scandinavian, and Dutch, University of Minnesota

Bianca Theisen, Department of German, Johns Hopkins University

Rochelle Tobias, Department of German, Johns Hopkins University

Hans Rudolf Vaget, Department of German Studies, Smith College

Luciana Villas-Bôas, Department of Germanic Languages and Literatures, Columbia University

Janet Ward, Department of History, University of Nevada, Las Vegas

Sean Ward, Independent Scholar, Fayetteville, Arizona

Lindsay Waters, Harvard University Press

Klaus Weimar, Deutsches Seminar, University of Zurich

David E. Wellbery, Departments of Germanic Studies and Comparative Literature and Committee on Social Thought, University of Chicago

Horst Wenzel, Institut für Deutsche Literatur, Humboldt-Universität Berlin

Hansjakob Werlen, Department of Modern Languages and Literatures, Swarthmore College

Christopher J. Wild, Department of Germanic Languages, University of North Carolina at Chapel Hill

Geoffrey Winthrop-Young, Department of Central, Eastern and Northern European Studies, University of British Columbia

Peter Wollen, Department of Film and Television, University of California, Los Angeles

Elisabeth Young-Bruehl, Columbia Center for Psychoanalytic Training and Research, New York

Jan Ziolkowski, Department of the Classics, Harvard University

Index